PUBLIC PAPERS OF THE PRESIDENTS
OF THE
UNITED STATES

PUBLIC PAPERS OF THE PRESIDENTS
OF THE
UNITED STATES

William J. Clinton

1995

(IN TWO BOOKS)

BOOK I—JANUARY 1 TO JUNE 30, 1995

UNITED STATES GOVERNMENT PRINTING OFFICE
WASHINGTON : 1996

Published by the
Office of the Federal Register
National Archives and Records Administration

For sale by the
Superintendent of Documents
U.S. Government Printing Office
Washington, DC 20402

353.035
C641p
1995
v.1

Foreword

The first half of 1995 was a time of challenge and change. The election of a new Republican Congress set the stage for a fundamental public debate over the role of government, the country's values, and the way we could move forward as one people. Throughout this debate, I remained firmly committed to this ideal: America is strong only when America is united, and when we leave no one behind.

As I made clear in my State of the Union Address, we have an obligation to offer the American people a new kind of government for new times. My Administration recognizes that there isn't a program for every problem, but that we can produce a government that works better and costs less. We launched a top-to-bottom overhaul of Federal rules in an effort to bring common sense to often complex regulation. We streamlined the regulatory process by abolishing 16,000 pages of regulations. We reformed environmental workplace safety and pharmaceutical regulation and we trimmed red tape and business burdens, without hurting public safety and health. We eliminated the 10,000 page Federal personnel manual and we cut 136,000 positions from the Federal work force.

As we celebrated the 50th anniversary of the end of World War II in Europe, we reaffirmed our commitment to lead for peace and freedom. At a summit meeting in Russia, I joined the Russian leader in advancing the security of our people and the world—by deepening our common efforts to reduce the nuclear threat, agreeing to improve our cooperation against terrorism, and pledging to work as partners for an undivided Europe. In Haiti, I thanked our troops for securing the transition from dictatorship to democracy. And at the 50th anniversary of the United Nations, we took stock of half a century of achievement and pledged to adapt the UN for the challenges of the 21st century.

Pursuing our mission to create a safer world, the United States led the international effort among 170 countries to secure the indefinite and unconditional extension of the Nuclear Non-Proliferation Treaty. And by applying steady, patient pressure to North Korea, we secured an agreement that froze its dangerous nuclear program.

In furthering our commitment to open markets and expand opportunities for U.S. exports, we reached an historic agreement with Japan to open further its automotive market to potentially billions of dollars worth of American cars and parts.

In April, our Nation was shaken by the tragic terrorist bombing of the Alfred P. Murrah Federal Building in Oklahoma City. One hundred sixty-eight Americans lost their lives. But moments of tragedy often bring out the best in people, and thousands of Americans turned their energy and prayers toward helping the people of Oklahoma endure and overcome their enormous loss.

Finally, in June, I introduced a balanced budget plan that reflected the values of the American people: opportunity, responsibility, the duty we owe one another, strong families, a strong America. This plan built on our success in reducing the deficit by nearly one half during the first two and one-half years of my Administration. This reflected an attempt to reach out to the Congress and find common ground on the budget. And it set the stage for a climactic debate: not about whether to balance the budget, but how.

William J Clinton

Preface

This book contains the papers and speeches of the 42d President of the United States that were issued by the Office of the Press Secretary during the period January 1–June 30, 1995. The material has been compiled and published by the Office of the Federal Register, National Archives and Records Administration.

The material is presented in chronological order, and the dates shown in the headings are the dates of the documents or events. In instances when the release date differs from the date of the document itself, that fact is shown in the textnote. Every effort has been made to ensure accuracy: Remarks are checked against a tape recording, and signed documents are checked against the original. Textnotes and cross references have been provided by the editors for purposes of identification or clarity. Speeches were delivered in Washington, DC, unless indicated. The times noted are local times. All materials that are printed full-text in the book have been indexed in the subject and name indexes, and listed in the document categories list.

The Public Papers of the Presidents series was begun in 1957 in response to a recommendation of the National Historical Publications Commission. An extensive compilation of messages and papers of the Presidents covering the period 1789 to 1897 was assembled by James D. Richardson and published under congressional authority between 1896 and 1899. Since then, various private compilations have been issued, but there was no uniform publication comparable to the Congressional Record or the United States Supreme Court Reports. Many Presidential papers could be found only in the form of mimeographed White House releases or as reported in the press. The Commission therefore recommended the establishment of an official series in which Presidential writings, addresses, and remarks of a public nature could be made available.

The Commission's recommendation was incorporated in regulations of the Administrative Committee of the Federal Register, issued under section 6 of the Federal Register Act (44 U.S.C. 1506), which may be found in title 1, part 10, of the Code of Federal Regulations.

A companion publication to the Public Papers series, the Weekly Compilation of Presidential Documents, was begun in 1965 to provide a broader range of Presidential materials on a more timely basis to meet the needs of the contemporary reader. Beginning with the administration of Jimmy Carter, the Public Papers series expanded its coverage to include additional material as printed in the Weekly Compilation. That coverage provides a listing of the President's daily schedule and meetings, when announced, and other items of general interest issued by the Office of the Press Secretary. Also included are lists of the President's nominations submitted to the Senate, materials released by the Office of the Press Secretary that are not printed full-text in the book, and proclamations, Executive orders, and other Presidential documents released by the Office of the Press Secretary and published in the *Federal Register*. This information appears in the appendixes at the end of the book.

The Public Papers series also includes volumes covering the administrations of Presidents Hoover, Truman, Eisenhower, Kennedy, Johnson, Nixon, Ford, Carter, Reagan, and Bush.

The Public Papers of the Presidents publication program is under the direction of Frances D. McDonald, Managing Editor, Publications and Services Group. The series is produced by the Presidential and Legislative Publications Unit, Gwen H. Estep, Chief. The Chief Editor of this book was Karen Howard Ashlin, assisted by Scott Andreae, Brad Brooks, Anna Glover, Margaret A. Hemmig, Carolyn W. Hill, Maxine L. Hill, Rachel Rondell, Cheryl E. Sirofchuck, and Michael J. Sullivan.

The frontispiece and photographs used in the portfolio were supplied by the White House Photo Office. The typography and design of the book were developed by the Government Printing Office under the direction of Michael F. DiMario, Public Printer.

Richard L. Claypoole
Director of the Federal Register

John W. Carlin
Archivist of the United States

Contents

Cabinet

Secretary of State .... Warren M. Christopher

Secretary of the Treasury .... Robert E. Rubin
(effective January 10)

Secretary of Defense .... William J. Perry

Attorney General .... Janet Reno

Secretary of the Interior .... Bruce Babbitt

Secretary of Agriculture .... Richard Rominger
(acting, effective January 1)
Dan Glickman
(effective March 30)

Secretary of Commerce .... Ronald H. Brown

Secretary of Labor .... Robert B. Reich

Secretary of Health and Human Services .... Donna E. Shalala

Secretary of Housing and Urban
Development .... Henry G. Cisneros

Secretary of Transportation .... Federico Peña

Secretary of Energy .... Hazel Rollins O'Leary

Secretary of Education .... Richard W. Riley

Secretary of Veterans Affairs .... Jesse Brown

United States Representative to the
United Nations .... Madeleine Korbel Albright

Administrator of the Environmental
Protection Agency .... Carol M. Browner

United States Trade Representative .... Michael Kantor

Director of the Office of Management
and Budget .... Alice M. Rivlin

Chief of Staff .... Leon E. Panetta

Counselor to the President .... Thomas F. McLarty III

Chair of the Council of Economic
Advisers .... Laura D'Andrea Tyson

Director of National Drug
Control Policy .... Lee Patrick Brown

Administrator of the Small Business
Administration .... Philip Lader

Director of Central Intelligence .... John M. Deutch

Administration of William J. Clinton

1995

Remarks on Arrival in Little Rock, Arkansas
January 2, 1995

Hello. I want to thank you so much for coming out to see us. It's wonderful to be home. We're looking forward just to spending some personal time visiting with our friends, saying hello to people, driving around the State a little bit. And I'm even going to have a few hours tomorrow where I have nothing on the schedule, for the first time in years and years, to go off——

[At this point, the President's microphone failed.]

So what, I didn't want to give a speech anyway. Hello. *[Laughter]*

NOTE: The President spoke at 12:13 p.m. at Adams Field.

Statement on Additional Steps To Prevent Violence at Abortion Clinics
January 2, 1995

In America, the heart of constitutional government is the rule of law. Today, our commitment to the rule of law is being tested by those who believe that their opposition to abortion gives them the right to commit acts of violence, even murder, against their fellow citizens who seek only to exercise their constitutional right to choose or to assist others in exercising that right.

I recognize and respect the range of deeply felt beliefs Americans hold on abortion. A continued vigorous debate over abortion is proper. Violence against those who hold differing opinions is not.

Last year, Congress passed and I signed a law prohibiting violent interference with Americans who exercise their rights in this area. Because of continued violations of this law and the Constitution, I have today instructed the Department of Justice to: (1) direct each United States Attorney immediately to head a task force including Federal, State, and local law enforcement officials to formulate plans to address clinic security for all clinics in their jurisdiction; and (2) direct each U.S. Marshal to consult with all clinics in their jurisdiction to ensure that the clinics have all the information they need to communicate with appropriate Federal, State, and local law enforcement officials on a timely basis about potential threats. I have also asked the Attorney General to consult with law enforcement officials on any further steps that might be taken to address this serious problem.

I applaud Americans of conscience who differ in their convictions on abortion but who stand united in their opposition to violence. As we begin a new year, let us all reaffirm our devotion to the rule of law and our respect for the diversity of opinion that rule protects.

Letter to Congressional Leaders on Trade With Bulgaria
December 30, 1994

Dear Mr. Speaker: (Dear Mr. President:)

On June 3, 1993, I determined and reported to the Congress that Bulgaria is in full compliance with the freedom of emigration criteria of sections 402 and 409 of the Trade Act of 1974. This action allowed for the continuation

1

of most-favored-nation (MFN) status for Bulgaria and certain other activities without the requirement of a waiver.

As required by law, I am submitting an updated Report to Congress concerning emigration laws and policies of the Republic of Bulgaria. You will find that the report indicates continued Bulgarian compliance with U.S. and international standards in the areas of emigration and human rights policy.

Sincerely,

WILLIAM J. CLINTON

NOTE: Identical letters were sent to Thomas S. Foley, Speaker of the House of Representatives, and Albert Gore, Jr., President of the Senate. This letter was released by the Office of the Press Secretary on January 3, 1995.

Letter to Congressional Leaders Reporting on Iraq's Compliance With United Nations Security Council Resolutions
December 30, 1994

Dear Mr. Speaker: (Dear Mr. President:)

Consistent with the Authorization for Use of Military Force Against Iraq Resolution (Public Law 102–1), and as part of my effort to keep the Congress fully informed, I am reporting on the status of efforts to obtain Iraq's compliance with the resolutions adopted by the U.N. Security Council.

The crisis precipitated in early October when Iraq moved significant numbers of ground forces toward its border with Kuwait has been largely resolved. Since my last report, Iraqi Republican Guard forces have redeployed north of the 32nd parallel, including some Republican Guard units that were south of the 32nd parallel prior to the crisis. Six Iraqi regular army divisions which were located in the south prior to the crisis continue to be deployed there. U.S. forces deployed to the Gulf in response to Iraq's actions will redeploy to the United States over the next several weeks. Some forces—primarily aircraft—will remain in the theater to deter further acts of Iraqi provocation and aggression. In order to enhance significantly our ability to strike at Iraqi tanks south of the 32nd parallel, Kuwait has agreed to permit us to base a squadron of 24 Air Force A–10s in Kuwait. We also have plans to increase the amount of prepositioned equipment in the Gulf which will be sufficient to outfit a division, thereby enhancing our ability to rapidly deploy a significantly larger and more capable ground force. To this end, Kuwait has agreed to permit the prepositioning of additional equipment to complete the armored brigade set that is already on the ground in Camp Doha.

The United Nations Security Council, in Resolution 949 of October 15, 1994, condemned Iraq's military deployment toward the border with Kuwait and demanded that Iraq: 1) immediately withdraw all military units recently deployed to southern Iraq; 2) not again use its military or any other forces to threaten its neighbors or U.N. operations in Iraq; 3) not redeploy to the south those forces to be withdrawn or take any other action to enhance its military capacity in southern Iraq; and 4) cooperate fully with the U.N. Special Commission (UNSCOM). In order to ensure that Iraq fully understood our intentions, Ambassador Albright met with Iraq's UN Ambassador, Nizar Hamdun, and explained in precise terms what would constitute an Iraqi violation of Resolution 949. She also left no doubt that our response to any such violation would be swift and firm.

This recent episode is yet another indication that Iraq remains unwilling to comply with the will of the international community. We shall continue to insist that Iraq not threaten its neighbors or intimidate the United Nations and that it take steps to ensure that it never again possesses weapons of mass destruction. The sanctions will be maintained until Iraq complies with all relevant provisions of U.N. Security Council resolutions.

On November 10 the Iraqi government, in an unqualified and irrevocable way, recognized the Iraq-Kuwait boundary demarcated by the relevant U.N. demarcation commission and the sovereignty, territorial integrity, and political independence of the State of Kuwait. This action represented a significant victory for the Security Council, which has resolved to accept nothing short of full compliance with the demands it has placed on Iraq. Although the Security Council welcomed this development, it has also made clear that it will follow closely Iraq's implementation of its decision and will also continue to keep under review Iraq's actions to complete its compliance with all relevant Security Council resolutions.

Iraq has still not complied with Security Council demands to resolve the issue of Kuwaiti MIAs, return Kuwaiti property stolen during the occupation, and renounce terrorism. Iraq has also not met its obligations under resolutions concerning Kuwaiti and third-country nationals it detained during the war and has taken no substantive steps to cooperate fully with the International Committee of the Red Cross (ICRC), beyond agreement to participate in a technical committee being organized by the ICRC. Iraq has also failed to comply with resolutions calling for the end of repression of segments of its civilian population, cooperation with international relief organizations and the equitable distribution of humanitarian relief supplies.

Cooperation by Iraq with the United Nations since 1991 has been meager, sporadic, selective and opportunistic. Taken as a whole, Iraq's record represents a stunning failure to meet the standard set by the Security Council when it set the terms for ending the Gulf War in Resolution 687: to assure the world community of its "peaceful intentions." The purpose of the drafters of Resolution 687—to ensure that Iraq could never again pose a threat to its neighbors or to regional peace and security—remains unfulfilled. On November 14 the Security Council, for the 22nd time, unanimously decided that existing sanctions against Iraq should not be modified.

Despite the lack of cooperation from the Government of Iraq, UNSCOM and the International Atomic Energy Agency have continued their efforts, with the assistance of the United States and other supporting nations, to implement a comprehensive and effective monitoring regime for Iraq. In consultation with UNSCOM Chairman Ekeus, the U.N. Security General reported on October 7 that this regime is "provisionally operational." This effort must be carefully designed to ensure that Iraq cannot rebuild its weapons of mass destruction (WMD) programs, including a convert nuclear program, as

it did before the Gulf War, when it claimed to be in compliance with the Nuclear Nonproliferation Treaty. Continued vigilance is necessary because we believe that Saddam Hussein is committed to rebuilding his WMD capabilities.

Indeed, significant gaps in accounting for Iraq's past programs for WMD continue. There are unresolved issues in each of the four weapons categories (nuclear, long-range missile, chemical, and biological). This has been particularly true in the chemical and biological weapons areas, where Iraq claims to have destroyed large amounts of documentation. Therefore, it is extremely important that the monitoring regime be effective, comprehensive and sustainable. A program of this magnitude is unprecedented and will require continued, substantial assistance for UNSCOM from supporting nations. Rigorous and extensive trial and field testing will be required before UNSCOM can judge the program's effectiveness.

Of increasing concern is UNSCOM's dire financial situation. Chairman Ekeus reports that UNSCOM will have to shut down if funds are not forthcoming immediately. Without more cash, UNSCOM will have to begin phasing down its operations in December and completely disband by mid-February 1995. Some countries in the region have agreed to provide partial emergency funding. While this may take care of the immediate crisis, lack of funding will be a chronic problem.

Chairman Ekeus has told Iraq that it must establish a clear track record of compliance before he can report favorably to the Security Council. We strongly endorse Chairman Ekeus' approach and reject any attempt to limit UNSCOM's flexibility by the establishment of a timetable for determining whether Iraq has complied with Security Council Resolution 715.

The U.N. resolutions regarding Iraq do not prevent the shipment of food or medicine to that country. Between January and August of this year, the U.N. Sanctions Committee received notifications of $2 billion worth of food and $175 million worth of medicine to be shipped to Iraq. During the same period, the Committee approved shipments of $2 billion worth of other items deemed to be for essential civilian needs. Meanwhile, the Government of Iraq has asked the Sanctions Committee for permission to import luxury goods such as liquor, video recorders, leather jackets, brass beds and expensive automobiles. The Iraqi government has continued to maintain a full embargo against its northern provinces and has favored its supporters and the military in the distribution of humanitarian supplies throughout the country.

The Iraqi government has refused to sell up to $1.6 billion in oil as previously authorized by the Security Council in Resolutions 706 and 712. Talks between Iraq and the United Nations on implementing these resolutions ended unsuccessfully in October 1993. Iraq could use proceeds from such sales to purchase foodstuffs, medicines, and materials and supplies for essential civilian needs of its population, subject to U.N. monitoring of sales and the equitable distribution of humanitarian supplies (including to its northern provinces). Iraq's refusal to implement Security Council Resolutions 706 and 712 continues to cause needless suffering.

Proceeds from oil sales also would be used to compensate persons injured by Iraq's unlawful invasion and occupation of Kuwait. Of note regarding oil sales, the Security Council has engaged in discussions with Turkish officials concerning the possible flushing of Iraqi oil now in the Turkish pipeline that extends from Iraq through Turkey. The objective would be to prevent physical deterioration of the Turkish pipeline, which is a unique asset. Such a flushing of the pipeline, if conducted in a manner consistent with the U.N. sanctions regime, would produce the added benefit of financing the import of needed food and medicine into Iraq. However, the Government of Iraq has refused to implement the flushing because it rejects international monitoring of the distribution of humanitarian goods.

The no-fly zones over northern and southern Iraq permit the monitoring of Iraq's compliance with Security Council Resolutions 687 and 688. Over the last three years, the northern no-fly zone has deterred Iraq from a major military offensive in the region. In southern Iraq, the no-fly zone has stopped Iraq's use of aircraft against its population.

Nonetheless, the Iraqi government continues its harsh campaign against its perceived enemies, throughout the country. Baghdad's campaign of economic warfare against the people of northern Iraq continues. In September, the Iraqi regime cut electrical power to the Aqrah/Shirwan districts of Dohuk Governorate. Three hundred fifty thousand people in those districts now confront a lack of water, sanitation, and hospital services. Approximately one million persons in Dohuk Governorate are now reliant on temporary generators for electricity, due to such systematic power cut-offs by the Government of Iraq. Also in northern Iraq, in the vicinity of Mosul, we are watching Iraqi troop movements carefully since Iraq's intentions are still unclear. In the south, Iraq's repression of the Shi'a population, and specifically the Marsh Arabs, and the implementation of a policy of environmental devastation represent a clear intent to target a specific area for reprisals without regard to the impact on innocent civilians. Further, Iraqi forces still wage a land-based artillery campaign in the marshes, and the shelling of marsh villages continues. In the last few years, the population of the region, whose marsh culture has remained essentially unchanged since 3500 B.C., has been reduced by an estimated three-quarters and will soon disappear altogether. The Special Rapporteur of the U.N. Commission on Human Rights (UNHRC), Max van der Stoel, continues to report on the human rights situation in Iraq, particularly the Iraqi military's repression against its civilian populations in the marshes. In his November interim report to the General Assembly, the Special Rapporteur noted the widespread phenomena of political killings, mass executions and state-sponsored terrorism throughout Iraq. He also reported the introduction by the Government of Iraq of new forms of torture, including the amputation of ears and hands and the branding of foreheads for certain economic crimes and for desertion from the military. The Special Rapporteur asserted in previous reports that the Government of Iraq has engaged in war crimes and crimes against humanity, and may have committed violations of the 1948 Genocide Convention. Regarding the Kurds, the Special Rapporteur has judged that the extent and gravity of reported violations place the survival of the Kurds in jeopardy. He also noted the extent to which the Government of Iraq represses and terrorizes the Shi'a clergy in southern cities. The Special Rapporteur has noted that there are essentially no freedoms of opinion, expression or association in Iraq. The Special Rapporteur continues to repeat his recommendation for the establishment of human rights monitors inside Iraq to improve the flow of information and to provide independent verification of reports. We continue to investigate and publicize Iraqi crimes against humanity, war crimes and other violations of international humanitarian law. We will continue to insist that the Government of Iraq allow human rights monitors to be stationed inside Iraq, as called for by the Special Rapporteur.

Examples of Iraqi noncooperation and noncompliance continue in other areas. There have been several incidents in which merchant vessels have entered the Shatt-al-Arab bound for Iran but subsequently have proceeded to Iraqi ports where they have onloaded Iraqi oil. Upon exiting the Shatt-al-Arab these vessels have been diverted by the Maritime Interception Force and their embargo violations have been confirmed. Gulf states are being encouraged to take action against the vessels and oil, with the proceeds eventually being paid to the UN Escrow Account referred to in Security Council Resolution 778.

For more than three years, the Baghdad regime has interfered with relief operations, threatened and harassed relief workers, and refused to issue visas to such workers. We have persuasive evidence that the regime has offered "bounties" to persons willing to assassinate international personnel. U.N. and other humanitarian relief workers, as well as international journalists reporting on the humanitarian situation, have been the victims of car bombs, drive-by shootings and execution-style killings. Ten persons have been injured and two have been killed in such attacks this year.

There is also persuasive evidence linking the Government of Iraq to the July death, under suspicious circumstances, of a noted Shi'a religious figure and three members of his family. These acts are indicative of Iraq's continuing disdain for the United Nations and, in our view, also constitute violations of Security Council Resolutions 687 and 688.

We are monitoring closely the plight of the civilian population everywhere in Iraq. We will persist in our demand that the Government of Iraq comply with the relevant U.N. resolutions so that humanitarian assistance can reach all segments of the society, instead of only the supporters of Saddam Hussein. Our bilateral assistance program in the north will continue, given our access to the north and our ability to ensure that relief reaches vulnerable populations. We also will continue to make every effort, given the numerous practical constraints, to assist the populations in southern and central Iraq through U.N. humanitarian programs. Finally, we will

continue to explore with our allies and Security Council partners the most effective means to compel the Government of Iraq to cooperate on humanitarian and human rights issues.

The U.N. Compensation Commission (UNCC) has received approximately 2.4 million claims thus far, with another 100,000 expected. The United States Government has filed a total of 3,100 individual claims with a total asserted value of over $215 million. Earlier this year, one panel of UNCC Commissioners submitted its report on the first installment of individual claims for serious personal injury or death. The UNCC Commissioners' report recommended awards for a group of about 670 claimants, of which 11 were U.S. claimants. The Governing Council of the UNCC approved the panel's recommendations at its session in late May. This past summer the first U.S. claimants received compensation for their losses. A second group of claims involving death and serious personal injury is expected to be reviewed in the December Governing Council session. At its October session, the Governing Council approved the first set of awards for claimants who were forced to depart suddenly from Iraq or Kuwait during the invasion and occupation. Of the approximately 53,000 claims, close to 200 were from U.S. claimants. However, these awards cannot be paid at this time because there is not enough money in the Compensation Fund. The Governing Council began consideration of the first report and recommendations from the panel of commissioners reviewing itemized individual losses for amounts up to $100,000 (e.g. lost salary or personal property). Due to the importance and complexity of the issues involved, the Governing Council deferred final action on the recommendations until its December session. The Governing Council also decided not to accept additional filings of late individual claims after January 1, 1995.

The United States Government also submitted a total of approximately $1.5 billion in corporate claims against the Government of Iraq, representing about 140 business entities. Those claims represented a multitude of enterprises ranging from small family-owned businesses to large multinational corporations. In addition, in late July the United States Government filed five U.S. Government claims with the UNCC. The five claims were for nonmilitary losses, such as damage to U.S. Government property (e.g., the U.S. Embassy compound in Kuwait) and the costs of evacuating U.S. nationals and their families from Kuwait and Iraq. These U.S. Government claims have an asserted value of about $17 million. In the future, the United States Government also expects to file one or more additional U.S. Government claim(s) involving the costs of monitoring health risks associated with oil well fires and other environmental damage in the Gulf region. The UNCC expects to begin processing corporate claims and government claims in 1995.

Iraq may rejoin the community of civilized nations only through adherence to basic norms of international behavior, adoption of democratic processes, respect for human rights and equal treatment of its people. Iraq's government should represent all of Iraq's people and be committed to the territorial integrity and unity of Iraq. The Iraqi National Congress espouses these goals, the fulfillment of which would make Iraq a stabilizing force in the Gulf region.

In summary, Iraq continues to be a threat to regional peace and security. The oil embargo and other sanctions must remain in place until Iraq demonstrates its peaceful intentions over a sustained period by fully complying with all relevant U.N. Security Council resolutions.

I appreciate the support of the Congress for our efforts, and I will continue to keep the Congress fully informed regarding this important matter.

Sincerely,

WILLIAM J. CLINTON

NOTE: Identical letters were sent to Thomas S. Foley, Speaker of the House of Representatives, and Robert C. Byrd, President pro tempore of the Senate. This letter was released by the Office of the Press Secretary on January 3, 1995.

Letter to Congressional Leaders Transmitting a Report on Loan Guarantees to Israel
December 30, 1994

Dear Mr. Speaker: (Dear Mr. President:)

Enclosed is an unclassified report on the Loan Guarantees to Israel Program and on economic conditions in Israel, as required by section 226(k) of the Foreign Assistance Act of 1961, as amended (Pub. L. 87–195), and section 1205 of the International Security and Development Corporation Act of 1985 (Pub. L. 99–983).

I hope this report will be of use to you.

Sincerely,

WILLIAM J. CLINTON

NOTE: Identical letters were sent to Thomas S. Foley, Speaker of the House of Representatives, and Albert Gore, Jr., President of the Senate. This letter was released by the Office of the Press Secretary on January 3, 1995.

Letter to Congressional Leaders Transmitting a Report on Haiti
December 31, 1994

Dear Mr. Speaker: (Dear Mr. President:)

Attached, pursuant to Section 3 of Public Law 103–423, is the third monthly report on the situation in Haiti.

Sincerely,

WILLIAM J. CLINTON

NOTE: Identical letters were sent to Thomas S. Foley, Speaker of the House of Representatives, and Robert C. Byrd, President pro tempore of the Senate. This letter was released by the Office of the Press Secretary on January 3, 1995.

Exchange With Reporters After Duck Hunting Near Cotton Plant, Arkansas
January 3, 1995

The President. Good morning, everybody.

Q. Was it a fair fight?

The President. Two for two. We only saw two.

Q. You've got two there?

The President. Yep.

Q. Is that the limit?

The President. No, but it was our limit today because it's all we saw.

Q. And are you responsible for their demise, sir?

The President. Yes, I shot them both. They let me shoot them, so I shot them.

Q. It's cold and it's wet out there. Where's the fun part?

The President. Well, the most fun part is just being out there when the light comes up and seeing the ducks come across. We had a lot of geese, too. You know, the geese fly in these huge V formations; they're really beautiful.

And we all shot them with weapons, I might add, that were not affected by the crime bill, except they were protected.

Q. What kind of weapons?

The President. We all had our different shotguns. But I just want to make that point to all the sports men and women who are watching this. Contrary to what some of them were told in the last election, we're all still hunting and nobody has lost their gun. And we did the right thing to ban the assault weapons.

But I had a great time out there today. The best thing, like I said, about it today was just watching—on a cloudy day like this the ducks can see the hunters, so they're less likely to come down in large numbers, but we saw a huge number of them flying around. It was quite beautiful.

Q. Are they fooled by the duck calls?

The President. On a clear day, the duck calls help.

Q. Can we hear your technique?

The President. The duck call? No. I got this—this duck call is made in Stuttgart, Arkansas, which is close to here, where they have the international duck calling championship every year. And the man that made this call is now the mayor of the city.

Q. Does it work?

The President. It works fine.

Q. Six dollars at the Wal-Mart.

[*At this point, a reporter blew a duck call.*]

The President. Do it! Do it! [*Laughter*]

Q. What do you think?

The President. A little more down here. [*Laughter*]

Q. I'm from Brooklyn.

The President. For Brooklyn, it's good. [*Laughter*]

Q. Do you feel like you're really on vacation now, sir?

The President. Yes—well, I wish I had a little more time to spend. But it was wonderful. We had a great time out there, and I'm here with some old friends.

Q. The male bonding kind of thing?

The President. Well, the guys I was here with, the ones I was here with today, we bonded a long time ago. They may be interested in unbonding. [*Laughter*]

Q. Do you eat the ducks?

The President. Oh, yes. Yes, we're just trying to figure—I'm sitting here trying to figure out how I can get them back to the White House.

Q. Do you clean them?

The President. No, not lately I haven't. When I was younger I did that. I probably—maybe I'll do it again.

Q. How far off are they when you shoot them?

The President. How far were these away?

Hunter. The white one was a long way.

The President. One of them was—how far were they, Bob?

Bob Robinson. Oh, anywhere from 70 to 80 yards. The President made two great shots.

The President. I got lucky today.

Q. And who retrieves them?

The President. Actually, Bob went out and—no, you didn't go. They went out—we had a boat and got them today. Sometimes you have dogs get them but today we—people retrieved them in a flat-bottom boat. But it was a wonderful morning.

[At this point, the President left the reporters to speak with his fellow hunters. He then resumed speaking with reporters.]

The President. We didn't see many today, but we got two shots. There were a couple more that came in close, but they came in so fast that we weren't ready. But these were really the only two we could shoot at. And I had the charity—this crew over there, they all sat there and let me shoot at it. *[Laughter]*

Q. Are you glad to be home?
The President. Yes. I really started feeling like a person when I was about 5 minutes out on the water today.

NOTE. The President spoke at approximately 9 a.m. at the Robinson farm. A tape was not available for verification of the content of this exchange.

Exchange With Reporters at Cotham's Mercantile Store in Scott, Arkansas
January 3, 1995

The President. We have a lot of people who come in who still use it as a country store, but as you can see, a lot of people come in and eat every day. We have people drive every day from Little Rock. But it's a regular pharmacy.

Q. It reminds me of the stores along that one street in Plains, Georgia, where Jimmy Carter lived. They had stores like this.

The President. They've even got a little museum here that I helped them put together, Plantation Museum. You saw that land coming back, all that farm land you saw, this is the heart of our rice country. We grow about 40 percent of America's rice on the land that we came across today.

Q. Forty percent?
The President. Yes.
Q. Wow.
The President. Arkansas is the number one rice-producing State in the country, more than California or anyplace. And you can see why, because of all the little—you see all the little rivers and creeks and everything.

Q. You've got the paddies.
The President. Yes. Good topsoil, and it's also a lot of high-tech stuff. They literally flood those rice fields. They have a little laser beam that they go down and throw that laser beam across that rice field to make sure the water level is just right, not too low so that the crop—*[inaudible]*—not too high so it rots. Just right. It's amazing.

Anyway—and we also went through—did you see the cotton field we went through?

Q. Sure did.

The President. And the name of the nearest town to where we were hunting today was Cotton Plant.

Q. Right. In fact, that's the dateline on all our stories.

The President. And cotton was a big crop here, but closer to the river, going back before the Civil War, but back here all the way up to the point. But that land, most of that land we saw today, we drove across was hardwood forest until the twenties. The timber companies came in and tore all the hardwood down. But because the topsoil was so thick, because the water was so great, it became great agriculturally. Fifty-three percent of this State is still covered with timberland. You couldn't tell that from today. It's a very different place. But anyway, that's——

Q. You sound homesick for——

The President. This was all a big part of my political base, all these places we've been through here today. I never lost—this State.

Q. *[Inaudible]*—county?

The President. Woodruff County. Benton County is the next——

Q. Woodruff County is where we were this morning.

The President. Woodruff County.

Q. Do you have a recommendation for us for lunch?

The President. All of our counties here have big sportsmen, like Tom's sponsor of Ducks Unlimited. With all these ducks, the sky is full of ducks and geese, and they come down from Canada down what's called the Mississippi Flyway, right down the river. And the reason that they're now here is that it's gotten colder up north. The colder the weather is, the more birds fly south.

Q. Will they winter here or move on? They'll winter here?

Q. The President. No, they'll go further.

Q. Do you do any other kind of hunting here?

The President. Yeah. I usually go hunting—when I was living here—my ears are bad so I don't hunt very much. But I'd usually go hunting—I'd usually go duck hunting once a year and usually do something else once a year.

Q. Do you have pheasant hunting here?

The President. No. Turkey hunting, a lot of turkeys, a lot of deer, quail—lot of quail.

Q. Good fishing around here, too, isn't there?

The President. Wonderful, wonderful. Bass, trout.

I don't know if you guys saw the—when we were coming up, there were hundreds of ducks just like that. That's illegal to stop along the side of the road and shoot them.

Q. Because it's not fair or——

The President. Because it's not fair and because you can't just stop on the road and shoot them. And of course, there's a limit. You can only shoot two mallards a day.

Q. Do you ever feel like a sitting duck resting on the water sometime? [*Laughter*]

The President. Yes, I do——

Q. I think that's a political——

The President. [*Inaudible*]

Q. What is the deal with—our driver said if you shot the female first, that was it; you don't get to shoot anymore. How can you tell what you shoot first?

The President. You can tell when you go pick them up. [*Laughter*] There are different rules for different kinds of ducks, too. It changes every year. But one of the things that—one of the best organized things in America is the wildlife preservation. The hunters and fishermen are, in a way, the best conservationists in the country. They worked hard on this whole way of replenishing the duck species. You can see it—primarily, in America you see it here on the Mississippi Flyway. And then where we are, over on the Eastern Shore of Maryland you see a lot where the ducks fly down that way, along the coast, you see a lot of that. But there's been an enormous amount of money invested, some through public funds, largely through private funds, for things like that to replenish the species. And the length of the season, the timing

of the season, and the daily limits are carefully calibrated to allow maximum enjoyment of the sport while keeping the supplies replenished.

When I was Governor, I used to have a picture on my wall of a place in this country about 20 miles from here, back in the thirties, one of those open ponds with all the stumps like you saw today. Literally a hundred thousand ducks covered it, blanketed as far as you could see. And the population went way down. Now it's all been—[*inaudible*]—I don't think it will ever be able to—[*inaudible*]—we do the same thing with the deer population, very carefully managed. And it's a big deal. We still have factories that close——

Q. [*Inaudible*]—selection of the duck stamp each year now?

The President. No, I know that—my role in all this when I was Governor was to stay up—[*inaudible*]—fish commission. In a State like ours, it's an enormously important thing. Over half the adults in the State have a hunting or a fishing license.

Q. And you do, too, sir?

The President. I have a lifetime license. After I served as Governor for 10 years—you still have to buy the stamps every year, which we did. We're legal today. You still have to buy the stamps every year. But I've got a—they gave me a lifetime hunting and fishing license. Sort of like a gold watch—get to use it.

Q. Really. That's quite a perk.

Q. When is the last time you had this much fun?

The President. Oh, I don't know.

Q. Never. [*Laughter*]

The President. It's been a while. I had a good time. And the people I was hunting with today, they've been my friends for 20 years. That makes a difference. They're good people, farmers, people I've known for a long, long time.

Q. You said you felt like a real person.

The President. Yes, I liked it there. Old Bobby Robinson, he came out and talked to you——

Q. He was great.

Q. Yes, he was great.

The President. He's the salt of the Earth.

Q. He was bragging up his wife's breakfast. Was that pretty good?

The President. Unbelievable. I told Bobby, when I come over to see her I don't—it doesn't matter to me what happens, as long as she feeds me. [*Laughter*]

Q. Is it a combined license in Arkansas?

The President. You can. You can buy combined; you can buy separate. You can buy licenses—in the hunting season you can buy a hunting license, or you can buy a license to hunt separate things by season if you want. And also, you can buy different fishing licenses. We have a lot of people coming in on weekend fishing trips, tourists and all that, so there is a whole—the game and fish commission has a whole different menu of things depending on what it is you want to hunt, whether you want to hunt or fish, what you want.

Q. [*Inaudible*]

The President. That's "American Gothic." Have you ever seen it?

Q. Oh, yes, the original. I hadn't seen this version of it.

The President. That's just sort of a tongue-in-cheek thing that an Arkansas artist did.

Q. Your favorite?

The President. Yes, yes. We've got one. We've got the original back at the White House. And they've got an old Governor's picture of me, and another one about 10 years old, unsigned.

Q. When you only hunt once a year, how do you keep your timing to be able to lead a duck?

The President. I hit the one. It was on the fly. And the other one I hit at a very long distance. It was almost—but it was a very long distance. I just—it was a good gun. I had a good gun. It was a little Remington with a shorter barrel, three-shot limit.

That's another interesting thing about this assault weapons deal. Some of these people that were opposing the 10—magazine limit on the assault weapons overlooked the fact that they were very happy to have a three-shot limit on the semiautomatic for shooting ducks. That's the law today. And when I was in Maryland last year, I was laughing—some of the folks up there——

Q. You can only put in three cartridges?

The President. Yes. You put in three, and you've got to—if they hold four, you put in three instead of four.

Q. Are you tickled about the school dedication tomorrow?

The President. Oh, yes. Yes, I'm real happy about that.

[*At this point, the President finished his lunch and then went outside, where he again spoke with reporters.*]

Q. You're ducking us. [*Laughter*]

Q. Thanks, Mark [Mark Knoller, CBS Radio]. Now you've wrecked his mood. [*Laughter*]

The President. I'll tell you what, I heard you on that duck call, it was like a magnet—[*laughter*]—come flying into the pond. [*Laughter*]

Q. We went out shopping last night. We had to go to three stores to get them. We went to Montgomery Ward, and they were sold out of duck calls.

The President. Well, they would be, here.

Q. Well, they were.

The President. This is our pastime at this time of year. But you can buy—you can have a duck call, pay anywhere from $5 to $125.

Q. We saw that, $40 for a duck call. The one around your neck looked like an expensive one, too.

The President. Yes. Well, like I said, those are hand-made. And the guy that hand-made that is the mayor of Stuttgart, which is where they have the international duck calling championship.

Q. [*Inaudible*]

The President. Oh, yeah. You know, I've worked like a dog for the first 2 years. I worked every weekend. I worked at night. And I think I need to do a little more of this. And I'm glad I did the work, and I'm glad we got done what we did, but I also think it's important to kind of keep your batteries charged, your roots watered.

Q. Batteries charged for the start of a Republican Congress tomorrow?

The President. I'm looking forward to it.

Q. Somebody has to ask that question, right?

The President. I'm looking forward to it.

Q. Not dreading it?

The President. No. I just don't want to talk about it until tomorrow. [*Laughter*] I want to enjoy my——

Q. So much for the duck call.

Q. Got everything?

The President. No, no. These guys don't have their hamburgers yet. They said 5 minutes they'd have everybody's. I'm sorry, I thought you all had been fed.

Q. It's been a great day, Mr. President. Thank you.

The President. It has. I'm sorry it's raining on us. I guess I'd better not go play golf. [*Laughter*]

Q. [*Inaudible*]—worse than when you played golf in Martha's Vineyard on Labor Day?

The President. Yes, I've played golf in a lot worse. I've played golf here in 35 degrees sleet. But I had my uniform. It takes a special uniform for that.

Q. You can't golf in a duck uniform, is that it?

The President. You know, Hillary gave me a great Goretex suit that you can wear in the rain. It's rain-repellent. I've played a lot of golf in it.

Q. Doesn't it restrict your movement?

The President. No, because it's a double extra large. It's too big, so you can just swing away. [*Laughter*] But it's a—yes, it cuts down on your distance. But when you're out there in a hailstorm, you don't expect to hit it very far. [*Laughter*]

Are we ready?

Q. Can we get one picture?

The President. Oh, sure. This young lady made it all the way from here to Mount Vernon College. Good for you. Good luck to you. What do you teach?

Q. English, 12th grade.

The President. Hang in there.

Q. Are you going to go to the Plantation——

The President. I'm going to go home and put on some different duds and talk to Hillary about it. Then I'll go down to the Plantation Museum. Did you see it down there?

NOTE: The President spoke at approximately 11:50 a.m. A tape was not available for verification of the content of this exchange.

Question-and-Answer Session With Students at William Jefferson Clinton Elementary Magnet School in Sherwood, Arkansas
January 4, 1995

The President. Well, good morning.

Students. Good morning.

The President. It's cold out there, isn't it?

Students. Yes.

The President. But it's warm in here.

Students. Yes.

The President. Do you like your new school?

Students. Yes.

The President. I want to congratulate you on being in positions of leadership in this school. I want to say how glad I am to be in this media center and how pleased I am it's named for my wife, who did a lot of work to try to help make sure we created schools like this magnet school that children and their parents could choose to come to, and it could give you very special learning opportunities. I'm very, very happy about that. And I'm glad to see all of you.

Hillary Clinton. I'd like to ask how many—are there any kindergartners here? Good. Now, this is your first year of school, and you're already going to be helping to lead the school. That's great.

How many first-graders do we have? Congratulations, first-graders. How about second-graders? That is wonderful. Now, some of you who are in first and second grade, you were at different schools last year, right? So you're here. That's good. You get to help create the school.

How about third-graders? Ah, third-graders, that's really important. And I see a T-shirt that goes with the school. That's nice.

The President. Stand up, and let's look at that T-shirt.

Hillary Clinton. That's really nice. How about fourth-graders? Where are the fourth-graders? You have a lot of responsibility, I know. How about fifth-graders? Fifth-graders—great. I can see we get more and more as we move up the classes. And then, how about sixth-graders?

Well, thank you. This is really an exciting opportunity to help start a school, which is what all of you are doing, and to try to make sure it gets on the right track. So I want to thank you for doing that. It's a big responsibility.

I once was in the first class of a new school when I was in high school, and you really have a lot of chances to set the standards for everybody who comes after you. So thank you for doing that.

The President. Are you excited about starting a school?

Students. Yes.

The President. Someday all of you will know more about me than I do. [*Laughter*]

Hillary Clinton. I know. We wanted to be sure if you had any questions for us, you'd have a chance to ask, okay? My goodness! We won't be able to answer every question. [*Laughter*]

The President. Let's take—shall we start in grades, going backwards? A sixth-grader. Go ahead.

Q. How do you deal with criticism?

The President. How do I deal with criticism? Better on some days than others. [*Laughter*] I think the important thing about criticism is to try to take it very seriously; that is, can we learn from criticism? Benjamin Franklin, one of our Founding Fathers, said, "Our critics are our friends for they show us our faults." And since no one is perfect, your critics can help you learn to do better. But it's important not to take criticism personally. That is, a lot of times people try to hurt you personally, and you can't let that happen.

So if someone criticizes you, ask yourself, "Is it true what they're saying?" And if it's true, then say, "Well, I'm going to try to improve. I'm going to try to do better." Don't let anybody put you down as a person. Too much criticism today is designed to hurt people personally and to hurt them in the eyes of other people. That's wrong. But criticism itself can be very good.

Hillary Clinton. That's a good question, because I would bet that as all of you who are on the student council and are ambassadors make decisions, you will get some criticism. You'll have friends who will say, "Why did you do that?" or "I don't like you anymore," or "I don't agree with that." So that was a very good question to ask.

Of course, the best way to handle criticism is to remember the Golden Rule. You all remember the Golden Rule?

Students. Yes.

Hillary Clinton. From church and Sunday school? If you can treat other people the way you want to be treated, then you can learn from criticism but not get pulled down by it, not be upset by it.

The President. And you should think about that, too, not only how you deal with criticism but if you're going to criticize. If you want to be a critic, that is, if you see something in school you don't like or you see someone doing something you don't like, think about how you're

going to say that so they will be able to listen and hear you, but you won't be hurting them.

So you go up and say, "You're doing something I disagree with. I think you're a good person, but I don't agree with what you're doing. Here is what I think you should do." Do it like that, instead of saying, "I don't like you anymore. You're not a good person. Goodbye." [*Laughter*] You see what I mean? So you can do it. It's important to receive criticism, but it's also important to give it in a good spirit.

Is there a fifth-grader with a question? Let's see, go ahead.

Q. Why is it important to swear in when you become President?

The President. To swear in?

Q. Yes.

Hillary Clinton. When you become President.

The President. That's a very good question. Because when the President swears the Oath of Office, when he puts his hand on the Bible and swears before God and all the American people to uphold the Constitution and laws of the United States, that increases the obligation the President feels inside, in his heart, to do the job. All the American people see the President making that promise, and they then, no matter who they voted for—whom they voted for—come together as a people and see that the President is now the President. And that seals the decision of the election and makes it more than an election, it makes it a matter of law and also makes it a matter of conviction to the American people. It's a very important symbolic thing.

Is there a fourth-grader with a question?

Q. Why didn't you let your goal down of being President?

Hillary Clinton. I'm sorry, we couldn't hear you.

Q. Why didn't you let your goal down of being President?

The President. I didn't. What do you mean? I don't understand the question, I'm sorry. Say it again.

Q. Why didn't you let your goal down of being President?

Hillary Clinton. Oh, how did he have the goal of being President all the time he was growing up, and why didn't he give up or why didn't he quit?

The President. Oh, why didn't I give up on my goal of being President? Is that what you're asking? That's a very good question. There are some days when I still ask myself that. [*Laughter*] That's a very good question.

Well, when I started running for President and I started having the elections, you know, to run—because you have to go and run in a lot of different States to get the nomination of your party, and then you run in the general election—there were a lot of times when I got discouraged, and a lot of difficult things happened.

But I was able to hold on to the goal by always remembering why I wanted to be President, that I wanted to help people like you have a better future. I wanted to help your parents have more jobs and better opportunities. I wanted to help our country solve its problems and take advantage of all the wonderful opportunities that are out there for us. So whenever I would get really discouraged and really down, I would always remember why I was doing the work.

And you should remember that, because if you set a goal for yourself, particularly if it's a high goal and especially if you can't do it tomorrow, if it takes next week or next month or next year or years ahead, a lot of things will happen in life to discourage you. People will criticize you. You will honestly make mistakes. There will be times when you wonder whether you're smart enough or strong enough or sometimes even whether you're good enough to achieve your goal. And you just have to keep remembering in your mind and in your heart a good thing you want to do—why do you want to achieve this goal?—and keep that deep inside. And if you do that, then you won't be discouraged. You can take all the disappointments and just keep right on going.

Okay? That's a very good question.

Is there a third-grader with a question? Go ahead.

Q. What made you want to become the President?

The President. I wanted to become the President because I thought the President has a unique opportunity. There's no job like it in the United States. In a way, there's no job like it anywhere in the world. And I thought at this time in our history, in the history of the United States, the President had a unique opportunity and a unique responsibility to try to make our economy strong again, to try to improve our education system, to try to make sure our country could lead the world to be a more peaceful

place, to be a more free place, to be a more prosperous place, and to also secure for you the American dream, the dream that if you work hard, if you obey the law, if you develop the abilities God gave you, you can do anything you want to do, you can be anything you want to be.

And I wanted to make sure that you had that dream. That's the dream I had when I was your age, and I wanted to make sure you had it. That's why I ran for President.

Hillary Clinton. And we hope all of you have dreams and goals, too.

The President. You don't have to have the same dream I did or the same dream Hillary did, but you should have your own dream. Always you should be thinking about: What do I want to do when I grow up? What do I want to do when I'm in high school? What do I want to do in grade school here? How do I want to be treated as a person, and how do I want to treat other people?

Think about how you want your life to be, and then go out and do what you think about. You can do it. It's not easy, and you'll mess up now and again. We all do. Everybody's not perfect; no one is perfect. But you have to have your dreams.

Is there a second-grader with a question? Go ahead.

Q. Why is the White House in Washington, DC? Why did they build it in Washington, DC?

The President. That is a great question: Why is the White House in Washington, DC? Well, when our country got started, there were 13 States. Now how many are there?

Students. Fifty.

The President. Fifty, that's right. There were only 13 when we started. And these States were very jealous of one another. That is, the main thing they had in common, the 13 States, was that they all wanted to be independent of Great Britain. And the Revolutionary War was fought to make them free of Great Britain, and they all joined together in this fight. But for a long time they couldn't agree on what their relationship to each other would be. That is, would all these States be more or less independent and just get together every now and then to do certain things, or would they join together in one country with one government?

Well, finally they decided they would join together in one country, with a National Government, but the States would keep their separate governments, and they would have control over how many cities and counties they had in each State. Well, they needed a Capital for the National Government, but they didn't want to give the Capital to any particular State, see, because they had all been very jealous of each other. They all had been independent. And each State, even little Delaware or Rhode Island, thought they were as important as big New York or Pennsylvania. So no one wanted to give the Capital to any particular State.

So they set aside a piece of land where Washington is now and created the District of Columbia as an independent entity, a creation, if you will, of the National Government, and put the Capital there. And they put the White House there. And those were the first two big buildings in Washington, DC, the Capitol of the United States and the President's house, where the President lives and works.

Hillary Clinton. And we hope you can all come visit us.

The President. Would you like to come see it?

Students. Yes.

Hillary Clinton. We'd love to show you.

The President. Well, I hope you can come someday.

Is there a first-grader with a question?

Q. How old are you?

The President. How old am I? How old do you think I am? [*Laughter*] I'm very old. [*Laughter*] I'm 48.

Hillary Clinton. Forty-eight years old.

The President. And I'll be 49 on August 19th. And Hillary is younger than I am. [*Laughter*] Anybody else have a birthday on August 19th? You do?

Hillary Clinton. In August? Is your birthday August 19th?

Student. February.

Hillary Clinton. February? [*Laughter*] That's when Chelsea's birthday is. Chelsea has a birthday in February.

The President. Is there a first-grader with a question? We did first grade. Kindergartner? Go ahead.

Q. Would you like any visitors?

The President. Would I like visitors?

Hillary Clinton. We'd love to have you come visit.

The President. We love visitors, and we especially love visitors from home. We love it when people from Arkansas come up and see us. But we have visitors from all the States, and we have visitors from all over the world. And in the morning we start tours in the White House, on most days. People can come and see the White House where the President lives. They just come in and see. Very often I stop and talk to them and see people from all over America there.

Well, should I ask the principal if we can continue? How are we doing, Ms. Parker?

Jackye Parker. Well, I think it's about time for us to have to leave.

The President. Well, I wish I could answer all your questions.

Hillary Clinton. You have good questions.

The President. You guys ask great questions. And I want you to have a wonderful day. I want you to remember what we said about your dreams. Will you do that?

Students. Yes.

Hillary Clinton. Oh, we have 4-year-olds here.

The President. Oh, 4-year-olds. Is there a 4-year-old with a question?

Hillary Clinton. Are you a 4-year-old? Here's a 4-year-old with a question.

The President. What's your question?

Q. Does your cat, Socks, sleep in the White House?

Hillary Clinton. Yes, our cat, Socks, does sleep in the White House. And if you come to visit, maybe you'll get to see Socks, because when he's not in the White House he's outside of the White House. And the President's office is called the Oval Office, and Socks hangs out outside the Oval Office. [*Laughter*] And then he travels everywhere; he visits everywhere. You know, Socks gets letters. If you want to write to Socks, Socks gets letters, and he sends back a picture.

The President. With a paw print on it.

Hillary Clinton. Right, that he has signed. [*Laughter*] So I will tell him that you were asking for him, okay?

The President. Yes, I can see Socks every day. We put him right outside my office. I can turn around, look outside the window, and there he is.

Hillary Clinton. Thank you all so much.

The President. Have a wonderful day.

Hillary Clinton. And a wonderful year, too.

The President. Bye. I'll see you later.

NOTE: The President spoke at 8:53 a.m. in the Hillary Rodham Clinton Media Center of William Jefferson Clinton Elementary Magnet School.

Remarks at the Dedication of William Jefferson Clinton Elementary Magnet School in Sherwood
January 4, 1995

Thank you very much. First of all, I want to thank Mario. He gave a pretty good speech, didn't he? I mean—[*applause*]—give him a hand. He looked fine. He spoke with confidence and strength. And he was brief. He's going to win a lot more elections if he keeps doing that. [*Laughter*]

Jackye Parker, thank you for making Hillary and me and all of us feel so welcome today. Reedie Ray, thank you for your leadership on the school board and for your comments. To my old friend Bobby Lester, thank you for your heartfelt remarks and for your lifetime of devotion to the children of our State. To the teachers and the parents, the district officials, all of you who are here; to the mayors of Little Rock and North Little Rock, of Jacksonville and Sherwood; to the county officials, I'd like to say a special word of welcome and thanks for their attendance. To Governor and Mrs. Tucker, thank you for being here and for your leadership of our State. I thank my dear stepfather, Dick Kelley, for coming here today. I am glad to have him and the Clinton connection here. And I thank my pastor, Reverend Rex Horn, for coming. Thank you for being here, and many others I probably should introduce.

I just was in the media center named for Hillary, and we met with a representative group of students who asked us questions, everything from whether Socks really sleeps in the White House to how I handle criticism. So if I forgot to introduce someone, we'll see how I handle criticism when this is over. [*Laughter*]

This is a wonderful way for us to start the new year. I've had a great stay at home, and this is a great way for me to leave Arkansas to go back to begin work with the new Congress and facing our new future.

You know, I was apprehensive when I heard that you were going to name this school after me. Most people don't have a school named

after them until they're not around anymore. [*Laughter*] And here I am, apparently healthy and able to enjoy it and very, very happy about it and proud of it. I'm proud of it because so much of my work as Governor of this State and so much of my work as President of our country is tied to education and to the absolute necessity for all of our people to be able to learn and learn and learn.

I thank you for making this dedication a family affair, for naming the multipurpose room for my mother, and especially for naming the library and media center for Hillary, because as Mr. Lester especially knows, she worked very, very hard to take all the districts in our county here out of court and put them back in the business of teaching our children and to help create these magnet schools which could be a magnet for the imagination and the potential of all the children of this area without regard to their race or their background or their family circumstances.

I thank you for your mission, which is a real picture of America's future, core knowledge, technology with a special emphasis on communications. If you think about it, we all need more core knowledge in a society where success is based on what you know and not just how hard you work. We all need to master technology because our society is changing so fast. When these children are our age, they will be dealing with things in technology that we cannot even imagine now.

And we all need to learn how to communicate with one another better, because while we want to be independent, we know that we are dependent on one another for our common success. And unless we can understand each other and communicate our deepest feelings and values and convictions, we won't be successful.

You know, when I was a Governor here, I had a very clear sense that Arkansas needed to work on two things above all others. One is to create more jobs and to be more competitive in getting jobs into this State. The other was to provide for the education of our children and the training of our adults so that we could compete and win in this tough global economy. It took a long time to do it. I am very proud of the work that Governor Tucker and the others at our State level and all the folks at the local are still doing in that regard.

The day before yesterday I heard something that was music to my ears when one of the Governor's economic development officers told me that the toughest problem they're facing now in recruiting new industry is trying to convince people from other States and other countries that there really will be enough people here to fill those new jobs, because we have the lowest unemployment rate we've had in nearly 20 years. That is a wonderful, wonderful circumstance.

And I want every one of you to know, as I'm sure you do, that that didn't happen overnight. The credit goes to thousands, indeed tens of thousands of people, who worked for years and years and years to turn our State around economically and to build our State up educationally.

If you think about where America is today, poised on the 21st century, that is what we need to be doing in the United States. And we need to understand that just as our State couldn't turn all of its challenges around overnight, neither can the United States. But unless we begin and unless we stick at the task and unless we refuse to be diverted, to be jerked from one end of the spectrum to the other, and keep our eye on the future, we cannot succeed.

These children deserve a future that is worthy of the work being done by the teachers, the parents in this school. That's what they deserve, and we've got to give it to them.

I have worked hard for 2 years to try to clean up some of the problems I found when I became President. We have taken now $11,000 in debt off of the family—every family in Arkansas by reducing the deficit—$11,000 off of these children's future. We have expanded the ability of Americans to sell our goods and services to other countries, more than ever before. And we now have more than 5 million new jobs in our country.

But we know that a lot of folks are still struggling with the same problems we dealt with here for so many years: how to get and keep a good job, how to provide health care and education and other necessities for their families, how to make sure their children have a good education. And so, as I leave to go back to Washington, I'm going back to challenge the Congress to do what is necessary to guarantee the future of the next generation of Americans, and this present—of this generation of Americans as we move into the 21st century. I want them to adopt what I call a middle class bill of rights, to keep the American dream alive by promoting education and strengthening family. And I hope the Congress will adapt and accept that challenge.

You know, anybody can come up and say, "I want to give you a tax cut," and make people happy in the short run. What I want to do is reduce taxes for people to invest in the education of their children and their own training and skills, so we can go forward and grow this economy.

So I say to all of you—I got a question from one of the students today that I want every grownup here to think about as we think about what we want for our country. One of the students asked me when we were in the other room meeting, he said, "How did you not give up on your dreams of being President?" So I ask all of you, first of all, do you have a dream, and second, how are you going to not give up on it, just like the young student asked me?

My dream for our country is that when we go into this next century we will still be the strongest country in the world, leading the world toward peace and freedom and democracy and prosperity. My dream for America is that the American dream will still be alive, the middle-class dream that if you work hard and obey the law you can make the most of yourself, you can do anything you want to do.

When I was born in this State right after World War II and nearly everybody in Arkansas was very poor, mothers and fathers were giving their children that dream. And we ought to give it to this generation of children.

So I say to all of you: Let's take the lessons of the children. Let's pay attention when people are talking to us. Let's listen to all sides of the argument. Let's be good citizens and discuss the great challenges facing our country. Let's discount all the politics of personal destruction and enhance our ability to think about what is true, what is fair, and what is important. Let us take responsibility for the future of this country and commit ourselves to economic opportunity and to education and to doing that in a way that strengthens the American community, so that we come together instead of being more and more divided.

To the students I say: This is a beautiful building. I am honored that my name is on it. I am honored that a room is named for my mother and that a room is named for my wife, who worked so hard for your education. But the really important thing about the building is you. It's what you do here every day. I want you to learn and learn and learn.

I want you to say no to the bad things that will face you. Say no to violence and no to drugs and no to people who want to take your future away from you.

But more importantly, I want you to say yes: Yes, I have a dream for what I can be. Yes, I'm going to live out my dream. Yes, I'm going to do everything I can in this school to learn and to grow, to be a good person, to have a great life. That's what education is all about. I want you to be good people and have great lives. Then, having my name on this school will be the greatest honor any person could ever have.

Good luck. God bless you, and thank you very much.

NOTE: The President spoke at 9:44 a.m. in the cafetorium. In his remarks, he referred to Mario Hood, president of the student council; Jackye Parker, principal; Reedie Ray, president of the board of education; and Bobby Lester, superintendent of schools.

Remarks and an Exchange With Reporters on the Legislative Agenda
January 5, 1995

The President. I want to welcome the new congressional leadership and congratulate them. I was pleased with what I heard and saw yesterday, and I think that we're off to a good start. The real work is now beginning.

I note that there are several areas where I believe that we can work together and where I hope we can work rapidly, congressional reform, the line-item veto. I hope we can do something on lobbying reform and on campaign finance reform. I believe that there are areas we can work together on welfare reform, on health care reform. We can do a lot of things.

I think we all know that we're expert in stopping things. What we want to do is prove now we can work together to make things happen. And I'm encouraged by what I've heard and seen.

I also think there is a consensus in this country that we shouldn't do anything that would increase the deficit, hurt the middle class, hurt poor people who are trying to work their way into the middle class, or do anything that would undermine our economic recovery. So on that basis, I think we can look forward to a good Congress. I'm excited about it and ready to go. And I'm glad they're here.

Q. Is it like a compromise—between you and me—[*laughter*]—is it going to be compromise or combat?

The President. My answer to that is, Mr. Gingrich will whisper into your right ear, and I will whisper into your left ear. [*Laughter*]

NOTE: The President spoke at 10:13 a.m. in the Cabinet Room at the White House, prior to a meeting with congressional leaders. A tape was not available for verification of the content of these remarks.

Remarks on the Appointment of Michael D. McCurry as Assistant to the President and Press Secretary and an Exchange With Reporters
January 5, 1995

The President. This is a live event. Now listen, you all have to be respectful. I just saw CNN describe this as a live event. [*Laughter*]

To none of your surprise, I am very pleased to announce the appointment of Mike McCurry as the Assistant to the President and the White House Press Secretary. He has done a very fine job representing our administration at the Department of State since I took office. He has dealt with the wide range of very sensitive, complicated, and difficult issues, and he's done it very well.

He has almost two decades of experience here in Washington, but to give you an idea of the kind of person he is in spite of that, the only pictures on his wall are the pictures of his wife and his two children. And they have a third one on the way. Debra and Mike told me on the way out here that they were the embodiment of the family values of this administration. [*Laughter*] And let me say I appreciate the personal sacrifice that both of them are making for Mike to do this job.

Legislative Agenda

Before I turn the podium over to Mr. Panetta and officially welcome Mike McCurry, let me say that, as all of you know, I had my first meeting today with the new bipartisan leadership of the Congress. I was very pleased with it in terms of tone and substance. I congratulated them in the House on passing the bill that requires Congress to live under the laws it imposes on the private sector. That bill passed the House last year by a similar margin, but it didn't pass the Senate. I hope it will this time, and I pledge to sign it quickly.

I'd also like to see further movement on political reform in areas where we clearly agree: the line-item veto, the unfunded mandates issue. We can do a lot of business together for the benefit of the country.

The other thing that happened in the meeting today that really impressed me was an acknowledgement by the Members of the Congress who have been here for years and years in both parties that they made a mistake back in 1981 to adopt a bidding war in the tax cuts that gave us what became known as "trickle-down economics" and quadrupled the national debt. And they agreed that we ought to have a limit to how much we cut revenues, determined by how much we can pay for that with spending cuts, so that there is going to be, apparently, no attempt to go back to what I call trickle-down economics, to exploding the deficit and a ratification of the work of the last 2 years in reducing the deficit by $700 billion, which is about $11,000 a family in this country. I was happy with that result.

I think there will be a lot of other things we can do, but I hope now that the House has taken one vote in the reform area, they will keep on going with the line-item veto, with the unfunded mandates legislation, and hopefully, too, with lobby reform and other reforms. I'm sorry the lobby reform legislation didn't pass yesterday, but it can pass on its own merits, and it's a very important part of what we need to do to restore the confidence of the American people in our Government here.

Thank you very much.

Q. President Clinton, it almost sounds as if you're saying that the country is better off because Republicans won the majority in Congress.

The President. No. The country is better off because we reduced the deficit, produced 5 billion jobs, expanded trade by record amounts, and did some things to help ordinary people deal with their lives. But people are living through a time of great uprooting, with great changes in their lives. They voted to give the majority control in Congress to the Republicans.

My job is not to do what they did. My job is not to stand in the way and be an obstructionist force. My job is not to practice the politics of personal destruction. My job is to work with them to try to help build this country. And that's what I'm going to do.

If they want to keep bringing the deficit down, that's something we started. If they want to reduce the Government, that's something we began. If they want to pass welfare reform, if they want to deal with health care reform, if they want to deal with these governmental reform issues that I have supported for years, like the line-item veto, the country can be better off. Yes, the country can be better off if we work together than if we don't.

But that should be taken in no way as a diminishing in my eyes of what happened in the last 2 years, which was terrific. Even if the voters didn't agree or didn't even know about it, it was good for the country, and the country's better off. So the country's better off today than it was 2 years ago.

What our moral and legal obligation is, is to make sure that the country will be better off 2 years from now. I think the people are sick, literally sick of seeing all this partisan infighting up here. I just showed up here 2 years ago, and I was bewildered by it. I was astonished by it. And I was revolted by it. And I think the American people are, too.

Now, the others who were in that room with me today, starting with Speaker Gingrich and Senator Dole, they've been part of the Washington scene for a lot longer than I have, for decades. And I understand that. But they said they wanted to see an end to the partisan infighting. The Democrats, to their everlasting credit, said that they had learned from the Republicans how to stop things, but they thought that was not their job. Their job was to make things happen. So that's what we're trying to do. And I'm going to do my best to make good things happen for America. I do not want to see a series of partisan battles.

We need first to identify what we can agree on and move this country forward. And we ought to start with lobby reform and these other reforms. Then we ought to move on to responsible tax reform that I hope will focus on the middle class bill of rights and giving people education deductions because that will build the economy.

This is Mike McCurry's press conference, and I've already said enough.

Thank you.

NOTE: The President spoke at 1:46 p.m. in the Briefing Room at the White House.

Letter to Congressional Leaders on the Agenda for the 104th Congress
January 5, 1995

Dear _____:

We have an opportunity to make historic change in the way that Washington works and the government does the people's business.

This week, the Congress has begun to take important and positive steps to change its operations for the better. Shrinking the number of committees, reducing staff, and other measures are valuable, and long overdue. The passage of legislation that would apply to Congress the laws that apply to the public is only fair, is simple common sense, and is also long overdue. I hope that this time, unlike the last session of Congress, the Senate follows the House's action. I congratulate you on these steps.

But true congressional reform must reduce the power of lobbyists and special interests. The power of organized money in Washington hurts the middle class, bloats spending and the deficit, and blocks needed change. Today, some 90,000 people in Washington are associated with lobbying Congress on behalf of specific interests, which too often are able to manipulate the con-

gressional process to insert spending projects or tax provisions in legislation that do not serve the larger public's interest. Lobby power coupled with the ever-escalating cost of campaigns, which has risen fourfold over the past two decades, gives wealthy interests and wealthy candidates disproportionate influence in decision-making.

These are not partisan concerns; they are American concerns. I urge you, as you undertake the task of reforming Congress, to take on these real political reform issues.

First, as you enact legislation to apply general laws to Congress, it is vital that professional lobbyists be barred from giving gifts, meals and entertainment to members of Congress—just as they are now barred from giving these benefits to executive branch officials.

Second, Congress should also quickly enact legislation to bring professional lobbyists into the sunlight of public scrutiny. The current lobby disclosure statute is cumbersome and antiquated. Lobbyists should disclose who their clients are, what bills they seek to pass or block, and how much they are paid.

Third, I am pleased that the Congress wants to pass a line item veto authority for the President, something that I have consistently supported before and during the 1992 campaign and since. The line item veto authority will help us cut unnecessary spending and reduce the budget deficit. It is a powerful tool for fighting special interests, who too often are able to win approval of wasteful projects through manipulation of the congressional process, and bury them in massive bills where they are protected from Presidential vetoes. It will increase the accountability of government. I want a strong version of the line item veto, one that enables the President to take direct steps to curb wasteful spending. This is clearly an area where both parties can come together in the national interest, and I look forward to working with the Congress to quickly enact this measure.

Finally, we must clean up political campaigns, limit the cost of campaigning, reduce the role of special interests, and increase the role of ordinary citizens. Real campaign finance reform, too, should be an area of bipartisan cooperation. Requiring broadcasters to provide time to bona fide candidates would cut the cost of campaigning and ensure that voters hear all arguments, regardless of candidate wealth. Strong proposals for free TV time have been introduced in previous years by Senator Dole and by the new chair of the House Commerce Committee, Rep. Thomas Bliley; these proposals should be the basis of agreement on reform.

I look forward to working with the Congress to achieve results that are bipartisan, bold, and give the government back to the people.

Sincerely,

BILL CLINTON

NOTE: Identical letters were sent to Newt Gingrich, Speaker of the House of Representatives; Richard K. Armey, House majority leader; Richard A. Gephardt, House minority leader; Robert Dole, Senate majority leader; and Thomas A. Daschle, Senate minority leader.

Remarks on the Economy
January 6, 1995

The President. Good morning, everyone. We are here and anxious to get to work, but I wanted to make an announcement this morning and chart our course for the year ahead.

Two years ago, I formed a partnership for prosperity and opportunity with the Democratic leadership in Congress. Along with then Speaker Foley and Majority Leader Mitchell, the Democrats put together majorities that we needed in both the House and the Senate to make the hardest choices Washington has made in over a generation: to cut Federal spending deeply; to raise revenues, largely from income tax increases on the top 1½ percent of our people and corporations with incomes of over $10 million; to reinvent and restructure the Government so that it would be much smaller and still work better; and to invest in education, research, and technology, and tax relief for working families of modest incomes.

Most important of all, the Congress chose to do the right thing, rather than the political thing, because they believed it was more important to make real life easier for Americans than it was to make political life more comfortable for people here in Washington. As a result, there was a huge increase in investment and economic growth, building on the productivity of American workers and American businesses.

This morning I am pleased to announce that the recovery of which our economic plan was such a large part has brought paychecks to more than a quarter million more Americans in December alone. And compared with an unemployment rate of over 7 percent when I took office, we now see an unemployment rate in December of 5.4 percent. We have grown the private economy as we have cut Government. That's a real recovery and a real bargain for the American people.

A real recovery means that in 1994 alone our economy created 3.5 million new jobs, the most created in one year by the private sector in a decade. In '93 and '94 combined, our economy has produced 5.6 million new jobs. A real recovery means that after losing 2 million manufacturing jobs in the previous 12 years, in 1994 alone 292,000 manufacturing jobs were added to the economy, and manufacturing jobs grew in every month of last year for the first time since the 1970's. It means working people can look to the future with more hope and more optimism now, especially if we move to protect the economic expansion and to get to work to match the expansion with income growth increases for ordinary American working people.

We're ready to build on the progress we've made in cutting spending and the size of the Federal work force. As I announced last year, the reduction and reinvention of Government will continue with the budget I will submit next month. But I will stand against any effort to roll back or to rock the foundations of the recovery by proposals that explode the deficit or gimmicks that undermine the integrity of the budget we have worked so hard to put in place. And to ensure that incomes grow, which is, after all, the most important thing to ordinary American working families, we have to pair that with the economic growth by arming America's families with the tools they need to increase their own prosperity.

Our middle class bill of rights will do just that by ensuring more investments in better education and more disposable income for hardworking families who deserve some benefits from this recovery. We will do it by rewarding investments in education; in the rearing of children; in paying for education, health care, retirement costs; paying for training. These are things that will generate economic opportunity as well as tax fairness. They will ensure that the work ethics and the work efforts of the middle class are rewarded with growing incomes.

We've had a good first 2 years. It's time now to make a commitment to keep it going. We, the Democrats, stand ready to work in partnership with the Republicans. We want to make sure that we can do as well in the next 2 years as we have in the first 2. And I think that they will have the same attitude.

Thank you very much.

Q. Mr. President, can you tell us what your message to Boris Yeltsin is?

The President. I want to talk about jobs today. I already discussed that——

NOTE: The President spoke at 10:20 a.m. in the Oval Office at the White House, prior to a meeting with congressional leaders.

The President's Radio Address
January 7, 1995

Good morning. Now that the holidays are over, it's back to business around the country and back to the people's business here in Washington.

I'm looking forward to working with the new Congress. If they'll put politics as usual aside and put the American people and our future first, we've got a great opportunity to make progress on our mission: restoring the American dream of opportunity to all Americans and making sure we enter the next century, now just 5 years away, still the strongest and greatest nation in the world.

Earlier this week, I met at the White House with Republican and Democratic congressional leaders. I challenged them to work with me and with each other, and they assured me that they are willing to cooperate.

Many of the toughest decisions we made in the last 2 years are paying off for us now. We've reduced the deficit by $700 billion; that's $11,000 in less debt for every family in America. We've cut the Federal Government, eliminating over 100 programs, and there are already 100,000 fewer people working for the Federal Government than when I took office.

We've taken the savings and invested in the American people, in their education and training by expanding Head Start and apprenticeship programs and making college loans more affordable to 20 million people, providing the opportunity for national service to thousands of others.

Just yesterday, we saw new evidence that this economic strategy that has been pursued with such discipline over the last 2 years is still working. Unemployment is now down to 5.4 percent from over 7 percent when I took office; 5.6 million new jobs have been created in the almost 2 years since I became President. Nineteen ninety-four was the best year for job growth in a decade, and the vast majority of these new jobs are in the private sector. This was the first year that manufacturing jobs increased in every month since 1978. These new jobs are a testament to what can be accomplished when we combine the phenomenal ability and productivity of American businesses and workers with responsible and visionary political leadership willing to make tough choices. I will work with the new Congress to keep this recovery going. I will not go back to the failed policies of the past, which may have short-term attraction but will undermine our economic future.

We've still got a lot more to do, things that we must do in the months ahead, because for all the good statistics and all the legislative accomplishments of the last 2 years, the average American simply is not receiving enough benefit from this recovery. And Republicans and Democrats have to work together to change that.

Here's the problem: For about 20 years, the incomes of Americans without college educations have been stagnant. They've been working harder for the same or less income. Their benefits are less secure. What caused this? Technology and the global competition that we face mean that even when the economy is growing, inflation is low, and that's good. But wages often don't go up either, and that's not. There's a bigger educational premium than ever before. That is, workers who have more education are more likely to have higher incomes compared with workers without than at ever before in our history.

What's the answer to this dilemma? First, we have to create more high-wage jobs. I'm heartened that in 1994 we had more high-wage jobs coming into our economy than in the previous 5 years combined. But second, and even more important, we have to get more education and training opportunities to all of our people and an increase to take-home income of middle class Americans.

That's why I want Congress to adopt what I call the middle class bill of rights, four new ideas to help middle class Americans build a future that lives up to their dreams. Like the GI bill of rights after World War II, the middle class bill of rights will help people go to college, raise their children, and build a future. Like

the best of all Government programs, the middle class bill of rights offers opportunity, not a guarantee; it emphasizes personal responsibility; and it's open to all so that it can help build the strength of our entire American community.

Now, anybody can say, "I want to give you a tax cut," and make people very happy in the short run. What I want to do is cut taxes so that people can invest in the education of their children and in their own education in training and skills. That will raise incomes and lead to a stronger America. I want our people to have more than a quick fix. I want them to have the resources they need to fulfill their hopes and dreams over the long term.

Here's what's in the middle class bill of rights: first, a tax deduction for the tuition costs, up to $10,000, of all education after high school, for college, community college, graduate school, professional school, vocational education, or worker training for families with incomes of $120,000 or less; second, for families with incomes of $75,000 a year or less, a tax cut phased up to $500 for every child under 13; third, for those with incomes of under $100,000, the ability to put $2,000 a year, tax-free, into an individual retirement account, but also the ability to withdraw that money, tax-free, not just for retirement but for education, for health care, for the care of an elderly parent, or to buy a first home. Finally, the middle class bill of rights will take the billions and billions of dollars Government now spends on a variety of job training programs and consolidate that money and instead make it directly available to working Americans, so that when people are eligible for the funds, because they lose a job or because they're training for a better job, they'll be able to get the cash and spend it where they want in the education program of their choosing.

Every single penny of this middle class bill of rights proposal is paid for by dramatic cuts in Government that I've proposed. We have led the way to the largest 2-year deficit reduction in the history of our country, and I will not allow anyone to destroy this progress in reducing the deficit and to threaten our economic recovery. We've already seen that progress is possible in Washington this year. The House of Representatives this week voted to apply the laws that apply to the rest of America to Congress. That's long overdue. They did that last year, but the Senate didn't follow suit. I hope the Senate will follow suit now.

But we have to do more to change politics as usual. We desperately need to pass lobbying reform. The lobbyists didn't go away with the last election, and we still believe that they shouldn't be allowed to give gifts, entertainments, or trips to lawmakers. Unfortunately this week, the new majority in Congress voted not to enact lobby reform, at least for now. It's not too late for them to do it, and I urge them to do it as quickly as possible. If we want middle class Americans to benefit from what we do, then the public interest, not those of special interest, should have the loudest voice in Washington.

That's why I'll apply one simple test to every policy, every piece of legislation that comes before me: Does it advance the interests of average American families—does it promote their values, build their future, increase their jobs and incomes? If it passes that test, I'll support it, and if it doesn't, I won't.

If we work together to do the job the American people hired us to do, 1995 will be a terrific year for all Americans who work hard and play by the rules. We've seen for too long how people in Washington can obstruct progress for partisan gains. Now, sincerely, we must prove that we can work together to keep our country moving forward for America's gain.

Thanks for listening.

NOTE: The President spoke at 10:06 a.m. from the Oval Office at the White House.

Remarks at Carl Sandburg Community College in Galesburg, Illinois
January 10, 1995

Thank you for that wonderful and warm welcome. It is wonderful to be here. Thank you, Dr. Crist, for making me feel so much at home. Thank you, Congressman Evans, for coming down, and Congressman Poshard, delighted to see you. And Mayor Kimble, thank you for making me feel welcome here. The representatives of Knox College and Blackhawk Community College as well as Carl Sandburg Community College, I'm glad to see all of you here.

I'm glad that Secretaries Reich and Riley came with me, and I understand they have already spoken, which makes anything I say perhaps redundant. [*Laughter*]

I met a college president the other day. He looked at me and said, "I've got a lot of sympathy with you. Being President is just like running a cemetery. You've got a lot of people under you, and nobody is listening." [*Laughter*]

I want to begin by saying how very, very happy and proud I am to be here today. I believe as strongly as I can state that community colleges represent the very best of America in 1995 and where we need to go as a country with all of our institutions, community based, flexible, committed to quality, opportunity for everyone, with a real sense of community. I'm honored to be here, and I'm honored to have all of you here.

I'd also like to recognize the people who were with me just a few moments ago who participated in our little roundtable, who have had some experience with this institution. I'd like to ask all of them to stand up that were in my private conversation because I want to thank them. [*Applause*] Thank you. They're employers of people who came out of this community college. They're students. They're former students. They're people who have taught here. They are a picture of America.

I came here to talk about America, about where we are and where we're going. And I don't think we could have picked a better place. This place is so steeped in our national history, just as this community college is so representative of the best of our present and our future. The Underground Railroad came through Galesburg, and as all of you know and as you saw just a few moments ago, over 135 years ago, Abraham Lincoln and Stephen Douglas met here for one of their famous debates. How'd they do just a few minutes ago? [*Applause*] Thank you. I met them outside, and they were still arguing about who really won. [*Laughter*]

I identified with what President Lincoln said. He performed so brilliantly in those debates, but he lost the Senate race anyway. And he said that it hurt too much to laugh, and he was too old to cry. And then he said something I have always kept with me. In fact, I've got a copy of the exact quote on the wall in my private office in the White House. He said after Douglas defeated him for the Senate, he was walking home, and it had been raining that day and the path was muddy, and one of his feet slipped and hit his other foot and knocked his footing out from under him. But just before he fell, he righted himself and he smiled, and he said, "This is a slip and not a fall." Well, I think we all ought to try to keep that in our own minds as we deal with life's challenges and adversity.

The Lincoln-Douglas debates, as you just heard for a few moments, were about the course of our country and the proper role of government in a time of great change. In 1858, of course, the issue was slavery. Lincoln believed that it was a national issue. Long before he believed the Government could abolish slavery, he at least believed the Government could stop it from expanding. Douglas believed it was not a national issue, that it should be just up to the States or to the territories; if they wanted to keep slavery, they could vote for it and then come on into the Union.

The Republican Party was born out of a conviction that even though we are a country deeply devoted to limited government, there are some things that the times demand national action on and that at that moment the times demanded, first, national action to stop the spread of slavery and, then, national action to stop slavery.

About a half a century earlier, the Democratic Party was born in the Presidency of Thomas Jefferson, who passionately believed in limited government. I was driving across the beautiful Illinois farmland today, feeling very much at home, thinking about how Jefferson loved being on his farm more than he liked being at the White House and how he wanted to limit government. But when he became President, he knew there were certain things that he had to use the power of the National Government to do because the times demanded it.

He bought the Louisiana Purchase, $15 million—peanuts, really, to us for all that land. I like it because it included Arkansas. So if he hadn't done it, I could never have been an American, much less President. [*Laughter*] But at the time it was a stunning, sweeping thing. The price of Louisiana was the entire budget of the National Government for a year. Can you imagine what you'd think of me if I wanted to spend that much on any piece of real estate? [*Laughter*] But he did.

Both believed in limited government. Both approved of action by the National Government to meet the demands of the time, to do what the people needed. Our Founders established this great country under a Constitution that limits government. Mostly it limits what government can do to private citizens and gives us a lot of elbow room to think what we please and say what we please and go where we please and worship God as we please. It also limits government in other ways, dividing it at the State and local as well as the national level, the President, the Congress, the courts. But it was set up to allow all of us to pursue life, liberty, and happiness. And it was set up with enough flexibility so that over time we could have the kind of government that we needed as a people, not the kind of people that the Government needs but the kind of government that we need as a people.

Now we're at another great sea-change period of American history. Everyone knows we are moving from an information age—I mean, to an information age from an industrialized age in which all organizations were bigger, more hierarchical, more bureaucratic, to a time which is more flexible, more rapidly changing, more full of opportunity and uncertainty. And so we will have to have some changes in what we expect our Government to do, but we have to be clear about our purpose.

I think our purpose has to be to keep the American dream alive for all the people in this country into the 21st century and to make sure we cross the threshold of the next century still the strongest country in the world, still a force for freedom and peace and democracy at home and around the world.

Every American who works hard and obeys the law should be able to get ahead in this new world. It should not be a province of opportunity for a few. To get that done we face enormous challenges. Most of the people who are at a community college know better than I that for the last 10 or 15 years the majority of our people have worked longer and longer work weeks for the same or lower wages, that in the last year alone over a million Americans in working families lost their health insurance.

This is quite a new phenomenon for us. From World War II until 1978, the American economy grew, and all income groups grew at about the same rate that the American economy did. So we were rising together. For the last 15 years, the top 20 percent of Americans had a dramatic increase in their income; the next 20 percent, a modest increase; the next 20 percent were stagnant; the bottom 40 percent had declines in their incomes. We're talking now about working people, not people who are on welfare.

So if a lot of Americans, about half of us, are working harder for lower wages—and actually, we also know now, sleeping a little less at night—it's no wonder that there's a lot of stress in this country. We also know that this is a time of great change. It's not just the workplace that's changing; the nature of our communities are changing. Our families are under great stress. Life seems to be too random and too insecure for too many people. And yet, we have to admit there is no country in the world that has remotely an economy as strong as ours, as full of opportunity, as full of hope.

So what's the trick to bridge the gap, to make sure that everybody who wants to do the right thing has a chance to make that leap into the economy of the future and succeed? That must be the mission of the United States in these last 5 years of this century.

I told these folks that were good enough to spend about 45 minutes visiting with me that I probably enjoyed it more than they did because before I became President, when I was a Governor, I did this sort of thing all the time. I knew that my mission was to generate more jobs and increase the education and skills of our people. And I lived in a place that was small enough where it was more possible for people to talk about political life in nice, calm terms, instead of what normally tends to dominate the debate today. But I couldn't help being just overcome almost in my admiration for their individual stories, which wouldn't be all that much different from your individual stories.

I ran for President because I wanted to do just what you clapped for. I do not believe that we have to go into the future taking advantage of all these opportunities for some and letting others fall behind and becoming more divided. But I think, as I have said now for more than 3 years, we must do three things. We've got to have a new economic policy designed to help the American people compete and win in a global economy in which the Government is a partner with people in their private lives and in private business in expanding opportunity.

In the first 2 years, that meant that we had to cut the deficit because we spent the 1980's dealing with our economic problems, trying to spend our way out of them, and exploding the deficit. Now, I know that's not very popular. It's kind of like going to the dentist. Everybody's for going to the dentist, in general. Did you ever see anybody who wanted to do it in particular when it came their time to go to the dentist? That's the way the deficit is. Everybody says—you take a poll; people will say, "Yes, cut the deficit." But then we have to do the things to do it. It's not very popular. It's like going to the dentist. So I had a drill in your tooth the last 2 years. But we cut the deficit by $700 billion, thanks to the help of those two gentlemen. And that's $11,000 a family. That's not a small piece of change.

And we expanded trade, and that was controversial. A lot of my best supporters said, "Why are you trying to do all these trade deals? The more we trade, the more we have low-cost products from low-wage countries coming into America, putting pressure on American wages." That's true, but it's only half true. Now, if we don't do anything, that's happening. That's been happening for years. And it is true that some of our people have either lost their jobs or can't get wage increases because they're competing with products from overseas, produced by people who work for wages we can't live on. That's true. It's also true that when we sell things to other countries, on balance the people who make the things and the services we sell to other countries make wages above the national average. So if we don't do the trade deals, we'll get the downside of the trade war. The reason I fought for the trade agreements was so we could create more high-wage jobs in America by selling more world-class American products around the world. And it's working. So we need a new economic policy. We've got to sell. We've got to produce. We've got to be productive, and it has to be a partnership.

The second thing we need is what I called during my Presidential campaign a New Covenant, a new approach to our society. It was then, it has been for 2 years, and it will always remain my contract with you. But it's about more than a tax cut, although cutting taxes are part of it. I believe what this country needs on a national basis is what I see at the community college here. What those of us in the position to do so ought to be doing is expanding opportunity but only for those who will exercise the personal responsibility to make the most of those opportunities.

You build a community with opportunity and with responsibility, with rights and responsibilities. You can't have one without the other and last for a long time. You can't have people being responsible all the time and never getting anything for it. Pretty soon they get tired. But neither can you have people getting things all the time and never giving anything back. Pretty soon the well runs dry.

So that's what we've been trying to do. That's what the crime bill was all about. We cut the Government bureaucracy over 5 years by 270,000 people and gave all the money back to local communities to hire police, to build prisons, to drug treatment programs, to do things that would lower the crime rate at the grassroots level for people who use the money right and were responsible.

That's what I hope this welfare reform debate that we're ginning up again after a year will be all about in Washington. I do not believe that most Americans really want simply to reduce welfare so that we can punish poor people. I think what most Americans want is a welfare system that puts an end to welfare, that puts people to work and lets them be responsible parents instead of just having kids. I think that's what we want.

And that's why we have invested so much in education, because education by definition is part of a covenant. You cannot educate somebody who will not be educated. All you can do is throw the lifeline of opportunity out there, and someone either does it or not. They either exercise their own responsibility or not.

So we worked to expand Head Start and to set standards that are great for our Nation's schools and to have new partnerships for young people that don't go to college to get further education. And we reformed drastically the college loan program so we could cut the costs and string out the repayments and make it something that could really be used by people instead of just another headache. And that's all made a difference I think. So a new economic policy, a New Covenant, a new social policy.

The third thing we've tried to do is to give you a different kind of Government, to have the Government in Washington change, the way the economy is changing, to have it be smaller, yes, but also more effective; to literally reinvent Government, to use the Vice President's phrase, by cutting the bureaucracy to its smallest size in 30 years but increasing our ability to solve problems that the Federal Government needs to solve. There are 100,000 fewer people working in Washington, DC, or for the Federal Government today than there were on the day I was inaugurated President, but we have solved a lot of problems that were left too long. And I would just give you one or two examples.

Small business people used to have to fill out a multipage form that took them hours to fill out to get an SBA loan. We've taken that down to one page, and you can get an answer in 3 days now. So that's an example of what we're trying to do to reinvent the Government.

I don't know if the Secretary of Labor mentioned this, but at the end of last year, we reformed the Pension Benefit Guaranty Corporation—that's a mouthful. That's the group in Washington that's supposed to keep your pension well. And it's going to help save the pensions of 8½ million Americans whose retirement was at risk after years and years and years of hard work.

There are problems the Federal Government still should be solving. And when the floods were raging here, the 500-year flood, up and down in Illinois and Iowa, after years in which the Federal Emergency Management Agency was the goat of the Federal Government and everybody complained about it, I think you saw by the way they showed up and the way they performed that it is working now. It is effective. It is doing its job.

So we're moving in these directions. But it is not enough. What are the results of the first 2 years, not from our point of view in what we did but from your lives. Well, we have 5.6 million more jobs, and that's a good thing. And the unemployment rate has dropped very low by historic standards, although not low enough to suit me. It's still dropped quite a bit, by more than 2 percent. And 5.6 million new jobs is nothing to sneeze at.

And manufacturing jobs went up in every month in 1994 for the first time since 1978, which means that manufacturing is not inconsistent with the information age. It helps our manufacturing come back when we increase productivity and use computers and educate our workers. So that's good; that's all good. But most folks still haven't gotten a pay raise out of this recovery. Many people are still worried about losing their jobs. Another million Americans lost their health insurance. Why is that? That is because the wages are still set in an environment that is highly competitive because of technological changes and foreign competition.

So if we want to raise incomes, the only way you can do it is to get more high-wage jobs in this country, take less out of working people's pockets, or increase their education and training. There is no other way to do it. And that's what we have to do. So what I want to do now is—we worked hard to get the fundamentals fixed for 2 years—I want to spend 2 years working on lifting incomes and prospects and optimism and real hope for the future among people who are carrying the load in this country. That's what we can do. And that's what the middle class bill of rights is all about.

I might as well have called it the bill of rights and responsibilities, because it doesn't do anything for anybody who's not already doing something for himself or herself. Anybody can give a tax cut, but what I want to do is cut taxes in a way that strengthens families and raise incomes. That's what we need to be doing in this country: We need to strengthen families; we need to raise incomes.

Fifty years ago, the GI bill of rights helped transform a wartime economy into the most successful peacetime economy in history. It literally built the great American middle class, helping them get houses and education and to raise their kids. And now what I want to do is to implement this middle class bill of rights, these ideas that will help us move into the 21st century with the American dream alive for everyone.

Now, if you agree with the analysis I just gave you, I hope you will agree with the particulars. First of all, I think people ought to be able to deduct the cost of education after high school from their taxes. If you think about it, you can deduct the interest on your home. Why? Because we want people to buy homes; we want people to be homeowners. We think it's a good thing. It's important to being an American and having a solid life. Well, in the 21st century, and in 1995, and with all the people I just finished talking to, having a decent education is also important to being in the middle class. And you may not get to the homeownership stage if you don't have an education

in the first place. So we ought to let people deduct the cost of an education.

Secondly, we ought to try to support working families more, and so I recommended a tax credit, or a tax reduction, of $500 a child for every child under 13 in families with incomes of $75,000 a year or less. In 1993, we cut taxes an average of $1,000 a year for working families who were on really modest incomes and having a hard time making ends meet. It's now $26,000 a year or less will get an average of $1,000 tax cut below what the taxes were when I took office. But this will help people raise their children.

Third, I believe we ought to bring back the IRA, the individual retirement account, let people put $2,000 in it. But under our proposal, you could take the money out in any year, tax-free, as long as you spent it on education, health insurance, buying a home for the first time, or the care of an elderly parent. This would empower people to solve their own problems. It's something that government can let you do for yourself. It requires no bureaucracy. It requires no program. It requires nothing, just letting you withdraw money you save, tax-free, to solve a problem for yourselves and for the United States.

Finally, finally, we propose to take the literally billions of dollars the Government now spends on dozens, literally dozens, of different training programs and consolidate those programs and make that money directly available to people who are now eligible for it. That is, today, people who are unemployed can get help from a Government training program. And people who are on quite modest incomes who are eligible, for example, to participate in the Job Training and Partnership Act training programs can get help through a training program. But there are literally dozens of these programs. You've got to figure out what you're eligible for, what the criteria are, where the program is, are you going to be in it. I mean, by the time you get through fooling with it, it may seem like it's not worth the trouble. We discovered that we could collapse 50 of these programs and just give you the money if you're eligible for it, and it would make people who are eligible able to get a chit, a voucher for education only, worth up to $2,600 a year for 2 years.

Now, that's better than having a Federal bureaucracy. It's better than giving the money to a State bureaucracy. Everybody in America, just about, is within driving distance of a community college now. We do not need all these separate Government programs telling people what to do. We ought to just give you the money if you're eligible for it and let you bring it here and get a good education. That's the fourth element of our program.

I like this middle class bill of rights a lot because it furthers all three objectives that I had when I ran for President. It helps us build a new economy. The more people we educate, the more powerful our Nation will be, the stronger our economy will be. It helps us build a New Covenant. We offer more opportunity to people if they exercise the responsibility to take it, they have the power to improve their own lives. All of you do. You know that, or you wouldn't be here today.

And it changes the way Government works. Government is still being used to help expand opportunity but in a less bureaucratic, less mandatory, more empowering way. I like it, and I hope the Congress will like it as well. And I hope you will help them like it by telling them that you like it.

Under this last proposal—let me just give you one example. If we want to set up centers where what the Government does is make sure you have information on the jobs that are available in an area and the educational opportunities that are available in one place, you could show up at the local one-stop center and find out, for example, here about jobs opening up at Maytag because of the new $164 million retooling project they've got underway. Then you could figure out whether you could get the skills needed to be a part of that project in this place. And if you could, if you qualified, you could simply take your certificate, show up here, and start to school. Much better than having to enroll in some sort of program.

Here at this community college—and this is true all over the country, maybe not quite this good, but this is typical—there is an extraordinary job placement rate of over 94 percent at an average wage of nearly $12 an hour. And believe me, that's a lot better than a lot of people are facing who have no education and training and who have been left behind by the changes that are going on in our economy.

This is the kind of opportunity that I believe the middle class bill of rights can help create. This will enable us to finish the job. Yes, we have laid the foundations of a disciplined, re-

sponsible economic policy. Yes, we have taken a strong stand against crime. Yes, we know—and I hope we'll have a bipartisan consensus on what to do about problems like welfare. But until we know that we have done everything we can to use the power of this country to give every American the opportunity to win in this global economy, the job will not be finished. That, more than anything else, can keep the American dream alive in the 21st century.

So, as I go back to Washington, I ask all of you, Republicans and Democrats, to tell the people who represent you in Washington to adopt the same attitude about these challenges that you have. If you think about it, in every new time our country faces, there are new problems that have no necessary partisan solution. And the problems fall over everybody and the opportunities come to people without regard to their party, their philosophy, their race, or their region today. We should be united in tackling these problems. They are America's problems and America's opportunities.

You have seen over and over and over again, probably enough to make you scream, that people in Washington know how to stop things for partisan gain. It's now time for us to join together and do things for the people's gain. That's what you expect us to do. That's what we need to do. That's what will take us into the next century with the American dream alive and well, stronger than ever, and America stronger than ever.

I am convinced—I am convinced—having traveled the world now on your behalf, having seen what is going on in Europe, having seen what is going on in Asia, having met with the leaders of all the Latin American countries, having a feel for what is happening in this world, I am convinced more than ever in my life that the best days of this country are still ahead of us if we remember that there are no guarantees.

The Founders gave us the right to pursue life, liberty, happiness. That's what they gave us the right to do. Over 70 years ago, your namesake here, Carl Sandburg, wrote a poem inspired by the Washington Monument. And I want to close with the line from that poem that meant the most to me: "Nothing happens unless, first, a dream." More than anything, more even than our Constitution and laws, this country is a dream. And it is our job to renew it.

Thank you very much, and God bless you all.

NOTE: The President spoke at 12:44 p.m. in the gymnasium. In his remarks, he referred to Don Crist, president of the college, and Mayor Fred Kimble of Galesburg.

Remarks to Students at Galesburg High School in Galesburg
January 10, 1995

The President. Thank you. Wow! Thank you. Thank you very much. I don't know where everybody else in Galesburg is today, but I'm glad you're here. I'm glad to see you all. [*Applause*] Thank you. Thank you. Thank you so much.

I would like to begin by paying my compliments to the band. Didn't they do a good job? I thought they were terrific. [*Applause*]

I also want to thank—I understand that you all heard the speech I gave. Is that right? No, yes? No? Somebody is saying yes; somebody is saying no. Anyway, I was over at the community college, as you know, and I met there with about 20 people who had either been students there or are now students there or who taught there or who hired people who graduated from there. And I went there to talk about education with the Secretary of Labor, who is not here with me, and the Secretary of Education, Dick Riley, the former Governor of South Carolina, who is here with me, and your fine Congressman, Lane Evans. I'm glad to see him. Give him a hand. [*Applause*]

I would like to say, first of all, on behalf of myself and all of those who came with me from Washington today, we have had a wonderful welcome in this terrific community. And we're very grateful to all of you for that.

I must say, when I landed at the airport and they told me that I couldn't take the helicopter to Galesburg, I'd have to drive, I was actually kind of happy because I got to drive across the farmland. And I looked at all the land, and it kind of made me feel—no, I liked it. It made me feel right at home. That's where I grew up.

I would like—I want to say a couple of things about what I came here to talk about today, since some of you heard what I said and some of you didn't. I'll be brief, but I want to talk about it because I think it's important.

When I ran for President in 1992 and I came here to Illinois and I went up and down the State——

Audience member. To Peoria.

The President. Yes, to Peoria and other places—I always knew it was a very big State, but when I visited Southern Illinois University in the southern part of the State, I looked at a map, and I realized I was south of Richmond, Virginia. And I said, this is a very big State and a very beautiful one and, of course, my wife's home. So I like it a lot.

I believed then and I believe now that we are going through a time of great change which, if we do the right thing, will lead us to America's greatest days. I think the young people here in this school can live in the most peaceful, most exciting, most prosperous, most exhilarating times this country has ever known if we do the right thing.

And if you look at what's going on in America today, it just reinforces in my mind the things I have always wanted to do. I worked as a Governor for 12 years, and I knew what my mission was in this global economy: I had to improve the schools, improve education for people of all ages, and get more jobs into my State.

If you look at where we are as a country now, I ran for President committed to doing three things. I wanted a new economic policy so that the Government would be working with ordinary working people and with business so that we would be able to compete and win in a global economy, we'd be able to get good jobs and keep them.

I wanted to change the way the Federal Government works. I wanted the Government to be smaller but more effective. I wanted it to be able to solve people's problems but to be flexible and creative and not waste money. And I thought we could do that, and I've come back to that. I think we've done a good job of making those changes.

And the third thing I wanted to do was to institute what was my version of the Contract With America. I called it the New Covenant. I believe that we need a new sense in this country that the Government's job is to do what it can to provide more opportunity, but we need more responsibility from our citizens as well. If we're going to rebuild the American community, we have to have more rights and responsibility. And you can't have one without the other. If people go around being responsible and no opportunities ever come their way, they get tired and quit. But if you just give people things and they never act like responsible citizens, the whole country comes apart at the seams. What we need is more of both: more opportunity and more responsibility. And if we have it, we can rebuild America.

Now, after 2 years, I can make this progress report to you. We had to first work on the economy. We had to bring the deficit down. We had to open some markets around the world to our goods and services because we were seeing people selling things in America who worked for wages we couldn't live on. We saw people losing jobs here and losing incomes. We had to open those markets around the world. Well, after 2 years, we've reduced the deficit by $700 billion. That's $11,000 a family in less debt for you and your future, $11,000 a family. And we've had more opening of markets to American products and services than in any period in our history. So we're moving. What have we got to show for it: 5.6 million new jobs, the lowest unemployment rate in Illinois in 20 years. We are moving in the right direction.

Now, we've changed the way the Government works. There are 100,000 fewer people working for the Federal Government today than there were working for the Federal Government on the day I became President. We are going to reduce the Government now by over 300,000. It will be the smallest it's been since John Kennedy was President, but it's doing things. It's doing things. When you had the terrible floods here, the Federal Emergency Management Agency, which had been condemned for years as an ineffective agency, showed up here and was ready to serve the people in the middle of the worst emergency you've had in a long time. It delivered. It worked. That's the kind

of Government we need, smaller but effective and strong and there.

Third, and maybe most important, we tried to expand opportunities for communities and individuals in a way that would enable people to take responsibility for their own lives. That's what our crime bill is all about. The crime bill that Lane voted for will reduce the size of the Federal Government by 270,000 over 5 years and take every penny of that money and give it back to you and your local community to hire more police, to have drug treatment and drug education programs, to do things that will lower the crime rate. And everywhere I go in America, law enforcement officers or mayors come up to me and say, "We're going to lower the crime rate because of that crime bill. Thank you very much." That's the kind of thing we ought to be doing.

And I hope, let me say, I hope when the new Congress gets around to debating welfare reform, that's what I hope they'll do with welfare reform. The problem with welfare is not that it is so costly; it's only about 3 percent of our national budget. The problem is that it encourages dependence instead of independence, encourages welfare instead of work. What we want is not a program that punishes poor people but that requires poor people to take those steps that will enable them to move from welfare to work, to be responsible parents and responsible workers, not punishment but reward.

So we did that for 2 years, but there's still a real problem in America. Why are a lot of people not very happy? Because most Americans still have not felt any personal benefit from this economic recovery. This is a new thing in our history, and all the young people here should listen to this. We created all these new jobs in America with these productive American industries. Why aren't people happy? Because their wages aren't going up, right? And because a lot of people still feel uncertain about their jobs, and because another million Americans lost their health insurance last year who are in working families, and because millions of Americans are worried about their pensions. All these changes are going on, and people don't feel secure even when we create more jobs.

Now, how do you raise wages? There are only three ways to raise wages: You have to get more high-wage jobs in the economy. You can take less out of the pocketbooks of middle class wage earners and let them keep more of the money they do earn. Or you can increase the education and skill level of people.

Now, let me say, we're getting more high-wage jobs into the economy. And I want to support a middle class tax cut like the one I have outlined in the middle class bill of rights that will give people more take-home pay. But the most important thing of all is to do it in a way that will support the mission of education and training, not only for our schoolchildren but for the adults I met at that community college today, because we know now that for the first time in history, we're going to have economic recovery and job creation that don't benefit ordinary people unless we can raise the education levels of all the people in the United States in the work force, the adults. That means we've got to get more people to the colleges, more people back to the community colleges. We've got to help people work and train and raise their kids at the same time. That's what I talked about today.

Whether you are a Democrat or a Republican, I hope you will support these ideas because they're American ideas. Let's give a tax deduction for the educational expenses that people have after high school, whether they're in a college or a community college. Let's let working people invest in an IRA, an individual retirement account, but be able to withdraw money from that tax-free for education, for health care, for caring for their folks. Let's give tax relief to working people for their children in their homes so they can help be successful parents and successful workers. And finally, I propose to take all these Government programs that are paid to train people and consolidate the money. And if you qualify because you're unemployed or because you're a low-income person, if you want to go to school, I propose, in effect, letting

you send a check to the local community college and not having to go through all these Government programs and redtape. Just go to school, get the education, go forward. Just do it.

Now, folks, these are good ideas. They're American ideas. I don't care who gets credit for it, but I want us to do them. There is no party label that will change the reality that the most important thing we can do for Americans is to give everybody a good education, give people the skills to compete and win in this global economy, and give not only our schoolchildren but their parents and their grandparents, if they need it, the ability to go back to these community colleges and get the skills to have a better life and a stronger life and do a better job for themselves and the rest of this country. That is the most important thing we can do to lift the income of the American people.

So, that's what I said over there, but I took about 5 minutes longer to say it. I care about you and your future. My job is to make sure that when all these young people get out of this high school, the American dream is alive and well; this is still the strongest country in the world; we are still a force for peace and freedom and opportunity. But in order to do it, you, every single one of you has got to make a commitment that we are going to develop the capacity of our people. That's how we're going to win. That's how we're going to get wages up. That's how we're going to bring security back. That's how we're going to bring this country together again. That's how we're going to do it. And we can with your help.

Thank you, and God bless you all.

NOTE: The President spoke at 2:23 p.m. in the gymnasium.

Statement on Disaster Assistance for Floods in California
January 10, 1995

Tonight I have declared that a major disaster exists in California caused by the damaging floods in northern and southern California. I have directed Federal Emergency Management Agency Director James Lee Witt to oversee the Federal response in the recovery.

FEMA officials are already working closely with State and local officials to ensure a quick response to this flood. Director Witt is in California making sure disaster funds begin to flow quickly to help the people affected by the flood damage. These funds will help to begin the process of recovery.

Californians have a resilient spirit and great sense of community. You have shown over the past year during the earthquake, the fires, and now the current floods that you are a people that come together in times of crisis. The American people support you as you would them in a similar time of need. Our hearts are with the thousands of victims affected by the floods and the family members of those who have died.

NOTE: This statement was included in a White House statement announcing disaster assistance for California.

Radio Address to California Flood Victims
January 11, 1995

Last night I declared a major disaster in the State of California. The necessary assistance will be made available to thousands of victims of the flooding in both northern and southern California.

The Federal Emergency Management Agency, FEMA, is working closely with State and local officials to ensure a quick response to the flood. FEMA Director James Lee Witt is in California to ensure that disaster funds begin to flow quickly to the State. These funds will help to begin the process of recovery, and we'll be with you for the long haul.

I want to say a special word of thanks to all the young volunteers from AmeriCorps, our national service program, for the quick and good work they have done. Californians have proven over the last few years that they have a resilient spirit and a great sense of community. You have shown in the earthquake and the fires and now in these floods that you are a people who come together in times of crisis. The American people are with you.

Hillary and I send our thoughts and prayers to the thousands of victims, and we wish you well.

NOTE: The address was recorded at approximately 9:20 a.m. in the Oval Office at the White House for later broadcast.

Exchange With Reporters Prior to Discussions With Prime Minister Tomiichi Murayama of Japan
January 11, 1995

California Floods

Q. Mr. President, we know you're having this meeting, but can you help us with any comments on the situation in California?

The President. We're going to have a press conference after our lunch. I'd be happy to talk about it then. I talked with Mr. Witt last night at 1 a.m. in the morning our time, so I'm up to date. But I'd rather defer questions until our lunch, until our press conference after the lunch.

Japan

Q. Can you tell us if you do expect to make some progress here today given the political situation in Japan?

The President. When the Japanese press come through here, they may say, "Do you expect to make some progress here given the political situation in the United States?" [*Laughter*] Of course I do.

Q. [*Inaudible*]

The President. Do you want to—what did you say? Sure. Should we have a handshake? It's a big table, but—[*laughter*].

[*At this point, the President and the Prime Minister shook hands. Then one group of reporters left the room, and another group entered.*]

California Floods

Prime Minister Murayama. I wish to extend my sincere condolence to the victims of the torrential rain and the flood in California.

The President. The people of California have suffered a lot in the last 2 years. They've had earthquakes, fires, and now floods. It's a very— it's a wonderful place to live, but they bear a great burden.

NOTE: The exchange began at 11:28 a.m. in the Cabinet Room at the White House. Prime Minister Murayama spoke in Japanese, and his remarks were translated by an interpreter. A tape was not available for verification of the content of this exchange.

The President's News Conference With Prime Minister Tomiichi Murayama of Japan
January 11, 1995

The President. Good afternoon. I am delighted to welcome Prime Minister Murayama here for his first official visit. It comes at a very important time, a time when we are beginning to mark the 50th anniversary of the end of World War II, a time when we must move to strengthen the vital partnership between our peoples for the 21st century.

We are starting this year in exactly the right way, working together as representatives of two great democratic nations, committed to solving the problems we face together. We know America has no more important bilateral ties than those with Japan. In a dramatically changing world, we look to Japan as an unwavering friend, one devoted, as are we, to promoting peace and advancing prosperity.

Recently, the vitality of our relationship has been illustrated again by our cooperation to diffuse the danger of nuclear weapons on the Korean Peninsula. Working together with our South Korean allies, we have confronted the nuclear threat and stopped it. The agreement we reached with North Korea already has frozen their nuclear program in a way that is verifiable. North Korea will be giving up control of nuclear materials that could be used in bombs. Construction of new and dangerous reactors has stopped. Ultimately, this program will be dismantled. And all of this is being done, as I said, with strict outside monitoring and verification.

Prime Minister Murayama and I talked about our two countries' roles in implementing the North Korean nuclear agreement, including some activities each of us will undertake. I want to express my appreciation for Japan's strong support for this agreement, including its willingness to play a significant financial role. I reaffirmed my intention to Prime Minister Murayama that the United States will also continue to play a leading role in implementing the agreement.

This year, the United States and Japan will also work together to develop a comprehensive blueprint for liberalizing trade among the rapidly growing Asian-Pacific economies. We're confident that during its chairmanship of APEC, Japan will show the leadership necessary to chart the course and fulfill the goals of the agreements announced in Indonesia in November. Free and fair trade in Asia will deliver more high-paying jobs for American workers, and those are exactly the jobs that will give more Americans a chance to pursue the American dream.

The Prime Minister and I discussed our bilateral economic relationship. Under our framework agreement, I'm pleased to announce that this week we reached an accord that will open up Japan's financial services sector to American businesses. Over the past 4 months, we have also forged agreements to open Japanese Government procurement as well as Japan's glass and insurance markets to American companies. These agreements must, of course, be fully implemented to ensure that real results are achieved, and more remains to be done. But in the last calendar year, we have reached 8 separate agreements and a total of 14 in the 2 years I have been in office.

Still, Japan's current account surplus is too high, largely because it is just coming out of a period of recession. But further progress must be made, especially in the areas of autos and auto parts, which make up the bulk of our trade deficit with Japan. Negotiations there are set to resume soon. I am firmly committed to opening the market in this and other areas. We must redouble our efforts to assure further progress.

Finally, let me say that the Prime Minister and I will release today the first report detailing the tremendous achievements that have been made in a range of joint projects on global issues. In programs that address such problems as explosive population growth and AIDS, the eradication of polio and the battle against the drug trade, our common agenda for cooperation is making great strides in confronting issues that know no national boundaries.

These are just a few of the projects that our nations are working together on, and they are proof of a relationship that no one could have dreamed of 50 years ago or perhaps even 20 years ago. Today, we have every confidence that the extraordinary bonds between Japan and the United States will only grow stronger in the years, the decades, and the new century to come.

Mr. Prime Minister.

Prime Minister Murayama. At the beginning of the year marking the 50th anniversary of the end of World War II, President Clinton and I confirmed the importance of Japan-U.S. relations today, which have been built by the peoples of Japan and the United States over 50 years. And we agreed to further develop Japan-U.S. relations towards the future.

I took this opportunity to express my gratitude for the magnanimous assistance which the United States had provided Japan after the war. Both our Governments share the view that it is important for Japan and the United States to firmly maintain the Japan-U.S. security arrangements. We reaffirmed that both our countries would further advance cooperation for the peace and prosperity of the Asia-Pacific region.

Japan will cooperate with the United States towards the success of the APEC meeting in Osaka to be held this autumn. We'll also further advance the common agenda which emphasizes the Asia-Pacific region. Today the joint report on the common agenda was submitted. During

this summit meeting, we agreed to add women and development as a new area under the common agenda. In my talks with the President, I stressed the importance of advancing exchanges between the peoples of our countries and cited the exchange of students as a specific example.

We also exchanged our views on international issues of common interest. The Government of Japan strongly supports last year's agreed framework between the United States and North Korea. I stated that to ensure the success of the light-water reactor project, which directly relates to the security and stability of the northeast Asian region, including Japan, the Government of Japan intends to play a significant financial role in the LWR, or light-water reactor project, under an overall project scheme in which the Republic of Korea is expected to play the central role.

As regards the economic aspects, since the end of September last year, discussions have been concluded on the flat glass and financial sectors, and agreement was reached to resume the automobiles and auto parts talks. We commended such progress and confirmed that we would continue to seriously engage ourselves in the Japan-U.S. framework talks.

During this pivotal year, I'm resolved to make efforts to advance the Japan-U.S. creative partnership together with President Clinton, building on today's meetings as a good starting point. Furthermore, I look forward to welcoming President Clinton to Japan as a state guest this autumn.

Thank you.

The President. Thank you. We'll alternate between the American and the Japanese press. Terry [Terence Hunt, Associated Press], go ahead.

Japan-U.S. Trade

Q. Mr. President, Japan's trade surplus is running at more than $60 billion. Last year at this time, you said that you'd rather admit failure than accept an empty agreement or try to paper over differences. Where do things stand now? Do you think that you've made any breakthrough with these agreements that you've mentioned, or are things pretty much about where they are?

The President. I do. I think I would point out two things. First of all, in the last calendar year, we have reached eight agreements. If they're all implemented fully and in good faith, there's going to be a timelag between the time those specific market sectors are opened and we begin to feel the benefits of it here in the United States.

The second point I would make is that at any given time, the trade relationships between two countries will depend upon the state of the economies in those two countries. We had the good fortune of coming out of our recession more quickly than did Japan. Our growth rate has been higher for the last 2 years. Theirs is now picking up again. I would expect it would be very strong.

One thing I can say to you is that imports and exports increased equally in the last 2 years, that is, by the same percentage. It was an 11 percent increase—I mean, excuse me, in this last year there was an 11 percent increase in imports from Japan and an 11 percent increase in exports to Japan. If we can implement these agreements that we have reached and if we see the Japanese economic growth rate coming up to about the American rate, then I think you will see a tightening of that trade deficit.

The final point I would like to make is that it will never be in rough parity unless we continue to strengthen and discipline our own economy and, most important, unless we make some progress on autos and auto parts, because that's about 60 percent of the trade deficit. So that's a part of our framework agreement. We're about to start the talks again there. That's all in the private sector in Japan, but that's what's going to be necessary to finally get this relationship where it ought to be.

But I don't think you can overread the figures from this year because of the impact of the recession and because of the time delay in implementing the eight agreements we made in '94 and their impact. We're clearly making progress, but not enough, and we have to move on auto parts and autos.

World War II Commemorations

Q. Mr. President, how are you going to commemorate the 50th anniversary of the end of the war? Did you, or are you going to invite the Prime Minister to some ceremony which will be held later this year?

The President. Well, there will be a number of commemorations, as you probably know, throughout the Pacific. But we have not yet decided precisely what I will do and how we will do it.

Let me say this: I know there's a debate going on in Japan about this whole issue now and how it should be handled. I can only say that the last three leaders of Japan have expressed in the sincerest terms their regret about the war. We have had a remarkable relationship, a partnership, and a growing friendship with Japan. And I would hope that we could mark this year by saying this is something that civilized nations can never permit to occur again. But looking toward the future and what our responsibilities and what our opportunities are in the future by working together to change the world for the better, that is what I think we should do. And I hope that all these areas of cooperation that the Prime Minister mentioned that will be in the report we're mentioning today, we're releasing today will be at the forefront of what people in the world think about the United States and Japan in the years ahead.

Mexico

Q. Can you tell us something more about what the United States is doing to help stabilize the Mexican economy, what effect the crisis there is having on the U.S. economy or what effect it may have? And can you answer people who are beginning to say that this proves that getting involved, further involved with Mexico and Latin America in treaties like NAFTA may have been a mistake?

The President. Let me—there's two separate questions; let me answer them both. First of all, let me say again I have confidence in the long-term future of Mexico. What we have now is a short-term liquidity crisis. There was inevitably going to be some correction in the Mexican currency value because they had run a rather high budget deficit. But they have had stable political leadership, a good economic direction, a commitment to the right kind of future. And they have shown real discipline. President Zedillo's latest moves will require genuine sacrifice from the Mexican people.

And so the United States is committed to doing what we can to help Mexico through what I believe is and should be a short-term crisis. We have considered a number of options. We have consulted with people in our Government and, obviously, among the leadership of Congress. I spoke with President Zedillo myself last evening again. And we are watching this closely and may have more to say specifically in the days ahead.

But I think it's—this is very important to us. Mexico is our neighbor and has been a constructive partner, has tried to work with us on issues ranging from the drug trade to immigration, as well as on our economic issues. Mexico is sort of a bellwether for the rest of Latin America and developing countries throughout the world. So we have to work on the confidence and the liquidity crisis. And I think that it's in our interest to do so.

Now, let me say on the second question, the people who were opposed to NAFTA made exactly the reverse argument. What they said was that the Americans would be taken to the cleaners, and Mexico would get rich off NAFTA, and America would be greatly disadvantaged. As it turned out, because of our high levels of productivity, the recovery of our economy, and the particular needs of the Mexican economy and the Mexican people now, we did quite well under NAFTA for the last 2 years.

And what has happened is something that no one really foresaw. But I would think this should reaffirm our determination to try to have both democracy and progress, not only in Mexico but throughout Latin America. And for those who can remember what it was like for the United States when Latin America was in depression and when Latin America did not have democratic governments, I think there's no question that it is better for us to have the sort of atmosphere and the sort of reality we saw at the Summit of the Americas. So I just disagree with those who make the second assertion.

Anyone have a question for the Prime Minister?

Q. Mr. President, following Mexico, I want to know if you can tell us the amount of the increase in the credit facility you're going to announce and when, and second, if you plan to keep your support for the candidacy of President Salinas for the WTO over this international criticism for his role in this grand monetary crisis in Mexico?

The President. The answer to the first question is no, I can't give you a specific answer. The answer to the second question is yes, I still support President Salinas.

Is there a Japanese journalist who has a question, a Japanese journalist, a question for the Prime Minister?

North Korea

Q. [*Inaudible*]—support for the light-water reactor project, the President mentioned there was a strong support by Japan, and the Prime Minister mentioned Japan intends to play a significant financial role. I wonder what specific commitment you gave to the President? Also, since you've mentioned Japan intends to play a significant financial role, I wonder if there was any specific ratio indicated, any number given to that financial role? And now there is some criticism with regard to the rather ambiguous solution reached in that agreed framework, and I wonder if there was any comment on that?

Prime Minister Murayama. Well, with regard to the resolution of the North Korean nuclear issue, I would like to say that this issue has a bearing not just on Japan and the neighboring areas but for Asia-Pacific region as a whole. And we've watched very carefully the progress in the U.S.-North Korean talks. And thanks to the tenacious efforts made by the United States, agreement has been reached, and we appreciate that very highly.

In relation to that nuclear issue, we're now discussing the light-water reactor project. As I mentioned earlier, the Government of Japan intends to play a significant financial role in relation to that LWR project. That is what I told the President. However, we have not decided on the specifics of that financial role. For example, we have not commented on how much that financial role is going to be. It is not merely that the Government of Japan intends to cooperate; rather we take this issue as a matter of—for itself as well. And I think it's with that very engaged attitude that we have to address the problem.

The President. Rita [Rita Braver, CBS News]. We'll take, I think, one more each.

Minimum Wage

Q. Mr. President, your aides have said that you are definitely considering a raise in the minimum wage in this country. Have you signed off on that? What's the area in which you're talking about raising it, and when do you think you'll have a final decision? And are you worried about Republican opposition already building?

The President. Well, I have not—let me say, number one, I haven't received a recommendation yet on that from my economic advisers. So I don't want to comment on it until I do.

I think we should look at three things, basically, in making this decision. First of all, the minimum wage is at a 20-year low. Second, inflation is at a 30-year low. And then we need to analyze whether—so there's an argument—and thirdly, the number one mission of the country in this recovery is to raise incomes.

Now, you can argue, well, there are a lot of people on the minimum wage who are actually young people who live at home with parents, and they're not low-income people, and they don't need it. You can argue, there are also a lot of people who are contributing to the support of their children.

Two years ago we attempted to do something really significant about this through the dramatic increase of the earned-income tax credit, which was made refundable, so that today working families in America with an income averaging $25,000, $26,000 a year or less will get an average of a $1,000-a-year tax cut below what their tax rates were before I took office. For those on the low end of the wage scale, that was in part designed to offset the fact that the minimum wage had fallen so far behind inflation and had not kept up with wage growth. There are those who argue that the structure of the American economy has changed so much that this would be burdensome. That's what my economic advisers are evaluating now. They will give me a recommendation.

But my goal, the reason I focused on the earned-income tax credit and the reason I've said we ought to pass the middle class bill of rights, is that we have to raise incomes. Ultimately, the way to raise incomes in America is to increase the skills of the American work force, which is why the most important thing we can do, more than anything else, is to pass the bill of rights: the education tax deduction, the IRA with education withdrawals, and the training voucher program I've proposed to let all the training programs be collapsed and let American workers have up to $2,600 a year in just cash money to get training. That will raise their incomes.

But I will seriously consider this recommendation when I get it. I have simply not received it yet.

Q. Any idea what the—[*inaudible*]—rate would be?

Japan-U.S. Security Arrangements

Q. On Japan-U.S. security arrangements, I understand that you reaffirmed the importance. Now, with regard to host-nation support, I wonder how Japan intends to address that issue? What did you tell the President? And also, with regard to the future, was there any discussion of the possibility of cooperation between the two countries on PKO under the United Nations?

Prime Minister Murayama. The necessity, the need for Japan-U.S. security arrangements was discussed, and we see eye-to-eye with each other completely. Although the cold war structure has disappeared, regionally there still remain numerous unresolved issues. And we believe we should look at the Japan-U.S. security arrangements not simply as something for Japan and the United States. The role that the setup plays for the security and stability of the Asia-Pacific region as a whole is very significant. And therefore, we have to continue to maintain that relationship.

And we should take that security relationship or security setup as the pivot and not simply build on that in the security area but also in the other areas as well. And I think that is very important. And we would like to, therefore, continue to strengthen that relationship from that vantage point.

Your second question was on peacekeeping operations. As you know, Japan is a country that has a constitution, a peace constitution, and therefore we cannot provide cooperation that involves the use of arms. However, we have already sent our self-defense forces to Rwanda and other parts of the world for humanitarian purposes. And for such humanitarian purposes and within the extent that the Japanese Constitution will allow, we have been saying consistently that Japan is willing to cooperate with the world. And I think there is full understanding between the two countries on that.

Japan-U.S. Trade

The President. Let me say that the Prime Minister has to leave. And before he does, I want to make a presentation. Yesterday for the first time, the Japanese market was opened to apples from the United States. And as the Prime Minister left, he was telling me the marketplaces were being filled with the apples, but he didn't have a chance to get any. Now, shortly, the

American market will be open to apples from Japan. And we're looking forward to them. I personally like them a great deal. But since the Prime Minister left before the markets opened, I want to give him a basket of Washington State apples to take home to Japan with him. [*Laughter*] This is the symbol of our progress.

Prime Minister Murayama. The Japanese people are enjoying the taste of American apples, and I hope that American people will enjoy the taste of Japanese apples.

Thank you very much.

NOTE: The President's 84th news conference began at 2:05 p.m. in the Grand Foyer at the White House. Prime Minister Murayama spoke in Japanese, and his remarks were translated by an interpreter.

Remarks to California Flood Victims
January 11, 1995

Good afternoon. I want to speak to you today about the ferocious floods now battering California.

In recent times, unrelenting rains have ravaged many places across our great country, rains that have destroyed people's homes, devastated families, carried away the fruits of many, many years of hard work. There can be no greater challenge to a community than facing down these terrifying tides. Yet that is what Americans can do so well. And that is what you, the people of California, are doing at this very minute.

I want you to know that you have my support and the support of our administration to fight this battle the way it has to be fought. Late last night, I declared a major disaster across California and asked James Lee Witt, the Director of the Federal Emergency Management Agency, to oversee our efforts to quickly provide the necessary assistance and to get you moving on the road to recovery. At 1 o'clock our time last night, he assured me that that is exactly what he would do. We're working closely with Governor Wilson, Senator Boxer, and Senator Feinstein, with all the local, State, and Federal officials to fight the flooding.

Let me say a special word of thanks to all the young volunteers from AmeriCorps, our national service program, and the other volunteers for the quick and good work they have done and are doing. Californians have proven over the last few years they have a very resilient spirit. And in a great sense of community, with the earthquakes and the fires, you have shown that you're a people who can come together in times of crisis and overcome those crises.

Our administration has stood with you. Almost a year ago, those of you in the Los Angeles area were awakened by that terrible quake. We stood by you then, by making available billions of dollars and thousands of workers to help in the rebuilding effort, and we'll stand with you again.

Hillary and I send our thoughts and our prayers to the families whose loved ones have died and the thousands of you whose lives have been disrupted. We wish you well. We'll get through this in good American style.

NOTE: The President spoke at 3:02 p.m. by satellite from the Roosevelt Room at the White House.

Statement on the Economic Situation in Mexico
January 11, 1995

I have spoken with President Zedillo and conveyed our continued support for Mexico.

The Mexican President has outlined a comprehensive economic program, which has won the support of the International Monetary Fund.

We have a strong interest in prosperity and stability in Mexico. It is in America's economic and strategic interest that Mexico succeeds.

We are in close touch with the Mexican authorities. I have instructed the Treasury, working closely with the Federal Reserve, to continue to take appropriate steps to help Mexico get through these short-term financial pressures and build on the strong foundation for economic growth created in recent years.

If appropriate, I am prepared to authorize the extension of the maturity of our existing credit facility and to increase those commitments to assist Mexico in meeting its short-term financial obligations.

I am calling on the international financial institutions to work quickly to put in place a substantial lending program to support Mexico's economic program.

Statement on the Democratic National Committee
January 12, 1995

Later this month, at the Democratic National Committee (DNC) meeting in Washington, I will formally ask DNC members to support the appointment of two capable and committed party advocates for general chairman and national chairman. I have asked Senator Chris Dodd (D–CT) and Don Fowler to accept these assignments, and I am enormously grateful that they will be my partners in strengthening the Democratic National Committee.

With their help, we will return to the important business of electing Democrats at all levels of government, and assuring that the voices of the people who work hard and play by the rules—our constituents—are heard and heeded at the seats of government throughout our land.

Senator Chris Dodd is one of Congress' most eloquent and effective advocates for children and working families. He wrote both the Family and Medical Leave Act and the child care and development block grant, 1990's landmark child care legislation. He has also been a leader in the Senate on foreign policy and business issues. As general chairman, Senator Dodd will complement his Senate duties by serving as our spokesman and as a leading strategist for the party.

A little more than 30 years ago another gentleman from Connecticut named John Bailey helped direct our party to victory in landmark elections, and I am convinced that my friend Chris Dodd will repeat that precedent in the elections of 1995 and beyond.

Don Fowler of South Carolina, a DNC member since 1971, will serve as national chairman, doing the hard but important work of running

a political party. In the past, Don has served as chairman of the South Carolina Democratic Party, president of the Association of State Democratic Chairs, and CEO of our convention in Atlanta in 1988. No one knows more about our party's operations and strategy, and no one is more serious or qualified than Don to guide and direct Democrats to win elections. He will also be a leading strategist and will be the operational head of the DNC.

While many organizations and entities contribute resources and ideas that make our party stronger, it is the Democratic National Committee that works to elect the local, State, and Federal elected officials who serve the working people of our country.

As we move toward the next century, and as we face the challenges of expanding middle class participation in the recovery, reforming Government, restoring values and decency in our society, and holding fast to the principles of justice and fairness, retaking the Congress and electing Democrats to office is the work of our party committee, and its work must be successful. I thank Chris and Don for taking on this challenge.

I know they join me in thanking Debra DeLee for her service as Democratic Party chair since November. She was remarkable in giving her energy, her commitment, and her strength to sustaining the party at a challenging time in its history. We have asked her to take on another assignment as CEO of the party's nomination convention in Chicago in 1996, and I am thrilled that she will be serving in that capacity.

Statement With Congressional Leaders on the Economic Situation in Mexico
January 12, 1995

We agreed that the United States has an important economic and strategic interest in a stable and prosperous Mexico.

Ultimately, the solution to Mexico's economic problems must come from the people of Mexico, but we are pursuing ways to increase financial confidence and to encourage further reform in Mexico.

We agreed to do what is necessary to restore financial confidence in Mexico without affecting the current budget at home.

NOTE: This statement was announced jointly with Newt Gingrich, Speaker of the House of Representatives, Robert Dole, Senate majority leader, Thomas Daschle, Senate minority leader, Richard Armey, House majority leader, and Richard Gephardt, House minority leader.

Message to the Senate Transmitting the South Korea-United States Legal Assistance Treaty
January 12, 1995

To the Senate of the United States:

With a view to receiving the advice and consent of the Senate to ratification, I transmit herewith the Treaty Between the Government of the United States of America and the Government of the Republic of Korea on Mutual Legal Assistance in Criminal Matters, signed at Washington on November 23, 1993, with a related exchange of notes signed the same date. Also transmitted for the information of the Senate is the report of the Department of State with respect to this Treaty.

The Treaty is one of a series of modern mutual legal assistance treaties that the United States is negotiating in order to counter criminal activities more effectively. The Treaty should be an effective tool to assist in the prosecution of a wide variety of modern criminals, including members of drug cartels, "white-collar" criminals, and terrorists. The Treaty is self-executing.

The Treaty provides for a broad range of cooperation in criminal matters. Mutual assistance available under the treaty includes: (1) taking testimony or statements of persons; (2) providing documents, records, and articles of evidence; (3) serving documents; (4) locating or identifying persons or items; (5) transferring persons in custody for testimony or other purposes; (6) executing requests for searches and seizures; (7) assisting in forfeiture proceedings; and (8) rendering any other form of assistance not prohibited by the laws of the Requested State.

I recommend that the Senate give early and favorable consideration to the Treaty and give its advice and consent to ratification.

WILLIAM J. CLINTON

The White House,
January 12, 1995.

Remarks in Cleveland, Ohio, at the White House Conference on Trade and Investment in Central and Eastern Europe
January 13, 1995

Thank you very much. Mayor White, Congressmen Stokes and Sawyer and Brown, distinguished officials here from Cleveland and Cuyahoga County. Secretary Brown, thank you for your kind introduction. That was an illustration of Bill Clinton's second law of politics, that introduction: Whenever possible, be introduced by someone you've appointed to high office. You always get a good one. [*Laughter*]

I do want to say here that I believe, in the history of the Department of Commerce, there has never been a better Secretary than Ron Brown. I am grateful to him for his dedication to the American business community and to the growth of the American economy and for his commitment to international outreach.

I thank the Commerce Department and the Business Council for International Understanding for organizing this conference. You've assembled an impressive and diverse group: delegations from Central and Eastern Europe, business leaders from the United States and Europe, American ethnic leaders from all around our country, and so many outstanding State and local officials. I thank you all for being here.

I have to say, I'm especially pleased that we're meeting in Cleveland. Many of the men and women who made this great city a foundation of America's industrial heartland came to our shores from Central Europe. With just a little money but lots of determination and discipline and vision, they helped to build our great Nation. And now their children and their grandchildren are leaders in Cleveland and in dozens of other American communities all across our country. Strong bonds of memory, heritage, and pride link them today to Europe's emerging democracies. So it's fitting that we should be meeting here.

I also chose Cleveland because people here know what it takes to adapt to the new global economy. Whether you're in this great State or in Central Europe's coal and steel belt, meeting the challenges of change are hard. But Cleveland, Cleveland is transforming itself into a center for international trade. And it is a real model for economic growth throughout our country. Already, Cleveland exports $5.5 billion worth of

goods every year. And that trade supports 100,000 jobs. Cleveland was one of the cities to recently win a highly competitive effort to secure one of our empowerment zones. And Cleveland was selected because of the remarkable partnership that has been put together here between the public and private sectors. So I'm very glad to be here.

I came to this office with a mission for my country that involves all the countries represented here today. I came because I believed we had to make some changes to keep the American dream alive in the United States, to restore a sense of opportunity and possibility to our people in a time of great and sweeping change, and to give us a clear sense of purpose at the end of the cold war, as we move toward the 21st century. But I also wanted us to move into that new century still the world's leader for peace and democracy, for freedom, and for prosperity. This conference symbolizes both those objectives.

We have worked hard in the United States to get our economy going again, to get our Government deficit down, to invest in our people and the technologies of the future, to expand trade for our own benefit. We have been fortunate in this country in the last 2 years in generating over 5½ million new jobs and having a new sense that we could bring back every important sector of our economy. But we know that over the long run, our success economically in America depends upon our being true to our values here at home and around the world.

And so I say to you that I came here today because I know that America must remain engaged in the world. If we do so, clearly we have an historic opportunity to enhance the security and increase the prosperity of our own people in a society that we hope will be characterized forever more by trade and culture and learning across national lines than by hatred and fighting and war.

Many of you in this room are proving that proposition every day. The new partnerships that you are forging between America and Central Europe bring tangible benefits to all the people involved. Increased trade and investment promotes our exports. It gives our people new skills and creates good jobs—but not only for us, for our trading partners as well. And it plays another very important role: It gives us a dividend by helping the nations with which we trade, and especially the nations in Central Europe, to consolidate their hard-won democracy on a foundation of free enterprise and political freedom.

In all of our countries, we stand at the start of a new era, an era of breathtaking change and expanding opportunities. The explosion of trade and technology has produced a new global economy in which people and ideas and capital come together more quickly, more easily, more creatively than ever before. It is literally true that the end of the cold war has liberated millions of Europeans and introduced both free markets and democracy to countries not only there but on every continent of the globe.

But this promise is also clouded by fear and uncertainty. Economic uncertainty, the breakdown of the old rules of the social contract is a problem in every advanced Western democracy and in wealthy countries in the East, like Japan. And beyond that and even deeper, aggression by malicious states, transnational threats like overpopulation and environmental degradation, terrible ethnic conflicts, and the proliferation of weapons of mass destruction, all these problems beyond our own borders make it tempting to many Americans to retrench behind our borders, to say, "Look, we've got a lot of possibilities, and we've got more problems than we can handle here at home, so let's just forget about the rest of the world for a while. We did our job in the cold war. We spent our money to keep the world free from communism. And we are tired, and we've got plenty to do here." There are many people who believe exactly that in this country and in our Congress.

But the very fact of democracy's triumph in the cold war, while it has led some to argue that we ought to confine our focus to challenges here at home and to say we cannot afford to lead anymore, in fact imposes on us new responsibilities and new opportunities. And I would argue that we cannot benefit the American people here at home unless we assume those responsibilities and seize those opportunities.

Those who say we can just walk away have views that are shortsighted. We must reach out, not retrench. I will continue to work in this new Congress with both the Republicans and the Democrats to forge a bipartisan coalition of internationalists who share those same convictions. The agreement we reached yesterday with congressional leaders from both sides of the aisle to help Mexico restore full confidence in its economy demonstrates the potential of a coalition committed to America's interests in the world of tomorrow. And I will do everything in my power, as I have done for 2 years now, to keep our country engaged in the world. I won't let anyone or anything divert the United States from this course. The whole future of the world and the future of our children here in the United States depend on our continued involvement and leadership in the world.

History teaches us, after all, that security and prosperity here at home require that we maintain a focus abroad. Remember that after World War I the United States refused the leadership role. We withdrew behind our borders, behind our big trade barriers. We left a huge vacuum that was filled with the forces of hatred and tyranny. The resulting struggle to preserve our freedom in World War II cost millions of lives and required all the energy and resources we could muster to forestall an awful result.

After the Second World War, a wise generation of Americans refused to let history repeat itself. So in the face of the Communist challenge, they helped to shape NATO, the Marshall plan, GATT, and the other structures that ensured 50 years of building prosperity and security for America, for Western Europe, and Japan.

Ultimately, the strength of those structures, the force of democracy, and the heroic determination of peoples to be free produced victory in the cold war. Now, in the aftermath of that victory, it is our common responsibility not to squander the peace. We must realize the full potential of that victory. Now that freedom has been won, all our people deserve to reap the tangible rewards of their sacrifice, people in the United States and people in Central Europe. Now that freedom has been won, our nations must be determined that it will never be lost again.

The United States is seizing this moment. History has given us a gift, and the results are there to prove it. Because of the agreements we reached with Russia, with Belarus, with Kazakhstan, with Ukraine, for the first time since the dawn of the nuclear age, Americans can go to bed at night knowing that nuclear weapons from the former Soviet Union are no longer pointed at our children.

Our patient but hardheaded diplomacy has secured an agreement with North Korea on nuclear issues that is clearly and profoundly in our interest. The critics of that agreement are wrong. The deal stops North Korea's nuclear program in its tracks. It will roll it back in years to come. International inspectors confirm that the program is frozen, and they will continue to monitor it. No critic has come up with an alternative that isn't either unfeasible or foolhardy.

Our troops, who maintain their preparedness and their enormous capacity to stand up for freedom as the finest fighting force in the world, have stood down Iraq's threat to the security of the Persian Gulf. They caused the military regime in Haiti to step down peacefully, to give the Haitians a chance at democracy. We're using our influence constructively to help people from the Middle East to southern Africa to transform their conflicts into cooperation.

We have used our ability to lead on issues like GATT and NAFTA and the Asian-Pacific Economic Cooperation council and the Summit of the Americas to help to create a new trading system for the next century. Already trade is becoming more free and more fair and producing better jobs for our people and for others around the world.

In Central Europe, as elsewhere, the United States has moved aggressively to shape the future. The reasons are simple: Helping Central Europe to consolidate democracy, to build strong economies is clearly the best way to prevent assaults on freedom that, as this century has so painfully demonstrated, can turn quickly into all-consuming war. A healthy and prosperous Central Europe is good for America. It will become a huge new market for our goods and our services.

America is also engaged with Central Europe because it's the right thing to do. For four and a half decades, we challenged these nations to cast away the shackles of communism. Now that they have done so, surely we have an obligation to work with them—all of you who are here—to make sure that your people share with our people the rewards of freedom that the next century and the new economy can bring.

Some argue that open government and free markets can't take root in some countries, that there are boundaries, that there will necessarily

be boundaries to democracy in Europe. They would act now in anticipation of those boundaries by creating an artificial division of the new continent. Others claim that we simply must not extend the West's institution of security and prosperity at all, that to do so would upset a delicate balance of power. They would confine the newly free peoples of Central Europe to a zone of insecurity and, therefore, of instability.

I believe that both those visions for Europe are too narrow, too skeptical, perhaps even too cynical. One year ago this week, in Brussels, in Prague, in Kiev, in Moscow, and in Minsk, I set forth a vision of a different Europe, a new Europe that would be an integrated community of secure and increasingly prosperous democracies, a Europe that for the first time since nation-states came into existence on the European Continent would not be subject to a dividing line. With our engagement with the countries of Central Europe and the former Soviet Union, we can help to make that vision a lasting reality.

First, Europe must be secure. The breakup of the Soviet Union has made the promise of security more real than it has been for decades. But reform in Russia and all the states of the former Soviet Union will not be completed overnight, in a straight line, or without rocky bumps in the road. It will prove rough and unsteady from time to time, as the tragic events in Chechnya remind us today. Chechnya is part of the Russian Federation, and we support the territorial integrity of Russia, just as we support the territorial integrity of all its neighbors. But the violence must end. I call again on all the parties to stop spilling blood and start making peace.

Every day the fighting in Chechnya continues is a day of wasted lives and wasted resources and wasted opportunity. So we again encourage every effort to bring to a lasting end the bloodshed. We encourage the proposals put forth by the European Union and the Organization for Security and Cooperation in Europe. These proposals deserve to be heard and embraced.

Some have used this conflict in Chechnya to question continued American support for reform in Russia. But that conflict, terrible though it is, has not changed the nature of our interest. We have a tremendous stake in the success of Russia's efforts to become a stable democratic nation, and so do all the countries represented here today. That is why the United States will not waver from our course of patient, responsible support for Russian reform. It would be a terrible mistake to react reflexively to the ups and downs that Russia is experiencing and was bound to experience all along and will continue to experience in the years ahead, indeed, perhaps for decades, as it undergoes an historic transformation.

If the forces of reform are embattled, we must renew, not retreat from, our support for them. So we will continue again to lead a bipartisan effort here at home and an international coalition abroad to work with Russia and also with the other New Independent States of the former Soviet Union to support reform, to support progress, to support democracy, to support freedom.

We are well aware, too, of Central Europe's security concerns. We will never condone any state in Europe threatening the sovereignty of its neighbors again. That is why the United States protected Baltic independence by pressing successfully for the withdrawal of Russian troops.

In this period of great social and political change, we want to help countries throughout Central Europe achieve stability, the stability they need to build strong democracies and to foster prosperity. To promote that stability, the United States established the Partnership For Peace. And we have taken the lead in preparing for the gradual, open, and inevitable expansion of NATO. In just a year, the Partnership For Peace has become a dynamic forum for practical military and political cooperation among its members. For some countries, the partnership will be the path to full NATO membership. For others, the partnership will be a strong and lasting link to the NATO alliance.

Last month, clearly and deliberately, NATO began to map out the road to enlargement. Neither NATO nor the United States can today give a date certain for expansion, nor can we say today which countries will be the first new members. But let me repeat what I have said before: The questions concerning NATO expansion are not whether NATO will expand, not if NATO will expand, but when and how. And when expansion begins, it will come as no surprise to anyone. Its conditions, its timing, its military implications will be well and widely known and discussed in advance.

NATO membership is not a right. We expect those who seek to join the alliance to prepare themselves, through the Partnership For Peace, for the obligations of membership; they are important. Countries with repressive political systems, countries with designs on their neighbors, countries with militaries unchecked by civilian control or with closed economic systems need not apply.

And let me say once again: Only the 16 members of NATO will decide on expansion. But NATO expansion should not be seen as replacing one division of Europe with another one. It should, it can, and I am determined that it will increase security for all European states, members and nonmembers alike. In parallel with expansion, NATO must develop close and strong ties with Russia. The alliance's relationship with Russia should become more direct, more open, more ambitious, more frank.

European security embraces a democratic Russia. But for Central Europe to enjoy true security, its nations must also develop not only military ties and security arrangements but also successful market economies. If we have learned anything about the new century toward which we are moving, it is that national security must be defined in terms that go far beyond military ideas and concepts. That's why we're all here. From Tallinn to Tirana, people must have good jobs so that they can provide for their families and feel the self-confidence necessary to support democracy. They must have the tools to adapt to this rapidly changing global economy. They must have economic confidence, in short, to believe in a democratic future.

Since the fall of the Berlin Wall, the United States has played an important role in promoting these goals. We have strongly supported Central Europe's integration into the European Union. We have taken significant steps to improve access to our own markets, and we have provided Central Europe with financial aid, with technical support, and with debt relief. This assistance has been used for a staggering array of projects, from helping the Czech Republic draft a modern bankruptcy code, to training commercial bankers in Slovakia, to advertising and equipping modern and independent media throughout the region.

But for all our Government has done and will continue to do, the fact remains that only the private sector can mobilize the vast amounts of capital and the human skills and technology needed to help complete the transformation of Central Europe's free markets.

President Walesa put it to me this way last July: "What Poland needs," he said, "are more American generals, like General Electric and General Motors." [*Laughter*] That's not a commercial; I could have advertised the other auto companies, the other electric companies. Congressman Stokes reminded me that Lincoln Electric here in Cleveland just got the Secretary of Commerce's E Award last night. But the point is that President Walesa's comment defines national security for Poland in a broader context and demonstrates an understanding of what it will take for democracy and freedom to flourish.

In just 5 years, most of the countries in Central Europe have undertaken many of the difficult reforms necessary to build credibility with investors and trading partners, to make themselves attractive to the General Electrics and the General Motors. Bold economic reform works. Countries that have pursued it with the greatest conviction have rebounded most quickly from the recession. They are among Europe's fastest growing economies. And they are drawing the most foreign trade and investment.

More trade and investment is good for Central Europe. But make no mistake about it, it's also very good for the United States. For all of us, it means more jobs, higher wages, an opportunity to learn the new skills we need to succeed in the new global economy. And I say again, it means more real security.

Consider the benefits of just two recent American ventures in Central Europe: The International Paper Company of New York bought a major mill in Poland, retrained its work force, modernized the mill, and turned it into a thriving exporter. It also acquired a strong presence in the competitive European market that will generate $30 million in American exports in support of hundreds of jobs back here at home.

Denver-based US West will soon bring nationwide cellular phone service to Hungary. That will give Hungarians, who now wait an average of 12 years to get a phone, immediate access to modern communications. And it will produce $28 million in United States exports and support hundreds of jobs here in the United States. I have to say, sort of off the record, that we'll also soon make the Hungarians as frayed around the edges and overbusy as Americans are with their cellular phones. But if they want it, we should help them have it. [*Laughter*]

I am very proud that these and literally dozens of other projects went forward with the help of loans and insurance and other guarantees from the United States Government. But I know what our trade and investment in Central Europe could do if we were all to make the most of the opportunities that are there. Our involvement should be much greater. American companies and investors are second to none in identifying good opportunities. But they will reject a project if roadblocks to getting it done efficiently and fairly are too high, especially given the fierce competition for trade and investment from Latin America and Asia.

Our companies need to be sure that when they make a deal, it won't be arbitrarily reversed. They look for full information and reasonable regulation. They want clear commercial tax and legal codes. And of course they want private sector counterparts, the driving force of Central Europe's economies, with whom they can do business.

One of the most effective roles the United States can play is to promote continued reform and to help businesses do business, which of course is what this conference is all about. But our efforts did not begin and will not end here in Cleveland. Already we have concluded investment and taxation treaties with many of the countries represented here. The Trade and Development Agency has identified thousands of business opportunities throughout Central Europe. Peace Corps volunteers are teaching business, banking, and finance skills to new entrepreneurs. Our Export-Import Bank is promoting the use of America's products for major infrastructure projects and for bringing environmental technology and expertise to Central Europe. And today I am pleased to announce that the Overseas Private Investment Corporation has set up two new equity funds that, together with funds OPIC already supports, should leverage more than $4 billion in private investment.

Every United States economic agency is working hard to help American business, big and small, to take advantage of the opportunities in Central Europe and around the world. And I want to say that what I said about Secretary Brown and the Commerce Department could also be said about the Export-Import Bank and the Overseas Private Investment Corporation. It is the strongest economic team the United States has ever put in the field of international business, and we intend to see it keep working until we make a success of the ventures like the one we're engaged in here today.

All of their teamwork has proved that Government can work for the American people, a proposition very much in doubt in our country today. I know how difficult and unsettling this period of change is for so many people all over the countries represented in this room and here at home, as well. Sometimes it seems that the more you open your eyes to the world around you, the more confusing it becomes. But we must not lose sight of the fact that even greater forces of history are working for the development of human capacities and the fulfillment of human dreams than the forces working to undermine them.

And if we use these great positive forces, if we guide them, if we shape them, if we remain committed to making them work for us, we can make our people more secure and more prosperous. Look at what is happening in Central Europe. Every day, open societies and open economies are gaining strength. Every day, new entrepreneurs and businesses are spurring growth and are creating jobs in their own coun-

tries and for us back here in America as well. It is in our national interest to help them succeed. We cannot afford to do otherwise.

Just 6 years ago, the countries of Central Europe were still captive nations. Now, 120 million people have the freedom to speak their own minds, to create, to build, to prosper, to dream dreams and try to fulfill them. This new freedom is the fruit of Europe's struggle and America's support. We owe it to those who brought us this far—more importantly, we owe it to ourselves and to our children—not to turn our backs on their historic achievement or this historic moment. That is why this administration will not retreat. We will continue to reach out, working together, trading together, joining together. We will fulfill the great promise of this moment.

Thank you very much.

NOTE: The President spoke at 10:15 a.m. in the Grand Ballroom at the Stouffer Renaissance Hotel. In his remarks, he referred to Mayor Michael R. White of Cleveland.

Statement on Investment Funds for Central and Eastern Europe
January 13, 1995

In Prague last January, I promised we would create investment funds for Central and Eastern Europe. This January we have four of them. They can mean billions of dollars in capital investment to help fuel economic development in the region while creating jobs for Americans at home.

NOTE: This statement was included in a White House statement announcing new Overseas Private Investment Corporation loan guaranty commitments for two privately owned and managed equity funds.

Statement on Bilateral Investment Treaties With Albania and Latvia
January 13, 1995

These bilateral investment treaties put in place a strong foundation for expanded U.S. trade and investment with the reforming democracies of Central and Eastern Europe. They are another step toward integrating Europe's new democracies with an expanding transatlantic

community. Americans and Central Europeans alike will benefit through the increased business.

NOTE: This statement was included in a White House statement announcing the signing of the treaties.

Statement on Disaster Assistance for California
January 13, 1995

Today I am sending to the State of California $10 million from the disaster relief fund. These funds will be used by the State and local governments in the flooded areas to remove debris and to take protective measures to ensure the health and safety of their residents.

At this time, I have approved Federal assistance for 34 California counties stricken by the disastrous floods. Our hearts go out to the people who have suffered losses in these disastrous floods. I have asked James L. Witt, the Director of the Federal Emergency Management Agency, to make certain that all appropriate resources of the Federal Government are applied to assist the State of California in helping their citizens to begin to recover from this disaster. The action I have taken today will be a start for California residents down the difficult road to recovery.

Statement on the Dispute Between Bridgestone-Firestone and the United Rubber Workers
January 13, 1995

I have long supported legislation to prevent companies from permanently replacing their striking workers. Unfortunately, last year a minority of Senators prevented the full Senate from voting on the bill.

Now Bridgestone-Firestone's use of permanent replacements shows exactly why this protection is necessary. By bringing in permanent replacements for their workers who are on strike, while refusing to come to the bargaining table, the management of Bridgestone-Firestone is flagrantly turning its back on our tradition of peaceful collective bargaining to solve labor disputes. When companies replace their workers under these circumstances, they sow seeds of distrust and resentment which can extend far beyond their company, undermining labor-management relations across the land. Bridgestone-Firestone should get back to the bargaining table with the United Rubber Workers to reach a fair settlement. Secretary Reich and the Federal Mediation and Conciliation Service stand ready to help. Let's get on with it.

The President's Radio Address
January 14, 1995

Good morning. Let me begin by saying that Hillary and I send our prayers and our good wishes to all the families who are suffering in the terrible California floods. Our administration is doing everything in our power to make sure you get the relief you need. And I pledge to you that the American people will stand by you in this time of crisis as they have in the past.

On Monday, we'll all celebrate the life of Dr. Martin Luther King on what would have been his 66th birthday. Dr. King was one of the great moral prophets of our time. He never held public office, but no one ever did more to redeem the promise of American life or stir the soul of our Nation.

One of Martin Luther King's greatest lessons was that every American deserves a piece of the American dream, the chance to pull ourselves up and work our way into the middle class. He taught us that we have more uniting us than dividing us, that no matter our race, our religion, our income, we all share the same hope of building better lives for ourselves and our children.

The most important civil right is the right to dream the American dream and to have the opportunity to live it. I ran for President because I feared we were in danger of losing that right. At a moment of great change in our history, as we move from the industrial age into the information age, as we end the cold war and move into the global economy of the 21st century, I believe our purpose has to be to keep the American dream alive for all Americans.

To do that, I have fought for three things: first, a new economic strategy to help our people compete and win in the new global economy; second, a New Covenant with the American people that offers more opportunity to everyone willing to assume personal responsibility for their own lives; and third, a new kind of Government, a leaner but not a meaner Government that cuts yesterday's programs and bureaucracy to make room for tomorrow's solutions, rooted in responsibility, empowerment of our citizens, the strength of our communities.

In 2 years we've made a good start. We have a strong economy with 5.6 million new jobs. We've made historic cuts in the deficit, enough to take $11,000 in debt off of every family's future. We've cut the size of Government. There are 100,000 fewer people working for the Federal Government than there were on the day I became President. And we've made lots of programs more efficient and more effective. And we've offered the American people new opportunities that demand more responsibility, from more affordable college loans to the family leave program to giving our local communities the resources they need to lower the crime rate.

But despite this progress, too many Americans are still working harder for less. They don't have the security they need and deserve because they work hard and play by the rules. As we face the challenges of the 21st century, too many Americans remain in danger of falling behind or fear that they will still be left behind as they have been in years past.

That's why I proposed the middle class bill of rights, which might be better called the middle class bill of rights and responsibilities. It gives Americans the chance to arm themselves for the new economy and to lift their incomes. It gives middle class families the opportunities they need to raise their children, pay for college, save money for the things families need, and get the training and skills they need to prosper.

It offers a tax deduction for all education after high school. It offers lower taxes for families with young children. It offers an individual retirement account with tax-free withdrawals for costs other than retirement that are devoted to the future, costs for education, for health care, for care of an elderly parent, for buying a first home. And it offers a training account of over $2,600 for those who are unemployed or who are lower wage workers who want to get more skills to improve their own futures.

This program furthers all three of my objectives. It helps all of us to meet the challenges of the new economy. It helps us to build that New Covenant of opportunity in return for responsibility. And it cuts Government and changes the way it works to make it more modern, less bureaucratic, more flexible, more focused on personal empowerment. I hope the new Congress will pass the middle class bill of rights, and I welcome anyone else's ideas that advance these same goals.

In the new Congress, my test will be: Does an idea expand middle class incomes and opportunities? Does it promote values like family and work, responsibility and community? Does it contribute to strengthening the new economy and to building a better future for all of us? If it does, I'll be for it, no matter who proposes it. And if it doesn't, I'll oppose it.

One of the best examples of what we're trying to do is something we've already begun to do, our national service program, AmeriCorps. It helps those who help themselves in America. It says, take responsibility to serve your country at the grassroots level, and we'll give you the opportunity to get the education you need to build a better future for yourself. Already there are 20,000 AmeriCorps volunteers serving their communities while earning money for college. There are more people now in AmeriCorps in this year than ever served in the Peace Corps in a single year.

On Monday, Martin Luther King Day, I've called for a national day of service. And AmeriCorps volunteers will be hard at work all cross our country rebuilding a school in Atlanta, rebuilding housing in Memphis, helping the flood victims in Los Angeles. I hope you will join them because the idea and the ideal of service, service to country, service to community, service to our fellow citizens, is central to our Nation's future.

Dr. King's most profound lesson was that in America, "me" depends on "we." As he said, "We are all caught in an inescapable network of mutuality tied into a single garment of destiny." In the end, we will rise or fall together. Martin Luther King knew that we all have to do our part. What he wanted was for all Americans to have not a handout but a hand up. That's what the national day of service is all about.

Of course, there are no guarantees that the future will be easy for all of us. We will face great challenges. But if we'll all join together and do our part as citizens, we can—we can receive the American dream that Martin Luther King envisioned.

Thanks for listening.

NOTE: The address was recorded at 5:43 p.m. on January 13 in the Oval Office at the White House for broadcast at 10:06 a.m. on January 14.

Remarks Honoring Martin Luther King, Jr., in Denver, Colorado
January 16, 1995

The President. Thank you. It is wonderful to be back in Colorado, to be back in Denver, and to be in this great spot which holds such a warm memory for me. The last time I came here we had a vast crowd. I was asking for the opportunity to serve as your President. And I must say, when I came before, I had Sinbad with me as the warmup act, and I thought that was responsible for the crowd. Today I am honored to be here with all these fine people on the platform and with all of you.

I thank my friend Governor Romer for what he said and for his leadership and for his long friendship. I thank Senator Campbell and Congresswoman Schroeder for coming all the way back from Washington to be here with me and, most important, to be here with you today. I thank Secretary Peña for his outstanding service as our Transportation Secretary, working to make this country a safer place. And of course, I am grateful to the mayor and to Mrs. Webb for their leadership in this stunning event and for allowing me to be a small part of this.

We come here today to celebrate the life of Martin Luther King. We know that he would have been 66 years old today. To me, it seems only yesterday when he was 39 and laying down his life for what he believed. Mayor Webb said that the life of Martin Luther King had special relevance for African-Americans because of what he meant. Let me tell you that his life should have special impact for every American, for he freed the rest of us, too, of our hatred, our bigotry, of the illusion which still crops up from time to time that we can somehow lift ourselves up by putting others down, that somehow, if we can just find someone to look down on, we can feel like we're being looked up to.

Martin Luther King knew better than that. I ask you today, my fellow Americans, to think about why he lived and what he laid his life down for, to think about what ought to be driving our lives, our individual lives and our lives as citizens.

You heard earlier Dr. King's famous "I have a dream" speech. I saw a sign held up earlier, when I came in, saying that they had a dream for America; did I have a dream for America—the people holding the sign up there. Remember what Martin Luther King said? He said, "My dream is deeply rooted in the American dream." What did he mean by that? The Founders said: We hold these truths to be self-evident, that all are created equal and endowed by their Creator with certain inalienable rights, and among these are life, liberty, and the pursuit of happiness.

Today, my fellow Americans, I want to talk to you about our common right to life, liberty, and the pursuit of happiness. I ask you to think today of Government but to think beyond Government to people. I ask you to think today of the programs and the work of Government but to think beyond that to the lives of people. I ask you to remember today that, more than anything else, Martin Luther King's life was a life of service. Even as he marched all across this land and took that vast throng to Washington, DC, and asked the Government to act, he knew that in the end, what was in the heart and the spirit and the mind of the average American citizen was even more important.

49

And that is why he always said that all of us had a responsibility to do our part and to serve. Martin Luther King said, "Everybody can be great because everybody can serve." He said, "If all you do is sweep the streets, then sweep them just as well as Michelangelo painted the Sistine Chapel." Be the best streetsweeper that ever lived; serve and serve.

I was asked the other day, of all the things that had happened in the last 2 years, was there one achievement I could say I was most proud of? And I said, I think it was the creation of the national service program. And some of them are here today. Why? Because these young people are committed to service. And if we all are committed to the idea that we are bound up with one another, then we can all be great and our country will be great.

When I came here in 1992, I was worried about the direction of this country. I was concerned about the economic problems of America. More importantly, I was concerned that we seemed to be drifting and divided and that we had no clear role for how we might work together to build a better future, to reclaim that dream for which Martin Luther King gave his life. And I told you that I would seek, for my part, to do three things: one, to give this country a new economic policy that would bring down the deficit and bring up employment and bring us forward toward the next century; two, a different way of governing, that I would reduce the size of the Federal Government and increase its creativity, its effectiveness, its relevance to your life. And we have done both those things. We have restored a sense of economic direction and opportunity to this country, and the Government is smaller and yet still more effective. No one exemplifies that any better than Denver's Transportation Secretary, Federico Peña.

But I knew then and I say again now that that would be fine but not enough, that we literally had to change our relationship in America as citizens to our Government and, most importantly, to each other. It was what I called then and what I say now is a New Covenant, the idea that you have a right to certain opportunities, but in return you must exercise personal responsibility in return for those opportunities to make the most of your own life, the life of your family, the life of your community, and the life of your country. That is what this is all about.

That's why when people talk about something like welfare reform, I don't think about punishing poor people, I think about ending welfare so poor people can work and be good parents and have a better life and look to a better future. That's why, when we passed the crime bill, I thought it was a good thing just to give money to local communities to hire more police officers and also to have opportunities to give our children something to say yes to as well as something to say no to, so that we could show responsibility even as we seized opportunities.

If you think about it, that is the great debate we should be having today: What is our responsibility to ourselves, and what is our responsibility to each other? If you have rights without responsibility, pretty soon people lose their rights because they don't behave responsibly. If you go around telling people to be responsible all the time and there never is an opportunity coming forward, pretty soon they get tired of being responsible.

What we have to do today, if we want hope, if we want the dream to live again, is to say to each other: We will have a new commitment to creating opportunity and to being responsible. We will say no to violence and yes to hope. We will say no, no to the idea that we can get anywhere by being divided against one another and yes to the idea that our diversity is a strength.

I am telling you, we can have all the economic growth in the world, but until we face the fact that we are going up or down together and we'd better get after the business of working together to make the most of all our potential, we will never be what we ought to be as a country.

Now, I know we have more to do in Washington. I know that a lot of people are working harder and still not having a raise. I know, as the pastor prayed, that another million Americans in working families lost their health insurance last year. I know there are problems there. That's why I have said that in this coming session of Congress I will devote myself to what I call the middle class bill of rights, which could be called the bill of rights and responsibilities, because it offers you the right to pursue happiness, not the guarantee of happiness. I believe with all my heart that if we're going to worry about lowering taxes, we ought to lower taxes to help people educate themselves and their children and strengthen their families, so we can move forward together and grow together.

And so I have said, let's do four things that the Government can do to help people exercise more responsibility and take control of their own lives: tax deductions for all the cost of education after high school; lower the tax burden for parents with young children so they have more money to spend on raising the kids; let people save money in an individual retirement account, but let them withdraw it without a penalty for education or health care or taking care of their parents when they're sick; when people are unemployed or working hard for low wages and they're willing to get new skills, give them the funds they need to get education and training so they can grow into what God meant them to be.

But I say to you again: We can pass that program. We can have the crime bill work perfectly. But unless in Denver, Colorado, you do what the Governor challenged you to do, we will not be what we ought to be.

This country cannot go on with children shooting children. This country cannot go on with so many kids just giving up on their lives. This country cannot go on with more and more little babies being born into unstable situations where the mothers are children, too, and the future looks bleak. We can turn this around. But we have got to turn it around, and we have got to do it together by lifting each other up.

You know, the reason I said what I did about the service corps—and all the young people in the Denver national service corps raised their hands—I want to tell you why I did that. I did that because to me that represents everything I wanted to do. These young people are building the new economy because when they work on solving problems in Denver, they earn some money to go to college. And they're changing the way the Government works because there is no bureaucracy at all; they just have a project here and apply for the opportunity for young people to work in it. This is not a Government bureaucracy. But most important of all, most important of all, this is creating that new relationship of opportunity and responsibility, building up a community by people giving and getting and giving and getting and giving and getting, until pretty soon lives are changed and futures are changed.

Today, to celebrate Martin Luther King's birthday, there are young people like this all over America. They're rebuilding schools in Atlanta as we talk today. They're rebuilding homes in Memphis. They're helping people work their way out of the flood in California. And they're here today in Denver, building this country, doing what we ought to do.

I was told a day or so ago that in this new Congress there may be a move to abolish the national service corps to save money to pay for tax cuts.

Audience members. No-o-o!

The President. Well, let me say, I know about cutting Government spending. We've taken $11,000 in debt off of every family in America by reducing the deficit. We have reduced the size of the Federal Government to its smallest size since Martin Luther King visited John Kennedy in the White House. I know about that. But the purpose of all this is not to wreck the Government, not to give us a mean-spirited Government. It is to give us a lean Government that will help us to work together to solve our own problems. That's what we should be committed to do in Washington and in Denver and in every community throughout this great land.

So let me ask you to think about this. Look at all the young people in this audience. Look at the fine young people in their band uniforms. Look at the young people around the choir and the young kids here. Look at all the children here, all different colors and backgrounds. What is the American dream? It is the right to pursue happiness. It requires a certain equality and a certain respect. It requires us to listen as well as to talk.

I know the American people are often angry and frustrated today. But let me tell you something, folks, this is a very great country, and there is nothing that cannot be fixed if we will rely on our hearts and our spirits and what we know to be true. I have traveled this whole world on your behalf. I have seen many different places. I have dealt with many different opportunities and problems. I am more convinced today than I was on the day I took the oath of office that the greatest days of America lie in front of us if we have the courage to live the dream of Martin Luther King.

But remember, what he lived and died for was for every one of you to have the right to do good and to be good and to make the most of your own life. It was no living and dying for the freedom to shoot people, no living and dying for the freedom to shoot up, no living and dying for the freedom to hate people, no living and dying for the freedom to ignore the responsibilities of parenthood and the obligations of our children. That is not what this was about. And there was no living and dying to advance the proposition that we are all just isolated individuals out here, we don't need anybody helping anybody else, and everything we do as a Government is intrinsically bad. That idea is wrong, too.

So I say to you, as you look to the next century, let's make Denver and the West the frontier of the next century by proving that you can be a rugged individual, you can do everything you want in your individual aspirations, but only if you build a new community where everybody has a chance to rise up and everybody has a chance to be respected and every child has a chance to be loved and to be important. That is what this is all about.

And let us look for ways every day, every day, to say the dream of Martin Luther King depends upon what I do inside and how I relate to my fellow men and women and to all the little boys and girls.

Twenty-seven years ago, April 4th, Martin Luther King was killed. Only such a young man, but he gave his life willingly so that we might become all God meant for us to be. We can still do it. We will have more opportunities than ever before. But you look at this sea of people, and you think about what the Founding Fathers said over 200 years ago: life, liberty, the pursuit of happiness, together.

Thank you, and God bless you all.

NOTE: The President spoke at 12:34 p.m. in the Amphitheater. In his remarks, he referred to Gov. Roy Romer of Colorado and Mayor Wellington Webb of Denver and his wife, Wilma.

Remarks Honoring Martin Luther King, Jr., in Los Angeles, California
January 16, 1995

The President. Thank you. Are you having a good time?

Audience members. Yes!

The President. Well, so am I. And I'm glad to be here again. I want to thank all the people who are here, all the elected officials and the clergy and the people on the board of Community Build. I thank Brenda Shockley for her fine work. Yes, give her a hand. She's great. [*Applause*] I thank Marla Gibbs and Robert Hooks for their work tonight. And I thought Linda Hopkins was great; I was back there listening to her sing behind the curtain. And it's wonderful to see Rosa Parks and Cicely Tyson here. I'm honored to be in their presence, as always. I want to thank the young people behind me who met with me for a few moments before I came out here: Charles Rousseau, who is one of our Faces of Hope; my friends from the playground; and all the others who are back there who told me about what this effort is all about, who talked to me about Community Build in terms that anybody could understand.

Ladies and gentlemen, when I ran for President and I came here to south central L.A., I, first of all, knew my way around a little bit because I had actually come here before I ever dreamed of running for President, just because I was interested in what was happening to you and how we were going to build with the challenges we face.

And I said that I thought my job, if you would let me be President, was to do three things: first, to try to get the economy going again; second, to try to have a Government that worked in a way that made sense for people at the grassroots level and would take us into the 21st century. It would be less bureaucratic. It could even be smaller, but it would be able to do more in partnership with people where they live, so that when you pay your taxes you would think you were getting your money's worth for a change. But the third and most important thing that I thought we had to do as a people that the President had to be a part of was to create a new agreement between the people and their Government and between the people, themselves, what I called a New Covenant, a commitment to extend more opportunity in return for people assuming responsibility for their own lives, their own families, their own communities, for changing the things that have to be changed. That's the only way we're ever going to straighten this country out is if we have more opportunity and more responsibility, if people really believe that we can make a difference.

You know why I like being here? Because these people have proved that they can change their lives. And if they can do it, we can change America.

I work with Maxine Waters and with Mayor Riordan on a lot of things, and you are fortunate to be represented as you are. I tell you, the mayor just showed up, and he's had an earthquake, a fire, and a flood. [*Laughter*] I asked him if he thought God had hidden a volcano somewhere in Los Angeles County, and then you could become a new tourist mecca as a full-service disaster area. [*Laughter*] You know why we can laugh about that? Because you keep coming back. You've got good leadership and good grassroots folks and a spirit that won't quit.

And I was looking at Congresswoman Waters up here giving her talk tonight, and I was thinking, I wonder if those people have any idea how she worries the President to death in Washington until he does what she wants him to do? [*Laughter*] The first time she looked at me like that—the way she can look at you if she thinks you're not going to do the right thing—after I became President, I said, "Maxine, I'm the President; you don't have to look at me like that anymore." She said, "Oh no, I have to look at you more like that now." [*Laughter*]

I'm proud of the fact that the Labor Department put $7 million in this project, because I think that Community Build and the Youth Fair Chance Plus programs represent all three of the things that I set out to do:

We're helping people become part of the economy, and that's important. Work gives dignity to life. People need an education. They need a job. They need a future, to give dignity to life.

And we're changing the way the Government works. We're reducing the size of Government, and we've taken $11,000 in debt off of every family in America by reducing that deficit, and that gives our kids a better future. But we also have to prove that we can change the present,

and that's what this program does. And the Federal Government should be involved in programs like this, nonbureaucratic people programs that build people up instead of tearing them down.

And I like it because it does build that New Covenant. It says, "Okay, here's your opportunity." But you know, we can be spending $700 million here, and if people like these guys behind me hadn't decided they were going to change on the inside and do differently, the money would not make any difference. So we've got it all going in the right direction.

I say to you tonight, my friends, that if Dr. King could be here—and I think he is here, in a way—he'd be pretty pleased with what we're doing here. I know that much remains to be done. I know that in the atmosphere of the present where people have been told that everything the Government does is bad, it will be hard to continue.

But let me tell you something: Los Angeles and the cities around here and California and America are better off because of programs like this and better off because we're giving communities more funds to help deal with the crime problem, not only to hire more police officers but also to give young people some activities they can be engaged in that are positive so they have something to say yes to as well as something to say no to. These things matter. And we can make a difference. I know we must do more, but we should do more in ways that make sense.

I'm proud of the fact that this week it was announced that we not only have seen over 5½ million new jobs come into this economy since I became President but the unemployment rate among African-Americans is at a 20-year low. I'm proud of that. Now, that's the good news. The bad news is that the unemployment rate among young people is still very high, over one in three, and that among people who do not have much education, the unemployment rate is very high and the wages of those that work tend to be low and to stay there. So in the coming year, with this new Congress, I'm going to say to them, "You say you want the free enterprise system to work. You say you want more business people in minority communities. Well, so do I. Let's begin with passing my middle class bill of rights."

If we're going to cut people's taxes, let's cut them for education and for raising children, to do things that will strengthen all the American people and build this country up from the grassroots up. And if we're going to cut spending, let's cut things that will free up money to build up people. Let's don't cut programs like this one. Let's don't cut programs like the national service program. Let's don't cut programs like Head Start. Let's don't make it more expensive for people to go to college; let's make it cheaper for people to go to college and more affordable.

In other words, the role of Government should not be to pretend that we can solve problems that people have to solve for themselves, often inside their own heart. But the role of Government should not be to be heartless, either, and to walk away. The Government should be a partner. The Government should help people to acquire the tools they need and the means they need and the education they need and the belief and the hope they need to make the most of their own lives. That is what we're here to celebrate today. That is what Martin Luther King wanted us to do.

You know, when Dr. King gave that famous "I have a dream" speech, he said that his dream was deeply rooted in the American dream. What is the American dream? The Founders of our country said it over 200 years ago: We hold these truths to be self-evident that all are created equal, endowed by their Creator with certain inalienable rights, that among these are life, liberty, and the pursuit of happiness. Life, liberty, the pursuit of happiness—no, not a guarantee of happiness but not death, destruction, and the end of hope, either—the means of working together to achieve the God-given potential of every person in this room, every person in south

central Los Angeles, all the people in this country.

It is not a dream rooted in race. Race became a factor when people could not see behind their own prejudice. And I tell you today, my friends, that when we realize what a resource we have in America, that we come from so many different racial backgrounds, that we come from so many different ethnic backgrounds, that we come from so many religious backgrounds, in a global society where the world is smaller and smaller and smaller, we are the world's richest country because of our differences. Now we must find common ground and build up all people. And no, we don't have a person to spare. All these children have a role in our future, every one of them.

So I'm glad to be back in south central Los Angeles. I want these young men to help me find the secret to get people like this all across America to say no to violence and no to drugs and no to the life of the street with no tomorrow and yes to a better future. We can do this. We can do it if we work together. We can do it if we talk together. We can do it if we believe in one another's potential. That is the American dream.

Thank you, and God bless you all.

NOTE: The President spoke at 5:41 p.m. at Community Build, Inc. In his remarks, he referred to Brenda Shockley, executive director, Community Build, Inc.; masters of ceremonies Marla Gibbs and Robert Hooks; civil rights activist Rosa Parks; actress Cicely Tyson; and Mayor Richard Riordan of Los Angeles.

Remarks at California State University at Northridge
January 17, 1995

Thank you. What a great day. Thank you very much. Thank you so much, Mayor Riordan. Thank you for your outstanding leadership, for being such a good working partner, for putting the interest of all the people of this community first. Thank you, Dr. Wilson, for your leadership and for hosting this wonderful event on this beautiful campus with its beautiful buildings, all standing, thank goodness. I'm glad to see you all here. I thank Congressman Berman and Con-

gressman McKeon, Lieutenant Governor Davis, Supervisor Yaroslavsky, and of course, the people who are here with me today. I'd like to introduce them all: the Secretary of Transportation, Federico Peña; the Secretary of Housing and Urban Development, Henry Cisneros; and the Director of the Federal Emergency Management Agency, James Lee Witt. They have done a great job for you.

Ladies and gentlemen, even as we recall the devastation here today, we know that nature has struck again here at home in California with the floods and with extraordinary fury in the earthquake in Japan. I know all of you join with me in extending our profound condolences to the families of those in the Osaka-Kobe area of Japan who have suffered such a tremendous loss in the last day.

We have spoken with the Japanese Government and, with their agreement, based on our experiences here, I have ordered a high-level team that includes representatives of the Federal Emergency Management Agency and the Department of Transportation to leave for Japan shortly to see if anything we learned here can be helpful to them there. The Chairman of the Joint Chiefs of Staff, General John Shalikashvili, is in Japan now, and he has already stated that our military forces there are also available to help them in any appropriate way.

You know what they're going through. So I'd like to ask, before I begin my remarks, if we could just have a moment of silence for the victims of the flood here in California and the victims of the earthquake in Japan.

[*At this point, a moment of silence was observed.*]

Thank you.

I am so glad to be here at Cal State Northridge. You are now the symbol of the ability of the people of this State to keep coming back after adversity upon adversity, as well as the symbol of California and America's future because of the educational opportunities open to all kinds of people from all walks of life and all different backgrounds here at this fine institution.

The most damaging earthquake ever recorded on our continent destroyed a great deal here when it hit a year ago. But as the mayor said, even though it shook you, it didn't break you. It didn't break your faith in the future. How else can you explain the fact that here there is a baseball team known as the Earthquake Kids? I want to ask them to be recognized here in a minute, but I do want to note, as the spring slowly approaches, that they did something the pros couldn't: They kept baseball going. And they won the national championship in the Little League World Series. Let's give them a hand. Would the team stand, please? [*Applause*]

You know, you might think that Californians have had too many opportunities to show heart. [*Laughter*] The wonderful, sainted Mother Teresa once said that she knew God wouldn't give her any more than she could bear; she just wished God didn't have such confidence in her sometimes. [*Laughter*] That's the way I feel about you from time to time. I told the mayor last night that I hope that there would be no simmering volcano uncovered around here— [*laughter*]—anytime in the future. Fires, earthquakes, and devastating floods are quite enough.

But in these disasters where lives are lost and others are shattered, I know it's not easy to keep going and to keep your heart. A year ago I said that we would not leave you to pick up the pieces alone, that we would stay on until the job was done. We have kept that pledge today, and today I renew that pledge into the future.

Since the flooding began a few days ago, I have been working closely with Governor Wilson and Senator Boxer and Senator Feinstein and your other officials to help fight the flooding. The disaster I declared across California and the work of FEMA and other agencies are already helping to move on the road to recovery.

This afternoon I'll have a chance to go to northern California to view some of the damaged areas there. But I say again to the victims of this disaster: You are not alone. We will work with you to help you reclaim your lives, as the earthquake victims have been reclaiming theirs.

Who would have thought a year ago that the highways and bridges could be rebuilt and reinforced in just a fraction of the time the experts had predicted and the time the law allowed until we changed the way things worked. The Santa Monica Freeway was reopened on April 11th, the Golden State Freeway on May 17th, the Simi Valley Freeway partly opened in February and fully opened in September. I could go on and on. Who would have thought this campus would reconvene classes in one month? The main section of the library behind me was reopened in 64 days, a job that would normally have taken a year, a great tribute to your president and to all of the leaders of this fine institution.

I just verified with James Lee Witt what strikes me as an astounding statistic: There were 5,600 school buildings damaged a year ago, and today all but 40 are open, doing business, educating our children, and giving them something to look forward to.

This happened because we put aside politics and worked on being partners, partners as citizens, as businesses, as government, partners in the person of people like Ramona Sanches Vega, a volunteer who sought out families living in their cars because their homes were too damaged. She helped them to get housing. People like your own college president, who did make the impossible possible on this campus. People like so many of you in this audience who did countless things for your friends and for total strangers that will never be recorded anywhere except in the minds and hearts of those whom you touched.

For Government's part, 27 Federal departments and agencies worked with State and local officials in unprecedented ways to produce, as Mayor Riordan said, the most efficient and effective disaster operation in American history. So far, over $11.5 billion in aid has come to California to help to deal with the aftermath of the earthquake. But in addition to that, the whole system was literally reinvented, with new technologies, ways found to cut business-as-usual and the bureaucracy that too often goes with Government assistance. Decisions were based on need, not paperwork and rules. More than 270,000 homeowners received Federal grants to help repair their homes. More than half a million people were given grants or low-interest loans for disaster housing.

I know there are those today who say that Government is inherently bad, always gets in the way, and never amounts to anything. Well, I say, look at the difference it made in dealing with the disaster. It can work if we put people first and think about how to make it work.

But this institution is another example of how Government can work. We can't wait for disaster to strike to deal with our long-term challenges. Every day millions upon millions of Americans fight other kinds of struggles, to get and keep new jobs, to provide health care for their families, to deal with the struggles of modern life, and to strengthen the ties of community when there are so many pressures that divide us one from another. And anytime an American loses one of those fights, it's a disaster for our future as well.

Everyone knows that we live in an era of enormous change, a time of great uprooting of things both good and bad. As we change from what has popularly been called the industrial age to the information age, from the cold war of global division to a globe united in economic cooperation and one which must unite to deal with the common threats to all of us in terrorism and ecological destruction—in this era of change, our biggest challenge is to simply keep alive the American dream for all of our people, to make sure that we go into the next century just 5 years away still the strongest country in the world, the most profound force for peace and freedom, and still with the American dream alive for all people, regardless of their race, their region, their religion, their background, the capacities they came into this world with.

My simple belief is that in this time, we know that the Government cannot really solve problems for people, but I think we know that the Government cannot walk away, either. The role of Government in this age is to be a partner, to help give people the tools they need to solve their own problems, to fulfill their own dreams, to make their own future. And I am determined to see that the rest of your Government works as well as the disaster team did in the California earthquake. That is a good standard for all of us to meet.

I believe, my fellow Americans, that we need to do three things: We need a new economic strategy that I have fought for, for 2 years, appropriate to the new world we're all going to live and compete in. We need a new form of Government that is smaller, less bureaucratic, more creative, more oriented toward flexibility in solving people's problems, but one that is an effective partner, not a disabled or a mean participant on the sidelines just telling people what to do instead of helping people to do it.

And third and most important, I think we need what I call and have for 3 years now called—my contract with America—a New Covenant, one that says here are certain opportunities and here are your responsibilities. How are we going to rebuild the American community to look like this crowd does unless we all have opportunity and we all assume responsibility? If all you do is assert rights and there are no responsibilities, pretty soon nothing good happens. If all people do is go around being responsible and they're never rewarded for it, pretty soon they get tired of it. We need both, more opportunity and more responsibility in this country. And that's how we're going to rebuild America and keep the American dream alive.

We have made a good beginning. We have 5.6 million more jobs. We have a lower Federal deficit. We've taken $11,000 in debt off of every family in America, and that means a brighter future. We have the smallest Federal Government we've had in over 30 years, but we're doing things more effectively. We're also offering opportunities to people that demand that they assume more responsibility, from expanding Head Start to making college loans more affordable for more people.

But we all know that there is a lot more to be done. More than half the adult work force in America is working harder today for lower wages than they were making 10 years ago. Another 1 million Americans in working families lost their health insurance last year. Millions of American workers wonder if their retirement is secure, and we're working hard on that.

We see a lot of upheaval. There are still a lot of people who don't feel safe on their streets, in their neighborhoods, in their schools. Even though the crime rate is coming down where people have done what has been done here in Los Angeles—to put more police on the street and to work on projects like the Community Build project that we supported that the mayor and I visited yesterday, where ex-gang members are teaching other kids to lead the gangs to turn away from violence, to go to education and work and away from things that are destructive—we have a long way to go.

That's why I so strongly hope that we can, together, without regard to party, make a commitment that, in this year, we will go back when the Congress is in full session and working and adopt what I call the middle class bill of rights. Let's don't just have indiscriminate tax cuts, let's control the deficit and focus tax relief on the people who need it most, on strengthening families and making education more available to all American people. That will get us into the next century.

I think we should lower taxes on families with young children. I think we should make all Americans able to save money in an IRA and then withdraw it, tax-free, to pay for their own education or health care or to help them care for their parents. I think we should give people who need more training because they're unemployed the right not just to sign up for a Government program but to get a check which says, this check can be spent at the educational institution of your choice to raise your income. That's what I think we should do.

But more important than anything else, in the next century in the information age, having an education will have more to do with income and options and choices than ever before. And so I believe that we should finally—and we should have done it long ago—we ought to make all educational expenses after high school tax deductible. That's important.

We made interest paid on home mortgages tax deductible decades ago. Why? Because owning a home was important to the idea of the American dream. In the 21st century we may not get to homeownership if we don't have an education. Let's make that tax deductible. That's important to our future.

And I might say, that is the essence of what we ought to be about, because you cannot take advantage of that opportunity without being responsible. People can offer you an education, but you have to get it. That is what we ought to be doing, giving opportunity in return for responsibility.

The New Covenant comes down to this: We deserve opportunity, but we have to earn success. And that is what the people of California have shown over and over and over again.

Let me close with this. The great writer Wallace Stegner called this part of America "hope's native home." It was built by people he called, and I quote, "The stickers, not just those who pillage and run but those who settle and love the life they have made and the place they have made it in."

Today we salute all of you, the stickers, the settlers, the rebuilders of this great State. Let us take what you have done here and use it as a model for our entire beloved country into the 21st century.

Thank you, and God bless you all.

NOTE: The President spoke at 10 a.m. at the Northridge Oviatt Library. In his remarks, he referred to Mayor Richard Riordan of Los Angeles, CA; Blenda Wilson, president, California State University at Northridge; Lt. Gov. Gray Davis and Gov. Pete Wilson of California; and Zev Yaroslavsky, a Los Angeles County supervisor.

Remarks to the Community in Roseville, California
January 17, 1995

Well, good afternoon, everyone. Let me say, first of all, I'm very glad to be here. I want to thank all of the people in this community who have shared their experiences with us. I'm here with Congressman Doolittle, Congressman Fazio, Lieutenant Governor Gray Davis, and members of our administration, including the Secretaries of Transportation Federico Peña and Housing and Urban Development Henry Cisneros and, of course, our ever-present FEMA Director James Lee Witt, who is virtually a taxpaying citizen of California, thanks to floods, fires, and earthquakes.

And we've been walking around the neighborhood today, talking and listening to people. I want to especially thank the Hayes family and the Merenda family for taking me into their homes and showing me the flood damage and explaining in very gripping and human terms what this means to all of you and to your lives and your hopes and your dreams.

I also want to thank all the people who have worked here to try to help put the community back together and try to help people put their lives back together. I'd especially like to say something about the young people in the California Conservation Corps. I admire that group so much, and they've done a lot of very, very good work. The California Conservation Corps receives several million dollars every year from our national service program. It's one of the affiliate programs. And I was very impressed when Richard Merenda told me that he is about to go to work for the California Conservation Corps in Klamath. He's going to work on firefighting, salmon restoration, and flood control. He's very well prepared for the last category now as a result of this. But I'll tell you, I hope he never has to come home and work on this again.

I want to thank again all of you and especially the young people who worked so hard on this. Mr. Hayes told me that—I forget how many hours he said had already been put in by volunteers helping him with his home, something over 600, I think.

I want to say a special word of appreciation to the local and the State officials and, of course, all the Federal officials, that we're trying to work efficiently together. I have heard about some of the things that we should be doing, and we're going to try to improve and try to make sure everybody knows what they're entitled to and get as much help as we can.

You know, 38 of your counties have now been declared disaster areas as a result of the flood. We've released $10 million from FEMA last week for cleanup, and more than 13,000 people have registered for assistance. In this community, I think of the 338 or so homes that were severely damaged, I think there are still almost 100 people who have not yet registered. So we've got some work to do here, and we're going to do it. But of the 13,000 people who have already registered, I know that a couple of hundred thousand dollars in checks have already been sent out. So we're going to move this process along quickly and get you as much help as possible. I know a lot of people are living in motels or trailers or with friends or family and have very, very difficult short-term personal situations, so we're going to try to fix them.

I'm also happy to say today that we're going to release another $15 million in emergency funds from the Federal Highway Administration. Rodney Slater, the Administrator of the Federal Highway Administration, is here. That's a part of the Department of Transportation. We have some significant road damage here we're going to do our best to deal with. The Federal Government will pay 100 percent of the costs of the emergency highway repair, and we're going to try to get everybody back to business as quickly as possible.

Let me say one thing on a very personal note. A lot of people have said to me today, "Well, I'm glad you came out here, Mr. President. This is a little town, and I appreciate you taking time to come." But if you look at what we're seeing today, or you've dealt with a disaster beyond your control, I think I can say for everybody that came with me, we were deeply moved by what we saw, by the unity and the spirit in this community, by the devotion of people to their homes and their families, but especially by the devotion of people to each other.

I wish I could bottle what I have seen and heard here today and spread it out in every community in America. We could solve about half the problems of this country in a very short time if I felt the kind of devotion and commitment everywhere that I sensed here on the streets of this community today. And I just want to urge you not to give up and not to be discouraged.

When that earthquake hit southern California a year ago, there were 5,600 school buildings damaged. Today, a year later, we celebrated the one-year anniversary; all but 40 of those buildings are open, out of 5,600, educating kids. And that shows you what you can do if everybody pulls together and works together.

I know that a lot of you have really painful stories now about work you've done in your home that seems to be wiped away and family furniture that may be lost forever and a lot of things that are a very important part of your past. But I would just urge you not to lose the optimism, the resilience, the strength that I have sensed here from all of you today. Don't give up. We will look at the long-term problems that I've been asked to look at. I know this is the second time this has happened in 10 years, and you're getting sick of waiting for the water to come every time the thunder claps overhead. So we'll look at that.

But meanwhile, let's all pull together and work together and follow the lead of these fine young people and the families I had the privilege to visit with today.

Thank you, and God bless you all.

NOTE: The President spoke at 2:46 p.m. at the corner of Tina Way and Elisa Way.

Statement on Action on Congressional Accountability Legislation
January 17, 1995

I want to commend the Congress for passing the Congressional Accountability Act of 1995 today. It is about time that Congress lived by the same laws it places on the private sector. Passage of this bill fulfills a campaign commitment of mine.

However, while this legislation is an important political reform, it is only the first step in what must be a greater effort to change business-as-usual in Washington. Therefore, I reiterate my call for Congress to act swiftly on several much needed reform proposals including real campaign finance reform and the gift ban and a strong version of the line-item veto.

Remarks on Loan Guarantees for Mexico
January 18, 1995

Thank you very much, Secretary Rubin and Ambassador Kantor.

Ladies and gentlemen, we wanted to be here today to make the clearest public case we can for the proposal which has been developed by the administration and the bipartisan leadership in Congress for dealing with the present situation. We have worked hard with an extraordinary group of people who have joined forces because all of us realize how important this proposal is, not only to the people of Mexico but also to the United States and to our workers.

We are acting to support the Mexican economy and to protect and promote the interests of the American people.

As Ambassador Kantor said, and as all of you know very well, we live in an increasingly global economy in which people, products, ideas, and money travel across national borders with lightning speed. We've worked hard to help our workers take advantage of that economy by getting our own economic house in order, by expanding opportunities for education and training, and by expanding the frontiers of trade, by doing what we could to make sure there was more free and fair trade for Americans. And we know, and all of you know, that those efforts are creating high wage jobs for our people that would otherwise not be there.

Our goal, our vision must be to create a global economy of democracies with free market, not government-run, economies; democracies that practice free and fair trade, that give themselves a chance to develop and become more prosperous, while giving our own people the opportunity they deserve to reap the benefits of high-quality, high-productivity American labor, in terms of more jobs and higher incomes.

We have pursued this goal with vision and with discipline, through NAFTA, through the Summit of the Americas, through a number of other international endeavors like GATT and the Asian-Pacific Economic Cooperation group. But we have pursued it especially here in our own hemisphere, where we are blessed to see every nation but one governed in a democratic fashion and a genuine commitment to free market economics and to more open trade.

We have to know that the future on this path is plainly the right one, but as with any path, it cannot be free of difficulties. We have to make decisions based on a determined devotion to the idea of what we are pursuing over the long run. We know that, given the volatility of the economic situation in the globe now, there can be developments that for the movement are beyond the control of any of our trading partners, themselves developing nations, which could threaten this vision and threaten the interests of the American people.

Mexico's present financial difficulty is a very good case in point. Of course, it's a danger to Mexico, but as has already been said, it is plainly also a danger to the economic future of the United States.

NAFTA helped us to dramatically increase our exports of goods and services. It helped us to create more than 100,000 jobs here at home through increased exports to Mexico. But over the long run, it means even more. It means even more opportunities with Mexico. It means the integration of the rest of Latin America and the Caribbean into an enormous basket of opportunities for us in the future. And we cannot—we cannot let this momentary difficulty cause us to go backward now.

That's why, together with the congressional leadership, I am working so hard to urge Congress to pass an important and necessary package to back private sector loans to Mexico with a United States Government guarantee. Let me say, I am very gratified by the leadership shown in the Congress on both sides of the aisle.

By helping to put Mexico back on track, this package will support American exports, secure our jobs, help us to better protect our borders and to safeguard democracy and economic stability in our hemisphere, because America and American workers are more secure when we support a strong and growing market for our exports, because America and American workers are more secure when we help the Mexican people to see the prospect of decent jobs and a secure future at home through a commitment to free-market economics, political democracy, and growing over the long term, and because we're more secure when more and more other countries also enjoy the benefits of democracy and economic opportunity, and perhaps most important over the long run, because we are more secure if we help Mexico to remain a strong and stable model for economic development around our hemisphere and throughout the world.

If we fail to act, the crisis of confidence in Mexico's economy could spread to other emerging countries in Latin America and in Asia, the kinds of markets that buy our goods and services today and that will buy far more of them in the future. Developing these markets is plainly in the interests of the American people. We must act to make sure that we maintain the kind of opportunities now being seized by the Secretary of Commerce and the delegation of American business leaders who have had such a successful trip to India.

If you take Mexico, just consider the extraordinary progress made in recent years. Mexico erased a budget deficit that once equalled 15 percent of its gross domestic product. It slashed inflation from 145 percent a year to single digits. It sold off inefficient state enterprises, dramatically reduced its foreign debt, opened virtually every market to global competition. This is proof that the Mexican Government and the Mexican people are willing to make decisions that are good for the long run; even if it entails some short-term sacrifice for them, they know where their future prosperity and opportunity lie.

Now Mexico, of course, will have to demonstrate even greater discipline to work itself out of the current crisis. Let me say, though, it's important that we understand what's happened. And the Secretary of Treasury and I and a lot of others spent a lot of time trying to make sure we understood exactly what had happened before we recommended a course of action.

It is clear that this crisis came about because Mexico relied too heavily upon short-term foreign loans to pay for the huge upsurge in its imports from the United States and from other countries. A large amount of those debts came due at a time when, because of the nature of the debts, it caused a serious cash flow problem for Mexico, much like a family that expects to pay for a new home with the proceeds from the sale of its old house only to have the sale fall through.

Now, together with the leadership of both Houses, our administration has forged a plan that makes available United States Government guarantees to secure private sector loans to Mexico. The leadership in Congress from both sides of the aisle and the Chairman of the Federal Reserve Board developed this plan with us. It is something we did together because we knew it was important, important enough to the strategic interest of the United States to do it in lockstep and to urge everyone without regard to party or region of the country or short-term interests to take the long view what is good for America and our working people. We all agree that something had to be done.

Now, these guarantees, it's important to note, are not foreign aid. They are not a gift. They are not a bailout. They are not United States Government loans. They will not affect our current budget situation. Rather they are the equivalent of cosigning a note, a note that Mexico can use to borrow money on its own account. And because the guarantees are clearly not entirely risk-free to the United States, Mexico will make an advanced payment to us, like an insurance premium. No guarantees will be issued until we are satisfied that Mexico can provide the assured means of repayment. As soon as the situation in Mexico is fully stabilized, we expect Mexico to start borrowing once again from the private markets without United States Government guarantees.

The U.S. has extended loans and loan guarantees many, many times before to many different countries. In fact, we've had a loan mechanism in place with Mexico since 1941. And Mexico has always made good on its obligations.

Now, there will be tough conditions here to make sure that any private money loaned to Mexico on the basis of our guarantees is well and wisely used. Our aim in imposing the conditions, I want to make clear, is not to micromanage Mexico's economy or to infringe in any way on Mexico's sovereignty but simply to act responsibly and effectively so that we can help to get Mexico's economic house back in order.

I know some say we should not get involved. They say America has enough trouble at home to worry about what's going on somewhere else. There are others who may want to get involved in too much detail to go beyond what the present situation demands or what is appropriate. But we must see this for what it is. This is not simply a financial problem for Mexico; this is an American challenge.

Mexico is our third largest trading partner already. The livelihoods of thousands and thousands of our workers depend upon continued strong export growth to Mexico. That's why we must reach out and not retreat.

With the bipartisan leadership of Congress, I am asking the new Congress to cast a vote, therefore, for the loan guarantee program as a vote for America's workers and America's future. It is vital to our interests. It is vital to our ability to shape the kind of world that I think we all know we have to have.

No path to the future—let me say again—in a time when many decisions are beyond the immediate control of any national government, much less that of a developing nation, no path to the future can be free of difficulty. Not every stone in a long road can be seen from the first step. But if we are on the right path, then we must do this. Our interests demand it. Our values support it, and it is good for our future.

Let me say again that the coalition of forces supporting this measure is significant; it may be historic. The new Republican leaders in Congress, the leadership of the Democratic Party in Congress, the Chairman of the Federal Reserve Board, why are they doing this? And I might say, I was immediately impressed by how quickly every person I called about this said, "Clearly, we have to act." They instinctively knew the stakes.

Now in the public debate questions should be properly asked and properly answered. But let us not forget what the issue is. Let us not read too little into this moment or try to load it up with too many conditions unrelated to the moment. The time is now to act. It is in our interest. It is imperative to our future. I hope all of you will do what you can to take that message to the Congress and to the American people.

Thank you very much.

NOTE: The President spoke at 3:49 p.m. in the Cash Room at the Treasury Department.

Remarks on the Retirement Protection Act of 1994
January 19, 1995

Thank you very much, Mr. Secretary. After that kind introduction I'm loath to say what I was about to say, which is I'm afraid the headline on this story will be "Reich comes out for playing hard." [*Laughter*] But I think people who work hard should also be able to play hard. [*Laughter*]

I want to thank Paul Wood for his story and Marvin Clarke for his testimony in his long battle to make sure the country did something to help people so that there wouldn't be other people in the situation he finds himself in. I want to thank the steelworkers and the senior citizens groups and all the others who were mentioned by Secretary Reich. I'd like to especially thank someone who is not here, my longtime friend J.J. Pickle, who retired from the Congress and who left this as his last legacy in a long career of helping people with their own lives. I'd like to thank another longtime friend of mine who is still here—that's maybe a disability in this town, but Marty Slate has done a wonderful job at the Pension Benefit Guaranty Corporation. I'll never forget the first time Hillary told me about Marty Slate. She said, "That's the smartest guy I ever met in my life. He'll find a way to solve any kind of problem." And you have done a fine job, and we're grateful to you.

And I'd like to thank someone whose name I don't know and I've been trying to find out before this moment. I'd like to thank the person in the Richmond debate in 1992 who asked President Bush and Ross Perot and Bill Clinton about the problems of underfunded pensions and first got my attention on this issue. I wish—I don't know who that person was, but I am deeply indebted, and now so are several million other Americans, to that person for bringing this issue personally to me in a very direct way.

Two years ago from tomorrow, I became President, with a commitment to try to restore the American dream for all Americans and to make sure that we enter the next century as the strongest country in the world, a force for peace and freedom and democracy, but most important of all, as one which in a very different world would keep the American dream alive for all of our people.

When I signed the Retirement Protection Act into law last month, it was almost completely unnoticed because at the end of the year it had to go through in the comprehensive legislation that involved the passage of the GATT trade agreement. And we wanted to do this today because this act was so profoundly important to so many millions of Americans and it says a lot about what we are trying to do here in Washington.

This is part of a new economic policy designed to help the American people stay ahead in a world economy that is changing so rapidly that, while it offers vast new benefits to people, it also is very frightening to a lot of people and causes too much insecurity and unsettling for people who have worked hard and done the right things all their lives. It gives the American taxpayers a more effective, more efficient, and more disciplined Government. And this bill furthers what I have called my own contract with America, the New Covenant. It says that people who act responsibly should be rewarded.

The Retirement Protection Act says that people deserve a pension system that they rely on. They deserve employers who take actions to be worthy of their own trust and the labor that they give them, year-in and year-out. They deserve a Government that will protect them and stand by them, a Government that is their partner.

It says to employers that they can no longer gamble with the retirement savings of their own employees, allowing pension plans to become dangerously underfunded, expecting taxpayers to bail them out. It means that responsible businesses with well-funded plans will no longer have to carry an unfair share of the burden of the insurance costs for businesses who do not do the same.

As a result of the new law, the funding level of large, underfunded pension plans will be increased dramatically so that the benefits can be paid as they were promised. The National Pension Insurance System will remain secure. Employees will get better information warning them when their plans could be at risk.

In stabilizing the Federal insurance system, we used the power of Government to avert a potential crisis, protecting millions of retirees, corporate pension plans, and the taxpayers from huge potential losses.

Today we can be grateful that the security of our pensions are strong and growing stronger, thanks to the Retirement Protection Act and the work of all of you in this room who did so much to make it happen.

Thank you very, very much.

NOTE: The President spoke at 12:34 p.m. in the Roosevelt Room at the White House. In his remarks, he referred to Marvin D. Clarke of Moundsville, WV, who lost one-third of his pension, and Paul E. Wood of Griffin, GA, who feared losing his pension. The Retirement Protection Act of 1994 appears in title VII of the Uruguay Round Agreements Act of 1994, approved December 8, 1994 (Public Law No. 103–465).

Message to the Congress Transmitting the Estonia-United States Fishery Agreement
January 19, 1995

To the Congress of the United States:

In accordance with the Magnuson Fishery Conservation and Management Act of 1976 (16 U.S.C. 1801 *et. seq.*), I transmit herewith the Agreement between the Government of the United States of America and the Government of the Republic of Estonia Extending the Agreement of June 1, 1992, Concerning Fisheries Off the Coast of the United States. The Agreement, which was effected by an exchange of notes at Tallinn on March 11 and May 12, 1994, extends the 1992 Agreement to June 30, 1996.

In light of the importance of our fisheries relationship with the Republic of Estonia, I urge that the Congress give favorable consideration to this Agreement at an early date.

WILLIAM J. CLINTON

The White House,
January 19, 1995.

Letter to Congressional Leaders Transmitting a Plan for Consolidation of International Broadcasting
January 19, 1995

Dear Mr. Chairman:

Pursuant to the requirements of section 310(a)(2)(B) of the United States International Broadcasting Act of 1994 (title III, Public Law 103–236), I am pleased to transmit a Plan for the Consolidation of United States Government International Broadcasting.

The Plan reflects my continued strong commitment to the use of international radio and television as methods for advancing democracy and enlarging the community of free-market nations.

I look forward to working with the Congress on this and other issues in the months ahead.

Sincerely,

WILLIAM J. CLINTON

NOTE: Identical letters were sent to Jesse Helms, chairman, Senate Committee on Foreign Rela-
tions; Mark O. Hatfield, chairman, Senate Committee on Appropriations; Benjamin A. Gilman, chairman, House Committee on International Relations; and Bob Livingston, chairman, House Committee on Appropriations.

Exchange With Reporters on Loan Guarantees for Mexico
January 20, 1995

Q. Mr. President, what do you say to Congressman Leach, who suggests that the partisanship, the bickering over Speaker Gingrich's book deal is poisoning the atmosphere and not allowing this Mexican package to go through?

The President. Well, of course, he has been in Washington many more years than I have, but in the 2 years that I have been here, I have seen an unusual amount of partisan bickering. But it didn't stop us from passing GATT, from dealing with NAFTA, from dealing with the urgent problems in Russia that we confronted when I came here early on, and from pursuing a course in the Middle East that is having a very positive result, from doing any number of other things that were critical to the national interest. And it can't stop us now.

We have to do what we always do in these cases. We have to act, act quickly, act with dispatch, and put the national interest first. That's what we all have to do.

NOTE: The exchange began at 11:44 a.m. in the Roosevelt Room at the White House, following the taping of the President's radio address.

Message on the Observance of National African American History Month, February 1995
January 20, 1995

Warm greetings to everyone celebrating African American History Month, 1995.

Hillary and I join you in marking the brave efforts of the countless Americans throughout our nation's history who have demanded justice, declared an end to segregation, and fought to ensure that every individual has the opportunity to build a brighter future for themselves and their families.

Today, there is a renewed sense of hope in America—a hope based on the idea that our great diversity can unite rather than divide our society. It is the same hope that has inspired African Americans since our country's beginnings to dream of a nation in which all people enjoy the freedom to make their own lasting contributions to our world. If we are truly to build on history's rich lessons, we must always remember these pioneers' pivotal roles in American history.

Ours can be a land of unprecedented peace and prosperity in the twenty-first century if we have the faith that Martin Luther King described, the faith to "transform the jangling discords of our nation into a beautiful symphony of brotherhood." We must never cease striving to bring people together across racial and cultural barriers. This is our generation's most solemn calling and most important challenge.

I urge everyone, during African American History Month and throughout the year, to take up this challenge and to learn more about the black Americans who have made this country great.

BILL CLINTON

Statement on the Death of John White
January 20, 1995

Hillary and I were deeply saddened to learn of the death of former Democratic National Committee Chairman John White. Our prayers are with Nellie and his family at this difficult time. I am proud to have had the opportunity to work with him and learn from him. His decency, perseverance, and humor are a model for all of us who face the challenges and possi-bilities within our political system to move ideas forward and improve people's lives. John dedicated his life in service to the Democratic Party and this Nation. As Democrats gather from across the country to formally elect new leadership this weekend, memories of his sharp wit and tireless commitment will be in our hearts.

The President's Radio Address
January 21, 1995

Good morning. I know I speak for all Americans this week when I send my condolences to the victims of the terrible earthquake in Japan. And to the families of the American victims of that tragedy, let me say, our thoughts and prayers are with you.

If there's any consolation to be found in this kind of disaster, it's that nature's worst brings out humanity's best. I'm proud of the many Americans who joined the massive Japanese relief effort, like the engineers from the University of California at San Diego who flew to Osaka on their own dime and then walked to Kobe to pitch in. They're a fine example of the American inclination to reach out when others are in need.

This week, we as a nation were called upon to address a different kind of crisis closer to home, the financial crisis in Mexico. We had to act not just for Mexico's sake but for the sake of the millions of Americans whose jobs and livelihoods are tied to Mexico's well-being and to the well-being of other nations around the world that could be affected by the difficulties in Mexico.

I'm grateful to the leadership in Congress from both parties. They shared my sense of urgency in assembling a support package that will prevent this crisis from spreading and help to put Mexico back on a stable and prosperous course.

Every American should understand what's at stake and why it's in the interest of working men and women all across our country to sup-port Mexico. Mexico is our third largest trading partner. And already the goods and services we sell there support 700,000 American jobs. Helping Mexico remain a strong and growing market for our exports is vital to our ability to help create the kind of high-paying jobs that give people their shot at the American dream.

At the same time, we share a 2,000-mile boundary with Mexico and a common concern to stem the flow of illegal immigrants to America. By supporting Mexico, we'll help Mexican workers see the prospect of a decent job and a secure future in their home, not across the border.

Finally, Mexico serves as a model for developing countries from Latin America to Asia that are completing the transition to free markets and democracy. If we allow the crisis in confidence in the Mexican economy to continue, it could spread to those other countries whose emerging markets are buying a huge and growing share of our own exports and supporting millions of jobs here at home.

So you see, we've got a lot at stake. But Mexico's problems can be overcome. And with our help they will be. As serious as the crisis is, it represents a temporary detour from the path to prosperity and stability that Mexico has been on for the past decade. What's happened in these past few weeks is that Mexico ran into a cash-flow crunch, much like a family that expects to pay for a new home with money from the sale of the old house, only to have the sale fall through.

The support package we're proposing will back private sector loans to Mexico with a U.S. Government guarantee. That's like the Government cosigning a note that Mexico will use to borrow money. The package will relieve the squeeze on Mexico and help it to get its economy back on solid footing.

I want to be clear about this: This support package is not foreign aid. It's not a gift. It's not a bailout. It's not a Government loan. It won't affect our current budget deficit a bit. We will attach strict conditions to make sure that any money Mexico does borrow on the basis of our guarantees is well and wisely used. And those guarantees will be backed by Mexico's oil revenues.

Now, along with Republican and Democratic leaders in the House and the Senate, I call upon the Congress to do the right thing and cast a vote for America and our workers. For 200 years, we've always had our partisan fights, and we always will. But when our national interest is on the line, we all must rise above partisanship and act for our Nation.

President Bush put it very well in the strong statement he issued supporting this proposal when he said, and I quote, "If there ever was a time for a strong bipartisan support for a foreign policy initiative, it is now."

Passing this program will help to preserve a critical export market, support thousands of our jobs, stop more illegal immigration, and give countries all around the world confidence that open markets and democracy are the best guarantees for peace and prosperity.

I hope all of you listening today will tell your Representatives that you support this plan and you want them to support it as well. This package is good for Mexico, but even more important, it's right for America.

Thanks for listening.

NOTE: The address was recorded at 11:42 a.m. on January 20 in the Roosevelt Room at the White House for broadcast at 10:06 a.m. on January 21.

Remarks to the Democratic National Committee
January 21, 1995

The President. You remember what Mark Twain said, "The reports of our demise are premature." I could have listened to Al Gore talk all day about that. [*Laughter*]

The Vice President. You thought you might have to. [*Laughter*]

The President. Do you know what he said? He said, "For a while you thought you might have to." [*Laughter*] He was waxing eloquent, you know. He kept saying all that stuff, and I thought, well, why didn't we win last November? [*Laughter*] I've got some ideas about that, too, I'll share in a moment.

Let me begin by thanking all these people who are here on the head table and all of you. It is wonderful, wonderful to see you and to see you in good spirits and with a strong heart.

And let me also say a special word of thanks to Don Fowler and to Chris Dodd. I need one of those Don Fowler stickers. I've known Don Fowler since 1972. You think we're in trouble now, you should have been there then. [*Laughter*] And I owe Don Fowler a lot. I mean,

he ran that convention in '88. He wrote the speech I gave in 1988. [*Laughter*] I was supposed to talk about the future here today, but instead I decided to finish that speech. So you all relax, and I will. [*Laughter*] I wish you hadn't laughed so hard at that. [*Laughter*]

I want to thank Chris Dodd, who has been my friend for a long time, almost that long. I've known him about 15 years now. And I remember when we were young men in public life back in 1980 when I went to the Democratic Convention in Connecticut to give the keynote speech and he was about to go to the Senate. And I have watched him, and I wanted him to do this job because I don't think our country has a stronger voice for the values, the ideas of the Democratic Party and because he's not afraid to fight. I wanted Don Fowler because I thought we ought to have somebody in the leadership who does not have an accent—[*laughter*]—and because, whether the South knows it or not, we're a lot better for most of them than the other guys are.

So I feel very good about this team. I thank Debbie DeLee for all of her work and for her leadership. I thank David Wilhelm in his absence.

David and Degee brought young Luke by to see me yesterday. And I sat him on the desk in the Oval Office. And they're already saving up for the Inaugural gown for when Luke's inaugurated in 40 or 50 years. [*Laughter*]

I'd like to say a special word of thanks, too, in honor, in homage—I know there is something on the program about this later, but I'd like to tell you all personally how sad I am about the passing of John White and how much I appreciate him. He was the cochairman of our campaign in 1972 in Texas, and I've known him a very long time. He was a great Democrat, a great leader for our party. And I know all of you join me in wishing his wife, Nellie, well and in thanking him from the bottom of our hearts for being such a loyal and effective leader for our party for so very long.

You know, I was listening to the Vice President talk—I say first I need to thank all three of them who spoke. I thank Tipper Gore for being basically, on many occasions, the continuing spark plug of our team, for fighting for the rights and the interests of people who need better mental health opportunities in this country. I do believe that Al Gore will go down in history as the most effective Vice President in the history of the Republic and the person who has exercised the most responsibility.

And I want to say this to my wife. I never really thought when we started this she would become quite the target she has been. It's funny, when we lived in Arkansas, which is supposed to be more conservative and traditional than the country as a whole, most people thought it was a pretty good thing when the Governor's wife tried to get kids an education or make sure they didn't go to bed sick at night if it could be helped. And I'll tell you something else—[*applause*]—I'd like to say something else. When I look at her at night, I think there's a lot worse things that could happen to you in life than to get caught redhanded trying to give health care to 40 million Americans who don't have it.

I come here today in a curious role: as the leader of the party I love but also as the President of a country that includes both Democrats and Republicans, a fair number of people that don't think either party amounts to much and

just kind of go with the flow of election after election.

I do regret, in all candor, that any administration that could have done as much as we have done, and any group of Members of Congress that could have supported that, did not find greater favor in the election of November. And I thought, well, maybe there's a lot of reasons for this. There are, objectively, a lot of reasons. First of all, it takes a while for the laws you pass to be actually felt in the lives of people. And secondly, there are all kinds of reasons today why it's hard to get good news out, and it's almost harder if there's more of it. And thirdly, there are a lot of people in this country today who, in the midst of this great recovery, don't feel more secure. And they really don't. And they're our friends and we are their friends, but they may not have known it in the last election, given what they had to listen to.

But the truth is that a whole bunch of folks in America, even in spite of the fact that we've got over 5½ million new jobs in the last 2 years, are working harder for less money than they had 15 years ago. Their wages have not kept up with inflation. Another 1.1 million Americans lost their health care last year, and they were in working families. They were not people on welfare.

I just signed a bill a few days ago—we celebrated it this week—to try to stabilize the pensions of 40 million Americans who depend upon the Government guarantee system and who were in danger of being let down; 8½ million of them were in trouble in their pensions. People know that.

More and more workers feel like they're just sort of dispensable products that can be thrown away in this new rapidly changing global economy, and they feel great anxiety.

And not all the problems of this country are economic. A lot of people feel insecure on their streets. And they don't like what they see happening to our families and our communities. And they're vulnerable to the siren songs they heard in the last election: Promise them anything; tell them what they want to hear; tell them the Government is their enemy.

But let me tell you something else right on the front end, folks. When people say change is hard and you have to be strong and you have to be willing to take unpopular positions, that isn't just rhetoric, that's true. I used to carry a bunch of—about nine rules of politics around in my billfold when I was Governor, Clinton's rule of politics. And one of them was, "Everybody is for change in general, but against it in particular." [*Laughter*]

I remember a story our junior Senator, David Pryor, told me one time about going to a birthday party for a guy who turned 100. And he said to this guy who had just passed a century of life, he said, "You know, it's remarkable; you have all your faculties about you. You can really—you speak clearly; you hear me when I speak to you." He said, "Yeah." And he said, "You're thinking just right." He said, "That's right." He said, "You must have seen an amazing number of changes in your lifetime." He said, "Yes, son, and I was agin every one of them." [*Laughter*]

And that's what I see sometimes—you think about it. The last time we had a period of really profound change like this was at the end of the Second World War. We had a President named Harry Truman. He had an 80 percent approval rating on the day that he dropped the bomb on Japan. Two years later, when he sent national health insurance to the Congress for the second time, and he'd gone through 2 years of reverse plastic surgery from the organized interest groups pounding against change, he was at 36 percent approval. But he fought for change because it was necessary. And he reached out and worked with the Republicans when he could to build the structure of the post-cold-war world. He did what was right, and eventually they were able to get it across.

So I say to you, the number one lesson is not to be cynical, not to give up, not to turn back but to bear down and go forward and do what is right by the American people. It will come out all right in the end if we stand up for what is right and do what is right.

You know, I have been very interested in what the new Republican leaders in Congress have said in the last few days. The Speaker, quoting Franklin Roosevelt at length, has basically said, "Well, the Democrats did do almost every good thing that was done in the 20th century; give them that. But in the information age, they're irrelevant. We thank them. They did a good job; give them a gold watch and send them home. And put us in in the information age because in the information age, well, Government is just intrinsically a part of the problem. It is intrinsically bad. And those Democrats, they think there's a program for every problem. They think Government can

solve the problems. They are wrong. They are irrelevant. Throw them away."

It's a funny world, that world they're sketching, a world in which Big Bird is an elitist and rightwing media magnates are populists. [*Laughter*] It's an interesting world. I'm still trying to get it, but I'm working at it real hard.

But I say to you, my friends, we have an obligation that is more than contesting the other party, and certainly I do. I do not believe there is a program for every problem in the information age. I do not believe Government can solve all the problems. But I do not believe that Government is inherently bad. Our Founders created Government at a time of limited Government. And I still think what they said it was for is the best statement we could ever make: We hold these truths to be self-evident, that all men are created equal, endowed by their Creator with certain inalienable rights, and among these are life, liberty, and the pursuit of happiness. And Government was instituted to help the American people pursue those ends. That is what I believe.

And you know, in times of sweeping change, times of great uprooting, times which are uncertain and insecure for people, it is more important than ever that we work hard not only to do the right specific things but to define that, to say what we believe. So will we have a different form of Government in the 21st century? You bet we will. And will it be less bureaucratic and more entrepreneurial and more creative? You bet; it must be. But does it still need to be on the side of average Americans to help empower them, to give them the tools, to give them the means so that they can survive and do well and have the American dream in their own lives and rid themselves of this gripping insecurity that still dominates the lives of so many million American families? I say yes, that is our job.

And so I challenge the leaders of the other party: You won a piece of responsibility; exercise it. Stop the politics of demonization and division, and let's think about exercising joint responsibility. You say you want to restrain Government spending; so do I. Without help from them, we took $11,000 in debt off of every family in this country. We reduced the size of Government, as the Vice President said. We have begun to reinvent it to make it work. Nobody looks the other way now when there's an emergency and the Federal Emergency Management

Agency comes, like they did when the Republicans were in power. They now say, "Bring them on. They're our friends. They're our helpers. They get things done." When California had their terrible earthquake, we got that highway rebuilt in about half the time—the busiest highway in America—they said they could do. If you go into the Small Business Administration now, you can fill out a one-page form for a loan and get an answer in 3 days. You don't have to wait months after going through page after page. I talked to university administrator after university administrator who tells me that they are saving weeks of time now in college loan applications because they like our new college loan program, our direct loan program that cuts costs to the taxpayers and cuts costs to the students and gives people a better way to pay back their college loans and cut out bureaucracy.

They say they want to help us. I say, come on. We need the help. We'd like to have some support. We've been carrying this burden for 2 years, reducing the Government, reducing the bureaucracy, making it work better. We would like to have a partner; you are welcome. Let's go, let's talk about positive ideas for our future.

They say we have to do something about immigration. They're right; there are too many illegal immigrants in America. But we have increased the number of border guards. We have accelerated the deportation of people convicted of crimes. We have faced these problems after they were ignored by the people who were here before. If they want to help in a responsible and fair way, I say, come on.

They say they're for welfare reform. Well, in the last 2 years, we gave 24 States permission to get around Federal rules and regulations to find new ways to put people to work, to give them a chance in life. So I say, okay, come on; help.

They say they want to be tough on crime. Most of them voted against the crime bill that put 100,000 police on the street, passed "three strikes and you're out," gave our people some prevention programs—and law enforcement, community leaders—to give kids something to say yes to and a better future. But we want help in these areas, and I say, come on.

They say they want to give tax relief to working people. So do we. In the last 2 years, as the Vice President said, we not only made 90 percent of the small businesses eligible for tax

cuts, but for working families under $26,000, their taxes this year will be, on the average, $1,000 lower than they would have been if this administration had never come to office. That's under the laws that are already there. So let's look at what we can do.

But let's look at what we should not do. In the last 2 years, a lot of the important things we did were opposed by somewhere between a majority and 100 percent of the members of the other party. Now they're in the majority. But I don't think we should repeal the family leave law. I don't think we should repeal the tax cuts for working families on low income to keep them off welfare. I don't think we should repeal the Brady bill. And I don't think we should repeal—and I know it may have cost us the House of Representatives, and most people who studied it closely believe it did, but I don't believe we should repeal the assault weapons. You don't need them. I'm not sure about this; you may need assault weapons to hunt giraffes, but you can go with ducks just fine with an ordinary shotgun.

This is a serious thing. Policemen lay down their lives every day in this country because of the upsurge in assault weapons. Talk to people who run the emergency rooms of our hospitals about the increasing mortality rate of people with gunshot wounds, and you know what they'll tell you? It's happening because there's more bullets in people's bodies who are shot with guns, on average, than there used to be. A lot of good Democrats laid down their careers to give our children a chance to stay alive on the street, give our police officers a chance to stay alive while they do their duty. We must not go back on that.

I'll tell you something else. We shouldn't repeal the law that will make it possible to immunize all the kids in this country against serious diseases who are under 2 years old. We shouldn't repeal the national service law. We should not do that. You know, on Martin Luther King's birthday, those national service volunteers were building houses in Atlanta, repairing tattered housing in Chicago, and helping people fight the floods in California. And they're earning money to go to college, which is important to their future and ours. And we shouldn't repeal it. We shouldn't repeal it.

I guess what I want to say to you is that I don't think the Government in any given time is intrinsically good or bad. Is it relevant? Is it working? Does it reflect our values and our interests? That is the question. There are many areas in which we can find agreement, and we must be big enough to seek those areas. Even though in so many places they turned away from the same opportunity in the previous 2 years, we have to let that go. Our job is to think about the people out there in America, those who are left behind in this global economy who need help to work their way from the under class to the middle class. We need to think about people out there who are working harder and falling further behind who deserve to have the American dream in a swelling opportunity middle class.

We need to be true to many of you in this room who are successful people, who are winning in the global economy but who know that your ultimate success and that of your children and your grandchildren depends upon our ability to go forward together. And you haven't left the Democratic Party, because you believe that America is one country and one community and we're going forward together. We have to be true to those people.

And so we have to work together. I hope that we will get bipartisan support for the administration's middle class bill of rights, which could just as well be called the bill of rights and responsibilities. It reflects all three things that I sought to do from the day I came here: to create a new economic policy, a new way of governing, and a New Covenant of rights and responsibilities.

If we give a tax deduction for education after high school, if we let people withdraw tax-free from an IRA for educational purposes, we are helping to rebuild our economy, we're having a nonbureaucratic governmental effort to help people grow, and we are establishing rights and responsibilities because you cannot be given an education, all you can be given is an opportunity to get an education for yourself. You have to do that for yourself.

Anybody can offer a tax cut. We saw that for the 12 years before we showed up. You know, you can quadruple the debt of the country, increase inequality, and claim you gave everybody a tax cut, even if it wasn't a fair one.

What we ought to do is to give hardworking, middle class Americans the benefit of this economic recovery by having a tightly disciplined tax relief focused largely on middle class Americans in ways that are paid for so that we do not explode the deficit. That should be our goal, and that will be my goal.

We're gunning with another round of reinventing Government proposals. We want there to be bipartisan support for that. We also think there ought to be some more political reform. I applaud the Republicans for supporting the law applying to Congress the same laws that are applied to the private sector. I think that's a good idea. And we should be for that; everybody should be for that. But we ought not stop there. We ought to also pass lobby reform and require disclosure and ban the gifts and the trips and let the American people know that there is no special political class in this country forgetting about them.

The Democrats ought to keep pushing until we get lobby reform and responsible campaign finance reform and the things that will move us forward as a people in increasing the trust of the voters in their Government. We ought to be doing that and say, "Join hands with us and do that, too. We like what you did, let's go further." That's the attitude that we ought to have.

And we ought to also be for more welfare reform. But I want to say something about this. I may be the only President who ever actually spent a lot of time talking to people on welfare. I may be the only President who ever, when he was a Governor, actually went into a welfare office, not just one but many, and watched how they work. We need to change this system. And our goal should be to move from welfare to work, from dependence to independence, from just proving you can biologically have children to responsible parenting. That ought to be our goal.

But our goal ought to be to liberate the energies and capacities of people to be good parents and to be good workers, not to punish people because they happen to be poor. And there will be some strong differences that need to be debated here, because I believe the American people desperately want a change in the welfare system. I believe they do not like the direction of our culture in terms of the breakup of families and the rising number of our children born out of wedlock. But I do not believe they want to punish parents and children just because they're poor or because they've made some mistakes in their lives.

I think we ought to require a system that promotes parenting, that promotes education, that promotes work. And we can do it in a way that builds people up, not tears them down. We can do it in a way that unites this country, not divides it. And the Democrats ought to take it as their solemn mission to make sure that that is exactly the kind of welfare reform we have in this country when I sign a bill on it.

Finally, let me make this point. Both parties and all candidates bear some responsibility for the fact that our public life has deteriorated in recent years, by treating the voters as if they were purely consumers in two senses: first, consumers in the sense that all they care about is economics. That's not true. There are other ways of defining our common security. And second and most importantly, perhaps, for us as a party, that we would treat them as consumers of politics, not participants in it. Who's got the best 30-second ad? Who rushes most quickly to define his or her opponent as a bad person? Who answers the ad best? And the American people become political couch potatoes, very often no more involved in politics than they are in the Super Bowl.

We've got an excuse, I do, for being a couch potato at the Super Bowl: I'm not good enough to play or young enough or strong enough. But we're all good enough to play in citizenship. And one of the reasons that we were successful in 1992 is that we got rid of a bunch of that. We did all those town meetings; we got on those buses and rode across the country; we stopped in little crossroads where nobody had ever been before. And we treated people like they had good sense and could be involved in a dialog about our country's future.

We must not draw the wrong lesson from the recent election. We must not think that the only answer is for us to have better negative ads than they do. Because we have obligations to the people of this country as well as to the party we love. And I am telling you—Andy Jackson, one of the founders of our party, said that the answer to every problem of democracy is more democracy. So we have to do a better job of reconnecting our citizens to our enterprise. The people cannot respond to us just because we pass a lot of bills in Congress. They have to be a part of that. Their lives have to change.

You know some of the happiest people I've seen in America since I've had the honor of being your President? People who are fighting disasters. I remember when that 500-year flood hit the Middle West, I met a little girl named Brianne Schwantes, who had brittle-bone disease, down in Iowa—lived in Wisconsin, came down to Iowa—the child had all kind of broken bones—fighting the flood, knowing that she could break a lot of her bones again, because it was a great enterprise and it made her feel that she could give something. And all the other people were just the same.

When I was in California last week, we were celebrating the one-year anniversary of the earthquake. They had 5,600 damaged school buildings a year ago; all but 40 are open today. And they are brimming with pride about what they did.

They're dealing with the floods. I flew to northern California; I went to a little unincorporated town in Congressman Fazio's district, Rio Linda, where Rush Limbaugh had his first radio program. And I was in this little Methodist church with all the volunteers in this flood. And this lady comes up to me—we were all standing around in a circle, and we were going to say a prayer—and she puts her arm around me, and she said, "Well, I'm a Republican, Mr. President, but I think I'll stand here with you anyway." Why? Because she was an American first. She was proud of what she was doing. She was helping people in trouble. And she felt more like a person who mattered.

And whether it's right or wrong, whenever our party, that has labored so long and so hard to lift up ordinary people and give them a chance to live out their dreams, suffers a reversal, it's because a lot of them don't think we think they matter. And what we have got to do, in addition to all these things we're doing here in Washington, is to change the way we are conducting politics, to make citizenship matter again, to let people become actors, not couch potatoes, in the great drama that is unfolding.

I am telling you, the next century will be the most exciting time this country ever had. Our best days are still ahead of us. We will have opportunities for people to move from total deprived circumstances into real success because of the technological changes that are occurring if we have the courage to make the right decisions and if we do it together so that people feel they matter. This party would not be here after 200 years unless at every critical juncture in our history, we had been able to do that.

So I tell you, when I say our job is to create opportunity but to provide responsibility and an opportunity to exercise it, it begins with the work of citizenship. When you go home, I want every one of you to think about that. What can you do with the State party? What ought you to do with the Republican Party in your State? What kind of debates can you sponsor? What kind of ways can you reach out and touch people? We must make people matter again.

You know, we'll win some elections in the future if none of this happens. We'll be smarter, and we'll get cleverer, and the next time this happens we'll do better. But what the country needs is to take these incredible technological changes that are going on and use them to connect people together again, not continue to drive them apart. You just think about that.

Why do people think they matter more in adversity than in creating a future that we can all be a part of? Why does there have to be a flood or a tornado before everybody who walks the streets, without regard to their income, their education, their race, their background, or their politics, feels like they are first and foremost an American? That is what we have to give back to them. And if we do, we'll be doing fine because we will remember that the most important thing is whether the American people do fine.

Thank you, and God bless you all.

NOTE: The President spoke at 12:50 p.m. at the Hilton Hotel and Towers. In his remarks, he referred to the following Democratic National Committee officers: Donald Fowler, national chairman; Senator Christopher Dodd, general chairman; Debra DeLee, former interim chair and 1996 Democratic Convention CEO; and David Wilhelm, former chair, and his wife, Degee. He also referred to the Retirement Protection Act of 1994, which appears in title VII of the Uruguay Round Agreements Act of 1994, approved December 8, 1994 (Public Law No. 103–465).

Statement on the Terrorist Bombing in Israel
January 22, 1995

I condemn in the strongest possible terms this horrendous act of terrorist violence. Once again, the enemies of peace have struck down innocent people in an evil effort to destroy the hopes of peaceful coexistence between Israelis and Arabs.

I call on all those who have chosen the path of peace to condemn this act and redouble their efforts to achieve a secure and lasting peace. The perpetrators of terrorism and their sponsors are determined to stop us from achieving this goal. I repeat what I said to them in the Middle East last October: "You cannot succeed. You will not succeed. You must not succeed, for you are the past, not the future."

On behalf of the American people, I extend our condolences and deepest sympathy to the families of the victims.

NOTE: The statement referred to the January 22 suicide bombing which killed 19 people at a military bus stop near Nordiya, Israel.

Message to the Congress on Disaster Assistance to Japan
January 20, 1995

To the Congress of the United States:

I have directed the Secretary of Defense to provide appropriate disaster assistance to the Government of Japan in response to the devastating earthquake of January 17, 1995. As required by section 404 of title 10, United States Code, I am notifying the Congress that the United States commence disaster relief operations on January 18, 1995, at 11:06 p.m., eastern standard time. To date, the U.S. military has provided 37,000 blankets. In addition, the following information is provided:

1. Disaster relief assistance is being provided in response to an earthquake affecting Kobe and Osaka, Japan.
2. Reports indicate at least 3,100 people have died, nearly 900 are missing, over 16,000 are injured, and an estimated 240,000 are homeless. The destruction of basic physical infrastructure poses a threat to the lives of the survivors.
3. Currently, U.S. military involvement has been limited to 15 U.S. Air Force C–130 Hercules sorties. Further requests for U.S. military assistance in the form of transportation, supplies, services, and equipment are unknown at this time.
4. Switzerland is providing search and rescue dog teams. Assistance by other countries is unknown.
5. Anticipated duration of disaster assistance activities is unknown.

WILLIAM J. CLINTON

The White House,
January 20, 1995.

NOTE: This message was released by the Office of the Press Secretary on January 23.

Remarks on Signing the Congressional Accountability Act of 1995
January 23, 1995

Good morning, everyone. I'm delighted to be joined this morning by Senator Nickles, Senator Ford, Senator Lieberman, Senator Grassley, and Senator Glenn and by Congressman Armey, Congressman Fazio, Congressman Shays, Congressman Gutknecht, and also by former Congressman Dick Swett and former Speaker Foley, who were instrumental in supporting this legislation in the previous session of the Congress where it passed the House but not the Senate.

Let me say that I am extremely pleased, and I think the American people are extremely pleased, that we are beginning the new year with a reform that requires Congress to live under the laws it imposes on the American people. I'm encouraged that we've begun this year with the White House and Congress, with Republicans and Democrats working together on a reform that has long been needed.

Most Americans are actually surprised when they learn that some of our most basic laws don't apply to Congress and their staffs. This legislation ensures that we'll change that. It guarantees that the cafeteria workers and the police who work in Congress and who help millions of tourists every year will have the same rights as all Americans do to a safe environment, to collective bargaining, to civil rights protection.

It does something else that's very important. Over the years, Washington has too often isolated itself from the everyday experience of ordinary Americans. It's become remote from the consequences of the actions Congress takes. I want to end this. Congress clearly wants to end this. Now when Congress passes a law, it will immediately know the consequences of the law if it affects private employers as well.

This will help us reconnect Government to the lives of ordinary Americans. That's why I supported this change when I ran for President and why I have supported it as President. It will help us to do what we must do to continue to fight to bring a reality check to Washington. That's why I worked to cut the White House staff, to eliminate the executive dining rooms, to cut back the widespread use of Government limousines, to reduce the deficit, to shrink the Federal bureaucracy to its smallest size in 30 years.

I'll admit that last year when this reform didn't pass I was disappointed. But I am very happy today. I want to thank all the Senators who are here, Senators Lieberman, Glenn, and Grassley, Senator Nickles, for what they all did. I thank Congressman Shays and Congressman Hoyer, who is not here, and the other Members of the House for all the work that they did. And again I say, I thank those who worked on this last year when it passed the House.

Already this year, Congress has enacted other important reforms, like reducing the staff and the number of committees. I want to congratulate the Members of Congress on these steps and, in particular, Majority Leader Dole and

Speaker Gingrich, the Senate Democratic leader, Tom Daschle, and the House Democratic leader, Dick Gephardt.

These changes I hope are the beginning of something that will continue for the next several years. We must use this impetus to make much deeper changes in the culture of Washington that has too often disconnected it from ordinary Americans. The American people, for example, know that lobbyists frequently get access to Congress they can never hope to get. They know the voices of special interests still sometimes ring too loud. They know too much of what goes on here goes on behind closed doors. Congress should ban the practice of gifts and meals and travels and entertainment from lobbyists. It should pass the strongest possible version of the line-item veto, lobby disclosure reform, and real comprehensive campaign finance reform.

I want to discuss these matters in detail tomorrow evening, but this is a job we must finish. This bill demonstrates the common resolve of people here that those in power should not lose touch with those who sent them here. Now we've got to go on. We must make this system more open, more fair, and less elitist. That's the goal we all share. I look forward to working with all of the Members here and all the Members of the Congress in both parties to achieve that goal.

Now I want to get on with signing the bill.

NOTE: The President spoke at 10 a.m. in the Oval Office at the White House. S. 2, approved January 23, was assigned Public Law No. 104–1.

Message to the Congress on Terrorists Who Threaten To Disrupt the Middle East Peace Process
January 23, 1995

To the Congress of the United States:

Pursuant to section 204(b) of the International Emergency Economic Powers Act, 50 U.S.C. 1703(b) and section 301 of the National Emergencies Act, 50 U.S.C. 1631, I hereby report that I have exercised my statutory authority to declare a national emergency with respect to the grave acts of violence committed by foreign terrorists that threaten to disrupt the Middle East peace process and to issue an Executive order that:

—Blocks all property, including bank deposits, of foreign persons or organizations designated in the Executive order or pursuant thereto, which is in the United States or in the control of United States persons, including their overseas branches; and

—Prohibits any transaction or dealing by United States persons in such property, including the making or receiving of any contribution of funds, goods, or services to or for the benefit of such designated persons.

I have designated in the Executive order 12 foreign organizations that threaten to use violence to disrupt the Middle East peace process. I have authorized the Secretary of State to designate additional foreign persons who have committed, or pose a significant risk of committing, acts of violence that have the purpose or effect of disrupting the Middle East peace process, or who assist in, sponsor, or provide financial, material or technological support for, or services in support of, such acts of violence. Such designations are to be made in coordination with the Secretary of the Treasury and the Attorney General.

The Secretary of the Treasury is further authorized to designate persons or entities that he determines, in coordination with the Secretary of State and the Attorney General, are owned or controlled by, or acting for or on behalf of, any of the foreign persons designated under this order. The Secretary of the Treasury is also authorized to issue regulations in exercise of my authorities under the International Emergency Economic Powers Act to implement these measures in consultation with the Secretary of State and the Attorney General and to coordinate such implementation with the Federal Bureau of Investigation. All Federal agencies are directed to take actions within their authority to carry out the provisions of the Executive order.

I am enclosing a copy of the Executive order that I have issued. The order was effective at 12:01 a.m., eastern standard time on January 24, 1995.

I have authorized these measures in response to recurrent acts of international terrorism that threaten to disrupt the Middle East peace process. They include such acts as the bomb attacks in Israel this past weekend and other recent attacks in Israel, attacks on government authorities in Egypt, threats against Palestinian authorities in the autonomous regions, and the bombing of the Jewish Mutual Association building in Buenos Aires, as well as the car bomb at the Israeli Embassy in London.

Achieving peace between Israel and its neighbors has long been a principal goal of American foreign policy. Resolving this conflict would eliminate a major source of instability in a part of the world in which we have critical interests, contribute to the security and well-being of Israel, and strengthen important bilateral relationships in the Arab world.

Attempts to disrupt the Middle East peace process through terrorism by groups opposed to peace have threatened and continue to threaten vital interests of the United States, thus constituting an unusual and extraordinary threat to the national security, foreign policy, and economy of the United States.

Terrorist groups engaging in such terrorist acts receive financial and material support for their efforts from persons in the Middle East and elsewhere who oppose that process. Individuals and groups in the United States, too, have been targets of fundraising efforts on behalf of terrorist organizations.

Fundraising for terrorism and use of the U.S. banking system for transfers on behalf of such organizations are inimical to American interests. Further, failure to take effective action against similar fundraising and transfers in foreign countries indicate the need for leadership by the United States on this subject. Thus, it is necessary to provide the tools to combat any financial support from the United States for such terrorist activities. The United States will use these actions on our part to impress on our allies in Europe and elsewhere the seriousness of the danger of terrorist funding threatening the Middle East peace process, and to encourage them to adopt appropriate and effective measures to cut off terrorist fundraising and the harboring of terrorist assets in their territories and by their nationals.

The measures we are taking demonstrate our determination to thwart acts of terrorism that threaten to disrupt the Middle East peace process by attacking any material or financial support for such acts that may emanate from the United States.

WILLIAM J. CLINTON

The White House,
January 23, 1995.

NOTE: This message was released by the Office of the Press Secretary on January 24. The Executive order of January 23 is listed in Appendix D at the end of this volume.

Address Before a Joint Session of the Congress on the State of the Union
January 24, 1995

Mr. President, Mr. Speaker, Members of the 104th Congress, my fellow Americans: Again we are here in the sanctuary of democracy, and once again our democracy has spoken. So let me begin by congratulating all of you here in the 104th Congress and congratulating you, Mr. Speaker.

If we agree on nothing else tonight, we must agree that the American people certainly voted for change in 1992 and in 1994. And as I look out at you, I know how some of you must have felt in 1992. [*Laughter*]

I must say that in both years we didn't hear America singing, we heard America shouting. And now all of us, Republicans and Democrats alike, must say, "We hear you. We will work together to earn the jobs you have given us." For we are the keepers of a sacred trust, and we must be faithful to it in this new and very demanding era.

Over 200 years ago, our Founders changed the entire course of human history by joining together to create a new country based on a single powerful idea: "We hold these truths to be self-evident, that all men are created equal, . . . endowed by their Creator with certain unalienable Rights, and among these are Life, Liberty and the pursuit of Happiness."

It has fallen to every generation since then to preserve that idea, the American idea, and to deepen and expand its meaning in new and different times: to Lincoln and to his Congress to preserve the Union and to end slavery; to Theodore Roosevelt and Woodrow Wilson to restrain the abuses and excesses of the industrial revolution and to assert our leadership in the world; to Franklin Roosevelt to fight the failure and pain of the Great Depression and to win our country's great struggle against fascism; and to all our Presidents since to fight the cold war. Especially, I recall two who struggled to fight that cold war in partnership with Congresses where the majority was of a different party: to Harry Truman, who summoned us to unparalleled prosperity at home and who built the architecture of the cold war; and to Ronald Reagan, whom we wish well tonight and who exhorted us to carry on until the twilight struggle against communism was won.

In another time of change and challenge, I had the honor to be the first President to be elected in the post-cold-war era, an era marked by the global economy, the information revolution, unparalleled change and opportunity and insecurity for the American people. I came to this hallowed Chamber 2 years ago on a mission, to restore the American dream for all our people and to make sure that we move into the 21st century still the strongest force for freedom and democracy in the entire world. I was determined then to tackle the tough problems too long ignored. In this effort I am frank to say that I have made my mistakes, and I have learned again the importance of humility in all human endeavor. But I am also proud to say tonight that our country is stronger than it was 2 years ago. [*Applause*] Thank you.

Record numbers of Americans are succeeding in the new global economy. We are at peace, and we are a force for peace and freedom throughout the world. We have almost 6 million new jobs since I became President, and we have the lowest combined rate of unemployment and inflation in 25 years. Our businesses are more productive. And here we have worked to bring the deficit down, to expand trade, to put more police on our streets, to give our citizens more of the tools they need to get an education and to rebuild their own communities.

But the rising tide is not lifting all boats. While our Nation is enjoying peace and prosperity, too many of our people are still working harder and harder, for less and less. While our businesses are restructuring and growing more productive and competitive, too many of our people still can't be sure of having a job next year or even next month. And far more than our material riches are threatened, things far more precious to us, our children, our families, our values.

Our civil life is suffering in America today. Citizens are working together less and shouting at each other more. The common bonds of community which have been the great strength of our country from its very beginning are badly frayed. What are we to do about it?

More than 60 years ago, at the dawn of another new era, President Roosevelt told our Nation, "New conditions impose new requirements on Government and those who conduct Government." And from that simple proposition, he shaped the New Deal, which helped to restore our Nation to prosperity and define the relationship between our people and their Government for half a century.

That approach worked in its time. But we today, we face a very different time and very different conditions. We are moving from an industrial age built on gears and sweat to an information age demanding skills and learning and flexibility. Our Government, once a champion of national purpose, is now seen by many as simply a captive of narrow interests, putting more burdens on our citizens rather than equipping them to get ahead. The values that used to hold us all together seem to be coming apart.

So tonight we must forge a new social compact to meet the challenges of this time. As we enter a new era, we need a new set of understandings, not just with Government but, even more important, with one another as Americans.

That's what I want to talk with you about tonight. I call it the New Covenant. But it's grounded in a very, very old idea, that all Americans have not just a right but a solemn responsibility to rise as far as their God-given talents and determination can take them and to give something back to their communities and their country in return. Opportunity and responsibility: They go hand in hand. We can't have one without the other. And our national community can't hold together without both.

Our New Covenant is a new set of understandings for how we can equip our people to meet the challenges of a new economy, how we can change the way our Government works to fit a different time, and, above all, how we can repair the damaged bonds in our society and come together behind our common purpose. We must have dramatic change in our economy, our Government, and ourselves.

My fellow Americans, without regard to party, let us rise to the occasion. Let us put aside partisanship and pettiness and pride. As we embark on this new course, let us put our country first, remembering that regardless of party label, we are all Americans. And let the final test of everything we do be a simple one: Is it good for the American people?

Let me begin by saying that we cannot ask Americans to be better citizens if we are not better servants. You made a good start by passing that law which applies to Congress all the laws you put on the private sector, and I was proud to sign it yesterday. But we have a lot more to do before people really trust the way things work around here. Three times as many lobbyists are in the streets and corridors of Washington as were here 20 years ago. The American people look at their Capital, and they see a city where the well-connected and the well-protected can work the system, but the interests of ordinary citizens are often left out.

As the new Congress opened its doors, lobbyists were still doing business as usual; the gifts, the trips, all the things that people are concerned about haven't stopped. Twice this month you missed opportunities to stop these practices. I know there were other considerations in those votes, but I want to use something that I've heard my Republican friends say from time to time, "There doesn't have to be a law for everything." So tonight I ask you to just stop taking the lobbyists' perks. Just stop. We don't have to wait for legislation to pass to send a strong signal to the American people that things are really changing. But I also hope you will send me the strongest possible lobby reform bill, and I'll sign that, too.

We should require lobbyists to tell the people for whom they work what they're spending, what

they want. We should also curb the role of big money in elections by capping the cost of campaigns and limiting the influence of PAC's. And as I have said for 3 years, we should work to open the airwaves so that they can be an instrument of democracy, not a weapon of destruction, by giving free TV time to candidates for public office.

When the last Congress killed political reform last year, it was reported in the press that the lobbyists actually stood in the Halls of this sacred building and cheered. This year, let's give the folks at home something to cheer about.

More important, I think we all agree that we have to change the way the Government works. Let's make it smaller, less costly, and smarter; leaner, not meaner. [*Applause*]

I just told the Speaker the equal time doctrine is alive and well. [*Laughter*]

The New Covenant approach to governing is as different from the old bureaucratic way as the computer is from the manual typewriter. The old way of governing around here protected organized interests. We should look out for the interests of ordinary people. The old way divided us by interest, constituency, or class. The New Covenant way should unite us behind a common vision of what's best for our country. The old way dispensed services through large, top-down, inflexible bureaucracies. The New Covenant way should shift these resources and decisionmaking from bureaucrats to citizens, injecting choice and competition and individual responsibility into national policy. The old way of governing around here actually seemed to reward failure. The New Covenant way should have built-in incentives to reward success. The old way was centralized here in Washington. The New Covenant way must take hold in the communities all across America. And we should help them to do that.

Our job here is to expand opportunity, not bureaucracy, to empower people to make the most of their own lives, and to enhance our security here at home and abroad. We must not ask Government to do what we should do for ourselves. We should rely on Government as a partner to help us to do more for ourselves and for each other.

I hope very much that as we debate these specific and exciting matters, we can go beyond the sterile discussion between the illusion that there is somehow a program for every problem, on the one hand, and the other illusion that the Government is a source of every problem we have. Our job is to get rid of yesterday's Government so that our own people can meet today's and tomorrow's needs. And we ought to do it together.

You know, for years before I became President, I heard others say they would cut Government and how bad it was, but not much happened. We actually did it. We cut over a quarter of a trillion dollars in spending, more than 300 domestic programs, more than 100,000 positions from the Federal bureaucracy in the last 2 years alone. Based on decisions already made, we will have cut a total of more than a quarter of a million positions from the Federal Government, making it the smallest it has been since John Kennedy was President, by the time I come here again next year.

Under the leadership of Vice President Gore, our initiatives have already saved taxpayers $63 billion. The age of the $500 hammer and the ashtray you can break on "David Letterman" is gone. Deadwood programs, like mohair subsidies, are gone. We've streamlined the Agriculture Department by reducing it by more than 1,200 offices. We've slashed the small business loan form from an inch thick to a single page. We've thrown away the Government's 10,000-page personnel manual.

And the Government is working better in important ways: FEMA, the Federal Emergency Management Agency, has gone from being a disaster to helping people in disasters. You can ask the farmers in the Middle West who fought the flood there or the people in California who have dealt with floods and earthquakes and fires, and they'll tell you that. Government workers, working hand in hand with private business, rebuilt southern California's fractured freeways in record time and under budget. And because the Federal Government moved fast, all but one of the 5,600 schools damaged in the earthquake are back in business.

Now, there are a lot of other things that I could talk about. I want to just mention one because it will be discussed here in the next few weeks. University administrators all over the country have told me that they are saving weeks and weeks of bureaucratic time now because of our direct college loan program, which makes college loans cheaper and more affordable with better repayment terms for students, costs the Government less, and cuts out paperwork and bureaucracy for the Government and for the universities. We shouldn't cap that program. We should give every college in America the opportunity to be a part of it.

Previous Government programs gathered dust. The reinventing Government report is getting results. And we're not through. There's going to be a second round of reinventing Government. We propose to cut $130 billion in spending by shrinking departments, extending our freeze on domestic spending, cutting 60 public housing programs down to 3, getting rid of over 100 programs we do not need, like the Interstate Commerce Commission and the Helium Reserve Program. And we're working on getting rid of unnecessary regulations and making them more sensible. The programs and regulations that have outlived their usefulness should go. We have to cut yesterday's Government to help solve tomorrow's problems.

And we need to get Government closer to the people it's meant to serve. We need to help move programs down to the point where States and communities and private citizens in the private sector can do a better job. If they can do it, we ought to let them do it. We should get out of the way and let them do what they can do better. Taking power away from Federal bureaucracies and giving it back to communities and individuals is something everyone should be able to be for.

It's time for Congress to stop passing on to the States the cost of decisions we make here in Washington. I know there are still serious differences over the details of the unfunded mandates legislation, but I want to work with you to make sure we pass a reasonable bill which will protect the national interests and give justified relief where we need to give it.

For years, Congress concealed in the budget scores of pet spending projects. Last year was no difference. There was a $1 million to study stress in plants and $12 million for a tick removal program that didn't work. It's hard to remove ticks. Those of us who have had them know. [*Laughter*] But I'll tell you something, if you'll give me line-item veto, I'll remove some of that unnecessary spending.

But I think we should all remember, and almost all of us would agree, that Government still has important responsibilities. Our young people—we should think of this when we cut—our young people hold our future in their hands. We still owe a debt to our veterans. And our senior citizens have made us what we are. Now, my budget cuts a lot. But it protects education, veterans, Social Security, and Medicare, and I hope you will do the same thing. You should, and I hope you will.

And when we give more flexibility to the States, let us remember that there are certain fundamental national needs that should be addressed in every State, North and South, East and West: Immunization against childhood disease, school lunches in all our schools, Head Start, medical care and nutrition for pregnant women and infants, all these things, all these things are in the national interest.

I applaud your desire to get rid of costly and unnecessary regulations. But when we deregulate, let's remember what national action in the national interest has given us: safer food for our families, safer toys for our children, safer nursing homes for our parents, safer cars and highways, and safer workplaces, cleaner air, and cleaner water. Do we need common sense and fairness in our regulations? You bet we do. But we can have common sense and still provide for safe drinking water. We can have fairness and still clean up toxic dumps, and we ought to do it.

Should we cut the deficit more? Well, of course we should. Of course we should. But we can bring it down in a way that still protects our economic recovery and does not unduly punish people who should not be punished but instead should be helped.

I know many of you in this Chamber support the balanced budget amendment. I certainly want to balance the budget. Our administration has done more to bring the budget down and to save money than any in a very, very long time. If you believe passing this amendment is the right thing to do, then you have to be straight with the American people. They have a right to know what you're going to cut, what taxes you're going to raise, and how it's going to affect them. We should be doing things in the open around here. For example, everybody ought to know if this proposal is going to endanger Social Security. I would oppose that, and I think most Americans would.

Nothing has done more to undermine our sense of common responsibility than our failed welfare system. This is one of the problems we have to face here in Washington in our New Covenant. It rewards welfare over work. It undermines family values. It lets millions of parents get away without paying their child support. It keeps a minority but a significant minority of the people on welfare trapped on it for a very long time.

I've worked on this problem for a long time, nearly 15 years now. As a Governor, I had the honor of working with the Reagan administration to write the last welfare reform bill back in 1988. In the last 2 years, we made a good start at continuing the work of welfare reform. Our administration gave two dozen States the right to slash through Federal rules and regulations to reform their own welfare systems and to try to promote work and responsibility over welfare and dependency.

Last year I introduced the most sweeping welfare reform plan ever presented by an administration. We have to make welfare what it was meant to be, a second chance, not a way of life. We have to help those on welfare move to work as quickly as possible, to provide child care and teach them skills, if that's what they need, for up to 2 years. And after that, there ought to be a simple, hard rule: Anyone who can work must go to work. If a parent isn't paying child support, they should be forced to pay. We should suspend drivers' license, track them across State lines, make them work off what they owe. That is what we should do. Governments do not raise children, people do. And the parents must take responsibility for the children they bring into this world.

I want to work with you, with all of you, to pass welfare reform. But our goal must be to liberate people and lift them up from dependence to independence, from welfare to work, from mere childbearing to responsible parenting. Our goal should not be to punish them because they happen to be poor.

We should, we should require work and mutual responsibility. But we shouldn't cut people off just because they're poor, they're young, or even because they're unmarried. We should promote responsibility by requiring young mothers to live at home with their parents or in other supervised settings, by requiring them to finish school. But we shouldn't put them and their children out on the street. And I know all the arguments, pro and con, and I have read and thought about this for a long time. I still don't think we can in good conscience punish poor children for the mistakes of their parents.

My fellow Americans, every single survey shows that all the American people care about this without regard to party or race or region.

So let this be the year we end welfare as we know it. But also let this be the year that we are all able to stop using this issue to divide America. No one is more eager to end welfare— [*applause*]—I may be the only President who has actually had the opportunity to sit in a welfare office, who's actually spent hours and hours talking to people on welfare. And I am telling you, the people who are trapped on it know it doesn't work; they also want to get off. So we can promote, together, education and work and good parenting. I have no problem with punishing bad behavior or the refusal to be a worker or a student or a responsible parent. I just don't want to punish poverty and past mistakes. All of us have made our mistakes, and none of us can change our yesterdays. But every one of us can change our tomorrows. And America's best example of that may be Lynn Woolsey, who worked her way off welfare to become a Congresswoman from the State of California.

I know the Members of this Congress are concerned about crime, as are all the citizens of our country. And I remind you that last year we passed a very tough crime bill: longer sentences, "three strikes and you're out," almost 60 new capital punishment offenses, more prisons, more prevention, 100,000 more police. And we paid for it all by reducing the size of the Federal bureaucracy and giving the money back to local communities to lower the crime rate.

There may be other things we can do to be tougher on crime, to be smarter with crime, to help to lower that rate first. Well, if there are, let's talk about them, and let's do them. But let's not go back on the things that we did last year that we know work, that we know work because the local law enforcement officers tell us that we did the right thing, because local community leaders who have worked for years and years to lower the crime rate tell us that they work. Let's look at the experience of our cities and our rural areas where the crime rate has gone down and ask the people who did it how they did it. And if what we did last year supports the decline in the crime rate— and I am convinced that it does—let us not go back on it. Let's stick with it, implement it. We've got 4 more hard years of work to do to do that.

I don't want to destroy the good atmosphere in the room or in the country tonight, but I have to mention one issue that divided this body greatly last year. The last Congress also passed the Brady bill and, in the crime bill, the ban on 19 assault weapons. I don't think it's a secret to anybody in this room that several Members of the last Congress who voted for that aren't here tonight because they voted for it. And I know, therefore, that some of you who are here because they voted for it are under enormous pressure to repeal it. I just have to tell you how I feel about it.

The Members of Congress who voted for that bill and I would never do anything to infringe on the right to keep and bear arms to hunt and to engage in other appropriate sporting activities. I've done it since I was a boy, and I'm going to keep right on doing it until I can't do it anymore. But a lot of people laid down their seats in Congress so that police officers and kids wouldn't have to lay down their lives under a hail of assault weapon attack, and I will not let that be repealed. I will not let it be repealed.

I'd like to talk about a couple of other issues we have to deal with. I want us to cut more spending, but I hope we won't cut Government programs that help to prepare us for the new economy, promote responsibility, and are organized from the grassroots up, not by Federal bureaucracy. The very best example of this is the national service corps, AmeriCorps. It passed with strong bipartisan support. And now there are 20,000 Americans, more than ever served in one year in the Peace Corps, working all over this country, helping people person-to-person in local grassroots volunteer groups, solving problems, and in the process earning some money for their education. This is citizenship at its best. It's good for the AmeriCorps members, but it's good for the rest of us, too. It's the essence of the New Covenant, and we shouldn't stop it.

All Americans, not only in the States most heavily affected but in every place in this country, are rightly disturbed by the large numbers of illegal aliens entering our country. The jobs they hold might otherwise be held by citizens or legal immigrants. The public service they use impose burdens on our taxpayers. That's why our administration has moved aggressively to secure our borders more by hiring a record number of new border guards, by deporting twice as many criminal aliens as ever before, by cracking down on illegal hiring, by barring welfare benefits to illegal aliens. In the budget I will present to you, we will try to do more to speed the deportation of illegal aliens who are arrested for crimes, to better identify illegal aliens in the workplace as recommended by the commission headed by former Congresswoman Barbara Jordan. We are a nation of immigrants. But we are also a nation of laws. It is wrong and ultimately self-defeating for a nation of immigrants to permit the kind of abuse of our immigration laws we have seen in recent years, and we must do more to stop it.

The most important job of our Government in this new era is to empower the American people to succeed in the global economy. America has always been a land of opportunity, a land where, if you work hard, you can get ahead. We've become a great middle class country. Middle class values sustain us. We must expand that middle class and shrink the under class, even as we do everything we can to support the millions of Americans who are already successful in the new economy.

America is once again the world's strongest economic power: almost 6 million new jobs in the last 2 years, exports booming, inflation down. High-wage jobs are coming back. A record number of American entrepreneurs are living the American dream. If we want it to stay that way, those who work and lift our Nation must have more of its benefits.

Today, too many of those people are being left out. They're working harder for less. They have less security, less income, less certainty that they can even afford a vacation, much less college for their kids or retirement for themselves. We cannot let this continue. If we don't act, our economy will probably keep doing what it's been doing since about 1978, when the income growth began to go to those at the very top of our economic scale and the people in the vast middle got very little growth, and people who worked like crazy but were on the bottom then fell even further and further behind in the years afterward, no matter how hard they worked.

We've got to have a Government that can be a real partner in making this new economy work for all of our people, a Government that helps each and every one of us to get an education and to have the opportunity to renew our skills. That's why we worked so hard to increase educational opportunities in the last 2 years, from Head Start to public schools, to apprenticeships for young people who don't go to college, to making college loans more avail-

able and more affordable. That's the first thing we have to do. We've got to do something to empower people to improve their skills.

The second thing we ought to do is to help people raise their incomes immediately by lowering their taxes. We took the first step in 1993 with a working family tax cut for 15 million families with incomes under $27,000, a tax cut that this year will average about $1,000 a family. And we also gave tax reductions to most small and new businesses. Before we could do more than that, we first had to bring down the deficit we inherited, and we had to get economic growth up. Now we've done both. And now we can cut taxes in a more comprehensive way. But tax cuts should reinforce and promote our first obligation: to empower our citizens through education and training to make the most of their own lives. The spotlight should shine on those who make the right choices for themselves, their families, and their communities.

I have proposed the middle class bill of rights, which should properly be called the bill of rights and responsibilities because its provisions only benefit those who are working to educate and raise their children and to educate themselves. It will, therefore, give needed tax relief and raise incomes in both the short run and the long run in a way that benefits all of us.

There are four provisions. First, a tax deduction for all education and training after high school. If you think about it, we permit businesses to deduct their investment, we permit individuals to deduct interest on their home mortgages, but today an education is even more important to the economic well-being of our whole country than even those things are. We should do everything we can to encourage it. And I hope you will support it. Second, we ought to cut taxes $500 for families with children under 13. Third, we ought to foster more savings and personal responsibility by permitting people to establish an individual retirement account and withdraw from it, tax-free, for the cost of education, health care, first-time homebuying, or the care of a parent. And fourth, we should pass a "GI bill" for America's workers. We propose to collapse nearly 70 Federal programs and not give the money to the States but give the money directly to the American people, offer vouchers to them so that they, if they're laid off or if they're working for a very low wage, can get a voucher worth $2,600 a year for up to 2 years to go to their local community colleges or wherever else they want to get the skills they need to improve their lives. Let's empower people in this way, move it from the Government directly to the workers of America.

Now, any one of us can call for a tax cut, but I won't accept one that explodes the deficit or puts our recovery at risk. We ought to pay for our tax cuts fully and honestly.

Just 2 years ago, it was an open question whether we would find the strength to cut the deficit. Thanks to the courage of the people who were here then, many of whom didn't return, we did cut the deficit. We began to do what others said would not be done. We cut the deficit by over $600 billion, about $10,000 for every family in this country. It's coming down 3 years in a row for the first time since Mr. Truman was President, and I don't think anybody in America wants us to let it explode again.

In the budget I will send you, the middle class bill of rights is fully paid for by budget cuts in bureaucracy, cuts in programs, cuts in special interest subsidies. And the spending cuts will more than double the tax cuts. My budget pays for the middle class bill of rights without any cuts in Medicare. And I will oppose any attempts to pay for tax cuts with Medicare cuts. That's not the right thing to do.

I know that a lot of you have your own ideas about tax relief, and some of them I find quite interesting. I really want to work with all of you. My test for our proposals will be: Will it create jobs and raise incomes; will it strengthen our families and support our children; is it paid for; will it build the middle class and shrink the under class? If it does, I'll support it. But if it doesn't, I won't.

The goal of building the middle class and shrinking the under class is also why I believe that you should raise the minimum wage. It rewards work. Two and a half million Americans, two and a half million Americans, often women with children, are working out there today for $4.25 an hour. In terms of real buying power, by next year that minimum wage will be at a 40-year low. That's not my idea of how the new economy ought to work.

Now, I've studied the arguments and the evidence for and against a minimum wage increase. I believe the weight of the evidence is that a modest increase does not cost jobs and may even lure people back into the job market. But the most important thing is, you can't make a living on $4.25 an hour, especially if you have children, even with the working families tax cut we passed last year. In the past, the minimum wage has been a bipartisan issue, and I think it should be again. So I want to challenge you to have honest hearings on this, to get together, to find a way to make the minimum wage a living wage.

Members of Congress have been here less than a month, but by the end of the week, 28 days into the new year, every Member of Congress will have earned as much in congressional salary as a minimum wage worker makes all year long.

Everybody else here, including the President, has something else that too many Americans do without, and that's health care. Now, last year we almost came to blows over health care, but we didn't do anything. And the cold, hard fact is that, since last year, since I was here, another 1.1 million Americans in working families have lost their health care. And the cold, hard fact is that many millions more, most of them farmers and small business people and self-employed people, have seen their premiums skyrocket, their copays and deductibles go up. There's a whole bunch of people in this country that in the statistics have health insurance but really what they've got is a piece of paper that says they won't lose their home if they get sick.

Now, I still believe our country has got to move toward providing health security for every American family. But I know that last year, as the evidence indicates, we bit off more than we could chew. So I'm asking you that we work together. Let's do it step by step. Let's do whatever we have to do to get something done. Let's at least pass meaningful insurance reform so that no American risks losing coverage for facing skyrocketing prices, that nobody loses their coverage because they face high prices or unavailable insurance when they change jobs or lose a job or a family member gets sick.

I want to work together with all of you who have an interest in this, with the Democrats who worked on it last time, with the Republican leaders like Senator Dole, who has a longtime commitment to health care reform and made some constructive proposals in this area last year. We ought to make sure that self-employed people in small businesses can buy insurance at more affordable rates through voluntary purchasing pools. We ought to help families provide long-term care for a sick parent or a disabled child. We can work to help workers who lose their jobs at least keep their health insurance coverage for a year while they look for work. And we can find a way—it may take some time, but we can find a way—to make sure that our children have health care.

You know, I think everybody in this room, without regard to party, can be proud of the fact that our country was rated as having the world's most productive economy for the first time in nearly a decade. But we can't be proud of the fact that we're the only wealthy country in the world that has a smaller percentage of the work force and their children with health insurance today than we did 10 years ago, the last time we were the most productive economy in the world. So let's work together on this. It is too important for politics as usual.

Much of what the American people are thinking about tonight is what we've already talked about. A lot of people think that the security concerns of America today are entirely internal to our borders. They relate to the security of our jobs and our homes and our incomes and our children, our streets, our health, and protecting those borders. Now that the cold war has passed, it's tempting to believe that all the security issues, with the possible exception of trade, reside here at home. But it's not so. Our security still depends upon our continued world leadership for peace and freedom and democracy. We still can't be strong at home unless we're strong abroad.

The financial crisis in Mexico is a case in point. I know it's not popular to say it tonight, but we have to act, not for the Mexican people but for the sake of the millions of Americans whose livelihoods are tied to Mexico's well-being. If we want to secure American jobs, preserve American exports, safeguard America's borders, then we must pass the stabilization program and help to put Mexico back on track.

Now let me repeat: It's not a loan. It's not foreign aid. It's not a bailout. We will be given a guarantee like cosigning a note, with good collateral that will cover our risks. This legislation is the right thing for America. That's why the bipartisan leadership has supported it. And I hope you in Congress will pass it quickly. It is in our interest, and we can explain it to the American people because we're going to do it in the right way.

You know, tonight, this is the first State of the Union Address ever delivered since the beginning of the cold war when not a single Russian missile is pointed at the children of America. And along with the Russians, we're on our way to destroying the missiles and the bombers that carry 9,000 nuclear warheads. We've come so far so fast in this post-cold-war world that it's easy to take the decline of the nuclear threat for granted. But it's still there, and we aren't finished yet.

This year I'll ask the Senate to approve START II to eliminate weapons that carry 5,000 more warheads. The United States will lead the charge to extend indefinitely the Nuclear Non-Proliferation Treaty, to enact a comprehensive nuclear test ban, and to eliminate chemical weapons. To stop and roll back North Korea's potentially deadly nuclear program, we'll continue to implement the agreement we have reached with that nation. It's smart. It's tough. It's a deal based on continuing inspection with safeguards for our allies and ourselves.

This year I'll submit to Congress comprehensive legislation to strengthen our hand in combating terrorists, whether they strike at home or abroad. As the cowards who bombed the World Trade Center found out, this country will hunt down terrorists and bring them to justice.

Just this week, another horrendous terrorist act in Israel killed 19 and injured scores more. On behalf of the American people and all of you, I send our deepest sympathy to the families of the victims. I know that in the face of such evil, it is hard for the people in the Middle East to go forward. But the terrorists represent the past, not the future. We must and we will pursue a comprehensive peace between Israel and all her neighbors in the Middle East.

Accordingly, last night I signed an Executive order that will block the assets in the United States of terrorist organizations that threaten to disrupt the peace process. It prohibits financial transactions with these groups. And tonight I call on all our allies and peace-loving nations throughout the world to join us with renewed fervor in a global effort to combat terrorism. We cannot permit the future to be marred by terror and fear and paralysis.

From the day I took the oath of office, I pledged that our Nation would maintain the best equipped, best trained, and best prepared military on Earth. We have, and they are. They have managed the dramatic downsizing of our forces after the cold war with remarkable skill and spirit. But to make sure our military is ready for action and to provide the pay and the quality of life the military and their families deserve, I'm asking the Congress to add $25 billion in defense spending over the next 6 years.

I have visited many bases at home and around the world since I became President. Tonight I repeat that request with renewed conviction. We ask a very great deal of our Armed Forces. Now that they are smaller in number, we ask more of them. They go out more often to more different places and stay longer. They are called to service in many, many ways. And we must give them and their families what the times demand and what they have earned.

Just think about what our troops have done in the last year, showing America at its best, helping to save hundreds of thousands of people in Rwanda, moving with lightning speed to head off another threat to Kuwait, giving freedom and democracy back to the people of Haiti. We have proudly supported peace and prosperity and freedom from South Africa to Northern Ireland, from Central and Eastern Europe to Asia, from Latin America to the Middle East. All these endeavors are good in those places, but they make our future more confident and more secure.

Well, my fellow Americans, that's my agenda for America's future: expanding opportunity, not bureaucracy; enhancing security at home and abroad; empowering our people to make the most of their own lives. It's ambitious and achievable, but it's not enough. We even need more than new ideas for changing the world or equipping Americans to compete in the new economy, more than a Government that's smaller, smarter, and wiser, more than all of the changes we can make in Government and in the private sector from the outside in.

Our fortunes and our posterity also depend upon our ability to answer some questions from within, from the values and voices that speak to our hearts as well as our heads; voices that tell us we have to do more to accept responsibility for ourselves and our families, for our communities, and yes, for our fellow citizens. We see our families and our communities all over this country coming apart, and we feel the common ground shifting from under us. The PTA, the town hall meeting, the ball park, it's hard for a lot of overworked parents to find the time

and space for those things that strengthen the bonds of trust and cooperation. Too many of our children don't even have parents and grandparents who can give them those experiences that they need to build their own character and their sense of identity.

We all know that while we here in this Chamber can make a difference on those things, that the real differences will be made by our fellow citizens, where they work and where they live and that it will be made almost without regard to party. When I used to go to the softball park in Little Rock to watch my daughter's league and people would come up to me, fathers and mothers, and talk to me, I can honestly say I had no idea whether 90 percent of them were Republicans or Democrats. When I visited the relief centers after the floods in California, northern California, last week, a woman came up to me and did something that very few of you would do. She hugged me and said, "Mr. President, I'm a Republican, but I'm glad you're here." [*Laughter*]

Now, why? We can't wait for disasters to act the way we used to act every day, because as we move into this next century, everybody matters. We don't have a person to waste. And a lot of people are losing a lot of chances to do better. That means that we need a New Covenant for everybody.

For our corporate and business leaders, we're going to work here to keep bringing the deficit down, to expand markets, to support their success in every possible way. But they have an obligation when they're doing well to keep jobs in our communities and give their workers a fair share of the prosperity they generate.

For people in the entertainment industry in this country, we applaud your creativity and your worldwide success, and we support your freedom of expression. But you do have a responsibility to assess the impact of your work and to understand the damage that comes from the incessant, repetitive, mindless violence and irresponsible conduct that permeates our media all the time.

We've got to ask our community leaders and all kinds of organizations to help us stop our most serious social problem, the epidemic of teen pregnancies and births where there is no marriage. I have sent to Congress a plan to target schools all over this country with antipregnancy programs that work. But Government can only do so much. Tonight I call on parents and leaders all across this country to join together in a national campaign against teen pregnancy to make a difference. We can do this, and we must.

And I would like to say a special word to our religious leaders. You know, I'm proud of the fact the United States has more houses of worship per capita than any country in the world. These people who lead our houses of worship can ignite their congregations to carry their faith into action, can reach out to all of our children, to all of the people in distress, to those who have been savaged by the breakdown of all we hold dear. Because so much of what must be done must come from the inside out and our religious leaders and their congregations can make all the difference, they have a role in the New Covenant as well.

There must be more responsibility for all of our citizens. You know, it takes a lot of people to help all the kids in trouble stay off the streets and in school. It takes a lot of people to build the Habitat for Humanity houses that the Speaker celebrates on his lapel pin. It takes a lot of people to provide the people power for all of the civic organizations in this country that made our communities mean so much to most of us when we were kids. It takes every parent to teach the children the difference between right and wrong and to encourage them to learn and grow and to say no to the wrong things but also to believe that they can be whatever they want to be.

I know it's hard when you're working harder for less, when you're under great stress, to do these things. A lot of our people don't have the time or the emotional stress, they think, to do the work of citizenship.

Most of us in politics haven't helped very much. For years, we've mostly treated citizens like they were consumers or spectators, sort of political couch potatoes who were supposed to watch the TV ads either promise them something for nothing or play on their fears and frustrations. And more and more of our citizens now get most of their information in very negative and aggressive ways that are hardly conducive to honest and open conversations. But the truth is, we have got to stop seeing each other as enemies just because we have different views.

If you go back to the beginning of this country, the great strength of America, as de Tocqueville pointed out when he came here a long time ago, has always been our ability to

associate with people who were different from ourselves and to work together to find common ground. And in this day, everybody has a responsibility to do more of that. We simply cannot want for a tornado, a fire, or a flood to behave like Americans ought to behave in dealing with one another.

I want to finish up here by pointing out some folks that are up with the First Lady that represent what I'm trying to talk about—citizens. I have no idea what their party affiliation is or who they voted for in the last election. But they represent what we ought to be doing.

Cindy Perry teaches second graders to read in AmeriCorps in rural Kentucky. She gains when she gives. She's a mother of four. She says that her service inspired her to get her high school equivalency last year. She was married when she was a teenager—stand up, Cindy. She was married when she was a teenager. She had four children. But she had time to serve other people, to get her high school equivalency, and she's going to use her AmeriCorps money to go back to college.

Chief Stephen Bishop is the police chief of Kansas City. He's been a national leader—stand up, Steve. He's been a national leader in using more police in community policing, and he's worked with AmeriCorps to do it. And the crime rate in Kansas City has gone down as a result of what he did.

Corporal Gregory Depestre went to Haiti as part of his adopted country's force to help secure democracy in his native land. And I might add, we must be the only country in the world that could have gone to Haiti and taken Haitian-Americans there who could speak the language and talk to the people. And he was one of them, and we're proud of him.

The next two folks I've had the honor of meeting and getting to know a little bit, the Reverend John and the Reverend Diana Cherry of the A.M.E. Zion Church in Temple Hills, Maryland. I'd like to ask them to stand. I want to tell you about them. In the early eighties, they left Government service and formed a church in a small living room in a small house, in the early eighties. Today that church has 17,000 members. It is one of the three or four biggest churches in the entire United States. It grows by 200 a month. They do it together. And the special focus of their ministry is keeping families together.

Two things they did make a big impression on me. I visited their church once, and I learned they were building a new sanctuary closer to the Washington, DC, line in a higher crime, higher drug rate area because they thought it was part of their ministry to change the lives of the people who needed them. The second thing I want to say is that once Reverend Cherry was at a meeting at the White House with some other religious leaders, and he left early to go back to this church to minister to 150 couples that he had brought back to his church from all over America to convince them to come back together, to save their marriages, and to raise their kids. This is the kind of work that citizens are doing in America. We need more of it, and it ought to be lifted up and supported.

The last person I want to introduce is Jack Lucas from Hattiesburg, Mississippi. Jack, would you stand up? Fifty years ago, in the sands of Iwo Jima, Jack Lucas taught and learned the lessons of citizenship. On February 20th, 1945, he and three of his buddies encountered the enemy and two grenades at their feet. Jack Lucas threw himself on both of them. In that moment, he saved the lives of his companions, and miraculously in the next instant, a medic saved his life. He gained a foothold for freedom, and at the age of 17, just a year older than

his grandson who is up there with him today—and his son, who is a West Point graduate and a veteran—at 17, Jack Lucas became the youngest Marine in history and the youngest soldier in this century to win the Congressional Medal of Honor. All these years later, yesterday, here's what he said about that day: "It didn't matter where you were from or who you were, you relied on one another. You did it for your country."

We all gain when we give, and we reap what we sow. That's at the heart of this New Covenant. Responsibility, opportunity, and citizenship, more than stale chapters in some remote civic book, they're still the virtue by which we can fulfill ourselves and reach our God-given potential and be like them and also to fulfill the eternal promise of this country, the enduring dream from that first and most sacred covenant. I believe every person in this country still believes that we are created equal and given by our Creator the right to life, liberty and the pursuit of happiness. This is a very, very great country. And our best days are still to come.

Thank you, and God bless you all.

NOTE: The President spoke at 9:14 p.m. in the House Chamber of the Capitol.

Remarks at Kutztown University in Kutztown, Pennsylvania
January 25, 1995

The President. Thank you very much. You all sit down and relax. Cold outside, warm in here. I want to thank Dr. David McFarland for that introduction and for making me feel so very welcome here at Kutztown. I've had a great time already.

I know that before I came out, your mayor, Mayor Schwoyer, and Congressman Holden, who came up from Washington with me today, Secretary Reich, and Secretary Riley talked, and I thank them for what they said. And I thank, especially, my colleagues Congressman Holden and Secretary Reich and Secretary Riley for what they have done for the cause of education.

I am so happy to be here with all of you today. There are a lot of reasons I came here. One is, I'm beginning to feel old, and I heard

that you've got a guy my age on your football team, and I wanted to—where is he? Where is Chuck Roseberry? Where is he? Stand up. Where are you? *[Applause]* I know he's here somewhere. Where are you? Yes. That's good. You know, it's all I can do every morning to get up and go jog, and I resent you. I can't believe it. But I'm impressed.

I'm also glad to be joined here by your former Congressman, Gus Yatron, and your former Senator, Harris Wofford. I thank them both for being here along with Catherine Baker Knoll, our State treasurer. Thank you, Catherine Baker Knoll, for coming—our State treasurer. I'm glad to see you, too. And our neighboring Congressman, Paul McHale, wanted to come but he could not. There's a very important vote this afternoon in the Congress, and Congressman Holden has already gone back; besides, he's heard this speech before. [*Laughter*]

I want to say how very proud I am to be here, because this is a time of great challenge for our Nation, and I believe that this institution represents a big part of the answer to that challenge.

You know, just a few months ago, I had a brief roundtable with a lot of your community leaders, business people, teachers, and students, who are associated with the efforts of this fine institution to help solve the problems of this area, to get an education to people, to help the businesses grow, to help start new businesses.

I wanted to come here because I was very, very impressed with your entrepreneurial development and global education center, the work you've done for small businesses, the work you've done for minority businesses, the work you've done to try to bring together people of all ages and all backgrounds who want to get an education and who want to serve and who want to help. And I'd like to ask all these folks who just met with me to stand up, because I learned a lot from them, and I'm grateful for what they did. Would you all stand up, please? Thank you very much. [*Applause*]

There's one other group of people I'd like to acknowledge who are here who represent a lot of what I talked about last night, who are young people trying to serve our country at the grassroots level by helping people solve their problems. They are the members of the Pennsylvania Service Corps, part of AmeriCorps. [*Applause*] They're working to help people build housing, to reduce neighborhood violence, to clean up the local environment, to help people with AIDS. Busloads of them are here, and you just heard from them. [*Laughter*] I thank them for their enthusiasm, their devotion to their country, and for symbolizing what I think all of us have to do more of: learn and gain by serving and giving.

You know, this is a beautiful rural area. I understand I am the first President since 1948 to come to this county, and the first person ever to visit this community as President. And I am delighted to be here.

Pennsylvania as a whole and this area have been through dramatic and sweeping economic changes in the last several years. The economic opportunity that made Pennsylvania one of the great manufacturing States of America and one of the great economic powers of the entire post-cold-war world have changed; those forces have changed dramatically. And as those of you who are younger enter your adult years and look forward to the future, you know that we have moved from an industrial age to an information age; you will hear it everywhere.

What you may not hear is that it does not mean that manufacturing will be less important. Quite the contrary, if we do it right, it means that America will continue to be the leading manufacturing country in the world. But more and more and more, manufacturing will require more knowledge, higher skills, a better education, fewer people producing more things, which means that education will be important, and it will also be important for us to continually be able to start more and more new businesses.

Big enterprises are like the Federal Government: We're downsizing. We're making the Federal bureaucracy smaller so we can give the money back to you to educate people, to provide tax relief, to bring the deficit down, to fight crime. That's what we're doing. That is very, very important. It matters to your future that Federal debt is now $10,000 a family less than it would have been if our deficit reduction plan had not passed. It matters that the economic programs have helped to contribute to this enormous rise in productivity in America. And we have over 6 million new jobs in our country now in the last 2 years, with low inflation and with every prospect of continuing our growth.

But what's going to enable us to solve our problems over the long run is the ability and strength of the American people to solve their problems at the local level, to make the most of their own lives, and to work together in communities. I said last night in my speech, and I will say again today, that I believe what our country needs is a New Covenant based on an old idea, the idea that, with opportunity must come responsibility. They have to go hand in hand. If you don't have both, you can't solve the problems of America.

If you tell people to be responsible all the time and they never get any benefit out of it, pretty soon they get tired and quit. But if people just always say, I want my rights, and we don't think about what responsible conduct is for ourselves and our friends and neighbors, then pretty soon our society comes apart. We have to have both. And we have to base our efforts in community after community after community where people can sit down, the way these people did with me today, and talk to each other and work with each other to develop the God-given potential of all of our people.

In the world we are moving into, the success of the United States as a whole will be more dependent than ever before on the success of every community to educate and develop the capacities of every person who lives in the community, everywhere and everyplace. We don't have a person or a community we can walk away from and turn our backs on.

That's why, even though we've been cutting Government spending—and last year for the first time in 25 years, we cut both defense and domestic spending, except for Medicare and the health programs of the Government and Social Security, of course—we cut domestic and defense spending for the first time in 25 years to deal with the deficit.

But we did not cut education. We expanded Head Start. We expanded our efforts to help our public schools achieve educational excellence. We set up a program to try to support networks like the ones I saw today, for businesses to work with schools to help young people who don't go to 4-year colleges at least get some education and training after high school, so they can get better jobs and have higher incomes. We reformed the college loan program so that student loans now are less costly to middle class students, have better repayment terms, and they actually cost the Government less in terms of tax dollars. It is a good program.

And with all of that, let me remind you of what the fundamental facts are in this economy and why these efforts are so important. Even though we had 6 million new jobs in the economy in the last 2 years, even though we had more high-wage jobs coming back into our economy in 1994 than in the last 5 years combined, most Americans are working a longer work week than they were working 15 years ago for about the same income once you make adjustments for inflation.

Most of our people have found that this new exciting global economy, which moves with lightning speed and opens up vast opportunities for people who can take advantage of it, has left them working harder for less, with less security. All these changes are great if you can always get a new job, but if you're the one losing the job, the change doesn't look very good.

So what our job is, is to make more success stories, like the programs I see here. It is to empower more schools to do what this one did, to drop their categories and open their walls and reach out to all kinds of people, and make education a community enterprise and a lifetime enterprise. That is what we must do.

And that is why I say to the American people and to the Congress, we have gotten the deficit down, and we have gotten the economy going, and there are more cuts we can make in Government spending, and we can afford to provide some more tax relief to hard-working Americans, but we should do it with a focus on education so that we can raise people's incomes who have worked harder for less in the short run with the tax relief, but in the long run with better education, which is the only way to raise people's incomes over the long run.

You think about the things that this country's done in our past that really did something for the economy. I think you can make a compelling case that, at the end of World War II, the passage of the GI bill did more to explode the American economy than any other single action, because it made it possible for our returning servicemen to go back to school and to get an education. And that money has repaid itself many times over.

So I have said that that's the kind of thing we ought to focus on now. The middle class bill of rights that I proposed last night to the American people and to Congress—and as I said, it might better be called a middle class bill of rights and responsibilities because you, by definition, have to be responsible to take the benefits of it—focuses heavily on education in three ways, and I want to emphasize them.

First of all, I think you ought to be able to deduct the cost of education after high school from your taxes. You think about it: If you own a home, you can deduct interest from your taxes. And in the early years of a home mortgage, it's almost all interest. Why do we do that? Because we want people to be able to own their homes. If you run a business and invest in new equipment, you can deduct the cost from your taxes. Why do we do that? Because we want our businesses to modernize. You know, the stories I heard over here before I came out were, the cost of equipment is going up dramatically, but now we can produce more with fewer people. We've got to support that.

But if our people today can't get an education—not everybody needs a 4-year college degree—but if they can't get an education, if the systems aren't there for that education, they may not get to the homeowning. They may not have the American dream that we want. So I say, if education is the most important thing for personal success in the 21st century, we ought to permit people to deduct the cost of it from their taxes: Raise your income in the short run; raise your income in the long run.

Audience member. That's right, Bill!

The President. That's right. You know, we flew that person up here from Washington, and I was beginning to think they weren't going to say anything. [*Laughter*]

The second thing I want to say is, we want to broaden the number of Americans who can invest tax-free in an IRA, an individual retirement account, but we want to let people withdraw from the IRA, tax-free, to pay for education expenses, so that you can take better care of yourself.

The last education component is, we want to take about 70 different programs the Federal Government runs in training, which require enormous administrative costs, collapse them and give the money to the American people who are eligible for them. So if a person loses a job and is on unemployment, or if a person is in a lower wage job so they're eligible for Federal training help, instead of having to figure out which of 70 programs you qualify for, you just get a voucher of $2,600 a year—up to that—for 2 years, and you take it to this school or take it to a local community college or take it wherever you choose if you're eligible to get it. It's a kind of a "GI bill" for American workers. It will make a huge difference. And it's the kind of thing Government ought to be doing: less bureaucracy, more direct help to people to get the education and training they need to grow and to learn.

I want all of you to help me do this for you. We are trying to change the focus of the National Government to the grassroots of America. There are a lot of other things that I will be talking about over the next few weeks that are part of this New Covenant, welfare reform, what we're going to do in crime to lower the crime rate and implement the crime bill, what we're going to do to try to grow the economy, and other ways. But nothing, nothing can make a bigger difference than trying to get more edu-

cation to more people in more ways. So I hope that you will do two things: first, I hope you will say, with your voices, without regard to your party, "Cut the deficit. Cut spending. Reduce the size of the Federal bureaucracy. Keep on doing what you're doing, but do not cut education. Increase investment and education so we can grow this economy and grow America." And I hope you will support the middle class bill of rights, and I hope you will support the AmeriCorps program in Pennsylvania, and I hope you will support the programs at this school to develop entrepreneurs because they're all grassroots community-building programs that develop the ability of people to fulfill their own dreams and bring us together across the lines that divide us.

You know, I don't have an—literally, I don't have a clue about which of the people I was sitting and talking with this morning were Democrats, which were Republicans, who was an independent. I don't have any idea who they voted for in the last election. I probably should have checked. [*Laughter*] I mean, I don't. Why? Why? Because they are organized around developing the potential of the people here. They have built a community of interest where everybody wins by helping everybody else. Now, that's what makes America go. That's what makes America grow. I see it when I visited these community services programs.

I see it, as I said last night in my speech, when I go out after a disaster. I mean, it's a terrible thing to say, but if you go to one of these places where they're putting sandbags on a levee against a flood or where they're trying to help people deal with the aftermath of the fires, as I saw in California, the earthquakes, people have their shoulders back and their heads held high, and their eyes are clear, and their voices are strong. Why? Because they know they matter. And when Americans get in trouble, you know, we would take the shirt off our back for people. And we fight, and we work in these things, because we know we matter, because we're doing something that makes us feel better and stronger and we're helping other people as well. We have to return that spirit to our country every day, in every way, in all of our activities. That is what this is all about, and we can do that.

So what I want to say to you is, we've got a lot of economic challenges, and we've got some profound social problems. But we can deal with them, we can solve them, we can move on them. I see it—I have seen all over this country. I am telling you, there is not a problem this country has that is not being addressed in a way that all of you will be proud of by somebody, somewhere. What we have to do is to figure out a way to galvanize and organize and energize all of that work so that it spreads across our whole country.

The New Covenant is a way of thinking about that. Responsibility in return for opportunity, building this country at the community level, that's what I'm committed to doing. My role in that will be in this coming Congress to try to pass the middle class bill of rights, to try to emphasize education, to try to keep downsizing the Federal Government and controlling the deficit and cutting unnecessary spending, but building up those things which will enable people to make the most of their own lives. That is my job.

Your job is to support institutions like this to get all the education you can to break down the walls between business and government and education at the grassroots level and to try to help me pass this. Would you do that? I need you. I hope you will, and I want your support for it. [*Applause*]

Folks, the best days of this country are still before us. This is the most exciting era we have ever known. You are going to see opportunities in the next 20 years for people to make a living in exciting and interesting ways that we could not have imagined 20 years ago. But our job is to make sure that, as President Kennedy said,

"the rising tide lifts all boats." We can't have an America where 20 or even 40 percent of us are the only ones that really do well in this global economy, and it need not be that way.

But if we want our best days to lie ahead, we have got to—we have got to say we are going to get an education for all of our people. It's going to be a lifetime project. Our educational institutions are going to become the center of our communities. We're going to tear down the walls that divide us. We're going to make education available to everybody, and we're going to use the power of Government not to expand or create a new bureaucracy but to empower people at the grassroots level to chart their own future and to make their own lives in this new and exciting age.

That is our mission. If we do it, our best days are ahead. I want that more than anything for you, for our children, and our grandchildren and our country. And I can tell you, the world still needs that. There are a lot of things out there in the rest of the world that are still a threat to decency and humanity and progress. You saw this terrible terrorist attack in the Middle East the last couple of days. The world needs a strong America, and Americans deserve it. And we're going to get it with your help.

Thank you, and God bless you all.

NOTE: The President spoke at 12:36 p.m. in the fieldhouse. In his remarks, he referred to David McFarland, president of the university, and Mayor James Schwoyer of Kutztown.

Remarks to University Presidents
January 26, 1995

Well, good morning. I'm delighted to see all of you, and most of you, I'm delighted to see you again. We're glad to have you at the White House. As all of you know, in the State of the Union, I did my best to restate my vision for our country and the role of education and educational institutions in that vision.

The job of every American at the close of the 20th century is to do what we can to guarantee that, as we move to the next century, the American dream will be available to all of our

people, and that our country will remain the world's strongest force for freedom and democracy. That means, to use my formulation, that we have to make some profound changes in our country which will require a New Covenant of commitment to opportunity and to responsibility, a commitment to the strength of our communities and the work of citizenship. We have to empower our people to make the most of their own abilities. We have to expand opportunity without expanding bureaucracy in the information age, and we have to enhance our security at home as well as abroad.

The work of education does all that and helps us to strengthen our communities at the grassroots level. And as I said the other night, the middle class bill of rights I've proposed should be called the bill of rights and responsibilities, because as all of you know well, you can't give somebody an education, you can only give them the opportunity for an education. It's something that people have to seize for themselves.

In the last 2 years, we've made remarkable progress on the education front, from expanding Head Start to passing the Goals 2000 program. It's promoting reforms within our public schools, like charter schools and the character education movement that the Secretary of Education has done so much to promote, to promoting the partnerships from school to work for the young people who don't go to universities, to dramatically changing the student loan program in ways that have lowered the cost of the loans, improved the repayment options for students, cut down on the paperwork for institutions of higher education, and miraculously lowered the cost of Federal Government as well.

I'm very pleased with all this, but as all of you know, we still have a lot to do. I want to talk a little bit today about the middle class bill of rights and a couple of other issues that are very, very important. To emphasize the importance of the bill to me, I'd just ask us all to remember that, as exciting as this new world is for all of us, most Americans are still working a longer work week for the same or lower wages than they were making 15 years ago. There is an education premium in this new economy that is greater than has ever been the case in the entire history of the Republic, ever. And your work, your mission and your opportunities, therefore, are greater than ever before.

It's also true, as I have seen recently with Dr. Wilson at Cal State Northridge or yesterday at Kutztown University in Pennsylvania or at the Carl Sandburg Community College in Illinois, that the institutions of higher education themselves are probably the most significant institutions in America today for rebuilding a sense of community and effective citizenship at the grassroots level, because I see it over and over again: People from all ages, all income groups, all walks of life, all political backgrounds, all races meet together, tear down the walls between them, and work to solve problems.

I had a fascinating, fascinating session yesterday at Kutztown talking with the business leaders and immigrants and students about what they were doing to prepare their area to succeed in this new time.

The middle class bill of rights does something we should have done a long time ago: It gives a deduction for the cost of education after high school. It provides for tax-free withdrawals from an IRA and gives a broader number of people access to an IRA for the cost of education. It collapses about 70 of our education and training programs into one block and lets people, not local governments but people, draw down a voucher worth $2,600 a year for up to 2 years for education and training programs of their choice. These programs, a lot of these training programs were organized and established at a time when there weren't as many grassroots community options as there are now.

And so all these three things, it seems to me, have a major contribution to make to increasing the number of our people who are in educational programs, increasing the strength of our communities and the strength of our economy. And we need the help of every university and college administrator and executive, professor and student in this country to pass this program.

There is a great push for a middle class tax cut in this Congress, and it is appropriate because of the stagnant incomes of most middle class Americans and because we have succeeded in getting control of the deficit and in getting the economy going again. The middle class bill of rights is paid for fully by spending cuts. In fact, we will offer in our budget more than twice as many spending cuts as the tax relief costs, so that we'll have further deficit reduction and pay for the middle class bill of rights. I would urge you to support that concept, too. We have our responsibilities here, and we ought to pay for whatever we do.

I'd like to make two further points. One is, I know that all of you are working on this and worried about it, and I know the demographic changes in our country have put great pressures on you. But in the 1980's, the cost of a college education was the only thing that went up more rapidly than the cost of health care in the market basket of families' essentials. So one of your responsibilities in this is going to be to try to hold down the costs. Cynics are saying that if we provide tax relief for the cost of a college education, that a lot of college executives will simply raise the cost of education to deal with problems at home. We cannot let that happen. We've got to send a signal to America that if you do this, we will use this opportunity to put more people in our institutions and give more people opportunity.

The last point I want to make before introducing the Vice President is—and he will talk about this at greater length—is that we do not want to lose the ground we have gained. We do not want to see overall cuts in education programs. Our budget will reduce the deficit, dramatically cut the budget, and not cut education programs.

We do not need to see a cap in the direct loan program. The direct loan program is saving the Government money, saving the student money, and saving the institutions time and money. We do not want it—if you don't want to join it, that's your business, but you ought to have the opportunity to do it. The Government should not tell you, you cannot become part of this.

The Secretary of Education has done a superb job in administering this program and we don't want to back off of it. There are other programs, as you know, which are profoundly important to you, the work study program, the Pell grants, and others. We are committed to keeping them intact. So I ask you for your support for the middle class bill of rights. I ask you to make it clear to the Congress that you will not take advantage of this by using it basically to increase costs for the same services; this is going to be used to expand educational opportunity, and I ask you to fight to keep the reforms that we've put in place and the programs that you've relied on over the years. We can do these things, and if we do, we will truly be moving forward in a dramatic way for all of our people.

[At this point, the Vice President and Secretary of Education Richard Riley made remarks.]

The President. Thank you very much, Secretary Riley. Before I turn the microphone over to President Kelly of Tulane, I wanted to just emphasize two other points, if I might.

First, one of the things our administration has tried to do is to make sure that we all work together to do what was necessary here in Washington make sense of our common efforts. And Tom Glynn is here from the Labor Department, and I want to say a special word

of appreciation to the cooperation of the partnership that the Education and the Labor Departments have had on all these issues; Secretary Shalala, from the Department of Health and Human Services, who used to be in your line of work and some days wishes she still were— [laughter]—Joe Duffey, who used to be in your line of work and who probably almost never wishes he still were—[laughter]—because he had such a good job at the USIA; Sheldon Hackney, who used to be in your line of work and I think it just depends on what day it is— [laughter]—done a great job at the National Endowment for the Humanities; and of course, our wonderful adviser and leader on science and technology, Jack Gibbons, is here; Carol Rasco, the Domestic Policy Council Chief in the White House; and others. We're all honored to be here with you.

There is one other point I wanted to make that none of us mentioned. And that is, I want to begin by thanking you for responding so well to the call I issued in a letter to all of you last September on national service. And I asked you to support the AmeriCorps program and the whole concept of service for students and do what you could to enhance that. I got hundreds of letters back, literally hundreds of letters back. It was a very rewarding exchange. And there are even three colleges, Hampshire in Massachusetts, Loyola of Chicago, and Earlham in Indiana, that have agreed to match the $4,725 educational grant that every AmeriCorps student earns in a year with a grant from the college to double the impact of it. And so, doubtless, they'll be getting more AmeriCorps students than some places. But that's a very good thing to do.

There are those who believe that we ought to eliminate the AmeriCorps program. I think that would be a terrible mistake because it— it again, it does all the things that I think we should be doing. It promotes education, it promotes citizenship, it strengthens community bonds, and it is totally nonbureaucratic. It involves people helping others, one on one, in established grassroots organizations.

So we understand that the new Congress— many of the Members came in with a commitment to slash spending, and we've been slashing spending. We'd like to have some help. And we understand that they came in with a commitment to reduce the size of the Federal bureaucracy. We've been doing that. There are 100,000 fewer people here today than there were on the day I became President. We'd like to have some help doing that.

We just don't believe that raising the cost of going to college, reducing access, undermining national service, is the way to do it. And we want to work with them in good faith, but we think we have to have your help in supporting the right kind of tax cuts that raise incomes in the short run and in the long run, through education, and the right kind of budget cutting. Those are the two requests we ask of you. Help us get the right kind of tax cuts, the right kind of budget cuttings; let's do it in a way that will increase the incomes and the opportunities of the American people so that we really do expand access to the American dream.

Thank you.

NOTE: The President spoke at 9:16 a.m. in the Indian Treaty Room at the Old Executive Office Building. In his remarks, he referred to Blenda Wilson, president, California State University, Northridge, and Eamon Kelly, president, Tulane University.

Remarks to the World Economic Forum
January 26, 1995

Good evening, and thank you, Professor Schwab, for that introduction. I'm pleased to join all of you, especially Secretary-General Boutros-Ghali, Councillor Cotti of Switzerland, and Prime Minister Carlsson of Sweden. And I'm delighted to have this opportunity to speak to the World Economic Forum.

Let me begin by saying I've very much enjoyed listening to the questions you asked the Secretary-General and to his answers. I was profoundly moved by the wisdom of his answer about the media. I wrote it down, and now I will use it in the next press conference. I noted you also talked about the academic wisdom and the media power represented in your group. I hope also there is academic power and media wisdom in your group.

The thoughts that you shared and the projects that grow out of your meetings clearly are going to play a vital role in determining the issues that dominate all of our international agenda. Your opinions will play a key part in shaping the debate on some of the most important issues of our time.

Two years ago, I took office with the strong conviction that the American people, as all the people of the world, were facing a new and rapidly changing global economy. I believed then, and I believe more strongly now, that the incomes and living standards of Americans are tied directly to what happens outside our borders. It is now impossible to separate international and domestic economic concerns. As soon as our administration began its work, we devised a detailed strategy to set a new direction. And during the last 2 years, we have devoted ourselves to preparing our country and our people for this global economy and to creating an international system of free and expanding trade that benefits not just the American people but all the world's people.

We've made good strides. The essential first step for us was to put our own house in order. Let's not forget that, 2 years ago, it was a very open question whether the United States could summon the political will to cut our deficit significantly. But as many of you who specialize in global economics had urged for years, we changed that dynamic. We did the hard work. We cut the deficit dramatically, more than $600 billion, or about $10,000 for every family in our country.

This year, the deficit will shrink for the third year in a row, for the first time since Harry Truman was the President of the United States. Cutting the deficit has helped us to create almost 6 million new jobs in the last 2 years, to keep the inflation to 2.7 percent and to boost our exports by 11 percent. The combined measure of unemployment and inflation is at its lowest point since 1968. In fact, a survey of your own members last year concluded that the United States is now the most competitive economy on Earth, and we appreciate that, and we're going to do our best to keep it that way.

To ensure that, we know we must continue to invest in our own people, to empower individuals to take advantage of the opportunities of the global economy and to make the most of their own lives. Today, when exports account for so many of our high-skill, high-wage jobs and when what we earn depends so directly on what we know and what we are capable of learning, education is more important than ever before.

That's why I proposed as part of my middle class bill of rights, that we make education and training more accessible than ever before in the United States, through a range of tax cuts for students of all ages and through a system of cash vouchers for people who have been laid off and must be retrained. Another part of our strategy has been to lay the foundation for a new era of global growth and open markets in the century to come.

Already, after 7 years, we've made some real progress by adopting the GATT treaty. Those negotiations were begun here in the United States under Presidents Reagan and Bush. They were completed, they were approved by Congress, and I was proud to sign them into law last year. That's the most ambitious trade agreement ever.

We also brought the NAFTA treaty into force with support from both Democrats and Republicans, and since then, trade with our NAFTA partners have accounted for 100,000 new American jobs. On the basis of the agreement forged at the Summit of the Americas last month, we've begun to create a free trade zone for our own hemisphere. And finally, we've extended our efforts to the booming economies of the Asia-Pacific region. At the APEC summit in Jakarta, we forged an agreement to create a vastly more open trade area there by 2020. All told, these 2 years in the United States have been one of the most intense and productive periods of economic innovation, both domestically and internationally, in recent times.

But while the promise of these new arrangements is clearly enormous, their benefits will not simply fall into our lap. Indeed, with the completion of this array of trade agreements, we're entering a new and difficult phase of the global economy. Now, we face the challenge of turning visions into concrete realities, a time for painstaking efforts, for dismantling the old barriers and creating the new arrangements, brick by brick, for implementing these new trade pacts and completing the architecture of the international economy.

It's also a time for careful reform. We must reexamine the international institutions that have played such an important role in the post-war era and consider how they are adapting to the new realities. These institutions have served us well for nearly half a century. In many respects, they still do. They have evolved with the changing world economy, discarding old missions and assuming new ones.

But as all of you know, change in the world economy has taken on astonishing dimensions. Globalization has met the growth in interdependence on a scale that would have been inconceivable a decade ago, that richly rewards good decisions and good policies. But we've also seen that 24-hour markets can respond with blinding speed and sometimes ruthlessness that the statesmen of the Bretton Woods era never would have imagined.

And for that reason, at last year's summit in Naples, my G–7 colleagues and I saw the need to review our international economic institutions, identifying new needs and evaluating how best to adapt the institutions to meet the tremendous challenges of the 21st century. This review will be a central part of our discussions at the Halifax summit in June.

In just the last few weeks, the crisis in Mexico has reminded us that the road ahead will have its difficult stretches. Mexico today has an economy with strong fundamentals and a capacity to grow and to meet its obligations. But partly because Mexico relied on too many short-term foreign loans, a fallen market confidence turned into a dangerously self-fulfilling prophecy.

I am confident that the guarantee program we are putting together to put Mexico back on track will win approval in our Congress and will make a difference in the world economy. The combined leadership of the U.S. Congress, the Chairman of the Federal Reserve Board, and the Secretaries of Treasury and State are constructing a creative and unprecedented package. Some have said it's just foreign aid and a bailout. Well, they're not right. It's the kind of response to address a problem before it spreads that the new world economy demands.

Failure to act could have grave consequences for Mexico, for Latin America, for the entire developing world. More important, our approach will safeguard hundreds of thousands of Americans whose livelihoods are now tied to Mexico's well-being. So it's the right thing to do for the rest of the world, but it's also the right thing to do for America.

The crisis in Mexico has helped to show us again just how much smaller our world has become and how our stake in what happens in other countries has dramatically increased. This is not just true for economic affairs but also for a whole range of other problems, like attacking the capital movements by drug cartels and organized crime, dealing seriously with the interconnection of global terrorisms or environmental policies that have regional impact or social policies that bear on the global population issue.

The challenge before us is to adapt our international institutions, to deepen the cooperation between nations so that we can confront a new generation of problems that know no national borders. Indeed, the job of constructing a new international economic architecture through our trade agreements and the revitalization of our institutions is, for our generation, as pressing and important as building the postwar system was to the generation of the Marshall plan and Bretton Woods, the heroic generation of Dean Acheson and Jean Monnet. Then, they had the immense job of proving that democracy and capitalism could provide for fulfilling and meaningful lives in the aftermath of war and in the face of the rival system of communism. Today, our job again is to persuade people that democracy and free markets can give all people the opportunity to live out their dreams, but we must do so without the prod of a rival political system to contend with or the fresh memory of war to spur us on.

Today, as never before, we can see the extraordinary possibilities that lie before us in the 21st century. It promises to be an era in which free people, working across open borders, will have a chance to create growing prosperity, economic security, to fulfill their God-given potential and their dreams as never before in human history. But it won't happen without hard work, real dedication, and clear vision.

I am glad to be speaking to this group at Davos because you are exactly the kind of people who must help make certain that the international system we build works fairly and safely. We must rise to the example of our predecessors. We must forge a system that will benefit the people of all walks of life and all parts of the globe, not just those for whom the global economy now holds the very richest opportunities.

We must do it because it's the right thing to do, because it's the fair thing to do, and because, ultimately, it is clearly in all of our best interests.

Thank you very much.

NOTE: The President spoke by satellite at 12:47 p.m. from Room 459 of the Old Executive Office Building to the meeting in Davos, Switzerland. In his remarks, he referred to Klaus Schwab, World Economic Forum founder; United Nations Secretary-General Boutros Boutros-Ghali; Falvio Cotti, Chief, Department of Foreign Affairs, Switzerland; and Prime Minister Ingvar Carlsson of Sweden.

Interview with Tom Brokaw of NBC Nightly News
January 26, 1995

State of the Union Address

Mr. Brokaw. Mr. President, your Chief of Staff, Leon Panetta, said that your State of the Union speech the other night was the most important one of your Presidency. When you got back to the living quarters and you were alone with Hillary, how did the two of you critique it?

The President. Well, I thought it was effective in the sense that I got a chance to get back to the basic values and the basic ideas that got me into the race for President in the first place, really that drove my whole public service career before I became President. It was a little longer than I wanted it to be, partly because I was frankly not anticipating that the Congress and especially the Republicans would respond as positively as they did to some of the things that I said. And I appreciated it, but it lengthened the speech some.

That was a good problem to have. That was what my friend Mack McLarty calls a high-class problem.

Mr. Brokaw. Well, I always get the impression, though, that once you get up there and get into a roll, so to speak, it's pretty hard for you to sit down; you love the art of political oratory so much.

The President. Well, I like—the State of the Union I like because it really gives the President an opportunity that's not there at any other time of the year to talk both to the Congress and to the American people in a way that goes way beyond ordinary politics and partisanship and at least gives the opportunity to go to the heart of the problems and the challenges and the opportunities of the country.

President's Strength of Conviction

Mr. Brokaw. Mr. President, we did a poll that began really shortly after the State of the Union speech. Good news and bad news for you in it. Your job performance rating is 51 percent positive, 40 percent negative. Those people who agreed with the goals of the State of the Union speech, 58 percent; only 9 percent disagreed. But then this question: Bill Clinton, do you think that he's a man of strong convictions, or is he easily swayed? Those who felt that you had strong convictions, 31 percent; easily swayed, 61 percent. That's a continuing problem for you.

The President. It is, but it's obviously a problem of perception rather than reality. If you look at all the strong opponents I've got, I wouldn't have them if I didn't have strong convictions. No other President, while sitting in office, has ever taken on the NRA. I did, at great cost. We reversed 12 years of trickle-down economics and reversed this deficit in a brutal fight where we prevailed by only one vote in each House, largely because the Members knew they would be angering the wealthiest and most powerful people in our society by raising the income taxes in the top 1.2 percent. I took on the strongest constituencies in my own party, including my friends in the labor movement, to pass the Brady bill. I took on the banking interests of the country to reduce the costs of the student loan program and lower the cost of it. So I clearly am a person of strong convictions who has taken on brutal, tough fights. I went forward with the Haiti mission when nobody was for it.

So it's clear that (a) I'll take on unpopular things, (b) I'll make enemies, and (c) I'll fight until I win. But we live in an environment in which I think maybe because of the way it's covered and maybe because of my style—because naturally I don't talk in ways that try to threaten people; I like to try to bring people together—maybe I've contributed to my own problem.

But the historic record is that we have taken on tough fights others ignored and walked away from; we got results because we fought through to the end. And that, it seems to me, if you just take the four examples I gave you, will be the enduring truth. And my job now is to show the American people as this new Congress meets that I will work with them in a reasonable way. I don't think they want me to be hardheaded and totally uncompromising, but there are some things that I will draw the line on and fight for.

New Covenant

Mr. Brokaw. But with all due respect, Mr. President, you used that phrase the other night—the New Covenant was a phrase that you used in your acceptance speech, but then once you took office, you didn't put many of those issues front and center until the Republicans just beat your brains in on November 8th, like the middle class bill of rights, for example, talking more about leaner Government, a higher minimum wage, school prayer you even made some references to.

The President. Now wait a minute, let's go back. That's simply not true. What did I do when I first got here? What was in the first economic plan? I said to the American people, "We've got to bring the deficit down and get the economy going first. So I cannot afford to give all the middle class a tax cut. We're going to start with a working families tax cut that this year will lower taxes $1,000 a family, for every family with an income of under $26,000." Now, we did something miraculous. In the whole history of American politics, nobody has ever given a tax cut to 15 million American families and kept it a secret. But somehow I succeeded in doing that. We made 90 percent of our small businesses eligible for a tax cut. We gave a tax cut to people who start new businesses. We made a good first step. And I said in '93, "Let me get the deficit down. Let's get the economy going. Let's give these people a tax cut. Then we'll come back and do the rest."

In terms of reducing the Government and the bureaucracy, they didn't start that, my goodness, we did. When the Republican administrations were here—we've now got 100,000 fewer people working for the Federal Government than we did on the day I became President. If the Republican Congress passes no other bill, we will have 250,000 fewer people working here at the end of my 4-year term. We'll have the smallest Government since Kennedy was President. Now, that's stuff we did. We did that. I may be a poor communicator of it, but that was at the centerpiece.

I sent welfare reform legislation to the Congress last year, and when they didn't pass it, we just kept on giving States permission to get around the Federal rules to move people from welfare to work and to support responsible parenting, 24 States, more than were given waivers from the Federal rules in the previous 12 years combined.

So I believe what I said in the State of the Union Address is consistent with what I've been trying to do. I think a lot of people, in all candor, thought that the health care program was against that because they were convinced it was a big Government program. I don't think it was a big Government program, but I did bite off more than I could chew. I tried to do too much too quick.

But if you look at what we've done, it's consistent with the New Covenant message all along.

Minimum Wage

Mr. Brokaw. Part of the case against Bill Clinton that will be made even by your friends from time to time is that you talk the talk but don't walk the walk. Take minimum wage. Our polls shows that there is an overwhelming majority for it. But you've made it clear from the White House that you're not going to go up and make the fight to the last breath on Capitol Hill for minimum wage.

The President. That is not at all what I have done. First of all, who reversed 12 years of flagrant deficit spending? We did, by one-vote fights in both Houses in the most brutal fight anybody can remember. We did that. We walked the walk and took a lot of grief for it.

And one of the reasons the Democrats lost this last session in this last election is because the Republicans convinced the voters that we raised everybody's taxes when what we did was raise taxes sharply on the top 1.2 percent, and a lot of those folks funded those campaigns.

We took on the NAFTA fight. It was deader than a doornail when I became President, and we brought it back to life. We took on the NRA on the Brady bill and the assault weapons ban. You may agree or disagree; no other sitting President had ever done it. So this "walk the walk" business is a bogus charge.

On the minimum wage, Senator Kennedy, clearly a big supporter of the minimum wage, suggested to me before the State of the Union Address, he said, "Instead of putting a number in there, why don't you challenge the Congress in a bipartisan fashion to come up with a reasonable number? If you say a specific number on your own, even though everybody knows you want to go to $5, if you say it, then the Congress, the Republicans may feel that they have to be for something else. Let them take credit for it."

Now, I don't know who told you in this White House that I'm not going to push for it, but I'm going to push very hard for it. But I think—if you look at realistically where we are, we have a majority in both Houses in the hands of the Republicans. We have leaders in the Republican Party—the Republican majority leader says we ought to abolish the minimum wage altogether.

I have to create the conditions in which we can raise the minimum wage if I possibly can. I want the Congress to do it in a bipartisan fashion. I want them to have a full share of credit for it. I will work very hard for it. But I don't want to waste a lot of time making strong posturing and undermining the chance that we can raise it. I want to raise it. I want it to get done.

And I think in the end—Theodore Roosevelt said, who was a very good speaker, that in the end the measure of what we do should be what we do, not what we say. So I'm doing my best to actually get it raised.

Entitlement Programs

Mr. Brokaw. It seems to me, Mr. President, that one of your greatest challenges in the next year or so is to reconnect to those middle and working class families that have traditionally voted Democrat that have strayed now from the fold. Their children are going to be saddled with great debt as a result of the entitlements that are building up year after year. Why don't you take on entitlements, including Social Security and Medicare, in terms of getting the cost under control by not eliminating them and not reducing the benefits but maybe cutting back on the COLA's, the cost of living increase, taxing the wealthy more for Medicare, and saying to the country candidly, we have to do something about this?

The President. Well, let's look at the record. First of all, in 1993, in that budget battle that passed by one vote, we did take on Social Security. We asked upper income Social Security recipients to pay a little more on their income to bring them in line with private pensions. And it was a big issue in the last election. The Republicans ran against us on it. They said we were wrong. It was the responsible thing to do.

We lowered the rate of Medicare increases by taking disciplined steps to bring the cost under control. And I said all along that I thought that upper income Medicare recipients, people with incomes of $100,000 a year or more, might have to pay more for it in order to fund health reform and bring the cost under control over the long run.

But I do not believe that we should mislead the American people. Let's just take Social Security. Social Security has produced a surplus for this budget for years and years, ever since the Social Security reform in the mid-eighties. We take in more every year than we pay out in Social Security. Social Security payments are the same percentage of our income today that they were in 1972. Now, it is today not a problem for the deficit.

Medicare and Medicaid, the medical programs, have been a big problem. We have got to get them down. We have got to control the inflation rate there. And we are working on it. And I think that it has to be taken on. I met with Senator Kerrey the other day, and I told him we would have to continue to work on these things.

But I think it's very important that we understand what we're doing and what we're not doing. I don't think we have to hurt the vast number of Medicare recipients. I don't think we have to pretend that Social Security is contributing to the deficit when it's not.

Mr. Brokaw. Yes, but it will be if we continue at the projected rate.

The President. That's right. It will be by the year 2019 or something. And we will have to have, at some point in the future, another effort like we had in 1983 to take a hard look at it and deal with it. And we have to preserve the integrity of the system, and the American people plainly are willing to see us do some things. We're now raising the retirement age gradually, as you know, under the law passed years ago, from 65 to 67, and we'll look at that.

Mr. Brokaw. But it's——

The President. But the main thing we have to do—let me just say this—the main thing we have to do is to get health care costs more in line with inflation and continue to control other spending. We have brought the deficit down a lot. We can bring it down some more, but we need to do in a way that is really—that is fair and disciplined. That's why I've challenged the Republicans: Let's work together on this. Let's try to—you want to help now. We had to do it all alone with one party for 2 years; now we can do it in a two-party way, and I think it will be good.

Mr. Brokaw. But in your speech the other night and most remarks from the Republican side as well, they say, "Well, Medicare will be off the table. Social Security will be off the table." We've learned in the last couple of weeks about what a hot button, for example, veterans' benefits are. We can't get to where we need to get to without dealing honestly with these entitlements, can we?

The President. Well, first of all, we're dealing dramatically where we need to get—the deficit of this country, as a percentage of our annual income, is much lower than it was when I took office. We've taken $10,000 in national debt off every family in the country. We're moving in the right direction.

The issue is not, do we have to deal with health care costs in Medicare and Medicaid; the issue is, how do we deal with it? How do we deal with these other problems, and what is the fair way to do it? What I said was that I didn't think we should have Medicare cuts to pay for tax cuts. I thought that was wrong. I think the American people think that is wrong.

You know, we are working very hard, and we'll have some more proposals to control the rising costs of Medicare. But I think the American people want us to do it in a way that doesn't take benefits away from needy senior citizens who have paid into this program and are entitled to be taken care of. And I think we can do it.

You know, we're moving in the right direction. The economy is coming up. The deficit is going down. We're moving. The basic components of the deficit now are interest on the debt accumulated between 1981 and 1993 and rising health care costs. And so we have to understand that it's going to take a while to get that down. Most of the burden we're paying now on the deficit is because of those two things. And we can solve them. We have to solve them with discipline. We can also continue to cut other programs. We're cutting a lot of other Government spending in this budget, $140 billion in spending cuts.

Balanced Budget

Mr. Brokaw. Your Labor Secretary, Robert Reich, says that a balanced budget is not a high priority for your administration. Is that a fair statement?

The President. Well, it's not a high priority maybe for the Labor Secretary. What is a high priority is continuing to control the deficit and moving it down, driving it, driving it. What he meant, I think, was that no one believes you can do it overnight or in the next year or two and that if we adopt a balanced budget amendment before the people vote on it, they're entitled to know, does this mean their taxes are going up? Does this mean they're going to cut Medicare and Social Security across the board? What is the price of it? Will you get the same economic benefit if you take the deficit down to 2 percent of our annual income or one percent? What are we trying to do?

The Kerrey commission itself said that the long-term goal of the country should be to at least have the annual deficit down at about 2 percent of our income because we're investing that much every year and we'd be more or less like a State government or a private business running their books and balancing them.

Education and Retraining

Mr. Brokaw. Mr. President, in the course of your administration, it is indisputable that more than 5 million new jobs have now been created. But unfortunately, once you get just below the

senior management level, purchasing power has stayed flat at best. It has not declined.

The President. Absolutely.

Mr. Brokaw. You've put a big emphasis on job retraining and so on. But given the new technology of the workplace, aren't we going to get to a situation in this country where we are fixed? Those who are extremely well educated will do well; the rest are going to have to scramble for their working lifetime.

The President. I wouldn't characterize it quite that way, but you've put your finger on the biggest problem of the economy. If your goal is what my goal is, which is to open the American dream to all Americans who are willing to work for it, and you recognize that in a knowledge-based economy as opposed to the old industrial economy, education is the key to income, then it becomes more understandable how we could have had 5.6 million new jobs in 2 years, the lowest inflation in 30 years, the lowest combined inflation and unemployment in 20 years, the lowest African-American unemployment in 20 years, and still, no income increases for most people. It's because, in the global economy and with all of this technology changing, it tends to depress wages except for those who are educated.

That's why I think the middle class bill of rights is the right answer: Encourage people to get a tax cut by investing in education, in theirs and their children's, and take these Government training programs and collapse them and just give a check or a voucher to people to go back to school.

I think—you know, I've been going to these community colleges, these other colleges that are community-based. I think that you're going to see the educational institutions of the country become the focal point for business and labor and small business people getting together to train and educate and raise incomes. That is the only thing we can do, over the long run, to restore the American dream. So my view is, give people the tools they need to take care of themselves by lowering their tax burden now and raising their income in the long run.

It is going to be a challenge—this, by the way, is going on in every industrial country—but we have the capacity to do it, because we've got so much grassroots strength in these community educational institutions if we can get people to take advantage of it.

Mr. Brokaw. But isn't this whole problem of job creation in America going to ultimately prove to be a great frustration for welfare reform, because we've talked so much about making welfare recipients go to work and learn to get a job when there are not jobs out there for people right now that pay a living wage who are not even on welfare?

The President. Well, but there are two issues here, and let's separate them, because for the first time in our country's history in this new age, they are separate. There's creating jobs and raising incomes. We're creating jobs and more high-paying jobs, but the income levels generally are not rising.

What we have to do is to raise the basic income level, which is what the working family tax cut and the minimum wage increase is all about, get people from welfare to work, but we also have to raise incomes knowing that creating jobs won't necessarily raise everybody else's income. They're two separate things. That's why we need both welfare reform and the minimum wage increase and the middle class bill of rights to pass. They're two different things. We can do them. Is it going to be easy? Of course not. If it were easy, it would already be done. But if we work together, we can make a difference. We can change the course of our future if we work at it.

President's Safety

Mr. Brokaw. Let me ask you about a couple of other issues. Another man has been arrested today for making a threat on your life. There have been all kinds of incidents here at the White House, a plane crashing into it, a man firing off rounds from Pennsylvania Avenue. Has this made you more uneasy as, essentially, the target who lives here?

The President. No.

Mr. Brokaw. Really?

The President. No. I think—I have two reactions to all of it. First of all, some of it may be coincidental. These things happen from time to time and may run in waves. Secondly, throughout our history, any leader who raised strong hopes and wanted to make big changes has tended to spark an adverse reaction too, just almost like a law of physics. If you're moving strongly in one direction, you will have an equal and opposite force in the other direction.

And I do think, as I said the other night in the State of the Union speech, there is a

certain level of frustration and anger in the country that is being channeled in ways that often makes us see each other as enemies rather than just opponents in a certain sense. And I think that's bad. I think that—what I have to do and what I tried to do in the State of the Union speech is to say, we're all Americans. We've got to look at each other in ways that enable us to build people up. And I hope we can change the atmosphere and make it more positive.

But for me, personally, I don't ever think about it. You can't afford to think about it. You realize that—I mean, every day I just have a certain number of hours in the day. I have this job for a certain amount of time. I've got to focus on what I can do for the American people. And the Secret Service is very good. They do a terrific job. They're better at it today than they were last year. They get better all the time. And you can't have perfect protection. You can't be perfect. So I don't think much about it.

Hillary Clinton

Mr. Brokaw. Will Hillary have as active a role and as public a role in the second half of the first term as she has had in the first half?

The President. I think she will plainly have an active role and a public role. In many ways—today as we speak, she's out at the University of California at San Diego dedicating the Eleanor Roosevelt College there and visiting, again, a hospital to emphasize her concern about having more women take advantage of mammographies under Medicare, something that is a big concern to both of us not only because of what happened to my mother but because so many women suffer from breast cancer. And she can't not do that.

You know, when I met Hillary, she was already involved in the problems of families and children. When we were in law school, she took an extra year to work on children and family problems. And when we went home to Arkansas we always worked together on these family problems and these health care problems. It's the work of her life, and she'll keep on doing it, and I would encourage her to do it.

Speaker of the House

Mr. Brokaw. Mr. President, what do you think of Newt Gingrich?

The President. I think he's a very interesting fellow. I think he's got a lot of good ideas. I think he's open to looking at things in new and different ways.

Mr. Brokaw. Do you think he plays fair?

The President. Well, you know, let me say, I think for right now what I want to say is, we need to focus on playing fair with the American people in the future. And we differ on some things, and I'm sure we'll have our fights and arguments, but my commitment to him is a commitment to the American people. The American people gave the Republicans the majority in the House and Senate. The people who were there elected their leaders. He has made some clear statements that he wants to change the country in ways that are positive and in ways that I think we can work together on. So I'm going to get out there and try to work with him.

Where I disagree with him, I will disagree. I am strongly committed to national service. I don't want to see us do away with it. I hope I can change his mind on that, and if not, I hope I can prevail. There are other areas where we disagree, but if we're going to work together to reduce the bureaucracy and expand opportunity in this country, then we ought to do it, and we ought to look to the future, not to the past.

Baseball Strike

Mr. Brokaw. Mr. President, is there anything that you can do about the baseball strike?

The President. I'm certainly trying. You know, I have named Mr. Usery the mediator, and I talked to him this morning. I asked him to get the parties back together in the strike and to give me a report by February 6th, and if he couldn't get them to agree, he should actually make a proposal and tell them what he thinks they should do based on having heard all sides.

Mr. Brokaw. Would you throw out the first ball on a game that was being played by so-called replacement players?

The President. Well, I believe the players and the owners ought to come back together and give us a baseball season. I think they ought to give us spring training. You know, they have this feeling that baseball is always a game, not just a business. There are communities in spring training areas all over the South that are dependent on them for income and opportunity. But there are people—there's still a significant percentage of the American people, probably you and I among them, who really believe baseball is something special. And you know, there's a few hundred owners and a few hundred more players, and baseball generates $2 billion worth of revenues every year; about a thousand people ought to be able to figure out how to divide that up and give baseball back to the American people, and I hope they'll do that.

Loan Guarantees for Mexico

Mr. Brokaw. You've also been working very hard this week on Mexico, pressing for a $40 billion fund to help prop up the peso. Even the most casually informed American taxpayer is going to say, "Wait a minute. Why do we want to risk $40 billion of my money for Mexico, when you look at the experience of the last 15 years in South America when some very sophisticated banks and other investors simply got burned by putting dollars down there?"

The President. Well, they did, but we're not going to risk it. That's the difference. And I want to point out, one, we should help Mexico because it's in our interest. They're our third biggest trading partner. We've got $40 billion at risk and three quarters of a million jobs in America. Secondly, we have other interests at risk. We have the prospect of a new flood of illegal immigration if there's an economic collapse in Mexico. Thirdly, if Mexico has an economic collapse, we know from what we've seen already that it will bleed off into Argentina and all these other countries that are supporting our move to support more democracy and more free market economics in Latin America. So we have interests there.

Now, this is not foreign aid. It's not a loan. It's not a gift. We are cosigning a note. That's what the loan guarantee is. And we will only do it if we have good collateral. Mexico has never failed on any of its financial obligations to us in the past, and this will be something where we will cosign a note with good collateral. I think it's in our interest. I know it's not popular, but it's in our interest clearly, and we should do it.

Russia

Mr. Brokaw. Do you think that Boris Yeltsin is in charge of Russia every day?

The President. I think he is in charge of Russia.

Mr. Brokaw. Every day?

The President Well, if he's in charge, he's in charge every day. I think he's running the government. He's the elected President. He's been much more vigorous in the last few days in his assertion of policy with regard to Chechnya. The United States supports the territorial integrity of Russia and all of its neighbors, but we want to see an end to the violence there and a political reconciliation. I do believe he's in charge. And he's the elected President, and we've worked with him, and our country is better off. There are no Russian missiles pointed at America now for the first time since the dawn of the nuclear age. We're destroying 9,000 nuclear weapons and ways of delivering them. We're moving in the right direction there.

Super Bowl XXIX and the 1996 Election

Mr. Brokaw. Mr. President, I want to conclude with two scorecard questions. Who do you like in the Super Bowl, and who do you most want to run against in 1996?

The President. I want the Republicans to decide who I'm going to run against, and I'll abide their judgment and gladly receive them. And I'm for the team from California.

Mr. Brokaw. Now, Mr. President, there's a northern California and a southern California. [*Laughter*] One has a lot more votes than the other.

The President. They do.

Mr. Brokaw. You're not going to get off by just saying California.

The President. Both those communities voted for me. And I'm going to be for them. [*Laughter*]

NOTE: The interview began at 11:42 a.m. in the Roosevelt Room at the White House, and it was embargoed for release until 4 p.m.

Statement on the Baseball Strike
January 26, 1995

America has been living without baseball for far too long. Now, as the strike drags on, it threatens the start of the 1995 season. It could well damage the economies of the spring training States. It is imperiling the livelihoods of tens of thousands of workers whose jobs depend on baseball. And it is trying the patience and depressing the spirits of millions of baseball fans—including me. It is time for this strike to end.

It has always been my belief—and it continues to be—that the baseball strike, like any labor dispute, should be settled through good-faith bargaining between the parties. It was with this principle in mind that I endorsed the Secretary of Labor's proposal to appoint the best mediator around—former Labor Secretary Bill Usery—to help the parties sort out their differences.

Over the last 2 days, I have spoken with Secretary Reich and with former Secretary Usery about the status of the strike negotiations. We discussed all of the alternatives. I remain convinced that the best way to get baseball back for America is for the parties to reach their own settlement. But we cannot wait indefinitely.

This morning, I asked Bill Usery to bring the owners and the players back to the table and to step up the pace and intensity of his mediation efforts.

I have asked him to report back to me by February 6 with the progress they have made. If the parties have not reached an agreement by then—or are not on track towards a speedy settlement—I have asked Mr. Usery, if he believes it appropriate, to put forth his own recommendations for a proposed settlement between the parties.

I hope it doesn't come to that. I urge the owners and the players to give their full support to this mediation effort and to settle this unfortunate dispute themselves. It is time to put behind us the rancor and cynicism that are shadowing the American ideal of baseball. It is time to let all the excitement that the 1995 season can offer sweep away that tarnished image. It's time to "play ball."

Remarks on Welfare Reform and an Exchange With Reporters
January 27, 1995

O.J. Simpson Trial

The President. Is everyone in? This is a big pool today.

Q. The O.J. trial is not on——

The President. The O.J. trial hasn't started yet today, has it? Thank goodness it's in California or you all wouldn't pay any attention to what we're doing. [*Laughter*]

Q. Have you been watching it?

The President. I've seen a little of it. I saw a little of the argument last night.

Welfare Reform and the Economy

I think all of you know, as I said in my State of the Union, perhaps the most important legislative issue Congress will take up this year is welfare reform. And I strongly believe we have to end the welfare system as we know it. Tomorrow I'm having a working session with Members of the Congress, with representatives of State and local government.

But I wanted to begin this process by meeting with four people here who made the decision to choose work over welfare. I thank these women for coming in to meet with me, and I thank them for the work they've done to make the most of their own lives.

When we meet tomorrow, we need to be mindful of how this system has worked, what works about it, what doesn't work about it, what the human impact's going to be, and how we really can foster work and independence and good parenting. And that will be the focus of our discussion today and the focus of our discussion tomorrow.

One other point I'd like to make is that today we had the economic report on 1994, and we see now that last year we had the strongest economic growth in 10 years and the best combined rates of high growth and low inflation in 30 years. So we're moving in the right direction—or, 25 years. We're moving in the right direction.

And as we take up these decisions in the Congress over the budget and over the things that we are going to do, I would say we have to keep in mind that the most important social program is a job. And the most important thing that we can do to get to the New Covenant

of more opportunity and more responsibility is to make sure as we are working to legislate and to create more responsibility at the grassroots level, we also keep opportunity in mind. And so we've got to keep the economic recovery going. We've got to pass responsible welfare reform. And those are the two things that I want to emphasize today.

Q. Mr. President, what worries you about some of the welfare remedies that are being proposed by Republicans in Congress?

The President. Well, some of them seem to say that we should cut people off of assistance without regard to what will happen to their children and without regard to whether they will have an opportunity to get the skills they need to move into the work force. And I think that's the thing that bothers me most of all.

The other thing I wanted to do is to make sure that as we give more responsibility to the States, which is something I strongly support— we've given two dozen States permission to get out from under Federal rules and regulations to try their own remedies; no one of us has all the answers to this; nobody does, otherwise the problem would be solved—but I want to make sure that we do not do it in a way that strongly disadvantages some States and helps others. I think we have to be fair to all States. Not every State at every point in time in the future will have the same percentage of its citizens eligible for welfare.

The third thing I want to point out is, I think it's important that we do not forget that a lot of people who go on public assistance will only do it one time in their lives and do it because they hit a bump in the road—they have a marriage that breaks up, they lose a job, they have some personal misfortune. They're there for 4 or 5 months, 6 months, and then they get off. Their lives are stabilized; it never happens again. I think as we try to deal with the problem of long-term welfare dependency, we shouldn't forget and we shouldn't do anything that unduly burdens the people that never were in danger of being long-term welfare dependent but do need some short-term help.

Those are the three things that bother me most as we get ready to go into this debate.

I think that there is a genuine consensus across party lines, regional lines, income lines, racial lines that we ought to promote work and education and responsible parenting. I just want to make sure we don't fall into those other traps.

Q. Mr. President, what do you think of the balanced budget?

Q. Would your plan cost more at the beginning, though?

The President. The plan I presented last year cost somewhere in the beginning—I think we underestimated the savings. The more you invest in putting people to work, the quicker you will reduce long-term taxpayer costs. The more people are put into the work force, even if you have to spend some money to do it—for example, we gave Oregon permission to take the welfare checks and actually use it by giving it to employers as a wage supplement. They wanted to try it, and we said, "Have at it." I'm going to be very interested to see whether that works. Maybe a lot of States will do that. The Government can't afford a lot of public service jobs. Maybe the answer is to let the welfare checks go as employer supplements, to pay those wage supplements.

But the point is that however we do it, the more we focus on work and giving people a living wage and an opportunity to work, the better off we'll be. That's another good argument for raising the minimum wage.

Balanced Budget Amendment

Q. Mr. President, what do you think of the House passing the balanced budget amendment? Are you for it?

The President. I'm glad they adopted the Stenholm amendment.

Q. Are you?

The President. Absolutely, it makes the bill much better. I still believe that if it's going to be presented to the country, they ought to tell the country what's involved—what's involved. Let's have—there's a right to know here. I'm all for open Government, and I think there's a right to know what is involved. Let the people know what is involved, both in the short run what will have to be cut and what, if any, downsides there are, what's going to happen when we get into a recession, how will that be impacted? The people need more information about this before the legislators vote on it. If it's going to be sent out there, there ought to be a cover sheet showing how it would be done.

Thank you very much.

NOTE: The President spoke at 10:30 a.m. in the Oval Office at the White House, prior to a meeting with welfare recipients. A tape was not available for verification of the content of these remarks.

Remarks to the U.S. Conference of Mayors
January 27, 1995

Thank you very much. I'm delighted to be here. I see that half of the Cabinet is here. I guess they've already answered all your questions, solved all your problems. Now they can come solve ours. [*Laughter*]

Mayor Ashe and distinguished members of the organization, I'm delighted to see all of you. Is Mayor Grant from East Providence here? Your wife told me this was your birthday. Happy birthday, happy birthday. Just wanted you to know I was checking up on you. [*Laughter*]

Let me begin by saying congratulations to all of you on the overwhelming passage of the unfunded mandate legislation by the Senate today, 86 to 10 the bill passed. I have not had a chance

to look at the final version of the Senate bill. It just passed a little while ago. But I know some very good amendments were added, and I want to congratulate Senator Glenn and Senator Kempthorne. We worked very hard on this bill last year, and I was sorry we didn't pass it then. Both of them did very, very good work. And I believe the bill is a very strong one as it goes to the House. But I have not seen its final form, but I heard it was in good shape. And it must have been pretty good if it passed 86 to 10. And I think that should be reassuring to you; it certainly is to me.

I want to thank you for the resolution you passed on the baseball strike and the action we are taking. We will work very hard on that. I know how important it is to you. I sometimes think that the full economic implications of this whole thing have not been evaluated, not just for the cities that have major league teams but also for the cities that host spring training. This is a big deal, and we're working on it.

I want to thank your international committee for the vote you took on the Mexican stabilization package that we have offered. As you know, this is not the most popular issue in America today, but it's important. And I thank you for your support. It's in the interest of our working people and our economy. And it's not a gift; it's not foreign aid; it's not even a loan. It's cosigning a note with good collateral. So it's in our interests, and I thank you for that.

When I came here 2 years ago with a mission to restore the American dream for all of the people of this country and to make sure we moved to the next century still the strongest force in the world for freedom and democracy and peace and prosperity, I said then and had said all during my campaign that I wanted a new partnership for the American people. I called it a New Covenant of more opportunity and more responsibility, recognizing that unless we had more of both, we could not hope to do the things that have to be done.

I have sought to essentially focus on three things that I think are critical to making sure we succeed in this new economy: empowering our people to make the most of their own lives, expanding opportunity but shrinking the Federal Government bureaucracy, giving more authority to State and local governments and to the private sector. And I have sought to enhance the security of our people at home and abroad. In all those things you have been very helpful and supportive, both of the specific initiatives of this administration and of your own efforts which fit so well into that framework.

As all of you know, in the last 2 years we've had a lot of successes. We now have the figures in on 1994's growth rate. We know it was the best economic year our country had since 1984. We know that the combined rates of unemployment and inflation are the lowest they have been in 30 years. We know that we have inflation at a 30-year low. We know that, among other things, the African-American unemployment rate went into single digits for the first time in 20 years.

So there is a lot—[*applause*]—we've tried to expand more authority to our States and to our cities, and we're bringing the Federal Government down in size and reach where it's appropriate. We already have 100,000 fewer people working for the National Government than we did when I became President. And if nothing else is done, it will shrink by another 170,000. And of course, in terms of security, the most important things we did were to pass the Brady bill and the crime bill, which you were active in and supportive of, and I thank you for all that.

As we look ahead in this year, which promises to be somewhat unpredictable but exciting and I think could be very productive for our country—and I must say this passage of this bill today and the reasonable deliberation in the Senate and the way the amendments were debated in good faith is quite encouraging to me—there are some things that I think we have to do. In terms of empowering our people to meet the challenges of this age, we have to realize our job is still to expand the middle class and to shrink the under class. And the two main initiatives our administration has this year are the middle class bill of rights and raising the minimum wage.

We want to pass this middle class bill of rights, not only to give tax relief to middle class people who have been working harder for lower wages, or for at least no wage increases, but to do it in a way that will raise incomes in the short term and in the long term. That's why the focus is on a tax deduction for all educational expenses after high school and an IRA with tax-free withdrawal for education expenses or for health care expenses or for the care of a parent or purchasing a first-time home, and why we seek to consolidate the 70 various training programs into one huge block and let people get directly a voucher that they can use if they're unemployed or, if they have a low-wage job and they're eligible for training, to take to the local community college or wherever else they wish to take it to get the education and training of their choice.

I think it's important to raise the minimum wage because if we don't, next year the buying power of the minimum wage will be at a 40-year low. And the evidence is clear that if you raise the minimum wage a modest amount, it doesn't cause increased unemployed and indeed may bring people back into the job market who otherwise are not willing to come in and go to work. So I would hope you would support both of those things.

In the area of expanding opportunity and shrinking the bureaucracy, we're coming back with a second round of reinventing Government proposals—and perhaps Secretary Cisneros has already talked to you about what we're proposing for HUD—to collapse the 60 programs into 3. I want to emphasize that we're doing this to strengthen the mission of HUD and to strengthen the partnership that we have with the cities of this country, not to gut the Department's partnership or its capacity to help you do your job. And so I hope that you will help us as we debate this on both parts, say that you want to support a reduction in the size of the Federal bureaucracy but you do not want to see the mission of HUD as carried out by the mayors of this country undermined and weakened because you have a job to do.

Finally, let me say some things about the crime bill. I very much hope that we will be able to work through, in this session of Congress, a good faith carrying forward of the crime bill that was passed last year. It became unfortunately embroiled in politics; you know that better than I do. And I think you also know that the prevention programs that were passed were programs that were recommended to us in the strongest possible terms not only by mayors, not only by community leaders but by the leaders of the law enforcement community and that a lot of those prevention programs that were later labeled as pork were cosponsored, the first time they came up, by people who later said they were pork.

Well, all that's behind us now, and the only thing that matters now is, what is the best thing for the people of this country? What will keep our streets safer? What will reduce the crime rate more? What is the most likely approach to actually make the American people feel more secure? We must enhance our security at home. At the end of the cold war, I think it's fair to say that most Americans put their children to bed at night more worried about their security concerns at home than abroad.

So what we should seek to do, without regard to party or region of the country, is that which is most likely to make us most safe and to lower the crime rate. Many of you—I'll bet even a majority of you here—have recorded declines in the crime rate in the last year or so because of the strategies that mayors are adopting with community policing, with prevention programs, with using citizens to work with law enforcement to do things that will reach people in ways that will prevent crime as well as catch criminals more quickly. We have to take these lessons into account.

So as we enter into a second round of debate about the crime bill, I would say there are two or three things that we ought to keep in mind. First, as I said in my State of the Union Address, we should not repeal the assault weapons ban. We should not do that. [*Applause*] This issue, as you can hear from the response, is not a Republican-Democratic issue, it is not a liberal-conservative issue, it is overwhelmingly an urban-nonurban issue. And what we have to do is to convince all the people I grew up with—[*laughter*]—that we don't—we don't want to fool with anybody's hunting rifles. We don't want to stop anybody from going to shooting contests. We don't want to interfere with anybody's legitimate pursuit of happiness in the exercise of their right to keep and bear arms. But there is nothing in the Constitution that prevents us from exercising common sense. And people who live in urban settings know that the mortality rate in the emergency rooms of urban hospitals from gunshot wounds has gone up dramatically in the last 15 years because the average body has more bullets in it when it's wheeled into the emergency room. You do not have to be a genius to figure out what's happening.

And so I hope that we can put an end to this war. This is a phony war among the American people. And those of us that respect people's right to hunt and to engage in other appropriate conduct, those of us that enjoy it ourselves, we ought to be able to ask each other again: What's best for America? And what good is it to pretend that it's a matter of principle to maintain the right of a bunch of teenagers to have Uzis on the streets of our cities.

So I hope you will talk about this in a nonpartisan, nonpolitical way and realize this is one of those cultural problems that's gripping America. We got too many of them. They're keeping us apart. But we need to say to the nonurban folks in our society, this is something that—we've got to work this out. This is a fair deal. This is a balanced bill. There are 650 weapons enumerated in this bill that cannot be infringed on by the Government in any way, shape, or form. And so let's let this alone and go on about the business of the country.

I also think we ought to emphasize that at least the Attorney General is doing her dead-level best to make sure that the administration of the crime bill that passed is nonbureaucratic, nonpolitical, and efficient. If you look at what's happened so far, in October, not even 2 weeks into the new fiscal year, we had already funded 392 policing grants that went unfunded last year. Last month, at your recommendation, we gave 631 larger cities the go-ahead to begin recruiting and training more than 4,600 new officers. So they know the money will be there when their applications are handed in.

For the smaller cities, we've streamlined the application process, allowing them to apply more quickly for police with a simple one-page application. I don't know how many one-page applications we've got in the Government now, but I know you can ask for an SBA loan or a policeman with one page. You ought to be able to do more things with one page.

This COPS program has now helped more than 1,000 communities to put more than 10,000 more police officers on the street in all 50 States. Within a week, when the announcement is made of the winners of the COPS FAST program, that total will be close to 15,000, well on the way to the 100,000 goal of the crime bill. That would be a 20 percent increase in the strength on the streets.

Now, the crime bills now being considered in Congress have some things that I think may be superficially appealing but need to be thought through. If you scrap the $8.8 billion COPS initiative, as some suggest, and replace it with a $10 billion block grant which also has to include prevention programs, the good news is you'll have a block grant. The bad news is there'll be a lot less money in it than was provided for.

And keep in mind, to all those who say it wasn't funded, we did not raise one red cent in taxes to pay for the crime bill. We did not take one red cent away from any other program. We simply dedicated all the savings to be gained from reducing the size of the Federal bureaucracy to giving it back to local communities to use to fund the crime bill. That's what was done.

Now, to make matters worse, some have suggested that the $10 billion block grant to fund police and prevention could only be funded if we first fund $10 billion in new prisons. So

that's a decision that some would make against the unanimous advice of every police officer in the country who has testified. If we make that decision, that would be like people saying, "We don't care what lowers crime; we don't care what makes people safer; we don't care what people in law enforcement who vote Republican and Democrat say. This is what we're going to do. It will make us feel better, and we can claim that it was the best thing to do."

We should not do that. This ought not to become a political issue. That crime bill had a balance of police and prevention and prisons. We shouldn't take all the prevention money away through the back door and put it into prisons. And we shouldn't say that the prisons are more important than the police and the prevention. I had no objection to getting into the business of helping States with their prison construction, even though it was totally unprecedented, but there is no evidence that that is the way to lower the crime rate. The American people want to be safer at night; they want their kids to be safer on the streets and at school. And we ought to be driven by what is best for the American people.

I would also say, just parenthetically, that even last year I was concerned when the crime bill passed that the conditions on getting that Federal money for prison construction were so restrictive and required such a large State match that a lot of that money might never be used. We cannot permit a cruel hoax to then be written into the law saying, well, you can get this block grant for police and prevention but only after the prison money is spent and then have conditions on spending the prison money so strict that it will never be spent in the first place.

So I urge you to just go up there without regard to your party or region and say, look, let's do what will lower the crime rate; let's do what will keep people safer. The American people will figure that out. They will trust their local leaders; they will trust their local law enforcement people; they will trust them. We can share responsibility now. There need be no characterization that is negative when this process is over. There need be no name-calling. There needs to be no anything. We just need to do what is right to lower the crime rate. And all of us have worked so hard on this.

Again, I would say this is like the assault weapons issue. We've got big issues to deal with.

This unfunded mandates is one. Welfare reform is another. How we're going to lower the deficit and provide tax relief is another. There are major positive issues that we're going to have to face. We don't need to reopen an issue and make it worse. So I ask you to help us on that.

Now, let me say one final thing about the baseball strike, if I might. I asked Bill Usery, the Federal mediator, to get the sides back together and report to me by February 6th. Anybody know what February 6th is? It's Babe Ruth's 100th birthday. So it struck me as a good day to settle the baseball strike. I identify with Babe Ruth. He's a little overweight. [*Laughter*] And he struck out a lot—[*laughter*]—but he hit a lot of home runs because he went to bat. You are the people in this country who go to bat. You have to deal directly with people. You have to be accountable, not only for the rhetoric of your speeches but the reality of your actions.

And so I ask you to take this opportunity to join with us, and let's make the decision the American people made last November a good decision by making it one of shared responsibility. Let's move what we can back to the State and local level. Let's work to empower people. Let's reduce the burden of Government and increase the opportunity it creates. We can do these things, but it is very important that we not fix what ain't broke and that we not become diverted by issues that can only divide us when there is so much we can do that will bring us together.

Thank you very much.

NOTE: The President spoke at 4:36 p.m. in Room 450 of the Old Executive Office Building. In his remarks, he referred to Mayor Victor Ashe of Knoxville, TN, president, U.S. Conference of Mayors, and Mayor Rolland R. Grant of East Providence, RI.

Remarks on Welfare Reform
January 28, 1995

Good morning. I am on my way to Blair House to host an all-day meeting that is a bipartisan working session on welfare reform. We will have Members of Congress, Governors, and local officials there from all across our country. I am determined to work with them to pass welfare reform. I think it is perhaps the most pressing social problem we face in our country, and the time has come for Congress to act.

As I said in the State of the Union, what we need in welfare reform is a New Covenant of opportunity and responsibility. People on welfare who can work should go to work. Parents who owe child support should pay it. Governments don't raise children; people do. And we must have a national campaign against teenage pregnancy and births outside marriage.

If we're going to end welfare, let's do it right. We should require work and responsibility, but we shouldn't cut people off just because they're poor or young or unmarried. We should promote responsibility by requiring young mothers to live at home or in proper supervised settings and to finish school. But we shouldn't put them or their children out on the street. I have

worked on this issue since 1980. I know that the people who want to change welfare most are those who are trapped on it.

Yesterday, in preparation for this meeting, I met with four former welfare mothers who have managed to free themselves from the system. I listened again to the stories of people who have had great difficulty in trying to get the kind of support they need to get off of welfare, people who did not want to go on in the first place and were anxious to be off of it. I know that most people who are trapped in welfare will gladly take the work options if we can work out the system in the proper way. I also know that those who don't want to do the responsible thing must be required to do so.

But our job in the end is not to tear anybody down and not to use this issue to divide America, but to build people up, to liberate them, to give them the capacity they need to compete and win in this new economy. The American people want us to put politics aside and to get this done for our country. I am committed to doing it, and I believe the people who are coming to this meeting this morning are committed as well.

Wish us well. Thank you very much.

NOTE: The President spoke at 8:12 a.m. at the South Portico of the White House.

The President's Radio Address
January 28, 1995

Good morning. I want to talk to you today about the New Covenant I discussed in the State of the Union. My mission as President is to restore the American dream to all of our people. In the new economy of the 21st century, that requires a New Covenant between the people and their Government and among the people themselves.

This is something I've been talking about for many years, since I ran for President. The New Covenant is grounded in an old idea that all Americans have not just a right but a responsibility to do the hard work needed to rise as far as their talents and determination can take them and to give something back to their community and to their country in return. Opportunity and responsibility, they go hand in hand. We can't have one without the other, and we can't have a strong community without both.

We've worked hard to create more economic opportunity for our people in the last 2 years, bringing the deficit down, investing in education and new technology, expanding trade. We've gotten more than 6 million—or almost 6 million new jobs, the fastest growth in 10 years, and the lowest combined rate of unemployment and inflation in 25 years. That's good news.

But America's still got a lot of problems. There are still interests of people and values of people that are not being furthered. And there's really no better example of the need for us to build a New Covenant together than the failed welfare system. Today's welfare system doesn't provide enough opportunity, and it certainly doesn't require enough responsibility. It's a system so badly broken that it undermines the very values, work, family, and responsibility, people must have to put themselves back on track. We've got to return those values front and center. Our job in Government is to expand opportunity, not bureaucracy, and then to empower people to make the most of their own lives. We must not ask, and Government should

not provide, what we really must do for ourselves.

I've worked on this issue of welfare reform for a very long time now, since I first became Governor of Arkansas over 15 years ago. I know there are a lot of different ideas about what we should do. But everyone agrees the system is broken and it needs to be fixed. I'm committed to making welfare what it was meant to be, a second chance, not a way of life. I'm committed to making sure that the only goal of the welfare system is to help people get off of it, into a job where they can support themselves and their families. I believe we should give people the opportunity to move from dependence to independence, providing job training and child care if that's what they need for up to 2 years. At the same time, we must demand that people accept responsibility for themselves. After 2 years, anyone who can work must work. And if a parent doesn't pay child support, that person should be forced to pay. People who have children must be prepared to take responsibility for them.

We should require work and responsibility, but we shouldn't cut people off just because they're poor or young or unmarried. We should promote responsibility by requiring young mothers to live at home with their parents or in appropriate supervised settings and to finish school, but we shouldn't put them and their children on the street. I don't believe we should punish people because they happen to be poor or because of past mistakes. And absolutely, we shouldn't punish children for their parents' mistakes. All of us have made our mistakes, and none of us can change our yesterdays. But every one of us can change our tomorrows. That's what welfare reform should be all about.

And one more thing, Washington doesn't have all the answers. In fixing welfare, as on so many other issues, we have to shift resources and decisionmaking back to States and local communities. The welfare system shouldn't be centralized in Washington, dispensing services through large bureaucracies. We've got to shift more responsibilities back to the citizens of this country.

We've made a good start on this over the last 2 years. We've already given 23 States the right to slash through Federal rules and regulations to reform their own welfare systems. Last year, we introduced the most sweeping welfare reform plan ever presented by an administration. Today at the White House, I'm hosting an all-day working session on welfare reform including Governors, Members of Congress, Democrats and Republicans, people on welfare, and people who have worked their way off. I'm determined to work with all of them to pass welfare reform, and I hope we can make some progress today.

This is a complex and sometimes divisive issue. But if we put partisanship aside, we can come together and solve it around some simple and important values: moving from dependence to independence, from welfare to work, from childbearing to responsible parenting. Let this be the year we end welfare as we know it. And let it also be the year we are all able to stop using this issue to divide America. That should be our commitment. The American people deserve nothing less.

Thanks for listening.

NOTE: The address was recorded at 6:08 p.m. on January 27 in the Roosevelt Room at the White House for broadcast at 10:06 a.m. on January 28.

Statement on the Death of Jim Grant
January 28, 1995

It was with deep sadness and regret that Hillary and I learned today of the death of Jim Grant, executive director of UNICEF. Throughout his long career, Jim Grant was a visionary leader, one of the most distinguished international public servants of our time. It was in recognition of Jim Grant's lifelong contributions that I was honored to present him with the Presidential Medal of Freedom last August.

Under Jim Grant's 15 years of leadership, UNICEF has earned a reputation as one of the most effective and esteemed U.N. agencies. UNICEF retains its special place in the hearts of all Americans.

We will remember Jim Grant most for his tireless advocacy on behalf of the world's children and for pioneering low-cost, simple techniques for alleviating disease, poverty, and suffering among the neediest of children. One measure of his legacy lies in the fact that today 80 percent of children in the developing world receive immunizations, compared with 20 percent in 1980 when Jim Grant assumed leadership of UNICEF.

Today we have lost a personal friend, an American hero and champion of children throughout the world. We will all miss him.

Remarks at the National Governors' Association Dinner
January 29, 1995

Good evening, ladies and gentlemen, and welcome to the White House, again for many of you and for the first time for some. This is always one of my favorite evenings of the year, one of Hillary's favorite evenings, a chance to see old friends and think about old times and look to the future.

Two years ago, when I had the opportunity for the first time to host this dinner, after having been on the other end of it for 12 years, I pledged to you that I would take the experiences that we had shared together and strive to form a new partnership with the Governors and with the States. After 2 years, I think it's fair to say that we have made good on that pledge.

And tonight, I want to renew that pledge as we debate the astonishing range of opportunities and challenges that are ahead of us.

I also want to thank those of you who have gone out of your way to give me the opportunity to make good on the pledge when you thought we were slipping a little. [*Laughter*] And I want to thank those of you who have acknowledged what you thought we were doing right. In particular, two of the Governors, not of my party, who went through the line tonight and complimented the partnership of the Federal Government and various agencies, I appreciate very much.

I think every American now wants Government to expand opportunity and to shrink bureaucracy, to empower people to make the most of their own lives, to enhance our security but not to do those things which it ought not to do. Working in partnership with us, many of you have pioneered ways to reform health care and to reform welfare, free of Federal rules and regulations which had previously encumbered you. We have done our part to be good partners. We have reduced the deficit; we have reduced the size of the Government; we have reduced regulation in important areas.

We have also done what we could to improve our performance. I cited in the State of the Union, and I cite again, something that those of you who have had the misfortune to have disasters know, which is that the Federal Emergency Management Agency and all those who work in the disaster area, the Department of Transportation, HUD, and others, are no longer a disaster when disaster occurs. They are there working in partnership with you, and we want to do more of that.

In that spirit now, we begin a new year of debates, working on welfare, perhaps the most important thing we can do from the point of view of all the people of all of our States, without regard to party or region or race or income. We had a very, very good meeting yesterday with a bipartisan group of Governors, local officials, Members of Congress, and I thank those of you who participated.

The Vice President will also be presenting a second round of reinventing Government proposals which will cut further spending and reduce the Federal role and give more responsibilities to the State. And as you know, we are proposing a tax relief package which focuses primarily on education and giving people tax reductions in return for educating their children and themselves.

I hope as we go forward, we can agree on the things which we don't think the Federal Government should be doing. And I hope we'll also be agreeing on some things we think we should do. There is a plain national interest in protecting the essential needs of the children of this country. We clearly can do some things right in a nonbureaucratic, creative way. And I think the best example of that is AmeriCorps, our national service program, which has worked closely with many of you in this room tonight.

I want to close by saluting your distinguished chair, Governor Dean, and Judy, and all of you for all you have done. For those of you who have worked with Hillary and with me over the years and with the members of our Cabinet, particularly those who are former Governors—and I see Governor Babbitt and Governor Riley here—let me say that there is no more rewarding experience than being able to reach across the lines that divide us to feel that we are really making a difference in peoples' lives, that we are giving the American people a government that is leaner but not meaner, one that really does help them make the most of their own lives. I think that's why we all got into this work, and if we'll just keep that in mind, I think when we're all done, we'll be very proud.

I'd like to propose a toast to the chair of the National Governors' Association and to his fine wife and to all the Governors and their spouses tonight.

To the Governors and their families: Thank you.

NOTE: The President spoke at 8:41 p.m. in the State Dining Room at the White House. In his remarks, he referred to Gov. Howard Dean of Vermont, chair of the National Governors' Association, and his wife, Judith.

Remarks in a Telephone Conversation Congratulating the Super Bowl Champion San Francisco 49ers
January 29, 1995

The President. Eddie, can you hear me?

Eddie DeBartolo. Yes, Mr. President, I can.

The President. It's nice to hear your voice. Congratulations.

Mr. DeBartolo. Thank you so much, sir.

The President. I want to say to you and to George and Carmen and to all your wonderful players, it was a—the whole season was thrilling for all of us, and I think the best thing I can say about the 49ers is, I haven't met a single fan anywhere in America who resents all the success you've had. And that's a rare thing. And it's a real tribute to you, to the coach, and to the players in the way you've won and the way you've conducted yourself. We're all happy and proud of you tonight.

Mr. DeBartolo. Well, Mr. President, I can't thank you enough for taking this time, and I know from a very busy schedule. And we're all your backers, and I thank you so much from the bottom of my heart.

The President. Thank you. Congratulations to all of you.

Mr. DeBartolo. Thank you very much.

The President. I liked seeing George without his glasses. He looks good.

NOTE: The President spoke at 10 p.m. from the Residence at the White House. In his remarks, he referred to San Francisco 49ers football team owner Eddie DeBartolo, head coach George Seifert, and team president Carmen Policy.

Remarks at the National Governors' Association Gala
January 29, 1995

Thank you. Well, we want to thank John and Jonathan and Mary Chapin Carpenter. And at least from my part, I know how hard it is to do anything when you're hoarse. [*Laughter*]

It doesn't get any better than this. You were wonderful. We thank you. It's been wonderful for Hillary and for me to have all of you here. There will be music out in the foyer and a little dancing if you have a little of that spirit.

I will say this: For all of us who come from small towns all across America, I wish I had a nickel for every time I drove through that town you sang about tonight. [*Laughter*]

Thank you all. God bless you, and good night.

NOTE: The President spoke at 10:48 p.m. in the East Room at the White House. In his remarks, he referred to singer Mary Chapin Carpenter and her accompanists, John Jennings and Jonathan Carroll.

Remarks to the National Governors' Association
January 30, 1995

Good morning. First, I want to welcome you back to the White House. For those of you who were here last night, Hillary and I enjoyed having you; it was a great dinner and we enjoyed the conversation and the entertainment and the fellowship.

There are two or three things I'd like to speak about this morning before turning the microphone over to Governor Dean and Governor Thompson and the Vice President. First, let me thank the executive committee for its vote yesterday on our stabilization measure for Mexico.

And let me urge the NGA as a whole to support that executive committee recommendation.

The United States has a lot at stake in Mexico. We have hundreds of thousands of jobs that are tied to the success of the Mexican economy. It is now our third largest trading partner—several billions of dollars a year. Our future cooperation and our ability to manage some very significant immigration problems could be affected by what is going on there, and the efforts that we are making to cooperate on the drug issue could obviously be affected by what is going on there.

I want to emphasize that the stabilization initiative is not a gift, not a loan, not a bailout; it is a loan guarantee. We are cosigning a note. We'll have good collateral. We're doing it because it's in the interest of the United States. I worked on it extensively this weekend, and I realize that it's not politically popular back home, it's a rather complex issue, but it is clearly in the interest of American workers, American businesses, and the United States as a whole. So I thank the executive committee for your vote, and I hope the NGA as a whole will follow the recommendation of the executive committee.

The second thing I'd like to talk about is, very briefly, is the commitment that I made 2 years ago to have a better, stronger partnership with the States, to regulate less, to empower more, to try to push more responsibilities down to the State and local level. The Vice President will say a little more about that, and then tomorrow at the NGA I'll have a chance to speak in greater detail.

But we have worked not simply to reduce the size of the Federal Government, although we have by over 100,000 already; not just to reduce the burden of regulation, although we have in banking and intrastate trucking and a number of other areas; not just to reduce the cost, although we did—last year was the first time in 25 years when the Congress voted to reduce both domestic and defense spending, obviously except for Social Security and the health care programs—but also to try to move more responsibility to the States.

In the last 2 years, our administration, for example, granted more waivers in the area of health care and welfare reform than in the previous 12 years combined. And we want to do more of that. We also have worked very hard to try to help work through problems that have

existed in the past with specific governmental agencies, and we want to do more of that. And as I said, the Vice President will have more to say about that.

We are strongly supporting the move to get unfunded mandates legislation passed in the Congress and are encouraged by the work that was done in the United States Senate where, as I remember, the bill passed 86–10 last week, after a really open and honest discussion of all appropriate amendments. The legislation is now moving through the House. I think there are about 100 amendments pending, but I think they will move through it in a fairly expeditious way, just as the Senate did.

With regard to the balanced budget amendment, it has passed the House; it is now in the Senate. I will say again what I've said all along here. It seems to me that the State legislators, the people, and the Governors have a right to know what is entailed in the time line if the effort is made. And I would hope that we would continue to take that right-to-know position. You have a right to know what happens. You have a right to know what happens if we protect Social Security. You have a right to know what happens if we protect Social Security and Medicare. You have a right to know what happens in the details of this.

We have cut $600 billion-plus off this deficit. I am going to give a budget in early February to the Congress which will take over $140 billion more in cuts. We have eliminated 100 programs; we have cut hundreds and hundreds of others. I want to keep bringing this deficit down, but I think we ought to all go into a change in the fundamental document of this country with our eyes wide open and knowing what the consequences are.

The third thing I'd like to talk about, briefly, is welfare reform. For those of you who were present at the Saturday meeting, I want to thank you again for being there. It reminded me very much of the process that we went through in 1987 and 1988 when we had a Republican President and a Democratic Congress and a bipartisan group of Governors. And we worked in '87 and '88 toward the passage of the Family Support Act.

I thought it worked then; I think it will work now, if we all work in good faith. We agreed that welfare has to be reformed, that the most important thing is to change it from a system which fosters dependence to one that fosters work and independence, that we ought to support education where it is needed, and that we ought to support responsible parenting.

We agreed that as we try to put more of the operational decisions back to the State and local level, there must be some strong national steps taken on child support enforcement because so many of those orders are multistate in their impact and because we are doing such a bad job as a country now in collecting child support which should properly be paid to children.

We agreed that there must be more State and local flexibility; we agreed that there ought to be an effort to reduce teen pregnancy and out-of-wedlock pregnancy generally. Governor Carper gave a very moving presentation of what is going on in Delaware, and as you know, I announced in my State of the Union that we would make a national effort on this which we'll have more to say about in the next few days.

We did not reach final agreement on the questions of how the partnership should be structured, what the implications of a block grant would be, and what, in specific terms, the national interest is in preserving the welfare of the children of this country. I have to say that I basically am in favor, as I always have been, of maximum flexibility for the States. I was a strong supporter of the community development block grant program, for example, when I served as a Governor. But we do have a national interest in protecting the welfare and the possibilities of our children.

In 1985, for the very first time in our history, at least since we've been keeping such statistics, the elderly became less poor than the rest of the population because of the cost-of-living ad-justments and Social Security, because of supplemental security income, because of Medicare. That is something I think we're all proud of.

The flip side of that is that the poverty population itself has stayed the same, or has actually increased, and almost all the poor now are little children and their not very well educated parents, by and large. So we do have a national interest in the welfare of these children and in changing the welfare system so that it promotes responsibility and lifts people up without punishing children who were not the cause of the problems that they face in life. That, it seems to me, is the dividing line that we have to be animated by as we try to forge this new partnership. I'm excited about it; I think we can do it.

We must pass welfare reform this year, and it has got to be real, meaningful, different, and better and broader than anything we've ever done before. And it ought to give you a great deal of flexibility out of—if nothing else, out of a sense of sheer simple humility that no one has all the answers to deal with these difficult riddles that threaten the stability of our families and the future of our kids.

So I am encouraged by where we are. I thank you again for the executive committee resolution on Mexico. We are going to work with you to further the partnership between the States and the Federal Government. And we must pass welfare reform this year, but it ought to be the right kind with the right results.

NOTE: The President spoke at 9:58 a.m. in the East Room at the White House. In his remarks, he referred to Gov. Tommy G. Thompson of Wisconsin.

Remarks and an Exchange With Reporters Prior to Discussions With President Mircea Snegur of Moldova
January 30, 1995

The President. Let me say, first of all, it's a real pleasure and an honor for me and for the United States to welcome President Snegur here and the whole delegation from Moldova. They have been a real model of commitment to democracy and to economic reform. And we have been deeply impressed by the work they have done, the progress they have made. And I'm looking forward to my visit with him.

I also want to thank him for sending me the nice Moldovan wine last Christmas, which was very much appreciated here at the White House.

Mexican Loan Guarantees

Q. Mr. President, will you have a Mexico bailout bill ready today? The peso and the bolsa are dropping sharply.

The President. We certainly hope so. I worked yesterday for several hours on this and secured again the reaffirmation of the commitment of the leadership of both parties in both Houses to go forward. And we have put out more strong statements today about it.

I think we just—this is something we have to do. The time is not a friendly factor, and I realize that the Congress had other important measures to debate last week, the unfunded mandates legislation in the Senate, the balanced budget amendment in the House. But this can be resolved fairly quickly, and it needs to be.

Q. Mr. President, there's a suggestion by some leaders that support is eroding for the package rather than increasing. Do you—is that the case?

The President. Well, I think it will increase again once people look at the facts, if we get a bill out there. We need to—the bill needs to go in. And Secretary Rubin has and others have negotiated in great detail and in good faith with the appropriate leaders in the Congress, the committee chairs and others. And I think they're ready for a bill to go forward. And it's time to get it in and go forward.

Q. What do you think of critics who say it's a bailout for Wall Street?

The President. It isn't a bailout for Wall Street. There are—first of all, helping the econ-omy stay strong down there is more important than anything else for our working people and our businesses on Main Street that are doing such business in Mexico. If they want to continue to grow and to have that as a market, we can't let the financial markets, in effect, collapse the Mexican political and economic structure. Secondly, there are a lot of pension plans and ordinary Americans that have their investments tied up there. Thirdly, we have immigration and narcotics cooperation and control issues here involved. This is something for ordinary Americans. It's very much in our interest, and we don't want to let it spread to other countries and, indeed, to developing countries throughout the world. We're trying to promote countries that are moving toward market reforms and moving toward democracy, not to undermine them. And it's very much in our personal interest to do so. It is not a Wall Street bailout, it's in America's interest to build the kind of future we want.

Q. Are you optimistic you'll get a package this week or next?

The President. I'm optimistic that we'll pass it because more often than not in very difficult issues the Congress does the right thing. And we've got a new and different Congress, but I think they'll do the right thing.

NOTE: The President spoke at 12:08 p.m. in the Oval Office at the White House. A tape was not available for verification of the content of these remarks.

Joint Statement With President Mircea Snegur of Moldova
January 30, 1995

At the invitation of President Clinton, President Mircea Snegur of the Republic of Moldova made a working visit to Washington. During their discussions on January 30, the two leaders welcomed the strong state of U.S.-Moldovan relations, which have expanded considerably since diplomatic contacts were established in 1992.

President Snegur described the substantial progress made toward economic and democratic reform in Moldova. He mentioned that prices in Moldova have been completely liberalized, and reaffirmed his government's commitment to reduce government subsidies and privatize commercial enterprises. Noting Moldova's success over the past year in reducing inflation and maintaining the value of its currency, President Snegur pledged to continue working closely with international financial institutions such as the International Monetary Fund and the World Bank. The Moldovan President reviewed the democratic parliamentary elections conducted in February 1994, and the adoption of a new constitution enshrining respect for democratic government and fundamental human rights.

President Clinton praised Moldova's economic and political development, which has placed that country at the forefront among the new independent states of the former Soviet Union, and reiterated continued U.S. support for Moldovan reforms. President Clinton announced that Moldova will receive $22 million in technical assistance in fiscal year 1995, targeted primarily on privatization, economic restructuring, health and exchanges. This brings the total of U.S. assistance to Moldova since 1992 to well over $200 million. President Snegur expressed his appreciation for U.S. assistance over the past three years and cited the important impact this aid has had on the success of reform in Moldova.

President Clinton and President Snegur discussed the inauguration of new programs in 1995 to assist Moldova in creating its first stock exchange, to help emerging small businesses in the regions outside Chisinau, to expand a program of technical assistance and training in agribusiness development, and to establish a permanent office of the Western NIS Enterprise Fund in Chisinau. President Snegur requested that the United States further its efforts to promote U.S. investment in Moldova, underlining that a favorable legal framework has been established to achieve this goal. The Peace Corps will initiate an Economic Development Program, expanding its current work to include volunteer advisers for small businesses and local entrepreneurs.

Moldova and the U.S. Department of Agriculture are finalizing an agreement for $10 million in concessional food sales in 1995, and an additional $2 million in food donations. The Department of Agriculture will also fund at least 16 Moldovan participants in the Cochran Fellowship Program for 1995, which provides training programs in the United States for selected agricultural specialists. President Clinton announced the United States will seek beneficiary status for Moldova under the Generalized System of Preferences (GSP). Such a step is designed to promote greater bilateral trade through tariff reductions on various commercial items. During his visit to the White House, President Snegur and Vice President Gore signed the Globe Bilateral Agreement for Cooperation. The Globe program, initiated by the United States, is an international environmental science and education program that will bring students, teachers and scientists together to study the global environment.

President Snegur discussed with President Clinton the status of negotiations toward a peaceful settlement of the separatist dispute in Moldova's eastern Transdniester region. He assured President Clinton of his commitment to a peaceful, negotiated settlement of the dispute in accordance with international standards and in cooperation with the international community, including the Organization for Security and Cooperation in Europe (OSCE). President Snegur described recent progress in negotiations to reestablish economic links between the communities on both sides of the Dniester River, and to formulate a special status for the Transdniester region within a unified Moldovan state. President Clinton lauded President Snegur for Moldova's exemplary approach toward peaceful resolution of this internal political dispute. He reaffirmed the United States' support for the independence, sovereignty and territorial integrity of Moldova and applauded its positive human rights record, particularly its treatment of national minorities. President Clinton reiterated that the United States would continue to promote a settlement of the Transdniester dispute, including through its cooperation with the OSCE.

President Snegur reviewed the status of negotiations between Moldova and Russia concerning the withdrawal of the Russian 14th Army, noting the importance of the October 1994 framework agreement establishing a three-year withdrawal timetable. President Clinton expressed his expectation that Russia and Moldova would implement the terms of the agreement expeditiously and comprehensively, paying particular attention to the withdrawal of military equipment. The two presidents welcomed the OSCE's constructive role in following the implementation of the withdrawal agreement and searching for a lasting political solution of the problems in the eastern part of Moldova, as called for in last month's OSCE Budapest Summit.

President Clinton and President Snegur noted the great strides made in recent years toward overcoming the division of the European continent and opening the way for closer cooperation among the European states. During President Snegur's visit to the Pentagon, he and Defense Secretary William Perry signed a Joint Statement on Future U.S.-Moldovan Defense and Military Relations. President Clinton welcomed Moldova's decision to participate in the Partnership for Peace, an important component in an emerging new security concept for Europe. Under the Warsaw Initiative, the United States will seek to provide Moldova assistance in the next fiscal year to complement Moldova's own resource commitments for Partnership activities. The two leaders reaffirmed their support for coordinated international efforts, through such structures as the OSCE and the United Nations, to promote peaceful solutions to regional conflicts.

President Clinton and President Snegur expressed the belief that the visit by President Snegur contributed greatly to further strengthening bilateral relations. President Snegur expressed his warm appreciation to President Clinton and the people of the United States for the opportunity to visit.

NOTE: An original was not available for verification of the content of this statement.

Remarks to the National Association of Home Builders
January 30, 1995

Thank you very much. Thank you, Tommy, for your introduction, and thank you for all of the hard work you've done as president and the work you've done with us. I also want to send my best wishes to your new president, Jim Irvine. I look forward to working closely with you, Jim, and with your entire association.

Let me begin by doing something I wasn't supposed to do. You know, my staff told me I didn't have time to stay and answer questions, and then the gentleman who preceded me didn't get a chance to answer the question. So I'll answer it the best I can here off the top of my head with regard to the deficit, because it will set up what I want to talk about in a moment.

When you make your income tax check out in April, about—well, over a third of it will go to pay interest on the national debt, and about 28 cents of it will go to pay interest on the debt accumulated between 1981 and 1993 in January when I took office, in just that 12 years alone.

To give you some idea of the contrast: only about a nickel of your income tax check would be required to pay for welfare and foreign aid put together. So it is a very serious problem. We estimate within a couple of years interest on the debt will be more costly than national defense every year, which is why I've worked so hard on it.

I thought I'd start by answering a question to see if I could get your attention. I was thinking that, as I was being introduced, of a joke I was told by a college president over the Christmas holidays, when she said that she iden-

tified with me when someone said that being a president was a lot like running a cemetery: There are a lot of people under you, but nobody's listening. So I thought I could answer your question and maybe you would.

Let me thank each and every one of you in the National Association of Home Builders for the support you've given to our administration's efforts to get this economy going and to bring the deficit down. Working together, we have made a real difference in the lives of the American people, and I want you to know I appreciate all your hard work to make sure we're a stronger nation as we move into the 21st century and to preserve the American dream, including home ownership for all of our people.

I know Secretary Cisneros spoke with you on Saturday, and I'm especially glad you had a chance to hear from him on my behalf. The efforts he's made at the Department of Housing and Urban Development have been a crucial part of what we've all done together to build up America. Our work is a prime example of the kind of partnership I've tried to build between the public and the private sectors throughout our country. Together, our job is to build a foundation upon which American families can build up their own futures, share in economic prosperity, and keep the American dream alive for another generation.

Our partnership is part of what I have called the New Covenant. When I ran for President, the New Covenant was at the center of my campaign. It's a call for more opportunity and more responsibility, recognizing that you can't really have one without the other and that unless we have more of both, we can't hope to stay strong at home and remain the strongest force for peace and freedom throughout the world.

To build that New Covenant, I've focused on three things that are critical to making sure we succeed in the new global economy: first, empowering our own people to make the most of their own lives; second, expanding opportunity and shrinking and redirecting the Federal bureaucracy to meet the needs of our people today and tomorrow; and finally, shifting more authority to the State and local levels and to the private sector over those things that they can do better than the Federal Government.

The National Association of Home Builders has been a strong partner in many of these efforts. Throughout the life of our Nation, nothing has been more important as a building block of the American dream than home ownership. And that's been especially true in the second half of this century.

Together, we've worked hard to reinforce that foundation and provide new building blocks, and the results show that our partnership is working. Think about your industry first. America had nearly 1.5 million housing starts last year, the best since 1988. Single-family starts totaled nearly 1.2 million; that's a 13 percent increase over the previous year, the best year of performance since 1979.

Beyond the homebuilding industry, we see strong evidence that our partnership is working as well. In contrast to the 4 years before I took office, we've had almost 6 million new jobs in this economy in just 2 years. Nineteen eighty-four gave us the fastest growth in 10 years and the lowest combined rate of unemployment and inflation in 25 years. And for the first time in nearly a decade, America was rated as having the world's most productive and competitive economy.

We're doing all of this because, first and foremost, we've worked to put our economic house in order. Just 2 years ago, it was an open question whether we would find the strength to cut the deficit that had exploded out of control during the previous 12 years and had driven our interest rates up and our economy down.

Together, thanks to people like you, we were able to change that course. We passed an economic package that's bringing the deficit down by more than $600 billion. That's about $10,000

for every family in America. And it's going down 3 years in a row for the first time since Truman was President.

You were one of our biggest supporters in deficit reduction because you knew it would bring down interest rates and you knew it would get our economy going again, and I'll always be grateful for your help on that.

Getting the deficit under control was only a beginning. We've also cut the size of Government and focused its efforts where it can really make a difference in meeting today's and tomorrow's challenges. We've already cut the bureaucracy by more than 100,000, and we're on our way to cutting 272,000 positions over a 5-year period without regard to anything else that happens in this Congress. So the Federal Government is already going to be at its smallest size in 30 years.

Look at HUD. We closed all the regional offices, eliminating an entire layer of bureaucracy. We cut the Department's work force by 10 percent to make their work, and we hope your work, more efficient. And HUD wasn't the only Department. We're closing 1,100 Agricultural Department offices and doing a lot of other things that I think all of you would approve of.

But cutting the Government is only part of the job. We're also making the Government we have work better for our people. We've streamlined many, many programs and given local communities more flexibility to solve problems at the grassroots where they can get the job done most effectively. In the area of welfare reform alone, for example, we have given two dozen States permission to get around cumbersome Federal regulations, to try new and exciting ways to move people from welfare to work.

In the housing field, under the leadership of Secretary Cisneros, the Federal Housing Administration has already lowered costs and changed rules to help home buyers. After the reforms FHA has made, today it takes just 3 to 5 days, not 4 to 6 weeks as it used to, to get an FHA single-family loan endorsement. That's why FHA insured 1.3 million new loans last year, including 450,000 for first-time buyers. That's the second best year in its 60-year history.

Now we're moving to strengthen our efforts. We propose to consolidate 60 different narrowly focused housing programs into three flexible funds. We want to transform the Federal Housing Authority into an entrepreneurial, Government-owned corporation. And we propose phasing out direct subsidies to housing authorities and to end public housing as we know it. Instead of subsidizing bureaucracies, we want to give money directly to residents so that they have the opportunity to take more responsibility for their own lives. This is progress all of us can be proud of. Our partnership is working.

But as much progress as has been made, you and I know it's not enough. Too many people are working harder for less. They have less security, less income, less certainty they can even afford a vacation, much less the downpayment on a new home. That's why I proposed a middle class bill of rights, which could be called and probably should be called the middle class bill of rights and responsibilities because for every opportunity it offers, it requires responsibility in return.

The middle class bill of rights is about ensuring that the American dream stays alive for everyone willing to take responsibility for their future. It will help with your piece of the American dream and with a lot of others as well. To foster more savings and personal responsibility, the middle class bill of rights will enable people to establish individual retirement accounts and then to withdraw from them, tax-free, for the cost of education, health care, the care of a parent, and to buy a first home.

Because of our work in the last 2 years, we've already seen the home ownership rates for young families actually go up for the first time in more than a decade. The middle class bill of rights will help even more Americans to buy a home. It says to our young couples in particular, owning a home is not out of your reach. There is a reason to save and real hope that your hard work and responsibility will pay off for your family.

Education is another critical building block in the strong foundation for our country. And the middle class bill of rights also includes a deduction for education and training costs after high school. That eases the burdens on families by helping them to educate themselves and their children. Furthermore, the middle class bill of rights offers a $500 tax break for families with young children and collapses nearly 70 different Federal job training programs into a grant which will provide for direct vouchers to unemployed workers or low-wage workers who are willing to go back to school and learn more skills so they can earn more money.

Now, all of this will be an important part of keeping the American dream alive. And I should emphasize that this middle class bill of rights is fully paid for by spending cuts and that I will send Congress more than twice as many cuts as are necessary to pay for the middle class bill of rights, so we can keep driving the deficit down.

In the housing field, we want to do even more. As you know, I set a national goal of boosting home ownership to an all-time high by the end of the century, to forge a national home ownership strategy. Secretary Cisneros has been doing a great job to put those goals into action, working with you, with mortgage lenders, with Fannie Mae and Freddie Mac, with the U.S. Conference of Mayors and the National League of Cities, and with national civic organizations and advocacy groups. The strategy will aim to lower regulatory barriers so we can step up construction of starter homes. It will give communities more power to rebuild themselves. And it will give citizens more information so they can take hold of their opportunities.

Secretary Cisneros will submit the strategy to me in March, and I look forward to working with you to act on it and to make the dream a reality for more Americans. The key to our success with this new strategy will be strengthening the same partnership that has served us so well, so far. We've shown how we can succeed for the American people when we work together to bring the deficit down and get the economy going again.

I was eager to talk with you today because I believe that we must recommit ourselves to building a stronger America and to giving our people even more opportunities in the years to come. That's what the new national home ownership strategy is all about. It's what the middle class bill of rights is all about. It's what the New Covenant is all about.

We have to keep the recovery going; we have to increase opportunity; we have to support more responsibility from all of our people. These building blocks will build a stronger future for our children. Together, we've built a strong foundation. This country's in better shape than it was 2 years ago. Now, let's move forward to finish the job for America and for the American people.

Thank you, and God bless you all.

NOTE: The President spoke by satellite at 1:02 p.m. from Room 459 of the Old Executive Office Building to the association's annual convention in Houston, TX. In his remarks, he referred to association president Tommy Thompson.

Message to the Congress Transmitting the Report on Radiation Control for Health and Safety
January 30, 1995

To the Congress of the United States:

In accordance with section 540 of the Federal Food, Drug, and Cosmetic Act (21 U.S.C. 360qq) (previously section 360D of the Public Health Service Act), I am submitting the report of the Department of Health and Human Services regarding the administration of the Radiation Control for Health and Safety Act of 1968 during calendar year 1993.

The report recommends the repeal of section 540 of the Federal Food, Drug, and Cosmetic Act that requires the completion of this annual report. All the information found in this report is available to the Congress on a more immediate basis through the Center for Devices and Radiological Health technical reports, the Radiological Health Bulletin, and other publicly available sources. This annual report serves little useful purpose and diverts Agency resources from more productive activities.

WILLIAM J. CLINTON

The White House,
January 30, 1995.

Message to the Congress Transmitting the Report of the National Institute of Building Sciences
January 30, 1995

To the Congress of the United States:

In accordance with the requirements of section 809 of the Housing and Community Development Act of 1974, as amended (12 U.S.C. 1701j–2(j)), I transmit herewith the annual report of the National Institute of Building Sciences for fiscal year 1993.

WILLIAM J. CLINTON

The White House,
January 30, 1995.

Remarks at the Democratic Governors Association Dinner
January 30, 1995

Thank you very much. I appreciate your enthusiasm. Chris Dodd has that effect on everyone. [*Laughter*] Governor Carnahan and Jean, thank you very much for your service here and for your success tonight. I really would like to say a special word of thanks to my neighbor Mel Carnahan. He helped me when I ran for President. He helped me even when he was in the midst of a tough primary when it could have done him no good at all to be for anybody running for President. But he survived me, and he got elected—[*laughter*]—and then I got elected. We worked together fighting floods, reforming welfare, doing a lot of things, and I am honored to be his friend and his partner.

I want to say a special word of appreciation, too, to the DGA vice chair, Governor Caperton, and Rachel. I have been their friend for a long time, and I'm looking forward to working with them.

I also want to say a personal word of appreciation to your outgoing chair, Evan Bayh, and to Susan. They did unbelievable work with the help of a lot of you in a very, very difficult year, and I will never forget all the efforts Evan Bayh made. And you know, where I grew up, we always say, "It's a long road that doesn't turn." And when the road turns, don't forget that Evan Bayh was there for us when it was tough, and he did his part.

I thank Katy Whelan and Mark Weiner for the wonderful work that they have done for the DGA. They have really been terrific.

I'm sure glad to see all of you. And you're so quiet. You know, over New Year's I was talking to a lot of interesting people, and a lady came up to me who was a college president, and she said, "You know, I really identify with you. Being president is just like running a cemetery. There's a lot of people under you, but nobody's listening." [*Laughter*] Well, I've had that feeling for the last couple of years from time to time, but I think that also is beginning to change. Lord knows, I gave it a good test last Tuesday night in the State of the Union—[*laughter*]—and it turned out the American people were listening.

I want to express my appreciation also to Chris Dodd and to Don Fowler, to Debbie DeLee for leading our Democratic Party. I thank Chris and Don especially for being willing to come on at this time and to help us remember who we are and why we are Democrats and what it is we're supposed to do now, and I thank them. They've done a wonderful job.

You know, there are days when I really miss being a Governor. I loved it. I mean, we also had public housing and security, and people called us by something other than our first names. But nobody ever sprayed the front of the Governor's mansion with an assault weapon or tried to land a plane in my back yard. [*Laughter*] But most days, I am profoundly happy to have the chance to wage these battles, and every day I am honored for the opportunity and the obligation to do it.

You know, it's kind of fashionable now for our colleagues in the other party to quote Franklin Roosevelt. They like his words, you know; it's optimism and hope and everything. And when they do it, they have a little spin on it. They say, "Now, Roosevelt was the right person for his time, and the Democrats were right for their time." If you really read between the lines, they basically say, "Okay, okay, everything that was worth doing in the 20th century, the Democrats did." I agree with that. But their line is something like, "Well, the reason that's so is that in the 20th century we had an industrial age dominated by large, powerful organizations, and we needed a Democratic Party that was the party of National Government to protect the common people and the little children and the elderly and others from abuse by large private organizations. But in the 21st century, the world will be very different. It will be more rapidly changing, more entrepreneurial, less bureaucratic, the age of the PC, not the mainframe." You've heard all that stuff. "And therefore, we don't need the Democrats any more. They're an anachronism. But we like Roosevelt's words."

Well, I say to them, I know the world is changing, and I know we need to reduce the size and reach of much of the Federal Government's activities. As a matter of fact, we started forward with it. But the issue facing America is the issue that has faced America from the beginning and, certainly, the issue that has faced America repeatedly in the 20th century, as we stand at the dawn of a new era. It is still: Can we really guarantee the American dream for all Americans willing to work for it? And can we find ways with all of our incredible differences to come together as a people to do what we have to do? If you go back through the 219 years of American history since the issuance of the Declaration of Independence, you find those challenges over and over and over again. Will we do what it takes to expand the American dream and keep it alive for all of our people? Can we find a way, with all of our differences, to come together, because we know that's the only way we're ever profoundly strong? I say to you that there is still something for the Democratic Party to do.

Consider, consider the differences in their Contract and our Covenant. Consider what is good about what they want to do and what is good about what we want to do and what is sort of open to question, and you will see where we should go. Because there is no question that if we really want to guarantee the American dream in this new economy for all of our people, what we have to do is to empower people to make the most of their own lives, to find a way to continue to enhance opportunity even as we shrink the bureaucracy, and to strengthen our sense of citizenship and community as a fundamental condition of America's security, opportunity, and responsibility.

Yes, yes, yes, we must change the Government. Yes, we have to shrink it. There's 100,000 fewer people working for the Federal Government than there were on the day I became President, and there'll be another 170,000 more leaving if no new laws are passed by this Congress. But what about empowerment? Which party wanted family and medical leave? Which party wanted to immunize all the children in this country against serious disease? Which party said, "We can't afford to keep wasting money on the college loan program. Let's cut the cost of it, make it available to more Americans, and make it cheaper for students"? The Democratic Party did that.

Yes, we should reduce the tax burden on people that are paying all they can afford. You know, that's the only secret I kept from the press the last 2 years. We cut taxes on 15 million working families, kept it a total secret from the American people. [*Laughter*] I'm still trying to figure out how we did it, but it's not too late to let them know.

Yes, we have to do better. But there is the right way to do it. Our middle class bill of rights could more properly be called the bill of rights and responsibilities because you can't get the tax break unless you're trying to raise your kids or educate them or educate yourselves or take care of your families. In other words, we reward, by reducing the tax burden, people who are carrying on the work of citizenship and making the country stronger for everybody. We lower people's taxes and raise their income in the short run in a way that will also raise their income in the long run. That's why we ought to have a tax deduction for education costs after high school. That's why we ought to have an IRA that can be drawn on for education or health care or care of an elderly parent. That's why we ought to lower the cost of raising young children. That's why we ought to collapse all these terrible plethora of programs, and instead of letting people sign up for a Government program, give them a chit worth cash that they

can take to the local community college when they're unemployed or they need job training. Yes, we have some good ideas. Let's cut the taxes, but let's do it in a way that raises the economic power of America in the long run and helps middle class families to build their lives.

And while we're at it, let's not forget that the last time the country got in a total fever over tax cutting, we overdid it, and we wound up with a terrible burden. And the Democrats are not blameless, because then there was a Republican President and a Democratic Congress. And when power is divided, one of two things can happen: You can either share the responsibility and say both have to be responsible and move forward, or you can point the finger of blame and hope that everybody can escape responsibility.

Well, we tried it the second way, folks, and it didn't work out very well. When you make out your checks to the Federal Government to pay taxes in April, remember this: Interest payments on the Federal debt will require the amount equal to 36 percent of your personal income tax. And 27 percent of it, 27 cents, more than a quarter of every dollar you pay to the Federal Government in personal income taxes, will be required to pay interest on the debt run up between 1981 and the day I became President.

So yes, it's okay to cut taxes if we do it in the right way, but let's pay for these tax cuts with spending cuts. Let's don't put more debt on our children and more burdens in that budget.

So, we have an agenda: to empower people, pass the middle class bill of rights and raise the minimum wage and reform the welfare system so people can go to work. And we have an agenda to reduce Government more. The Vice President's coming back with another round of reinventing Government. And we're going to make it smaller, and we're going to have it do better.

Look at the way the emergency management programs work now. I just talked to the homebuilders today in Houston, and I reminded them that Henry Cisneros, since he's been head of the Housing and Urban Development Department, has reduced the size of that Department by 10 percent, eliminated all the regional offices, and cut the time for loan processing from 4 to 6 weeks down to 3 to 5 days. That's a Democratic way of reinventing Government that serves better with less.

You can say, "Well, maybe this won't work." Well, maybe it won't, but it's worked pretty well for 2 years. We have almost 6 million jobs more than we had 2 years ago. We've reduced the debt on our families by over $600 billion, about $10,000 a family. We've seen in the last week that 1994 was our best year economically in terms of growth and in terms of personal income increases in 10 years. And we also had the lowest combined rates of inflation and unemployment—what President Reagan used to call the misery index—the lowest in 1994 it's been in 25 years.

But we have a long way to go, because we all know that our rising tide is not lifting all boats. We know that a lot of people are not doing better economically. We all know there are still challenges ahead. But let's keep our eye on the goal: What's best for the American people? Empower them to compete and win. Do what we can to give them a Government that offers more opportunity with less bureaucracy. And finally, let's not forget that for those who are willing to be responsible, this country is best when it works together, when there's a sense of partnership, a sense of citizenship, a sense of community.

We have worked with innovative Governors in this room and their predecessors in health care, in welfare reform. We've worked with Governors like Governor Chiles, Governor Kitzhaber, Governor Dean on health care reform, and we're not through with that issue. We plead guilty to wanting to get the 40 million Americans, most of them in working families, who can't have health insurance—we think we ought to have it for them, and we think there must be a way to do it that all Americans can agree on. We plead guilty to believing that when people change jobs, they ought not to lose their family's health insurance. We believe that. That's what we believe. And we can do these things in ways that build our community.

Watch the debate on welfare reform. Should we require responsibility? You bet we should. Should we just give people a check forever and a day, no matter how they behave or what they do? No, we shouldn't. No, we shouldn't. But the focus ought to be on liberating people, moving them from welfare to work, moving them from having children to being the best possible parent. It should not be on punishing people

because they're poor or because they made a mistake. If that were the criteria, a bunch of us were once poor, and all of us have made mistakes, and none of us want to be punished for either one.

So, let us approach this welfare debate with a sense of excitement and determination but also a little bit of humility. If anyone knew the answer to this problem, it would have been fixed by now. But the welfare debate embodies all the things that are going on in our culture now: our worry that Government doesn't give us our money's worth; our fear that our profoundest problems are really cultural, not political or economic, that something is amiss in our society and we've got to get our values right again; our deep understanding that we don't really have anybody to waste and when people aren't being as productive as they ought to be, it hurts the rest of us and our economic future as well. All of this is there in this debate.

Now, Saturday we had a very good meeting with Republicans and Democrats from the Congress, from the Governors, from the local governments around the country. And on Friday, I got ready for that meeting by spending an hour with four women who had worked their way off welfare. And I'm telling you, what I heard Friday is what I have heard now for 15 years. The people who know how broke the system is, best, are those who've been on it, who've been trapped by it, who regret it, who've resented it, who struggled and worked and slaved to get out of it. It is that that we should tap into.

We are the party of change. We brought the deficit down. We reduced the size of the Government. We put welfare reform and health care reform and aggressive, expansive trade on the world's agenda and on America's agenda. It was our administration that first had a Commerce Secretary like Ron Brown that went around selling American products all over the world, not the Republicans.

So I say, let's extend the hand of partnership to those in the other party. Let's say, "We hear you. You want to reduce the size of Government? You want to reduce regulation? You want to give more authority to the States? You want to privatize those things which can be privatized? So do we."

But our contract is a covenant. We want to create opportunity, not just bash Government. We want children to have a future no matter where they come from, what their roots are, what their disabilities are by virtue of their birth. We believe that America works best when everybody's got a chance at the brass ring. That is our credo, and it will always be. And that's why the Democrats are coming back.

Thank you, and God bless you all.

NOTE: The President spoke at 9:06 p.m. at the Omni Shoreham Hotel. In his remarks, he referred to Gov. Mel Carnahan of Missouri and his wife, Jean; Gov. Gaston Caperton of West Virginia and his wife, Rachel; Gov. Evan Bayh of Indiana and his wife, Susan; Katherine Whelan, executive director, and Mark Weiner, treasurer, Democratic Governors Association; Gov. Lawton Chiles of Florida; Gov. John Kitzhaber of Oregon; Gov. Howard Dean of Vermont; and Democratic National Committee officers Senator Christopher Dodd, general chairman, Donald Fowler, national chairman, and Debra DeLee, former interim chair.

Letter on Withdrawal of the Nomination of Robert Pastor To Be Ambassador to Panama
January 27, 1995

Dear Bob:

I received with regret your request that I not resubmit your nomination as Ambassador to Panama to the Senate. I am certain that you would have served your country with great distinction and honor in that important post.

Throughout your career you have made important contributions to American foreign policy in Latin America and the Caribbean. During your service on the National Security Council, you helped to fashion a human rights policy consistent with fundamental American values that advanced the cause of freedom throughout the hemisphere. At the Carter Center, you have continued to foster democracy and peace with great skill and dedication, most recently contributing to the restoration of democracy in Haiti.

I applaud you for these outstanding contributions and look forward to your continuing advice and assistance.

Sincerely,

BILL CLINTON

NOTE: This letter was released by the Office of the Press Secretary on January 31.

Message to the Congress on Libya
January 30, 1995

To the Congress of the United States:

I hereby report to the Congress on the developments since my last report of July 18, 1994, concerning the national emergency with respect to Libya that was declared in Executive Order No. 12543 of January 7, 1986. This report is submitted pursuant to section 401(c) of the National Emergencies Act, 50 U.S.C. 1641(c); section 204(c) of the International Emergency Economic Powers Act (IEEPA), 50 U.S.C. 1703(c); and section 505(c) of the International Security and Development Cooperation Act of 1985, 22 U.S.C. 2349aa–9(c).

1. On December 22, 1994, I renewed for another year the national emergency with respect to Libya pursuant to IEEPA. This renewal extended the current comprehensive financial and trade embargo against Libya in effect since 1986. Under these sanctions, all trade with Libya is prohibited, and all assets owned or controlled by the Libyan government in the United States or in the possession or control of U.S. persons are blocked.

2. There has been one amendment to the Libyan Sanctions Regulations, 31 C.F.R. Part 550 (the "Regulations"), administered by the Office of Foreign Assets Control (FAC) of the

Department of the Treasury, since my last report on July 18, 1994. The amendment (59 Fed. Reg. 51106, October 7, 1994) identified Arab Hellenic Bank (AHB), an Athens-based financial institution, 4 other entities, and 10 individuals as Specially Designated Nationals (SDNs) of Libya. (In addition to the recent SDN action against AHB, the Greek central bank has recently announced that AHB's banking license has been revoked.) Included among the individuals are three Italian shareholders in Oilinvest (Netherlands) B.V., who increased their positions in the Libyan government-controlled firm shortly before United Nations Security Council Resolution (UNSCR) 883 directed a freeze on certain Libyan assets owned or controlled by the Government or public authorities of Libya.

Pursuant to section 550.304(a) of the Regulations, FAC has determined that these entities and individuals designated as SDNs are owned or controlled by, or acting or purporting to act directly or indirectly on behalf of, the Government of Libya, or are agencies, instrumentalities, or entities of that government. By virtue of this determination, all property and interests in property of these entities or persons that are in the United States or in the possession or control of U.S. persons are blocked. Further, U.S. persons are prohibited from engaging in transactions with these individuals or entities unless the transactions are licensed by FAC. The designations were made in consultation with the Department of State and announced by FAC in notices issued on June 17 and July 22 and 25, 1994. A copy of the amendment is attached to this report.

3. During the current 6-month period, FAC made numerous decisions with respect to applications for licenses to engage in transactions under the Regulations, issuing 136 licensing determinations—both approvals and denials. Consistent with FAC's ongoing scrutiny of banking transactions, the largest category of license approvals (73) concerned requests by non-Libyan persons or entities to unblock bank accounts initially blocked because of an apparent Government of Libya interest. The largest category of denials (41) was for banking transactions in which FAC found a Government of Libya interest. Three licenses were issued authorizing intellectual property protection in Libya.

In addition, FAC issued eight determinations with respect to applications from attorneys to receive fees and reimbursement of expenses for provision of legal services to the Government of Libya in connection with wrongful death civil actions arising from the Pan Am 103 bombing. Civil suits have been filed in the U.S. District Court for the District of Columbia and in the Southern District of New York. Representation of the Government of Libya when named as a defendant in or otherwise made a party to domestic U.S. legal proceedings is authorized by section 550.517(b)(2) of the Regulations under certain conditions.

4. During the current 6-month period, FAC continued to emphasize to the international banking community in the United States the importance of identifying and blocking payments made by or on behalf of Libya. The FAC worked closely with the banks to implement new interdiction software systems to identify such payments. As a result, during the reporting period, more than 210 transactions involving Libya, totaling more than $14.8 million, were blocked. As of December 9, 1994, 13 of these transactions had been licensed to be released, leaving a net amount of more than $14.5 million blocked.

Since my last report, FAC collected 15 civil monetary penalties totaling more than $76,000 for violations of the U.S. sanctions against Libya. Nine of the violations involved the failure of banks to block funds transfers to Libyan-owned or -controlled banks. Two other penalties were received for corporate export violations. Four additional penalties were paid by U.S. citizens engaging in Libyan oilfield-related transactions while another 76 cases of similar violations are in active penalty processing.

In October 1994, two U.S. businessmen, two U.S. corporations, and several foreign corporations were indicted by a Federal grand jury in Connecticut on three counts of violating the Regulations and IEEPA for their roles in the illegal exportation of U.S. origin fuel pumps to Libya. Various enforcement actions carried over from previous reporting periods have continued to be aggressively pursued. The FAC has continued its efforts under the Operation Roadblock initiative. This ongoing program seeks to identify U.S. persons who travel to and/or work in Libya in violation of U.S. law.

Several new investigations of potentially significant violations of the Libyan sanctions have been initiated by FAC and cooperating U.S. law enforcement agencies, primarily the U.S. Customs Service. Many of these cases are believed to involve complex conspiracies to circumvent the various prohibitions of the Libyan sanctions, as well as the utilization of international diversionary shipping routes to and from Libya. The FAC has continued to work closely with the Departments of State and Justice to identify U.S. persons who enter into contracts or agreements with the Government of Libya, or other third-country parties, to lobby United States Government officials or to engage in public relations work on behalf of the Government of Libya without FAC authorization. In addition, during the period FAC hosted or attended several bilateral and multilateral meetings with foreign sanctions authorities, as well as with private foreign sanctions institutions, to consult on issues of mutual interest and to encourage strict adherence to the U.N.-mandated sanctions.

5. The expenses incurred by the Federal Government in the 6-month period from July 7, 1994, through January 6, 1995, that are directly attributable to the exercise of powers and authorities conferred by the declaration of the Libyan national emergency are estimated at approximately $1.4 million. Personnel costs were largely centered in the Department of the Treasury (particularly in the Office of Foreign Assets Control, the Office of the General Counsel, and the U.S. Customs Service), the Department of State, and the Department of Commerce.

6. The policies and actions of the Government of Libya continue to pose an unusual and extraordinary threat to the national security and foreign policy of the United States. In adopting

UNSCR 883 in November 1993, the Security Council determined that the continued failure of the Government of Libya to demonstrate by concrete actions its renunciation of terrorism, and in particular its continued failure to respond fully and effectively to the requests and decisions of the Security Council in UNSCRs 731 and 748, concerning the bombing of the Pan Am 103 and UTA 772 flights, constituted a threat to international peace and security. The United States continues to believe that still stronger international measures than those mandated by UNSCR 883, possibly including a worldwide oil embargo, should be imposed if Libya continues to defy the will of the international community as expressed in UNSCR 731. We remain determined to ensure that the perpetrators of the terrorist acts against Pan Am 103 and UTA 772 are brought to justice. The families of the victims in the murderous Lockerbie bombing and other acts of Libyan terrorism deserve nothing less. I shall continue to exercise the powers at my disposal to apply economic sanctions against Libya fully and effectively, so long as those measures are appropriate, and will continue to report periodically to the Congress on significant developments as required by law.

WILLIAM J. CLINTON

The White House,
January 30, 1995.

NOTE: This message was released by the Office of the Press Secretary on January 31.

Remarks to the National Governors' Association Conference
January 31, 1995

Thank you very much, Governor Dean, Governor Thompson, fellow Governors, and ladies and gentlemen. It's a pleasure for me to be back here. I have enjoyed our visits in this meeting. I was delighted to have you at the White House on Sunday evening, and I have very, very much enjoyed our discussion yesterday, our discussions of welfare reform and a whole range of other issues.

Last year, you may remember, when I was here, Governor Carroll Campbell and I both

lost our voices before our talks, making collectively millions of people in both parties happy. [*Laughter*] Unfortunately for you, I am fully recovered this year, and I would like to begin, if I might, by thanking you for your vote just a few moments ago on the Mexico stabilization package. I want to underline the critical nature of the financial problem in Mexico. All of you understand it, and I applaud your vote across party and especially across regional lines, because a number of you are not in the moment as directly affected as others are.

This crisis poses, however, great risks to our workers, to our economy, and to the global economy, and it poses these risks now. We must act now. It has gotten worse day by day since I asked for legislative action about 2 weeks ago. Rather than face further delay, I met with the congressional leadership this morning and told them that I will act under my executive authority, and I have asked for their full support. We cannot risk further delay, and I tell you today, frankly, that your strong support is very, very helpful and very welcome.

The situation in Mexico continues to worsen. But the leadership advised me that while they believe Congress will or, at least, might well eventually act, it will not do so immediately. And therefore, it will not do so in time. Because Congress cannot act now, I have worked with other countries to prepare a new package. As proposed now, it will consist of a $20 billion share from the United States Exchange Stabilization Fund, which we can authorize by executive action without a new act of Congress; $17.5 billion from the International Monetary Fund; and in addition to that, there will be a short-term lending facility of $10 billion from the Bank of International Settlements. That means that in the aggregate we will be able to have an action that is potentially even more aggressive than the $40 billion one I originally proposed, with more of the load being taken by international institutions and our trading partners around the world, which I applaud, but with a significant part of the burden still being borne by the United States.

This is in the interest of America, contrary to what some have said, not because there are large financial interests at stake but because there are thousands of jobs, billions of dollars of American exports at stake, the potential of an even more serious illegal immigration problem, the spread of financial instability to other countries in our hemisphere and indeed to other developing countries throughout the world, and the potential of a more serious narcotics trafficking problem. All these things are at stake in the Mexican crisis, and therefore, I will act to protect our interests. I have asked the bipartisan leadership of Congress to support these actions, and I hope and believe they will at some later point today.

The risks of inaction are greater than the risks of decisive action. Do I know for sure that this action will solve all the problems? I do not. Do I believe it will? I do. Am I virtually certain that if we do nothing, it will get much, much worse in a hurry? I am. This is the right thing to do. You have understood it, and I thank you very, very much for your vote a few moments ago.

Since our first meeting 2 years ago, we have enjoyed unprecedented cooperation, which have included 7 major waivers in the health care reform area and 24 in the welfare reform area, a partnership and a successful fight for the crime bill last year which, as you know, reduces the Federal Government and gives all the money back to State and local communities to fight crime at the grassroots level. We have had innovative and more comprehensive agreements with the States of West Virginia and Indiana in the area of children and families and the remarkable agreement that we signed recently with the State of Oregon and seven of our Cabinet Secretaries, ending Federal micromanagement across a whole range of areas in return for the statement by the State of Oregon of clear goals and performance measures for the future.

This is the kind of thing that we need to be doing more of. It is the kind of thing that I believe we are in the process of doing on welfare reform. I was informed of the Speaker's remarks just a few moments before I came here, and I applaud them, and I think we have a real chance now to have a partnership between the White House and the Congress, the Governors, and others who care deeply about this issue.

Our next goal must be to dramatically restructure the relationship between the Federal Government and the States, to create a stronger partnership on behalf of our people that goes to the heart of what I have called the New Covenant of opportunity and responsibility. I believe the Federal Government's job is to expand opportunity and shrink bureaucracy. And therefore, I think it is clearly the thing for us to do to try to shift more responsibility to the States, to the localities, and where appropriate, to the private sector and therefore give you the opportunity to solve problems, working with your people, that have eluded all of us for too long.

The system we inherited was based, fundamentally, on a kind of a benign distrust, from an era when, let's face it, in decades past, States might not have always done what they should have done to protect their citizens. As a Southerner, I can tell you that I don't know what we'd have done if the Federal Government hadn't been willing to take some of the actions that it took in civil rights and in some other areas to help poor children in my State and others.

So we cannot and we need not condemn the past to say that the whole nature and character of State government, the expertise that's there, the knowledge that's there, the connections that are there with volunteer groups, with community groups, with the nonprofit groups, is totally different than it used to be. And the nature of the work to be done and the problems to be solved are different than they used to be. Therefore, the system we have inherited needs a searching re-examination, and where it is yesterday's Government and not tomorrow's, it ought to be changed.

We have tackled this problem with energy and with some success. We have done it with real support from the Cabinet and some opposition from some within the bureaucracy that have been there through Republican and Democratic administrations alike and some in our Congress who have questions about what we are doing.

But I have spent too many years of my life around this table to have forgotten what I learned there. I think I came to this office with a profound understanding of the challenges that you have faced in working with the Federal Government. To build on that understanding is part of the reinventing Government initiative. The Vice President, who came with me here today for this announcement because he's worked so hard to make it possible, has talked literally to thousands of State and local government workers, and they have been among the most helpful in shaping our reinvention blueprint.

The message is loud and clear: They want us to stop the micromanagement, trust them to do their jobs, hold them accountable for results where Federal money and national interests are involved. That's why we wish to create a new Federal Government and a new partnership, based on trust and accountability. You know better than anyone that a great deal of what our National Government does is already

carried out by States, by counties, by cities. That's why we must change the relationship and trust them more. I believe we should ship decisionmaking, responsibility, and resources from bureaucracies in Washington to communities, to States, and where we can, directly to individuals.

Part of my job is to keep pushing the focus of the National Government back to grassroots America, where we can solve so many of our problems more effectively. We have begun that work first by cutting the size of the Federal Government. We have already cut over a quarter of a trillion dollars in spending, more than 300 domestic programs, more than 100,000 positions from the Federal bureaucracy. Those cuts will ultimately total, if no more laws or budgets are passed, more than 270,000, making, when the process is finished, your Federal Government the smallest it has been since the Kennedy administration.

But cutting Government isn't enough. We also have to make it work better, and we've done that too, in many ways. We streamlined the Agriculture Department, closing 1,200 field offices. We've moved FEMA from being a disaster to helping people in disasters. The Department of Transportation worked with private businesses and helped to rebuild southern California's fractured freeways in record time and under budget, also with a partnership from the State, by changing the laws and the procedures and making it work. We've cut an SBA loan form from an inch thick to a single page. We've cut the time it takes to get an FHA loan endorsement from 4 to 6 weeks to 3 to 5 days. We've reformed the procurement system of the Government so that Governments can buy the way businesses do, putting an end to the Vice President's opportunity to go on the Letterman show and break $10 ashtrays that ought to cost a dollar and a half. [*Laughter*] We have reformed the college loan system. The direct loan program will literally save the taxpayers billions of dollars, lower interest rates and fees, and improve repayment schedules for students, and lower paperwork, bureaucratic time for our institutions of higher education.

Much of this work is simple common sense. The Bureau of Reclamation used to require 20 people to sign off on building special fish ladders in northern California, taking 3½ years. The fish were dead by then. But at least the ladder was approved. Well, we removed 18 approval layers and cut the time down to 6 months, in time for the fish to spawn, to their great relief. [*Laughter*] I say this to make the point that a lot of this is common sense and an enormous amount of this still remains to be done.

I suppose I have gotten more comments from you in these last 2 days, pro and con, about the process of Federal regulation than anything else. Some of you have said, "Well, I'm getting better cooperation from the EPA than ever before. Thank you very much." Others have said, "What the policy is sounds good, but there's nothing happening in our State to make it better." And we have a long way to go, but we can do this. And we ought to do it not simply with general rhetoric but also taking these issues one by one by one, until we make it right.

I've asked the Vice President in phase two of his review to continue to shrink Federal departments, and we're making sure that the remaining Government will be more economical, more entrepreneurial, less bureaucratic, and less dictatorial.

A year ago I signed an Executive order to encourage creative partnerships with the private sector in the ownership, financing, and construction of infrastructure, responding to your insistence that you needed the same kind of flexibility the private sector has when you raise funds for major infrastructure projects. Today I'm happy to say that Secretary Peña is announcing a series of 35 new infrastructure projects in 21 States that will mobilize almost $2 billion in investment capital to build roads, bridges, and other infrastructure, relying on trust and accountability, not rules and bureaucracy.

Tens of thousands of new jobs will be created this year, not by rocket science but by simply adopting the financing techniques the private sector uses all the time. We wouldn't have any of these projects if we followed the old rules and allowed them to get in the way of innovation. In the budget I'm submitting to Congress, I will propose turning this approach into national policy by building performance partnerships with State and local governments. We want to consolidate categorical funding and call on you to take responsibility for meeting the performance standards. Trust and accountability are the foundation of these new partnerships. We have to trust you, our partners, to make the right choices in spending public funds. And even though you'll have more flexibility to solve your

problems, you must be held accountable for how you spend the Federal money.

I'm excited because this approach gives us a new opportunity to work together, to move forward. On Saturday, Governor Engler captivated the Nation by rolling out a list of 335 programs on parchment, sacred programs he wanted to put in the block grant, that he could write on a piece of notepaper. He didn't know it, but next week, we want to announce plans that we've worked on for months to consolidate 271 programs into 27 performance partnerships. And a lot of those were on Governor Engler's list. I'd like to help him cut it shorter. [*Applause*] Thank you.

One of those I've already announced is the new performance partnership for education and job training, part of our middle class bill of rights. We propose to collapse 70 separate programs to make them more efficient and effective, a "GI bill" for America's workers, who need new skills to meet the demands of changing times. State and local governments will have broad flexibility to help meet those needs, but we propose not just to give this money back to State training programs but instead to let the workers themselves get a voucher and choose where they want to go. Almost every American is now within driving distance of a community college or some other kind of high training program with a proven rate of success far better than anything we need to design. So we ought to put more power not only back to the local level but also directly into the hands of citizens for the purposes that are plainly in the national interest.

In public health, we want to consolidate 108 programs into 16 performance partnerships, to abolish a dozen environmental grants and give you more power to achieve environmental goals. And I guess in parenthesis, I thank Governor Carper for his repeated lectures to me on that subject, citing the Delaware example. We want to continue to combine the 60 HUD programs into 3. The Federal Government has worked in one way for decades. Now it is time to try a new way, a way that is proven in its performance in the private sector. It's time for these and other changes, and many of them are drawn directly from your own experience in your own laboratories of democracy.

When our country was founded, the Founders rejected Government based on central control and distrust of people. Our Constitution provides a few profound guiding principles. It puts deep trust in the American people to use their common sense to create a shared vision, not a centralized vision, and to give life to those ideals. We have to take advantage of this rare moment to renew that idea, to reshape the relationship between the National Government and the States. The American people have voted twice in the last two elections for dramatic change in the way our country works. They want more for their money: better schools, safer streets, better roads, a clean environment. But they want a greater say in how this work is done, and they don't want the Federal Government to do what can better be done by private citizens themselves or by government that is closer to them.

They also have a deep feeling about our national commitment and our national responsibilities and our national interest, the things like the welfare of our children, the future of our economy, our obligations to our seniors. They know that we can meet these national obligations and pursue our national interest with a dramatic devolution of power and responsibility and opportunity to the State governments of this land. I look forward to making all this happen with you.

Thank you very much.

NOTE: The President spoke at 11:15 a.m. at the J.W. Marriot Hotel. In his remarks, he referred to Governors Howard Dean of Vermont, Tommy G. Thompson of Wisconsin, Carroll W. Campbell of South Carolina, John Engler of Michigan, and Tom Carper of Delaware.

Statement With Congressional Leaders on Financial Assistance to Mexico
January 31, 1995

We agree that, in order to ensure orderly exchange arrangements and a stable system of exchange rates, the United States should immediately use the Exchange Stabilization Fund (ESF) to provide appropriate financial assistance for Mexico. We further agree that under Title 31 of the United States Code, Section 5302, the President has full authority to provide this assistance. Because the situation in Mexico raises unique and emergency circumstances, the required assistance to be extended will be available for a period of more than 6 months in any 12-month period.

The United States will impose strict conditions on the assistance it provides with the goal of ensuring that this package imposes no cost on U.S. taxpayers. We are pleased that other nations have agreed to increase their support. Specifically, the International Monetary Fund today agreed to increase its participation by $10 billion for a total of $17.8 billion. In addition, central banks of a number of industrial countries through the Bank for International Settlements have increased their participation by $5 billion for a total of $10 billion.

We must act now in order to protect American jobs, prevent an increased flow of illegal immigrants across our borders, ensure stability in this hemisphere, and encourage reform in emerging markets around the world.

This is an important undertaking, and we believe that the risks of inaction vastly exceed any risks associated with this action. We fully support this effort, and we will work to ensure that its purposes are met.

We have agreed to act today.

NOTE: The statement was announced jointly with Newt Gingrich, Speaker of the House of Representatives; Bob Dole, Senate majority leader; Thomas Daschle, Senate minority leader; Richard Armey, House majority leader; and Richard Gephardt, House minority leader.

Statement on the Terrorist Attack in Algeria
January 31, 1995

The United States condemns in the strongest possible terms the terrible atrocity in Algiers yesterday which took the lives of dozens of innocent Algerians and wounded hundreds more. On behalf of the American people, I want to express my deepest sympathy to the Government of Algeria and to the families of the victims. Such indiscriminate and senseless terror cannot be excused or justified. It can only serve to deepen the profound crisis and increase the suffering through which Algeria is now living.

This outrage comes just one week after a similar terrorist bombing in Israel. Whether in Netanya or Algiers, extremism, violence, and terror must not silence the voices of those who work for peace and reconciliation. It is our profound hope that reason and dialog can transcend violence and hate and that a better future can be realized for all the people of Algeria.

Statement on the Observance of Ramadan
January 31, 1995

I want to offer my greetings and sincere best wishes on the occasion of the holy month of Ramadan.

The crescent moon symbolizes Islam and with the sighting of the crescent which heralds Ramadan millions of Americans will join Muslims around the world in observing this most sacred of times. During the next month, those who follow the Islamic religion will fast and abstain from the normal routines of life in order to better devote themselves to understanding and following their faith. It is a time not just for inward reflection but for rededication to the needs of the wider community and the requirement of service to others.

At this time of spiritual peace, when recognition of the ties which bind people of good will is paramount, it is fitting to recall the strides which have been taken to bring peace to the Middle East. As enemies reconcile and dialog replaces confrontation, this is a time for reflection on the hopes and dreams of a better life and a better world shared by those of all faiths.

Let us take pride in what has been accomplished toward realization of this noble vision. But for the sake of our children—our future—let us all renew our determination and work to make this moment of peace a lasting testament to a more peaceful world for all.

NOTE: Ramadan began on February 1.

Remarks and a Question-and-Answer Session With the Mayor's Youth Council in Boston, Massachusetts
January 31, 1995

The President. Let me just begin by—let me make a couple of comments, and then I'll answer your questions. First, I want to congratulate all of you and the mayor on this remarkable project. I wanted to do this for a couple of reasons, but one is I think this might spread across the country as more people, through the news media, hear about it. I think this is a wonderful idea that every city in the country could profit from copying.

I also want to say I'm glad to be here with your mayor, with Mrs. Menino, but also with Senator Kennedy and Senator Kerry, who flew up here with me from Washington. We're going to dinner tonight, but they wanted to come over here and see you. And I think that's a great tribute to you and what you're doing.

Let's talk about the dropout rate a little bit and especially as it applies to teen parents. This is a big issue. We've just been discussing this down in Washington now as a part of what we call the New Covenant. You mentioned that. The New Covenant is, for me, the obligation that we have to create more opportunity and people and citizens have to exercise more responsibility. It means that we in Government have to try to help give you the tools you need to make the most of your own lives and then all of you have to do the most you can with your lives and help your fellow citizens. That's the big reason I wanted to come here today, because I think it's so remarkable that you're committed to doing this.

Now, we know that a lot of people who have children drop out of school, and one of the things I said to the Nation and to the Congress the other night in my speech is that as we reform the welfare system our goal ought to be to prepare people to go to work, to get them in jobs, to keep them in jobs, and to do it in a way that helps them be better parents. So what I'm trying to do is to work with the States all across the country to structure welfare systems where there are always incentives for young people to stay in school and, if they have little children, that the children should be given appropriate child care and other kinds of support.

And I think one of the things that you can do is to hammer home to people that if they can, if they have enough to get by, they ought to stay in high school before they leave and go to work, because in the world that we're living in, all the people who live in Boston and all the people who live in Massachusetts are competing with people all around the world for jobs and for income. And there's been a huge decline in the earnings of younger workers who are high school dropouts. When you make adjustments for inflation and the cost of living going up year in and year out, younger workers without a high school education are making probably 20 percent less than they were just 10 or 15 years ago.

So you need to go out and tell people, look, I know it's hard right now, but you need to be thinking about the long run. One of the things we've got to do that you can do for your peers, for other young people, that I can't do

as well as you can, is say to people, "Hey, the future is not what happens in an hour, it's not what happens tomorrow, it's not what happens next week. It's what happens 5 years from now or 10 years from now." And you'll always have to think about not just now but the future. You've got to always be thinking about your future. That's what you have to do when you're young. And I know it's hard when you've got a lot of responsibilities and a lot of problems, but we have simply got to get more of our young people to realize that if they don't stay in school, then the future won't be what it otherwise could be.

[*At this point, a participant stated the need for stronger laws to punish people who sell guns to children.*]

The President. Well, in the crime bill that we passed last year we stiffened penalties under Federal law for all gun-related offenses, particularly those that affect young people. And I see it already, we get reports, I get reports from the U.S. attorneys around the country that they're beginning to bring cases under all these new laws with stronger penalties. What I think you need to look at is the fact that most laws that deter crime are passed in the State level, by the State legislature. And most laws then have to be implemented as a matter of policy by local police organizations. So what I think you need to do is to have someone who knows more about that than I do give you a report on what the laws are in Massachusetts and evaluate whether you think the laws are strong enough, then look and see if you think they're being properly enforced.

And let me make one other point, because this goes back to something you can do. I've worked in the area of law enforcement longer than most of you have been alive. I was elected attorney general in my State in 1976. I took office in January of 1977. And I have seen the crime wave rise and fall and rise and fall in my home area.

I lived in a neighborhood, a real old neighborhood in Little Rock when I was the Governor of my State. And I saw the crime rate rise and fall, rise and fall. And the most important thing that drove the crime rate down was neighborhood councils like this council. If there were citizens groups working the neighborhood, working with the police, calling the police when there were strangers in the area, calling police when they said there are people here selling guns to kids, there are people here pedaling guns out of the back of their cars, it was amazing how much the crime rate could be driven down.

So I think you should look at the laws at the State level, talk to the mayor's people here at the local level about how they're being implemented but also see whether or not the young people are willing to organize themselves in these neighborhood councils in the high-crime areas. I'm telling you, it does more than anything else I've ever seen to lower crime.

[*A participant asked how the President could help influence the media to present a more positive image of young people.*]

The President. I don't know that I'm the best one to ask about negative portrayals. [*Laughter*] I tell you—well, one thing about being here, I think it helps, and I came here because you're doing something positive, and it's newsworthy, and it's different. If you want some advice about it, I'll tell you—I'll give you my advice. I think you have to follow the same advice that Senator Kennedy or Senator Kerry or Mayor Menino or the President has to follow. You have to always be looking for new ways to manifest the idea that most young people are good, most young people are in school, most young people are obeying the law, most young people care about their friends and neighbors. And every time you do something to manifest that, then that's new. That is—let me just give it to you in crass terms, because you can't blame them for this. If you start a program and it's a good program and you do it every day for 2 years, it's an important thing to do, but it may only be news the day you start it and then when you have your anniversary. But every time somebody holds up a liquor store or shoots somebody on the street, that's a new and different story. See what I mean?

So you may—you've got a lot more good people, but it might not be a new thing. So I think one of the things you ought to do is to think about, in this youth council, how many different things are now going on in Boston that are good news, that show young people in a positive light. And how many of them have been written about in the papers? How many of them have been on the local news? What can you do to get the positive story out there?

And you ought to have one person on your council who's job it is to always be thinking of some new thing you're doing that hasn't yet been portrayed. And what you will find is that over time—you can't turn this around overnight—but over time, if you're steady about it, you will slowly balance the scales, and people will say, "Hey, we've got a problem, but most of our kids are good kids."

[*A participant asked if the President would give priority to school-to-work programs.*]

The President. The answer is, I will. And you have to ask the Congress to do the same. Senator Kennedy and Senator Kerry and I were talking on the way up here. We have cut a lot of spending from the Federal budget, a lot. But we've tried to spend more money on education and on job training programs, starting with Head Start and including more affordable college loans and these school-to-work programs, which train young people to move into jobs and get education while they're doing it. And we're just now—we just started that program last year, and we're just now expanding it. And I'm really hoping that the new Congress will agree to this approach. Cut the inessential spending, but put more money into education, because that's really the key to our economic future as a country.

[*A participant stated that many afterschool programs to keep children away from drugs and gangs were oriented toward boys rather than girls and asked about planned support for such programs.*]

The President. Well, most of those decisions have to be made by the local school districts and the local communities. What we do is to try to provide the funds, like, for example, in the crime bill, one of the more controversial parts of the crime bill were the funds that Congress voted for and that I supported to provide cities, for example, monies that they could use in afterschool programs and other preventive programs, to try to give young people something positive to do.

The content of those programs, exactly whether there are enough programs for girls and they're as good and fair as the ones for boys and all that, all those are things that you have to work out here. So my answer to you is, that's what this youth council's for. You should—if the city controls the programs, talk to the city about it. If there are local groups who make the decision, but they don't work for the mayor, call them into your council and ask them to come testify. Tell them what you don't like about the program.

In other words, use the power of this council. You're talking about making news; you've got a forum now. Next time you call a council meeting, these folks will come cover you. I won't have to be here. [*Laughter*] The mayor won't have to be here. And bring them in and say, "Look, these afterschool programs are fine, but they're not good enough. There's this preconception that only boys need it, and girls do, too, and here's what we need." You ought to use the power of this council. You ought to think about everything you would change in here, in this community, if you could wave a magic wand, and remember that you have a public forum to do it. Now, that's what the mayor's giving you.

Q. Mr. President, I was just wondering if you—I was recently accepted at Oxford, and I was just wondering if you could tell me what it's like over there. [*Laughter*]

Mayor Thomas Menino. Tell him what high school you went to. Tell them the background of high school.

Q. I go to ACC, Another Course to College, which is a high school—[*inaudible*]——

The President. And you're going to—and you're to start over there next year?

Q. Yes.

The President. What college will you be in?

Q. [*Inaudible*]

The President. Good for you. I know right where it is. I think you'll like it a lot. They're very nice people. The programs generally involve more reading and more essay writing and less conventional classroom work than the American programs do, so that young people coming out of American high schools, even out of very good programs, sometimes have to work harder to sort of discipline themselves to do more reading alone. So you'll have to find some friends and make sure that you do all that, because in general the system requires you to do more work on your own. But when you come back you'll be a greater writer. You'll be able to write real well.

[*Mayor Menino asked the participant to explain the ACC program.*]

The President. What do you want her to say, Mayor? [*Laughter*]

[*The mayor indicated that the participant was reluctant to talk about her accomplishment.*]

The President. You're being very modest, that's what he's saying.

[*The mayor stated that the young woman had achieved a goal that few students attain. Another participant then described the ACC program.*]

The President. So they did prepare you well, didn't they? [*Laughter*]

Who's next?

[*A participant stated the need for more police officers trained to deal with the various cultures in the cities. The mayor then thanked the President and the Massachusetts Senators for obtaining funding for a program to put bilingual police officers in Boston.*]

The President. It's a huge challenge, though, because a lot of our urban areas now have so many different racial and ethnic groups. Los Angeles County, our country's biggest county, in one county alone, have people from over 150 different racial and ethnic groups.

So it's going to be a big challenge for us to make sure we train our police officers not just in the language but also in the ways of thinking of people, because it's so easy for people who have different ways of relating to each other to misunderstand one another. And it's very important that our police officers get that kind of training. We're going to have to work hard on that.

[*The mayor discussed several city programs teaching English as a second language. A participant then conveyed her father's message regarding the November 1994 elections, "This too shall pass."*]

The President. I'm glad to hear that. Tell your dad he can send me a message anytime. [*Laughter*]

[*The participant asked the President to urge colleges to create scholarship programs targeting inner-city youth, as Northeastern University had done in Boston. The mayor then described Northeastern's participation in and enhancement of a city financial aid program.*]

The President. First of all, let me say I applaud Northeastern for doing it, because the cost of a college education has gone up quite a lot in the last several years. And I'm doing what I can to make it more affordable.

Let me tell you the two things that we have done and what we've tried to get others to do as well. The first thing we did was to take the existing student loan programs and Congress passed a bill that enables us to let that student loan program be administered in a different way, directly by colleges like Northeastern, so that the interest rates would be lower, the costs would be lower, and your repayment terms would be better. A lot of young people don't want to borrow money to go to college because they think, gee, if I get out and I just make a modest wage, I won't even be able to repay the loan. So under the new rules, you can borrow money to go to college, and then you can limit the amount of your repayment every year to a certain percentage of your income. So we've made available more loans.

In addition to that, through the national service program—you see a lot of these young people in the city or around here, some of them are affiliated with our national service program, and they're earning almost $5,000 a year for every year they work in the service program for their college education. Now, what we've done is to try to challenge the colleges and universities around the country to match that. And this year, I'm trying to pass, and I hope the Congress will pass, a bill that provides for the deduction from a person's income taxes for the cost of paying tuition to any institution of education after high school, 2-year or 4-year.

So these are the things I'm trying to do to make college more affordable. When we do these things, that makes it more possible for colleges like Northeastern to go out and take their own initiatives and to do more. Like that has to be done basically State by State and college by college, because as the President, what I have to do is to try to set up a network of things that will work everywhere in the country.

[*The mayor indicated that many law firms in Massachusetts had set up programs to help young people go to college.*]

The President. It's the best money you'll ever spend.

[*A participant thanked the President for his efforts to help college-bound youth obtain financial aid.*]

The President. Well, I thank you. But let me just say one other thing about this. You know,

I said this before in a different way. Having a college education has always been an advantage. When Senator Kerry and Senator Kennedy and I went to college, it was an advantage. But it's a much bigger advantage today than ever before, because in the information age, there are fewer jobs that you can perform with no education and just a willingness to work hard.

It's also true—I want to emphasize this because one of you talked about this earlier—even for the young people who don't go to 4-year colleges, they need to be in the school-to-work program. There needs to be something that gives almost everybody, nearly 100 percent of the young people, the incentive to get out of high school and then get 2 more years of some sort of education and training.

And meanwhile we'll keep doing everything we can to make college more affordable, because I think the great advantage this Nation has, and Boston has certainly seen it because you have such a wonderful array of institutions of higher education, is that we have a higher percentage of our people going to these institutions of higher education than any other country in the world. And they're higher quality. And what we've got to do is figure out how to make it possible for young people to know about it, to believe in themselves, and then to have money necessary to go.

Q. Thank you, Mr. President.

Mayor Menino. We have—Marcos' birthday is today.

The President. It's your birthday, right? Your 18th birthday?

Mayor Menino. You'll register to vote today, too, right? [*Laughter*] We need you next time.

The President. Good for you. Happy birthday.

Mayor Menino. This woman here has a question, Mr. President. Ask the question.

Q. You just put me on the spot. Actually, I do have a question. Do you actually see letters—well, besides the—[*laughter*].

Q. She was worried all this afternoon. [*Laughter*]

The President. The answer is, as you might imagine, with a country with 250 million people I do not see personally all the letters that come in. And we have so many letters coming into the White House that it requires literally—we have hundreds of volunteers working at the White House who help to sort our mail, who help to read our mail. A lot of retired military people come in every day and help us. We have a whole group of people who know my positions on certain issues, who help to write our letters when people write us about certain issues.

But, what happened to your letter is this: I have—I mean, before I was coming here, what happened to your letter is I have a—in my correspondence operation, every week they pull out a certain number of letters that are either especially moving because of the personal stories involved or that represent a large number of letters I'm getting on a certain subject, so that even though I'm President and I've got, you know, millions of people writing to me all the time, I have a good feeling for what's going on.

I also get a summary every week of how many letters came in, what the subjects were about, what people said, whether they were pro or con a certain issue. But the most—the thing— every week, I love reading the mail that I get sent. And I read the letters and sign them and in that way try to really stay in touch with what people are thinking.

Mayor Menino. Why don't we have Kristy read the letter.

[Kristy Foster then read a letter she had written to the President, thanking him for answering her previous letter about violence and for showing that he cared. Another participant asked if the President would videotape a message for their youth summit in March.]

The President. Sure.

Q. If there's any way possible for that.

The President. Were you trained in Senator Kennedy's office? *[Laughter]* Yes. I'd be happy to. We'll do it while we're here, maybe we can do that.

Mayor Menino. Is there any other—you have the President now. *[Laughter]* How many young people of America have the President in front of them? What's the other—any other question you have to ask, really would like to ask?

Q. I have really a general question.

The President. What's your name?

Mayor Menino. Catch up with this guy here.

Q. He wants your job. *[Laughter]*

The President. Some days I'd like to give it to you. *[Laughter]* But not most days.

Q. As President of the United States, most of us know and we've heard the story of how you wanted to shake President Kennedy's hand.

What advice would you offer to other young adults that are aspiring to become involved in politics?

The President. I would recommend that you do three things. You're probably doing all three of them already. I would recommend, first of all, that you do everything you can to develop your mind, that you learn to think, and you learn to learn. That is, some of you may be strong in math, maybe you're strong in science, maybe you like English, maybe you like history. There's no—contrary to popular belief, in my view, there is no particular academic discipline to get, to have to be a successful public servant. But it's important that you learn to learn because you have to know about a lot of different things that are always changing.

The second thing I would recommend you do is more what you're doing here. I don't think, over the long run, people do very well in public service unless they like people and are really interested in them, different people, people who are different from you. Find out what you have in common, what your differences really are.

And the third thing I would recommend that you do is look for opportunities to be a leader, working in this group, working in your school, working for people who are running for office, working in the mayor's next campaign.

These things really matter. That's what I did. I mean, I came from a family with no money or political influence, particularly. I had a good education. I had a lot of wonderful friends. I was interested in people. I had a chance to work in campaigns and to do other things that gave me a chance to get started. This is a great country that is really open to people of all backgrounds to be successful in public life. But you need to learn, you need to care about people, and then you just need the experience.

[At this point, Eugenia Kiu, chair of the council, presented the President with a cap and a sweatshirt.]

The President. Now, let's get everybody up here.

Q. Oh, I have something to say. I would like for you and Mr. Menino to sing me "Happy Birthday."

The President. Let's do it.

[The group sang "Happy Birthday."]

The President. Well, it wasn't the sweetest sound I ever heard. [*Laughter*]

NOTE: The President spoke at 4:11 p.m. at Parkman House.

Remarks at the New England Presidential Dinner in Boston
January 31, 1995

Thank you very much. You know, for a President who has been derided from time to time on the pages of the Wall Street Journal and other places for being too concerned with diversity, I feel that I should apologize tonight for giving you such an overconcentration of Irish blarney in the last three speakers. [*Laughter*] I hardly know what to say. And even if I do, I'll just repeat something. [*Laughter*]

They were wonderful. I want to say first to Senator Kerry, I thank you for your leadership and your wise counsel to me on so many things; for your occasional constructive criticism, which is always helpful—[*laughter*]—and for always thinking about how we can reach out to people who aren't in this room and who have been vulnerable to the siren's song of the other party. We should do more of that, because we're working hard to represent them and to help them.

I also want to say that when you introduced Teresa tonight, I was sitting here thinking that next only to the President of the United States, you're about to become the most over-married man in the whole country. [*Laughter*] And I congratulate you both, and I wish you well and Godspeed.

I want to say how elated I was to be a part of a couple of events for Senator Kennedy up here in the last campaign. Whatever labels you put on Democrats, the truth is that all elections are about two things: whether a majority of the people identify with you and think you're on their side and whether you've got a message for the future. In this last election, without apology, with great energy and gusto and courage, when all the national trends were going the other way and when no one could any longer seriously claim that Massachusetts was just a different State, Ted Kennedy told the people of this State what he stood for, what he had done, and most importantly of all, why he wanted another term. He made the election about the future and the people of Massachusetts, and he won. And if the Democrats will make the

elections of 1996 about the people of the United States and the future of our country, we will win as well.

I want to thank Alan and Fred and all the others on the committee. They're the only people I know who are more indefatigable than I am when it comes to trying to push our party's agenda and move this country forward. They're the sort of "Energizer bunnies" of the national Democratic Party, and I am grateful. [*Laughter*]

I wish I could put them on television the way Mario Cuomo and Ann Richards were. Did you all see them on the Super Bowl? I don't know about you, but I've had three dozen bags of Doritos since then. [*Laughter*] I can hardly walk. And I want them to stay on. I mean, write Doritos and tell them you ate lots of those Doritos and that's the only way we can get equal time with the Republicans on the airwaves. [*Laughter*]

I want to thank your party chair, Joan Menard, and Reverend Charles Stith, my longtime friend; your secretary of state; president Billy Bulger; Speaker Flaherty; and the attorney general; all the others who are here; and a special word of thanks to your wonderful mayor, Tom Menino, for making me feel so welcome here today.

You know, when Senator Kerry and Senator Kennedy and I went with the mayor to meet with that youth council today and they had a young person from every part of this great city, from all different ethnic backgrounds, and obviously different sets of personal conditions, and we were sitting there just having a family conversation about what these young people were interested in. And they kept asking me, "Well, here's a problem." But they didn't ask me, "What are you going to do about it?" They said, "What do you think we can do about it?" It was astonishing. Over and over, "What do you think we can do about it?" And I thought to myself, if we got enough kids like this all over America, our country is in pretty good shape. And it's a great tribute to Boston and to the ethic of citizenship and service, which is vibrant and alive and burning here.

I was so glad to—appreciate what Senator Dodd said about the national service program. I know all of you must be very proud of Eli Segal from Boston for the way he has run that program. It is a brilliant thing that is lining up possibilities all across our country: immunizing children in south Texas; rebuilding housing projects in Detroit; helping people in all the natural disasters in California; restocking the salmon in the Pacific Northwest. You cannot imagine what those young people are doing all across this country. And I have to tell you that if it hadn't been for Eli Segal I'm not sure we ever could have done it, the way he conceived it and executed it. And the next time he comes home to Boston give him a pat on the back, because he's been magnificent.

I want to thank my longtime friend Don Fowler for agreeing to join this team with Senator Dodd. The real reason Don came up here tonight is so there would be two southern rednecks book-ending all these Irish guys when they were talking. [*Laughter*]

Don understands what part of our problems are. Everybody talks about change, but Clinton's ninth law of politics is, everyone is for change in general but against it in particular. [*Laughter*] Everybody is for lowering the deficit. The problem is when you have to lower it—that's what Senator Kennedy was talking about—we didn't get much help when we actually had to do it. It's kind of like everybody is for going to the dentist, but if I tell you I made you an appointment for 7:30 in the morning, you'd have second thoughts. [*Laughter*]

So to whatever extent I bear a responsibility for some of our party's difficulties because I had a drill to the tooth of America for the last 2 years, trying to whip this thing back in shape, I regret that. But I don't regret the fact that we do have the economy back on track; we do have the deficit coming down; we do have this country in a position now where we can think about how to give tax relief to hardworking Americans and invest in education and still continue to bring the deficit down. I don't regret that. It was tough. It was hard. And I thank the people of the Congress who did it.

You know, Don and I come from part of the country where it's been hard to be a Democrat for over 20 years now. And part of it is

this whole deal, everybody is for change in general but against it in particular. One of my favorite stories from my previous life as Governor of Arkansas was going to the 100th birthday party of somebody with my junior Senator, David Pryor. We went up to this guy. We were amazed at what good shape he was in—astonished. I said, "You know, you have all your faculties. You hear well. You see well. You speak well." He said, "Yeah." And I said, "You're really just in great shape, aren't you?" He said, "I am." And I said, "Boy, I bet you've seen a lot of changes." He said, "Son, I sure have, and I've been against every one of them." [*Laughter*] The more you think about that, the sadder it'll get. But anyway, there it is.

There is some of that out there. But our people also really do want change. They want us to stick up for the principles of the Democratic Party, but they also want us to reach out a hand of partnership. And as your President, I have to be the leader of our party and the leader of our country. I feel very indebted to Chris Dodd and to Don Fowler for being willing to put aside a lot of their other activities to take the time to help to rebuild and reinvigorate and revitalize our party.

I know in my bones, I can feel it, that if we can stay true to our principles and clarify our vision for the American people and say what we are doing and where we want this country to go, that the fact that we honestly represent and care more about the vast majority of the American people will manifest itself, not simply in Massachusetts but throughout the United States within the next 2 years. And that should be our common commitment and our common cause.

The whole purpose of politics, after all, is to improve the life of people. Read the Declaration of Independence. As I said in the State of the Union, nobody's really done any better than that. We pledge our lives and our fortunes and our sacred honor to the idea that all of us are created equal and endowed by God with the rights of life, liberty, and the pursuit of happiness, not a guarantee of happiness but the right to pursue it, the right to succeed, the right to fail.

For 200 years, we've had to work to refine that phrase like a piece of steel. And we reach a certain point and we realize, oh, we've got a whole new set of circumstances or our understanding was painfully limited. That's what the Gettysburg Address was all about.

I don't know if you read Gary Wills' terrific book "Lincoln at Gettysburg," but he basically argues that Mr. Lincoln rewrote the Constitution with the Gettysburg Address by making the spirit of the Constitution the letter. That's what it was all about. He said: How could we be so dumb to have slavery and say all people are created equal? So from now on, that's what this means.

And you look what happened when Theodore Roosevelt and Woodrow Wilson tried to redefine the obligations of our National Government to protect the American people from the abuses of the industrial age, or when Franklin Roosevelt ran on a platform of limited government and balancing the budget but realized that he couldn't let the country go into the tubes, that he had to lift people's spirits and lift their circumstances and give them ways to work together.

If you look at some of our most difficult times, they're the times of transition when we're moving from one era to another and people can't give you a clear road map. In the middle of the Depression, I remember my grandfather telling me as poor as people were, there was a certain happiness of spirit people felt after Roosevelt got in, and everybody knew that they were working together and they were going somewhere.

I told a lot of people over the last month I'd just been astonished every time I go to California and I see those poor people. They've had an earthquake. They've had floods. They've had fires. Some of the happiest people I've ever met are people in those relief shelters in California. They get together from all walks of life. I was in one of those flood relief shelters the other day in northern California in a little unincorporated town called Rio Linda where Mr. Limbaugh had his first radio program. [*Laughter*] And I was in a little Methodist church talking to all these people and this old gal came up to me and put her arm around me, and she said, "Mr. President, I'm a Republican, but I'm sure glad to see you." Like I was going to fall out or something. Why? Because they were there, they didn't care what their party was or their philosophy. They were there trying to do something good. And they felt that they were part of something bigger than themselves.

In a period of transition like this, we're going from the cold war era and the industrial age to the post-cold-war era and an information age. We're going through enormous changes in the way work is organized and the way the society works. We've got all these cultural tensions in our country just eating people up. In times like this, people tend to be disoriented and out of focus. And it is difficult for them to do the work of citizenship and to believe that we can come together and do the things we ought to do. And we have to find ways to recreate in ordinary, normal circumstances the spirit that I see when adversity strikes America. That's what the mayor did by bringing those kids into that youth council today. And that's what we have to do as Americans.

The Democrats need to forthrightly say, we believe, even in the 21st century, even in the information age, even when we trade in our mainframes for our PC's, there is a role for us working together as a people; that the market is a wonderful thing and we want it to work, but it won't solve all the problems; that we still need the public sector to expand opportunity even as it shrinks bureaucracy, to empower people to make the most of their own lives no matter what their circumstances, to enhance our security at home and abroad.

And we don't have all the answers, because a lot of the problems are new. But we know that if we are guided by what I call the New Covenant, the idea that we will create opportunity and challenge the American people to be more responsible and that's how we'll build our communities and restore citizenship, we can do quite well.

It's amazing how many things I've had to do as President that I knew would be unpopular, like that economic plan. It wasn't unpopular in Massachusetts because Ted Kennedy defended his vote. And if everybody else had done that, they'd have found the results more satisfactory. I remember when—but we had to do that. We couldn't just keep ballooning the deficit. We'd never have gotten interest rates down in 1993. We would never have gotten this economy going again. We had to do it. And we have to continue to do things that are unpopular.

It was unpopular to say that the time had come for the dictators in Haiti to go, but it had to be done. We had to stand up for freedom in our hemisphere. We couldn't deal with the consequences of walking away from that and the commitment we had made. We had to do it. It was unpopular, but it had to be done.

And I know the surveys say that by 80 to 15, or whatever they said, the American people either didn't agree or didn't understand what in the world I'm up to in Mexico. But I want to say to you, it might be unpopular, but in a time of transition it's the right thing to do. Today, 2 weeks and a few days after the Mexican crisis presented itself, after meeting with the leaders of both parties in the Congress, I decided to commit to a loan guarantee of $20 billion, not $40 billion, from the Emergency Stabilization Fund, something within the control of the President, with the support of the leaders of Congress of both parties.

We've now gotten countries, other countries through the International Monetary Fund, to kick in about half what we need, which is a good thing. But we couldn't wait for 2 more weeks of congressional debate. I don't blame the Congressmen for wanting to ask questions. I don't blame them for not wanting to vote on this. It's a hard sell. It's pretty hard to explain in south Boston or up in Dover, New Hampshire, why this is a good deal for people in New England.

But here's the basic problem. Those folks got into a little economic trouble, but they didn't deserve as much as they got, because a lot of the international financial markets today are controlled by a hundred thousand different forces and when a speculative fervor starts in one direction, sometimes it's hard for it to stop when there's been some proper economic balance struck. But they've got a good democracy. They believe in free market economics. They buy tons of our products. They're our third biggest trading partner.

Why is this in the interest of the people of New England? Well, New Hampshire's unemployment rate was 7.4 percent when I took office, and it's 3.8 percent now. And a big reason is they're exporting more. That's just one example.

So our third biggest trading partner is in trouble. And they didn't ask us for a grant. They didn't ask us for a loan. They didn't ask us for a bailout. They said, "Would you cosign this note? And by the way, if we get in trouble and can't pay, we've got a whole bunch of oil and we'll give you some. You can sell it and put the money in the bank." That's pretty good collateral. Near as I can figure, even 10 years

from now we'll still be burning oil. We'll be able to use it. We'll be able to turn it into money. It will be worth something at the bank. And they said, would you help? So we got a $40 billion trading arrangement. It's jobs for Americans, folks. Those who say, "Well, Clinton is just bailing out rich investors on Wall Street; most of them will do just fine." But if we lose markets, if we lose possibilities—a lot of people here have built factories and shut them down. They're hard to start up again when you've shut them down. You've got to go through up and down times, but it's an important thing. It's American jobs.

We share a vast border down there. We have problems along that border, illegal immigration and narcotics trafficking. This government's trying to help us with both. If you have an economic and a political collapse, we have more illegal immigration, more narcotics trafficking, more misery on the streets of America, more anxiety for American taxpayers.

This is the right thing to do, and I was glad to take responsibility for it. And I know it's not popular, but in a time of change not all decisions which have to be made when they have to be made can possibly be popular. So I hope you will support it anyway. It's in the interest of building the future of the United States. [*Applause*] Thank you. Thank you. Thank you very much.

So much has been said tonight; there's not much more for me to say. But I want to make a couple of points about what I hope to achieve this year in this new environment for all of our people. And I'd like to begin by telling you a story.

When my last Secretary of the Treasury, Lloyd Bentsen, was at his last Cabinet meeting, preparing to go home to Texas after more than three decades of public service to a well-deserved retirement, with the reputation of being not only one of the wealthiest members of my Cabinet but one of the most conservative—a man who inspired great confidence all over the world for his policies and his personal strength—he said to us as he left, "You know what I'm most worried about? Here I am in my seventies, having had the chance to work for my country all these years, having enjoyed all the successes America could bring in the private sector and the public sector. You know what I'm most worried about? I'm worried about the growing inequality in America and the fact that so many Americans are working harder and harder and harder and falling behind. And I don't know how we can preserve our country as we know it unless we can figure out a solution to this problem. And I wish that I had left you with one before I retired." Everybody in that Cabinet room was just almost dumbstruck. What did he mean? He meant that something has changed since President Kennedy said, "A rising tide lifts all boats." It doesn't.

I'm honored by the fact that in 1994 we had the best growth in 10 years, the best personal income growth in 10 years, the lowest combined rates of unemployment and inflation in 25 years. That is a very good thing. We should be proud of that. And the economic management and discipline of this administration certainly had something to do with it. And the dramatic improvements in productivity of American businesses and working people had the lion's share to do with it. And the fact that we're opening new trading opportunities had something to do with it. And the fact that our Commerce Department and others, as has been said, are trying to sell American products and services—it all had something to do with it.

But the hard, cold fact is, people say, "Well, why doesn't the administration get credit for this?" Senator Kennedy alluded to it. Well, one reason is a lot of people are still working a longer work week than they were 15 years ago. They're spending more for the essentials of life, but their wages haven't kept up with inflation. Another million Americans in working families lost their health insurance last year, once again making us the only—and I reiterate—the only advanced country in the world with a smaller percentage of working families with health insurance today than had health insurance 10 years ago.

There was even a study last week that said the average working adult is spending an hour a night less at sleep. So if you have less time for leisure, if you're not sure you can even afford a vacation, much less send your kids to college, and you keep reading how great the statistics are, and all the rest of your information you get from some more negative source, it's not hard to understand how people are a little disoriented. Plus, the fundamental fact is we are moving from one time to another, and we aren't there yet, in our minds and in our experience.

Therefore, it should not be surprising, and we should not complain if those of us in public life sometimes become the object of resentment when we can't figure out how to explain in clear, unambiguous terms that cut through the fog of the national debate what is going on and what we are trying to do about it and what the people have to do about it.

That is the great challenge we face today. But we should be optimistic about it. With all my heart, I believe the best days of this country are ahead of us. But we have to find a way for the American tide to lift every boat in America. We have to find a way for everybody willing to work hard to do well. We have to find a way to keep the American dream alive for everyone, to grow the middle class and shrink the under class. We have to find a way to rebuild our sense of security.

I can think of no better way to explain it than what I have been trying to say for 3 years now: Our job is to create more opportunity and to challenge the American people to assume more responsibility. We have tried to do that. We are now in a position where it is my judgment that what we need to do in this coming session of Congress is, first of all, to keep the recovery going; secondly, not to let the deficit explode; thirdly, not to permit the fever for cutting Government and cutting regulation undercut the fundamental social compact in this country.

One of the reasons people are so torn up and upset is they're not sure what the deal is anymore. The harder they work, the more insecure they feel.

So I say, you want to cut spending, to our friends in the Republican Party, let us have at it. We have cut $255 billion in spending. I'm going to send you another $140 billion in spending cuts. I am all for it. But let's not cut Head Start for children or the school-to-work program for the non-college bound kids. Let's not cut the nutrition programs and the food programs that keep our people alive. Let's don't do that. You want to cut taxes? That's all right. I'm for that. But let's not cut more than we can pay for. Let's not play funny numbers. Let's not pay for tax cuts by cutting Medicare. Let's cut spending that we can do without. We can do that. Let's do that.

And more importantly, in my judgment, is let's not fool people. What we're trying to do is to raise incomes. A tax cut raises incomes in the short run. We ought to do it in a way that raises incomes in the long run. That's why I favor—in this education State, it ought to be popular—finally giving the American people a tax deduction for all education expenses after high school. We ought to do that. Why? Because that lowers taxes and raises income in the short run, but far more important, it raises income in the long run, and not only the incomes of the people claiming a tax deduction but the incomes of every single American, because we have to do a better job of getting more education for everybody.

We also ought to raise the minimum wage. Senator Kennedy is right about that. Now, I just want to say a word about this. I know that there's a conventional theory that, well, most people on the minimum wage are young people in middle class households, going home to nice homes at night, and they don't need a raise. Well, the statistics show that about 40 percent of the gains of the minimum wage go to people in the middle 60 percent. But about 45 percent go to people in the lower 20 percent of our income brackets. There's a lot of women out there raising children on a minimum wage, and people can't live on $4.25 an hour.

And the other night on our television in Washington there was a little snippet on some people who were working in a factory in a rural area not very far from Washington. And a television interviewer went out and interviewed these ladies that were working in this operation. And this wonderful woman was interviewed. And he went through all the economic arguments against raising the minimum wage: "They say they're going to, if we raise the minimum wage, take your job away and put it into a machine." And she looked at the camera, and she said, "Honey, I'll take my chances." [*Laughter*] And I'll tell you what, I'll bet you if anybody in this room were working for $4.25 an hour, you'd take your chances. Let's give them the chance. What do you say? I think we ought to.

I want welfare reform. I met last Saturday with Republicans and Democrats. Senator Kennedy was there. We talked about the welfare system. People that hate welfare most are the people that are trapped on it. I may be the only President that ever had the privilege of spending hours talking to people on welfare. It doesn't work.

But what should our goal be? Should our goal be to say we are frustrated, we think there are a lot of deadbeats on welfare, and we want to punish them? Or should our goal be to say there ought to be a limit to this system; we want to move people from welfare to work and we want to move people to the point where they can be good parents and good workers, and the system we have has all the wrong incentives; let's change them? That's what our goal ought to be. We can liberate people. If we're going to shrink the under class, we have to reform the welfare system, but the goal of it ought to be how to train for a job, how to get a job, how to keep a job, and how to be a better parent. And that is going to be what drives me in this debate.

So that's what I hope we'll do: go for the middle class bill of rights; pass the minimum wage; pass welfare reform; let's keep cutting the size of the Government. You know, if we don't do anything else—I got tickled when Senator Kennedy was up here talking about it—but if we don't pass another law, in 3 years the Federal Government will be the smallest it's been since John Kennedy was President of the United States because of reductions voted by Democrats 100 percent. And I'm proud of that.

We should never be the party of yesterday's Government. We should never be the party of undue regulation. We should never be the party of things that don't make sense. The average person, when they pay money in April, thinks that they don't get their money's worth when they send their check to the Federal Government. That's what they think. And too often they have been absolutely right. We shouldn't defend that. We should be in the forefront. But when we are, as we have been for the last 2 years, we shouldn't keep it a secret. We need to tell it. We need to make sure people know it.

But I also will tell you that I have challenged the Republican leadership in Congress to make some move on health care. We lost another million Americans last year. The health care costs have moderated, thanks to what a lot of you in this room are doing who are in health care. But we still have serious problems with the costs going up more rapidly than inflation, and we still cannot continue in the face of plain evidence that every year we'll go on being the only successful country in the world to lose working people from the rolls of the health insured. We can't continue to walk away from this problem.

So maybe we did bite off more than we can chew last year. But as I said so many times, I'm still proud of the First Lady for trying to give health care to everybody in this country. And I don't think we should be ashamed of it. [*Applause*] Thank you. So I think we've got a lot to do.

Let me close with reminding you of this: The most important work of all still must be done by citizens. You know what we're doing here tonight? We're celebrating the right of citizens to have a say in their Government. That's what this fundraiser is. And most of you are unselfish. You know darn well if you were at one of their fundraisers, it probably would get you a bigger tax cut. Most of you are here because you believe in your country, because you want everything to go better for everybody, and because you know you'll do better in the long run if we have the discipline to bring the deficit down, to put in sensible economic policies, and to take care of the children of this country. That's why you're here. You're here because your view of your self-interest goes beyond tomorrow or the next day. You're here because, for whatever reason, you haven't become so disoriented in this time of change that you're stopping thinking about the long run. And I value that; I thank you for that.

What we've got to do is to spread that to other people. The spirit I saw of those young children in the Mayor's council today, we have to spread that to other people. We can't allow resentment to take over. I don't know if you saw the—I was very gratified by the results of the public opinion survey today about Massachusetts voters. It was in the press today or yesterday, whenever it was. But—[*applause*]—before you clap, let me tell the rest of it. [*Laughter*] But that's a fascinating commentary. You know, my wife took a lot of hits when she fought for health care, and a lot of people said, well, she's got no business doing that, and all that stuff you heard. And so the survey said there's a dramatic difference between what women and men thought, particularly working women thought about what she had done. Now, why is that? Why would there be such difference? Because we're going through a period of real change, and people are disoriented, and it's tough out there. And this so-called angry white

male phenomenon—there are objective reasons for that. People are working harder for less, and they feel like they're not getting what they deserve. They worry whether they're letting their own families down. And it's easy to play on people's fears and resentments. It's easy to build up people's anger. The hard work, the right thing to do, what we have to do is to channel all that frustration and anger into something good and positive. What we have to do is to say what we say to our children, "Okay, be mad. Be angry. Scream. Let off steam, but what are you going to do? What about tomorrow, how are you going to change your life? What are we going to do together?"

That is our job, every one of our jobs. And no President, no Congress, no program, nothing can change what citizens can change if we are determined to see one another as fellow citizens instead of enemies. Even when we're opponents, we shouldn't be enemies.

So I ask you—there's enough brain power and education and understanding in this room to move Boston all the way to Washington, there's enough energy and innovation and creativity here. And I thank you for being here, and I thank you for supporting us. But tomorrow and the next day, look all your fellow citizens in the eye; when you drive to work and drive home, when you walk the streets, seek out people who are different, who have different views. Imagine what their lives are like.

This is a difficult time. We're moving from one place to another. And we need to find our bearings. We cannot do it with division. We cannot do it with demonization. We cannot do it with the politics of destruction. We cannot do it just by giving vent to frustration. We have to build. Every time this country has gone through a period like this, every time, we are simply doing the work that has been done for 200 years: We are redefining what we have to do so that all of us can pursue life, liberty, and happiness.

We should be proud that we have the chance. We shouldn't be deterred by momentary adversity. If we keep our eyes on the prize, which is the human potential of every single American, we're going to do just fine.

Thank you, and God bless you all.

NOTE: The President spoke at 8:56 p.m. at the Park Plaza Hotel. In his remarks, he referred to Senator John F. Kerry and his fiance, Teresa

Heinz; Senator Edward M. Kennedy; Alan Leventhal and Fred Seigel, fundraisers, Democratic National Committee; Mario Cuomo, former Governor of New York; Ann Richards, former Governor of Texas; Joan M. Menard, chair, Massachusetts Democratic Party; Rev. Charles Stith, who gave the invocation; Massachusetts State officials William Galvin, secretary of state, William Bulger, senate president, Charles Flaherty, house speaker, and L. Scott Harshbarger, attorney general; and Mayor Thomas Menino of Boston, MA.

Remarks Prior to a Meeting With Military Leaders and an Exchange With Reporters
February 1, 1995

[*The President's remarks are joined in progress.*]

Defense Budget

The President. ——I'm especially glad to have this chance to be here. And a lot has changed and a lot has happened since we met last year. I want to get a good briefing on the readiness issues and on the quality of life issues that are implicit in the request that we're making in the defense budget. We've got to maintain our preparedness; we've got to maintain our readiness. I also want to emphasize how important my supplemental recommendation is to the Congress. We need to get that approved as quickly as possible. I know it's important to all of you. And Secretary Perry and Deputy Secretary Deutch talk to me about it all the time. We're working hard on that supplemental, and we're going to do our best to get it passed.

Baseball Strike

Q. Mr. President, the baseball negotiators—changing the subject—[*laughter*]——

The President. National security. [*Laughter*]

Q. On a subject dear to many Americans, after 40 days they are starting to talk again today in Washington. And you have imposed this February 6th deadline for some progress. Is there anything you can do personally to get baseball off the—to get it going again?

The President. I am doing whatever I can do personally. But the less I say about it, the better. We're all working. This administration has worked hard. But I think Mr. Usery, our mediator, should be given a chance to work through this last process to try to come up with an agreement between the parties. If they don't, I've urged him to put his own suggestions on the table. We'll just keep working through this until we get to a—hopefully get to a successful conclusion.

Mexican Loan Guarantees

Q. Mr. President, what do you think about the international response to your Mexico decision so far?

The President. So far I'm encouraged. I think it was the right thing to do, and I'm encouraged. I hope we have another good day today. Yesterday was very encouraging, good for our country, good for our jobs, good for the stability of the region.

NOTE: The President spoke at 10:18 a.m. at the Pentagon. A tape was not available for verification of the content of these remarks.

Remarks at the National Prayer Breakfast
February 2, 1995

Thank you, Martin Lancaster, for your incredible devotion to this prayer breakfast and for all the work you have done to make it a success. To Vice President and Mrs. Gore and to the Members of Congress and the Supreme Court, the Governors, the distinguished leaders of previous administrations, and of course, to all of our foreign guests who are here and my fellow

Americans: Hillary and I look forward to this day every year with much anticipation. It always gives me new energy and new peace of mind. But today has been a special day for me.

It's always wonderful to see our friend Billy Graham back here. This is the 40th of 43 prayer breakfasts he has attended. I'd say he's been faithful to this as he has to everything else in his life, and we are all the richer for it.

It was wonderful to be with Andy Young again. He stayed with us last evening at the White House, and we relived some old times and talked about the future. None of us could fail to be moved today by the power of his message, the depth of his love for his wonderful wife, who blessed so many of us with her friendship. And I'm sure he inspired us all.

I also want to say a special word of thanks to my friend Janice Sjostrand for coming here all the way from Arkansas. You know, one of the greatest things about being Governor of my State is I got to hear her sing about once a month instead of once in a blue moon. And I miss you, and I'm glad to hear you today. Thank you.

We have heard a lot of words today of great power. There is very little I can add to them. But let me say that, in this age, which the Speaker of the House is always reminding us is the information age—an exciting time; a time of personal computers, not mainframes; a time when we are going to be judged by how smart we work, not just how hard we work—the power of words is greater than ever before. So by any objective standard the problems we face today, while profound, are certainly not greater than they were in the Great Depression, or in the Second World War, or when Mr. Lincoln made those statements when he left his home in Illinois to become President that Governor Engler quoted, or when George Washington suffered defeat after defeat until, finally, we were able to win by persistence our freedom. No, they are not, these times, as difficult as they are, more difficult than those.

What makes them more difficult is the power of words, the very source of our liberation, of all of our possibility and all of our potential for growth. The communications revolution gives words not only the power to lift up and liberate, the power to divide and destroy as never before—just words—to darken our spirits and weaken our resolve, divide our hearts. So I say, perhaps the most important thing we should

take out of Andy Young's wonderful message about what we share in common is the resolve to clear our heads and our hearts and to use our words more to build up and unify and less to tear down and divide.

We are here because we are all the children of God, because we know we have all fallen short of God's glory, because we know that no matter how much power we have, we have it but for a moment. And in the end, we can only exercise it well if we see ourselves as servants, not sovereigns.

We see sometimes the glimmer of this great possibility: When, after hundreds of years, the Catholics and Protestants in Northern Ireland decide that it may be time to stop killing each other; when after 27 years, Nelson Mandela walks out of his jail cell and a couple of years later is the President of a free country from a free election; when we see the miraculous reaching out across all the obstacles in the Middle East. God must have been telling us something when he created the three great monotheistic religions of the world in one little patch and then had people fight with each other for every century after that. Maybe we have seen the beginning of the end of that, in spite of all the difficulty. But it never happened unless the power of words become instruments of elevation and liberation.

So we must work together to tear down barriers, as Andy Young has worked his whole life. We must do it with greater civility. In Romans, St. Paul said, "Repay no one evil for evil, but take thought for what is noble in the sight of all; do not be overcome by evil, but overcome evil by good." There's not a person in this room that hasn't failed in that admonition, including me. But I'm going to leave here today determined to live more by it.

And we must finally be humble, all of us, in whatever position we have not only because, as Andy reminded us, we're just here for a little while, not only in our positions but on this Earth, but because we know, as St. Paul said in Corinthians, that we see through a glass darkly and we will never see clearly until our life is over. We will never have the full truth, the whole truth. Even the facts, as Andy said—I thought that was a brilliant thing—the flesh and blood of our lives, the facts we think we know, even they do not tell us the whole truth. The mystery of life.

So, my fellow Americans and my fellow citizens of the world, let us leave this place renewed, in a spirit of civility and humility, and a determination not to use the power of our words to tear down.

I was honored to say in the State of the Union last week that none of us can change our yesterdays, but all of us can change our tomorrows. That, surely, is the wisdom of the message we have heard on this day.

Lastly, let me ask you to pray for the President that he will have the wisdom to change when he is wrong, the courage to stay the course when he is right, and somehow, somehow, the grace of God not to use the power of words at a time in human history when words are more omnipresent and more powerful than ever before to divide and to destroy but instead to pierce to the truth, to the heart, to the best that is in us all.

Thank you all, and God bless you.

NOTE: The President spoke at 9:20 a.m. at the Washington Hilton Hotel and Towers. In his remarks, he referred to Martin Lancaster, chair, National Prayer Breakfast; evangelist Billy Graham; former United Nations Ambassador Andrew Young; and singer Janice Sjostrand.

Interview With Religious Affairs Journalists
February 2, 1995

The President. Well, I'm glad to see you all and welcome you here, for many of you, for the first time. As you know, in the State of the Union Address I issued a challenge, and as part of my explanation of the New Covenant in challenging citizens to be more responsible, to people of faith and to religious leaders specifically to help us to deal with those problems that we have to deal with person by person and from the inside out, to help us to deal with the problems of teen pregnancy and out-of-wedlock birth, to help us to deal with the challenges of excessive violence, to help us to deal with the things that have to be organized and dealt with literally one by one at the grass-roots level. And while I think we have to be more tolerant of all people, no matter what their differences are, we need to be less tolerant of conditions that are within our power to change.

And as you know now, for 2 years, ever since I took this job, I've been trying to find ways to galvanize the energies of people of faith to work together on a common agenda that nearly all Americans would agree on and, at the same time, to try to respect the differences of opinion and views. Our administration strongly supported the Religious Freedom Restoration Act, and we've worked very hard to implement it in a good faith way. And I think an awful lot of people from right across the spectrum of religious affiliations in our country would agree that we have done that.

Anyway, if you have any questions, I'd be glad to answer. But the other thing I was going to say today—what I said today was that the problems our country faces today are quite profound, you know, the fact that a rising tide is not lifting all boats; that a lot of people, in spite of this remarkable recovery, have not gotten a raise and they're more vulnerable with their health care, their pensions; and the fact that a lot of people find their values violated and their security violated by crime and violence and the breakdown of the social order. It would be very hard to assert that there are more profound difficulties than the problems of previous days, than the problems that George Washington or Abraham Lincoln or Franklin Roosevelt confronted.

The difference is that in the information age, which gives us these vast new opportunities because the creation of wealth is based on knowledge and that these people have access to more knowledge than ever before, it's also a great burden because words have greater power today than ever before, not only to build up but also to tear down, to divide, to destroy, to distract. And therefore, in a very profound sense in the modern world, it is more important that people be striving for the kind of spiritual presence of mind and peace of mind that will lead you to use words to build up and to unify, instead of to divide and tear down. And I really do believe that. I think that it's clearly different from any previous time. Words have always been able to wound in letters or speeches or whatever. But the omnipresence of information today and the fact that we're buried in it, it seems to me, imposes an even greater responsibility on people in positions of respect and trust and power to use those words more carefully.

Personal Morality

Q. An awkward question, sir. The moral crusade elements of the State of the Union Address, teenage pregnancy, as an example, sits well, except that there are investigations into your own conduct which some people say leaves an impression. Is this interfering with your ability to lead that type of crusade?

The President. Not in my own mind. That's up for other people to determine. But the one thing that I would say today—we live in an age where anybody can say anything and, unlike in previous times, it gets into print. And even if they admit they took money to say it—which is what happened in my case a couple of times—it still gets wide currency. So there's not much I can do about that.

I can tell you this: The work I've tried to do to reduce teen pregnancy and out-of-wedlock births generally is something I've been involved in for many years. And I think it's a very serious matter. The life of these young people was very, very different than my life was when I was their age. Their temptations, their travails, it's very, very different and much more difficult for them. And I think we've got to try to find a way to help them walk back from what is now happening.

Interestingly enough—this is a statistical comment I'm making now—there is some evidence that the efforts may be beginning to have some impact. The actual numbers of out-of-wedlock births have stabilized in the last 2 or 3 years. The rate of illegitimacy is going up because the rate of childbearing by couples who are young and successful is going down, which is another problem for another discussion. But anyway, I don't see that we have any choice as a people to deal with it, and it's—and you know, if folks want to use that as another excuse to attack me, that's their problem, not mine.

Welfare Reform and Abortion

Q. Related to that, some people suggest that both your welfare reform proposals and the Contract With America's welfare reform pro-

posal takes such Draconian measures against these unwed teen mothers in terms of limits that what it's likely to do is to drive up the abortion rate, not stop the unwanted pregnancy rate but drive up the abortion rate. Do you see that happening?

The President. Well, I don't agree with that in my proposal, and obviously I don't know what would happen in the others, but let's look at that.

The abortion rate has been going down in America. And I think it's been going down for—maybe because of all the protest against abortion. But I also think that most Americans have deeply ambivalent feelings. That is, I believe that a majority of Americans are pro-choice and anti-abortion. That is, they don't believe that the decision should be criminalized because there are too many different circumstances where most of us feel that decisions should be left to the people who are involved rather than having a totally legal prohibition. On the other hand, most people think in most circumstances that abortion is wrong and that it shouldn't be done.

So the abortion rate is going down in America. It's still very much too high, and we've tried to do some things to make adoption more attractive. And there was a law signed last year, that's gotten almost no notice because it was part of the Elementary and Secondary Education Act, to try to remove the prohibitions or the discriminations in courts across the country in cross-racial adoptions to try to do whatever we could to just encourage more adoptions.

But let me back up to your question and to explain, if I might, why I don't agree that our position would cause more abortions. There are basically three different approaches, with a zillion different limitations, but three different approaches in this welfare debate. There is the Contract approach which is deny benefits to the second welfare child born out of wedlock. And then this extreme version is deny benefits to any teenager who has a child out of wedlock and to that child for up to 18 years. That's what—then there's the people who say, turn it over to the States and let them do whatever they want, which could include that.

Our position is give the States a lot more flexibility, but don't punish the children; take care of their basic needs. And we say don't cut the parents off of public assistance unless, number one, they're bad parents or, number two, they do things which will undermine their ability to either be successful workers or successful parents.

So for example, the way our plan works is if you're a teenager and you have a baby, in order to draw the public assistance in a normal way you'd have to stay in school, you'd have to live at home with your parents, and if you lived in a bad home you'd have to live in some other supervised setting. You'd have to cooperate and help identify the father so we could attempt to get the father to pay child support and support the child. If at the end of your education period and training, if 2 years have elapsed and you haven't gone to work, then you would have to go to work if there were a job available. And if you turned down a job, you could lose your benefits. Under their proposal, the second problem is, you'd be cut off after 2 years whether there's a job there or not.

So the two differences are, I say cut people off after a limited amount of time if there's a job there. They say cut them off altogether. I say only take benefits away from people if they misbehave as parents or in their own responsibilities. They say if you have a child out of wedlock and you're a teenager, you should never get benefits and neither should your child.

I'll leave it to you to conclude what impact that might have on the abortion rate; I don't know. But I don't believe ours would. I think ours is responsible. You have to have more requirements on people; you can't just continue to perpetuate the present system. But I don't think you should punish the children or punish people for their past mistakes. You should deal with their present conduct.

Child Health and Welfare

Q. What about the suggestion that, particularly of Speaker Gingrich, that the churches and the charities should be able to take over much of the responsibility, including the financial responsibility that the Government now has for foster children and various other tough social situations? Is that an appropriate way for these problems to be taken care of, for these people to be cared for? And if so, how should the money get there?

The President. Well, I think the churches could well be involved in more activities. For example, I think that you might—and one of the things that I want to do is to give more

flexibility in how to implement welfare reform to State and local government. If they want to involve the church, particularly, for example, in developing supervised settings for young girls and their children who can't, and shouldn't, be living in their homes because of the problems in their homes, that's the sort of partnership that I would certainly not oppose.

But I don't think you can say from that that there's no national interest which should command some taxpayer support to make sure that these children have minimal levels of nutrition and medical care and just the basic things that it seems to me we've got an interest in doing, because we don't want to lose any more of these kids than we have to.

The welfare benefits themselves, by the way, are not a problem. The real welfare benefits are about 40 percent lower than they were 20 years ago. So nobody goes on welfare for the check. It's the child care; it's the food stamps; it's the medical care for your children. Therefore, nearly anybody who can will get off and go to work if they can take care of their children and their children won't lose their health care.

But do I think the churches should do more? I do. And one of the things that we want to do is to give more operational control of this program to the States and let them use churches or community organizations or others to do whatever they can to repair the families.

Q. Much of what the churches already do—for instance, Catholic Charities, their money comes from contracts through Federal agencies. In essence, what some of the Republican proposals are asking them to do is to continue doing the sort of work but without those contracts, without the money.

The President. Well, it will just be harder for them, won't it? I mean, I think—I mean, Fred is a good example. The Government does not—we are not a particularly generous country in terms of social welfare. The thing—I don't think the American people object to spending tax money on poor people. I think what they object to is spending tax money on a system that perpetuates destructive conduct and irresponsible conduct. I think that the issue is—for example, I don't think most Americans really think that it would be a great idea to cut out all spending on poor children in order to afford a capital gains tax cut. I don't think that's where they would come down. On the other hand, would they rather have a tax cut or just waste money on any program, including a program that perpetuated dependency? I think they would—or reduce the deficit or whatever.

So I think the—what my goal is, is to say there's a national interest in the health and welfare of our children. I think it requires some investment of taxpayer money in the areas of particularly basic health care and nutrition and immunization of children against serious diseases. But the systems are dysfunctional. So I think we ought to try to fix them.

Response to Criticism

Q. In a meeting of Baptist leaders back in October you were asked a question about some of your critics who were attacking you with unsubstantiated charges. I'm thinking specifically of Reverend Falwell pushing a video on his TV program. And your response to the question was that you were busy running the country and didn't want to respond to your critics, but you were surprised that the Christian community wasn't taking these men on.

Since that time, I know American Baptist Tony Campollo was asked for equal time on his show to try to defend you. But do you know of any other attempts like that, or anything since that time to try to answer some——

The President. There have been an awful lot of attempts—I think there have been a lot of press stories refuting some of the specific allegations. But I would just say again, in the world we're living in—I'll say what I said at the prayer breakfast today—there is an inordinate premium put on the use of words to destroy or to distract people. And it takes away from my ability to be President, to do the job with a clear head and a clear heart and to focus on the American people, if I have to spend all my time trying to answer charges about what people say that I did years ago. And I just can't do it; I just can't do it.

I do the very best I can. Sometimes you can actually disprove something someone says about you. A lot of times, some people could lie about you in ways that you can't disprove. You can't always disprove every assertion. So insofar as whatever happened, I can't change yesterday, I can only change today and tomorrow. So I've just got to keep going. I think it is—I think I have—if I'd done anything, even though I've tried not to deal with it at all, I think whatever time I've spent kind of trying to absorb those blows since I've been President has been time

and effort and energy, emotional as well as intellectual energy, has taken away from the American people. And I'm not going to cheat them anymore; I'm just not going to do it. I'm tired of letting other people say things that require me to deprive the American people of the best effort I can make. They'll have to make whatever evaluation of this they want to.

There is a difference between reputation and character, and I have increasingly less control over my reputation but still full control over my character. That's between me and God, and I've just got to try to be purified by this.

I also noticed, Winston Churchill said—I ran across this the other day—that just because someone strays from the truth in criticizing you doesn't mean you can't learn something from their criticism. So I've decided that I'll try—need to learn a little something from my critics, even if what they say is not so. None of us are perfect, and I'm certainly not. But I just can't—I really think I made the right decision to try to just tune it out and go forward.

Q. Is there a place in the Scriptures where you find a source for the kind of faith you talked about earlier and stillness in facing these things, a story or a parable or a reading that you've turned to?

The President. Well, it's interesting, I just finished reading the entire Psalms. I also read—this is ironic—Lloyd Ogilvie's book on the Psalms that I didn't—I read it before he was selected to be Chaplain of the Senate. And there are a lot of the Psalms where David is sort of praying for the strength to be sort of purified in the face of adversity and in the face of his own failures.

There are a lot of the Proverbs which talk about the importance of keeping a quiet tongue and at least not getting in your own way, which I've done a lot in my life and which I've tried, even still, to grow out of. And I've spent a lot of time dealing with that over the last 2 years, as you would imagine I would have to.

I think the important thing, and I find this in the Scriptures over and over again, the important thing that I have to keep focusing on is what am I going to do today, what am I going to do tomorrow, how can I be free to call on the power of God to make the most of this job that I have for a little bit of time in the grand sweep of things. And that's just what I keep focusing on every day.

But I think—you'd be amazed how many people write me little fax notes, from friends of mine on a daily basis, saying look at this Scripture, look at that Scripture, look at the other Scripture. During this difficult period, a lot of people were giving me different Psalms to read—it was amazing—and so I did.

Negativism in Politics

Q. Sir, when you talk about destructive language, if you—you refer to personal attacks on yourself. But what about some of the uncivil language which has been so much in the news over the past months that has been in Congress? Are you including that in——

The President. Oh, sure. I said today at the prayer breakfast, I don't think anybody in public life, including me, is blameless. I think it's that there are general—excuse me, genuine differences that people have on issues, and they ought to express them. But our public life needs more of the spirit of reconciliation, it needs more civility, it needs more humility. Sometimes we think we know things we don't.

And I think on debates over public issues, that is true as well. The American people very much want us to—they respond to these negative things, but they don't like it. The reason it keeps happening is because they respond to it. The politicians read polls, you know, and they know very often that the negative campaigns work and elect people. And they know that if you just constantly demean and run down people, like, after a while it sticks. They know that, so they keep on doing it. And the people respond to it, but they hate it. It's almost saying, "I wish you'd lock this liquor store up so I couldn't drink anymore."

And so somehow we have to crawl back off of this wedge because it has, as I said, it's— today people get more information that is sort of argumentative and editorial and often less accurate, and then get in a more negative context than ever before. And it is a function of the information explosion. And so I do believe that I and others have a heavier responsibility even than we might have had in a former time, when in order to just get people's attention, you might take a little license with your language, you know.

Politics and Religion

Q. [*Inaudible*]—proven through the words and your actions that you are a genuinely reli-

gious person, since you were very young, and your wife as well. And a lot of religious people I talk to don't seem to accept that, who don't seem to feel it's genuine, feel that you're using it in the course of making politics. And I'm wondering why, if you believe that, too, and if you—any analysis as to why that is and what it might say about the role of religion in politics, whether they really ought to be bound together——

The President. Well, I don't think they should be bound together. I mean, I think the First Amendment is a good thing for our country, that we protect the right of everybody to be faithful to whatever they believe by not uniting church and state. But I don't think you can change people or who they are. They have the convictions they have. They have the beliefs they have.

And what I've tried to do is to draw the proper balance by encouraging people of all faiths, including people who disagree with me, to be activist citizens. I think the—the book that Stephen Carter wrote on that, he makes a better statement about that than I can make, in terms of why they don't accept that about me. I think it's hard to make a case that I have tried to use this. I've never tried to say that—for example, I never tried to say that there was a Christian coalition behind anything I did, you know, that God had ordained us to do these following things and I knew it, and anybody that didn't was seized by the Devil. I never said that.

I've said that like every other person, I consider myself a sinner because I believe I consider myself forgiven. I consider—you know, I need the power of God. This is a humble thing for me. But it's an important part of my life and has been for a long time, but especially again in recent years and before I became President. And the same thing is true for Hillary.

I think the truth is that there are people who don't believe it's genuine because they disagree with me politically. They don't believe that you could be a committed Christian and not want to criminalize all abortions. "I just don't believe you can be"—that's what they think. They don't believe that you could be a committed Christian and believe that—take the position that I took on gays in the military. They thought—think the Bible dictated the previous policy on gays in the military, even though we fought two World Wars, Korea, and Vietnam with a different policy. But they don't believe that. That's their conviction.

So then I think there are people, once they disagree with you so much, who will believe—who will believe in perpetuating anything anybody says about you, and so they think that's evidence of that. But—you know, the Bible is full of refutations of the latter point. All they had to do was read the Scripture to know better than to make that argument. But I can't worry about them; that's their problem. Let them think what they want.

I literally—you know, the one thing I realize is, is I wasted too much time when I got here, and it caused me to be a less effective President, either being hurt by or paying a great deal of attention to what people said about me in the past. And I've just got to try to keep going and fight against it, because the people that wanted to really blow that up either wanted to do it for their own purposes or wanted to do it literally without regard to whether the Government of the United States functions or the public interest is furthered. It's just a crazy way to behave; you can't do it. It never happened before in our history to this extent, and it shouldn't be happening now. And if it is happening, I can't control it. So what I should do is just do my job and shut it out; that's what I have to do.

Q. Sir, do you think that religious groups such as the Christian Coalition risk their credibility by wholesale endorsement of the Contract With America?

The President. Well, I think that's for others to judge, I think, but I would say this: You know, I think that they will come to be seen more and more like a political party with an agenda, rather than people who are driven into politics based on one or two issues that they believe the Bible dictates a position different from the present policy of the United States.

And there are a lot of European political parties with the name "Christian" in them, the Christian Democratic Party in Germany, Helmut Kohl's party. Nobody considers him to be, how should I say, sacrilegious because he's part of a party called the Christian Democratic Party that has religious roots, but no one anymore seriously believes that every position they take

is rooted in their reading of the Scripture. And I think that the Christian Coalition is long since at that point.

Now, the thing I do think they have to be careful about with their credibility is the very, very hard hits they put on office holders who don't do as they believe. I remember one of the Members of Congress who lost in the last election told me of an encounter with a Christian Coalition minister who said to this Member, "Well, you want to see what we're going to put out in our churches on Sunday, tomorrow?" And she said, "Yes, I'd like to see it." And she went to these ten items; she said, "But these two things aren't true." He said, "So, it's generally true. So what?"

So I think that that could hurt their credibility more than anything else, the idea that they're using the emotions of people of faith who are deeply disturbed for good reasons with what's going on in our country today and channeling those emotions into convictions about people in public life that aren't true. Now, that could hurt their credibility.

But I think just taking positions on these other things, I think everybody knows that they basically are an arm of the Republican Party and that they're going to take all these positions. I don't see that there's anything wrong with them doing it. And I agree with some of them, too. You know, I don't disagree with everything in that Contract; I agree with some of it.

Did everybody get a question? I'm glad to see you.

Q. It's good to see you.

The President. Thanks. Do you ever wish you were back in Conway?

Q. Almost every day when I'm driving out to Fairfax County for that hour and a half. [*Laughter*]

The President. It's pretty out there. I had a woman today from Lonoke come sing at the prayer breakfast. It made me so homesick I could hardly stand it.

NOTE: The interview began at 11:46 a.m. in the Oval Office at the White House. A tape was not available for verification of the content of this interview.

Remarks Announcing the Nomination of Henry W. Foster, Jr., To Be Surgeon General and an Exchange With Reporters
February 2, 1995

The President. Thank you very much, Madam Secretary, and let me say it's a pleasure to have Mrs. Foster and Senator Frist, Congressman Clement here.

The Surgeon General of the United States has enormous responsibilities. As the public face of our Public Health Service, he or she really is the people's doctor, the person responsible for promoting good health practices and alerting the Nation when health threats exist. To fill this post, I wanted someone who is both a top-flight medical professional and a strong leader and effective communicator. Dr. Henry Foster is such a person. And I am pleased today to announce my intention to nominate him as the Surgeon General of the United States.

He is widely respected in the world of medicine and science. After serving his country for 2 years as an Air Force medical officer, he became chief of obstetrics and gynecology at Andrew Memorial Hospital at Tuskegee University.

For the past 21 years, he has worked at Meharry Medical College in Nashville, Tennessee. As the dean of the school of medicine and its acting president, he helped Meharry to lead the way to meeting the health needs of the poor and the underserved. At the moment, he is a visiting senior scholar at the Association of Academic Health Centers here in Washington.

In the communities he's served, Dr. Foster has won hearts and minds for his innovation and his dedication to saving the lives of young people and vulnerable people. He's received numerous honors for his work in obstetrics and dealing with sickle cell anemia and, very notably, in the prevention of teen pregnancy.

He has shown us how one person can make a difference. Eight years ago he developed and directed the "I Have A Future" program at Meharry to help stop teen pregnancy. It has been an unqualified success. Working with young people that others might think beyond help, he built up their self-esteem. He taught them job skills. He encouraged them to stay in school. Most important, he told them to be responsible for themselves. Thanks to Dr. Fos-

ter, these young people have a chance to live a good, full life.

I want Dr. Foster to use what he's learned to help America attack the epidemic of teen pregnancies and unmarried pregnancies. We know Government can only do so much. So large a part of Dr. Foster's job obviously will be to use his enormous skills of persuasion to reach out to people in the private sector, in the religious, education, entertainment, sports, and other communities in this country. As I said in the State of the Union, when I challenged all sectors of our society to help us deal with these problems that must be dealt with one by one, we have to have help everywhere. I am convinced Dr. Foster is the person to galvanize this help and lead this charge. We want everyone to do their part to find the solution to this problem.

I want Dr. Foster now to say a few words, but as I introduce him, I want to thank him for taking on a task in public service at a time when public service sometimes has prices that are clearer than rewards. I thank him for his willingness to serve, to try to make a difference in the health care of the people of this country and especially to try to make a difference in the future of the people of this country.

I thank his friends and colleagues for supporting him, the marvelous letter we received from Donna Shalala's predecessor, Dr. Lou Sullivan, the letter we received from the head of the American Medical Association, and of course, the support you have from your Congressman, Bob Clement, and from Senator Frist, who just told me that he's the first doctor elected to the United States Senate since before the Depression.

So I would say it is time. Now, I'm going to try to keep from feeling so poorly I need his help in any way other than a legislative sense.

Dr. Foster, the podium is yours.

[At this point, Dr. Foster thanked the President and made brief remarks.]

Teen Pregnancy

The President. You just hit the high point. Now you have to answer questions. [*Laughter*]

Q. Dr. Foster, do you think that at the— your programs about teen pregnancy in Nashville can be applied on a national scale?

Dr. Foster. I certainly do, and there have been efforts already to replicate the program. There is no doubt about it, it can be——

Q. I hear a lot about personal commitment, but I don't hear anything about official commitment. Mr. President, does your plan to combat teen pregnancy carry any new money with it? How do you intend to do that, or is it going to be done primarily by the private sector?

The President. We have a whole plan we've been working on for months, and Dr. Foster and I are going to get together and go over the outlines that we had worked on before he agreed to come on, and we will finalize that. I expect we'll be announcing it sometime in the very near future, and we'll talk about then how we intend to do it.

Q. Will it take more Federal money?

The President. Well, I think the main thing we have to do is to galvanize the resources that are there now, spend the money that's there now better, and get—I have been led to believe by many people all across this country that there will be an enormous amount of support for this effort in the private sector if they have confidence that it's a serious, disciplined, organized effort that is likely to work.

I might let Dr. Foster say more about that.

Dr. Foster. No, the only thing I would add that didn't come out, we are going to also utilize greatly the volunteer efforts. There is an emerging middle and upper black class that's doing everything now to give back. This has only developed among African-Americans since World War II. And I'm surely certain that the same sort of emergence is occurring with Hispanics and other ethnic groups in this country.

Q. Mr. President, does he have same license to be as outspoken and blunt as Dr. Elders did, or some areas—did you caution him that there are some areas that he shouldn't be talking about?

Dr. Foster. No comment. [*Laughter*]

The President. I can't do better than that. [*Laughter*]

Q. Mr. President, some conservatives have already said that they plan to oppose the nomina-

tion because of Dr. Foster's support for distribution of contraceptive devices in public schools and his stand on abortion. Do you anticipate a problem—in this confirmation?

The President. No. I'll tell you, the policy of the administration is that we should have appropriate education policies in schools, that we should encourage abstinence among our young people, that the question of contraception is one that should be resolved at the local level involving all sectors of the local community. There is no national policy on that, and there will not be.

In terms of the other issues that could be raised, I am confident that thoughtful conservatives will have the same view of Dr. Foster as Senator Frist does when they have the same opportunity to review his whole record. I think that—you know we got an endorsement from the head of the American Medical Association already and from President Bush's HHS Director, Dr. Sullivan, who went to medical school with Dr. Foster, and I think there will be many others coming forward. So I feel good about it.

Deficit Reduction

Q. Mr. President, the budget that is going to be released on Monday, are you calling for a smaller deficit decrease than you had originally hoped for?

The President. A smaller deficit——

Q. Are your efforts to decrease the deficit——

The President. Our efforts to decrease the deficit—let me say this—I'm calling for twice as much in budget cuts as I am for the cost of the middle class bill of rights, the tax relief for the middle class. So my tax cuts are paid for, and there is further deficit reduction in our budget. And we will keep a tight rein on the budget deficit.

The one thing that we have no control over in the budget deficit is the impact of higher interest rates on the deficit. The American people should know that whenever interest rates are raised by the Fed, among other things, the cost of carrying the Nation's debt goes up. So we can't do anything about that. And in that sense, the deficit will not go down as much as I had hoped, because the interest rates have gone up. You can't overcompensate for that. There's nothing to be done about it.

But we're doing a better job in controlling inflation and health care than I thought we would a year or so ago; the whole country is. I don't mean just the Government; the people in health care and the people in business are working harder on it. We have a lot of budget cuts that are very important and significant in this budget, and I'm looking forward to working with Congress to see how we can do even better. And I think that I'm encouraged by what they said, that they want to pay for their tax cuts. So I think that this—when I submit the budget, I think it'll be the beginning of a very positive thing. I don't have bad feelings about it.

China

Q. What's your reaction to China saying that your human rights report is indiscreet and meddling in their own affairs?

The President. Well, that's always been their view, and we disagree. I mean, we believe there are international standards for human rights.

The Human Rights Assistant Secretary is charged by law with submitting a report every year. All he did was fulfill his legal responsibility to tell the truth as he saw it, and I support what he did. I think Mr. Shattuck's done a good job, and I think it's a very—it's by far, by the way, the most comprehensive report ever filed by the State Department on human rights, and it covers far more than China. China was not singled out. We evaluated every country in every part of the globe with any issue in this regard.

Thank you very much.

Baseball Strike

Q. How are the baseball talks going? Have you gotten feedback?

The President. We just—we're in it. That's all I can say. Not up, not down—we're in it.

NOTE: The President spoke at 2:10 p.m. in the Oval Office at the White House. In his remarks, he referred to Dr. Foster's wife, St. Clair Foster.

Statement on Naming Aircraft Carriers for Presidents Truman and Reagan
February 2, 1995

Today I approved Secretary of the Navy John Dalton's recommendation to name CVN–75 and CVN–76, Nimitz-class aircraft carriers currently authorized for construction, the U.S.S. *Harry S. Truman* and U.S.S. *Ronald Reagan*, respectively. Protecting our Nation's security—our people, our territory, and our way of life—is a President's foremost constitutional duty. It is therefore most appropriate to name two great warships after two former Presidents who exemplified the ideals of patriotism, camaraderie, and courage found in the service men and women they led as they discharged their highest duty.

Our military today is the best equipped, best trained, and best prepared fighting force in the world. These two aircraft carriers represent my pledge to ensure our security is underpinned with military forces that are ready to fight. But our Nation can only address this era's dangers and opportunities if we remain actively engaged in the world. The two Presidents we honor today knew that there is no security for America in isolationism, no prosperity in protectionism. They worked with a Congress led by the other

party in order to foster the broad, bipartisan understanding and support necessary to sustain U.S. international engagement.

As President Truman said, "We face a clear-cut choice between two courses of action. We can either isolate ourselves from the rest of the world, or we can take constructive steps to build lasting world peace." And that is exactly the same challenge we take up today. It is therefore most appropriate to name CVN–75 in honor of the President who courageously led us out of the Second World War and prepared us to win the peace through international engagement. It was the courage and wisdom of President Truman's decisions which provided the foundation for 40 years of peace and stability throughout the cold war.

I also find it most fitting to name CVN–76 in honor of President Ronald Reagan, an American leader unsurpassed in his boundless patriotism and love for the Armed Forces and someone who still inspires us with his courage and grace. As I said in my State of the Union Address, Ronald Reagan exhorted us to carry on until the twilight struggle against communism was won.

It is because of their enduring contributions in protecting our Nation's security that we honor these two Presidents of different parties and different times. These two aircraft carriers will bear their names overseas as an instrument of power behind our determined diplomacy. Once again, the names Truman and Reagan will lend themselves in pursuit of our national security in an effort to secure the peace they won during the cold war. Together, they will join the finest forces this Nation has ever known.

Statement on Appointments to the Commission on the Roles and Capabilities of the United States Intelligence Community
February 2, 1995

I am announcing today appointments to the congressionally mandated Commission on the Roles and Capabilities of the United States Intelligence Community. The Commission will be chaired by the current Chairman of my Foreign Intelligence Advisory Board, Les Aspin. Former Senator Warren Rudman will serve as the Vice Chairman, and I have asked General Lew Allen, Jr., Zoe Baird, Ann Caracristi, Stephen Friedman, Anthony S. Harrington, Robert J. Hermann, and Ambassador Paul Wolfowitz to serve as well.

These distinguished Americans will join the eight members appointed by the leadership of the 103d Congress. They are Tony Coelho, David Dewhurst, Representative Norm Dicks, Senator James Exon, former Senator Wyche Fowler, Representative Porter Goss, General Robert Pursley, and Senator John Warner.

Intelligence remains a critical element of our national power and influence. For over 40 years bipartisan support for the work performed by U.S. intelligence has been essential to the creation of an intelligence capability that is second to none. While the world has changed in dramatic ways, our need to retain the advantage that U.S. intelligence provides our country remains constant.

With the end of the cold war we must renew and reinvigorate this bipartisan support. The foundation for this support must begin with a thorough assessment of the kind of intelligence community we will need to address the security challenges of the future. Our objective is to strengthen U.S. intelligence, to ensure it has the management, skills, and resources needed to successfully pursue our national security interests through the next decade and beyond. It is an effort to which I attach the highest personal priority.

I am confident that Les Aspin, Warren Rudman, and the other outstanding members of this Commission will work cooperatively with the leadership of the intelligence community and the Congress to ensure continued bipartisan support for this critical mission. And I know that their effort will ensure the continued trust of the American people in the outstanding and often unheralded work performed by the men and women of U.S. intelligence.

NOTE: Biographies of the appointees were made available by the Office of the Press Secretary.

Letter to Congressional Leaders on Major Narcotics Producing and Transit Countries
February 2, 1995

Dear Mr. Chairman:

In accordance with section 490(h) of the Foreign Assistance Act of 1961, as amended, I have determined that the following countries are major illicit drug producing or drug transit countries: Afghanistan, The Bahamas, Bolivia, Brazil, Burma, China, Colombia, Dominican Republic, Ecuador, Guatemala, Haiti, Hong Kong, India, Iran, Jamaica, Laos, Lebanon, Malaysia, Mexico, Nigeria, Pakistan, Panama, Paraguay, Peru, Syria, Taiwan, Thailand, Vietnam, and Venezuela. These countries have been selected on the basis of information from the April 1, 1994, International Narcotics Control Strategy Report and from other United States Government sources.

While it is an important cannabis producer, Morocco does not appear on this list since I have determined that its estimated 30,000 hectares of illicit cannabis cultivation are consumed mostly in Europe and North Africa as hashish and do not significantly affect the United States. (Under section 481(e)(2)(C) of the Foreign Assistance Act, as amended by the International Narcotics Control Corrections Act of 1994, the term "major illicit drug producing country" is defined to include countries in which 5,000 hectares or more of illicit cannabis is cultivated or harvested during a year, unless I determine that such illicit cannabis production does not significantly affect the United States.)

This year the Dominican Republic, Haiti, Taiwan, and Vietnam have been added to the list and Belize has been removed for the following reasons:

Dominican Republic and *Haiti.* These countries share an important location astride one of the key transit routes for drugs moving from South America to the United States. Over the past few years, there has been continuing evidence that Colombian traffickers use the Dominican Republic to transship cocaine bound for the United States. A number of metric ton cocaine seizures in Puerto Rico were delivered in small craft proceeding from Dominican ports. In March 1993, the U.S. Coast Guard seized 756 kilograms of cocaine just south of the Dominican Republic. In June 1993, Dominican authorities seized another 784 kilograms on the country's northern coast. As of November 29, 1994, Dominican authorities had seized 2.6 metric tons of cocaine this year. These record seizures represent an increasingly active and effective counternarcotics effort on the part of the Dominican government in 1994. We look forward to building upon this cooperation in the coming year.

There is strong evidence that much of the cocaine passing through the Dominican Republic was originally delivered on the Haitian side of the island, where until September a chaotic political situation provided an environment for drug trafficking. Before the U.S. intervention, Haitian authorities reported seizing 716 kilograms of cocaine. Accurate measurement of the volume of drugs moving through Haiti, however, was difficult because of the minimal cooperation from the military regime.

Since the intervention, measures taken by the Aristide government, as well as improved cooperation between the Haitian and United States Governments, appear to have drastically reduced trafficking through the Haitian part of Hispaniola. We expect that the return of democratic government will make it harder to move drugs through Haiti, but its geographical location will continue to offer a convenient transshipment point for U.S.-bound drugs. We plan to work closely with Haitian authorities to develop even more effective antidrug programs in the months ahead.

Taiwan. Taiwan has become an important point for the transshipment and repackaging of heroin and should be included on the list on that basis. The recordbreaking U.S. seizures of nearly half a metric ton (486 kilograms) of heroin in 1991 was transshipped through Taiwan. Heroin seizures in Taiwan have risen from 240 kilograms in 1991 to more than one metric ton (1,114 kilograms) in 1993, confirming Taiwan's role as a point of major activity in the heroin trade. Taiwan authorities are aware of the heroin trafficking problem they face and have mounted a vigorous drug enforcement campaign that is responsible for the recent high volume of seizures.

Vietnam. We have no official United States Government estimate of opium cultivation in Vietnam, but the Government of Vietnam and the United Nations Drug Control Program (UNDCP) agree that cultivation far exceeds the 1,000-hectare threshold that requires inclusion on the list as a drug producing country. According to the UNDCP, over 14,000 hectares of opium were cultivated in the 1992/93 growing season, 10,000 of which were eradicated and 4,000 harvested. A Government of Vietnam source stated that 3,770 hectares were cultivated in the 1993/94 season. Vietnam also has a worsening drug addiction problem and a growing role as a transit and trafficking point for Southeast Asian heroin.

Belize. Belize was originally listed as a major cannabis producer at a time when the country's marijuana exports were having an impact in the United States. Since joint eradication efforts have effectively reduced cannabis to negligible amounts. Belize has been removed from the list of major drug producing countries. We will be watching to determine whether it becomes a major transit point for drugs moving to the United States.

Although Cambodia and Cuba have not been added to the list during this cycle, their strategic location along major trafficking routes makes them logical prospects for inclusion as major drug transit countries. We do not yet have sufficient information to evaluate either country's importance in the transit of U.S.-bound drugs. We will be observing them closely with the possibility of adding one or both to the list in the future if the circumstances warrant.

In my letter of January 3, 1994, to your predecessors, setting forth last year's list of major illicit drug producing and drug transit countries, I noted that we were examining the possibly significant illicit cultivation of opium poppies in Central Asia and anticipated completion of our assessment by 1995. Because of technical and resource limitations, we do not yet have useful survey results on opium cultivation in Central Asia. We hope to be in a better position to assess the situation by late 1995.

Sincerely,

WILLIAM J. CLINTON

NOTE: Identical letters were sent to Jesse Helms, chairman, Senate Committee on Foreign Relations; Mark O. Hatfield, chairman, Senate Committee on Appropriations; Benjamin A. Gilman, chairman, House Committee on International Relations; and Bob Livingston, chairman, House Committee on Appropriations. The related memorandum of February 28 is listed in Appendix D at the end of this volume.

Remarks on the Minimum Wage
February 3, 1995

Good morning. When we scheduled this out here, we had a different forecast. [*Laughter*] But here we are, the hardy party. [*Laughter*]

Today marks the completion of 2 full years of economic reports in our administration. This morning the Department of Labor reported that nearly 6 million jobs have come into our economy since I took office 2 years ago; 1994 was the best year for job growth in a decade. The unemployment rate has dropped 20 percent in the last 2 years, and the combined rates of unemployment and inflation are at a 25-year low. Ninety-three percent of this job growth has been

in the private sector. That's the highest percentage of private sector jobs created in any administration in half a century, 8 times as many per month as during the 4 years before I took office. The majority of these jobs have been created in higher wage occupations. And in the 12 years before I took office, while our economy lost 2 million manufacturing jobs, in the last 17 months we have gained 300,000 manufacturing jobs.

I'm proud of this record, but I am also keenly aware of the fact that not all Americans have benefited from this recovery, that too many

Americans are still in what the Secretary of Labor has called the anxious class, people who are working harder for the same or lower wages.

From the end of World War II until the late 1970's, the incomes of all Americans rose steadily together. When the wealthiest Americans did better, so did the poorest working Americans in roughly the same proportion. But since 1979, the income of the top 20 percent of our people has grown significantly, while the income of the last 80 percent grew barely at all or not at all or actually dropped. Much of the problem in the widening income gap among working Americans depends upon whether they have skills or not to compete in the global economy.

A male college graduate today earns 80 percent more than a person with only a high school degree. That's why we've pursued the far-reaching education agenda that the Members here on this platform have been so actively involved with, making it easier and more affordable to get college loans. That's why I proposed the middle class bill of rights to help parents with their children's education and with their own and to improve the way we provide help to workers who are trying to get retraining skills.

But another no-less-important part of this problem is the declining value of full-time wages for many, many jobs. I believe if we really honor work, anyone who takes responsibility to work full time should be able to support a family and live in dignity. That is the essence of what I meant in the State of the Union Address and what I have talked about for 3 years now with the New Covenant. Our job is to create enough opportunity for people to earn a living if they'll exercise the responsibility to work.

That's why we fought so hard to expand the earned-income tax credit, a working family tax cut for 15 million families in 1993; precisely why we're calling on Congress today to raise the minimum wage 90 cents to $5.15 per hour. The only way to grow the middle class and shrink the under class is to make work pay. And in terms of real buying power, the minimum wage will be at a 40-year low next year if we do not raise it above $4.25 an hour.

If we're serious—let me say this, too, emphatically—if we are serious about welfare reform, then we have a clear obligation to make work attractive and to reward people who are willing to work hard. I hope more than anything that we will have a genuine bipartisan, well-founded welfare reform legislation this year that will encourage work and responsible parenting and independence. But we cannot hope to have it succeed unless the people we are asking to work can be rewarded for their labors.

Let me close with one observation about recent history. In 1990, Congress raised the minimum wage according to the exact same schedule I proposed today, 45 cents a year for 2 years. That increase was passed by overwhelming majorities in both Houses with, let me emphasize, majority support from both parties. This has always been a bipartisan issue.

If in 1990, because the minimum wage had not been raised in such a long time, a Republican President and a Democratic Congress could raise the minimum wage, surely, in 1995, facing the prospect that work, full-time work could be at a 40-year low in buying power unless we act, a Congress with a Republican majority and a Democratic President can do the same for the American people.

Thank you very much. And thank you all.

NOTE: The President spoke at 9:35 a.m. in the Rose Garden at the White House.

Message to the Congress Reporting on the National Emergency With Respect to Haiti
February 3, 1995

To the Congress of the United States:

1. In December 1990, the Haitian people elected Jean-Bertrand Aristide as their President by an overwhelming margin in a free and fair election. The United States praised Haiti's success in peacefully implementing its democratic constitutional system and provided significant political and economic support to the new government. The Haitian military abruptly interrupted the consolidation of Haiti's new democ-

racy when, in September 1991, it illegally and violently ousted President Aristide from office and drove him into exile.

2. The United States, on its own and with the Organization of American States (OAS), immediately imposed sanctions against the illegal regime. Upon the recommendation of the legitimate government of President Aristide and of the OAS, the United Nations Security Council imposed incrementally a universal embargo on Haiti, beginning June 16, 1993, with trade restrictions on certain strategic commodities. The United States actively supported the efforts of the OAS and the United Nations to restore democracy to Haiti and to bring about President Aristide's return by facilitating negotiations between the Haitian parties. The United States and the international community also offered material assistance within the context of an eventual negotiated settlement of the Haitian crisis to support the return to democracy, build constitutional structures, and foster economic well-being.

The continued defiance of the will of the international community by the illegal regime led to an intensification of bilateral and multilateral economic sanctions against Haiti in May 1994. The U.N. Security Council on May 6 adopted Resolution 917, imposing comprehensive trade sanctions and other measures on Haiti. This was followed by a succession of unilateral U.S. sanctions designed to isolate the illegal regime. To augment embargo enforcement, the United States and other countries entered into a cooperative endeavor with the Dominican Republic to monitor that country's enforcement of sanctions along its land border and in its coastal waters.

Defying coordinated international efforts, the illegal military regime in Haiti remained intransigent for some time. Internal repression continued to worsen, exemplified by the expulsion in July 1994 of the U.N./O.A.S.-sponsored International Civilian Mission (ICM) human rights observers. Responding to the threat to peace and security in the region, the U.N. Security Council passed Resolution 940 on July 31, 1994, authorizing the formation of a multinational force to use all necessary means to facilitate the departure from Haiti of the military leadership and the return of legitimate authorities including President Aristide.

In the succeeding weeks, the international community under U.S. leadership assembled a multinational coalition force to carry out this mandate. At my request, former President Carter, Chairman of the Senate Armed Services Committee Sam Nunn, and former Chairman of the Joint Chiefs of Staff Colin Powell went to Haiti on September 16 to meet with the *de facto* Haitian leadership. The threat of imminent military intervention combined with determined diplomacy achieved agreement in Port-au-Prince on September 18 for the *de facto* leaders to relinquish power by October 15. United States forces in the vanguard of the multinational coalition force drawn from 26 countries began a peaceful deployment in Haiti on September 19 and the military leaders have since relinquished power.

In a spirit of reconciliation and reconstruction, on September 25 President Aristide called for the immediate easing of sanctions so that the work of rebuilding could begin. In response to this request, on September 26 in an address before the United Nations General Assembly, I announced my intention to suspend all unilateral sanctions against Haiti except those that affected the military leaders and their immediate supporters and families. On September 29, the U.N. Security Council adopted Resolution 944 terminating U.N.-imposed sanctions as of the day after President Aristide returned to Haiti.

On October 15, President Aristide returned to Haiti to assume his official responsibilities. Effective October 16, 1994, by Executive Order No. 12932 (59 *Fed. Reg.* 52403, October 14, 1994), I terminated the national emergency declared on October 4, 1991, in Executive Order No. 12775, along with all sanctions with respect to Haiti imposed in that Executive order, subsequent Executive orders, and the Department of the Treasury regulations to deal with that emergency. This termination does not affect compliance and enforcement actions involving prior transactions or violations of the sanctions.

3. This report is submitted to the Congress pursuant to 50 U.S.C. 1641(c) and 1703(c). It is not a report on all U.S. activities with respect to Haiti, but discusses only those Administration actions and expenses since my last report (October 13, 1994) that are directly related to the national emergency with respect to Haiti declared in Executive Order No. 12775, as implemented pursuant to that order and Executive Orders Nos. 12779, 12853, 12872, 12914, 12917, 12920, and 12922.

4. The Department of the Treasury's Office of Foreign Assets Control (FAC) amended the Haitian Transactions Regulations, 31 C.F.R. Part 580 (the "HTR") on December 27, 1994 (59 *Fed. Reg.* 66476, December 27, 1994), to add section 580.524, indicating the termination of sanctions pursuant to Executive Order No. 12932, effective October 16, 1994. The effect of this amendment is to authorize all transactions previously prohibited by subpart B of the HTR or by the previously stated Executive orders. Reports due under general or specific license must still be filed with FAC covering activities up until the effective date of this termination. Enforcement actions with respect to past violations of the sanctions are not affected by the termination of sanctions. A copy of the FAC amendment is attached.

5. The total expenses incurred by the Federal Government during the period of the national emergency with respect to Haiti from October 4, 1991, through October 15, 1994, that are directly attributable to the authorities conferred by the declaration of a national emergency with respect to Haiti are estimated to be approximately $6.2 million, most of which represent wage and salary costs for Federal personnel. This estimate has been revised downward substantially from the sum of estimates previously reported in order to eliminate certain previously reported costs incurred with respect to Haiti, but not directly attributable to the exercise of powers and authorities conferred by the declaration of the terminated national emergency with respect to Haiti.

Thus, with the termination of sanctions, this is the last periodic report that will be submitted pursuant to 50 U.S.C. 1703(c) and also constitutes the last semiannual report and final report on Administration expenditures required pursuant to 50 U.S.C. 1641(c).

WILLIAM J. CLINTON

The White House,
February 3, 1995.

Message to the Congress on Trade With Armenia, the Bahamas, and Israel
February 3, 1995

To the Congress of the United States:

The Generalized System of Preferences (GSP) program offers duty-free treatment to specified products that are imported from designated beneficiary countries. It is authorized by the Trade Act of 1974, as amended.

I am writing to inform you of my intent to add Armenia to the list of beneficiary developing countries for purposes of the GSP program. I have carefully considered the criteria identified in sections 501 and 502 of the Trade Act of 1974. In light of these criteria, I have determined that it is appropriate to extend GSP benefits to Armenia.

I am also writing to inform you of my decision to terminate the designation of The Bahamas and the designation of Israel as beneficiary developing countries for purposes of the GSP pro-gram. Pursuant to section 504(f) of the Trade Act of 1974, I have determined that the per capita gross national products of The Bahamas and of Israel have exceeded the applicable limit provided for in section 504(f). Accordingly, I have determined that it is appropriate to terminate the designation of The Bahamas and Israel as GSP beneficiaries.

This notice is submitted in accordance with sections 502(a)(1) and 502(a)(2) of the Trade Act of 1974.

WILLIAM J. CLINTON

The White House,
February 3, 1995.

NOTE: The related proclamation is listed in Appendix D at the end of this volume.

Letter to Congressional Leaders Transmitting the Report on Science, Technology, and American Diplomacy
February 3, 1995

Dear Mr. Speaker: (Dear Mr. Chairman:)

I am pleased to transmit this annual report on Science, Technology and American Diplomacy for fiscal year 1994, in accordance with Title V of the Foreign Relations Act of Fiscal Year 1979, as amended (Public Law 95–426; 22 U.S.C. 2656c(b)).

Prevention and resolution of conflicts that threaten U.S. interests continues to be a key goal of U.S. foreign policy. National and regional stability, broadly defined, are preconditions for the growth of democracies, economies, and markets. By supporting international science and technology collaborations, the United States has reaped significant economic benefits, promoted goodwill, and helped maintain the peace.

The 1994 Title V report describes the role of international science and technology cooperation in the implementation of U.S. policy. As in previous years, the report focuses on a few selected areas of science and technology cooperation of particular importance to the United States, in addition to the detailed country narratives.

The report reviews the steps U.S. agencies take to advance U.S. technology and competitiveness interests through international efforts. These fall into three broad categories: monitoring foreign science and technology developments; conducting strategic international collaborative initiatives and programs to take advantage of opportunities for mutual gain, sometimes done in conjunction with the private sector; and the elimination of international barriers that impede technology development or trade. International collaboration in science and technology is also critical to U.S. efforts to help address population stabilization and the improvement of women's health. The 1994 Title V report provides an in-depth description of efforts underway in U.S. agencies to address these broad themes.

We face the challenge of seeking greater world stability at a critical time in our history. Finding creative solutions to global problems that impact Americans can be accomplished, in part, through interactions with scientists around the globe. We must continue to ensure that our country maintains world leadership in science and technology, and that international cooperation continues to advance our broad policy interests.

Sincerely,

WILLIAM J. CLINTON

NOTE: Identical letters were sent to Newt Gingrich, Speaker of the House of Representatives; Jesse Helms, chairman, Senate Committee on Foreign Relations; and William V. Roth, Jr., chairman, Senate Committee on Governmental Affairs.

The President's Radio Address
February 4, 1995

Good morning. This week marked the completion of 2 full years of economic reports during our administration. Since I took office 2 years ago, nearly 6 million new jobs have come into our economy. The unemployment rate has dropped more than 20 percent. Nineteen ninety-four was the best year for economic growth in 10 years in the United States. And the combined rates of unemployment and inflation are the lowest they've been in 25 years.

Ninety-three percent of our new jobs are in the private sector. That's the highest percentage of private sector jobs created in any administration in 50 years and 8 times as many each month as were created during the 4 years before I took office. The majority of these jobs are in higher wage occupations. And while the economy lost 2 million manufacturing jobs in the 12 years before I took office, we've gained back 300,000 of those manufacturing jobs in the 17 months since our economic plan went into effect.

I'm proud of this record. But I am very aware that far too many Americans have not benefited from this economic recovery. It used to be that a rising tide did lift all boats. From the end of World War II until the late 1970's, the incomes of all Americans rose steadily together. But since then, too many Americans are working harder and not getting ahead. Since 1979, the top 20 percent of our country has done quite well. But incomes from the rest of us have barely grown at all, or have actually dropped.

Why has this happened? Pressures from the new global economy and the constant demand for new skills put a huge premium on education and training and make it harder and harder for people without the necessary skills to compete for rising incomes. This has had an impact on nearly every one of our families, making it harder to guarantee job security, harder to get a raise.

That's why we push so hard to improve educational opportunities, including college loans for middle class people that are more affordable and easier to pay back. That's why I've proposed the middle class bill of rights which will increase income in the short and long runs by cutting taxes and promoting education and training, by giving a tax deduction for the cost of education after high school, by letting people withdraw tax-free from their IRA's for education costs, by making available to lower wage workers and unemployed people cash vouchers of up to $2,600 a year for more training.

But even as we help Americans to gain the tools they need to compete and to raise their incomes, we have to reward their work by improving the wages of people who work full-time. I've worked hard to get higher paying jobs into our country through trade and increased investments and technology, but we have to do more. If we're really going to honor work, we have to show that anyone who takes responsibility and works full-time can support a family and can live in dignity.

Those are the values at the heart of the New Covenant I've talked about for the last 3 years. Our job is to create opportunity for those who take responsibility to work hard and lift themselves up. Those are the values that have always sustained us and kept us a great nation.

That's why we fought so hard for the earned-income tax credit in 1993, a working family tax cut for 15 million families with incomes under $26,000. And that's why I now call on Congress to raise the minimum wage 90 cents, to $5.15 an hour, over the 2 years. In terms of real buying power, the minimum wage will be at a 40-year low next year if we don't increase it above where it is now at $4.25 an hour.

As I told the Congress, already just this year, in one month of work, Members of Congress have earned more than full-time minimum wage workers earn all year long. Nobody can live on $4.25 an hour, and yet 2.5 million Americans are working for just that amount, and many of them have children to feed. Millions more are just above the minimum wage.

The only way to strengthen the middle class and shrink the under class is to ensure that hard work pays. Increasing the minimum wage is an important part of our strategy to do that. Congress is considering other economic strategies now as well. The test for all of these ideas should be: Do they reward work? Do they grow the middle class and shrink the under class? Do they build economic opportunity in America?

I believe, for example, if we're really serious about welfare reform, increasing the minimum wage will plainly help. More than anything, I want to give a genuine bipartisan welfare reform effort the best chance it can to produce a bill that we can all be proud of, a bill that will encourage work and responsible parenting and independence. But welfare reform can't possibly succeed unless the people we expect to leave welfare and go to work are rewarded for their labors.

In 1990 Congress raised the minimum wage, just as I propose to do, 45 cents a year for 2 years. Then, overwhelming majorities in both Houses with majority support from both political parties did that.

If in 1990 a Republican President and a Democratic Congress could get that job done, surely in 1995 a Republican Congress and a Democratic President can do the same, to uphold the value of hard work for the American people.

Thanks for listening.

NOTE: The address was recorded at 1:30 p.m. on February 3 in the Oval Office at the White House for broadcast at 10:06 a.m. on February 4.

Remarks on the 1996 Budget
February 6, 1995

Good morning. Today I am pleased to announce our administration budget for fiscal year 1996. This budget, of course, is not a beginning but a continuation, the next important step in our coordinated economic strategy to bring discipline back to Government and to help strengthen the American dream for all of our people.

I want to thank the economic team which has worked so hard to put this budget together. The Vice President, Secretary Rubin, CEA Chair Tyson, and Director Rivlin will talk today, but there are others who have also worked very, very hard on this budget.

This budget, like the two that preceded it, is based on the New Covenant I advocated when I ran for President. We're creating a leaner, not a meaner, Government, one which offers more opportunity to those who are taking responsibility for themselves, their families, and their communities.

None of this was being done when we came here 2 years ago. At that time, we faced slow economic growth, inadequate investment, very low levels of job creation, a deficit that was nearly $300 billion and projected to go over $400 billion a year by the end of the decade. The annual deficit and the total national debt had quadrupled in the 12 years before I took office.

In 2 years, we have turned that around. In 1993, we passed the single largest deficit reduction package in American history, reducing the deficit over 5 years by $505 billion. When you take into account improved performance of the economy and reduced interest rates in 1993, the deficit reduction will exceed $600 billion over this 5-year period.

We did it by returning something to Washington that had been missing for too long, real discipline and honest numbers in the budgeting process. We did it, unfortunately, last year and the year before without any votes from members of the other party. And I hope now we will be working together to keep the deficit under control and keep the economic growth going.

We cut the Federal Government by more than 100,000 positions in the last 2 years. We're on the way to reducing it, with laws already

passed, by 272,000 positions, making it the smallest it's been in more than 30 years. We cut taxes for 15 million working families, with 40 million Americans in it, about an average of $1,000 apiece for families of four with incomes under $26,000 this year. We made 9 of 10 of our small businesses eligible for tax reductions. We invested in the tools our people need, in education, in training and technology. We did more to open markets in the last 2 years than in any previous period in a generation.

The results are clear. The deficit that 2 years ago was projected to be over $400 billion a year by the end of the decade is now under $200 billion. It's going down for 3 years in a row for the first time since Truman was President. The economic plan we have already passed will cut the deficit in half as a percentage of our economy. We have almost 6 million new jobs, the biggest year in economic growth in 1994 in a decade, with 93 percent of those jobs in the private sector. That's the largest percentage of private sector job growth in 50 years. We have the lowest combined rate of unemployment and inflation in 25 years. I am proud of this record, and the budget we send today builds on that foundation.

In the third year of our strategy we are adding $81 billion more to deficit reduction. That's nearly $600 billion in real deficit cuts. And in addition to that, of course, there is more, as I said, coming as a result of the economic growth of the last 2 years.

This budget provides more than a dollar in deficit reduction for every dollar that goes into the tax cuts I will discuss in a moment. If Congress gives me the line-item veto, I will find even more cuts.

The budget already provides $144 billion in hard budget savings. Behind me, you can see in black and white the 400 programs that this budget will eliminate or consolidate: the termination of about 130 programs here and over here, the consolidation of 270 more—those 271 programs will be distilled down into 27. We are also restructuring five major agencies as part of the second round of reinventing Government the Vice President will discuss in a moment, to save $23 billion. And our reinventing Government effort is looking at all the other agencies for further opportunities that might emerge in the course of the budget debate this year.

Now, we're not cutting Government blindly. We're clearing away yesterday's Government to make room for the solutions to the problems we face today and tomorrow. We still have to keep investing to raise the living standards of our people. Despite all the progress we have made, there are still too many Americans who are working harder for less. That's why the centerpiece of this budget for me is the middle class bill of rights. It will help keep the American dream alive for everyone, by lowering taxes in ways that encourage investment in the future. It will increase the incomes of people who have not benefited from this recovery in both the short term and the long term.

There are four provisions: first, a tax deduction for the cost of education and training after high school; second, a $500 tax cut for children under 13; third, the ability to put money into an individual retirement account and withdraw the money tax-free for education, for health care costs, for the care of an elderly parent, for the purchase of a home for the first time; and fourth, the proposed "GI bill" for American workers, which collapses 70 Federal training programs, gets rid of the bureaucracy that goes with them, and instead gives a voucher worth $2,600 a year in cash to workers who are unemployed or who have low wages and are eligible for Federal training assistance so that they can take the money to the nearest approved training program that they choose.

This budget also continues our investments in other crucial areas, from education and training, including more money for Head Start and our investments in technology and our continued expansion of the national service program, which has done so much good in a completely non-bureaucratic way. It strengthens our fight against crime. It does not cut overall spending from the commitments of the crime bill last year. And it provides the most comprehensive immigration plan to fight illegal immigration that any administration has produced. It stiffens our enforcement. It increases our capacity to deport illegal immigrants, particularly those who commit crimes. It increases our ability to move in the workplace and to identify those who are in the workplace who should not be.

It provides critical resources to keep America engaged in the world. And it helps us to continue to maintain the finest military in the world. As all of you know, a few weeks ago I asked that we increase defense spending over the next 6 years by $25 billion to improve our training and quality-of-life components in the Department of Defense budget. We need to do that to support a strong and steady military.

This budget supports our efforts to reduce the risk of nuclear war and the proliferation of weapons of mass destruction. It provides funding to promote peace and to maintain democracy and free markets in crucial places throughout the world. It provides funds to continue our efforts to break down barriers to the international trading system, which mean more and better jobs if we succeed.

The only way to make these investments in our future is to make tough choices, and this budget makes them specifically and clearly. Every single one of these proposals is paid for with specific spending cuts. Anyone can offer a tax cut or propose investments. The hard part, of course, is paying for them.

I challenge the leadership of the Congress to do what we have done, to provide the taxpayers with specific and real details about the proposals they make, and then to work with us to get a budget that furthers the interests of all the American people.

Americans deserve to know. It is their futures, their families that are at stake. They deserve to know what will happen to programs they care about, like Social Security and Medicare; what their opportunities will be for educating their children and whether they'll be enhanced or reduced; what we're doing about the poorest and most vulnerable children in our society— are we increasing our investment in their Head Start, in their nutrition programs, or not?

My budget cuts spending, cuts taxes, cuts the deficit, and does not cut education or Social Security or Medicare. That is a good budget. It continues to reduce the deficit without undermining the things that I believe the Federal Government should be doing. And I wish to work with the new Congress to achieve these objectives. I hope that they will submit budgets which do the same.

Our test should be, as we go into this budgeting process: Do our decisions expand opportunities and incomes for the vast mass of middle class Americans? Do our decisions promote the values of responsibility and family and community? Do our decisions contribute to strengthening the American economy in the new global economy? If we propose a tax cut, have we paid for it?

I am proud to say that this budget meets all those tests. And I call on the 104th Congress to give it serious consideration and to enact it.

Now I'd like to ask the Vice President to come forward and talk about the specific cuts and consolidations that we have recommended. Thank you very much.

NOTE: The President spoke at 10:35 a.m. in Room 450 of the Old Executive Office Building.

Teleconference Remarks With the Crew of the Space Shuttle *Discovery* and an Exchange With Reporters
February 6, 1995

The President. Hello.

Comdr. James Wetherbee. Good afternoon.

The President. Good afternoon. I didn't know you were on the line. Congratulations.

Commander Wetherbee. Well, thank you very much, sir. And it's an honor to be talking to you. Thanks for calling.

The President. I'm glad to do it. We're all following you with great anticipation, and we're all so impressed. You know, this really proves, I think, that Russians and Americans can work together and that we can make this international space station project successful. And I can't tell you how much I appreciate all the work that all of you have done to that end.

Commander Wetherbee. Well, we agree, sir. What I kept thinking as we were rendezvousing on *Mir* was it's a great world. They have a beautiful spaceship, and we have a beautiful spaceship built by Americans. We met the people that built their spaceship. They love their space program, and we love our space program, and I think together it will be a lot better.

The President. Well, we're confident that it will. As you know, this whole mission is a number of firsts. You're the first person to ever command our efforts to rendezvous with a Russian space vehicle, and I know that Eileen Collins is the first woman ever to pilot a space shuttle.

So Eileen, I suppose you have literally shown young women all across the world they can fly as high as their dreams will take them.

Astronaut Eileen Collins. Yes. I'd like to say I think this is one of the greatest jobs in the world. And for any young people out there, if you work hard enough, you can always, always reach your dreams.

The President. Well, you certainly proved that. Look at that. We enjoy watching the microphone there. [*Laughter*]

I want to ask Dr. Harris to pick it up as it flies toward him. I want to—he's going to set another milestone by becoming the first African-American to walk in space. So you'll be floating on air, but be sure you come back.

Astronaut Bernard Harris, Jr. I'm really looking forward to that a couple of days from now, but I know I won't be—I may be the first, but I won't be the last.

The President. No, you won't be the last. We'll have a lot more if we have you as an example.

I'd also like to say something to our Russian partner in space, Vladimir Titov, who is one of the world's most experienced space travelers, and he's the first cosmonaut to see the *Mir* from an American spacecraft. So I'd like to give you a chance to say anything you'd like to the American people, Mr. Titov.

Cosmonaut Vladimir Titov. And good day, Mr. President. Thank you very much. And I'm very happy of the possibility to have this great flight. And right now, our press conference, our organization listened on the Station *Mir*, and the crew on board Station *Mir* sent for you great hello.

The President. Well, thank you very much. I want to say to all of you again, this is very exciting for us. You know, the Vice President's here with me, along with Dan Goldin, and our Science Adviser, Dr. Jack Gibbons, and we have supported this space program so strongly. And it's been, as you know, somewhat controversial in the United States in the past, but I think that people all over our country and all over the world will be seeing you today and will say, "You know, this is something worth doing." All of you have made us very proud. I can't thank you enough.

Commander Wetherbee. Well, we thank you very much for your support, Mr. President. We know you've done a lot of work over the last several years in getting us this far. There's a lot of people around our country and a lot of people in Russia that we owe a great deal of thanks, and of course it starts right at the very top. So thank you very much for your support.

The President. You're welcome. And of course we want to say hello to Michael and Janice, too, with whom we haven't talked. We're proud of all of you. Have a wonderful time, and come home safe and sound.

Give a speech. We're all——

Astronaut Janice Voss. Thank you. As you saw today, Jim Wetherbee does a great job of flying this vehicle, and we're looking forward to seeing his landing.

The President. I'll bet you are. [*Laughter*]

Commander Wetherbee. Sir, it will be a very good one, I'm quite sure.

The President. Well, come home to us. We're proud of you. Goodbye.

Commander Wetherbee. Yes, sir. Thank you very much.

[*At this point, the teleconference ended, and the President took questions from reporters.*]

The President. That's the best connection we've had, I think. Wasn't it?

Q. Would you like to be up there?

The President. You know, I would. That's pretty impressive.

Surgeon General Nominee Foster

Q. How are you going to salvage Dr. Foster's nomination?

The President. Oh, we're going to have hearings, and he's going to go forward. If the facts are no different than I understand them to be, I don't understand why he would even be in trouble.

Q. How hard are you willing to fight for his confirmation?

The President. Well, I'm going to fight for him. Like I said, if the facts are as I understand them to be, here's a man who has delivered, what, 10,000 babies, who was recognized by President Bush for his work in fighting teenage pregnancies and, in the process, reducing the number of abortions. If what he has done is what he has said he has done, I don't think that is disqualifying. And it is, after all, the law of the land.

So I'm going to be—I'm going to be very interested to see how the hearings unfold and what arguments people would give against the person who has plainly devoted his life to bringing babies into the world in a healthy and happy condition and then try to make sure they live successful lives, that they do not have children prematurely, that they do not engage in the kind of conduct that's caused so much trouble in our society today. I'm impressed with his career and with his record, and I think he'll do well.

Baseball Strike

Q. What do you hear from baseball?

The President. We're working—I just keep telling them to play ball. It's time to go. You know, it's just a few hundred folks trying to figure out how to divide nearly $2 billion. They ought to be able to figure that out in time for the rest of America to enjoy this baseball season.

Q. Do you have any hope that it will be finished tonight?

The President. I just don't know. I don't know. I don't have a recent enough update to know that. But they're working, at least, and talking, and that's hopeful.

NOTE: The President spoke at 4:52 p.m. from the Oval Office at the White House. In his remarks, he referred to Daniel S. Goldin, Administrator, National Air and Space Administration, and *Discovery* astronaut C. Michael Foale. A portion of these remarks could not be verified because the tape was incomplete.

Message to the Congress Reporting Budget Rescissions
February 6, 1995

To the Congress of the United States:

In accordance with the Congressional Budget and Impoundment Control Act of 1974, I herewith report 23 rescission proposals of budgetary resources, totaling $1.1 billion. These rescissions, when combined with other discretionary savings proposals contained in the FY 1996 Budget, will reduce FY 1995 budgetary resources by $2.4 billion.

The proposed rescissions affect the Departments of Agriculture, Commerce, Education, Health and Human Services, Housing and Urban Development, Labor, and Transportation; the Environmental Protection Agency; the National Aeronautics and Space Administration; the Small Business Administration; the Chemical Safety and Hazard Investigation Board; and the National Science Foundation.

WILLIAM J. CLINTON

The White House,
February 6, 1995.

NOTE: The report detailing the proposed rescissions was published in the *Federal Register* on February 15.

Remarks on the Immigration Policy Initiative and an Exchange With Reporters
February 7, 1995

The President. Good morning. Two years ago, when I took office, I was determined to do a better job of dealing with the problem of illegal immigration. About 2 years ago this week, when I discussed with Janet Reno the possibility of her becoming Attorney General, we had a talk about this, and for the last 2 years we have been hard at work to try to fix a system that everyone agreed had serious problems.

The Vice President and I have just been briefed by Attorney General Reno; Doris Meissner, the Commissioner of Immigration and Naturalization Service; our Secretary of Labor, Bob Reich; Maria Echaveste, the Director of the Wage and Hour Division of the Labor Department; Silvestre Reyes, Chief Border Patrol Agent of the El Paso Sector; Gus de la Vina, the Director of the Western Region of the Immigration and Naturalization Service; Doug Crum, the U.S. Border Patrol Chief; and George Weise, our Customs Commissioner.

After our meeting, I signed a Presidential directive to the heads of all executive departments instructing them to very quickly expand and strengthen our program to reduce illegal immigration in four key areas: first, protecting our borders; second, protecting the interests of our workers in the workplace; third, removing more

criminal aliens; and fourth, providing more assistance to the States which are burdened with the problem of illegal immigration.

For example, I've asked the Attorney General to increase those elements of our Border Patrol strategy that are proving most effective, including the use of helicopters, night scopes, and all-terrain vehicles. I've asked the members of the Cabinet to create for the first time a national detention and removal plan to dramatically increase the identification and removal of deportable illegal aliens. These are just a few examples, and of course you'll get more in a moment when the people behind me give a more extensive background briefing.

One of the cornerstones of our fight against illegal immigration has been a get-tough policy at our borders. We initiated Operation Hold the Line at El Paso, Operation Gatekeeper in San Diego, and Operation Safeguard in Arizona, all with one clear intention, to secure the Southwest border. As we speak, these initiatives are making a substantial difference. Illegal immigration is down; crime is down. And my budget in immigration strategy builds on that success. Here are the elements of the initiative:

First, I have asked Congress for an additional $1 billion to fight illegal immigration in the coming fiscal year. I want to emphasize that while most of the talk yesterday was about cutting the budget, and we do have $140 billion in budget cuts, there are some things we should spend more money on. We recommended spending more money on education, on medical research in AIDS, on crime, in the community policing bill, on veterans interests. And we recommended a billion more dollars to fight illegal immigration. Under the budgets already passed, we've added 1,000 new Border Patrol agents just in the Southwest. By the end of 1996, our administration will have increased overall border personnel by 51 percent since 1993.

Second, I've asked for more funds to protect American jobs by increasing the number of workplace investigators by 85 percent. Our administration will begin to test different methods of helping employers verify a worker's employment authorization. This was, as I'm sure you'll remember, one of the key recommendations of the Jordan commission. Barbara Jordan wanted to be here with us today, but in pursuit of that commission's work, she is traveling the country. She has sent us a letter endorsing the proposals in this package.

The fact is that employer sanctions have been in the law on illegal immigration since 1986, but no prior administration has made a serious attempt to enforce them. With this budget and with legislation I will soon be sending to Congress, we will be able to crack down on employers who knowingly hire illegal immigrants. If we turn off the employment stream for illegal workers, far, far fewer of them will risk the difficult journey here.

Incidentally, our financial support package for Mexico will also, over the long run, reduce pressure on illegal immigration. With a healthier economy, the Mexican people will find more opportunities for jobs at home.

Thirdly, I have asked for new funds to double the deportation of criminal aliens next year and to triple them by 1996.

And finally, ours is the first administration to reimburse States for a share of the costs that they bear related to illegal immigration, including the incarceration of illegal aliens. I've asked Congress for a total of $550 million for State reimbursement; that more than doubles the fund that now exists.

Whether through the budget, the directive I've just signed, or the legislation I will soon send to the Congress, our goals are the same: tougher border enforcement, more protection for American workers, faster deportation of criminal aliens, additional assistance to the States. That's a comprehensive strategy that is already beginning to work and that will work much better if this plan is implemented by the administration and by the Congress. We need help from the Congress to implement this plan.

I want Congress to move quickly on this issue, just as we have moved quickly on a number of fronts. I am proud at the speed that the INS showed recently in moving 62 Border Patrol agents in 24 hours to Nogales, Arizona, to reinforce that border. In the future, if our budget becomes law, that kind of movement won't be necessary. For the first time ever there will be a rapid response team to enable the Border Patrol to react quickly to buildups at any particular border spots.

We've accomplished a lot in just 2 years. As I said in the State of the Union, we are a nation of immigrants, and we should all be proud of it. But we're also a nation of laws. It is wrong and ultimately self-defeating for a nation of immigrants to permit the kind of abuse of our immigration laws that we have seen in recent years. There is too much of it, and we must do much more to stop it.

Thank you very much.

Surgeon General Nominee Foster

Q. Mr. President, have you cleared up the conflicting statements about Dr. Foster and abortions?

The President. I believe that they've been cleared up, and I certainly support him.

NOTE: The President spoke at 11:23 a.m. in the Roosevelt Room at the White House. The memorandum is listed in Appendix D at the end of this volume.

Remarks and an Exchange With Reporters on the Major League Baseball Strike
February 7, 1995

The President. Good evening. Sorry to keep you here so long tonight. I had hoped that tonight I'd be coming out to tell you that baseball was coming back in 1995, and for a good while this evening, I thought that that might well be the case. Unfortunately, the parties have not reached agreement.

The American people are the real losers, the major league cities, the spring training communities, the families of thousands of Americans who won't have work unless there's a baseball season, and of course, the millions of fans who have waited now for 6 long months for the owners and the players to give us back our national pastime.

I have done all I could to change this situation. At my request, Bill Usery, the highly respected former Secretary of Labor, has been working very hard in mediating this dispute. He has certainly gone the extra mile, and we all owe him our thanks. But the players and owners still remain apart on their differences. Clearly they are not capable of settling this strike without an umpire. So I have now concluded, since I have no legal authority in this situation, as all of you know and have known for some time, that I should send to the Congress legislation seeking binding arbitration of the baseball dispute.

This is not a request for a congressionally imposed solution. It is a request for the only process we have left to us to find a solution through neutral parties. And the only way to do this appears to be for Congress to step up to the plate and pass the legislation. Unless they do, we may not have baseball in 1995.

I know that the people in Congress say they have other pressing business, and they certainly do have other pressing business. I regret very much having to send this legislation there, but spring training is just 9 days away, and I think many Americans consider this pressing. At least when the bill goes to the Congress, the American people can make themselves heard one way or the other on the legislation and Congress can consider it.

Clearly, the best solution is still one that is voluntary. I still call again on both sides to work

with Mr. Usery to narrow their differences. Hopefully, they can reach agreement. If not, then Mr. Usery's recommendations as to where the parties are at the time can be made available to the arbitrators.

I urge the parties to embrace this course themselves. And as I said, I had hoped for a while tonight that they would. We have done the best we can. The American people have been frustrated by the strike. I think all the parties who were here tonight have now been frustrated by the strike.

There is something the American people can do. They can tell their Senator or Representative whether they feel this is a proper case for binding arbitration. Last fall, for the first time in 90 years, there was no World Series. If something goes on for that long without interruption, seeing our Nation through wars and dramatic social changes, it becomes more than a game, more than simply a way to pass time. It becomes part of who we are. And we've all got to work to preserve that part.

So again I say, I call on the players and the owners to go back, to keep talking, to work through this. There is still time. I will send the legislation to Congress with the full expectation that Congress will consider it in light of what they believe their constituents want, which their constituents will have the opportunity to tell them.

Q. Mr. President, you've met now with the players and the owners. In your opinion, who is more to blame for this impasse? And why don't they simply accept voluntarily binding arbitration?

The President. Well, I think both sides have their share of blame, and I think it would be wrong for me to characterize it at this time. I don't think that would help to settle the suit. You should ask them why they won't accept what they won't accept. They will both have different explanations for that, and I will leave it for them to put it out there. I did urge that course strongly.

Q. Mr. President, what gave rise to the optimism you felt during the course of the evening that a settlement might be possible?

The President. Well, I don't want to do anything to weaken either side's position or characterize it in a way they might later think is unfair. Let me just say, I thought that we were about to get agreement on a process which would permit the next season to be played, that would permit spring training to occur, and that would lead to the resolution of these issues. I thought that we had worked our way through—there were some new ideas presented tonight as we discussed, as we talked.

That's why, you know, when they didn't reach agreement, when they came over here at 4:30 p.m., I thought I was going to come out and make the statement I just made to you. But then I said we ought to try one more time. And the Vice President sat with Mr. Usery and both sides, and then about 7 p.m. I began to meet with them. Now, we've worked hard for more than 3 hours now, and we could not agree on a process that both sides thought was fair to their interest which would immediately permit me to announce that baseball would be played this season. But we did have some new ideas offered that had not been on the table before that I thought would lead to that. Unfortunately, it did not, at least it has not tonight.

Q. Mr. President, when will you send up your legislation? And are you asking Congress to make this their top priority, putting aside their other business until they complete action on this?

The President. I'm going to send it up tomorrow, and I would like to have it considered expeditiously, yes. I haven't looked at the congressional calendar; I don't even know what their options are for that. But I think it should be considered expeditiously. I think, obviously it can't be done in a day or two, anyway, so the Congress will have time to hear from the American people, pro and con. This is an unusual request; I realize that. There is no baseball commissioner. We lost the World Series. Millions upon millions of dollars in lost income is at stake, and a lot more as well. So I hope they will consider it expeditiously. I think that's the only way it could lead to a season in '95.

Q. How do you compare this, Mr. President, to, say, President Kennedy acting on steel prices and former uses of the office and the Oval Office for labor dispute?

The President. Well, I think it's a little different in the sense that the steel price issue could have sent inflation through the economy and shut the economy down. I've tried to explain that if it weren't for the unusual nature of this case, I would not be intervening in the baseball case because the economy of the country won't go down as a result of it. The inflation rate of the country won't go up as a result of something that could or couldn't happen.

This is far more in the nature of a unique set of circumstances where there isn't a commissioner and there should have been to resolve this, and where there is immediate substantial threat to a large number of communities affected by spring training and the communities that have baseball teams, and where I think the country would be well served by resolving this. So it is different in that sense.

I was looking at the history of Presidential action in these areas, going back to the first one, which I believe was under President Theodore Roosevelt, which unfortunately was also unsuccessful. Just 3 years before he settled the Russo-Japanese War and won the Nobel Peace Prize, he found difficulty in settling a labor dispute here in the United States.

I still think this can be settled. The parties are just going to have to decide whether they want to have a baseball season in '95 and what the long-term damage to baseball will be and therefore the economics of both sides if it doesn't happen.

Q. Mr. President, if the season begins with replacement players, would you throw out the first ball?

The President. I am encouraging these parties to go back and work out their differences. Until I am convinced that they have exhausted all opportunities to do that, the less I say about all other issues, the better we're going to be. I do not want to be yet another force undermining the possibility of an agreement. I want to be a force to create an increased likelihood of an agreement, and that's what I've done so far. I'm sorry I don't have a success to report tonight. I'm not sorry I tried, and we'll keep working at it.

NOTE: The President spoke at 10:51 p.m. in the Briefing Room at the White House.

Remarks Announcing Community Policing Grants
February 8, 1995

Thank you so much, Sheriff Kelly. He spoke so well I hardly want to say anything. [*Laughter*] Chief Viverette, thank you very much for your work and for coming here and for what you said. I thank Attorney General Reno and Lee Brown for their outstanding work for our country. I'm very proud that they're a part of our administration. And I thank Chief Brann and John Schmidt for the work they have done on this police program, and of course, the Vice President for what he said and for what he does and for clarifying the nature of public spending under the LEAA program. If they bought me an airplane I'd still be Governor. [*Laughter*] I want to thank the Members of Congress who are here for what they did on the crime bill last year. And I want to thank many who are not here, but I would be remiss if I did not acknowledge Senator Biden, without whom we might never have had this crime bill. I thank him especially in his absence.

This is security week at the White House, I think you could say. We talked about immigration yesterday and the need to protect our borders from illegal immigration. Today we're releasing our drug control strategy and talking about police officers. I'd like to put it briefly in the context of what I have been trying to achieve here.

I ran for this office with a vision that at the end of this century we need to be preserving the American dream for all of our people and making sure that as we move into the next century we're still the strongest country in the world. I think our strategy should be what I have called the New Covenant, creating more opportunity but insisting on more responsibility and strengthening our communities at the grassroots level.

The role of government and specifically the role of the Federal Government at this time, it seems to me, is to do three things: to expand opportunity while shrinking bureaucracy, to empower Americans to make the most of their own lives, and to enhance our security at home and abroad.

In ways that are obvious, the crime bill we passed and the drug strategy we pursue furthers all of those objectives. We are working hard to help communities to arm themselves to fight crime and violence. We are working hard to help people to defeat the scourge of drugs, both by enforcement as well as prevention and education and treatment. The crime bill makes the most of the resources that we have achieved by shrinking the Federal bureaucracy dramatically, to the point where, when we finish, it will be the smallest it's been since President Kennedy was in office.

Now, that leaves a lot up to you. It's up to all of you to hire and train the police officers. It's up to you to deploy them as you see fit. It's up to every citizen in every community in America to take responsibility to join the fight.

I am all for more flexibility for States and localities. This crime bill, particularly as it was changed—and I want to thank some of the Republicans who are here for your contribution for that—we said, "Hey, we ought to give the local communities more flexibility in deciding which prevention programs to fund; they know what works and what doesn't." That was the wisdom of the Congress, but there is a national interest in having 100,000 more police officers. There is a national interest in doing that because we know enough to know that when crime triples—violent crime—over 30 years, and the size of our police forces only increase by 10 percent over 30 years, and more police get off the street and into the cars, that becomes a national problem. And when all the police groups in the country come to us and say this is in the national interest, then we have to respond to that as well.

Today we are here to award grants to over 7,000 new police officers in over 6,600 small cities, as the Attorney General said. It's an astonishing thing to me that more than half the communities in our country said, "We want to be a part of this." If ever there was evidence that there is a national interest here, that is it.

I wish that violence were a stranger to small towns. I wish that this really could have been just a problem for big cities where all the criminals in the country are congregated. But we all know that's not true. Indeed, we all know that most of our big cities have seen a decline

171

in the crime rate in the last couple of years, even though it's still at a horrendously high level. But many of our smaller communities are dealing with the aftermath. Indeed, I have many law enforcement officers tell me that they are now dealing with the consequences of being near bigger cities that have gotten more effective in combating crime, and some criminals are looking for greener pastures and more poorly armed police forces in smaller communities all across America.

All of you know that I grew up in small towns in my home State. I can still remember when we never locked the car or the house and we never gave any thought to whether we were walking outside in the night or in the daytime. I wish that that were the case for all Americans today, but it isn't. And until it is again, we have to continue to work with you to restore those conditions and to fight the people who are keeping them from occurring.

Police officers on the street are still the best protection we know for not only enforcement but for prevention, for all the ways that the chief spoke about and all the ways that all of you know. We also know that police officers on the street need the help of people in their communities. That's why in the State of the Union Address, I tried to emphasize the role of citizens.

When I lived at home in Little Rock, we lived in an area that was very mixed in every way, racially, economically, and in terms of the citizens who lived there. And our crime rate went up and down and up and down over the decade I lived in the Governor's mansion. And the biggest difference was whether the citizens in our neighborhood were participating in the neighborhood crime watch and helping the police in our neighborhood to do their job.

So we are well aware, we are well aware that we need the help of the citizens. But unless we follow through on our commitment to have 100,000 police officers on the street, the United States Government will not be doing its job and exercising its responsibility to give you the opportunity to make the streets safer. We need 100,000 more badges.

Just before I came out here, someone gave me a police badge from a neighboring State of Arkansas. I saved them, along with all the military coins I have from the units I've met. So now I have another one to put back on my desk. I want 100,000 more of these on the

street. That's in the national interest, and the Congress and the country should not back away from that. We should stay right with it until we have 100,000. That's what all these people lobbied for, and we should stay all the way.

I want to thank again all of those, but especially those in the Justice Department, who worked so hard to create a nonbureaucratic way for these police officers to come out. And that's been discussed. And I want to say again, I'm working hard to give more flexibility to State and local governments. I'm working hard to turn more authority back to States and local governments, even to the private sector where that's appropriate. I support the changes that were made in the last crime bill to give more flexibility in the area of prevention. But I will oppose any attempt to undermine the capacity of the crime bill to produce the 100,000 police officers that we promised the American people, that you came up here and lobbied for, and that you worked so hard for. We must not do that.

You know, one of the things that I've never read in all these biographies or accounts of my career is I actually once participated in the LEAA programs; I taught law enforcement officers. I taught constitutional law and criminal procedure. I was proud to do it, and it was a good program. But it didn't obscure the fact that we also have problems in the LEAA, as the Vice President outlined. And more importantly, it doesn't obscure the fact that we have a national interest and now a national solemn responsibility to take the money we save by reducing the Federal work force to go forward with 100,000 police.

I also want to emphasize—I saw a lot of you nodding your head out there when Lee Brown was up here talking—our crime bill and our national drug control strategy are intimately related. With the help of the crime bill, this year's drug controls budget is the largest in the history of the Federal Government. Last year, for the first time in 25 years, I submitted to Congress a budget—and Congress largely adopted it—which reduced both domestic and defense spending in an attempt to get control of this terrible deficit. For the first time in 25 years, the only things that went up were interest on the debt and the medical costs of the Government and the cost of living for Social Security. The aggregate spending, otherwise, went down. And I am proud of that. This year I have submitted to Congress a budget with another $140 billion in spending cuts.

But remember our objectives here. The Federal Government's job is to increase the ability of people to make the most of their own lives and to enhance security. So we're spending more on education and training and children and their future in our budget. We're also spending more on security, not only abroad but at home: more to fight the drug war, more to fight crime, more to do things that will make people more secure in their homes, in their schools, on their streets, in their workplaces. That's why this drug control strategy is important. And it's also important to note that it, too, is funded in the crime bill. A big part of the prevention section of the crime bill is an antidrug strategy, to take this country's commitment to fighting drugs to new heights.

I thank Lee Brown for his leadership, and I am going to do everything I can to implement the 1995 drug control strategy that has four steps: We propose to work more closely with foreign governments to cut drugs off at the source. We propose to boost community efforts to educate young people about the dangers and penalties of drug use, something that is very important. We see fresh and disturbing efforts—evidence that a lot of young people are no longer afraid that they will get sick, that they can die, that they can become addicted if they have casual drug use. We will work to break the cycle of crime and drugs by providing treatment to hardcore drug users who consume most of the drugs and cause much of the crime and health problems. And we will punish people who break the law more severely.

This strategy gives your communities more resources to fight drugs as well, and more flexibility, as I said, in the use of those resources.

I want to work with the new Congress to build on this crime bill, but we should not move backwards. We shouldn't undermine our ability to implement the drug control strategy. We shouldn't walk away from our commitment to provide 100,000 police officers. And we shouldn't let this become a partisan political issue. The crime bill passed with bipartisan support; it should be maintained with bipartisan support.

I have no idea what political party the law enforcement officers standing up on this platform belong to, and I don't care. It's enough for me that they're all willing to put on a uniform and put their lives on the line to make the people of this country safer and give the kids of this country a better chance.

We should listen to the experts in law enforcement and do what is right and keep this above politics. Above all, we must keep it above partisan politics. Let us listen to the evidence and do what is right for America. That should be our only test.

Thank you very much.

NOTE: The President spoke at 11:40 a.m. in Room 450 of the Old Executive Office Building. In his remarks, he referred to Gene Kelly, sheriff, Clark County, OH; Mary Ann Viverette, police chief, Gaithersburg, MD; Joseph Brann, Director, Community Oriented Policing Services program (COPS); and Associate Attorney General John Schmidt.

Remarks Announcing the Nomination of Michael Carns To Be Director of Central Intelligence and an Exchange With Reporters
February 8, 1995

The President. Ladies and gentlemen, I'm delighted to see you all here. I thank the Members of Congress especially for being here, Senator Thurmond, Senator Specter, Senator Leahy, Congressman Dicks. Is Congressman Gilman here?

It is my pleasure and honor today to announce my intention to nominate General Michael Carns to be the next Director of Central Intelligence.

General Carns will face a challenge whose difficulty is matched only by its importance. The cold war is over, but many new dangers have taken its place: regional security threats; the proliferation of weapons of mass destruction; terrorists who, as we have seen, can strike at the very heart of our own major cities; drug trafficking; and international crime. The decisive advantage United States intelligence provides this country is, therefore, as important as it has ever been.

As President, I've had the opportunity to appreciate just how important that intelligence is to our national security. Most Americans never know the victories our intelligence provides or the crises it helps us to avoid, but they do learn about its occasional setbacks. And as we prepare our intelligence community to face new challenges, we must not forget its many successes.

General Carns' broad experience and exceptional qualities make him the right leader for our intelligence community in this time of challenge and change. He's distinguished himself as a fighter pilot, a military commander, and a manager. He's a proven innovator, open to new ways of doing business and skeptical of conventional wisdom. He understands the critical importance of intelligence because he's had to rely on it when the lives of Americans and the security of our country were on the line. He's taking this critical assignment after having already dedicated a whole lifetime of outstanding service to our country. I thank him and his wife for that decision.

After graduating from the Air Force Academy in 1959, he went on to fly over 200 combat missions in Vietnam, where his heroism earned him the Silver Star and the Distinguished Flying Cross. He served as director of operations for the Rapid Deployment Task Force, deputy commander-in-chief of the United States Pacific Command, vice chief of staff of the Air Force, the office he held before entering a very short-lived retirement last September. And somewhere along the line, he even found time to get an MBA from Harvard, something for which I have already forgiven him. [*Laughter*]

General Carns also served as director of the Joint Staff during Operations Desert Shield and Desert Storm. Both Admiral William Crowe and General Colin Powell, who relied on General Carns to get the job done when our Nation was at war, know and appreciate the full measure of this fine man.

His exceptional accomplishments are rooted in a tradition of patriotism and service instilled in him by his father, Major General Edwin Carns of the Army, and by his mother, Jan, whom I had the privilege of speaking with yes-

terday. Mike and his wife, Victoria, have carried on this tradition and passed it along to their own children, Michelle, a cadet at the United States Air Force Academy, and Mark, who serves in the Air Force. Let me say to their entire family, the country is proud of your service. And I am, I say again, especially grateful to you, Victoria, for supporting this move today.

General, your mission will be greatly helped by the distinguished commission, led by our former Secretary of Defense Les Aspin and former Senator Warren Rudman, that I have asked to review the missions and structure of our intelligence community. Together, and with the help of the Congress, you can build a strong consensus for reinvigorating U.S. intelligence so that it pursues clear priorities and puts its resources behind the core missions that will continue to give our Nation the most timely, relevant, and honest intelligence in the world.

As we look to the future, I also want to thank the outgoing Director of Central Intelligence, Jim Woolsey, for his service. Thank you, Jim, and we're delighted to see you here today. No one has been a more forceful advocate for the intelligence community, in my own case, beginning long before I became President. His efforts to streamline collection systems and improve the quality of analysis will pay off for our country for many years to come.

I'd also like to express my deep appreciation to our Acting Director, Bill Studeman, who has served our Nation admirably for 32 years now. Both of you have earned our Nation's gratitude.

Finally, to the men and women of our intelligence community whose work often goes unheralded, let me say on behalf of all of us and all Americans, your country owes you a debt which can never be fully repaid, but we respect it and we appreciate it. What we can do, and what General Mike Carns and I will vow to do, is to work with you, to support you, and to challenge you as we build an intelligence community for the next century.

General Carns.

[*At this point, General Carns thanked the President and made brief remarks.*]

The President. This is the first test of his centralized intelligence. [*Laughter*]

Any questions?

Central Intelligence Agency

Q. Are you going to find any spies around?

General Carns. I think I recognize that voice. [*Laughter*]

Q. Do you think that the CIA needs an overhaul? I mean, they've made a lot of mistakes recently, haven't they?

General Carns. I would be happy to respond to your questions as soon as I am confirmed. In the meantime, I will keep my counsel.

The President. Let me just say one thing. I think recently they deserve a lot of credit for uncovering mistakes that were made in the past. After all, the Ames problem developed before the recent history—it was uncovered in recent history. They deserve credit for solving problems. The same thing with that big building out there.

Q. It took a long time.

The President. Well, we've only been here 2 years. I'm pretty proud of what Mr. Woolsey did and what the CIA has done. I think they deserve credit for solving problems.

Baseball Strike

Q. Mr. President, on another topic, there's been a lot of talk on Capitol Hill today, and a lot of opposition from Republicans to your suggestion that Congress get involved in the baseball strike. Can you tell us about that?

The President. I'll send the legislation up there. I think that this is—they should be reluctant; I was reluctant; we're all reluctant. If we had a baseball commissioner, we wouldn't—none of us would have been in here. I respect their reluctance. What I think will happen is, I'll send the legislation up, they'll hear from the American people, and they'll make their own decision. Meanwhile, I hope that the—last night I really began to hope that they'd work it out on their own. That's still what ought to happen, that's the best thing, and I hope they'll do it.

Q. Do you have any regrets about getting involved in the first place?

The President. No, because if I hadn't named a Federal mediator, without a baseball commissioner, then I would have felt that we hadn't gone the last mile to try to help resolve it. So I'm glad I named Mr. Usery. He did the very best he could. And I still hope they'll work it out.

Thank you.

Surgeon General Nominee Foster

Q. What are you hearing from the Hill about Dr. Foster? What are you hearing about from the Hill——

The President. I don't know. I haven't heard much from them, but I had lunch with a number of House Members today who said that, based on what they knew, they were for him, and so am I. I think he's a good man. You read the editorial from his hometown newspaper, the Nashville Tennessean, that came out in the last couple of days; his colleague, the only physician in the United States Congress, the doctor from Tennessee, Republican doctor from Tennessee, who stood up here with him when we announced him. He is a good man who has delivered thousands of babies and devoted his life to trying to prevent the kind of problems that he's now being criticized for. I believe he should be confirmed, and I believe he will.

Thank you.

Q. Do you think this is just a tactic to get people to defeat him because he has favored abortion rights?

The President. I think he's a good man, and when he has his hearings the American people will think so, too.

NOTE: The President spoke at 2:20 p.m. in the Roosevelt Room at the White House. In his remarks, he referred to Dr. Bill Frist, Senator from Tennessee. The Office of the Press Secretary also released a biography of the nominee.

Message to the Congress Reporting on the National Emergency With Respect to Iraq
February 8, 1995

To the Congress of the United States:

I hereby report to the Congress on the developments since my last report of August 2, 1994, concerning the national emergency with respect to Iraq that was declared in Executive Order No. 12722 of August 2, 1990. This report is submitted pursuant to section 401(c) of the National Emergencies Act, 50 U.S.C. 1641(c), and section 204(c) of the International Emergency Economic Powers Act, 50 U.S.C. 1703(c).

Executive Order No. 12722 ordered the immediate blocking of all property and interests in property of the Government of Iraq (including the Central Bank of Iraq), then or thereafter located in the United States or within the possession or control of a United States person. That order also prohibited the importation into the United States of goods and services of Iraqi origin, as well as the exportation of goods, services, and technology from the United States to Iraq. The order prohibited travel-related transactions to or from Iraq and the performance of any contract in support of any industrial, commercial, or governmental project in Iraq. United States persons were also prohibited from granting or extending credit or loans to the Government of Iraq.

The foregoing prohibitions (as well as the blocking of Government of Iraq property) were continued and augmented on August 9, 1990, by Executive Order No. 12724, which was issued in order to align the sanctions imposed by the United States with United Nations Security Council Resolution 661 of August 6, 1990.

Executive Order No. 12817 was issued on October 21, 1992, to implement in the United States measures adopted in United Nations Security Council Resolution 778 of October 2, 1992. Resolution No. 778 requires U.N. Member States temporarily to transfer up to $200 million apiece in Iraqi oil sale proceeds paid by purchasers after the imposition of U.N. sanctions on Iraq, to finance Iraqi's obligations for U.N. activities with respect to Iraq, such as expenses to verify Iraqi weapons destruction, and to provide humanitarian assistance in Iraq on a nonpartisan basis. A portion of the escrowed funds will also fund the activi-ties of the U.N. Compensation Commission in Geneva, which will handle claims from victims of the Iraqi invasion of Kuwait. Member States also may make voluntary contributions to the account. The funds placed in the escrow account are to be returned, with interest, to the Member States that transferred them to the United Nations, as funds are received from future sales of Iraqi oil authorized by the U.N. Security Council. No Member State is required to fund more than half of the total transfers or contributions to the escrow account.

This report discusses only matters concerning the national emergency with respect to Iraq that was declared in Executive Order No. 12722 and matters relating to Executive Orders Nos. 12724 and 12817 (the "Executive orders"). The report covers events from August 2, 1994, through February 1, 1995.

1. There has been one action affecting the Iraqi Sanctions Regulations, 31 C.F.R. Part 575 (the "Regulations"), administered by the Office of Foreign Assets Control (FAC) of the Department of the Treasury, since my last report on August 2, 1994. On February 1, 1995 (60 Fed. Reg. 6376), FAC amended the Regulations by adding to the list of Specially Designated Nationals (SDNs) of Iraq set forth in Appendices A ("entities and individuals") and B ("merchant vessels"), the names of 24 cabinet ministers and 6 other senior officials of the Iraqi government, as well as 4 Iraqi state-owned banks, not previously identified as SDNs. Also added to the Appendices were the names of 15 entities, 11 individuals, and 1 vessel that were newly identified as Iraqi SDNs in the comprehensive list of SDNs for all sanctions programs administered by FAC that was published in the *Federal Register* (59 Fed. Reg. 59460) on November 17, 1994. In the same document, FAC also provided additional addresses and aliases for 6 previously identified Iraqi SDNs. This *Federal Register* publication brings the total number of listed Iraqi SDNs to 66 entities, 82 individuals, and 161 vessels.

Pursuant to section 575.306 of the Regulations, FAC has determined that these entities and individuals designated as SDNs are owned or controlled by, or are acting or purporting to act directly or indirectly on behalf of, the Government of Iraq, or are agencies, instrumentalities or entities of that government. By virtue of this determination, all property and interests in property of these entities or persons that are in the United States or in the possession or control of United States persons are blocked. Further, United States persons are prohibited from engaging in transactions with these individuals or entities unless the transactions are licensed by FAC. The designations were made in consultation with the Department of State. A copy of the amendment is attached to this report.

2. Investigations of possible violations of the Iraqi sanctions continue to be pursued and appropriate enforcement actions taken. The FAC continues its involvement in lawsuits, seeking to prevent the unauthorized transfer of blocked Iraqi assets. There are currently 38 enforcement actions pending, including nine cases referred by FAC to the U.S. Customs Service for joint investigation. Additional FAC civil penalty notices were prepared during the reporting period for violations of the International Emergency Economic Powers Act and the Regulations with respect to transactions involving Iraq. Four penalties totaling $26,043 were collected from two banks, one company, and one individual for violations of the prohibitions against transactions involving Iraq.

3. Investigation also continues into the roles played by various individuals and firms outside Iraq in the Iraqi government procurement network. These investigations may lead to additions to FAC's listing of individuals and organizations determined to be SDNs of the Government of Iraq.

4. Pursuant to Executive Order No. 12817 implementing United Nations Security Council Resolution No. 778, on October 26, 1992, FAC directed the Federal Reserve Bank of New York to establish a blocked account for receipt of certain post August 6, 1990, Iraqi oil sales proceeds, and to hold, invest, and transfer these funds as required by the order. On October 5, 1994, following payments by the Governments of Canada ($677,756.99), the United Kingdom ($1,740,152.44), and the European Community ($697,055.93), respectively, to the special United Nations-controlled account, entitled "United Nations Security Council Resolution 778 Escrow Account," the Federal Reserve Bank of New

York was directed to transfer a corresponding amount of $3,114,965.36 from the blocked account it holds to the United Nations-controlled account. Similarly, on December 16, 1994, following the payment of $721,217.97 by the Government of the Netherlands, $3,000,891.06 by the European Community, $4,936,808.84 by the Government of the United Kingdom, $190,476.19 by the Government of France, and $5,565,913.29 by the Government of Sweden, the Federal Reserve Bank of New York was directed to transfer a corresponding amount of $14,415,307.35 to the United Nations-controlled account. Again, on December 28, 1994, following the payment of $853,372.95 by the Government of Denmark, $1,049,719.82 by the European Community, $70,716.52 by the Government of France, $625,390.86 by the Government of Germany, $1,151,742.01 by the Government of the Netherlands, and $1,062,500.00 by the Government of the United Kingdom, the Federal Reserve Bank of New York was directed to transfer a corresponding amount of $4,813,442.16 to the United Nations controlled account. Finally, on January 13, 1995, following the payment of $796,167.00 by the Government of the Netherlands, $810,949.24 by the Government of Denmark, $613,030.61 by the Government of Finland, and $2,049,600.12 by the European Community, the Federal Reserve Bank of New York was directed to transfer a corresponding amount of $4,269,746.97 to the United Nations-controlled account. Cumulative transfers from the blocked Federal Reserve Bank of New York account since issuance of Executive Order No. 12817 have amounted to $157,542,187.88 of the up to $200 million that the United States is obligated to match from blocked Iraqi oil payments, pursuant to United Nations Security Council Resolution 778.

5. The Office of Foreign Assets Control has issued a total of 533 specific licenses regarding transactions pertaining to Iraq or Iraqi assets since August 1990. Since my last report, 37 specific licenses have been issued. Licenses were issued for transactions such as the filing of legal actions against Iraqi governmental entities, legal representation of Iraq, and the exportation to Iraq of donated medicine, medical supplies, food intended for humanitarian relief purposes, the execution of powers of attorney relating to the administration of personal assets and decedents' estates in Iraq, and the protection of preexistent intellectual property rights in Iraq.

6. The expenses incurred by the Federal Government in the 6-month period from August 2, 1994, through February 1, 1995, that are directly attributable to the exercise of powers and authorities conferred by the declaration of a national emergency with respect to Iraq are reported to be about $2.25 million, most of which represents wage and salary costs for Federal personnel. Personnel costs were largely centered in the Department of the Treasury (particularly in the Office of Foreign Assets Control, the U.S. Customs Service, the Office of the Under Secretary for Enforcement, and the Office of the General Counsel), the Department of State (particularly the Bureau of Economic and Business Affairs, the Bureau of Near East Affairs, the Bureau of Organization Affairs, and the Office of the Legal Adviser), and the Department of Transportation (particularly the U.S. Coast Guard).

7. The United States imposed economic sanctions on Iraq in response to Iraq's illegal invasion and occupation of Kuwait, a clear act of brutal aggression. The United States, together with the international community, is maintaining economic sanctions against Iraq because the Iraqi regime has failed to comply fully with United Nations Security Council resolutions. Security Council resolutions on Iraq call for the elimination of Iraqi weapons of mass destruction, the inviolability of the Iraq-Kuwait boundary, the release of Kuwaiti and other third-country nationals, compensation for victims of Iraqi aggression, long-term monitoring of weapons of mass destruction capabilities, the return of Kuwaiti assets stolen during Iraq's illegal occupation of Kuwait, renunciation of terrorism, an end to internal Iraqi repression of its own civilian population, and the facilitation of access of international relief organizations to all those in need in all parts of Iraq. More than 4 years after the invasion, a pattern of defiance persists: a refusal to account for missing Kuwaiti detainees; failure to return Kuwaiti property worth millions of dollars, including weapons used by Iraq in its movement of troops to the Kuwaiti border in October 1994; sponsorship of assassinations in Lebanon and in northern Iraq; incomplete declarations to weapons inspectors; and ongoing widespread human rights violations. As a result, the U.N. sanctions remain in place;

the United States will continue to enforce those sanctions under domestic authority.

The Baghdad government continues to violate basic human rights of its own citizens through systematic repression of minorities and denial of humanitarian assistance. The Government of Iraq has repeatedly said it will not be bound by United Nations Security Council Resolution 688. For more than 3 years, Baghdad has maintained a blockade of food, medicine, and other humanitarian supplies against northern Iraq. The Iraqi military routinely harasses residents of the north, and has attempted to "Arabize" the Kurdish, Turcomen, and Assyrian areas in the north. Iraq has not relented in its artillery attacks against civilian population centers in the south, or in its burning and draining operations in the southern marshes, which have forced thousands to flee to neighboring States.

In 1991, the United Nations Security Council adopted Resolutions 706 and 712, which would permit Iraq to sell up to $1.6 billion of oil under U.N. auspices to fund the provision of food, medicine, and other humanitarian supplies to the people of Iraq. The resolutions also provide for the payment of compensation to victims of Iraqi aggression and other U.N. activities with respect to Iraq. The equitable distribution within Iraq of this humanitarian assistance would be supervised and monitored by the United Nations. The Iraqi regime so far has refused to accept these resolutions and has thereby chosen to perpetuate the suffering of its civilian population. More than a year ago, the Iraqi government informed the United Nations that it would not implement Resolutions 706 and 712.

The policies and actions of the Saddam Hussein regime continue to pose an unusual and extraordinary threat to the national security and foreign policy of the United States, as well as to regional peace and security. The U.N. resolutions require that the Security Council be assured of Iraq's peaceful intentions in judging its compliance with sanctions. Because of Iraq's failure to comply fully with these resolutions, the United States will continue to apply economic sanctions to deter it from threatening peace and stability in the region.

WILLIAM J. CLINTON

The White House,
February 8, 1995.

Message to the Congress Transmitting a Report on the Operation of the Andean Trade Preference Act
February 8, 1995

To the Congress of the United States:

I hereby submit the first report on the Operation of the Andean Trade Preference Act. This report is prepared pursuant to the requirements of section 203 of the Andean Trade Preference Act of 1991.

WILLIAM J. CLINTON

The White House,
February 8, 1995.

Letter to Congressional Leaders Transmitting a Report on Haiti
February 8, 1995

Dear Mr. Speaker: (Dear Mr. President:)

Attached, pursuant to Section 3 of Public Law 103–423, is the fourth monthly report on the situation in Haiti.

Sincerely,

WILLIAM J. CLINTON

NOTE: Identical letters were sent to Newt Gingrich, Speaker of the House of Representatives, and Strom Thurmond, President pro tempore of the Senate.

Statement on the Apprehension of Ramzi Ahmed Yusuf
February 8, 1995

This evening in New York, Ramzi Ahmed Yusuf, one of the world's most sought after suspected terrorists, was placed in Federal detention. Yusuf is under indictment as a key figure in the 1993 bombing of the New York World Trade Center. He was on the FBI's Most Wanted List.

Yusuf was recently arrested by Pakistan and turned over to U.S. authorities in accordance with the requirements of international law.

I especially want to thank all involved in this important process. This arrest is a major step forward in the fight against terrorism. Terrorism will not pay. Terrorists will pay. We will continue to work with other nations to thwart those who would kill innocent citizens to further their own political aims.

The Executive order I signed last month to stop fundraising for Middle East terrorist groups and my proposed omnibus antiterrorism act will greatly strengthen our abilities to act quickly and decisively against this threat to peace. The budget I submitted earlier this week maintains the vigorous law enforcement, intelligence, and diplomatic capabilities the United States requires to act effectively against terrorism on all fronts.

We and other members of the international community will continue to dedicate ourselves to the cause of peace and to unite against those who threaten innocent lives.

Remarks Welcoming Chancellor Helmut Kohl of Germany
February 9, 1995

Chancellor Kohl, members of the German delegation, distinguished guests, on behalf of the American people, it is a distinct honor to welcome back to Washington the leader of one of our closest allies and one of the preeminent statesmen of our time, Chancellor Helmut Kohl.

Today marks another stride in our extraordinary journey together, one that has lasted nearly half a century. It began with reconstruction after one devastating war and a common effort to deter another. Today, Germany and the United States enjoy the fruits of our perseverance and our friendship. Because our nations have stood shoulder-to-shoulder for so long, last summer Chancellor Kohl and I could walk through the Brandenburg Gate together without checkpoints, without armed sentries.

Now our two nations must continue our journey together with the same resolve we have shown in the past. Today we renew and reaffirm our vital partnership. Together we will work to support continued reform in Russia and the Newly Independent States, a cause in which Chancellor Kohl has shown such extraordinary leadership. We will consider how to move toward NATO's expansion to Europe's new democracies and how to adapt the international institutions to serve us for the next 50 years. Working together to solve the new problems we face and to create a truly integrated Europe, this is exactly how two great democracies should mark their successes and look toward the future.

Chancellor Kohl, in the spirit of friendship and gratitude and with great hope for the future, it is a personal honor on behalf of all the people of the United States to welcome you back to the White House.

NOTE: The President spoke at 10:11 a.m. on the South Lawn at the White House.

Exchange With Reporters Prior to Discussions With Chancellor Helmut Kohl of Germany
February 9, 1995

1996 Presidential Campaign

Q. Mr. President, have you heard that former Vice President Quayle has decided not to run for the Republican nomination?

The President. I was literally—I was informed of that 3 minutes ago.

Q. What do you think about it?

The President. I'm a little surprised. But it's a hard decision, and it's an intensely personal one. I wish him well. I know it must have been a difficult decision for him.

Death of J. William Fulbright

Q. Do you have anything to say, sir, about Senator Fulbright?

The President. Yes. As you know, he was a very close friend of mine. And if it hadn't been for him, I don't think I'd be here today. I had a wonderful visit with him and with Mrs. Fulbright over Christmas. They came to the White House to see the decorations, and we had a great, great visit. And I was in his home a few weeks before that. So I've kept in close touch with him in these months of his illness.

He made an amazing contribution to the life of our country and, of course, to our home State. And he was a great inspiration to thousands and thousands of us who were young when he was a Senator and serving. And the country is in his debt.

Q. Do you think you'll go to his funeral?

The President. I certainly hope so. We're— I was informed early, early this morning that he had died during the night, and I told the folks to try to work it out.

Surgeon General Nominee Foster

Q. What do you think of Dr. Foster's performance on "Nightline"?

The President. I'm sorry to say I didn't see it because I went to bed early last night; I was very tired. But I heard he did quite well.

And I think he's a good man. I think he just needs to keep talking about his life and his record and what he wants to do. I'm looking forward to the hearings.

[At this point, one group of reporters left the room, and another group entered.]

Russia

Q. Mr. President, may I ask a question? Do you see eye to eye with the Chancellor when it comes to supporting Boris Yeltsin?

The President. I think we are almost completely in agreement on our positions. Now, we haven't had a chance to talk; we've just arrived. But certainly over the last 2 years since I've been President, our positions have been the same. And we have worked very hard to try to promote democracy and progress within Russia. And we have done it together, and I think we will continue to work together on this.

Q. Do you support economic sanctions because of the situation in Chechnya?

The President. I don't think—we just started, and we haven't had a chance to have a conversation yet. We'll have a press conference later, and we'll all answer questions then.

NOTE: The exchange began at 10:40 a.m. in the Oval Office at the White House. A tape was not available for verification of the content of this exchange.

The President's News Conference With Chancellor Helmut Kohl of Germany
February 9, 1995

The President. Good afternoon. Please be seated. It's a pleasure for me to welcome Chancellor Kohl to the White House again. For more than 12 years American Presidents have looked to Helmut Kohl for insight and cooperation, for friendship and support on the most pressing issues of the day. Thanks to his wisdom and leadership, the relationship between Germany and the United States has strengthened and grown, becoming a force for positive change in the post-cold-war world. America has no better friend than Chancellor Kohl.

The Chancellor's visit comes at an important time. One of the most vital issues we discussed today is building a more integrated Europe in the wake of this new era. The Chancellor and I reaffirmed our intention to press ahead with the enlargement of NATO to include Europe's new democracies. The current deliberations are moving at the right pace. We agreed that the inevitable process of NATO expansion will be gradual and open, that there will be no surprises. Its conditions, timing, and military implications must be well and widely known in advance.

We also agreed that in parallel with expansion, NATO must develop close and strong ties with Russia. Chancellor Kohl and I will consult closely on the form this new partnership will take.

We share a vision of European security that embraces a democratic Russia, and we will continue to reassure President Yeltsin that an expanded NATO will pose no threat to a democratic Russia.

Recent events in Russia were an important part of our discussions today, especially the tragedy in Chechnya. Chancellor Kohl and I are in full agreement: The violence there must end, and negotiation must begin. Every day the fighting continues, more innocent civilians fall victim. In response to international appeals, the United States will offer up to $20 million in humanitarian and refugee assistance to alleviate their distress.

In our conversations with President Yeltsin, we have both made clear our fears about the corrosive effect the conflict in Chechnya can have on democratic, market-oriented reform in the Russian Republic. But the conflict has not changed the nature of our interests, namely that Russia's efforts to become a stable, democratic nation must succeed.

Today the Chancellor and I remain determined to stick to our course of patient, responsible support for Russian reform. But help can only be extended if Russia stays on the course and continues the hard work of building democratic institutions and implementing market-oriented reforms.

The Chancellor and I also discussed a broad range of other issues, including our efforts through the Contact Group to reach a negotiated settlement in Bosnia. Both of us believe it's essential to do what we can to support the Muslim-Croat Federation, which ended hostilities between two of the three parties to that conflict. We believe that strengthening the Federation will provide a concrete, positive step toward an eventual peace agreement.

I also want to thank the Chancellor publicly for Germany's role in assembling the stabilization package for Mexico, which helped to avert a larger and far more dangerous financial crisis. The Chancellor and I support efforts in the G–7 to review our international institutions, a necessary step to ensure that they are fit for the challenges of the next half century.

Finally, we're in full agreement that the United Nations should not lift sanctions on Iraq until that country meets all the conditions set forth in the U.N. resolutions, something so far Iraq has failed to do.

As you can see, in a short time we covered a great deal of ground. Once again we've discovered much common ground. Our nations share a vision of an integrated Europe, of strong bonds across the Atlantic, of a world that continues to grow more peaceful and more prosperous. Our agenda is ambitious, and the tasks ahead are not small. But I'm convinced that working together we will be equal to the challenge.

Chancellor.

Chancellor Kohl. Thank you very much, Mr. President. Mr. President, ladies and gentlemen: Permit me to preface my actual statement by a brief remark. What I'd like to do, Mr. President, is to offer my special respect and my special condolences to you, Mr. President, and to the American people on the occasion of the death of Senator Fulbright. I'm saying this as a member of a generation who, even when they were students, wanted nothing more than to obtain a Fulbright scholarship. Few men and women who enter politics ever succeed to have their names affiliated once and for all with a specific program. For many Germans, for many Europeans, Senator Fulbright was a man who we did not know personally, but he was someone who gave a signal after the Second World War and after the end of the Nazi barbarism—

and I'm saying this very pointedly this year, when on May 8th we will be looking back to 50 years—the name that was closely related with openness, with friendship, and with people striving together. I think it's only fitting that I, the German Chancellor, being here today, should offer my condolences as I just did.

Mr. President, thank you and thank your staff, especially the Vice President, for the very warm and cordial reception we were given, as usual. These talks, which many might find boring, are talks which took place once again in an exceedingly friendly and warm atmosphere. And we aren't done with them; we will be continuing them. These talks of ours make a great deal of sense, even though we do talk on the phone regularly and frequently. But there's a difference between telephone conversations and conversations eye to eye. And that is why I am especially happy to be able, once again, to be here in Washington with my delegation.

I need not add much to what the President said in his preface. We are in full agreement as far as the topics and our views on them are concerned. It's very important to me, personally, to make very clear in public for the benefit of all Americans that the German policy and the policy that I, as the Federal Chancellor, am pursuing be proceeding in close coordination with the President of the United States.

We are living in radically changing times, times of dramatic changes; everybody knows that. We are finding out today that Germany is increasingly feeling how the situation has changed. Many of our countrymen no longer live under a regime that subjugated them for 40 years, and at this point, the question of stability is more urgent than ever before. And that is why to us, the Germans and the Europeans, NATO and the transatlantic security alliance with the United States be preserved because they guarantee our future.

This alliance is one that in a changing world will increasingly have to shoulder responsibility for stability throughout Europe. I fully agree with President Clinton in that the preparatory work for extension of NATO we should proceed in accordance with the program we outlined in Brussels last year. It is a gradual process, and when I say gradual, I mean step by step. It's entirely possible that some of these steps will be larger than others.

It is a process which we in Europe and in Germany will possibly be doing in parallel with the full expansion of the European Union, although they are not directly connected. The expansion of NATO is part of an overall security concept which is intended to make sure that we do not get new boundaries within Europe, and that is why a close partnership with Russia and Ukraine is especially important. NATO and the European Union have to combine their strengths, to combine their forces in pursuit of the common goal that we have with a view to what used to be called, in a simplified fashion, the Warsaw Pact countries. We must join forces to further democracy in the Central and Eastern European countries. And I want to urge everyone here to realize that this process will require a great deal of patience.

As a German, I am more aware than others how difficult it is to take a country where people speak the same language and bring two parts of it together after 40 years of complete isolation. I know the misunderstandings that can arise on simple, everyday matters. And if I try to imagine, and by God I do, what it means that since 1917 Russians lived under the Communists—being aware that the Romanovs weren't exactly a picnic either—when you look at all these facts, you can appreciate how difficult the process is that is going on in Russia at this time.

And since that is the case, we agreed, the President and I and our governments are agreed, that we should encourage Russia to pursue the course of reform. What that means is that we have a vital interest—the Germans in particular, because we are close neighbors—we have an elemental interest in furthering reforms and cooperating with Russia.

I would like to underline that I still support President Yeltsin, as I've always done. And I do it with the objective of enabling reforms in Russia, enable them to introduce market economy and create a state based on the rule of law. As I say that, I'm stating very clearly that we will support Russia in its legitimate efforts to preserve the territorial integrity of its country, but that does require that Russia also stand by its commitments in the area of human rights and other international standards that they have committed themselves to, making Russia a country open to reform.

I support what the President said regarding events in Chechnya, but let me add that our shared wish is to have a peaceful situation, in the best sense of the word, return to Chechnya.

We wish for the authorities in that country to pursue their responsibilities in the manner I tried to outline just now.

And now, let me state very briefly that we are in full agreement that we all must try to diminish and end the horrible suffering of people there. We shall jointly pursue that matter. It's an area where hundreds of years of histories have led to the situation that we have now, but that shouldn't discourage us. We must do the best we can. Time is running out. Winter will soon be over. That means at the end of winter, which generally has a paralyzing effect on fighting, the full armed conflict might once again rear its head in that area. There is no alternative to the combined efforts of the Americans and the Europeans in the Bosnian area.

Thank you very much, Mr. President, for the kind welcome you have extended to us. And now both of us, as we are required, are looking forward to the many questions that you will doubtless have.

The President. Let me say just before I recognize the first question, I'd like to thank the Chancellor for his expressions. I think he could speak not only for the people of Germany but for the—largely, for the people of the rest of the world, of condolences on the death of Senator Fulbright.

As many of you know, this is a sad day for me personally. We'd been friends for more than 25 years. And I'm just profoundly grateful today for the conviction that he imparted to me when I was a young man that we could make peace in the world if we seek better understanding, if we promote the exchanges among people, if we advance the cause of global education. And for what you said, Chancellor, I am very grateful.

Surgeon General Nominee Foster

Q. Mr. President, how do you respond to criticism from Republicans and Democrats that the White House badly fumbled Dr. Foster's nomination? And how can you convince skeptical Senators about his credibility and allay their concerns about his abortion—[*inaudible*]?

The President. Well, first of all, I think the question about how it was handled was answered yesterday as well as can be answered. Dr. Foster represented himself last night on television, I thought, rather well.

I have confidence in him. I do not believe that anything I have heard about him disqualifies him from serving as Surgeon General. It is, it seems to me, an unfair characterization, but perhaps too typical of the appointments process generally, to try to define him in the way that those who believe that all abortions should be criminal have tried to define him. I mean, here's a man who's delivered thousands and thousands and thousands of babies and devoted the rest of his time in the last several years to trying to end the scourge of teen pregnancy and illegitimacy in our country and thereby to reduce the number of abortions and to solve one of our most profound problems.

He was recognized by President Bush for that effort. He has been endorsed by Dr. Sullivan, the HHS Director in the Bush administration, as well as by a host of others. I have confidence in him. I think he's a good man. I think he'll be a good Surgeon General. And I think that that ought to be the issue.

And I do not believe that we should be under any illusion here. This is the—the Senate will have an opportunity to decide on his qualifications and his life and his work. And I think to allow a man like this who has lived the life he has and has garnered the endorsements he has from the people who have known him and worked with him of both parties for 40 years would be a grave mistake.

I support him. I want him to have his hearings. I believe the Senate will support him. And I think we should not back away from this.

Now, I know that those who believe that we should abolish the right to choose and make conduct which is now legal, criminal, will try to seize upon this nomination to negate the work of a man's life and define him in cardboard cut-out terms, but I think that is wrong. And I am for him, and I think the American people will be for him when they hear him.

Russia

Q. Chancellor, Mr. President—[*inaudible*]— President Yeltsin, after the events in Chechnya, as being a stable force and a trustworthy partner for peace?

Chancellor Kohl. Well, you know, I am probably just as much as anyone in the world not able to actually make any predictions, any safe predictions, about the future of the Russian country or about the office of the President of Russia. It's a dramatic—it's a country that currently undergoes dramatic changes. And I tried to explain this in my introductory remarks.

And my position and the position, I believe, of the President is rather easily defined. We— I personally have experienced Boris Yeltsin as a man on whom one can rely absolutely, as a man who, to the last dotting of the "i's" and crossing of the "t's," has fulfilled his obligations. When they withdrew the Soviet troops from Germany, he completely adhered to what he promised. And obviously I know that in Russian military circles there were quite different forces at work at the time. Still, they kept their promises.

And I believe that in supporting him and in showing a spirit of friendship towards him, we should not only see support for reforms and the building of democracy, the building of the economy, introducing the rule of law, but this friendship should also give us the right to tell him quite clearly that he must not deceive our hopes and that, although we do have understanding, a certain amount of understanding for certain setbacks occurring, but still reforms have to go on.

And I'm saying this not in the sense of actually making any conditions, but for me at least, that would be a prerequisite for continuing support of the aims that he pursues, democracy and rule of law and all of that. There are people who consider themselves to be particularly intelligent and particularly wise and who now say, "Well, it can't work, so let's not get involved in that." Then there are other people, and they exist also in Germany, they think to be even more intransigent; they think they can ride this wave of disappointment, of bitterness, in view of the pictures that are related to us every day from Chechnya and who want to push this man into a corner and want to deal with this matter quite differently. I can only warn people to adopt such a course.

I don't know whether what I'm suggesting here today will be successful, but I'm absolutely sure, absolutely convinced that if we were to push the forces of reform and the President into a corner, isolate them, and say, "We give up on you. There's nothing that we can do here," that this will immediately bring us back to the old, bad structures of the past. And I don't want in a few years ahead to be facing the accusation that had we acted in time and reasonably, we could have prevented this.

The President. I have confidence in President Yeltsin. Every time he has given me his word, he has done what he said he would do, withdrawing troops from the Balkans, for example—I mean, from the Baltics, and carrying through on all of our nuclear agreements, and all the things that we have worked on.

I think that all of us knew—and before I met with Boris Yeltsin the first time in April of '93, the first time I'd met with him as President, I tried to caution everyone that Russia was facing a difficult and a challenging period, the road would not always be even, and we wouldn't always agree with every decision that was made and everything that happened. But should we continue to work with President Yeltsin and to support democracy and reform and to say honestly where we have concerns and disagreements? I think that's what mature countries do. And that's what people who are struggling for a goal like democracy where it has long been denied and prosperity and reform where it has long been absent, that's what people have to do. You have to be willing to deal with the rough spots in the road, say where you disagree and stay on course. And the United States and Germany must do that. We have to keep on course. And I believe we're doing the right thing.

Helen [Helen Thomas, United Press International].

Welfare Reform

Q. Mr. President, there is a Republican move afoot on Capitol Hill to deny the disadvantaged who now receive welfare benefits their guaranteed benefits. What do you think of that and all of the other moves that are—would deny rights under the Constitution against searches without a warrant, repealing the crime bill, not guaranteeing there won't be cuts with the balanced budget—what does all this mean?

The President. It's hard to know what it means. No bill has passed yet, but there's been a lot of moving around. I said yesterday in this room what I thought about the crime bill, and I had—all the law enforcement officers in the country were symbolically represented here. We don't believe it should be changed in ways that weaken our commitment to putting 100,000 police on the street, and basically spend more money on prisons and less money on police and prevention.

With regard to the welfare reform, I think that I owe it to them to review the substance of the bill, and I will. You know what my position is. My position is we should change the

system in ways that promote more work, more responsible parenting, give more flexibility to the States but have a strong, strong protection for the interests and welfare of the children of this country. There is a national interest in making sure that the food, the nutrition, the health care of the children of this country are protected. That is not a State-by-State interest; that is a national interest. Now, I'm willing to go a long way toward letting the States implement and design their own welfare reform programs. We should.

The other issue I want to—I didn't see in the summary today is that the Republican Governors were very strong in saying that they did think the one area where we needed stronger national action was in the area of child support enforcement, that the States were not capable of having the kind of tough child support enforcement that we need because fully more than a third of the orders today that are not enforced involve more than one State.

So I want to review all these details, but I think, let's keep the principles in mind. I will evaluate their proposal by those principles. And if it promotes work and family and protects children, then I will be favorable toward it, even with a lot more flexibility to the States; I want that. But I want all those criteria protected. So I'm going to have to look very closely on the, it sounds to me like on the child protection issue, and I will do that.

Mexican Loan Guarantees

Q. Chancellor Kohl, you did not respond to President Clinton's comments about aid to Mexico. Now, your government's representative at the IMF abstained on the vote last week extending $17.8 billion in credits to Mexico. Are you now satisfied with the way the Clinton administration handled the multilateral aid package, and do you have assurances that in the future you'll be consulted more extensively?

The President. I thought you were a German on that side. [*Laughter*] Go ahead.

Chancellor Kohl. I am content. I'm satisfied with the result. After all, we did agree on the road to that decision one or the other hurdle could have been taken more elegantly. But, you know, these kinds of things happen, once we sway to one side, once we sway to—another time be swayed to another. If you want to try and drive a wedge between us on this question, you're not going to be successful.

185

Bosnia

Q. Mr. President, in a couple of weeks Congress is probably going to vote to lift the arms embargo against Bosnia. If such a demand comes up, will you comply with it? Will you change your policy? And Chancellor, if the Congress votes to lift the arms embargo, what will be the reaction of Germany and what will be the reaction of the Europeans?

Chancellor Kohl. Well, I think we should talk about that when we get that decision. Today, I'm going to be on the Hill. Later on I shall be talking to Senators and Congressmen, and I'm going to advise that we do as much together as we can, that we closely coordinate things.

The President. I'm not sure that's going to happen. I certainly don't think it should happen. You know what my position is.

North Korea

Q. Mr. President, there are some reports that the nuclear agreement with North Korea is beginning to unravel. Is that the case? And are you confident that it can go forward as you had originally——

The President. Absolutely. I'm under—I have no information that it's beginning to unravel. And I think it can go forward. I think it should go forward. I think it must go forward. It is a major part of our strategy to protect the world from nuclear proliferation. And I feel very strongly about it. We must go forward.

Is there a German question?

World Bank

Q. Mr. Chancellor, President Clinton talked about reviewing the tasks of the international institutions. Following the difficulties here you mentioned regarding the Mexico package, do you think the Federal Republic is going to insist on reviewing the credit lines and the credit award lines at the World Bank?

Chancellor Kohl. I'm in favor of that, not simply because of this particular experience; I think we should review our work from time to time at regular intervals. I hope that we'll be dealing with a very peaceful problem when you talk about financing developments in the Middle East. That's one example which I do hope will turn into a really peaceful challenge for us, assuming the peace process actually succeeds. Other than that, I'd be willing to stop and think at every stage whether the structures we had hitherto been using are the best ones.

Let me add that these are things one has to talk about. They need not be announced to the public before coordination has been achieved. We should simply talk to one another.

Terrorism

Q. Mr. President, what can you tell us about the arrest of this terrorist suspect in Pakistan? And what are the ramifications, in your opinion, for terrorist cells or networks or the breakup of these groups here in the United States and abroad?

The President. I can tell you that I'm very pleased about it, and that—obviously, there are some things that are better left unsaid, but I would refer back to the statement that I issued. This country is serious about combating terrorism. We are going to put a lot of resources and effort into it. The Attorney General today is releasing the legislation that we are sending to the Hill that we very much hope will pass with bipartisan support. And this should be further evidence that we take this problem very seriously, for ourselves, and for our friends, and the friends of freedom around the world. And we continue to stay after it. And I'm very pleased about it.

Q. Will his arrest, sir, to follow up, lead to the possible breakup of other groups here in the States or abroad?

The President. I think that it is better that I not say anything else about his arrest other than what has already been in the paper at this time.

Is there another German question?

Q. Can I follow up on that?

The President. Yes, sir. The normally suave and confident—[*laughter*]—is suffering technology breakdown. [*Laughter*]

German Exports to Iran

Q. Mr. Chancellor, they couldn't drive a wedge between you and the President in Mexico. How about on Germany's exports to Iran? There are growing concerns, you know, among U.S. officials that Germany may be doing with Iran what it did with Iraq before the Gulf war, inadvertently helping it develop weapons of mass destruction. Is Germany involved? Are you taking another look at some of the exports that you're providing to Iran, which has been accused, as you know, by the United States as being a source of international terrorism? And

President Clinton, how concerned are you about Germany's exports to Iran?

Chancellor Kohl. First of all, I think your statement is incorrect. What you just said about Iraq is wrong. If you read the complete report that came out, not just the little passage about Germany, then you'll find that Germany was not number one. I know that this rumor is cropping up in Washington time and again, but I'd like to use this opportunity to say that that is wrong.

As far as Iran specifically is concerned, we are in agreement. We are not willing to support any policy in Iran which might entail the danger of fundamentalism, which to me is one of the greatest dangers we are facing today. We are not willing to add any support to fundamentalism. We have cut back economic relations with Iran considerably. Those were longstanding relations which we have cut back considerably.

And if I'm not mistaken, Time magazine, being a respectable news magazine, has said quite a number of things this week about American oil companies, not German oil companies, mind you. And if you take a look, you'll have to conclude that these oil companies export into other countries, not our country.

We feel that, with a view to the peace process in the Middle East in which we, as Germans, have a special interest, a process in regard to which we fully support the President's policy in wanting that process to succeed, that this is a very important step indeed. We're talking about Israel here, among other things. And if a German Chancellor, 50 years after Auschwitz, talks about Israel, you may believe him when he says that he has a great interest in that process being successful and that we would not dream of supporting any policy in any part of the world which might in any way impede Israel's prospects for a peaceful future. And that is why we are most certainly going to act along the lines I pointed out in regard to economic relations as well.

We are in a somewhat different situation because, following the developments of the past years, we have become a country that has very few regulatory controls, that is quite open to the outside. And in the past—and this has, time and again, been our problem, also vis-a-vis Iraq—we have been one of the major suppliers of chemical products because we had a superb chemical industry. And then we time and again got a situation where one of those chemical companies supplied a product, exported a product that could be used for many purposes, mostly of course for peaceful purposes but which could be abused, which could be misused and used for other purposes.

I talked to German industry and we agreed that we would do everything we can in order to make diversion impossible. Or to put it differently, we are not talking simply about law enforcement here; we are going to make sure that the reputation of our country is not damaged. So it's not only a matter of criminal pursuits but it's a matter of maintaining our country's reputation, which I find important.

NOTE: The President's 85th news conference began at 1 p.m. in Room 450 of the Old Executive Office Building. In his remarks, he referred to Ramzi Ahmed Yusuf, alleged mastermind of the 1993 bombing of the World Trade Center in New York City. Chancellor Kohl spoke in German, and his remarks were translated by an interpreter.

Statement on the Death of J. William Fulbright
February 9, 1995

I am deeply saddened by the death of former Senator William Fulbright. Both Hillary and I send our condolences to his wife, Harriet, and to their daughters, Elizabeth, Roberta, Heidi, Evi, and Shelby. Our prayers are with them at this difficult time.

I am also grateful today for the conviction Senator Fulbright imparted to me when I was a young man. He taught me that we could make peace in the world if we seek a better understanding, if we promote exchanges among people, and if we advance the cause of global education.

Senator Fulbright's legacy was about heart as much as brains. He made us feel that we could amount to something in our lives, that education could lift us up and lift this country up. He made us believe that we had an obligation to develop our God-given abilities to their fullest and then use them to engage in the passions of our day. He believed in reason and that, in the end, democracy would only prevail if we had the courage to seek the truth.

One of his greatest legacies, the Fulbright scholarships, will celebrate their 50th anniversary in 1996. So far, 70,000 Americans and more than 200,000 people worldwide have participated in this program in more than 150 countries. Senator Fulbright left his mark on the lives of all the people who have benefited from those scholarships—and on many, many more of us along the way. We are all in his debt.

Message to the Congress Transmitting Proposed Legislation To Settle the Major League Baseball Labor Dispute
February 9, 1995

To the Congress of the United States:

I am pleased to transmit for your immediate consideration and enactment the "Major League Baseball Restoration Act." This legislation would provide for a fair and prompt settlement of the ongoing labor-management dispute affecting Major League Baseball.

Major League Baseball has historically occupied a unique place in American life. The parties to the current contentious dispute have been unable to resolve their differences, despite many months of negotiations and the assistance of one of this country's most skilled mediators. If the dispute is permitted to continue, there is likely to be substantial economic damage to the cities and communities in which major league franchises are located and to the communities that host spring training. The ongoing dispute also threatens further serious harm to an important national institution.

The bill I am transmitting today is a simple one. It would authorize the President to appoint a 3-member National Baseball Dispute Resolution Panel. This Panel of impartial and skilled arbitrators would be empowered to gather information from all sides and impose a binding agreement on the parties. The Panel would be urged to act as quickly as possible. Its decision would not be subject to judicial review.

In arriving at a fair settlement, the Panel would consider a number of factors affecting the parties, but it could also take into account the effect on the public and the best interests of the game.

The Panel would be given sufficient tools to do its job, without the need for further appropriations. Primary support for its activities come from the Federal Mediation and Conciliation Service, but other agencies would also be authorized to provide needed support.

The dispute now affecting Major League Baseball has been a protracted one, and I believe that the time has come to take action. I urge the Congress to take prompt and favorable action on this legislation.

WILLIAM J. CLINTON

The White House,
February 8, 1995.

Remarks at a Dinner Honoring Chancellor Helmut Kohl of Germany
February 9, 1995

Chancellor Kohl, members of the German delegation, members of the diplomatic corps, distinguished guests: On occasions like this, I normally rise to say how very much I've enjoyed spending time with a distinguished head of state. I enjoyed today, but after all, it was Helmut Kohl's third visit to the White House since I have been President. He's been here so many times during his 12 years as Chancellor that, on his last trip here, he took me to his favorite restaurant in Washington. [*Laughter*] I'm happy to announce that after this dinner, Chancellor Kohl will be conducting tours of the White House. [*Laughter*]

Helmut Kohl has become a good and trusted friend of mine, as he has been a good and trusted friend of the United States for as long as he's been in public life. Hillary and I were deeply touched last summer by the famous Palatinate hospitality which he and Mrs. Kohl showed to us when he took us to his hometown of Oggersheim. I must say, I felt right at home when we turned down the street on which the Kohls live and the whole neighborhood turned out to say hello. I hope that Chancellor Kohl feels at home here, and I hope someday I'll have the opportunity to take you to my home. Believe me, the whole neighborhood will show up. [*Laughter*]

Even before Helmut Kohl became Chancellor, American leaders were drawn to Rheinland-Pfalz. In 1788, a couple of years before Helmut became Chancellor, Thomas Jefferson traveled along the Rhine. He loved the paintings he saw in Dusseldorf, but he was annoyed that the Westphalians thought they were the only people who smoked their hams; they didn't know Virginians did it, too. When he traveled farther south to the Palatinate, he said he had entered what he called "our second mother country" because so many people from that region had settled in America and their customs had become American ones. History does not record whether Thomas Jefferson sampled that famous regional dish *Saumagen*, but I have, thanks to Helmut Kohl.

When Hillary and I went home with the Kohls, I was remembered that real leadership does not begin in theories but in places and lives like those I saw in Oggersheim, in the homes that we love and the people and the customs that make us who we are. We are all proud of the ties that bind us together. The German language sums up the richness of those bonds in a single almost untranslatable word, *Heimat*. Here in the United States, my attachment to my roots has become somewhat legendary, but no world leader has more love for his *Heimat* than Helmut Kohl. A leader who keeps his *Heimat* in his heart will always remember what people want most, the certainty that their children will inherit a more peaceful, more prosperous, more rich world in terms of the human spirit. Today we worked hard to advance those shared goals, goals which have bound our people together for nearly 50 years now and goals which will take us together into the 21st century.

Ladies and gentlemen, let us raise a glass to the friendship between the people of the United States and the people of Germany, and to the Chancellor who has done so much to make it better.

NOTE: The President spoke at 8:05 p.m. in the State Dining Room at the White House.

Message to the Congress Transmitting the Report of the National Endowment for the Humanities
February 9, 1995

To the Congress of the United States:

I am pleased to present to you the Twenty-ninth Annual Report of the National Endowment for the Humanities (NEH), the Federal agency charged with fostering scholarship and imparting knowledge in the humanities. Its work supports an impressive range of humanities projects.

These projects can reach an audience as general as the 28 million who watched the documentary *Baseball*, or as specialized as the 50 scholars who this past fall examined current research on Dante. Small local historical societies have received NEH support, as have some of the Nation's largest cultural institutions. Students from kindergarten through graduate school, professors and teachers, and the general public in all parts of the Nation have been touched by the Endowment's activities.

As we approach the 21st century, the world is growing smaller and its problems seemingly bigger. Societies are becoming more complex and fractious. The knowledge and wisdom, the insight and perspective, imparted by history, philosophy, literature, and other humanities disciplines enable us to meet the challenges of contemporary life.

WILLIAM J. CLINTON

The White House,

February 9, 1995.

NOTE: This message was released by the Office of the Press Secretary on February 10.

Message to the Congress Transmitting Proposed Legislation To Combat Terrorism
February 9, 1995

To the Congress of the United States:

I am pleased to transmit today for your immediate consideration and enactment the "Omnibus Counterterrorism Act of 1995." Also transmitted is a section-by-section analysis. This legislative proposal is part of my Administration's comprehensive effort to strengthen the ability of the United States to deter terrorist acts and punish those who aid or abet any international terrorist activity in the United States. It corrects deficiencies and gaps in current law.

Some of the most significant provisions of the bill will:

- Provide clear Federal criminal jurisdiction for any international terrorist attack that might occur in the United States;
- Provide Federal criminal jurisdiction over terrorists who use the United States as the place from which to plan terrorist attacks overseas;
- Provide a workable mechanism, utilizing U.S. District Court Judges appointed by the Chief Justice, to deport expeditiously alien terrorists without risking the disclosure of national security information or techniques;
- Provide a new mechanism for preventing fund-raising in the United States that supports international terrorist activities overseas; and

- Implement an international treaty requiring the insertion of a chemical agent into plastic explosives when manufactured to make them detectable.

The fund-raising provision includes a licensing mechanism under which funds can only be transferred based on a strict showing that the money will be used exclusively for religious, charitable, literary, or educational purposes and will not be diverted for terrorist activity. The bill also includes numerous relatively technical, but highly important, provisions that will facilitate investigations and prosecutions of terrorist crimes.

It is the Administration's intent that section 101 of the bill confer Federal jurisdiction only over international terrorism offenses. The Administration will work with Members of Congress to ensure that the language in the bill is consistent with that intent.

I urge the prompt and favorable consideration of this legislative proposal by the Congress.

WILLIAM J. CLINTON

The White House,

February 9, 1995.

Note: This message was released by the Office of the Press Secretary on February 10.

Statement on Argentina's Accession to the Nuclear Non-Proliferation Treaty
February 10, 1995

I warmly welcome Argentina's accession to the Nuclear Non-Proliferation Treaty (NPT) this morning. In joining the NPT, Argentina has taken an historic step to reinforce its own security and to unite with 170 other NPT parties in the global effort to stem the spread of nuclear weapons. I salute President Menem and his government for their foresight and courage in making Argentina a champion for nonproliferation in Latin America and around the world. In the State of the Union Address, I pledged that the United States would lead the charge for indefinite extension of the NPT when the treaty's future is considered this April. Argentina's NPT adherence will help us reach that goal.

The President's Radio Address
February 11, 1995

Good morning. Today I've asked Attorney General Reno and Drug Control Director Lee Brown to join me here at the White House. I want to discuss the crime and drugs that plague almost every community in our country.

I ran for President because I believe it's the responsibility of our generation to work together to preserve the American dream for all Americans and to ensure that we move into the next century still the strongest country on Earth. The best way for us to do that is by building a new partnership in our country between Americans and their government, and especially between Americans and each other. I call that partnership the New Covenant.

Essentially that means the Government's responsibility is to expand opportunity while shrinking bureaucracy, to empower people to make the most of their own lives, and to enhance our security not just abroad but here at home, too. At the same time, it means we must demand more responsibility from every citizen in return, responsibility for our country, for our communities, for our families and ourselves.

Part of our job here in Washington is to help arm the American people to fight crime and violence. During the Presidential campaign I promised the American people that I would cut 100,000 Federal bureaucrats in Washington and use those savings to put 100,000 new police officers on America's streets. Last year, Democrats and Republicans joined together to pass the crime bill to keep that promise. We've been working ever since to put that crime bill into effect. It's been only 4 months since the crime bill became law, but already we've awarded over 16,000 new officers to half the police departments in America. We're under budget; we're ahead of schedule.

Police departments all around the country are putting this effort to work, hiring, training, and deploying officers as fast as we can give a go-ahead. The last thing your local police department needs is Congressmen in Washington playing politics with their safety and yours. But the astonishing thing is, despite the urgent need for more police on our streets, despite our success in getting them there, some Republicans in Congress actually want to repeal this effort. They want to replace an initiative guaranteed to put 100,000 police on the street with a block grant program that has no guarantees at all.

The block grant is basically a blank check that can far too easily be used for things besides police officers. That's why the law enforcement steering committee, representing over 450,000 police officers, is absolutely opposed to this block grant approach or to any other change that weakens our commitment to put 100,000 police on the streets.

Undermining this commitment to law enforcement is not acceptable. I didn't fight to cut 100,000 Federal bureaucrats so we could trade them in for an old-fashioned pork-barrel program. I fought to trade 100,000 bureaucrats for 100,000 police officers. Last year, Republicans and Democrats passed the 100,000 cops bill, and I signed it. I made a commitment, a promise to put 100,000 more police on our streets, because there is simply no better crimefighting tool to be found. And I intend to keep that promise. Anyone on Capitol Hill who wants to play partisan politics with police officers for America should listen carefully: I will veto any effort to repeal or undermine the 100,000 police commitment, period.

Of course, as crucial as these 100,000 police officers are, they can't do the job alone. Every citizen in America has to help in this fight, because no amount of police officers can replace people taking responsibility for their own lives and for their communities.

This week, I announced our administration's 1995 drug control strategy. It involves cutting off drugs at the source, stiffer punishment for drug dealers, more education and prevention, and more treatment. But perhaps the most important part of this strategy will be to boost efforts to educate our young people about the dangers and penalties of drug use. Our children need a constant drumbeat reminding them that drugs are not safe, drugs are illegal, drugs can put you in jail, and drugs may cost you your life.

Community-based education programs work. I saw them work in school when my daughter was younger. This morning I've been joined by some police officers who participate in community education programs and especially in the national drug abuse education and resistance program that you probably know as D.A.R.E. Every American should follow their example and accept the responsibility to join the fight against drugs and crime and violence.

Parents must teach their children right from wrong. They must teach that drugs are bad and dangerous. And make no mistake about it, parents must set a good example for their children. Young people must have the courage to do what's right and stand up for what's right. That means not using drugs, staying out of gangs, studying hard, avoiding violence. It also means telling friends that drugs and gangs and guns aren't cool, and children that are involved in those things aren't going to be your real friends.

That's what the New Covenant is all about: more opportunity, more responsibility. We've got to do our part here. But each and every one of you must take responsibility to join us. We can only win this fight together.

Thanks for listening.

NOTE: The President spoke at 10:06 a.m. from the Oval Office at the White House.

Remarks at a Meeting With Middle Eastern Leaders
February 12, 1995

Thank you, Mr. Secretary. And thank you, all of you, for coming to this very important meeting. It is no secret to anyone in the world that we are at a critical moment in the peace process. We cannot allow the rise of terror again to threaten this peace, or as Chairman Arafat said the other day, we cannot allow it to kill the Palestinian dream.

We are prepared in this country to redouble our efforts to get the peace process back in full gear. We are doing what we can on our own and with others to deal with the problem of terror.

I want to begin by saying a special word of appreciation to President Mubarak for the Cairo summit. He has been involved in this process all along, and I think that the Cairo summit produced a clear statement by the leaders of all of you here represented that we are not going to let terror hold sway, that we are not going to let the peace process collapse. Today it is for us to begin to take the specific steps necessary to have the message of peace and renewed commitment carried out.

I think it's clear that we have to complete phase two of the Israel-Palestinian Agreement. I think it's clear that we have to fully implement the peace treaty between Jordan and Israel. I think it is clear that we have to bring some economic benefits of peace as quickly as we possibly can.

And the United States is prepared to do its part on that. For example, if you agree to establish industrial zones in the West Bank and Gaza and elsewhere, I am prepared to go to Congress and seek approval for extending duty-free treatment to products coming out of those zones. Of course, in the end, the economic and political cooperation among all of you will be the most important thing in reaping economic progress. But I want to do our part.

I know our Russian partner feels the same. I think that many others around the world will also help. But I am absolutely convinced that we need to move as quickly as we can to prove that there are some economic benefits to peace.

Let me say also that, even though we must have enhanced security to create enhanced economic benefits, it is obvious that our attempt to do that is impaired when the movement of goods is limited by boycott, by closure, by any other action. So we're all going to have to work hard to make progress on the peace front, on the security front, and on the economic front at the same time. And we all have to recognize that there are difficult decisions to be made in this area.

The negotiations that you have already concluded have built a framework for peace. What we have to do now is to have specific achievements, lasting achievements. We will do our part. We are as committed today as we have

ever been to a comprehensive peace. I wish the representatives of Syria and Lebanon were around this table; they are not here only because there has been no peace agreement signed with them. But I know you all join me in saying that our work will never be completed until we are all around a table as partners working for peace.

Now, there are many other things I could discuss today, but I mostly want to say to you, the United States is still committed to this, more strongly than ever. We are ready to do our part. We are ready to do our part economically. We are certainly ready to do our part in fighting terror. But we all have to do this together. And I hope that this meeting will produce further specific steps that we can all take to keep doing it together. We cannot let people believe that they can disrupt the rational, humane, decent course of history by terror.

Mr. Secretary.

NOTE: The President spoke at 12:30 p.m. at Blair House. The following officials and their respective peace delegations attended the meeting: Secretary of State Warren Christopher; Foreign Ministers Atef Sedky of Egypt, Shimon Peres of Israel, and Abd al-Karim al-Kabariti of Jordan; and Nabell Sha'ath, Minister of Planning and International Cooperation for the Palestine Authority.

Radio Address to the People of Burundi
February 13, 1995

The recent violence in Burundi demonstrates that extremists want to reverse your remarkable progress toward democracy. The United States rejects those who reject peace. We stand with those who are against violence and for tolerance and peace. Burundi has suffered enough.

Your historic elections in 1993 promised to open a new, peaceful chapter in your nation's history. The American people and supporters of democracy around the world watched with high hopes as Burundi embarked on a new course. Despite tragedy and suffering, the vast majority of your people have worked for lasting peace, security, and freedom.

I say to the people and the leaders of Burundi: Do not go back. You deserve to live in peace and without fear. Democracy will help you build a better future for yourselves and your children. Say no to violence and extremism. Say yes to peace and reconciliation.

NOTE: The address was recorded on February 11 at approximately 10:15 a.m. in the Oval Office at the White House, and it was released by the Office of the Press Secretary on February 13. A tape was not available for verification of the content of this address.

Remarks on the Economic Report of the President and an Exchange With Reporters
February 13, 1995

The President. As you know, we are here to receive the annual Economic Report of the President. So I want to begin by thanking the Council of Economic Advisers: Dr. Laura Tyson, our Chair; Dr. Joseph Stiglitz; and Dr. Martin Baily.

This economic report is an important milestone for me. It measures our success in fulfilling the mission that I brought to the Presidency. I ran for this office to help to restore the American dream and to guarantee its availability for all Americans into the 21st century, to make sure that the middle class would still be growing and that work would still be rewarded. The best way to do that is by building a new partnership between Americans and their Government and Americans and each other, the partnership that I have called the New Covenant.

Essentially, it means that our responsibility here in Washington is to expand opportunity while shrinking bureaucracy, to empower people to make the most of their own lives, and to enhance our security, not only abroad but here at home as well. At the same time, it means that we must demand more responsibility from every citizen, especially those who seek the benefits of Government action, responsibility for our country, for our communities, for our families, and for ourselves.

These responsibilities have defined our economic strategy. We have pursued deficit reduction to make more of our Nation's resources available for private investment, growth, and jobs. We have reduced the size of the Government's bureaucracy, cutting the Federal work force to its lowest level in 30 years. We have expanded trade to provide more opportunity for jobs and higher incomes. And we have invested in the American people, from Head Start to the Goals 2000 program, to the program to help young people who don't go to college but do need further training, and of course, what we've done in national service and student loans.

We've done all of that to help our people get the skills they need so that they can grow and prosper in a global economy. And now, 2 years into our administration, we can see the positive results of this strategy: almost 6 million new jobs, the lowest core rate of inflation in 30 years, the deficit reduced by over $600 billion.

It's not enough. Too many of our people are still working harder for less, with less security. So today I'm sending Congress two new bills that are the next installment in our comprehensive effort to raise the wages and the incomes of working Americans and to give them more opportunity in return for their responsibility of learning and working. These bills reward work. They raise living standards. They allow people to invest in themselves and to make the most of their own lives.

The "Working Wage Increase Act" would increase the minimum wage by 90 cents over 2 years. This would benefit over 11 million workers and their families. It would be the equivalent of an $1,800 raise or about 7 months of groceries for a family.

The middle class bill of rights has four provisions that will also benefit those who are working to help themselves: a $500 tax cut for families with children under 13; a way to allow more families to invest in an IRA and withdraw those investments, tax-free, to pay for education, health care, purchase of a first home, or the care of an elderly parent; a voucher to improve worker skills worth $2,600 a year for 2 years for people who are unemployed or who are working for wages low enough to qualify for Federal training; and of course, I think, over the long run most importantly, a tax deduction for the cost of education beyond high school.

The success of the United States is clearly dependent upon our ability to educate and develop the capacities of every one of our citizens. That's what the middle class bill of rights is all about. It goes with our previous efforts to expand Head Start, to work to help public schools achieve excellence, to move people into the work force who don't go to college, and of course, to expand the student loan program.

This Economic Report of the President shows that this strategy is working. We should not abandon it. Instead, we should build on it. We should deepen it. When you're doing something that's working, you shouldn't turn around and do something else. You should do what you're doing better, do more of it, keep going in the same direction. That's what we're trying to do. We're reducing Government spending. We're cutting Government bureaucracy. But we are increasing our investment in the American people. The middle class bill of rights, raising the minimum wage, these are things we ought to do. The evidence that we ought to do them is in the success of the last 2 years' strategy in the Economic Report to the President.

I thank Dr. Tyson and the others and, of course, all of those on our economic team and all of those in the Congress and throughout the country who've done so much to make this report a reality.

Thank you.

Minimum Wage

Q. What do you think the chances are of getting the minimum wage, Mr. President?

The President. Well, I think they should be pretty good. The more we see the evidence— you know, there was a very moving piece in one of the papers yesterday on that community in North Carolina that has such a high percentage of minimum wage workers. I saw a television interview the other night with a lady working, I believe, in southwest Virginia, who gave an answer to the question that has become the battle cry for the minimum wage around here when she said, "Well, some people say if we raise your minimum wage, that you could lose your job because more of the work will be done by machines," and she looked at the interviewer and said, "Honey, I'll take my chances." [*Laughter*] That's sort of become our battle cry around here for the minimum wage.

I will say this, in 1989, or the last time the minimum wage was raised, whatever year it was, '91, the bipartisan support was truly impressive. It ought to be there again. Half of this minimum wage increase is necessary just to bring the minimum wage back up to the point where it was when it was raised the last time. The other half would be a modest increase in the living standards of people who are working hard to support themselves and often their children. So I'm going to keep fighting for it. I'm going to keep working for it. And my instinct is, we've got a pretty good chance to pass it.

Deficit Reduction

Q. Mr. President, you've taken a lot of criticism for your budget, and a lot of people are saying that you haven't done enough to reduce the deficit in the coming 5 years, that you actually have stopped doing what we were doing before. I think Speaker Gingrich today said that maybe your budget was even—that it could even be a factor that would tip the country into recession. What do you say to these critics?

The President. Well, let me just say, first of all, all those people, including the Speaker, were here for 12 years when we had a bipartisan conspiracy to quadruple the debt of this country. With Republican Presidents and Democratic Congressmen, they quadrupled the debt of the country. If it weren't for the interest we have to pay on the debt that was accumulated between 1981 and 1993, we would have a balanced budget next year and a surplus thereafter. And we have cut the deficit more than it has ever been cut before in history, I might say, with no help—no help—not a single vote from the Republicans.

Now, they're in the majority, and it's their turn. If they don't like my budget, let's see what theirs is. They promised—they made promises that would make the deficit bigger with all the tax cuts and spending increases they talked about. Now the real world is crowding in on them. I have done my duty. I have sent a budget to the Congress that contains another $140 billion in spending cuts, that pays for the middle class bill of rights, including the education tax deduction, that reduces the deficit by $80 billion more, and that does it without cutting Social Security, Medicare, veterans, or education. It is time for them to take a little responsibility.

They were here during the years of the eighties when we created this deficit problem. America was never buried in a deficit problem until 1981. They voted and voted and voted and voted. I got here 2 years ago. I have been fighting this as hard as possible. I have welcomed them to give me their ideas. I have said, I will work with you to reduce the deficit more. And I will do that, but let's see what they want to do to do it. They have some responsibility, too. Where is their budget? What are they for? Let's see what they're for. I want to work with them.

You know, I find it amazing that people who are here every year, digging the country in the hole I've been digging us out of, are now saying I'm not getting this out quick enough. I mean, where were they, and where are they? It's time for them to suit up and show up.

Surgeon General Nominee Foster

Q. Are you going to the mat on Dr. Foster?
The President. Yes.

Q. Mr. President, there are some who would argue now that you're going to be spending so much time trying to get Dr. Foster confirmed, it's going to detract from your other priorities, because this looks like it's going to be one hell of a fight. Are you prepared for that right now?

The President. Yes, but I want to say, just because you've spent a lot of time talking about it, doesn't mean it's going to take us a lot of time to do it. [*Laughter*] We've got a lot of folks that work here and a lot of things to do. And every day we may only be talking about one or two things, but we're working on a lot of things. It will not in any way undermine the impact of the Presidency on the other work we have to do.

And let me also say—let me go back to that other question. I don't see how anybody could seriously say that our budget would cause a recession. They caused the recession before I ever showed up here. Since I have been here, we have reduced the deficit, we have grown the economy. After we presented our budget, the markets had a very positive response to it: Long term interest rates dropped; the stock market went up. It was seen as a very prudent budget. Now, if they can do better, then we ought to get beyond the politics and let them put their proposal on the table and let us work through. At some point, they have to vote. They've got to get beyond the talking. I've gotten beyond the talking. I've given a budget. Let's see theirs.

Entitlements

Q. Why haven't you taken on entitlements, Mr. President?

The President. I did take on entitlements. The Republicans ran an ad against me the last time. Don't you remember that, in '94? And don't you remember all the surveys that said, "Democrats losing their edge among elders" because the Republicans, the people now in the majority in Congress, launched those vicious ads claiming that we had tried to tax Social Security recipi-

ents, when in fact the upper 13 percent of Social Security recipients were only asked to pay taxes on their Social Security on the same basis that private pensioners were.

We took on entitlements. We had savings in Medicare. We had savings in Medicaid. We did that. And the Republicans said they hated that. Now let's see what they do. It's their turn. They're in the majority in Congress. It is time— I don't have a vote; let them do it. Do you remember when Ronald Reagan—they protected him for years. They said—President Reagan and President Bush, in 12 years between them, vetoed one appropriations bill because it didn't spend enough money and got away with blaming the Congress for raising the deficit. It beat anything I ever saw.

Now, I have tried to work with the Congress. I have tried not to be political. I have tried to say, "Here's my budget. If you've got a better idea, you put your ideas up. Then we'll work together." So far their reaction is, "It hurts us too much to put our ideas forward. We think we'll criticize yours." The American people are sick of this. They want us to work together.

White House Conference on the Economy

Q. Why are you going to have an economic conference in March?

The President. What?

Q. Why are you having an economic conference in March?

The President. Because I think it would be a good thing to get those people back together that gathered 2 years ago, not only to review the progress that has been made but, more importantly, to look at the thorny problems that remain. The middle class still feels squeezed in the midst of a recovery.

And I want us to focus on the challenges that we face for the 21st century in terms of ordinary middle class people. What can we do to raise living standards and increase security for people who are working harder and harder? How are we going to spread the benefits of economic recovery to the middle class? How are we going to grow the middle class and shrink the under class and still keep this marvelous environment for entrepreneurs in which so many people are doing better than they ever had before? That is a separate set of questions.

Two years ago when that group gathered, we had to focus on just getting the economy out of the recession, getting the deficit down, getting the overall growth up. That has happened. Now we need to focus on what still needs to be done to make sure we're solidifying and strengthening and growing the middle class instead of dividing and shrinking it.

Republican Party

Q. Mr. President, is the Republican Party being taken over by extreme right-wing, anti-abortion elements? [*Laughter*]

The President. Well, I hope not, but that's up to them, isn't it?

Surgeon General Nominee Foster

Q. Do you have the votes for Dr. Foster now, Mr. President?

The President. He hasn't even had a hearing yet. I haven't even canvassed them.

Q. Do you think you'll have the votes?

The President. I think if he's judged on his life's work, on the merits, I think he'll be confirmed. I think that if he gets the kind of hearing I would expect him to get from a fair-minded Senate, I think he'll be confirmed.

Border Crossing Fees

Q. Mr. President, are you going to change your border crossing fees? Some Texans saw advisers of yours today and thought—[*inaudible*]—Mr. Panetta was going to take a closer look at it.

The President. I certainly think we have to look at it.

1996 Presidential Campaign

Q. Are you happy that Speaker Gingrich is not going to run against you for the Presidency?

Q. They're dropping like flies, Mr. President.

The President. Did he say that today? They're dropping like flies? Is that what you said? I notice there are still a few. [*Laughter*] I wish the absence of Republican opposition was my main worry, but I don't think it is. Somebody will show up, sure as the world. [*Laughter*] Thank you very much.

NOTE: The President spoke at 2:23 p.m. in the Oval Office at the White House.

Message to the Congress Transmitting Proposed Middle Class Tax Relief Legislation
February 13, 1995

To the Congress of the United States:

I am pleased to transmit today for your immediate consideration and enactment the "Middle-Class Bill of Rights Tax Relief Act of 1995." I am also sending you an explanation of the revenue proposals of this legislation.

This bill is the next step in my Administration's continuing effort to raise living standards for working families and help restore the American Dream for all our people.

For 2 years, we have worked hard to strengthen our economy. We worked with the last Congress to enact legislation that will reduce the annual deficits of 1994–98 by more than $600 billion; we created nearly 6 million new jobs; we cut taxes for 15 million low-income families and gave tax relief to small businesses; we opened export markets through global and regional trade agreements; we invested in human and physical capital to increase productivity; and

we reduced the Federal Government by more than 100,000 positions.

With that strong foundation in place, I am now proposing a Middle Class Bill of Rights. Despite our progress, too many Americans are still working harder for less. The Middle Class Bill of Rights will enable working Americans to raise their families and get the education and training they need to meet the demands of a new global economy. It will let middle-income families share in our economic prosperity today and help them build our economic prosperity tomorrow.

The "Middle-Class Bill of Rights Tax Relief Act of 1995" includes three of the four elements of my Middle Class Bill of Rights. First, it offers middle-income families a $500 tax credit for each child under 13. Second, it includes a tax deduction of up to $10,000 a year to help middle-income Americans pay for postsecondary education expenses and training expenses. Third, it lets more middle-income Americans make tax-deductible contributions to Individual Retirement Accounts and withdraw from them, penalty-free, for the costs of education and training, health care, first-time home-buying, long periods of unemployment, or the care of an ill parent.

The fourth element of my Middle Class Bill of Rights—not included in this legislation—is the GI Bill for America's Workers, which consolidates 70 Federal training programs and creates a more effective system for learning new skills and finding better jobs for adults and youth. Legislation for this proposal is being developed in cooperation with the Congress.

If enacted, the Middle Class Bill of Rights will help keep the American Dream alive for everyone willing to take responsibility for themselves, their families, and their futures. And it will not burden our children with more debt. In my fiscal 1996 budget, we have found enough

savings not only to pay for this tax bill, but also to provide another $81 billion in deficit reduction between 1996 and 2000.

This legislation will restore fairness to our tax system, let middle-income families share in our economic prosperity, encourage Americans to prepare for the future, and help ensure that the United States moves into the 21st Century still the strongest nation in the world. I urge the Congress to take prompt and favorable action on this legislation.

WILLIAM J. CLINTON

The White House,
February 13, 1995.

NOTE: A fact sheet on the "Middle-Class Bill of Rights Tax Relief Act of 1995" was also released by the Office of the Press Secretary.

Message to the Congress Transmitting Proposed Legislation To Increase the Minimum Wage
February 13, 1995

To the Congress of the United States:

I am pleased to transmit for your immediate consideration and enactment the "Working Wage Increase Act of 1995."

This draft bill would amend the Fair Labor Standards Act to increase the minimum wage in two 45 cents steps—from the current rate of $4.25 an hour to $4.70 an hour on July 4, 1995, and to $5.15 an hour after July 3, 1996. The pattern of the proposed increase is identical to that of the last increase, which passed the Congress with a broad bipartisan majority and was signed by President Bush in 1989. The first increment of the proposal simply restores the minimum wage to its real value following the change enacted in 1989.

If the Congress does not act now, the minimum wage will fall to its lowest real level in 40 years. That would dishonor one of the great promises of American life—that everyone who works hard can earn a living wage. More than 11 million workers would benefit under this proposal, and a full-time, year-round worker at the

minimum wage would get a $1,800 raise—the equivalent of 7 months of groceries for the average family.

To reform the Nation's welfare system, we should make work pay, and this legislation would help achieve that result. It would offer a raise to families that are working hard, but struggling to make ends meet. Most individuals earning the minimum wage are adults, and the average worker affected by this proposal brings home half of the family's earnings. Numerous empirical studies indicate that an increase in the minimum wage of the magnitude proposed would not have a significant impact on employment. The legislation would ensure that those who work hard and play by the rules can live with the dignity they have earned.

I urge the Congress to take prompt and favorable action on this legislation.

WILLIAM J. CLINTON

The White House,
February 13, 1995.

Remarks and an Exchange With Reporters Prior to Discussions With President Zhelyu Zhelev of Bulgaria
February 13, 1995

The President. I'd like to tell you how delighted I am to welcome President Zhelev and the representatives of his government here. The United States supports the democratic and economic transformation of his country, and we're looking forward to having this visit and then signing a declaration of principles and a common agenda together. We look forward to working together. And we're very, very pleased to have him and the Ambassador and leaders of the Government here.

Q. Is Bosnia at the top of your agenda, and the lifting of the embargo? Any move toward that?

The President. Well, I imagine we'll discuss that and a number of other things. But we just started.

Q. What is this declaration of principles? Is it just a friendship kind of thing?

The President. It sort of—it outlines the basic principles that will govern our relationship and also sets forward an agenda for how we can work together so that we can support their successes, which is something we want to do.

Q. Thank you.

Q. Life in the old corral.

The President. What did she say?

The Vice President. She said, "Life in the old corral." [*Laughter*]

The President. I don't know; you haven't stayed rounded up too well, Helen [Helen Thomas, United Press International]. This corral analogy has got its limits. [*Laughter*]

[*At this point, one group of reporters left the room, and another group entered.*]

The President. We are honored to have President Zhelev and the leaders of the Bulgarian Government here today, and I look forward to our conversations and to continuing the support of the United States for the democratic and economic transformations in the country. We are also going to sign a joint declaration in a few moments, setting forth the principles and the specific agenda that we will follow in working together. And I am very, very pleased that the President and the leaders of the Government are here.

NOTE: The President spoke at 5:54 p.m. in the Oval Office at the White House. A tape was not available for verification of the content of these remarks.

Joint Statement on Relations Between the United States of America and the Republic of Bulgaria
February 13, 1995

At the invitation of President Bill Clinton, President Zhelyu Zhelev visited Washington, meeting with President Clinton at the White House on February 13.

President Clinton and President Zhelev stressed the value of the close cooperation established over the past five years in maintaining regional stability and supporting Bulgaria's democratic and market economic transformation. They agreed that relations between the two countries rest on the values of democracy and human rights. President Clinton noted that the security of Bulgaria and the other Central Euro-

pean democracies is inseparably linked to that of the United States and praised Bulgaria's balanced and constructive policy in the Balkans.

Both Presidents noted the importance of continued implementation of Bulgaria's market economic reforms. In this context, they noted the need for Bulgaria to solidify its efforts at stabilization, to accelerate implementation of privatization and to complete the legal and regulatory conditions necessary to a market economy. President Clinton offered continued U.S. assistance to support Bulgaria's efforts in this direction. As part of the planned 1995 $30 million

U.S. foreign assistance program in Bulgaria, President Clinton told President Zhelev of a new $7 million loan program designed to support small and medium-sized private businesses, especially in rural areas.

Recognizing the significant cost to Bulgaria of enforcing United Nations sanctions against Serbia/Montenegro, President Clinton and President Zhelev agreed about the continuing importance of sanctions as a key tool to resolving peacefully the conflict in the former Yugoslavia.

President Clinton reaffirmed that the United States will remain engaged in efforts to improve regional transportation infrastructure in the southern Balkans, including Bulgaria. The two Presidents agreed that such projects can help mitigate the interruption of trade routes and promote regional stability and democracy. President Clinton noted that he has asked Congress for $30 million for this regional project.

The United States and Republic of Bulgaria affirmed their determination to enhance regional and European stability through support of the OSCE, United Nations and Partnership for Peace.

Both countries will work to advance Bulgaria's integration into international and Euro-Atlantic economic and security institutions. President Clinton and President Zhelev affirmed support for the Partnership for Peace as the path for all countries of Central Europe and other Partners who wish to work toward NATO membership. President Clinton stated that under his Warsaw Initiative the United States will seek $5 million in security-related assistance for Bulgaria to support the purposes of the Partnership for Peace plus additional resources to support security cooperation.

Recognizing the international dimension of many crimes, the two Presidents agreed to deepen cooperation between their respective law enforcement agencies in the struggle against terrorism and organized criminal activities including narco-trafficking, money laundering and smuggling of cultural and historical objects.

The two leaders agreed to encourage and promote trade and investment between their countries, based on market principles. The two nations intend to work together to create the conditions necessary for such market cooperation, taking into account such issues as protection of investments and new technologies, adequate and effective protection of intellectual property and other elements necessary to a friendly investment environment. Agreements concerning trade and investment have already been signed, including a Trade Agreement and Bilateral Investment Treaty, and the two Presidents placed high priority on the conclusion of a Treaty on the Avoidance of Double Taxation. Following the announcement of a new Central Europe Initiative by the U.S. Export-Import Bank, the Presidents agreed to work to establish a cooperative financing arrangement to support Bulgarian exports that also involve U.S. goods and services to third country markets. The two Presidents agreed that this initiative could help create jobs in both Bulgaria and the United States.

President Clinton recognized the importance of the removal of Bulgaria from application of the provisions of Title IV of the U.S. Trade Act of 1974 (the Jackson-Vanik Amendment). The U.S. Administration has made determinations that Bulgaria is in full compliance with Title IV criteria and will consult with the U.S. Congress concerning legislation to remove Bulgaria from application of Title IV at an early date.

Both Presidents agreed to support ongoing educational and cultural projects such as the American University in Blagoevgrad and to seek to conclude and implement a Science and Technical Agreement.

Through cooperation to advance common political, economic, security and humanitarian interests, the United States and the Republic of Bulgaria continue to build a strong and enduring relationship.

NOTE: An original was not available for verification of the content of this joint statement.

Letter to Congressional Leaders Transmitting a Report on Reform of United Nations Peacekeeping
February 13, 1995

Dear Mr. Chairman: (*Dear Member:*)

There have been few times in history when mankind has had such an opportunity to enhance peace. The founding of the United Nations fifty years ago was one such opportunity. The victorious Allies put in place an institutional mechanism that could be used to enhance peace. Unfortunately, it was not used properly, and Cold War replaced peace.

Now, with the Cold War behind us, we have another important opportunity. Around the world, old enemies are coming together in the Middle East, South Africa, Haiti, Ireland, Central America, and across the great rift that divided Europe for almost five decades. This is a unique period. It can be, as was written in Ecclesiastes, a time for peace.

Peace, however, does not come easily or quickly. Numerous threats remain to our own and our allies' security.

For our generation to seize this opportunity for wider global peace, America must stay engaged. We must also be prepared to pay our fair share of the price of peace, for it is far less than the cost of war.

One of the tools we have to build this new peace is that institution created fifty years ago, the United Nations. As the Cold War ended, the previous Administration turned to the UN and its peacekeeping mechanism to deal with many of the conflicts left over from the superpowers' competition. As a result, the number of UN peacekeepers and their cost sky-rocketed, overburdening the capabilities of the UN system.

I have made UN peacekeeping reform a key goal, working to reduce costs and improve efficiency, using UN peacekeeping when it will work and restraining it when the situation is not ripe. More needs to be done to make UN peacekeeping realize its potential and more effectively serve U.S. interests. It is in the U.S. interest to ensure that UN peacekeeping works and to improve it, because peacekeeping is one of the most effective forms of burdensharing available. Today, other nations pay more than two-thirds of the costs of peacekeeping and contribute almost 99 percent of the troops. Troops from seventy-seven nations are deployed throughout the world in the service of peace.

The UN, once a forum for anti-American debate and propaganda, now is a vehicle for promoting the values we share. Throughout the world, the UN is promoting democracy and providing security for free elections. Its agencies are the chief instruments in the battle against proliferation of nuclear arms and other weapons of mass destruction. UN forces have assumed roles that once had been performed by American troops—in Kuwait, Somalia, Rwanda and soon Haiti. They stand on battlements in places of great importance to us: on Israel's border, and Iraq's, in the Mediterranean between two NATO allies, in Europe on the border of the Former Yugoslav Republic of Macedonia to deter a wider Balkan conflict, and in the Caribbean. The UN recently completed and closed successful operations in numerous places, including in our own backyard in Central America, Cambodia, Namibia and Mozambique.

Were the UN not engaged in promoting peace and security, we would have to invent it. If we did so, it might not look precisely as it has now evolved. The U.S. assessment share would be less. It would be able to respond more rapidly to disasters and do so more economically and effectively. These and other improvements we seek can be achieved only if the U.S. stays engaged in the world and we remain a member of the United Nations in good standing.

I look forward to working with the Congress, as we continue the task of reforming UN peacekeeping and the mission of building and consolidating world peace.

The enclosed report is submitted pursuant to Section 407(d) of the FY 1994/1995 Foreign Relations Authorization Act (PL 103–236).

Sincerely,

WILLIAM J. CLINTON

NOTE: Identical letters were sent to Jesse Helms, chairman, and Claiborne Pell, ranking member, Senate Committee on Foreign Relations; Mark O. Hatfield, chairman, and Robert C. Byrd, ranking member, Senate Committee on Appropriations;

Benjamin A. Gilman, chairman, and Lee H. Hamilton, ranking member, House Committee on International Relations; and Robert L. Livingston, chairman, and David R. Obey, ranking member, House Committee on Appropriations.

Remarks to the American Council on Education in San Francisco, California
February 14, 1995

Thank you very much. Thank you, Juliet, and thank you ladies and gentlemen. Your welcome was worth the 5-hour plane ride. [*Laughter*] I want to congratulate you all on this meeting, and I want to thank Juliet for her leadership and also say to Frank Jenifer, whom I know will carry on the Council's outstanding work and strong leadership in higher education, I wish you well, and I'm delighted to see you again.

I want to thank the entire American Council on Education Board of Directors for endorsing our middle class bill of rights. It will build education and training across America, and I want to say a little more about it in a few moments. You will have to play an important role in making it a reality, and I know that you'll be interested in what I think you have to do, along with what I have to do.

Let me say at the outset what an honor it is for me to be here with my longtime friend, our Secretary of Education, Dick Riley. He has really done a wonderful job, and I am very, very proud of him. And he is responsible for the fact that we had the most successful year last year in promoting advances in education in the Congress in at least 30 years in the United States, and I thank him for that.

I'm also glad to be here for the second straight year and to have Juliet's suggestion that maybe I should think about becoming a college president when I am once again unemployed. [*Laughter*] Now, before we came out here, she gave a slightly earthier description of why I should think about that. She reminded me that President Kennedy, when asked why he wanted to be President, said that the pay was pretty good, a nice house came along with the job, and you work close to home, and that was like a lot of college presidents' jobs. [*Laughter*]

Over New Year's I met a college president who told me that we had a lot in common with people who run cemeteries. He said, "You know, if you run a cemetery, you've got a whole lot of people under you, but nobody's listening." [*Laughter*] On the hard days, when you're about to cry, you can think of that and laugh a little bit about it.

We have more in common than that. You are the keepers of a great trust of this Nation, the most diverse network of learning in the entire world. It's a spur for our economy and a magnet for our people and for people and ideas from all around the globe. I come today as someone who spent some of the happiest years of his life teaching in colleges and universities, as someone who worked as a Governor tirelessly to advance the cause of education, and now in this job, as your partner in a very important mission at a very important time in our country's history.

Our job, yours and mine together, is to redefine the partnership to empower our people through education and through training to face the demands of this age. That's really why I ran for President. I believe it is the responsibility of our generation to work together to preserve the American dream for all Americans and to ensure that we move into the next century still the strongest country in the world.

And I think the best way for us to do that is by building a new partnership in our country between Americans and their Government and between one another. I've called that partnership the New Covenant, more opportunity in return for more responsibility and a renewed sense of citizenship and community. In that New Covenant, Government's responsibility is to expand opportunity while shrinking bureaucracy, to empower people to make the most of their own lives, and to enhance our security abroad but here at home as well. At the same time, we have to demand more responsibility from every citizen in return, more responsibility for our country, for our communities, for our families, and for ourselves.

As we end this century, we are facing dramatic changes in our economy, our Government, and our daily lives. As we move away from the cold war into the information age, we face a world that is both exciting and very challenging, a world where knowledge is the basis of wealth, creation, and power, and where technology accelerates the pace of change. In a world like that, those who have the skills to prosper will do far better than any generation of Americans has ever done. But those who lack the ability to learn and to adapt may be left behind no matter how hard they work.

That is part of the frustration of America today, that there are so many of our fellow Americans who are working harder and harder and harder and never feeling that they're rewarded, feeling that they're falling further behind, having less time for their children, having less time for their spouses, having less time for the things that we know as the quality of life, and just plowing ahead. It leads to people having too much anxiety and too little hope, and it leads to special responsibilities for all of us.

At the heart of all three of the responsibilities that I said the Federal Government has—expanding opportunity, empowering people, enhancing security—is your work, education. It is, indeed, the essence of the New Covenant. Now more than ever, education and training are the keys to opportunity for every American, and the future will only make that more true. They will only work, of course, if individuals also assume the responsibility for themselves to get themselves educated and to impart the value of education to their children, to their families, and throughout their communities. But it is clear that the key to opening the American dream for all Americans as we move into the next century is our ability to broadly spread the benefits of education.

For more than two decades, I have not budged from this conviction. I had, as it turns out for this job, the good fortune of growing up in a State which itself was burdened, in America's greatest explosion after World War II, for lack of education. And I have worked now for about 20 years, relentlessly, to constantly change the role of Government so that it wastes less money and does fewer things it shouldn't, but so that at the same time it serves people better, it insists on accountability, it promotes excellence, but it especially emphasizes educating people.

America now must do that if we have any hope of preserving the American dream in terms of all of our people, in terms of an expanding middle class instead of one that is shrinking and constantly being divided between the haves and have-nots, not in terms of money but in terms of education. As a Governor, I invested more in education and in higher standards for our students, for our teachers, and for our schools and in trying to make it easier for our young people in my State to go to college.

The "Nation At Risk" report, back in 1983, confirmed the crying need for changes in our public schools, and I was glad to work on trying to change the conditions in ours. At the end of the decade, I was proud to be one of the Governors who reached out across party lines to work with the governors association and with President Bush and his White House to craft anew national education goals, goals which we then wrote into law in the Goals 2000 program and which we are doing our best to help schools all across America to achieve on their own.

From the first day I became President, we have been committed in this administration to reinventing Government in all areas but especially in education. Our approach is not—and I repeat, is not—to micromanage anything. We have deregulated the Federal Government's role in education, in the public schools and elsewhere. We have worked to inspire reform at the grassroots level. We have recognized that our job is to define a road map, clear standards of excellence, and then to work to empower everyone in this society to reach those standards through education, to support the educational institutions all across this country, to support the students and the families to help them to reach those standards of excellence.

Instead of defending the status quo, we have worked to change it. We've abolished 13 of the education programs we inherited. We have cut another 38 programs that we thought were less than essential. We have consolidated 70 more programs in the budget I have just sent to Congress. And all of this is designed to empower students and working people, not educational bureaucrats; to help teachers to do their job, not to help the Federal Government to regulate more.

Others have talked about such things, but our administration has actually cut over a quarter of a trillion dollars in Federal spending. We have reduced more than 300 domestic programs. We have eliminated more than 100,000 people from the Federal payroll, and we have used the savings from the payroll reduction to put 100,000 more police officers on our streets in community policing settings, not run by the Federal Government but people who work at the grassroots level on the problems they confront every day. We are on our way, if no other law passes, to cutting more than a quarter of a million people from the Federal payroll and putting all those resources back into making our communities more secure.

And the budget I have just sent to Congress proposes another $144 billion in spending cuts. But my strategy is eliminating yesterday's Government to meet the demands of today and tomorrow, to give us a leaner but not a meaner Government, to cut Government to reduce the deficit and to increase our investments in the future, in education, in technology, in research, things like Head Start and Goals 2000 and the defense conversion programs we supported and the medical research programs we supported. These things make us stronger as a people. They build opportunity, and they demand responsibility, and they are good for America.

We should be discriminating in this work we are doing. We should move beyond rhetoric to reality. Let others talk about cutting spending. We have done it, and we'd like some more help. But we have to realize why we're doing it. We're doing it to lift the country up and bring the country together and move the country forward, not to find some way to divide us in a new and different way so we have more rhetoric, more hot air, and less progress. Let that be our commitment: to do better.

Now, I admit that some in the new Republican Congress see education in another way. They think education at the national level is just another area to cut and gut. Their proposals will cut investments in our future and increase the cost of student loans to our neediest students to fund tax cuts for the wealthy. They will limit the availability of lower cost direct loans to middle class students to increase profits for the middlemen in the student loans, even though that means a higher deficit. Indeed, the only thing they have proposed spending more money in education on are funds going to middlemen by limiting the amount of the direct loan program, by cutting it off just as it's becom-

ing more and more successful. And some of them don't want to reinvent the Department of Education as I have done to make it stronger and leaner and more effective. They want to abolish it altogether. Well, I think Dick Riley's worth the money. And so, I want you to know that to all of this, I will say no. I will fight these proposals every step of the way. And I want you to join me in fighting them, too.

The fight for education is the fight for the American dream. It is the fight for America's middle class. It is the fight for the 21st century. It should therefore—and I emphasize—it should therefore be a bipartisan fight. When we passed the elementary and secondary education act last year, drastically reducing regulation, emphasizing more help to poor children in need, giving teachers and school principals more flexibility, it had bipartisan support.

Look, I want to work with this new Republican Congress to help America. We support many of the same initiatives. I supported them when they passed the bill to apply to Congress all the laws they put on private employers. I have supported our common efforts to reduce the burden of unfunded mandates on State and local governments. I have supported giving more flexibility to the States in pursuing welfare reform and health care reform. I've supported the line-item veto. But we clearly have our differences.

Look at the student loan reforms. We eliminated the middlemen and got the funds directly to the schools and the borrowers which meant, unbelievably, lower fees, lower interest rates, easier repayment choices for students. It meant less paperwork, less redtape, less bureaucracy to administer the programs for colleges and universities, and it meant much, much lower costs to the taxpayers.

Our proposal, when fully implemented, will save the taxpayers $12 billion over a 6-year period, while lowering the cost of college loans to the student and reducing the hassles to you. That is reinventing Government at its best. That is the new Democrat approach. It ought to be the new Republican approach, but instead they want to cap these loans. I want to expand them. I want to include all the schools and all the students who want to be a part of this program by 1997. Your choice, but I'll be darned if I want to cut it off from you when I know that it will help you.

They want to pay for the tax cuts in their contract for America by eliminating the student loan subsidy so that we start charging interest on the loans to our poorest students while they're in college. That costs $2 billion a year. That adds 20 percent on the average to the cost of going to college for some of our neediest students to pay for tax cuts. It is not right. That would be the biggest cut in student financial aid in the history of the United States.

Our approach is to help students and their hard-working parents, to cut bureaucracy, to reduce the deficit by not subsidizing noncompetitive middlemen. I might add that those who wish to compete for student loans are now doing it in many places for lower cost than they were providing when the Government was giving them a lock-down guarantee, because of the competition from the direct loan program.

Now, that is our approach. The other approach would increase the cost of education, would keep the bureaucracy and the redtape, and would increase the deficit by guaranteeing billions and billions in no-risk funds to middlemen in the student loan system. It is wrong. It is wrong. And we should not stand for it. And I hope you won't stand for it. I hope you'll stand up and fight for it.

Now, as you well know—and I want to emphasize—we are not talking about a give-away. This Department of Education has gotten tougher on enforcing laws against default. And the default rate has dropped by one-third. The net annual cost to the taxpayers has fallen by almost two-thirds since we have been in office, from $2.8 billion to $1 billion, because we're enforcing the laws against default. I think it is wrong to default on your student loan. This Department of Education has gotten tough with scam operators masquerading as higher education. And every one of you wanted us to do that. Now, with this progress, I hope we can continue to remove the regulatory burdens from many of the strong institutions with proven records of responsibility. That's what you want us to do. That's his valentine present to you.

But that's the way we ought to be doing this. Secretary Riley will work with you to find a better way of balancing the flexibility you want with our obligations to the taxpayers. But the point is, other people talk about this stuff, but when I showed up in town 2 years ago, I found a student loan program that was too costly, helping too few people, gave too few options to

the borrowers with a redtape headache to you, and the taxpayers were being ripped off. And we've tried to change it.

Now, when we proposed these direct student loans, our opponents and those who wanted to protect the status quo said that the Federal Government was completely incapable of administering a loan program. Well, they weren't right. They were wrong.

I got a letter that was sent to Terry Hartle by Jerome Supple, the president of Southwest Texas State in San Marcos. It's a big school now. It has 21,000 students. It distributes grants and loans in excess of $23 million. President Supple wrote about what direct lending has meant to his school. He also wrote to me, but Dick Riley gave me this copy of his letter to Terry Hartle, and I like it better than what the speechwriters put in, so I'm going to write what he actually said. [*Laughter*]

This is what he said: "We are aware of the concern of some members of the financial community about the shift to direct lending and can understand the concern for a loss of revenue. However, the savings to the Government and the improved service to other students offered by direct lending are of greater importance. The other argument that the Federal Government cannot effectively administer such a program and must rely on the expertise of the private sector is counter to our experience."

Listen to this: "The results have more than met our expectations. We have gone from an institution that was scrambling to meet our students' need, often after classes have started, to an institution that was one of the first in the State to get awards out last fall, so early, in fact, that it had a positive effect on our admissions program.

"While the direct lending program must share some of the credit for the improvement of our financial aid services with our hard-working and talented staff"—there's a good politician— [*laughter*]—also true—"there is no doubt that direct lending allows us to serve our students better. And finally," he says, "it is legitimate to express concern about the ability of the Department of Education to manage the direct lending program at full capacity, but the experience to date suggests that it can do this very well. It is rare that the Federal Government creates a program that both saves money and improves service to its constituents."

Listen to what the students say. I got a letter from Marie Lyons, a 40-year-old student—rather more typical these days. She wrote to me to say that she had given up hope on going to college. But with our loan reforms, she's been able to go to Murray State University in Kentucky, studying criminal justice. She'll be the first person in her family to graduate from college.

You know, we can't take hope away from people like Marie Lyons and all the other people now that are flooding back into your institutions, into the community colleges, into the 4-year institutions, because they know—they're way ahead of the politicians—they know what they need to do to make good lives for themselves, and they're coming to you. They're coming to you in record numbers. But people like that deserve the best opportunity we can give them. They are very responsible. They are working hard. They are people from all races and income groups and backgrounds with a million different life stories, but they are chasing a common dream. Because of people like that, we should not abolish the Department of Education, either. We should not do that.

You know, everybody talks about this being the information age. The White House and now the House of Representatives are in this little friendly contest to see who can do the most high-techy stuff on Internet, and call us on the computer and see what we have to offer, read the administration's budget. But if this is true, if the new economy really is based more than ever before on knowledge and skills, we have to do more of education. And undercutting education at this time, saying that this is not a national concern, that would be like undercutting the Department of Defense during the cold war. We won the cold war because we stayed strong. And we will win the fight for our own future and a place in the 21st century if we stay strong with education. That is what we should do.

You know our future depends upon it. You know, as President, as has already been said, I've worked pretty hard for us to do well in this new war for the minds and hearts of our people and for the future. And I do think one of the smartest things I ever did was to appoint Dick Riley as the Secretary of Education. One of the reasons is, I find that once you become President, sometimes people, even people you think know you very well, all of a sudden don't

really tell you what's on their minds. It drives me nuts since I don't mind hearing what's on people's minds. Sometimes they don't want to hear what's on mine in return when they tell me, but it's okay. [*Laughter*] But one of the things you need to know about the Secretary of Education is, we've been friends since I was barely old enough to shave. He always tells me what's on his mind—[*laughter*]—and what's on his mind is you and your students and the future of this country.

So I'll say again, we're cutting inessential education programs. We've saved more money by going to the direct student loans than they can save by cutting out the people who work at the Department of Education. Who are we trying to kid here? He is worth the investment; the other people who work there are worth the investment.

We are not running education, but we are trying to energize it and create opportunity and shine a light to the future. This is a classic battle, and we ought to fight it and win it together, not just the battle to save the Department of Education, not just the battle for the direct loan program, not just the battle against increasing the cost of student loans but the larger issue. And I will say again, this ought to be a bipartisan battle that we fight so that we can meet our responsibility to prepare our children for the 21st century and so that we can make the most of our own lives.

For 2 years, we have done everything we could do to prepare our people for the new economy. Last year when I came before you, I presented a comprehensive agenda for lifelong learning. I'm proud to report that with the last Congress, we did produce a tremendously successful record in achieving that agenda. We reformed Head Start and expanded it by 30,000 more children. And next year, I want to expand it again by at least that many. That's why we're cutting inessential programs, not only to reduce the deficit but to put the money where the people need it. I think the taxpayers want the Head Start program expanded.

We passed the Goals 2000 program, and for the first time we spell out a national understanding of what our young people must learn to compete in the world. This goes right to the heart of the whole approach of the national role in education, not trying to tell people how to teach or regulate how they spend every day and every hour or control them through a blizzard of paperwork but to set national standards and then give State and local governments the control, the power, the opportunity, and, where we can, the resources to get the job done, to give them the flexibility through waivers of complex Federal rules and reforms like charter schools and public school choice, and to do it with no new Federal regulations to diminish State and local control. I'm proud of that.

The way we're running that program is the way the Federal Government ought to relate to the States in the area of public education. We are raising the bar for everyone. All of our young people are going to have to do better. I think we all know that. All of our parents and grandparents are going to have to help our young people to do better. All of you in this room now accept as a truism that we have the best higher education system in the world, but that we have to do better in our school systems K–12, and we are all going to have to teach to higher standards, to work to higher standards, to learn to higher standards.

Our communities, our businesses, they're going to have to pitch in and do more. And our young people, we know—and let me say this with all sincerity and convictions—we know that too many of them are still trying to learn in atmospheres that are too dominated by violence and drugs. If they can't walk down the halls or learn in the classrooms because they're afraid for their safety, then all the reforms will not be successful. That's why making our school environment safe and disciplined and drug-free are important to all the other standards being achieved, and why we have worked so hard in this administration and in this Department of Education to make sure that all of our legislative efforts included the safe schools initiatives.

You know, some young people—I ought to emphasize, too, because I know who all is out here—don't plan to go on to 4-year colleges. And that's fine. If they don't plan to do that, we also have to make sure that they have the academic strength and skills they need to compete.

That's what our School-to-Work Opportunities Act was all about, to reinvent the relationship of high school to the world of work and the work of post-high-school education with high standards that enable our students to learn in class and to begin to reach out into the real world. Along with their classroom learnings, they are learning real jobs, dealing with real people, and we expect them to go on for some post-high-school education as well.

We're not doing this with a big national bureaucracy. We're doing it with grants and advice and help and support to let every State set up a flexible network, working with employers and schools and the postsecondary educational institutions to make sure that we fill this enormous gap in the American system. There are too many of our young people still who neither get a 4-year college degree or at least have a good school-to-work transition the way many of our competitors do.

These reforms, every one of them, will make sure that more capable students are coming into your institutions, which means you'll have to spend less time bringing them up to speed. I know that would be a relief to all of you. A lot of us have been working on it for years and years, but I believe it will make a difference.

Something else we did last year that I'm very proud of that two or three of you have already mentioned to me today is our national service program, AmeriCorps. It already has 20,000 Americans taking responsibility for improving their country at the grassroots level and earning some money to go to school. It is a very, very important thing for this country, and I am very proud of it.

Americans like the 16 members at the University of California at Berkeley, who have 750 of their classmates tutoring middle school students and helping four local police departments set up neighborhood watch programs. Now, that's just one example of hundreds I could give you of what a modest Federal investment can do to get a big result. Eighty-nine members of AmeriCorps in Texas immunized—listen to this—104,000 infants in Texas two summers ago. In Simpson County, Kentucky, AmeriCorps members are teaching second-graders to read, and they've already raised the reading levels there from 2 years behind the official standard to 1 year ahead of it.

Now again, some people in the new Republican Congress say that AmeriCorps is a waste of money, bribing people to do service, an expensive way to send people to college. I say it's about the best thing that's happened to this country in a long time. I'm going to fight to keep it, and I hope you'll fight for that, too. And for all of you that have had AmeriCorps projects on your campuses and with your students, I thank you, and I hope more of you will ask to do it.

We've got a lot more work to do. We have to protect the Pell grants, and as Juliet said, my budget raises the maximum grant by 12 percent. We all know the Pell grant program got in trouble, and we had to make it solvent again, and it hasn't kept up with the economy. But this is a good step in the right direction.

We've got to preserve the work-study program, the other campus-based programs that we all know are important to the students on your campuses. And we've got to keep moving forward on university-based research with expanded investments and less redtape. I do not believe that it is the right thing to do to take universities out of the partnerships we now see forming. In defense conversion, for example, where we are doing remarkable things with the decline of the defense budget, taking some of that decline and putting it into partnerships between universities and private companies with some Federal investment and a whole lot of private investment. Again, there are some in the new Congress who say, let's get rid of all that. That's our competitive edge, research, development, mind work, making connections, moving forward.

All of this is an agenda that works. In his state of American education address earlier this month, to which Secretary Riley alluded, he said that America is turning the corner from being a nation at risk in education to being a nation on the move. Well, you've got my word: I will fight for the education and training reforms that will keep us on the move. And I want you to fight for them, too, and we will win because the American people are for us.

Now, that's why I have proposed this middle class bill of rights, because I want to emphasize what we still have to do. We can't just preserve what we've got. We've got to keep going forward. All over this country there are people who are saying, "Well, I read about this recovery, and I know we've got 6 million new jobs, but it's not affecting me. I still feel insecure and uncertain, and I haven't gotten a raise. The middle class bill of rights, I think should be called the bill of rights and responsibilities because, like all the other things we've been talking about today, you can't take advantage of it unless you act responsibly. It does offer a tax cut for people, but only if they're behaving

responsibly, raising their children, educating themselves or their children.

From your point of view, the most important parts of it are a tax deduction for the cost of education after high school; an IRA that you can withdraw from tax-free for education and for other purposes like buying a health insurance policy; and the collapse of 70 of the Government's training programs into a program which a person who's eligible for Federal training help because he or she is unemployed or working for a very low wage can draw on and just take the money, up to $2,600 a year, to an institution of his or her choice, getting around the Federal bureaucracy, getting around all the programs and going direct to a lot of you.

Now, this is a good thing, and I thank you for endorsing it. But I need your help to make it happen. Why is it a good thing? It's a good thing, first of all, because it will lower the cost of living for hard-working people who have gotten no benefit out of this recovery yet. But instead of just giving them a quick fix, it lowers their cost of living because it increases their standard of living over the long run by putting the money into education. It is the right way to give tax relief to the middle class. It is consistent with long-term control of the deficit. It is consistent with a commitment to long-term economic growth. And I ask each of you to do what you do best now—to help teach people about this, to talk about it; because this resolution is really nice, but what we really need is for every Member of Congress to hear from every college president, every dean of students, every member of every board of trustees, every student body president, every student organization in the country, "Hey, don't take the interest subsidy away." "Hey, don't stop us from getting the direct loans." "Hey, pass the middle class bill of rights."

Education is the key to our future. It ought not to be a partisan issue. If there is one thing in the wide world that ought to unite us on the way to the next century, it should be our common commitment to explode the potential of our people. I need your help. I want your help. You can do it. But the resolution has to be a first step, not the last step. Be heard in every office of every Member of Congress in the United States, and we will have a great victory. I need you. I want you to do it. I'm confident you will.

Thank you very much.

NOTE: The President spoke at 11:45 a.m. in the Hyatt Regency Embarcadero Hotel. In his remarks, he referred to Juliet Garcia, chair, Franklyn Jenifer, incoming chair, and Terry Hartle, vice president for government relations, American Council on Education.

Remarks at San Bernardino Valley College in San Bernardino, California
February 14, 1995

Thank you for that wonderful, wonderful welcome. Thank you, Dr. Singer, for your introduction. I know the Secretary of Education, Secretary Riley, has already spoken. I'm glad to be here with him. And I thank the mayor for being here and Dr. Bundy. And let's give the Etiwanda High School Band a hand. Didn't they do a great job? Great job. Thank you. When I heard them playing "Hail to the Chief" outside I thought they'd transported the Marine Band from the White House here, they were so great. They were great.

I'd also like to recognize a couple of other groups that are here. First of all, I want to thank the members of our national service program, AmeriCorps, who are here. They're over there. And I want to thank a representative group of incredible people who just spent about an hour with me, talking to me about this institution, how it has affected their lives and your community and the remarkable partnerships that are being made and the dreams that are being made to come true. I'd like for all the people who were just in the little roundtable discussion with me to be recognized. They're over here somewhere. Where are they? There they are. [*Applause*] Thank you. They were great. I feel that I know a lot more about you now because I listened to all of them, and believe me, they put you all in a very good light.

I want to talk to you today about the importance of this community college and education in general, not only to your future but to the future of our country, what it means and what we should be doing about it. I met a lot of folks already here today that represent what I think America is all about, people who are coming together around the idea of education without regard to their race, their income, their background, what country they were born in, what situation they're in now just because they want to make the most of their own lives and make a contribution, live up to the fullest of

their God-given abilities. And I really think that's what we ought to be supporting.

The reason I worked so hard for the national service program that you see all these young people in is because I believe that we ought to be helping young people to find ways to earn money for education and contribute to the strength of their communities at the same time.

I ran for President because I was worried, as we come to the close of this great century, that we wouldn't be able to guarantee the American dream for all people moving into the 21st century and we wouldn't be able to make sure America was the strongest country in the world, and I believe those are the two jobs the President has to do. And I believe the way we should do that is what I have called the New Covenant. We should create more opportunity; we should insist on more responsibility from all of us; and we should work to build our communities at the grassroots level, where the real strength of America is.

Now, there's been a lot of debate in our country now in two separate elections, in 1992 and 1994, about what the role of Government is and whether Government is bad or good inherently. My answer to you is that we need a different kind of Government for the 21st century and that your National Government has three major jobs. One is, we should expand opportunity while shrinking the Federal bureaucracy and the burden it imposes. Two, we should recognize that the Government can't support everybody, but it should work to empower people to make the most of their own lives. And three, we should work to enhance the security Americans feel not only in terms of what goes on beyond our borders but here at home as well. More opportunity, more empowerment, more security: that is what we should be about in the National Government.

Now, if you look at what this national service project does, they're working in the San

Bernardino forest, people who are helping to clean up the forest, maintain it, strengthen it, keep it there for our children and our grandchildren, make sure it's an important resource. Last year there were 89 young people in this program in south Texas who immunized 102,000 infants to help them live, and all of them earned money on their education. Sixteen of these young people work at Berkeley, helping 750 of their classmates to tutor middle-school students. These are the kinds of things that are going on all over America, and I think it emphasizes what I'm saying. For a small amount of Federal money we have increased opportunity with no bureaucracy. This is all done at the grassroots level.

We have certainly empowered these young people to make more of their own lives, and we are clearly going to be a stronger country because we have more people getting an education and more people preserving the environment, making our kids healthier, making our country stronger at the grassroots level. That is what I am trying to do. And I want to talk to you today about what that means for education in general, and especially for community colleges like this one, which are the key to the future of the American economy and the ability to preserve the American dream for all people.

Let me give you an example of what we're trying to do in another area on security, and then I'll come back to education, because I want to make sure that you understand exactly how I'm thinking about this. I welcome the call of the new Republicans in the Congress to cut the Government, but I—now, wait a minute, you all don't get into a partisan fight already; wait until the end of the speech. [*Laughter*] For the last 2 years, we've been doing it without any help. I'd like some help. I'd like some help. But what is the purpose of this? That's what I want you to think about.

Now, there are now over 100,000 fewer people working for the Federal Government than there were the day I took office. We have shrunk the Federal Government. If they don't pass a single law this year, we will reduce the size of the Federal Government by over a quarter of a million because of the budgets adopted in the first 2 years of my term, and we'll make the Federal Government the smallest it's been since John Kennedy was President.

Now, what do we do with the money? What are we doing with the money? We cut, already,

over $600 billion from the deficit, and we're going to cut more. I've just sent a budget to the Congress that cuts more spending from the deficit. What are we doing with the money? We propose, first, to reduce the deficit and, secondly, to increase investments in the areas that I mentioned, to increase investments that would create more opportunities—jobs; that would empower people more—education; and that would enhance security—things like the crime bill.

If you just take the crime bill, for example, I said when I ran for President—I came to California and campaigned—"Vote for me, and I will reduce the size of the Federal bureaucracy by 100,000 and we'll put another 100,000 police officers on the street." And that's exactly what we've done, except we reduced the size of the Federal Government by 270,000 and used it to pay for police officers, prisons, and prevention. We passed that crime bill last year with a bipartisan majority. After 6 years of partisan haggling and scrapping around and people throwing words at each other, we actually passed a bill. And since October, we have put—but I only was there a year and a half, you understand—[*laughter*]—but since October, we've put 16,000 police officers out, 16,000. And we've got 17 right here in San Bernardino, new police officers.

Listen to this: We did it with a one-page form, eight questions that could be faxed in; nobody had to hire consultants. And of all the communities in America with police officers, every size, including those with just one, one-half of all the communities in America have already applied for help under this program because it's a good program, it works, and there's no hassle in it. That's the kind of Government we ought to have, a leaner, not a meaner Government that makes sense and makes people more secure. We're under budget, ahead of schedule, moving forward.

It took 6 years to pass the bill. I started working on it when I got elected; we got it done. In only 6 weeks of this new Congress, the new majority in the House of Representatives is trying to wipe out the crime bill and pass two block grants, to cut back on the money that goes to police and to prevention, to put it all in one package, send it to the States and say, you all do whatever you want to with it, and to put more money into the prison system. Now, here's the interesting thing—wait a minute, don't get into a partisan fight, just listen to me make my piece. [*Laughter*] Every police organization in the country, including those that are overwhelmingly Republican, has endorsed our position to leave it alone and let it work. This is not a partisan issue.

So the people in the House said, "I don't care what the police said. I don't care what the people working in the community said. I don't care what the evidence shows. This is what we're going to do. We're determined not to spend any money on prevention. If the States want to do it and not put police on the streets, that's their business. And here's the money, build the prisons, or else." Now, what I believe is that we still have a chance to keep this a bipartisan issue. And I'm going to do my best to go into the Senate and to work with people who understand law enforcement, who will listen to people who are out here on the streets every day trying to save these kids and save our communities and save our streets and keep this bill intact so we can put the police on the street and have the prevention programs.

But I will not—I will reiterate what I said Saturday—if I have to, I will veto any bill that attempts to undermine the commitment that we made last year after 6 years. But it need not be a partisan issue. It ought to be an American issue. And that's what I say to you about education. What are we going to do in this day and time? What is our job in Washington that affects you way out here in the Inland Empire when it comes to education? What is our job when it comes to helping to raise middle class incomes and let people in the under class work themselves into the middle class? What is our job, and what is the problem?

You know, if anybody told me 2 years ago that we would be able, in the space of 2 years, to bring the deficit down over $600 billion and have a hand in creating almost 6 million new jobs, I would have been very happy to hear that. In 1994, we had the best year for economic growth in a decade and the first year in a long time when all 50 States, including California that's been through so much, had economic growth. What is the problem?

The problem is, a whole lot of people have jobs but their incomes aren't going up. They don't feel secure at work. They're afraid they can't keep their health insurance, or they don't have it now. We had 8.5 million people worried about their retirement until we passed a reform

of the retirement guaranty system late last year. So in this global economy the good news is, there are more people in America becoming millionaires than ever before. That's good news. The good news is, there are more people with an education doing exciting things than ever before. The bad news is, if you don't have the skills you need, you can work harder and harder and harder for less and less and less, right?

So when you have a good news-bad news story, you have two choices. You can tell a joke about it, but if you're President, that doesn't seem to be a particularly good option. [*Laughter*] The other choice you have is to try to make more good news and less bad news. And the only way to do that, I would argue to you, is to make sure we give all of our people access to the education and training they need to compete and win in this global economy, so when they work harder, they'll be rewarded for it and not punished for it. That is what we have to do.

Now, I want you to focus with me just for a minute, therefore, on two big issues, what we ought to do in this year and what we should not do. I think we ought to give some tax relief to hard-working middle class people who haven't felt the benefit of the recovery. But the question is, what kind, and will we pay for it? I do not think we should increase the Federal deficit. That's been a big problem. We've gotten it down. We ought to keep bringing it down, not exploding it.

Secondly, I think that the best tax relief is embodied in what I call the middle class bill of rights because it rewards work and family. It gives tax relief for people raising young children, and it gives tax relief for the cost of all education after high school, which I think is important. You think about it, you can deduct the cost of interest on your home if you have a home. But in the information age, if you don't have an education, you may never get to a home. So why shouldn't we let people deduct their education costs? It's a good investment. We also propose to let more people get an IRA, an individual retirement account, and withdraw from it tax-free for the cost of education. I think that's what we ought to be doing.

And finally, I had a lot of questions earlier about unemployment; one gentleman talked about his father being unemployed. We have scores of different Federal training programs that you have to wonder, are you really qualified for or not? And what we propose to do is to create a "GI bill" for America's workers by taking 70 of these programs, putting them in one big pot and saying, "If you're unemployed or if you're working for a really low wage and you're eligible for Federal help, instead of having to figure out how to enroll in one of these programs, qualify, we'll send you a voucher. Show up at this community college. We'll send them a check." That's the way it ought to be done.

We're also taking the savings from cutting out all of these programs. In the Education Department alone, Secretary Riley has abolished 13 programs, reduced 38 others, and consolidated 70 more, in the Education Department. We took the savings and put it into more funds for Head Start, more funds for apprenticeship programs for people who don't go on to 4-year colleges.

I met a young woman today, and a police officer who is working with her, who's in one of these programs that we now see people desperately trying to set up all over the country, training young people in high school, giving them work experience, letting them see what it's like, giving them a chance to look forward to a job in the workplace.

You know, not everybody has to go to a 4-year college, but everybody needs to get out of high school and have access to at least 2 years of further education. And one way to do it is to abolish the artificial distinction between learning and work by bringing the workplace into the school, the education into the workplace, and doing it everywhere in America. So we've put some more money into that.

The other thing we have sought to do is to make available college loans on better repayment terms and lower costs to more people, through the so-called direct loan program.

This is an amazing thing. I want you all to— this is an amazing thing. When I became President, I discovered that we were spending about $3 billion a year in your money because of people defaulting on their college loans. I discovered we were spending a fortune because the college loan program was a guarantee program. So you'd go to a bank, and if you qualified, the bank would give you a note. And if you didn't pay it back, we'd give them the money. So they didn't have much incentive to see that you paid it back, because we were going to give them the money.

And we discovered if we started loaning the money to people directly, these good things would happen if it could be properly managed: We discovered we could loan the money sometimes at lower interest rates and always at lower fees. We discovered that we could give people a lot of options about how they repaid it so that when you get out of school, if you take a job that doesn't pay much money and you've got a lot of loans, you could pay it off as a percentage of your income instead of having to pay an amount you couldn't afford to pay. We discovered we could cut the bureaucratic paperwork and hassle for the colleges by more than half. And we discovered, miracle of miracles, if we didn't have to pay a middleman and we started collecting on these student loans, we could actually lower the cost to the taxpayers.

It almost doesn't make sense: lower costs to students, lower costs to taxpayers. But this plan has already saved in the budget about $5 billion, and if we can send it to all colleges and universities in the country, it can lower the deficit by $12 billion and lower the cost of loans to every student in America with a student loan. That's one of the most important things we have done, and we need to do it.

Now, here's the political problem that you need to be a part of. We're having a big debate up there: Everybody wants to cut the size of Government, everybody wants to reduce the deficit, and everybody has got a different idea for a tax cut. But some people in the new Congress believe that one of the ways they can reduce the deficit is by increasing the cost of student loans to people who don't have to pay interest on the loan while they're in school now. You know about the loan subsidy; a lot of you are probably eligible for that. That will add 20 percent to the cost of student loans.

I'm against it. That is not the way to cut the budget. That is not the way to pay for a tax cut, to increase the cost of going to college to people. We need more people going to college at lower cost, not fewer people going to college at higher cost. And I hope you will support that.

The other idea—this is unbelievable to me— is we got this program working to lower the deficit, lower the cost of student loans, and there are some people in the Congress who want to limit the number of students in this country who can get these direct loans to 40 percent of the colleges in America. Why? Because the people that are in the middle who get the money don't like losing it. I mean, it's not a bad deal: I loan you money; you don't pay me back; I get a check from the Government. But it didn't work very well.

Secretary Riley, since he's been there as Secretary of Education, has cut the cost to the taxpayers of college loan defaults from $2.8 billion a year to $1 billion a year. We're collecting the loans. We're doing it right, and we ought to keep going.

So what I want to ask you to do is, without regard to your party, and maybe—especially if you have never voted before—I want to tell you something: You've got a big stake in this debate that's going on in Washington. And it is a good and healthy debate in some ways. We do need a less bureaucratic, more creative, more entrepreneurial, more flexible Government in Washington as we move into the 21st century. We do need more responsibility put down to the State and local levels. What's the best institution you know? The community college. No-

body from Washington is telling you what programs to have, what to do, who to sign up for—nobody. You're doing this. It's a community-created institution. We do need to change the nature of the Federal Government. We do have to keep cutting Federal spending.

But the key to our future is whether we educate everybody, so we don't need to cut investment in education. And we do need to do things, I will say again, that enhance security, empower people to make the most of their own lives, and expand opportunity. That is education, education, education. We should not turn back on it.

Thank you very much. God bless you. We need your help. Please support it. Thank you.

NOTE: The President spoke at 5:45 p.m. in the Snyder Gymnasium. In his remarks, he referred to Dr. Don Singer, president, San Bernardino Valley College; Mayor Tom Minor of San Bernardino; and Stuart Bundy, chancellor, San Bernardino Community College District.

Letter to the Speaker of the House on Emergency Supplemental Appropriations Requests
February 14, 1995

Dear Mr. Speaker:

My Fiscal Year 1996 Budget requests $10.4 billion in supplemental appropriations for the current fiscal year. Much of the request is for emergency requirements, such as contingency operations of the Department of Defense and disaster relief provided by the Federal Emergency Management Agency. My Budget also proposes to reduce low-priority spending in FY 1995 by $2.4 billion, primarily to pay for nonemergency supplemental requests.

I was disappointed to receive your February 7, 1995 letter indicating your intent to delay action on several of these emergency requests until the Administration proposes offsets. I am particularly concerned about my request for $6.7 billion for FEMA Disaster Relief, all of which is properly designated as an emergency, under the terms of the Budget Enforcement Act of 1990.

The Budget Enforcement Act established the authority for the President and Congress to exempt certain spending from the statutory caps, specifically for the purpose of meeting emergency, unanticipated requirements. This joint designation by the President and Congress has been used over the last four years to provide critical assistance in response to earthquakes, hurricanes, floods, extreme cold and agricultural disasters, and for other purposes.

President Bush and Congress approved $10.2 billion as emergency spending in response to Hurricanes Andrew and Iniki in Florida, Louisiana and Hawaii. In fact, from 1991–1992, President Bush and Congress provided emergency funding for 100 accounts, totalling $12.3 billion.

I worked with Congress to provide $6.8 billion in emergency funding to aid the victims of the Midwest floods in nine states. I also reached agreement with Congress to designate emergency spending for the Northridge earthquake.

The emergency designations were appropriate because the human and physical costs of these disasters were extraordinary and the economic effects were truly national in scope.

Of the pending $6.7 billion FEMA request, $4.9 billion is related to the Northridge earthquake. Over 700,000 people were affected. Approximately 120,000 structures, including schools, hospitals, municipal buildings and private residences, were damaged. Almost 40 miles of roads and freeways were rendered impassable.

Following the January 17, 1994 earthquake, I responded with a request for emergency supplemental funding on January 26. Congress quickly responded to the urgent needs of the Southern California region and I promptly signed the emergency legislation on February 12, just 26 days after the earthquake.

The nation should be proud of our rapid response. All of the damaged highways were reopened to traffic within 10 months. Virtually all of the 6,000 school buildings that were damaged have reopened. Over 113,000 loans have been made to small businesses and homeowners, and FEMA disaster housing assistance has been provided to over 400,000 households.

Because of the need to respond quickly to the earthquake, FEMA's damage estimates were necessarily preliminary. Our revised request is based on the more detailed studies that are required of damaged structures.

If action on our request is delayed, FEMA will, beginning in May, be unable to allocate funds to meet any new disaster requirements, unless money reserved for the 40 states currently receiving disaster assistance is cut. For example, emergency appropriations provided in FY 1994 are currently being used to fund assistance to people, businesses and local governments impacted by Tropical Storm Alberto in Georgia, the Midwest floods, the Texas floods and the recent floods in California. If action is further delayed until July, FEMA will run out of money.

While I share your concern for reducing the deficit, I do not believe we should delay assistance to victims of natural disasters. I am proud of my Administration's record for reducing the deficit, while providing prompt assistance to the victims of natural disasters. When responding to crises, America has traditionally come together without regard to politics or region. In that spirit, I urge you to reconsider your decision.

Sincerely,

BILL CLINTON

Interview With Dick Enberg of NBC Sports in Palm Springs, California
February 15, 1995

Mr. Enberg. Well, a historic foursome. How do you put this group together to play a game of golf?

Bob Hope. Well, it's damned lucky, I think, you know. Because I called President Clinton and asked him, and he finally said, "Yes, I'd like to do that." Then I got President Ford, President Bush, and we got—and me. Three Presidents and a hacker. [*Laughter*]

Mr. Enberg. Mr. Clinton, your ambitions as a golfer—have you set any goals?

President Clinton. I'm just trying to get my handicap in single digits. That's my goal. It seems unlikely in my present position. But I love to play, and I was gratified when Bob called me the other day. He said that he liked my State of the Union Address, but I could speak a lot better if I come out here and played in his tournament. It would put me in a better frame of mind.

Mr. Enberg. You're without your 35-year-old putter. I hope the rumors aren't true that Mr. Ford confiscated that. [*Laughter*]

President Gerald R. Ford. Well, Dick, I've played here 17 years with Bob, and it's always a great, great thrill. He's kind of a scoundrel, but he's fun to play with, and it's a great cause.

Mr. Enberg. And your thoughts, Mr. Bush?

President George Bush. Just to try to get it in the air. [*Laughter*]

President Clinton. We're going to try to stay out of—we're going to avoid out of bounds, he and I are. We're not going to go too far right or too far left. We're going to play political golf today. [*Laughter*]

Mr. Enberg. Have you been in this close an association in recent terms, or have you played before?

President Clinton. We've never played golf together before, but President Bush has been good enough to support a lot of things we've done together on trade and issues, for example, things he started that I tried to finish. So we've been together on several occasions.

Mr. Enberg. Any interesting wagers as you go around today?

President Bush. I don't know. We haven't gotten to that.

President Clinton. We're on the same side. We want somebody to bet with us and these other foursomes.

Mr. Enberg. Well, how about that on this side?

President Ford. Well, Bob and I will take the young fellows on. [*Laughter*]

Mr. Hope. Yes, sir.

Mr. Enberg. Well, Mr. Hope, this event becomes bigger and better every year. It's a great testimony to your love for——

Mr. Hope. Well, I'll tell you, we've drawn a crowd here today. I don't remember seeing anything like this. It's a beautiful thing to have happen for golf, you know, because you can't do any better.

President Clinton. Absolutely.

Mr. Enberg. Isn't it interesting that in these complicated times, this sport brings this unusual group together?

President Clinton. One of the nicest things about golf is that it's really becoming a sport for every man and woman in America. All kinds of people, all these new courses coming up, public courses, people able to play who never could have played 10, 20 years ago. And that's very rewarding, because it's a sport that you can play throughout your life and at all different skill levels. It's really a perfect sport for our people.

Mr. Enberg. Well, you gentlemen are used to high pressure. I can't think of anything in sports that has more anxiety and pressure than that first hit. [*Laughter*]

President Clinton. We are nervous as cats. We were just talking about it. We're just as nervous as we can be. [*Laughter*]

President Ford. Dick, I would advise people they should stay behind us. [*Laughter*]

Mr. Enberg. Gentlemen, thank you very much, President Bush, President Clinton.

President Clinton. Thank you very much.

NOTE: The interview was taped at 9:56 a.m. for later broadcast at the Indian Wells Country Club, where the President participated in the Bob Hope Chrysler Classic golf tournament. A tape was not available for verification of the content of this interview.

Statement on Petroleum Imports and Energy Security
February 16, 1995

I am today concurring with the Department of Commerce's finding that the Nation's growing reliance on imports of crude oil and refined petroleum products threaten the Nation's security because they increase U.S. vulnerability to oil supply interruptions. I also concur with the Department's recommendation that the administration continue its present efforts to improve U.S. energy security, rather than to adopt a specific import adjustment mechanism.

This action responds to a petition under Section 232 of the Trade Expansion Act of 1962, which was filed by the Independent Petroleum Association of America and others on March 11, 1994. The act gives the President the authority to adjust imports if they are determined to pose a threat to national security. The petitioners sought such action, claiming that U.S. dependence on oil imports had grown since the Commerce Department last studied the issue in response to a similar, 1988 petition.

In conducting its study, the Department led an interagency working group that included the Departments of Energy, Interior, Defense, Labor, State, and Treasury, the Office of Management and Budget, the Council of Economic Advisers, and the U.S. Trade Representative. The Commerce Department also held public hearings and invited public comment. Following White House receipt of the Commerce Department's report, the National Economic Council coordinated additional interagency review.

As in the case of its earlier study, the Commerce Department found that the potential costs to the national security of an oil import adjustment, such as an import tariff, outweigh the potential benefits. Instead, the Department recommended that the administration continue its current policies, which are aimed at increasing the Nation's energy security through a series of energy supply enhancement and conservation and efficiency measures designed to limit the Nation's dependence on imports. Those measures include:

—Increased investment in energy efficiency.
—Increased investment in alternative fuels.
—Increased Government investment in technology, to lower costs and improve production of gas and oil and other energy sources.
—Expanded utilization of natural gas.
—Increased Government investment in renewable energy sources.
—Increased Government regulatory efficiency.
—Increased emphasis on free trade and U.S. exports.
—Maintenance of the Strategic Petroleum Reserve.
—Coordination of emergency cooperation measures.

Finally, led by the Department of Energy and the National Economic Council, the administration will continue its efforts to develop additional cost-effective policies to enhance domestic energy production and to revitalize the U.S. petroleum industry.

Message to the Congress Reporting on the Proliferation of Chemical and Biological Weapons
February 16, 1995

To the Congress of the United States:

On November 16, 1990, in light of the dangers of the proliferation of chemical and biological weapons, President Bush issued Executive Order No. 12735, and declared a national emergency under the International Emergency Economic Powers Act (50 U.S.C. 1701 *et seq.*). Under section 202(d) of the National Emergencies Act (50 U.S.C. 1622(d)), the national emergency terminates on the anniversary date of its declaration unless the President publishes in the *Federal Register* and transmits to the Congress a notice of its continuation.

On November 14, 1994, I issued Executive Order No. 12938, which revoked and superseded Executive Order No. 12735. As I described in the report transmitting Executive Order No. 12938, the new Executive order consolidates the functions of Executive Order No. 12735, which declared a national emergency with respect to the proliferation of chemical and biological weapons, and Executive Order No. 12930, which declared a national emergency with respect to nuclear, biological, and chemical weapons, and their means of delivery. The new Executive order continued in effect any rules, regulations, orders, licenses, or other forms of administrative action taken under the authority of Executive order No. 12735. This is the final report with respect to Executive Order No. 12735.

This report is made pursuant to section 204 of the International Emergency Economic Powers Act and section 401(c) of the National Emergencies Act regarding activities taken and money spent pursuant to the emergency declaration. Additional information on chemical and biological weapons proliferation is contained in the annual report to the Congress provided pursuant to the Chemical and Biological Weapons Control and Warfare Elimination Act of 1991.

The three export control regulations issued under the Enhanced Proliferation Control Initiative are fully in force and continue to be used to control the export of items with potential use in chemical or biological weapons (CBW) or unmanned delivery systems for weapons of mass destruction.

During the final 6 months of Executive Order No. 12735, the United States continued to address actively in its international diplomatic efforts the problem of the proliferation and use of CBW.

At the termination of Executive Order No. 12735, 158 nations had signed the Chemical Weapons Convention (CWC) and 16 had ratified it. On November 23, 1993, I submitted the CWC to the Senate for its advice and consent to ratification. The United States continues to press for prompt ratification of the Convention to enable its entry into force as soon as possible. We also continue to urge those countries that have not signed the Convention to do so. The United States has remained actively engaged in the work of the CWC Preparatory Commission headquartered in The Hague, to elaborate the technical and administrative procedures for implementing the Convention.

The United States was an active participant in the Special Conference of States Parties, held September 19–30, 1994, to review the consensus final report of the Ad Hoc Group of experts mandated by the Third Biological Weapons Convention (BWC) Review conference. The Special Conference produced a mandate to establish an Ad Hoc Group whose objective is to develop a legally binding instrument to strengthen the effectiveness and improve the implementation of the BWC. The United States strongly supports the development of a legally binding protocol to strengthen the Convention.

The United States maintained its active participation in the Australia Group (AG), which welcomed the Czech Republic, Poland, and Slovakia as the 26th, 27th, and 28th AG members, respectively. The Group reaffirmed members' collective belief that full adherence to the CWC and the BWC provides the only means to achieve a permanent global ban on CBW, and that all states adhering to these conventions have an obligation to ensure that their national activities support these goals.

The AG also reiterated its conviction that harmonized AG export licensing measures are consistent with and indeed actively support, the requirement under Article I of the CWC that States Parties never assist, in any way, the manufacture of chemical weapons. These measures also are consistent with the undertaking in Article XI of the CWC to facilitate the fullest possible exchange of chemical materials and related information for purposes not prohibited by the Convention, as they focus solely on preventing assistance to activities banned under the CWC. Similarly, such efforts also support existing nonproliferation obligations under the BWC.

The United States Government determined that one foreign individual and two foreign commercial entities—respectively, Nahum Manbar, and Mana International Investments and Europol Holding Ltd.—had engaged in chemical weapons proliferation activities that required the imposition of trade sanctions against them, effective on July 16, 1994. A separate determination was made and sanctions imposed against Alberto di Salle, an Italian national, effective on August 19, 1994. Additional information on these determinations will be contained in a classified report to the Congress, provided pursuant to the Chemical and Biological Weapons Control and Warfare Elimination Act of 1991.

Pursuant to section 401(c) of the National Emergencies Act, I report that there were no expenses directly attributable to the exercise of authorities conferred by the declaration of the national emergency in Executive Order No. 12735 during the period from November 16, 1990, through November 14, 1994.

WILLIAM J. CLINTON

The White House,

February 16, 1995.

Message to the Congress Reporting on the Proliferation of Weapons of Mass Destruction
February 16, 1995

To the Congress of the United States:

On September 29, 1994, in Executive Order No. 12930, I declared a national emergency under the International Emergency Economic Powers Act (IEEPA) (50 U.S.C. 1701 *et seq.*) to deal with the threat to the national security, foreign policy, and economy of the United States posed by the continued proliferation of nuclear, biological, and chemical weapons, and their means of delivery. Specifically, this order provided necessary authority under the Enhanced Proliferation Control Initiative (EPCI), as provided in the Export Administration Regulations, set forth in Title 15, Chapter VII, Subchapter C, of the Code of Federal Regulations, Parts 768 to 799 inclusive, to continue to regulate the activities of United States persons in order to prevent their participation in activities that could contribute to the proliferation of weapons of mass destruction and their delivery means.

I issued Executive Order No. 12930 pursuant to the authority vested in me as President by the Constitution and laws of the United States of America, including the IEEPA, the National Emergencies Act (NEA) (50 U.S.C. 1601 *et seq.*), and section 301 of title 3 of the United States Code. At that time, I also submitted a report to the Congress pursuant to section 204(b) of the IEEPA (50 U.S.C. 1703(b)).

Executive Order No. 12930 was revoked by Executive Order No. 12938 of November 14, 1994. Executive Order No. 12938 consolidates a number of authorities and eliminated certain redundant authorities. All authorities contained in Executive Order No. 12930 were transferred to Executive Order No. 12938.

Section 204 of the IEEPA requires follow-up reports, with respect to actions or changes, to be submitted every 6 months. Additionally, section 401(c) of the NEA requires that the President: (1) within 90 days after the end of each 6-month period following a declaration of a national emergency, report to the Congress on the total expenditures directly attributable to that declaration; or (2) within 90 days after the termination of an emergency, transmit a final report to the Congress on all expenditures. This report, covering the period from September 29, 1994, to November 14, 1994, is submitted in compliance with these requirements.

Since the issuance of Executive Order No. 12930, the Department of Commerce has continued to administer and enforce the provisions contained in the Export Administration Regulations concerning activities by United States persons that may contribute to the proliferation of weapons of mass destruction and missiles. In addition, the Department of Commerce has conducted ongoing outreach to educate concerned communities regarding these restrictions. Regulated activities may include financing, servicing, contracting, or other facilitation of missile or weapons projects, and need not be linked to exports or reexports of U.S.-origin items. No applications for licenses to engage in such activities were received during the period covered by this report.

No expenses directly attributable to the exercise of powers or authorities conferred by the declaration of a national emergency in Executive Order No. 12930 were incurred by the Federal Government in the period from September 29, 1994, to November 14, 1994.

WILLIAM J. CLINTON

The White House,
February 16, 1995.

Message on the Observance of Presidents' Day, 1995
February 16, 1995

Greetings to Americans across the country celebrating Presidents' Day, 1995. As citizens gather to reflect upon our nation's rich history, I am proud to salute our former Presidents for the legacy of leadership they have built in this nation.

From the bold example of George Washington to the timeless courage of Abraham Lincoln—the Presidents whose birthdays we commemorate today—each President, in his own way, has sought to use the power of the American government to make our country better, stronger, and truer to the ideals of its charter. Fueled by the mission of our nation's citizens, Presidents of each generation have aspired to serve the common good, recognizing that whether we Americans choose to rise or fall, move forward or backward, we will all do so together. On this special occasion, and in honor of that great tradition, I ask each of you to join in rededicating yourselves to maintaining the freedoms we hold most dear, for ourselves and for the generations to come.

Best wishes for a wonderful holiday celebration.

WILLIAM J. CLINTON

Remarks at a Memorial Service for J. William Fulbright
February 17, 1995

Mrs. Fulbright, the children and grandchildren of Senator Fulbright, all of his family and friends here assembled, we come to celebrate and give thanks for the remarkable life of J. William Fulbright, a life that changed our country and our world forever and for the better. In the work he did, the words he spoke, and the life he lived, Bill Fulbright stood against the 20th century's most destructive forces and fought to advance its brightest hopes.

He was the heir of Jefferson in our time. He believed in the American idea, but he respected others who saw the world differently. He lived with passion tempered by reason. He loved politics, but cautioned against the arrogance of power. He cherished education as the answer to our common problems and our personal dreams. But he knew there would always be more to learn.

Time and again for 32 years as a Congressman, a Senator, chairman of the Foreign Relations Committee, he worked for progress and peace, often against great odds and sometimes at great personal cost: expanding opportunities for the people of his beloved Arkansas and other Americans who needed help to make the most of their lives; leading the way to found the United Nations; taking a long, lonely stand against Joseph McCarthy; expanding the reach of our culture as the driving force behind the Kennedy Center; fighting to change our course in Vietnam; reminding us that the forces of freedom would win the cold war if we could avoid nuclear war, what he called his generation's power of veto over the next; and of course, in a cold dawn only 2 weeks after Hiroshima, calling for the creation of the international exchange program that will live as his most profound legacy.

The Fulbright Scholarship Program is a perfect example of Bill Fulbright's faith, different kinds of people learning side by side, building what he called "a capacity for empathy, a distaste for killing other men, and an inclination

for peace." Next year will be the 50th anniversary of that program. Now it includes as its alumni Nobel Prize winners, Members of Congress, leaders for peace and freedom the world over, and many not so famous people who went home to live out the faith of Senator Fulbright. More than 120,000 from other countries have come here and more than 90,000 Americans have gone overseas to study, to learn, and to grow. No matter what their native tongue, all of them are now known by the same name, Fulbrights.

In a way, a lot of us here, especially those of us from Arkansas and those who worked for him in other ways over the years, are also in our own way Fulbrights. Those of us who knew and loved him, who worked for him, who learned from him, each of us have our indelible memories, some of them serious, some of them quite funny.

I must say that I was a little reluctant to accept the request that I speak today because I once attended a funeral with Bill Fulbright, and I know how much distaste he had for highly formalized rituals. If he were giving me instructions, he'd say, "Bill, say something nice, be brief, and try to get everybody out so they can enjoy this beautiful day."

But let me tell you that those of us who understood and shared his roots in the Ozarks, those of us who knew what his life was like as a young person growing up and playing football and becoming the president of a university, those of us who understood later in life what he learned when he had the chance first to travel overseas and study in England and see the insanity that resulted from the squandering of the victory in World War I, those of us who saw firsthand the enormous anguish he felt, as I would see him early in the morning and late in the evening in the Senate office building, in the great struggles over the Vietnam war, those of us who saw him in his campaign in

1968, when this country was being literally torn apart, still trying to learn, trying to understand, and trying to be understood, we will never forget the debt that we owe him and the debt the country owes him.

When Mrs. Fulbright spoke last year in Germany, in recognition of the Senator's receipt of a distinguished award from the American Chamber of Commerce there, she quoted from a letter Senator Fulbright received 30 years ago. I'd like to leave it with you, so that you can remember something of what he did and the times in which he did it.

She said, all this talk of leadership, freedom and education may seem simple, self-evident and commonplace to you now, but there was a time when it was considered radical, even dangerous. Thirty years ago, Senator Fulbright was called names I wouldn't dream of putting on paper, much less pronouncing to a respectable audience. He got emotional letters full of praise and hate. There was one which affected him far more deeply than all the rest. And after reading it, he closed his office doors, ordered all the calls held, and wrote in longhand an answer which he did not copy. I will read you the letter:

"Dear Senator Fulbright: I have never voted for you. I have never missed a chance to belittle you. But deep inside me, there was a nagging suspicion that I have been wrong. As this world plunges headlong toward what well may be its destruction, it gets increasingly harder to hear lonely voices, such as yours, calling for common sense, human reason, and the respect for the brotherhood of man. But be of good cheer, my friend, keep nipping at their heels. This old world has always nailed its prophets to trees, so don't be surprised at those who come at you with hammers and spikes. Know that those multitudes yet unborn will stand on our shoulders. And one among them will stand a little higher because he is standing on yours."

We owe a lot to Bill Fulbright, some of us more than others. Let us all remember the life he lived and the example he set.

A few years ago, Senator Fulbright came home to Fayetteville, and we celebrated a Fulbright Day. I was then the Governor, and after the official event, we went back to his hotel room and watched the football game. And when the young player for one of the teams kicked a field goal, he looked at me and he said, "You know, I used to do that over 60 years ago. I don't know what happened to all those years. They sure passed in a hurry." I think we can all say that they also passed very well.

Senator Fulbright's lesson is captured on the statue in the Fayetteville town square in these quotes: "In the beauty of these gardens, we honor the beauty of his dream, peace among nations and free exchange of knowledge and ideas across the Earth." Bill Fulbright also left us the power of his example, always the teacher and always the student.

Thank you, friend, and Godspeed.

NOTE: The President spoke at 10:25 a.m. at the Washington National Cathedral. In his remarks, he referred to Harriet Fulbright, widow of the Senator.

Remarks at a Salute to African-American Veterans
February 17, 1995

Ladies and gentlemen, Secretary Perry, Secretary Brown, General Shalikashvili, General Powell, General Davison, Admiral Gravely, Ossie Davis, Colonel Earley.

I hate to throw any cold water on this magnificent night, but I'm just sitting here thinking whether as Commander in Chief I should dismiss or simply demote whoever it was who arranged for me to speak after Colonel Earley. [*Laughter*] If ever there was an embodiment of what we came here to celebrate tonight, if ever there was evidence that this celebration is occurring at least 50 years too late, it is Colonel Earley.

Tonight we celebrate the extraordinary history of patriotism of our Nation's African-American citizens, whose courage and devotion to country helped to raise the consciousness of a nation, and through years and decades and centuries to reverse a tragic legacy of discrimination. History records their great deeds, and we have honored them tonight.

We can only marvel at the dedication that they manifested year-in and year-out, war-in and war-out, from the first days of the Republic, in spite of all that they were denied under the Constitution and laws. In spite of being treated as second-class soldiers, segregated from their peers, with second-class training, too often with rifles that jammed or misfired, sometimes shamefully harassed by comrades, still they served:

Peter Salem, who fired the shot that killed the leader of the British forces at Bunker Hill, served in the Revolutionary War.

Sergeant Alfred Hilton, under the withering fire outside Richmond during the Civil War, picked up the Union flag from its fallen bearer and carried it further into battle until he, too, fell, mortally wounded. You should know that today, that soldier's great-grandnephew, Steve Hilton, upholds his tradition of service to the country as a captain in the Army Reserve and a member of the White House senior staff.

The 369th Infantry Regiment in France during the First World War, whose French commander said they never lost a prisoner, a trench, or a foot of ground.

But it was during World War II, as we saw tonight, when our country was forced to marshal all its resources, to call forth every ounce of its strength, that African-Americans in our Armed Forces made contributions that would literally save the world from tyranny and change the course of our Nation at home. Time and again, from the far reaches of the Pacific to the very heart of Europe, the more than one million African-Americans in uniform distinguished themselves as P–40 fighter pilots and Navy Seabees, Sherman tank drivers, orderlies, and engineers.

You've heard the stirring story of Dorie Miller, a steward aboard the USS *Arizona* at Pearl Harbor, who saw his captain fall wounded and pulled him to safety. And then, despite the fire, he manned a machine gun and downed two enemy planes.

At Iwo Jima, the African-American marines of the 16th Field Depot, working as stretcher bearers, braved shells and bullets and mines to pull their comrades back from the frontlines when they were wounded.

At the Battle of the Bulge the men of the 3496th Truck Company hauled weapons, soldiers, and prisoners down roads that the rain had turned into rivers of mud and ice. They unloaded their 2½-ton trucks as mortars fell all around them. And even today, 50 years later, their commander, Colonel Benjamin Layton, says he can still feel the driving snow and the deadening cold of the Ardennes. He's with us tonight, and we honor him and those like him who served their Nation so well. Thank you, Colonel Layton.

And I, too, must say just a word about the legendary Tuskegee Airmen, who flew over 1,500 combat missions and never lost a single bomber under their escort. Some of them are here with us tonight, including Second Lieutenant Luther Smith, who was forced to bail out over Yugoslavia after a successful attack on an ammunition dump, where he was captured and interned as a POW in Austria. He entered that camp weighing 150 pounds. Six months later when the British forces liberated him, he was down to 70 pounds. But he survived, and he's here. God bless you, sir.

After the war, after winning the victories over fascism and intolerance, these heroes came home to a nation that still could not shed its habits of hatred and bigotry. A mayor and a city marshal pulled a young black sergeant from a bus in South Carolina and beat him blind. A mob gang in Georgia dragged a newly returned veteran and his wife from their car and shot them so savagely they could scarcely be identified. These and other horrible acts of violence done to our African-American veterans moved President Truman to desegregate the military and put forward the most sweeping civil rights legislation our country had then known.

So it was that in Korea and Vietnam, African-Americans were able to serve shoulder to shoulder with soldiers of all races for the first time. Beamed by television into America's living rooms, images of their camaraderie and shared sacrifice helped our Nation to act on a truth too long denied: that if people of different races could serve as brothers abroad, putting their lives on the line together for this country, surely, surely at last they could live as neighbors at home.

It is a measure of the progress we have made as a people that today many of our most revered military leaders are African-Americans. Admiral Gravely and General Davison came in with me tonight. I was proud to look up here at the beginning of the program and see the Commander of our district here, General Gorden. And of course, we heard the 220-year saga tonight that led from Crispus Attucks to General Colin Powell.

Today I say to you ladies and gentlemen who have served us in uniform, at last our children, without regard to their race, see in you nothing more and nothing less than what you are: American heroes in the proud tradition of George Washington, John Pershing, and George Marshall. You have earned their way into the Nation's hearts, and you are there now forever and ever.

Tonight let me salute you for many things but most of all for never giving up on America. Finally, finally, in the military your country is worthy of you, worthy of the words of the Constitution and the Bill of Rights, worthy of the sacrifice that you and your forebears have given. Let us never forget it. And let us now say: Wouldn't it be nice if the rest of America worked together as well as the United States military?

Thank you, and God bless you all.

NOTE: The President spoke at 8:13 p.m. at Constitution Hall. In his remarks, he referred to Gen. Colin Powell, USA, Ret.; Maj. Gen. Frederick Davison, USA, Ret.; Vice Adm. Samuel L. Gravely, Jr., USN, Ret.; Ossie Davis, narrator of the salute; Mrs. Charity Adam Earley, former Lieutenant Colonel, Women's Army Corps; and Maj. Gen. Fred Gorden, Commander, Military District of Washington.

The President's Radio Address
February 18, 1995

Good morning. I'm joined today by the Houston Rockets, last year's National Basketball Association champs. I'm glad they're here to have their recognition and take their tour of the White House, not only because of what they've achieved but because I believe team sports reflect America at its best.

And in America, as in team sports, anyone can rise as far as his or her God-given talents and hard work will take them. That doesn't mean everyone can lead the NBA in scoring. The American dream doesn't guarantee results for anybody. But it does mean that opportunity is there if you're willing to work and struggle and do your very best. At the same time, for teams to succeed, people have to work hard and work together. Hakeem Olajuwon would probably be the first to admit that stars can break records but only teams win championship rings.

That's what I mean when I talk about a New Covenant in America. It's about teamwork, partnership among all of our people.

In this country at this time, as we move into a new century and a new economy, the Government's job is to expand opportunity while shrinking Government bureaucracy, to empower people to make the most of their own lives, and to enhance our security, not just abroad but here at home on our streets, too. At the same time, we must demand more responsibility from every citizen in return, not just for ourselves and our families but responsibility for our communities and our country. We're all in this together—more opportunity and more responsibility.

I know the American people want us to practice that here in Washington, and I've reached out to the Republican Congress. At the end of the cold war as we move into this information age, there are many areas where we can work together to improve the lives of hard-working Americans: reducing the size of the Federal Government, reducing the burden of unfunded requirements on State and local governments, requiring Congress to live under the same laws it imposes on people in the private sector, the line-item veto to control unnecessary spending, and giving more flexibility to States to reform their welfare and health care systems.

But we still have our differences as well. And when we do, I'm going to judge a policy not on whether it's a Republican or a Democratic one but on whether it's best for the American people. If it is, I'll support it, fight for it, sign it into law. But if it isn't, I will oppose it.

Just this week, we've seen where some of these differences lie. When I ran for President,

I pledged to cut 100,000 Federal bureaucrats and use the money to put 100,000 new police officers on the street. I did it because one of the jobs of the Federal Government is to enhance our security at home and because crime and violence is a problem all over America, in communities small and large.

Well, we're keeping that promise. Last year's crime bill reduces the Federal bureaucracy and takes all the money and gives it to our communities to fight crime. It provides explicitly for 100,000 new police officers. Just since the 4 months since the crime bill took effect, police departments in America have been able to hire over 16,000 police officers. That's in just 4 months. We're going to make the 100,000 goal.

And just so you'll know how much that is, there are only 550,000 police officers in America. So with these 100,000 all going on the streets, that's about a 20 percent increase in the police forces of America to keep our people safer.

Incredibly, Republicans in the House of Representatives voted to replace our guarantee of 100,000 police with a blank check that has no guarantees at all, with money that can be used for all kinds of things other than police. Now, I'm all for cutting bureaucracy; under our plan, communities can apply for police with a one-page, eight-question application. But I know the American people want more police on the street, and I know the law enforcement officers of this country know it's the best crime-fighting tool there is. I'm going to work with the Senate to fix this proposal. But I will veto any effort to repeal or undermine our promise.

Some are saying that this change is necessary because police departments won't hire 100,000 people because we require them to come up with a little of the money, too. To them I say, in only 4 months, one-half of all the communities in the entire Nation have written to us asking for more police. This is popular in the country, and it ought to stay the law here in the Congress.

As we enter the 21st century, the keys to opportunity for every American are education and training. That's another one of our jobs here in Washington, to give people the tools they need to make the most of their own lives. That's why we reformed the student loan system, eliminating middlemen and actually cutting the cost to the taxpayers and making college loans more affordable for all kinds of middle class students all across this country, lower cost and easier to pay back. We also expanded the Head Start program by 30,000 children and made it apply to younger kids. We're helping young people who don't choose college learn the skills they need to get and keep high-paying jobs.

In the last Congress, many Republicans supported these things as well as Democrats. But in this Congress, some Republicans want to limit the reach of our college loans so over half the students in the country can't get them. They want to slow down or stop or reverse a lot of these other educational gains.

But creating opportunity for people who take responsibility for themselves is exactly what the Government should be doing at this time in our history. Some of these Republicans see education as just another place to cut and gut. I want to cut Government. I have cut Government. There are already more than 100,000 fewer people working here than there were the day I became President. But I don't want to do it at the expense of our children's skills and education and our future.

Finally, this week our administration opposed Republican efforts in the House of Representatives to force the Government to spend billions on a Star Wars-type defense system, diverting those resources from high priority national security areas and threatening our Antiballistic Missile Treaty. I was gratified that the Democrats and some Republicans who joined them had the courage to defeat this unacceptable and unconstitutional infringement on the President's authority. America's security must never be about Republicans and Democrats, about who happens to be President and who happens to control Congress. Our national security should never be a partisan issue. And I will not allow Congress to jeopardize that security by making it one. After all, our job, no matter what our party is, is to work together to move America forward and to preserve the American dream for all Americans in the new global economy.

That's why I proposed the middle class bill of rights, to cut taxes for ordinary people to help them invest in their families and in their education; why I want to raise the minimum wage, so people who will take the responsibility to work full-time and stay away from welfare can earn a decent living for themselves and their children while they're doing it.

I will fight for every idea, every proposal, every piece of legislation that strengthens the American dream. And I'll keep doing everything in my power to fight against anything that weakens it.

Thanks for listening.

NOTE: The President spoke at 10:06 a.m. from the Oval Office at the White House.

Remarks Congratulating the 1994 National Basketball Association Champion Houston Rockets and an Exchange With Reporters
February 18, 1995

The President. Good morning, everyone. I am delighted to be here with the Houston Rockets; along with NBA Commissioner David Stern; Congresswoman Sheila Jackson-Lee; the owner of the Rockets, Leslie Alexander; and of course, Rudy Tomjanovich, the head coach.

I want to congratulate the Rockets formally on their championship last year. We've been trying to find a time for them to come to the White House and make their official visit for some time, and as you know, they played the Bullets here last night, and I'm glad to have them here.

I enjoyed last season immensely. I enjoyed watching the Rockets win. It was the first-ever major championship in sports for a Houston team. It opened the season with 15 straight wins, tying an NBA record. And the victories, the number of victories they had was the best in the team's history. So it was a great season for them. And you all know, I kind of liked basketball last year anyway. And I'm beginning to like it better this year as it goes along.

It occurs to me that basketball is a lot like my work around here: You get behind; you get ahead; you never know whether you're going to win until the end of the game. But the most important thing is that you keep playing and doing the best you can and working on the teamwork.

Coach Tomjanovich did a great job in leading the Rockets to victory last year. He's been with the Rockets for 24 years. And I might say that's sort of a rarity in professional athletics today. But it's the kind of loyalty to an organization that I think we need more of all across America, in every walk of life.

I was just told that, before I came in here, that Hakeem Olajuwon's name in Arabic translates into "always on top." [*Laughter*] I would say that even for the NBA's most valuable player and defensive player of the year, it helps to be on top if you're 7 feet tall. And he's really done very, very well.

Let me say in closing, I think all Americans enjoy athletics, and I think it's a very healthy thing. But as I said in my radio address today, the thing I like best about basketball is that it is, every play, in every way, a team sport. And it requires a team mentality, even with a lot of stars, to win. You can't win without great players, but you can't win without good teamwork either. And that's what our country needs more of. And I'm delighted to have the Houston Rockets here.

I'd like now to ask the NBA Commissioner, David Stern, to come forward and say a few words.

[*At this point, Mr. Stern made brief remarks and presented the President with a jacket.*]

The President. What do you think this will do for my image, guys? [*Laughter*] I love this. I love this.

Mr. Stern. It's an extra large, Mr. President. [*Laughter*]

The President. I need an extra large. That's great. [*Laughter*]

Mr. Stern. With that, I'd like to introduce the owner of the Houston Rockets, Les Alexander. Les.

The President. Thank you.

Mr. Alexander. Thank you, Mr. President, for having us here today. I'd like to present you with a championship ring with your name on it, and it says, "To the number one fan in America, from the Houston Rockets."

The President. Thank you so much. That's beautiful. Thank you.

Mr. Alexander. Now I'd like to introduce one of the great coaches in the world, Rudy Tomjanovich, and of course the greatest player in the world, Hakeem Olajuwon.

Mr. Tomjanovich. Thank you, Mr. President, for taking time and making this a very special day for us. It's a day we'll always remember. And I would like to present to you a Rocket jersey with your name on the back and the number one.

The President. That's great.

Mr. Tomjanovich. You're the number one man on the number one team in the world.

The President. You know, I've got a basketball court down here in the backyard. Do you think I should wear this? [*Laughter*] Good length, too, don't you think? [*Laughter*]

Mr. Olajuwon. Well, I would just like to thank Mr. President for this, an honor for us as a team and also to have this opportunity to visit the White House. And we're so glad you're the President. And thank you so much for inviting us. And we would like to come back next year as the champion. [*Laughter*]

The President. Will you come back next year? Thank you very much.

It's all aired up. I may go down and——

Q. All you need is trunks. [*Laughter*]

The President. Yes. A shot might help—if I had a shot. [*Laughter*] I still need a shot.

Thank you very much. It's good to see you. It's great.

Meeting With President Boris Yeltsin of Russia

Q. Mr. President, have you put off a summit with Yeltsin in May?

The President. No. I don't know what the—let me just say this. I don't know what the source of that story is, but I want to make it very clear: We have made no decision about the May schedule. And there are lots of issues involved, because there are lots of 50th anniversary events on celebrating the end of World War II. And we literally would not had a meeting on that. So it would be wrong to draw any inference one way or the other. There has literally been—I've gotten no recommendations from my staff on it. We've had no meeting. Tony Lake and I had our first passing conversation about it last night about 6 p.m. So we'll make a decision quite soon and announce it, but there has been no decision made.

Q. Well, you wouldn't go, would you, if there's a war on in Chechnya?

The President. I have said, there is no decision made. I have made no decision. I've had no meeting. And when I do, I'll let you know.

Secretary of Commerce Ron Brown

Q. Mr. President, does Ron Brown still have your support?

The President. He's the best Commerce Secretary we've ever had. And he's gotten more results. That ought to be the test. He's a good Commerce Secretary. The questions that have been raised about what happened before he became Commerce Secretary are being looked into in an appropriate fashion. And meanwhile, he's on the job, and I'm supporting him in that.

No Commerce Secretary has ever done more than he has to create jobs for Americans and to support the interest of American business. And that is the test. And he should go forward and do his job. That's what I want him to do.

Thank you all.

NOTE: The President spoke at 10:47 a.m. in the Roosevelt Room at the White House.

Interview With Brian Lamb of C-Span
February 19, 1995

Former U.S. Presidents

Mr. Lamb. Mr. President, we're talking in and around President's Day, so I want to see if you could tell us the purpose of having this little thing on your desk that involves another President, "Dewey Defeats Truman."

The President. Well, of course, that's the famous headline from the Chicago Tribune. I got it when I was in Independence, Missouri, at the Truman Library. And I'm a big admirer of President Truman. He was my neighbor—you know, Arkansas and Missouri border each other—and I always—I like having that on my desk. It reminds me that things are not always what they seem and that it's important to keep fighting. I look at it every day; I have it right there on the desk.

Mr. Lamb. If you could talk to any past President—and I know you just got off the golf links with a couple of them—who would it be, and what would you want to talk to him about?

The President. Well, it's difficult to say which one President I would talk to. For myself, personally, I would talk to Lincoln because I admired him so much, personally, and because I believe he grew so much in the job. His personal growth in the job was extraordinary, and his ability to distill all the forces at work into clear and powerful language was so great.

But there are others. Jefferson, I would like to speak with because he carried around in his very soul the ideals of the Founders. And he found himself in the same position to some extent I find myself in, in a very different historical context, in that he believed deeply in limited Government, he didn't want Government to oppress people, but he felt that there were occasions in which the national interest demanded a level of activism. In Jefferson's case, he purchased Louisiana, for example, which cost the equivalent of one year's Federal budget. So I think Jefferson understood the kind of complexity that we're facing today. He had a fertile, complex mind, and he understood how to reconcile the bedrock principles and apply them to the facts of the case at hand, and I like that.

I wish I could have a long conversation with Truman, because the time we're living in today somewhat parallels the period after the Second World War in the sense that we're going through a period of transition, things are being redefined. The size of the Government is being reduced, but there's still a mission for the Federal Government to advance the cause of ordinary citizens in America. There is a new security reality in the world, and we have to adapt to that. So the times that we live in now are quite a lot like those times.

Mr. Lamb. Do you read the Presidents now, since you've been in the White House, their words?

The President. Yes, I just read—interestingly enough, I just read Benjamin Thomas' biography of Lincoln, which was written in the fifties, I think, and it's a biography I had never read. You see over there on my desk I've got a new

biography of Jefferson, the Randall biography of Jefferson I'm about to get into. I just read Doris Kearns Goodwin's magnificent biography of Franklin and Eleanor Roosevelt during the war, "No Ordinary Time." It's a terrific book. So I read quite a bit about it. I read August Heckscher's biography of Woodrow Wilson last year, something which I should have read before, I guess, but I had never gotten around to reading.

Mr. Lamb. As you're reading, do you delve in and see yourself in any of those positions and learn anything that you can change, or is that another period?

The President. Of course you do. You can't help imagining how you would have done in their time, how they would do in your time, what strengths did they have that you could perhaps develop, what errors did they make that you could perhaps avoid, how different is it?

Mr. Lamb. What's the first thing you'd ask Jack Kennedy if you could talk to him today?

The President. I would ask for his advice about what we could do to restore at least a measure of the optimism and the sense of trust that existed when he became President, because he had more space, in some ways, to govern and to be President, even though there were terrific conflicts. In fact, he had much more difficulty with the Congress than I did in the 2 previous years. But there was a sense of confidence in the American people and a sense of trust in their elected leaders and a willingness to look at things in a more balanced way, I think, than exists today. And I would ask for his advice about how we could get some of that back.

Mr. Lamb. Did you change your mind at all about F.D.R. after you read Doris Kearns Goodwin's book?

The President. No, I just appreciated him more. I was sad for him in a way, personally. I was sad—I knew that his life was somewhat difficult and that Mrs. Roosevelt's was. But they had a remarkable positive impact on this country, and I'm grateful for that. But I didn't change my opinion of him. He was, in many ways, the most adroit politician who ever occupied this office. And he was a person who was fortunate enough to be there at the right time for him. The country sometimes brings us the right people for the right times, and he was, I think, really perfectly suited, temperamentally and by means of experience, to the times in which he governed.

Mr. Lamb. You know, a lot is written about the criticism of you at this point in your Presidency. When you read the history, do you find that other Presidents were hit about by their critics as much as you are?

The President. Well, they were subject to the same criticism, but by and large, it wasn't nearly as intense or public. There wasn't as much news. And the news rules were different then; they were different.

I suppose Jefferson——

Mr. Lamb. Like what?

The President. Well, they just didn't have the—you know, Roosevelt could have off-the-record press conferences. Roosevelt could debate matters and take months deciding issues without having 100 commentarians talk about how indecisive he was.

I got tickled the other day—I read an analysis of decisionmaking and record that was done in "The American Prospect," which said that I was—in which the author argued that I was much more decisive in difficult situations than President Roosevelt had been early on in his term and that I had paid a bigger political price for it, in other words, arguing that Roosevelt was viewed as being sly and canny. But that's just—part of it is just the times, you know, the times change. And the nature of coverage of politics today and the sort of instantaneous commentary about every issue and the obsession with process over product and with politics over policy, I think these things just give a President less space. They require you to affect an almost arbitrary way of decisionmaking because of the heavy tilt in the way your decisions are characterized to the American people.

Mr. Lamb. There have been a half dozen books already written about your Presidency.

The President. It's crazy.

Mr. Lamb. The latest one was the David Maraniss book.

The President. It's just crazy. I mean, how can you possibly reflect on someone—I mean, you know, I've given a lot of thought to—that's another thing, Kennedy had Arthur Schlesinger in the White House, you know. But you didn't have people out there writing books about his administration until it was over, until they had some time to reflect and get some fairness or balance in it. It's amazing now, it's sort of—

it's just the difference in the time in which we live.

Mr. Lamb. Do you read any of those books?

The President. What I—normally I look at them. I don't spend a lot of time reading them, just because I think that what I need to be doing is I need to focus on today and tomorrow. I can't do anything about yesterday. And particularly if I read a little and I think, you know, somebody's got an angle and a line, and all the facts are going to fit into the angle and the line, I try to figure out what that is, and then I just go on and go about my business.

Golf Tournament With Former Presidents

Mr. Lamb. I've got the Christian Science Monitor here from Friday, and they've got a picture of you on the front page with George Bush. And then they have an editorial, "Presidents and the Links," and this one line I wanted to ask you about. It says, "He at least appears as though he's enjoying the job" now. The "now" is mine, but that's the essence of what they're saying. Are you——

The President. Absolutely.

Mr. Lamb. ——enjoying it?

The President. Yes, I had a great time. And I had a great time out there playing golf with President Ford and President Bush and Bob Hope. Even though it was the worst golf game I've had in about 3 years, I still had a great time.

Q. What did you talk about?

The President. We talked about golf and what was going on. We talked a little about Bob Hope and what an amazing man he was—astonishing that he could be 92 and out there playing golf. Still has a great swing; he made some great shots that day. It was all light and friendly. I think we share some common concerns about some of the issues being debated today, but I just thought it was inappropriate to bring it up on the golf course.

Mr. Lamb. So you didn't have any——

The President. No——

Mr. Lamb. ——didn't seek any advice or——

The President. Well, I do talk to them from time to time and ask their advice about other things. But on this occasion, it just seemed like we ought to be out there having fun. And the crowd was great. There was a vast crowd there, and they were very nice to all of us, and they wanted to talk and chat and visit. So it just wasn't an appropriate thing to discuss business.

I thought they needed the day off, and I knew I did. So we all took it.

Media Coverage

Mr. Lamb. You talk about the, you know, being difficult when people are writing books about you and you're only in here 2 years. I brought with me a Time magazine cover story in January. One of your favorite people is on the cover, Rush Limbaugh. But inside there's an article by Bob Wright about hyperdemocracy. And the headline is, "Hyperdemocracy: Washington Isn't Dangerously Disconnected From The People; The Trouble May Be It's Too Plugged In." What about that, just that headline? Is this whole town too plugged into every moment of your life?

The President. Well, there's something to be said for that. I mean, the argument is, of course, that every decision can become the subject of instant analysis and communications and that Congress can be paralyzed by a blizzard of faxes, not F-A-C-T-S, F-A-X-E-S, and that you can just have a stampede based on the emotion of the moment. I think there's something to that.

But Andrew Jackson once said that the cure for any problem of democracy was more democracy. I mean, you know, look what we're doing here. C-Span is exactly the reverse. It's plugged in, but you just cover everything the way it is and people can make their judgments about Bill Clinton or Newt Gingrich or Bob Dole or whomever they wish to evaluate. And they can hear the ideas; they can assess the people. And I think even, you know, talk radio can be a very positive thing if it's a conversation rather than a weapon.

I remember—I just went today, before this interview started, as you know, to the memorial service for Senator Fulbright. And I remember 20 years ago—and he's been gone from the Senate for 20 years—coming on his last campaign, he was complaining about how the Members of the Congress then, by his standard, had to travel around too much, had to be almost too accessible, didn't have the time they needed to think and absorb and then discuss with their constituents in an unhurried way what the great issues of the day were. Well, that's 10 times more true today then it was then. So what I think we need to do is not recoil from the democracy, the hyperdemocracy, but try to work through the more irrational and destructive aspects of it to have a national conversation again.

You know, when I was running for President, we had all these town hall meetings, and I just loved them. And I—particularly when I attracted no notice—I never had to worry about whether I could have a meeting with 400 people and answer 40 questions, and then if one of them turned out to be a controversial question, that would then be on the evening news and 100 million people would see that, and only 400 would have heard the regular things. So I could go around and carry on this democracy. And we just have to find ways to do more of that and to show things whole and balanced and not twisted.

Presidential Debates

Mr. Lamb. As you know, we were a part of reenacting the Lincoln-Douglas debates this last summer.

The President. It was great.

Mr. Lamb. But it was 3 hours. Could you ever see yourself, either in a conversation or in a debate, spending 3 hours with an opponent or somebody that you could go through the issues with?

The President. Oh, sure. I don't know if people would watch it that long, but I think they would watch them for an hour. Look at the Presidential debates in the election. They were watched for a long time. And I think, you know, having discussions with people, including people of different perspectives, I think it would be a very good thing. And the American people would get a good feel for it.

Mr. Lamb. Where you'd have just two people instead of a moderator?

The President. Sure, I could conceive of that. You know the—I met Lincoln and Douglas; your Lincoln and Douglas came to Galesburg, Illinois, when I was there at Carl Sandburg Community College, and they warmed up the crowd for me. And I thought it was—you know, when they did that, they were both on an equal footing, they were both running for the Senate, and they both were speaking of issues that had both local and national impact. I think it did a great service to the country. I don't know that—as I said, I don't know how much of an audience you could get for a 3-hour debate now, but for an honest discussion I think you could get a good hour.

Mr. Lamb. Right over your shoulder is a copy of the Lincoln-Douglas debates on your shelf over there.

The President. Yes.

Mr. Lamb. Have you ever read them?

The President. I've never read the whole thing, but I've read extensive passages of them to try to understand the evolution of Lincoln's thinking, because he started with the proposition that slavery should not expand. And even in his first Inaugural Address, he made a commitment not to try to abolish slavery. And then he, for a long time, had all kinds of legal problems about how much he could do and how far he could go.

My staff actually gave me that. You know, I collect old books about America. And in '93 for my birthday, my staff gave me the first campaign biography of Abraham Lincoln written in 1860. And then last year, they gave me the Lincoln-Douglas debates.

The Presidency

Mr. Lamb. Based on what you've learned after being here 2 years and—assume you run again next time around, would you do something different?

There was a lot written, for instance, when you went on MTV and somebody asked you what kind of underwear you wore, and then for weeks afterwards it was written about all the time. Are there things like that you're to avoid, or did that bother you?

The President. Oh, I think you have to avoid them. I think one of the things I would do is, I wouldn't stop doing these town meetings; I think they're important. But I would be much more careful before I do them, not to do them at a time when I'm very busy, preoccupied with other things, and maybe a little overtired. Because then, sometimes you just simply answer questions when you shouldn't or you say things you shouldn't say.

I think with the Presidency, there is a fine line which has to be walked between being really responsive to people and listening to them and not giving up the dignity and strength of the office. So I would—you know, I have a much greater appreciation now than I did before I took this office about the symbolic impact of every word you say and everything you do.

It isn't like being a Governor, for example, where people really do have a chance to see you as a whole person and evaluate your whole record, and they don't necessarily look for great, symbolic significance in everything you say or every suit you wear or, you know, that sort of stuff. When you're President, you're just so far removed, on the one hand, from the people and, on the other hand, you bear the responsibility of carrying the idea of America. So it requires a different level of care and understanding, and it's something I've learned quite a lot about, I think, in the last 2 years.

Media Coverage

Mr. Lamb. Back to that piece in Time magazine. Bob Reich quotes a lot of Madison, and the issue is whether or not this is a representative Government or whether it's a direct democracy. And back to this theme of hyperdemocracy, is it anywhere close to being ungovernable with all this attention every day to——

The President. I wouldn't say that, but one of the frustrations is that what is going on—in a funny way, you don't have either one. Because if you had direct democracy, at least people would then want to take real time and have real debates and assume real responsibility. But what happened—what is happening often now, particularly to us in the first 2 years, where the Democrats had the Congress but not a controlling majority—that is, the Republicans could kill anything but a budget in the Senate—and I was in the Presidency, the culture of criticism took over. I mean, the people could say anything and not have to be responsible and not even be held accountable, and very often the mainstream media even would not pay any attention to what was being said on talk radio or by my political opponents because, after all, it didn't affect decisions. But the impact of this was that the people tended to understand the criticism more than the record of what was done. It's an almost stunning disconnect between what you're actually doing and what is being talked about and understood out there.

So that's why I say the cure for this is not to try to undo it. You can't undo it; you can't go back the other way and abolish technology and abolish opportunities to communicate. We have to look at where we are now as a stop along the way, and we have to keep working through it so that people don't just use their information as an instrument of anger and frustration and so they know when they're being manipulated by people who have an ax to grind and they have access to things they care about, to hear both sides, evaluate the facts, and then go forward.

So we just have to keep working through it, and we'll get there.

Administration Accomplishments

Mr. Lamb. This Parade magazine—I don't know if you've had a chance to see your picture——

The President. I saw the copy. It comes out Sunday, I think.

Mr. Lamb. It does, and by the time people hear this, they will have already read it, but there was just one line in there I wanted to ask you to explain. You said, "I think we did a good job of doing things," meaning your first 2 years, "but not a very good job of communicating." What do you mean by that, and how can you improve that?

The President. Well, I think in some ways we did almost—you might argue we did too many things. But when I say I think we did a good job of doing things, I think it's quite obvious. You know, we passed the biggest deficit reduction package in history. We passed the biggest expansion of trade in history. We had, therefore, a major positive impact on the growth of the economy and almost 6 million new jobs.

We had, in 1994, the best year for educational opportunity in 30 years, with expansion of Head Start and apprenticeships for young people who don't go to college and more affordable college loans for millions of people. We passed the family leave bill. We passed a major crime bill. We launched a rigorous effort to reinvent Government so that we were not only creating opportunities for Americans but we were actually downsizing the Government, reducing regulation, reducing the size and burden of Government, giving more power to the States—everything the Republicans said they were going to run on, things we did. And along the way, 15 million American families with incomes of under $25,000 a year or less got an average tax reduction of $1,000.

And people didn't know those things, and in many surveys when people were given those facts, they just refused to believe it. They said, "That's just not true. If that had happened, I would know it."

Mr. Lamb. How do you break through, then?

The President. I think—that doesn't mean I didn't make any mistakes, and I don't want that to be read—I mean, I think I have also made mistakes. But on balance our record was very, very strong, and it was only the third time since

World War II that a Congress had enacted over 80 percent of a President's initiatives in 2 years; it only happened three times since World War II. And I don't believe any American—that's counter to the experience of—Americans, when they hear it, they say, "Well, why don't I know that?" I think that when you get into the business of making decisions and taking responsibility, if you're not careful you become the captive of the language of incumbency and you look like a defender of Government, even though you're trying your best to change it and warring against the forces you don't agree with. And I think when you do a lot of things, then as soon as you lay down one fight, you take up another, and there's not enough time to really impress upon the American people what has been done.

I also think that one weakness I had was that I didn't easily keep the language of my campaign in the office of the Presidency, particularly in the first year. I think I did exactly what I said I'd do, and one Presidential scholar says I've kept a higher percentage of my commitments than the last five Presidents have averaged keeping theirs.

But I think that there is an enormous obligation on the President, again, in an atmosphere of hyperdemocracy and also, quite apart from politics, hyperinformation—you think about just the blizzard of stuff coming at the average American voter every day, and the average America voter is working harder, sleeping less, more stressed out, buried in information. To get a message through there requires enormous discipline and focus and concentration. And I simply believe that I've spent massive amounts of my time and effort trying to get things done, which was my first job. But I didn't organize and deploy the resource properly to make sure that we had communicated what we had done and how it fit into the vision that I ran for President to pursue.

Then of course, when we got into the health care debate and we had all that vast array of resources against us, telling the American people I was trying to have the Government take over the health care system and all that kind of stuff—it wasn't true, but that's what they were told—that cut against the image that I was trying to reduce the size of Government and expand opportunity while shrinking bureaucracy, which was the message I ran for President on.

Presidential Reelection

Mr. Lamb. This is an amateur count, so those professional counters out there may get me on this one, but I counted last night that there have been 11 Presidents, out of 41 men, who have been elected to 2 terms and served those 2 terms. The law of averages there aren't very good, one in four.

The President. They've gotten worse here lately, I mean, in the last——

Mr. Lamb. Yes.

The President. That tends to go up and down. If you look at it, in wartime we tend to stick with the people that we've got, and that's Lincoln, Wilson, Roosevelt. And we tend to stick with war heroes, Grant and Eisenhower. And then when times are good, we tend to reelect when people feel good, when people feel secure; that's Kennedy, Johnson. You know, if Kennedy had lived, I believe he would have been reelected, but it's the Kennedy-Johnson thing. Truman defied the odds, because he was coming at the end of the New Deal, he was in a period of historic change when people were disoriented and looking for a new way. He did it by staying at the job, doing the task at hand, and then fighting like crazy. But I think if you go back, Teddy Roosevelt did it by being relevant, vigorous and relevant, to the times in which he lived. He didn't serve two full terms, but you know, he did serve 7 years, virtually two terms.

So I think the lesson is, it has a lot to do with the times in which you live and a lot to do with how people feel about those times. But I can't worry about that. What I've tried to do in my public life is to help people make the most of their own lives and to deal with the challenges of the moment. And that's what I'm trying to do now.

Opportunities for Communication

Mr. Lamb. Based on your experience watching what happened over the 2 years, when does your message get through the best, at what kind of thing you do—either an Oval Office speech here, a speech out on the hustings, an appearance on a television show? What have you found?

The President. Well, the State of the Unions. There's no question they're far and away the best, because that's the only time the President has to talk about all the things that he's doing and put it into some context. So I don't think

there's any question that those audiences are listening and giving you a shot and listening to you.

I like the prime time press conferences. I have talked to the Nation on occasion, as you know, on national television when we did Haiti and when I spoke in December about how I was going to try to relate to the new Congress and what kind of tax relief I would propose for the middle class, that I wanted to tie it to education so we could raise people's incomes in the long run and not just have a tax cut. But on balance, I would say the State of the Union.

I love the town hall meetings, and they're the best forum, because you have an honest dialog with people. But in candor, the difficulty with the town hall meetings is, if there are 40 questions and 38 are positive and 2 are negative and you're slightly off, the real hazard of the town hall meetings is that one then becomes the evening news story and 100 million people hear one thing, and then maybe one million people hear the town hall meeting. I like doing more of those, though, because it's good for me. It reminds me it's too easy for Presidents to get isolated and see all issues in terms of their combatants. Most Americans are not combatants; they want you to be fighting for them. And so I like those.

State of the Union Address

Mr. Lamb. Did you know, by the way, that speech was going to be an hour and 21 minutes long?

The President. No, it should have been about my standard length. We thought it would be about 45 minutes, 50 minutes.

Mr. Lamb. How did it get so long?

The President. Well, for one thing, they were very nice to me. The Congress was much more receptive than I thought they'd be. I think there were 90 interruptions, and it added a little more time than I thought. And then I think I probably—at the end, I was so exuberant about all those people, I probably maybe elongated it a little bit, you know, talking about the folks at the end. I wanted them to come because they symbolize what I think is important here.

You know, in this time where we've got to create more opportunity and have more responsibility, the Government can only do so much. We can expand opportunity. We can shrink bureaucracy. We can empower people to make more of their own lives. We can enhance security through being tough on crime at home and taking care of foreign policy concerns. But we need a different sort of citizen action. We need more people who are engaged and who are involved, so that the hyperdemocracy, to use your phrase, become a positive force, not a negative one. So it's not just composed of people who are either political couch potatoes on the one hand or inflamed about one issue on the other but by people who are really trying to engage their fellow citizens, and that's why I did that at the end.

1996 Presidential Election

Mr. Lamb. Go back to when you're talking about all of the different Presidents and the different scenarios. What kind of a scenario do you think yours will be when you run again, and will people be saying, oh, he's doing the Truman strategy or he's doing the Eisenhower strategy or——

The President. I don't know, I think it would be a mistake to draw too tight an historical analogy. This time bears some relationship to Truman's time, but it is very different in many ways, too, in terms of what the issues are and the facts are and the political forces. But the larger historical fact is there, that it's still a period of great change. It depends on what happens, partly, this year. You know, I'm making a good-faith effort to work with this new Congress. I think that's what the American people want me to do. And a lot of what they want to do are things I want to do. I want to downsize the Government. I want to reduce the burden of unnecessary regulation. I want to have more discipline in the budget. So I don't have any problem with that.

But I don't want to do things that will undermine the economic recovery, undermine the ability of the President to protect the national security interests of the country. And most importantly, I don't want to do things that will undermine our responsibilities to try to give middle class people economic opportunity and educational opportunity and give poor people the opportunity to work themselves into the middle class.

So I think what happens this year will dictate, to some extent, what happens in the election. You know, I'm going to keep doing what I said I'd do when I ran in '92. I'm going to try to keep moving the country forward. I'm going to

try to be less partisan. The biggest disappointment, I guess, in the first 2 years I had was how bitterly, bitterly partisan it turned out to be.

The image I think the people had was that the Democrats weren't necessarily sticking with me in the Congress. But the facts are that they voted with me more loyally than they voted for Kennedy or Johnson or Carter, something that would again, I think, based on the coverage, I think would surprise people.

The Republicans opposed me more than any opposition party had opposed any President since World War II. And they were rewarded for it because of the times in which we live and maybe because I didn't make the best case I could have to the American people or maybe because of the things that happened in the congressional races.

But now, that's water under the bridge, and we've got a country to see after. We've got a people to attend to, to work with, to challenge. So I hope it'll be less partisan.

Presidential Libraries

Mr. Lamb. About out of time. Let me just ask you a couple of off-the-subject questions. The last time we were here, I asked you about Presidential libraries and whether you had thought much about that. And you said no, but since then I understand that you've had somebody out and about checking out the other libraries. Have you got any plans yet?

The President. Well, I expect to have one, but that's all I can say about it. I mean, I like the idea of them; I think they've served the country well. I've been at President Nixon's for his service. I've been at President Carter's. I've been at President Johnson's. And I strongly support the concept.

I did talk briefly to President Ford about that at the golf course; it was, I guess, the only substantive thing. He just mentioned to me that he sure thought the Archivist ought to be somebody that supported the Presidential library system. So I like them. But I'm worried about doing this job, and then I'll worry about what's in the library when I finish the job. But I believe in the system, and it's served the country well.

Of course, I've been to the Truman Library and the Roosevelt Library, so I guess I've been to most of them.

Mr. Lamb. We're out of time, and I thank you.

The President. Thank you. I enjoyed it.

NOTE: The interview was recorded at 12:45 p.m. on February 17 in the Oval Office at the White House for release on February 19.

Remarks Commemorating the 50th Anniversary of Iwo Jima in Arlington, Virginia
February 19, 1995

Thank you, ladies and gentlemen. I think we should give Colonel Barber a round of applause for his remarks and for his service. [*Applause*]

General and Mrs. Mundy, Secretary and Mrs. Brown, honored veterans and families, distinguished guests, my fellow Americans. Today on this wonderfully quiet morning, within sight of so many of our Nation's great monuments and on the edge of our national cemetery, where some of those whom we honor today are buried, we recall the fury of war and a landmark in our history that is one of both loss and triumph. We gather in the company of heroes, those who served at Iwo Jima. Many of them do rest nearby, but we thank God that many are still here today.

Fifty years ago, with their lives before them, they left everything, their families, their loved ones, the serenity and security of their homes, to fight for a just cause. They departed on a journey to places they had never heard of to confront dangers they could not have imagined. But they never wavered or faltered. And when they were done, our liberties and our homes were safe again.

Last year at Normandy, I was privileged to say something I would like to say again because I think that the rest of us can never say it enough: To all of you who served at Iwo Jima, we are the children of your sacrifice, and we are grateful. On behalf of a grateful nation, I would like to ask all of those here who served at Iwo Jima to stand and be recognized. [*Applause*]

Today the dimensions of their struggle still stagger us. As we have heard, when they attacked Iwo Jima, the enemy was so deeply dug in as to be invisible and all but impregnable. The carnage on the beaches was almost unimaginable. The sands were black and deep and so soft that one man said it was like walking on coffee grounds. Trying to claim just a few hundred yards, troops were raked by gunfire and pinned down. And as Secretary Brown said, on the first day 2,400 were killed. On hearing of the casualties, President Roosevelt was reported to have gasped with horror for the first time since Pearl Harbor.

Securing Iwo Jima was supposed to take less than 2 weeks, but it took 5. Progress was a yard's advance. But never were the words "issue in doubt," the call for withdrawal, uttered. The 75,000 who went ashore pulled together. Privates rose and took command. In just one case of many, a platoon suffered so many casualties that command passed to 12 different marines. Navy corpsmen saved one life after another, pulling the wounded from battle. The Seabees did their vital construction work under constant fire.

But 13 days into the battle, the first crippled B–29 touched down on an island landing strip. And eventually more than 2,200 of those B–29's made emergency landings on their return from bombing runs. Nearly 25,000 airmen owed their lives to the troops who secured Iwo Jima.

Admiral Nimitz put it perfectly: "Among the Americans who served on Iwo Jima, uncommon valor was a common virtue." Our country saw the true definition of courage. Everyone who waded ashore on Iwo Jima shared that quality.

Captain Robert Dunlap scrambled to an exposed position 200 yards ahead of our lines at the base of Mount Suribachi. Amid constant enemy fire, he directed the attack on pillboxes and emplacements, not for 1 or 2 hours but for 48 hours. His extraordinary action helped to make it possible for the marines to sweep through the island's western beaches. "All in a day's work," he said.

Douglas Jacobson, a private first class from Rochester, New York, showed what real strength of body and spirit can do. When a fellow marine was shot, he grabbed the man's bazooka and sprinted through the area called "Meat Grinder," destroying 16 positions before he ran out of ammunition. The bazooka, by the way, that he had was a two-man weapon, but he shouldered it alone.

Captain Joseph McCarthy showed us the meaning of determination. With his company under merciless fire from several enemy strongholds, he charged through an open field to one of them and knocked it out with a carbine and grenades. He then repeated the feat three more times, using his bare hands when necessary. He cleared an essential ridge on the way to one of the island's airstrips.

And Jack Lucas, whom I had the privilege of introducing at the State of the Union Address, was 17 years old when he threw himself on two grenades to save the lives of his comrades. Not long ago he said, "It didn't matter who you were or where you were from, you relied on one another. And you did it for your country."

These are just a few of the countless feats of heroism from that distant place in time, deeds all of you who served performed for your Nation. And these stories are just 4 of the stories of the 27 Medal of Honor winners on Iwo Jima, the largest from any single battle in American history. We are honored to have these four winners today with us. And I ask them to be recognized at this time. [*Applause*] Thank you. Thank you.

This is their legacy. This is the legacy of all of you who served. To those in the units that took Suribachi, to the nurses and doctors who worked under constant fire on the beachfronts, to the sailors on the hundreds of support ships, to the African-American Montford Point marines who fought off the last desperate attack by the enemy, to the families who so courageously endured at home, this is the legacy of bravery and dedication you have given us.

To be worthy of that sacrifice, we must determine in this time to remain the strongest nation in the world so that our freedom is never again threatened. And we must work to create a nation worthy of the generation that saved it for our freedom. We must do it together.

Ultimately no lesson from Iwo Jima looms larger than the one behind me. This image of the flag-raising over Mount Suribachi, known around the world from Joe Rosenthal's picture and captured before us in Felix de Weldon's great bronze memorial, tells it all. Instantly it became the symbol of our effort in World War II. It was published and republished until every American could see it with his eyes closed. Six men straining together, giving all they have, faces turned to the task of planting our flag: Block, Sousley, Hayes, Bradley—the Navy corpsman—Gagnon and Strank. A real picture of America, a Texan and Kentuckian, a Wisconsin farm boy, a Native American, a New Englander of French Canadian stock, a kid from the coal country of Pennsylvania.

Hard men wept when they saw the flag fly over Suribachi. President Roosevelt wanted the flag-raisers brought stateside as heroes to boost morale on the homefront. But three of them never got the chance. They were on Iwo Jima, their faces still turned to the task, when they were killed days later. They gave us still forever this picture of common purpose of striving together, of the unity that our Nation forged out of the many who make it up.

For all Americans today, for those who still defend our liberty in uniform and those who fight for decency and civility in our towns and communities, the men and women of Iwo Jima will forever stir our hearts, spur our conscience, and summon us to action. With our eyes closed, we can all still see the flag rising atop the hill.

May God bless them all, and may God bless America.

NOTE: The President spoke at 11:25 a.m. at the Iwo Jima Memorial. In his remarks, he referred to Col. William Barber, USMC (Ret.), Iwo Jima veteran; Gen. C.E. Mundy, Jr., USMC, Commandant, Marine Corps; and Secretary of Veterans Affairs Jesse Brown.

Remarks on Regulatory Reform
February 21, 1995

Thank you very much. I want to begin by thanking the Vice President for his leadership on this issue. When we formed our partnership back in 1992, and we talked about all the things we wanted to do, and we had a series of long, fascinating conversations in which he talked to me about science and technology and the environment, and I talked to him about education and economic development and reinventing Government. And I told him that when I was a Governor, every couple of years we'd eliminate an agency just to see if anybody noticed. [*Laughter*] And normally, they didn't. And they never did complain when they did notice.

And I asked him if he would—then after we actually won and came here, I asked him if he would get involved with this and really try to make it work for the American people, because I was convinced that there was so much justifiable anxiety out there among our people about the way Government operates, that unless we could change that we'd never be able to maintain the faith of the taxpayers and the integrity of the Federal Government.

I also asked him to do it because he was the only person I could trust to read all 150,000 pages in the Code of Federal Regulations. [*Laughter*] At this very moment, Tipper is being treated for insomnia at the Georgetown Hospital—[*laughter*]—but he's just about through.

I also want to thank all of you who are here who represent really the future of the Federal Government and the future of its ability to maintain the confidence of the American people that we're protecting and promoting their interest and doing it in a way that reinforces instead of defies common sense.

I believe very strongly in the cause of regulatory reform. And as the Vice President said, we've been working at it for about 2 years now. I also believe that we have to hold fast to certain standards. I believe we can bring back common sense and reduce hassle without stripping away safeguards for our children, our workers, our families.

There are proposals pending in the Congress today which go beyond reform to roll back, arguably even to wrecking, and I oppose them. But I believe we have the burden of reform.

And that means we have to change in fundamental ways the culture of regulation that has permeated this Government throughout administrations, from administration to administration, from Republicans to Democrats occupying the White House.

The Federal Government to many people is not the President of the United States. It's the person who shows up on the doorstep to check out the bank records or the safety in the factory or the integrity of the workplace or how the nursing home is being run. I believe that we have a serious obligation in this administration to work with the Congress to reduce the burden of regulation and to increase the protection to the public. And we have an obligation on our own to do what we can to change the destructive elements of the culture of regulation that has built up over time and energize the legitimate and decent things that we should be doing here in Washington and, more importantly, that should be being done all across the country.

I thank those who have come here today as examples of the progress which has been made. We do want to get rid of yesterday's Government so we can meet the demands of this new time. We do want results, not rules. We want leaner Government, not meaner Government. At a time when I have said our obligation should be to create more opportunity and also to provide more responsibility, our responsibility here is to expand opportunity, empower people to make the most of their own lives, enhance security, and to do it all while we are shrinking the Federal bureaucracy, to give the people a Government as effective as our finest private companies, to give our taxpayers their money's worth.

Now, everybody has talked about this for years now, but in fact, we have taken steps in the right direction. Already, we have reduced Federal spending by over a quarter of a trillion dollars, reduced the size of the Federal payroll by over 100,000. We are on our way to a reduction in excess of 250,000 in the Federal work force, which will give us by the end of this decade the smallest Federal Government since the Kennedy administration.

235

Vice President Gore's leadership in the reinventing Government initiatives have already saved taxpayers $63 billion. Some of the more visible changes have been well-noted: the reduction of offices in the Agriculture Department by more than 1,200, throwing away the Government's 10,000-page personnel manual. I haven't heard a single soul complain about it. Nobody has said, "You know, I never thought about the personnel manual, but I just can't bear to live without it now." [*Laughter*] I haven't heard it a single place.

We've worked hard to solve problems that had been long ignored: reforming the pension benefit guarantee system to secure the pensions of 8½ million working Americans whose pensions and retirement were at risk, reforming Government procurement so that the days of the $500 hammer and the $10 glass ashtray are over, turning FEMA from a disaster into a disaster relief agency, breaking gridlock on bills that hung around in Congress for years, 6 or 7 years, like the family leave law, the motor voter law, the Brady bill, and the crime bill.

But maybe the most stubborn problem we face is this problem of regulation. How do we do what we're supposed to do here? How do we help to reinforce the social contract and do our part to work with the private sector to protect the legitimate interests of the American people without literally taking leave of our senses and doing things that drive people up the wall but don't make them safer?

We all want the benefits of regulation. We all want clean air and clean water and safe food and toys that our children can play with. But let's face it, we all know the regulatory system needs repair. Too often the rule writers here in Washington have such detailed lists of do's and don'ts that the do's and don'ts undermine the very objectives they seek to achieve, when clear goals and operation for cooperation would work better. Too often, especially, small businesses face a profusion of overlapping and sometimes conflicting rules. We've tried to set up an effective procedure here for resolving those conflicts, but it drives people crazy. I had somebody just yesterday mention being subject to two directly conflicting rules from two Federal agencies.

We have to move beyond the point where Washington is, to use the Vice President's phrase, the sort of national nanny that can always tell businesses, consumers, and workers not only what to do but exactly how to do it, when, and with a 100-page guideline. And as has already been said, we have begun to take the first steps in doing this.

You've heard about what the Comptroller of the Currency has done. I can tell you one thing: When I was out in New Hampshire in 1992, I heard more grief about the regulation of the private sector by the Comptroller of the Currency than any other single thing. And now every time I go to New England, they say, "We're making money. We're making loans, and we can function, because we finally got somebody down there in Washington who understands how to have responsible and safe banking regulations and still promote economic growth." I hear it every time I go up there, and I thank you, sir, for what you've done on that.

We've got industry and environmentalists alike supporting Carol Browner and the EPA's Common Sense Initiative and our proposed overhauls of the Superfund and the safe drinking water laws which I pray will pass in this session of Congress, and I believe they will, would increase both flexibility and improve results for consumers. We've slashed the small business loan form from an inch thick to a single page.

We haven't had to wait for legislation to streamline all regulations. We've asked regulators and instructed them to use market mechanisms whenever possible and to open up the regulatory process to more public scrutiny and involvement.

HHS has cut its block grant application form in half for maternal and child health programs. EPA is exploring using enforceable contracts instead of regulation to eliminate potential risk. The FAA is reviewing all of its rules to identify those that are out of sync with state-of-the-art technology practices. And there's nothing more maddening to a businessman than being told one thing on Monday by one governmental agency and another thing on Tuesday by another.

Our Labor Department did something unusual about that as it relates to regulations that affect both labor and the environment. They talked to EPA before issuing their asbestos rules, a stunning departure from past practices. So that at least there, there are now no contradictory instructions.

We're also trying to bring common sense in other ways, targeting high-risk areas, focusing, for example, on lead in day care centers rather than aircraft hangars. We're making school lunches more nutritious but reducing the forms the local schools have to fill out to qualify for the program.

Today we're attempting to work with Members of both parties in Congress to further reform regulation. Soon the Congress will pass legislation so that Washington won't order States to solve problems without giving them the resources to do it. We're working together to pass legislation that ensures that regulation is especially sensitive to the needs of small businesses and to reduce paperwork. But we must clearly do more. We must ask ourselves some questions that are very, very important. And I want to emphasize those here.

Would you take the card down? This is why I asked all of you here, not just to be between me and the press corps. [*Laughter*]

Today, this is what we are now going to do. I am instructing all regulators to go over every single regulation and cut those regulations which are obsolete, to work to reward results, not redtape, to get out of Washington and go out into the country to create grassroots partnerships with the people who are subject to these regulations and to negotiate rather than dictate wherever possible.

We should ask ourselves—let me go through each one—on the regulations, we should ask ourselves: Do we really need this regulation? Could private businesses do this just as well with some accountability to us? Could State or local government do the job better, making Federal regulation not necessary? I want to really work through these things, and I want you, all of you, to review all these regulations and make a report to me by June 1st, along with any legislative recommendations you need to implement the changes that would be necessary to reduce the regulatory burden on the American people.

Second, I want every one of you to change the way we measure the performance of your agencies and the front-line regulators. I love the comment the Vice President had about people in Customs being evaluated about how many boxes they detain. I believe safety inspections should be judged, for example, by how many companies on their watch comply, not by how many citations our regulators write. We ought to be interested in results, not process.

Third, I want you to convene immediately groups consisting of the frontline regulators and the people affected by their regulations, not lawyers talking to lawyers in Washington or even the rest of us talking to each other in Washington but a conversation that actually takes place around the country, at our cleanup sites, our factories, and our ports. Where this has been done, as we saw here, we have seen stunning results. Most people in business in this country know that there is a reason for these regulations, for these areas of regulations. And most people would be more than happy to work to find a way that would reduce hassle and still achieve the public interest we seek to achieve.

Fourth, I want to move from a process where lawyers write volumes to one where people create partnerships based on common objectives and common sense. I want each regulatory agency head to submit to the White House a list of pending procedures that can be converted into consensual negotiations.

Now, I want to say this again. This is very important. By June 1st, I want to know which obsolete regulations we can cut and which ones you can't cut without help from Congress. We want a system that will reward results, not redtape. We want to get out of Washington and talk to people who are doing the regulating and who are being regulated on the frontline. That is the only way we will ever change the culture that bothers people. We could stay here from now to kingdom come in this room, and we would never get that done.

And finally, we need to look for the areas in which we can honestly negotiate to produce the desired results rather than dictate.

Finally, the Vice President has been conducting a serious review of regulation in the areas of greatest concern. In the coming months, he will present to me a series of recommendations for regulatory reform on the environment, on health, on food, on financial institutions, on worker safety. And when appropriate and necessary, I will present them to the Congress.

This is what we are going to do, and it is high time. But let me also emphasize what we are not going to do. We have to recognize that, done right, regulation gives our children safer toys and food, protects our workers from injury, protects families from pollution, and that when we fail, it can have disastrous consequences.

The American economy is the envy of the world, in part because of the public health protections put in place over the last 30 years. Toxic emissions by factories have dropped by more than 50 percent, and lead levels in children's blood have dropped by 70 percent in three decades. Lake Erie, once declared dead, is now teeming with fish. One hundred and twelve thousand people survived car crashes because of auto safety rules. Workplace deaths are down by 50 percent since OSHA was created. Our food is safer, and we know its true nutritional content because the Government stood up for public interests.

These protections are still needed. There's not too little consumer fraud. Toys are not too safe. The environment is still not able to protect itself. Some would use the need for reform as a pretext to gut vital consumer, worker, environmental protections, even things that protect business itself. They don't want reform; they really want rigor mortis.

Some in Congress are pushing a collection of proposals that, taken together, would bring Federal protection of public health and safety to a halt. Later this week, the House will vote on an across-the-board freeze on all Federal regulations. It sounds good, but this stops in its tracks Federal action that protects the environment, protects consumers, and protects workers. For example, it would stop the Government from allocating rights to commercial fishermen. A person who's worked with those folks in Louisiana is here today. It would stop the Government from authorizing burials at Arlington Cemetery. It would stop good regulations, bad regulations, in-between regulations, all regulations. No judgment—sounds good but no judgment. It would even cancel the duck hunting season. That gives me some hope that it will not prevail. [*Laughter*] It would stop new protection from deadly bacteria in our drinking water, stop safer meat and poultry, stop safer cars, stop final implementation of the law that lets parents take a leave to care for a sick child. It would undermine what we're trying to do to promote safety in commuter airlines. If a moratorium takes effect, all these benefits will be on hold for the foreseeable future. Therefore, to me, a moratorium is not acceptable.

I agree with the Republicans in Congress on many things. We do need to change this system. We have been working for 2 years to change it, and believe you me, I know we've got a long way to go. But there is a right way to do it and a wrong way to do it. We can agree on many things, but I am convinced that a moratorium would hurt the broad interests of the American people and would benefit only certain narrow interests who, in the moment, think they would be undermined by having this or that particular regulation pass.

The best thing to do is to change the culture of regulation, to do the four things that I have outlined, not to put these things on hold but to put these things in high gear. That is the right way to do this. I still believe that, working together with Congress, we can achieve real and balanced regulatory reform. But we shouldn't go too far. For example, we want all agencies to carefully compare the cost and benefits of regulations so that we don't impose any unnecessary burdens on business.

But the Contract With America, literally read, could pile so many new requirements on Government that nothing would ever get done. It would add to the very things that people have been complaining about for years—too many lawsuits, everything winds up in court. The contract, literally read, would override every single health and safety law in the books; distort the process by giving industry-paid scientists undue influence over rules that govern their employers; in the name of private property, could literally bust the budget by requiring the Government to pay polluters every time an environmental law puts limits on profits.

These are extreme proposals. They go too far. They would cost lives and dollars. A small army of special interest lobbyists knows they can never get away with an outright repeal of consumer or environmental protection. But why bother if you can paralyze the Government by process? Surely, after years and years and years of people screaming about excessive governmental process, we won't just go to an even bigger round of process to tilt the process itself in another direction. We cannot strip away safeguards for families in this country.

Here in our audience today are real people on whose behalf we act or we might have acted. There's a father in this audience whose son died from *E. coli* bacteria in food that might have been discovered if our proposed rule had been in effect when his son ate the contaminated food. There are people here whose lives were saved by air bags. Let's not forget these people as we cut redtape and bureaucracy. There's a woman here who is a breast cancer survivor who lost a child to cancer, who lives in an area unusually high in the density of people who suffer from cancer. Let's not forget the kind of work that still needs to be done.

At every stage in the history of this country, our Government has always had to change to meet the needs of changing times. And we need to change now. We need a Government that's smaller and more entrepreneurial, that provides a lot less hassle, that realizes that there are an awful lot of people out there in the private sector who have enlightened views and they want to do the right thing and they need to be helped instead of hindered in that.

I would never defend the culture of this community when it is wrong. But let us also not forget that as we strive for a Government that is costing less and is more flexible, that is producing better results and not more rules, that we have a job to do for the American people and that people are entitled to protection. So I echo again what the Vice President said earlier: Reform, yes. Bring it on. Roll back, no. There is too much good to do to turn this noble enterprise into something that we would live to regret. Let us instead work to do what must be done.

Thank you very much.

NOTE: The President spoke at 12:40 p.m. in Room 450 of the Old Executive Office Building.

Remarks Announcing the Appointment of Laura D'Andrea Tyson as National Economic Adviser and an Exchange With Reporters
February 21, 1995

The President. Good afternoon. I am pleased to announce today my decision to appoint Dr. Laura Tyson, the Chair of the Council of Economic Advisers, to be the new Special Assistant to the President for Economic Policy and the chair of the National Economic Council.

When I became President I believed that to have a sound economic policy, our economic policymakers had to work together as a solid and carefully coordinated team. To that end, I established the National Economic Council to play a coordinating role in economic policymaking, similar to the role the National Security Council has played in defense and foreign policy for 47 years. I believe that was clearly the right decision. It added discipline, direction, and strength, as well as sweep to the administration's economic policymaking.

For 2 years, under the leadership of Robert Rubin, now the Secretary of the Treasury, we did work together as a team. We had talent. We had discipline. We had common vision, and we have produced results. We had an economic strategy that focused on the expansion of trade, technology, and educational opportunities and the reduction in the Government deficit and the size and sweep of adverse governmental policies. We had $600 billion plus in deficit reduction to which we have proposed another over $80 billion in deficit reduction. We've done more to open the world's markets to our products and services than any administration in a generation. We have reduced taxes on 15 million American working families and made tax cuts available to 9 out of 10 small businesses that invest more in their business. The economy in the last 2 years has created about 6 million new jobs, with the lowest combination of inflation and unemployment in 25 years.

Reversing the economic policies of the previous 12 years did not come easily. It required tough choices. Many of them were unpopular in the short run, but the results have clearly been felt. We were able to make those choices and follow through on them in the face of relentless predictions that they would produce recessions and produce disasters, because of the hard work of the outstanding members of our economic team.

One of the most important members of that team was Laura Tyson. She came to our administration from the University of California where she's a professor of economics and business administration. I found when I met her in the Presidential campaign that she had an exceptionally analytic mind and an understanding of the underlying global economic and political realities affecting our ability to compete and our economic future. She has been a very credible voice for us on the economy, and I have appreciated especially her unfailingly frank, direct, and principled advice. She has been a consensus builder and an honest broker without in any way compromising her own views in the inner councils and when we discussed economic policy.

We'll miss her at the Council of Economic Advisers, and I will appoint a new Chair in the near future. But I am confident she will be a worthy successor to Bob Rubin at the National Economic Council. I'm glad she's taking on this new job. I think it will help us to keep taking on the job of keeping the American dream alive.

I also want to say again how important this is. I think when the history of this administration is written, one of the most significant organizational changes we will have made, and one that I predict all future administrations will follow, is the creation of a National Economic Council and the development of a coordinated, disciplined national economic policy for global economy.

I'd like to now introduce Dr. Tyson and let her make a few remarks. Thank you for doing this. Congratulations; no condolences. It's going to be a good change.

Thank you.

[At this point, Dr. Tyson thanked the President and made brief remarks.]

Contract With America

Q. Mr. President, tomorrow's day 50 of the Republican Contract With America. Do you find yourself in the position now, as you criticized the Republicans the first 2 years of simply saying no to many of your initiatives, that you are saying no, consistently threatening vetoes to many of the Republican initiatives? Is there a way around this so that there can be some bipartisanship in the next 2 years?

The President. There can be a lot of bipartisanship. First of all, I have not said consistently no. I strongly supported applying to Congress the laws that apply to the private sector. I have supported limiting the ability of Congress to impose unfunded mandates on State and local government. I support the line-item veto. I support significant reform in the Federal regulatory process.

But where I do not agree with the extreme elements of the contract—and I might add, where also a number of Republican Senators do not agree with it and where, apparently,

some Republican House Members no longer agree with it—Star Wars, eroding the 100,000 police commitment, cutting Medicare to pay for tax cuts. On those things, I think I'm obligated to say where I don't agree. And that's what I'm doing. I'm trying to be as clear as I can be, hoping we can work together, hoping we can get legislation out of this.

I have not done what was done frequently in the previous 2 years, which is to say, "We're walking away from this no matter what it is, even if we have to change our position on it," which is what they did on the crime bill.

So I'm looking forward to this. We're still going to make some good things happen, and we can still do it. But I owe it to the American people to protect them. They did not, in my judgment, ratify every extreme element of the contract as defined in every piece of legislation there. I am not trying to thwart them; I am trying to give them an opportunity to know exactly where I stand and to work with them.

This is Dr. Tyson's day, and I want to let her answer questions.

Thank you.

Mexican Loan Agreement

Q. To both of you, sir, Mexican markets took quite a tumble today on the news of the agreement reached here, which I think was probably considered surprising in some quarters. I wonder if both you and Dr. Tyson could comment on why you think that is and any worries you may have that the cure here may turn out to be worse than the disease.

Dr. Tyson. Well, I don't want to comment on specifics of the agreement, simply because there was a comment made by Secretary Rubin at luncheon because, frankly, I just got off an airplane and haven't been fully briefed on the agreement. What I will say is that we believe that the path that we've gone down is the correct path, and that we've worked hard to reach an agreement which we believe to be a sensible agreement which will do the trick.

Q. Mr. President?

The President. I don't know; I don't have an opinion. I think it may have something to do with the other decisionmakers than the United States and Mexico. We'll just have to see, but I would not overreact to it. We have done the right thing. Mexico is taking some very courageous steps, difficult steps for them. They have followed the proper economic path in general, and the United States has great interest there. There are many jobs tied up in it, our whole strategy of promoting democracy and free markets throughout Latin America. I think we did the right thing, and I believe it very strongly, and I think that time will bear us out. And if it doesn't, then we have very good collateral on this deal, so we have done the right thing by the American taxpayers and the American people as well.

Thank you.

NOTE: The President spoke at 4:39 p.m. in the Briefing Room at the White House.

Remarks Following a Meeting With Congressional Leaders and an Exchange With Reporters
February 22, 1995

The President. Good morning. Everyone here? I had an excellent meeting this morning with the House Democratic Caucus. We discussed a wide range of issues. I complimented them; I compliment them again on the work they are doing to remain unified in pursuit of the best interests of the people of this country.

I reaffirmed my willingness and desire to work with the Republican leadership in the Congress to advance the cause of the American people but that there are things which we simply disagree on and where we feel very strongly. I think it is ironic that here, on the 50th day of this 100-day effort that they are making to put in their contract, the single most important issue in the world to them seems to be to cut the School Lunch Program and end it.

An old conservative adage used to be, "If it ain't broke, don't fix it." Here's a program that isn't broke, that's done a world of good for millions and millions of children of all races and backgrounds all across our country, and I think it would be a terrible mistake to put an end to it, to gut it, to undermine it. And I hope that my party will stand against this. I do not agree with it. I do not think it is right, and it seems to me that this is one of the things that we hired on to do, to stick up for the interest of children, for the vast middle class, and for our future. And I intend to do that, and I believe the Congress will, as well— at least those in our party will, as well.

Mr. Leader.

[At this point, Representative Richard A. Gephardt made brief remarks.]

Tax Cuts

Q. Mr. President, as Republicans look at balancing the books now, support for a big tax cut is supposedly softening and may very well wither and die on the Senate vine. Do you still feel that it's responsible to have some kind of tax cut?

The President. Yes, I didn't—of course, I always thought their tax cuts were too big and couldn't be paid for. The one that I offered was, I think, roughly less than a third in aggregate costs of what theirs was. And of course, in the second 5 years, if theirs had passed, it would have been much greater. So I'm glad to see a sobering of attitudes about that.

But I do believe, again, that our main mission here has to be to try to advance the cause of the American people. And we have to continue to bring the deficit down, but we also have to recognize that there is out there in this country what Secretary Reich has called an anxious class, people who are working harder and for whom more jobs in the American economy have not meant more security.

If we allow a deduction of the cost of education after high school, especially if we couple that with a minimum wage increase, and continuing to increase the college loans and the investments in education, we will increase those folks' incomes in the short run in ways that will increase their incomes in the long run, increase their ability to pay taxes, and strengthen the American economy.

So I believe a carefully targeted tax relief to the middle class, tied to education in ways that will grow the economy and grow jobs, is an appropriate thing to do. I'm glad to hear the talk of abandoning tax cuts of the size that were being proposed. I tried to tell the American people in the campaign there was no way in the wide world that could be done, and I welcome that talk.

Democratic Congressional Support

Q. Does this 50-day point mark some sort of turning point for you in terms of shoring up, taking a firm stand on things, trying to present the Democratic side as a unified side against the Republicans?

The President. Well, I think they've been doing a good job on that. There have been two or three issues here lately where the Democrats have really rallied: first, in the national security area, where they basically were responsible for not going back to Star Wars, which would have been a big mistake and, secondly, where they voted against abandoning our commitment to the American people to put 100,000 more police officers on the street. And I believe they will be even more unified against an attempt to destroy the School Lunch Program. So I feel good about that.

But I also think we have been willing to work with the Republicans. You know, the bill to apply to Congress the laws that applies to the private sector passed overwhelmingly in the House of Representatives with the same level of Democratic support as Republicans support. The bill to reduce the burden of unfunded mandates on State and local governments received large Democratic support.

So we want to work with the Republicans. But we have no intention of abandoning the American people to unproven theories and extreme positions. We're the people party, and we're going to stick up for the people. And when we can do that in good conscience by working with them to reduce the burden of Government, we want to do that, and we should do that. But I'm excited by the opportunity that this new period offers us to stand up for what we believe in.

Q. Where will you draw the line?

Deputy Press Secretary Ginny Terzano. Thank you.

The President. What did you say? Thank you? You want me to quit? [*Laughter*]

Thank you.

NOTE: The President spoke at 10:50 a.m. at the Capitol.

Statement on the Peace Process in Northern Ireland
February 22, 1995

I welcome today's announcement by Irish Prime Minister Bruton and British Prime Minister Major of the launching of a joint framework document outlining their shared proposals for inclusive talks on the future of Northern Ireland. The publication of this document marks another significant step forward in the peace process. I congratulate both Prime Ministers, former Irish Prime Minister Albert Reynolds, Irish Foreign Minister Dick Spring, and British Secretary of State for Northern Ireland Sir Patrick Mayhew, all of whom have worked hard and risked much in the search for a new path forward to reconciliation and lasting peace.

The framework document lays the foundation for all-party talks among the British and Irish Governments and the political parties in Northern Ireland. The talks are intended to be all-inclusive, with all issues on the table. As the Irish and British Governments have emphasized, the document is designed to assist discussion and negotiation on Northern Ireland and will not be imposed on any party. The clear wish of the people of Northern Ireland is for a lasting peace. We call upon all the parties to examine the document carefully and move forward on the basis of it.

The guns and bombs have been silent in Northern Ireland for almost 6 months. The benefits of peace are obvious to all, and I urge the parties to seize this opportunity. I will continue to strongly support the peace process in Northern Ireland and to work with the Governments of Ireland and the United Kingdom to build on today's courageous step forward toward lasting peace. In addition, I look forward to our Trade and Investment Conference to be held this May as a way to underscore the tangible benefits to peace.

Statement on Compensation for Persian Gulf Conflict Veterans
February 22, 1995

Today, the country takes a long-overdue step to recognize the sacrifices of these Persian Gulf veterans. We are taking an unprecedented approach to assisting these veterans by providing compensation for conditions that have defied conventional diagnoses. We encourage any Persian Gulf veteran who is sick to file a claim, and we will automatically reopen previously denied claims as a result of this new law.

I felt that we could not wait on science. For some Persian Gulf veterans like Michael Sills, medical science does not have answers today, but we must not and will not give up.

Michael Sills and veterans like him who served their country honorably have earned our gratitude. And when they are sick, we must do what is right.

NOTE: This statement was included in a White House statement announcing that the President met with Michael I. Sills, one of the first recipients of a compensation check awarded to Persian Gulf conflict veterans with chronic disabilities resulting from undiagnosed illnesses.

Message to the Congress Reporting Budget Rescissions and Deferrals
February 22, 1995

To the Congress of the United States:
In accordance with the Congressional Budget and Impoundment Control Act of 1974, I herewith report one revised deferral, totaling $7.3 million, and two revised rescission proposals, totaling $106.7 million.

The revised deferral affects the Department of Health and Human Services. The revised rescission proposals affect the Department of Education and the Environmental Protection Agency.

WILLIAM J. CLINTON

The White House,
February 22, 1995.

NOTE: The report detailing the proposed rescissions and deferral was published in the *Federal Register* on March 7.

Remarks to the Business Council
February 22, 1995

Thank you very much. Ed, you did such a good job, I was thinking there wasn't much more for me to say. I'll just—what if I say I agree and sit down and get a free meal? [*Laughter*] I'm delighted to be back here with this group, and I'm glad to see many old friends.

I've tried to make a couple of the tables, and afterward, I want to go around to say hello to everybody I missed.

I, more than anything else, want to say, too, I appreciate the receptivity that many, many members of this group have had to working with me and with the members of our administration. I have many members of the Cabinet here and sub-Cabinet members, and we've worked on a whole range of issues.

As a gesture of good will, I left my golf clubs home tonight—[*laughter*]—so none of you are in danger of being hit by errant balls. Actually, I didn't hit anybody last week, either. I didn't hit it far enough to hit anybody. I was trying, but I couldn't get the ball up in the air.

I've given some thought to what we ought to talk about tonight. There are several issues I want to speak about. Maybe I should try to do pretty much what I did last year, which is to just give you an update as big stockholders in America on where I think we are and where we have to go.

I'd like to begin by thanking you for the work we've done together in trade, particularly, and the support many of you have given to our deficit reduction and budget control and Government reduction efforts over the last couple of years and the involvements we've had in building new and, in many ways, unprecedented partnerships with the private sector to try to promote American products and services around the world.

But even more fundamental than that, I'd like to say that perhaps the thing we have most in common is not that we run big operations. Some of you may have heard the story I've been telling about the college president who told me over New Year's that being president was like running a cemetery. You had a lot of people under you, but nobody was listening. [*Laughter*] And sometimes you may feel that way as well.

But what we really have in common is that we've had the chance, each of us in our different ways, to live the American dream. We've had opportunities to do what we want to do, to live out the dreams of our childhood, to be rewarded for our labors in ways that very few people in this country and in this world have had. And it may be just because we're eminently deserving, but I'm sure we'd all admit we've been the beneficiaries of good fortune and a lot of help along the way as well. I know that I certainly feel that way.

And I think we have a peculiar obligation at this moment in our country's history when there is so much change going on to try to make sure that we preserve the dream that we've lived for all the people that are coming after us. That's really the mission that I think we should all be on at the end of the 20th century.

As you look ahead to the future, it is so full of excitement and opportunity and unimaginable benefits. But it is also full of a range of changes and challenges to ordinary people that are truly intimidating. And these challenges, these great opportunities that are sweeping across our country as we hurdle into the global economy of the 21st century are having very uneven impacts out there in America, even among people who are all trying to do the right thing as hard as they can. All the downsizing and rightsizing and changing all the challenges and all the rewards that come to people who meet the education premium of the knowledge society, they all have a different side which brings upheaval and uncertainty and insecurity to an awful lot of our folks.

And at a time like this, it's very important that the people who are out there, trying to make sense of what's going on in the world as it affects their lives, at least know that those of us who are in positions of leadership and who have responsibility for capturing and keeping and preserving and passing on the American dream are doing our dead-level best to do that and to keep a world in which, if you're in this country and you're doing the right things, you've got a good chance to be rewarded for your efforts in making a successful career and raising a successful family.

I ran for President because I thought we were running away from too many of our major challenges, because it was too easy to play the politics of the moment. There is, as we find repeatedly, a price for taking the long view and doing things that are difficult and unpopular, but nonetheless, that's work that has to be done.

When I got here, we began by passing the biggest deficit reduction package in history, one that would reduce the deficit by $600 billion-plus over 5 years. We cut or eliminated outright more than 300 programs, reduced the Federal Government already by over 100,000 positions and, if no new laws were passed by the new Congress, the size of the Federal Government would be shrunk by 272,000 now over 5 years, making it the smallest it's been since Mr. Kennedy was the President of the United States.

In that budget, we were able to give tax relief for working families with incomes of under $26,000 a year, increase the expensing provision for the small businesses of our country in ways that benefited large numbers of them, and of course, we've worked together to lower export barriers and to pass NAFTA and GATT, to get the APEC nations to agree to a free trade zone in Asia early in the next century, and at the Summit of the America's, we've agreed to work on a free trade zone here in our own back yard.

We've had the most active and aggressive efforts on behalf of American interests by the Export-Import Bank and the Overseas Private Investment Corporation, at least in all of my experience, and I think of that of most of yours. We've tried to harness the power of science and technology and the downsizing of the defense budget to make them opportunities for us to develop new commercial products that we can sell around the world.

It is important in all these things to realize that we have made a fundamental choice as Americans, a choice we've been making now for many decades, and that is that we're going to compete and win in the world; we're not going to run away from it; we're not going to attempt to hide behind barriers; we're going to face the very vigorous challenges that global competition presents; and we're going to make them work for the American people and for our future.

Not everyone believes that that's a course we should take. That has not only economic implications but also security implications. And so I ask that those of you who understand that support the decisions that we will have to make that may be unpopular in the short run.

Many of you have already written to me or called me, supporting the action that I took with regard to the financial crisis in Mexico. I appreciate that. It is an important issue for the workers and the business interests of this country long-term and, as many of you know, not simply because of Mexico but because of Argentina and Brazil and all of Latin America and, indeed, the developing world at large. We have a stake in seeing that people who are committed to democracy and to free market economics and to open trade have a chance to succeed in a difficult world. And we should not be surprised when there are certain rocks in the road, when the path is uneasy and uneven. And so I hope that all of you believe that I did the right thing, but I do want to say for those of you who have expressed your support, I appreciate that.

The second point I want to make is that this is not just an economic issue. The burdens of leadership, if we want to benefit from them, also require us to be involved in the world in foreign policy issues, require us to take the lead, for example, in trying to resolve the nuclear issue with North Korea, require us to do things that are wildly unpopular in the short term but are in our long-term interest, like restoring democracy in Haiti and require us to continue to support responsible operations in the United Nations.

Now, in this new Congress, there will be many debates designed basically to try to withdraw the United States from a role of world leadership. And I understand why people who voted for both parties in the last congressional election are overwhelmingly preoccupied with their own problems at home. But what you understand is, we cannot solve our problems at home unless we remain a leader in the world. It is a false choice.

And so, I urge you to engage the new Congress in a constructive debate from your perspective about our responsibilities to maintain the leadership of the United States in economic affairs, in support of freedom and free markets, and in security affairs. And the two things go hand in hand. We should be prudent. We should be restrained. We should not be involved in every conflict. We cannot solve every problem. But where we can make a difference, where it is plainly in the interest of the United States, we must be in a position to do so, in terms of our economic interests and our security interests. So that's the first request I would make of you in our common obligation to preserve the American dream into the next century.

The second thing I'd like to say is that we have cut Government, and we've made it work better. We've tried to do things that other people talked about. We've deregulated much of the banking operations. We've deregulated intrastate trucking. We have lowered dramatically export controls on high-tech products. We've reformed the Federal procurement system, which was an unbelievable mess and which the Vice President liked because it got him on the David Letterman show, breaking up $10 glass ashtrays. [*Laughter*]

We cut the SBA loan form from an inch thick to a page long and the response time to nearly nothing. We did the same thing with FHA processing. We are working hard with this new Congress in many ways that I think all Americans support. I was glad to sign the law applying to Congress any requirements it imposes on private employers, and I think that will make the Congress think a while when they start passing laws that affect you, when they have to consider how it will affect them.

We are working now to pass a bill that will reduce the burden of unfunded Federal mandates on State and local governments, and I think we should. We are trying to resolve the conflicts in Federal regulations that have often occurred between one agency and another, and we are making some specific progress there in getting the Labor Department and the EPA to work together.

All of these things have been part of an economic strategy that, when combined with your remarkable efforts and those of American business people, large and small, and American workers all across this country, booming productivity, all these things together have given us the lowest combined rate of unemployment and inflation in 25 years, nearly 6 million new jobs, 93 percent of them in the private sector, the highest rate of private sector job growth in any recovery in the last 20 years. For the first time in 9 years, last year our country's economy was voted the most productive in the world.

We've reduced our deficit to about half the percentage of our national income it was when I became President. And the Council of Economic Advisers gave me an interesting chart the other day which showed the annual deficit of the country, except for interest on the debt—to show you what a problem that is, you take away interest on the accumulated national debt—the last time we had an operating surplus in the Federal budget was in Lyndon Johnson's term, and it was tiny. In the Kennedy-Johnson term, it was larger. In our first 2 years, our operating surplus, without interest on the debt, is as large as it was in the Kennedy-Johnson term, the first time in 30 years that's been the case through Republican and Democratic administrations alike. So we have worked hard to control Government spending, but the accumulated burden of interest on the debt has changed the dynamics rather dramatically of managing that problem.

We had to make some tough decisions to get to this point. They were characterized by our opponents in the last election in ways that benefited them politically and burdened us. Peo-

ple accused us of raising their taxes when we didn't and accused us of expanding the Government when we were contracting it.

But the important thing is not the results of any particular election but that we did the right thing and that the country is moving in the right direction, and we must continue to do that and take on the jobs that are still ahead. We know we've got a lot more work to do in changing the way the Federal Government works. And I believe now more than anything else, we are in place and on the way to eliminating and consolidating any number of Government programs. In this new budget, we cut or eliminate another 400 and consolidate them.

We've proposed the "GI bill" for America's workers, which I hope every one of you will support, which would consolidate 70 Federal training programs into one program and give an unemployed worker or a worker with a wage so low that he or she qualifies for Federal training funds the right to a $2,600 a year voucher to take to the nearest community college or to any other approved training program to get whatever training they need. So that instead of having all these piecemeal Federal programs of uncertain impact, we just put the money in a pot and use it to educate and retrain workers who are moving between jobs. That will increase the productivity of the work force, reduce the time of unemployment, and increase the earning capacity of a lot of workers.

Those are the kinds of things we're working on. I think perhaps the most important thing we can do, to go back to something Ed said, is to try to change this sort of culture of regulation which has accumulated over the last 30 or 35 years in both Republican and Democratic administrations, unrelated to whether the objectives of the regulation are in conventional terms, if you will, liberal or conservative.

We have regulators who have not wanted to be arbitrary, so they've tried to think of every conceivable circumstance that could happen in a certain area and then write rules with overwhelming precision, the impact of which was to be so incapable of understanding that the administration of them was as arbitrary as if you had written something very general.

We have other rules which focus too much on the process rather than the end product. Instead of saying, "This is the clean air standard that State X must meet," they say, "Here are the 25 things you have to do because they will produce the clean air standard," whether they will or not.

We have too many rules where the process of enforcing the rules is evaluated more than the results. We've found, for example, that we had Customs officials who were evaluated on their jobs based on how many shipments of imported toys they commandeered. Well, not surprisingly, we had more toys than other products in certain Customs places, because that's how you determine whether you were doing a good job, not whether there was anything wrong with the toys or not. We have other places where people are qualified and evaluated for promotions based on the volume, the number of fines that they write, not whether or not they eliminate the problem which causes people to get fined in the first place.

So this whole culture, it seems to me, needs a thorough reexamination. Yesterday, the Vice President and I made an appearance before all of the Federal regulators from all of the agencies and introduced some of our success stories, a banker from Oklahoma who came to talk about how the Comptroller of the Currency was dealing with banks from his point of view better than anybody had in decades. We also introduced some reminders of why we need regulation, a man whose wife was saved by air bags, a man whose son was lost to *E. coli* poisoning because the rule we now have in place on meat inspections was not there when his son ate contaminated food. And we talked about the changes we were going to try to make.

I instructed these regulators to review every single regulation they have by June 1st and make a report to me by June 1st based on which ones they thought could be scrapped altogether, which ones could be modified, and whether any of the regulation could better be done at the State and local level or by some self-policing mechanism. I asked them to look for new measures of success that focused more on results as opposed to process.

Finally, the Vice President's conducting a review of all of the regulations covering food, health, the environment, worker safety, and financial institutions to make further recommendations for reforms in those areas.

I want to work with the Republicans in this area to try to help to break and change a culture of regulation that makes people hate the Federal Government when they think it is grinding on them in ways that don't make sense and which

don't necessarily—the culture often doesn't necessarily give us better regulation and better results. And I hope that we can work together to do this, but I don't think we ought to roll back or wreck things that do work or walk away from our obligation to elevate the quality of life in this country.

One of the reasons our economy is strong, in my judgment, is that we have found a way to pursue economic growth and pursue environmental protection. We have found a way to pursue increasing productivity, and we have seen a reduction in injuries in the workplace.

So I don't think most people believe we ought to walk away from our obligation to have safe food or safe toys or clean air or clean water. I don't believe that it's wrong to make sure that our cars are safe or that mammograms are accurate. I think that these safeguards really work. The question is, how can we change them in ways that really make sense?

I find that a lot of the things we have to do, like a lot of the things you have to do, are not particularly sexy, flashy changes; they require hard work. And the impact of them accumulates over time. It's just like these 102,000 employees that don't work for the Federal Government anymore. A lot of people are genuinely surprised because they didn't see any of them leaving on the news at night. And they didn't, because we managed the process in a very disciplined way to try to minimize disruption in people's lives, the same way you would manage the process.

Now, the temptation is always to try to do something that will make a statement that will pierce the public consciousness even if it's not the right remedy. That's what we're facing on regulation now, from my point of view. Some of the people in the Republican Congress are proposing that we freeze all Federal regulations for an extended period of time in a way that would override every single pending health and safety law on the books. To me, that's not acceptable. And there are a whole lot of pending regulations that we have people in this room who want to go through. And it will create unimaginable headaches. The last time we did it, every single analysis was that it cost more money than it saved, that it led to lawsuits, that it turned out to be a headache.

I know we need to change the way the Federal Government regulates. We have already done it in some areas. We have not done nearly what we need to do. We have a process in place that we've been working on for months to do it. But I ask you to help us do it in the right way. I also hope that when we get into this whole budget, we will be able to proceed in the right and responsible way.

A lot of you here, for example, have argued in the past and have testified in the Congress for expanding Head Start, for the Women, Infant, and Children program, for continuing to invest in the education and training of our people. We know that the only way to raise incomes in America and the global economy is to improve the education and training of the work force and to improve the overall productivity and wealth-generating capacity of the economic system itself. We clearly have an obligation there. And so, I would hope that the second thing I would ask you—the third thing, after the regulatory issue—support regulatory reform, insist on it, demand on it, demand it, give us your ideas, but let's don't do something that looks good that will have a perverse impact.

And the third thing I would ask is that you would support an investment budget for the Federal Government that gives people the chance to make the most of their own lives. It gives people the chance to get the education and training they need.

You know, one of the best things we've done is this direct student loan program. When I ran for President—and I had been a Governor for a dozen years; I had listened to students who dropped out of college; I listened to people who couldn't go to college; I listened to older people who wanted to go back. And one of the things I kept hearing complaints about was the loan program and how a lot of people wouldn't go to school or would drop out because they didn't want to borrow so much money and they didn't think they could pay it back. So under our system now, people who borrow money, number one, get it at lower cost and, number two, have the option of paying the money back as a percentage of their income, so that if they get out of school and take a modestly paying job, they can still pay their loans back no matter what the burden is.

And believe it or not, because we went to direct loans and got out of the middle-man system where we essentially guaranteed student loans to banks who made them so that there was no risk and very little incentive on collecting and no incentive to go to court to collect, be- cause we were going to pay anyway, we actually have cut the cost of the student loan program by over $5 billion over a 5-year period and increased the volume of loans and lowered its cost.

These are the kinds of things, it seems to me, we ought to be doing. And by the way, every now and then the Government does something right. When I became President, you were paying out $2.8 billion a year in tax money because of loan defaults. We've cut that to $1 billion a year. We've cut it by almost two-thirds, the costs.

So these are the things, it seems to me, we ought to be doing. And so I would say to you that on this last point—this is very important— it's not only important for us to say what the Government should not be doing—and I will support this new Congress, as I said, in many ways; we're going to have a big fight on the line-item veto, and a lot of people in my party aren't for it, but I am strong for it; I think we ought to have it; I will support it—but there are some things we should be doing, things that we do right. And I hope that you, of all people, who understand the critical importance of education and training for a lifetime, will support a responsible Federal role here.

Let me just tell you that this is not an idle discussion I'm having. Just today, just for example, the chairman of the relevant House committee introduced a bill that would eliminate the Federal commitment to food and nutrition for children, throw the money into two block grants and send it to the States and freeze the money, which will effectively mean the end of the School Lunch Program. Now, that has been a remarkable success. It feeds 25 million kids every day. It has a low administrative overhead, and we are in the process of simplifying the ability of the schools to participate in the program, cutting their costs, cutting their hassles.

We have done everything we could, by the way, to make flexibility the order of the day for States. We've granted more waivers in welfare reform and health care reform than the two previous administrations put together, so that States who were serious about changing their own systems could get around all these Federal rules. But doing away with the School Lunch Program is not my idea of reinventing Government or saving tax money.

When I was growing up, a conservative was somebody who said, "If it ain't broke, don't fix it." And now we've got lots of folks in Washington—there are all these things that are broken we ought to be fixing, and they're running right by them, trying to fix things that are working just fine. The School Lunch Program does not need to be destroyed in our common lust to reduce the Federal Government where it has to be reduced.

In 1991, as I said, there were five major CEO's who appeared before Congress to say that the WIC program, the Women, Infants and Children, was a good idea. Three of them are here tonight: Bob Allen, John Clendenin, and Bob Winters. They said WIC was, I quote, "a triple-A rated investment in the future." They were right then; they're right now. At that time, a bipartisan group in the Senate, led by Senator Leahy and Senator Dole, helped to save that program. We have expanded that program, and we're going to have healthier children and a stronger future as a result. So I ask you please to stand up for that.

Lastly, let me say that a lot of you supported, a lot of you opposed, and a lot of you sat on the sideline and scratched your head when we had the big health care debate last year. I want to put this issue before you. As has always been the case, at least since President Nixon first tried to do it in '72—I don't know what happened when Harry Truman did it; I know what happened to him, but I don't know what happened to health care costs—but there was a dramatic moderation of health care costs last year. More people are going into managed care plans. But there are still serious problems with it.

The only part of the Federal budget that's going up at faster than the rate of inflation are Medicare, Medicaid, and interest on the debt. We've now had 2 years in a row where we have reduced both defense and domestic discretionary spending and produced what I said before, an operating surplus, except for interest on the debt.

The only responsible way to deal with the entitlements problem over the long run is to keep working to help to solve the health care problem. And in spite of the moderation in health care costs, you should know that another million Americans in working families lost their health insurance last year. We're the only country in the world with an advanced economy that has a smaller percentage of people under 65 with health insurance today than had it 10 years

ago. And most of you represent companies that are paying for that, because these people do get health care when they're too sick and it's too late and they show up at the emergency room, and you get the bill in indirect costs. You know that.

So as I have said in the State of the Union Address, we bit off more than we could chew last time. We tried to do too much. But piece by piece, we need to have some insurance reforms. We need to think about people whose families are without insurance when they're unemployed. We need to think about what we can do to put some pieces in place that will stop the cost-shifting and allow some long-term reform of this system and bring the Medicare and Medicaid programs within line of inflation without having even more costs passed along to you.

Those are things that I can report to you, this country's in better shape than it was 2 years ago, but these are things that we need to work on. We need to maintain America's economic and security leadership in the world. We need to continue to work to downsize the Government and to change the culture of regulation in the right way. We need to stand up for what is necessary and appropriate from our National Government in terms of preserving the quality of life and, more important than anything else, empowering people to make the most of their own lives. And we need to keep working at this entitlement/health care problem piece by piece so that we can help the economy to grow, help the deficit to be controlled, and provide health care to the people who deserve it. If we do those things, we will be doing what we should do to give the next generations of Americans the American dream that brought us all here tonight.

I think it is a very exciting time to be here. I enjoy it. I enjoy working with the new Congress, and I don't mind the disagreements with the new Congress. But the most important thing is, this is not a game, and it is not a dress rehearsal. We are taking the American people into the next century, and we owe it to them to do it in a way that gives countless generations that come behind us the chance to be in rooms like this for generations from now and to do whatever they want to live up to their God-given ability.

Thank you very much. Thank you. Ed, tell them to go serve dinner, and I'll go shake hands. [*Laughter*] Thank you.

NOTE: The President spoke at 7:40 p.m. at the Park Hyatt Hotel. In his remarks, he referred to Edgar S. Woolard, Jr., chief executive officer, E.I. du Pont de Nemours & Co., Inc.; Robert E. Allen, chairman and chief executive officer, AT&T Corp.; John L. Clendenin, chairman and chief executive officer, BellSouth Corp.; and Robert C. Winters, chairman emeritus, Prudential Insurance.

Remarks on Arrival in Ottawa, Canada
February 23, 1995

Governor General and Mrs. LeBlanc, Chief of Protocol Lederman, Ambassador and Mrs. Blanchard, Ambassador and Mrs. Chrétien, ladies and gentlemen: *Je salut nos voisins, nos alliés, nos amis.* I salute our neighbors, our allies, our friends.

I must say that on this beautiful day I can't help recalling the wonderful visit that Vice President and Mrs. Gore enjoyed here last July. I thank you for the hospitality you showed them. And I also want to tell you what I told the Vice President, Governor General: The next time, I get July and he gets February.

I come to Ottawa to celebrate the vital friendship and the partnership between Canada and the United States and the work to make it even stronger. Our relationship is centered on a shared continent, shared values, shared aspirations, and real respect for our differences. Its very success makes it easy to take for granted, but we must never take it for granted.

In a world in which too many nations still choose conflict over cooperation and erect barriers instead of bridges, our partnership has been and must ever be a model for others and the foundation on which to build a common future.

Over the years, our alliance has been enriched by strong leadership from Canada, and I have come to appreciate that firsthand. Prime Minister Chrétien possesses an extraordinary breadth of experience in government and a passion for this great nation from Halifax to Vancouver. He has forcefully advanced Canada's interests. Fair in settling our differences, he has been a true friend in working with me on the dozens of concerns our countries share.

Our nations have forged the most comprehensive ties of any two nations on Earth. They bind not only our Governments but also our economies, our cultures, and our people. From NORAD to NAFTA, Canadians and Americans have seized opportunities to provide for our common security and prosperity. We've tackled tough problems from acid rain and water pollution to differences over beer and grain in the spirit of friendship and in pragmatism.

We've grown so close that some Americans find it uncomfortable that your Blue Jays have won the last two World Series. We hope and we believe they will not be the last World Series, and we were grateful for a little equal time when our Rangers got bragging rights to the Stanley Cup.

This week we'll focus on commerce between our countries, which last year exceeded $270 billion. It is the largest bilateral trading relationship in the world. It supports millions of good jobs, and thanks to NAFTA, it's growing by more than 10 percent every year. It sends a powerful message around the world that open markets can be the key to greater prosperity. Now, to take greater advantage of the opportunities free trade offers our people, we'll sign a new aviation agreement that makes it easier for passengers and cargo to travel between our countries.

The work we're doing to better the lives of people within our borders will also benefit from our leadership beyond our borders. From making peace in the Middle East to restoring democracy and keeping the peace in Haiti, we are working together to spread freedom and tolerance and civility. From expanding NATO to revitalizing the G-7, which Canada will host in Halifax this June, we are preparing the world's major organizations to meet the challenges of the 21st century.

At a time when some tell us to retreat from our problems abroad rather than to reach out to make the world more peaceful and more prosperous, Canada's strong internationalist tradition is an inspiration to those of us in America and to countries around the world.

Addressing your Parliament 50 years ago, President Truman declared that the success of the U.S.-Canadian relationship was due to, and I quote, "one part proximity, and nine parts good will and common sense." Good will and common sense remain the foundation of our friendship. This week we will go forward to strengthen it, a friendship in which all of us take real and just pride, and from which all of us draw strength, and for which all of us, Canadians and Americans, should be very, very grateful.

Thank you.

NOTE: The President spoke at 10:59 a.m. in Hangar 11 at McDonald-Cartier International Airport. In his remarks, he referred to Governor General Romeo LeBlanc of Canada, and his wife, Diana Fowler-LeBlanc; Canadian Chief of Protocol Lawrence Lederman; U.S. Ambassador to Canada James J. Blanchard and his wife, Janet; Canadian Ambassador to the United States Raymond Chrétien and his wife, Kay; and Prime Minister Jean Chrétien of Canada.

Remarks at a Luncheon in Ottawa
February 23, 1995

Governor General LeBlanc, Mrs. LeBlanc, Prime Minister and Mrs. Chrétien, ladies and gentlemen: Hillary and I are honored to be your first official guests, humbled to be reminded of the results of the last two World Series—[*laughter*]—grateful to be reminded of the results of the last Stanley Cup. [*Laughter*]

I have to say for the benefit of the American press corps traveling with us and especially for my often beleaguered Press Secretary, Mr. McCurry, who's over there, the Governor General, I learned in preparation for this trip, in a former life was the Press Secretary to two previous Canadian Prime Ministers. So there is life after the labors, Mr. McCurry. [*Laughter*]

It's a great pleasure for me to be here in this beautiful Rideau Hall to celebrate the friendship of our two nations. It is fitting that not far from here two rivers come together to form the powerful Rideau Falls, much like the strength of our two nations increase as we join together. Shared history, shared borders, they are the foundation of our unique and intensely productive relationship, an alliance the likes of which the world has really never seen before.

From the Canadians who helped slaves to freedom on the Underground Railroad, to the battalions who fought side by side on the beaches of Normandy, to the United States astronaut who used a Canadian-made robotic arm on the space shuttle 2 weeks ago, Americans are grateful to our neighbors for helping us along the way.

When President Kennedy visited Ottawa here over 30 years ago, he said, "Geography has made us neighbors. History has made us friends. Economics has made us partners. And necessity has made us allies. Those whom nature has so joined together, let no man put asunder." So President Kennedy proclaimed our wedding vows—[*laughter*]—and I am here to tell you we should reaffirm them. The bond that the President described so well must continue to deepen. Together we have pushed open the doors of commerce and trade. We have found common ground to preserve the beauty and the natural resources of our lands. We have walked as one in our efforts to make the world beyond North America more secure and more free.

I thank you for your support of our common endeavors in Haiti. I admire you for your faithfulness in seeking peace in the former Yugoslavia. And I thank you most recently for your support in the action we have taken to try to stabilize the situation in Mexico, our partner and friend.

Today, instant communication has made our world so much smaller that some say the entire globe is our neighborhood. Yet, the ties that bind these two nations, Canada and the United States, remain unique. And as we move into the next century, let us, both of us, resolve

251

to help make those ties grow in spirit, grow in harmony. The times demand it. Our children deserve it. The world is depending upon it.

Thank you for welcoming me to this beautiful city and this wonderful country.

I would now like to offer a toast to Canada, to the Governor General and to Mrs. LeBlanc.

NOTE: The President spoke at 12:21 p.m. at the Governor General's residence. In his remarks, he referred to Prime Minister Jean Chrétien and his wife, Aline.

Remarks to the Canadian Parliament in Ottawa
February 23, 1995

Mr. Prime Minister and Mrs. Chrétien, Mr. Speaker of the Senate, Mr. Speaker of the House of Commons, honorable Senators and Members of the House of Commons, distinguished members of the diplomatic corps, ladies and gentlemen: I have pondered for some time the differences between the Canadian political system and the American one, and when the Prime Minister pointed out the unanimous resolution you passed yesterday, I realized that in one respect, clearly you are superior. We do not control the weather in Washington, DC— [*laughter*]—and I am grateful that you do.

I also thank the Prime Minister for his history lesson, I have never believed in the iron laws of history so much as I do now. [*Laughter*]

I thank the Prime Minister and all of you for welcoming me to this magnificent capital city. The Prime Minister first came to this Chamber to represent the people of Canada when President Kennedy was in the White House. I resent that, because when President Kennedy was in the White House, I was in junior high school—[*laughter*]—and now the Prime Minister has less gray hair than I do. [*Laughter*] And he does, in spite of the fact that since that time he has occupied nearly every seat in his nation's Cabinet. The first time I met him, I wondered why this fellow couldn't hold down a job. [*Laughter*]

I can tell you this: We in the United States know that his service to this nation over so many years has earned him the gratitude and the respect of the Canadian people. It has also earned the gratitude and the respect of the people of the United States.

I know it is traditional for American Presidents, when they address this body, to speak of their affection for, their ties to the Canadian

people. On behalf of the United States, let me stay with that tradition and say, *l'amitié solide* [solid friendship].

But let me say to you that it is a big part of our life. I remember so well more than a decade ago when Hillary and I, with our then very young daughter, came to Canada to celebrate the New Year. And we started in Montreal, and we drove to Chateau Montebello. And along the way, we drove around Ottawa, and we watched all those wonderful people skating along the canal. I came from a Southern State; I couldn't imagine that anybody could ever get on skates and stand in any body of water for very long. [*Laughter*] And I could see that always—Hillary has had in the back of her mind all this long time how much she would like to be skating along this canal. And I think tomorrow Mrs. Chrétien is going to give her her wish, and we are looking forward to that.

My wife has visited Toronto, and we had a wonderful, wonderful family vacation in Western Canada in Victoria and Vancouver back in 1990, one of the best times that all of us have ever had together anywhere. We are deeply indebted to your culture. Our daughter's name was inspired by Canadian songwriter Joni Mitchell's wonderful song "Chelsea Morning."

And all of you know that in the spring of 1993, the first time I left the United States as President, I came to Vancouver for the summit with President Yeltsin. Both of us at this time were under some significant amount of stress as we tried to reaffirm our relationship and solidify democracy in Russia. And I can say without any equivocation, the reception we received from the people of Canada, as well as from the Government and the Prime Minister, made it very, very easy for us to have a successful meeting. And for that we are very grateful.

I come here today to reaffirm the ties that bind the United States and Canada in a new age of great promise and challenge, a time of rapid change when both opportunity and uncertainty live side by side in my country and in yours, a time when people are being lifted up by new possibilities and held down by old demons all across the world. I came here because I believe our nations together must seize the opportunities and meet the challenges of this new age. And we must—I say again—do this together. From the oil from Alberta that fires factories in the United States to the silicon chips from California that power your computers, we are living proof of the value of partnerships and cooperation. Technologies produced in your nation save lives in our hospitals, while food from our farms line your supermarkets.

Our horizons have broadened because we have listened in the United States to the CBC. And our culture is much richer because of the contributions of writers like Robertson Davies, whom Hillary had the pleasure of meeting last week after reading him for years, and Margaret Atwood and because of the wonderful photography of Josef Karsh, whose famous picture of Churchill I just saw. He took some pictures of Hillary and me that aren't so distinguished, but I love them anyway. [*Laughter*] And as a musician, I have to thank you especially for Oscar Peterson, a man I consider to be the greatest jazz pianist of our time.

Ours is the world's most remarkable relationship—the Prime Minister said, whether we like it or not. I can tell you that on most days I like it very, very much. We have to strengthen that relationship. We have to strengthen it for our own benefit through trade and commerce and travel. And we have to strengthen it because it is our job to help to spread the benefits of democracy and freedom and prosperity and peace beyond our shores. We're neighbors by the grace of nature. We are allies and friends by choice.

There are those in both our nations who say we can no longer afford to, and perhaps we no longer even need to, exercise our leadership in the world. And when so many of our people are having their own problems, it is easy to listen to that assertion. But it is wrong.

We are two nations blessed with great resources and great histories, and we have great responsibilities. We were built, after all, by men and women who fled the tyranny and the intolerance of the Old World for the New. We are the nations of pioneers, people who were armed with the confidence they needed to strike out on their own and to have the talents that God gave them shape their dreams in a new and different land.

Culture and tradition, to be sure, distinguish us from one another in many ways that all of us are still learning about every day. But we share core values, and that is more important: a devotion to hard work, an ardent belief in democracy, a commitment to giving each and every citizen the right to live up to his or her God-given potential, and an understanding of what we owe to the world for the gifts we have been given.

These common values have nourished a partnership that has become a model for new democracies all around this world. They can look at us and see just how much stronger the bonds between nations can be when their governments answer the citizens' desires for freedom and democracy and enterprise and when they work together to build each other up instead of working overtime to tear each other down.

Of course, we have our differences. And some of them are complex enough to tear your hair out over. But we have approached them directly and in good faith, as true friends must. And we in the United States come more and more every day to respect and to understand that we can learn from what is different about your nation and its many peoples.

Canada has shown the world how to balance freedom with compassion and tradition with innovation in your efforts to provide health care to all your citizens, to treat your senior citizens with the dignity and respect they deserve, to take on tough issues like the move afoot to outlaw automatic weapons designed for killing and not hunting. [*Applause*] And I might say, since you applauded so, you are doing it in a nation of people who respect the right to hunt and understand the difference between law and order and sportsmanship.

Those of us who have traveled here appreciate especially the reverence you have shown for the bounty of God's nature, from the Laurentians to the Rockies. In a world darkened by ethnic conflicts that literally tear nations apart, Canada has stood for all of us as a model of how people of different cultures can live and work together in peace, prosperity, and respect.

The United States, as many of my predecessors have said, has enjoyed its excellent relationships with a strong and united Canada, but we recognize, just as the Prime Minister said with regard to your relationships to us a moment ago, that your political future is, of course, entirely for you to decide. That's what a democracy is all about.

You know, now—[*laughter*]—now, I will tell you something about our political system. You want to know why my State of the Union Address took so long—[*laughter*]—it's because I evenly divided the things that would make the Democrats clap and the Republicans clap. [*Laughter*] And we doubled the length of the speech in common enthusiasm.

I ask you, all of you, to remember that we do look to you, and to remember what our great President of the postwar era, Harry Truman, said when he came here in 1947. "Canada's eminent position today," he said, "is a tribute to the patience, tolerance, and strength of character of her people. Canada's notable achievement of national unity and progress through accommodation, moderation, and forbearance can be studied with profit by sister nations." Those words ring every bit as true today as they did then.

For generations now, our countries have joined together in efforts to make the world more secure and more prosperous. We have reached out together to defend our values and our interests, in World War I, on the beaches of Normandy, in Korea. Together we helped to summon the United Nations into existence. Together we stood fast against Communist tyranny and prevailed in the cold war. Together we stood shoulder-to-shoulder against aggression in the Gulf war.

Now our nations have stepped forward to help Haiti emerge from repression and restore its democracy. I thank the Prime Minister for what he said about that. When it was not popular anywhere in the world to worry about poor, beleaguered, abandoned Haiti, Canada was truly a friend of Haiti.

In one international forum after another, we stand side by side to shape a safer and a better world. Whether it is at the World Population Conference, pushing together for an indefinite extension of NPT, in any number of ways, we are working together.

Now, we know that for Canada, this history of action is a matter of deep tradition and personal conviction. The tradition runs from Lester Pearson to Jean Chrétien. It says we must be engaged in the affairs of the world. You have always shown the wisdom of reaching out instead of retreating, of rising to new responsibilities instead of retrenching. Your tradition of engagement continues to this day, and believe you me, it earns respect all around the world from people of all races and ethnic groups and political systems.

In places like Cyprus and the Sinai, Canadian troops have played an invaluable role in preventing more violence in those critical hot spots. Today, your 2,000 peacekeepers in the former Yugoslavia are courageously fulfilling their mission in the midst of one of the most intractable, difficult problems in our lifetime.

For a half century, the United States has shared your philosophy of action and consistent exercise of leadership abroad. And I am determined, notwithstanding all the cross currents in our country, that we shall preserve that commitment. These times may be turbulent, but we have an historic opportunity to increase security and prosperity for our own people and for people all around the world. And I want you to know that I intend to do everything in my power to keep our country constructively involved in the problems that we must face if we're going to guarantee that our children will live in a peaceful, sane, and free world.

Imagine what the Persian Gulf would look like today if we had not risen to the challenge of Iraqi aggression. Imagine what tariffs and barriers would plague the world trading system if we hadn't worked so hard together over such a long period of time from the end of World War II to the events the Prime Minister described, to NAFTA, to GATT, to the Asian-Pacific Cooperation, to the Summit of the Americas that was held in Miami in December. Imagine how different it would have been. Imagine how much worse the horrible tragedy in Rwanda would have been if we had not been there to try to provide essential help in those refugee camps to keep people alive.

We cannot let anyone or anything break this great tradition of our nations. In our partnership, we will find the key to protecting our people and increasing their prosperity and the power to reach beyond our shores in the name of democracy and freedom, not only because it is right, because it is our interest to do so.

Just before we came down here, the Prime Minister and I agreed again that if we were going to meet these new challenges in the 21st century, we must adapt the institutions that helped us to win the cold war so that they can serve us as well in the 21st century. We have to do that.

Some have evolved with the changing world. Some have clearly already discarded their old missions and assumed new roles. But we have also seen that the end of the East-West conflict, the advent of 24-hour financial markets, sudden environmental disasters, the rise of international terrorism, the resurgence of ancient ethnic hatreds, all these things have placed new demands on these institutions that the statesmen of 50 years ago simply did not imagine. The 21st century will leave behind those who sit back and think that automatically these problems will be solved. We simply have to face these challenges and ask ourselves what do we have to change and how are we going to do it.

For example, to meet the security needs of the future, we must work together to see that NATO, the most successful military alliance in all of history, adapts to this new era. That means that we must make certain that the inevitable process of NATO expansion proceeds smoothly, gradually, and openly. There should be no surprises to anyone about what we are about. And we will work so that the conditions, the timing, the military implications of NATO expansion will be widely known and clearly understood in advance.

And to parallel the enlargement of NATO, we have to develop close and strong ties with Russia. I have worked hard for that, and so has the Prime Minister. We must continue working together at the United Nations, where our nations have together taken the lead in efforts to reform our peacekeeping operations, to control costs, to improve information gathering, to make sure we have the right kind of command-and-control system before the young people who put on our uniforms are put in harm's way.

We have to continue also to work at reforming the international economic institutions. We've already made some great strides in reshaping the new global economy with the passage of GATT, which is the most comprehensive trade agreement in history. But the work is only beginning. At the upcoming G-7 summit in Halifax, which we're very much looking forward to, we will be working to ensure that our international trading institutions advance the cause of trade liberalization in ways that produce tangible gains for the people of the countries involved.

We also have to reexamine the institutions that were created at the time of Bretton Woods—the IMF, the World Bank—to make sure that they're going to be able to master the new and increasingly complex generation of transnational problems that face us, problems like explosive population growth and environmental degradation, problems like those that we have been facing together in Mexico and throughout Latin America in the recent financial crisis.

Real progress on all these areas will depend not only on our willingness to be involved but our willingness to lead as partners. Together, Canada and the United States are striving to seize all the advantages the new global economy has to offer.

Trade produces high-wage jobs, we know that, the kind of jobs that give our people the opportunity to care for their families and educate their children and to leave the next generation better off than they were, a dream that has been called into question in many advanced economies in the last few years. The success of NAFTA, which is generating new jobs and creating new markets from Monterey to Medicine Hat, is the proof. And now, as the Prime Minister has said so well, we in NAFTA are on our way to becoming the Four Amigos. That phrase will go down in history. I wish I'd have thought of it. We'll soon start our consultations with Chile for accession in NAFTA, and they will be a very good partner. The addition of that thriving economy will only continue to increase the benefits for all of us.

I want to take another moment here to thank Canada for its recent support and help in the financial crisis in Mexico. You understood what we had on the line, that more than Mexico was involved, that jobs and trade and the future and our support for democracy and stability throughout Latin America was at issue. You understood it, and we are grateful. Because we stood shoulder-to-shoulder, we have a chance to preserve this remarkable explosion of democracy that we saw at the Summit of the Americas, and we should continue to do that.

I want to say a word if I might about the environment. As we expand trade, we have to remember we must defend that which we have inherited and enhance it if we can. The natural riches of this continent we share are staggering. We have cooperated to such great effect on our continent in the past: Our air quality agreement is solving the acid rain problem; the Great Lakes are on the road to recovery; the eagles have returned to Lake Erie. Now we have to build on those accomplishments.

With the NAFTA environmental commission located in Montreal, your country will play a key role in ensuring that we protect the extraordinary bounty that has been given to us for our children and our grandchildren. NAFTA is only one of the several fronts on which we can work together to both increase our prosperity and protect our environment. But we must do both.

Our nations are building on the progress of last year's Summit of the Americas, as well. It will create a free trade area embracing the entire hemisphere. Across the Pacific, as the Prime Minister said, we paved the way of new markets and for free trade among the dynamic economies in the Asian-Pacific area. That was a very important thing for us to do because they are growing very fast, and we did not want this world to break up into geographical trading blocks in ways that would shrink the potential of the people of Canada and the United States for decades to come.

All these efforts will only enhance what is now the greatest trading relationship, yours and ours. Every day, people, ideas, and goods stream across our border. Bilateral trade now is more than a billion Canadian dollars every day—I learned to say that—[*laughter*]—and about 270 billion United States dollars last year, by far the world's largest bilateral relationship. Our trade with each other has become an essential pillar in the architecture of both our economies. Today, 4½ million Americans have jobs that involve trade between our two countries. Those are the concrete benefits of our partnership. Between 1988 and 1994, trade between our nations rose about 60 percent. Last year alone, it increased by 15 percent.

But the statistics don't give the human reality behind the flourishing exchange of goods and ideas. Our trade is creating real jobs for real people. In Boscawen, New Hampshire, just for example, a small company called Secure Care

Products produces monitoring systems for patients in nursing homes. Recently, Secure Care began exporting its products to Canada. Sales there are already growing fast, and the company expects them to triple this year. And so Secure Care is hiring people like Susan Southwick, the granddaughter of Quebecers, the mother of two, and now the company's 26th employee. Giving Susan and her husband a shot at the dream which Canadians and Americans share, that's what this partnership is all about.

Much further away from you in Greensboro, North Carolina, another small company called Createc Forestry Systems is showing how our trade helps people turn their hopes into realities. It was founded by a man named Albert Jenks in his family's kitchen. Createc makes hand-held computers that track lumber mill inventories. Those computers help managers assess their needs better so fewer trees are cut unnecessarily. A few years ago, Createc began to export to Canada, and now those sales accounts have risen to nearly 20 percent of their total business. That means a more secure future for the company, for Mr. Jenks, for his son, Patrick, who works with his father in the family business. That shows how our trade can increase our prosperity and protect the environment as well.

Your companies are thriving in our markets, bringing tangible benefits to Canadians. Whether it's repairing the engines of some of the U.S. Air Force's largest planes or manufacturing software to manage our natural resources or building some of the Olympic Village for Atlanta's 1996 games, Canadian firms are a strong presence in the United States. Their successes there help your people to turn their hopes into facts and their dreams into reality.

The example of our biggest industry shows another side of this remarkable story. Working together, U.S. and Canadian companies have integrated North America's auto industry and staged one of the most remarkable comebacks in all the history of the industrial revolution. We have drawn on each other's strengths, and today, our companies work so closely that we do not speak any longer of U.S. or Canadian content in these vehicles but of North American content, whether it's a Chrysler minivan made in Windsor or a Chrysler Jeep made in Detroit. [*Applause*] I think that was the Ambassador from Michigan—I mean from the United States clapping down there.

Productivity and employment have risen to such a point that when I visited Detroit last fall, the biggest complaint I heard in a State that was given up as lost economically a decade ago—the biggest complaint I heard from the autoworkers was that they were working too much overtime. Now, where I come from, that is known as a high-class problem. [*Laughter*]

The auto industry now provides more than one million jobs in our countries. To reinforce our commitment to NAFTA and to dramatically expand an important market, tomorrow our nations will sign an agreement to open the skies between our two nations. This agreement, which allows for a dramatic expansion of U.S. and Canadian service to each other's nations, will create thousands of new jobs and billions of dollars of economic activities in our cities, yours and mine. We've reached a fair solution that will make life easier for travelers on both sides of the border, that will profit both Canadian and U.S. airline carriers, that will increase the mutual travel and interconnections of our people. That we have done so amicably provides yet another model of how neighboring nations can settle their differences.

Friendship, engagement: Canada and the United States have shown the best there is in partnerships between nations, all the great potential that awaits all the free peoples of this Earth if they can join in common cause. We are, as the monument at the St. Lawrence Seaway declares, "two nations whose frontiers are the frontiers of friendship, whose ways are the ways of freedom, whose works are the works of peace.

Every day we see the enormous benefits this partnership gives us in jobs, in prosperity, in the great creative energy that our interchanges bring. But we have only seen the beginning. For the Susan Southwicks who want a chance to build better lives and the companies like Createc that are trying to build solid businesses that will last, this partnership of ours holds a great promise with vast horizons, as vast as our great continent.

Together we've turned our energies toward improving the world around us for now nearly a century. Today, more than ever, let us reaffirm and renew that great tradition. Let us engage and confront the great challenges of the end of this century and the beginning of the next. We must sustain our efforts. We must enhance our efforts. We must maintain our partnership. We must make it stronger. This is our task and our mission. Together, we will be equal to it. The border separates our peoples, but there are no boundaries to our common dreams.

Thank you, and God bless you all.

NOTE: The President spoke at 3:23 p.m. in the House of Commons at the Parliament. In his remarks, he referred to Gilbert Tarent, Speaker of the House of Commons, and Geldes Malgat, Speaker of the Senate.

Remarks at a Gala Dinner in Ottawa
February 23, 1995

Prime Minister and Mrs. Chrétien, Ambassador and Mrs. Chrétien, Ambassador and Mrs. Blanchard, ladies and gentlemen: Let me begin by thanking the Prime Minister for his generous words and by thanking Prime Minister and Mrs. Chrétien and all of our Canadian hosts for making Hillary and me feel so at home here today in our first day of this wonderful visit.

We all have so much in common, so many roots in common. I couldn't help thinking, when we shared so many jokes in the Parliament today and so many good laughs, of all the things I might have said. One of the things that is most fascinating to Americans about Canada is the way you blend your cultures. I understand, now that we've come across the river from Ottawa to Hull, everything is first in French and then in English. And I'm trying to accommodate to all this. And I thought about a true story that I would share with you.

One of the members of our official party today came all the way from Georgia, Mr. Gordon Giffen, who's sitting out here, but he was born in Canada. And you should know that Georgia, in the heart of the American South, has a Lieutenant Governor named Pierre Howard. He was very self-conscious about running with a name like Pierre in the South. And in desperation one day, he said, "Well, you have to understand, Pierre is French for Bubba." [*Laughter*] And you all know that I come from Arkansas. I can say to you with absolute confidence that if any person from my State were here tonight, he or she would say, "*Je me sens chez moi au Canada* [I feel at home in Canada]."

The Prime Minister and I have a lot in common. We have smalltown roots and modest backgrounds, his in Shawinigan in Quebec. Did I say that right? Shawinigan? Shawinigan. Better? And mine in Hope—I have a hometown that's easier to pronounce. We began early in political life. He entered the Parliament, I think, when he was 29. I tried to enter the Congress when I was 28. I failed, and I have been grateful for it ever since. [*Laughter*]

Our political persuasions and our programs are so similar that one magazine called me a closet Canadian. I think that is a compliment, and I take it as such. We talk a lot about our humble roots. At home when our friends wish to make fun of me, they say that if I talk long enough I will convince people that I was born in a log cabin I built myself. And that's what I thought the first time I met Prime Minister Chrétien. [*Laughter*]

We've had a few agonizing political defeats, and we've managed a comeback. As I think about it, I can only think of one thing that separates me from the Prime Minister: about 15 points in the public opinion polls. [*Laughter*] I resent it, but I'm doing what I can to overcome it.

Mr. Prime Minister, one of the glories of Ottawa is the wonderful old canal that winds through this community. It's protected by sweeping and weeping willows in the summertime, and it's, as I saw today, animated by skaters in the winter. As I understand it, the canal was constructed about 150 years ago by a British engineer to help defend Canada from the United States. Thankfully, I'm told that if you ask most Canadians today why the canal was built, they can't say. The fact that the canal's origin is unremembered speaks volumes about the unique relationship between our two countries: neighbors, allies, friends. Each of us is blessed to share with the other the bounty of this magnificent continent.

Over the years the partnership we have forged has produced many tangible benefits for our people, as you pointed out. We have a joint defense program that protects our skies and makes us more secure. We have a shared commitment to our environment that improves the quality of the air we breathe and the water we drink. We have economies that are so complementary we enjoy the world's largest trading relationship in ways that create jobs and raise incomes on both sides of our border. We have a common passion for democracy that has united us in trying to protect freedom and peace and democracy and enterprise far from our own lands.

The interests and values we share have allowed us to recognize and respect our differences as well. Canada has shown the world how to build a gentler society with a deeply felt concern for the health and well-being of all its citizens. It has shown the world that strength and compassion are not incompatible. There is much in your country from which Americans can and do draw inspiration.

And so tonight, in celebrating all that unites us, let us also remember that which is unique in our countries. Hillary and I enjoyed very much our all-too-brief tour of this magnificent tribute to your unique culture. Let us resolve to work together to bring out the best in each other as we move forward together as partners and as friends. Long live this great nation.

Mr. Prime Minister, one of your most illustrious predecessors, Lester Pearson, put it well when he said, "I now accept with equanimity the question so constantly addressed to me, 'Are you an American?' and merely return the accurate answer, 'Yes, I am a Canadian.'"

And so tonight, in celebrating our countries and what unites us, let us work together and let us say: Long live Canada! *Vive le Canada!*

NOTE: The President spoke at approximately 8:35 p.m. in the Grand Hall at the Museum of Civilization. In his remarks, he referred to Prime Minister Jean Chrétien and his wife, Aline; U.S. Ambassador to Canada James Blanchard and his wife, Janet; and Canadian Ambassador to the United States Raymond Chrétien and his wife, Kay.

Remarks at a Breakfast With Business Leaders in Ottawa
February 24, 1995

Thank you very much, Mr. Prime Minister, Ambassador Chrétien, Ambassador Blanchard. Ladies and gentlemen, Ambassador Blanchard's introduction of me is a sterling illustration of what is known in our little circle of friends as Clinton's third law of politics, which is, whenever possible, be introduced by someone you have appointed to high office. They'll lie about you every time. [*Laughter*]

I want to thank Jim Blanchard for the wonderful job that he has done representing the United States in Canada and representing Canada to the United States. I want to say the second half of that again, Mr. Prime Minister: representing Canada to the United States. Sometimes he comes to see me in the White House and he works me over for 10 or 15 minutes about one of these rather complicated issues that we are trying to discuss between our two countries, and I look at Jim and I say, "Now, whose side are you on, anyway?" which is, I think, the best compliment I could give him in being part of the cement that holds this remarkable relationship together.

I want to welcome all the business leaders here from Canada and the United States. Thank you for coming today. I'd also like to thank you, madam, for hosting us in this magnificent, magnificent hall in this wonderful facility. It's a tribute to the vision of the people of Canada in building it for all of the citizens here and others who visit.

I ran for President of the United States primarily because I wanted to help get our country's economic policy back on track, because I felt that unless we had a strategy for moving into the 21st century in ways that would give all of our people a chance to be rewarded for their work and succeed as workers and as members of families, we were going to have a very difficult time in preserving the magic of the American dream.

And we have worked very, very hard for the last 2 years in our administration, in our country to try to do the things that, it seems to me, are critical to pursuing that mission: to increase trade, to diminish the deficit, to increase the level of partnership between the public and private sectors, to advance the cause of American interests around the world, to improve our investment and the quality of our investment in the education and training of our people—to do those things, in short, which would increase the productivity of the American work force in ways that would actually generate not only more jobs but higher incomes.

Canada has almost exactly the same challenges because all the advanced economies of the world face the same challenges in the global economy of the 21st century. One key to that for us is making the most of our relationship. And Jim Blanchard mentioned that when we first met 12 years ago when we were both young Governors, I had—even though I was a long way from Canada, I was asked to be one of the Governors that promoted the interest of what subsequently became NAFTA, the first agreement between the United States and Canada, among the Governors and then tried to sell it in the Congress and especially among those who were somewhat more protectionist in our Congress. I was glad to be able to do that.

And since then, I am pleased with the progress that we have made working with Canada and NAFTA, which has increased our bilateral trade by about 15 percent last year alone; in the GATT agreement; in the Asian Pacific Economic Cooperation group that we're a part of that's now agreed to open markets in Asia early in the next century, something very, very important to those of us here in the West; and of course in the Summit of the Americas, trying to open the markets in Latin America to all of us. And Latin America, as all of you know, is the second fastest growing set of economies in the world and an enormous opportunity for all of us here, as well as an enormous responsibility in terms of what we should be doing in preserving democracy and open markets in that part of the world.

I am pleased with all of that. I'm especially pleased that a few months ago, for the first time ever in our country, there was a survey which said that more people saw trade as a source of hope than as a threat for the first time since we had been taking such public opinion surveys. That is very important. My premise is that unless all of us intend to just close our markets, we will get the downside of global trade and global economics just by living and getting up every day. And the only way we can get the upside is to aggressively push these trade agreements and then work on having the kind of arrangements necessary to expand the frontiers of opportunity. So I feel very, very strongly about all of that. And I hope that all of us can be working on that in the years ahead.

In the meanwhile, let's not forget that there's something to be said for doing more to make the most of what's right here in front of us, our own relationship. And the aviation agreement that we're going to sign in a few minutes is an example of that. It will make it easier for businesses to do business by significantly expanding passenger and cargo services between our two countries. It will mean billions of dollars in new business activity and thousands of new jobs on both sides of our border. Now, the only bad news is for those of you with frequent flier accounts; it means you'll earn fewer miles because it will be so much easier and quicker to get back and forth between Canada and the United States. That's also a high-class problem in this context. [*Laughter*]

Let me say one other thing. This summer the Prime Minister is going to host the G–7 nations in Halifax. And one of the questions we will be dealing with there is a question, it seems to me, that's central to the economic future of our nations in the 21st century. And no one at least with whom I have talked has the answer to this question, but I invite you to ponder it. What we are trying to determine is whether or not the institutions that were developed for the global economy after the Second World War, the IMF, the World Bank, all the others, can adapt within the terms in which they must now operate to the challenges of the 21st century.

We're very mindful of that here in the United States and in Canada now because of the recent financial challenges that Mexico faced and how we saw that reverberating throughout Latin America, the impact in Argentina, the impact in Brazil, the kinds of things that could happen just as we're building up democracy and free markets and real opportunities for us there.

And so, the last point I want to leave you with is this: We are getting the enormous benefits of the market, and we are pushing those benefits as aggressively as we know how. But in the end, what sustains support for democratic

governments and market economics is that they work for ordinary people. That's what sustains them in the end.

Every day, whether the sun shines or not, no matter who's in the White House or giving the speeches in Ottawa, most of our folks get up every day and go to work and do the very best they can and live out their dreams as best they can and raise their children as best they can. And they must believe that if they do this, that somehow they will be rewarded; that in our system, if they work hard, if they play by the rules, if they're the best workers, the best mothers, the best fathers they can possibly be, then a good society will give them a chance. The same thing must be true in these developing countries that we're trying to bring into our way of believing about politics and economics. They have to believe that if they do the right thing, they will be able to build a better life.

And all the institutions that we developed at the end of the Second World War had certain assumptions about the way the world economy would work that are no longer accurate. They are trying to adapt to this new world. Whether they can or not is the question we will deal with in Halifax. The Prime Minister's been very active in pushing this debate. I have tried to be active in pushing this debate. We invite all of you to be a part of this debate because, after all, your interests, your future, your companies, your workers, their families will be very much affected by what we do.

In the meanwhile, I am absolutely confident that our common endeavors to make the most of our own relationships may be the most important thing we can do in the near term to further the dreams of all of our people.

I'd like now to close by inviting Prime Minister Chrétien up here, by telling you that as the President of the United States, one of the most important responsibilities I have and one of the great joys of my job is getting to know a huge number of the leaders of the countries of the world. And it's no small comfort to me— I must say this 20 times a year after I have a meeting with somebody from somewhere— I say, you know, now that I've met him or her, I understand it's no accident that this person got to run that country. The selection systems in all these nations tend to produce people who have the capacity to do what they're supposed to do at the time they're required to serve. But I can tell you that in many, many years in public life I have rarely met anybody that I thought had the particular blend of strengths that Prime Minister Chrétien has, a man who cares passionately about ordinary people and the problems that they face and is also terrifically engaged in the great intellectual challenges that governing in this new time presents and that has the practical sense to build the bridges between the great challenges of the time and the ordinary concerns of real citizens. He is a very, very good leader for this time, and I am very glad to have him as our partner in trying to build our dreams for the 21st century.

  Prime Minister.

NOTE: The President spoke at 9:56 a.m. in the Great Hall at the National Gallery of Canada. In his remarks, he referred to Prime Minister Jean Chrétien; Canadian Ambassador to the United States Raymond Chrétien; U.S. Ambassador to Canada James J. Blanchard; and Shirley Thomson, director, National Gallery of Canada.

Exchange With Reporters in Ottawa
February 24, 1995

Secretary of State Christopher

  Q. Mr. President, how did you find Secretary Christopher?

  The President. He was doing well this morning. I had a great talk with him. And he feels good, and he's going to go home with us this afternoon.

  Q. Will he be able to get back to work soon?

  The President. I'm encouraged.

  Q. Would it affect the Mideast trip at all, sir?

  Q. *[Inaudible]*—that's what gave him the ulcer? *[Laughter]*

  The President. Gee, I hope not. *[Laughter]*

NOTE: The exchange began at 10:30 a.m. at the Parliament. A tape was not available for verification of the content of this exchange.

The President's News Conference With Prime Minister Jean Chrétien of Canada in Ottawa
February 24, 1995

Prime Minister Chrétien. Ladies and gentlemen, this concludes a great meeting between the President of the United States and myself, members of his Cabinet, and members of my Cabinet. As I had the occasion to say many times, the relations between our two countries is an example to the world. We have some problems, but we are able to work on them and find solutions.

  I'm delighted, Mr. President, that the Canadians appreciate very much the relations between Canada and the United States at this moment. It was some years ago only 25 percent were happy with the quality of our relations. Now 53 percent are happy. So it's probably more because of you than of me, but—*[laughter]*—I just want to say to you that it's been, for my wife and I, a great occasion to receive your wife and you. And the bond between our two nations, I'm sure, are better because you came here.

[At this point, the Prime Minister spoke in French, and his remarks were translated by an interpreter.]

  It is always for us a great pleasure to welcome our neighbors to the south. We share a continent. We share history. If there have been difficulties between the United States and Canada a century and a half ago, today we are able to sit down together and to find solutions that bring about a better understanding between two neighbors where mutual respect resides and neighbors who understand that it is in working together that we can go forward.

[*The Prime Minister resumed speaking in English.*]

The last 15 months that I have been the Prime Minister I have had many occasions to meet with the President. It's probably the ninth time that we are together, and we speak on the phone. But I can see the influence that the Americans have on the world scene at this moment. And it's extremely important to keep the leadership in the world. In my traveling in Latin America, in my traveling in Asia the last few months, I realize that we've made some fantastic progress.

For me to see that all these countries in Asia want to be part of APEC and now of a free trade arrangement by the year 2010, and they want to work in a market economy and break down barriers and specialize and take share of the market in the best way, the way that we have developed in America and Canada over the last century is fantastic. But probably, the most significant thing that I've lived was when I was in Latin America and I saw this democracy, as I said this morning, getting better now and all these leaders very anxious to develop our values in the era of dictatorships in these areas and talk and be open about trade, but mostly about democracy and about human rights was a great satisfaction.

And they all were telling me to tell you that they need America to be involved. And it's why I'm happy to say that publicly at this moment, because, Mr. President, you are respected by the leaders of the world, and they want the United States of America to remain the champion of democracy and human rights and economic and social progress.

Thank you.

The President. This morning the Prime Minister and I had a fine and wide-ranging discussion with many members of his Cabinet and members of our administration. I want to begin by thanking again Prime Minister Chrétien and Mrs. Chrétien and all the Canadian people for making Hillary and me and all of our group feel so welcome here in Canada. We have had a wonderful trip. Everything we've done has been immensely enjoyable and productive. And I'm very grateful for the chance that we all had to come here and have this meeting.

I thank the Prime Minister for the statement he made about the role of the United States in the world. There are many debates now going on in our country about what we should be doing. It is clear to me that my ability as President to work with our people to open up economic opportunity and to give all Americans the chance to be rewarded for their labors and to solve their own problems and to have a good life for themselves and their children as we move into this next century requires an aggressive leadership on our part—prudent, to be sure; restrained, to be sure—but still American leadership involved in the world and working with real partners like the Canadians on a whole range of issues. And I thank him for that.

I'd like to say a special word of appreciation, too, about the agreement we have just signed to open the skies between our two countries. It will strengthen our partnership. It will create thousands of new jobs and billions of dollars of economic activity. As I said this morning, the only losers in this will be the people who have been piling up frequent flier miles; they'll be a little short because now it will be a lot easier to get back and forth between Canada and the United States. Nearly as I can figure, everybody else involved in this agreement comes out way ahead. And nonstop flights from many major cities in the United States to places like Montreal and Toronto and Vancouver are now going to be more available. And I am very encouraged because today we've agreed to throw out the 30-year-old rules that have suffocated business and wasted time and money for millions of travelers. The travel time on many major routes will now be cut in half because of this agreement. Passengers on both sides of the borders can look towards dramatically expanded services at more competitive prices. Canadian and American airlines will now be able to actually advertise and be telling the truth when they say you can get there from here. [*Laughter*]

Letting market demand, not Government regulation, determine the number and destination of flights between our two nations is a big step forward. It's consistent with what we've being doing in NAFTA, which has led to a big increase in bilateral trade in just the last year alone. And I believe it's consistent with the larger vision that Prime Minister Chrétien and I have shared and worked for with NAFTA, with the GATT agreement, with the agreement with the Asian-Pacific nations, with the agreement at the Summit of the Americas to open those markets.

I want to say a special word of thanks to the Transportation Minister of Canada, Doug Young, and our Transportation Secretary, Federico Peña, for what they have done here.

Finally, let me say, Mr. Prime Minister, I'm looking forward to coming back to Halifax this summer. We have a lot of work to do to examine the questions that you and I put forcefully on the table in Italy last year. Are the institutions which were established at the end of the Second World War to promote growth and developing trade, are they adequate to meet the challenges of this new age? When so many people in the world are struggling for democracy and are struggling to support enterprise, are they going to be rewarded for those efforts? And if they're going to be rewarded for those efforts, what do we have to do to make sure that the movement to democracy and the movement to enterprise, that that is not derailed with the inevitable kinds of crises that will arise from time to time, such as the recent one in Mexico?

I am confident that we can meet that challenge, and I'm glad we're coming back to Halifax because you've been such a leader in that regard. And I thank you, sir.

Thank you all very much, and we'd be glad to answer questions. Thank you.

Q. Mr. President, you've said some admirable things about Canada, Mr. President. Can I ask you——

Prime Minister Chrétien. No, no. You don't ask—[*inaudible*]—in Canada, French and English. So I will use my privilege to—[*laughter*]

[*The Prime Minister concluded his remarks in French, and a translation was not provided. The next question was then asked in French, and a translation was provided by an interpreter.*]

Canadian Unity

Q. Mr. Chrétien, I would like to ask you if you're satisfied with the winks in favor of Canadian unity from the President?

Prime Minister Chrétien. Is it to me or to him?

Q. To both.

Q. First, Mr. Clinton, you said yesterday that Canada's future was for Canadians to decide. After having met with Lucien Bouchard, can you tell us if you consider, if the Quebecers were to vote yes in the upcoming referendum, in favor of pulling out from Canada, would you consider this from an American perspective as a minor or a major disturbance or no disturbance at all?

The President. You already said I winked yesterday. I was never consciously aware of having winked at Prime Minister Chrétien. That will, doubtless, be a story at home. [*Laughter*] Look, I came here to celebrate, not to speculate. I'm celebrating the relationship we now have. I said everything I had to say yesterday, and I think that most reasonable people reading or hearing my words knew what I said and processed it accordingly. And I don't think that I have anything to add to what I said yesterday about this.

Q. Can you just help us with this interpretation? Since you said so many admirable things about Canada, can one assume that you would like to see it stay united, that would be your preference?

The President. You can assume that I meant what I said yesterday. [*Laughter*]

Affirmative Action

Q. Mr. President, is it true that you have ordered a review of affirmative action programs? And does it mean that you are backing off from giving a leg up to disadvantaged from past eras?

The President. No, it's not true that I'm backing off—it's not true that I'm backing off from giving a leg up. It is true, as I have said publicly now for some time, that I believe that we should not permit this affirmative action issue to degenerate into exactly what is happening, just another political wedge issue to divide the American people.

I believe that every American would acknowledge that there are affirmative action programs which have made a great deal of difference to the lives of Americans who have been disadvantaged and who in turn have made our country stronger. The best examples of all, I believe, are the people who have served in the United States military, who, because of the efforts that have been made to deal with disadvantaged minorities who had not been given a change to rise as high as their abilities could take them. In education, training, leadership, development, the military today is a model; it looks like America, and it works.

I, furthermore, think that it is time to look at all these programs which have developed over the last 20 to 25 years and ask ourselves: Do they work? Are they fair? Do they achieve the desired objectives? That is very different from trying to use this issue as a political wedge one way or the other. I think it would be a great mistake.

So we have been talking for, oh, months now with people about this issue, people who have participated in these programs, people who are knowledgeable about them, people who have both philosophical and practical convictions about them. I think we need to have a national conversation not only about affirmative action but about what our obligations are to make sure every American has a chance to make it. And I'm going to do my dead-level best—and some of you may try to get in the way of it, but I'm going to try to stop this from becoming another cheap, political, emotional wedge issue. This country—our country has been divided too often by issues that, substantively, were not as important as the political benefit that the dividers got. And that——

Q. You don't think that we have equality in our country, do you?

The President. I absolutely do not, and I think we—we don't have equality. We may never have total equality. But we need—and we don't have—we don't even guarantee equality of results. What we need to guarantee is genuine equality of opportunity. That's what the affirmative action concept is designed to do. And I'm convinced that most Americans want us to continue to do that in the appropriate way. But we shouldn't be defending things that we can't defend. So it's time to review it, discuss it, and be straightforward about it.

Relationship With Prime Minister Chrétien

Q. Mr. Prime Minister, during the election you talked about not wanting to go fishing with the President of the United States in case you looked like the fish and things like that. [*Laughter*] Can I ask you—your relationship has been pretty close during this visit—are you referring to the President by his first name, or is it still Mr. President? How would you describe your relationship?

Prime Minister Chrétien. You know, he is Mr. President when there is another person in the room. And when we're alone, I don't call him William J., I call him Bill. [*Laughter*]

The President. Thank you.

Q. Mr. President——

The President. I'd be honored to put the bait on his pole if he wanted to go fishing. [*Laughter*]

Balanced Budget Amendment

Q. Mr. President, back home the balanced budget drive is picking up steam. Two more Democratic Senators came out in favor of it. Is this an idea whose time has come, or are you going to try to stop this or get on the bandwagon? What's your position on it now?

The President. Well, my position on it is the same thing it was last year. I don't think it is a good idea. And I don't think it's a good idea in part because of the judicial review provisions which means that, basically, we're allowing—it's ironic to me that the Republicans, who have lambasted the Federal courts and lambasted the courts running our lives for years, are now willing to let the Federal budget be determined in Federal court. I find that astonishing, first of all. Secondly, we don't need this balanced budget amendment to reduce the deficit. And what it really does is give the minority the power to decide what's in the budget and maybe to increase the deficit. Thirdly, the Republicans still don't want to give us the right to know. They dance around Social Security; they dance around the other details. I think they have given us a little right to know with the rescission package they've presented, which is basically making war on the kids of the country. So I hope that it will be—that the Congress will not go along.

And I have talked to some Senators; I intend to talk to some more. But this is a decision most of them will make based on their own convictions, I think. We do need to keep bringing this deficit down; I am committed to doing that. I don't think this is the right way to do it. That's my position.

[*The following question was asked and answered in French, and a translation was provided by an interpreter.*]

Q. Prime Minister, are you sensitive to President Clinton's budgetary intent, that is, to give the middle class a break? I'd also like to hear the President. Has he tried to convince you that a fiscal break for the middle class of Canada is a good thing?

Prime Minister Chrétien. Obviously, everyone wants a taxation system that is beneficial to the middle class. But we haven't really discussed this problem between us. We had other questions to deal with, the President and I. So we did not deal with our respective budgets. But both of us, no doubt, want to provide very good administration to our respective countries and balance the books at some point.

Spending Cuts

Q. Yesterday, a number of House subcommittees proposed cuts in housing and rental assistance and EPA water projects and your own national service program. With all of this coming at once, what's your strategy to oppose these cuts? And isn't there something to what was said by one of the local newspapers, that, in a way, because of what's going on in Congress, you come here almost more as a titular head of government than as a real chief of state?

The President. Well, near as I can tell, ma'am, we've been here 50 days under this new regime, and they've only sent me one bill and I was proud to sign it. I mean, congressional committees can vote whatever they want; the House can pass whatever it wants. Unless I missed my guess, a bill doesn't become law unless I sign it or it passes over my veto. [*Laughter*] Now, last time I checked the Constitution, that was the rule.

What they're doing is showing what I tried to tell the American people last October and in September. What they should—look at their rescission package. What they want to do is to make war on the kids of this country to pay for a capital gains tax cut. That's what's going on. And the people will figure that out, and I think the Senate will figure it out. And I still believe we can make some real progress here. And meanwhile, I'm going to pursue my agenda and get done as much as I can.

I still believe we can make some real progress. But I do not think the American people expect nor support these radical right-wing measures that are coming out of these House committees. And we'll just see whether they do or not. We've got a constitutional system, and we've got a chance to see it work. I hope they can send me some more bills that in good conscience I can sign. I'm still waiting for the unfunded mandates, the line-item veto, all these things that will help us control unnecessary spending. But their definition of unnecessary spending apparently is the Women, Infant and Children program and Head Start and all these programs. I disagree with that, but we knew that to start with.

We've got to go through the Senate and go through conference. So I don't consider myself

a titular head of state, and until there is some evidence to the contrary, you shouldn't either. [*Laughter*]

Currency Fluctuations

Q. Thank you, Prime Minister. President Clinton, in terms of North American free trade—and as usual on visits like this, a lot was said about trade—are you concerned about the value of the Canadian dollar being about 71 cents, the decline of the peso—who knows what it is today—and at what point does your administration lose patience with this and at what point do you have concerns that your many friends in Congress will say, we're at the losing end of this because of the value of the dollar?

The President. You mean because when the value of your currency goes down it changes the trade relationship? Well, the truth is that all of us have not—something less than 100 percent control over the value of our currency. And the Prime Minister and I are dealing in part with the accumulated problems that we found when we took office. That is, I was stunned last year when the value of the American dollar went down. When we were having 4 percent growth, the best economic year in 10 years, we had the lowest combined inflation and unemployment rate in almost 30 years, the value of the dollar is dropping. Why? Because we had to borrow a lot of money to finance the accumulated debt of the years before I took office.

So these are problems that we have to work through. But I am not concerned about it. I did what I thought was right in Mexico. I knew it wasn't popular, but I thought it was right because I think, long term, Mexico's on the right path. They are committed to democracy and enterprise. And I don't see how anybody could look at Canada today and believe that it was not—that this country is not a country of massive potential, moving in the right direction, one of the most successful countries in the world by any measure.

And you're going to have these fluctuations in the currency. They're going to happen, and often they're happening because of market forces that were rooted in developments before we showed up. So I'm not impatient. We're just going to work together and work through these things and make the best of the situation and seize the opportunities that are out there.

Administration Accomplishments

Q. Speaker Gingrich gave a speech in Washington this morning. He said on ethics, he's a victim of a systematic smear campaign. He said, Democrats are the guys who smear mud, Republicans are the guys who pass legislation. [*Laughter*] Your reaction, please.

The President. I think the laughs in the audience are a better reaction than anything I can say about that. I don't have any comment about that. We had—the record was largely lost, I think, on the public, but the fact is that in the previous 2 years, more constructive bills were passed in more areas to get more done than in any time in the previous 30 years.

After 2 years of talking about what wasn't happening, I noticed in one of the news magazines a tiny chart after the elections were over that said, "Oh, by the way, we neglected to say this before, but this was the third Congress since World War II that passed more than 80 percent of a President's proposals in both years." So I think our record for passing laws is pretty good.

And secondly—I mean, on the other deal, I hardly know what to say. I think that it would be better, since I hope we can work together to pass some laws that are good for the American people, it would be better if I didn't say too much about that.

Canadian Unity

Q. Prime Minister, could you tell us, please, if you think that anything that President Clinton has said during this trip has helped your cause of promoting national unity in Canada? And if I might also ask the President, when Lucien Bouchard said that he wanted to meet with you, he said that one of the things he hoped to achieve was to let you meet a separatist in flesh and blood. So what were your impressions of him, and do you feel he was a good ambassador of separatism?

Prime Minister Chrétien. I will reply first. You know, the President has stated the obvious, that Canada is a great example to the world. So there it is—it was a statement of fact. And I was very disappointed when you talk about the values of moderation and sharing and compassion and the ability to live together with our differences, that it could not be applied to the Bloc Quebecois because I know that the

Quebecers share these values and they want—that it's very dear to them. That is my comment about what the President said. I was not present at the meeting between Mr. Bouchard and the President; that was another Chrétien there. [*Laughter*]

The President. My answer to you, sir, is that, as you know, I'm sure, whenever I go abroad as President, I meet with opposition leaders. I do that quite frequently in democratic parliamentary countries. I have very often done that.

I met with Mr. Bouchard because he was the leader of the opposition. He happens to be a separatist, and he stated his case clearly and articulately. I think the people who agree with him would have been pleased with the clarity with which he expressed his position.

Spending Cuts

Q. Some of the Republicans on Capitol Hill who are involved in legislation about which you spoke say that, contrary to being cut, the child nutrition programs, about which you and members of your administration have spoken so strongly in recent days, that funding for those programs will actually be increased, though not at as great a rate as had previously been anticipated. In light of that, sir, I wonder if you might think that "war on children," and some of the other phrases have been perhaps a bit extreme?

The President. Well, it's my understanding, Brit [Brit Hume, ABC News], that they wanted to block-grant the School Lunch Program and therefore flat-fund it for 5 years. If that's not what they want to do then I'll—then I need to know what the facts are. My understanding is that they wanted to flat-fund it. And my understanding is that in their rescission package, they have proposed to reduce funding already approved for WIC. They proposed, it's my understanding, to eliminate the summer jobs for children, which will make our streets a little steamier in the summer for the next 2 years, and to do a number of other things that are cuts from the budget that is already approved. If I'm wrong about that, then I'm wrong. But I don't believe I am wrong; I believe that's what they want to do.

Prime Minister Chrétien. Merci beaucoup. Thank you very much.

NOTE: The President's 86th news conference began at 12 p.m. in the Reading Room at the Parliament. In his remarks, he referred to Lucien Bouchard, leader of the separatist Bloc Quebecois in the Canadian Parliament.

The President's Radio Address
February 25, 1995

Since I became President, I have worked hard to fulfill our responsibility, in this time of dramatic change, to preserve the American dream for all of our citizens and to make sure this country enters the next century still the strongest nation on Earth.

Much of what we have to do, creating jobs, raising incomes, educating all of our citizens, promoting work over welfare, much of this work is harder because in the 12 years before I became President, Government made the problem worse, promoting inequality by overtaxing the middle class and not asking the wealthiest of our citizens to pay their fair share; reducing investments in our future, things that would grow jobs and incomes; and unbelievably, quadrupling the national debt.

We have to be responsible with our tax dollars. If we don't have a responsible budget, nothing else can get done. That's why with each budget I've submitted to Congress, we've cut Government, cut the deficit, and still invested more in the American people so that they can make the most of their own lives.

Two years ago when I submitted my first budget, some argued that it was impossible to dramatically reduce the deficit, increase investment in education and training and jobs, and create economic opportunities. Well, 2 years later, the facts have silenced the naysayers. We cut the deficit by over $600 billion; our new budget cuts it another $80 billion. Our 1993 economic plan cut over 300 domestic programs; this new budget eliminates or consolidates 400 more. And still we invested more in education, training, and jobs. Since I took office, the economy has created almost 6 million new jobs.

I remain committed to cutting the deficit further and to moving toward a balanced budget. The question is, what's the best way to do it? The United States Senate is about to vote on the so-called balanced budget amendment. The amendment doesn't really balance the budget, it simply requires Congress to come up with a drastic combination of cuts and tax hikes and to cram them in by a date certain, no matter what the other economic impacts might be, unless 60 percent of both Houses vote to continue to deficit spend. Now, there are some serious problems with this approach, and I'd like to mention three of them.

First, we're fortunate that today our economy is strong. But it won't always be, and when the economy is weak, many people need a little extra help to get back on their feet. Now, when more people are out of work, Government spending on things like job training goes up, and tax revenues go down because there aren't as many taxpayers. At a time like this, the last thing the American people need is a tax hike or a cut in job training or an arbitrary cut in our national defense. But the balanced budget amendment will force us to make just those decisions every time the economy is weak. That kind of extreme fiscal policy makes a small recession worse. In its most exaggerated form, it's what helped to turn the economic slowdown of the 1920's into the Great Depression of the 1930's. According to the Treasury Department, if a balanced budget amendment had been in effect in 1992 during the height of the last recession, another one and a half million Americans would have been out of work.

The second problem is this: The Constitution clearly establishes that budgetary choices should be made by elected representatives. But under this balanced budget amendment, budget decisions could end up being made by Federal judges, who certainly aren't elected. That's why an army of constitutional scholars from every part of the political spectrum, from conservative Robert Bork to liberal Laurence Tribe, have advised the United States Senate to defeat this amendment. We do not want budget decisions affecting tens of millions of Americans being made by unelected Federal judges.

The third problem is this: Interest payments on our debt, run up between 1981 and 1993 before I took office, are so big now that paying our interest will soon be a bigger part of the budget than the defense budget. What that means is that every time the Federal Reserve raises interest rates to hold down inflation, that increases the deficit. Since this economic recovery got going, there have been seven interest rate increases; the last few have added more than $100 billion to our deficit. Now, this balanced budget amendment, therefore, could give the unelected Federal Reserve the power not only to raise your interest rates but also to cut spending on things like Head Start, childhood immunization, and educational opportunities for all of our children. I don't think that's a very good idea.

We do need to keep reducing the deficit. We need to bring the budget into balance on a regular basis. What does this require? It requires tough decisions. Our administration has made those decisions. Except for the interest payments we're making on the debt, our administration is running a surplus for the first time in over 25 years. We are going to have a balanced budget for the first time in over 25 years next year, except for the interest payments on the debt run up just between 1993 and 1981, in the 12 years before I came here. That's because we've made tough decisions. Do we need to make some more? You bet we do.

This new Congress has been here over 50 days, but there is still no serious explanation of how the budget is going to be balanced by 2002 coming out of the new leadership, even though they support balancing the budget by then. Why is that? That's because these decisions are tough. It's not easy to make the cuts we've already made. It's not going to be easy to make the cuts we've proposed. It's not going to be easy to go beyond that. But we have to do it.

The Federal budget is a statement about our priorities as a nation. The American people have a right to know what's going to be cut, how it's going to affect them. They have a right to know that before a balanced budget amendment is adopted. They have a right to know it if we don't adopt a balanced budget amendment and we keep doing the responsible thing to reduce the deficit. Only recently has the new Republican Congress started to make its priorities clear. I want to work with them on this, but I believe some of their intentions run counter to the best traditions and the best interests of our people.

Many of these Republican leaders seem to be saying that we ought to cut programs for children to pay for a capital gains cut for upper income people. I don't believe we should reduce the School Lunch Program, but some Republicans have proposed to do exactly that. Just to take that program for an example, it's done a world of good for millions of kids from all backgrounds, all across America, since Harry Truman was President. "If it ain't broke, don't fix it." That used to be the conservative credo; it ought to be again.

We shouldn't dramatically increase the cost of college tuition for millions of students either. But Republicans have proposed to eliminate the student loan subsidy and start charging interest on loans to low-income students while they're still in college. That could increase the cost of their college education by more than 20 percent. We need more people going to college at lower cost, not fewer people going to college at higher cost.

And finally, we must uphold our responsibility to care for elderly Americans. It's important to me and most people in our country to do this. But Republicans are suggesting dramatic cuts in Medicare and other services to our elderly citizens.

These are some of the targets for cuts if a balanced budget amendment is adopted. I don't think they're the right choices for America. I came here to stand up for our children, for people who work hard to make the most of their lives, for people who've worked hard and played by the rules all of their lives. I don't intend to let them down.

We must continue to reduce the deficit and to strengthen our economic security. We must continue to cut Government and make it work better. But we must be careful, not careless; lean, not mean. The only way to preserve the American dream for our children is to make tough choices and hard decisions. We can't avoid our responsibility by legislating those choices away and giving them to people who were not elected to make these decisions.

Thanks for listening.

NOTE: The President spoke at 10:06 a.m. from the Oval Office at the White House.

Statement on the Trade Agreement With China
February 26, 1995

I am pleased that the United States and China today signed an agreement on intellectual property, culminating months of hard work by our negotiators and their Chinese counterparts.

This is a strong agreement for American companies and American workers. China will undertake immediate steps to crack down on piracy, enforce intellectual property rights, and provide more open access for U.S. exporters to the burgeoning China market. This agreement will eliminate practices that have cost Americans over $1 billion a year in high value exports. It will mean thousands of jobs for Americans in key industries, including computer software,

pharmaceuticals, agricultural and chemical products, books and periodicals, and audio visual products.

U.S. action in China is part of the broader economic strategy of my administration to create high paying jobs for Americans. On behalf of U.S. workers, we have used every tool at our disposal to fight foreign barriers to competitive U.S. exports.

This new agreement also promotes broader goals in China. Greater respect for rule of law and greater access to intellectual property products both promote a more open Chinese society.

Remarks on Signing the Executive Order To Facilitate Payment of Child Support and an Exchange With Reporters
February 27, 1995

The President. I'm glad to be joined here by the members of this administration who are active in child support enforcement and by advocates of tougher child support enforcement.

Today the Executive order I have just signed is another important step in our efforts to bring the Federal Government in line with the basic values of ordinary Americans. People who bear children and bring them into this world have an absolute responsibility to do their best to take care of them. And any parent who isn't paying child support should be required to pay.

The action I'm taking today builds on the work we've been doing for the last 2 years to step up child support enforcement. Just last week, the Department of Health and Human Services reported that we collected a record $703 million in delinquent child support enforcement in 1993 by garnishing income tax returns of parents who failed to pay. That is a 13 percent increase in child support collection. It helped almost one million families.

The Executive order I just signed will make the Federal Government a model employer in the area of child support enforcement. It will make it easier for us to find Federal employees who don't meet their obligations to their chil-

dren. It will speed up our ability to garnish wages and force them to pay the child support they owe.

Any parent who is avoiding his or her child support should listen carefully: We will find you. We will catch you. We will make you pay.

Children should not suffer for their parents' mistakes. Too many children in this country do suffer because of their parents' irresponsible behavior. We can't let them be punished any longer. When parents don't provide the child support they owe, their children pay forever, and in more ways than financial.

The toughest enforcement measures ever proposed for child support were part of the welfare reform legislation I sent to the Congress last year. Our plan said to absent parents, if you're not paying your child support, we'll garnish your wages, suspend your license, track you across State lines, and if necessary, require you to work off what you owe. Child support enforcement is essential to the welfare reform effort, and Congress should include these tough child support enforcement measures in the proposed welfare reform legislation. We should be tough on deadbeat parents, not on innocent children.

Again, I thank all the people who have helped to put together this child support enforcement order. We will proceed to aggressively implement it.

Balanced Budget Amendment

Q. Mr. President, What's your reading on the balanced budget amendment in terms of passage?

The President. I think it's a close vote.

Q. How close?

Q. Have you talked to Senator Nunn yet?

The President. I've talked all the undecided Senators, to the best of my knowledge. I've talked to several, anyway.

Q. You think Nunn will hold out?

The President. I think I should let him speak for himself.

Q. What is it going to take to defeat it tomorrow?

The President. I think it depends upon what those undecided Senators believe is the right thing to do.

Q. Are you going to be meeting with any of them today or tomorrow, Mr. President? What will you be doing to try and head this thing on?

The President. I'm not sure. I've had extensive conversations with all of them. I don't know what else I'll be doing.

Chelsea Clinton's Birthday

Q. How are you going to celebrate Chelsea's birthday? Just a little offbeat.

The President. Well, we're going to have dinner tonight. You know, it's a school day. You don't get your birthday off at school. [*Laughter*]

Q. You're not going to be a deadbeat father, are you? [*Laughter*]

The President. I got up this morning, and we had a nice visit this morning for her birthday. But we're going to have—we're going to have a dinner. We're going to have a family dinner tonight to celebrate her birthday. And then after the press of her school activities clears, we'll probably have a little party for her. But she didn't want one tonight, so we're just going to have a family dinner.

Q. Can you raise a teenager in the White House? [*Laughter*]

The President. Well, I think she's doing very well. She's doing very well.

Thank you very much.

Lincoln-Douglas Sculpture

Q. And what are you doing with Lincoln and Douglas on your desk? Does that portend something?

The President. When C-Span came in here and did the interview for President's Day, they gave me that. I liked it a lot. And I met the people who played Lincoln and Douglas in the Galesburg, Illinois, debate when we were out there. I just liked it. I thought it looked good on the desk. Besides that, it reminds me that this town has always been about argument. [*Laughter*]

Thank you.

NOTE: The President spoke at 9:14 a.m. in the Oval Office at the White House. The Executive order is listed in Appendix D at the end of this volume.

Remarks at the American Red Cross
February 27, 1995

Thank you very much, ladies and gentlemen, and thank you, Elizabeth Dole. Thank you for your remarks, and thank you especially for the strong leadership you have given to the Red Cross. In my own experience, I have watched you give it through hurricanes and earthquakes, through fires and floods, and I am delighted to be the honorary chairman of the American Red Cross and to be here at the start of the 1995 community campaign.

You know, when I became President, I spent a great deal of time early trying to make sure that the Federal Government could do its part in dealing with natural disasters. There had been so much criticism of the Federal disaster relief program before I took office. And we worked hard, and I think that everyone in America would admit that the Federal Emergency Management Agency is doing the best job it has perhaps ever done. But I can tell you this: We never could have done what needed to be done for the American people had it not been for the Red Cross, in the floods in the Middle West, in California, all across the country.

I also can't help saying that on the way in here, Elizabeth, who never misses a chance to get you to do something else for the Red Cross—[*laughter*]—said, "Oh, by the way, on the way out, we're a little short in our blood drive, and would you mind making a public service announcement?" [*Laughter*] And I said, "No, I also wouldn't mind giving blood, and I think I should catch up." As a matter of fact, it occurred to me that I ought to—I could really require everyone—[*laughter*]—I could really require everyone at the White House to contribute, since they give blood every day every way. [*Laughter*] They might as well give it to the Red Cross and do some good.

I want to say, again, a special word of thanks to all of you who have been involved in the work of the Red Cross. I have, for several years now, said I thought what our country needed, in thinking about how we relate to each other, is the idea of a New Covenant, that we are entitled to more opportunity but we owe, each of us, more responsibility. We've got to build this country at the grassroots level, and that means we have to do it primarily as citizens, as private citizens with public spirits. That's what the Red Cross is all about. I have seen the Red Cross workers in Florida and in California and all those terrible States that were devastated in the Middle West.

I'm reminded of the example of Debbie Blanton, the head of the Red Cross chapter in Albany, Georgia. When the floods struck last summer there, her home was literally buried by water. But she and her husband, Joe, went to work right away, and the very next morning after the floods struck, they had already opened the first shelter in their area, even though they couldn't get to their own home. When I went down to Georgia a few days later, I met a lot of people, but I didn't meet her because she was too busy working on relief work. I'm happy to report that she and her husband moved back into their home just 4 days before Christmas.

Time and again I have seen the work of the Red Cross, as I said, all across the country. I remember what I saw in the flood-devastated areas in California recently. I saw the Red Cross there feeding families from mobile kitchens,

passing out blankets and emergency clothes, running shelters for displaced families.

As awful as they are, these natural disasters have a funny way of bringing out the best in us, neighbors helping neighbors to rebuild their communities and restore hope. If you go back to the beginning of our country or back to the wonderful writings of Alexis de Tocqueville, you see that the keenest observers of America have always said that our ability to associate with people different from ourselves to work for common purpose is the great strength of this country. For more than a century, the Red Cross has led the way in that endeavor. I only wish that we could find a way to do on a daily basis what the Red Cross helps us to do when disaster strikes.

For service men and women the world over, the Red Cross means a helping hand or a word from home. For hospital patients, it means the world's safest blood supply. For people in need, it means a hot meal, a warm bed, a hope for a better future. So for many others, the Red Cross is terribly important not just in times of disaster but when problems strike them or needs plague them day-in and day-out.

I want to take a moment, if I might, to recognize two young people who are here today who represent the strong partnership in disaster response between the Red Cross and AmeriCorps, our national service program. Johnny Jones and Beverly Beyer were trained by you, the Red Cross. They've worked side by side with the Red Cross when disaster struck in Idaho during fires and Houston after the flood. I'm proud of them and the spirit of voluntarism they represent. I'd like them to raise their hands and be recognized. There they are. Thank you very much. [*Applause*]

Now I have to do what Elizabeth sent me here to do, the sales pitch. [*Laughter*] Because the truth is that for all the work the Red Cross does, none of it can happen without the generous support of the American people, without the million and a half volunteers, the millions of financial contributors, and yes, the blood donors.

So I urge all Americans to keep up your support, to give your time, to give your money, to give your blood, because, as the saying is this year, "Help Can't Wait." I hope the American people will continue to live out the ideals of the Red Cross and be good neighbors every day.

Thank you very much, and God bless you.

NOTE: The President spoke at 11:26 a.m. on the lawn at Red Cross headquarters. Following his re-marks and a tour of displays, he signed the American Red Cross Month proclamation, which is listed in Appendix D at the end of this volume.

Remarks Commemorating the First Anniversary of the Brady Law and an Exchange With Reporters
February 28, 1995

The President. Thank you very much. Mr. Vice President, Mr. Secretary, Madam Attorney General, Commissioner Lovitt, and my friend Jim, congratulations. Happy anniversary.

You know, I'd like to begin by saying a special word about Jim Brady. He dedicated his life to public service. In no small measure because of that dedication, 14 years ago his life was in danger and his life changed forever. In spite of all the hardship and the pain that followed, he never looked back but instead decided he should fight on, determined to do his part to prevent the tragedy that struck him from striking other people. More than any other person in the United States, we celebrate today the courage and determination of Jim Brady, and we are in his debt.

Thank you, sir.

James Brady. Thank you, sir.

The President. You know, Jim and Sarah Brady represent in so many ways the kind of citizen action I talked about in the State of the Union Address, the New Covenant: moral responsibility along with more opportunity and people sparking grassroots movements across this country. I am committed to this law and committed to what it represents. You know, our big problems here in Washington often stem from the fact that we don't think about what promotes responsibility and what creates opportunity and what enables people to make the most of their own lives. The Brady bill does all that.

A crucial part of our job here in Washington is to help arm the American people, through our police officers, to fight crime and violence. The Brady law, in that sense, is one of the things that I'm proudest of that has happened since I have been President. We put an end to 7 years of politics-as-usual, of people saying one thing and doing another, when the Brady law passed. It's not a complex piece of legislation, but it took 7 years, 7 years, to pass Congress.

And all the naysayers talked about how terrible it would be. Well, now we know that, as the Secretary said, over 40,000 convicted felons, fugitives, drug dealers, gang members, stalkers, were prevented from purchasing handguns in the Brady law's first 11 months. I should point out that the real national number is bigger than that because, as you know, there are some States that have companion laws that go along with that. And the estimates are that, nationwide in the States with Brady-like laws and the Brady law, the total is more like 70,000.

A recent study says that, as the Secretary said, that that's only 3.5 percent of all the people who buy handguns. And as he said, it's kind of like airport metal detectors. I think 97 percent of us should be willing to wait a while, so that the 3 percent of us who are trying to buy guns for the wrong reasons can be stopped. Three percent of the American people buying guns for the wrong reasons can do a phenomenal amount of damage, and stopping them can do a phenomenal amount of good, can keep a lot of citizens alive, and it can keep an awful lot of law enforcement officials alive.

There are thousands of examples around the country, but let me just cite one or two. In March of 1994, the Brady law stopped a handgun purchase by a man in Kansas under a restraining order for allegedly stalking his wife and threatening to kill her. In April, the law led to the arrest of a suspected drug dealer in Texas with outstanding warrants for possession of cocaine and heroin with intent to distribute. In November, it helped to catch two gang members, both convicted felons, who traveled all the way from California to Nevada to purchase weapons.

These are the people the law was meant to stop. Law-abiding people are those the law was meant to protect. The test was simple: Will it save a life? Will it protect one child walking home from school, so he or she could feel a little safer? Will it spare one woman from abuse? If it could, we all thought the law would be a success. Now we know that it has done that thousands of times over in just one year. The Brady bill has become the Brady law with flying colors.

After years of the same old politics-as-usual, the last Congress stood up to the special interests and stood up for the American people. They heard the pleas of the victims, and they thought through to the end, past all the rhetoric that was in their way. When they passed this bill and when they banned 19 deadly assault weapons and their copies, many of them paid a terrible price. Some of them laid down their seats in Congress to stand up with the law enforcement officials of this country and with Jim Brady. But America is safer because of their courage. And I think now, after one year of the Brady law's impact, the entire American electorate will see that those who attacked it were wrong and those who stood up for it were right.

You know, today there's a lot of concern in our country and a lot of interest in the news media about the balanced budget. And next week there will be another issue, and the week after that there will be another issue, and 6 months after that there will be another issue. And people may forget what Jim Brady went through for 7 years, and people may forget why some of those Members of Congress lost their seats last November. But from now until the end of this country's existence, every year there will be more people alive because of Jim Brady and because of what the Congress did.

And so I just want to say this: For all the other things that will be debated, you can mark my words, the Brady law and the assault weapons bill are here to stay. They will not be repealed.

Thank you, Jim, and thank you, ladies and gentlemen.

Republican Crime Bill

Q. Mr. President, does that mean you're reaffirming your veto threat for the Republican crime bill and the——

The President. I will stay with what I said all along. We ought not to repeal the Brady bill, we ought not to repeal the assault weapons ban, and we certainly ought not to back off the 100,000 police commitment. And I will do everything I can to protect that.

But let me be fair to this new Congress. Remember, there are two Houses in this new Congress. The Senate has not yet acted on the crime bill or any of these other bills. And I'm confident that we have at least a chance of working out a better bill in the Senate and in the conference process.

I have made clear my veto position on 100,000 police, and I reaffirm it. But I want to emphasize that I still am committed to trying to make good things happen in this Congress, and I have not in any way or shape given up on that. The bill has still got to go to the Senate, and we'll see what happens.

Q. Why do you have so much faith?

The President. I'm just a cockeyed optimist and always have been. [*Laughter*]

Balanced Budget Amendment

Q. Mr. President, does that extend to what's coming on the balanced budget amendment today? Do you have anything that you'd like to say to the Senate as they approach that?

The President. Well, I have two things. I made a little note here. I asked somebody to give me this. Obviously, I don't support it. But I support the impulses that are giving rise to it, that is, the American people understand that something went terribly wrong about 14 years ago. In the 12 years before I got here, we quadrupled the national debt. And before that, in almost 200 years as a country, we didn't have permanent deficits. We've raised the debt when we needed to, and we ran a surplus when we needed to.

Now, I don't believe we need to change the Constitution to overcome the 12 years before I got here and the mistakes that were made. We've already lowered the deficit for 3 years in a row, and we can do more. But I want to say this. You know what I think is wrong with it. What I think is wrong with it is that it may give a little extra impetus to our reducing the deficit, but it also runs the risk of turning recessions into near depressions and of turning Federal judges into budgeteers—they're not elected—and of giving the Federal Reserve the power, in effect, to wipe out all of our education programs, because when they raise interest rates, they'll raise the deficit. So there are a lot of problems with this automatic mechanism.

But let me say this: Whatever happens today, the real question should be, what are we going to do tomorrow? What are we going to do tomorrow? You know, I'm very proud of the fact that my budgets are the first budgets in 30 years which run surpluses, exclusive of interest on the debt. That is, no President since the Johnson years has introduced a budget and passed a budget through Congress which runs a surplus with all the operating programs of the Government, exclusive of interest on the debt. I'm proud of that. That shows that we've done what we could to bring down unnecessary spending, to reinvent Government under the Vice President's leadership, and to move in the right direction.

Now, I have been here now waiting for 770 days—770 days—for the members of now the majority party in Congress to both propose and vote for a budget that actually reduces the deficit. And I am willing to work with them. But this balanced budget amendment does not reduce any spending. And the American people still don't know what's going to happen to Social Security. They still don't know what's going to happen to education. They still don't know what's going to happen to Medicare. They still don't know anything about what the details are.

So the real question is: Whatever happens today—and it's obviously in the hands of the sponsors in the Senate, because they know what they have to do to get the votes to pass. They have to make it less bad; they have to fix at least the judicial—they have to fix the idea of giving the Federal judges the power to raise taxes and cut spending. And what are we going to do tomorrow? That's what I want them to think about. I'm willing to work to do more, to cut more of the deficit, but we need a partnership here, and we need to go beyond posturing.

So I do not think it's a good idea, but that decision is in the hands of the Congress, and we'll just have to see what they do. But whatever happens today, the real question is, what are we going to do here tomorrow?

Q. It sounds like you're throwing in the towel.

The President. No, I'm not. No, I think——

Q. You sound very——

The President. I have worked—it's just that I know where those five people are that are

undecided, and I know that there are changes that the majority could make in the Senate to get the votes. You know, if they would—for example, they plainly could pass it if they said that they weren't going to give Federal judges the power to raise taxes and cut spending and they weren't going to use Social Security in trying to resolve this, they weren't going to put Social Security into the balanced budget calculation. Then the thing would clearly pass.

The only point I'm trying to make is, it's up to them now whether it passes or not, because I've talked to all five of those folks. Others have talked to them. They've made their positions public. They've made it clear where they stand. Those five Democrats are all people who, like me, have worked hard to try to bring down the deficit. So we'll just have to see what happens.

No, I'm not sure it's going to pass, see, because I don't know what's in their minds. Some of the cynics believe that they want it to lose so they can continue to blame the Democrats.

Q. You don't seem to have put much energy in it.

The President. That's not—I have made my position very clear. I don't have a veto, as you know, in this process. I've made my position clear. I've had extensive talks with undecided Members. I've done everything I could. Our administration has testified on it. But what I think happens is that a lot of the Members of Congress are frustrated because of what's happened in the previous 12 years before we showed up here, and they see this mountain of debt that's piled up. But I don't believe the amendment is the way to solve it, because I think of the whole history of America. I know we could fix this without a constitutional amendment.

And if we fix the big structural deficit and we're stuck with this amendment, then what happens the next time we have a recession? Are we going to make it worse? In a recession, are we going to be raising taxes and cutting job training programs? What happens the next time the Federal Reserve has to raise interest rates? Are we going to come back and cut Head Start and college loans?

So we need to continue to work on this. We need strong action. I'm just afraid that the American people have not been told the full implications of this for Social Security, for education, and for the economy. And I think that it's regrettable, but understandable, that the supporters did not want to comply with the right-to-know suggestion. But they're going to have to, anyway. They're going to have to before the States vote on it. They're going to have to tell people what the consequences are.

Q. Is there anything they could change to make you go along with it with this point of view that it's such a bad idea to change the Constitution?

The President. I think that changing—I think if you change the Constitution without some sort of an economic emergency—that's my problem. That is, my problem is, if you read Senator Moynihan's three lectures on this, three speeches in the Senate, he did a wonderful job, Moynihan did, of laying out the whole history of our budgeting and pointing out how this problem that we're saddled with is a new problem in American history. It arose from 1981 to 1993. It did not exist before in our country. And the point he made is, we can fix it without amending the Constitution if we have the will to do it and if we'll work together in a bipartisan fashion.

And if we amend the Constitution and we fix it, then the next time it takes effect, it'll be destructive, because we'll be in a recession and it will make the recession worse. That's what I'm worried about. I don't know how they could fix that. I understand one of the Senators had some sort of an economic emergency amendment that would fix that. But that's what I see as the real problem.

You know, I guess when you come down to it, the best argument for it is the drunk in the liquor store argument: Every time I drive by, I'm going to go in and buy a fifth; you better board it up. I mean, near as I can tell, that's the argument for it. And I just think that we should have a bipartisan determination to keep bringing that rascal down without amending the Constitution in ways that 10, 15 years from now are likely to hurt our children and our grandchildren.

Thank you.

NOTE: The President spoke at 9:32 a.m. in the Roosevelt Room at the White House. In his remarks, he referred to Secretary of the Treasury Robert Rubin; Jerry Lovitt, Kentucky State police commissioner; former White House Press Secretary James Brady, who was wounded in the 1981 assassination attempt on President Ronald Reagan; and Mr. Brady's wife, Sarah, head of Hand Gun Control, Inc. Public Law 103–159, "To provide for a waiting period before the purchase of a handgun, and for the establishment of a national instant criminal background check system to be contacted by firearms dealers before the transfer of any firearm," approved November 30, 1993, took effect on February 28, 1994.

Exchange With Reporters Prior to Discussions With Prime Minister Wim Kok of The Netherlands
February 28, 1995

Iran

Q. Mr. President, are you concerned about Iran placing antiaircraft missiles at the mouth of the Persian Gulf?

The President. I think that I'll wait until later to answer any questions.

Q. Even the ones—the Republicans saying that they're willing to change the balanced budget amendment so that the courts cannot raise taxes or cut spending?

The Netherlands

Q. And about The Netherlands—[laughter]——

The President. It's a great country and a great ally of the United States.

[At this point, one group of reporters left the room, and another group entered.]

"Apache" Helicopters

Q. Mr. President, how will you react if the Dutch Government decides not to buy *Apache* helicopters?

The President. Well, that's a decision for the Dutch Government to make. Obviously, I hope that that will be the decision because I think on the merits, it's the best product. But that's a decision that the Government has to make.

Q. Mr. President, are you trying to sell the Prime Minister on the benefits of the *Apache* helicopter?

The President. I've already done that. I've already made my pitch, if you will.

Prime Minister Kok. And Mr. President, if we don't buy them, we remain a great country.

The President. That's right. We have—you know, our relationship with the Dutch, it's a very—it's a deep and broad and complex one. There are a lot of things involved in it, and this is just one part of it. We are allies in every sense of the word, in so many ways. And we have to continue to work together. There are a lot of problems in Europe and beyond that require our cooperation and our mutual support. And of course, we have a terrific commercial relationship as well. So we have a lot riding on this relationship, and no single element of it can be allowed to define it.

United Nations Peacekeeping

Q. [*Inaudible*]—about U.N. peacekeeping forces that may be in jeopardy because of the attitude of the Republican Party?

The President. Well, I don't agree with the attitude of the party with regard to the peacekeeping forces in Bosnia and with regard to at least some of what I've seen in the House of Representatives on peacekeeping generally. I believe the United States should participate in peacekeeping. I think we should pay our way. I think we should continue to be a strong force there.

With regard to Bosnia, I think we should—the United States should support the Contact Group and should support those countries that do have their soldiers on the ground and at risk there. And we have said, for example, if we had to withdraw, if UNPROFOR collapsed, we would try to do our part to help people get out of Bosnia safely. But I think it would be a mistake for the United States to go off on its own and start making independent Bosnia policy. We don't have our soldiers there. The Europeans do have soldiers there; the Canadians have soldiers there. They have put their lives at risk. We have spent a lot of money in Bosnia, and we have supported from air and sea and from our hospital in Croatia, and a lot of other ways we've supported the operation of the U.N. in Bosnia.

Q. So you're with our Prime Minister and against the Republicans in this matter?

The President. That's correct. That's essentially——

Q. [*Inaudible*]

The President. [*Inaudible*]—Constitution——

Q. [*Inaudible*]

The President. There has to be a difference of opinion in the United States or you're on the long end of it—you're in the right position. [*Laughter*]

NOTE: The exchange began at 10:27 a.m. in the Oval Office at the White House. A tape was not available for verification of the content of this exchange.

The President's News Conference With Prime Minister Wim Kok of The Netherlands
February 28, 1995

The President. Please be seated. Welcome. It's indeed a pleasure to welcome Prime Minister Kok to the White House. Since the days of our Revolutionary War when The Netherlands gave shelter to John Paul Jones' ships, The Netherlands has consistently been one of our most valued and trusted allies.

I also have warm personal recognition, Mr. Prime Minister, of your country. I last visited it a few years ago when I was Governor of Arkansas, and I hope I have a chance to visit

it again. In the meanwhile, I'm glad we had the opportunity to return the hospitality today.

The Prime Minister comes here at a very important time, when we are seeking to work together to meet the challenges of the post-cold-war era. One of the most vital issues we discussed is the effort to build a more integrated, more secure Europe, to ensure that democracy and prosperity grow strong in the years ahead. We reaffirmed our intention to press ahead with the enlargement of NATO to include Europe's new democracies.

The Netherlands is playing a leading role in building bridges to these new democracies. It was the first NATO nation to host a Partnership For Peace exercise on its own soil, something for which we are very appreciative.

We also agreed that in parallel with this expansion NATO must develop close and strong ties with Russia. We share a vision of European security that embraces a democratic Russia.

The Prime Minister and I discussed a broad range of issues, including our interest in continuing to expand trade between our two nations. Not many people know just how rich our partnership is. The Netherlands is our eighth largest trading partner. And the Dutch people obviously think the American economy is a good bet because they have invested more in the United States than anyone except Britain and Japan. I hope this trading relationship will continue to grow with our friendship in the years ahead.

During our talks, we also agreed on the importance of indefinite extension of the Nuclear Non-Proliferation Treaty to prevent the spread of nuclear weapons. We reviewed our joint efforts in the Caribbean where we are working together to combat narcotics trafficking.

I want to thank the Prime Minister and all the people of The Netherlands, especially, for the support they have given to our common efforts to restore democracy in Haiti, a truly remarkable success story to date. No other European nation has been as forthcoming at every stage of this endeavor, from sending ships for sanctions enforcement, to the police monitors in the multinational force, to the Dutch Marines, who are part of the U.N. mission. Like their involvement in the peacekeeping in the former Yugoslavia, this vital help to the people of Haiti writes yet another chapter in the great Dutch tradition of supporting humanitarian relief efforts and human rights around the world.

When I spoke 2 weeks ago at the Iwo Jima Memorial commemoration, I admired once again the wonderful gift that The Netherlands gave us in thanks in part for our part in liberating their country in World War II, the wonderful Netherlands Carillon. Today, I want to thank the Prime Minister and the people of The Netherlands for renovating and updating the Carillon, which is now receiving a 50th bell. This is the gift that I have here. Now, as the Prime Min-

ister reminded me, some of the bells are as big as he and I are. But this 50th bell, which I assure you—it's been over in the Oval Office for a day or so, and we have all lifted it. It's quite heavy and quite wonderful, and we thank him for this.

Bells have rung out the news of victory and liberty for centuries. As we move forward to meet the challenges of this new century, it is fitting that we and our Dutch friends will be reminded of the common cause we shared 50 years ago by the sound of this beautiful new bell. May it also be sounding 50 years from now and even beyond.

Mr. Prime Minister.

Prime Minister Kok. Thank you very much, Mr. President. Let me, first of all, express my gratitude and the gratitude of Minister for Foreign Affairs Van Mierlo to be here. Having been here at this official working visit, this visit underlined once again the close links and the excellent cooperation and relation between our two countries, both on a bilateral basis and also in the international framework. And so I want to thank you for that occasion.

You said a few words about this bell. Indeed, this is one of the smallest ones we have, but it's number 50, number 50 on a row. And this symbolizes, with the words "Freedom" and "Friendship" on it, it symbolizes how grateful we still are and ever remain for the way in which the United States and the United States soldiers participated in liberating our continent, liberating our country. And I will be proud to see and to hear from far away, from in The Netherlands when, on the 5th of May of this year——

The President. We will ring——

Prime Minister Kok. ——at the day where, 50 years ago, The Netherlands were freed, that the bells will ring, all the bells will ring, and that symbolizes then, again, our friendship.

Coming back to the main purpose of our talks and our visits, the President indicated the subjects that have been discussed. I think we live in a world where cooperation, partnership, and leadership is more necessary than ever before. In this world, we in The Netherlands participate in European cooperation. We want to strengthen the European Union. We want to expand the European Union. We want to offer perspective to the peoples of the Central and Eastern European countries that they can be part of our integrated European Union. And we want to work on the security architecture together with the United States.

We are convinced—Europeans—but I'm even more convinced that without transatlantic cooperation, European integration at the end will not be successful. So we need each other. We need the United States in that role, and we want to strengthen our identity in Europe also in this field, foreign policy, security policy, but together with the United States.

And I want to end by saying that especially in this time, the role in which you, Mr. President, use the word "leadership," the way in which you are prepared to take the lead in going the way into the right direction in the universal context is impressive and encouraging, because we need each other. We need strong and good cooperation between Europe and the United States. We need leadership.

Sometimes I'm a little bit concerned about tendencies in American society where you get the impression—but I'm only here for a few days—you get the impression that there is a certain tendency towards isolationism, stepping somewhat back from the international scene. And that would be very riskful, to put it mildly. That would be very riskful, because responsibility and leadership is a necessity now and forever.

Thank you very much.

The President. We'll begin with one question from an American journalist, and then we'll alternate between the American and the Dutch journalists who are here.

Iran

Q. Mr. President, what can you tell us about the presence or nonpresence of missiles at the opening of the Persian Gulf?

The President. I can tell you that basically what General Shalikashvili said is accurate, and it's a situation that we're monitoring very closely. The missiles are rather old. As you know, they've been here for some time, in the possession of the Iranians. And we are monitoring them, trying to evaluate exactly everything we need to know about them. But we're on top of the situation, and we think there is no undue cause for concern at this moment.

United Nations Peacekeeping

Q. I have a question for the Prime Minister and the President. First, the President. The Prime Minister has expressed deep concern about the debate in this city of scaling down the American contribution to U.N. peacekeeping operations. Especially the Republicans are pushing hard this idea. But when it comes to this point, who is responsible, though, the Republicans on Capitol Hill, or the President of the United States?

And to the Prime Minister: Which Washington did you like the best, the Washington of Dole, who you met yesterday, or the Washington of President Bill Clinton?

Prime Minister Kok. I will have to think about my answer. So, first, perhaps the President. [*Laughter*]

The President. You asked him the right question in the wrong way, so I'll try to fill up some time so he thinks of a clever answer. [*Laughter*]

Well, let me say our Congress has voted already. It's a matter of American law to reduce our peacekeeping contribution from 31 percent down to 25 percent, more in line with our world share of GDP, although it's smaller than that.

Nonetheless—and that was done before the last elections. And it was a part of an agreement I reached with the Congress that at least secured the money that we owed when I became President in back debts to the U.N. The United States was the biggest debtor to the U.N. We owed money, and I was trying to get the money and trying to move forward.

Now, we have been very active in supporting reforms of U.N. practices, in which I think we are in accord with, with The Netherlands on that. And we wanted to pay our dues, and we want to stay active in peacekeeping—at least our administration does. I appreciated what the Prime Minister said. A lot of Americans are understandably concerned about their own problems in the economic and other challenges we have here at home. But we cannot afford to walk away from not only the obligations but the opportunities to work together with other countries to solve problems before they get more severe and before the United States could be dragged in at greater costs in treasure and in human life.

So I very much support the comments the Prime Minister made. I have tried to keep the United States actively engaged with Europe, with Asia, with Latin America, and indeed with the entire globe in pursuing an aggressive strategy of promoting democracy and freedom and peace and prosperity. And that will continue to be my policy. It is a policy that under our

Constitution I can pursue as long as I am the President. But the Congress does have the ability to appropriate or fail to appropriate money. That is their job under our Constitution.

So that will answer most of your questions when you think about these conflicts coming up and what the United States can and cannot do. If I have a difference of opinion with them, if it relates to the appropriation of money, that's their first job. If it relates to the conduct of foreign policy under the Constitution, that's my primary job.

Prime Minister Kok. Now comes a difficult question. Well, let me tell you this. I'm not here to compare. I'm here to listen and to debate. And I'm grateful that the President of the United States explains his policies and his position in the way he did in our meeting.

In addition to this, I want to say this: We, to a certain extent, also see in other parts of the world, including The Netherlands, these tendencies of—in the period where the old enemy, communism, is not there anymore, after the cold war—certain tendency where perhaps a responsibility for international solutions of international problems is not always put high enough on the agenda. So it's not just an American discussion. Of course, in America, the discussion is more important than elsewhere because of the size of your country, you're a continent in itself, and because of the consequences if the United States would abstain from playing that active and prominent role.

So the lesson I draw from this short visit, and also from the short meeting yesterday with Senator Dole, is that we have to discuss and debate much more also with the Republicans, because I could imagine that quite some Senators and Members of the House are just a little bit unaware of the responsibility that has to be taken in order to solve the number of huge international problems.

Perhaps some Senators and Members of the House are not fully aware of what is the real situation in former Yugoslavia, what the situation, for example, of Dutch troops, Blue Helmets, is, and what the consequences would be of a unilateral arms embargo lift, where of course we are here again today heard that the American President would not agree with.

But I think this type of debate, of debate with the Americans, also the Americans from the Republican side, is necessary. And I'm ready with my government to invest also in that type

of contact, because the wrongest solution for problems is drawing your back to each other. We have to discuss. And I'm glad, as I said before, that between the President of the U.S. and the Dutch Government there's a close similarity in view, vision, and perspective.

Q. Mr. President——

The President. One, two, three. I'll get to all of you. Go ahead. [*Laughter*]

Balanced Budget Amendment

Q. Virtually every major economist, with the exception of Milton Friedman, has said, in effect, that the balanced budget amendment is, in effect, a crackpot idea that could bring back the kinds of policies that triggered the Great Depression. Yet it seems to be benefiting from a political stampede on Capitol Hill. How do you account——

The President. Not yet, hasn't passed yet. It's hanging in the balance.

Q. If it does pass in the Senate later today, will you lead a campaign to block ratification by the States?

The President. Well, first of all, I will say— I will keep on saying what I've been saying. The only argument for it is the argument that many people who helped to create the problem we've got are making, which is that we can't help ourselves unless the Constitution makes us make a change.

We never had a chronic deficit problem before 1981. Our country was not into the business of permanent deficits, although we slipped into—we were undisciplined in the seventies, but not chronically so. Then in '81 and '82, and then again in '86 we made a series of decisions which gave us a permanent deficit. That needs to be corrected. We've made major steps in the last 2 years in correcting it.

The American people are right to want it corrected. But if we solve the so-called structural deficit problem, the permanent deficit problem, with the balanced budget amendment, then the next time we have a recession, it could make it much worse. That's why all the economists of all political stripes are against it.

And I'll just keep making that point and keep urging the Republicans—tomorrow, what happens tomorrow, however this vote comes out today? I've been here 770 days, and I want the members of the other party to propose and vote for something that will reduce the deficit. That has not happened yet. And I want them to work with me. I will work with them in good faith to do more. That's what we ought—that's what the people hired us to do. They want us to make the decisions. If we do that, we can demonstrate that the amendment is not needed, but that we must get rid of this sort of permanent deficit that we built into our economy starting in the early eighties.

United Nations Peacekeeping

Q. Mr. President, I have a question on balanced budget of the United Nations. The obvious question of your leadership in foreign policy will be whether you will veto that nation that will diminish contribution to a U.N. peacekeeping. Will you do that?

The President. First of all, it's already in our law that we cannot—that we must ratchet down our contributions on a regular basis. Now, we also do other things, like what we did in Haiti with the multinational force, that we don't believe should be counted against that. But I will do everything I can to keep the United States involved in the United Nations in peacekeeping and to keep us supporting an active role in the world.

I believe the American people understand that we're better off having these burdens shared with all the nations of the world, trying to nip these problems in the bud and that if we walk away, as some suggest we should in our Congress, and don't spend any money on this, all we're going to do is make the world's problems worse, make other countries behave in a more irresponsible way, and wind up dragging American soldiers and American wealth into deeper and deeper problems that could be avoided if we have a responsible, disciplined approach to burden sharing and peacekeeping. So that's what I'm going to try to do.

Iraq

Q. I wonder if you've had a chance to talk about the sanctions against Iraq and whether or not there's a sense out there that the international community is willing to stand with the U.S. to keep them in place, especially because of what we're hearing from Russia and France on pulling back.

The President. Actually, we did not discuss that today.

Prime Minister Kok. No.

The President. You know what my position is. My position is that there are a whole set of rules that Iraq must comply with before the sanctions could be lifted, and they haven't been. They shouldn't be lifted. That's what my position is.

"Apache" Helicopters

Q. Mr. President, did you convince the Dutch Prime Minister that The Netherlands should buy the *Apache* helicopter? [*Laughter*] And Prime Minister, have you already made a decision after your talks with the President?

The President. Well, maybe I can let him off the hook. He said that the decision had not been made, and I reaffirmed my conviction about two things: one, the high quality of the American helicopters, and second, the importance of having very good and interoperable equipment for NATO allies generally. I made the appropriate points in the appropriate way. The Prime Minister listened, made some good responses and made it clear that no decision had been made yet.

Bosnia and Croatia

Q. Did you assure the Prime Minister that the U.S. would take part in any possible withdrawal of U.N. peacekeepers from Croatia, if necessary?

The President. Croatia and what?

Q. Croatia with U.S. troops? Would U.S. troops help bring them out, if necessary?

The President. Let me, first of all, say, we did not discuss that explicitly. You know, the United States has—I guess we ought to get this clear—the United States has committed explicitly and has a plan for helping on the troops in Bosnia. And one of the reasons that the Dutch have been so strong in believing we should not unilaterally lift the arms embargo is that they have troops in and around Srebrenica, I think——

Prime Minister Kok. Right.

The President. And perhaps the most vulnerable of all of the United Nations troops are the Dutch. They have really been brave. They've stuck their necks out. They have prevented much more bloodshed and saved a lot of lives. And that's why they're against the unilateral lift of the arms embargo, because they know what could happen not only to their own troops but, if they are compelled to withdraw, what could happen in that fragile area. And we all remember when it wasn't so long ago when that whole area was given up for lost and now hasn't been.

Now, we have gone through that. We're still doing our best to preserve the U.N. mission and presence in Croatia. We may not be able to persuade President Tudjman and his government to do that. We have, therefore, not articulated a clear position. Obviously, we feel a great obligation to all of our allies who are in UNPROFOR who are in vulnerable positions. But I want to say that we have not at this moment explicitly embraced a plan, consulted with the congressional leadership, and ratified it. But obviously, we are just as concerned about the U.N. forces in Croatia as those in Bosnia, but the decisionmaking process is at a different point.

Foreign Policy

Q. The Prime Minister is very concerned about what he perceives as isolationist tendencies in American society. Do you share those concerns? Do you think there is a danger that the United States may abdicate its role as a world leader?

The President. Yes, I share the concerns. No, I don't think the United States will abdicate its role as a world leader. I share the concerns because—for two reasons: One is, a lot of our people here know that the cold war is over, know that most Americans have worked hard for more than a decade now without any appreciable increase in their living standards, and would like to see us focus on our problems here at home in ways that make progress on our economic and social problems.

I believe that we have to make progress on our economic and social problems, but I don't believe that over the long run we can really solve our own problems at home unless we are also operating in a world that's more peaceful, more democratic, and more prosperous. The only way a wealthy country like The Netherlands or the United States grows wealthier is if there is growth in the world, and we trade into it, and we work our way into it.

So we have a very clear personal interest that does not permit us to be isolationists. And if we—we could get away with being isolationists for a couple of years, and then pretty soon we'd be spending even more of our money on military involvement, cleaning up foreign problems and dealing with the consequences of our neglect.

So I believe that we will resolve these tensions and debates by reaffirming America's leadership in the world. And that is my determination. That is what I'm committed to doing and why I'm so grateful for the Prime Minister's presence here in the United States and for his words and for the leadership and the example that The Netherlands have set in this area.

Thank you very much.

NOTE: The President's 87th news conference began at 12:55 p.m. in the Cross Hall at the White House. In his remarks, he referred to President Franjo Tudjman of Croatia.

Message to the Congress Transmitting the National Security Strategy Report
February 28, 1995

To the Congress of the United States:
    As required by section 603 of the Goldwater-Nichols Department of Defense Reorganization Act of 1986, I am transmitting a report on the National Security Strategy of the United States.

WILLIAM J. CLINTON

The White House,

February 28, 1995.

NOTE: This message was released by the Office of the Press Secretary on March 1.

Statement on the Food Stamp Program Antifraud Initiative
March 1, 1995

I am very pleased that USDA is presenting this comprehensive proposal to Congress today.

With this package, we are saying to the Congress that we expect the Food Stamp Program to continue to get food to people who need it but that we will not tolerate criminals who defraud the system and seek to profit from the hunger of others.

Over the past 2 years, this administration has made restoring public trust in Government a top priority. As part of our comprehensive strat-

egy to reinvent the Food Stamp Program, we are today asking Congress for broad new powers, comprised of 13 specific items, to counterattack those who have exploited the program.

This administration has made clear our opposition to block grants for our nutrition programs. With this tough, workable antifraud initiative, we are ensuring that the Food Stamp Program will earn the public trust, and continue to help people who need it.

Message to the Congress Transmitting the Report of the Department of Transportation
March 1, 1995

To the Congress of the United States:

In accordance with section 308 of Public Law 97–449 (49 U.S.C. 308(a)), I transmit herewith the Twenty-seventh Annual Report of the De-

partment of Transportation, which covers fiscal year 1993.

WILLIAM J. CLINTON

The White House,
March 1, 1995.

Message to the Congress Transmitting the Energy Department Report
March 1, 1995

To the Congress of the United States:

In accordance with the requirements of section 657 of the Department of Energy Organization Act (Public Law 95–91; 42 U.S.C. 7267), I transmit herewith the 13th Annual Report of

the Department of Energy, which covers the years 1992 and 1993.

WILLIAM J. CLINTON

The White House,
March 1, 1995.

Letter to Congressional Leaders on Deployment of United States Troops to Somalia
March 1, 1995

Dear Mr. Speaker: (Dear Mr. President:)

On February 27, 1995, at approximately 3:00 p.m. e.s.t., 1,800 combat-equipped U.S. Armed Forces personnel began deployment into Mogadishu, Somalia, to assist in the withdrawal of U.N. forces assigned to the United Nations Operation in Somalia (UNOSOM II). The U.S. forces were accompanied by approximately 500 Italian marines. A total of 14,000 multinational personnel are participating in this operation. The U.S. forces include the USS *Essex* Amphibious Readiness Group, the USS *Belleau Wood*, the Special Marine Air-to-Ground Task Force, and Special Operations forces including four AC–130 gunships.

The U.S. Armed Forces entered Somalia in December 1992, pursuant to United Nations Security Council Resolution 794, with the mission of establishing a secure environment for humanitarian relief operations. Upon completion of this mission in 1993, responsibility for maintaining the environment created by the U.S.-led operation was transferred to UNOSOM II. Almost all U.S. military forces were withdrawn from Somalia on March 31, 1994, and the few remaining U.S. forces were subsequently withdrawn on September 15, 1994.

The U.S. forces have returned to Somalia to support the U.N. withdrawal as part of the U.S. long-standing commitment to U.N. humanitarian efforts in Somalia. The withdrawal operation is a coalition effort consisting of forces from Italy, the United Kingdom, France, Pakistan, Malaysia, Bangladesh, and the United States. We do not intend that U.S. Armed Forces deployed to Somalia become involved in hostilities. Nonetheless, these forces are equipped and ready to take such measures as may be needed to accomplish their mission and defend themselves, if necessary; they also will have the support of any additional U.S. Armed Forces necessary to ensure their safety and the accomplishment of their mission. It is my intention that this will be an operation of short duration whose only purpose is to assist in the withdrawal of UNOSOM II forces.

Over the course of the U.N. operations in Somalia, various items of U.S. equipment (helicopters, tanks, and armored personnel carriers) were leased to the United Nations to support operations in Somalia. It is our intention to assist the United Nations in withdrawing this equipment, to prevent its falling into the hands of those who might use it to cause further harm to the Somali people.

I have taken this action pursuant to my constitutional authority to conduct U.S. foreign relations and as Commander in Chief and Chief Executive.

I remain committed to ensuring that the Congress is kept fully informed regarding significant employments of the U.S. Armed Forces. Accordingly, and consistent with the War Powers Resolution, I am providing this report on the U.S. military actions described above. I appreciate your continued support as we complete this operation.

Sincerely,

WILLIAM J. CLINTON

NOTE: Identical letters were sent to Newt Gingrich, Speaker of the House of Representatives, and Strom Thurmond, President pro tempore of the Senate.

Remarks to the Nixon Center for Peace and Freedom Policy Conference
March 1, 1995

To Tricia and John Taylor and all the people from the Nixon Center; our distinguished guests from Germany and from Russia; of course, to Henry Kissinger—I was thinking when he said we both spoke with accents, judging from the results of the last election, his native country is still claiming him more than mine is claiming me. [*Laughter*] But I'm a big one for reconciliation—[*laughter*]—and there's plenty of time to achieve it.

I am honored to be here tonight. Just a month before he passed away, President Nixon wrote me the last letter I received from him about his last trip to Russia. I told some people at the time that it was the best piece of foreign policy writing I had received, which angered my staff but happened to be the truth. [*Laughter*] And as with all of our correspondence and conversations, I was struck by the rigor of his analysis, the energy of his convictions, and the wisdom of the practical suggestions that he made to me.

But more than the specifics of the letter, which basically argued for the imperative of the United States continuing to support political and economic reform in Russia, I was moved by the letter's larger message, a message that ran throughout Richard Nixon's entire public life and all of his prolific writings. President Nixon believed deeply that the United States simply could not be strong at home unless we were strong and prepared to lead abroad.

And that made a big impression on me. When I was running for President in 1992, even though there was this little sticker up on the wall of my campaign headquarters that said, "It's the economy, stupid," I always said in every speech that we had to have two objectives. We had to restore the American dream for all of our people, but we also had to make sure that we move into the next century still the strongest nation in the world and the world's greatest force for peace and freedom and democracy.

Tonight I want to talk about the vital tradition of American leadership and our responsibilities, those which Henry Kissinger mentioned so well, those which President Nixon recognized so well. Our mission especially I want to discuss: to reduce the threat of nuclear weapons.

Today, if we are going to be strong at home and lead abroad, we have to overcome what we all recognize, I think, is a dangerous and growing temptation here in our own land to focus solely on the problems we face here in America. I want to focus on the problems we face here in America—I've tried to do it for the last 2 years; I look forward to working with this new Republican-led Congress in the next 2—but not solely. There is a struggle now going on between those of us who want to carry on the tradition of American leadership and those who would advocate a new form of American isolationism, a struggle which cuts curiously across both party and ideological lines. If we're going to continue to improve the security and prosperity of all our people, then the tradition of American leadership must prevail.

We live in a moment of hope. We all know that. The implosion of communism and the explosion of the global economy have brought new freedoms to countries on every continent. Free markets are on the rise. Democracy is ascendant. The slogan says, "after victory." Today more than ever before, people across the globe do have the opportunity to reach their God-given potential. And because they do, Americans have new opportunities to reach theirs as well.

At the same time, the post-cold-war world has revealed a whole web of problems that defy quick or painless solutions: aggression of rogue states, transnational threats like overpopulation and environmental degradation, terrible ethnic conflicts, and economic dislocation. But at the heart of all these complex challenges, I believe, lies an age-old battle for power over human lives, the battle between the forces of freedom and tyranny, tolerance and repression, hope and fear. The same idea that was under attack by fascism and then by communism remains under attack today in different ways all across the world, the idea of the open society of free people.

American leadership is necessary for the tide of history to keep running our way and for our children to have the future they deserve. Yet, there are some who would choose escapism over engagement. The new isolationists oppose our efforts to expand free trade through GATT or NAFTA, through APEC and the Summit of the Americas. They reject our conviction that democracy must be nurtured with investment and support, a conviction that we are acting on from the former Soviet Union to South Africa. And some of them, being hypocritical, say that we must trumpet the rhetoric of American strength, and then at the same time, they argue against the resources we need to bring stability to the Persian Gulf or to restore democracy to Haiti or to control the spread of drugs and organized crime around the world or even to meet our most elemental obligations to the United Nations and its peacekeeping work.

The new isolationists both on the left and the right would radically revise the fundamentals of our foreign policy that have earned bipartisan support since the end of World War II. They would eliminate any meaningful role for the United Nations, which has achieved, for all of its problems, real progress around the world, from the Middle East to Africa. They would deny resources to our peacekeepers and even to our troops and, instead, squander them on Star Wars. And they would refuse aid to the fledgling democracies and to all those fighting poverty and environmental problems that can literally destroy hopes for a more democratic, more prosperous, more safe world.

The new isolationists are wrong. They would have us face the future alone. Their approach would weaken this country. And we must not let the ripple of isolationism that has been generated build into a tidal wave. If we withdraw from the world today, mark my words, we'll have to contend with the consequences of our neglect tomorrow and tomorrow and tomorrow.

This is a moment of decision for all of us without regard to our party, our background, or our accent. This is a moment of decision. The extraordinary trend toward democracy and free markets is not inevitable. And as we have seen recently, it will not proceed easily in an even, uninterrupted course. This is hard work. And at the very time when more and more countries than ever before are working to establish or shore up their own freedom in their fragile democracies, they look to us for support. At this time, the new isolationists must not be allowed to pull America out of the game after just a few hours of debate because there is a modest price attached to our leadership.

We know now, as President Nixon recognized, that there must also be limits to America's involvement in the world's problems, limits imposed by clear-headed evaluation of our fundamental interests. We cannot be the world's policemen. We cannot become involved in every problem we really care about. But the choices we make must be rooted in the conviction that America cannot walk away from its interests or its responsibilities.

That's why, from our first day in office, this administration has chosen to reach out, not retreat. From our efforts to open markets for America, to support democracy around the world, to reduce the threat posed by devastating weapons and terrorists, to maintaining the most effective fighting force in the world, we have

worked to seize the opportunities and meet the obligations of this moment.

None of this could have happened without a coalition of realists, people in both Houses of Congress and, importantly, people from both parties; people from coast to coast in our towns and cities and communities who know that the wealth and well-being of the United States depends upon our leadership abroad. Even the early leaders of our Republic, who went to great pains to avoid involvement in great power conflicts, recognized not only the potential benefits but the absolute necessity of engaging with the world.

Before Abraham Lincoln was elected President, our farmers were selling their crops overseas, we had dispatched the trade mission all the way to Japan trying to open new markets—some problems don't go away—[*laughter*]—and our Navy had already sailed every ocean. By the dawn of this century, our growing political and economic power already imposed a special duty on America to lead, a duty that was crystallized in our involvement in World War I. But after that war, we and the other great powers abandoned our responsibilities, and the forces of tyranny and hatred filled the vacuum, as is well-known.

After the Second World War, our wise leaders did not repeat that mistake. With the dawn of the nuclear age and the cold war, and with the economies of Europe and Japan in shambles, President Truman persuaded an uncertain and weary nation, yearning to shift its energies from the frontlines to the homefront, to lead the world again.

A remarkable generation of Americans created and sustained alliances and institutions, the Marshall Plan, NATO, the United Nations, the World Bank, the IMF, the things that brought half a century of security and prosperity to America, to Europe, to Japan, and to other countries all around the world. Those efforts and the special resolve and military strength of our own Nation held tyranny in check until the power of democracy, the failures of communism, and the heroic determination of people to be free consigned the cold war to history. Those successes would not have been possible without a strong, bipartisan commitment to America's leadership.

Senator Arthur Vandenberg's call to unite our official voice at the water's edge joined Republicans to Truman's doctrine. His impact was all the more powerful for his own past as an isolationist. But as Vandenberg himself said, Pearl Harbor ended isolationism for any realist.

Today, it is Vandenberg's spirit that should drive our foreign policy and our politics. The practical determination of Senators Nunn and Lugar to help Russia reduce its nuclear arsenal safely and securely, the support from Speaker Gingrich and Leader Gephardt, from Chairman Livingston and Representative Obey for aid to Russia and the Newly Independent States, the work of Senators Hatfield, Leahy, and McConnell, and Chairman Gilman, and Representative Hamilton for peace in the Middle East; the efforts of Senator Warner to restructure our intelligence: all these provide strong evidence of the continuing benefits and vitality of leadership with bipartisanship.

If we continue to lead abroad and work together at home, we can take advantage of these turbulent times. But if we retreat, we risk squandering all these opportunities and abandoning our obligations which others have entrusted to us and paid a very dear price to bring to us in this moment in history.

I know that the choice to go forward in a lot of these areas is not easy in democracies at this time. Many of the decisions that America's leaders have to make are not popular when they're made. But imagine the alternative. Imagine, for example, the tariffs and barriers that would still cripple the world trading system for years into the future if internationalists coming together across party lines had not passed GATT and NAFTA. Imagine what the Persian Gulf region would look like today if the United States had not stepped up with its allies to stop Iraqi aggression. Imagine the ongoing reign of terror and the flood of refugees at our borders had we not helped to give democracy a second chance in Haiti. Imagine the chaos that might have ensued if we had not moved to help stabilize Mexico's economy. In each case, there was substantial and sometimes overwhelming majority opinion against what needed to be done at the moment. But because we did it, the world has a better chance at peace and freedom.

But above all now, I ask you to imagine the dangers that our children and grandchildren, even after the cold war is over, still can face if we do not do everything we can to reduce the threat of nuclear arms, to curb the terrible chemical and biological weapons spreading around the world, to counter the terrorists and

criminals who would put these weapons into the service of evil. As Arthur Vandenberg asked at the dawn of the nuclear age, after a German V–1 attack had left London in flames and its people in fear, "How can there be isolation when men can devise weapons like that?"

President Nixon understood the wisdom of those words. His life spanned an era of stunning increases in humankind's destructive capacity, from the biplane to ballistic missiles, from mustard gas to mushroom clouds. He knew that the atomic age could never be won but could be lost. On any list of his foreign policy accomplishments, the giant steps he took toward reducing the nuclear threat must stand among his greatest achievements.

As President, I have acted on that same imperative. Over the past 2 years, the United States has made real progress in lifting the threat of nuclear weapons. Now, in 1995, we face a year of particular decision in this era, a year in which the United States will pursue the most ambitious agenda to dismantle and fight the spread of weapons of mass destruction since the atom was split.

We know that ours is an enormously complex and difficult challenge. There is no single policy, no silver bullet, that will prevent or reverse the spread of weapons of mass destruction. But we have no more important task. Arms control makes us not only safer, it makes us stronger. It is a source of strength. It is one of the most effective insurance policies we can write for the future of our children.

Our administration has focused on two distinct but closely connected areas, decreasing and dismantling existing weapons and preventing nations or groups from acquiring weapons of mass destruction and the means to deliver them. We've made progress on both fronts.

As the result of an agreement President Yeltsin and I reached, for the first time in a generation Russian missiles are not pointed at our cities or our citizens. We've greatly reduced the lingering fear of an accidental nuclear launch. We put into force the START I treaty with Russia that will eliminate from both our countries delivery systems that carry more than 9,000 nuclear warheads, each with the capacity to incinerate a city the size of Atlanta.

START I, negotiated by two Republican administrations and put into force by this Democratic administration, is the first treaty that requires the nuclear powers actually to reduce their strategic arsenal. Both our countries are dismantling the weapons as fast as we can. And thanks to a far-reaching verification system, including on-site inspections which began in Russia and the United States today, each of us knows exactly what the other is doing.

And again, through the far-sighted program devised by Senators Nunn and Lugar, we are helping Russia and the other Newly Independent States to eliminate nuclear forces and transport, safeguard, and destroy nuclear weapons and material.

Ironically, some of the changes that have allowed us to reduce the world's stockpile of nuclear weapons have made our nonproliferation efforts harder. The breakup of the Soviet Union left nuclear materials dispersed throughout the Newly Independent States. The potential for theft of nuclear materials, therefore, increased. We face the prospect of organized criminals entering the nuclear smuggling business. Add to this volatile mix the fact that a lump of plutonium the size of a soda can is enough to build a bomb, and the urgency of the effort to stop the spread of nuclear materials should be clear to all of us.

That's why from our first day in office we have launched an aggressive, coordinated campaign against international terrorism and nuclear smuggling. We are cooperating closely with our allies, working with Russia and the other Newly Independent States, improving security at nuclear facilities, and strengthening multilateral export controls.

One striking example of our success is Operation Sapphire, the airlift of nearly 600 kilograms of highly enriched uranium, enough to make dozens of bombs, from Kazakhstan to the United States for disposal. We've also secured agreements with Russia to reduce the uranium and plutonium available for nuclear weapons, and we're seeking a global treaty banning the production of fissile material for nuclear weapons.

Our patient, determined diplomacy also succeeded in convincing Belarus, Kazakhstan, and Ukraine to sign the Non-Proliferation Treaty and give up the nuclear weapons left on their territory when the Soviet Union dissolved. One of our administration's top priorities was to assure that these new countries would become non-nuclear nations, and now we are also achieving that goal. Because of these efforts, four potential suppliers of ballistic missiles, Russia, Ukraine,

China, and South Africa, have all agreed to control the transfer of these missiles and related technology.

Pulling back from the nuclear precipice has allowed us to cut United States defense expenditures for strategic weapons by almost two-thirds, a savings of about $20 billion a year, savings which can be shifted to vital needs such as boosting the readiness of our Armed Forces, reducing the deficit, putting more police on our own streets. By spending millions to keep or take weapons out of the hands of our potential adversaries, we are saving billions in arms costs and putting it to better use.

Now, in this year of decision, our ambition for the future must be even more ambitious. If our people are to know real lasting security, we have to redouble our arms control, nonproliferation, and antiterrorism efforts. We have to do everything we can to avoid living with the 21st century version of fallout shelters and duck-and-cover exercises, to prevent another World Trade Center tragedy.

In just 4 days we mark the 25th anniversary of the Non-Proliferation Treaty. Nothing is more important to prevent the spread of nuclear weapons than extending the treaty indefinitely and unconditionally. And that's why I've asked the Vice President to lead our delegation to the NPT conference this April and to work as hard as we can to make sure we succeed in getting that indefinite extension.

The NPT is the principal reason why scores of nations do not now possess nuclear weapons, why the doomsayers were wrong. One hundred and seventy-two nations have made NPT the most widely subscribed arms limitation treaty in history for one overriding reason: It's in their self-interest to do so. Non-nuclear-weapon states that sign on to the treaty pledge never to acquire them. Nuclear-weapon states vow not to help others obtain nuclear weapons, to facilitate the peaceful uses of atomic energy, and to pursue nuclear arms control and disarmament, commitments I strongly reaffirm, along with our determination to attain universal membership in the treaty.

Failure to extend NPT infinitely could open the door to a world of nuclear trouble. Pariah nations with rigid ideologies and expansionist ambitions would have an easier time acquiring terrible weapons, and countries that have chosen to forgo the nuclear option would then rethink their position. They would certainly be tempted to reconsider that decision.

To further demonstrate our commitment to the goals of the treaty, today I have ordered that 200 tons of fissile material, enough for thousands of nuclear weapons, be permanently withdrawn from the United States nuclear stockpile—200 tons of fissile material that will never again be used to build a nuclear weapon.

A second key goal of ours is ratifying START II. Once in effect, that treaty will eliminate delivery systems from Russian and American arsenals that carry more than 5,000 weapons. The major reductions under START I, together with START II, will enable us to reduce by two-thirds the number of strategic warheads deployed at the height of the cold war. At my urging, the Senate has already begun hearings on START II, and I am encouraged by the interest of the Senators from both parties in seeking quick action. I commend the Senate for the action taken so far, and I urge again the approval of the treaty as soon as possible.

President Yeltsin and I have already instructed our experts to begin considering the possibility, after START II is ratified, of additional reductions and limitations on remaining nuclear forces. We have a chance to further lift the nuclear cloud, and we dare not miss it.

To stop the development of new generations of nuclear weapons, we must also quickly complete negotiations on a comprehensive test ban treaty. Last month I extended a nuclear testing moratorium that I put into effect when I took office. And we revised our negotiating position to speed the conclusion of the treaty while reaffirming our determination to maintain a safe and reliable nuclear stockpile.

We will also continue to work with our allies to fully implement the agreement we reached with North Korea, first to freeze, then to dismantle its nuclear program, all under international monitoring. The critics of this agreement, I believe, are wrong. The deal does stop North Korea's nuclear program, and it does commit Pyongyang to roll it back in the years to come. I have not heard another alternative proposal that isn't either unworkable or foolhardy or one that our allies in the Republic of Korea and Japan, the nations most directly affected, would fail to support. If North Korea fulfills its commitment, the Korean Peninsula and the entire world will clearly be less threatened and more secure.

The NPT, START II, the Comprehensive Test Ban Treaty, the North Korean Agreement, they top our agenda for the year ahead. There are other critical tasks we also face if we want to make every American more secure, including winning Senate ratification of the Chemical Weapons Convention, negotiating legally binding measures to strengthen the Biological and Toxin Weapons Convention, clarifying the ABM Treaty so as to secure its viability while permitting highly effective defenses against theater missile attacks, continuing to support regional arms control efforts in the Middle East and elsewhere, and pushing for the ratification of the Convention on Conventional Weapons which, among other things, would help us to reduce the suffering caused by the tens of millions of antipersonnel mines which are plaguing millions of people all across this world.

My friends, this is a full and challenging agenda. There are many obstacles ahead. We cannot achieve it if we give in to a new isolationism. But I believe we can do no less than make every effort to complete it.

Tonight let us remember what President Nixon told the joint session of Congress when he returned from his historic trip to Moscow in 1972. He said, "We have begun to check the wasteful and dangerous spiral of nuclear arms. Let us seize the moment so that our children and the world's children can live free of the fears and free of the hatreds that have been the lot of mankind through the centuries."

Now it is within our power to realize the dream that Richard Nixon described over 20 years ago. We cannot let history record that our generation of Americans refused to rise to this challenge, that we withdrew from the world and abandoned our responsibilities when we knew better than to do it, that we lacked the energy, the vision, and the will to carry this struggle forward, the age-old struggle between hope and fear.

So let us find inspiration in the great tradition of Harry Truman and Arthur Vandenberg, a tradition that builds bridges of cooperation, not walls of isolation; that opens the arms of Americans to change instead of throwing up our hands in despair; that casts aside partisanship and brings together Republicans and Democrats for the good of the American people and the world. That is the tradition that made the most of this land, won the great battles of this century against tyranny, and secured our freedom and our prosperity.

Above all, let's not forget that these efforts begin and end with the American people. Every time we reduce the threat that has hung over our heads since the dawn of the nuclear age, we help to ensure that from the far stretches of the Aleutians to the tip of the Florida Keys, the American people are more secure. That is our most serious task and our most solemn obli-

gation. The challenge of this moment is matched only by its possibility. So let us do our duty.

Thank you very much.

NOTE: The President spoke at 9:15 p.m. at the Mayflower Hotel. In his remarks, he referred to Tricia Nixon Cox, daughter of former President Richard Nixon; John Taylor, Director, Richard Nixon Library and Birthplace; and former Secretary of State Henry Kissinger.

Remarks on Senate Action on the Balanced Budget Amendment
March 2, 1995

Good afternoon. I have a statement I'd like to make about the vote on the balanced budget amendment and what happens now. And I look forward to taking your questions tomorrow. We're going to have a press conference then, and so I'll just read the statement now.

The balanced budget amendment has been defeated because Republicans could not provide enough Democratic Senators with the simple guarantee that Social Security would be protected in any balanced budget amendment procedures.

Let me begin by simply congratulating the people on both sides of this issue who argued with great depth of conviction and sincerity and people on both sides who want to bring down the deficit and eliminate unnecessary spending but who differed on the consequences and the necessity of using an amendment to the Constitution to do it.

The question we must all face now is, what happens tomorrow? We all know that there is no real requirement of a constitutional amendment to reduce unnecessary Government spending and to reduce the deficit. For 12 years before I took office, Washington allowed the deficit to explode. Organized interests did well, but the public interest and the future suffered. Washington, during this entire period, spent too much time on rhetoric and gimmicks and too little time making hard, smart, specific budgetary decisions.

Then, just 2 years ago, Democrats acting alone had the courage to pass the largest deficit reduction package in the history of the United States, now over $600 billion. Our annual deficit

at that time was about 5 percent of our income. It has now dropped to just over half that and is scheduled to go down much lower.

A month ago, we added to that historic deficit reduction with a budget that cuts spending, cuts the deficit even more, and provides for modest tax cuts to the middle class for education and childrearing. I am as ready as ever to work with the Congress to make further reductions in the deficit. As I have said repeatedly, it must come in the context of responsible health care reform because it is only the health care costs of the country that are going up in our budget. All other costs are flat or declining.

Now the process of reducing the deficit while investing in our future must go forward. There is a legal process for doing just that. In 1993, though I had never before been a part of Government in Washington, we presented our budget plan only 27 days into our administration. It has now been 57 days since the Republicans took control of the Congress. And even though their leadership has been here many, many more years, they have still not presented their budget. We passed the budget resolution for our plan before the legal deadline of April 15th. Now they must follow that process as well, telling the American people how they are going to keep the promises of their contract on balancing the budget and paying for their tax cuts by the legal deadline of April 15th.

When the Republicans do present their budget plan, we will carefully consider it. We owe them that, and we must. I have shown my commitment to reducing the deficit and to investing in our future. And I will continue to do that.

I believe we can reduce the deficit without compromising our commitment to education and to our children and without undermining our commitment to our seniors in Social Security and basic Medicare needs. I believe we can do that. I believe we can do it while continuing our commitment to provide 100,000 police officers for this country, a program that is already fully paid for by spending cuts. We do not need to allow any of those things to be used as a bank to cut taxes for upper income Americans.

There are other things we can do right now, things that I agree with the Republican leadership on, and let me just close with this one.

Let us now immediately take up in the Senate the line-item veto, and let's pass it. We can cut millions, tens of millions, hundreds of millions of dollars in spending with the line-item veto. So I urge the Senate to proceed immediately to take that up. And I will work as hard as I can to persuade members of both parties to support it and to continue the important work of reducing the deficit.

Thank you.

NOTE: The President spoke at 3:17 p.m. in the Briefing Room at the White House.

Letter to Congressional Leaders on Child Support Enforcement
March 2, 1995

Dear Mr. Chairman:

I am writing to reiterate my firm belief that Congress must pass tough child support enforcement measures as part of welfare reform. When absent parents don't provide support, the inevitable result is more welfare, more poverty, and more difficult times for our children. It is essential that all Americans understand that if they parent a child, they will be held responsible for nurturing and providing for that child.

I am doing everything in my power to crack down on child support enforcement. In 1993, we collected a record $9 billion in child support—a 12 percent increase over the previous year. Last week, I signed an Executive Order to ensure that federal employees who owe child support live up to their responsibilities as parents, and that the federal government will do its utmost to help find parents with delinquent child support claims. Our welfare reform plan included the toughest child support measures ever proposed. If absent parents aren't paying child support, we will garnish their wages, suspend their licenses, track them across state lines, and if necessary, make them work off what they owe.

Parental responsibility should not become a partisan issue. At the bipartisan national Working Session on Welfare Reform that I hosted at Blair House, Republican and Democratic leaders from around the country and every level of government agreed that we should enact the toughest child support enforcement measures possible.

I hope the committee will not shy away from its responsibilities on this issue. A number of bills similar to our plan could serve as the foundation for any effort to reform child support—including the one offered by Representatives Barbara Kennelly, Nancy Johnson, and others. Critical elements include denying welfare benefits to any unwed mother who does not cooperate fully in identifying the father, powerful measures for tracking interstate cases, and serious penalties—including license suspension, and if necessary, requiring work—for parents who refuse to pay what they owe. We must also include both the performance incentives and resources states need to do the job right.

It is time to get serious about child support in this country. I look forward to working with Congress to get it done.

With best wishes,

Sincerely,

WILLIAM J. CLINTON

NOTE: Identical letters were sent to Bill Archer, chairman, and Sam Gibbons, ranking member, House Committee on Ways and Means. An original was not available for verification of the content of this letter. The Executive order of February 27 is listed in Appendix D at the end of this volume.

The President's News Conference
March 3, 1995

The President. Good afternoon. Ladies and gentlemen, now that the vote on the balanced budget amendment has passed, it is time for Congress to go forward to write a disciplined budget that brings the deficit down, cuts unnecessary Government spending, and continues to invest in our future.

Two years ago, 27 days after I became President, I presented such a budget to the Congress. It has succeeded in reducing our deficit by over $600 billion, while still increasing our investment in our children, in education, and in our economic growth.

As of today it has been 58 days since the new Republican majority took office. Congress has a deadline for passing a budget resolution of April the 15th. The American people now are entitled to see this work go forward. When the Congress proposes their budget and passes their resolution, of course, I will work with them. As I have said repeatedly, we can get more deficit reduction in responsible health care reform, but I learned last year that that is clearly something we must do working together with both parties.

The debate that is going on in Washington today is about more, obviously, than simply the deficit and the budget. It is also about the role of Government. And you can see it running through every issue, from the laws being debated now in the Congress to the question of the rescission legislation before the Congress. The old Washington view, I think it's fair to say, is that the Federal Government could provide solutions to America's problems. The Republican contract view reflects in many cases an outright hostility to governmental action, although in some cases a curious willingness to increase the Federal Government's control over our daily lives.

My view, what has loosely been called the new Democratic view or the New Covenant view, is to be skeptical of Government but to recognize that it has a role in our lives and a partnership role to play.

We have made the Government smaller. We have given more power to States and localities and to private citizens. Our proposals would further accelerate those trends. We have, as you learned here in this room just a few days ago, been working for months on a serious effort to reduce the burden of unnecessary regulation.

But we believe Government has important work to do, to expand opportunity, to give people the tools they need to make the most of their own lives, to enhance our security. That's why we support adding 100,000 police. That's why we support more affordable college loans. That's why we supported the family leave bill. That's why I support the minimum wage legislation now before Congress and why I do not want to reduce our investment in education in our future.

The Republicans now have proposed to cut education, nutritional help for mothers and schoolchildren, antidrug efforts in our schools, and other things which to me appear to target children in order to pay for tax cuts for upper income Americans. I do not believe that that is consistent with our interests as we build America into the 21st century and we move into this new global economy.

So my job, it seems to me, is to continue to push my view, what I believe is the essence of the New Covenant: more opportunity, more responsibility; reform welfare but don't punish people, require work. This is the sort of thing we need more of. And I look forward to this debate. I think it's healthy. I think it's good for the American people.

And I would like to begin now by answering your questions. Helen [Helen Thomas, United Press International].

Senator Ben Nighthorse Campbell

Q. Mr. President, did you try to talk Senator Campbell out of jumping ship? What does it portend for the Democratic Party, and what does it mean in terms of your leadership?

The President. Well, I talked to him this morning because he called the White House and said he wanted to talk to me. And so I called him. And we had a good conversation, and he pointed out that he had voted with me over 80 percent of the time in the last 2 years, that he essentially supported our economic policies, our education policies, and our social policies, and that he would not change that. It was obvious to me that there were some Colorado-specific factors at work. I wish he hadn't done it. I think it was a mistake. But I hope he will continue to vote in the way he has in the past.

Q. Do you think there will be more defectors?

The President. No. I have no reason to believe it. He'd been talking about this for some time, we had heard, because of—apparently because of some things that happened out there that I'm not fully familiar with. I wish he hadn't done it, but it's done. All I can do now is hope that he'll keep voting the way he has the last 2 years. If he does, it will make a contribution to moving the country forward.

Russia

Q. Mr. President, there are growing strains in relations with Russia over the crackdown in Chechnya and the planned sale of nuclear technology to Iran. Does U.S. aid to Moscow give us any leverage on these problems? Is it time to consider an alternative to Boris Yeltsin, as Bob Dole says, that you've got too much invested in? And have you finally decided on the timing of a summit with Mr. Yeltsin?

The President. The answer to the last question is, no, we have not determined the exact date. As you know, we committed to meet with each other on a rotating and regular basis, so I have to sustain that commitment in the first part of this year. He asked me to come at the time they are celebrating the 50th anniversary of the end of World War II. There are some scheduling complications here. We're working through it. It shouldn't be long before you have an answer.

Let me respond to the second set of questions. First of all, I don't think it's fair to say the United States or that our administration has a Yeltsin-centered policy, or that it is time for the United States to determine to deal with someone else. What we want is a democratic Russia which continues to support reform within the country and respects the borders of its neighbors. That is what we want. We want a Russia that helps us to reduce further the nuclear threat in the world. Those are our fundamental interests.

Boris Yeltsin has been elected the President of a country that has a Constitution and a democratic system. He has a term of office. He is fulfilling that term of office. I think it would be curious, indeed, if the United States were to say that we have a separate set of rules for these new democracies: When things don't go the way we want or they follow some policy we don't like, well, then, we decide that we should invest ourselves in some other person.

We should support the elected representatives of the people, who are duly produced by constitutional judgments in a democracy. That's what I believe, and that's what I'm doing. When we differ with Russia, we say so. When they differ with us, they say so. But on the whole, let's not forget that a remarkable amount of progress has been made in that country and a remarkable amount of progress has been made in our relationship. They have no troops in Eastern Europe. They have no troops in the Baltics. They have helped us to implement START I. We are working on ratification of START II. We are working across a whole range of issues.

Do we have differences with them? Of course we do. But on balance, this relationship is one that is in the interest of the United States to continue to support.

Brit [Brit Hume, ABC News].

Social Security

Q. You indicated yesterday agreement with the Democratic Senators who balked on the balanced budget amendment because of their objections to the current and continuing practice of borrowing surplus Social Security funds to offset the deficit. In light of your attitude on that, sir, I wonder if you're prepared to take a lead on that issue by proposing that that practice be stopped and by revising, if necessary, your budget and your budget projections to take account of the change.

The President. Well, wait a minute, there are two issues in which that works. There are two ways in which the Social Security thing works. The first is that we clearly have been using payroll taxes for 12 years now, long before I ever came here, to minimize the size of the deficit exclusive of the payroll tax, so that from 1983 forward, previous Democratic Congresses and Republican Presidents made judgments that it was better and politically more palatable to tax payroll than income, even though it's a burden on working people and small businesses.

The other issue, however, Brit, to be fair, was that were we going to cut Social Security benefits to reduce the deficit and count that against deficit reduction. And that's what I have been emphasizing. That is, if Social Security is producing a surplus today as it is and if it's going to have to be reformed on its own terms for the 21st century when all the baby boomers retire, then I did not believe it was right for us to effect cuts in Social Security simply to reduce the deficit. I do not think that is right. I think that is wrong. So that was my position.

I have presented my budget. I stand behind my budget. I see that there are some specific cuts the Republicans have suggested that I also would think about, I see in their rescission package. But I am going to wait now until they do their constitutional duty, which is to present a budget, which is something that has not happened. Then I will work with them.

The key on this is not to reduce Social Security benefits. The key is to reduce health care costs.

John [John Palmer, NBC News]. Welcome back.

Affirmative Action

Q. Thank you, sir. I'd like to ask you a question, if I might, about affirmative action. I know your administration is now reviewing all of those affirmative action regulations, but there's some concern that this might be the prelude to a backing off of those policies. In fact, Jesse Jackson earlier this week expressed the opinion that maybe if you did, he might even run against you. But my question, really, on that issue is, what about the many Americans who really feel they have been punished by affirmative action? And I'd like to get your comments on that.

The President. Let me tell you about the review I've ordered and comment on the affirmative action thing. First of all, our administration is against quotas and guaranteed results, and I have been throughout my public career. I have always been for trying to help people develop their capacities so they could fully participate. And I have supported things—when I was a Governor, I supported, for example, minority scholarship programs—in my public life, I have done that.

I want to make a couple of comments here. First, I have asked for a review of all the Federal Government's so-called affirmative action programs because I think it's important that we analyze, number one, what they do and what—a lot of times people mean different things when they use affirmative action. For example, I take it there is virtually no opposition to the affirmative action programs that are the most successful in our country, which are the ones adopted by the United States military, which have not resulted in people of inferior quality or ability getting preferential treatment but have resulted in an intense effort to develop the capacities of everybody who joins the military so they can fully participate and contribute as much as possible and has resulted in the most integrated institution in our society.

So I want to know what these programs are, exactly. I want to know whether they are working. I want to know whether there is some other way we can reach any objective without giving a preference by race or gender in some of these programs. Those are the three questions we need to ask.

And let me make a general observation. I asked myself when this debate started, what have we done since I've been President that has most helped minorities? And I think that—I would say that the things we have done that have most helped are things that have benefited all people who needed them: expanding the Head Start program; expanding the college loan program; expanding the earned-income tax credit, the working families tax credit which has given an average tax cut of $1,000 to families with incomes under $25,000; the empowerment zones—and one of them, one of the empowerment zones went to an all-white area in Kentucky, but the disproportionate impact was on people who'd been left behind in our cities; and one thing that the rescission package would take away, the community development banks—which I think would be a terrible mistake—which is designed to empower people through the free enterprise system to make the most of their own lives.

So I would say to you, where we can move ahead based on need we ought to move forward, and we shouldn't move backward. There's still a lot of people who aren't living up to their capacity in this country, and it's hurting the rest of us. And so, I want this analysis to finish. I will then make a decision in a prompt way, and I'll tell the American people what I think, and I will proceed to act in the context of the Government.

Meanwhile, I urge all of you to read the history—in light of the other, the political comments you made—to read the history of how these affirmative action programs got started and who was on what side when they began. It's very interesting to go back through the last 25 years and see all the twists and turns.

The American people want an end to discrimination. They want discrimination, where it exists, to be punished. They don't want people to have an unfair break that is unwarranted. We can work this out, and I'm determined to do it.

Rita [Rita Braver, CBS News].

Balanced Budget Amendment and 1996 Presidential Election

Q. Mr. President, it seems like every day another Republican is jumping into the Presidential race. It also seems like every day we are reading about your election campaign and who is in and who is out. I wonder if you could tell us a little bit about the kind of organization that you're putting together.

And I also wanted to ask you about a comment that Senator Dole made yesterday when he was asked about why he didn't meet the Democrats' demands to take Social Security out of the fight over the balanced budget amendment. He said, "You have a President who has abdicated his responsibility. If you had a real President down there, we might think about it." What's your response to that in the context of his Presidential aspirations?

The President. My response to that is that Senator Dole's been part of Washington for 30 years, and he hasn't always been in the minority. And when I got here, policies supported by his Presidents and deficits run up under Republican administrations—remember, they had this town 20 of the last 26 years; they were making all these proposals—had given this country a $4 trillion debt, quadrupled—quadrupled—in the 12 years of Republican ascendancy.

And since I've been President, we've got a lower deficit, a lower unemployment rate, a lower inflation rate, a higher growth rate. We have cut the size of the Federal Government, something they did not do, and still found a way to invest more in the education of our children. And I might add, we have expanded trade more than they did, supported democracy, and supported a reduction of the nuclear threat. So we've got a safer world and a stronger economy. Now, I think that's a pretty good record, and I'll be glad to put it up against all that kind of name-calling and all of the stuff they want to do.

But you know, what I really want to say is, we've got to stop all this. It's March of 1995. I mean, I was a Governor, and I was at a severe disadvantage, and I didn't even announce for President until October of '91. I mean, we can't have everybody all torn up and upset about playing politics here for the next 6, 7 months. We've got a lot of work to do, and I think we should relax and do it.

I will, in an appropriate way, organize and proceed with my own efforts, but I've already given you my speech. We've got more peace, more prosperity, and fewer problems than we had when I showed up. And meanwhile, I'd like to work with them to continue to make progress. We can do things together.

And I think that that Social Security remark is—you know, they could have had the balanced budget amendment if they had done what the Democrats wanted on Social Security, and they chose the political issue instead. That was their judgment. They made their judgment, so they shouldn't blame someone else for a decision that they made. It was a decision they made, not me.

Q. Are you putting together an organization, though, yourself now?

The President. Well, I'm not actively involved as they are, but I will organize and proceed. As I told you, I intend to run for reelection. But I think—I can see right now, every day, everybody that wants to run for this job is going to be trying to make some remark or some move that runs everybody else halfway up the flagpole. And we've got enough politics in this town on a regular basis without injecting that into it. I wish—I want everybody to relax, take a deep breath, and go back to work. Let's try to do something for the American people for a year, and then we can have an election. We'll have plenty of time for the politics.

Go ahead.

Value of the Dollar

Q. Mr. President, are you concerned that the value of the dollar is falling again? And would you like to see the Fed do more to boost it?

The President. You know, one of the things I've learned since I've been here is that anything I say on this subject is wrong. [*Laughter*] So the Treasury Department is taking appropriate action today, and I don't think I should say anything else.

Go ahead, Mara [Mara Liasson, National Public Radio].

Affirmative Action

Q. Just another question on affirmative action, Mr. President. When you announced your review you said, we have to stop defending things that are not defensible. Do you think that rules that mandate a certain percentage of Federal contracts be set aside for minority firms—are those still necessary, and isn't that guaranteeing results, the kind of thing you say you're now opposed to?

The President. Well, I want to look at how they're implemented. For one thing, if you look at the rules and what they mean, it's difficult to draw a conclusion about whether they even do what they were supposed to do in the first place. But I want—I will make comments—I am almost done with this review, and I will make comments when I finish about what I think we should do. And then I will do whatever it is that I can do within my executive authority to go forward.

I do not—I want to continue to fight discrimination where it exists. I want to continue to give people a chance to develop their capacities where they need help. I want us to emphasize need-based programs where we can because they work better and have a bigger impact and generate broader support. But let me finish what we're doing here, and then I will try to answer all the details.

Q. Mr. President——

The President. Yes, Sarah [Sarah McClendon, McClendon News].

Teen Pregnancy

Q. Sir, we hear a lot of talk these days about these teenage pregnant women, most of them are poor and black and that sort of thing. Well, that's peanuts, the cost of that program, compared to what we are spending on arms sales around the world, making wars, and then we have to go and clean up when the famines that come along afterwards. And we're buying untested weapons. Why don't we work on the billions of war and have a little peace?

The President. Well, we should do that, but we should also work on reducing teen pregnancy.

Go ahead.

Mexico

Q. Mr. President, Mexico is going through very difficult times. The Republicans are asking for more and more information from you on the Mexican crisis. How do you see the election situation right now? And do you think things are working there or——

The President. Well, I think—first of all, it seems that President Zedillo is working very hard to try to develop a program, an economic program that will balance two interests: his desire to continue to be able to make Mexico attractive to investors outside the country, which is necessary for the long-term growth, and the need to keep Mexico strong enough and responsive enough to the domestic business interests and the working people of the country.

This is a difficult period. I think everyone would admit who has worked on this that the problems turned out to be more difficult and of long—more duration, more thorny than had originally been thought back in December and January. But I believe that he's moving in the right direction. And Mexico plainly has moved toward more democracy, more openness, and more market economics. And I did what I did because I thought it was good for America's jobs and America's long-term interest. I still believe that. And I believe it's in our interest to support that movement toward democracy and openness throughout Latin America, beginning with Mexico.

Deborah [Deborah Mathis, Gannett News Service].

Affirmative Action

Q. Mr. President, forgive me for pressing you on this, but if I'm not mistaken, you've always been in favor of affirmative action, and in fact, you have practiced it. Why now the hesitation?

The President. I have always—that's right. I'm glad you asked. I have always practiced it. But let's look at how I practiced it. Look at my appointments to the Federal bench, ones for which, I might add, I've been regularly and roundly attacked for trying to achieve diversity here in this community. I read something in the paper about once a month, people jumping on me because I've appointed more women and more minorities to the Federal bench than my predecessors combined at this point in our terms—my last three predecessors combined. And oh, by the way, they sometimes say, his appointees also have the highest rating from the American Bar Association of the last three Presidents.

I have practiced affirmative action here the way that I perceive the United States military has practiced it. I have made an extra effort to look for qualified candidates who could serve with distinction and make a contribution to this country and make the Federal bench reflective of the American population. I have not done it with any quota system in mind, and I have not guaranteed anybody a job. I have made an extra effort to do that.

The military starts before that. They have made an extra effort to develop the capacities of people who come to them with great raw ability, but maybe a disadvantaged background. Is that wrong? I don't think it is. And I'm not backing off of that.

The question is—here is the narrow question—the question is: If we're not for quotas in results, and we are for developing everybody's capacities, what do we do with all those rules and regulations and laws that really are in a gray area, that are really in a gray area where there is, let's say, a minority scholarship or a contracting set-aside that Mara asked about, that really is often got around because of the way they are written? I want to review those. I do not want to see us stop trying to develop the abilities of all Americans. I do not want to see us move away from trying to concentrate our resources in the areas of greatest need.

But I would say again, I think most minorities have been helped most by the programs in this country that have been targeted toward broad-based needs. And ironically, if you go back to the beginning of this whole affirmative action debate, it started in the late sixties, and many civil rights leaders at the time argued against affirmative action programs because they thought we'd wind up in the debate we are now having 25 years later.

I think we need to look at the programs, look at the facts, and ask the questions I just asked: How does this work? Is it fair? Is it necessary? Is there an alternative way to achieve the objective? But in terms of taking aggressive initiatives to develop the capacities of people, should we keep doing that? You bet we should. How should we do it in the law, that's the question.

George [George Condon, Copley News Service].

Illegal Immigration

Q. Mr. President, in the past you have bragged on Operation Gatekeeper. Governor Pete Wilson last week said that was a failure,

and the numbers from the INS seem to back that up. Are you rethinking in any way your approach to——

The President. How can you say that? Because——

Q. In the first 5 months.

The President. Yes, but what happened was, we had big problems in immigration when the Mexican economy started to go down, as I told everyone. But we have a lot of evidence, too, from what has been done in El Paso and in other places that we are stopping more people.

I think the key is—my answer is, we need even more border guards, we need to accelerate the deportation of people who have been found through the criminal justice system or otherwise who are illegal aliens, and we need to accelerate our ability to find people primarily in the workplace. And if we do that—that's part of the budget that I have submitted to the Congress. And if we do that, we will reduce the number of illegal immigrants, and we will accelerate rapidly the pace by which we are deporting those who have come here illegally.

So my answer to Governor Wilson is, the problem got bigger during the last 5 months because of the problems in Mexico, but we have made a difference. That's my first answer. My second answer is, it's a lot more than was done before I got here by the previous administration and by the United States Senate when he was a part of it. So I want him, instead of criticizing me for doing more than they did, he ought to keep working with us so we can do even more. That's what my budget does; I hope the Congress will adopt it.

Yes.

Administration Ethics

Q. Mr. President, you have an independent counsel investigating yourself and your wife. You have another independent counsel investigating your former Agriculture Secretary. The Justice Department is soon about to make decisions on whether independent counsels should investigate your Secretaries of Commerce, Housing, and Transportation.

Two questions: One, if any of those three are going to be subject to an independent counsel investigation, would you like to see them resign to take care of that? And two, combining the independent counsels with those others, like Webster Hubbell and Roger Altman, who have resigned after some ethical problems, how can you explain what's happened to your administration after you came into office promising the most ethical administration in history?

The President: Well, first of all, let's look at each one of them. The only people—Roger Altman resigned even though the finding was that he had violated no law and no rule of ethics. And he made a major contribution to this country. Let's just look at that.

Secondly, all the other examples—Secretary Espy was the single person who resigned because the subject of his activity involved things he had done as Secretary of Agriculture, which, I might add, in the aggregate, amounted to a few thousand dollars, all of which he has reimbursed, in return for which he got a special counsel with 33 lawyers and a historian.

All these other things—including mine—I would remind you, I am the first President in history ever to have a special counsel involving activities that have nothing to do with my work as President, nothing to do with the campaign for President, that all predated that, and that arose when there had not been a single, solitary serious assertion that I had done anything illegal. But I said, "Fine, we'll look into it. If it makes people feel better and to have more confidence, I'll be glad to do it."

We live in a time now where the first thing people call for is a special counsel. I don't know if you saw Susan Estrich's article in USA Today yesterday, but I commend it to all of you to read. I mean, we really have to ask ourselves whether we are creating a climate here in which a lot of people will be reluctant to serve. I saw the U.S. News essay on Dr. Foster. I commend them for that. It was a—I was quite moved by it. Now that I say it, the rest of you will probably jump on them since I said it. [*Laughter*]

But I'm just telling you, I think—no one has accused me of abusing my authority here as President. Everybody knows that I have tougher ethics rules than any previous President. For example, when we had the controversy where the Speaker misspoke about the drug usage in the White House and we found out that it was absolutely wrong, we found out that I have much, much tougher rules than the Congress does on random drug testing for employees, for example. So if you look at the rules and you look at the facts instead of the number of investigations, then there's no way to control that under that new law. All you've got to do is

have a certain number of Members of Congress ask, and then it triggers this prospect.

I want to just point out, again, if you look at the work that people have done in their public capacity since I have been President, you would be hard-pressed to cite examples that constitute abuse of authority.

Secondly, I have continued to argue for lobbying reform and campaign finance reform, two things which I see are still apparently very low on the priority list of the new Congress. If you want to clean Washington up, what we ought to do is to reform the lobbying rules. That's the best thing we can do.

START II

Q. Earlier this week, the Central Intelligence Agency went up to the Hill and said that the prospects for the START II, the Strategic Arms Reduction Treaty, in the Russian Duma are getting dimmer every day. Number one, I'd like to know if you agree with that intelligence estimate. Number two, have you conferred with President Yeltsin about what could be done to salvage the treaty in Russia, or what President Yeltsin could do to salvage it, if, in fact, it fails on the initial vote?

The President. Well, first of all, ever since we started dealing with the former Communist countries with elected Parliaments, both they and we have been hearing how our Congress or their Parliaments wouldn't take the next step, whatever the next step was. I remember all the people who said there was no way in the world we'd get the Ukrainian Rada to ratify the Non-Proliferation Treaty. And there have been all these sort of gloomy predictions about what this Congress would do. But in the end, the democracies normally wind up doing the right thing and moving forward on these issues.

Therefore, do I believe that eventually the Duma will adopt START II? I do. And that's one of the reasons that I think it's important that we continue to engage with Russia and I continue to work with the Yeltsin administration and with President Yeltsin to try to get things like that done.

But look, look at all the things that have happened here in the last 2 years. It's not predictable what parliamentary bodies are going to do in these tumultuous times. But do I think we'll prevail on that? I do.

Karen [Karen Ball, New York Daily News].

Whitewater Investigation

Q. Following on what you said about independent counsels, Newt Gingrich has called for Democrats attacking him on ethics to pay his legal bills and reimburse the Government if the charges prove groundless. You face $2 million in legal bills. Whitewater is probably going to cost taxpayers at least $5 million. Following on what Gingrich says, do you think Republicans should have to pay for this if Whitewater is groundless?

The President. You know, I don't want to personalize it. I really tried to just cooperate and go along with this thing and not talk about it at all. I've told the American people I didn't do anything wrong, and I've told the truth. We'll just see what happens. But I don't want to personalize it.

What I meant to say is that, looking forward, what I think we should ask ourselves is, is this really the way we should be running a democracy, the way this operates. But I don't want to—anything I say about my own situation I think is not helpful. I think that I should be treated—I don't want to be involved in it that way. I want to think about what's good for America after the Whitewater investigation is over. Let's look forward. Forget about me; let's let this thing unfold that involves me in an established way.

Yes.

Bosnia and Croatia

Q. Mr. President, if we could come back to foreign policy. Are you prepared to send American troops to Croatia at the end of the month to help in the withdrawal of U.N. peacekeepers if President Tudjman sticks to his deadline? And can you foresee beyond that any circumstances in which you would keep those troops there or expand the number of American ground troops in the region to help avert the wider war that so many people fear?

The President. Well, the United States has sent troops, as you know, to Macedonia as part of the United Nations effort to try to limit the scope of the Bosnian War. And we have committed to help get the U.N. peacekeepers out of Bosnia if the UNPROFOR mission in Bosnia collapses. We have done everything we could do to persuade President Tudjman not to suspend the U.N. mission in Croatia because we fear that it will lead to a wider war there. We

feel a strong responsibility to our U.N. and many of them our NATO allies as well, to try to help them, and we are trying to work through whatever plans would be appropriate to give that sort of assistance. But I do not foresee— I have worked very hard to avoid the long-term commitment of American ground troops in that region, and I will continue to do that.

I think that this is something that has to be handled through the United Nations. I have offered NATO support, and I have been willing to work with our allies who were willing to put their troops on the ground there because they thought it was an area in which Europe ought to take the lead. And that's generally the system I think we should continue to observe.

Yes.

Health Care Reform

Q. Mr. President, you mentioned health care reform yesterday and again today as one way you could achieve deficit reduction. I wonder if we're going to see any concrete proposals from you in this legislative session on health care reform.

The President. Yes, I think you will see concrete proposals in this legislative session.

Q. From you?

The President. From me, yes. But I want to do it, insofar as I can, with the Congress. As I said in the State of the Union Address, I think last time I bit off more than I could chew. They saw that, and then they decided to back away from their proposals and just take the political position they would kill anything we propose. And I think I made a mistake, but I think they did, too. And what I hope we ought to do now—what I think we ought to do now, is to figure out a way to help Americans get more affordable health care and to solve this problem. And if we do it in the right way, we will continue to substantially lower the costs of Medicare and Medicaid in the out-years.

Let me say something that almost nobody has noticed in this budget I presented, and that is that this budget reflects $94 billion less in health care costs over the next 5 years than last year's budget. Why? Because of the increasing use of managed care in the Medicare program, because more seniors are voluntarily going into managed care programs in Medicaid, and because of the general efforts in both the private and in the public sector to bring down health care costs. Now, the reason it hasn't reduced the deficit $94 billion is that interest rate increases have added to the cost of carrying the debt.

But we are lowering the cost of health care from what it was when I took office. And we can do that some more in a responsible, fair way. But we've got to do that together. I mean, we just—you know the Congress is a Republican majority Congress; I can't pass a health care bill unless they want to work with me on it.

Q. Are you saying you'll only do it with them then? I mean, are you inviting them to work on——

The President. No, what I'm saying is, I've been talking to Senators and Congressmen, House Members, in both parties for some weeks, and I'm very flexible about when to put what out and all that, but the point is, unless we have some agreement about how we're going to proceed, we won't pass a bill. If we do pass a bill, we can both help to make progress on health care for the American people, which is a thing they really want, and we can lower our future costs in health care.

First Lady's Travel

Q. Mr. President, Mrs. Clinton is about to visit a number of foreign countries, and I wonder, is there a diplomatic element to this at your behest, or what is the purpose of her visits, particularly to the South Asian nations?

The President. Well, she has been invited to go there, number one. And number two, I believe that the United States has given insufficient attention for some years now to South Asia; India has the biggest middle class in the world, for example. And there are two reasons for this. One is our historic ties to India were strained during the cold war because of what the geopolitics of that area did to their foreign policy. And secondly, there are these thorny problems between India and Pakistan which we have sought to help resolve through several administrations and without success. And it's not something that I can do right now. But we had a number of Cabinet members going there. She was invited, and I thought she ought to go. I encouraged her to go.

The trip to Copenhagen, she was invited to speak to the nongovernmental organizations about issues being dealt with at Copenhagen that she's been involved with for 25 years, and I was very glad she did that.

Wolf [Wolf Blitzer, Cable News Network].

Foreign Policy

Q. Mr. President, a two-part question on international issues. When you attack the new isolationists, specifically, who do you have in mind, by name? [*Laughter*]. And the second part of the question, as you know, the French Government has accused five CIA agents listed as diplomats in France of activities incompatible with their diplomatic status, which is a euphemism for espionage. Are they telling the truth? What does this mean?

The President. Let me take the second question first. I believe that we have resolved this matter with France, and as a practical matter, I have followed the policy of every President not to publicly discuss intelligence-related questions.

Secondly, I just got through saying, I think we're getting into too much name-calling in Washington, and I don't want to exacerbate that. I made it very clear what I said in my speech at the Nixon Center the other night. There are understandable tendencies all across the world— the gentleman just asked me the question about the Russian Duma—there are understandable tendencies all across the world to look inward in these democracies and in all countries where popular pressure is saying, "Let's shut the world out. This is a complicated world. We don't have control over all this. We've got enough problems here at home. We've got to walk away from them." And they are working on people, everywhere in the world. They are working on people here in the United States.

I do not want us to become either economically or politically isolated. That's what I mean by isolationist. Therefore, as you know, I believe that since we have no intention of just closing our borders—we're getting all the downside of global trade in terms of having people in vulnerable jobs being dislocated. Expanding trade gives us the upside, gives us the chance to win, to promote democracy and stability abroad and to get more high-wage jobs here. I think it would be a bad mistake for us to restrict the power of me—this President or any future President in peacekeeping, in all those areas.

So you know who's on what side on all these issues, and you know how I feel about it. And I don't think that us getting into name-calling will further that.

Peter [Peter Maer, Westwood One] and then Anne [Anne Compton, ABC News].

Russia

Q. Mr. President, returning to the issue of Russia, given the continued fighting in Chechnya and the apparent stall in Russian reforms, can you give us some measure of your confidence level in Boris Yeltsin or your lack of confidence? And how do you read his failure to conclude this situation in Chechnya?

The President. I think it's obviously a very difficult problem for him. And I think that— I hesitate to comment on it in great detail because I'm not sure I know everything there is to know about it. We and every other country in the world outside Russia and all of his allies— I know Chancellor Kohl and many others in Europe have said, "You ought to slow down the fighting. You ought to bring an end to the violence. You ought to bring the OSCE in there to be observers, to make sure there are no human rights violations, and this thing ought to be negotiated."

And so, the ambivalence between the military solution and the political solution and the fact that you obviously have 1.2 million or however many there are of very determined people in Chechnya with a decades-long history of resentment against the central government makes this thing just sort of hanging there. It's like a thorn in their flesh.

Now, I believe that he has made the major policy decisions there. I think he is in control of the policy there. And I have dealt directly with him in urging a change and a moderation of policy there, and I will continue to do that. My confidence level in him is strong. If you ask me do I think he is still the effective President of Russia, and is he making those decisions, yes, that's what I believe is the case.

I'll take one more. Anne, and then I'll go.

1996 Presidential Election

Q. Back on politics, you say it's too early for you to become consumed by reelection talk. It might not be too early for someone within the Democratic Party who might choose to challenge you. Do you expect a challenge from within your own party, and do you think that would be destructive for Democrats?

The President. I don't expect it. I don't not expect it. I don't know what will happen. I hope there won't be one. I think it would be a mistake for the Democratic Party. And again I would say, what would the issue be? What would the issue be? The unemployment rate is lower. The inflation rate is lower. The growth rate is higher. The world is more peaceful. We have a slew of problems out there. We can stay here for 3 or 4 hours and talk about it. There are a bunch of problems out there. The country is in better shape than it was 2 years ago.

I get tickled—I laugh every time I see one of the Republican—when the Republicans have a big fundraiser and they give them a bunch of money because a lot of them are angry that we raised income taxes on the top 1.2 percent of people to bring the deficit down. But I'll bet you almost everybody going to those fundraisers for those Republicans is doing better under our economic policies in the last 2 years than they were before.

So my job is just to do the best job I can, reward work, support families and communities, offer opportunity, demand responsibility in these changes, and keep moving forward. That's what I'm going to do. And this is a difficult, tumultuous time, but this country is doing better. And I am determined to keep fighting for the interests and the values of middle class people. And I'm going to let the election take care of itself, as I believe it will.

Thank you.

NOTE: The President's 88th news conference began at 1 p.m. in Room 450 of the Old Executive Office Building. In his remarks, he referred to civil rights leader Jesse Jackson, Surgeon General nominee Henry Foster, President Franjo Tudjman of Croatia, President Boris Yeltsin of Russia, and Chancellor Helmut Kohl of Germany.

Statement on the Death of Howard Hunter
March 3, 1995

Hillary and I were saddened to learn of the death of Howard Hunter and we extend our deepest sympathy to his family. President Hunter provided great moral and spiritual leadership to all Mormons as well as the entire country. His message of the need for greater kindness, gentleness, tolerance, and forgiveness is an important one for all of us.

Remarks at the National Public Radio Reception
March 3, 1995

Thank you very much, Carl. I have all these notes, and then I have all these things I really want to say. [*Laughter*] What can I tell you— I'm just sort of an NPR-kind of President. [*Laughter*]

President Kennedy, many of you will remember, in 1962 hosted a dinner here of the Nobel Prize winners and said it was the most stunning array of talent ever to dine in the White House since Thomas Jefferson ate here alone. Well, tonight you did Thomas Jefferson one better. You joined him with Abraham Lincoln and Teddy Roosevelt and Harry Truman and Mark Twain and George Bernard Shaw and Click and Clack. [*Laughter*] And you all did very well.

I want to tell you that Hillary and I are particularly grateful that you spared us from all the things you said that were not true and from the things you said that were. [*Laughter*]

I thank you for giving America this wonderful history lesson of the White House. Those of you who may or may not have known, the things they told you were really true, all those wonderful little history lessons, everything except what Jane Curtain said. This is "Friday Night Live." [*Laughter*]

I am honored to have all of you here at the White House as we celebrate NPR's 25th anniversary. You should know that NPR is alive and well in the real White House. We are members of both the NPR stations in Washington, DC, Hillary and I are. And when we lived at home in Arkansas, Hillary helped to bring the full range of NPR programming to our State. In fact, we woke up every morning to NPR at 6 a.m. We had one of these little radios that ticks on, and instead of an alarm clock, we had NPR. Some days it was so soothing, we didn't wake up. [*Laughter*] But still it was a lot better than talk radio. [*Laughter*] At least on those days we did wake up, we were able to eat breakfast. [*Laughter*]

Let me say that there were a lot of interesting things said tonight. And I have to shorten my speech because of all those things you heard about, nature's call and how there was only one restroom in the White House for the longest— [*laughter*] Well, guess what? There's still no restroom on this floor. So just take a deep breath, I'm nearly done. [*Laughter*]

Public radio stations are partners in America, partners in things that are worth doing. They offer reading services to the blind, town meetings on violence, information on health care and voting. They team up with schools and libraries. They help our children learn. They bring more than issues and news, from live classical and jazz performances to radio drama and, of course, that car advice. And you get it all for 29 cents a citizen a year, about the price of a day's newspaper.

I know it's fashionable today to condemn everything public, but it seems to me that public radio has been a good deal for America. You know, I've done a lot of work here as President trying to build up the private sector, and we've got a lot more people working in it than we had 2 years ago, and I'm proud of that. But we're having this great debate in Washington about what the role of the Government should be as we come to the end of this century, and I'm glad we are. But I think it's important that we not forget that we have some great challenges here. How are we going to get into the next century with a country where everybody still has a chance to make it? And how are we going to deal with all this diversity in ways that bring us together instead of tear us apart? And how are we going to learn enough as citizens to make good decisions about those issues that don't fit very well into the screaming and the clamoring, cutting us up in little pieces and making our blood boil instead of our hearts open and our heads clear? NPR can play a role in all that, for 29 cents a person a year. It's a good deal.

I'm glad that one of the many fights we're going to be waging this year for ordinary Americans is the fight to preserve National Public Radio.

Hillary and I are deeply honored to have every single one of you here tonight, honored by the generosity, especially, of our performers who came here, who have been so gifted and who have shared their gifts with us tonight. We thank you for doing it, and mostly we thank you for the purpose for which you have done it. We thank you for caring about your fellow Americans, who really need this great institution to be here 25 years from now celebrating the 50th anniversary of National Public Radio. Let that be our dedication on this wonderful night.

God bless you, and thank you.

NOTE: The President spoke at 9:05 p.m. in the East Room at the White House. In his remarks, he referred to Carl Kasell, newscaster, NPR News.

The President's Radio Address
March 4, 1995

Good morning. I always like to hear from young people across our country. After all, they're at the heart of our efforts to build America up, to face the demands and the challenges of the 21st century. The responsibility of my generation is to leave those young people a better world and to make sure that they're prepared to succeed in that world.

I was especially touched by a letter I recently received from a 15-year-old girl named Melissa, who lives in a small town in the Midwest. Even though she's only 15 and she lives in America's heartland, she's a recovering drug addict. She's been drug-free for 2 years now, but she still sees other children going down the road to drug abuse, and she's very worried.

This is what she wrote to me: "It seems there's just not enough help, and when there is help, there's not enough money to do what needs to be done. Let's help this problem so it's not so big for the next generation." We ought to listen to Melissa. From our smallest towns to our biggest cities, millions of our children face the temptation of illegal drugs every day in their schools. Surveys show that unfortunately more and more of our adolescents are using illegal drugs. Kids today are somehow not getting the message. They are beginning once again to think that it's all right to use drugs,

that they're not really dangerous. But they're wrong. Too often, they're dead wrong.

Now, think about what this means for our communities and for our country, for all the rest of us. Illegal drugs go hand in hand with violence. They foster fear. Schoolchildren stay home by the thousands every day because they are afraid. And in this kind of environment, even the best behaved young people have a tough time learning. That means our standards of education are being undermined by drugs and violence. And that hurts our ability as a nation to compete and win. So we all pay a price.

The first line of defense, of course, has to be in our communities, with our parents and teachers and our neighbors, other role models in law enforcement and the religious community, telling our young people in no uncertain terms that drugs and violence are wrong and helping them to stay away or to get off. I know that.

But we here in Washington have a responsibility, too. All of you know there's a big debate going on in Washington now about what the role of the Government ought to be. The Republican contract says we should cut just about everything to pay for big tax cuts that go mostly to upper income people. Well, I think we should cut Government. We have. There are over

150,000 fewer people working here than there were when I took office. I think we ought to reduce the burden of unnecessary regulation, and we are.

But I think we need a Government that's lean and not mean, one that offers opportunity and challenges people to be more responsible, one that's a partner in increasing opportunity, empowering people to make the most of their own lives and providing more security for our people. The fight against drugs and the fight for safe schools does all of that.

After all, leaders of both parties have seen this as a problem that can't be ignored in Washington. President Reagan and President Bush invested in initiatives for drug-free schools. And last year, working with Members of Congress of both parties, our administration expanded the safe and drug-free schools program to include violence prevention and security. We passed legislation that sends $482 million to the States, enough for efforts in over 90 percent of our school districts.

Communities are using this money in a lot of different ways. They are using it to pay for police officers and metal detectors to keep our schools safer, to train teachers, staff, and students on how to resolve conflicts without violence, to help guide young people in fighting peer pressure to use drugs, to help instruct parents on the warning signs of drug use. All of this is a very good and sound investment for our future. It's Washington being a good partner with people building their communities at the grassroots level.

The schools taking part wouldn't give up these safeguards. If anything, they want more help. But now, some Republicans in Congress want to completely eliminate our safe schools and antidrug efforts. Right now, Congress is considering a rescission bill that cuts out the money we passed last year for all these programs.

I am concerned that the Republicans are willing to sacrifice our children's safety and our ability to learn in secure environments to pay for these tax cuts for upper income Americans. That's not a good deal for American's children, for America's future. It's not a good deal for upper income Americans. It's not putting people first. It won't help to restore the American dream, to advance the economic interests of the middle class to support mainstream values. They're trying to cut other things that I don't support, either. They're trying to cut the crime bill we passed last year to provide 100,000 police on our streets and to cut other education programs.

Now, I know we've got to reduce the deficit. We've already brought it down by over $600 billion under the tough plan we passed last year and the year before. And I've given Congress a budget that has another $140 billion of spending cuts. I'll work with them to find more but not in education or jobs or the safety of our children. We need to be expanding opportunity up here, not restricting it. We need to be giving our people the tools they need to make the most of their own lives, not taking them away. We need to enhance our security, not undermine it.

And where our children are concerned, we've got to give them the best chance we can to develop their God-given abilities so they can do the rest. They've got to stay in school, stay out of trouble, stay off drugs and off the streets. But young people, given a chance, can overcome great obstacles.

Look at young Melissa. Now she's gotten herself a second chance to become a first-class citizen. We need more young people like her for their strength, their intelligence, their humanity. We don't have a one to waste. And our young people need us to have the vision and the strength to do what's best for their futures today.

Thanks for listening.

NOTE: The President spoke at 10:06 a.m. from the Oval Office at the White House.

Memorandum on Regulatory Reform
March 4, 1995

Memorandum for Heads of Departments and Agencies

Subject: Regulatory Reinvention Initiative

Last week, I announced this Administration's plans for further reform of the Federal regulatory system. This is a central part of reinventing our Government. All Americans want the benefits of effective regulation: clean water, safer workplaces, wholesome food, sound financial institutions. But, too often the rules are drafted with such detailed lists of dos and don'ts that the objectives they seek to achieve are undermined. Clear goals and cooperation would work better. Too often, businesses, especially small ones, face a profusion of overlapping and sometimes conflicting rules.

We have already made real progress in reforming regulation. This memorandum will build on the regulatory philosophy set forth in Executive Order No. 12866 of September 30, 1993, "Regulatory Planning and Review," which is premised on the recognition of the legitimate role of government to govern, but to do so in a focused, tailored, and sensible way.

In the year and a half since that order was signed, we have opened the rulemaking process to the public, we have increased cooperation and coordination among the Federal agencies, and we have seen good processes produce good decisions.

However, not all agencies have taken the steps necessary to implement regulatory reform. To reaffirm and implement the principles of Executive Order No. 12866, regulatory reform must be a top priority.

Accordingly, I direct you to focus on the following four steps, which are an integral part of our ongoing Regulatory Reform Initiative.

First: Cut Obsolete Regulations

I direct you to conduct a page-by-page review of all of your agency regulations now in force and eliminate or revise those that are outdated or otherwise in need of reform. Your review should include careful consideration of at least the following issues:

- Is this regulation obsolete?
- Could its intended goal be achieved in more efficient, less intrusive ways?
- Are there better private sector alternatives, such as market mechanisms, that can better achieve the public good envisioned by the regulation?
- Could private business, setting its own standards and being subject to public accountability, do the job as well?
- Could the States or local governments do the job, making Federal regulation unnecessary?

This review should build on the work already being done by your agencies under section 5 of Executive Order No. 12866.

Your regulatory review task force should be headed by one of your appointees who should be given your full support and should, to the extent practicable, be freed of other duties.

I further direct you to deliver to me by June 1 a list of regulations that you plan to eliminate or modify with a copy of the report sent to Sally Katzen, Administrator of the Office of Information and Regulatory Affairs (OIRA). The list should distinguish between the regulations that can be modified or eliminated administratively and those that require legislative authority for modification or elimination.

Second: Reward Results, Not Red Tape

I direct you to change the way you measure the performance of both your agency and your frontline regulators so as to focus on results, not process and punishment. For example, Occupational Safety and Health Administration (OSHA) inspectors should not be evaluated by the number of citations they write, nor should officials of the Consumer Product Safety Commission be judged by the number of boxes of consumer goods that are detained in shipment. This change in measurements should involve a two-step process.

First, you should identify appropriate performance measures and prepare a draft in clear, understandable terms, of the results you are seeking to achieve through your regulatory program. The draft should be circulated to frontline regulators for review and comment. This is the same work needed to meet the requirements of the Government Performance and Results Act of 1993.

Second, you should evaluate and reward employees based on the realization of those measures/goals.

By no later than June 1, I direct you to (a) eliminate all internal personnel performance measures based on process (number of visits made, etc.) and punishment (number of violations found, amount of fines levied, etc.), and (b) provide to the National Performance Review (NPR) staff a catalogue of the changes that you are making in existing internal performance evaluations to reward employees. You should also provide material describing shifts in resource allocation from enforcement to compliance.

Third: Get Out of Washington and Create Grassroots Partnerships

I direct you to promptly convene groups consisting of frontline regulators and the people affected by their regulations. These conversations should take place around the country—at our cleanup sites, our factories, our ports.

I further direct you to submit a schedule of your planned meetings to the NPR staff by March 30 and work with NPR in following through on those meetings.

Fourth: Negotiate, Don't Dictate

It is time to move from a process where lawyers and bureaucrats write volumes of regulations to one where people work in partnership to issue sensible regulations that impose the least burden without sacrificing rational and necessary protections. In September 1993, I asked each of you to identify at least one rule that could be conducted through negotiated rulemaking (or to explain why such could not be done) in order to promote consensual rulemaking as opposed to the more traditional rulemaking that has dominated the regulatory arena.

I now direct you to expand substantially your efforts to promote consensual rulemaking. To this end, you should submit to OIRA, no later than March 30, a list of upcoming rulemakings that can be converted into negotiated rulemakings. I have directed Sally Katzen to review your lists with a view toward making clear

to the regulated community that we want to work together productively on even the most difficult subjects.

To facilitate our ability to learn from those affected by regulation, I will amend Executive Order No. 12838 (which requires agencies to reduce the number of advisory committees that they use and to limit the future use of such committees) to allow for advisory committees established for negotiated rulemakings.

I also intend to take additional steps to increase our ability to learn from those affected by regulation. While many laws and rules that limit the ability to regulators to talk with those being regulated were imposed to curb abuse, they now often serve as a barrier to meaningful communication between the regulators and the regulated. To address this problem, and to promote consensus building and a less adversarial environment, I direct you to review all of your administrative *ex parte* rules and eliminate any that restrict communication prior to the publication of a proposed rule—other than rules requiring the simple disclosure of the time, place, purpose, and participants of meetings (as in Executive Order No. 12866). We will also begin drafting legislation that will carve out exemptions to the Federal Advisory Committee Act to promote a better understanding of the issues, such as exemptions for meetings with State/local/tribal governments and with scientific or technical advisors.

I also ask you to think about other ways to promote better communication, consensus building, and a less adversarial environment. Please send your ideas to the Office of the Vice President.

As I said on Tuesday, February 21, 1995, you are to make regulatory reform a top priority. Good government demands it and your full cooperation is crucial.

WILLIAM J. CLINTON

NOTE: This memorandum was released by the Office of the Press Secretary on March 6.

Remarks to the Veterans of Foreign Wars Conference
March 6, 1995

Thank you very much, Commander Kent, for that introduction. Ladies and gentlemen, I can tell you from firsthand experience that the VFW is very lucky to have a leader as forceful and as thoughtful as Gunner Kent. I also want to acknowledge the presence here of Secretary Brown and Deputy Secretary Gober; General Sullivan; your adjutant general, Larry Rivers; Charles Durning, who rode over here with me and regaled me with experiences. How lucky we are to have him going out and setting an example, visiting our hospitalized veterans all across the United States. And I appreciate the reception you gave him. I want to recognize the president of your ladies auxiliary, Helen Harsh. I also want to recognize these young people over here from the Voice of Democracy contest, the winners there. I'm glad to see them. I thank you for your support of the young people of this country and for this project. I very much enjoyed having my picture taken with the young people just before we came out, and I got to shake hands with all of them. And they took about 10 years off my life, so I feel pretty spry standing up here. [*Laughter*] I want to thank whoever organized this for putting the delegates from my home State of Arkansas up here close where I can keep an eye on them during my speech. [*Laughter*] And they were all pretty well-behaved when I walked out. I was glad to see that. Thank you very much, ladies and gentlemen.

I want to recognize two veterans of the VFW, Jimmy Gates of Alabama, who has given more than 50 years of service to this organization, and your past national commander, Bob Merrill of California. People like Bob Merrill, who piloted biplanes in World War I and devoted their lives to fighting for their fellow veterans, who have helped the VFW to make a difference in the lives of so many Americans, those are the kinds of people that I think that we ought to keep in mind when we make the decisions that are being made here in Washington about what is in the interest of the veterans of the United States.

It also gives me great pleasure to tell you that just as soon as it comes across my desk, I will sign the bill that will allow the VFW to reform its charter and expand your membership even further.

This year we mark the 50th anniversary of the end of World War II. Many of you fought in that great struggle. Meeting some of the men and women who sacrificed so much for our freedom, whether I met them on the windswept beaches of Normandy, between the crowded rows of the cemetery in England or Italy, or inside the tunnels of the rock of Corregidor in the Philippines, meeting those people has been one of the greatest privileges I've had as President. America owes to them and to all of you a debt that we cannot fully repay.

With their lives before them, the World War II veterans left everything, family, loved ones, home, to fight for a just cause. From the Aleutians to Okinawa, from the Mediterranean to the North Sea, they watched so many of their friends fall. We lost more than 400,000, and 700,000 more were wounded. But still, our veterans never faltered. They gave everything so that future generations of Americans might be free. And we are all profoundly grateful.

But to honor their deeds and those of all the veterans who fought for freedom in World War I, Korea, Vietnam, the Persian Gulf, and all around the world in between, gratitude and ceremonies are not enough. We must protect the benefits you have earned, address fully the dangers imposed by modern warfare, and preserve what you fought for: the American dream at home and our leadership around the world.

I've said a lot in other places about preserving the American dream at home in this new global economy, and I won't talk a lot about it today, except just to say that it is going to be a constant struggle for us to make sure that in the next century every American has the chance to get a good education, to have a good job, to do better than their parents, to pass along the values of opportunity to their children. And I'll be saying more about that in other places. Today I want to talk a little about the tradition of America's leadership because that tradition is under siege.

If the new isolationists in our Nation have their way, America would abandon policies backed by Republicans and Democrats that have guided us for half a century, policies that won the cold war and that won us unparalleled prosperity here at home.

I know that at this time we have to spend more attention and more energy and more investment on the problems we have at home. And goodness knows, that's what I have been working to do for the last 2 years. But there are those who would back away from any of our commitments abroad. They would back away from institutions like the United Nations, which promotes stability around the world. They would have us give up our support for peacekeeping and for fragile democracies, support which enables others to share the burden with us, and which undermines the risks that we have to bear and makes us safer. They would cut deeply into our support for emerging market democracies. Even some would put our efforts to make peace in the Middle East on the chopping block.

Now, no one knows better than the veterans the grave dangers of simply withdrawing from the world. The last time isolationism held sway, during the years after World War I, Europe and Asia slid into catastrophe, and we had to fight a Second World War because we walked away from the world at the end of the First World War. Now, those of you in this room, whenever you served, wherever you served, you know what could happen if we retreat from today's turbulent world.

Yes, it is true that the cold war is over, that the nuclear threat is receding. And I'm going to do everything I can to push it back even further this year, with a whole series of ambitious and aggressive efforts to push back the nuclear threat. Yes, nations on every continent are embracing democracy and free markets. But open societies and free people still face many enemies. You know it as well as I do: the proliferation of other kinds of weapons of mass destruction; aggression by terrorists, by rogue states; threats that go across national lines, like overpopulation and environmental devastation, drug-trafficking and other organized crime activities; terrible ethnic conflicts; and as we've seen recently in Mexico, just the difficulties that poor nations are going to face when they try to embrace democracy and free-market economics and relate well to the rest of the world.

Now, we cannot intervene everywhere; we can't be involved in solving all these problems. We shouldn't be. But we must be able to protect our own vital interests. And we must be able to work with other countries through multinational organizations to keep the world moving in the right direction. It is not an automatic. It is not given that 20 and 30 and 50 years from now we'll have more democracy, more prosperity, more peace, and less danger. It is not an accident; we have to keep working for it.

Just think about the recent history. Consider what might have happened in the last 2 years alone if we had abandoned our responsibilities. If we hadn't pushed for expanding trade, trade wars could have erupted without our leadership on the GATT World Trade Agreement, which will open great new markets to America, generate hundreds of thousands of jobs, but also give people all around the world a chance to work together in peace. Think what would have happened if we had not moved to try to help stem this crisis in Mexico, what could have happened on our borders in terms of an increase in illegal immigration and reduced ability to continue to fight the drug-trafficking that we fight every single week. Think what might have happened if we hadn't stood up in Haiti for democracy and against the military dictators. We could have had thousands and thousands more immigrants at our borders, people with no place to go because they couldn't stay home, living under oppression. Peace might not even have caught a foothold in the Middle East if we hadn't had the constant political and economic support there for the parties in the Middle East.

These events and others prove the timeless wisdom of the words Franklin Roosevelt set down in the last speech he wrote, when he said, "We have learned in the agony of war that great power involves great responsibility." President Roosevelt observed, "We as Americans do not choose to deny our responsibility, nor do we intend to abandon our determination that within the lives of our children and our children's children, there will not be a third world war."

Your devotion and the service of millions and millions of other veterans has helped to prevent that war and helped to bring an end to the cold war. You helped to stop the spread of Communist tyranny across the globe. You helped democracy and prosperity to grow for our allies in Europe and beyond. And when dictators raised their heads, you stood up and you stopped them.

We must be clear about this: In the understandable desire of millions of Americans to look first to our problems at home which are real, your legacy is being threatened, a half a century of American leadership that you worked for and that you fought for. At all costs, we must preserve America's leadership so that our children can have the future they deserve. We simply cannot be strong at home unless we are also strong abroad. There is no dividing line in this global economy. There is no dividing line when terrorism and ethnic conflicts and economic problems and organized crime and drug-trafficking spread across national lines. There is no place to walk away from.

As Commander in Chief, I have done everything in my power to protect and build on the legacy that you have left your country, to make certain that our country moves into the next century still the strongest nation in the world, still the greatest force for freedom and democracy. And that's exactly what we have to keep doing.

We will meet that goal only if first we protect and strengthen the Armed Forces. More than anything else, our Armed Forces guarantee our security and our global influence. They're the backbone of our diplomacy. They ensure our credibility.

Just take, for example, the Persian Gulf. Last year, where our troops deployed swiftly and convinced Saddam Hussein not to make the same mistake twice, we would not have been able to do that had it not been for the lessons we learned from the Gulf war, the pre-positioning of our equipment, our continued efforts to be able to move our troops quickly and rapidly around the world wherever they needed to be.

Take Haiti, for example, when the news that our forces were poised to invade convinced the generals that they had to go. If it hadn't been for the military, for the year of planning for the most truly jointly planned military operation in American history, and for the planes in the air, it would not have happened. Or in the last few weeks, when our troops showed such great professionalism in transferring Cuban refugees from Panama to Guantanamo and covering the safe withdrawal of United Nations peacekeepers from Somalia.

Time and again, the American military has demonstrated its extraordinary skills. As I pledged from the beginning of our administration, the United States will have the best

equipped, best trained, best prepared military in the world. We are keeping that promise every day.

Our forces are ready to fight. But to maintain that high state of readiness and to keep our military strong, I have asked the Congress to increase defense funding by $25 billion spread over the next 6 years. We have fewer troops today, and yet we ask them to perform more and more different missions than ever before. So our combat pilots must fly as often as they need to fly to be properly trained. Our sailors must get the hands-on experience they deserve. Our ground forces must train so they can be at peak levels. And we also have to deal with the strains that all of these different missions put on the people who are in uniform today.

So some of this money will be used to raise military pay and to provide better housing and child care for those who serve and the families who stand by them. We simply must improve the quality of life in the military if we want to continue to draw educated and motivated Americans who can be trained into the high professionalism that we have sometimes come almost to take for granted from the American military. Our men and women in uniform, some of them your sons and daughters, are clearly the finest fighting force in the world. And we must all be determined to keep them that way.

We must also recognize another simple truth: the troops of tomorrow will only be as good as our commitment to veterans today. The people in uniform look to us to see how we relate to you. Long after you have shed your uniforms, not just for a few months or a few years, but for your entire lives, our Nation must meet its solemn obligations to you for the service you gave.

When I sought this office, I vowed to fight for the interests of our country's veterans, and our administration has kept that pledge. The White House doors have been open to veterans as never before. Ask Commander Kent, who came to visit me recently, to discuss the case for protecting your benefits. We have consistently looked to veterans to help shape our policy for veterans. Much of your influence is due to the outstanding work of Secretary Jesse Brown. I thank him for that.

We've protected veterans' preference for Federal jobs when your national commander wrote us last year and said it was in danger. When interest rates fell, we reached out to veterans all around America to tell you about opportunities to refinance homes bought under the GI bill. We made sure that military retirees received their full cost-of-living adjustments when Congress approved them 6 months later than for civilian retirees. And of course, we have worked to improve health care for veterans. We expanded long-term care programs and established comprehensive care centers for women veterans. And we're working to process claims faster so that you can get the benefits you're owed.

Last year, we sent to Congress the only health plan that would have expanded your choices of health care, improved veterans health facilities, and given those facilities the flexibility to serve you better. We have confronted head-on the long-neglected problem of Agent Orange. We have reached out to 40,000 veterans who were exposed to Agent Orange and told them about expanded benefits now available to them. We made certain that when a U.S. delegation visited Hanoi, representatives of the VFW and other veterans groups were there to discuss the painful issues of MIA's. And we have continued to press for the fullest possible accounting for those lost while serving our Nation.

Our administration has brought the voices of veterans to the highest councils of government, protected your interests when they've been threatened, and worked hard every day to improve the services you receive. We have done this even as we have cut the Federal deficit by more than $600 billion, shrunk the Federal Government faster than at any time in modern history.

In the last 2 years, we have cut more than 150,000 positions from the Federal bureaucracy. We have cut spending in more than 300 Federal programs. And this year, while we cut the budget of almost every Federal agency, we still are able to say we are going to the mat for America's future and America's obligations to the past, for Head Start for our children, for the School Lunch Program, for nutrition for pregnant women and their children, for immunizing kids in their early years, for programs for young people who don't go to college but do need good training to get good jobs, for more affordable loans for middle class young people, for 100,000 new police on our streets, for military readiness, and, yes, for better health care for America's veterans.

Our administration is pushing for $1.3 billion more for the Department of Veterans Affairs over the next 5 years, $1 billion of that to the veterans health care system. That means care for 43,000 more veterans, 2 new hospitals, 3 new nursing homes, and other major improvements.

Sadly, some in Congress see that the need to improve your health care services is not very important. Indeed, legislation approved by the House Appropriations Committee just last week, if passed by the Congress, will cut very deeply. They seek to eliminate more than $200 million for veterans health, including money for veterans' outpatient clinics and millions of dollars for new medical equipment for veterans health services. And their cuts would also abolish a successful Department of Labor program that reintegrates homeless veterans by providing them with temporary housing and with help with job training and job placement.

Now, I believe these cuts are unwise and unnecessary. They would harm the veterans who need their nation's help the most. I pledge to you today that I will fight for those interests and for you every step of the way. But we need your help. You have to speak up. You have to speak out. Only your voices will make it clear. Caring for veterans is not a national option or a partisan program. It is a national tradition and a national duty.

Let me say again that fulfilling that duty means more than just meeting the promises of the past. It also means today making every effort we can to respond to the needs of today's soldiers.

Michael Sills of Villa Park, Illinois, is one of those soldiers. He's 34 years old, a veteran of America's victory in the Persian Gulf. He has a disabling illness. But neither he nor his doctors know how he got it. There are thousands of veterans like Michael Sills, thousands who served their country in the Gulf war and came home to find themselves ill. And neither they nor their doctors know how they got it.

Even though in so many of these cases we do not know the causes of their symptoms, we know their problems are real and cannot be ignored while we wait for science to provide all the answers. And that's why last year I supported and signed landmark legislation that for the first time in our history pays benefits to disabled veterans with undiagnosed illnesses that have not been scientifically linked to their military service, when we know good and well that's what happened.

Two weeks ago I met with Michael Sills, one of the first veterans to get benefits under this new law. I sat with him in the Oval Office for several minutes as I listened to his description of what happened to him and how he began to get sick and what the symptoms were and how it had affected his family. And then I listened to his plans about how he wanted to get on with his life. And I did my best to assure him that we will keep looking for the answers that he and his comrades deserve.

In the past few weeks, the First Lady has visited Gulf war veterans at Walter Reed and the Washington V.A. Medical Center. Some of them are here today. She met with Gunner Kent and Bob Currieo of the VFW and other groups to discuss these illnesses and what must be done.

When she was working on health care over the last 2 years, she kept getting letters from people all across America, saying, "Mrs. Clinton, please look into this, there's something wrong here. I love my country. I wouldn't fake an illness. I don't want anything I'm not entitled to." We've read and reread so many of these letters from veterans, the accounts of the unexplained illnesses, of the breathing problems, of the joint and muscle pain, of the persistent headaches, of the memory loss. We received a letter from Dylan and Theresa Callahan, of Hampton, New Hampshire, who referred to Dylan's undiagnosed illness as the, quote, "never-ending nightmare," and added simply, "Our lives may be in your hands."

From the beginning of our administration, we have listened to these veterans' messages. Working together with Democrats and Republicans in Congress, we determined the treatment for these veterans couldn't be delayed as it was for Vietnam veterans who were exposed to Agent Orange. That's why we moved to provide medical care and to compensate fully and fairly these Gulf veterans while making every effort to find the answers.

Today, as a result of these actions, Gulf war veterans are receiving comprehensive exams and treatment at VA and DOD medical facilities. Those on active duty receive specialized care in military hospitals. VA and DOD have opened specialized care centers that focus on veterans who are especially difficult to diagnose. Tens of thousands of Gulf veterans have received free physical exams, and those who are ill are getting free medical care. VA and DOD have registered more than 55,000 Gulf veterans with health concerns to help avoid the kinds of problems that delayed care and compensation for those exposed to Agent Orange.

We've enlisted some of our finest scientists and more than 30 research projects aimed at determining the causes of these veterans' illnesses. Research topics include the possible impact of oil fires and diseases common in the Gulf area. The Defense Department is declassifying all documents related to the possible causes of these illnesses. And both VA and DOD have set up toll-free hotlines to provide Persian Gulf veterans easy access to information about care.

Still, with all this, I believe we must do more. That is why I am announcing today the creation of a Presidential advisory committee to review and make recommendations to me regarding Government efforts aimed at finding the causes and improving the care available to Gulf war veterans. This committee will be made up of scientists, doctors, veterans, and other distinguished citizens. It will work closely with the Secretaries of Veterans Affairs, Defense, and Health and Human Services, and report through them to me. In the year ahead, we will also step up our treatment efforts and launch new research initiatives. The Departments of Veterans Affairs, Defense, and Health and Human Services will spend up to $13 million on new research. Projects will examine the possible causes of Gulf veterans' illnesses, including the potential effects of pesticides and other environmental toxins, antitank ammunition containing depleted uranium, and drugs used to protect against chemical and biological weapons.

VA will begin to survey 30,000 veterans and active duty personnel to learn more about the frequency and nature of Persian Gulf illnesses. The study will also examine whether illnesses have been transmitted to spouses and to children. Data including information regarding cancers and other serious illnesses among Gulf war veterans will continue to be made more accessible to the public. And the Defense Department will strengthen future training for troops on the risks of toxic exposure and will follow up and document information about troops when they return from their service.

We must listen to what the veterans are telling us and respond to their concerns. Just as we relied on these men and women to fight for our country, they must now be able to rely on us to try to determine what happened to them in the Gulf and to help restore them to full health. We will leave not a stone unturned. And we will not stop until we have done everything we possibly can for the men and women who, like so many veterans throughout our history, have sacrificed so much for the United States and our freedom.

Last month at the Iwo Jima commemoration, we heard two Latin words repeated again and again: *semper fidelis*, always faithful. The Marines' noble motto is one which serves well for a great branch of our military service but also for our whole Nation. Being faithful to one another and faithful to our traditions, these are tied together. Being true to our tradition of leadership in the world means reaching out across the oceans to support democracy and freedom and all the benefits they bring back home to us. Being faithful to one another requires us to keep faith with our veterans as we keep faith with our future.

You know better than anyone what these bonds of reliance are. As Dan Pollock, an Iwo Jima veteran and a member of the VFW, recalled just last month, and I quote his words, "You never had to watch your back," he said, "because in the midst of terrible battle, you belong to," what he called, "a band of brothers." Whether it's five decades later for the World War II veterans or just 4 years later for the Gulf war veterans, you should know that your Nation will never forget your service and will always, always, need your support for America's strength and leadership.

As long as I am President, the sacred tradition of protecting our veterans will continue and a strong America will march forward. You put your faith in America. America will continue to keep faith with you.

Thank you, and God bless you.

NOTE: The President spoke at 11 a.m. at the Sheraton Washington Hotel. In his remarks, he referred to Allen F. (Gunner) Kent, commander in chief, VFW; Gen. Gordon R. Sullivan, Chief of Staff, U.S. Army; and actor Charles Durning, Chair, Department of Veterans Affairs 1995 Salute to Hospitalized Veterans.

Statement on the 25th Anniversary of the Nuclear Non-Proliferation Treaty
March 6, 1995

March 5 marked the 25th anniversary of the Nuclear Non-Proliferation Treaty (NPT). This historic arms control agreement—to which 172 nations have now adhered—is the foundation of international efforts to stem the spread of nuclear weapons.

Last week, in a speech at the Nixon Center, I reaffirmed this Nation's commitment to the goals and obligations of the NPT. This treaty strengthens our security and that of all nations. It creates a dependable security environment that makes other arms control and disarmament measures possible. For these reasons, the United States strongly supports universal NPT membership.

Six weeks from now, an international conference in New York will consider extension of the NPT. The United States is firmly committed to the indefinite extension of the NPT without conditions. We will work closely with other parties to the treaty to achieve this objective.

The indefinite and unconditional extension of the NPT tops an ambitious global arms control agenda. Implementation of the START I treaty is already yielding dramatic reductions in nuclear forces. We seek early ratification of START II and the Chemical Weapons Convention. We have taken steps to accelerate the conclusion of a Comprehensive Test Ban Treaty and are pushing for a global ban on the production of fissile material for weapons. We seek to strengthen the Biological and Toxin Weapons Convention. These and other steps will significantly reduce the nuclear threat to America's cities and citizens.

Message to the Congress Transmitting the Report on Floodplain Management
March 6, 1995

To the Congress of the United States:

It is with great pleasure that I transmit *A Unified National Program for Floodplain Management* to the Congress. The Unified National Program responds to section 1302(c) of the National Flood Insurance Act of 1968 (Public Law 90–448), which calls upon the President to report to the Congress on a Unified National Program. The report sets forth a conceptual framework for managing the Nation's floodplains to achieve the dual goals of reducing the loss of life and property caused by floods and protecting and restoring the natural resources of floodplains. This document was prepared by the Federal Interagency Floodplain Management Task Force, which is chaired by FEMA.

This report differs from the 1986 and 1979 versions in that it recommends four national goals with supporting objectives for improving the implementation of floodplain management at all levels of government. It also urges the formulation of a more comprehensive, coordinated approach to protecting and managing human and natural systems to ensure sustainable development relative to long-term economic and ecological health. This report was prepared independent of *Sharing the Challenge: Floodplain Management Into the 21st Century* developed by the Floodplain Management Review Committee, which was established following the Great Midwest Flood of 1993. However, these two reports complement and reinforce each other by the commonality of their findings and recommendations. For example, both reports recognize the importance of continuing to improve our efforts to reduce the loss of life and property caused by floods and to preserve and restore the natural resources and functions of floodplains in an economically and environmentally sound manner. This is significant in that the natural resources and functions of our riverine and coastal floodplains help to maintain the viability of natural systems and provide multiple benefits for people.

Effective implementation of the Unified National Program for Floodplain Management will mitigate the tragic loss of life and property, and disruption of families and communities, that are caused by floods every year in the United States. It will also mitigate the unacceptable losses of natural resources and result in a reduction in the financial burdens placed upon governments to compensate for flood damages caused by unwise land use decisions made by individuals, as well as governments.

WILLIAM J. CLINTON

The White House,
March 6, 1995.

Letter to Congressional Leaders Transmitting a Report on Cyprus
March 6, 1995

Dear Mr. Speaker: (Dear Mr. Chairman:)

In accordance with Public Law 95–384 (22 U.S.C. 2373(c)), I submit to you this report on progress toward a negotiated settlement of the Cyprus question. The previous report covered progress through November 30, 1994. The current report covers December 1, 1994, through January 31, 1995.

On January 5, I appointed Mr. Richard I. Beattie as my U.S. Special Presidential Emissary for Cyprus. Emissary Beattie will work closely with all parties to promote an overall solution that will be fair, just, and permanent. He and Special Cyprus Coordinator James Williams traveled to Cyprus on January 23 for extensive meetings with the leaders of both communities. The two leaders expressed their desire to reach a settlement. In addition, Mr. Denktash reiterated his commitment to a bizonal, bicommunal federation with a single sovereignty and single citizenship. Emissary Beattie and Special Cyprus Coordinator Williams will consult in Ankara during March to continue their efforts to facilitate agreements on concrete steps towards a solution.

Throughout the period, my representatives continued to work for comprehensive progress, both on concrete steps such as the confidence-building measures and on overall settlement issues. The Greek-Cypriot side endorsed this approach provided a common basis for an overall settlement has been established; the Turkish-Cypriot side urged we proceed incrementally

from measures to overall talks. We will continue to pursue further efforts to establish such a common basis for a settlement.

Sincerely,

WILLIAM J. CLINTON

NOTE: Identical letters were sent to Newt Gingrich, Speaker of the House of Representatives, and Jesse Helms, chairman, Senate Committee on Foreign Relations.

Message to the Congress Transmitting the Report of the National Endowment for Democracy
March 6, 1995

To the Congress of the United States:

Pursuant to the provisions of section 504(h) of Public Law 98–164, as amended (22 U.S.C. 4413(i)), I transmit herewith the 11th Annual Report of the National Endowment for Democracy, which covers fiscal year 1994.

Promoting democracy abroad is one of the central pillars of the United States' security strategy. The National Endowment for Democ-

racy has proved to be a unique and remarkable instrument for spreading and strengthening the rule of democracy. By continuing our support, we will advance America's interests in the world.

WILLIAM J. CLINTON

The White House,
March 6, 1995.

Remarks to the National Association of Counties
March 7, 1995

Thank you very much. Thank you, Randy, for the T-shirt and for the sentiment which it represents. I thank all of you for having me here. I'm glad to be here with Secretary Shalala and Doug Bovin and Michael Hightower, Randy Johnson, John Stroger, my old friend from Arkansas by way of Chicago—[*laughter*]—Doris Ward, and Larry Naake.

Let me begin by congratulating you on this program this morning. I was impressed that you had our longtime friend Marian Wright Edelman, who gave my wife her first job after law school in the Children's Defense Fund. And I'm glad the Speaker got to come back and give his talk today—[*laughter*]—and I thank you for hearing him.

You know, I've done a lot of work over the years with the ACORN group and they stood

for a lot of good things in my home State. But I think everyone deserves to be heard. And we need people debating these important issues in Washington. This is a very exciting time, and it's important that all the voices be heard and that people like you especially that have to live with the consequences of what is done here hear the ideas that are being debated and also that you be heard.

I am always glad to be with people whom I think of as being in the backbone of public service in America. You serve at the level where you can have the greatest impact. When I was a Governor, nothing mattered more to me that just being in direct contact with the people who hired me to do my job. And I have to tell you, as President, perhaps the most frustrating thing about the job is that I don't have as many opportunities as you do to be in direct contact with the people who hired me to do this job. That's not good for me, and sometimes it's not so good for them as well.

When I was Governor, people used to make fun of me and say that I was basically a courthouse Governor, which meant that I loved to go to the country courthouse in the rural areas of my State and sit for hours and talk to the officials and also visit with the people who would come in. But I know this: I know that one of the things that our Government in Washington has suffered from for so many years is being too far from the concerns of ordinary Americans.

You see in personal terms, with names and faces and life histories, the struggle now going on to keep the American dream alive. And you know as well as any the importance of reconnecting the values of the American people to their Government. I ran for President because that American dream and those values were threatened in the face of the huge changes that are going on here in the United States and all around the world and because I thought that too often our Government was simply not prepared to deal with those challenges or, in some cases, actually making them worse.

Now, for 2 years I have worked hard to help ensure that our people have the tools they need to build good lives for themselves as we move into the 21st century and that we cross that great divide still the strongest and most secure country in the world, still the greatest force for peace and freedom and democracy.

We're about two-thirds through the first 100 days of this new Congress. On Saturday, March 4th, we had the 62d anniversary of President Franklin Roosevelt's inauguration as President and the start of the original first 100 days. On that day, Franklin Roosevelt began to restore our Nation and to redefine the relationship between our people and their Government for half a century. And a lot of things he said then are still accurate today. In his Inaugural he said, "The joy and moral stimulation of work must no longer be forgotten. These dark days will be worth all they cost us if they teach us that our true destiny is not to be ministered unto but to minister to ourselves and our fellow men."

Today, we face different challenges, but our job is much the same. We have to keep the American dream alive for ourselves and our children during a time of great change. And we have to do that while we maintain the values that have always made us strong: work, family, community, responsibility for ourselves and for the future of our children.

As all of you know—and you're now seeing it played out this morning—we're engaged in a great debate here in Washington about how to do that. The old Washington view is that the Federal Government can provide big solutions to America's big problems. The new Republican contract view reflects often an outright hostility to almost any Federal Government involvement, unless the present majority in Congress disagrees with what's going on in the States, and then there is a curious desire to increase the Federal Government's control over those aspects of our lives.

Now, my view is very different, really, from both. It reflects the years and years that I lived like you live now, when I was a Governor out there working among the American people and seeing these problems that people talk about in sound bites with names and faces and life histories.

The New Covenant that I want to forge with the American people for the future says we need both more opportunity and more responsibility, that we don't have a person to waste, so we have to have very strong communities that unite us instead of divide us. We do need very big changes in the way Government works. We don't need big, bureaucratic, one-size-fits-all Government in Washington.

But we do have common problems and common opportunities which require a partnership, a partnership with a limited but an effective Government; a Government committed to increasing opportunity in terms of jobs and incomes, while shrinking Government bureaucracy; a Government committed to empowering people through education and training and technology to make the most of their own lives; a Government committed to enhancing our security all around the world and here at home on our streets as well.

Now, this kind of Government will necessarily send more decisions back to the State and local governments and to citizens themselves. It will cut unnecessary spending, but it will invest more in jobs, incomes, and educations. It will, in short, as I said in 1992, put people first. It will insist on more personal responsibility, and it will support stronger communities. It will be a partner, but it won't be a savior, and it won't sit on the sidelines. Either extreme is wrong.

Now, I see this debate about the role of our Government as terribly important. And you can see it now playing out on every issue now before the Congress. We see it being debated in terms of how we should best educate our children, how we should train our workers, how we should make our communities safe again, how our civil justice system should work, what is the right way to fix the broken welfare system. I want you to watch it play out this year. Underneath it all will be, what is the responsibility of the Government in Washington, what is your responsibility at the grassroots level, how can it best be met.

As we debate these matters, I will keep working to change the way Washington does business, to achieve a Government that gives taxpayers better value for their dollar, to support more jobs and higher incomes for the middle class and to shrink the under class, and to reinforce mainstream values of responsibility, work, family, and community.

You know, for the 12 years before I came here, Washington allowed the deficit to quadruple and didn't do much to shrink the size or change the role of Government. Organized interests did very well, but the public interest suffered. In the last 2 years, we've begun to change that. We've cut the Federal deficit by $600 billion, shrunk the Federal Government faster than at any time in memory. We've cut more than 300 domestic programs and consolidated hundreds of others. We've got more than 150,000 fewer people working for the Federal bureaucracy today than on the day I became President, and we are on the way to reducing it by more than a quarter of a million, so that the Federal Government will be the smallest it has been since President Kennedy took office.

In the process, we have done a lot to shift power away from Washington to States, counties, cities, and towns throughout the country. Our reinventing Government initiative has already saved the taxpayers $63 billion under the leadership of the Vice President, and we will save more.

We have cut regulations that make it harder on business and local Government to create opportunity, but we will do more. And all of this has made a difference in the work and the lives of the people you serve. The economy has created almost 6 million jobs since I became President, the combined rate of unemployment and inflation is at a 25-year low.

But clearly, we still have more to do. Most people are working harder, without a raise, even though we've got a recovery. We're the only advanced country in the world where the percentage of people in the work force with health insurance is smaller today than it was 10 years ago. We still have a lot of economic problems out there, and you know that.

I am ready to work with the Republicans, especially in areas that will give you more power to do what you have to do. Together, we have moved forward legislation in the Congress that will keep Congress from imposing unreasonable new mandates on you without paying for them. We've got a few issues left to work out on that, but a bill has passed the House and a bill has passed the Senate, and I encourage all sides to work in a bipartisan way to resolve them soon. In particular, though—and I want you to weigh in on this, I hope you will—I think the bill ought to be made effective immediately. For reasons I don't understand, Congress seems to want to make it effective toward the end of this year or at the beginning of next year. If it's going to be a good idea then, it will be a good idea now. Let's go on and get it done.

As we have worked to cut yesterday's Government, we've also invested in our people to help them solve their own problems. We have approached that work, too, as a partner with people at the local level. For example, last year we had the most productive year in passing education reform legislation, from expanding Head Start to making college loans more affordable to the middle class in 30 years. But our education reforms set world-class standards for our schools and yet give to educators and parents much more say than the Federal Government used to about how to meet these standards and how to improve out children's education.

We tried to be good partners with local government on the crime bill. I want to thank all of you at NACO for helping us to pass it. After 6 years of rhetoric and hot air in Washington, we finally passed the crime bill. You told us you wanted an end to gridlock, and you helped us get it. And we are providing what you told us you wanted, you and other local officials all across the country, resources for 100,000 new law enforcement officers, smarter prevention efforts, tougher punishment, like "three strikes and you're out," a hard-won ban on assault weapons.

We are working with you now to implement this crime bill. The Justice Department and the Attorney General are working very, very hard. This is an amazing thing. I hear those who criticize this crime bill say that we have imposed this on local government, and they really don't want it, and they can't afford to pay any match. But do you know, since October, over half the police departments in the United States of America have already applied for assistance under the police grants—over half. And in this 5-year program, we have already released funds just since last fall to our 17,000 new law enforcement officers, including over 1,000 deputy sheriffs.

Now, sadly, some people in Congress think we ought to reverse this. I agree that we have to continue to cut the deficit. My new budget cuts $140 billion more in Federal spending. We have reduced the rate of health costs growing by about $100 billion over the next 5 years. We had about $250 billion in budget cuts in our last budget.

But how are we going to do this? I do not believe we should sacrifice our safety and not put 100,000 police on the street. I do not believe that we should not keep working for education. Instead, I think it's clear that our security and our ability to pay our way in the world depends upon educating and training our people for the new global economy. That includes a stronger Head Start program, serving more children. It includes more affordable college loans for middle class students. It includes a whole range of educational initiatives.

I don't think we should limit our efforts to make college loans more affordable, especially when you consider the fact that this administration has reduced your costs in delinquent college loans from $2.8 billion a year down to a billion dollars a year. We cut it by two-thirds, the loss to taxpayers. So we're collecting on the student loans; let's give more loans to young people to go to college to make America stronger.

I don't agree that we should eliminate the national service project, AmeriCorps. It's doing a world of good out there at the grassroots level. A lot of you are using it. And I certainly don't agree—with drug use on the rise among young people, who seem to have forgotten that it is not only illegal, it is dangerous—I certainly don't

agree that we should eliminate the provision for drug education programs and for security programs against drug problems in our public schools, which will now cover 94 percent of the schools in this country but if the proposal now in Congress passes will be wiped out. That is not the way to cut the budget. We do not have to do it that way.

It depends on how you look at it. Some in Congress want to cut the School Lunch Program. You know what we did instead? We closed 1,200 regional offices in the Department of Agriculture. I think we did it the right way.

So my view of this is that yes, we've got to cut the budget, but we should expand opportunity, not restrict it. We should give people the tools they need to make the most of their own lives, not take them away. We should enhance security, not undermine it. Those are my standards, and I need your help. You can make it clear to Washington that America wants us to get our house in order. They like it when we reduce the deficit. We have to cut the spending, but there is a right way and a wrong way to do this work.

And I'd like to ask your help in particular on an issue of concern to a lot of you. I know it differs from State to State in how it's implemented, but every American citizen has an interest in ending welfare as we know it. Like it or not, we have a welfare system that doesn't further our basic values, and like many of you, I have worked on this problem for years. Those of us who work in it know it's a little more complicated than people who just talk about it. I have spent countless hours in welfare offices talking to case workers, talking to people on welfare. For years and years now, about 15 years this year, I have been working on this problem as a Governor and as a President. I have seen this great drama unfold.

You know, when welfare started under President Roosevelt, the typical welfare recipient was a West Virginia miner's widow, who had a grade school education, was never expected to be in the workplace, and had orphaned children that needed help. And everybody thought this was the right thing to do. Then, we had people on welfare who just hit a rough patch but who got off welfare in a couple of months. And believe it or not, nearly half the people who go on welfare today are still in that category. Welfare actually works for them; we shouldn't forget that. There are a lot of folks who hit a rough patch in life, and they get on welfare, and then they get themselves off.

Then, there are those whom all the American people, without regard to party or philosophy, are justifiably concerned with, people who are trapped on welfare in cycles of dependency that sometimes become intergenerational, that are plainly rooted to the explosion of teen pregnancy, out-of-wedlock births, coupled with low levels of education, inability to pierce the job market, inability to succeed as both workers and parents. What ought to be the greatest joy of life, giving birth to a child, has now become a great social drama for us, in which we all worry that our values are being regularly violated and that's being reinforced by the way a Government program works. And we are worried about it.

Many of our people are worried because they don't have enough money to pay for their own kids and they think their tax money is going down the drain to reinforce values they don't support, to create more burdens on their tax money in the future.

And nobody wants to get off the welfare system, I can tell you, any more than the people who are on it. All you've got to do is go out and sit in any welfare office in the country and talk to people. I had four people who had worked their way off welfare into the Oval Office to see me the other day, and it was just like every story I've heard for the last 15 years, people talking about how they were dying to get off welfare.

Now, our country has been engaged in a serious effort to try to address this problem for some years now. This is not a new issue. In the late 1980's, along with then-Governor and now-Congressman Mike Castle from Delaware, I represented a bipartisan group of Governors in working with the Congress and the Reagan administration to pass the Family Support Act of 1988. It was a welfare reform bill designed to promote work and education and to move people from welfare to work through having the States do more with education and training and job placements and requiring that people participate in these programs.

And many of us who were Governors at the time used the Family Support Act to move people off welfare. But everybody who worked with it recognized that more had to be done if the welfare system was going to be changed. There were still a lot of people who said, "Well, if

I move from welfare to work, I'll lose my kid's child care," or "I'll lose medical coverage for my child after a few months." There are others who still could kind of get through loopholes in the program because we didn't cover everybody. So to reflect our country's values of work and education and responsible parenting, we knew we needed to do more.

We also knew that we needed more State flexibility in tackling this problem. If somebody knew how to fix this, it would have been done a long time ago and people in politics would be talking about something else. Right? That's what this whole State flexibility's about. The framers were pretty smart wanting the States and the localities to be the laboratories of democracy, because they knew that there would be thorny problems involving complex matters of economics and social organization and human nature that no one would know all the answers to.

So I'm glad the Republicans chose to make welfare reform part of their contract for America. It's always been part of my contract with America. Now, let's see if there's some things we can all agree on.

I think we should demand and reward work, not punish those who go to work. I think we should demand responsibility from parents who bring children into the world, not let them off the hook and expect the taxpayers to pick up the tab for their neglect. I think we must discourage irresponsible behavior that lands people on welfare in the first place. We must tell our children not to have children until they are married and ready to be good parents.

Now, in the last 2 years we've made some progress in pursuing these goals. In 1993 when the Congress passed the economic reform plan, one of the provisions gave a tax break averaging $1,000 a year to families with incomes of under $25,000 to 15 million working families to send this message: If you work full-time and you have children in the home, you should not be in poverty. And there should never be an incentive to stay on welfare instead of go to work. That's what the earned-income tax credit expansion was all about.

Last year I sent to Congress the most sweeping welfare reform plan ever presented to the United States Congress. It was prowork, proeducation, proresponsibility, and pro-State flexibility. It did not pass, but I still hope it will be the basis of what ultimately does pass.

We are collecting child support at a record level from delinquent parents, $9 billion in 1993. And last week I signed an Executive order to crack down on Federal employees who owe child support to require them to pay as well.

For the last 2 years, we have granted welfare reform waivers from Federal rules to two dozen States, more than the last two administrations in 12 years combined, giving States flexibility to try out their ideas without being stifled by Washington one-size-fits-all rules. Today I am proud to announce that Ohio has become the 25th State to receive a waiver to reform its welfare system.

Now, here's what Ohio wants to do. I think it's an interesting idea. They want to take some of their welfare and food stamp money to subsidize jobs in the private sector, including an initiative with our new empowerment zone in Cleveland. That's not a bad idea. Some people say, "Well, we don't have enough money to create government jobs for all these folks, and the private sector won't hire them if they have limited skills." So Ohio and Oregon and a couple of other States say, "Would you let us use the welfare check to give to employers, say, 'Okay, you're going to pay whatever you're going to pay at this job. This will replace some of what you'll have to pay.' Put these people to work. Give them work experience. Give them a chance. Give them a chance to earn something."

Secretary Shalala thought it was a good idea, and so do I. These are the kinds of things being done all across America. Half the country today, as of this day with this waiver, now half the States are carrying out significant welfare reform experiments that promote work and responsibility instead of undermining it. Ten States are strengthening their child support enforcement. Nineteen are finding ways to insist on responsible behavior in return for help. Twenty States are providing incentives to families to go to work, not stay on welfare.

I think we should go further and abolish this waiver system altogether in the welfare reform. Instead, we should give all States the flexibility to do all the things that our waivers allow 25 States to do today, so people don't have to come to Washington to ask.

But I would like to say in this debate and for your benefit, especially those of you who have county responsibilities in this area, we shouldn't forget that the need for flexibility doesn't stop at the State level. We need it at the local level as well.

So we're making some headway on this welfare reform. But we've still got a lot of work to do. In January, I called a meeting at the White House with leaders from both parties and all levels of government to press Congress to get moving on welfare reform legislation. I spoke about it in the State of the Union Address. I wanted the people who will write the legislation to hear from people like you, so we had representatives from local government at this meeting. I wanted them to hear from folks who will have to put this legislation into action on the front lines.

We all know the old system did too little to require work, education, and parental responsibility, that it gave the States too little flexibility. The original Republican contract proposal did give the States more flexibility, with some exceptions, in return for substantial reductions in Federal payments in future years. But like the present system and unlike my proposal, the original Republican contract proposal was weak on work and parental responsibility. And in terms of denying benefits to all welfare parents under the age of 18 and their children, it was also, in my view, very hard on children.

Now, the present bill in the Congress, as it stands today, as we speak, contains real improvements from the original contract proposal in the areas of work and parental responsibility. But I think there are still significant problems with it which could undermine our common goals. And in my view, they still make the bill too tough on children and too weak on work and responsibility. I'd like to talk a little about that, again, because there's a debate still to be had in the House and then when the bill goes to the Senate.

When we met in January, we agreed, Democrats and Republicans alike, that the toughest possible child support enforcement must be a central part of welfare reform. If we collected all the money that deadbeat parents owe, we could move 300,000 mothers and over half a million children off the welfare roles immediately, tomorrow, just with child support collection.

So at that meeting, people from every level of government and both parties agreed that while generally we want to move more of these decisions back to the State, we need national action on child support enforcement and national standards because 30 percent of the cases where parents don't pay cross State lines.

The original child support provisions in the contract of the Republicans left out a lot of the most effective means for finding delinquent parents, which were in our welfare reform bill, including a system to track them across State lines. But to the credit of the Republicans, they have recently included almost all our tough child support measures. And I appreciate it.

There is more that we ought to do, I think, together. Our plan calls on States to deny drivers and professional licenses to people who refuse to pay their child support. Now, I know that's a tough idea, but let me tell you, 19 States are doing that today, and they're collecting a lot more child support as a result of it. So I hope that the Congress will join us to make this provision also the law of the land. We've got to send a loud signal: No parent in America has a right to walk away from the responsibility to raise their children. That's the signal; we've got to send it.

Secondly, all of you know that the hardest and the most important part of welfare reform is moving people from welfare to work. You have to educate and train people. You've got to make sure that their kids aren't punished once they go to work by losing their health care or their child care. And then you've got to figure out where these jobs are coming from. I'm doing my best to lower the unemployment rate, but still, if there's unemployment in a given area, where will the jobs come from? Will the Government provide them? If not, you have to do things like I described in the Ohio waiver.

But this work has always been at the core of my approach. I think what we want for every American adult is to be a successful parent and a successful worker. When I proposed my plan last year and when I was running for President, I said, if people need help with education, training, or child care so they can go to work, we ought to give them the help. But after 2 years, they should be required to take a job and get a paycheck, not a welfare check, if there is a job available. There should not be an option. If you can go to work, you must.

Now, I know in their hearts this is really the position that most of the Republicans in the Congress agree with. Last year, 162 of 175 House Republicans, including Speaker Gingrich, cosponsored a bill that was similar to our plan on work in many ways. But the plan that they

are currently considering in the House doesn't do much to support work. It would actually make it harder for many recipients to make it in the workplace.

Now, they wisely abandoned an earlier provision which basically allowed a welfare recipient to get around the work requirement literally by submitting a resume. But their new plan gives the States a perverse incentive to cut people off welfare. It lets them count people as working if they were simply cut off the welfare rolls for any reason and whether or not they have moved into a job. Now, when people just get cut off without going to work, we know where they're likely to end up, don't we? On your doorstep. That's not welfare reform. That's just shifting the problem from one place to another.

Now, we know that an inordinate number of people also who get off welfare without work skills, without child care, wind up right back on welfare in a matter of a few months. Yet, the current Republican plan cuts child care both for people trying to leave welfare and for working people who are working at low incomes who are trying to stay off of welfare.

Equally important, this new plan removes any real responsibility for States to provide education, training, and job placement, though that is at the heart of getting and keeping people off welfare. In other words, these provisions on work effectively repeal the Family Support Act of 1988 which was passed with the support of President Reagan and substantial Republicans in the Congress and actually did some good where the States implemented it in good faith. Why? Because basically the new provisions are designed to allow the Federal Government to send less money to the States over time, and in return for saving budget money, they're willing to walk away from the standards necessary to move people from welfare to work. It's like a lot of things you can do around here: It may feel good for a year or 2, but 5 years from now we'll be hitting ourselves upside the head, saying why have we got a bigger welfare problem than we had 5 years ago.

Now, besides the need to support work and tough child support enforcement, I also think there are some other questions here, questions of the treatment of children and addressing the problems of teen pregnancy. Three-quarters of the unwed teen mothers in this country end up on welfare within 5 years. We clearly need a national campaign against teen pregnancy that sends a clear message: It is wrong to have a child outside marriage. Nobody should get pregnant or father a child who isn't prepared to raise the child, love the child, and take responsibility for the child's future.

I know the Republicans care about this problem, too. This is not a partisan political issue. It is not a racial issue. It is not an income issue. It is not a regional issue. This issue is eating the heart out of this country. You don't have to be in any particular political camp to know we're in big trouble as a society if we're headed toward a day when half of all the kids in this country are born outside marriage.

But some aspects of this current plan in Congress could do more harm than good. Our plan sends a clear message to young men and women that mistakes have consequences, that they have to turn their lives around, that they have to give their children a better chance. We want teen fathers to know they'll spend the next 18 years paying child support. We want teen mothers to know they have to stay at home with their parents or in an appropriate supervised setting and stay in school. And they have to implement—or identify the fathers. They don't have a separate check to go out on their own.

Now, the Republican plan in Congress sends a different message to young people that's both tougher and weaker. It says, "If you make a mistake, you're out on your own, even if it means you are likely to end up on welfare for life and cost us even more money down the road."

Now, in recent weeks, we've narrowed our differences, the Republicans and the administration, in response to concerns that have been raised by people within the Republican Party. But their bill still denies—now listen to this—their bill still denies any assistance to teen mothers under the age of 18 and their children until they turn 18, and then leaves the States the option of denying those benefits permanently, as long—to anybody who was under 18 when they had a child.

Now, I just believe it's a mistake to cut people off because they're young and unmarried and they make a mistake. The younger you are, the more likely you are to make mistakes, although I haven't noticed any absence of errors from those of us who get older. [*Laughter*] I think it's wrong to make small children pay the price for their parents' mistakes. I also think it's counterproductive. It's not in our interest. It will

cost the taxpayers more money than it will save. It's bound to lead to more dependency, not less, to more broken families, not fewer, to more burdens on the taxpayer over the long run, not less.

Now, our plan is different, but it is tougher in some ways. It would say, "If you want this check and you're a teenager, you've got to live at home. And if you're in an abusive home, you must live in another appropriate supervised setting. You must stay in school. You must identify the father of the child." So we're not weaker, but we're different.

We also want a national campaign against teen pregnancy, rooted in our local communities, that sends a clear message about abstinence and responsible parenting. That is the clue, folks. If we could get rid of that, we wouldn't have a welfare problem, and we'd be talking about something else in the next couple of years.

Now, there are other provisions in this bill that I think are unfair to children—and let me just mention, for your information, I think they're really tough on disabled children and children in foster homes—and I think they ought to be modified. And finally, it is important to point out that under the guise of State flexibility, this plan reduces future payments to States in ways that make States and children very vulnerable in times of recession or if their population is growing more than other States. So basically, if we adopt this plan the way it is, it will say to you in your State, if times get tough, you're on your own.

I don't think we should let budget-cutting be wrapped in a cloak of welfare reform. We have a national interest in the welfare of our children. Let's reform welfare. Let's cut the deficit. But let's don't mix up the two and pretend that one is the other. Let's put our children first.

Let me say that I have come here today in the spirit of good faith to try to outline these specifics. You may not agree with me; you may agree with them. But I want you to know what the points of debate are. Again, I am glad we're discussing this. This is a big problem for America. And I believe in the end we can work it out together as long as we remember what it's really about—again, the way you think about problems, you have a name, a face, and a life history. That's what we sometimes lose up here in Washington.

I just want to close with this story. When I was Governor, I was trying to get all the other Governors interested in welfare reform. I once had a panel at a welfare meeting in Washington. And I didn't even know how many Governors would show up. Forty-one Governors showed up to listen to women on welfare, or women who had been on welfare, talk about their lives.

There was a woman there from my State, and I was asking her questions, and I didn't know what her answers were going to be, letting her talk to the Governors. And I said, "Do you think it ought to be mandatory for people on welfare to be in these education and job placement programs?" She said, "Yes, I do." I said, "Why?" She said, "Because a lot of people like me, we lose all our self-confidence. We don't think we amount to much, and if you don't make us do it, we'll just lay up and watch the soaps." But then I said, I asked her to describe her job, and she did. And I said, "What's the best thing about having a job?" She said, "When my boy goes to school, and they ask him, what does your momma do for a living, he can give an answer."

So I want you to help us, because whether you're Republicans or Democrats or black, brown, or white, or liberals or conservatives, you have to deal with people with names, faces, and life histories. We're up here dealing in sound bites trying to pierce through on the evening news. It's a big difference. It's a big difference.

This debate is about more than welfare. It's about who we are as a people and what kind of country we'll want to pass along to our children. It's about the dignity of work, the bond of family, the virtue of responsibility, the strength of our communities, the strength of our democratic values.

This is a great American issue. And I still believe that all of us working together can advance those values and secure the future of our children and make sure that no child in this country ever has to grow up without those values and the great hope that has made us, all of us, what we are.

Thank you, and God bless you.

NOTE: The President spoke at 10:15 a.m. at the Washington Hilton Hotel. In his remarks, he referred to Randall Franke, president, Douglas Bovin, first vice president, Michael Hightower, second vice president, Randy Johnson, third vice president, John Stroger, immediate past president, and Larry Naake, executive director, National Association of Counties; Doris Ward, San Francisco County Assessor; Marian Wright Edelman, president, Children's Defense Fund; and ACORN, the Association of Community Organizations for Reform Now.

Statement on the Terrorist Attack in Pakistan
March 8, 1995

The attack on American diplomatic personnel in Pakistan today outrages all Americans. I have instructed relevant U.S. Government agencies to work with the Government of Pakistan to apprehend the perpetrators of this cowardly act. I want to thank the Government of Pakistan for the excellent cooperation it has already provided.

Our hearts go out to the families of Gary Durell, a communicator, and Jacqueline van Landingham, a consulate secretary, who were killed. We pray for the speedy recovery of Mark McCloy, a consulate spouse, who was wounded.

Attacks such as these should make the international community rededicate itself to efforts to stamp out terrorism everywhere.

Message on the Observance of Saint Patrick's Day, 1995
March 8, 1995

Warmest greetings to everyone celebrating Saint Patrick's Day.

More than 1500 years ago, Saint Patrick escaped the bonds of slavery and brought his message of faith and opportunity to the Emerald Isle. His extraordinary courage and conviction inspired the Irish people and heralded a new era of enlightenment and peace for his adopted homeland. Today, Saint Patrick's legacy continues to endure, in Ireland and beyond, as we strive for the hope embodied by his teachings and his life's work.

On this feast of the patron saint of Ireland, we rejoice in our Irish heritage and honor the Irish Americans who have made immeasurable contributions to our nation and our culture. Since the earliest days of our republic, the sons and daughters of Ireland have symbolized the American dream. Overcoming political, economic, and social struggles, Irish Americans have achieved tremendous success in all realms of American life—from politics to education, business to the arts.

This Saint Patrick's Day has a special importance to all friends of Ireland for it is the first in a generation to occur in a peaceful Northern Ireland. Let us today join together to build on the progress of the past year and advance the cause of peace and reconciliation.

Across our country today, in parades, in classrooms, and in churches, millions of Irish Americans will celebrate the spirit of Saint Patrick that lives on in all of us. Best wishes to all for a wonderful holiday.

BILL CLINTON

Message to the Congress Transmitting a Report on Railroad Safety
March 8, 1995

To the Congress of the United States:

I transmit herewith the 1993 annual report on the Administration of the Federal Railroad Safety Act of 1970, pursuant to section 211 of the Act (45 U.S.C. 440(a)).

WILLIAM J. CLINTON

The White House,
March 8, 1995.

Message to the Congress Transmitting the Report of the Federal Council on the Aging
March 8, 1995

To the Congress of the United States:

In accordance with section 204(f) of the Older Americans Act of 1965, as amended (42 U.S.C. 3015(f)), I transmit herewith the Annual Report for 1994 of the Federal Council on the Aging. The report reflects the Council's views in its role of examining programs serving older Americans.

WILLIAM J. CLINTON

The White House,
March 8, 1995.

Message to the Congress Transmitting Trade Reports
March 8, 1995

To the Congress of the United States:

As required by section 163 of the Trade Act of 1974, as amended (19 U.S.C. 2213), I transmit herewith the 1995 Trade Policy Agenda and 1994 Annual Report on the Trade Agreements Program.

WILLIAM J. CLINTON

The White House,
March 8, 1995.

Letter to Congressional Leaders Reporting on Iraq's Compliance With United Nations Security Council Resolutions
March 8, 1995

Dear Mr. Speaker: (Dear Mr. President:)

Consistent with the Authorization for Use of Military Force Against Iraq Resolution (Public Law 102–1), and as part of my effort to keep the Congress fully informed, I am reporting on the status of efforts to obtain Iraq's compliance with the resolutions adopted by the U.N. Security Council.

The October 1994 provocation by Iraq is emblematic of Iraq's failure to demonstrate the "peaceful intentions" called for by the Security Council in Resolution 687, which ended the Gulf War. Indeed, since its recognition of Kuwait last November, Iraq has done nothing to comply with its numerous remaining obligations under Council resolutions. At its bimonthly review of Iraq sanctions in January, the Security Council voted unanimously to maintain the sanctions regime on Iraq without change. We shall also insist that the sanctions be maintained until Iraq complies with all relevant provisions of U.N. Security Council (UNSC) resolutions.

The December 1994 report to the Council by the U.N. Special Commission on Iraq (UNSCOM) makes clear how far from full compliance Iraq remains in the area of weapons of mass destruction (WMD). Continued vigilance is essential because we believe that Saddam Hussein is committed to rebuilding his WMD capability. While UNSCOM has made progress in setting up the mechanics of monitoring (e.g., installing cameras, tagging equipment, and establishing the Baghdad monitoring center), the regime continues to withhold evidence of its past weapons programs in violation of the resolutions. Indeed, in the report, UNSCOM Chairman Ekeus expressed his conviction "that important documentation (on past weapons programs) still exists and that the Iraqi authorities have taken a conscious decision not to release it freely to the Commission." In the same report, Chairman Ekeus makes clear that this information is necessary for a comprehensive weapons monitoring program.

In addition to noncompliance with the WMD provisions of Security Council resolutions, the regime remains in violation of numerous other Security Council requirements. The regime has failed to be forthcoming with information on hundreds of Kuwaitis and third-country nationals missing since the Iraqi occupation. In January, the Kuwaiti government submitted to the Secretary General a list of the military equipment looted from Kuwait during the War. Iraq has taken no steps to return this or other Kuwaiti property stolen during the occupation, with the exception of initial preparations for the return of one Kuwaiti airplane. During the January review of sanctions, Ambassador Albright presented to the Council evidence acquired during Iraq's troop movements last October that proves that hundreds of pieces of Kuwaiti military hardware are now in the arsenals of Saddam Hussein's Republican Guard.

The UNSC resolutions regarding Iraq do not prevent the shipment of food or medicine to that country. Yet the Iraqi government continues to maintain an embargo against its northern provinces and to divert humanitarian supplies to its supporters and the military. The Iraqi government also still refuses to sell up to $1.6 billion in oil as previously authorized by the Security Council in Resolutions 706 and 712. Iraq could use proceeds from such sales to purchase additional foodstuffs, medicines, and supplies for civilian needs. Instead, Iraq's refusal to implement Security Council Resolutions 706 and 712 causes prolonged and needless suffering.

The no-fly zones over northern and southern Iraq continue to deter Iraq from using its aircraft against its population. However, the Iraqi government continues its brutal campaign against its perceived enemies throughout the country. Iraqi forces periodically shell villages in the south and the north with artillery. In the south, Iraqi repression of the Shi'a population, and specifically the Marsh Arabs, continues, as does a policy of deliberate environmental devastation. In the last few years, the population of the marsh region has fallen sharply as Iraqi military operations have forcibly dispersed residents to other areas and thousands of Shi'a refugees have sought refuge in Iran. The traditional lifestyle of Iraq's marsh Arabs, which has endured for centuries, may soon disappear altogether. In early February, Iraqi Shi'a oppositionists based in southern Iran launched a cross-border attack against Iraqi forces near Al-Qumah but were repelled.

The Special Rapporteur of the U.N. Commission on Human Rights (UNHRC), Max van der Stoel, continues to report on the human rights situation in Iraq, including the Iraqi military's repression against civilian populations and the widespread phenomena of political killings, mass executions, and state-sponsored terrorism. He has reported the recent use by Iraq of new forms of punishment, such as the amputation of ears and hands and the branding of foreheads. The U.N. General Assembly condemned these mutilations in a December 1994 resolution. Clearly, the Government of Iraq has not complied with the provisions of UNSC Resolution 688 requiring it to cease repression of its own people.

The Special Rapporteur has asserted that the Government of Iraq has engaged in war crimes and crimes against humanity and may have committed violations of the 1948 Genocide Convention. The Special Rapporteur continues to call on the Government of Iraq to permit the stationing of human rights monitors inside Iraq to improve the flow of information and to provide independent verification of reports of human rights abuses. We continue to support Mr. van der Stoel's work and his call for monitors.

Baghdad's attempts to violate the U.N. sanctions continue unabated. Since the last report, 12 maritime vessels have been intercepted and diverted to Gulf ports for attempting to smuggle commodities from Iraq in violation of sanctions. Gulf States have cooperated with the Multinational Interdiction Force in accepting diverted ships and in taking action against cargoes in accordance with relevant U.N. Security Council resolutions, including Resolutions 665 and 778.

For more than 3 years, the story has not changed; the Baghdad regime flouts the sanctions, demonstrates disdain for the United Nations and, in our view, engages in actions that constitute continuing violations of Security Council Resolutions 686, 687, and 688.

We are monitoring closely the plight of the civilian population throughout Iraq. Our bilateral assistance program in the north will continue, to the extent possible. We also will continue to make every effort, given the practical constraints, to assist the populations in southern and central Iraq through support for the continuation of U.N. humanitarian programs. Finally, we will continue to explore with our allies and Security Council partners means to compel Iraq to cooperate on humanitarian and human rights issues.

Security Council Resolution 687 affirmed that Iraq is liable under international law for compensating the victims of its unlawful invasion and occupation of Kuwait. The U.N. Compensation Commission (UNCC), has received 2.5 million claims worldwide, with an asserted value of $160 billion. The United States has submitted 3,200 claims, with an asserted value of $1.7 billion.

To date, the UNCC Governing Council has approved 59,000 individual awards, worth about $240 million. About 500 awards totaling $11.4 million have been issued to U.S. claimants.

The UNCC has been able to pay only the first small awards for serious personal injury or death ($2.7 million). Unfortunately, the remainder of the awards cannot be paid at this time, because the U.N. Compensation Fund lacks sufficient funding. The awards are supposed to be financed by a deduction from the proceeds of future Iraqi oil sales, once such sales are permitted to resume. However, Iraq's refusal to meet the Security Council's terms for a resumption of oil sales has left the UNCC without adequate financial resources to pay the awards. Iraq's intransigence means that the victims of its aggression remain uncompensated for their losses 4 years after the end of the Persian Gulf War.

In sum, Iraq is still a threat to regional peace and security. Thus, I am determined to maintain sanctions until Iraq has fully complied with all its obligations under the UNSC resolutions and will oppose any discussions of the relaxation of sanctions until Iraq has demonstrated its overall compliance with the relevant Security Council resolutions. Ambassador Albright is traveling to Security Council capitals to convey my determination on this vital matter.

As I have made clear before, Iraq may rejoin the community of civilized nations by adopting democratic processes, respecting human rights, treating its people equally, and adhering to basic norms of international behavior. The Iraqi National Congress espouses these goals, the fulfillment of which would make Iraq a stabilizing force in the Gulf region.

I appreciate the support of the Congress for our efforts, and will continue to keep the Congress informed about this important issue.

Sincerely,

WILLIAM J. CLINTON

NOTE: Identical letters were sent to Newt Gingrich, Speaker of the House of Representatives, and Strom Thurmond, President pro tempore of the Senate. This letter was released by the Office of the Press Secretary on March 9.

Letter to Congressional Leaders Transmitting a Report on Haiti
March 8, 1995

Dear Mr. Speaker: (*Dear Mr. President:*)

Attached, pursuant to section 3 of Public Law 103–423, is the fifth monthly report on the situation in Haiti.

Sincerely,

WILLIAM J. CLINTON

NOTE: Identical letters were sent to Newt Gingrich, Speaker of the House of Representatives, and Strom Thurmond, President pro tempore of the Senate. This letter was released by the Office of the Press Secretary on March 9.

Remarks at Patrick Henry Elementary School and an Exchange With Reporters in Alexandria, Virginia
March 9, 1995

The President. First of all, I want to thank all the people here at Patrick Henry for making us feel so welcome. I thank Principal Leila Engman for making me feel right at home here, and these five young students who have been terrific. They took me to lunch today and introduced me to some of their classmates. We played "Where's Waldo?" and had a great lunch. And I thank them for that.

I want to thank Senator Robb and Congressman Moran for coming with me and, of course, our distinguished Secretary of Education, Dick Riley, and Ellen Haas, the Under Secretary of Agriculture for Food, Nutrition and Consumer Services. Mayor Ticer, we're glad to be here in your community; thank you. And I'm glad that Dr. Jim Moller is here, head of the American Heart Association and a strong supporter of the effort for healthy meals in our public schools throughout the country. I thank Maxine Wood, the superintendent of schools, and Bernadette Johnson-Green, the vice chair of the school board, and the other representatives of this school system who are here.

I'm glad to be here today to participate for the first time in quite a few years in a school lunch program. I ate at my school cafeteria for most of my years in grade school and junior high and high school, but it's been quite a few years since I've had a chance to do this, except with Chelsea on occasion over the years.

Over 25 million young schoolchildren in this country eat school lunches daily. And for many of them it's their only nutritious meal in the day. This program has been around since the year I was born, 1946, when President Truman signed it into law as a matter of national security, to ensure that our children are properly fed.

For 50 years, this program has had strong bipartisan support. In 1969, President Nixon said, "A child ill-fed is dulled in curiosity, lower in stamina, distracted from learning." I received a letter from a woman from California who said, and I quote, "I'm glad there were free and reduced lunches for children; otherwise my kids would have starved." And she was working full-time as a nurse's aide while her children were in school.

This week's newspapers, of course, are full of similar stories. Yesterday, I read about a cafeteria worker who said she sees kids every day who are so hungry they practically eat the food from other children's plates.

School lunches have always been seen by both Democrats and Republicans as an essential part of student education. Last year, with the leadership of Ellen Haas, we took some further steps to make meals more nutritious, to increase their vitamin and mineral content and reduce their fat and sodium content, and the Congress ratified that in a piece of legislation passed last year. Unfortunately, this year, some Members of the new Congress have decided that cutting this program would be a good way of cutting Government spending and financing tax cuts for upper income Americans. This is penny-wise and pound-foolish. While saving some money now, these nutrition programs for schoolchildren and for women and for infants save several dollars in social costs for every dollar we spend on them. The American people want a Government that works better and costs less, not a Government that works worse and costs more.

These Republican proposals will cost us dearly in the health of our children, the quality of our schools, and the safety of our streets. I have done everything I could for the last 2 years to fight for the economic interests of middle class Americans, to help poor people to work their way into the middle class, and to support the values of responsibility, family, work, and community. This proposal undermines that. We have to give our children more support so they can make the most of their own lives.

This school lunch proposal, of course, is not the only thing in the Republican rescission proposal that is penny-wise and pound-foolish, that sacrifices enormous future prosperity and health for America for present, short-term gains. The rescissions would deprive 15,000 people of the opportunity to serve in AmeriCorps; 100,000 educationally disadvantaged students would lose their special services. Drug prevention programs that will now go to 94 percent of our schools would be eliminated. Drug prevention funds that go for security measures, for police officers, and for education and prevention efforts would be eliminated. And of course, 1.2 million summer job opportunities for young people would be eliminated.

This is hardly what I call "putting people first." This will advance not the economic interests of the middle class. It will not restore the American dream. It will not help the poor to work their way into prosperity. It will simply achieve some short-term gains in order to finance either spending cuts or tax cuts to upper income Americans.

I know we have to reduce the deficit. Last year, with the help of Senator Robb and Congressman Moran—in 1993, excuse me—we cut the deficit by $600 billion. I've given Congress $144 billion in further budget cuts. I will work with them to find more, but not in the area of education or health or nutrition for our children and our future.

We ought to be here expanding opportunity, not restricting it. But let me say, again, to Patrick Henry, to the school, to the school leaders, and most of all to these fine students, you have given me and Senator Robb and Congressman Moran and Dr. Moller a wonderful experience, and you have also helped once again to tell the American people that the School Lunch Program should not be put on the chopping block. Let's go out there, let's defend it, let's keep it, let's invest more in education and find other ways to cut the deficit.

Thank you very much.

Budget Priorities

Q. Mr. President, are there any rescissions that the Republicans have been proposing in the House that you would support?

The President. We're going through them. There may well be. But they know which ones I don't support. And let me just say, we're about to move into the debate on the line-item veto, which gives us a permanent mechanism to get rescissions, if you will, every year. And if they will pass the line-item veto, I'll work with them. We'll cut spending, and we'll continue to reduce this deficit.

But we don't need to reduce our investment in education, in child health, in medical research and technology, and in efforts to keep people off drugs and protect our children and our schools from the drug problem.

I am more than—I have proved that I will cut spending and I will cut some more. But look at the Agriculture Department. They want to cut the School Lunch Program; we closed 1,200 Agriculture Department offices instead. That's the kind of decisions we need to make, and we'll make the right decisions if we'll work together. And I think I speak for all of us here in saying there is a way to restore our country's fiscal health and still support our children and our future. That's what we're committed to.

Thank you.

NOTE: The President spoke at 12:22 p.m. in the cafeteria. In his remarks, he referred to Mayor Patricia S. Ticer of Alexandria.

Message to the Congress on Nuclear Cooperation With EURATOM
March 9, 1995

To the Congress of the United States:

The United States has been engaged in nuclear cooperation with the European Community (now European Union) for many years. This cooperation was initiated under agreements that were concluded in 1957 and 1968 between the United States and the European Atomic Energy Community (EURATOM) and that expire December 31, 1995. Since the inception of this cooperation, EURATOM has adhered to all its obligations under those agreements.

The Nuclear Non-Proliferation Act of 1978 amended the Atomic Energy Act of 1954 to establish new nuclear export criteria, including a requirement that the United States have a right to consent to the reprocessing of fuel exported from the United States. Our present agreements for cooperation with EURATOM do not contain such a right. To avoid disrupting cooperation with EURATOM, a proviso was included in the law to enable continued cooperation until March 10, 1980, if EURATOM agreed to negotiations concerning our cooperation agreements. EURATOM agreed in 1978 to such negotiations.

The law also provides that nuclear cooperation with EURATOM can be extended on an annual basis after March 10, 1980, upon determination

by the President that failure to cooperate would be seriously prejudicial to the achievement of U.S. nonproliferation objectives or otherwise jeopardize the common defense and security, and after notification to the Congress. President Carter made such a determination 15 years ago and signed Executive Order No. 12193, permitting nuclear cooperation with EURATOM to continue until March 10, 1981. Presidents Reagan and Bush made similar determinations and signed Executive orders each year during their terms. I signed Executive Order No. 12840 in 1993 and Executive Order No. 12903 in 1994, which extended cooperation until March 10, 1994, and March 10, 1995, respectively.

In addition to numerous informal contacts, the United States has engaged in frequent talks with EURATOM regarding the renegotiation of the U.S.-EURATOM agreements for cooperation. Talks were conducted in November 1978; September 1979; April 1980; January 1982; November 1983; March 1984; May, September, and November 1985; April and July 1986; September 1987; September and November 1988; July and December 1989; February, April, October, and December 1990; and September 1991. Formal negotiations on a new agreement were held in April, September, and December 1992;

March, July, and October 1993; June, October, and December 1994; and January and February 1995. They are expected to continue.

I believe that it is essential that cooperation between the United States and EURATOM continue, and likewise, that we work closely with our allies to counter the threat of proliferation of nuclear explosives. Not only would a disruption of nuclear cooperation with EURATOM eliminate any chance of progress in our negotiations with that organization related to our agreements, it would also cause serious problems in our overall relationships. Accordingly, I have determined that failure to continue peaceful nuclear cooperation with EURATOM would be se-riously prejudicial to the achievement of U.S. nonproliferation objectives and would jeopardize the common defense and security of the United States. I therefore intend to sign an Executive order to extend the waiver of the application of the relevant export criterion of the Atomic Energy Act until the current agreements expire on December 31, 1995.

WILLIAM J. CLINTON

The White House,
March 9, 1995.

NOTE: The Executive order is listed in Appendix D at the end of this volume.

Letter to Congressional Leaders Transmitting a Report on International Agreements
March 9, 1995

Dear Mr. Speaker: (*Dear Mr. Chairman:*)
Pursuant to subsection (b) of the Case-Zablocki Act (1 U.S.C. 112b(b)), I hereby transmit a report prepared by the Department of State concerning international agreements.
Sincerely,

WILLIAM J. CLINTON

NOTE: Identical letters were sent to Newt Gingrich, Speaker of the House of Representatives, and Jesse Helms, chairman, Senate Committee on Foreign Relations.

Message to the Congress on the Financial Crisis in Mexico
March 9, 1995

To the Congress of the United States:
On January 31, 1995, I determined pursuant to 31 U.S.C. 5302(b) that the economic crisis in Mexico posed "unique and emergency circumstances" that justified the use of the Exchange Stabilization Fund (ESF) to provide loans and credits with maturities of greater than 6 months to the Government of Mexico and the Bank of Mexico. Consistent with the requirements of 31 U.S.C. 5302(b), I am hereby notifying the Congress of that determination. The congressional leadership issued a joint statement with me on January 31, 1995, in which we all agreed that such use of the ESF was a necessary and appropriate response to the Mexican financial crisis and in the United States' vital national interest.

On February 21, 1995, the Secretary of the Treasury and the Mexican Secretary of Finance and Public Credit signed four agreements that provide the framework and specific legal arrangements under which up to $20 billion in support will be made available from the ESF to the Government of Mexico and the Bank of Mexico. Under these agreements, the United States will provide three forms of support to Mexico: short-term swaps through which Mexico borrows dollars for 90 days and that can be rolled over for up to 1 year; medium-term swaps through which Mexico can borrow dollars for up to 5 years; and securities guarantees having maturities of up to 10 years.

Repayment of these loans and guarantees is backed by revenues from the export of crude oil and petroleum products formalized in an agreement signed by the United States, the Government of Mexico, and the Mexican government's oil company. In addition, as added protection in the unlikely event of default, the United States is requiring Mexico to maintain the value of the pesos it deposits with the United States in connection with the medium-term swaps. Therefore, should the rate of exchange of the peso against the U.S. dollar drop during the time the United States holds pesos, Mexico would be required to provide the United States with enough additional pesos to reflect the rate of exchange prevailing at the conclusion of the swap.

I am enclosing a Fact Sheet prepared by the Department of the Treasury that provides greater details concerning the terms of the four agreements. I am also enclosing a summary of the economic policy actions that the Government of Mexico and the Central Bank have agreed to take as a condition of receiving assistance.

The agreements we have signed with Mexico are part of a multilateral effort involving contributions from other countries and multilateral institutions. The Board of the International Monetary Fund has approved up to $17.8 billion in medium-term assistance for Mexico, subject to Mexico's meeting appropriate economic conditions. Of this amount, $7.8 billion has already been disbursed, and additional conditional assist-

ance will become available beginning in July of this year. In addition, the Bank for International Settlements is expected to provide $10 billion in short-term assistance.

The current Mexican financial crisis is a liquidity crisis that has had a significant destabilizing effect on the exchange rate of the peso, with consequences for the overall exchange rate system. The spill-over effects of inaction in response to this crisis would be significant for other emerging market economies, particularly those in Latin America, as well as for the United States. Using the ESF to respond to this crisis is therefore plainly consistent with the purpose of 31 U.S.C. 5302(b): to give the United States the ability to take action consistent with its obligations in the International Monetary Fund to assure orderly exchange arrangements and a stable system of exchange rates.

The Mexican peso crisis erupted with such suddenness and in such magnitude as to render the usual short-term approaches to a liquidity crisis inadequate to address the problem. To resolve problems arising from Mexico's short-term debt burden, longer term solutions are necessary in order to avoid further pressure on the exchange rate of the peso. These facts present unique and emergency circumstances, and it is therefore both appropriate and necessary to make the ESF available to extend credits and loans to Mexico in excess of 6 months.

WILLIAM J. CLINTON

The White House,
March 9, 1995.

Remarks on the Administration's Economic Strategy and an Exchange With Reporters
March 10, 1995

The President. Good morning. Today's employment report shows that the economic strategy pursued by our administration has worked for the last 2 years, thanks not only, of course, to our economic policies but also to the dramatic increases in productivity by American businesses and American workers.

The new unemployment rate of 5.4 percent is the lowest in almost 5 years. We have the

lowest combined rates of unemployment and inflation in 25 years. The fundamentals of this economy overall are healthier than they have been in a generation.

When I took office, we had had 12 years in which the deficit had quadrupled and investments in our people had been ignored. There was no job growth. That's not true anymore. Our disciplined plan to reduce the deficit, lower trade barriers to American products and services, and invest more in the future of our people through education, training, and technology, is working.

Let me underscore this: As of today the economy has produced 6.1 million jobs since I became President. And if Michael Jordan goes back to the Bulls it will be 6,100,001 new jobs. [*Laughter*] That includes, I might add, 14 straight months of manufacturing job growth, something almost unheard of in the modern era. And encouragingly for our biggest continuing economic problem, last year we had more high-wage jobs coming into the economy than in the previous 5 years combined.

Those are 6.1 million reasons for this country to stay committed to an economic strategy of opportunity and responsibility, disciplined commitment to investment in the future of our people through education, training, and technology, selling our products, and reducing our deficit. We have reduced the deficit by $600 billion, and of course, our new budget proposed another deficit reduction in excess of $80 billion.

It has now been 66 days since the new Congress came to town. We are still waiting for the leadership to propose their budget plan. But now we do see that there is a proposal for massive tax cuts which will benefit largely upper income Americans, tax cuts that will cost $188 billion in the first 5 years, but, if you look at the 10-year figure, will cost $700 billion. These are more than 3 times the aggregate amounts of the proposals that I made in my budget, which are heavily targeted to the needs of middle class Americans to raise their incomes, educate their children, provide for the basic health

care needs through an IRA, a tax deduction for the cost of education after high school.

And I want to emphasize furthermore, that I think what we ought to be working on now as we look ahead, are things that will continue to increase jobs. That means staying with deficit reduction, staying with investments in education and training and technology, staying with selling American products and things that will raise incomes.

The "GI bill" for American workers does not cost any money, but the Congress could pass it to consolidate all these training programs, to give vouchers to unemployed people and people on low wages. The Congress could pass the minimum wage increase, which is overdue and which will have an impact in raising incomes.

But the fundamental strategy is sound. We are producing jobs. Now we have to raise incomes. We have to stay with this strategy. There are 6.1 million arguments for why it is the right strategy.

Thank you.

Q. What about the capital gains tax? What do you think of that?

Interest Rates

Q. Mr. President, don't these numbers push interest rates up?

The President. Well, Chairman Greenspan hadn't said that yet. Let's—I don't want—every time I say something about the money it turns out to be wrong, so I'm not going to comment on it.

NOTE: The President spoke at 9:45 a.m. in the Briefing Room at the White House.

The President's Radio Address
March 11, 1995

Good morning. I ran for President to keep the American dream alive for the forgotten middle class and for all of those struggling to make it in our country, to make sure all Americans have the chance to live up to their God-given potential. Today in Washington, there's a great debate about how best to do that, and the choices we make will say a lot about who we are as a nation as we enter the new century.

On one side, there's the old one-size-fits-all Washington view that big Government can fix every problem. On the other, there's the Republican contract view that the Federal Government is the cause of every problem. Well, I have a different view. I believe the purpose of Government is to expand opportunity, not bureaucracy, to empower people through education to make the most of their own lives, and to enhance our security on our streets and around the world. I believe in a Government that is limited but effective, lean but not mean, not a savior but not on the sidelines, a partner in the fight for the future. I believe in a Government that promotes opportunity but demands responsibility and that understands that we need all Americans in strong grassroots communities. That's what the New Covenant is all about, opportunity and responsibility.

Let me give you two examples. First, with regard to welfare reform, I believe we should offer more opportunity in terms of education and work to people on welfare, but we must demand more responsibility, tougher child support enforcement, responsible parenting, and the requirement that to receive benefits, young people should be in school or working toward going to work.

Or take the college loan program. Our administration believes more people should go to college, so we've offered more opportunity to millions of young people, more affordable college loans with much better repayment terms. But we've insisted on more responsibility. The cost to you, the taxpayers, of delinquent college loans has gone down from $2.8 billion a year to $1 billion a year since I took office, opportunity and responsibility.

Look at the economy. When I took office, we had no economic strategy for putting people first. Instead, we'd had 12 years in which trickle-down economics had quadrupled the deficit and investments in our people had been ignored. There was less opportunity and less responsibility. Today, we're reducing the deficit by over $600 billion. The Federal work force is down by over 150,000 and will soon be the smallest since John Kennedy was President. We cut 300 programs in our first two budgets, and this year, we want to eliminate or combine 400 more. But while we've cut, we're also helping people to invest in their future: more for Head Start, to apprenticeships, to college loans, to training for adults. The results are clear: This strategy is working.

We have the lowest combined rate of unemployment and inflation in 25 years. Since I became President, we have 6.1 million more jobs. Now, there's more to do. More people want work, and too many people haven't gotten a raise and are living with economic uncertainty. We've got to keep cutting unnecessary spending and investing in growing our economy.

The old view resisted change, but the Republican contract view often goes too far. Let me give you another example. We want to save money and to change the Agriculture Department, and so do the Republicans. The old view just left the Agriculture Department alone, though agriculture has changed greatly. My approach was to close 1,200 offices and to shrink the bureaucracy. But the Republicans want to cut the School Lunch Program that's helped our children thrive for 50 years.

You'll see this debate played out in many areas. One involves AmeriCorps, our national service program. AmeriCorps is about opportunity and responsibility. You get a helping hand for your own education if you give one to your country. Our young AmeriCorps volunteers are partners with our communities, with nurses, pastors, police officers, doing work that won't get done any other way. They're walking police beats in Brooklyn, building homes in Georgia, fighting fires in Idaho.

Jamie Kendrick is one of these young people. He's here with me, along with some other AmeriCorps volunteers today. He works with disadvantaged children in Baltimore. And as he does, he's helping them to help others. Every week, he leads more than 90 troubled kids into a nursing home to visit older people. The seniors get companionship and a chance to share their wisdom. The children, many of whom come from broken homes, now know older people who care about them. And Jamie knows he's serving others as he earns tuition for college. This is a good deal for Jamie, for the seniors, for the young people, and for us, too. We get better citizens, stronger communities, and more education.

I want to keep AmeriCorps growing. Right now, Republicans in the House of Representatives are proposing to cut off opportunities in AmeriCorps for 15,000 people like Jamie. Then they want to end AmeriCorps altogether. But AmeriCorps isn't a bureaucracy, it's a grassroots partnership to build strong communities through opportunity and responsibility.

The House Republicans want to cut all this and more, including the safe and drug-free schools program, the summer jobs program, to pay for huge tax cuts costing $700 billion over 10 years and benefiting mostly upper income Americans. AmeriCorps, the School Lunch Program, the safe and drug-free schools programs, all together, they cost a tiny fraction of that.

Now, I believe we must keep cutting spending, and we should give middle class Americans tax relief to help pay for their education, their childrearing, their health care costs. But this proposal goes too far. The path to the future is through opportunity and responsibility.

Before I close, I want to emphasize that in spite of these differences, I think we can make real progress now. We don't have to give in to gridlock. I've already signed a bill to apply to Congress the laws it applies to private business, and we're about to complete a bill to limit the ability of Congress to pass mandates on the State and local government without paying for them.

There's more we can do to cut pork, not people, in the Federal budget. We're about to begin debate in the Senate on the line-item veto, an issue on which the Republican leaders and I strongly agree. We need to pass it and keep cutting unnecessary spending.

This can be a very good time for our country if we all remember our mission: to make life easier, not harder for middle income families; to grow the middle class and shrink the under class; to make the future brighter, not darker, for our young people; to promote opportunity and responsibility.

We must keep faith with the American dream. The Jamie Kendricks of our country will do right by all of us if we will do right by them.

Thanks for listening.

NOTE: The President spoke at 10:06 a.m. from the Oval Office at the White House.

Statement on the Withdrawal of Michael Carns and the Nomination of John Deutch To Be Director of Central Intelligence
March 11, 1995

It is with profound regret that I accept General Michael Carns' decision to withdraw his name from consideration for the position of Director of Central Intelligence.

I understand General Carns' concern that allegations made against him in the course of his background investigation could be misconstrued and complicate his confirmation. The sad truth is that we live in a time when even the most exemplary individuals, like General Carns, who already has given so much to his country, are deterred from serving by the fear that their records will be distorted, their achievements ignored, and their families maligned during the confirmation process.

General Carns' decision to withdraw is our country's loss. This man, who flew more than 200 combat missions over Southeast Asia and distinguished himself as a military commander and an innovative manager, was prepared to come out of retirement to serve America one more time in a vital mission. I deeply regret that he will not have that opportunity and that our intelligence community and the American people will not have the benefit of his broad experience, his intelligence, and his dedication.

Finding another individual with the exceptional skills and qualities needed to lead the intelligence community was no easy task. But in Deputy Secretary of Defense John Deutch, who I am pleased to announce my intent to nominate as the next Director of Central Intelligence, we have found such a man.

Deputy Secretary Deutch has served at the highest levels of academia and Government in a wide variety of positions, from assistant professor of chemistry at Princeton to provost at MIT, from Under Secretary of Energy under President Carter to member of the President's Foreign Intelligence Advisory Board under President Bush, from Under Secretary of Defense to Deputy Secretary of Defense in my administration.

Over the past 2 years, I've enjoyed an increasingly close personal and professional relationship with Deputy Secretary Deutch. Together with former Defense Secretary Aspin and Secretary Perry, I have asked Deputy Secretary Deutch to take on some of the toughest, most important assignments at the Pentagon.

Deputy Secretary Deutch has played a lead role in reviewing our nuclear force posture. He's overseen the modernizing of our weapons systems. And he has become intimately familiar with the workings of the intelligence community, especially its support for the military. The blueprint Deputy Secretary Deutch worked out to eliminate redundancies and duplication between our civilian and military intelligence demonstrates the kind of innovative thinking we need to meet the new challenges of the post-cold-war world.

Strengthening U.S. intelligence is an effort to which I attach the highest personal priority. To make that commitment absolutely clear and to underscore that he will be a full member of my national security team, I have decided to appoint Deputy Secretary Deutch to my Cabinet

if he is confirmed as Director of Central Intelligence.

In John Deutch, we have a dynamic, brilliant leader with all the necessary skills for this critical assignment and my highest trust and confidence. I look forward to working with him, the Aspin commission, and Congress in building an intelligence community that will meet our national security challenges well into the next century.

NOTE: A statement by Michael Carns was also made available by the Office of the Press Secretary.

Statement on Disaster Assistance for California
March 12, 1995

Today I am declaring that a major disaster exists in California. Federal funds will begin to flow to the individuals and communities affected by this latest terrible act of nature. California has been badly hit by Mother Nature during the last 2 years, wildfires, the Northridge earthquake, January's flood, and now this flooding. But California has not been beaten. That is because of the great fortitude, spirit, and can-do attitude of its people. I saw this spirit when I visited the town of Roseville in January, as neighbor helped neighbor cope with the tragedy of destroyed homes, possessions, and livelihoods.

I know these are difficult times for many Californians. My administration will do all that we can to help permit life to return to normalcy as soon as possible. James Lee Witt, our Federal Emergency Management Agency Director, has gotten all too familiar with California during the

last 2 years. I am directing Director Witt and his staff to begin the flow of programs and to continue to perform its tele-registration and other outreach functions with the same enthusiasm and customer service orientation that we are now used to. I met some of those outreach people in January. They make us all proud.

State and local officials are working around the clock to rescue victims and fight the floods. And the American Red Cross is providing food, comfort, and shelter to those in need. Most importantly, the thousands of volunteers in communities throughout California are all working together in this difficult time. This community spirit is truly the best America has to offer.

Hillary and I send our thoughts and prayers to the families of those who have lost their lives. The thoughts and prayers of the American people are with them as well.

Remarks to the NCAA Football Champion University of Nebraska Cornhuskers
March 13, 1995

Please be seated. Welcome to the White House on this beautiful morning. I am delighted to welcome all of the members of the national championship Nebraska Cornhuskers here, along

with Chancellor Spanier, your athletic director Bill Byrne, and of course, Coach Osborne and all the players. I welcome the Nebraska congressional delegation: Senator Exon, Senator Kerrey, and Representatives Barrett, Bereuter, and Christensen. I do want to say a special word of regret, too, that Bob Devaney couldn't be here today, but we all wish him a very speedy recovery.

I have been, since I was a very small boy, an ardent college football fan. I know that Coach Osborne's record alone justifies a national championship, an 820 percent winning percentage. Most of us would like to have that here. [Laughter] Cornhuskers have been to a bowl game in each of his 22 years, and as I said when I called him the night Nebraska won, nobody deserves it more.

I want to congratulate your three first team All-Americans, linebacker Ed Stewart, tackle Zach Wiegert, and guard Brenden Stai, and also your three first-team Academic All-Americans, tackle Terry Connealy, tight end Matt Shaw, and the Academic All-American of the Year, who I just understood has never made a B, Rob Zatechka. We could give him a job here at the White House. It's sort of like playing for pro football.

I want to thank this team and this coach not only for winning the national championship—that's obviously a great honor—but for the way that it was won and the character and teamwork and spirit that Coach Osborne has always displayed and that this team displayed. I think it inspired people all across the country who are fans of athletics, and I think even people

who are not great football fans or particularly knowledgeable about all the details, who read about the Nebraska team, who saw not only that you had three All-Americans but three Academic All-Americans, and who have followed the work of Tom Osborne over the years. It inspired them all to believe in the value of teamwork and sacrifice and discipline, and certainly you were rewarded in ways that were well justified.

I'd also like to say, I asked Coach Osborne on the way out if this was the largest football team ever to win a national championship, and he said, "Yes, but they're good students, too." I liked it because I felt this is the only—when those three guys walked out with me, this is the only football team in America that could make me look like a ballerina. [Laughter] I liked it.

So I welcome you here. I honor your achievement. We're delighted to have the players here. And I'd like to ask Coach Osborne to take the microphone now.

Coach?

NOTE: The President spoke at 11:51 a.m. on the South Lawn at the White House. In his remarks, he referred to Graham Spanier, chancellor, and Bob Devaney, athletic director emeritus, University of Nebraska. Following the President's remarks, Coach Thomas Osborne made brief remarks, and the team presented the President with a team jersey and an autographed football.

Remarks to the National League of Cities
March 13, 1995

Thank you very much, Carolyn, for that warm introduction. And thank you, ladies and gentlemen, for the wonderful welcome you have given me. I'm glad to be here on this podium with all your officers, including Mayor Lashutka of Columbus. Did I pronounce that right? Close? Lashutka.

I just had the Nebraska football team over at the White House, and so I had a lot of practice pronouncing names this morning. [Laughter] The Nebraska football team are so big, that's the only group of people in America I could stand with and look like the resident ballet dancer. [Laughter]

Mayor James, it's good to see you here, and all the other mayors who are here and all of the other representatives of the cities and towns of our country.

I like to come here and meet with you because you deal with people at the level where you can have the greater contact with them. When I was Governor, nothing was more important to me than actually being able to spend a lot of time with the citizens at the grassroots community level who were interested in solving the problems of people. And I've always said that one of the things I like most about the job I used to have and one of the things I like least about the job I have now is that the closer you get to the people, the less political the work is, and the closer you get to Washington, the more political it becomes.

The most frustrating thing about being President is that I don't get enough time to speak with ordinary Americans in terms that they can understand about what we're trying to do up here. Although I must say, when I was driving up here today, I thought, these local officials may be out of touch, too. This is the most beautiful day we've had in Washington in 6 months, and here you are listening to a politician inside. [*Laughter*] I don't know.

You have the opportunity to see people struggling to keep the American dream alive every day. And when you think of these issues, it must stun you at times what you hear in the news about what's going on up here, when it seems too rhetorical. Because I know when you think of these issues, you know a name, you see a face, you know a life story. That gives meanings to the problems that we are dealing with. And I think Washington has suffered grievously from losing that connection, losing that touch with the people who sent us here, and trying to communicate with people from such a long way away over the mass media, through so many millions of conflicting messages with high levels of rhetoric.

I want to try to move back from that today and just to speak frankly about the choices that we face here and the choices that you face in doing your job and how we both can make the right decisions. As we stand on the edge of a new century and a new millennium, I think there are two great tasks facing America and our generation.

The first is to make sure that we enter the next century with the American dream alive and well for all of our people, for the middle class whose interests are so often forgotten, for those who are struggling to make it in the global economy, for all the poor people in this country who are working hard to play by the rules and to live up to their God-given capacity.

The second thing we have to do is to make sure we enter the next century making sure that America is still the strongest country on Earth, still the greatest force in the world for freedom and democracy and opportunity.

There are two great threats to this endeavor. One is the stagnation of middle class economics. The other is the erosion of mainstream values.

And the third thing that I want to talk to you about is the fact that the Government has often made these problems worse, not better, in the last several years. So we have to ask ourselves, what can we do to restore middle class economics, the opportunity part of the American dream? And what can we do to restore mainstream values, the responsibility part of the American dream? And what kind of Government changes do we need here to make sure we're good partners with the American people where you live and work?

For the last 20 years, most people have worked the same hours or even longer hours for the same or even lower wages. There is a new class of permanently poor people, mostly young women and their small children, and they're growing. And the anxieties of people are pronounced, economically. Even in this time of economic recovery, people worry about downsizing everywhere and whether they really count in the workplace anymore. And there is a huge inequality growing among our workers, where those with good education and those capable of learning new skills tend to get good jobs with growing incomes and those without tend to be stuck in a rut forever.

We have all this good news. We had in 1993—we haven't gotten the '94 figures yet—in '93 we had the largest number of new businesses started in the United States of America in any year in our history, and that's something to be proud of. But we also see people struggling just to hold on and to maintain their lifestyle, even though in many families both the husband and the wife are working and having less and less time to spend with their children.

On the social front, the values we all cherish, work and family and community, are threatened as crime and violence and drug use rises all across America. And even when it falls, it's still too high. The rate of children that are born out of wedlock continues to go up. Our social problems, in many ways, seem more profound today than they have in a long time.

And you see the traditions of breakdown in family, community, rooted in a loss of allegiance to these mainstream values and a lack of opportunity. This is a dangerous erosion of the things that made America great and kept us strong for over 200 years.

We are now in the midst of a great debate here in Washington about what we ought to do about this. How can we make the good things more present, and how can we reduce the bad things in America? How can we do the things we need to do to keep the American dream alive and keep our country strong? How we answer these questions will say an awful lot about what kind of people we're going to be and what kind of country we're going to pass on to our children in the 21st century.

There is on one side of the debate, on the extreme, the old and now discredited Washington view that a big, bureaucratic, one-size-fits-all Government can provide big solutions to all America's big problems and maybe to some of America's not so big problems.

The other extreme is the view of the Republican contract, that Government is the source of all the problems, and if we could just get rid of it completely or at least reduce the Federal Government's spending role, every problem in America would miraculously solve itself.

I have a different view, and it's probably rooted in the fact that I didn't live and work here until 2 years ago. My view is rooted in the fact that my experiences as a Governor of a small State are much more like yours than they are like most of the people who make most of the decisions in this community. I think we have to chart a course between and beyond the old way of big Government and the new rage of no Government.

No great country can survive without a National Government that in the information age is more limited but is still strong and effective. We do have, after all, common problems as a people. We have common opportunities. And these require a common response. We need the Government, in short, to be a partner with people in their private lives as citizens, a partner with State and local government, a partner with all of us.

I believe in a Government that promotes opportunity and demands responsibility, that deals with middle class economics and mainstream values, a Government that is different radically from the one we have known here over the last 30 to 40 years but that still understands it has a role to play in order for us to build strong communities that are the bedrock of this Nation. That's what the New Covenant I talk about all the time is really all about, more opportunity and more responsibility.

Our job is to work together to grow the middle class, to shrink the under class, to expand opportunity and to shrink bureaucracy, to empower people to make the most of their own lives. We can't give any guarantees in this rapidly changing world, but we can give people the capacity to do for themselves. And we must do that; all of us must do it.

And finally, we have to work to enhance our security on our own streets and around the world. I believe, in short, that the role of this Government is to be a partner in the fight for the future, not a savior—it can't be that—but not a spectator on the sidelines either. We've tried that, and it didn't work out very well.

We must face the fact that we live in a certain historical period in which the economy is global. The information age means that the basis of most wealth in the future will be knowledge and that we can be far more decentralized and flexible than we ever have been before. No one will ever again have to rely on a distant bureaucracy to solve every problem in today's rapidly changing environment.

We have to focus more on equipping people with the resources they need to tackle their own problems and to give people the responsibility to determine how best to do that. We have to send more and more decisions back not only to State and local government but to citizens themselves.

We must cut spending. We must cut Government. But I believe we must also invest more in jobs, incomes, technology, education, and training. That's what will make us wealthy.

I ran for President because I felt these challenges were not being met, because I felt there was no economic strategy for putting our people first. We had 12 years of trickle-down economics in which the deficit quadrupled and our future was mortgaged. But we didn't invest in our people or our economy. We had both less opportunity and less responsibility. In Washington all I ever heard was the blame game. And it often reminded me of—I felt often when I was out there in the country like you, like people must feel in a jury box, you know, when two lawyers get in an argument with a judge over what they can say or not. All the jury wants to know is who did it. [*Laughter*]

And the American people, what they want to know is, what are we going to do? And are we going to do? And so I ran for this job because I was tired of a system in which both middle class economics and mainstream values were suffering. And the Government was doing well by special interests but not the public interest. I felt very strongly that we had to do something to stop the conditions in which most Americans were living, where people were working harder and harder and harder for less and less and less security. And I still believe that's what we ought to be about.

Now we have begun to change all that. We have begun to change all that. And it required some pretty tough decisions. Some of them were unpopular. Some of the people who made those unpopular decisions lost their seats in Congress last year, because people were told for years and years and years they could have a free lunch, that there were no tough decisions to be made.

Everything here operated at the level of rhetoric. We got down to business. They talked about cutting the deficit. We did, by $600 billion. And we did it with over a quarter of a trillion dollars in spending cuts, with income tax increases on the wealthiest 1.2 percent of our people, with discipline—not by the way, because I think that's a good thing to do but because they were the ones best able to pay. And those were the people who were benefiting most economically from the economy.

And at the same time, we were cutting 300 domestic programs. We were also providing tax relief for 15 million working families who were working at or near the poverty line to make sure that nobody who works 40 hours a week with children in their home should ever live in poverty. It's the biggest incentive to stay off welfare to know that if you work hard and you raise your kids, you're going to be able to make a living wage. These are the things that we worked on.

Now, we eliminated or consolidated or cut about 300 programs. And in this new budget that I've got—we'll talk more about that in a minute—we propose to eliminate or consolidate 400 more. We reduced the size of the Federal work force in 2 years by over 100,000. And if no new laws pass—[*applause*]—thank you. If no new laws pass, the work force will be reduced over a 6-year period to its smallest size since John Kennedy was President. It will be 272,000 fewer people working here than on the day I was inaugurated President. I'm proud of that.

We have shifted power away from Washington to more responsibility for States and counties and cities and towns. The Vice President has lead our reinventing Government initiative,

which has already saved the taxpayers $63 billion and will save more. We've already cut regulations in banking and intrastate trucking and many other areas that make it now easier for businesses to create jobs and create opportunities. And we must do more, and we will. We've worked hard to try to make it easier for you to do your jobs and to improve the lives of the people that we both serve.

Now, we've done a lot of other things as well that often get lost in the smoke around here. We passed the family leave law after 6 years of arguing about it. We passed the crime bill after 6 years of arguing about it. We expanded Head Start and provided for the immunization of all children under 2 by 1996. And we made lower cost, better repayment college loans available to 20 million young Americans so more people could go to college. We were busy around here in the last 2 years.

And along the way we were able to pass two major trade agreements, resolve major trade disputes with China and other countries, and expand trade by more than at any time in a generation—very important when you consider the fact that low-cost goods from other countries come into our open markets if we have no trade agreements, but the trade agreements open markets for high value-added American goods and American services and American jobs all around the world. I say this to point out how much different it is where you live than where we live. If you had done that, your voters would know it, right? [*Laughter*]

And all the nay-sayers said, "Oh, if they put this economic plan in, it'll be the worst thing that ever happened to the country. The economy will collapse immediately. Everything will be terrible." Now they're all going to New Hampshire and giving the same speech all over again. I heard it for 2 years. You know, since no country has permanent growth, if they keep predicting a recession, eventually we'll get around to it. [*Laughter*] They said, "Oh, this is a terrible thing, if they pass this program. Oh, it's terrible. The economy will just—it'll be terrible."

Well, what's happened in the last 2 years? We've got the lowest combined rate of unemployment and inflation in 25 years because we took it on. Over 6.1 million Americans have new jobs in the last 2 years. That is a good beginning.

Now, having said all that, let's face the facts. You live with these folks, and you know as well as I do, there are still profound problems out there. Most people still have not gotten a raise. Every year more and more people lose their health insurance even though they're in the work force. This is the only advanced country in the world that has a smaller percentage of people in the work force covered by health insurance in 1995 than had it in 1985. No other country can say that.

And we know these other problems are still with us. Half of all Americans are living on less money than they had 15 years ago. So we now have to focus not only on creating jobs but raising incomes and improving the security of working life and family life when people do the right thing. If we're going to strengthen the middle class and shrink the under class, we have got to do those things which will enable people to really feel the American dream. We've got to begin by equipping people with the skills they need to compete in today's economy. Even as we cut yesterday's Government, we must invest more in the education and training of our people. We must. We must.

We have tried to approach that work as the partner of people at the local level. Most folks around here think last year was the best year for education legislation passing through Congress in 30 years as we expanded Head Start and provided more funds for apprenticeships for young people who don't go onto college and made those college loans more affordable and wrote into Federal law the Goals 2000, the world-class standards for our schools.

But we changed the way we were making education law in Washington pretty dramatically. We didn't neglect our responsibilities to help create educational opportunity, but we didn't presume to tell the people at the grassroots level how to meet the standards as the Government had done so much in the past. Instead, we gave to local educators and to parents the power to decide how to meet global standards of excellence.

We said, "Here are some things that have to be done to improve our children's education. Here are things we'd like to do to help you do it. But you decide how to do it." In many ways, in dealing more directly with city government, our empowerment zones and enterprise communities are the embodiment of that kind of approach: to create opportunity, to shrink bu-

reaucracy, to demand more responsibility, and then let you decide what you want to do with it and how you can best create jobs and opportunities.

We said to distressed communities, "Give us a comprehensive plan to create jobs, to revitalize neighborhoods, to bring the community together, to involve the private sector. Find the solutions together. The opportunity you get will be some cash money and tax incentives to encourage investment and resources to deal with other problems, like transportation or safety. And we'll cut the redtape so you can apply those resources as you see fit." This is a partnership between government, the private sector, and communities to encourage investment, to create jobs in places where too many people have been left completely behind.

If you think about it, our country has had major initiatives in the last several years to invest in Latin America, to invest in the Caribbean, to invest in all different kinds of places. They're fine. But this is the first major initiative we've had to get people to invest in America, to create jobs and markets and our best opportunities.

And by the way, I hope that before this session is over we will see an expansion of that program, not a contraction of it, one that is paid for, one that is funded, but we ought to work to expand it, to involve more communities. We had hundreds of communities wanting to be involved in it who had good proposals that could not be funded. We have to recognize that if we want people to live by the work ethic, there must be work for them to do.

That also is something we should remember as we deal with the next issue that is coming in this session of Congress that affects some of you more than others, depending on how the system operates in your State, but all of you in some ways, and that is, how are we going to fix the welfare system? I believe we should offer more opportunity in the form of education and work to people on welfare and then insist on more responsibility, requiring work after 2 years, tougher child support enforcement, responsible parenting. I've been working on this issue for 15 years now, and I know that Washington doesn't have all the answers and neither does anybody else, or we'd have solved it by now.

But we have done our best here to give more and more and more authority to conduct sweeping welfare reform efforts to the States. We have given 25 States waivers from the Federal rules and regulations to pursue welfare reform. Today we will give a waiver to Oklahoma, the 26th State to pursue a welfare reform proposal. That is more combined shift of power from the Federal Government to the States than occurred under my two predecessors, combined. I believe in this. I believe in this.

I know that the Government shouldn't dictate all the rules from Washington. On the other hand, I don't think we should give States welfare money without any standards at all. We do have a national interest in promoting work and responsible parenting, the reduction of out of wedlock births. We have a national interest in doing this.

Last year, I sent to Congress the most sweeping welfare reform plan ever proposed by an administration. It included the toughest possible child support enforcement. Let me just mention child support for a minute. Do you know, if we collected all the money owed in this country by deadbeat parents, we could move 800,000 mothers and children off the welfare rolls immediately, 800,000.

Now, one of the things that we have reached agreement with the Congress on is that in this area there has to be some national standard setting, because 30 percent of these cases cross States lines. So even though we want to move decisions back to the States, when the Governors came to town, they said, "Look, we know we've got to have some national action on child support enforcement, otherwise we can't ever collect on these orders that cross State lines." Justice should not depend solely on geography.

Reforming welfare is now a top priority for both parties, and that's good news. And we've worked together to find common solutions, and that's good news. We still have our differences. My plan and the one our administration has been behind for over a year now sends a clear message to young people. It says, "Take responsibility to turn your life around." Teen fathers must pay child support. Teen mothers should stay at home or in other appropriate settings, and they have to stay in school if they want to get a check.

But the Republican plan sends a different message at some points. It says, for example, "If you make a mistake before you're 18, and you have a baby, you're on your own"—no benefits for teenagers and their children who have babies before they're 18, until they turn 18,

and then if the States want to keep them out of benefits forever, that's okay. I think that's a mistake. I think what we ought to be saying to people is, "You should not have done that. You made a mistake. We don't want anybody else to do it. But we're going to help you succeed as a student and a parent and a worker, and you have to help yourself by playing by these rules." I think that is a better approach.

And I think it's in your interest. Look, when people get—if we just cut people off without putting them to work or keeping them in school, without making sure they have child care, if we just end all this, well, the Federal Government will save a little money. And you know what will happen, don't you? They'll be on your doorstep. They won't be part of some Federal statistic, and people will say, "Oh, we're not spending money on that up here like we used to. We'll just give you the problem, and you figure out what to do with it."

Well, my own view is that just shifting the problem is not enough. Like many of the cuts currently being debated, I think it will ultimately be counterproductive. It will cost us more than we will save. The Federal Government, the cities, the States, the taxpayers all will pay more down the road if we do something that fundamentally undermines the health of our children, the future of our children, and our commitment to getting more Americans to live with the opportunities of middle class economics and the responsibilities of mainstream values. That's what I believe.

Now, yes, yes, we do have to continue to cut the deficit. We do have to continue to save money. My new budget cuts the deficit another $81 billion and has over $140 billion in spending cuts. And I want to work with the Republicans to do more. We have already reduced the rate of health care cost increases in the Federal budget over the next 5 years by $100 billion. We have to keep working on the deficit.

But we have to do it in the right way. One of the things that the Republican leadership and I agree on is the line-item veto. We're about to take up debate on the line-item veto in the Senate. I hope it will pass quickly because it will give the President the opportunity and the responsibility to look at every single line item in the budget for waste. It will give us the chance to cut pork without hurting people. And that is an important distinction.

Let me give you an example of what I mean. Everybody knows we have to shrink the Department of Agriculture. Ross Perot had the best line of any of the candidates in the 1992 election. It grieves me to say that, but he did. [*Laughter*] Ross Perot had this great line where he said, "Did you hear about the employee at the Department of Agriculture that had to go see a psychiatrist because he lost his farmer?" [*Laughter*] And what he meant by that was, of course, that the number of farmers was shrinking and that technology and the modern world had reduced the need for some of the size and scope of organization of the Agriculture Department. So we all wanted to do that. Everybody knows we've got to save money.

One of the reasons I fought so hard for that GATT world trade agreement is so we could cut agricultural subsidies here without hurting our farmers in the global market. So my budget cuts agricultural subsidies, but now our competitors have to cut theirs more to give our people a fair break.

I'll give you another example. We wanted to cut the Agriculture Department, so we just closed 1,200 offices, 1,200. That's a lot of money. I do not think the way to cut the Agriculture Department is to freeze the School Lunch Program and send it to you, which means we're going to cut school lunches as the price of food goes up and the number of kids goes up. I don't agree with that.

And you cannot make me believe with all the poor kids in this world today and in this country who show up hungry to school every day, whose only decent meal occurs in school, you cannot make me believe that we cannot find a way to eliminate unnecessary spending from the Government budget without cutting the School Lunch Program. We can, and we will. We will.

I'll give you another example that affects a lot of you here. Some in Congress want to eliminate our community development bank initiative. Most of you probably have never heard of that, but let me tell you what it does. It's an initiative that would spend $500 million to either establish or support banks that are set up in economically distressed areas, whose primary purpose is to get lower income people in high unemployment areas into the free enterprise system.

Now, I found out about this a few years ago when I was in Chicago, when I had a friend working for the South Shore Development Corporation. And we set up a community development bank in Arkansas when I was Governor that operated in a rural area, and it did amazing things. People got credit who could never get credit from any bank before, and they set up businesses, and they started working, and they started hiring people. And it changed lives for a lot of people in these communities.

So when I ran for President, I said here's a good idea that came out of grassroots America. We could put a little money in it and make a lot of difference. It is estimated that the $500 million that we could spend on the community development bank initiative in your communities all over the country will generate $22 billion in activity in the free enterprise system in places that have no enterprise today. So I think it would be a mistake to eliminate it. That's what I believe.

Believe you me, there's a lot of Government programs that don't have that kind of return. And keep in mind, what is the purpose of the Government? It's to empower people to make the most of their own lives, to enhance their security, and to help create opportunity as a partner. That's what this does.

I'll give you another example of the things that I don't think should be cut. Our national service project, AmeriCorps, is all about opportunity and responsibility. A lot of you have AmeriCorps projects in your communities. Young people get a helping hand with their college in exchange for helping people solve their problems at the local community. Thousands of young people now are participants, as partners, as nurses, as teachers, working with pastors, working with police officers at the grassroots level. They walk police beats in Brooklyn. They build homes in Georgia. They fight fires in Idaho.

But some people in the House want to cut this effort, to deny 15,000 young people the chance to participate in it. Now, I've offered spending cuts, and I'll find some more. But I think it is a mistake to cut AmeriCorps because it's a good deal. It gives us better citizens, stronger communities, more education for limited money. And it enables a lot of people to do things in their communities that simply would not get done any other way.

Ironically, one other area where we're having a big difference of opinion is in college loans. There's some in the Congress who want to severely limit the reach of the so-called direct loan program that we started which, believe it or not, lowers the cost of the loans to the students, cuts the time of paperwork and bureaucracy to the colleges, and saves money for the taxpayers because we get around the middle-man. So here's one area where we can do more to send people to school for lower cost and actually save money. We've offered millions and millions of young people the opportunity to take these loans out and then pay them back as a percentage of their income.

But I want to emphasize that we've also been more responsible than Government was before. When I took office it was costing you as taxpayers, $2.8 billion a year to pay tax money for defaulted loans. We have cut that $2.8 billion down to $1 billion. We've cut it by nearly two-thirds and made more loans available so people can go to college. That's the approach we ought to be taking. That is the way to save money on the program.

Now, one last thing in this area that I'm very concerned about, in the education area, and that is that one of the things in the House list of rescissions to cut is all the money for safe and drug-free schools that would go to 94 percent of the schools in this country. And that's very important to me, personally. I invested a lot of time in fighting the problem of drugs when I was a Governor. We have worked hard to get more investment to fight drugs in every area in which we fight it here, since I've been President. And we see disturbing signs that in parts of our population, among young people, drug use is going up again, more casual drug use, young people thinking, after a decade of it going down, that somehow it's maybe not dangerous anymore, forgetting that it's illegal. And a lot of our schools are still not safe because of the root problems of drugs and violence. Now this money gives schools the ability to hire police officers, to put up metal detectors, but also to have drug education programs, the programs like the D.A.R.E. program that so many of you have had in your schools and others that try and help these kids stay off drugs. I think it would be a mistake to cut this money out.

Let me remind you that this money got into the crime bill, which you worked so hard for, because I gave the Congress, for the first time, a plan to cut the size of the Federal Government by 270,000. So we didn't raise any taxes. We didn't take any money away from anybody.

We shrunk the Government and gave the money to the communities of this country to fight crime, including the safe and drug-free schools money. We should not eliminate that. We should fight for it, not fight to cut it out.

As we are trying, you and I, to make responsibility a way of life in this country again, to teach young people the value of work, I think that all of us are going to have to say, first of all, without regard to our party, we agree with that.

Now that brings me to one other point I want to make beyond education. When I was a child, my mother used to say, "Idle hands are the devil's workshop." You're going to have a whole lot more idle hands this summer if we cut out those 600,000 summer jobs for our young people. And is it worth it to deny 1,000 young people in Louisville or 1,600 young people in Boston—I met with a young—the Mayor's Youth Council up there not very long ago, 2,000 in the San Jose area. Is it worth it to deny them the chance to work, to be around responsible adults, to learn what it's like to sort of show up on time, put a day's work in, how you relate to other people at work? I mean, this goes way beyond the little amount of money you get out of this.

Now, I have proposed, I will say again, to consolidate 60 programs and eliminate 4,000 bureaucrats to save money in the Housing and Urban Development Department, for example. I have proposed to do a lot of things like that.

I told you about the Agriculture Department. We're coming with more. Hold on; every week, there will be more. I am not here to defend the way Government has operated in the past in Washington. But we have to make judgments here. We get hired to make judgments and the right decisions and not to throw out the baby with the bath water.

Take the HUD Department, for example, I'm all for—I'm consolidating 60 programs. We're getting rid of 4,000 people. We're phasing the Department down. But I don't believe in the proposed cut to housing assistance that helps 63,000 families—women with small children, low-income senior citizens.

What we ought to do is to look at the right kind of cuts. This whole rescission package does some interesting things. We're supposed to be passing responsibility back to you, but not undermining your ability to do your job. I think it's smarter to streamline programs and cut bureaucrats than to put families on the street or to leave you to deal with the problem.

Many of the people willing to pass you the buck are talking about ending unfair burdens on local government. I do want to say this: I think—and the Speaker probably said this earlier today—it looks like we may have an agreement now among all of the conferees and the administration and everybody on this unfunded mandate bill. I am very strongly in favor of that. It is a good thing to do. It's something we should do.

It is long since past time to stop imposing those mandates on you without paying for them. I spent a decade in the Governor's office in Arkansas, writing checks for decisions other people made. Now, I'm excited about that. That bill just passed the House a few weeks ago. It passed the Senate. It's a good, good thing.

But look at this: The rescission package that's moving through the Congress actually cuts off funds to help you comply with present Federal requirements, including safe drinking water, lead paint, and asbestos removal. So that makes them, I guess, not unfunded, but de-funded mandates. [*Laughter*] So we eliminate burdens on the one hand and create new ones on the other. I think that is an error.

Let me mention just one final area where we worked closely last year. We passed the crime bill after the people who were here before just talked about it for 6 years, played politics with it, and the rhetoric was so juicy on both sides they could never get around to passing a bill. That's what always happens, you know?

Every one of these issues are tough. If they were easy, somebody would have done them. And you could pick either side and say it in a way that a majority is for you, right? I mean, you can. Are you for a balanced budget? Yes. Do you want to cut Social Security? No. [*Laughter*] See what I mean? So both sides win, right? Meanwhile, you're like the jurors listening to the lawyers' argument. Well, what's going to happen? Who did it? So we've got to work on this.

But I want to say this about the crime bill. We finally did that. And what we did largely was what was recommended by law enforcement officials and community leaders around the country: money for prevention with a lot of flexibility for people at the local level; tougher punishment, but help for States that would adopt tougher punishment, to build more prisons; and

of course, more police, 100,000 more police on the street.

We did that because of two things. First of all, the law enforcement people said, we need more police. They also said they wanted a prevention fund. Secondly, we did it because of the evidence of what happens when community policing is properly instituted in the cities of our country.

From over about the last 30 years, the number of police in our country had grown by only about 10 percent, while the violent crime rate tripled. Clearly, there is a connection between those two statistics. And yet, still we've seen in place after place, where more police are put on the street in community policing modes, the crime rate will drop. That's why every major law enforcement organization supported that.

Now, the congressional bills and the crime bill are different from the House and Senate, but I ask you to look at the system we have now and the work it did, not only to catch criminals but to prevent crime. In New York City, the police commissioner implemented an aggressive community policing program that helped to significantly reduce serious crimes last year: auto thefts down 15 percent, robberies down 16 percent, murder down 19 percent. Not just in big cities: The mayor of Odessa, Texas, wrote to tell me that in 1991 and '92, they had a very high crime rate. Then they implemented community policing, and 3 years later, serious crimes have dropped a total of 43 percent. Union City, Tennessee, calls for help from the police went down by 30 percent and arrests went up by 35 percent with community policing.

That's why this crime bill was a partnership to help communities willing to take the responsibility to invest in their own security be more secure. An opportunity that is buried in redtape can hurt more than it helps. I don't know how many times I've seen little towns in my State have to hire consultants to figure out how to get Federal money, and it cut the margin of benefit dramatically.

What we did was to set this police program up so that cities and counties can apply directly to the Federal Government, using a one-page application with eight questions, awarding police resources directly to you. Now, I think that's a pretty good deal. I know one of those bills wants to add another layer to that. I don't think that's a very good idea, either. I think that we ought to have an opportunity for communities to apply directly and get the funds directly for law enforcement. My fellow Governors may disagree with that, but that's what I think.

Now, in just the last few months since the crime bill took effect last fall, half the police departments in America have already received authority to hire almost 17,000 new police officers. We are ahead of schedule, and we're under budget. Some people who criticize our bill said that local governments wouldn't really want it; it was too much of a burden; it's an imposition; they can't afford to pay any match. All I know is, we have already received almost 11,000 applications representing over 60 percent of the police departments in America. Somebody thinks it's a good idea, and I think we ought to stay with it.

Here's the bottom line: The crime bill now on the books guarantees 100,000 new police officers. The alternative proposal doesn't guarantee a single one. We do give more flexibility and responsibility to you. Some of their proposals add bureaucracy and cut funds at the same time. So I say to you, if it ain't broke, don't fix it.

We should never, never close the door to writing new laws that will make us more secure in the fight against crime. And it should never be a partisan issue again. I was sick when I got here 2 years ago and I realized they'd been fooling around with that crime bill for 4 years because each side could figure out how to gain rhetorical advantage. And small differences obscured large agreements. So I want to continue to work on this problem.

But this police initiative is a better deal for you and a better deal for the American people.

And as I have said repeatedly, if necessary, I will veto any effort to repeal or undermine it.

But let me say this, what we need is not more vetoes. What we need is more action. What we need is for people here to behave the way you have to behave or you couldn't survive. Half of you come from places so small that if you made people declare their party every time they walked through the door to see if they got anything done or not, you'd be run out on a rail within a week. [*Laughter*]

So, the veto is a useful device and an important thing on occasion. But what the country really needs is action. We need action. We need to remember these problems have faces, names, and life histories. We need to pull together. We're doing it on the unfunded mandates. We can do it on the line-item veto. We can do it on all these other areas if we will exercise simple common sense and recognize what our mission is. We've got to keep the American dream alive: middle class economics, mainstream values, jobs, incomes, work, and family. We've got to make sure this country stays strong.

And I'm telling you, it takes action, not just words. You live where the action is. If you don't do anything else while you're here, give us your energy and tell us you want action.

Thank you, and God bless you all.

NOTE: The President spoke at 1:02 p.m. at the Washington Hilton Hotel. In his remarks, he referred to Carolyn Long Banks, president, National League of Cities; Mayor Greg Lashutka of Columbus, OH; and Mayor Sharpe James of Newark, NJ. A portion of these remarks could not be verified because the tape was incomplete.

Remarks and a Question-and-Answer Session With the National PTA Legislative Conference
March 14, 1995

The President. Thank you very much, Kathryn. Thank you, ladies and gentlemen. I am delighted to be here with you. More importantly, I am delighted to have you here with me. I need all the help I can get. [*Laughter*] I feel like reinforcements have just arrived.

I want to say, too, a special word of thanks to the PTA for presenting Secretary Riley the

PTA Child Advocacy Award tomorrow. He's here with me. And I think he's done a magnificent job. And I thank you for giving him that award.

Such a beautiful sort of premature spring day outside. I almost feel that we should be having recess instead of class. [*Laughter*] But unfortunately, events compel us to have class, for we are in danger of forgetting some of our most fundamental lessons.

I want to start by thanking a kindergarten class taught by Linda Eddington from Jackson Hole, Wyoming, for the wonderful letters they sent up here with her. I reviewed the letters. I had some favorites. Charlie Wheeler said, "You are a good paper-writer, because you practice." My favorite letter, regrettably, was unsigned, otherwise I would be writing a letter back. It said, "You're one of the best. I never have seen you, but I like your speeches." I am sending to the Congress today a proposal to lower the voting age to 5. [Laughter] We might get better results.

I want to thank the PTA for now nearly 100 years of help to children and to parents and to schools. The PTA has meant a lot to me personally. I have been a member of the PTA— Hillary and I both were active when I was the Governor of Arkansas. Essie used to come sell me my membership every year. [Laughter] And I actually paid and actually—[laughter]. You know how Presidents never carry any money anywhere they go? I brought some money today, because I knew she was going to be here. [Laughter] I did. I also, besides being an active member of the PTA and spending a lot of time at Chelsea's school, had a chance to work with the PTA for a dozen years in my State and throughout the country as we worked to implement the recommendations of the "Nation at Risk" report, starting in '83. And then we worked up to the national education goals in '89. And then, of course, ultimately culminating in my service as President in the last 2 years.

At a time when many of our most important citizenship organizations have been suffering and civic institutions generally are often in decline, the PTA has grown as parents have come back in droves to understanding that they had to do more to make their children's education work and that they had to be involved. PTA embodies the three ideas that I have talked about so much for the future—opportunity, responsibility, and community—what we call the New Covenant.

This is a period of profound change in the life of America and in the lives of Americans. There are many things going on which are wonderful, exhilarating, exciting, and others which are profoundly troubling. The biggest challenges we face on the eve of this new century relate to our economic and social problems, which threaten the middle class economics of the

American dream and the mainstream values of work and family and community. We see it everywhere in every community. About half of the American people are making the same or less money than they made 15 years ago. We have an enormous divide opening up within the great American middle class based largely on the level of education. And in spite of the fact that— and I'm very proud of the fact—that we've had an economic recovery that has produced the lowest rates of unemployment and inflation combined in 25 years and 6.1 million new jobs, a whole lot of Americans are still worried about losing theirs or losing the benefits associated with their job, their health care, their retirement, or never getting a raise. And in spite of the progress we are making on many fronts, there is still an awful lot of social turmoil in this country from drugs and violence and gangs and family breakdown. And these things are profoundly troubling to the American people.

So we have a lot of good news and a lot of bad news. And a whole lot is happening. In 1993 we had the largest number of new businesses started in the United States in any single year in the history of the country. So we're all trying to work through this as a people, as we must. I believe our common mission must be to keep the American dream alive for all of our people as we move into the next century and to make sure our country is still the strongest force for peace and freedom and democracy in the world. To do that, we've got to have a strong economy. We've got to be able to grow the middle class and shrink the under class. We have to support all these wonderful entrepreneurial forces that are bubbling up in our society. We have to dramatically change the way Government works. But our goal must be always, always the same: to make sure that every American has the chance to live up to his or her God-given potential. And that is what the PTA is all about.

Education has always been profoundly important in American life, from the very beginning. Thomas Jefferson talked about it a lot. But it has never been more important to the prosperity and, indeed, to the survival of the America we know and love than it is today, never.

Now, as we move away from the cold war and the industrial age into the post-cold-war era and the information age where most wealth generation is based on knowledge and technology is changing things at a blinding pace, we know that there will be big changes and there must be in the role of Government. There's a huge debate going on here in Washington, which can be seen in almost every issue, about exactly what the role of the Government should be as we move toward the 21st century. On the one side is the largely rejected view that Washington still knows best about everything and that there is a one-size-fits-all big answer to every big problem in the country. On the other side is what you might call the Republican contract view, which is that the Government is the source of all the problems in the country, and if we just had no Government, we'd have no problems, and—unless something is going on at the State and local level that they don't agree with, in which case they want Federal action. But, basically, that's the argument stated in the most extreme forms.

I believe that the truth is somewhere both in between and way beyond that. I believe we have common problems that require common approaches. I believe we need a Government in Washington that is leaner but not meaner, one that does not pretend to be the savior of the country but does not presume to sit on the sidelines, either, one that, instead, is a partner in working with the American people to increase opportunity while we shrink bureaucracy, to empower people to make the most of their own lives, and to enhance the security of the American people, both here at home on our streets and around the world. I believe that such a Government would promote both opportunity and responsibility. And I believe that such a Government should have clear priorities that put the interests of the American people first, the interests of all the American people.

Now, there are strong feelings on both sides of this debate. And a lot of what is said may be hard to follow. But I think it's important that we keep in mind what is really the issue. The issue is, how are we going to get this country into the 21st century? How are we going to give our children and our grandchildren a chance to live out the unlimited aspirations of the human spirit and to fulfill the traditions of America.

Now, let's look at this thing on an issue-by-issue basis. There is broad agreement that we should cut the size of Government, that we should send more responsibility back to the State and local level, and that we should work more in partnership directly with citizens, with

businesses, with other organizations and less in a regulatory Government-knows-best way. There is broad agreement on this. Indeed, we started this movement.

But the question is, how do you implement these challenges, and what does the Government still have to do? For example, I believe we should downsize the Government, but I think we should invest more in education, training, technology, and research. Why? Because I think it's in our interest. It looks to me like walking away from our opportunities to succeed in the global economy and to develop the capacities of all of our people at a time when we have so much diversity in our country and the world is getting smaller, so all this racial and ethnic diversity is a huge advantage to us. At a time when we have people who have phenomenal abilities who live all over the country in tiny, tiny places and big, big cities, to walk away from our common objective of developing their capacities, it seems to me, is not very smart. I just don't think it makes much sense. And I don't think that any theory of what we should or shouldn't be doing should be allowed to obscure the clear obligation we all have to help our people get into the next century. This is about a fight for the future.

Now, let me put it another way. It seems to me like trying to cut back on education right now would be like trying to cut the defense budget in the toughest days of the cold war. Because that's what—our competition for the future, our security now is going to be determined in large measure by whether we can develop the capacities of all of our people to learn for a lifetime. That is it.

For the 12 years before I came here, there was this political tug of war where Government was regularly bashed but the deficit quadrupled and we walked away from our obligations to invest in our future. For the 4 years before I came here, we had the slowest job growth in America since the Great Depression. For 2 years, we have worked very hard here to both create more opportunities and insist on more responsibilities. And we're making progress. The deficit is down. The Federal Government is smaller by over 100,000. We're on our way to the smallest Federal Government since Mr. Kennedy was the President. We have more jobs, more police on the street, more prosperity than when I took office. And we have invested more in our children.

In the last 2 years, we have, I believe, had the best year in terms of legislative advancements for education that we've had in 30 years. And I might say it was done in a largely bipartisan way. We expanded and reformed Head Start. We passed an apprenticeship program for young people who don't go on to 4-year colleges but do want to move into good jobs after high school. We made college loans more affordable and the repayment terms better for millions and millions of middle class and lower income students. We made a new commitment to help you to get drugs and guns out of our schools and to end the mindless violence that too many of our children still suffer from. And of course, with your help, we passed Goals 2000, something that was very, very important to me and very important to you. And it's a clear example of Government as a partner, not a savior and not on the sidelines.

No one disagrees with the fact that education is largely a State matter when it comes to funding and a local matter when it comes to teaching and learning. But global education and global competition will go hand in hand. There must be some idea in our country of the world-class standards of excellence we need to really meet the challenges of the future.

As Secretary Riley reminded me, when we were Governors working together and the "Nation at Risk" report came out—that's what the name of the report was, and it came out in a Republican administration. It was "A Nation at Risk," not one place here and another place there and not somebody somewhere else. It was "A Nation at Risk." And Goals 2000 responds to that. It sets those standards reflecting the national education goals that were adopted by the Governors in 1989, working with President Bush and the Bush administration, plus a commitment to continuing development of our teachers, plus the very important parental involvement goal that the PTA got in this—[applause].

If it was a good idea last year with bipartisan support, it didn't just stop being a good idea because we had one election. We worked for 10 years on this in a bipartisan way. It didn't stop being a good idea because we had an election. That is not what the election was about. It was not about turning our backs on world-class excellence in education and a partnership to make our schools better and the support that

you need to succeed in all of your communities. That was not what was going on.

The success we've had in the last 2 years is building on what has been done in the last 10 years. You know, after all, I think it's important to remember that there's been a lot of progress in our schools in the last 10 years. To hear these folks talk about it, you'd think that it's all gotten worse and only because we had a Department of Education in Washington—ran the whole thing into the ditch. [*Laughter*] I don't know what they're doing in Idaho today, carrying the burden of the Department of Education around all day long in their schools. [*Laughter*] That's the kind of talk we've got.

The truth is that kids are staying in school longer, more of them are going to college, math and science performance is up, because we emphasized, we worked on those things. We did it together. Are there a lot of problems? You bet there are. But this country is the most remarkable experiment in diversity of all kinds in all of human history. And we are doing better because we are working together and setting goals and working as partners. And that's what we should continue to do.

Dick Riley in a way has been perfectly suited to be the Secretary of Education at this time. I can't imagine why anybody would want to abolish his job after watching him do it for a couple of years. I'd just like to point out something to the people who say on the other side that the answer to our problems in education is to abolish the Department of Education. I noticed one of the Republican leaders said the other day that they had actually—the Department of Education actually made things worse.

Well, here are the facts. There are fewer people working in the Department of Education today than were working for the Federal Government in education when it was part of the Department of Health, Education and Welfare in the seventies. It's an inconvenient fact for the people who want to abolish it.

Here's another interesting fact. Secretary Riley has proposed to end in this present rescission package that we sent up, or in the coming budget, 41 programs and to consolidate 17 others, 58 of the 240 programs in the Department of Education—inconvenient facts for those that are saying that it's terrible and they're throwing money away. It happens to be true.

But we don't agree with what they're trying to do in the House, to cut $1.7 billion from education, to eliminate all the funds for the safe and drug-free school program, all the funds at a time when, disturbingly, young people are beginning to use drugs casually again, forgetting that they're dangerous and illegal, when schools still need the funds to help them be literally more secure in difficult areas. They want to eliminate all the funds in that bill for teaching homeless children, all the funds for the parent resource centers, which you know are very important. We're dealing with a lot of parents, folks, who want to do a better job by their kids but need some help and some support from people like you who have been showing up in the PTA for years, some of you for decades. They need it. [*Laughter*] Well, your kid stays in school. [*Laughter*] Listen, I got to keep laughing. Otherwise, we'll be in tears thinking about this.

They want to eliminate much of the money for computers and new technologies. The amount they propose to cut from Goals 2000 is equal to all the funds now allocated for poor and rural communities and all the funds necessary to help 4,000 schools raise their academic standards. And they want, of course, to cut back on the School Lunch Program.

Now, how are we going to cut? Dick Riley found a way to cut 41 programs without doing this. This School Lunch Program is a mystery to me. Everybody wants to cut funds in the Agriculture Department because the number of farmers is smaller. You know what we did? We finally concluded a world trade agreement so that our competitors would have to cut agricultural subsidies, so we cut agriculture subsidies. And then we realized we had basically an outdated structure in the Agriculture Department. The best line in the '92 Presidential campaign was Ross Perot's line about the employee at the Department of Agriculture who had to go to the psychiatrist because he lost his farmer. [*Laughter*] Because the number of farmers had gone down.

So what did we do? We closed 1,200 agricultural offices. They want to cut the School Lunch Program. I think we know how to cut better than they do. I think that's the way to do it.

So let me say again, every effort we had in the last 2 years, from Head Start to apprenticeships, to Goals 2000, to the reformation of the Elementary and Secondary Education Act, ev-erything we did was done in a bipartisan way. And now we see education becoming both a partisan and a divisive issue again. We cannot walk away from this. You need to be here. You are the reinforcements for America's future, and I want you to go up there today and say that, say this $1.7 billion in a $1.5 trillion budget is a drop in the bucket and it should not be eliminated to pay for $188 billion in tax cuts. It should not.

You know, I want us to have the right framework here so that you can go back home and do your job. I've done everything I could and Secretary Riley's done everything he could to devise Goals 2000 so that we would really have a partnership. We'd say, here are some resources, here are the goals, here's what we know; you decide how to implement. We want more responsibility for principals and teachers and parents at the grassroots level. We want less control of education in Washington. We have done a lot in the legislation that we have passed to reduce the degree of Federal control and rulemaking below that which previous administrations imposed. But we don't want to walk away from the kids and the future of this country.

I want to just mention one other thing. I want to thank Secretary Riley again for taking the lead in creating the National Family Involvement Partnership for Learning. It includes many members of the private sector, more than 100 organizations, including the PTA. He's been proposing seven basic steps for all parents to take. And I like them so much that I want to repeat them for every parent now here at the PTA meeting, because if these things are not done, then our efforts won't succeed. And if these things are done, then our efforts here become even more important to support the parents who are doing them: find more time to spend with your children; read with them; set high expectations for them; take away the remote control on school nights; check their homework, check their grades; set a good example; and talk directly to your children, especially to your teenagers, about the dangers of drugs and alcohol and the values you want them to have. Thank you, Mr. Secretary. That's about as good as it gets.

Let me say again in closing my remarks, I am doing my best to work in good faith with this new Congress. There are deep trends going on here which can make this a positive time if we stop posturing and put our people first. We do have to change the way Government works. We need dramatic reform in the Government, and we are working hard to get it.

But what is the purpose of all this? The purpose of all this is the same purpose that you have: to elevate the potential of the American people to make the most of their own lives, to keep the American dream alive, and to guarantee a future for their children. So go up there on Capitol Hill and remind everybody that we need to work together, tone down the rhetoric, and put the kids of this country and our future first.

Thank you, and God bless you.

[At this point, Kathryn Whitfill, president, National Congress of Parents and Teachers, thanked the President for his support and voiced her concern about program cuts and block grants. She then introduced a participant who spoke about the President's reaction to elimination of the Department of Education.]

The President. Well, for one thing, you have to ask yourself, why would they do this? First of all, there's a burden—why would you do it? And there are only two reasons to do it, to save money or because you think it's doing bad things or it's useless. And I noticed the other day that the majority leader of the Senate said that it was one of those departments that had done more harm than good.

Now, most of the time it's been in existence the Department of Education has been under control of Republican Secretaries of Education. Maybe they did do more harm than good—*[laughter]*—I hadn't really thought so until he said it. But maybe we need to reexamine that. But Secretary Riley has not done more harm than good. He's done more good than harm by a good, long ways.

And I think that it's just sort of fashionable now. I think the truth is that there have been big commitments made in terms of tax cuts, mostly for upper income people, and big commitments made in other areas. And so they are looking for ways to save money. But this is not a good place. This is not the right thing to do. And we have worked very hard to have what I consider to be the appropriate level of partnership.

Now, on the block grant issue, generally, let me just say I'm not against all block grants. I strongly supported the community development block grant, for example, which the States get and which bigger cities get, and then they get to decide how they're going to use it to develop the economy and make reports on an annual basis to Federal Government. I think that's fine.

We supported in the crime bill last year more block granting, more flexibility to States and localities in prevention on crime and crime prevention programs because programs that work in one community may not work in another. They know what works best there. We've now given 26 States waivers from Federal rules to implement welfare reforms in their own States, because they know more about it.

But let's not kid ourselves, the School Lunch Program was proposed for block granting just to save the money, because it works the way it is. And we've made some significant improvements in the School Lunch Program. Last year, with your support, as you know, we got the nutritional standards up; we made some changes. The only reason it was proposed for block granting is because block grants are in; they're fashionable; they're a la mode today. And that's the way they could save some money.

If you add all this money up, it's just not very much money in this big Federal budget. And you could argue that we should be doing much more for education, but I think it's very hard to argue that we should be spending less.

[A participant asked how the PTA could become more involved in efforts to make schools safer.]

The President. Well, I think the first thing I would say about that is that in the absence of security, not much learning is going to occur. You know that. We know that there are thousands of children who stay home from school every day because they are afraid of what might happen to them in school. We see constantly examples of violence both in school buildings and then in the near vicinity of schools.

Now, what we tried to do with the safe and drug-free schools act, because there was violence in the schools and in the perimeter, is to provide some funds for things like security devices, metal detectors, things like that, but also more enforcement officers in the outside of school. Then I think you must have—the PTA, and all the other committed groups in the country that care about the schools, but especially the PTA, has to work with every school district to make sure that there really is a functioning security policy.

You know, there are schools that are very safe environments in very high-crime areas in this country. So it's simply not true that there are no schools in high-crime areas that are safe. There are schools that are quite safe in very high-crime areas because of the security policies they have and because of the leadership and the discipline and the organization of resources that have been adopted and because they've gotten a lot of parental help often.

And so my recommendation is that you identify the schools that you think have done the best job in the most difficult circumstances, figure out what they did, and make sure every PTA chapter in the country has access to that knowledge, and then if we can get these funds and help out there, that you spend them in a way that will maximize the security in the schools in your area.

It's a huge deal, and there's no way—this is the kind of partnership we need. I mean, there's no way in the world the Federal Government can tell anybody how they should secure one, two, or three schools, because they all have different circumstances.

[*A participant asked what State and local school officials could do to help protect the school-to-work initiative from future budget cuts.*]

The President. Well, the Federal school-to-work initiative essentially tries to build on the work that's being done in States now. When I ran for President, I was fond of talking about the fact that we were the only advanced country in the world that had no real system for dealing with all the young people who finished high school but didn't go on to 4-year colleges and that, while most jobs in the 21st century would not require 4-year college degrees, most jobs would require at least 2 years of some sort of education and training after high school. And we already saw in the difference between the '80 and the '90 census what's happening to the earnings of people who don't have post-high school education and training.

Therefore, in terms of the long-term stability of a middle class lifestyle in America, that is, the idea that if you work harder and smarter, you might actually do a little better year in and year out, this school-to-work system, the idea of putting in to some sort of apprenticeship development system in America, may be the

most significant thing we can do to raise incomes. And so what our system does is to provide funds to States to help to build their own systems according to the best information we have and to build on the systems that States are working on.

And you're right. I did a lot of work on this at home because I became so alarmed, even as we got the college-going rate up, that, though we increased it quite a lot, there are all these people out there that were still just cut loose after high school. And we have to put an end to that. The best way to protect that program here is to—for every State to aggressively get with the Department of Education and begin to participate as quickly as possible.

That's the same thing with the Goals 2000. Secretary Riley's probably going to talk about this tomorrow, but I think we're on track for over 40 States to be involved in that pretty soon. And so the more States get involved, the more people get involved at the local level, the more it's Democrats and Republicans and independents—it's not a political deal, it's education—the more likely we are to continue to go forward with this.

[*A participant asked how future cuts in entitlement programs that affect children could be prevented.*]

The President. Well, I think, first of all, it's important for me to point out to all of you, if you talk about the entitlements, that an entitlement—let me say, an entitlement is a program in which there is no predetermined amount of money to be spent. That is, if you need it under certain circumstances, the money will flow. A nonentitlement is a program where the Congress appropriates a certain amount of money every year and you spend that and it runs out and you don't spend anymore.

Entitlements basically fall into three categories. One is—the best example is agricultural entitlements, where the farm programs are set up like that because the farm economy will change from year to year, you know, based on not only weather conditions and crop conditions in the United States but all around the world. And it's necessary to sort of even out the farming cycle.

The other programs, and by far the biggest entitlements today, are Medicare and Medicaid, the medical programs. And the main problem with the Federal budget today is not discretionary spending and education, is not defense spending—both discretionary spending and defense spending have been going down for the first time in 25 years—it's entitlements in health care, health care costs going up by more than the rate of inflation, and the accumulated interest payments on the debt run up between 1981 and 1993, when I took office. That's basically what the big problem is with the budget.

The other entitlements are entitlements basically for poor people, generally. And except for Medicaid, they, by and large, have not kept up with inflation, but they do provide a safety net. So if there is going to be a move away from those entitlements, the burden is on those who would move away to say, how are you going to care for these poor children?

Now, I like the Women, Infants and Children program; I like the School Lunch Program. I think these programs have worked pretty well for us over time. And we have an interest, all of us do, in not going back to the days when children were basically living in very brutal conditions. And I think there is a national interest in the welfare of the children.

I'm all for having the States have more flexibility about how to do these things, but I think there is a national interest in helping States to keep a floor under the lives of our children. Not every State is as wealthy as every other State. Not every State has the same priorities.

So, having a system that uniformly says we ought to have a quality of life for our poor children, that we believe that all of our children ought to have a chance to get to the starting line is pretty important.

What does the first education goal say?

Audience members. Ready to learn.

The President. Yes. Every kid ought to show up ready to learn, right? Not just intellectually but physically able to learn. My argument is, if I were making your strategy, I would say that we represent the PTA, and our schools can't succeed if, by the time our kids show up for school, their deprivations have already been so great that they will never overcome them, and that the rest of us will pay a whole lot more in tax money and social misery later on down the road if we back away from our obligation to get these kids to school ready to learn.

[*Ms. Whitfill thanked the President for participating and presented him with a paperweight.*]

The President. Thank you very much. Thank you. Bless you.

NOTE: The President spoke at 9:15 a.m. at the Washington Renaissance Hotel. In his remarks, he referred to Essie Middleton, president of the Arkansas PTA and member of the board of directors, National Congress of Parents and Teachers.

Statement on the Nomination of Lieutenant General Charles C. Krulak To Be Commandant of the Marine Corps
March 14, 1995

I am pleased to nominate Lt. Gen. Charles C. Krulak, U.S. Marine Corps, for appointment to the grade of general and as Commandant of the Marine Corps, succeeding Gen. Carl E. Mundy, Jr., who is retiring.

I have asked the Secretary of the Navy to announce my decision today in ceremonies at Iwo Jima commemorating the 50th anniversary of the battle.

General Krulak currently serves as Commander, U.S. Marine Corps Forces Pacific, and Commanding General, Fleet Marine Force Pacific. In this capacity, he is responsible for Ma-

rine Corps units and activities throughout the Pacific theater. During his distinguished career, General Krulak served two command tours in Vietnam, oversaw the Marine Corps logistic efforts during Desert Storm, and was responsible for significant and innovative changes in military doctrine and organization. He brings to the job of Commandant a dynamic vision of the Marine Corps' future, a wealth of experience, and a highly effective leadership and managerial style.

General Krulak assumes the post of Commandant of the Marine Corps at an important time in the U.S. Marine Corps' history. I will depend on him to continue General Mundy's superb efforts in ensuring that the Marine Corps remains fully ready and able in carrying out its important responsibilities under our national security strategy.

Statement on Secretary of Housing and Urban Development Henry Cisneros
March 14, 1995

Henry Cisneros' service as Secretary of Housing and Urban Development has been outstanding, and I know him to be a man of integrity and character. The Attorney General has determined that the facts warrant the appointment of an independent counsel to inquire into a question she believes is a "close and difficult factual and legal issue."

Secretary Cisneros is a good man and an effective public servant. He says he regrets any mistakes he has made. So do I. But that does not outweigh the excellent work he has been doing and will do as Secretary of Housing and Urban Development. I look forward to his continued valuable service.

Remarks at the Radio and Television Correspondents Association Dinner
March 14, 1995

Thank you very much. Thank you very much, Bill. I can't think of anything better for a politician than to be introduced by a guy named "Headline." [*Laughter*]

Hillary and I are delighted to be here. I am told that this is by far the largest group of radio and television correspondents ever assembled this far from a Los Angeles courtroom. [*Laughter*] You know, the press is always asking me if I'm watching the O.J. trial, and Mike McCurry always has to say, "Oh, he's so busy with affairs of"—of course I watch it. [*Laughter*] And the other day I was watching it, and the camera zoomed in to Judge Ito's computer monitor. You've seen that, haven't you? There was an E-mail message on it from Wolf Blitzer begging for a recess. [*Laughter*]

You know, every year when I come here, even though I've only been here a couple of years, I recognize more and more faces. And now I'm getting so good at it I can tell when people are missing. [*Laughter*] This year, thanks to Mr. Armey and others, PBS couldn't afford a ticket for both MacNeil and Lehrer. [*Laughter*] I know that because Louis Rukeyser told me that when he checked my coat when I came in. [*Laughter*]

I'm trying to figure out what's going on here. I guess the rest of you are, too. I have puzzled over this Republican assault on affirmative action. You know, the Republicans started affirmative action under Mr. Nixon. I think the reason that they don't like it anymore is because the Democrats are now a minority. [*Laughter*] I have decided to adopt their position on another important issue: term limits. I'll settle for two. [*Laughter*]

You know, this campaign is amazing. It's gotten so heated up that when I called L.L. Bean last week they told me they're back-ordered on red flannel shirts for several months. Because I'm President, they promised to send me mine by June. [*Laughter*]

Look, in spite of this campaign, I want to tell you that I am going to keep doing the job the American people elected me to do. I'm going to let the rest just take care of itself. I'm still working on Saturdays. I mean, I was working on Saturday a couple of weeks ago, trying to do the things that a President really doesn't have time for during the week. I was reinventing my filing system according to Gore, adding up my own frequent flier miles on Air Force One. I even did a little spackling in the Roosevelt Room. [*Laughter*] And I noticed—

I looked outside and there was the Vice President mulching the environment in the Rose Garden. [*Laughter*] So I invited him in, and we—there we were, all alone on a Saturday, a beautiful Saturday, and we got into this deep discussion about the new ideas we needed for reinventing Government. I said, "You know, we've got to have exciting ideas, breakthrough ideas, third-wave ideas." And so, we began to think. Right off the bat in this drive to downsize Government, we discovered that there was a useless extra "C" in the FCC, and we got rid of it right away. [*Laughter*]

Then we asked ourselves, in our lust for consolidation, "Do we really need North and South Dakota?" [*Laughter*] But when we thought of how frugal and inexpensive they were, and when we remembered the votes on the balanced budget amendment, we said, "Yes, we do." Furthermore, for economy's sake, we intend to propose a Central Dakota for this Congress. [*Laughter*]

The Vice President, ever the humble public servant, suggested that this year we could save money by doing away with the White House Christmas tree, and we could just hang the ornaments on him. Now, he approved that joke, I want you to know. [*Laughter*]

Then Leon Panetta came in, and we had, finally, at last, three people in the same room in the White House who were over 45. [*Laughter*] And we decided that we could consolidate our staff further by replacing fifteen 30-year-olds with five 90-year-olds. [*Laughter*] Then the rest of the staff came in. They all trooped in, and we were talking about new ideas, these exciting breakthrough ideas. We discussed an opportunity for entrepreneurship in dealing with the deficit, which I know the Republicans will agree with. Next week I intend to propose that we put the President and the Congress on commissions. Then we'll turn a profit in no time. All your programs will be gone, but we'll do well. [*Laughter*]

This is a serious proposal. Instead of getting rid of all these domestic observances that we have, all these domestic programs, why don't we do what all the athletic events are doing, you know, like the Mobil Cotton Bowl? Let's get corporate sponsorships for Government. Like, we could make February 12 Lincoln-Mercury's birthday. [*Laughter*]

And you all tell me all the time I need to do better marketing. So we have a new idea.

We're going to put Ed McMahon's picture on the IRS refund checks. Just imagine, when you get your envelope from the Treasury Department, up in the corner it says, "You may already be a winner." [*Laughter*]

Two other ideas we had—somebody in one of these meetings—you know, even the Democrats go too far sometimes on downsizing Government. One of them said we ought to turn the Pentagon into a triangle. And I said, no, I am going to hold the line with a veto threat for a rhombus. [*Laughter*] Then it was suggested that the greatest consolidation we could do is to consolidate the Bureau of Indian Affairs and the Joint Chiefs of Staff into the Joint Chiefs. [*Laughter*] You know, I was afraid that was politically incorrect, but it got by. It got by. [*Laughter*]

Now, this is the most important thing I'm going to say tonight. I came here to offer a way to make peace with our Republican friends on this heated school lunch issue. Al Gore and I have discovered a reinventing Government way, Mr. Armey, to get around this terrible rhetoric we've been flinging at you on school lunches. We have a way to save money through streamlining that does not require us to deprive our children of food. Instead of cutting food, we're going to cut the cutlery. And here's how: with a spork. [*Laughter*] Now, you know, I don't know how many of you know this, I've been eating off these things for years. I never knew they were called sporks. But that's what they are. This is the symbol of my administration. This is a cross between a spoon and fork, no more false choice between the left utensil and the right utensil. This is not an ideological choice. This is a choice in the middle and a choice for the future. This is a big, new idea, the spork. [*Laughter*]

Now, when we get by that, I'm going to reach a breakthrough agreement with Senator Dole to cut down on the commuting costs of Congress by moving the Senate sessions to New Hampshire. [*Laughter*] I'm hoping even to get Senator Gramm's vote for that. [*Laughter*]

Also, we decided to do something for that group of constituents that's supposed to be so alienated from the Democratic Party. We want to combine the Bureau of Alcohol, Tobacco and Firearms with both the Bureau of Fisheries and the Interstate Trucking Commission. We're going to call it the Department of Guys. [*Laughter*] And if you don't like it, there ain't a place for you in the Democratic Party anymore. [*Laughter*]

Finally, I have decided to support the most controversial Republican idea in the legal reform area, "loser pays," but only if we tie it to campaign finance reform and make it retroactive to 1992. [*Laughter*]

Now, that was what Al Gore and I did on just another Saturday afternoon at the White House. So even though all the action's with the Republicans on the Hill, I just wanted you to know you're still getting your money's worth out of us. [*Laughter*] It shows you the kind of great thinking you get out of a bunch of highly motivated people who don't get enough sleep at night. [*Laughter*]

Well, I could go on like this forever, but you know that, don't you? [*Laughter*] Let me say, for 51 years, all of you have gotten together and invited others to join you in celebrating the best of the electronic media. And while the times change and the rules change and the practices change, I really believe that most of us in this room, like the people who came here 51 years ago, want what's best for our country and do what we do in the hope that we're doing it well enough to advance the interests

of the United States and to keep the American dream alive.

This is an unusual and difficult time for all of us because of all the challenges out there in the country today, but it's a very, very exciting time, not only to be covering events in Washington but to be a part of it. I thank you for the work you do, and I thank you for having us here tonight.

I do want to say that I'm a little apprehensive; the next speaker, Bill Maher, has a TV show named "Politically Incorrect." Out of respect for him, I've tried not to be politically incorrect tonight. Out of respect for me, I hope he won't try to be presidential tonight. [*Laughter*]

Thank you all, and good night.

NOTE: The President spoke at 9:42 p.m. at the Washington Hilton. In his remarks he referred to Bill Headline, chair, Radio and Television Correspondents Association; CNN News reporter Wolf Blitzer; Representative Richard K. Armey; Robert MacNeil and James Lehrer, co-anchors of the MacNeil/Lehrer Newshour; economic commentator Louis Rukeyser; and television host Ed McMahon.

Remarks at the Welcoming Ceremony for King Hassan II of Morocco
March 15, 1995

Your Majesty, Your Royal Highnesses, members of the Moroccan delegation, distinguished guests: On behalf of the United States, it is my honor to welcome back to Washington a good friend of America and one of the Islamic world's most respected leaders, King Hassan II.

Your Majesty, the ties that link our two nations go back to the dawn of our independence. Before the cornerstone of this White House was laid, President George Washington and your ancestor, Sultan Mohammad III, signed a treaty of peace and friendship.

In the decades since, our two nations have sought to live up to that treaty's ideals by building on our friendship and working for peace and prosperity in your region and throughout the world. Now, much of what we have labored for and dreamed of is closer than ever to be-

coming reality, thanks in good measure to your wisdom and to your vision.

Your Majesty, you have worked tirelessly to secure a lasting and comprehensive peace in the Middle East, from helping to arrange President Sadat's historic journey to Jerusalem to building trust through quiet diplomacy, from establishing ties with Israel to hosting the Casablanca economic summit. Now we must accelerate the momentum for peace in the Middle East, the momentum which you have done so much to nurture and sustain.

As Morocco and the United States work for peace, we are also forging stronger bonds of commerce between our peoples. Morocco has embraced free markets, and today your economy stands poised to reap the benefits of this wise decision. Your Majesty, I look forward to discussing new opportunities for trade and investment which will support good jobs and create wealth in both our nations.

Your Majesty, under your leadership, Morocco has served as a force for tolerance and progress rooted in Islamic values. At a time when cooperation and moderation are taking hold in more countries than ever before but when violence and extremism still threaten all that we are working for, your example and your commitment to peace are more important than ever before.

Your Majesty, the United States is glad to have you as a friend, honored to have you as a partner as we work to shape the world for the better. Welcome to the White House. Welcome to America.

NOTE: The President spoke at 10:46 a.m. on the South Lawn at the White House.

The President's News Conference With King Hassan II of Morocco
March 15, 1995

The President. Good afternoon. His Majesty King Hassan and I have just concluded a very productive and wide-ranging meeting. We apologize for talking a little longer than the scheduled time, but we had much to discuss. Let me begin by thanking him for his visit, and continuing the tradition that he first began with President Kennedy of providing wise counsel to American Presidents.

Of course, we talked about how we can best support and accelerate the momentum for peace in the Middle East. His Majesty's visit comes at a time of renewed hope. As a result of Secretary Christopher's intensive discussions in the region, we now have an agreement to resume direct talks between Israel and Syria. This is a very encouraging development. Combined with the new energy we see in the Israel-Palestinian discussions and continued progress in implementing the Jordan-Israel peace treaty, I believe there is now a real opportunity to secure a durable resolution to the Arab-Israeli conflict.

The promise of peace owes much to King Hassan's vision and courage. He helped to arrange President Sadat's historic trip to Jerusalem. He undertook a direct dialog with Israel at a time when doing so was difficult. His quiet diplomacy facilitated talks between other Arab leaders and Israel. And Morocco continues to lead the effort to build a new Middle East.

His Majesty and I agreed that one key to peace is bringing tangible economic benefits to the people of the Middle East, a change in the quality of their daily lives so that they can develop a real stake in peaceful cooperation. That's why the process begun under King Hassan's leadership at the Casablanca summit last October is so important in order to expand economic integration and encourage private sector growth and investment.

His Majesty and I reviewed the next step in this process, including the Amman business summit this fall. We also discussed taking down barriers to trade and investment, such as the Arab League boycott of Israel that had denied the Middle East its full place as a dynamic participant in the global economy.

We discussed our shared interest in fighting the spread of weapons of mass destruction, which pose a threat to the entire Middle East and, indeed, to the world. I emphasized the importance the United States attaches to securing the indefinite extension of the Nuclear Non-Proliferation Treaty as a vital part of this effort.

We are also working to build closer economic ties. Today we will sign a trade and investment framework agreement to expand bilateral commerce and investment and to provide a framework for further trade liberalization. And Morocco announced plans to establish a counterpart in the United States to the U.S.-Morocco Joint Committee on Trade and Investment.

Later this afternoon, His Majesty will preside over a protocol signing with the Overseas Private Investment Corporation. OPIC will guarantee $200 million in U.S. Government support for a $1.5 billion powerplant being built by an American company near Casablanca. Morocco's decision to welcome foreign participation in privatizing its state-owned power sector made this project possible. Together with similar ventures in the future, it promises to generate jobs and exports for the United States and to provide Morocco with the electricity it needs to power its own industrial growth.

Finally, I'd like to express my own gratitude to the King for his enlightened leadership of the Organization of the Islamic Conference. I share his conviction that Islam can be a powerful force for tolerance and moderation in the world and that its traditional values—devotion to family and to society, to faith and good works—are in harmony with the best of Western ideals.

As I said in my speeches to the Parliaments of Jordan and Israel, the United States has great respect for Islam and wishes to work with its followers throughout the world to secure peace and a better future for all our children.

Throughout the course of our long friendship, which goes back to the very beginning of this country, Morocco and the United States have worked together to shape the world we live in for the better. King Hassan and I are committed to continuing that great partnership for progress well into the future. And I thank him for the contributions he has made to that today.

Your Majesty.

King Hassan. To begin with, I'd like to reiterate my thanks to Mr. President for the warm welcome with which we have been surrounded ever since we have tread the soil of this country.

We have spoken about many issues, Mr. President and myself. Now, we did not have the opportunity of knowing each other personally before, but we have come to know each other through the messages that we have exchanged in the past and also by means of the various positions that were taken by Mr. President concerning the peace in the Middle East. I think that Mr. Clinton should be proud of his balance sheet after 2 years in the White House.

We have also talked about bilateral issues, and thanks to God, we have come to realize how much harmony exists between the positions of our two countries. However, in the modern world in which we live today, there can be no schizophrenia in any healthy relationship. There is absolutely no justification for us to have such excellent political relations on the one hand and then on the other hand to have economic relations that are not up to the same level.

Up to now, we have been a one-legged man in our mutual action. And I hope that in the future we will be able to walk on two feet,

that is, hand-in-hand towards the prosperity and the success we are hoping for both countries.

Obviously, the United States of America has its own vision of matters because it deals with international issues. And therefore, the analysis of matters have to be to that proportion.

Morocco, though modest the way it is, has its own vision of things. Thanks to God, during our talks, we had absolutely no differences concerning our principles, ideals, and the aims that are to be attained. But considering that Mr. President and myself are perfectionists, we have to devise the most appropriate strategy in order for us to reach the aims that both countries have in mind.

Mr. President, once again I want to thank you for your warm welcome, but I would like also to thank you for the open heart with which I have been received here in the White House.

Middle East Peace Process

Q. Mr. President, you spoke this morning of the need to accelerate the peace process. What can the United States do to break the impasse when Syria and Israel resume negotiations next week?

The President. Well, of course, we're doing what we can with the Secretary's trip to the Middle East and with the work that Mr. Ross and others are doing. What we have sought to do, always, is to facilitate the conditions within which both parties will feel secure in making peace. That has always been our role. We cannot make a peace for the parties, and we're doing what we can, once again, to make our best case to both sides about what things will make them secure in making the decision.

As you know, when they discuss matters of this kind, it's best to let them deal with the details and make the decisions. So the less I say about the specifics, the greater the opportunity they have to make the peace.

Is there a question from Morocco?

North Africa

Q. Mr. President, you have spoken during the last visit you had made that you were concerned with stability—in Paris—that you were concerned with stability in North Africa. You have also spoken about the fact that Morocco is a point of stability and security in the region. Now, in your discussions with His Majesty, did you come to devise some kind of strategy in order to strengthen and sustain this idea of the security in the North African region?

The President. His Majesty and I spoke at great length about North Africa, and I asked him for his evaluation and for his advice with regard to a number of countries. And I think it's fair to say that he believes the United States is pursuing the right policy.

One of the things I think we have to do is to try to strengthen economically the forces of progress and tolerance, which is why I'm very pleased about the agreements that we have announced with Morocco today. We will continue to push to support elements of progress and tolerance in other nations as well.

Your Majesty, would you like to say anything about that question?

Middle East Development Bank

Q. The question is addressed to both you and His Majesty. What about the latest in the establishment of the Middle East development bank? The regional powers are anxious for it in the Middle East, but some European leaders are opposed to it. What is happening with it, and if so, what's the timetable on it?

The President. I don't know that I can give you a timetable. I can tell you that we are committed to it, as you know, and we are working with our allies in Europe. We're doing our best to set it up, and we'll do it as quickly as possible. I still think it's a good idea.

King Hassan and U.S. Presidents

Q. Your Majesty, you had the opportunity to meet seven Presidents of the United States. How did you find the President Bill Clinton different of the other? Thank you.

King Hassan. First, let me say no two men are alike. As a wise man once said, style is what defines the man. All the different Presidents that I've had the honor to meet here contribute together to the richness and the variety in the United States. Each time it has been a new style, a new inspiration, a new team.

The President. If His Majesty had not been a direct descendant of the Prophet, he might have become Morocco's greatest diplomat. [*Laughter*]

Egypt

Q. Thank you, Mr. President. Your Majesty, I'd like to ask you, sir, what you make of the increasing political difficulties that President Mubarak is said to be facing in Egypt and whether this subject arose between the two of you today? And also, Mr. President, I'd like to have your views on that as well.

King Hassan. Let me state, first of all, that this world in which we live cannot be without political crisis. Each country, on whatever continent and whatever the social-economic level and governance it has, confronts difficulties in economic, social, or employment areas. But it was not on our agenda to carry out a checkup on Egypt, so we did not take the time to devote to that particular issue.

The President. The only thing I would add is I thought His Majesty made a very important point when we discussed this briefly, which was that you cannot see the Egyptian difficulties solely in political terms and that they have to be seen in the context of the challenge that that nation and, I might add, many others are having around the world of sustainable development, of balancing a rapidly growing population, with all the pressures and problems that creates, with the need to provide for them food and shelter and education and a stable set of opportunities. And I appreciated that insight very much.

Middle East Peace Process

Q. Your Majesty, we would like to know what you are doing on the level of the peace process in the Middle East and what is your position about the Arab boycott of Israel? Are there any disagreements between Morocco and the United States regarding this issue?

King Hassan. Yes, indeed, we did discuss the issue of boycott—or that is, the boycott of the Arab States towards Israel. As I've said previously, I believe that man cannot walk on one leg. We are not looking into the peace process without looking into the economic peace process also. The boycott of which you have spoken is not a Moroccan-Israeli issue. It is a boycott on the part of all of the members of the Arab League and independently of whatever the view of any of the members of the Arab League is. Concerning this issue, I would say that there has to be a compromise among the members of the Arab League if the boycott is to be lifted.

As Mr. President has said previously, there are signs of good will that have been reported from Secretary Christopher's trip to Syria. And there is no doubt that the progress that is scored in the peace negotiations between Israel and

Syria will certainly bring about a collective decision on the part of all of the members of the Arab League concerning the lifting of the boycott.

The President. Thank you very much.

NOTE: The President's 89th news conference began at 1:17 p.m. in the Rose Garden at the White House. In his remarks, he referred to Dennis B. Ross, Special Middle East Coordinator. King Hassan spoke in Arabic and French, and his remarks were translated by an interpreter.

Message to the Congress on Prohibiting Transactions With Respect to the Development of Iranian Petroleum Resources
March 15, 1995

To the Congress of the United States:

Pursuant to section 204(b) of the International Emergency Economic Powers Act (50 U.S.C. 1703(b)) and section 301 of the National Emergencies Act (50 U.S.C. 1631), I hereby report that I have exercised my statutory authority to declare a national emergency to respond to the actions and policies of the Government of Iran and to issue an Executive order prohibiting United States persons from entering into contracts for the financing of or the overall management or supervision of the development of petroleum resources located in Iran or over which Iran claims jurisdiction.

The Secretary of the Treasury is authorized to issue regulations in exercise of my authorities under the International Emergency Economic Powers Act to implement these prohibitions. All Federal agencies are also directed to take actions within their authority to carry out the provisions of the Executive order.

I am enclosing a copy of the Executive order that I have issued. The order is effective at 12:01 a.m., eastern standard time, on March 16, 1995.

I have authorized these measures in response to the actions and policies of Iran including support for international terrorism, efforts to undermine the Middle East Peace Process, and the acquisition of weapons of mass destructions and the means to deliver them. We have worked energetically to press the Government of Iran to cease this unacceptable behavior. To that end we have worked closely with Allied governments to prevent Iran's access to goods that would enhance its military capabilities and allow it to further threaten the security of the region. We have also worked to limit Iran's financial resources by opposing subsidized lending.

Iran has reacted to the limitations on its financial resources by negotiating for Western firms to provide financing and know-how for management of the development of petroleum resources. Such development would provide new funds that the Iranian Government could use to continue its current policies. It continues to be the policy of the U.S. Government to seek to limit those resources and these prohibitions will prevent United States persons from acting in a manner that undermines that effort.

WILLIAM J. CLINTON

The White House,
March 15, 1995.

NOTE: The Executive order is listed in Appendix D at the end of this volume.

Remarks at a State Dinner Honoring King Hassan II of Morocco
March 15, 1995

Ladies and gentlemen, Your Majesty, Your Royal Highnesses, members of the Moroccan delegation, distinguished guests: Hillary and I are delighted to welcome you to America's home. I have been grateful for this opportunity to get to know Your Majesty and to appreciate the wise counsel you have given to every American President since John Kennedy.

In fact, your relationship with our country's leaders, I have learned, goes back even further than that. In January of 1943, at the height of World War II, you were present when your father, Mohammed V, hosted the Casablanca summit between President Roosevelt and Prime Minister Churchill. History does not record what advice you gave President Roosevelt and the Prime Minister, but I did note that, thereafter, the war turned decisively to the Allies' advantage. [*Laughter*] So, clearly, you gave good advice.

I also noted that when President Roosevelt and Prime Minister Churchill were in Casablanca, Mr. Roosevelt thought he had to come home and go to work, and Prime Minister Churchill made him stay in Morocco for 3 more days to see the beautiful sights. My staff never lets me do that. [*Laughter*] So we have not made progress in every respect since the 1940's.

Your Majesty, you have written that in the joyous moment following the declaration of Morocco's independence, your father pulled you aside and said, "We have passed through a difficult trial. But the road ahead will be long and hard. We do not have the right to disappoint the faithful and courageous people who have placed their trust in us." For the past 34 years, you have lived by your father's admonition. And by pursuing progress for the Moroccan

people and peace for all the peoples of your region, you have truly fulfilled his legacy.

The American people especially admire your steadfast devotion to securing a comprehensive peace among all the peoples of the Middle East. In a region where passion and hatred have so often overwhelmed cooler heads and clearer minds, yours has always been a voice of reason and tolerance. Quoting from the Koran, you have said, "If two groups of believers fight each other, endeavor to reconcile them." You have been tireless in your pursuit of reconciliation. You have helped the countries of the Middle East turn on the past and start a new chapter of peaceful coexistence.

Your Majesty, you have spoken of your beloved Morocco as a bridge between East and West, between Islam and the Judeo-Christian faiths, between respect for tradition and openness to the future. Under your leadership, that bridge, which runs from the tip of Europe to the sands of the Sahara and joins the Atlantic to the Mediterranean, that bridge has risen high as a beacon of hope.

And for all those reasons, ladies and gentlemen, honored guests, please join me in raising a glass to His Majesty, King Hassan II, to the Prince and the Princess who are here, and to the people of Morocco, who have done so much to build the bridges of understanding and peace.

NOTE: The President spoke at 8:45 p.m. in the State Dining Room at the White House.

Remarks on Regulatory Reform in Arlington, Virginia
March 16, 1995

The President. Thank you, Stu, and, ladies and gentlemen, thank you. Let me first of all say how delighted I am to be in this wonderful place. Among other things, they do their printing here with soy ink, and that's really why we're here, because I come from Arkansas, and my—[*laughter*]—my farmer friends grow a lot of soybeans, and we're always looking for new markets. And we're just trying to support responsible people who are using great ink.

This is a wonderful story today, and I thank all of these people for hosting us, Stu and all of his partners behind us, to make a point that,

to me, is very, very important. You heard the Vice President say that last month I called together the heads of the Federal regulatory agencies and told them to begin a root-and-branch examination of how we regulate the American people in all the various ways that we do.

I wanted to make this the next big part of the reinventing Government process that the Vice President has overseen so well for the last 2 years. And today, we want to announce the fruits of that process. But it's important to remember what the purpose is. Most Americans are honest people. The free enterprise system brings us great benefits. But we know we have certain things in common that we have to pursue through the Government that we all are responsible for.

The question is: How can we do it best? Today, we're announcing basically two sets of changes: First of all, some Government-wide regulatory reforms that will cut back on paperwork and trust honest business people as partners, not adversaries and, second, significant reforms in the way we protect the environment and the way we assure safe and high quality drugs and medical devices.

The philosophy that guided these changes is pretty simple: Protect people, not bureaucracy; promote results, not rules; get action, not rhetoric. Wherever possible, try to embrace common sense; it will confound your enemies and elate your friends. [*Laughter*]

Since I became President, I have worked hard on this. You know, I spent 12 years as a Governor of a State where I got to deal with the regulatory apparatus of the Federal Government as it related to both State Government and to every friend I had in every walk of life in my State. And I found that in the environmental area, for example, we often had both the environmentalists and the people who were in business both frustrated by some things that were going on. And I could give you lots of other examples, and all of you can, as well, from your own personal experience.

Our goal is to get rid of yesterday's Government so that we're capable of meeting the problems of today and the challenges of tomorrow. We want a Government that offers opportunity, demands responsibility, and shrinks bureaucracy, one that embodies the New Covenant I've been talking about, more opportunity and more responsibility with a less bureaucratic Government. I think Government can be as innovative as the best of our private sector businesses. I think Government can discard volume after volume of rules and, instead, set clear goals and challenge people to come up with their own ways to meet them. That kind of Government will be very different from the old one-size-fits-all bureaucracy. But it also would be different from the new proposals for one-size-fits-all deregulation and cutbacks.

I want to see a different approach. I want a Government that is limited but effective, that is lean but not mean, that does what it should do better and simply stops doing things that

it shouldn't be doing in the first place, that protects consumers and workers, the environment, without burdening business, choking innovation, or wasting the money of the American taxpayers.

We do need to reduce paperwork and unnecessary regulation. I don't think we want to freeze efforts to protect our children from unsafe toys or unsafe food. We do need to carefully analyze the risks, the costs, the benefits of everything we do, but I don't think it's a better approach to pile on dozens of new procedural requirements. That will only run up legal bills and weaken the public trust. Paralysis by process is not common sense.

So as I said before, reform, yes, and let's do it with a bipartisan flair, but let's don't roll back our commitment to the things that make life worth living here. We all want water we can drink and air we can breathe, food we can eat, and a place we can work in and feel safe and secure. But we know that the way we have sought these goals through Government often, often has frustrated the very goals we seek. The way our regulatory system has grown into a dense jungle of rules and regulations, precise lists of "do this" and "don't do that" can trip up even the most well-intentioned business person.

Can you imagine a fellow like this, running a shop like this on the cutting edge of the environment, is afraid to call the Federal Government for advice? There is no better example of what has been wrong. Here's a guy who's tried to do right, wants to do more right, and is afraid that if he does it, he'll be punished for doing it. It really is true that often in the Government no good deed goes unpunished. [*Laughter*] So it's time to stop doing things that drive people up the wall.

A few weeks ago, my good friend the Governor of Florida, who is also on this journey with us and has talked to me for more than— oh, I don't know—10 years we've been working on these issues, long before I ever thought of running for President, gave me this remarkable book that is now sweeping the country, "The Death of Common Sense." It makes an interesting point, the book does. It says that in our entirely understandable and necessary desire to protect the public, we have put in place a system that very often requires those who are carrying it out to defy common sense, unduly burden private taxpayers, and undermine the very objectives we are seeking to achieve.

Now, the author of that book, Philip Howard, has made a major contribution to the American debate on this. He's here with us today. He has done some work with the Vice President's National Performance Review, and I'd like to ask him to stand and be recognized. And thank you, sir, for doing this. [*Applause*]

Over the last 2 years, we've tried to get this Government of ours into some kind of shape. We have lowered the deficit by $600 billion, and we've reduced the size of the Federal bureaucracy by over 100,000. We're on the way to reducing the Federal work force by more than a quarter of a million. It'll be the smallest it's been since President Kennedy was here when our budgets are finally implemented.

Now, we've tried to do more than that. We've tried to do more than just cut. We've tried to change the way the Government works. We've tried to spend more money, for example, on education and training and research and technology, the things that we believe will raise incomes, offer more people opportunity, and protect the environment while we grow the economy. I don't think we should apologize for that. We should exercise judgment and common sense about what we cut and what we spend money on.

We also are trying to change the regulatory environment. I was proud to sign the first bill this new Congress passed, which applies to Congress most of the laws they impose on the private sector. I think that will have a very salutary impact on the deliberations of Congress.

We are about to get a bill out of the Congress which will restrict the ability of Congress to impose mandates on State and local governments that are unfunded; I think that is a good idea. And maybe most important of all, we're working hard, as the Vice President has said, to eliminate rules that are obsolete, to simplify rules that are too complicated, to cut paperwork wherever we can, in short, just to change the way Government works.

Most of the people I grew up with, who all write me with their great ideas now that I've become President, are just out there living in this country, making a living, raising their families, obeying the law, and doing the best they can. I believe their biggest objection to Government is not the size of it but the way it regulates, the way it operates in their own lives.

And I have done my best, relying on the extraordinary leadership of the Vice President and the National Performance Review staff and all the people who have been introduced here, particularly from the SBA and the EPA and the FDA and the Office of Management and Budget, to try to change this.

Let me just give you some examples. We want economic development. We've got the most active Commerce Department in American history. But the Commerce Department is also cutting the rules for businesses in half. That will also develop the economy. We want nutritious food, and the USDA has raised food safety standards, but they're also making it easier to import safe fruits and vegetables. We ought to repeal silly rules. The Department of the Interior just eliminated feather import quotas for exotic birds and a lot of other things as well.

So what are we going to do now? Today we're announcing the first big steps of what I assure you is just the beginning of a process that we intend to continue for as long as we have the public trust. First, we want to do something that recognizes that most of the businesses in this country are small, most of them want to do the right thing, and most of the new jobs are being created by them. We want to get our enforcers out of the business of mindlessly writing traffic tickets and into the business of achieving results. We're going to let these regulators apply common sense.

Two of the three problems Mr. Howard talks about in his book are addressed here today. One is that in our attempt to try to tell people how we think the Government should regulate, we have tried to imagine all conceivable permutations of things that could occur and then write rules to cover them. The other is that we've been far more obsessed—the Government has in the past—with process than results. That's the general problem I might add, of Washington, DC, not confined entirely to the Government. [*Laughter*]

Today we are ordering a Government-wide policy. Enforcers will be given the authority to waive up to 100 percent of punitive fines for small businesses so that a business person who acts in good faith can put his energy into fixing the problem, not fighting with a regulator. In other words, if they want to spend the fine money fixing the problem, better they should keep it and fix the problem than give it to the Government.

Similarly, regulators will be given the discretion to waive fines for small businesses altogether if it's a first-time violation and the firms quickly and sincerely move to correct the problem. Let me be clear: These changes will not be an excuse for violating criminal laws; they won't be an amnesty for businesses that harm public health; they won't enable people to undermine the safety of the public while their competitors play by the rules. But we will stop playing "gotcha" with decent, honest business people who want to be good citizens. Compliance, not punishment, should be our objective.

The second thing we want to do is to curb the Government's appetite for paperwork. We are going to have each agency allow regularly scheduled reports to the Government to be cut in half, unless there is some important public purpose that won't permit it. In other words, if people file quarterly reports, we want the agency to say file them twice a year; if they file them twice a year, file annual reports. The Vice President likes that. We'll leave more trees up, and we'll save more time for small business. Time is money. Time is the most important thing we have.

You know, we got rid of the Federal personnel manuals. I forget—the Vice President knows better than I do—I forget how many thousands of pages.

The Vice President. Ten thousand pages.

The President. Ten thousand pages. You know, I have yet to have the first Federal employee come up and attack me for that. [*Laughter*] I've yet to have the first citizen say, "How dare you waste my money. With this new arbitrary system, you got rid of these 10,000 pages. I can't sleep at night for thinking about it being gone." [*Laughter*] And believe me, nobody will notice this as long as we take care to protect the public health, the public safety, and the public interest.

The second thing I want to talk about are fundamental reforms in the area of the environment and drug and medical services. Environmental regulation touches every part of our lives. And this is a moment of transition in our environmental policy. The modern era began in 1970 with Earth Day, the passage of landmark legislation and the creation of the Environmental Protection Agency.

The results, we should never forget, are a great American success story, envied and copied around the world. Because we made a common commitment to protect the environment, people are living longer and living better, and we have a chance to pass the country along to our children and grandchildren in far better shape than would have been the case otherwise. But the methods that worked in the past aren't necessarily adequate to the present day.

Our environmental programs must work better and cost less to meet the challenges of the future. Today we are announcing a landmark package of 25 environmental reforms. Let me describe them in general terms.

First we recognize that market mechanisms generally make more sense than micromanagement by the Government. Letting utilities buy and sell their rights under the Clean Air Act, for example, has saved utilities and their customers $2 billion and given us cleaner air. Today we will dramatically extend this market concept to other areas of clean air and water protection.

Second, too many businesses are afraid to come to the EPA for help in cleaning up their act because they're afraid they'll be punished. That's the story you just heard. We're going to open compliance centers to help small businesses and say to them, "If you discover a problem, you'll have 180 days to fix it with no punitive fine."

And third, because you shouldn't need a forest full of paper to protect the environment, EPA will cut its paperwork requirements on businesses and communities by 25 percent, that is 20 million hours of work for businesses and communities that will be saved for other purposes next year.

While these steps will improve the current system, others will move well beyond it to a shift in the way we actually think about regulation. EPA will launch a pilot program called Project XL, excellence and leadership, which is simple but revolutionary. They will say to the companies in the pilot and, hopefully, eventually, the companies all across the country, "Here is the pollution reduction goal. If you can figure out how to meet it, you can throw out the EPA rulebook. You figure out how to meet the goal."

I want to say, especially here, how much I appreciate both the environmental groups and the business groups that are here. We know that pollution prevention pays. We know pollution prevention and reduction is a great source of job creation for America, as well as a guarantee for our children that this country will be worth living in.

We also ought to be smart enough to know that people who are living with the consequences of this might be able to figure out how to fix it better than folks who are writing rules about it. So we're going to see if we can figure out how to do it in this way.

The other set of major reforms we're talking about involve the realms of drugs and medical devices. When I was running for President, I don't know how many Americans I had come up to me and talk to me about this all over the country but especially in places where a lot of this kind of work is done. There was a time when consumers might find that their food was adulterated, their drugs were quackery or had dreadful side effects.

Today, Americans don't have to worry about the safety or effectiveness when they buy anything from cough syrups to the latest antibiotics or pacemakers. The Food and Drug Administration has made American Drugs and medical devices the envy of the world and in demand all over the world. And we should never forget that, either. And we are going to stick with the standards we have, the highest in the world. But strong standards need not mean business as usual in every area.

Today we are announcing a set of reforms that will make our high-quality drugs and medical devices available to consumers more quickly and more cheaply. First, FDA will stop using a full-blown review every time a biotech drug company makes a minor and risk-free manufacturing change in an established drug.

Second, FDA will stop requiring costly assessments on drugs that obviously have no significant impact on the environment.

Third, FDA will eliminate 600 pages of cumbersome regulations controlling the production of antibiotics and other drugs. And I'll give you $100 if anybody comes up to you and complains within the next 12 months—[laughter]—when you do that.

And finally, 140 categories of medical devices that pose low risk to patients, from finger exercisers to oxygen masks, will no longer need preapproval by FDA before they are put on the market.

These FDA reforms, and others we'll announce in the next few weeks, will keep quality at world-class levels and save industry and consumers nearly half a billion dollars a year. And I am pleased, again, to say that there are representatives from the drug and medical device industry here as well. We appreciate your support.

I am very, very excited about this. These changes, taken together, represent real and fundamental reform. Now, they lack the sledgehammer subtlety of a moratorium, but if we're going to be responsible, we ought to fix the problem, not just seek to freeze the problem. To go from yesterday's Government to tomorrow's Government we need movement, not paralysis. We need to continue our commitment to a Government that works better, costs less, reflects our values, and can make a difference and that doesn't drive us up the wall but drives us into the future together. That is common sense, and we can give it to the American people together.

Thank you very much.

NOTE: The President spoke at 10:47 a.m. at Custom Print, Inc. In his remarks, he referred to Stu McMichael, owner of the company.

Remarks to the National Conference of State Legislatures
March 16, 1995

Thank you, Jane Campbell, and thank you, Senator Lack, and thank you to the other leaders of the NCSL for meeting me outside. And welcome, all of you, to Washington. I know you just heard from Secretary Reich. He actually—he hasn't been here? [Laughter] That gives me something else to make fun of my staff about.

That's what it says. Let me try—what else does it say? Maybe I should put my glasses on, and it will come out differently. [Laughter]

Let me say, I am delighted to see all of you. I'm about as happy to see you as you acted like you were to see me. [Laughter] I loved the legislative process when I was Governor, and in Arkansas we had an interesting system. We were all there in our old State capitol, and the legislature was on the third floor, and I was on the second floor. And when the legislature was in session I just sort of kept open house. If a legislator showed up, I saw him or her. And we'd have morning planning meetings at 7:30 a.m. every morning, and half the time legislators just wandered in and sat at the administration's planning meeting. And I must say, I often think in the course of working here both for the last 2 years and for the last 2 months, if we wouldn't be better off as a country if we worked more like that up here. [*Applause*] Yes, you can clap for that. That's all right. That's a pretty good idea.

I've even met half a dozen of my State legislators since I've been gone from Arkansas who said they missed me, which is something I never thought I'd hear. [*Laughter*] Warmed my heart. We have a lot of former legislators in this administration, as I'm sure you know. I see the Deputy Secretary of Education out there, Madeleine Kunin, also the former Governor of Vermont. And Arthur DeCoursey of SBA was a State legislator in Massachusetts; Patrick McGowan with the SBA was a State legislator in Maine; Thomas Redder with the SBA was a State legislator in Colorado—all the other employees for the SBA were actually in small business at one time or another. [*Laughter*] Of course, Secretary Peña was as well, and Gary Blumenthal, the Executive Director of the President's Committee on Mental Retardation. So we're interested in what you're going through and in working with you.

I have said many places, but I'd like to have the privilege of repeating it here today, that I ran for this job because I felt the mission of this country at the end of the 20th century was to get us into the next century with the American dream alive and well and with America still the strongest country in the world, the greatest force for peace and freedom and democracy. Alive and well means that we have to have opportunities for more jobs and higher incomes. Half the American people are living on less money today when you adjust for inflation than they were making 15 years ago. That's one of the reasons a lot of people aren't happy in the recovery. We've got 6.1 million new jobs and the lowest combined rates of unemployment and inflation in 25 years, but a lot of folks'

incomes are not going up. And they feel uncertain, insecure.

I get letters all the time from people I grew up with in Arkansas who are nearing that magic age of 50 talking about the uncertainty they feel about their future, their children. Are they going to be able to educate their children? Are they going to be caught up in some great downsizing move, kind of the other side of this great churning change and all this opportunity that's out there?

The other part of the American dream is keeping our values alive, work, family, community, values you might put under the general heading of responsibility, so that we can pull back together. So I think we ought to offer more opportunity and more responsibility. I also think to do it here in Washington, we have to have a dramatic change in the way Government has worked. And I have been working hard at that for the last 2 years.

The old view was that there was kind of a one-size-fits-all—drove you nuts in the statehouses of the country, I'm sure—that there was a one, single big Government solution for every big problem in America. And half the time we told you what to do and didn't give you the money to do it with.

The other view that seems to have a lot of energy around here is that, basically, maybe there's nothing for the Federal Government to do except to give the problem to you and give you less money to deal with it, and the idea is that since Government would mess up a one-car parade, we just ought to walk away from all these problems.

My view is different from that, and I guess it's forged largely on my 12 years of experience as a Governor and the fact that before I got this job I actually used to be able to spend large amounts of time talking to real people every day. I don't mean that the people I talk to aren't real people; I mean that mostly the people I talk to have business before the Government or work for the President or in some event that I've set up. I don't get to walk the streets the way I used to and just visit with people in a more informal setting.

My view is that what we need is a Government that is very different, that has less bureaucracy, that is lean but not mean, that operates in a more entrepreneurial fashion, that gives more decision to the State and local governments and to the private sector, but that is an active partner in doing three things: promoting economic opportunities through jobs and incomes, empowering people through education and training to make the most of their own lives, and enhancing the security of our people, both in terms of safe streets and our security around the world.

And that's what I have worked to do so that if you believe that, it means that you have to have a smaller Government that is still effective, that does what it's supposed to do well and stops doing things that it shouldn't do, and that works more in partnership with you. Since I have been President, we have now given 26 States waivers from Federal rules to enact their own welfare reform proposals and 9 States waivers to do major, major health care reform, more States that the previous two administrations combined.

We've also done a lot to try to deregulate certain aspects of the private economy from undue Federal oversight. And we did a lot more about that today, and I'll say more about that in a minute. We have reduced the size of the Federal payroll by more than 100,000. We've reduced the size of the Federal deficit by $600 billion. We're on our way to the smallest Government in Washington since Kennedy was President and 3 years of deficit reduction in a row for the first time since Truman was President. We are changing the way things operate around here.

Now that the new Congress is here, we're having a huge debate about what the role of Government ought to be. And it can be a very healthy thing indeed. I must tell you, as all of you know, I have real differences as well as real agreements with this Congress. I have vigorous agreements and vigorous disagreements. I strongly agreed with the bill that applies to Congress the laws Congress imposes on the private sector. I thought it was long overdue and was elated to sign it. I campaigned on it in '92.

We're about to get a bill out of the conference and to my desk which will end unfunded mandates that are unreasonable and sharply reduce the ability of Congress to impose on you and on local governments requirements which we don't give you the money to pay for. And I think that is a very good thing indeed.

But I do not agree with the proposals that undermine our fundamental mission, more economic opportunity, empowering people through education and training, and increasing our security. Therefore, I don't agree with the proposal that would eliminate the 100,000 police commitment and the crime bill that we worked for 6 years for or cut school lunches or cut our education programs, the Goals 2000 program for 4,000 schools in America or the proposal for safe and drug-free schools.

Some of these proposals are embodied in the so-called rescission bill which was adopted by the House today. Some of them are embodied in their general budget. What they have in common is, in my view, is they cut too much of people and not enough pork.

The proposal passed today would virtually eliminate the AmeriCorps program, our national service program, which is not a bureaucracy, which many of you have worked with which, as you know, is helping police on the street, helping people to build houses, helping to fight fires in the West, doing work that wouldn't be done otherwise, and letting young people earn money to pay for their education. It is a great grassroots program. It should not be eliminated.

So as we move into the future and as these bills go to the Senate, we're going to have an interesting debate here. And a lot of it will affect you. I wondered when the unfunded mandate bill passed why it wasn't made immediately effective, because I'm strong for it. I'm for the line-item veto, too, and I hope we get that up here pretty soon. There's a lot of things Republicans want to do that I am strongly in favor of. But I said to myself, why aren't we making an unfunded mandates bill immediately effective? And I read that rescission bill, and I realized you're going to get some "defunded" mandates. If you look at some of those cuts to the States, the responsibilities are still on you, but the money is being taken back.

So I say to you, what kind of Government do we want? We knew we had to cut some money out of the Agriculture Department, just for example. You know, the Agriculture Department got real big. And the best line that came out of the 1992 Presidential campaign, I'm embarrassed to say—I wish it were mine, but it wasn't—was Ross Perot's line about the Agriculture Department employee that had to go see a psychiatrist because he lost his farmer. You remember that? I thought it was funnier than you did, apparently. [*Laughter*]

But anyway—so, we knew that we had to cut some money. What did we do? We closed

1,200 offices. What did they do? They propose cuts in the School Lunch Program. They say, "Well, they're not really cuts in the School Lunch Program." Well, yes, they are. If this proposal had been law in 1989, this year there would be one million fewer kids getting lunch at school. And a lot of these kids show up at school, and they don't have enough to eat at home. The meals they get at school is the only dad-gum good meal they get all day. There are children going to school in this country that never see a dentist until they are 16, 17, 18 years old. We want them to learn, and you know, everybody rails about the schools; I'm telling you, it's hard for a teacher to teach a poor kid who's hungry.

So I think there's a right way to do this and wrong way to do it. And it doesn't have to be a partisan deal. I told you, I'm for a lot of what they're trying to do. We do need to change the way we do business here. But we need to have the ability to bring common sense to bear in judgment, and we need to put our children and our educational system and our future first. We need to keep our eye on what is the mission, the mission to get the country into the 21st century still the strongest country in the world in a place where there's real opportunity.

Today we had a meeting about regulation. We've got a lot of regulatory legislation here, freeze all pending regulations for 6 months or a year or whatever and a lot of other things. Well, what I've been trying to do is not freeze it, I've been trying to fix it. Today we announced the following things in the regulatory area, something that I think is very, very important, that should be popular in every State here: We announced some dramatic changes for small business, in the environment, and in the area of drugs and medical technology.

We announced first of all, that small businesses who try to do the right thing but make a mistake will be given the opportunity not to pay their fine to the Government but to take the money in the fine they would have paid to the Government and fix the problem in the first place, and that small businesses who make a mistake for the first time can have their fines waived altogether if they have never had a record of bad behavior and who are obviously trying to do the right thing.

We announced today that all Government agencies, when it is consistent with the public interest—that is, public health and well-being— will cut in half the reporting requirements for small businesses. So whenever possible, if they have to report four times a year, now they can report twice a year. If they have to report twice a year, now they can report once a year. And we think it will make a big difference, and so does the Small Business Administration. We are trying to change things.

In the area of the environment we announced today that we would allow small businesses a grace period of 6 months to correct violations after they've been identified. We found out that a lot of people wouldn't call the Government and find out what the law is, because they were afraid that somebody would come see them and fine them. So we had a lot of people who were out of compliance because they were literally afraid to ask how to get in compliance.

We're going to cut environmental paperwork by 25 percent, which will save—get this—20 million hours of work per year for the American people. We are going to launch a pilot program with 50 businesses which will allow companies to reach a pollution reduction goal however they want. And if they can reach it, they can throw out the EPA rule book. Doesn't matter how they reach it, as long as they reach the production goals.

Same thing we tried to do for the schools, by the way, in the elementary and secondary education act, to give you more flexibility—here are the national goals, you figure out how to meet them—in the schools, the principals, the teachers. It's a very important policy change.

In the area of drugs and biotechnology, we have decided to stop doing a full-blown and very expensive review every time a biotech company makes a minor and insignificant change in one of its products. We're going to stop requiring very costly assessments on drugs that obviously don't have any impact on the environment. We're going to eliminate 600 pages of regulation. I'll bet you nobody will ever miss them, and it will save this industry, one of our most productive industries, $500 billion a year.

So this is the sort of thing we're trying to do. It will make a huge difference in the life of this country. But better to fix the problem than just to freeze it in place. Better to do something real than to do something that sounds good, that maybe causes more harm than good. We all want to have water we can drink and air we can breathe and food we can eat and a place to work we can feel safe and secure in. We can do this.

Now you have to decide, without regard to your party or your region what you believe our role is, too. To make a judgment about this debate that's unfolding here, you have to make up your own mind.

You know, I spent, when I was a Governor, I bet I spent more time cussing the Federal Government than most of you do. And since I've been President, I bet I've spent even more time doing it. [*Laughter*] But the fact is that this country has benefited by 25 years of effort to clean the environment up. This country has benefited by our common efforts to make people secure at work, to make toys safe for our children. This country has benefited from these efforts, but we have forgotten common sense in a lot of the way we do things. So the trick is to put common sense back into this and reestablish a partnership that makes sense between the National Government, those of you at the State level, people at the local level, and most importantly, private citizens, so that what we do makes sense, it achieves common goals, and doesn't waste taxpayer money.

That is going to be the great debate here. And to make the judgments, you have to move beyond the rhetoric to the reality of each issue here. Everybody is for cutting Government, but I think there's a real difference between closing 1,200 offices and cutting back on food stamps. I think there's a real difference between closing the regional offices at HUD and cutting back on a program for homeless veterans at the Department of Labor. I think there's a difference. I think it matters.

I don't think all Federal Government spending is the same. I think with drug use on the rise and among young people again, for reasons that are almost impossible to understand—young people thinking that it's no longer really dangerous to fool with drugs again, not to mention illegal—to cut out all of these programs that would give 94 percent of the schools in this country an opportunity to make their schools safer and more drug-free, whether it's metal detectors and police officers or more folks in there teaching prevention, is not common sense.

So I believe if we'll work together, check our rhetorical baggage, and try to get this country into the 21st century remembering our mission, we can cut a good deal more spending without cutting our kids and our future. We can absolutely dramatically reduce the unfair burden of regulation without undermining the quality of our environment or the safety of our lives.

In short, we can do what Americans have always done. We have always been philosophically conservative, pragmatic, operationally progressive people who got the job done and moved the country into the future. That's how we have performed. That's why we're still around after over 200 years. That is the genius of our constitutional system. That's how you pass a budget in your legislature every year.

So, since you're up here in a leadership conference, I would urge you without regard to your party or your region, to urge this course on the Congress. Urge this course on the Congress. You know, I don't need any lectures in the need to cut spending. We reduced the deficit $600 billion without a lot of help 2 years ago, and we're going to do it some more. But we cannot walk away from our responsibilities to our children and to our future. We have got to stop a lot of this crazy regulation, but we have got to do it in a way that leaves us not only more prosperous in the short run but leaves us with a safer and more secure environment and a healthier citizenry over the long run.

We can do this. We don't have to make a bunch of bogus choices. But we've got to act more like most people do at the State level and at the local level. We've got to be committed to solving problems, putting people first, checking the ideological baggage at the door. I hope you'll help us do that. If you do, we'll help you make America a better place.

Thank you, and God bless you all.

NOTE: The President spoke at 2:20 p.m. at the Hyatt Regency Hotel. In his remarks, he referred to Jane Campbell, president, National Conference of State Legislatures, and James Lack, New York State senator.

Statement on the Justice Department's Conclusion of the Investigation of Secretary of Transportation Federico Peña
March 16, 1995

This is good news for a Secretary of Transportation who's doing a great job. I'm pleased for Federico.

Remarks at a Saint Patrick's Day Ceremony With Prime Minister John Bruton of Ireland and an Exchange With Reporters
March 17, 1995

The President. Good morning. Please be seated. Happy St. Patrick's Day. It's a great pleasure for me to welcome the Prime Minister here. This is the Taoiseach's first visit to the United States since he assumed office. So on this St. Patrick's Day, I think we should begin with an appropriate greeting, *Ceade mile failte,* a hundred thousand welcomes.

Mr. Prime Minister, I think, in this symbolic ceremony, you should go first. So I want to turn the microphone over to you.

Prime Minister Bruton. Thank you very much. Mr. President, Mr. Vice President, Secretary of State, ladies and gentlemen: It's a wonderful honor for me to be received here as the leader of an Irish Government of a country, Ireland, that's now at peace, at peace after 25 years of violence.

I want to say that you, Mr. President, probably as much as any individual, have helped to bring that about. When you look back on your administration, I think the bringing of peace to Ireland will rank as one of your major personal achievements. The willingness that you showed, Mr. President, to take risks, to do things that many of us might have thought were foolhardy at the time, like granting a visa to Gerry Adams—it has been proven to be—you have been proven to be right. You made the right decision.

The results are there for all of us to see, because you gave that organization the sense of confidence in itself and a glimpse of the political dividend that was there for them by pursuing a peaceful rather than a violent path. That vista that you opened up to them by that decision enabled them, gave them the confidence to end their campaign and take a new road.

Others need to show similar courage and generosity. And I know that the United States will be willing to play the same crucial role in being a friend to all in Ireland and encouraging all in Ireland to be generous risktakers, as you have been, Mr. President, in your dealings with Ireland since the commencement of your administration.

My purposes in coming here today, on St. Patrick's Day, is to thank you very, very much, from the bottom of my heart, for what you have done and to look forward to working with you and your administration and, indeed, Congress on a bipartisan basis on building on this, your great achievement.

The President. Thank you.

Prime Minister Bruton. Now, Mr. President, it is my high honor to present you with some shamrocks to celebrate this great day.

The President. Thank you very much, Mr. Prime Minister, for the beautiful gift, the beautiful Irish crystal. I hope the shamrocks will bring us the luck of the Irish over the next few months. [*Laughter*]

Today we don't have to look much further than the green ties and the dresses in this room to be reminded of the bonds between the United States and Ireland, the common heritage we share and have shared since the beginning of our country's existence. Much of America's love of freedom has Irish roots, whether our ancestors were Catholics or Protestants. Four signers of the Declaration of Independence were born in Ireland. At least nine more were of Irish descent. And many of our bravest soldiers in the Revolutionary War were Irish-Americans.

367

Today the Irish are still fighting the good fight, the fight for peace in Lebanon and Somalia and the Balkans. Irish troops under U.N. command have braved great dangers in the quest for peace. Ireland has also opened a school to train U.N. peacekeepers from other nations so that we may all benefit from Ireland's experience.

Ireland has demonstrated its commitment to peace most powerfully, of course, in the efforts to end the violence in Northern Ireland. On this St. Patrick's Day, as the Taoiseach said, Northern Ireland is closer than at any time in a generation to a just and lasting settlement of the differences of the people who share that small country's land.

At this historic moment, I salute Prime Minister Bruton for his tireless efforts for peace and for continuing the work of his predecessor, Prime Minister Reynolds, in completing the joint framework document for Northern Ireland with the British Prime Minister, John Major, who also deserves our salutes for the brave risks that he has taken to make peace. This is a landmark step for all the parties to bring them together and forge a new partnership for reconciliation.

Today I want to take this opportunity, this St. Patrick's Day, once again to urge all the parties to look carefully at the framework, to accept it as the basis for moving forward. I call on all those who still resort to violence to end the beatings, the intimidations, the shootings. To those who have laid down their arms, I ask you now to take the next step and begin to seriously discuss getting rid of these weapons so they can never be used again and violence will never again return to the land.

I welcome the statement by Sinn Fein, reiterating its readiness to include the issue of weapons in the talks with the British Government. It must be included, and progress must be made.

As we have in the past, the United States stands ready to help those who are taking risks for peace. Our economic initiatives in Ireland are proceeding under the supervision of former Senator George Mitchell. In May we are hosting a White House Conference on Trade and Investment in Ireland. And there's tremendous interest in this conference from our private sector.

Mr. Prime Minister, the United States will continue to support your efforts and those of Prime Minister Major. You have done very

much to bring the prospect of a new day to Northern Ireland.

I'm also pleased to announce that beginning April 1st, Irish citizens visiting the United States on vacations or business will no longer require visas. This step is another demonstration of our confidence in the future of Ireland and the strong ties between our nations.

I finally want to say that I am very much looking forward to our reception tonight at the White House. I'm glad that you, Mr. Prime Minister, and Mrs. Bruton will join us. And we're going to have a high old Irish time. [*Laughter*]

In closing, let me thank the Secretary of State and our fine Ambassador to Ireland, Jean Kennedy Smith, for the work they have done in supporting the White House and the President in our efforts to help you bring peace.

Thank you all very much.

Northern Ireland Peace Process

Q. Mr. President, may I ask you, first of all, how you have reacted to what appears to be an implied British Government criticism of your decision to allow Mr. Adams to come into this country? And do you agree with those other Irish-Americans who seem to believe that the British Government and that John Major is being slow, too slow, in allowing his ministers to talk to Mr. Adams?

The President. Well, let me answer it in this way. First of all, I have had a good relationship during my Presidency with Prime Minister Major. And the United States has had a very unique and powerful relationship with Great Britain for a very long time. We may differ from time to time about the specific actions that each would take, but our goal is the same. And I think we all have to recognize the risks that Prime Minister Major has taken for peace within the context in which he must operate.

So I look forward to having a chance to visit with him in the next couple of days about this, and I'm basically very positive about it. And if you're the President of the United States, there are days when you're grateful for implied criticism. Most of it's expressed. [*Laughter*]

Q. Mr. President, you were asking for people who have guns and have used them in Ireland to take the next step. How soon do you think that next step might be taken by the IRA and Sinn Fein?

The President. Well, I know that it couldn't come soon enough for me. And this whole business about weapons decommissioning is, obviously, critical to the completion of the process. And we here in the United States have reached out not only to Sinn Fein but also to the Unionists. The Prime Minister has pointed that out. The Vice President and my National Security Adviser have, on more than one occasion, tried to establish contacts to make sure we were reaching out to everyone in Northern Ireland.

And the important thing to me is that we keep pushing this process and keep it going in the right direction. And I have every confidence that that will occur.

Wolf [Wolf Blitzer, Cable News Network].

Russia

Q. Mr. President, President Yeltsin announced that he's willing to eliminate military hardware from his V–E parade on May 9th in order to encourage you to join others in Moscow to celebrate the 50th anniversary of the end of World War II. Is that enough to encourage you to go to Moscow, and will you include a trip to Ireland after that? [*Laughter*]

The President. Well, I appreciate what President Yeltsin said today. And I expect to be making a decision about that whole set of issues very shortly. And when I do, I'll announce it.

Q. Mr. President, is Chechnya the stumbling block?

Northern Ireland Peace Process

Q. Mr. President, What pressures can the U.S. administration bring on Sinn Fein, particularly in regards to the decommissioning of arms? And was there a quid pro quo in that area for your granting a visa to Gerry Adams to fundraise in the United States?

The President. Well, certainly his prompt statement about the willingness of Sinn Fein to discuss arms decommissioning had an influence on my decision. I think it's important that the United States take some steps along the way, as the Prime Minister has said, to keep this process going. When others take appropriate steps, I think it makes it a lot easier for us to do the same thing.

Thank you.

NOTE: The President spoke at 10:40 a.m. in the Roosevelt Room at the White House. In his remarks, he referred to Gerry Adams, leader of Sinn Fein.

Memorandum on Federal Employees Affected by California Floods
March 17, 1995

Memorandum for the Heads of Executive Departments and Agencies

Subject: Excused Absence for Employees Affected by Widespread Flooding in California

I am deeply concerned about the devastating losses caused by widespread flooding in California and the impact on the well-being and livelihood of our fellow Americans who have been affected by this disaster. Many parts of the Federal Government have been mobilized to respond to this disaster.

As part of this effort, I request heads of executive departments and agencies who have Federal civilian employees in the areas designated as disaster areas because of the flooding to use their discretion to excuse from duty, without charge to leave or loss of pay, any such employee who is faced with a personal emergency because of the flooding and who can be spared from his or her usual responsibilities. This policy should also be applied to any employee who is needed for emergency law enforcement, relief, or clean-up efforts authorized by Federal, State, or local officials having jurisdiction.

WILLIAM J. CLINTON

Remarks to the 1994 National Hockey League Champion New York Rangers
March 17, 1995

Good afternoon. Please be seated. I'm delighted to see all of you here, and welcome to the White House and to the Rose Garden. You come on the first day that the trees are blooming, so you're bringing us all wonderful weather.

It's an honor for me to host the New York Rangers here, including the commissioner of the National Hockey League, Gary Bettman; the president and general manager of the Rangers, Neil Smith; coach Colin Campbell; and assistant coach Dick Todd. And I think Congressman Eliot Engel was supposed to be here, and he is unless they're still voting.

It was last June 14th when the Rangers won the Stanley Cup, finally breaking the infamous curse. The next day I got a letter from Senator Moynihan, a big Ranger fan, who said that since the Rangers brought the cup back to Madison Square Garden, I should bring the Rangers to the Rose Garden. I'm delighted you're finally here. We've been trying to arrange this visit for some time, but what's a few months compared to 54 years? [*Laughter*]

I can't tell you how much I personally enjoyed the playoffs. I really got into them. I tried to rearrange my schedule so that I could see the games. I enjoyed seeing Mark Messier predicting and delivering a victory when your backs were against the wall. I enjoyed Brian Leetch's MVP playoff performance, the first by an American-born player. And I especially enjoyed your goalie Mike Richter's acrobatic saves. All of us here in Washington can appreciate what goalies do because we have so many shots taken at us every day. And I was hoping maybe, in addition to a jersey, one of you could loan me a face mask for the next year or so. [*Laughter*]

I also want to say something that I observed watching these playoffs. Stars alone don't win championships; teams do. I remember your chant from last year, "Heave ho. Everybody pulling together." This year it's turned into "Heave ho. Two in a row."

The Stanley Cup is the oldest trophy competition by professional athletes in North America, the only trophy that bears the names of not only the teams but the individual players who won it. I'd also like to say a special word of appreciation because the Rangers boast the first four Russians ever to have their names engraved on the Stanley Cup, another sign of our increasingly interconnected global community and America's outreach to the rest of the world.

I also admire the tradition that the entire team shares the Stanley Cup. Each player gets to take it home to friends and to family. This team took that one step further, because the Rangers know that teamwork isn't only about the guys who lace up the skates, it's also about your fans, too. And if ever a team had great fans, you do. So you paid your fans back by remembering right after the victory a longtime fan who had passed away, by bringing the cup to sick children in the hospital and even by bringing the cup to restaurants and bars throughout New York—[*laughter*]—as well as to one of the Vice President's favorite hangouts, the David Letterman show.

For all that, I thank you. Your victory has shown us what is best about professional sports: perseverance, hard work, real commitment to working together. It's an example for which all of us in Madison Square Garden and the Rose Garden are very grateful.

Congratulations, and welcome again.

NOTE: The President spoke at 2:39 p.m. in the Rose Garden at the White House.

Remarks at a Saint Patrick's Day Reception
March 17, 1995

Is the microphone on? Now it is. Taoiseach and Mrs. Bruton, let me say again, welcome to the White House. *Ceade mile failte.*

We have been breaking out the green for many years on St. Patrick's Day, but this is truly an historic St. Patrick's Day. For the first time we have invited leaders of all the major political groups from Northern Ireland to join us, and I am delighted that so many are here tonight. Those who take risks for peace are always welcome under this roof.

President Kennedy, with his marvelous Irish understatement, once pointed out, and I quote, "The observance of St. Patrick's Day is almost as old in America as the Irish themselves. And some say they arrived in the 6th century." Actually, the first recorded mention of St. Patrick in America was in 1636, when an Irish ship bearing that name sailed into, where else, Boston Harbor. It, however, did not receive a warm welcome. The Puritans were not well disposed toward the Catholics, but as history shows, it was only a temporary setback as—*[laughter]*.

During the Revolutionary conflict, George Washington even paid his own compliment to the holiday in 1776. On March 17th, he ordered that the password of the day be "Boston," and the response, "St. Patrick." By the way, the Colonies' general at that time was a Sullivan.

A few months later, at least a dozen Irishmen signed the Declaration of Independence, and another, Mr. Dunlap of Philadelphia, printed the Declaration for the first time. He also lost the original copy. *[Laughter]* But that setback, too, was temporary because the Irish knew then how to back winners.

The Irish first became a force in our politics in the 1790's when they supported Thomas Jefferson. To their eternal credit, many of their descendants have seen fit to back his Democratic descendants in the years since. Taoiseach, as you know, I am on my mother's side Irish; her name was Cassidy. What you may not know was that the decisive battle for the nomination for President in 1992 was in Illinois and Michigan on St. Patrick's Day.

It is said that Ireland's greatest export is its people. No country has benefited more from that export, Catholic and Protestant, than the United States. These two traditions have been intertwined, and together have contributed immensely to our success as a nation and to our greatness as a people. More than a dozen Presidents descended from Irish ancestors, from Andrew Jackson, the son of immigrants from Carrickfergus near Belfast who was our first President of Irish-Protestant heritage, to John Kennedy, the great-grandson of a cooper who left County Wexford and was our first Irish-Catholic President. I might say we're honored to have his sister as our Ambassador to Ireland and his brother and two of his nephews in the United States Congress today. They're now seeking to expand their stranglehold; one of his nieces is the Lieutenant Governor of Maryland. The next thing you know they'll insist on a position on every city council in America. They have enough relatives to fill that. *[Laughter]*

In the fight for our independence and in the fight to preserve our Union, there were Irishmen from both traditions serving side by side in all-Irish units. In both wars, they were among the most feared warriors. They put freedom over faction, and they helped to build our Nation.

Finley Peter Dunne, the great Irish-American humorist, wrote that a fanatic is someone who is sure God would be on his side if only He knew all the facts. *[Laughter]* Today, with good humor but complete seriousness, I urge all our guests from Northern Ireland and all the parties concerned to put aside all extremism for the common good of peace.

The Prime Minister of Ireland and the Prime Minister of Great Britain, at no inconsiderable risk to themselves, have paved the way to a new era of peace. I urge all of you to follow that path. The tough tasks of compromise still lie ahead. The hard, unending work of democracy is never easy. Even here, after all these years, two centuries of it, we still have our difficulties from time to time, living with those who differ from us. But as you work to forge a new future, free of violence, free of intimidation, with the participation of all the people of Northern Ireland, the United States will stand by you.

American has received so many gifts from Ireland, so many people who have enriched our

Nation, people who continue to come to the present day. We perhaps have many to give back. Some are perhaps financial in nature, but maybe the most important thing we could give to Ireland and, indeed, to a very troubled world today is the example of what is possible when people find unity and strength in their diversity.

We know from our own hard experience, from the blood we have shed on our own land, from the struggles we have been engaged in for a long time and the joys that we draw every day from the increasing diversity of our people, that strength can be drawn from differences, differences which are celebrated, respected, ap-

preciated. That kind of strength can build a future worthy of all the people of Northern Ireland.

Tonight our hopes and our prayers are with all the people of Ireland and especially with you, Mr. Prime Minister, and with your fine wife and your family. We loved having you here. We love every St. Patrick's Day, but this one especially we will remember above the rest.

Thank you. Godspeed.

NOTE: The President spoke at 10 p.m. in the East Room at the White House.

The President's Radio Address
March 18, 1995

Good morning. This morning I want to talk about responsibility, the responsibility all parents have to support their children. I'm pleased to be joined by Gerri Jensen, the president of the leading child support enforcement group in America, along with six other conscientious parents who have struggled to raise their children without the child support they were entitled to.

Our generation, at the end of the 20th century, has two great responsibilities: first, to keep the American dream alive and well for all our children and, second, to help our country remain the strongest force for freedom and democracy in the world. We can't do that if we don't have strong families and responsible parenting.

In Washington we're having a great debate about what we ought to do here to support these goals. On one side is the old Washington view that big, bureaucratic, one-size-fits-all Government can provide big solutions to America's big problems. On the other side is the new extreme view that Government is the source of all our problems and if we just get rid of it every problem would go away as well.

I've got a different view based on practical experience. I think we have to chart a course between the old way of big Government and the new rage of no Government. I think Government's job is to expand opportunity while shrinking bureaucracy, to get more jobs and higher incomes with less burden from Govern-

ment, to empower people to make the most of their own lives through more education and training and technology and support for families and for work, and to enhance our security on our streets and around the world.

To achieve these ends, the Federal Government has to be a partner, a partner with the private sector, with State and local governments, with individual citizens to strengthen our communities, a partner in promoting opportunity and at the same time demanding more responsibility. That's what the New Covenant is all about.

Nowhere is the lack of values, the lack of opportunity and responsibility more apparent than in our own failed welfare system. We all agree we have to end welfare as we know it. I think to do it we'll have to offer more opportunity to move people from welfare to work and demand more responsibility in return, to have a requirement that anyone on welfare who can work must go to work, and to discourage irresponsible behavior that lands people on welfare in the first place by insisting on tougher child support enforcement and responsible parenting. We have to make responsibility a way of life.

I've been working on this issue for the last 15 years. Last year I sent Congress a sweeping welfare reform plan. Congress didn't act last year, but I applaud the new Republican majority and the Democrats, both of them, for making welfare reform a priority this year. Meanwhile, in the last 2 years, we've cut through Federal redtape to give 26 States, more than half the country, the authority to conduct their own welfare reform experiments. And Republicans and Democrats now agree on tougher child support enforcement. They all agree that we have to have national action on tougher child support enforcement because 30 percent or more of the child support cases that are delinquent cross State boundaries.

I've worked hard on this. Since I've been President, child support collections are up substantially. And I just issued a tough Executive order to crack down on delinquency by Federal employees.

If deadbeat parents paid all the child support they should in this country, we could immediately move over 800,000 mothers and children off welfare. Let me say that again: If deadbeat parents paid the child support they owe, we could move immediately over 800,000 mothers and children off welfare. This goes way beyond welfare. Millions of children of working parents would have more secure lives and much brighter futures if the errant parents, absent parents, paid what they owe.

The welfare reform plan I sent to Congress last year included five key provisions for tough child support enforcement: employer reporting of new hires to catch deadbeats who move from job to job, uniform interstate child support laws, computerized statewide collection to speed up payments, streamlined efforts to identify the father in every case, and tough new penalties, like driver's license revocation.

These reforms will work. According to a report issued today by the Department of Human Services—of Health and Human Services, if we crack down on deadbeat parents by making these five provisions the law all over America, child support collections would go up by $24 billion in the next 10 years.

I am pleased that the House Republicans have come our way on these child support enforcement issues. They have included four of the five steps I proposed in their welfare bill. But I think the fifth step is crucial as well. Our plan calls on States to deny driver's licenses and professional licenses to people who refuse to pay the money they owe for their own children. Nineteen States are doing that today, and they're collecting a lot more child support as a result.

So I hope the House Republicans will take a look at these new findings and join us to send deadbeat parents all across this country a loud signal: If you neglect your responsibility to support your children, we'll suspend your license, garnish your pay, track you down, and make you pay.

Eighteen years ago, Gerri Jensen's husband abandoned her and her two young sons. She held down several low-paying jobs but eventually was forced to turn to welfare because her ex-husband stopped paying child support altogether. She got so fed up with weak laws and bureaucratic runarounds that she launched a grassroots movement to crack down on deadbeat parents nationwide. We are all in her debt, and we all owe an obligation to all the people like her in America who are doing their dead-level best to be good parents. They deserve our support.

Gerri Jensen stood up and fought to make our laws reflect our values. No parent has a right to walk away from responsibility to his or her children. Now, if we work together, we can make this kind of responsibility the law of our land.

Thanks for listening.

NOTE: The address was recorded at 3:23 p.m. on March 17 in the Roosevelt Room at the White House for broadcast at 10:06 a.m. on March 18.

Statement on Proposed Line-Item Veto Legislation
March 20, 1995

The Senate is now debating the line-item veto legislation which passed last month in the House. I urge the Senate to pass the strongest possible line-item veto and to make it effective immediately. If the Members of Congress from both parties are serious about cutting the deficit, give me this line-item veto, and I will get started right away. This is one area where both parties can and should come together.

I have advocated the line-item veto for a very long time. When I was a Governor, I had a line-item veto and I balanced 12 budgets in a row. I advocated the line-item veto when I ran for President, and I have pushed for it since becoming President because it is a very effective tool for cutting wasteful Government spending and bringing down the deficit.

We have made great headway in cutting wasteful spending. We have already cut the Federal bureaucracy by 102,000 positions, on the way to cutting a quarter million. We are bringing the deficit down by more than $600 billion. My new budget calls for another $81 billion in deficit reduction.

But there is still too much waste in the Federal budget. This year I have proposed eliminating 131 programs altogether and consolidating 270 others. I proposed many of these spending cuts last year and the year before, only to have

Congress tell me I couldn't cut their pet projects. I tried to cut $16 million for the Small Business Administration's tree planting program, but Congress put it back in the budget. Congress even spent $12 million for a cattle tick eradication project.

Well, this year, if the Congress gives me the line-item veto, I will cut each one of these programs, and a whole lot more. I also think the line-item veto should be applied to the revenue as well as the spending sides of the budget, so I can curb wasteful tax and spending provisions.

This is really about closing the door on business-as-usual in Washington. If Congress is serious about changing the way Washington works and getting a handle on wasteful spending, they will put politics aside, stand up to the special interests, and pass the bill.

The President, no matter what party, needs the line-item veto to bring discipline to the budget process. I urge the Senate to pass it and make it effective right now.

Letter to Congressional Leaders on Welfare Reform
March 20, 1995

Dear Mr. Speaker:

This week, the historic national debate we have begun on welfare reform will move to the floor of the House of Representatives. Welfare reform is a top priority for my Administration and for Americans without regard to party. I look forward to working with Republicans and Democrats in both houses of Congress to enact real reform that promotes work and responsibility and makes welfare what it was meant to be: a second chance, not a way of life.

In the last two years, we have put the country on the road to ending welfare as we know it. In 1993, when Congress passed our economic plan, we cut taxes for 15 million working Americans and rewarded work over welfare. We collected a record level of child support in 1993—$9 billion—and last month I signed an executive order to crack down on federal employees who owe child support. In two years, we have granted waivers from federal rules to 25 states, so that half the country is now carrying out significant welfare reform experiments that promote

work and responsibility instead of undermining it.

I have always sought to make welfare reform a bipartisan issue. I still believe it can and must be. Unfortunately, the House Republican bill in its current form does not appear to offer the kind of real welfare reform that Americans in both parties expect. It is too weak on moving people from welfare to work, not as tough as it should be on deadbeat parents, and too tough on innocent children.

Last year, I sent Congress the most sweeping welfare reform plan any administration has ever presented. It did not pass, but I believe the principles and values at its core will be the basis of what ultimately does pass:

° First, the central goal of welfare reform must be moving people from welfare to work, where they will earn a paycheck, not a welfare check. I believe we should demand and reward work, not punish those who go to work. If people need child care or job skills in order to go to work, we should help them get it. But within two years, anyone who can work must go to work.

This is not a partisan issue: Last year, 162 of 175 House Republicans co-sponsored a bill, H.R. 3500, that promoted work in much the same way as our plan. But the current House Republican bill you will consider this week fails to promote work, and would actually make it harder for many recipients to make it in the workplace. It cuts child care for people trying to leave welfare and for working people trying to stay off welfare, removes any real responsibility for states to provide job placement and skills, and gives states a perverse incentive to cut people off whether or not they have moved into a job. When people just get cut off without going to work, that's not welfare reform. I urge you to pass a welfare reform bill that ends welfare as we know it by moving people from welfare to work.

° Second, welfare reform must make responsibility a way of life. We should demand responsibility from parents who bring children into the world, not let them off the hook and expect taxpayers to pick up the tab for their neglect. Last year, my Administration proposed the toughest child support enforcement measures ever put forward. If we collected all the money that deadbeat parents should pay, we could move 800,000 women and children off welfare immediately.

I am grateful to members in both parties for already agreeing to include most of the tough child support measures from our welfare reform plan. This week, I hope you will go further, and require states to deny drivers and professional licenses to parents who refuse to pay child support. We have to send a clear signal: No parent in America has a right to walk away from the responsibility to raise their children.

° Third, welfare reform should discourage teen pregnancy and promote responsible parenting. We must discourage irresponsible behavior that lands people on welfare in the first place, with a national campaign against teen pregnancy that lets young people know it is wrong to have a child outside marriage. Nobody should get pregnant or father a child who isn't prepared to raise the child, love the child, and take responsibility for the child's future.

I know members of Congress in both parties care about this issue. But many aspects of the current House plan would do more harm than good. Instead of refusing to help teen mothers

and their children, we should require them to turn their lives around—to live at home with their parents, stay in school, and identify the child's father. We should demand responsible behavior from people on welfare, but it is wrong to make small children pay the price for their parents' mistakes.

° Finally, welfare reform should give states more flexibility in return for more accountability. I believe we must give states far more flexibility so they can do the things they want to today without seeking waivers. But in its current form, the House Republican bill may impede rather than promote reform and flexibility. The proposal leaves states vulnerable to economic recession and demographic change, putting working families at risk. States will have less money for child care, training, and other efforts to move people from welfare to work. And there will not be any accountability at the federal level for reducing fraud or protecting children. We will not achieve real reform or state flexibility if Congress just gives the states more burdens and less money, and fails to make work and responsibility the law of the land.

While the current House plan is weak on work, it is very tough on children. Cutting school lunches and getting tough on disabled children and children in foster care is not my idea of welfare reform. We all have a national interest in promoting the well-being of our children and in putting government back in line with our national values.

I appreciate all the work that you have done on this issue, and I am pleased that the country is finally engaging in this important debate. In the end, I believe we can work it out together, as long as we remember the values this debate is really about. The dignity of work, the bond of family, and the virtue of responsibility are not Republican values or Democratic values. They are American values—and no child in America should ever have to grow up without them.

Sincerely,

BILL CLINTON

NOTE: Identical letters were sent to Newt Gingrich, Speaker of the House of Representatives, and Richard Gephardt, minority leader of the House of Representatives. This letter was released by the Office of the Press Secretary on March 21.

Remarks on the Appointment of Bonnie Campbell as Director of the Office of Violence Against Women
March 21, 1995

Thank you, Sarah, for your wonderful remarks and for the powerful example of your life. I was watching you speak today, thinking of your story, wondering how many other stories like yours there might have been if our society had responded more properly and how many more there will be now because we are going to do the right things.

I thank Attorney General Reno and Secretary Shalala, and of course, Senator Biden and Senator Hatch and Senator Boxer, Senator Harkin, Senator Kerry, Senator Moseley-Braun, Senator Wellstone—we've nearly got a quorum—[*laughter*]—Congresswoman DeLauro, Congresswoman Mink, Congresswoman Morella, Congresswoman Blanche Lambert Lincoln. I thank you all for being here.

This is an important day for me. This is an issue with which I have dealt as President, as a Governor, as an attorney general, as a citizen, going for years with my wife to the shelters in our State for battered women and their children, and as a human being. And I have looked forward to this day for a very long time.

We spend a lot of time in Washington, and we are now having a great and fascinating debate about what the role of this Government ought to be and how we're going to get into the next century and how we're going to create opportunity for all the American people. This is a good thing that we're doing. It's exciting, and I'm having a good time. But you know, let's be honest with each other. If children aren't safe in their homes, if college women aren't safe in their dorms, if mothers can't raise their children in safety, then the American dream will never be real for them, no matter what we do in economic policy, no matter how strong we are in standing against the forces that would seek to undermine our values beyond our borders. This is key to everything else we want to do.

So I applaud the Members of the Congress, and especially those who have been recognized already, especially Senator Biden and Senator Hatch, for recognizing that we had to take responsibility for trying to come to grips with issues that we ordinarily would think of as issues that belong to local law enforcement or local social agencies or even to the privacy of the home.

When we were fighting so hard last year to pass the crime bill, with the emphasis on more police and more punishment and more prisons and more prevention, one of the things that almost got lost was the Violence Against Women Act. I think it almost got lost for a very regrettable reason in this day and time: The Republicans and the Democrats weren't fighting about it. We really had a national consensus that we had to do something. And because we knew we had to do something and it passed, it was almost unnoticed.

But you know, domestic violence is now the number one health risk for women between the ages of 15 and 44 in our country. If you think about it, it's a bigger threat than cancer or car accidents. The incidence of rape is rising at 3 times the rate of the crime rate. The FBI estimates that a woman is beaten in this country once every 12 seconds. And we know, too, that often when a spouse is beaten, the children are beaten as well.

For too long, domestic violence has been considered purely a private matter. From now on, it is a problem we all share. What are we going to do about it? The first thing we have to do is do what we can to prevent violence. One part of the crime bill I am proudest of will help in our efforts to stop repeat offenses against women. It will prohibit individuals with a restraining order against them from purchasing or possessing a gun, no ifs, ands, or buts.

When crimes do occur, we must restore the rights of victims to their proper place. That means giving them the right to speak at sentencing hearings. And above all, it means helping victims rebuild their lives. We'll require sexual offenders to pay restitution to their victims. We must help people who suffer violence put their lives back on track and put the burdens on the criminals where they belong.

To help in prevention and in assisting victims, the crime bill establishes a Violence Against Women Office at the Department of Justice. Today I am pleased to announce that Bonnie

Campbell of Iowa will be the first Director of that office. As Iowa's first female attorney general, Bonnie Campbell helped to enact strong domestic violence and anti-stalking laws in that State. She worked with counties and college campuses to raise awareness about domestic violence. And she endorsed a victims' rights amendment to the State constitution. A big part of her new job will be helping States and communities to deal with domestic violence.

Today we are making available $26 million to help the States open rape crisis centers, to staff domestic violence hotlines, to provide victims advocates, to pay for more officers and more training. This is the first downpayment on a 6-year commitment of $800 million for this purpose.

This is part of a report I should make at least to these Members of Congress who are here about the crime bill. The work has already begun. In just 4 months we have awarded more than 16,000 police officers to half the police departments in America. We're taking guns and criminals off the streets. The "three strikes and you're out" law is being enforced in Iowa and in many other States throughout the country. In short, we are under budget and ahead of schedule. And I want more of that from our Government.

We passed this crime bill with bipartisan support. And I'd be the last person to say that it's the end-all and be-all, the ultimate answer to all the problems of crime in America. But I will not permit the crime bill to be undercut. It is just starting to make a difference in the lives of Americans. We have to keep going. We have to make a difference in the lives of everyone, but especially the women and the children we are called here today to pledge our allegiance to protect.

Let me begin this introduction of Bonnie Campbell and end it with a simple thank you. It's hard to get anybody with good sense to leave Iowa to come to Washington. [*Laughter*] And I thank her for doing it and for the shining example she has set in public service and for the excellent work I am confident she will do in this important position.

Bonnie.

NOTE: The President spoke at 1:11 p.m. in the East Room at the White House. In his remarks, he referred to Sarah M. Buel, Evelyn Green Davis fellow in law at Radcliffe College and 17-year activist on family violence issues. Following the President's remarks, Ms. Campbell made remarks.

Message to the Congress Transmitting the Report of the National Science Foundation
March 21, 1995

To the Congress of the United States:

In accordance with section 3(f) of the National Science Foundation Act of 1950, as amended (42 U.S.C. 1862(f)), I am pleased to transmit to you the Annual Report of the National Science Foundation for Fiscal Year 1993.

The Foundation supports research and education in every State of the Union. Its programs provide an international science and technology link to sustain cooperation and advance this Nation's leadership role.

This report shows how the Foundation puts science and technology to work for a sustainable future—for our economic, environmental, and national security.

WILLIAM J. CLINTON

The White House,
March 21, 1995.

Message to the Congress Reporting on Export Control Regulations
March 21, 1995

To the Congress of the United States:

1. On August 19, 1994, in Executive Order No. 12924, I declared a national emergency under the International Emergency Economic Powers Act (IEEPA) (50 U.S.C. 1701 *et seq.*) to deal with the threat to the national security, foreign policy, and economy of the United States caused by the lapse of the Export Administration Act of 1979, as amended (50 U.S.C. App. 2401 *et seq.*) and the system of controls maintained under that Act. In that order, I continued in effect, to the extent permitted by law, the provisions of the Export Administration Act of 1979, as amended, the Export Administration Regulations (15 C.F.R. 768 *et seq.*), and the delegations of authority set forth in Executive Order No. 12002 of July 7, 1977 (as amended by Executive Order No. 12755 of March 12, 1991), Executive Order No. 12214 of May 2, 1980, Executive Order No. 12735 of November 16, 1990 (subsequently revoked by Executive Order No. 12938 of November 14, 1994), and Executive Order No. 12851 of June 11, 1993.

2. I issued Executive Order No. 12924 pursuant to the authority vested in me as President by the Constitution and laws of the United States, including, but not limited to, IEEPA. At that time, I also submitted a report to the Congress pursuant to section 204(b) of IEEPA (50 U.S.C. 1703(b)). Section 204 of IEEPA requires follow-up reports, with respect to actions or changes, to be submitted every 6 months. Additionally, section 401(c) of the National Emergencies Act (NEA) (50 U.S.C. 1601 *et seq.*) requires that the President, within 90 days after the end of each 6-month period following a declaration of a national emergency, report to the Congress on the total expenditures directly attributable to that declaration. This report, covering the 6-month period from August 19, 1994, to February 19, 1995, is submitted in compliance with these requirements.

3. Since the issuance of Executive Order No. 12924, the Department of Commerce has continued to administer and enforce the system of export controls, including antiboycott provisions, contained in the Export Administration Regulations. In administering these controls, the Department has acted under a policy of conforming actions under Executive Order No. 12924 to those required under the Export Administration Act, insofar as appropriate.

4. Since my last report to the Congress, there have been several significant developments in the area of export controls:

Bilateral Cooperation/Technical Assistance

• As part of the Administration's continuing effort to encourage other countries to implement effective export controls to stem the proliferation of weapons of mass destruction, as well as certain sensitive technologies, the Department of Commerce and other agencies conducted a range of discussions with a number of foreign countries, including governments in the Baltics, Central and Eastern Europe, the Newly Independent States (NIS) of the former Soviet Union, the Pacific Rim, and China. Licensing requirements were liberalized for exports to Argentina, South Korea, and Taiwan, responding in part to their adoption of improved export control procedures.

Australia Group

• The Department of Commerce issued regulations to remove controls on certain chemical weapon stabilizers that are not controlled by the Australia Group, a multilateral regime dedicated to stemming the proliferation of chemical and biological weapons. This change became effective October 19, 1994. In that same regulatory action, the Department also published a regulatory revision that reflects an Australia Group decision to adopt a multi-tiered approach to control of certain mixtures containing chemical precursors. The new regulations extend General License G–DEST treatment to certain categories of such mixtures.

Nuclear Suppliers Group (NSG)

• NSG members are examining the present dual-use nuclear control list to both remove controls no longer warranted and to rewrite control language to better reflect nuclear proliferation concerns. A major item for revision involves machine tools, as the current language was accepted on an interim basis until agreement on more specific language could be reached.

• The Department of Commerce has implemented license denials for NSG-controlled items as part of the "no-undercut" provision. Under this provision, denial notifications received from NSG member countries obligate other member nations not to approve similar transactions until they have consulted with the notifying party, thus reducing the possibilities for undercutting such denials.

Missile Technology Control Regime (MTCR)

• Effective September 30, 1994, the Department of Commerce revised the control language for MTCR items on the Commerce Control List, based on the results of the last MTCR plenary. The revisions reflect advances in technology and clarifications agreed to multilaterally.

• On October 4, 1994, negotiations to resolve the 1993 sanctions imposed on China for MTCR violations involving missile-related trade with Pakistan were successfully concluded. The United States lifted the Category II sanctions effective November 1, in exchange for a Chinese commitment not to export ground-to-ground Category I missiles to any destination.

• At the October 1994 Stockholm plenary, the MTCR made public the fact of its "no-undercut" policy on license denials. Under this multilateral arrangement, denial notifications received from MTCR members are honored by other members for similar export license applications. Such a coordinated approach enhances U.S. missile nonproliferation goals and precludes other member nations from approving similar transactions without prior consultation.

Modifications in Controls on Embargoed Destinations

Effective August 30, 1994, the Department of Commerce restricted the types of commodities eligible for shipment to Cuba under the provisions of General License GIFT. Only food, medicine, clothing, and other human needs items are eligible for this general license.

• The embargo against Haiti was lifted on October 16, 1994. That embargo had been under the jurisdiction of the Department of the Treasury. Export license authority reverted to the Department of Commerce upon the termination of the embargo.

Regulatory Reform

• In February 1994, the Department of Commerce issued a *Federal Register* notice that invited public comment on ways to improve the Export Administration Regulations. The project's objective is "to make the rules and procedures for the control of exports simpler and easier to understand and apply." This project is not intended to be a vehicle to implement substantive change in the policies or procedures of export administration, but rather to make those policies and procedures simpler and clearer to the exporting community. Reformulating and simplifying the Export Administration Regulations is an important priority, and significant progress has been made over the last 6 months in working toward completion of this comprehensive undertaking.

Export Enforcement

• Over the last 6 months, the Department of Commerce continued its vigorous enforcement of the Export Administration Act and the Export Administration Regulations through educational outreach, license application screening, spot checks, investigations, and enforcement actions. In the last 6 months, these efforts resulted in civil penalties, denials of export privileges, criminal fines, and imprisonment. Total fines amounted to over $12,289,000 in export control and antiboycott compliance cases, including criminal fines of nearly $9,500,000 while 11 parties were denied export privileges.

• *Teledyne Fined $12.9 Million and a Teledyne Division Denied Export Privileges for Export Control Violations:* On January 26 and January 27, Teledyne Industries, Inc. of Los Angeles, agreed to a settlement of criminal and administrative charges arising from illegal export activity in the mid-1980's by its Teledyne Wah Chang division, located in Albany, Oregon. The settlement levied criminal fines and civil penalties on the firm totaling $12.9 million and imposed a denial of export privileges on Teledyne Wah Chang.

The settlement is the result of a 4-year investigation by the Office of Export Enforcement and the U.S. Customs Service. United States Attorneys offices in Miami and Washington, D.C., coordinated the investigation. The investigation determined that during the mid-1980's, Teledyne illegally exported nearly 270 tons of zirconium that was used to manufacture cluster bombs for Iraq.

As part of the settlement, the Department restricted the export privileges of Teledyne's

Wah Chang division; the division will have all export privileges denied for 3 months, with the remaining portion of the 3-year denial period suspended.

Storm Kheem Pleads Guilty to Non-proliferation and Sanctions Violations: On January 27, Storm Kheem pled guilty in Brooklyn, New York, to charges that he violated export control regulations barring U.S. persons from contributing to Iraq's missile program. Kheem arranged for the shipment of foreign-source ammonium perchlorate, a highly explosive chemical used in manufacturing rocket fuel, from the People's Republic of China to Iraq via Amman, Jordan, without obtaining the required validated license from the Department of Commerce for arranging the shipment. Kheem's case represents the first conviction of a person for violating section 778.9 of the Export Administration Regulations, which restricts proliferation-related activi-

ties of "U.S. persons." Kheem also pled guilty to charges of violating the Iraqi Sanctions Regulations.

5. The expenses incurred by the Federal Government in the 6-month period from August 19, 1994, to February 19, 1995, that are directly attributable to the exercise of authorities conferred by the declaration of a national emergency with respect to export controls were largely centered in the Department of Commerce, Bureau of Export Administration. Expenditures by the Department of Commerce are anticipated to be $19,681,000 most of which represents program operating costs, wage and salary costs for Federal personnel and overhead expenses.

WILLIAM J. CLINTON

The White House,
March 21, 1995.

Letter to Congressional Leaders on Deployment of United States Armed Forces to Haiti
March 21, 1995

Dear Mr. Speaker: (Dear Mr. President:)

On September 21, 1994, I reported to the Congress that on September 19, 1994, U.S. forces under the command of the Commander in Chief, U.S. Atlantic Command, were introduced into Haitian territory following an agreement successfully concluded by former President Jimmy Carter, Senator Sam Nunn, and General Colin Powell and as part of the Multinational Force (MNF) provided for by United Nations Security Council Resolution (UNSCR) 940 of July 31, 1994. I am providing this update of events in Haiti (Operation "Uphold Democracy") consistent with the War Powers Resolution to ensure that the Congress is kept fully informed regarding events in Haiti.

At their peak last September and into October, U.S. forces assigned to the MNF in Haiti numbered just over 20,000. Approximately 2,000 non-U.S. personnel from 27 nations also participated in the initial stages of the MNF. Over the last 6 months, U.S. forces gradually have been reduced, consistent with the establishment of a secure and stable environment called for by UNSCR 940, such that they currently num-

ber just under 5,300. Non-U.S. forces—both MNF and International Police Monitors (IPM)—currently number approximately 2,800. When the transition to the United Nations Mission in Haiti (UNMIH) authorized by UNSCR 975 of January 30, 1995, is complete on March 31, 1995, approximately 2,500 U.S. forces will remain in Haiti as the U.S. contribution to UNMIH's force structure. Following transition to UNMIH, non-U.S. forces will total approximately 3,500, for a total force of approximately 6,000. In addition, a U.N. civilian police monitor component of UNMIH will number approximately 900.

In January, the United Nations Security Council determined that a secure and stable environment had been established in Haiti, based upon assessments from the MNF Commander and the U.N. Secretary General, and recommendations from the MNF Member States. As to the duration of the deployment, it is anticipated that the entire U.N. security mission, including U.S. forces, will withdraw from Haiti not later than February 1996. Presidential elections are scheduled for November

1995 and the inauguration will be held February 7, 1996.

Overall, Haiti has remained calm and relatively incident-free since the deployment of U.S. and MNF forces. The level of political violence has decreased substantially since the departure of the *de facto* government. There is normal activity in the streets, and in stark contrast to when MNF forces first arrived, people are able to go outside at night due to a more secure environment. The number of weapons in Haiti also has been significantly reduced. Early in its deployment, the MNF took control of heavy and crew-served weapons belonging to the FAd'H (The Haitian Armed Forces). The MNF is also administering a weapons buy-back, seizure, and reduction program that has thus far yielded over 33,000 weapons, including hand grenades.

Thus far, there have been only five incidents involving attacks on or gunfire by U.S. forces. On September 24, 1994, a U.S. Marine Corps squad exchanged gunfire with members of the FAd'H at the police headquarters in Cap Haitien. One Marine was wounded, and ten Haitians were killed. On October 2, an unidentified individual fired shots over a wall in Les Cayes, wounding an American soldier. On October 14, a member of the FAd'H was wounded by U.S. Special Forces when he burst from his barricaded room and ran towards a U.S. soldier during a confrontation in Belladere. On December 26, U.S. forces came under fire during a demonstration by disgruntled former members of the FAd'H outside FAd'H General Headquarters. After receiving fire, the MNF fired on the Headquarters resulting in several Haitian, but no U.S. casualties. Finally, on January 12, 1995, a two-man Special Forces team was fired on at a toll booth south of Gonaives. One U.S. soldier was killed and another injured in the incident. The Haitian gunman was also killed.

I have taken the measures described above to further the national security interests of the United States. I have ordered the continued deployment of U.S. forces to the MNF pursuant to my constitutional authority to conduct foreign relations and as Commander in Chief and Chief Executive.

I remain committed to consulting closely with the Congress, and I will continue to keep the Congress fully informed regarding this important deployment of our forces.

Sincerely,

WILLIAM J. CLINTON

NOTE: Identical letters were sent to Newt Gingrich, Speaker of the House of Representatives, and Strom Thurmond, President pro tempore of the Senate. This letter was released by the Office of the Press Secretary on March 22.

Remarks on Signing the Unfunded Mandates Reform Act of 1995
March 22, 1995

I thank Governor Winter for his introduction and for the fine work he has done as head of the Advisory Council on Intergovernmental Relations. I want to welcome all of you here, especially the Members of the Congress. The Senate's been involved in business, and I think the House may still be voting. Representative Towns, I'm glad you made it. And I thank Senator Dole for coming. I want to say a special word of thanks to Senator Kempthorne, who picked a great first bill to pass in the United States Senate; to Senator John Glenn, who was the Democratic floor manager of this bill; Congressman Bill Clinger, the House sponsor; Congresswoman Cardiss Collins, the Democratic

floor manager; Congressman Gary Condit and Jim Moran, who both pushed this bill. And I welcome Governor Voinovich from Ohio here, who drew State and local governments together on this matter. We have many mayors here. I see Mayor Abramson and Mayor Daley and Mayor Lashutka. And there are representatives of the counties and the State legislatures here, other Members of Congress. I thank all of you for your work on this important piece of legislation.

I had the privilege in 1989—he may not remember this—of having dinner in Chicago with Mayor Daley just a couple of weeks after he took office. I learned that night, somewhere between salad and the main course, just how much Mayor Daley hated unfunded mandates. [*Laughter*] For those of you who would have been nice enough to let me get all the way to dessert, I welcome you here, too. [*Laughter*]

I share these concerns, having served as a Governor for a dozen years and witnessed the growth of many of the unfair burdens that unfunded mandates impose. Shortly after I became President, I signed an Executive order to prohibit Federal agencies from imposing nonstatutory unfunded mandates on State and local governments without full consultations first.

We have a few more Members coming. Come on in. Representatives Peterson and Tauzin, we're glad to see you.

This bill today extends that discipline to Congress. And I applaud Congress for passing it. It for the first time limits the ability of Congress to pass laws which impose unfunded mandates on State, county, local governments and tribal governments. Having been there as a Governor, I know this bill will make a big difference in the lives of our people.

We've made important progress this year in reforming Government already. The Congress passed a bill which I was proud to sign which requires Congress to live by the laws it imposes on the private sector.

Now this unfunded mandates law will be another model for how we have to continue to change the way Washington does business. The best ideas and the most important work that affect the public interest are often done a long way away from Washington. This bill is another acknowledgement that Washington doesn't necessarily have all the answers, that we have to continue to push decisionmaking down to the local level, and we shouldn't make the work of governing at the local level any harder than the circumstances of the time already ensure that it will be.

The other thing that this bill shows is that Republicans and Democrats can come together and break gridlock and do what the American people expect us to do. For all of you who are part of that cooperative effort and especially for the Members of the Congress, I thank you.

This is spring, and the roses are about to bloom here in the Rose Garden. This is a new beginning and a time for a new spirit of cooperation. I hope the Congress will move on from this to first pass the line-item veto, so we can bring more real discipline to our spending process, and then to pass welfare reform that promotes work and responsible parenting and tough child support enforcement.

We have got to build a true partnership with the American people, with a Government that gets rid of what's unnecessary for today and tomorrow and does what we have to do in a limited but effective way. We're trying to do that in reducing the deficit, the size of the Federal Government, reducing the burden of unnecessary regulation. This bill will make a real start.

Listen to this: Before 1964, the number of explicit mandates from the Congress on State and local governments was zero. But according to the National Performance Review, on the day I took office there were at least 172 separate pieces of legislation that impose requirements on State and local government. The Congressional Budget Office estimates the cost to States and localities of all the regulations imposed just between 1983 and 1990 is between $8.9 billion and $12.7 billion. After today, this should stop.

This bill requires Congress to show how much mandates over $50 million per year will cost State and local governments, to require Congress to identify a specific funding source for these mandates, and if it does not meet these criteria, Congress must explicitly waive the requirement that there be no unfunded mandate, something which I think will become increasingly rare with the passage of this law.

You know, our Founders gave us strong, guiding principles about how our governments ought to work, and they trusted us in every generation to reinvigorate the partnership they created with such wisdom so long ago. For 200 years, we've had to do that over and over and over, and about once a generation, we had to make some really big changes in the way we work together as a people, citizens in their private lives, local governments, State governments, and our Government here in Washington.

Today we are making history. We are working to find the right balance for the 21st century. We are recognizing that the pendulum had swung too far and that we have to rely on the initiative, the creativity, the determination, and the decisionmaking of people at the State and local level to carry much of the load for America as we move into the 21st century.

This bill will help to keep the American dream alive and help to keep our country strong. Every Member of Congress here who voted for it and every one who is not here deserves the thanks of the American people. And all of you from all over America who are here, from the cities, from the county operations, from the State legislatures and State Governments, we are all in your debt. I thank you, and I am honored to sign this bill.

Thank you.

NOTE: The President spoke at 12:45 p.m. in the Rose Garden at the White House. In his remarks, he referred to William Winter, former Governor of Mississippi; Gov. George V. Voinovich of Ohio; Mayor Jerry Abramson of Louisville, KY; Mayor Richard M. Daley of Chicago, IL; and Mayor Greg Lashutka of Columbus, OH. S. 1, approved March 22, was assigned Public Law No. 104–4.

Memorandum on the 1995 United States Savings Bonds Campaign
March 22, 1995

Memorandum for the Heads of Executive Departments and Agencies

The 1995 Federal U.S. Savings Bonds Campaign will soon be underway. Attached is a special message to all Federal employees who are eligible to take part in this campaign. Please give this letter appropriate distribution within your organization to enhance your campaign.

I encourage you to also generate a letter for each of your Department or Agency employees. Good luck on a successful campaign. I look forward to receiving your results later this year.

WILLIAM J. CLINTON

Memorandum on the 1995 United States Savings Bonds Campaign
March 22, 1995

Memorandum for All Federal Government Employees

Subject: 1995 U.S. Savings Bonds Campaign

The Federal Government will soon be conducting the 1995 Savings Bonds Campaign. This campaign is your chance to sign up for the Payroll Savings Plan for U.S. Savings Bonds or to increase your rate of saving if you are already participating.

Getting into the habit of saving money is not easy, no matter how hard you try. The Payroll Savings Plan for U.S. Savings Bonds is a convenient method of saving regularly that offers tax advantages and investment market-based interest rates for small sums of money. When you join the plan, you select an amount to be set aside from each paycheck to buy bonds. The rest is automatic; you save payday after payday without interruption.

In addition to their direct personal benefits, Savings Bonds also help reduce Federal spending. As members of the Government, we must set an example for all citizens to follow by establishing a high rate of participation in this excellent program.

Savings Bonds have helped millions of Americans purchase homes, finance college educations, guarantee secure retirements, and weather financial emergencies. When one of your fellow employees calls on you during the campaign, please consider how bonds can help you to achieve your own financial goals—then sign up for bonds.

WILLIAM J. CLINTON

Memorandum on Customer Service
March 22, 1995

*Memorandum for Heads of Executive
Departments and Agencies*

Subject: Improving Customer Service

In the first phase of this Administration's reinventing government initiative, I established the principle that government must be customer-driven. Executive Order No. 12862, "Setting Customer Service Standards," called for a revolution within the Federal Government to change the way it does business. The initial agency responses to that order, including the service standards published in September 1994, have begun the process of establishing a more customer-focused government. For the first time, the Federal Government's customers have been told what they have a right to expect when they ask for service.

In the second phase of reinventing government ("Phase II"), this effort should be continued and integrated with other restructuring activities. The first question agency restructuring teams should ask is whether a program or function is critical to the agency's missions based on "customer" input. To carry out this Phase II effort and assure that government puts the customer first, I am now directing the additional steps set forth in this memorandum.

Actions. The agencies covered by Executive Order No. 12862 are directed as follows:

1. In order to continue customer service reform, agencies shall treat the requirements of Executive Order No. 12862 as continuing requirements. The actions the order prescribes, such as surveying customers, surveying employees, and benchmarking, shall be continuing agency activities. The purpose of these actions will remain as indicated in Executive Order 12862—the establishment and implementation of customer service standards to guide the operations of the executive branch.

2. Agencies shall, by September 1, 1995, complete the publication of customer service standards, in a form readily available to customers, for all operations that deliver significant services directly to the public. This shall include services that are delivered in partnership with State and local governments, services delivered by small agencies and regulatory agencies, and customer services of enforcement agencies.

3. Agencies shall, on an ongoing basis, measure results achieved against the customer service standards and report those results to customers at least annually. Reports should be in terms readily understood by individual customers. Public reports shall be made beginning no later than September 15, 1995. Measurement systems should include objective measures wherever possible, but should also include customer satisfaction as a measure. Customer views should be obtained to determine whether standards have been set on what matters most to the customer. Agencies should publish replacement standards if needed to reflect these views.

4. Development and tracking of customer service measures, standards, and performance should be integrated with other performance initiatives, including Phase II restructuring. Customer service standards also should be related to legislative activities, including strategic planning and performance measurement under the Government Performance and Results Act of 1993, reporting on financial and program performance under the Chief Financial Officers Act of 1990, and the Government Management and Reform Act of 1994. Operating plans, regulations and guidelines, training programs, and personnel classification and evaluation systems should be aligned with a customer focus.

5. Agencies shall continue to survey employees on ideas to improve customer service, take action to motivate and recognize employees for meeting or exceeding customer service standards, and for promoting customer service. Without satisfied employees, we cannot have satisfied customers.

6. Agencies should initiate and support actions that cut across agency lines to serve shared customers groups. Agencies should take steps to develop cross-agency, one-stop service to customer groups, so their customers do not needlessly go from one agency to another. Where possible, these steps should take advantage of new information technology tools to achieve results.

The standard of quality we seek from these actions and the Executive order is customer service for the American people that is equal to the best in business.

Independent Agencies. Independent agencies are requested to adhere to this directive.

Judicial Review. This directive is for the internal management of the executive branch and does not create any right or benefit, substantive or procedural, enforceable by a party against the United States, its agencies or instrumentalities, its officers or employees, or any other person.

WILLIAM J. CLINTON

NOTE: This memorandum was released by the Office of the Press Secretary on March 23.

Remarks and a Question-and-Answer Session With the College Press Forum
March 23, 1995

The President. Thank you and welcome to the White House. This is, as I'm sure you agree, a fascinating time to be in our Nation's Capital. We are now having a great debate about how we can best assure the American dream for your generation and for your children well into the next century. The choices we make here will have a profound effect on all of your lives.

This is an historic era: We have the end of the cold war, the dawn of the information age, a globalized economy, an explosion of entrepreneurialism, an enormous amount of opportunity. At the same time, we have profound challenges. We have almost 20 years of stagnant incomes in the United States. We have growing inequality of incomes based primarily on educational differentials. We have deep strains within our society and still profound problems related to the breakdown of family and community and the rise of crime and violence. We have challenges abroad in terrorism, environmental destruction, population explosion, the proliferation of weapons of mass destruction.

The issue we are most debating around here now in many different ways is what is the proper role of the National Government in working with the American people to meet our challenges. The old view is that Government is inherently a positive force and that there is a one-size-fits-all, big Government solution for every big problem. The new view that's all the rage around here is that the Federal Government is the cause of every problem and if we just didn't have one we might not have any problems.

My view is different from both of these. I ran for President to advance that view, and I still believe it is the proper one. I believe Government does have a role to play as a partner in meeting the challenges of the future with all of the American people. I believe the role of Government is to increase opportunity as we shrink bureaucracy, to empower people to make the most of their own lives, and to enhance our security at home and abroad.

We have to work economically to expand the middle class and to shrink the under class. We have to work to promote mainstream values of work and family and future. We have to do it with a Government that is smaller and less bureaucratic but still effective. The key to our future is our ability to create more opportunity and, at the same time, the willingness of our citizens to assume more responsibility. That's what I have called the New Covenant.

I agree that we have to cut outmoded Government, and our administration has led the way. There are already more than 100,000 fewer people working here for the National Government than there were on the day I became President. We're on our way to the smallest Federal Establishment since President Kennedy worked here.

But I also believe that this Government should invest in your future and in your capacity to contribute and to live up to the fullest of your abilities. Therefore, I support more investments in education and technology and training and empowering people to make the most of their own lives.

I also believe that if you look at the end of 2 years, the evidence is pretty good that our approach is right. We have reduced the deficit 3 years in a row for the first time since Mr. Truman was here. We have 6.1 million new jobs, the lowest combined rates of unemployment and inflation in 25 years, the first time in 20 years the African-American unemployment rate has been under 10 percent. We have in 1993 the largest number of new businesses incorporated in any given year in American history. Finally, in 1994, we began to make some progress on the wage issue when we had more high-wage jobs coming into the economy than in the previous 5 years combined.

Notwithstanding that, the American people said they wanted a different sort of debate here in Washington last November, and so we are having it. Now, I believe that nothing will more clearly define the contours of this debate than what we decide to do in the area of education and training.

In the global economy into which we are moving, we can see what is happening to American jobs and incomes. Those who are able to grasp the high-wage jobs of the future are doing very well, indeed. We're going to have record numbers of millionaires created in this 4-year period. But we also see more and more and more Americans in the grip of insecurity as they work harder than they were working 20 years ago for wages that are the same or lower. And overwhelmingly, it is because technology and global economic competition have depressed wages in areas that are not high skilled, with the capacity to grow and learn for a lifetime.

Therefore, I do not agree that we should cut our investments in education and training, starting with the advances we made in Head Start, going through the School Lunch Program, all the way to the apprenticeship programs for young people who don't go to college, to college loans, to the subsidies for college loans for working young people—right the way through. I don't believe we should cut them, certainly not to pay for tax cuts and not even to reduce the deficit. We do not have to cut education to reduce the deficit.

The leaders of Congress have targeted two areas that I would like to mention—three, if I might, although only one reduces the deficit—or two. The first is the student loan program. We have, through our direct loan program, offered the opportunity for millions of young people to borrow money at lower costs on better repayment terms in a way that is less hassle for colleges and universities, less paperwork, and actually saves the Government money because we take out the middleman. We don't have guarantees to banks. We just make the loans

directly. That has actually reduced the deficit and reduced the costs of college loans. At the same time, we have gotten tougher on collecting delinquent loans, reducing the costs to the taxpayers of delinquent loans from $2.8 billion down to $1 billion. So, more loans, lower costs to the students, lower costs to the taxpayers, less hassle to the schools: It's a win-win deal.

The Republicans in the Congress want to change all of that. They, first of all, want to put a lid on the number of students who can participate in the direct loan program, which will add to the deficit. And then, they want to eliminate the student loan subsidy for 4 million college students and charge people interest on their loans while they're in college, even if they come from very modest backgrounds.

Interestingly enough, this cut in education will only replace the money that they want to keep giving middlemen in the old student loan program, so we could have the same reduction in the deficit by leaving the interest subsidy in place and making the direct loan program available to all the students in America. I think it's clear that our decision is a better one than theirs, and I hope that we will prevail. We are doing some things together, you know. We signed the unfunded mandates bill yesterday. We're about to get a bipartisan consensus for a line-item veto, which I have worked very hard for. So I hope that my view can prevail here, because it's very important to you.

The other thing that has happened in the House is that the Republicans have voted to cut the national service program, AmeriCorps, to the bone. I think that is a mistake. The AmeriCorps program is giving thousands of young Americans a chance to serve their communities, serve their country, and earn money for higher education. I don't believe we need to trade in our future for what is a piddling amount on the deficit but will have an enormous negative symbolic and substantive impact on what we're trying to do in this country.

There is an article in the Washington Post this morning by Mary McGrory, whom I see sitting in the back, who quotes a Georgetown student who happens to be a Republican who says, "I understand that taxpayers are heavily burdened, but if we give up what's best about America, what kind of legacy will we leave?"

So I will close with that. I urge you to think about this question. Yes, we have to continue to reduce the deficit, and we will. Yes, we have to move ourselves into the future economically. How can we do both? What are our other challenges?

One of the things we know is that the countries that do the best job of developing the full capacities of every one of their citizens will be the most successful in the 21st century. That's in all your interests, and that's what we should be debating here.

Thank you very much.

I'd like to now call on as many of you as we possibly can. I'd like to ask you when I recognize you, please, to say what your name is and what your school is. And we'll start here.

Education Legislation

Q. Jeff Glasser, from Yale. How do you plan to stop Congress from capping direct loans or cutting Pell grants or paying the interest on loans taken out during college? Are you willing to veto legislation if it comes across your desk?

The President. Well, of course I am in the areas of education, which are so important to me. But let me say again, what my first choice has been all along is to try to prevail in the debate in the Congress. We are making progress. As I said, we—I signed a bill yesterday that I strongly believe in, the unfunded mandates bill, which limits the ability of Congress to pass laws that require State and local governments to raise taxes or otherwise pay for things that we require. We're going to get the line-item veto, I hope and believe, which is a good way to cut out unnecessary spending. So maybe we can make some progress here.

I don't think there's as much enthusiasm in the Senate among Republicans, and I know the Democrats will oppose eliminating the subsidies, cutting the Pell grants, limiting the direct loan program. So I hope we can prevail in the Congress. But the veto pen is always there.

And this is a—look, I wouldn't be standing here today, no way in the world would I be standing here today if it hadn't been for the opportunities America gave me through education. When I was born in my State in 1946, the per capita income of my State was barely over half the national average. And my whole generation owes everything we have to the educational opportunities our country gave to us. And now education is even more important to the general welfare of America than it was when I was your age. I cannot sit by and watch it

go backward. We need to bear down and do more, not ease up and go back.

Yes.

President's Education

Q. Francine Friedman, from Georgetown. As a fellow Hoya about to graduate and start paying back my loans, I was wondering if you could share with us how you financed your Georgetown education.

The President. I had a $500—as I remember, it was a $500-a-year scholarship and a job; I worked in the Congress for 2 years. And when I went to Yale to law school I had a grant, a loan, a tuition postponement option—which works like the direct loan does now, that is, I paid it back as a percentage of my income— I had a national defense loan and six jobs. But never more than three at once. [*Laughter*]

NCAA Basketball Championship

Q. Kristal Adams, from the University of Arkansas at Little Rock. On a lighter note, I was wondering who do you have picked for the Arkansas-Memphis game, and do you think Arkansas will make it all the way to the championship game this year?

The President. Well, I feel somehow, after the last two games, there is some divine providence that keeps us going. [*Laughter*] So I'm more hopeful now than I was when they started the tournament. Thank you.

Affirmative Action

Q. Yes. My name is Peter McKay. I'm a sophomore at Florida A&M University. And my question deals with the White House review of affirmative action that's been going on for several weeks now. What is the status of the review, and what conclusions have you reached about affirmative action?

The President. Well, first, the status is ongoing. I'll talk a little about where we are now, but I want to emphasize that the review is still underway.

And let me urge you—I know there must be a lot of discussion about this on college campuses as it affects admissions policies. But I want to emphasize to begin with, if you spark a debate about this, it's important to know what people are talking about when they're talking about affirmative action. There are policies of the Government and policies in the private sector that affect admissions to colleges, availability of financial aid to schools, admissions to workplaces and promotional policies within the workplace, and access to contracts in the public sector and sometimes in the private sector as well, like big companies contracting with smaller ones. So you're basically talking about a range of programs.

When there is evidence of past discrimination, as found in a court, then there can be more strenuous rules and regulations. Otherwise, there are actually a lot of strictures on how far affirmative action can go in giving preferences to people based on race or gender.

But let me back up a little bit and again talk about a little history. When I was your age and I began to work in political campaigns—which I know was a long time ago, almost 30 years ago now, but it's not so long in the life of the country—there were still courthouses on squares in county seats in my State that had segregated restrooms. In my lifetime, when I was your age, in the mid-sixties, there were still older African-Americans in my State who did not know that they could vote without buying a poll tax, because it had only been abolished by the Supreme Court a couple of years before. I can remember when there were no women in any number of jobs now where we take it for granted that women will be.

The point I want to make to you is that we have made a lot of progress in this country. It has been inexact. It has been imperfect. There are still problems. We have made a lot of progress because we tried to take action to open up more opportunities to people without regard to their race or gender. And all of us, including white males, are better off because of that.

If you look at the countries around the world today that are being absolutely ripped apart because of violence based on ethnic or religious or racial disputes and sometimes also related to the role of women, if you look at the countries that are struggling to become modern today where there's still regularly violence against women—the general point I want to make to you is that it is in everyone's interest to see that everybody gets the best chance to live up to the fullest of their abilities.

On the other hand, it is in no one's interest to see that people get positions if they're completely unqualified to hold them. So the question is, how do we now go forward? And let me tell you the questions I've asked my folks

to answer. I've said, first of all, how do these programs work, and do they have a positive effect? Okay, that's the first question. Secondly, even if they work, are they sometimes, at least, unfair to others? Could you argue that in some cases there is reverse discrimination, and if so, how? Thirdly, are there now others in need who are not covered by affirmative action programs?

Keep in mind that's really what's fueling this whole thing. You've got 20 years in this country where most hourly wage earners have not kept up with inflation. Most Americans are working harder for lower wages than they were making 20 years ago. If so, how are we going to deal with them?

And finally, let's look at what clearly works, and I'll give you three examples. I don't think anybody in America would like us to suspend what we are doing in the military, the system that produced not only General Powell but countless other generals and colonels who are not only African-Americans and Hispanics and Asian-Americans but also women, doing things that never were available before. How does that system work? Why does nobody reject it? Because nobody thinks anyone unqualified gets promoted.

What do they do? They work as hard as they can to develop the capacities of everybody who signs up. They do their very best to see that at each level in the promotional pool, there is a mix of people that reflect the population in the rank just below. And then nobody, nobody gets promoted who is not qualified. But they really work hard to give everybody a chance and develop everybody's capacities.

A second example—this is self-serving, but I'll give it to you anyway—I have appointed at this point in my tenure, to this point in the 2 years, more judges to the Federal bench who were women or members of racial minorities than my three predecessors combined, I believe. But my judges have the highest ratings, on average, from the American Bar Associations of any of the last four Presidents. So no one suggests that I am not promoting quality in the Federal bench.

Fourth example: My Deputy Chief of Staff, Erskine Bowles, was, before he came to the White House, the head of the Small Business Administration. And he spent 20 years helping people finance small business. And I said, "We've got to bring enterprise into the depressed areas of this country. We have got to do it." So in one year, there was a huge increase in the volume of loans given to African-Americans, Hispanics, and women from the Small Business Administration without in any way discriminating against qualified white males, and every one of the loans was to a qualified person. Now, I don't believe any American would object to those three things.

The last thing I want to say is, I have also asked, where does discrimination still exist among people who are not poor or not economically distressed, in the traditional definition, based on race or gender? We just had the "Glass Ceiling" report issued this last week, which was originally initiated, I believe, by Senator Dole, which said that there is still evidence of discrimination in promotional practices in large enterprises.

So I want to review all this, I want to make the best decision I can, and I've given you the questions.

I want to close with just two points. I'm against discrimination. I'm against giving people opportunities who are unqualified. But we all have an interest, including white males, in developing the capacities of all of us to relate to one another, because our economy will grow quicker, it'll be stronger, and in a global society, our diversity is our greatest asset. We must not let this debate be another cheap political wedge issue to divide the American electorate. We can use this to come together, and that's what we ought to do.

Tell me your name and where you're from.

Preparation for Political Career

Q. My name is Lori Wiechman. I go to the University of Georgia. And in your first remarks, you had mentioned that you're really concerned about the future of us as college students and as—our children. And I was just wondering, looking back on your experience in politics, which areas would you suggest for the college students who attend all of the universities here who are wanting to go into politics to pursue before they begin their career?

The President. Well, first of all, I do not believe that there is a specific academic discipline that is necessarily better than another one to pursue a political career. If you are pursuing a degree in science or mathematics or economics, let's say, I would recommend that at least you take whatever electives you can in history

and in the social sciences, like political science, and in psychology. [*Laughter*] And then—but I think the most important thing is to develop your mind, is to learn to think.

And then the second thing I would say is, it's very important to spend your free time deciding whether you're interested in people as individuals and interested in public problems. Not everybody is, you know. And it's a good thing—I mean, a lot of wonderful work has been done in the world by people who didn't want to spend hours a day talking to people who were different from them.

But if you really want to make a positive difference, in my judgment, you have to be able to imagine what life is like for people who are very different from you, and you have to be willing to invest some time in listening to those people.

If you think about what's happening, even in—I read stories on college campuses that kids are sort of separating by race, at least younger people and—I'll give you something positive—one of the best things that's happened is a lot of older people are now coming back to schools, especially to community colleges but also to 4-year colleges. If you want to be effective in public life, you have to understand how other people view the world, and you have to be able to imagine yourself in their position.

And then, the third thing I would say is, you should get some experience in campaigns and in other public endeavors to find out both how hard and how exhilarating it is to get people together and try to work to change something. Those are the three pieces of advice. But there is no single academic discipline that's the best.

Illegal Immigration

Q. My name is Shafeeq Qaasim. I'm from Los Angeles Trade Technical College. As opposed to the budget that everybody's concerned about, and we have all of these illegal aliens that mostly—that affect all of us, including the taxpayers—I would like to know, considering we passed a proposal of Proposition No. 187 in California, and it's now somewhere in the Federal court system, what's being done, and how can it get back into the State where the voters have already voted?

The President. Well, the voters voted for it, and then like any law, it's subject to court challenge, and it's being challenged in the courts. Let me tell you what we've tried to do in the meanwhile. First of all, after I became President, I increased spending by 30 percent on programs designed to reduce the problem of illegal aliens. We have increased the number of border guards along the southern borders, assuming my next budget is adopted on this—I think it will be—by about 60 percent in 3 years. We are turning more people back.

We are also sending more people back home more quickly who come in contact with the criminal justice system. We are working to increase our ability to check workplaces for illegal immigrants, and we're trying to standardize identification so people can't give phony papers and stay in jobs. And we are trying to alleviate some of the costs that States face. We've given California, for example, more money to deal with their costs of imprisonment and health care and other things. And I asked the Congress to do even more than they voted to do. But I think that we should—as a matter of principle, no illegal immigrant is entitled to the expenditure of American people's tax dollars.

I did not support 187 for a very different reason. I don't think it's in the interest of the American people to have kids here and have them not in school. I don't think it's in the interest of the American people to have families here and not be able to get into a health clinic and maybe have them get seriously ill and spread whatever illness they have to the population at large. So my problem with 187 was in the details. We do not give welfare benefits, for example, to illegal immigrants, and we should not be spending our money there except where it is in the interest of our larger sense of self-interest. And I think schools and health care are.

But we've got to do a lot more to crack down on the borders, and we have to do a lot more to go into these workplaces and send people away. And I would hope again—this was a great wedge issue in the last election, but I'd like to remind you of where this issue came from, in part. A lot of the very same people that were out there for 187, just a few years ago when the California economy was booming, weakened the anti-immigration—anti-illegal immigration legislation pending in Congress, so they could get more illegal immigrants into workplaces in California who would work for lower wages, for their supporters. Now, that's the truth.

And what we need to do is crack down in the workplace, crack down at the borders, crack down in the criminal justice system, and not spend any money that we don't have to spend. And that's our policy and the one we're going to pursue.

Student Loans

Q. I'm from Ohio University in Athens, Ohio. My name is Joe Shaulis. We're represented by a freshman Republican in Congress who beat a freshman Democrat. His name is Frank Cremeans, and he says he opposes cuts in student aid, yet he says we need to look at your direct funding program—it needs to be cut or capped because it builds a billion-dollar bureaucracy here in Washington. Could you respond to that?

The President. It's just a—it's a myth. It's a myth. The direct lending program—the Secretary of Education is here with me—the direct lending program will save the taxpayers $12 billion over 6 years, the same amount of money they propose to save by eliminating the interest subsidy on student loan. Why is that?

You know how the student loan program works now under the old system? It's a 90-percent guarantee. So you go to the bank, and you borrow the money, right? And the Government guarantees 90 percent of it. And the bank gets payment in the middle. And then if somebody defaults on the loan, unless it's a huge amount of money, it's not worth it to the bank to go try to sue somebody and get the money back. Why? Because they're going to get 90 percent of it anyway. And they'll spend 10 percent or more on lawyer fees.

So what have we done? We have reduced the number of defaults. We have been tough on this, over and above the previous administrations who were here before me. We have reduced the loan defaults from a cost a year of $2.8 billion down to $1 billion. This direct lending program is far less expensive to run than the alternative. It is pure ideology to say, "It costs a little money to run the direct loan program, and we don't want to hire one Government employee; we'd rather pay billions and billions and billions of dollars to banks that could be going for lower cost college loans to more students."

This program is working. It saves money for everybody, and we shouldn't limit its reach. I think it is a real error.

Yes. Go ahead.

Diversity and Unity

Q. Margretta Sundelin, from Brigham Young University. It seems the United States is a nation founded on and prided upon its diversity. However, in the course of the last few years, it seems its diversity is dividing us. What I want to know is, in your Presidency, what have you done to bring cohesion back to the Nation and to settle the unrest?

The President. Well, I've tried to do many things, but let me emphasize two or three. The first thing I've tried to do is to focus on initiatives that would provide opportunities to all Americans, that would unite us in getting more opportunities by, first of all in economic terms, by bringing down the deficit and expanding trade opportunities for American products, by working to create more jobs for the American people. Secondly, in education, by increasing everything from Head Start programs to college loans, I have tried to offer broad-based opportunity.

The second thing I've tried to do is to demonstrate to the American people that you could have diversity and excellence at the same time—that's what I just mentioned—if you look at the people I've appointed to high public office, the people I've appointed to the Federal judgeships, and the things that I have tried to do that I think are important.

The third thing I have tried to do is to emphasize the importance of uniting the American people around shared values. That's what welfare reform is all about. That's what the attempts of the crime bill to clean up our streets from violence are all about. We should all be able to agree that we are going to pursue policies that promote family, that promote work, that strengthen communities, that look to the future. These are the things that I have tried to do.

And I believe that the American people would think more in these terms—I know that a lot of people are so bewildered by the changes and they feel so threatened by the changes going on today that it's easy to lash out at someone who is different from us. But if we would focus on those three things I think we'd come together more.

Technology and Education

Q. I'm Jaimee Silverstein, from Northwestern University. With the knowledge of computers and other types of technology becoming more crucial in order to succeed in the workplace, what steps is your administration taking to promote this type of education?

The President. Well, we are doing a number of things. First of all, I think you saw the White House on the Internet today, didn't you? We're trying to set a good example. But we're also promoting the availability of more computers and the use of more responsible computer education in our schools, starting in the earliest grades. It was a big part of the education reform legislation that Secretary Riley and I and the administration pushed last year.

One thing I note—Mr. Gingrich said the other day something that I really agreed with, and then he said maybe it was an unrealistic thing. But I don't think it is. He said it would really help to cure poverty if every poor child in America had a little laptop computer. And then I think he backed off of it. I don't think that's a bad idea at all. I think that if we had enough resources to teach every poor child in this country how to interact with the whole world of information that's available, if you can work that, it would be a very good thing.

So I believe we should continue to press technology. It is not an excuse—it's not a substitute for learning to read, for learning to write, for learning to express yourself clearly, for learning to reason and argue and think. But it is enormous leverage to us. And I think we should do more.

Homosexuals in the Military

Q. My name is Carrie Budoff. I'm from Rutgers University. Many colleges have policies of nondiscrimination. And your "don't ask, don't tell" policy for ROTC programs—it applies to ROTC programs, and it's an obvious conflict with the university's policy. The ROTC program in the case of Rutgers may lose funding because of this, because they are not abiding by the nondiscrimination policy. How can these programs—how can the ROTC program on college campuses deal with this if they have a nondiscrimination policy?

The President. Explain what you mean. I'm sorry, I don't understand it. Go ahead.

391

Q. Okay. The ROTC program at Rutgers University may lose scholarship funding because they are on the campus. And the "don't ask, don't tell" policy, which extends——

The President. Conflicts with Rutgers' nondiscrimination policy.

Q. Yes.

The President. Well, it's an act of Congress, so Rutgers will have to decide what to do about it. I mean, there isn't—I'll say this: If the policy were implemented in spirit and in letter the way it was really written, if you read the whole policy, I don't think it would be in conflict. But if you read the whole policy—I would urge you to go back and read the whole policy and see what it really says. I don't think it would be in conflict. But if Rutgers deems it's in conflict, then Rutgers will have to do whatever it decides to do, because that policy was written into law as an act of Congress and so it is not subject to change unless Congress changes it.

Education and Tolerance

Q. Christan Hanna, Western Michigan University. On our campus we had a nonviolent protest because a faculty member told a student that she asked "stupid—blank—questions." And instead of dealing with the problem of racism and talking about it on campus, the university's reaction has been to try to quell all of the surrounding problems instead of dealing with the issue, the main issue, which is the racism and problems that people have with that. What do you think the university's role in educating beyond your study, your area of study, is?

The President. Well, I think it's a very important role. I mean, if you have the luxury of going to college and you stay there for 4 years or, in the case of a community college, 2 years, it's maybe different if you've got a family to raise and a full-time job and all. But if basically you're a full-time student and you're in your formative years, some of the most important things that happen to you happen to you outside the classroom and involve things you don't get a grade on.

And I think one of the things—I've been really quite concerned about the challenges that both students and faculty members face in this so-called political correctness atmosphere. I think we need to encourage people to say what they really think but to do it in an atmosphere that is more tolerant. And I think universities

ought to be laboratories all across this country for people airing their real feelings and convictions but doing it in a way that other people can hear them and really being honest and forthright about it, because otherwise, then the universities can just become one more island of isolation for the American people. We don't need that. We don't need more islands of isolation. We need instruments to open us up to one another.

Health Care Reform

Q. Jim Buchanan, St. Louis Community College. Mr. President, I congratulate your efforts to try to bring about health care reform. And I wonder if you're going to try that again. And do you think a single-payer system might make it?

The President. The answer is, I am going to try to health care reform again this year. Obviously, the American people made a judgment, or at least the Congress did, and I think the American people did—that this was such a big issue, they didn't want me or anybody else to try to put together a program that purported to solve it all at one time. So I think we'll have to go back and take it a piece at a time.

My own view is that this is something—you need to know about this, by the way—the entire problem with the Federal deficit in 1995, 1994, 1993, now since our budget has come in, is interest on the debt and health care costs. Everything else is going down. Last year we reduced spending on both defense and domestic spending overall for the first time in 25 years. The deficit's going up because of interest on the debt and health care costs. So we have an interest in doing that.

The second thing you need to know is that your country is the only advanced country in the world where there are a smaller percentage of working families with health insurance today than had it 10 years ago. That is not true in any other advanced country in the world. So we have to do it. We have to—we should do it by reforming the insurance system, helping people when they're unemployed not to lose their insurance, giving incentives to cover children, and helping families with disabled kids or with parents who want care other than nursing homes and where that would be a cheaper, more affordable thing to do.

Let me give a little—go ahead, in the back there. I'll take a couple more. Go ahead. Yes, go ahead. [*Laughter*] You're great. You know, when they're here, they all stand up if I point in the general direction. [*Laughter*]

Scholarship Grants

Q. My name is Evan Koblentz, from Kean College of New Jersey. Much progress has been made in your administration for financially strapped or opportunity-privileged students to get grants and loans. What are you doing with the Republican Congress to get more grants available for merit-based and academic-based scholarships?

The President. Well, let me say, first of all, I'm not—I don't believe that that should primarily be the subject for the Federal Government. Historically, it hasn't been. And I'll come back to that in a moment. Secondly, let me emphasize that the direct loan program is not very much income-limited. It's really available to quite a broad range of young people to participate in. And since there are at least four different options for repayment, the idea is that you don't lose the right to get a loan even if you're a middle class student. And if you decide to take a job that doesn't pay a high wage, you can afford to pay it back if you want to be someone who's more interested in public service early on than higher incomes.

Now, on the merit-based scholarships, let me just say what I meant by that. There are many States—Georgia is one, I know we have some journalists here from Georgia—Georgia has now passed a law that says that if you have a B average in Georgia and you go to school there, you get a tuition scholarship. And I think you get some money for books as well. When I was the Governor of my State, I instituted a Governor's scholarship program that was similar to that. These programs are sweeping the country, but they are basically the province of State government.

Let me further state that this is the second year in a row when the economy of all 50 States has grown. So they're in a—if they don't do it, they're in a better position to do it than they were a couple of years ago. And that's one I would direct you to the State legislatures for.

The Middle Class

Q. Yes, all day we've been hearing—I'm sorry, Kelly McEvers, from the University of Illinois. All day we've been hearing about the growing

disparity between those in the upper echelon of income and those in the lower, those at the low poverty level. However, especially after the election in November, the rhetoric that seemed to be coming through, at least in the mainstream media, was solely toward the middle class. I guess one example is the middle class bill of rights. It seems to me that there's an attitude that we're becoming a classless society when, in fact, we're moving in opposite directions——

The President. We are——

Q. Is that because that's the class that goes to the polls?

The President. No. It's because—let me just say this. The argument of the Republicans in last November's election was, "The middle class should vote for us because all the Democrats do is take your taxes and spend it on poor people"—right?—or minorities or illegal immigrants or criminals or whatever. That was the basic argument, right? "Government's bad. Vote for us; we'll give you less government, lower taxes, and we'll be harder on all those groups."

And the voters bought it—wrongly, I think—at least those who voted—because we had done more for the middle class. But you have to understand what middle class is. Middle class is more than an economic designation in America. It's a statement about values. When we say middle class in America what we really mean is, everybody ought to have the chance to be rewarded for their work. If you work hard, raise your kids, obey the law, you ought to have a chance to do better.

And what is happening is we are becoming more stratified by economic class, but it's different than before. In other words—and I guess—I'm really glad you asked this, because I'll try to clarify the point I was trying to make before. We do have poor people in America. Mostly they're young women and their little children, but there are also a lot of working people who are poor, who are making the minimum wage or right near it, which is why I'm for raising the minimum wage. And then we have a lot of wealthy people in America, and our economy is producing more wealthy people, and that is good. Entrepreneurs—more entrepreneurs are becoming millionaires today than ever before, who started with nothing—not inherited wealth—but are making money. That is a good thing, not a bad thing.

But what is happening is that the middle class itself is splitting apart. That's the point I'm trying to make. The great American middle class, which basically rose more or less evenly with the poor and the rich in income from the end of World War II to the late seventies—everybody rose together about the same amount—the American middle class itself is now splitting apart, based largely on education, age, and job description. And if you don't have the skills and you're not in the place—in the workplace, where you can hook into one of these groups that is growing, then you tend to work harder every year for lower wages. That's what I'm pointing out.

So what do we try to do? In the economic plan in '93, we had one big tax cut. We cut taxes for working families with children to make sure nobody who was working 40 hours a week with children would be below the poverty line. That's what the earned-income tax credit was about. On average this year it's worth about $1,000 in lower taxes to families of four with income of under $26,000. Why do we do that? To reward work and family and lift people, keep trying to push people toward the middle class.

So this whole education thing—we know if our Government here can continue to follow responsible economic policies, we can create jobs, we can have growth. But we still—that will not raise incomes. And it won't overcome this inequality, this splitting apart of the middle class.

So that's what I'm saying. The middle class mentality, which has been—what made America great, requires us to follow policies that lift everybody's income.

I will close with just one thing. I had an interview with Money Magazine the other day. Do you all know Money Magazine? It's a—and they did a readers' survey, they told me. And they said—I guess I'm jumping my interview. They'll probably be mad at me, but—[*laughter*]. They said that their readers said that they recognize that we have lowered the deficit, created jobs, sparked an economic recovery, and two-thirds of them were still worried about their future. Right? "Yes, you lowered the deficit, created jobs, there's an economic recovery. Am I worried? You bet I am. Why? Because of all this churning instability in the global economy."

That is our challenge. We've got to find a way to keep the entrepreneurship, keep the growth going, but lift the middle class folks that are good people that have been left behind. That's why I'm glad to see some of the nontraditional students in the community college. That means that they're going to make the transfer from the middle class that might be left behind to the middle class that's surging ahead. And we need more of that, which is why we don't need to be in a position of reducing our commitment to education at the end of this century when the next century will trigger opportunity to education more than ever before.

Thank you very much. I have to go. Thank you.

NOTE: The President spoke at 1:05 p.m. in the East Room at the White House.

Statement on House of Representatives Action on Welfare Reform
March 23, 1995

I want to applaud Democrats and Republicans in the House of Representatives for approving an amendment this afternoon to require States to deny drivers and professional licenses to deadbeat parents who refuse to pay child support. This tough provision was a central part of the welfare reform plan my administration introduced last year and sends a clear signal: No parent in America has a right to walk away from the responsibility to raise their children.

I congratulate the sponsor of the amendment, Representative Marge Roukema (R–NJ), as well as Representative Barbara Kennelly (D–CT) and other Members who have worked across party lines to make tough child support enforcement a central part of welfare reform. With this amendment, the House welfare reform legislation now includes every major child support pillar of our welfare reform plan, which offered the toughest possible child support enforcement measures ever put forward.

These actions on child support enforcement prove that welfare reform can and must be a bipartisan issue. Unfortunately, the House Republican bill still does not offer the kind of real welfare reform that Americans in both parties expect. Welfare reform must be tough on work and tough on deadbeat parents, not tough on children.

I look forward to working with Republicans and Democrats in both Houses of Congress to enact real reform that makes work and responsibility a way of life.

Statement on Senate Action on the Line-Item Veto
March 23, 1995

The Senate tonight has taken another step toward passing strong line-item veto legislation. I hope the House and Senate will now get together quickly to resolve their differences and pass the strongest possible bill.

The sooner such a bill reaches my desk, the sooner I can take further steps to cut the deficit.

Message to the Congress on Trade With the West Bank and the Gaza Strip
March 17, 1995

To the Congress of the United States:

I am writing to inform you of my intent to designate the West Bank and Gaza Strip as a beneficiary of the Generalized System of Preferences (GSP). The GSP program, which offers duty-free access to the U.S. market, was originally authorized by the Trade Act of 1974.

I have carefully considered the criteria identified in sections 501 and 502 of the Trade Act of 1974. In light of these criteria, I have determined that it is appropriate to extend GSP benefits to the West Bank and Gaza Strip.

This notice is submitted in accordance with section 502(a)(1) of the Trade Act of 1974.

WILLIAM J. CLINTON

The White House,
March 17, 1995.

NOTE: This message was released by the Office of the Press Secretary on March 24. The related proclamation of March 17 is listed in Appendix D at the end of this volume.

Statement on House of Representatives Action on Welfare Reform
March 24, 1995

At a time when so many Americans without regard to party agree on the need for welfare reform, it's a shame the House of Representatives could not produce a real welfare reform plan that would promote work and responsibility and attract broad bipartisan support. I am disappointed that instead of joining in a real, bipartisan effort to move people from welfare to work, a narrow partisan Republican majority passed a bill that is weak on work and tough on children.

I am determined to work with Republicans and Democrats in Congress to produce the kind of welfare reform Americans, regardless of party affiliation, want and expect. To end welfare as we know it, we must be tough on work and trough on deadbeat parents not tough on children.

I commend the House of Representatives on one part of the bill that enjoyed true bipartisan support—tough measures on child support enforcement, including refusing drivers' and professional licenses to deadbeat parents who refuse to pay child support. The House passed every major child support element of our welfare reform plan, which will enable us to mount the toughest child support enforcement crackdown in history. It is time to demand responsibility from parents who bring children into the world, not let them off the hook and expect taxpayers to pick up the tab for their neglect.

Welfare reform can and must be a bipartisan issue. I look forward to working with Republicans and Democrats in the Senate to pass real welfare reform that will make work and responsibility the law of the land.

The President's Radio Address
March 25, 1995

Good morning. This morning I want to talk about how much we can accomplish when we work in a spirit of cooperation. Once again, this week demonstrated that Democrats and Republicans can come together to break gridlock when they put the American people first.

Our mission here is to keep the American dream alive for all our people; to grow the middle class and shrink the under class; to promote the mainstream values of work and family, community, and looking out for the future of our children; to reform Government to meet the challenges we face. There's a great debate here about how to change Government. On one side is the old view that big one-size-fits-all Government can fix all our big problems. On the other is the view that Government is the source of all our problems. In the real world that's a false choice.

We must go beyond the old way of big Government and the new rage of no Government to the idea of Government as a partner, a partner that works to expand opportunity while shrinking bureaucracy, to empower people to make the most of their own lives through education and training, and to enhance our security on our streets and around the world. That's what I believe. And I believe most Americans feel that way, too.

In short, I believe that Federal Government must be a savior—or cannot be a savior but must not sit on the sidelines. For our future we need a Government that helps us to create more opportunity but demands more responsibility from all our citizens. That's what I mean by the New Covenant: opportunity and responsibility.

Despite real differences between Republicans and Democrats, we see progress on three proposals I have supported for many years, proposals that I advocated when I ran for President. All of them impose more responsibility on the Federal Government. And it's high time.

First, Congress passed a bill, which I was proud to sign, requiring Congress to live by the laws it imposes on the private sector. Second, last week in the Rose Garden right outside the Oval Office where I'm speaking now, I was pleased to sign another bill which for the first time limits the ability of Congress to pass laws which impose unfunded mandates on State and local Governments. As a former Governor, I know this bill will make a big difference in the ability of State and local governments to improve the lives of our people without having Washington tell them how to spend the tax dollars you send them. Third, last week the Senate passed a line-item veto. I have favored this power for Presidents, no matter what their party, for a long time. It will bring more discipline to our spending process by enabling Presidents to veto particular projects which are unjustified but which today can be hidden in comprehensive bills the President has to sign. Now that the line-item veto in some version has passed both Houses of Congress, I urge Members from both parties to resolve their differences, pass a unified bill, and send it to me. Then the line-item veto can put our people ahead of pork.

Last week, we saw some progress on another crucial issue, welfare reform. We saw that we can find common ground, but we are not all the way there yet. In my radio address last week, I talked about the need to have tougher child support enforcement, to demand that parents take responsibility for their own children and not let parents off the hook or make the taxpayers pick up the tab for their neglect. If all the child support in America that is owed was paid, we could move 800,000 families off the welfare roll.

I'm pleased that Members of the House in both parties responded to my position on tougher child support enforcement. They voted by 426 to 5 to adopt a provision from my welfare reform bill that calls upon States to deny driver's licenses and professional licenses to deadbeat parents, people who owe child support and can pay it but don't. The House has now adopted every major child support element in my welfare reform bill. If the Senate will follow suit, we'll mount the toughest crackdown on deadbeat parents ever and will help more children, too.

But we have to do more to promote responsible parenting. Other provisions of the House bill would actually make it harder for many people to get off and stay off welfare. And the bill doesn't really do anything to promote work; indeed, it removes any real responsibility for States to help people gain the training and skills they need to get and keep jobs. It even cuts child care for working people struggling to hold down jobs and stay off welfare.

I commend the Democrats in the House for voting unanimously for an alternative bill sponsored by Congressman Nathan Deal of Georgia because it was tougher on work requirements, better for children, and did more to promote responsible parenting. I'm looking forward to working with Republicans and Democrats to really end welfare as we know it, making sure people earn a paycheck, not a welfare check, that they move from dependence to independence.

I also want to caution the Members of the House to try to tone down the rhetoric. It got a little rough last week and a little too personal and partisan. After all, all Americans want to change the welfare system; no American wants to continue a system that doesn't promote work and responsible parenting.

In everything we do we must be working to expand the middle class, to shrink the under class, and to promote these values of family and work, community, and looking out for the future of our kids. I hope we'll be back in the Rose Garden while it's still spring to sign even more bills into law that help us to do those things. Guided by the values that have always kept us strong, we can work together to help all our people earn a fair shot at the American dream.

Thanks for listening.

NOTE: The President spoke at 10:06 a.m. from the Oval Office at the White House.

Interview With Tony Bruno and Chuck Wilson of ESPN Radio
March 25, 1995

Mr. Bruno. As we continue on ESPN Radio, Tony Bruno and Chuck Wilson with you. And I've always wanted to do this, Chuck, when introducing a guest, but we've never had the opportunity so far.

Ladies and gentlemen, the President of the United States, Mr. Bill Clinton.

Mr. President, thanks for joining us on ESPN Radio. This is not a joke. People will think because I like to clown around that we're pulling a fast one on the American public, but we are not. And we appreciate you joining us.

The President. I'm glad to do it. And I'm glad to be in a conversation where the American people think someone else is pulling a fast one on them instead of the President. [*Laughter*]

NCAA Basketball Tournament

Mr. Wilson Mr. President, we have had an opportunity to see an outstanding NCAA tournament. I know you're a big basketball fan, and your Arkansas Razorbacks, they're still alive.

The President. They're an amazing team. You know, everybody they've played this year it seems has played their very best game against them, and in every game it seems they have a few minutes of mental lapse where they let the other team get back in. But they've got enormous heart. I'm really proud of them, just to keep coming back. They never give up, and I respect that. I respect that in life, and I certainly respect it on the basketball court.

Mr. Wilson They've kept you on the edge of your chair, haven't they? The one-point game with Texas Southern, 2 overtime games, 13 times this year they've had a game decided by 5 points or less, and they win 12 of the 13.

The President. It's amazing. They find a way to win. They keep getting themselves in trouble, but they find a way to win. Last night we had a watch party here at the White House, and we had a lot of folks from home there. And we had a cardiologist there—we were all glad he was there. We thought he was going to have to jumpstart half the crowd to get us through the end of the game. [*Laughter*]

Mr. Bruno. They also keep you up very late also because of these overtime games. Can't you control CBS and have them put them on earlier? [*Laughter*]

The President. No, I don't have any—you know, that's the first amendment; the President, more than anybody else in the country, has no control over the media.

Mr. Bruno. President Bill Clinton is joining us from the Oval Office.

Let's talk about—now the Arkansas Razorbacks are one more step—actually, they're one step away from the Final Four. You've got the Sunday game. Is this team going to all the way? I want the Presidential prediction here now.

The President. Well, I think they have the ability to do it and they have the heart to do it. They've got to find the right combinations and maintain their concentration. I think they tend to up their play. You know, the two best basketball games I saw all year were the two games they played against Kentucky. And one they won, and one they lost. So it's obvious that they have the talent and the heart to do it, and I think if they can really get to the end of the games mentally, I think they've got a good chance to make it.

I was—I must say I was very impressed with the game Virginia played against Kansas last night. They were exhausted with 7 or 8 minutes left to go. I didn't know if they could get through the end of the game, but they somehow found the strength and the reserve to hang in there and win that game. So they've got a hard game to get by Virginia before they get to the Final Four. But I do think they have a chance to win.

The Presidency

Mr. Wilson. President Clinton, frequently Presidents are accused of being out of touch with the people. They sit in the White House; they attend official functions. They don't get out with the regular people. You seemed to have really pushed very hard to be as normal as you can in the White House. Do you find it beneficial, even beyond the family aspects, to get out and to go to basketball games or a football game, that kind of thing?

The President. Oh, I do. I think it's beneficial whenever the President can be in more normal circumstances, for two reasons. First of all, it makes you remember that there's a real life beyond the White House and all the security apparatus that surrounds the President; it makes you feel better and kind of get back in touch with yourself. And secondly, it's important that the President see people in informal ways who are all kinds of citizens, that he relates to people without regard to their party or income or any other particular reason they might have to come to see the President in the White House. I think that's very important.

This is a wonderful opportunity. And it's important that the President be, to some extent, removed from the day-to-day things of life because you've got to keep looking for the long run. You've got to do a lot of things in this job that are unpopular because you believe them to be best for America in the long run. But still, the biggest danger is just being out of touch. So I try to fight it, and I enjoy trying to fight it.

Mr. Wilson. And it's tough to be normal in a sense because of all the security measures. You go to a game; it's not Bill Clinton going to the game, it's the President going to the game.

The President. Yes, and I—you know, I love to go to basketball games. I made one Georgetown game, my alma mater, and one George Washington game here in Washington this year. And I tried to do it in a way that would be as least disruptive as possible. I don't like to make other people wait on me to get out of a basketball arena. I don't like to make people wait in line while I'm getting in and getting seated. I really—I'm reluctant to go out to these events because I don't like to inconvenience other people. But it's certainly a great deal of fun when I get there.

Baseball Strike

Mr. Bruno. President Bill Clinton joining us from the Oval Office here on ESPN Radio, Tony Bruno and Chuck Wilson.

One of the things that we—none of us will be able to go to unless we want to go to replacement games is major league baseball. Mr. President, we all know the situation is now at a turning point. We would have liked a line-item veto a couple of weeks ago to eliminate some parties from the bargaining mix. [*Laughter*] Unfortunately, you weren't able to do that for us either.

The President. We're about to pass the line-item veto. We're going to get that done. I don't know if I can apply it to baseball negotiations. I think it only applies to budgets, but it's not a bad idea. It's not too late.

Mr. Bruno. Well, the American fans, almost are apathetic about this. We're a week away from opening day. The real games, obviously, aren't going to start, barring some miraculous development this coming week. What do you think is going to happen? Do you think that this thing will eventually be solved before the season is totally shot?

The President. Well, I still think there's a chance. Mr. Usery, the person I appointed to mediate this, is still working. And of course, there are some developments involving—in the courts—involving the NLRB decisions that could have an impact on this. But I have to say, I will say again, I think both the players and the owners have to be aware that ultimately this game depends upon the fans. And if the fans finally get sick of it and decide they'd rather do something else, that's not good for baseball. And in the end, that is the ultimate hazard, that if it becomes so painfully clear that it's no longer a sport and it's just a business, then the customers may decide to take their business elsewhere. And that's what I think they all have to be sensitive to. They're about to run out this string. They need to resolve this.

Mr. Wilson. The thing that is so frustrating is that this game is predicated so much on the history of the sport. And if we start the season with replacement ballplayers, it really puts a stain on the history of the game, doesn't it?

The President. Well, sure, it does. Just like the strike last year. We had a chance to break records that had stood for decades, both because we had some great hitters having great seasons

and, of course, because the expansion maybe spread the pitching a little thinner than the hitting. But for whatever reason, we were on the verge of having a shattering season in the best sense. And the American people were excited about it; they were into it. We had all kinds of people my age who hadn't thought about baseball in years that were back into it. And then, boom, all of a sudden there was the strike, and it was over.

So I think if you put that with a season of replacement players, I think there's going to be a lot of diminished enthusiasm. I think people will be more interested in their minor league teams, the teams in their own little leagues in their communities, than they are in major league baseball. It could become a community support again—sport again, almost the way soccer is, if they don't fix it.

Michael Jordan

Mr. Bruno. Mr. President, sooner or later baseball will be back; we all know that somehow, someway, will happen. Michael Jordan, though, returned recently now to the NBA, and Mike Tyson was just released from prison. So things aren't really all bad. We're seeing some of the big names in sports come back. Your thoughts on the return of Michael Jordan and Mike Tyson now back into the mainstream society.

The President. Well, I think Jordan has played very well, considering the pressure that's been on him and how long he's been out of basketball. You know, he doesn't quite have his shot back yet. But he's played very well, and I'm amazed that—I know he was training for baseball, but it's still—it's a different sport that requires different skills. I'm amazed at how well he's gotten back into the flow of the game. And he makes the Bulls a different team because he in effect makes all those other guys more potent weapons as well. So I think—I don't know how quickly they'll get it all worked out, but when they do they'll be humming again.

NCAA Basketball Tournament

Mr. Bruno. All right, Mr. President, before we let you go—and we appreciate your time this morning—we've got to get—we know you like Arkansas. We need the Final Four prediction from President Bill Clinton.

The President. I don't want to get into that. I'm devoted to Arkansas, and of course, the Oklahoma State coach, Eddie Sutton, is a very close friend of mine. He coached at Arkansas for many years. And he has done a brilliant job, I think, in getting that team as far as it's gone. So I think—you know, I thought when we started the tournament that there were eight or nine teams that could win. Last year, when Arkansas won, I think, realistically, there were only about four teams that had a good chance to win. This year there really are eight or nine teams. And of course, now we're down to eight, and I think every one of them—I can see a scenario where they could come out on top.

UConn and UMass are both playing much better than they were along toward the end of the season. And UCLA has been stunning, and Kentucky, I don't think they've missed a shot since they beat Arkansas in overtime. So

I wouldn't hazard a prediction. I think any of these teams that are left can win.

Mr. Bruno. President Bill Clinton, taking the safe political route here on ESPN. Mr. President, we——

The President. As long as you know who I'm for, I don't have to predict who's going to win. [*Laughter*] I'm unambiguously for—[*laughter*].

Mr. Bruno. Mr. President, thank you so much for joining us here on ESPN Radio. We appreciate it.

The President. Thanks, Tony. Thanks, Chuck. Bye-bye.

NOTE: The interview began at 10:57 a.m. in the Oval Office at the White House and was embargoed for release until 6 p.m.

Remarks on the National Performance Review
March 27, 1995

Thank you very much. Mr. Vice President, Chairman Hundt, Secretary Babbitt, to Phil Lader and Dan Goldin and James Lee Witt, ladies and gentlemen: I'm glad to be here. I'd go nearly anywhere to get a check that size. [*Laughter*]

And I have now—and with all of you as my witnesses—the Vice President publicly thanking me for asking him to take over this reinventing Government effort. [*Laughter*] That is enough to wipe away all the private reservations that we have had to go through over the last year and a half. I want to thank him and Elaine Kamarck and all the staff of the reinventing Government effort because they have worked so very hard to give our country the Government that it deserves, the Government for the future, one that costs less and works better and reflects the real values of our people.

You know, in Washington, we're engaged today in a great debate over what the role of the Government here ought to be. Just about everybody has rejected the past view that there is a big one-size-fits-all Government that can solve all the big problems of America. Now the rage in Washington is to argue that the Government is the source of all of our problems and if just there simply weren't one, we'd have no problems. Sooner or later, the American people

will come to agree, and I think they are quickly coming to agree, that the old one-size-fits-all view was wrong but the new rage of no Government is wrong as well, that we need a Government that can be a partner to our people, to help them to compete and prosper in a global economy which is changing very rapidly and which presents great opportunity but also real challenges as well.

I believe we need a Government that shrinks bureaucracy and increases opportunity, one that empowers people to make the most of their own lives instead of pretending that they can solve people's problems for them, and a Government that enhances security around the world, but here on our streets as well. The key to our future is to, therefore, create more opportunity but also to have all of us, each in our own ways, assume more responsibility. That's what I have called the New Covenant. It's basically an old-fashioned social compact about citizenship, citizenship for the 21st century, that requires us to get rid of yesterday's Government and replace it with a new Government.

A lot of the things that we have to do don't have a necessary partisan tinge to them, and I hope that we can keep this reinventing Government effort a broad-based bipartisan one. In that regard, I thank Congressman Boehlert for coming today, in spite of the results of the NCAA basketball tournament. I thank you, sir. We had a bet on the Syracuse-Arkansas game, and he paid his 5 dollars. And I told him that since God determined the outcome, he should give it to a church instead. [*Laughter*] But I thank you, sir.

Since we have been here, we have worked very, very hard to try to show discipline and order and direction. We've got the deficit down by $600 billion. We've reduced the size of the Government. It's on its way to being fewer than 2 million, for the first time since President Kennedy was here.

But we know we have to go beyond cutting, and even beyond restructuring, to literally reevaluate what we're doing. Are we doing it well? Should we be doing it at all? Should somebody else be doing it? Are we being as innovative and flexible as the most creative private organizations in this country? We should never, we should never be less creative or less entrepreneurial simply because we have a public, as opposed to a private, mission.

Today we see again the good that can come when we discard the old ways. The FCC didn't used to have auctions. In the past, a company that wanted the right to broadcast on certain frequencies filled out a stack of Government forms, then hired lawyers and lobbyists to shepherd the case through the process year after year. When all was said and done, the company had in fact paid a lot for the privilege of broadcasting, but only the lawyers and the lobbyists had collected, and the Government simply gave away the goods. More recently, the FCC did auction off the broadcast rights, but they did it for free. And the winners held auctions and profited—pocketed the profits.

When I say we want Government that works like the best private business, the first rule is, taxpayers don't want the Government to give any of their property away for free when it ought to be paid for. And last year the reinvented FCC started holding auctions of its own. We had hoped they'd be a success, but frankly, this $7.7 billion check for the American taxpayers by selling off parts of the wireless spectrum exceeds every expectation which was put out there, including our optimistic projections.

When we said this is what we're going to do, and this is how we're going to help get the deficit down, a lot of my colleagues on Cap-

itol Hill sort of rolled their eyes and said, "Yeah, sure." Well, they were wrong. We didn't raise just a few billion dollars. We raised a few billion dollars and then a few billion dollars more from this. And I want to compliment all those who had anything to do with organizing and carrying out these auctions. I'd also like to thank those who won the bids—[*laughter*]—and those who bid them up. This money goes straight to reducing the deficit, and there will be more such auctions in the future. So Chairman Hundt, on behalf of the American taxpayers, I thank you for that $7.7 billion. The dividend will go a good ways toward paying down our Government's deficit.

We have other things that we're working on as well. And again, I would say it's important not just to cut, not just to generate income for the American people but to do it in the right way. Yes, the United States Department of Agriculture must be shrunk. We think the right way to do it is to close agricultural field offices and to reduce subsidies after worldwide negotiations, not to cut school lunches. We don't need to take summer jobs away from young people who will be idle in some of the most difficult areas of our country if we take more full-time jobs away from Federal employees which we don't need anymore. We don't have to shut down national service or stop training our teachers if we trim the Government's overhead. We don't have to give up on making our children's schools safe and drug-free if we simply stop giving away commercial treasures, like these broadcast bands.

We have to do a lot more. We have to do a lot more. We still have to continue to get the deficit down and to free up the money we need to invest in our people and their future. So today we're announcing further changes in four agencies that are here with me today that will save over $13 billion and enable us to reduce the number of Federal bureaucrats by over 5,000 more.

At NASA, we have streamlined operations to take account of what the needs of today's space program are. It used to be that 42 senior managers supervised the space station program; NASA has reduced that number to 4. Now, we're going to build on this momentum by making the management of our most forward-looking agency our most modern as well.

At the Small Business Administration they're closing offices all around the country, even as they open partnerships with banks and retired business people to work to help small businesses. Once, when the SBA made a loan, a public employee did all the paperwork. Now they're working with 7,000 banks so that they bear the overhead cost of making the loans. That's more money for private investment and fewer taxpayer costs.

At the Department of the Interior, they're reducing the work force by 2,000 people and making this far-flung department work more like a business. We're allowing companies who have, for example, offshore oil leases to prepay the taxpayers. Believe it or not, a lot of them really want to do it. That brings in billions of dollars and means we don't need battalions of auditors to make sure we're getting our money's worth.

As I said on many occasions, under the leadership of James Lee Witt, we have transformed FEMA from being a disaster into being a model disaster relief agency. Now we're going to build new partnerships with our States to reduce the Federal micromanagement and help them prepare for emergencies at the local level.

All of these changes, indeed, the entire reinvention effort, has one overall goal: a Government that does only what it needs to do, but everything it must do, it does it well, efficiently, and at the lowest possible cost to the taxpayers.

Just consider this fact. Today we talked about the SBA; the entire budget of the SBA is less than the taxes paid last year by three companies that got their starts with SBA loans. Listen to the three: Apple, Intel, and Federal Express. I think an SBA that stays in business and helps more people get started is in the interest of the United States of America.

I should also say, as Chairman Hundt never tires of telling us, that there's a chart in the other room which documents the fact that these auctions generated more than 3 times the total budget of the Federal Communications Commission from its inception during the Great Depression to last year, which I also think is a pretty good bargain for the American taxpayers.

What this should remind us of is that you can reinvent Government, cut costs to the taxpayers without a mean spirit or a meat ax. We can do this in a way that brings the American people together instead of divides them. We can do this in a way that lifts the incomes and the job prospects of the American people instead of diminishes them. We can do it in a way that is humane and decent to our Federal employees, too. And I thank the Vice President and the REGO team for their work on the buyout package because it was the right and fair and decent thing to do.

We can do this, but it takes hard work. It takes a good, open mind. It takes consistent determination. And I hope we will continue to have broad, bipartisan support for the kind of thing we're celebrating today. If we do we're going to get rid of the deficit and build America for the 21st century.

Thank you very much, and bless you all.

NOTE: The President spoke at 12:40 p.m. at the Old Post Office. In his remarks, he referred to Reed E. Hundt, Chairman, Federal Communications Commission, and Elaine C. Kamarck, Senior Policy Adviser to the Vice President.

Message to the Congress Reporting on the National Emergency With Respect to Angola
March 27, 1995

To the Congress of the United States:

I hereby report to the Congress on the developments since September 26, 1994, concerning the national emergency with respect to Angola that was declared in Executive Order No. 12865 of September 26, 1993. This report is submitted pursuant to section 401(c) of the National Emergencies Act, 50 U.S.C. 1641(c), and section 204(c) of the International Emergency Economic Powers Act, 50 U.S.C. 1703(c).

On September 26, 1993, I declared a national emergency with respect to Angola, invoking the authority, *inter alia*, of the International Emergency Economic Powers Act (50 U.S.C. 1701 *et seq.*) and the United Nations Participation Act of 1945 (22 U.S.C. 287c). Consistent with

United Nations Security Council Resolution 864, dated September 15, 1993, the order prohibited the sale or supply by United States persons or from the United States, or using U.S.-registered vessels or aircraft, of arms and related materiel of all types, including weapons and ammunition, military vehicles, equipment and spare parts, and petroleum and petroleum products to the territory of Angola other than through designated points of entry. The order also prohibited such sale or supply to the National Union for the Total Independence of Angola ("UNITA"). United States persons are prohibited from activities that promote or are calculated to promote such sales or supplies, or from attempted violations, or from evasion or avoidance or transactions that have the purpose of evasion or avoidance, of the stated prohibitions. The order authorized the Secretary of the Treasury, in consultation with the Secretary of State, to take such actions, including the promulgation of rules and regulations, as might be necessary to carry out the purposes of the order.

1. On December 10, 1993, the Treasury Department's Office of Foreign Assets Control ("FAC") issued the UNITA (Angola) Sanctions Regulations (the "Regulations") (58 *Fed. Reg.* 64904) to implement the President's declaration of a national emergency and imposition of sanctions against Angola (UNITA). There have been no amendments to the Regulations since my report of September 20, 1994.

The Regulations prohibit the sale or supply by United States persons or from the United States, or using U.S.-registered vessels or aircraft, of arms and related materiel of all types, including weapons and ammunition, military vehicles, equipment and spare parts, and petroleum and petroleum products to UNITA or to the territory of Angola other than through designated points. United States persons are also prohibited from activities that promote or are calculated to promote such sales or supplies to UNITA or Angola, or from any transaction by any United States persons that evades or avoids, or has the purpose of evading or avoiding, or attempts to violate, any of the prohibitions set forth in the Executive order. Also prohibited are transactions by United States persons, or involving the use of U.S.-registered vessels or aircraft, relating to transportation to Angola or UNITA of goods the exportation of which is prohibited.

The Government of Angola has designated the following points of entry as points in Angola to which the articles otherwise prohibited by the Regulations may be shipped: *Airports*: Luanda and Katumbela, Benguela Province; *Ports*: Luanda and Lobito, Benguela Province; and Namibe, Namibe Province; and *Entry Points*: Malongo, Cabinda Province. Although no specific license is required by the Department of the Treasury for shipments to these designated points of entry (unless the item is destined for UNITA), any such exports remain subject to the licensing requirements of the Departments of State and/or Commerce.

2. FAC has worked closely with the U.S. financial community to assure a heightened awareness of the sanctions against UNITA—through the dissemination of publications, seminars, and notices to electronic bulletin boards. This educational effort has resulted in frequent calls from banks to assure that they are not routing funds in violation of these prohibitions. United States exporters have also been notified of the sanctions through a variety of media, including special fliers and computer bulletin board information initiated by FAC and posted through the Department of Commerce and the Government Printing Office. There have been no license applications under the program.

3. The expenses incurred by the Federal Government in the 6-month period from September 26, 1994, through March 25, 1995, that are directly attributable to the exercise of powers and authorities conferred by the declaration of a national emergency with respect to Angola (UNITA) are reported at about $50,000, most of which represents wage and salary costs for Federal personnel. Personnel costs were largely centered in the Department of the Treasury (particularly in the Office of Foreign Assets Control, the Customs Service, the Office of the Under Secretary for Enforcement, and the Office of the General Counsel) and the Department of State (particularly the Office of Southern African Affairs).

I will continue to report periodically to the Congress on significant developments, pursuant to 50 U.S.C. 1703(c).

WILLIAM J. CLINTON

The White House,
March 27, 1995.

Message to the Congress Transmitting the Report on the Health Care for Native Hawaiians Program
March 27, 1995

To the Congress of the United States:

I transmit herewith the Report on the Health Care for Native Hawaiians Program, as required by section 11 of the Native Hawaiians Health Care Act of 1988, as amended (Public Law 102–396; 42 U.S.C. 11701 *et seq.*).

WILLIAM J. CLINTON

The White House,
March 27, 1995.

Remarks to the Atlanta Committee for the Olympic Games in Atlanta, Georgia
March 28, 1995

The President. Thank you. This is a pretty lively crowd. Mayor Campbell, thank you for welcoming me back to Atlanta. I'm glad to be back. I'm glad to be here with Billy Payne and Andrew Fleming and all the leaders of the Olympics, LeRoy Walker and others.

You know, I was listening to Billy Payne talk, and I was thinking it really would have been a shame if the world had been deprived of all that energy and the Olympics had gone someplace else. My granddaddy used to say that people like Billy Payne are the kind of folks who sell hospitalization to shut-ins. [*Laughter*] I believe he could talk an owl out of a tree. The more you think about that the funnier it will get. [*Laughter*]

I'm glad to see my good friend Andrew Young here. He was a great ambassador for you, recently, when he spoke at the annual President's prayer breakfast, the congressional prayer breakfast in Washington, DC. And I thank him for all he has done over the years, especially on the Olympics.

This is a great endeavor. I can't imagine that Herbert Hoover refused to open the Olympics. That's probably why he was a one-termer. All this time we've been reading in our history books it was because of the Depression; turned out it was the Olympics. [*Laughter*]

I don't think—Herbert Hoover didn't like athletics very much because he was the first President who got a lower salary than a baseball player. [*Laughter*] Now the lowest paid baseball players make five times what the President

makes, but back then the priorities were different. Babe Ruth was the first baseball player who ever made more than the President. And they asked him—they said, "It's the middle of the Depression. You're making more than the President of the United States. What do you have to say about that?" He said, "I ought to be. I'm having a better year." [*Laughter*]

You know, a lot of things happen here in Atlanta. I saw the other night on television Michael Jordan had his first buzzer-beater since coming back, you know, in Atlanta. You didn't like that, but it was nice for the rest of us. [*Laughter*] Georgia is going to the Final Four of the Women's NCAA. Playing Tennessee. [*Laughter*] We have a ticket here—don't you think one of us ought to be for Georgia? [*Laughter*]

I am delighted to be here. I came here mostly to say a simple thank-you to all of you. You have no idea, I think, what you are doing for the United States. This is a great endeavor, and it is an endeavor that is just as much about cooperation as it is about competition. It's about cooperation because of the teamwork required to put this endeavor together. It's about cooperation because a lot of these sports are team sports. It's about cooperation because the competition, even in the individual sports, requires a rigorous adherence to certain ethical rules of conduct which make the competition honorable and honored when over. That is true for the Olympics, it is true for the Paralympics, and therefore, in what you are doing, you are upholding the very best in this country.

The facilities are great. The technology is great. Don't you like hearing the Vice President talk about technology? You know, I thought I was a policy wonk until I had Al Gore as Vice President and Newt Gingrich as Speaker. It's amazing. [*Laughter*] Now I feel like the linesman at the tennis match. I just—out, in, let. [*Laughter*]

I told them the other day—you know, we're up there, fighting about the School Lunch Program and the food stamp program, and I found a technological fix for them. We should scrap the School Lunch Program and substitute E-mail stamps that would give you virtual food that everybody could download on the Internet. They're going to explain to me next week why that won't work, when I get back. [*Laughter*]

I want to say, too, that I appreciate the Olympic force. You're going to have 50,000 volunteers working on this, and then you're going to have—you've got 770,000 people in this Olympic force working in community service projects. That's an amazing thing. Nothing like that has ever been done, take my word for it, around anything like this before. And it probably would only happen in the United States. But again, it reinforces the fact that if you have enough spirit and enough vision and you're willing to cooperate, you can get just about anything done you want to do.

And if you ask me what I hope would come out of this, it would be that. This is a remarkable endeavor. There will be some winners and some losers. There will be some things that don't go right. There will be occasional accidents. As the Vice President said, we offer our deepest condolences to the family and friends of Jack Falls, who was killed in the accident, working on the Olympic stadium, and to those who were injured, David Oakes and Bruce Griffin. But we know that in the course of human endeavor, if people work together and they try to bring out the best in each other and they play by rules that are honorable and clear and widely respected, that there is nearly nothing that cannot be done.

I'll bet you anything when all this is said and done, people look back and they celebrate the Olympics, and then they'll celebrate the incredible physical facilities you'll leave behind, which will be used by generations of people after most of us are even gone here. But one of the most enduring legacies will be the idea that over three-quarters of a million people actually got together to try to use the Olympics as a way of organizing around how to lift people up who live here. This spirit of partnership is, frankly, one of the reasons that our administration awarded one of only six highly coveted empowerment zones to the City of Atlanta, because of what you represented here.

I remember when I was a kid, I really admired Jesse Owens, and I watched those old films of Jesse Owens running in Berlin after Hitler promulgated all of his theories of racial superiority. And at the time, there was some question about whether Jesse Owens would be able to go and run; the Nazis were going crazy in Germany. And Jesse Owens ran his way into the hearts of the world and the history books of the Olympics and the United States.

He said something that has stayed with me. He said, "A lifetime of training for just 10 seconds." But the truth is that it's not that. You may feel that. You may feel like you're spending three lifetimes in the next 479 days just for 17 days. [*Laughter*] But it isn't that. It will endure.

This is an interesting time for the United States, and it could not be a better time in our history for us to have the Olympics. And I'll tell you why. Our economic system has produced, and just in the last 2 years, over 6 million new jobs. Other countries all around the world are asking us to come and help them set up the mechanisms of a market economy in former Communist countries: How do you regulate the banks; how do you set up a stock market; how do you get things so that they will work honestly and fairly and well, and free people can earn their way? We find people all over the world asking us to send the FBI in to help them deal with the problems of crime once they stop being dictatorships and they open up freedom, because we know that freedom can always be abused—always asking for America to do that. And when I go to these meetings, they say, "Well, gosh, you guys seem to be doing well. You've got your economy going and your deficit's down and things seem to be headed in the right direction." And yet, here at home, because there's so many changes going on, a lot of Americans still don't feel secure about their future.

In a global economy, the things that lift a lot of people in Atlanta up—make for the record number of new business starts we had in 1993 and the record number of people, hardworking Americans, becoming very wealthy—those same forces scare other people, with companies being downsized and all these changes happening.

And we need the Olympics in the United States—not just in Atlanta, not just in Georgia, not just in the New South that you are leading into the future—the United States needs the Olympics to remind us that every time we work together, we keep our eye on the future, we have a set of honorable rules by which we play, and we try to lift each other up, we do quite well. You will stun the world by your performance here. You will do that.

In doing that, and in working with all the people who are going to be doing all these volunteer projects, you have the capacity to remind America that just because the future is uncertain and rapidly changing, we do not need to be insecure. All we need to do is to do what we have always done when the chips were down and the stakes were high.

We are doing, as a country, better than virtually any other place in dealing with the challenges of the modern world, but we are not immune to those challenges, those problems, those anxieties. Now we're either going to hunker down or take a deep breath, throw our shoulders back, and walk right through them into the future. That is what you must do here. And when you do it, I'll make you a prediction: It will have an enormous positive impact on what Americans all over this country, from Alaska to southern Florida, from Maine to southern California, will believe we can do. And goodness knows we need it. And we're all going to do our best to make the most of it.

So thank you. Good luck, and Godspeed.

[*At this point, an ACOG representative and Mayor Bill Campbell of Atlanta presented commemorative bricks to the President and the Vice President.*]

The President. You have no idea how much this means to us—[*laughter*]—especially the way they were presented. We spend most of our time in Washington dodging these. [*Laughter*]

Thank you very much.

NOTE: The President spoke at approximately 5:40 p.m. in the Inforum Building. In his remarks, he referred to William Porter (Billy) Payne, chief executive officer, and Andrew Young, cochair, Atlanta Committee for the Olympic Games; G. Andrew Fleming, chief executive officer, Atlanta Paralympic Organizing Committee; and LeRoy T. Walker, president, U.S. Olympic Committee.

Remarks at Session I of the Southern Regional Economic Conference in Atlanta
March 29, 1995

Thank you very much. Thank you, Secretary Brown, for that introduction, and thank you for the magnificent job you have done as Secretary of Commerce, promoting the interest of American businesses and American workers throughout the United States and all across the world. As far as I know, there is no precedent for the efforts that you have made or the results you have achieved. President Chace, thank you for your remarks this morning, and thank you for hosting us. Governor Miller, as always, thank you for bringing us back to Atlanta and to Georgia. Thank you for giving me such a nice place to sleep last night.

You heard Secretary Brown talk about this economic conference in the context of the one we did 2 years ago in Little Rock. Let me say that that conference, I believe, was very successful and did play a major role in helping us to finalize the economic strategy that we have pursued for the last 2 years.

We wanted to come back now to the country and do some regional economic conferences for some reasons I will explain in a moment. We thought we should begin in the South and we should begin here in Atlanta. This city and this university are remarkable examples of where we ought to be going as a people. This is a place of opportunity and responsibility where people are working together. And I can say, I think, for all Americans, we can hardly wait for another

479 days to pass so the Olympics will begin here.

As the industrial age gives way to the information age and all of our economies are linked as never before, the South has really done a remarkable job of tapping into all the opportunities that are presented. Atlanta has become a magnet for worldwide corporate headquarters. Miami has become a financial center for all of the Caribbean and Latin America. South Carolina and Tennessee have become new homes for manufacturing operations from all around the world. Charlotte has become a new national home for banking. And obviously, three letters, CNN, prove that this part of our country is the center of a global information network.

This conference, as I said, is designed to be the first of several regional conferences to follow up on what has happened in the last 2 years. The remarkable group of people that came to Little Rock in 1992, some of whom are here today and are participating in this second round of conferences, really gave us a lot of ideas to take to Washington that were consistent with the things I had advocated in my campaign but in some ways went beyond them.

The strategy that we brought to Washington was fairly straightforward. We wanted to reverse the trickle-down economics and reverse the idea that the Government had no affirmative responsibility to be a partner in growing the economy, increasing the number of entrepreneurs, expanding the middle class, and shrinking the under class.

We did that with a strategy that was designed to reduce the deficit, expand trade, increase our investment in the education and training of our people in the technologies of the future, to help the areas that were left behind or that were subject to sweeping changes because of defense downsizing, for example, and to reform the Government, to make it cost less and do better.

The results, I think, are clear: We've had $600 billion in deficit reduction. We have already cut or eliminated 300 programs with 400 more on the way for our new budget. The Federal Government is at its smallest size in a long time. We have already reduced it by 100,000, and for the budget already adopted, over a 6-year period it will go down by 272,000, which will make it the smallest it's been since President Kennedy was in office.

Our economic plan changed the tax structure in ways that made it, I think, more fair and

more conducive for economic growth. While income taxes were raised on corporations with incomes of over $10 million and 1½ percent of our people, working families with modest incomes received a significant tax cut. This year the average family of four with an income of $25,000 a year or less will pay about $1,000 less in income taxes. That's 6 million families in the Southern States alone.

Ninety percent of the small businesses, the engine of economic growth, were made eligible for tax cuts by increasing the expensing provisions by 70 percent. We created empowerment zones and enterprise communities to give incentives for people to invest in areas that had been left behind. Four of the nine major empowerment zones, which got big tax incentives for private enterprise to invest in them, are located in the southern region, including Atlanta, the Kentucky Highlands, the Mississippi Delta, and the Rio Grande Valley of Texas.

Last year there were twice as many loans to small businesses in the SBA under the then leadership of Erskine Bowles from North Carolina and now under the leadership of Phil Lader from South Carolina. There were twice as many loans in the South from the SBA than in any succeeding year ever, including the year before I took office. That includes over 11,000 businesses in loans worth over $2 billion.

So that strategy was our economic strategy. It went with our strategy to expand trade: NAFTA, GATT, the Asian-Pacific region, the Summit of the Americas in Miami, the national export strategy that Secretary Brown has worked so hard on to sell more of our products and services around the world.

We increased investment in education, from Head Start to making more college loans available to people. And we certainly began not only to shrink the size of Government but to change the nature of Government, to let States have more say over welfare reform and health care reform, to move toward what we have now done in this year, reducing the unfunded mandates on State and local governments, and to change the nature of regulation under the Vice President's reinventing Government effort.

We have, for example, just announced that small businesses will be allowed, when they're first fined, not to pay the fine but instead to put the fine into correcting whatever the problem is with a Government agency; that Government agencies will be given the authority not even to impose a fine in the first instance, to waive it, on small businesses. The Environmental Protection Agency is reducing the paperwork burden by 25 percent. It will save 20 million hours of work for American citizens in the private sector this year.

So these are the things that we have worked so hard to do. What have been the results? Well, you heard them already, but I'd like to say again. We've had over 6 million new jobs in this economy, and 1993 was the best year in American history for small businesses and start-ups. The combined rate of unemployment and inflation is at a 25-year low. We have the African-American unemployment rate in the United States below 10 percent for the first time in 20 years. Unemployment in the South has dropped even more than in the country as a whole. The South has 30 percent of the population but has generated 40 percent of the new jobs that have come into this economy in the last 2 years.

Now, that is the good news. Why are we having this economic conference? Because the news is not all good and because we are under a great responsibility to try to keep this economic recovery going of high growth and low inflation.

Let me talk first about the news that's not all good. You may wonder with these numbers, which are better than we've had in decades, why poll after poll after poll says that people think the country is not going in the right direction. One reason is that over half the American people in spite of this recovery, are working longer workweeks for the same or lower wages than they were making 15 years ago. This is a new phenomenon in the global economy, that wages are stagnant.

The other thing is that nearly everybody knows someone who's been part of a restructuring, a downsizing, some market change in a larger economic unit, which means that even when times are good, people think things are changing so fast that their level of security, their sense of stability, of rootedness, of reward for work is more fragile than it has been in the past.

It's funny, you know, this economic strategy that I've tried to pursue basically grew out of my experience as a southern Governor, when the real southern strategy of the seventies and eighties in the South was better education, more jobs, and a closer partnership between the public and private sectors and between people of all races and backgrounds. That's the strategy, the real southern strategy that lifted the South from the sixties forward. And it's ironic that in the country now with this problem of wage stagnation and the splitting apart of the middle class, the challenge we have, in a funny way, is a lot like the challenge that I faced when I first became a Governor.

You know, most of us who were born in the South remember when nearly everybody was poor. Zell Miller gave that magnificent speech at the Democratic Convention about living in the house his mother built herself. When I was born in Arkansas, the per capita income of my State was 56 percent of the national average. And most of us who are natives to this region thought that a major part of our life's mission would be getting the American dream to all the people who lived in our region, without regard to their race or condition of birth.

Now, the challenge for America is whether or not, even in the midst of all our economic triumphs and when we are the world's only military superpower, we can preserve the American dream for all of our people. Can we avoid this wage stagnation? Can we avoid this increasing inequality in the United States that is gripping every advanced economy in the world as we become more globalized, as we become more dependent on technologies, as things change faster and education determines income more than ever before? That is the great challenge.

And that's why we are working now in Washington to continue what we've been doing for the last 2 years but also to focus on things like the middle class bill of rights, the education tax deduction, more training for workers who are unemployed or underemployed, raising the minimum wage, working on welfare reform, things we think will raise incomes and bring people together again.

So let me close with this. I hope that all of you think that this will be a day well spent. From my point of view, I think we should be focused intensely on three questions. One is: Even though all 50 States are growing now—it's the first time in a long time that's happened—what are the differences in the economies of the various States in this region, in this region, and the rest of the country? Are there specific things that ought to be done in the southern region or within the Southern States that are different from what we might be doing as a whole? Question one.

Question two: What is the proper role of the National Government in working with you to build this economy and to make it better? That's the great debate in Washington we're having today. It used to be the prevailing theory was there was a big-Government solution for every big problem. Now, the prevailing theory is the Government would mess up a one-car parade, and if it didn't exist, America wouldn't have any problems. Both theories are wrong and are contradicted by all experience everywhere in the world. Not Japan, not Germany, or any country ever became a great industrial power without trying to develop the capacities of the people and having a coordinated economic strategy and having a framework within which markets could succeed. So, what should we be doing? What should we be doing? What have we done that's right? What have we done that's wrong? What should we stop doing? What should we start doing? That's the second question.

The third great question is the one that I mentioned earlier, and it's the national question. And it is at the core of what we will have to be concerned about, I predict to you, for decades: How do you preserve the American idea that if you work hard and play by the rules, you can do better; that we will always be able to grow the middle class and shrink the under class and spark an unprecedented number of entrepreneurs? How do you preserve that American idea in the global economy? That is the great challenge of this era.

When this day is over, if we honestly address those three questions—are there still differences about the South or within the South that we need to be sensitive to; what's the role of the Federal Government; what can we do to raise incomes and increase stability for people who are working hard and playing by the rules— then I think you will believe your day was well spent.

In 1986, I was the chairman of the Southern Growth Policies Board, and I asked the former Governor of Mississippi, Bill Winter, to be the chairman of our project on the future of the South. Every 6 years, there's a report on the future of the South. The Secretary of Education, Dick Riley, issued one in 1980. We've been at this a long time. We called our report in 1986, "Halfway Home and A Long Way To Go," which captured the fact that the South was moving rapidly compared to the rest of the country but wasn't there yet. Now we're in one of the two Southern States that has a per capita income above the national average. We know the South is growing more rapidly than the rest of the country and moving quickly. But there are still differences, and there are profound challenges facing the United States.

So I would say to you, we're more than half-way home. The southern strategy has found its finest expression, perhaps, here in Georgia and with the administration of this Governor. I noticed—one thing I have to brag on him for— these HOPE scholarships so that any young person in Georgia who has a certain grade-point average gets a full tuition scholarship for 4 years to any institution in the State, public institution in the State—anybody. That's the kind of strategy and the kind of programs that we ought to be supporting everywhere in the United States.

So we've done very well, but these three great questions still have to be asked and answered. We're going to ask these questions all across the country, but I think we did the right thing to start here.

Let me close with this. In 2 weeks, on April 12th, we will honor the 50th anniversary of President Roosevelt's death in Warm Springs, Georgia, about 60 miles from here. On the day he died, Roosevelt was drafting a speech for Thomas Jefferson's birthday, a speech he obviously never got to deliver. The last words written in his own hands were these: "The only limit to our realization of tomorrow will be our doubts of today. Let us move forward with strong and active purpose."

One final problem we have are the doubts the American people have about today. If you look at what has been achieved in this State, in this region in the last 10 years, there is a lot more room for hope than for doubt.

Thank you very much.

Now, to provide an economic overview, I would like to call on the Secretary of the Treasury, Bob Rubin. As most of you know, he was, until he became the Secretary of the Treasury, succeeding Lloyd Bentsen, he was the President's National Economic Adviser and the head of the National Economic Council, a position now occupied by Laura Tyson, who was the Chairman of the Council of Economic Advisers.

One of the important things we did in our economic strategy, which has received virtually no attention but which I predict historians will credit for a long time to come, was to establish a National Economic Council, like the National Security Council, that met on a regular basis, included all the various actors in the Federal Government, and forced us to coordinate our economic policy in ways that had never been done before. It is obvious that a big part of our national security in a global economy depends upon our national economic strength.

I am convinced that that institution now will endure through future Presidencies of both parties and unforeseen developments. And I think one of the reasons it will endure is because Bob Rubin, as the first person to head the Economic Council, did such a good job in bringing people together and making it work. So I'd like to call on Secretary Rubin for a brief overview of the economy as we see it today.

Mr. Secretary.

NOTE: The President spoke at approximately 9 a.m. in the Cannon Chapel Building at Emory University. In his remarks, he referred to William M. Chace, president, Emory University, and Gov. Zell Miller of Georgia.

Remarks at the Closing Session of the Southern Regional Economic Conference in Atlanta
March 29, 1995

Let me close by once again thanking Emory University and its leadership for letting us be here. And thank all of you for giving us a day of your lives, which I will say again, I hope you think it has been well spent. I have been deeply moved by the stories I have heard. I have actually quite a lot more specific and clear sense than I did when the day started about the similarities and the differences of the southern economy as compared with the rest of the country and the differences within the States, which are still not insignificant.

I have a clearer idea of what all of you think, based on your personal experience, is the appropriate role of the Federal Government. And again I will say, it strikes me as not on the extreme that there is a Government solution for most problems or the extreme that it would be better if the Government went away and wasn't around anymore, but at somewhere not in the middle but way beyond that, much more sophisticated.

And I leave this meeting feeling more hopeful, as I always do when I get a chance to talk to the American people, but certainly to be here in a kind of a homecoming setting for me; there's a lot of you I've worked with for more than 10 years.

But I would say this, in view of what both Bill Winter and what Billy Payne said. You know, all of us have a scale inside us, I think, that's sort of a psychological scale about the way we look at the world, and some days there seems to be a little more weight on the positive, hopeful side of the scale, and some days somebody takes some of the weight off and it kind of gets off on the other edge. And we all battle it within ourselves, within our families, within our communities, within our work organizations. And one thing I said this morning I want you to remember: We cannot go on where we have a disconnect between our public conversation, which is so often oriented towards what divides us and how to get us to resent one another, and our public behavior, that is, the things we do together, which is what works—is what Billy said—is when we play by the rules, we work hard, we try to bring out the best in everybody, and we recognize we don't have a person to waste.

The South learned that lesson, I think, better than any other part of the country because of the horrible price we paid for our past. And I think that's why the economy is growing more rapidly than any other part of the country, why Atlanta is the perfect place to host the Olympics, and why we have a chance to see this region lead our country into a very bright 21st century. But we've got a lot of work to do, and I feel today that all of us, and I know the President, at least, has more energy for the tasks ahead and a better idea about how to approach them, thanks to you.

I thank you very much.

NOTE: The President spoke at approximately 5 p.m. in the Cannon Chapel Building at Emory University. In his remarks, he referred to William F. Winter, Chair, Advisory Commission on Inter-governmental Relations, and William Porter (Billy) Payne, chief executive officer, Atlanta Committee for the Olympic Games.

Remarks to Students at Emory University in Atlanta
March 29, 1995

The President. Thank you very much. Thank you, Laura Sawyer, for your warm and generous introduction. Thank you, President Chace, for what you said in reminding me of our generation's obligations to the students here present by recalling that day, now almost 32 years ago, when I met President Kennedy.

I have very much enjoyed this day at Emory. I thank the university and all responsible for making it possible for us to hold here the first of our conferences on the state of the American economy and where we go from here. I wish all of you could have been there today to hear the people who came to tell their stories, stories of struggle and triumph, stories, many of them against all the odds, what they had done to make their way in the economy of the 1990's and how they were looking forward to the next century.

I just have one question about this before I get too serious. Where is Dooley? I was told if he showed up, you all would get up and leave. [*Laughter*] I hope he waits until the end if that's true.

Let me say that I ran for the office of President because I was concerned about the direction of our country and the future of our children, basically because I believe the obligation of every generation of Americans is to preserve and nourish and deepen the American idea, the idea that if you work hard and play by the rules you can make the most of your God-given potential and live the life of your dreams and that you can do it without holding anyone else down, and indeed, the more people from all walks of life and all races and regions who are lifted up, the better off we'll all be. That is the American idea.

When I met John Kennedy and when I went off to college—I was the first in my generation to go to college. I was the son of fairly poor people in the South when I was born in Arkan-

sas right at the end of World War II. The per capita income of our entire State was only 56 percent of the national average. And for young people who were growing up in the South when I was about your age, the great question was whether we could become part of the great American mainstream, whether we could overcome our legacy of abject poverty and our legacy of racial discrimination to come together and learn and grow.

That is not at issue anymore. Now, two Southern States, Georgia and Virginia, have surpassed the national average in per capita income. Atlanta is the home to more international companies than any other city in the United States. You're doing a lot of things in the southern region that are the envy of the rest of the world. Thirty percent of America's people live in the South, but 40 percent of the new jobs created just since I've been President have been created in this region.

So the issue is not what it was a generation ago. There is a different issue today, which is whether we can keep the American dream alive for all our people in a global economy in the information age, which splits people apart based on their level of education and their skills, and at a time when the differences in our country and the differences throughout the world in race, religion, and other areas both serve as ways to unite us and to divide us. That is the great question of this time.

Now, when I became President, I wanted first to get the economy moving again, to give people some economic hope. And we had a distinct strategy: reduce the deficit, expand trade, increase investment in education and technology, reform Government, give lower income families a tax break so nobody would ever be punished for work instead of welfare, encourage small businesses and new businesses, reduce regulation and give the States more authority to experiment in tough areas like welfare reform and health care reform. That was our agenda.

After 2 years, we have a reduction in the deficit of $600 billion. This is the first time since the mid-1960's when your Government is running at least an operating surplus; that is, if it were not for interest on the debt accumulated before we came here, we would have a budget surplus today, so at least our operations do not exceed our revenues.

We have expanded trade by more than at any time in a generation. We have dramatically reformed the Government, already 100,000 fewer people working for the Federal Government if no new changes are made by the new Congress, which is unlikely. But if there were no changes made, the Government would be reduced in size over a 5½-year period by 270,000 people, to its smallest size since I went to Washington when John Kennedy was President.

And we have given vast new authority to the States to experiment in important areas. We have reduced regulation. We are trying to move forward. And perhaps most important of all, we have cut spending while increasing our investment in education, from expanding Head Start to apprenticeships for young people who don't go to college, to the Goals 2000 program to help our schools meet tough national standards with grassroots reforms, to expansion of the student loan program in ways that make our student loans now less costly with better repayment terms.

Now, these are important changes. The results are pretty clear. In the last 2 years, we've had 6.1 million new jobs. We have the lowest combined rate of unemployment and inflation this country has had in 25 years. We had, in 1993, the largest number of new business incorporations in the history of the United States. In 1994, the unemployment rate in America for African-Americans dropped below 10 percent for the first time in 20 years. The results speak for themselves.

I must say, since I'm trying to spark an honest and civil bipartisan discussion of this, I was honored to see on the front page of your newspaper today one of your most distinguished alumnuses, the Speaker of the House, acknowledges that the economic program has brought some good results to the United States of America, because it has. It was the right thing to do, and it is moving the country forward.

Now, so I ask you, if that's true and all that has happened, well, why isn't everybody happy? And why do they keep voting to change the way the Government's going if the policies are working? Well, I think there are a number of reasons, but let me offer a few, because they will affect your lives as Americans.

In the first place, the global economy and all the pressures of the global economy and the information revolution and all the dramatic changes it brings means that for the first time, even though we are having more jobs coming into this economy, wages are stagnant for most Americans. Half of the American people are working longer work weeks for the same or lower wages than they were making 15 years ago. And that is unheard of in our history.

In addition to that, there's more inequality among the middle class. That's why I say over and over again, my mission is to expand the middle class and to shrink the under class, to give poor people a chance to work their way into a good life. But today, the American middle class is splitting apart based on whether people have the education and training and skills necessary to compete in the global economy for a good job that pays a good wage with a good future.

The third thing that's happened is that—and a lot of your parents have probably been affected by this or at least work in companies that are affected by it—there is more instability in the work force today even when there is more prosperity: downsizing in government, downsizing in big companies, reorganizations that are constant, so that people are worried about whether they're going to have their job even when we have more jobs. And when people do lose their jobs, they tend to be unemployed for longer periods of times, and they tend to get a new job, not their old job back. All this is new in your lifetime.

This will be the pattern you will face, but if you described all this to somebody 10 years ago, they'd say it couldn't happen; there's no way, you cannot create 6 million jobs, drive down the unemployment rate, explode the economy, and not have wages go up. You can't do it. It's impossible. Well, it happened.

So what is our job economically? Our job is to lift the incomes and the sights and the aspirations of the American people. How are we going to do it? You have to get more high-wage jobs into this country, more trade, more focus on technology. You have to make sure our people can fill high-wage jobs. We have to educate everyone better, everyone, not just the college students, everyone. And thirdly, we have to have the right kind of Government. The great debate going on in Washington today is about what the proper role of our National Government is.

The old view was that there was a big-Government solution to every big problem and that people who were in need should be helped. The new rage in Washington is that the Government is the source of all the problems and we would have no social problems, no economic problems, no problems at all if we had no Government. If the Government went away, except for national defense, everything would be peachy keen. [*Laughter*] Now, the whole theory is that every problem—all the social problems we've got, from teen pregnancy to welfare dependency to the breakdown of life in our cities, was all because we had too much Government trying to help people.

Now, I have a different view from both those views. I don't think either one of those views is right. My experience as a Governor, my observation of other countries that are doing well, plain common sense, and the stories we heard today indicate that we need a limited but effective Government that costs less but does what it's supposed to do. And here's what I think it's supposed to do.

I believe the National Government is still essential in creating opportunity even while we're shrinking bureaucracy, creating opportunity by making sure we've got a level playing field, and creating opportunity by making sure that people can make the most of their own lives. We've got to empower people. You can't really help people past a certain point except to put food on their table and to get them through the tough times. But you can empower people, through education and technology, to make more of their own lives. That's what we have to do.

And the third thing we can do is, even in a very dynamic economy, in a dynamic society, we can enhance security in a legitimate way, without in any way undermining opportunity. We enhance security abroad when we make an agreement with the Russians so that, for the first time since nuclear weapons were invented, there are no nuclear weapons pointed at the people of the United States. That enhances our

security. But if we make progress toward peace in the Middle East, we are enhancing our own security because of the volatile impact of that area on the whole rest of the world.

But there are things we can do here at home that enhance our security as well. The family and medical leave law, which allows people to take a little time off when a baby is born or a parent is sick without losing their job, that enhances our security because it makes our families stronger while we keep our jobs. The crime bill, which puts more police officers on our street and gives our local communities the flexibility in choosing prevention programs that keep young people out of crime and off drugs, those things enhance our security. If we didn't have 2 million highly dysfunctional drug abusers in this country, the crime rate for violent crime would be about half what it is today. So it enhances our security when we have a safer society with lower crime rates. And that's—part of that role is a national responsibility. That's what I have tried to do.

Now, that leads us—and I want you to watch this debate unfold in Washington, and you've got to decide where you fit. And your old party label may not give you an answer to the present problems that we face, because Government can't fix it all, and Government cannot walk away from it all. And there are a lot of hard questions that have to be resolved.

But for example, my view is, there's a right and a wrong way to cut spending. I do think that the Agriculture Department had to be cut, but my view was not to reduce the School Lunch Program but close 1,200 offices, because we didn't need that many when we had fewer farmers and fewer problems.

I agree that we should have reduced expenditures in the Housing and Urban Development Department, but what we did was to get rid of a whole layer of regional offices and to consolidate a lot of those various programs that had been kind of encrusted with bureaucracy over the years. We didn't want to cut a program for homeless veterans or make it more difficult for poor elderly people to have a roof over their head. There is a difference in how you cut spending. And these are distinctions that have to be made.

Or in the area of education, we offered a way to cut the deficit and increase educational opportunities. I had student loans when I went to school, and I'm not ashamed of it. I'm proud of it. I'm grateful that I was able to get it from the previous generation. And when I got out of college, I paid them off. And I think when you get out of college, if you've got one, you ought to pay it off—[*laughter*]—because that's the way we're going to preserve it for the next generation.

So we have reduced student loan defaults. They no longer cost the taxpayers $2.8 billion a year. The cost is down to $1 billion a year. We've reduced defaults by nearly two-thirds. We're doing a better job of collecting. Now that's a lot better than getting rid of the interest subsidy and raising the cost of student loans. That is better. That is a better way to do that.

We found there were so many incentives in the old student loan program toward bureaucracy and paperwork and wasting money because basically you'd go to a bank and get the student loan. It was a 90-percent guarantee. So if you default on the loan, does the bank have an incentive to sue? No, because the Government will give you 90 percent and 10 percent will be at least what the lawyers would cost.

So we went into this direct loan program and we said, "You can have these loans at a lower interest rate with better repayment terms when you get out of college. If you've got a big loan burden, you can pay it off as a percentage of your income." And now about, oh, 40 percent of our universities have already enrolled. We just had people there from the University of Florida today, a man and his wife in medical school saying they would owe $140,000 between them. And when they go into residency, if they had to start paying off their student loan under the old system, it would take one-half of their disposable incomes. But because of the new program, we cut the cost, improved the repayment terms, and guess what? It saves the taxpayers $10 billion over 6 years. So if we can give people more loans at less hassle and save $10 billion, why would we instead say, no, let's keep the old system and save the $10 billion by adding to the cost of going to college? Our way is better, because it's pro-education, and it makes sense, and it will take us into the future.

I wish I had longer to listen to you and we could ask questions. I'd like to stay here 3 or 4 hours, but I've got to go to Florida. But I want you to think about this. Think about this debate. Every time you see an issue being debated in Washington, ask yourselves two questions: How can I cut through all the political

rhetoric to figure out how this is going to affect me and my friends and my generation and the future of this country and the children I hope to have? Don't think about it in political terms. Think about it in terms of how it's going to affect your life and the future you want for yourselves and your children.

And the second thing you ought to say is, now, what do I believe my country should be doing about this? Because we are going through this huge period of——

[*At this point, there was a disturbance in the audience.*]

What did they say? Prisons are not shelters? I agree with that. Why are you shouting at me? Sit down. I heard you. We heard you. We heard you. We heard you. Sit down. We heard you. [*Laughter*]

I like those guys. They believed in their free speech and mine as well. I appreciate that. Thank you very much.

Audience member. Why 100,000 more cops instead of more shelters?

The President. I'll tell you why we need 100,000 more police.

Now, wait a minute, let's don't start a flood here. Free speech—we'll listen. [*Laughter*] I'll tell you why; I'll tell you why we need 100,000 more police. Because the violent crime rate in America has tripled. And this is a big fight I'm in with the Congress. They just want a block grant. They want to cut the amount of money to the crime bill, block-grant it to the cities and States, and say, basically, spend it however you please. I say no, we've got to have 100,000 more police. Here's why. You're entitled to an answer to that.

The violent crime rate has tripled in the last 30 years. The number of police officers has increased by 10 percent. In every major city where more police officers have been trained not simply to catch criminals but to prevent crime, to work with friends and neighbors and help kids on the street, the crime rate has gone down. One of the little-known good things that is happening in America today is that in many, many, many places, the crime rate is going down because of community policing.

So I say we ought to have a 20 percent increase in the number of police forces, not only to catch criminals but to prevent crime from occurring. And a 30 percent overall increase in police is still not as much as a 300 percent increase in violent crime. I think we made the right decision on that. That's exactly the kind of debate that we ought to be having.

But I also believe—I also believe we have to do more for shelter. I also believe we have to do more for shelter. Our administration—you look at the record of Secretary Cisneros and HUD. We have tried our best to increase that. But none of this is answering the big questions. And you have to answer that. I want you, every one of you, without regard to where you're from, what your family's income is, what your race is, I want every one of you to believe that your tomorrows will be whatever you want them to be and whatever you're willing to work hard to make them to be.

I want you to be positively ecstatic at the prospect of bringing your own children into the world and this country and thinking about the 21st century being the most peaceful and prosperous and exciting time the world has ever known. That's what I want. And that is all that matters, in the end, is whether we do our part.

When I was your age, I had a professor of Western civilization who told me that the United States represented the finest expression of our civilization because it had embodied the two most important ideas: first, that the future can be better than the present, and second, that every single one of us has a personal, moral obligation to make it so. That is what I am trying to do in Washington. We're having a big debate about what the role of the National Government is. I want you to answer the debate by determining what is best for you and your future and the other people in this country.

This country's in better shape than it was 2 years ago. It's going to be in better shape 2 years from now if I have anything to say about it, but you will have more to say about it than anybody else. Stand up for education, and stand up for the future.

Thank you, and God bless you.

NOTE: The President spoke at 5:34 p.m. in the Woodruff Physical Education Center. In his remarks, he referred to Laura Sawyer, student council president.

Statement on Proposed Legislation To Establish a District of Columbia Financial Authority
March 29, 1995

I am pleased that Congressman Davis introduced legislation today to establish a financial oversight authority for the District of Columbia. My administration worked closely with the Congress in drafting the bill, and I hope we can continue the bipartisanship already at work to help the District return to fiscal health.

The financial crisis in the District is serious and demands immediate attention. Although other cities have suffered similar problems, Washington, DC, plays a uniquely important role in the Nation's life. It is the Nation's Capital and is important not just to the people who live there but to all citizens of the United States.

I care deeply about the District and its residents. They deserve a government that delivers municipal services efficiently and effectively.

My administration stands ready to work with Congress to determine what help is appropriate. At my direction, my Budget Director, Alice Rivlin, a DC resident for 38 years, is heading a senior level, interagency working group to monitor the District's problems and assist DC in meeting its responsibilities.

Statement on Senator Howell T. Heflin's Decision Not To Seek Reelection
March 29, 1995

I was sorry to learn of Senator Heflin's decision not to run for reelection. His strong voice, his solid belief in right and wrong and his sense of humor have helped the Nation confront some of our toughest issues head on, while his efforts in areas of education and race relations have changed the course of the country. Although we will miss his leadership here in Washington, I wish him all the best in Tuscumbia.

Statement on Senate Action To Reject a Regulatory Moratorium
March 29, 1995

I am deeply committed to regulatory reform that cuts redtape without undercutting the health and safety of the American people. Giving the Congress 45 days to consider regulations before they take effect would let lawmakers focus on the specifics of these issues and address real problems as they come up, without delaying necessary public protections. This approach, not the blunt instrument of a moratorium, is the right way to reform regulation. It's common sense.

Remarks to the Community in Tallahassee, Florida
March 29, 1995

Thank you, ladies and gentlemen. It's about to rain on us, but I won't melt. And I'm glad to be back in Florida and glad to be in Tallahassee, and I thank you.

I want to thank Governor Chiles and Lieutenant Governor McKay and your County Commissioner Malloy and, of course, your fine mayor, all of them for meeting me, and along with my EPA Director, Florida's own Carol Browner. I'm glad to have her back here.

Ladies and gentlemen, I am glad to be back in Florida, a State that embodies what I am trying to get done all across the country, a State that is committed to opportunity, committed to building strength out of diversity, and committed to our future. That's what America needs everywhere.

I wish you could have been with me in Atlanta today. We had the first of a number of regional economic conferences. I had all kinds of people talking about what's going on in the South and how we're going to get this country into the next century with the American dream alive, with opportunity and education and hope for every single citizen of this country. That's what I believe in.

I'm sure it has not escaped you that we're having a mild debate in Washington, DC, these days about what our Government ought to be doing. Now, on the one side there's people who believe that everything that's been done in the last 25 years is fine and that there's a big-Government solution for every big problem. I disagree with that.

But now all the rage in Washington is that everything the Government did was wrong and Government is the source of all of our problems and if Government would go away, everything would be like flowers blooming in the desert. I disagree with that, too.

Well, I believe, like Lawton Chiles believes, that we need a Government that is limited but effective, that is smaller, that regulates less, but that is committed to the following things: creating opportunity, empowering people through education to make the most of their own lives, and finally, enhancing the security of the American people, not only abroad as we have but also at home in our streets and in our schools and in our families. That is what we need a Government for.

And we have made a good beginning. We have reduced the deficit. We have expanded trade. We have 6 million more jobs in this country. We have the lowest combined rates of unemployment and inflation in 25 years. And I know that you know that Florida has grown more rapidly than the rest of the country. Since I became President, the unemployment rate in this State has dropped almost 3 percent. Governor Chiles whispered in my ear, said it's the lowest in 13 years, and I appreciate that.

Almost a million families in this State got an income tax cut because they're working hard for modest wages and we don't believe anybody who works full-time with a child in the house should be in poverty. We want people to leave welfare and go to work, and they shouldn't be taxed if they're working.

We have worked hard to deal with the problems of this State up and down, to maintain a strong military and a military presence in northern Florida and throughout the State. We've worked hard to make Florida a showcase of the future with the Summit of the Americas conference we had down in Miami in December.

And I know that apparently a few hours ago it leaked out that the Defense Department has just decided to move the command of the Southern Command for Central and South America away from Panama, as we're required to do under the Panama Canal Treaty, to Florida, to Dade County.

I want you to know that the Central Command, which as I said, covers all of Central and South America—I want you to know how important this is. They are working to promote democracy throughout our hemisphere, to promote cooperation with these countries, to help to defend the Panama Canal, and most important of all now, to help to protect the American people and the people of those countries from the scourge of drugs and the illegal thugs that purvey them all across our part of the world. And now the center of that effort will be in your State.

Sometimes I ask myself, well, if things are going this well, why aren't we all happy? And there's good reason. There is a good reason, because for the first time in our history, the global economy with all of its competition and the rise in technology with all of its ability to have fewer people do more work means that we have created 6 million jobs but our incomes aren't going up yet. This has never happened before, where half the American people are working longer without a raise, where there is more inequality in the middle class, with incomes splitting apart and uncertainty.

So I say to you, we've had 2 years to generate more jobs and get the economy going again. Now we've got to concentrate on growing the middle class and shrinking the under class and getting the incomes of the American people up again so they can look forward with confidence to the future.

Audience members. Four more years!

The President. Now—thank you. But let's talk about 4 more days for a minute. [*Laughter*]

Let me ask you this, we all know that we need a smaller and less bureaucratic Government. Lawton Chiles has got pictures in the paper all over America, being hoisted up to get rid of all those regulations. But there is a right way and a wrong way to do it.

I am proud of the fact that Carol Browner is getting rid of 25 percent of the paperwork of the EPA to save 20 million hours for the American people every year. I'm proud of that. I'm proud of the fact that a small business person in Florida can go to the SBA for a loan; instead of having to fill out a form an inch thick, it's just a page long, because we got rid of bureaucracy. I'm proud of the fact that we threw 10,000 regulations away in the Federal personnel manual. But I think you still want us to have clean water, clean air, a safe workplace, and a safe country.

If we're going to raise incomes, folks, we need a commitment to do things that will raise incomes, more good jobs. If we're going to give tax breaks, which I favor, let's give them to middle class people to educate their children so that that will lift incomes. Let's raise the minimum wage. It hasn't been raised in years, and it will help people's incomes. Let's reform welfare so that people go to work and raise their children and people who owe child support have to pay that child support to take care of their children.

And let's get rid of wasteful Government, but let's don't cut off our nose to spite our face. When we wanted to cut money out of the Department of Agriculture, we closed 1,200 offices; we did not cut the School Lunch Program.

When we wanted to cut money out of our efforts on housing, we got rid of all the regional HUD offices and consolidated these old bureaucratic programs. We didn't try to cut a program for homeless veterans. There's a right way and a wrong way to do this.

And here, with all this fine music that's been provided to us by the band and the choir from—what? From Florida A&M and Florida State, right? The last thing we need to do is to cut the college loan program and make it more expensive to go to college.

So I say to you, you stay with us. You engage in this great debate. Yes, we'll bring the size of the Government down. Yes, we'll reduce the burden of regulation. But let's remember, we've got to keep our people first. We've got to keep our eye on the future. We've got to invest in education. We've got to grow the economy. We've got to keep the American dream alive.

I want every young person, every young person here tonight, to be able to look to a future where you can do anything that your dreams and your efforts will permit you to do. I want every one of you young people to look forward with the same anticipation that all of us up here had in having your own children and raising your own families. I want you to believe in the promise of America. Let us commit to that and make sure it's real and alive here in Florida.

Thank you, and God bless you all.

NOTE: The President spoke at 7:30 p.m. at Tallahassee Regional Airport. In his remarks, he referred to Gov. Lawton Chiles and Lt. Gov. Buddy McKay of Florida; Rudy Malloy, Leon County commissioner; and Mayor Scott Maddox of Tallahassee.

Remarks to the Florida State Legislature in Tallahassee
March 30, 1995

Thank you very much. [Applause] I may stay all day, but not here behind the podium. [Laughter]

Mr. Speaker, thank you, and Mr. President, thank you. Mr. Speaker Pro Tem, Governor Chiles, Lieutenant Governor McKay, distinguished State officials and members of the Cabinet, members of the Supreme Court, members of the Florida Legislature, ladies and gentlemen: I am very pleased to be here. I've had a wonderful, brief stay in Tallahassee already—ran around Lake Ella this morning and the local park and met a lot of your fellow citizens and enjoyed that very much.

I have enjoyed nothing so much in a long time as listening to Elizbet Martinez play the national anthem. I was watching on the Speaker's closed-circuit television. It was very moving. I was moved by the letters I received from friends and supporters of hers when she was playing the national anthem in Guantanamo, and I just told her that, under the program which the Attorney General has supervised so ably, all the children from Guantanamo should be resettled in the very near future. And we thank you, young lady, for what you have done.

Elizbet gave me a beautiful little angel, and I told her I was going to put it on my table in the Oval Office and I wanted her to come see it. I think she ought to play that in the White House, and I hope she will.

I'm delighted to be here, along with Attorney General Reno and EPA Administrator Carol Browner, here in the Florida Legislature on the 150th anniversary of your statehood. This is the first State legislature I've had the privilege of addressing since I have actually been in office. And as a former Governor and as a Governor who had the privilege of being Governor during the 150th anniversary of our State's statehood, I am especially happy to be here today.

When I ran for President, I was determined to make a new partnership with the States and to be a good partner. We have worked hard on those things with Florida. And goodness knows we've had lots of opportunities, some of them positive and some of them just the problems that life brings. We've worked hard to turn FEMA around and to help you with the last of the hurricane relief, which occurred, of course, before I was elected, but a lot of the work remained to be done when I took office.

And we worked hard in the aftermath of the recent flooding. And I was pleased when I arrived at the Tallahassee Airport last night: Three different people told me they thought FEMA had done a good job handling the floods, which made me feel very good about that.

Attorney General Reno and the INS have worked hard to improve immigration laws, and the Customs Service has worked hard at the Port of Miami to clear the ships faster and step up our antidrug efforts at the same time. We've gone for more public-private partnerships, like the National Magnetic Lab here in Florida, and Carol Browner has worked very hard with many of you here in this room and people throughout the State on a responsible plan to save the Everglades.

The Summit of the Americas was hosted in Florida, and it was a triumph, and we are still feeling the vibrations of it throughout the hemisphere. And I thank all of you who had something to do with that.

Many of you worked hard with us to help to save the space station project. And I think now we have firmly anchored it as a part of America's future. And it's very important, and I can tell you that—I see Bill Nelson nodding his head—he's ready to go. [*Laughter*] I cannot tell you what an important part of our foreign policy it has become. It's given us a way of cooperating with the Russians in ways that cut through political differences and other problems and involve all of our other partners in the space station.

And of course, yesterday I had the privilege of announcing that the Department of Defense had selected Florida as the new headquarters for our Southern Command when it moves out of Panama to the State of Florida. [*Applause*] Thank you. [*Applause*] Thank you.

One thing I tried hard on that I wasn't so successful on to be a good partner with you was to get baseball started up again in time for a full spring training. But I can say that, as you know, there's a case in the courts now, and if the judge does uphold the injunction and the players do manifest their willingness to return to work as they have said they will, then I certainly hope there will not be a lockout. I hope we can have baseball this year, and I think all of you hope that as well.

Let me say to you that the experience that I had as a Governor in the seventies, the eighties, and the nineties—I served for 12 years

in all three decades—directly affected the decision I made to seek the Presidency and to do the things I have tried to do. I ran for President largely because I thought our country at the dawn of this new century was facing a whole set of challenges which did not fall easily into the political patterns into which Washington seemed to be frozen, the constant partisan battles, the constant attempt to divide every issue between whether it was liberal or conservative or left or right instead of determining whether it would move our country forward.

Most of the Southern States, and Florida most especially, did pretty well in the 1980's by following a different sort of southern strategy: focusing on educating all of our children and more and more of our adults, focusing on getting more jobs and economic opportunity into our States, focusing on getting people together across racial and other lines, and focusing on real partnerships between the public and private sector. That's what works in real life. It seemed to be a very small part of the political life of our Nation's Capital. And I ran because I wanted to change that. I wanted to try to break out of all the false choices that cloud the rhetoric we hear for years and years and years out of Washington, to try to move this country forward.

I really believe the great question facing our country on the eve of a new century, which will be characterized by breathtaking change brought on by the information revolution, the globalization of the economy in all of its manifestations, the end of cold war, and therefore the end of the need for people to sort of hunker down behind their barriers into two world camps, the great question is whether we can seize the opportunities this new time presents us without being undone by the problems that we confront; whether we can literally preserve the American idea that if you work hard and play by the rules, you can live up to your God-given abilities, that you can provide for your children and know they'll have a limitless future, that you can rely on your country being the strongest force in the world for peace and freedom and democracy in ways that help you at home. That is the great question.

And the answer to the question, indeed, the many answers to the question, in my judgment, do not fall easily within the sharp ideological partisan battles that have dominated our Nation's Capital for too long. Governors and legislators tend to be more practical people. Not that we don't have passion, not that we don't have principles, not that we don't have convictions but we know what works in the end is people working together, not finding ways to drive us apart.

And so I ask you today to spend a few minutes with me thinking about where we are, what we're going to do, what you expect your National Government to do, and how you expect it to relate to you as a citizen, as well as a member of the State government of Florida.

I believe that the role of the National Government in 1995 should be not to be a savior, not to be a Government-knows-best, a one-size-fits-all Government. Nobody believes that anymore. But I also don't believe in the new rage that Government is the source of all of our problems, and if we didn't have it, we wouldn't have any problems. That is contradicted by the experience of every country in the world today and every country the world has known since the beginning of the industrial revolution.

I believe the role of Government is to do the following things: Number one, to create opportunity with a minimum of bureaucracy; number two, to empower people to make the most of their own lives, not to solve their problems for them but to give them the tools to take care of themselves; number three, to enhance our security not just abroad but at home on our streets and in our schools, in our families, as well; and number four, to wage a relentless assault to change the Government that was appropriate for the industrial age but is too bureaucratic, too big, and too cumbersome for the information age and the 21st century.

Now, we've worked hard on that for 2 years. We had an economic strategy to create opportunity, reduce the deficit, and we did, by $600 billion. Indeed, the Government budget today, for the first time in 30 years, is actually in surplus in its operating costs; that is, except for interest on the debt, we have a surplus today, except for interest on the debt.

Now, of course, the bad news is that 28 percent of personal income tax receipts are required to pay the interest on the debt accumulated between 1981 and 1993. So that doesn't mean we can stop working on it. We have to do more, but we have done a very great deal, indeed.

We have expanded trade in ways that have clearly benefited Florida: NAFTA, GATT, the Summit of the Americas, reaching out to the Asian-Pacific region. We have increased our investment in infrastructure and technology. And we have done right well. We have sought to empower people from everything from expanding Head Start to providing more help to States to help them with people who don't go to college but do need some training after high school and apprenticeship programs, to providing more affordable college loans to millions and millions of students in every State in this country.

We have sought to enhance our security by doing a better job of protecting our borders, by fighting against the proliferation of weapons of mass destruction, by reaching agreements with the Russians and other states of the former Soviet Union to dismantle nuclear weapons. And for the first time since the dawn of the nuclear age, there are no nuclear missiles pointed at the children of the United States today. That is a good thing.

But we have also sought to enhance our security through the crime bill's attempt to put 100,000 more police on our streets through the safe and drug-free schools act, through the Family and Medical Leave Act, through giving tax relief to low-income working families so no one who works full-time with children in the home will still live in poverty. Those things relate to our security, as well.

And finally, we have sought to change the Government, to make it smaller, less bureaucratic, less of a problem, and more of a partner in the American adventure. The Government is now over 100,000 people smaller than it was when I became President. We are on our way to reducing it by 270,000 over 6 years. If no new actions are taken, that will give us the smallest Federal Establishment since John Kennedy was President.

We are cutting programs. We have already eliminated or reduced 300 programs. And in my new budget, I've asked Congress to eliminate or consolidate 400 more. We are deregulating important segments of our economy and trying to reduce the burden of regulation. I'll say more about that in a moment. And we are committed to giving more responsibility to the States, in very important ways that we've also been a good partner with Florida that I didn't mention earlier—the waiver you got from restrictive Federal rules to pursue health care reform, which has enabled small businesses in Florida that could not afford health insurance before finally to voluntarily insure their own employees.

And I'll say a little about this in a moment, but Florida was also one of now 25 States to receive a waiver from the cumbersome Federal rules governing the welfare system to try to help you move people from welfare to work. We've given more of these waivers in 2 years than the previous administrations, combined, in 12. I believe in shifting power back to the States to make their decisions to build the future of the people of the States, where you can do a better job.

Now, the preliminary results are hopeful. In the last 2 years, we've had sustained economic growth, over 6 million new jobs, a big drop in the unemployment rate, about a 3 percent drop in the unemployment rate here in Florida; the job growth rate here in the private sector about 4 times what it was in the previous 4 years. We are moving forward as a country. We have the lowest combined rates of unemployment/inflation in 25 years. That is the good news. But there are still many challenges, challenges that you confront every day, challenges in economics, challenges in the fabric of our social life, challenges in the way Government works.

We know, still, that in spite of this big recovery, most wage earners are working harder for the same or lower wages than they were making 10 or 15 years ago. We know that within the great American middle class the great challenge of our time is that we have more inequality, people splitting apart by income, mostly related to their own educational levels, something that we never faced before. From the end of World War II until the end of the 1970's, this country rose together. Almost every income group rose about 100 percent, just about double their income. The bottom 20 percent actually increased their income from the end of World War II until 1978 by about 140 percent. We were going up, and we were going together.

Now, since 1979, we have the bottom 60 percent of our country actually losing ground economically in real terms, the next 20 percent having a modest 5 percent gain, and only those of us in the upper 20 percent of the income brackets actually doing quite well. This is something you see in a lot of other countries, but it presents a special threat to the American idea that anybody, anybody who will work hard and play by the rules can live up to the fullest of

their ability. And it is a challenge we must face together. It is a new challenge. It has no simple partisan ideological solution.

We know, still, we have too many social problems. We are divided with too much crime and violence and drug abuse, too many of our children born out of wedlock, still too many things that are taking apart the fabric of our society. And we know that for all the changes we've made in Government, we sure have a long way to go there.

I know that Governor Chiles sent all of you a copy of the book "The Death of Common Sense." What you may not know is that he sent me one, too. [*Laughter*] In fact, he put it in my hot hand, and I read it within 48 hours. And we called Philip Howard, and we got him to come to Washington, and we asked him to work with us as he has worked with you.

So when we talk about cutting Government, I guess I'm singing to the choir and looking at the lead singer over here on my left. But I'd like to give you a report about what we are doing and what we propose to do. And I need your help and your involvement, without regard to your party, from your perspective at the State level about what the next steps are going to be. And so does the Congress.

Let me just tell you some of the things we've done already. We announced the other day that we're going to cut reports we require from the American people in half, unless there's some compelling public interest reason not to, so that people who have to file reports four times a year will go to twice a year; twice a year, once a year and so on.

We took the small business loan form from being an inch thick to a page long. Last year, we gave twice as many loans at lower cost to taxpayers than the year before I took office. We gave in Florida 1,200 loans, worth over $250 million, and under the leadership of our Vice President and the new head of SBA, we are now going to cut the SBA budget by 32 percent and increase the number of loans by 12,000 next year. That's what we ought to be doing for this Government: more performance, lower cost.

Under the able leadership of your former staffer Carol Browner, the Environmental Protection Agency is working through complicated problems from Florida to California that were mired in the courts for years. But she is doing it and, at the same time, cutting paperwork from the EPA by 25 percent. That will save 20 million hours of work for the American people every single year.

The Environmental Protection Agency is also opening compliance centers and telling people, if you wonder whether you're in or out of compliance, come to our center, and if you're out of compliance and you show up voluntarily, we will waive the fine for 6 months while you get in compliance. No more punishment for people who are trying to do the right thing.

We have changes in the Food and Drug Administration, where we've heard a lot of complaints about things taking too long. We've reduced the time lag and the cost for permitting drugs that have absolutely no possible danger to health or to the environment, for moving antibiotics on line, for moving medical devices on line that plainly present no problem. It will put another half a billion dollars a year into the American economy, just speeding up the 140 medical devices and getting rid of 600 pages of regulation. And I'll bet you right now $100 that a year from now there will not be a single American who will come up to the President and say, "What did you do with those 600 pages of regulation? I miss them so much. I can't stand it." [*Laughter*] We are moving in the right direction.

We have changed our approach to small businesses. If a small business violates a Federal rule for the first time now, every regulator is going to be given the authority to waive the fine altogether. And if any business violates a rule but does not do so flagrantly, instead of taking a fine away from the business, the business will be given the option of taking the fine and keeping it and spending it on correcting whatever the problem was instead of giving the money to the Government. This is the kind of commonsense direction I think we ought to follow.

We've changed rules for procurement in the Defense Department. It's going to save you billions of dollars a year as taxpayers. There's going to be no more $500 hammers and $50 ashtrays, and there won't be $50 on every transaction. The rules and regulations on procurement added $50 to the cost of everything the Defense Department bought that cost under $2,500.

We had Defense Department rules that required people in our military to buy computers at twice the cost with half the capacity that you could buy them off the shelf in a store

in Tallahassee. All that's been scrapped. We're moving in the right direction.

The new Congress and I have worked together on three things that I campaigned for President on that I think probably has wide support among members of both parties here that I'm very encouraged about. They passed a law that I was proud to sign that applies to Congress all the laws they impose on the private sector. High time. They passed a law that I signed last week that reduces the ability of Congress to impose upon States and local governments unfunded mandates to require you to raise taxes and change your priorities.

And both Houses of Congress have passed different versions now of the line-item veto, which I strongly support, and I believe we will reconcile them and come out with something that works, and I assure you I will do my dead-level best to use that line-item veto in a way that restrains unnecessary Government spending.

Now, here's where you come in, because we need to move to the next area where we're still having a big debate, because I think there is a right way and a wrong way to cut Government spending, a right way and a wrong way to relax regulation. And I want you to be a part of this process.

For example, we wanted to cut spending in the Agriculture Department. We closed 1,200 offices we didn't need. We think that's a better approach than reducing the School Lunch Program. We realized we had to cut some spending in the housing area. We got rid of the regional offices of HUD, and we consolidated a lot of old bureaucratic programs. We think that's a better approach than ending efforts to help homeless veterans, many of whom are still deeply troubled because of the experiences that they've had to come to grips with in their lives. We had the EPA cut regulation by 25 percent. We think that's a better approach than this "takings bill" before Congress, which 20 States in referendums have rejected because it undermines the ability of governments even to do basic zoning and could bankrupt the budget of any government that tried to implement it. So there are ways to do this that I think are right and wrong.

And let me just say one thing about the block grant proposal. When I was a Governor, I loved block grants, and I still think they're a pretty good idea in many areas. I haven't changed just because I've become President. I like the community development block grant, and I used it effectively. But I want to remind you it's worth about half or maybe less than half of what it was when it was given in the early eighties in the Reagan administration.

The Congress gives block grants primarily to save money. And now we're talking about block grants in areas that could be really painful to the high-growth States. So I ask you, think about what's attractive about it, but look at the details. Don't get caught in the rhetoric; look at the reality. It is not fair for the Federal Government to adopt a block-grant system which flat-funds big things that are very important to the quality of life, indeed, the ability to live a decent life for millions of our people. That may be just wonderful for States with no growth or declining population. They might even make money out of the deal. But for the growth States of the country, it can be a trap. So watch it, read it, look at the fine print, and stick up for your interests. [*Applause*] Thank you.

Now, I'd like to give you three examples of where I think we have done the right thing to reduce spending and help you and help your people. And again, let me say that we need to move beyond the labels of the past. We need to put the people of this country first, and we need to keep our eye on the future. And I'd like to give you three examples with three groups of people from Florida who are up there—and I'll recognize them each in turn—that, to me, symbolize the right way to cut Government, to make college loans more affordable, to end welfare as we know it, and to make our streets safer.

One of the most important things that our administration has accomplished is to make college loans more affordable for millions of Americans by eliminating the middleman in the old college loan system, lowering the cost, and offering better repayment terms. Believe it or not, we've actually reduced the deficit, made loans more affordable to young people all across the country, and cut the hassle to the colleges and universities involved.

We've also been very strict in enforcement. No opportunity without responsibility. It was costing you in 1991 $2.8 billion a year as taxpayers in delinquent loans, people who borrowed the money and wouldn't pay it back. We have cut that rate from $2.8 billion a year down to $1 billion a year by cracking down on people who won't pay their loans. People who borrow the money ought to pay it back.

But let me say again, we have found a way to lower the cost of the college loan program to the taxpayers, give out more loans at lower cost to the students, and cut the hassle to the colleges and universities in between.

I want to introduce some of the people that are up there. Michelle Bellamy, of Orlando, is a senior criminal justice major at Florida A&M here in Tallahassee. And Rebecca and Craig Cummins, husband and wife, are 4th-year medical students at the University of Florida. I'd like to ask them to stand up there. Now, yesterday I held a regional economic conference in Atlanta, and Rebecca and Craig came and testified. Rebecca said that when they got out of medical school they'd have combined debts of $140,000, that under the old student loan program it would have taken half of their income to pay their loan obligations when they went into residency at very low pay. Under the new student loan program, they can have their choice of ways to repay the loan. And one of their choices is to pay the loan off over a longer period of time as a percentage of their income.

This means that young people will never be discouraged from borrowing money to go to college because they know they'll never be bankrupted by paying it back, even though we're going to be tougher on requiring it to be paid back.

Their loan administrator said that she thought she had died and gone to heaven when she got into this program—literally, that's what she said—because there was no hassle. They didn't have to wait weeks and weeks and weeks to get the money. There was less paperwork. And I will say again, because we took out the middleman, it lowers costs to the taxpayer.

There are 502,000 Florida students and former students who now can take advantage of this direct college loan program. They and others are using this program today. There are some other students up there with them, and I'd like to ask them to stand. All the students that are up there, would you all stand together and be recognized.

So here's decision number one for you. I made a proposal to reduce the cost of education in the Federal budget, and there's another proposal in the Congress to reduce the cost of education in the budget. You decide which one you think is best. Right now we can make only

40 percent of our schools eligible to participate in this program. My proposal is, over the next 5 years let 100 percent of America's schools decide if they want to participate in the program. It will cut the deficit by $12 billion over 6 years and get a lot more people into college loans, get a lot more people into college, and people will be able to pay them back.

The other proposal is to cap the program right where it is, which will add $6 billion to the deficit over the next 5 years—by taking that money and giving it to the middlemen who are making the loans now and making a much bigger bureaucratic hassle—and to save that money, that $6 billion, by making the loans that young people get now more expensive, by charging them interest on the loans while they're already in college and adding $2 billion a year to the cost of the loans.

Now, I think common sense says that my way of saving money, which gets you more students at lower cost and better repayment terms, is better than the alternative proposal, which gives more money to the banks in the middle, runs the deficit up, gives you fewer students, and gives them more headaches at the colleges administering the program, and far more heartache to the students in repaying it. I think it's a clear choice.

But you need to be heard on it. It's not a partisan issue. It's a special interest against a public interest issue. It's an old Washington way of doing things against a new way of doing things issue. This is a big deal, and it's a clear choice. Both parties propose to reduce the deficit from education costs, but the choices are different.

Let me give you another example. Everybody in America wants to reform the welfare system. And good for them—because we know that some people on welfare, a significant percentage, are there because they're young, they have young children, they have no education, they don't have a particularly bright future if all they do is get a check from the Government to stay in the fix they're in, that the system for too many people does not promote responsible parenting, good work, or independence.

Most people also know that the system we have today is worse than it would be because we don't enforce our child support enforcement the way we ought to and that it's complicated for you because more than a third of the child

support cases in America today cross State lines, so your ability to do it is limited.

Now, last year I worked with Members of the Congress in both parties and sent a sweeping welfare reform proposal to the Congress. It was not passed. They didn't get to it, and I wish they had. This year we're going to get a welfare reform bill, and it's a good thing. It will give the States far more flexibility, no matter which system is passed.

One of the things that I think is that since we've now given 25 States, including Florida, waivers from all these Federal rules, I think every State in America ought to do anything that any State's already got the right to do. Why should you have to keep coming back to the Federal Government asking for permission to try innovative ways to change your welfare system? I don't think you should.

But I think what you've done here shows what works. And again, it's a choice we have to make. And this one is a little harder for you than the last one. But I want you to make a choice, and I want you to be heard.

In January of 1994, Florida received one of our first waivers to implement a family transition program, to accelerate the pace of moving people from welfare to work in Alachua County and Escambia County. The program reflects what we're trying to do, and I thought it was a good proposal. And apparently, it's working. It requires people to move from work to independence within 2 years, and it creates additional opportunities for people to do that by investing in education and training and child care.

And I might say, every time you interview a bunch of people on welfare, they'll always tell you, "If we had health care for our kids and child care and some way to go to work, we'll go to work." And the Florida program does that.

Now, what we want to do in the Congress is to pass a bill that will promote work, responsible parenting, and tough child support. The bill that passed the House of Representatives— I want to compliment it—does promote tough child support. We know today if we were collecting all the child support that is owed and could be paid, we could move 800,000 families off welfare today—if we were just collecting child support. And I compliment the House on passing that bill.

But the rest of the program, in my opinion, is deficient. I think it's weak on work and tough on kids. I don't think it does as much as—it certainly doesn't do as much as the Florida project does to move people from welfare to work. The attractiveness of it is it gives you a block grant. It says, "You do what you want, and what do you care what they do in Utah or Idaho or Maine." The problem is the block grant also has some strings attached and requires, for example, States to deny benefits to teenagers who have babies and to their babies until they reach the age of their majority—the mothers—and gives people the option to deny it altogether.

Now, it just seems to me that the better course is to give the States a great deal of flexibility, but to say, number one, if you have a growing caseload we shouldn't block-grant you. You can't help it if Florida is growing faster than some other States. And number two, we shouldn't punish children for the mistakes of their parents. And number three, what we really want is for people to go to work and be good parents, and we ought to have certain baseline requirements to do that.

Now, that's what I believe. And I'll tell you why I believe that. There are reasons up there, again, in the audience. Irene Marry is ending welfare as we know it. She is the mother of six from Escambia County. She participated in your program. Since joining the family transition program a year ago, she received her GED, she enrolled in training for a high-wage job as a heating and air-condition technician. She will earn a paycheck, not a welfare check. And I met some other ladies who are with her who are doing the same thing. This is your program. I think this is what America ought to do. I'd like to ask them to stand up. Please stand up, all three of you. [*Applause*]

Last example of the choice you have to make. No State in the country knows any more about crime and violence than Florida. We know that there are many reasons for crime. There are many causes of crime, and there are many proposed solutions to crime. After 6 years of partisan gridlock, last year we broke gridlock and passed the crime bill.

The crime bill had three major components: a lot of money for prisons for States that had tough sentencing provisions—you had to have certain tough sentencing provisions to get the Federal money to help build the prisons; a sub-

stantial but smaller amount of money for prevention programs—there were certain categories specified, but essentially States and local communities got to decide what worked best in prevention; and a substantial amount of money to help local communities and county jurisdictions and, to some extent, States hire law enforcement officials.

There was a total flexibility on the part of the States, virtually, in the prevention money, nearly none in the prison money, and some in the police money, but basically the money had to be used to hire police on the street and not behind desks.

Now, this bill was put together in complete cooperation with the law enforcement community. There were 11 major law enforcement groups that worked on this, along with the State attorneys general—General Butterworth knows, he was very active in this—the prosecutors association, all the law enforcement folks around the country. They told us, among other things, "You've got to have some prevention money in here. We can't jail our way out of this problem." People in law enforcement said that. And it was interesting, I mean, a lot of these folks were Republicans, and some were Democrats. But they said, "This is not a partisan deal. We live on the streets. Our badges are on every day. We cannot jail our way out of this. We have got to have some prevention money, as well."

The argument for the police was plain: Violent crime has tripled in the last 30 years in America. The number of police on the street has increased by only 10 percent. This is not high math. So we proposed to, in effect, increase by another 20 percent the number of police officers on the street. Why? Because one of the little known success stories in America in the last several years is that in community after community after community that has adopted an aggressive community policing system, the crime rate has gone down, not just because more criminals are being caught but because more crime is being prevented. There is evidence here. This is not some theory. There is evidence, city after city after city with crime rates declining where they have been able to implement aggressive community policing programs.

In Florida—and the Attorney General—I want to compliment the Attorney General on this. She set up—it used to be that law enforcement groups hated dealing with the Federal Government because they had to hire a consultant to figure out how to get through the web of the Justice Department. Janet Reno instituted for smaller communities a one-page, eight-question form to get a police officer, one page, eight questions.

And since October—you know, the people who are attacking this approach say, "Communities don't really want this. They can't afford to match it. They don't like it." All I know is, since October, over half of the communities in America have asked for police grants from the Justice Department on their one-page, eight-question form. And since October, we have already awarded over 16,000 new police officers to over half of the police departments in America, almost 1,000 new officers in Florida. The Escambia Sheriff's Office is putting 20 new officers on the street, and 14 of them are with us today. I'd like to ask them to stand because that's what you got for your money.

Again, you have a choice to make. There they are. My proposal is—and let me say what the—the crime bill was paid for by a trust fund, no tax increases, no money from anything else. The 272,000 people we're going to take out of the Federal bureaucracy, all of those savings go into a trust fund to pay for this crime bill. That's how it's paid for.

Now, the House bill says that, "No, no, we don't like this. We want to spend more money on prisons but only if you comply with our sentencing requirements." No State flexibility there. "We know how you should sentence people, and if you do it our way, you can have this money. And we want to spend less money on police and prevention, but—here's the deal—we'll put it in a block grant for you and you can do what you want to with it. You won't get as much, but you can do what you want to."

It's very seductive and very attractive. You have to ask yourselves from your perspective: Should there be less on prevention? Should there be less on police? Should we really walk away from this commitment to 100,000 police officers when violent crime has tripled, only a 10-percent increase in police, and every law en-

forcement group in America tells us we ought to do it?

I think the answer is clear. You may disagree, but you should know—again, on the block grants, you're a growth State and your opportunities are exploding. But your problems will grow, too. So I ask you to think about it and to make your voice heard. And for goodness sakes, do your best to talk about it in terms of what puts your people first, what gets us into the future. No partisan political rhetoric; let's look at what is right for the country and what is right for our State.

I think this is a very exciting time to be alive and to be in public service. This debate we are having about the role of Government is a good thing to have. But in the end, our mission has got to be to keep the American dream alive. The idea that this is a special country, where little girls who can play the violin can come and breathe the air of freedom and fight for it for all of those who are like her who don't enjoy it.

This is a special country. And there is never going to be a time—I thought about this when the minister was praying at the beginning of the session here—the Scriptures tell us there will never be a time when human existence is free of difficulties. They are endemic to our nature and to the condition of things on this Earth.

So we have vast new opportunities and profound new challenges. And the real question is, how are we going to meet them. With all my heart, I believe that the best days of this country lie ahead of us if we make the right decisions. In a new time, the right decisions cannot be made with old rhetoric that divides us when we need to be united.

Thank you, and God bless you all.

NOTE: The President spoke at 10:45 a.m. in the House Chamber at the State Capitol. In his remarks, he referred to James A. Scott, president, Peter R. Wallace, speaker, and Jack Ascherk, speaker pro tempore, Florida Legislature; violinist Elizbet Lorenzo Martinez; Bill Nelson, Florida treasurer and insurance commissioner; and Bob Butterworth, Florida attorney general.

Remarks to Students at Hillsborough Community College in Tampa, Florida
March 30, 1995

The President. Thank you very much, Bill Lanthripp, for that introduction. Thank you, President Paloumpis, and thank you, ladies and gentlemen, for making me feel so very, very welcome here today. I also want to thank those of you who brought the little children here; it's wonderful to see them—that little girl back there in her green dress and that little girl there, this young man there; you look great. Thank you.

I want to thank some of my partners in trying to make your future better who are here with me, your Governor and Lieutenant Governor, Lawton Chiles and Buddy McKay. I thank my friend Congressman Gibbons for being here, the speaker of the house, Peter Wallace, and your representative, the majority leader of the house, Jim Davis. I thank them all for being here.

I also want to say that I almost got here in time—I got here a day ahead of the new mayor's inauguration, so I want to thank, on the next-to-the-last day of her tenure, my long-time friend, your mayor, Sandy Freedman, for doing such a good job for Tampa. And I want to wish your new mayor, Dick Greco, all the best, and I look forward to working with you.

Ladies and gentlemen, if I could start on a more serious note, I just had the opportunity to meet at the airport with the families of the two Tampa police officers, Mike Vigil and Kevin Howell, who were shot and wounded last week. I also had the opportunity to meet an HCC student, Mike Meyer, who saved one of those officers' lives because he's a certified emergency medical technician. He told the police he was a paramedic, and they brought him there. He grabbed his bag and rushed to the fallen officers, and he did a very fine job. And I had a chance to thank him for that, and it's an encouragement to all of us to learn some of the skills that he knows. You never can tell when you will need them. I understand that Officer Vigil remains in critical but stable condition, but I was just informed by his family that the doctors say his chances are now better than 50–50 that he's going to make a good recovery.

I am delighted to be back in Florida. I had the opportunity to spend the night at the Gov-

ernor's mansion last night and to address the Florida Legislature today about the challenges facing our country and what we're going to do about it. Today I want to talk to you about your future. I spend a lot of time in community colleges like this one, because I think in many ways this is the most important institution in American society as we move toward the next century.

With all of the challenges we face, we basically know what works. What works is educating all of our people; what works is doing what it takes to generate more jobs; what works is bringing people together across racial and income and other lines; what works is a commitment to give more people a shot at the American dream, to grow the middle class and to shrink the under class, and to prepare for the future. And that's what community colleges do.

In a very real sense, what I have been trying to do as President is to bring that spirit and those ideas into the National Government. I've worked for a dozen years as a Governor, in which time I had the honor and privilege to spend countless hours in educational institutions, from elementary schools to community colleges, to vocational training schools, to our 4-year universities. And I found when I went to Washington that every reason that I worried about the country when I ran for President turned out to be true.

I ran because I thought this country was on the verge of a new century, dominated by the end of the cold war, the emergence of the global economy, wealth tied more to knowledge than ever before, when we had new opportunities but new challenges, and that Washington was in the grip of old-fashioned partisan political rhetoric, dividing us when we needed to be united, holding us back when we needed to go forward.

Now we are all engaged in a great debate which you hear every day on the news as you watch events unfold about what your Government should be doing in this moment. The old view was that there was a Government solution in Washington for every big problem in the country and that Government could actually help people with big problems. Well, we know that that's not exactly right; they're not one-size-fits-all, Government knows best, out of Washington. And we know that there are great limits on how much Government can help people to fulfill their abilities.

The new rage is to say that the Government is the cause of all of our problems and if only we had no Government, we'd have no problems. I can tell you, that contradicts evidence, history, and common sense. Now, the truth is—so the question is, what are we going to do? I can tell you what my view is, and it is different from either extreme.

I believe we need a Government that doesn't pretend to be a savior but that doesn't sit on the sidelines. I believe in a partnership. I believe that the National Government's mission at the end of this century is as follows: Number one, we ought to be creating opportunity and demanding responsibility. Number two, I think we ought to be doing everything we can to empower the American people through education for a lifetime to make the most of their own lives. Number three, I believe we ought to be enhancing the security of the American people, not only by making the world a safer place but by making our streets and our schools and our homes and our workplaces safer places. And number four, I think we have got to dramatically change the National Government to make it smaller, less bureaucratic, less meddlesome, but still helpful to move this country forward.

Now, if you look at the record in creating opportunity, we have brought down the deficit, we have expanded trade, we have increased our investments in new technology, and in the last 2 years our Nation has produced over 6 million new jobs. The unemployment rate in Florida has dropped 3 percent from 7.4 to 4.3 percent. We are clearly moving forward and creating more opportunity.

If you look at the empowerment issue, we have increased investments in education, everything from expanding Head Start to expanding the efforts of States to make apprenticeships for people who don't go to college, to dramatically—and I mean dramatically—increasing the availability of scholarships for middle class people to get a higher education.

If you ask, well, what have we done on security, well, look around the world. We are making progress in troublesome areas of the world like the Middle East, in bringing peace, and North-

ern Ireland. We have made agreements with Russia and with other countries in the former Soviet Union to drastically reduce the number of nuclear weapons. And for the first time since the dawn of the nuclear age, there are no nuclear missiles pointed at the children of the United States of America.

Now, if you ask what have we done to reduce the size of Government—and I want to compliment Governor Chiles for his leadership in this. Florida is one of the—really, the groundbreaking State in America, I think, in slashing unnecessary regulation, and I congratulate him on that.

What are we doing in Washington? Well, we've reduced the size of the Federal bureaucracy by 100,000. We're going to reduce it by 270,000 over 5 years. It'll be the smallest Federal Government since John Kennedy was President of the United States.

We have reduced the Government deficit so much that if it weren't for interest on the debt incurred in the 12 years before I showed up, we'd have a surplus today, not a deficit in the Government account. We're paying our operating bills.

We're now giving Government regulators the authority not to fine people the first time they make a mistake. And Carol Browner, from Florida, who's the head of the EPA, has opened up an office in which people, good, honest business people can go and say, "Look, I'm afraid I'm in violation of some environmental law," and instead of getting a fine they'll get 6 months to fix it. We have changed the rules so that now if somebody makes a mistake in good faith, our Federal agencies have the right not to fine people but to say, "You keep the fine if you'll spend it in fixing the problem, making the workplace safer, making the environment cleaner."

So we are moving forward. With this new Congress, we are finding some areas of agreement that are quite important. I signed a law that I campaigned for President to support that applies to Congress all the laws they put on the private sector. I think it's high time.

I signed a law the other day which limits the ability of the Congress to impose upon State governments and local governments so-called unfunded mandates, requiring them to raise your taxes because of something people in Washington want, instead of what you decided the mayor should do or the Governor and the State legislature should do. And it's high time.

And we're about to get agreement—we passed a line-item veto, which most Governors have, which allows a President to go into a big bill, where a lot of pork-barrel spending might be hidden with a lot of good things so you can't afford to veto the bill, and find the pork. And we're going to get that passed soon. And that's a good thing.

But there still are some disagreements. And the American people, without regard to their party, will have to be heard on these disagreements, because you have to decide what you think the main mission of our country is. Is the main mission to make sure there is no Federal Government, or is the main mission to grow the middle class, shrink the under class, and support family and community and the future of this country? I think that is what the main mission of this country is.

And let me give you some ideas. With all the cutting of the budget we have done—and last year, I gave the Congress the first budget in 25 years that cut defense and domestic spending together. Only medical costs went up because of inflation. Everything else was cut. But I did not cut, within that, education. We increased our investment in education. Why? Because—look around you—it is the future of America.

So are we going to grow the middle class, shrink the under class, and be a safer country if more poor little kids go through Head Start? I think we are. Are we going to grow the middle class if more kids who get out of high school but don't want to go to college at least get 2 years of some kind of training afterward in a community college, that type of thing? I think we are. Will we be growing the middle class and shrinking the under class if every person who wants to go to college can get a college loan at a lower cost and a better repayment schedule? I think we are.

So this is a big decision we have to make in Washington. Let me give you a clear, explicit example. I recommended that we could save some money and do a better job by our young people if we changed the college loan program, because it was a big bureaucracy. You know it was a guarantee, so the Government would guarantee a loan a bank would give you. The bank charges a fee; then if somebody doesn't pay it back, the bank gets 90 percent of the money from the Government. So they never sue, because the lawyer fee would cost more

than 10 percent. Right? We were spending, when I became President, $1.8—$2.8 billion a year of your money for delinquent loans, because people weren't paying their student loans.

Colleges and universities were complaining all over America that the paperwork was driving them bananas to process the student loans. The students were complaining that they couldn't get the loans in a hurry. And then when they had to repay them on a 10-year schedule, if you borrowed a whole bunch of money, you couldn't take a job that you might want if it has a salary so low you could never make your loan repayment. And it didn't just apply to people in what you call public service jobs.

Yesterday in Atlanta, I had an economic forum, and I had two married medical students, a husband and wife from the University of Florida, come and testify. They are 4th-year medical students. They will owe $140,000 when they get out of medical school. You say, "Well, doctors make a lot of money." They do, but not when they're residents. Right? They were going to literally have to spend one-half of their income, combined, paying off their students loans while they're residents working 60, 70, 80 hours a week. Under our plan, they can pay it off as a percentage of their income. So when they start making money, they pay more. But now they get to make a living and work and become doctors. It's a better system.

So how does this affect you? Today, 40 percent of American institutions are eligible to participate in that. What I said is, let's let everybody participate. We'll cut the fraud rate. We've already taken it from $2.8 billion down to $1 billion a year. We've cut the fraud by nearly two-thirds. We'll cut the cost of the program. We'll loan more money to more students. We'll be less trouble to the institutions of higher education, and the deficit will go down because we'll save $6 billion. That was my proposal.

Now, here is the other proposal in the Congress. The other proposal is: Leave the banks with the money; cap the number of colleges that can participate at 40 percent; and instead, make students start paying interest on their loans while they're in college—add $2 billion a year to the cost of college.

Audience members. No-o-o!

The President. To me, I don't think you have to be Einstein to conclude that does not make sense. Let's stay with our program. Let's save money and educate people and not go back to charging people more for student loans.

Let me tell you something else. There's a lot of talk about tax cuts in Washington today. There is a limit to how much we can cut taxes because the deficit's big. We need to keep bringing the deficit down. But I believe we should have a modest tax cut for middle class people, targeted to raising incomes and increasing the wealth of the country over the long run. Don't just write people a check. Give people who are playing by the rules some incentives to do more. That's why my bill says let's give people a tax deduction for the cost of education after high school. Get more people to get educated and do that. Why? Why? Because it's just like the GI bill after World War II: Everybody who goes to school is going to make a higher income and pay more taxes and run the deficit down and run the wealth of the country up. And if we keep it disciplined and small, we can afford it.

But we can't afford just to go out here with these huge tax cuts with the deficit of the country as big as it is. The reason the Florida economy dropped in unemployment by 3 percent is that we brought the deficit down and increased our investment and expanded trade. So we got interest rates down and business opportunities up and generated more jobs. The most important thing is to keep the American people working and get their incomes up. And that's what we have to do.

Now, you will see these debates over and over and over again. I want to mention two more, because they affect you. We're having a big argument about what to do about crime. Well, we finally passed a tough crime bill last year. Your mayor helped us pass it. Your Governor, your attorney general, your law enforcement official helped us pass it.

And what that crime bill does is it says—first of all, it was virtually written by law enforcement officials—it says that we should have the National Government do three things to help bring the crime rate down: Help the States build more prisons so we don't let dangerous criminals out too soon; help local communities give kids something to say yes to and not just something to say no to, so we prevent crime and keep people out of trouble; and have a 20 percent increase in the police forces of the country so we can catch criminals and prevent crime. Those are the three things we did.

Now, the Congress has proposed to reduce the amount of money we're spending on the crime bill, but require the States to spend more on prisons and spend less on police and prevention, and tell the communities, do whatever you want to with the money. And I'm opposed to that, and I want you to know why. Violent crime has tripled in the last 30 years, and we have to do something about it—all kinds of violent crime. I just announced last week that the former attorney general of Iowa, Bonnie Campbell, is going to head the first-ever division of the Justice Department on domestic violence, violence against parents and children. We have to do something about this.

Now, in 30 years, violent crime triples, but the police forces of the country increase by only 10 percent. You don't have to be a genius to figure out that there's some connection between a huge increase in crime and nearly no increase in the police force. How are they supposed to do what they're doing? Not to mention how much better armed the criminals have become—right?—which is part of the problem with these fine police officers.

Now, we know also that one of the good news stories that often does not get told in this country is—I have seen this with my own eyes—there's city after city after city where the crime rate has gone down because of strategies that have been adopted, like some of the strategies adopted right here in Tampa. When you put people out and you deploy police in the proper way and they work with people in the community, they not only catch criminals quicker but they also deter crime. I have seen it all across America. This is a good deal. Florida has already been awarded funds for more than 960 police officers, 18 of them right here in Tampa. We don't need to tamper with the crime bill. We ought to stay with it and implement it.

I'm just going to give you one last example, because we have to decide what kind of country we're going to be and what we're going to do together. These young people that were introduced over here, the AmeriCorps volunteers—and they clapped and I was glad to see them—they're part of our national service program. It's a program basically to bring the idea of the Peace Corps to the streets of America. It's a program designed to say, "If you will work, essentially, for minimum wage for a year, we'll give you about the equivalent college education benefit of the GI bill, if you'll help us to deal with our security problems here at home, help to volunteer and to rebuild America here at home."

Now, there are those who say, "Well, we can't afford this. It's too expensive." We have 20,000 young Americans in AmeriCorps today, thousands of more who want to get in, who want to work for minimum wage and earn this education credit and build up our country. There are more people in AmeriCorps today than ever served in the Peace Corps in any single year in its history since President Kennedy started it, because the American people are dying to get out there and do something to lift this country up.

Let me just give you a couple of examples. Two years ago, just 89 of our volunteers immunized 104,000 infants in poor areas in Texas. Believe me, they paid for the whole program in that one year. Here in Florida after the hurricane, our volunteers, working with Habitat for Humanity, built 75 homes, and they built them quicker and better because of that.

These AmeriCorps volunteers are from Pinellas County. They're members of three local law enforcement agencies involved in community police departments, the Clearwater department, the St. Petersburg department and the county sheriff's office. They're working together to make what I just talked to you about, community policing, a reality, to make the streets safer. They're out there doing things that uniformed officers don't have to do that lower the crime rate and make people safer. That is what we ought to be doing. I think it is worth the investment.

I'm cutting spending as quick as I can. We've cut more spending in the last 2 years than had been cut in a month of Sundays, and I will cut more, and I will work with the Congress to cut more. But it is not right to cut out AmeriCorps. We should be lifting up young people like this and giving them a chance to serve.

So I want you to be a part of this. America needs to work like the community colleges work: People get in, and they're just judged based on their merit, and everybody gets a fair shot.

And you know if you conclude the course, you've got a good chance to get a job and a better chance to live out your dreams. That's the way this country ought to work. It ought to be flexible, unbureaucratic, changing to meet the needs of a changing society, but it requires a partnership between the public sector and the private sector.

Your Government in Washington, I am doing my best to change it to make it more like this. But we are creating opportunity, we are empowering people, we are enhancing our security, and we are downsizing this Government. We are making America a better place together. And I urge you to enter this debate and tell everybody that you can, we do not need more of the old-fashioned, hot air, partisan political rhetoric. We need a strategy to move this country forward.

And let me say this in closing, I got a letter the other day from a guy I went to grade school with. And he said, "You know, Bill, one of the problems that you're having as President is that you're living out your dream. But too many people our age are living with broken dreams." I ran for this job because I wanted all the people my age to be able to live their dreams and because I want you younger people here to be able to look forward to a life that is full and rich as the one I've enjoyed. And those of you that are young and don't have any children yet, I want you to think about having children with an atmosphere of excitement and hope and conviction that your kids will see America's best days. And I'm telling you, if we will keep our heads on straight and think about how we can pull together instead of how we can be driven apart, we will do that.

God bless you, and thank you.

NOTE: The President spoke at 2:34 p.m. in the gymnasium at the Dale Mabry Campus. In his remarks, he referred to William Lanthripp, president, Dale Mabry Campus Student Government Association; Andreas A. Paloumpis, president, Hillsborough Community College; and student John Meyer.

Remarks on the Major League Baseball Strike and an Exchange With Reporters in Tampa
March 30, 1995

The President. Since I'm here in Florida, it might be appropriate to say something about the baseball situation. The judge is going to hand down a ruling, apparently, pretty soon. And I would just say, if the injunction stays and the players do again state their willingness to go back to work, then I hope they won't be locked out. I think it gives us a chance at least to start the baseball season in a good way and without the replacement players.

Ultimately, of course, they're still going to have to work this out, and they're going to have to do it by some mutual agreement. But we may be given an opportunity in the next couple of days to have a baseball season. And if that opportunity arises and the players are willing to go back, then I hope the owners won't lock them out.

CIA and Guatemala

Q. [*Inaudible*]—CIA covered up the murder in Guatemala?

The President. Well, we have no information to that effect. We are looking into all the allegations. And I have taken exceptional steps to make sure that there is a good investigation and to make sure that the records are secure. I think I should do that. As you know, this relates to events that occurred before I became President. But we need to know the facts, and we're going to do everything we can to find out the facts.

Haiti

Q. Is there any evidence that—any evidence that Aristide's people were behind the assassination?

The President. President Aristide immediately asked for help to investigate the action. Indeed, the people who were down there were working before to try to head off any political violence leading up to the handover this weekend. And as soon as the killing occurred, he asked for help, and we had dispatched immediately a substantial team from the FBI. So I think that is significant evidence that he wants to get to the bottom of this and that he's keeping his word not to support political violence.

There are many factions there. They've done a good job of keeping down political violence. They don't need to start it again. What they need to do is to keep things calm, maintain a low crime rate, continue to work with the United Nations, and rebuild that country. We only have, I think, 6,000 of the 35,000 factory workers who were working before the military coup back working. So we need to keep working on building the country. And that's what I'm going to say when I go down there.

Thank you.

NOTE: The President spoke at approximately 3 p.m. at Tampa Bay International Airport. In his remarks, he referred to President Jean-Bertrand Aristide of Haiti and to the March 28 assassination of President Aristide's political opponent Mireille Durocher Bertin.

Statement on the Major League Baseball Strike
March 30, 1995

For the first time in months there is reason for some optimism for those of us who are hoping for a 1995 baseball season with real major league players.

The players have agreed to return to work if the district court judge issues an injunction.

If the judge does grant the injunction, I hope the owners decide to let the players play ball.

In October, in an attempt to assist the parties, we appointed Bill Usery as special mediator with the hope that he could bring the owners and players together at the bargaining table, where ultimately this dispute must be resolved. He has done his best to get that job done and will continue to do so.

As the owners and players meet in these last few days before the scheduled start of the season, I hope they will give it their best shot, that they will bargain in good faith and be flexible and willing to compromise so that America's baseball fans again have a sport they can be proud of.

Like millions of other fans across the country, I want to see the Ripkens, Gwynns, Bonds, Mattinglys, and Cones in uniform on the playing field. We're getting down to the wire. Let's hope the owners and players see the light for the sake of the fans and bring back Major League Baseball.

Statement on Senate Action Confirming Dan Glickman as Secretary of Agriculture
March 30, 1995

I am pleased the Senate today overwhelmingly voted in support of Dan Glickman as the new Secretary at the Department of Agriculture.

Dan Glickman will be a strong voice and advocate for farmers, working families, and American agriculture.

During the past 2 years, the Agriculture Department has broken new ground on expanding trade opportunities, developing empowerment zones for distressed rural areas, and streamlining a major Federal agency that now runs more efficiently. However, our work is not done, and we must still tackle other important issues facing rural communities, farmers, and ranchers.

Next month will be especially important as we convene in Ames, Iowa, for the National Rural Conference to discuss the development of our Nation's economy, jobs, trade, and preservation of the family farm. It is important to hear firsthand from ordinary Americans, and I am pleased Dan is starting the job with his sleeves rolled up.

Message to the Congress on Science and Technology
March 29, 1995

To the Congress of the United States:

This Nation's future depends on strong public and private support for science and technology. My Administration's decision to make sound investments in science and technology even as the Federal Government cuts other spending is premised on three basic assumptions:

• Technology is the engine of economic growth.

• Scientific knowledge is the key to the future.

• Responsible government advances science and technology.

The Congress and the American people can find evidence of the Administration's dedication to responsible government support for science and technology in our defense and economic policies as well as our management of the science and technology enterprise. We have decreased the Federal deficit, helped to create millions of new jobs, and improved the tax treatment of small businesses and of investments in research and development. Hemispheric and global trade agreements as well as relaxation of outdated export controls have opened huge export markets to America's high-tech industries. My *National Security Strategy of Engagement and Enlargement* (February 1995) depends on farsighted and efficient science and technology investments. Our foreign policy and security interests are also supported by mutually beneficial international cooperation in science and technology.

We have consistently endorsed technology policies to increase prosperity and enhance environmental quality. In *Technology for America's*

Economic Growth (February 1993) and *Technology for a Sustainable Future* (July 1994) this Administration conveyed to the American people our plans for public/private partnerships to improve the business environment, enhance access to quality education and training, support development of information infrastructure, ensure continued excellence in health care, and strengthen America's global competitiveness.

Streamlined government based on strong partnerships—within the government, with the private sector, and among nations—is a hallmark of the Clinton/Gore Administration. The "virtual department" I created by establishing the National Science and Technology Council (NSTC) has cut bureaucratic red tape and produced a historic first: an integrated research and development budget that focuses on national goals. The NSTC has also produced large savings by enabling agencies to coordinate their efforts, divide tasks, and share resources.

My Committee of Advisors on Science and Technology (PCAST) provides critical links to industry and academia. Their oversight of NSTC activities, such as development of strategies for the management and disposition of fissile materials, promises to improve the Federal effort. So, too, do the forums and workshops that have drawn in thousands of experts and stakeholders to help develop priorities in areas as diverse as fundamental science; environmental technology; and health; safety; and food research.

I am also very proud of the steps we have taken to improve international cooperation in science and technology. Through the Gore-Chernomyrdin Commission we have used science and technology cooperation to ease the Russians' transition to democracy and a market economy. We have received valuable new technology and cultivated a crucial partner in global affairs through Russian participation in the international space station. We have used the Megasciences Forum of the Organization for Economic Cooperation and Development and other international forums to explore ways to share the increasing costs of cutting-edge research while maintaining our position of world leadership. Bilateral science and technology cooperation with other nations, including advanced industrial economies such as Japan, and big, emerging markets such as the People's Republic of China, serve us well in the global economy—giving us access to new ideas and new technologies while creating new opportunities for business.

Economists have estimated that the social rate of return on investments in research and development averages about 50 percent, or about double the average private rate of return. Clearly a solid Federal investment program is justified even in the leanest times. It is especially important for the Federal Government to maintain its investments in science and technology when the pressures of international competition are leading businesses to focus on shorter term payoffs at the expense of more basic, longer term, and riskier research and development.

In *Science in the National Interest* (August 1994), the Vice President and I reaffirmed our longstanding commitment to world leadership in science, mathematics, and engineering. Scientific discoveries inspire and enrich us. Equally important, science and mathematics education provides all Americans with the knowledge and skills they need to prepare for and adapt to the high-technology jobs of the future and to exercise the responsibilities of citizenship.

This Administration has articulated clear goals and established priorities for Federal spending, and our economic policies have improved the climate for private investment as well. We intend to work closely with the Congress to ensure the well-being of our children and grandchildren. These investments will prepare us for the challenges of the 21st century.

WILLIAM J. CLINTON

The White House,
March 29, 1995.

NOTE: This message was released by the Office of the Press Secretary on March 31.

Remarks to United States Troops in Port-au-Prince, Haiti
March 31, 1995

The President. Thank you.

Audience member. Go, Razorbacks!

The President. Who said, "Go, Razorbacks?" We should have had a longer promotion ceremony up here. [*Laughter*]

General Fisher asked me to take roll call. Are the 2d Brigade Warriors here? [*Applause*] The 65th Engineer Staffers? [*Applause*] The 1st of the 21st Gimlet? [*Applause*] The DISCOM Lightning Supporters? [*Applause*] The 1st of the 25th Aviation Bandits? [*Applause*] Special Forces Green Berets? Per person, they deserve applause. What about the 3d Squadron 2d ACR Wolfpack? [*Applause*] Are all the Light Fighters present and accounted for? [*Applause*]

I've been told that your lungs are as strong as your hearts and your hands.

Did I leave out anybody? Would you like to be heard? [*Applause*]

Audience members. Semper Fi!

The President. Good for you. [*Laughter*]

Every one of you who has taken part in Operation Uphold Democracy, on behalf of the American people, I am here to say thank you. Thank you for serving your Nation. Thank you for being democracy's warriors. Thank you for helping to bring back the promise of liberty to this long troubled land. You should be very proud of what you have done.

We gave you a tough and demanding mission which some said could not be done, and you proved them wrong. Look what you have accomplished. Seven months ago, a brutal military regime ruled Haiti, beating and torturing and murdering its citizens. Now the Haitian people are moving from a dark night of fear to a new day of freedom. You and all those who have served since last September helped to make that happen.

Seven months ago, thousands of migrants were streaming out of Haiti. Now tens of thousands of Haitians have come home, home to start to build a better life for themselves and their fellow country men and women. You helped to make that happen.

Seven months ago, the world wondered whether the United States could summon the will to protect democracy in this hemisphere. Now the world knows once again that the United States will honor its commitment and stand up for freedom. And you helped to make that happen. For all this, you should be very, very proud.

We gave our word, and the men and women of the Army, the Navy, the Air Force, the Marines, and the Coast Guard, you've kept our word. You have succeeded because you're the best trained, best prepared, best equipped fighting force in the world. Your reputation landed in Haiti before you did. And I am convinced that is one of the reasons that so much was done with so little bloodshed. The moment the military rulers learned that you were on the way, they got out of the way.

Since you've been here, you've been asked to do it all, and you have. You've taken thousands of guns off the street. You've helped to train a new Haitian police force. You've repaired roads and bridges. You've brought food and medicine to the farthest reaches of our country—to this country. And of course, you have literally turned the lights back on in dozens of towns.

You not only answered the call of duty, time and again you have gone beyond it. And that is what heroism is all about. Each of you in your own way has become a hero in Haiti. I'd like to mention a few of you whose stories I have learned about.

Sergeant 1st Class Steven Lamb, whose platoon conducted over 140 patrols, often under hazardous conditions: On one mission the platoon came across a mob using steel pipes to beat a man whose hands were tied behind his back. They dispersed the crowd, freed the man, treated his injuries. By stopping violence, confiscating weapons, and defusing problems before they got out of control, the platoon helped to give hundreds of Haitians a new sense of confidence and security. Thank you, Sergeant Lamb.

I met Sergeant 1st Class Michelle Howard of the Army: Many men and women under her command were overseas for the first time. Their morale was a little low without any mail from home, so she wrote the families of every single soldier in her platoon and told them to sound off in writing more often. Then the letters, postcards, and packages came in by the dozens. And now Sergeant Howard is called by the troops "Mother Teresa With a 9-Millimeter." Well, thank you, Mother Teresa, and thank you, Sergeant Howard.

I met 1st Sergeant Jose Garcia Apponte: And he and dozens of volunteers from all the service branches, on their free time and with no pay, started the School of Hope to teach Haitians English. Already the school has graduated more than 300 students. And now they'll return to their communities to share what they have learned. Thank you, Sergeant Garcia Apponte.

I met Private 1st Class John Firneno, a medic from the 32 ACR: He was on patrol about midnight last month when he came upon a young Haitian woman about to give birth. Now, that requires courage. [*Laughter*] As his comrades clustered around him with flashlights, he helped to deliver an 8-pound baby boy. Well, he didn't get a medical degree, but the boy now bears his name. Thank you, Private Firneno.

I want to thank the special forces who fanned out across the country and helped our local leaders learn the basics of government of, by, and for the people, good things like keeping the streets safe and holding town meetings and even some of the not so good things like collecting taxes.

Through these and dozens of other acts, big and small, you have defended democracy and made it stronger here. You have shown the Haitians what it means to be a soldier in a free society, working for the people, not against them. And when you go home, you must know that you have inspired a new generation of Haitians, supported by the United Nations mission, to carry on the never-ending struggle for freedom.

I know that for those of you who are preparing to leave, your loved ones are ready to welcome you home. General Sullivan, the Army Chief of Staff, recently visited in Hawaii with the families of the 25th Infantry Division soldiers. On my behalf, he thanked them for their sacrifice and the extraordinary support they have given to you. They and all of our military families have been heroes, too. And our country is in their debt, as well.

I'd also like to thank the soldiers from other countries who have been our partners in this remarkable endeavor. I know some of them are represented to my right here. Some of them

have shared this encampment with you, and some of them are in other places. I got to thinking about what a small world it can be when we are united for democracy and freedom.

Some of you may know that the First Lady is about to visit two of the countries represented here, Bangladesh and Nepal. Americans there, the First Lady and my daughter and others, Bangladeshis and Nepalese here, all standing for freedom all across the world, led by the United States, led by you. You should be very proud.

Even though, my fellow Americans, Haiti is democratic, free, and more secure than ever before, we know there is long hard work ahead. And we know that some of you will have a hand in it as part of the United Nations mission. In the end, of course, we all know the Haitian people themselves must rebuild their country and realize their dreams, just as we must in the United States. But now because of you, they have a chance to do so, just as we do in the United States.

The hand-painted signs seen all over Haiti say it all, "Thank you, America." Today America says thank you to the men and women of our Armed Forces who helped to give Haiti a second chance.

Whether you serve in an active unit, the Reserves, or the National Guard, we ask you to bear many burdens. We ask you to travel far from home. We ask you to stand in the face of danger. We ask you to be away from your families and your friends for a very long time. We ask you to protect your country and to defend democracy and freedom. We ask all these things. And time and again, you have risen to the challenge. Today, because of you, the Haitian people know why we call the United States "land of the free and the home of the brave."

You have allowed freedom to triumph over fear here. You have helped to remind the world that democracy is still on the march, even though it still has enemies. And you have stood up for a principle upon which our country was founded, that liberty is everyone's birthright.

Thank you, each and every one of you, and God bless America.

NOTE: The President spoke at 9:28 a.m. at Warrior Base. In his remarks, he referred to Maj. Gen. George A. Fisher, USA, Commanding General, 25th Infantry Division.

Remarks at an Arrival Ceremony in Port-au-Prince
March 31, 1995

The President. President Aristide, Mr. Secretary-General, distinguished guests, and citizens of a free and democratic Haiti, *bon-jour.*

I am deeply honored by President Aristide's invitation to speak with you today. In the many months we have known each other, I have learned firsthand of President Aristide's tremendous courage. His strength in the face of great challenge reflects the unbreakable will of the Haitian people. We respect him as the President you elected freely and fairly and for his leadership of all Haitians since his return.

Today we come together as friends. Today, once again, we give life to the ideals of democracy, justice, and freedom. Today we celebrate the restoration of democracy to your country. Never, never again must it be stolen away.

For centuries, the Haitian people have known little more than blood and terror. You have been robbed of opportunity and deprived of basic rights. Your children have grown up with too much violence. From Cite Soleil to the smallest village in the farthest corner of your land, you have sacrificed much in your quest for liberty. Now you stand on the brink of a new and more hopeful time. Now you have a chance to make real the dreams of those who liberated your nation nearly 200 years ago.

The tasks ahead will not be easy. Democracy does not flow naturally like the rivers, and prosperity does not spring full grown from the Earth. Justice does not bloom overnight. To achieve them, you must work hard, you must have patience, you must move forward together, with tolerance, openness, and cooperation. I believe you can do it, for as President Aristide has said, your challenge is great, but your will to succeed is greater.

Your democracy will be maintained and strengthened by free elections and respect for the rights and obligations enshrined in your Constitution. Your government, the United Nations, and the United States will do all we can to guarantee free, fair, and secure elections, first in June and then in December. We know from experience that when elections are free, fair, and secure, you will participate. That is what democracy requires of you, and we know you will do it.

Your nation has been stripped bare of many of its natural resources. But the most important of these resources, you, the people, have survived with dignity and hope. As the proverb says, *"Espwa fé viv."*

Now you have a chance to come together to make the rice fields come alive and harvest the corn and millet, to build the schools and clinics that promise a better future for your children. We, your neighbors, your allies, and your friends, will support your efforts to create jobs, to attract investment from beyond your borders, and to rebuild and repair your injured land.

In a few months, the program will begin to pave the 1,000 kilometers of your roads. And later this year I will send the American Peace Corps here to help to organize the planting of millions of trees. As the roads are built and the trees are planted, thousands of you will have jobs. As you begin this work, I urge your country men and women who fled the terror to return and to help you to rebuild your land and theirs.

Economic progress will demand much patience. But we will stand with you as you tackle the hard and sometimes painful work ahead. *Men anpil chay pa lou.*

There will be times of great frustration as you build your democracy and move toward prosperity. But today, Haiti has more friends than ever before. And so once again, I urge each and every citizen of this nation to come together in this spirit of unity that President Aristide has so eloquently promoted. I can do no better than to repeat his words, "Say no to vengeance, no to revenge, yes to reconciliation."

[Inaudible]—take the law into their own hands. Each of you must choose, as most of you have already chosen, to build up, not tear down. I congratulate you for the patience you have already shown.

History records that two centuries ago on the eve of your independence, and during my nation's Revolutionary War, more than 500 of your ancestors came from Haiti to my country and died in the fight to bring the United States to life. More than 200 years later, the United States is proud to have helped to give you a second chance to build your democracy and bring life to the dreams of your liberators.

I have been told that throughout your land, our soldiers, our diplomats, and our volunteers have been greeted by hand-painted signs with three simple words. These words go right to their hearts and to mine. They are: Thank you, America. Now it is my turn to say, *Merci à Haiti.* Thank you for the warmth of your welcome and your support for all who have joined hands with you. Thank you for embracing peace, for denying despair, for holding on to hope.

Because of your courage, because of your determination, freedom can triumph over fear.

Today we stand in the warm, bright light of liberty, and together we can say, *Kenbé fèm, pa lagé. Kenbé fèm, pa lagé.*

Merci, and thank you.

NOTE: The President spoke at 11:16 a.m. at the National Palace. In his remarks, he referred to President Jean-Bertrand Aristide of Haiti and United Nations Secretary-General Boutros Boutros-Ghali. A tape was not available for verification of the content of these remarks.

Exchange With Reporters Prior to Discussions With President Jean-Bertrand Aristide of Haiti in Port-au-Prince
March 31, 1995

Assassination of Mireille Durocher Bertin

Q. President Aristide, was your Interior Minister involved in the Tuesday assassination?

President Aristide. No.

Q. Have these allegations cast a damper over the President's visit?

President Aristide. No.

Q. Have you asked the FBI to look into the possibility that he might have been involved in the Bertin death?

President Aristide. We welcome help from the international community, from the United States in helping us finding proof of this violence for months—for days. And together we'll be working.

Q. Mr. President, are you satisfied the Interior Minister was not involved?

President Clinton. President Aristide asked the FBI to help investigate this. They are doing an investigation. I think we should applaud this quick and decisive action and let the investigation proceed and not presume its results.

This is a day of celebration, and nothing can cast a cloud on it. It's a day of mission accomplished for the United States, a day of celebration for Haiti and for the United Nations force, and a day for looking ahead for the work still to be done.

President's Visit

Q. How did you like your reception, Mr. President?

President Clinton. I liked it a lot. It was very nice. It was great.

Q. Must be a little bit tired—all the handshaking.

President Clinton. It was quite wonderful.

Q. [*Inaudible*]—was your idea?

President Clinton. No, but I liked it, though.

NOTE: The exchange began at 12:05 p.m. at the National Palace. A reporter referred to Interior Minister Gen. Mondesir Beaubrun of Haiti. A tape was not available for verification of the content of this exchange.

Remarks at the United Nations Transition Ceremony in Port-au-Prince
March 31, 1995

Mr. Secretary-General, President Aristide, members of the multinational force in Haiti, members of the United Nations mission in Haiti: We gather to celebrate the triumph of freedom over fear. And we are here to look ahead to the next steps that we will take together to help the people of Haiti strengthen their hard-won democracy.

Six months ago, a 30-nation multinational force, led by the United States, entered Haiti with a clear mission: To ensure the departure of the military regime, to restore the freely elected government of Haiti, and to establish a secure and stable environment in which the people of Haiti could begin to rebuild their country. Today, that mission has been accomplished, on schedule and with remarkable success.

On behalf of the United States, I thank all the members of the multinational force for their outstanding work, and pledge our support for the United Nations mission in Haiti.

Over the past 6 months, the multinational force has proved that a shared burden makes for a lighter load. Working together, 30 nations from around the world—from the Caribbean to Australia, from Bangladesh to Jordan—demonstrated the effectiveness and the benefits of international peacekeeping. And they helped give the people of Haiti a second chance at democracy.

The multinational force ensured the peaceful transition from the military regime to President Aristide. It removed more than 30,000 weapons and explosive devices from the streets. Through the international police monitors, led by Commissioner Ray Kelly, it trained and monitored an interim police force and worked side by side with them throughout Haiti. And it helped to prepare a permanent civilian police force that will maintain security and respect for human rights in the months and years ahead.

Let me say to the members of the new permanent police force who are with us here today: You are the guardians of Haiti's new democracy. Its future rests on your shoulders. Uphold the constitution. Respect democracy and human rights. Defend them. That is your sacred mission and your solemn obligation.

Now it is the United Nations mission's task to secure and stabilize the environment in Haiti and to help the government prepare for free and fair elections. The mission, with participants from 33 countries, has the tools it needs to succeed: a 6,000-strong military force under the command of United States Army General Joseph Kinzer; a 900-member international police force led by Chief Superintendent Neil Pouliot of Canada; and dozens of well-trained economic, political, and legal advisers.

The United Nations mission will end its work here in February 1996, after the election and inauguration of a new President. To all of you taking part in the U.N. mission, I know many challenges lie between here and there. Your work will be demanding and difficult. But the multinational force has set a strong foundation of success upon which to build.

Most important of all, the people of Haiti, have shown a powerful commitment to peace and to reconciliation. Working with them, you can help make real Haiti's reborn promise of democracy. I know you will do that.

Good luck, and Godspeed.

NOTE: The President spoke at 2:16 p.m. at the National Palace. In his remarks, he referred to United Nations Secretary-General Boutros Boutros-Ghali.

The President's Radio Address
April 1, 1995

The President. Good morning. I'm speaking to you this morning from the Gibbs Magnet School for International Studies in Little Rock, Arkansas. I'm happy to be joined by the principal, Dr. Marjorie Bassa, members of her staff, and 30 wonderful elementary students, their parents, and other interested citizens here.

Good morning, class.

Students. Good morning, Mr. President.

The President. What you just heard was the sound of America's future. This school and these people are living proof that the education reforms that were started when I was Governor of Arkansas and that are continuing now under the leadership of Governor Tucker are paying off.

The young people who attend this public school are getting a head start on the 21st century. Beginning in kindergarten, they learn about other cultures. They receive foreign language training. They're already acquiring the skills that will allow them one day to compete and win in the new global economy. They come from many different racial and cultural backgrounds, but they all have a shot at the American dream.

I want to spend a few moments telling you why I think education and training for all of our people is the most important thing we can do to keep the American dream alive in the 21st century.

You know Washington's in the midst of a great debate today about the proper role of our National Government. On one side is the old view that big, one-size-fits-all Government can provide the answers to all of our big problems. On the other side is the view that Government is the source of all of our problems. In the real world, that's a false choice.

Let's look at what started this debate. As we move toward the 21st century and the information age, jobs and incomes will depend more and more on what we know and what we can learn. That means that today, at the end of the cold war, we're able to create jobs, new businesses, new millionaires at a rapid rate, more than ever before. But at the same time, about two-thirds of our people are working hard for the same or lower wages and are quite insecure about their future. And we know we still have too many social problems we're not making enough headway on, crime and drugs, violence and family breakdown.

In the real world, we have to face the fact that we have to create opportunity but deal with these problems of economic stagnation and social disintegration. And we are stuck with a Government that's too organized to meet the problems of yesterday and not enough able to meet the problems of today and tomorrow.

I believe we have to chart a new course between the old way of big Government and the new rage of no Government, because I believe we need a Government that does four things: first, that creates economic opportunity—grow the middle class and shrink the under class; second, that enhances the security of the American people here at home, on our streets, in our schools, and abroad; and third, that reforms the National Government to make it smaller, less bureaucratic, to serve the interests of ordi-

nary Americans, not special interests, to serve the future, not the past, and to demand more personal responsibility of our citizens. Fourth, and most important, we need a Government that helps our people raise their education and skill levels so they can make the most of their own lives. That's what I call the New Covenant, a partnership between Americans and their Government that offers more opportunity in return for more responsibility.

Earlier this week, I convened a regional economic conference at Emory University in Atlanta with a group of economists, business and Government leaders. And working Americans discussed ways to strengthen our economy and to ensure a better future for our children. They were Republicans, Democrats, and independents. But the one thing we all agreed on was that the countries that will do the best job of developing the full capacities of all of their children and all of their adults will be the most successful in the 21st century. We all agree that higher education levels are essential if we're going to raise the incomes of working Americans, if we're going to grow the middle class and shrink the under class.

That's why I and my administration have worked so hard to expand Head Start, to set world-class standards for our schools, to give parents and teachers more resources to meet those standards but also to give them more authority at the school level to decide how best to achieve excellence. We've worked to establish apprenticeship programs to prepare young people who don't go on to college to get higher paying jobs. And we've worked hard to make college loans more affordable for more students, millions of them throughout the country.

By eliminating the middlemen in the college loan system, lowering the cost, and offering better repayment terms, our direct student loan program is giving more young people a chance to go to college while saving tax dollars at the same time. And we're demanding more responsibility in return. More students get loans at lower cost, but now they have to pay them back. Stricter enforcement of the student loan program has cut the cost of delinquent loans to taxpayers from $2.8 billion in 1991 to a billion dollars today. That's opportunity and responsibility.

Because we've focused on education, for the last 2 years we've been able to cut Government spending, cut the deficit, cut hundreds of programs and over 100,000 bureaucrats from the Federal budget, and still increase our investment in education.

Now, many in Congress think there's no difference in education and other spending. For example, there are proposals to reduce funding for Head Start; for public school efforts to meet the national education goals; for our national service program, Ameri- Corps, which provides scholarship money for young people who will work at minimum wage jobs in local community service projects; even proposals to reduce school lunch funding. There are proposals to eliminate our efforts for safe and drug-free schools altogether and, unbelievably, to cut the college loan programs.

These are not wise proposals. Here at Gibbs, where students are preparing for the 21st century, close to 50 percent of the students depend upon the School Lunch Program for a nutritious meal. And all these young people, not just those who have the money to afford it, should be able to go as far as their talents will carry them. And if that means they need scholarships, student loans, and the opportunity to do community service, we ought to give it to them.

Some in Congress want to cut education to pay for tax cuts for the wealthy. I want instead a middle class tax cut that helps families pay for education and training, a tax deduction for education costs after high school.

Now in the past, education and training have enjoyed broad, bipartisan support. Last year, with strong support from Republicans and Democrats, Congress enacted my proposals to help students and schools meet the challenges of today and tomorrow. Educational experts said we did more for education by expanding Head Start, expanding apprenticeships, expanding college loans than any session of Congress in 30 years.

Now in this new Congress, some want to cut education, and that's wrong. Gibbs Magnet School is a reflection of what we ought to be doing more of in America. I don't know what political party these children belong to, but I do know we need them all and they deserve our best efforts to give them a shot at the American dream. We must begin when they're young, training our people to succeed, preparing them for a lifetime of learning. The fight for education is the fight for the American dream.

Thanks again to all those people who are here with me today, especially our children. And thanks for listening.

NOTE: The President spoke at 9:06 a.m. from the Gibbs Magnet School for International Studies in Little Rock, AR.

Interview With Chris Fowler, Digger Phelps, and Dick Vitale of ESPN
April 1, 1995

NCAA Basketball Championship

Q. Last year President Clinton was the first Chief Executive to attend the Final Four in person. Right now we are honored; he is definitely the first President to ever join us on "Sports Center," from Little Rock. Mr. President, you're one for two today. The home State Razorbacks get in the championship game. Your good friend is defeated.

The President. Well, I'm very proud of both those teams. I'm of course proud of Arkansas. They played well. And you can never count the Tarheels out; Dean Smith coached a great game there down the stretch. And I'm glad we hung on, and it's a real tribute to those young men and to Coach Richardson.

And of course, I think Eddie Sutton had a great season, and I'm very proud of him. But UCLA has fabulous talent. And you've said it all night, but the point guard, Edney, was terrific at the end. He just took the game over.

Q. Well, Mr. President, you and I talked earlier today on the phone, and we were going through that first-half adjustment, and you said, "We need a big guy inside." Were you happy the second half?

The President. Real happy. You and I were talking—you know, they just had to get the ball to Williamson. They did, and he delivered just the way he's delivered all year. He's a real clutch player, and he played magnificently tonight.

Q. Mr. President, Dick Vitale. You look at the match-up now, UCLA, and you look at the match-up against Arkansas—how do they contain the little guy? You're a coach—should they zone? You told Mr. Jarvis to use the zone earlier this year against Massachusetts. Should they zone?

The President. Yes, I did. I think I'd start in the zone. I think Williamson will do well. I think that Thurman will do well. And I think that we've got enough skill, enough talent to beat them. But boy, they're deep, they're fast, and they're good. And we're going to have to play great defense to win that game. That's why they really got back in this game, I think.

Q. Mr. President, what has it been like as an Arkansas fan in this tournament? Game after game they've survived. They were dead against Syracuse before the timeout was called by Lawrence Moten. The average margin of victory, just four points. Has it been tough as a fan?

The President. It's been tough as a fan, but you know, every team this team has played has had their best game of the year against them. And it's been hard for them to get up. But the last two games they've been—they've been a different team in the second half of both the last two games. They've played like national champions, and they're going back to the final, and they deserve it. It's going to be a great, great game, I think.

Q. Well, Mr. President, now that you've gone through the weekend—and a little golf, a little basketball—do you have the urge to sneak out to Seattle Monday night?

The President. Oh, I do, but wherever I am, I'm going to be there cheering for them. And I'm really proud of them, and I'm excited. The fans will see a great game. UCLA's got a terrific team, and this will be a very, very exciting final, I predict.

Q. Mr. President, you better come out here, because word has it that John Wooden may be out here to give them a little bit of an edge. They need you.

The President. Well, I'm nowhere near in his class, but I'll be screaming my lungs out wherever.

Q. Thank you very much for joining us.

The President. Thank you.

NOTE: The interview began at 9:21 p.m. The President spoke by satellite from Doe's Eat Place in Little Rock, AR. In his remarks, he referred to University of Arkansas coach Nolan Richardson and players Corliss Williamson and Scotty Thurman; Oklahoma State University coach Eddie Sutton; University of California-Los Angeles player Tyus Edney and former coach John Wooden; George Washington University coach Mike Jarvis; and Syracuse University player Lawrence Moten. A tape was not available for verification of the content of this interview.

Statement on the Major League Baseball Strike Settlement
April 2, 1995

Today's decision is good news for the game of baseball, its fans, and the local economics of the cities where baseball is played.

While I am heartened to know this season will start with major league players, there are a number of underlying issues which still need to get resolved. I strongly urge the owners and players to meet and reach full agreement at the bargaining table so that another season won't be in jeopardy.

Remarks at the Dedication of the Dean B. Ellis Library at Arkansas State University in Jonesboro
April 3, 1995

Thank you very much. I think Molly Mayer did a great job, don't you? [*Applause*] I am delighted to be here today with so many old friends. I look out across this crowd and see a great portion of my life looking back at me, and I'm glad to see you all here.

I'm delighted to be back at ASU. I got myself a list from my staff—as I get older my memory begins to fade—I got my staff to pull up a list of all the times I have been here, at least in official capacity, to this campus as Governor, and we found—or as attorney general—we found a dozen times. I've been here a dozen more times, I know, just to see students and have meetings. But it is wonderful to be back here.

I was glad to see Gene Smith giving his speech. And I'm kind of glad you didn't let him retire. [*Laughter*] He looks young enough to keep working to me, and he's certainly done a wonderful job. I thank my friend John Trout for what he said. I cannot even begin to recount all the instances in which I worked with people from Craighead County and indeed from all of northeast Arkansas in trying to generate more economic opportunities here. I was very glad to be accompanied here today by two of your former presidents, Carl Whillock and, of course, Congressman Thornton.

And Rodney Slater and Mack McLarty and I all came up on a helicopter. We didn't mean to interrupt your ceremony, but anyway, it's not a bad sight to see us coming down. And we were all talking about all the changes that had occurred at ASU over the last several years and how much better things are. And for that I thank all the members of the board of trustees, Larry Ross and the others—and I'm glad to see a lot of people I appointed still serving; that's an immensely rewarding thing—as well as the members of the board of higher education.

I'd like to say a special word of thanks to Congresswoman Blanche Lambert Lincoln for what is literally a ferocious job of lobbying she does in behalf of the interest of the people of the First District. There is no Member of the House of Representatives who is on my doorstep more often for more different things. And when I complained about it one day, she said, "Well, that's just the way you used to behave when you were Governor." [*Laughter*]

Let me say a special word of thanks to the members of the Arkansas Legislature I see out here in the audience. One of them was in Washington the other day for a meeting, and he said, "You know, I kind of miss you, and I never thought I'd say that." [*Laughter*]

I remember coming here in 1977 when I was attorney general. This is how I really got interested in helping ASU. I came here to speak to a commencement. And it was supposed to be a beautiful day like this, and instead it rained, and we had to go inside to the old field house where there was no air conditioning. And the rain—you know how it is when it gets warm here; the rain just makes it worse. The humidity was sizzling around. No one could breathe. The faculty and the students were suffocating in their beautiful robes. And I gave a 6-minute speech. [*Laughter*] And I made up my mind that if God ever gave me the opportunity to serve long enough, I'd build us a place with air conditioning where I could give a longer speech. [*Laughter*] And that's how the Convocation Center got started.

I have enjoyed immensely being involved with this wonderful place, it was mentioned already, the Communications and Education Building and the Convocation Center and now this library. I'll never forget the first time I went to an event in the Convocation Center. I've seen a lot of games, a lot of athletics. I remember the first time Jonesboro got to host the AAU national championship basketball tournament. And I came and saw two high school kids play basketball, named Chris Webber and Grant Hill, who later had a pretty good career, all because they had the experience of playing basketball here when they were 16 years of age.

I'd also like to say a special word of appreciation to all of you who have run all of the programs here, the extracurricular programs here at the university. And I'd like to say a special word of appreciation to one of your students who became very, very famous this year in that remarkable, wonderful contribution to our understanding of American life, "Hoop Dreams." Arthur Agee has really been a great example of what we could do with our dreams.

I'd like to say one other word of introduction. I was profoundly pleased to know that a special part of this new library has been set aside for a Delta Studies Center. As has already been said, the delta region of our State has always had special meaning for me. When I was a boy coming home from college, I used to take a day of my Christmas vacation every year and just drive around in the delta. I never saw a place that was so poor economically and so rich in spirit and people. And when I was head of the Lower Mississippi Delta Study Commission, we made a common commitment to try to invest more in our people so that we could be rich in spirit and rich economically. And I know that this studies center will carry on the work of that commission and will continue its important mission.

I'd like to say also that—all of you know this, and it's already been said, but—I actually ran for Governor for a pretty simple and straightforward reason many years ago. I wanted to see the people of my State have the same opportunities as the people of the rest of this country had. And I believed that the only way we could do it was by concentrating on building the economy, maintaining our unique quality of life, and educating our people, and doing it in a spirit of partnership. All my life I had seen our State held down by public leaders who played on our fears and divided us one from another. And for a good long time here in Arkansas now we've been working in the opposite direction, developing our economy, educating our people, preserving our quality of life, and working together.

I think it's pretty clear that that course has been more successful. If you look at the faces of the young people here, if you look at all of you here, not only from the cities of eastern Arkansas but from the smallest little hamlets, who support Arkansas State University, if you look at the remarkable job growth our State has enjoyed just in the last few years after a decade of struggling to modernize our economy, it is obvious that we made the right decision as a people.

I ran for President because just as I thought Arkansas was going to catch up to the rest of the country, our country was clearly having problems getting into the next century with the American dream of opportunity for all alive.

We live in a very unusual time, indeed, almost without precedent I think, in human history, where our economy is growing but most of our people say they feel insecure. How can that happen? How could we have 2 years where we'd have over 6 million new jobs, a dramatic drop in the unemployment rate, the lowest rates of inflation and unemployment combined in 25 years, and still a majority of the American people say, "I am really worried about my future."

It has happened because of what America's role in the global economy is doing to the lives of ordinary Americans. It has happened because even as we create more jobs, most people haven't had an increase in their income, and there is increasing inequality in America.

From the year I was born at the end of World War II until the year I was elected Governor in 1978, America rose together economically. Every income group and every region was doing better, and they were rising together. But in the last 15 years, that's all changed. And it makes your mission even more important.

In the last 15 years, the wealthiest and best educated Americans have done right well as we've moved in the global economy. About a third of us are doing fine. But about 60 percent of us are working harder for the same or lower wages, so that even when we create jobs in America, many people wind up being insecure. They say, "Well, maybe I'll be one of the people laid off."

And as we move from big corporations to small businesses being our main employers, a lot of those big companies are laying people off. Is that cause for despair? Not at all. Don't you forget this, this is still the greatest country in the world. We've still got the strongest economy. We're still producing more jobs. We've still got the greatest ability to adapt. We still do better at relating to one another across racial and religious and ethnic lines than any multifaceted country in human history. You should be optimistic about the future.

But what it does mean is that we must now nationally do what we tried to do here. As a country we should be focused on growing our economy, maintaining our quality of life, educating our people, and doing it together. There is a huge debate today about what the Government in Washington ought to be doing.

And you know, ever since the beginning of this Republic, we've all loved to cuss the Government, especially at tax time. Every one of us can tell at least one and sometimes 50 stories that just prove beyond any doubt that the Government would mess up a one-car parade. [*Laughter*] But the truth is, if you look over the 200-year history of this country, we're still here, the longest lasting democracy in human history, because most of the time we did the right thing. Most of the time we met the challenges of the day and did the right thing.

Just parenthetically, I'll tell you, I wish all of you could have been with me in Haiti a few days ago to see all our young men and women in uniform who revolutionized a country that was mired in violence and did it with barely a shot fired. Those young Americans are the best that we have to offer. And if we look at them and what works there, that'll work for our country as well.

So now that I'm living in Washington instead of down here with you, every day I hear this big debate up there. And the popular thing, of course, is just to talk about how the Government would mess up a one-car parade and tell everybody they're against it and say, let's just cut everything. That's the new rage in Washington, "If there were no Federal Government, we'd have no problem." And the old rage was that the Federal Government could solve all the problems.

Well, based on my experience with you, I would say both ideas are wrong and present a false choice. The great things about this country are things that the Government can't reach. They have to do with how we behave personally and with our families and our communities and what we do in the workplace. But we need our Government as a partner. And I have tried to say I believe with all my heart, if you want us to do well in the 21st century, we've got to do four things: We've got to have more jobs and higher income; we've got to educate our people; we need a Government that is smaller and less bureaucratic, that's more oriented toward the future than the past; and we have to have more security, more security in a profound sense.

I am proud of the fact that since I've been President there are no Russian missiles pointed at the children of the United States for the first time since the dawn of the nuclear age. But I also know that our security is threatened

when there is too much violence on our streets, too much violence in our schools. Our security is threatened by drugs. Our security is threatened by the strains on families. And our security is threatened when families who work hard and do the right things by their children are mistreated and abused and don't have the chances they need to support a better future.

So I'd like to say to you in front of this library today, our country under Franklin Roosevelt began to create a safety net for the elderly. It was Social Security, and it included Medicare later. We developed a certain safety net for poor people. But in the future, if we are really going to become what we ought to be, we need a commitment to the middle class that will end this income stagnation, that will end this increasing inequality, that is a safety net for all Americans. And it is one word: education, education, education.

Today, the people who believe that everything the Government does is wrong want to cut everything, either to balance the budget or to give a tax cut. Well, I'm for doing both. We've reduced this deficit $600 billion since I've been President. We're going to have 3 years of declining deficits for the first time since Harry Truman was President. I am for cutting unnecessary spending. We ought to do that.

And I believe we ought to cut taxes for people in ways that will raise their incomes today and tomorrow. That's why I think the best thing we could do is to give people a tax deduction for the cost of all their and their children's education expenses after high school.

But let me say, Arkansas is not where it is today because we cut education. And if we'd started investing in education and improving education 10 or 20 years earlier than we did, we'd be further ahead today. There's not a person in this audience who doubts the truth of that statement. And therefore I say to you, you should say to all of us, "Get that deficit down. Get this economy going. Be fair to American taxpayers, but do not cut education."

In the last 2 years, we have expanded Head Start. We have given our schools the opportunity to meet national education goals and still have more flexibility than the Federal Government used to give them. We helped States to establish apprenticeship programs for young people who don't go on to college but who do want good jobs. And we have dramatically expanded the availability of affordable college loans with better repayment terms to the young people of this country. We have started the national service program to give young people the chance to earn money for college while working in their communities. And some of our volunteers are over here in the audience today. They've worked with migrant workers in Hope. They've helped to reduce school dropouts in Texarkana. They've done a lot of really wonderful things.

And there are people today in Washington who think the answer to our problems is to restrict the availability of student loans, to cut Head Start, to reduce our commitment to the national education goals, to destroy the national service program, even, believe it or not, to cut the School Lunch Program or to eliminate the program to make our schools safer and more drug-free.

My friends, this has never been a partisan political issue. When we were in Little Rock working on education, we had Republicans and Democrats working on it together. Last year and the year before, every piece of legislation we passed for education in Washington had the support of Democrats and Republicans. This has not been a partisan political issue, and we dare not let it become one. If we walk away from education when the 21st century depends upon what we know and what we can learn, it will be just as dangerous as it would have been for us to disarm in the middle of the cold war. We didn't do that, and we shouldn't do this.

So let me say in closing, you know, I'm feeling a little sentimental today. I'm sitting here wishing I could focus on the hundreds of people I've already seen that I've walked so many roads with. Those of you who were working for me in 1982 in these 11 counties in northeast Arkansas know that if it hadn't been for you then, I wouldn't be here now as President.

But let me say that in spite of all the sentiment and warm feelings I have, the main thing I want to say is when I look at you, I think you have good common sense. I think you love your communities, and you love your families, and you love this country. The people I know

up here have spent a lifetime trying to make things better for their families and their communities and their future. And I am telling you that we can't afford sentiment today because we've got to make some tough decisions.

Yes, we've got to cut unnecessary, wasteful, bloated Government. Yes, we have to get things under control in Washington. I've been working like crazy for 2 years to do it. But we dare not in the information age believe that the answer to America's growing insecurity about jobs and incomes is to undermine the very thing that will take us into the 21st century still the strongest country in the world, still the greatest country the world has ever known, still the home of the American dream that says no matter who you are or where you're from, if you work hard and play by the rules, you can live up to your God-given capacities and your wildest dreams. And that, my fellow Americans, is education.

Now, the country needs that strategy. And I ask you to support your Members of Congress, to support the people here, and to remind everybody that this is not rocket science, this is basic. And this is America's future.

I am delighted to be here. I'm honored to have played a role in this library and all the other things that are here at ASU. But the most important thing that's here at ASU is the speaker who introduced me and all the other students. They are our future. And all of us had better decide that our first commitment is to do right by them. If we do, the rest of us will do just fine.

Thank you, and God bless you all.

NOTE: The President spoke at 10:55 a.m. at the front of the library. In his remarks, he referred to Molly Mayer, student government president, and Eugene Smith, president, Arkansas State University; John Trout, Jr., editor and publisher, Jonesboro Sun; Rodney Slater, Federal Highway Administrator; and Thomas F. McLarty III, Counselor to the President.

Message to the Congress Transmitting a Report on Alaska's Mineral Resources
April 3, 1995

To the Congress of the United States:

I transmit herewith the 1994 Annual Report on Alaska's Mineral Resources, as required by section 1011 of the Alaska National Interest Lands Conservation Act (Public Law 96–487; 16 U.S.C. 3151). This report contains pertinent public information relating to minerals in Alaska gathered by the U.S. Geological Survey, the U.S. Bureau of Mines, and other Federal agencies.

WILLIAM J. CLINTON

The White House,
April 3, 1995.

Interview With Pat O'Brien, Mike Krzyzewski, and Quinn Buckner of CBS Sports
April 3, 1995

NCAA Basketball Championship

Mr. O'Brien. Good evening, Mr. President. How are you?

The President. Fine, Pat, how are you?

Mr. O'Brien. I'm fine. It sounds like you're having a nice time back there watching the game.

Your thoughts, sir, on the first half?

The President. I can't hear you, I'm sorry.

Mr. O'Brien. That's okay, that happens.

Your thoughts on the first half, sir?

The President. Well, I think that it's a—I'm glad we're just one point behind. We made a lot of unforced errors, and as you were saying, UCLA had very quick hands. They played great defense, and I'm looking forward to an exciting second half.

I think that our team and their team—it's a wonderful game so far. But you've got to give it to UCLA. They played great defense, and they got a lot of very good shots on offense. And I think that's why they're a point ahead.

Mr. O'Brien. I know you've tried to watch a few of Arkansas' games this season. Do you have any fingernails left? The games have been such nail-biters throughout the tournament.

The President. Yes, they always give us a lot of thrills. Basketball is exciting enough on its own, but they give us a little extra every game. We try to have a cardiologist at every watching party that we have. [*Laughter*]

Mr. Buckner. Mr. President, Quinn Buckner. Did you fill out your brackets this year?

The President. Did I what?

Mr. Buckner. Did you get a chance to fill out the brackets at the beginning of the tournament?

The President. No, I didn't, and I wish I had. But I would have been wrong on all accounts except I expected these two teams to be in the finals. Otherwise, there were a lot of surprises along the way.

Mr. O'Brien. Mr. President, we know you're very athletic and earlier this week, on Friday I think, you were in Haiti. And we have some film, a tape of you shooting buckets out there on the grass with some of our good troops down there. And there you put up a bank shot. I don't know if you called it or not. [*Laughter*]

The President. You've got to call that one. [*Laughter*]

Mr. O'Brien. Then you shot around at Arkansas State with Arthur Agee, from the documentary film "Hoop Dreams." And Mike Krzyzewski, who you rooted against last year, is going to go over your form on this. He's going to telestrate your form.

Mr. Krzyzewski. Well, if you don't mind——

The President. This is his chance to get even. [*Laughter*]

Mr. Krzyzewski. Mr. President, I'm sure you're accustomed to some criticism, so I'm going to critique you. [*Laughter*]

447

Here's Mr. President in the lane. He's not worried about 3 seconds. Good form. But he doesn't want to show that he's just an inside player; he goes outside. [*Laughter*]

And now he's in the outside. Watch that form. Take a look at his hand and the release. [*Laughter*]

Mr. O'Brien. Very good, Mr. President.

Mr. Krzyzewski. It's a very delicate release. And he puts it through.

Mr. O'Brien. What do you think, Mr. President?

Mr. Krzyzewski. That's not bad. What do you think?

The President. I think the feet were on the floor. [*Laughter*]

Mr. Krzyzewski. You know, quite honestly, sir, what did you take away from your visit with Arthur Agee today?

The President. Well, he's a remarkable young man, you know. And I—what I took away from it is, here's a young fellow that made up his mind he was going to make something of his life and try to live out his dream. He's committed to continuing his education until he gets his degree. He still wants to play pro basketball. But whatever happens to him, he's going to have a good life. And I hope that "Hoop Dreams" and I hope that Arthur Agee both serve as a kind of an inspiration to kids all across this country who are growing up in very hard circumstances. They can make it. They can be something. And I'm very grateful that he came down to Arkansas to go to college. He's a terrific young man, and I wish him well.

Baseball Strike

Mr. O'Brien. Mr. President, I know you're also very grateful that the baseball season will begin here at the end of April. I know you followed it very closely.

The President. You bet.

Mr. O'Brien. Would you like to throw out the first pitch at the end of April?

The President. I sure hope that I can do that. I'm looking forward to it. And I think it's going to be good for the country to get baseball back on track. I still hope they can get together and actually work out these differences. We don't need a cloud hanging over baseball for another whole season. And they ought to be able to do it. They're not that many people, and there's lots of money there. They can figure out how to divide it and give us the sport back.

President's Golf Game

Mr. O'Brien. Well, with the Masters coming up, Mr. President, I have to ask you, how many mulligans do you get when you play golf with your friends? [*Laughter*]

The President. Well, it depends, but I try not to take any anymore—maybe one off the first tee. [*Laughter*]

Mr. O'Brien. Okay, good for you. Good for you.

Mr. President, thank you. It's always a pleasure to talk hoops with you. Thank you for watching. We'll see you down the road.

The President. Thanks. Keep your fingers crossed. Bye-bye.

NOTE: The interview began at 8:34 p.m. The President spoke by satellite from Juanita's Restaurant in Little Rock, AR.

The President's News Conference With Prime Minister John Major of the United Kingdom
April 4, 1995

The President. Good afternoon. Please be seated. I am delighted to welcome Prime Minister Major back to the White House.

Throughout this century, the United States and the United Kingdom have stood together on the great issues that have confronted our people. Our common cause has been at the heart of our success in two World Wars and, of course, in the cold war. In just the last 2 years British-American cooperation has played an essential role in allowing us to reduce the threat of weapons of mass destruction, in promoting peace around the world, and certainly in expanding free trade.

Today we have continued working in that tradition. We've had excellent discussions. We've covered a broad range of issues. We have, as always, found much to agree about.

On security issues, we agreed that the inevitable process of NATO expansion must proceed smoothly, gradually, and openly, without any surprises. This is essential for extending stability, democracy, and prosperity throughout Europe. We believe that, in parallel with the enlargement of NATO, the alliance must develop and maintain close ties with Russia.

We affirmed our shared commitment to a political settlement in Bosnia, based on the Contact Group plan. The conflict is being prolonged because of Bosnian-Serb intransigence. Renewed fighting will not end the conflict but only lead to more bloodshed and continued stalemate.

The Prime Minister and I also vowed to continue working together to contain the Iraqi threat to stability in the Persian Gulf region. We are deeply concerned that Saddam Hussein could be regaining the ability to build weapons of mass destruction. We are determined that Iraq must meet all its United Nations obligations. This is no time to relax sanctions.

The Iraqi people are suffering tremendously under Saddam's tyranny, and they do deserve the help of the international community. But easing up on a regime that oppresses people will not help them. So while there can be no compromise, the United States, the United Kingdom, and Argentina have put forward new proposals in the United Nations to get food and medicine to the people of Iraq. We hope other nations will join these efforts and support our Security Council resolution and pressure Saddam Hussein to stop the needless suffering of his innocent citizens.

Prime Minister Major told me a great deal about his recent trip to the Middle East. We both strongly believe this is a hopeful moment for broadening the circle of peace. The United States and Europe must continue to fight the efforts to derail the peace process by those who prefer destruction to peace. It is clear that for peace to take root in the region, more economic assistance is vital. Peace and prosperity depend upon one another. I applaud the United Kingdom's investment program in the West Bank and Gaza, as well as its debt relief measures for Jordan. We must all continue to support those who take risks for peace.

Nowhere is this more true than in Northern Ireland. I salute the Prime Minister for the tremendous efforts he is making to bring an enduring peace to Northern Ireland. Today, Northern Ireland is closer to a just and lasting settlement than at any time in a generation, thanks in large measure to the vision and courage of John Major. He and Prime Minister Bruton of Ireland together introduced the Joint Framework, which provides a landmark opportunity to move ahead toward a political settlement, one that will be backed by both of Northern Ireland's communities. We also agreed that the paramilitaries of both sides must get rid of their weapons for good so that violence never returns to Northern Ireland.

And we must work to increase economic opportunity in that area. Their prospects have been blighted by bloodshed for too long. Next month our White House Conference on Trade and Investment in Ireland will help to expand the ties between the United States, Northern Ireland, and Ireland's border counties. Building those kinds of bonds will help to lead to a better life for all the people of the region.

The Prime Minister and I discussed some other issues. We agreed on the need for an indefinite extension of the Non-Proliferation Treaty at the review conference that begins this month. To further the cause of nonproliferation, the Prime Minister joins me in calling for full implementation of the framework agreement we negotiated with North Korea to end that country's nuclear program.

And we discussed the need to adapt our international institutions to the challenges of the next century at the G–7 summit in Halifax. I was particularly impressed by the thinking that the Prime Minister has done on this profoundly important issue. The United States and the United Kingdom, after all, helped to shape those institutions. They have served our interests for the last half century. With the extraordinary relationship between our two countries as important as ever, I am confident we can make the changes necessary and work together to advance our shared values and our common interests, to promote peace and democracy and prosperity in the years ahead and, of course, in the century ahead.

Finally let me say, we discussed the ceremonies that will mark the 50th anniversary of the end of World War II. Because of my prior commitments, I've asked the Vice President to represent me and all Americans in London on May 8th at services that will commemorate the great wartime bravery and sacrifice of so many Britons. And I look forward to seeing Prime Minister Major when we go together to Moscow on May 9th to pay our respect to the heroism of the Russian people in that conflict.

Mr. Prime Minister.

Prime Minister Major. Mr. President, thank you very much.

We've had the opportunity today for a good-humored, worthwhile, productive, and very far-reaching series of exchanges on a whole range of matters. The President has set out much of the agenda we discussed, and I won't reiterate what the President said, except to say that in his remarks he spoke not just for the United States but for the United Kingdom as well. I share the views he expressed, and I won't reiterate them.

We spent some time looking forward at two separate matters which I think are of some importance to both our countries and of wider importance as well. The first of them the President just touched on, and that was the review of the Bretton Woods institutions and the United Nations that we agreed with the other G–7 heads of government at Naples last year that we should undertake and return to at Halifax later this year.

We've given a great deal of discussion to that, and I think for a range of reasons the time is right to look at a fairly comprehensive reform of some of those institutions. And we exchanged some ideas today on precisely how we might do that and agreed that we would exchange further ideas before we came to the G–7 summit. I think there is scope to rationalize some of the international financial institutions.

We wish to look particularly, in addition to that, at the United Nations where there are a number of overlapping functions. I am a very strong supporter of the United Nations, and I wish to see the United Nations a successful organization for the year 2000. It does seem that, looking at it, some of the areas of the U.N. could well do with updating, refreshing, to make sure that they are entirely applicable to the problems they will have to face in the late 1990's and beyond the turn of the century. And I hope very much that we will be able to get together with some more of our ideas and float those in greater detail when we get to the Halifax summit later on this year.

We also spent some time looking at the commonality of interests that exists between the United Kingdom and the United States. There are a huge range of areas where there is common interest, and not just those that were discussed—the agreements that we have in terms of policy towards Russia, Iran, Iraq, the Middle East, Bosnia, and a range of other areas.

But beyond that, I think there's a commonality of interest in the future security and prosperity of the Central and East European states, and also with two other matters: First, the further extension of free trade, to which I wish to return in just a second; and second, with looking together and combating together some of the problems of instability, extremism, and terrorism that we can begin to see in parts of North Africa, parts of the Levant, and parts of the Middle East. And we spent some time considering how we might address some of those problems in the future. It was necessarily a discussion that dealt with problems that may arise and dealt in some cases, frankly, with generalities. But it was an opportunity to look forward, rather than to just discuss the immediate topical problems that we face at the moment.

One area of growing importance that we touched on was the possibility of seeing how we can build on the Uruguay round agreement of a year or so ago and see how we can move forward to deal with much freer trade in financial services, for example, removing many of the nontariff barriers that still exist between Western Europe and the United States, and seeing how, step by step, we can move forward to a much greater element of free trade between North America and the Western European nations. That is something that needs to be done. I think it's something that's of immense benefit. And I found our discussion on that immensely productive and it's one I know that we will both return to in the future.

So I found the discussion not just on contemporary matters of use, but I found the sharing of ideas about how we deal with the development of the transatlantic relationship to deal with the problems that are going to arise in the future and also the examination of the common transatlantic view on many of the international problems around the world to be a very worthwhile and a very refreshing discussion, and I'm delighted we were able to have it.

And I think the President and I will be happy to take any questions anyone may have.

The President. Terry [Terence Hunt, Associated Press].

Taxes

Q. Mr. President, I would like to ask you about two tax matters at home. Congress has sent you a bill that would provide health insurance tax deductions for self-employed people. But it also allows billionaires, a handful of billionaires, to avoid taxation by renouncing their citizenship. Will you sign or veto that measure? And secondly, the House tomorrow takes up the Republican tax bill that provides benefits to a range of businesses and also a $500 child tax credit for families earning up to $200,000 a year. I know you have your own approach, but can you live with the Republican approach?

The President. Well, as to the first question, I strongly support restoring deductibility to self-employed people for the cost of their health insurance. I think it's unconscionable to have a different standard for them than for corporations. And that was a big part of my health care reform bill last year. So I'm on record strongly in favor of that. As a matter of fact, I'd like to see it expanded.

I am deeply troubled that the conference committee took out a payment mechanism by simply asking billionaires who made their money as Americans and largely made their money in the United States to pay the taxes they owe and instead to let them evade American income taxes by giving up their citizenship now that they have it made. So I'm going to have to look at that very closely and examine whether there might be some other opportunities to achieve that objective. But it's just wrong for us to walk away from that. That's just wrong.

Now, on the second matter, you know what my views are on that. We have two objectives here. I support tax relief for the middle class. I support greater tax fairness. I think it should be much more focused on things that will raise incomes in the short term and in the long term, so I favor a sharp focus on educating people and raising children, on families and education. But we cannot afford a cut of that magnitude and do the right thing by the deficit. And we should not be cutting taxes in ways that benefit very wealthy Americans and require us in turn to cut education, which will weaken our country as a whole. Education is the middle class social safety net, if you will. It is the key to our economic future as well. So I think that's a big

mistake. I think it's too big. I think it is—we need to focus on the deficit, and we don't need to be cutting education and investment in our future to give tax relief to people who don't really need it.

Prime Minister Major. Don MacIntyre [The Independent].

Northern Ireland Peace Process

Q. Could I just ask the President whether he accepts the British Government's pronouncements that Sinn Fein has not yet gone quite far enough on decommissioning of arms to justify a ministerial talk? And also, could I ask the Prime Minister whether he's satisfied with the administration on that issue?

The President. Well, I think it's a decision entirely for the British Government to make when in negotiations with Sinn Fein, when ministerial talks are appropriate. I will say this: I was very clear when the Adams visa was granted with permission to fundraise that there must be an agreement, a commitment in good faith, to seriously and quickly discuss arms decommissioning. Without a serious approach to arms decommissioning, there will never be a resolution of this conflict.

And so I think that—I would hope that there would be no difference in our position on that because I think the Prime Minister is right about that; we have to deal with this arms decommissioning issue. And I know that there is an attempt by the government to work with the paramilitaries on both sides to achieve that objective, and that's what I think should be done.

Prime Minister Major. Let me just add to that point. We've already started discussions at ministerial level with the loyalists paramilitaries on decommissioning, and those discussions are proceeding. What we're seeking to do is to have exactly the same discussions on exactly the same terms with Sinn Fein.

Now, if Mr. Adams is serious about moving towards peace—and he has repeatedly spoken about it—then he needs to discuss with the British Government the question of the modalities of decommissioning the arms. We need to know how it can be done, when it can be done, what needs to be done, a whole series of details. That matter has to be discussed.

Now, I think it is right for that matter to be discussed at ministerial level with Sinn Fein. And we've made it perfectly clear that, providing they are prepared to discuss that matter—and we've suggested what an agenda might be, and we're in discussion with them about that—then I think it is right for us to move to ministerial discussion on decommissioning of arms.

What is absolutely clear is that unless we are able to make progress on decommissioning of arms, there will be no possibility of Sinn Fein sitting down with the democratic political parties, the other democratic political parties in Northern Ireland. They simply won't be prepared to talk about meeting a settlement until there has been progress on decommissioning of arms. So I very much hope Mr. Adams will embark upon those discussions speedily.

Iraq

Q. Mr. President, I just wondered if you could elaborate on something you said in your opening remarks about your concerns with Iraq and their apparent ability to build weapons of mass destruction.

The President. I didn't say they had the apparent ability. I said they could be regaining it. And what I mean by that—I want to be very specific about it—what I mean by that is, unless Mr. Ekeus and the international inspectors can certify that they're in full compliance with all the relevant United Nations resolutions, then we have no assurance that they are not regaining the capacity to move forward with weapons of mass destruction. That is what I mean, but that is all I mean about it.

Q. So you're saying you don't have evidence that they are actually——

The President. That they are doing that now? I do not. And I want to make clear—that's why I used the word "could be regaining."

The United States position, which the United Kingdom has supported and for which I am very grateful, is that we should not relax these sanctions until there is full compliance with the resolutions. The resolutions were not passed in a careless way. They are carefully worded resolutions designed to assure the international community that this cannot happen. And unless those resolutions are complied with, the international community cannot know that this cannot happen.

Q. Mr. Prime Minister, do you share that view?

Prime Minister Major. I share that view, absolutely. I think we need to await Mr. Ekeus's report. From all I hear, it's not going to be

satisfactory about the way Iraq is behaving. We are concerned about the humanitarian aspect of people in Iraq. There is a Security Council resolution, which I trust is going to be passed, which will open up a better possibility for Saddam Hussein to sell oil in order to feed people in Iraq. It's an option that will be there. I very much hope he'll take that option.

But on the general relief of sanctions, until he has met the Security Council resolutions, met the Security Council resolutions in full, and we have seen independent verification that he has met the Security Council resolutions in full, then we entirely agree that there could be no relief whatsoever from the sanctions that have been imposed.

Northern Ireland Peace Process

Q. Mr. President, having broken bread with Gerry Adams——

The President. It's Mr. Major's turn.

Q. Well, it's to both of you. Having broken bread with Gerry Adams, could you, person-to-person, man-to-man, recommend that he speak with Gerry Adams himself?

The President. That's a decision for the Prime Minister to make in the context of the peace process. I have said—I said on St. Patrick's Day when I spoke then, I will say again, we are where we are today because of the risks that John Major has been willing to take for peace—and they have been considerable risks to himself, to his party, to his government—because he knows that this matter must be resolved. And I applaud that. The details of the decision-making must be made by the participants. And that is a decision for him to make.

Helen [Helen Thomas, United Press International].

Prime Minister Major. Adam Boulton [Sky TV]—sorry.

The President. We didn't do a British—go ahead.

Prime Minister Major. No, no, no—go after Helen. Ladies first. Adam Boulton next. He will willingly wait, won't you, Adam? [*Laughter*]

U.S. Nuclear Weapons Policy

Q. Mr. President, with all due respect, your nuclear policy is filled with inconsistencies, replete. You want to stop Russia from building a nuclear reactor in Iran. You want to ease sanctions against Pakistan, which we believe is developing nuclear weapons. You want Egypt to sign the Nuclear Non-proliferation Treaty, and all other states in the area. And you never try to persuade Israel, which does have a nuclear arsenal, to sign the treaty. Can you explain?

The President. Well, first of all, I'm trying to remember if I can remember all those three things. [*Laughter*]

The United States does not want Russia to give the capacity to Iran because we don't want that to be the beginning of their increased capacity to develop nuclear fuel and technology for other purposes. And given their conduct, I think that is the right policy, and I don't have any problem with it.

With regard to Pakistan, the simple question there is whether the policy we have pursued in the last few years is achieving its objectives and whether we will be a stronger force for peace and reconciliation and ultimately for the defanging, in terms of weapons of mass destruction, in the area if we change our policy or if we stay with it. I think it's time for—I think we should seriously review the policy.

If you look at the number of people in those countries in South Asia, the potential they represent for the future and the powder keg on which they sit because of their problems, the United States, it seems to me, has an obligation to do the very best we can to bring about the best result and the most peaceful result. And that's all we're doing.

Q. [*Inaudible*]—even if it's producing weapons?

The President. We don't support that. We want everybody to be a member of the nonproliferation regime. We want everybody to do that. And that's why I said what I did to President Mubarak of Egypt. Our position is that we want the largest number of people possible to participate in the nonproliferation regime and to go forward with its requirements. And we want to keep as many states nonnuclear as possible. And we are doing our best to reduce the nuclear threat by reducing the number of nuclear weapons that we have, in agreement with the Russians and with the other former states—states of the former Soviet Union.

And I think that our policy is consistent if you look at what the objective is. The objective is to reduce the threat of nuclear war to the world in the future and to reduce the threat of other weapons of mass destruction. There still is no more significant obligation I have to

future generations, and that is the common thread running through all these policies.

Prime Minister Major. Adam.

United Kingdom–U.S. Relations

Q. Given that as Tories, Democrats are supposedly on the opposite side ideologically, and given that we understand Teddy Blair of Labour may be coming here soon, I wonder if I could ask you how important you think your personal relations are for the relations between our two countries?

Prime Minister Major. Do you want to have first crack at that? [*Laughter*]

The President. Well, first of all, I think that in foreign policy, the differences are not easily discernible by party. We have, as you heard today, broad overlap, and indeed, in our country the differences among us here in America as Americans in foreign policy don't tend to break down along party lines. For example, the Speaker of the House and the Senate majority leader supported the position I took on debt relief for Mexico, which was opposed by a number of members of their party and a number of members of mine.

So I think there is—at the end of the cold war in this country, and I sense throughout Europe perhaps, there are forces arguing for kind of an inward-looking approach, a little bit more, if not isolationist, disengaged approach. And there are others who believe we must still continue to broaden the frontiers of relationships, to expand trade, in order to support democracy and prosperity. I am in that latter group. Prime Minister Major's in that latter group. Last year at the G–7 meeting, we were the two strongest proponents of expanding opportunities for economic integration of the countries there. So I just don't believe that there is a necessary partisan breakdown to our common objectives in the world community.

Secondly, I think we've got a good personal relationship, and I feel very comfortable about where it is. And I think it's honest and open. And it endures occasional disagreements, but the agreements are far more numerous and over the long run should be the shaping factors of our relationship.

Prime Minister Major. The fact of the matter is that we know well enough—we know one another well enough and the relationship is good enough to have those disagreements. And it doesn't affect the broad sway of agreement that exists between the two countries. I was fascinated to see that you referred to differences between parties and not within parties. And I think that's a great advance. [*Laughter*] I'm delighted—I'm delighted you put it that way.

Let me just make a broader point, really, about the Anglo-American relationship. At almost any time there's probably an issue—be astonishing if there wasn't, if there wasn't some measure of difference on an issue between two sovereign governments, whether they happen to be Conservative or Labor in the United Kingdom, Democrat or Republican in the United States. But against that, I think you have to look at the huge range of things in which the instinctive outlook between the United Kingdom Government and the United States Government is exactly the same.

If you run down most of the great issues of the moment—relationship with Russia, relationship with the Middle East, relationship on terrorism, relationship with Iran, relationship with Iraq—you won't find a scintilla of difference—present policy on Bosnia—between the British Government and the United States Government. If you look at the two nations that were foremost in propounding a free trade agreement, the GATT agreement, and taking that forward, you'll find the same relationship, the British and the American Government.

As for looking forward, I spoke a few moments ago of two areas where we've actually been looking forward today, together, of what we might actually do in the future. But as to whether the relation is good enough, perhaps I can just give you a practical example. If you were to spend a weekend, Adam, on one of our nuclear submarines, you would find a *Trident* missile on it. I'm not sure you could travel on anyone else's submarine and find a *Trident* missile on it. And I hope very soon in the future that you'll be able to see *Tomahawk* cruise missiles in the United Kingdom armory. And I'm not sure anybody will have those.

Now, they're practical illustrations of the extent of the closeness of the defense, of the security and other relationships between the United Kingdom and the United States. And the fact of the matter is, it is sufficiently close and has been sufficiently close for a large number of years to enable the President and I to have the occasional disagreement if we want without any harm coming of it.

The President. Rita [Rita Braver, CBS News].

Press Secretary McCurry. Make this the last one.

Russian Nuclear Cooperation With Iran

Q. If I could get back to the issue of Russia, you said that you do not want the Russians to go forward with their plans to sell a nuclear powerplant to Iran. What, if anything, did you talk about in terms of putting some real pressure on them? Is there anything you can do at this point to stop it from going forward? And if they do go forward, will it put a damper on the Western relationship with Russia?

The President. Well, we're continuing to have negotiations and discussions with them about it. And I think that's all I can really say at this time because we're in the midst of our conversations.

I thought Helen was going to ask me the question I think you asked me the last time, which is, are we trying to discourage Russia from selling to Iran the technology we're trying to finance in North Korea. The difference is, when I became President, I found a full-blown nuclear program in North Korea, which I'm trying to take down. And I don't want to leave some future President in the United States and the people of Britain with a program in Iran that they have to try to take down. I'm going to do the best I can to deal with it.

Q. Well, a lot of Americans, sir, are questioning whether or not the United States can really rely on Russia in any way—[*inaudible*].

The President. Well, let's don't jump the gun here. We're having these serious discussions. We're working it through. We have a lot of interests in a democratic and a reformist Russia. And the Prime Minister and I talked about it at some length today. And I think that they have done better economically than either the Prime Minister or I thought they would a couple of years ago in terms of pursuing the path of reform. They have continued to honor their Constitution and their electoral system and obligations to democracy. And we're going to have differences from time to time, but I wouldn't assume we can't work this one out. We're going to keep working hard on it.

Prime Minister Major. Peter [Peter Riddell, Times of London].

Bretton Woods Institutions

Q. Mr. Prime Minister, the President mentioned your ideas on the Bretton Woods institutions and the U.N. How much have you worked that up in detail, and what would it actually involve? I mean, is it a fully—a several-page plan, or what?

Prime Minister Major. It's developing rather than being developed. We agreed last year that we needed to look at some of the overlap there was in the Bretton Woods institutions and see how we could look at making the—bringing the United Nations a little more up to date.

If I could just give you a couple of illustrations—if you mean have we yet got a detailed, worked-out position between the United Kingdom and the United States, the answer is no, we haven't. We've both been looking separately, as we agreed we would do at the G–7 summit last year, at the sort of ideas we might bring forward for discussion with partners at Halifax later on this year and the sort of things that we're looking at in—by "we" I now mean the United Kingdom—in terms of the financial institutions. You'll be aware of the idea we've had in the past of selling some IMF gold to help some of the poorer nations. That's still on the agenda as far as we're concerned. Looking at perhaps a greater degree of rationalization of some of the activities of the IMF, OECD, and the World Bank—that's an area we're looking at.

We'd like to look at the way in which poverty is dealt with through the U.N. There seem to us to be a number of overlapping agencies, a certain amount of duplication, which could credibly be looked at. In terms of trade, we'd like to see what can be done to bed down the

World Trade Organization satisfactorily. In terms of environment, I would suggest that there are some areas of overlap as well. The U.N. Environment Program and the Commission for Sustainable Development, there seem to be areas of overlap.

Now, they're just specimen samples of the sort of things we are looking at. I emphasize, we are in the early stages of that examination. We haven't reached any conclusions. But I think those are matters we must examine.

Other things I'd like to see us examine at the summit would be to look more comprehensively at crime, drugs, and money laundering. We had a G–7 task force on money laundering some time ago. That's been successful. I think we should revisit that, given the nature of the problem and given the problem that exists internationally with crime and drugs. And I think we'd like to look a little more carefully at what might be done in terms of conflict prevention.

Those are just broad headlines of some of the areas we're looking at. We shared them in general outline today. We will come to them in detail at the summit.

The President. Thank you very much.

NOTE: The President's 90th news conference began at 2:53 p.m. in the East Room at the White House. In his remarks, he referred to President Saddam Hussein of Iraq; Rolf Ekeus, chairman, United Nations Special Commission (Iraqi Weapons); Gerry Adams, leader of Sinn Fein; and President Hosni Mubarak of Egypt.

Statement on the Buyout Program for Federal Employees
April 4, 1995

More than 2 years ago, I promised to fix the Federal Government. I was firmly convinced that we could do more with less, that we could create a Government that was leaner but not meaner, and that we could make Government our partner rather than a problem.

I established the National Performance Review and put Vice President Gore in charge. He and his team have helped to transform Government, to cut bureaucracy and redtape, and to find ways to give the American people the

service they deserve. At the same time, my economic plan is bringing down the deficit by more than $600 billion, and we are proposing another $81 billion in deficit reduction in the budget I recently sent to Congress.

A major element of my strategy was my commitment to streamline and cut the Federal work force. For too long in Washington, we have had too many layers of bureaucracy, too many workers whose main job was to check on the work of other workers rather than to perform useful work themselves. As the National Performance Review noted, we had good people trapped in bad systems. I promised to cut the work force, and that's what I'm doing. Through our efforts, we have already cut the work force by 102,000 positions and we are on track to cut it by a total of 272,900 positions, bringing it to its smallest size since John Kennedy was President.

While committed to cutting the work force, we want to do it in a humane way. We faced the same dilemma that confronted many private companies; they needed to downsize but wanted to avoid firing large numbers of loyal employees. Many of them have given people an incentive to leave by offering "buyouts." We wanted to do the same.

Early last year, Congress approved my request to allow non-Defense agencies to offer buyouts of up to $25,000 a person. The Defense Department and a few other agencies already could offer buyouts under existing law. Because normal attrition will help us downsize in the future, we offered buyouts only until March 31, 1995, which was last Friday.

Looking back, I can safely say that our buyout program has been a huge success. It achieved what we had hoped: to help us cut the work force in a fiscally responsible and humane way.

To reduce the work force by 102,000 positions by the end of fiscal 1994, we offered about 70,000 buyouts. Several non-DOD agencies have offered deferred buyouts that will take place between now and March 1997. Defense will be using buyouts as it continues to downsize through 1999. Counting those, we expect to buy out another 84,000 workers through 1997 as we reduce the work force by a total of 272,900 positions.

The buyouts were not offered in a random fashion, however. We targeted them to reduce the layers of bureaucracy and micro-management that were tying Government in knots. We made sure that departments and agencies tied their buyout strategies to their overall plans to streamline their bureaucracies. As a result, almost 70 percent of our buyouts in the non-Defense agencies have gone to people at higher grade levels, such as managers.

I'm proud that our buyout program was so successful. It shows that we can, in fact, create a Government that works better and costs less.

Remarks to the National Conference of the Building and Construction Trades Department of the AFL–CIO
April 5, 1995

Thank you very much. Ladies and gentlemen, thank you for that wonderful welcome. Thank you, Bob Georgine, for that fine introduction, all the distinguished affiliated presidents up here on the platform, and all of you out there in the audience. And I thank those of you who brought your children. Since most of what we're doing and a lot of what I have to say is about them, I'm glad to see them here.

I forgive the person in the back who shouted, "UCLA." I told the Gridiron Dinner the other night at the Press Club—I said my worst nightmare was a final with Arkansas and UCLA, my worst nightmare, the team I love against a team with 54 electoral votes. [*Laughter*] It was a great tournament, a great game. They won it fair and square, and I congratulate them.

You know, a lot of us here have a lot in common. Bob and I have something in common.

We were both raised by strong mothers who believed in hard work and optimism and practiced what they preached and made sure that we practiced what they preached. It was our first lesson in organized labor. [*Laughter*]

I'm deeply honored to be here with you today. I want to thank you for the support that you have given to our programs to train America's workers for the future. I believe that good, strong unions and collective bargaining can help us to meet the challenges that are just ahead if all of us are willing to embrace those challenges and to do what has to be done to make sure that we compete and win in the global economy.

That's why one of the very first things I did as President was to rescind the anti-union Executive orders of the last 12 years and why last month I also signed an Executive order which bars Federal agencies from doing business with companies that hire permanent replacement workers.

I have been saying as I'm going around the country that we know what works in our own lives. What works in our own lives is when we are well-educated, well-trained, we work hard, and we work together. There is no future in this country in pitting management against labor. All of us are caught up now in a common destiny in the global economy. All of us will have more job security or more job insecurity, as the case may be, depending on how well we adapt to the challenges of today and tomorrow.

That is the way we have to look at this. We are going up or down together. And it is time we stop looking for ways to be divided, one from another, and start at looking harder for how we can resolve these divisions in an open and honest way so we can get about the business of building our future. That's what we ought to be doing in this country, and that's what I'm trying to do for you every day at the White House.

I look at the unions represented here, the carpenters, the painters, the bricklayers, the electricians, the others; you built our homes, our cities, our factories, the biggest industrial system in the world. You have built our country. And then you have had to rebuild our country. One of the greatest wonders I have seen since I have been President is the swift handiwork of your members who rushed in after the natural disasters, from Florida to the Midwest to California. You did a very good job. And we now are doing a better job with our Emergency Management Agency to try to make sure we do our part and the money gets out there to rebuild places who are torn down through no fault of their own.

Many of you have become heroes to folks whose lives were devastated in those disasters, who wouldn't have a bridge to cross a river or roads to get them to work or offices to work in or roofs over their head if you hadn't worked hard to make sure that the American dream could be restored.

All through 1992 when I was out running for President, I met a lot of people who wondered about the state of the American dream, including construction workers, farmers, office workers, mothers and fathers. I talked with them and listened to them; I worked with them. I walked a picket line with them, with the Cat-

erpillar workers in Illinois. What I found was that most people felt that they were out there on their own, struggling against forces that were bigger than they were without anybody very much concerned about what was going to happen to them.

I ran for President because I felt strongly that the end of the cold war and the dawn of the information age gave us opportunities for peace and prosperity, gave our children opportunities to live out their dreams never before known in human history, but that we also had some very, very profound challenges that unless they were faced, the American dream for all of our people would be at risk.

I wanted to make sure that middle class Americans and their children were not forgotten. I wanted to make sure that poor people would have a chance to work their way into the middle class. I wanted to make sure that we could keep alive opportunities for entrepreneurs to become wildly successful without forgetting that this country was built and this country will endure by the broad middle class and by the fact that they work hard, play by the rules, raise their children, and deserve to be rewarded for it, and must be rewarded for it if we're going to keep the American dream alive. That is why I ran for this job.

I also, very frankly, ran to challenge middle class America, because there are many things that Government cannot and should not do. The most important things in the world to us, our commitments, our values, our work, our family, our communities, by and large operate independent of the Government.

Today we're having a great debate here in Washington about what role our National Government should play and how far we can go in working together and moving together. Really, the debate has been going on for at least 15 years now, a debate that, frankly, I'm getting kind of tired of: an old debate that defends Government at every turn, a new debate that attacks Government at every turn; an old view that says we should spend more on everything, a new view that says we should spend less on everything; an old view that said we should do more of everything, a new view that says we should do less of everything. Both views defy our common experience, our common sense, and what we see about what's working, not only here in the United States but around the world.

What works is when the Government, in my judgment, focuses on four things. First of all, creating economic opportunity, jobs, working for better jobs and higher incomes, and demanding responsible behavior from citizens in return. I had an economic meeting in Atlanta last week, and Hugh McColl, from North Carolina, the chairman of NationsBank, pointed out that about that time, he said, "Tonight your basketball team and mine are going to have a basketball game. And the referee is going to throw the ball up, make sure the playing field is level, enforce the rules, and otherwise get out of the way. And that's about what the Government ought to do." But we have to make sure the playing field is level, that there are rules that are enforced, and we get out of the way.

The second thing that we have to pay attention to is the security of our people, our security from attack from abroad and our security from within. I'm proud of the fact that since I have been President, for the first time since the dawn of the nuclear age there are no Russian missiles pointed at the children of the United States of America. I am proud of that. But I know and you know that our security is also threatened by crime and violence and drugs on our streets. And our security is also threatened by the things which are breaking our families apart and punishing people who are doing their best to do the right things.

That's why we worked so hard to pass that crime bill with 100,000 police on the streets and with prevention programs to give our kids something to say yes to and why we should not walk away from our commitment to putting 100,000 police on the street. Violent crime has tripled in the United States in the last 30 years; the police forces have expanded by 10 percent. You don't have to be a rocket scientist to know that we could lower the crime rate if we did what city after city after city is doing now and put more police on the block, working with kids, trying to prevent crime and catch criminals quicker. And we must not back away from that commitment to our security.

And there is another element to our security, too. It's what happens to families. Are we really going to reward work? Are we going to permit people to be successful workers and successful parents? Most places today, whether they're single-parent or two-parent households, all the parents are working. That's why I fought so hard for the Family and Medical Leave Act—I saw

that as a question of family security; why I want to see all the children in this country immunized; why in the economic plan last year we insisted that we give tax breaks for families with incomes just above the poverty line so we would not encourage anybody to slip back into welfare, and because nobody who works full-time and has children in the home should live in poverty in this country. If you work hard, you ought to be able to have a decent life.

The third thing we have to do is to reform the Government. We do have to change it. It ought to be smaller. It ought to be less bureaucratic. We ought to give more decisions back to the State and local government. We ought to give more decisions back to private citizens in their own lives. We ought to have Government that meets tomorrow's problems, not yesterday's.

That's why we've worked hard at deregulation and why we have given more responsibility to States in the area of welfare and health care reform than—in 2 years—than the last two administrations combined did in 12 years. We have been the administration that has pushed the decentralization of authority for solving a lot of our problems. And we've reduced the size of Government. There are over 100,000 fewer people working for the Federal Government today than there were on the day I became President.

And we have also decided that we have to solve some problems too long ignored. In a little-known action at the end of the last Congress, there was a reform in the United States pension systems which saved the pensions of 8½ million working Americans who were in danger of losing their pensions and protected the pensions of over 30 million more. We still have work to do, and when we have to do it, we should do it well.

The fourth thing we have to do, and maybe the most important of all, is to help our people make the most of their own lives by making sure that everywhere—everywhere—we have a system of lifetime education and training that will permit people always to find work and always to compete and win in the global economy. That is what I think the job of Government is: create jobs, get better paying jobs, increase the security of the American people, make the Government smaller and less bureaucratic, but do the job that has to be done, and give people the skills they need to make the most of their own lives. That should be our road map.

If we could create opportunity and we can insist on more responsibility from the American people—and I believe that strongly. That's what welfare reform is all about. We'll help you if you're in trouble but not for a lifetime; you've got to go to work sometime. I think that's what child support enforcement is all about. If you've got the money, you ought to be taking care of your kid, not asking the taxpayers to do it. That's what enforcing the student loan program is all about. I increased the availability of student loans, but when I became President, it was costing you $2.8 billion a year because people weren't paying the loans back. We've cut that down to a billion dollars a year. If people borrowed money from the Government to go to college, they ought to pay it back when they get a job so other kids can borrow the money when they come along.

I have called this new arrangement the New Covenant. What it means to me is simple: The Government should try to create more opportunity, but the citizens of this country are going to have to behave more responsibly in seizing it. And if you put the two together, there will be no stopping the United States.

Now, if you look at what's been accomplished in the last couple of years, I think the most important thing is that we have changed the direction of economic policy in this country. We went beyond the old debate. There's no more tax and spend, but there's not more trickle-down, either. This is invest and grow economics. And look at the results.

Two years ago when we were fighting for the economic plan, the people who were against it said the sky would fall: "If the President's plan passes, the economy will be wrecked. Everything will be terrible." Some said I was cutting too much. Some said it was an error to raise taxes on the wealthiest Americans to put against the deficit because that would hurt the economy. Well, 2 years later, we have over 6 million new jobs and the lowest combined rates of unemployment and inflation in 25 years.

In reducing the deficit by $600 billion, we took $10,000 in debt off the future of every family in the United States. In cutting taxes for 15 million working families, this year, on average, families with two kids with an income of $25,000 a year or less will pay about $1,000 less in taxes than they would have if that economic plan hadn't passed. We made it possible for our country to say, "If you work 40 hours a week and you have a child in your home, you will not be in poverty." That is important, folks. If you want people to get off welfare, we have to reward work. And it's also why, by the way, we ought to raise the minimum wage, because people can't live on it.

And we didn't just spend more money on everything. We cut 300 programs, and the new budget I proposed cuts or consolidates 400 more.

We've also done what we could to help those of you in labor who have been taking responsibility all along. Last year, the AFL–CIO listed all the bills supported by organized labor that I signed into law. As of last fall, there were 32 of them—motor voter, family and medical leave, the assault weapons ban, to name just a few—laws that increased our security as workers, parents, and citizens.

But you know, in spite of all this, there's still a lot more to do. I have people all the time come up to me in kind of bewilderment and say, "Well, things are going well in my business. Things are going well for our country. This country is in better shape than it was 2 years ago. Why are people still so negative about the future of the country?" When you ask people what about the direction of the country, they say they are worried. I was interviewed by a magazine the other day saying their annual readers poll said that people understood that things were getting better, but they were more worried about their personal security than ever before. Why is that?

Well, there's a reason for that. The global economy has imposed new challenges and new burdens on our country and every wealthy country in the world and runs the risk in our country of literally splitting apart the American idea. Let me explain what I mean by that.

From the time I was born at the end of World War II until the year I was elected Governor of my State for the first time, 1978, the American people moved forward in absolute lock-step. That is, if you break the economy into people who are in the lowest 20 percent and the second and so forth on to the top 20 percent, all of them had about the same increase in their incomes. Incomes roughly doubled in America from 1950 to 1978 evenly across the board, except the poorest 20 percent had an increase of 140 percent. So we were all going forward, and we were actually coming together.

Since 1978, that's all changed. Wages have been stagnant and not kept up with inflation on average for hourly wage earners. And in the last 15 years, half of the American people are now living for the same or lower earnings that they were making 15 years ago when you adjust for inflation. Why? Because of the way the technology revolution and the global economy, where management and money and technology can fly across national borders, have divided opportunity, so that people with high levels of skill in growth industries tend to do well, and people with lower skill levels tend to get hurt. And then, if our Government walks away from its obligations to invest in our future, even more people get hurt.

The other thing that's happened is because the economy is changing so fast, even a lot of people that are doing well today think they're waiting for the other shoe to drop. So many big companies getting smaller all the time—you ought to read my mail about it, people my age, even young people I grew up with—not so young anymore—writing me, saying, "You know, I've worked for this company for 25 years. I've got to send my kids to college. We're doing great now, but what happens if they lay me off?"

So there is this uncertainty in our country today, even though we are clearly in better shape than we were 2 years ago. We've turned away from the false choice between tax and spend and trickle-down economics. We're moving in the right direction. The question is, how can we get everybody involved in the American dream? How can we reward everyone's work? How can we make people more secure in living with all these changes that are rifling through the world? That is the burden that I carry to the office every day, because I know—I know that if everybody in this country had a chance to live their lives the way most of you have lived your lives and raised your kids, this country would be fine, and our future would be unlimited.

The key to the 21st century, more than anything else, is clearly education for young people, lifetime job training for adults. It is clear that if we can raise the skill levels of our people, constantly and permanently, and continue to change the job mix so that we're always getting America's share of those high-wage jobs, we can keep the American dream alive, and we can stop the middle class from splitting apart, so

that everybody can grow and prosper. That is our great challenge, and that is the one we must not walk away from.

You have been working on this for years. You've had opportunities to train a new generation of builders. I want to especially commend the outreach programs that you've had with the Housing and Urban Development Department, reaching deep into our cities, taking thousands of young people from housing projects, teaching them the skills, and clearing away the obstacles to job opportunities. You have done some things that the Government could not do. And I thank you for that. I know that Bob really cares a lot about this outreach program because he spent his own early years in housing projects in Chicago. This is the kind of partnership we need more of.

For Government's part, we have to do more, as well. In 1994, the educational experts said that the United States Congress, in passing our education program, did more for education than had been done in Washington in 30 years. We expanded Head Start. We established the Goals 2000 program, which writes the national education goals into law but gives our local schools more flexibility in how they spend Federal money to achieve excellence. We dramatically increased the number of programs around our country for apprenticeships from young people leaving high school who aren't going on to college. And we expanded the availability of college loans to the middle class, at lower cost and better repayment terms.

And of course, our national service program, AmeriCorps, is now bigger than the Peace Corps ever was. And there are 20,000 young people all across America working in community service projects, doing things that need to be done and earning funds to go on to college.

Those are the kinds of things we must do more of. Those are the kinds of things that are important. That's why I said a moment ago that if we work on education and we work on incomes, the rest of this will pretty much take care of itself, I think. That's why I hope the Congress this year will not only raise the minimum wage, but with all this tax cut talk, we can't afford a lot of these tax cuts. We've got too big a deficit. But we ought to give the middle class a break. And the most important thing we could do is give people a tax deduction for any costs they or their children have for any education after high school, because that will raise incomes over the long run.

Let me just ask you one other thing I want you to think about. There are a lot of exciting things going on in this town these days. And as I said, we are debating the role of Government, but there must be a distinction made. If you don't believe in tax-and-spend economics and you don't believe in trickle-down economics and you do believe in invest-and-grow economics and you've seen how it is working the last 2 years, then you also have to reject this debate that we should spend more money on everything or we should spend less money on everything.

We have to make judgments up here based on what is important. Therefore, I would say, let's cut more spending. I have cut and cut and cut, and I want to cut some more. We've got to get this budget deficit down further. We can bring this budget into balance, and we can do it in a fair way. But we have to make judgments. We should not be cutting Head Start. We should not be cutting aid to the public schools. We shouldn't be cutting the apprenticeship programs. And we certainly shouldn't be limiting the availability of college loans to the middle class. We shouldn't be adding to the cost of college education for working families. These are proposals that I think are wrong. We shouldn't be eliminating national service. And we certainly shouldn't be doing all these things either to pay for a tax cut for the wealthiest Americans or because we refuse to find other things to cut. That is wrong. Let's make decisions, and let's do it right, and let's stick up for education and training.

And you have issues in this Congress—Bob referred to one of them, the Davis-Bacon law. We need to make this economy more competitive. But we need more high wages. We don't need a low-wage strategy; we need a high-wage strategy for the future. We need a high-wage strategy. Like every other law, it shouldn't be abused. We should not pretend it's something it's not. But it is a decent thing to say that the Government should stand on the side of good wages and the real wages in the community that are good and fair.

I've made appointments, like Bill Gould to the National Labor Relations Board and Fred Feinstein to be the General Counsel, who now have given you a board that believes in the process of collective bargaining and one that believes we can be fair to workers. These are

the kinds of things that we ought to do if you believe our future is in working together.

I'm not for repealing Davis-Bacon. I also believe that we should not walk away from our commitment to safety in the American workplace. In 1993 there were more than half a million construction injuries and over 900 fatalities. We can reform OSHA in ways that you feel better about it and employers feel better about it, where it works better and makes more sense and helps you get more jobs and gain more income and helps them make bigger profits. But we cannot walk away from the fundamental fact that before we were committed to worker safety, a lot more people died in the workplace, a lot more people were permanently maimed in the workplace, a lot of more people were hurt in the workplace. There is a right way and a wrong way to reduce the burden of Government.

I could just—let me mention one other thing that affects some of your industries. I believe with all my heart if we hadn't passed the environmental protection legislation in the 1970's, the air would not be as clean, the water would not be as pure as it is today, and the legacy we're going to pass along to our children would not be as good. I believe that. I also believe, like any Government bureaucracy, there are things about the EPA that ought to be changed. So we're going to more market-based incentives to give companies incentives to clean up the environment. And Carol Browner, our Administrator, is reducing by 25 percent the paperwork burden of the EPA. It will free up 20 million man-hours of work next year. That's a lot of time in a lot of industries that all of you work in.

We're trying to give small businesses a break. We're saying to small businesses—I was at a union print shop in Virginia a couple of weeks ago to announce this—if you worry about whether you've got an EPA violation and you're afraid to call because you're afraid they'll fine you, now we're going to set up a compliance center, and if you call there and ask, if you ask, you can't be fined for 6 months. And you're going to be given a chance to clean up the problems.

I think we can change the way Government regulation works to make it less nutty. But let's not forget that we have a common public interest in a safe workplace. We have a common public interest in a clean environment. And we have a common public interest in having a high-wage, high-growth partnership economy, not a low-wage, stagnant, divided economy.

So I say to you, engage the Members of Congress; tell them you welcome the debate about the role of Government. But Government has certain responsibilities: first of all, to change and get rid of the past stuff that doesn't work; to create more opportunity; to provide more security; to insist on more responsibility, but to give people the education and training and skills they need to make it in the 21st century.

I'm telling you that if we take advantage of this time, if we keep the economic strategy that we have adopted—that I hammered through the Congress by the narrowest of margins, with all the doubters saying, "Well, we had to either have tax and spend or trickle-down," and I knew this was the right thing to do—if we will stay with this economic strategy and then aggressively go after strategies to raise wages, raise incomes, educate and train people, and if we don't throw out the baby with the bath water, this country is going to do just fine.

I am looking for a future for America like the ones most of us who are my age in this audience used to take for granted. And we can give it to our kids, but only if we are tough enough and wise enough and compassionate enough to do what we know in our heart is right. You help, we'll do it.

Thank you, and God bless you.

NOTE: The President spoke at 10:20 a.m. in the Grand Ballroom at the Washington Hilton Hotel. In his remarks, he referred to Bob Georgine, president, Building and Construction Trades Department of the AFL–CIO.

Exchange With Reporters Prior to Discussions With President Hosni Mubarak of Egypt
April 5, 1995

President Clinton. Good morning, everybody. Good afternoon.

Q. Good morning. What's on the agenda today?

President Clinton. A lot of things. But we're going to have a press briefing afterwards, so you'll get to ask all the questions.

Q. That's what you said yesterday, Mr. President. [*Laughter*]

President Clinton. And we did it, didn't we?

Nuclear Non-Proliferation Treaty

Q. President Mubarak, will you support the extension of the Non-Proliferation Treaty?

President Mubarak. We were one of the founders who participated in the drafting of the NPT since 1968. So we support the NPT 100 percent. We have no problem with the United States, anyway, concerning the NPT.

Q. Do you have a problem with Israel?

President Mubarak. No, we would like to find a solution so as to keep our area free of all mass destructive weapons. That's all.

Q. It sounds like you're going to sign.

President Mubarak. I'm not going to tell you now anything.

Q. Was President Clinton persuasive?

President Clinton. We just met 2 seconds ago. We're going to have a press briefing soon.

Q. Thank you.

[*At this point, one group of reporters left the room, and another group entered.*]

President Clinton. Good afternoon.

Egypt-U.S. Relations

Q. How would you describe the Egyptian-American relations?

President Clinton. I think it's very good. I've enjoyed working with President Mubarak, and I'm looking forward to this discussion. And of course, afterward, we'll have an opportunity to take your questions.

Q. President Clinton, will you ask Israel to fulfill its obligation and to deploy its forces from the West Bank and Gaza?

President Clinton. I'll answer the questions in the press briefing after I visit with President Mubarak.

NOTE: The exchange began at 12:07 p.m. in the Oval Office at the White House. A tape was not available for verification of the content of this exchange.

Remarks to the United States-Egypt Presidents' Council
April 5, 1995

Let me begin by welcoming you all to the White House and here to the Roosevelt Room and thanking you for your willingness to participate in this council.

I think all of you know that the United States and Egypt have had and continue to have a very close relationship, and we believe that our future interests are very much bound up together. We believe we have to do more in the economic area. We need more partnerships and more success stories. And for my part, I am very, very committed to trying to further the work of increased economic interaction, bringing about more prosperity, more opportunity.

So I want to thank both the Americans who are here and the Egyptians who are here for your willingness to serve and commit the resources and the efforts of this Government to the success of this endeavor. And I know I speak for the Vice President, the Secretary of State, and of course, our Trade Ambassador and Secretary of Commerce. We are convinced that this is an important part of our common future.

Mr. President.

NOTE: The President spoke at 1 p.m. in the Roosevelt Room at the White House. A tape was not available for verification of the content of these remarks.

The President's News Conference With President Hosni Mubarak of Egypt
April 5, 1995

President Clinton. Good afternoon. Please be seated. As always, it's a great pleasure to have President Mubarak back at the White House. For 14 years, he has been a valued friend and partner to the United States. He was one of the first foreign leaders to visit me here after I became President, and I began my trip to the Middle East last fall by visiting him in Cairo to seek his counsel. Under his wise leadership, Egypt has been an ally, as well as a source of stability in the region and throughout the world.

In the last 2 years, we've witnessed the dawn of a new era in the Middle East. Without President Mubarak's tireless efforts on behalf of peace, these landmark achievements would not have occurred. Thanks to his persistence, the promise of Camp David, where Egypt took its stand against war, has been redeemed. In the months and years ahead, we will continue to look to President Mubarak to play a vital role in broadening the circle of peace. We're determined to do everything we can meanwhile to deepen our own partnership for peace and prosperity.

He and his government have already made great strides toward reforming and restructuring the Egyptian economy. I got a very impressive report on the progress that has been made at the luncheon we just concluded. But more is necessary to stimulate the economy so that it can provide good jobs and a future of hope for the hundreds of thousands of young people who enter the Egyptian work force every year.

The United States is committed to helping. Vice President Gore just returned from his second visit to Egypt in the last 6 months. On my behalf, he began a dialog for growth and development with President Mubarak that is unprecedented in its scope and ambition. Today he and I have taken another step forward in this partnership by meeting with the new members of our Presidents' Council at their first gathering. These top American and Egyptian businessmen will advise us on several vital issues: expanding the private sector, building stronger commercial ties between our peoples, creating better conditions to attract United States investment to Egypt.

We're also working together to bring more prosperity and stability to the entire region, efforts that are essential for peace to establish firm roots. We reaffirmed our support for greater regional cooperation and development, especially the economic initiative that began at the Casablanca summit. We also had a good discussion about the need to lift the boycott of Israel and ways to accomplish this as soon as possible.

Egypt and the United States share a determination to confront and to defeat all those who would undermine peace and security through the use of terror and weapons of mass destruction. President Mubarak told me of Egypt's regional proliferation concerns and of its commitment to a strong, universal Non-Proliferation Treaty and to a Middle East that is free of all weapons of mass destruction. The United States shares those goals.

To create the confidence and security that will make those aims a reality, we must continue to do all we can to bring a comprehensive and lasting peace to the Middle East. For the same reason, I believe we must ensure that the NPT is strong and as enduring as possible. Indefinite and unconditional extension of NPT is vital to achieving the goals that we both share.

When President Mubarak and I first met here 2 years ago, he told me that together we could help to make a just and comprehensive peace in the Middle East. He was right. We have worked side by side to fulfill that vision. Doing so, we have deepened the friendship between our two nations. Our goal is now within grasp, and America is proud to be Egypt's partner on this great mission.

Mr. President.

President Mubarak. Thank you. Once again I meet with my good friend President Clinton in order to pursue our joint endeavor for the benefit of our two nations.

We discussed all issues of mutual interest in the spirit of friendship, candor, and mutual confidence. Our views were similar on various issues. Our paramount commitment is to strengthen the structure of world peace and security and to promote cooperation among nations. Our two countries are destined to play a pivotal role throughout the world and in their regions, re-

spectively. We are determined to pursue our mission with vigor and determination. We realize that the challenge is awesome, but our commitment to our noble goals is firm, and quite firm.

President Clinton, together we worked tirelessly for decades to promote peace and security in the Middle East. We achieve tangible success year after year, and we remain determined to pursue this goal until a just and comprehensive peace is reached throughout the area. We should never allow enemies of peace to threaten the gains which were made in the recent past. We will never hesitate to condemn terrorism and all forms of violence. Our aim is to eliminate the sources of hatred and conflict.

As we move to cement the structure of peace and security in the Middle East, we should do our utmost in order to remove all potential threats. Our purpose is to build together a new future of hope and promise for this troubled region. With this in mind, I deemed it necessary to propose in 1990 the establishment of a Middle East free of all weapons of mass destruction. My objective was and still is to make every Arab and Israeli feel more secure and less worried about the future and that of his children.

I explained to President Clinton and his able assistants our position on the NPT. We remain among the most enthusiastic supporters of the treaty. We consider it one of the pillars of the stable world order. Hence, we would like to reinforce the moral authority of the NPT. By the same token, we have a certain concern which emanates from the existence of nuclear programs in our region.

Our view is that since peace is spreading throughout the region, all the parts ought to work together towards the elimination of the potential threats, especially the spreading of nuclear, chemical, and biological weapons. This is the true application of the principle of the universality and adherence to the NPT. All states of the region should realize that it serves in their own interests to accede to the treaty. Unless this is done, no one would have control over the spread of such lethal weapons in a fragile and vulnerable region which has suffered long enough from war and devastation.

We propose, for our common good, to achieve that through serious but friendly negotiations between Egypt, and perhaps other Arab countries, and Israel. It is our sincere hope that Israel will approach this issue in a positive and constructive spirit. The U.S., under the leadership of President Clinton, can help attain this objective.

Our bilateral relations, Mr. President, are excellent. We work together in various fields in harmony and mutual trust. As we have been partners in peace and security, we are establishing a new solid partnership for economic growth and development. Thanks to President Clinton and Vice President Al Gore, we have developed a new concept for this partnership. The idea is to stimulate growth and productivity. It is vital to create jobs for our young people. We shall do that through promoting trade and investment.

We have already begun the implementation of this concept, and we are determined to make it a success story. We are encouraging the private sector to play a major role in this endeavor. As you know, our economy is becoming more and more business-friendly. This is a cornerstone of our economic reform program. We are fully committed to pursue this reform until it bears fruit.

In conclusion, I would like to thank President Clinton for his warm reception and hospitality. We are most appreciative of the understanding and the cooperation we have been receiving from every American. We will leave this great country with a renewed assurance of the solidity of the friendship and the depth of our cooperation.

Thank you, Mr. President.

President Clinton. Thank you.

I'd like to alternate questions now between the American and the Egyptian press. We'll start with Ms. Santos [Lori Santos, United Press International].

Nuclear Non-Proliferation Treaty

Q. Mr. President, did President Mubarak assure you that he will sign the extension of the Nuclear Non-Proliferation Treaty and stop urging other Arab nations not to sign unless Israel does?

President Clinton. Let me tell you the position that I took on it. And I think I'll let President Mubarak speak for himself. We believe that the NPT should be universal. And we believe that the Middle East should be free of all weapons of mass destruction, nuclear, biological, chemical. We also believe that cannot be accomplished overnight and that Egypt and Israel, as the first two parties to make peace in the Middle East,

should work on this together. And I'm encouraged that the Foreign Ministers, Mr. Moussa and Mr. Peres, are going to meet soon on this issue.

The reason we believe, however, that we should vote for an NPT extension that is indefinite, without regard to whether every country in the world that we think should be in the NPT is in it, is that it seems to us that with the indefinite extension of the NPT, that will allay a lot of the security concerns of countries that are not in it and encourage them to get in it, whereas if we don't indefinitely extend it, then countries that are not fully participating may think they should hedge their bets for the future. So that's our policy; that's why we support it and why we hope it will prevail.

Mr. President, would you——

President Mubarak. I would like to say something about the NPT. In 1968, we were one of the 18 countries who participated in drafting the agreement of the NPT. We are supporting the NPT. We know that the NPT is for the welfare of the whole world in the new world order. And we know it's very important that all parties should join the NPT. We are working very hard for that, and we will never withdraw from the NPT—just to make sure of what you may mean that way.

Egypt-Israel Relations

Q. President Mubarak, the new peace between Jordan and Israel is warming up fast. The first peace between Israel and Egypt is still somewhat chilly. Will you come to Israel for the first time and personally warm it up so we can move ahead together?

President Mubarak. Jordan has about 3 million population, Egypt about 60 million. Jordan and Israel are living with each other, let us be very realistic and frank, long time ago. They have so many Palestinians here and there. But believe me, without the key of peace which was started by late President Sadat, I don't think that neither Jordan nor Palestinian would have the courage or would have thought of opening peace with this country.

Peace is not cold, as some people could say, but sometimes it's affected by a statement here or there. But believe me, there is much more progress on the cooperation with the Israelis between Israel and Egypt now. And this is the cornerstone.

President Clinton. Someone from the Egyptian press.

Q. Mr. President——

President Clinton. Go ahead.

Q. As the national security is top priority for the United States and Egypt and we are friends and allies, how can the United States help Egypt to secure its national security while there are nuclear weapons at its borders, a few kilometers from its borders? And my question is to both Presidents.

President Clinton. Well, I will restate what I said before. I believe that we—Egypt's security is best served in terms of what the United States can do in three ways, first of all, by continuing the general search to rid the entire region of all kinds of weapons of mass destruction. And we realize that we deal with the history and the facts of the countries as we find them, that it cannot be done overnight, but that that must be our goal and we must be working on that. And universal application of NPT is one of the ways we think that should be done.

The second thing is a comprehensive peace in the Middle East. If we can resolve the issues still outstanding among the other countries in the Middle East, that clearly will help to bolster Egypt's security.

Then the third thing I think we can do is what we are doing here by trying to strengthen our economic ties, so that the reform policies that have been adopted by President Mubarak and his government will be rewarded and people who live inside Egypt will feel more personally secure with their own opportunities.

I think all those things have to be pursued, but I don't think that we can—any of us can pretend that we can do it without regard to the past history of the countries involved.

President Mubarak. I think I agree to all of what President Clinton already mentioned, and I have nothing to add more than that.

Q. Mr. President——

President Clinton. Go ahead, Terry [Terence Hunt, Associated Press].

CIA and Guatemala

Q. Mr. President, the Senate is holding hearings today on CIA dealings in Guatemala, and I know that you've ordered an investigation. Can you say if the CIA's activities were appropriate in Guatemala, and were the White House and Congress kept fully and properly informed?

President Clinton. Well, I cannot answer the questions fully until I see the investigation. I think both those questions are—they're still open questions. I wish I could say absolutely yes to both of them. But because I can't say, with absolute conviction, yes to both of them, I have ordered an investigation that, as you know, is reasonably unusual in its scope and in terms of who's doing it. And so, I'm going to keep working until we get to the bottom of it. And then when I do, I'll give you the best answer I can.

Yes, ma'am.

Middle East Peace Process

Q. Egypt and the United States have played a pivotal role in the peace process since its inception. What, in your views, are—this is for both Presidents—the steps that should be taken by all parties concerned to further the peace process, especially that the Israeli and the American elections are soon, close?

President Clinton. Do you want to go first? [*Laughter*]

President Mubarak. As you like.

About the peace process, you know there is a Declaration of Principles, first of all, with the Palestinians, and we consider that, the Palestinian problem, the main problem in the whole Middle East issue.

The implementation may be a little bit lagging behind, because some terroristic action taking place—[*inaudible*]—and the Israelis are looking for their security. My proposal is—and I spoke with Mr. Arafat and Mr. Rabin—they should both cooperate. The two authorities should cooperate to avoid all this terroristic action, because if we surrender to these people, they will feel it is a success for them and the whole peace process will be a failure. I think both understand this very well, and I hope that they could do well in that direction and to continue the implementation of the Declaration of Principles.

If it is in the course of the Syrians, I know that the Syrians are now negotiating on the level of ambassadors here. I hope that there will be progress in the future. I am very sure that President Asad want reach a settlement to the problem and want sign—to reach an agreement, peace agreement with Israel.

President Clinton. I agree with the points that have been made. I would only make two other points. With regard to the Palestinians, it's also important that we try to resolve—as we resolve the security issues, that we try to work on getting economic investment back into Gaza and to Jericho, so that there is some opportunity for people there, some alternative to the destructive behavior that many are urging.

And with regard to the Syrians, I agree with what President Mubarak said, but—I think President Asad does want peace, and I think Prime Minister Rabin wants peace, but I think it is important that they reach an agreement fairly soon for the reasons that you said.

And let me say further, let me reiterate something I said in my opening statement. I think we've got a good chance to keep implementing the principles, with all the difficulties the Palestinians are having. I think we've got a good chance to reach an agreement with Syria and Israel. And I don't think either thing would happen if it weren't for the intense involvement of both the United States and Egypt.

Go ahead.

Nuclear Non-Proliferation Treaty

Q. This is a question for both of you. Are you saying that it would be acceptable if Israel would agree to sign the NPT at some point in the future, say, at the time a comprehensive Middle East peace is reached?

President Clinton. Well, I think President Mubarak should answer that, since it's really a question about whether it would be acceptable from his point of view. My position is that all countries should join the NPT; that the Middle East should be free of all weapons of mass destruction, nuclear, biological and chemical; that that objective will be more easily achieved, notwithstanding the differences between Israel and the other countries, if we have an indefinite extension. That is the position of the United States and the position that I strongly believe to be the correct one. At any rate, I hope we'll be able to prevail with that position when the vote comes with a healthy majority.

The President of Egypt has his own views and convictions, and what he said is absolutely true: Egypt has been a complete and consistent supporter of the NPT regime from its inception. So I think I should let him answer for himself.

President Mubarak. We have no problem even with the United States concerning the NPT, as I have already mentioned before. The NPT— as I said, we were one of the 18 countries who drafted, participated in the draft. The point is,

there is peace in the area. Egypt signed peace agreement, and we are in peace with Israel. Jordan signed peace agreement. Palestinian Declaration of Principles has been implemented now. Syria is on its way to reach an agreement. So there will be peace in the whole area.

So I don't think that Israel will be in need for any nuclear weapons in the future. But we are negotiating this issue to find any kind of formula to be agreed upon. We are not asking them to join the NPT now or tomorrow. We would like to know what we are going to do just for our national security. I think the ministers are going to meet tomorrow. I hope, with the help of the United States, we could narrow the gap and reach something concerning this issue.

Middle East Peace Process

Q. My question is for President Clinton. The Middle East continues to give rise to cynicism regarding the wider peace. Do you think that this might be due to lack of forceful American engagement?

President Clinton. Because of the continuing problems?

Q. Yes, because of the feeling that nothing is happening.

President Clinton. Well, first of all, a very great deal has happened in the last 2 years, and more than at any time in the last 15 years since the Camp David accords. So we have accomplished a great deal. We're about half of the way home toward a complete resolution of it.

The Secretary of State just got back from the Middle East. The Vice President has been to Egypt twice in the last 6 months. I am sending another envoy out today. I have been in regular and extensive contact with President Asad and Prime Minister Rabin, who was just here to see me recently. So we are working at it very, very hard.

I was concerned and, frankly, I would have agreed with a little bit of your question until about a month ago. About a month ago we got some new energy, some new direction, some new sense that both parties were really committed to trying to resolve this in the reasonably near future. So I'm more optimistic now, and I just think we have to keep working and people have to believe that there is not an unlimited amount of time within which to resolve this before other factors intervene.

Wolf [Wolf Blitzer, Cable News Network].

104th Congress

Q. Mr. President, if I could ask you a domestic question. The 100 days of the Republican Contract is about to end. Could you give us your assessment of these 100 days, what lessons have you learned, and where are you planning to go from here?

President Clinton. Well, I think, for one thing, I thought it got off to a pretty good start. From my point of view and my convictions, it's not ending as well as it started, because I don't agree with this tax bill. But it got off to a good start. The first three issues that were really taken up in earnest were issues that I also campaigned on: Applying to Congress the same laws they apply to the private sector—that's been passed and I've signed it; reducing the ability of the Federal Government to pass mandates on to State and local governments that cost the taxpayers there—I've signed that into law and I applaud the Congress for doing that; and both Houses have passed a version of the line-item veto, which I think is badly needed to control unnecessary spending. So those things I think are quite good.

In terms of a lot of the other measures which have made their way through the House, I think it depends on what the Senate does to them in terms of whether I think they're good for America. I do not believe that it's wise to have a tax cut of this magnitude where—with the deficit we've got and with our need to invest in our future and our children, where one percent of the people get 20 percent of the benefits and 12 percent of the people get half of the benefits, and in order to pay for it we run the risk of exploding the deficit or devastating our commitment to our children, to our educational system, and to our support for families, all of which are critical to our future economic growth.

I mean, we don't want to go back to trickle-down economics here under another term. The reason I ran for President was to get out of the old fight between tax-and-spend economics and trickle-down economics. I wanted to invest and grow the economy. So we reduced the deficit and increased our investment in education and technology and our efforts in trade. That economic strategy is working to lift Americans' incomes. Now we have to add an educational

component. And this tax approach is just wrong in my judgment.

So I'm going to keep working. Let's see what happens in the next 100 days and the 100 days after that and the 100 days after that. But our goals should be to lift the future prospects of the American people and grow the middle class again. And that's my assessment at this point.

Middle East Peace Process

Q. President Clinton, in the serious effort that your administration is dedicating to our Israeli-Palestinian peace, you are to be commended and your administration. And in the attempt to assist the Palestinian Authority in receiving the needed funds to build its infrastructure, can you please call, you and President Mubarak, on the Israeli Government and Mr. Rabin to end the closure of the Gaza Strip and the territories and allow more workers to enter Israel seeking employment as a way of injecting more funds in Gaza and the West Bank and all of the territories and help improve the economic conditions of the Palestinians that you are also working hard on that? Thank you.

President Clinton. We talked about this at some length together. I think it's the toughest issue, frankly, that we face between the Israelis and the Palestinians for this reason. When the borders were open, it made Israel more vulnerable to terrorism. When innocent people are killed, it undermines support in Israel for the peace process and weakens the government's ability to go forward. When the borders are closed, the incomes of the Palestinian people drop dramatically, and it makes young people more vulnerable to the appeals of the terrorists.

So it is an almost insoluble problem in that sense. It is the most difficult problem. And it is—obviously, the enemies of peace know this, and they seek to be rewarded whether the borders are open or the borders are closed. They think they will get their reward.

So I would say to you that I wish I had an easy answer. We are working on this problem. We are certainly talking to the Israelis about it. But it is the most difficult aspect of this process. And it is something that we have to be—I'm very sympathetic with the Palestinians who are within Gaza, and with the instability there, which undermines our ability to get, for example, Palestinian-Americans to invest there.

On the other hand, I understand Prime Minister Rabin's situation. I saw what it did to Israel when these acts of terror started occurring again, what it did to the psychology of the people, their feeling of confidence that peace could make a difference for them. So I won't presume to give you a final answer today, except to say I am very focused on this, and I know that this is the toughest part of the problem and that we're going to have to resolve it.

President Mubarak. I think what—we discussed this at length with President Clinton and we had long talks about it, realizing the situation will be much more difficult in Jericho and the Gaza because the income of the people nearly stopped. And we're wondering how are they going to live. And this may complicate the whole situation. That's why we have—already I have contact Mr. Rabin several times, and I spoke with Arafat. They should find a way for these people to have their income. Otherwise we'll return to terrorists, as the President already said, and it will be very difficult after that to solve the problem because complications will continue and the terrorist groups will feel that they succeed.

President Clinton. Brian [Brian Williams, NBC News].

President's Role in the Legislative Process

Q. Mr. President, one more domestic question. I'm curious as to your role over the next 100 days. Do you see it changing from that of dissenter to something, for lack of a better word, more proactive, more proactive legislatively?

President Clinton. Well, we were quite active in the—first of all, I agreed with—let me go back to the three areas which have passed. With regard to the bill applying to Congress the laws they put on the private sector, there was no activity for us to undertake, since I agree with the bill as it was drafted by the congressional leadership.

With regard to the bill on unfunded mandates, we were quite active in the Senate there and in the conference committee to try to get a bill which would permit us to protect the national interest and still give relief to State and local governments.

And with regard to the line-item veto, I personally lobbied a number of Democratic Senators very hard to make sure that we would be able to get a line-item veto through the Sen-

ate so we could go to conference and get one to my desk. Now, as I said, all three of those things I have worked very hard on.

All the other contract items that have passed with which I disagree, we are working in the United States Senate and we will work in the conference committee to try to get bills that are consistent with the principles that I hold to my desk so that I can sign them, not veto them. I do not want a pile of vetoes.

In the next 100 days, you're going to see a very exciting debate about welfare reform, something I've been involved in for 15 years. I have laid out my principles very, very clearly on that. You're going to see a debate about the larger budget that will run for the next 6 months, I think, in which I have very strong feelings about what we should be doing. I hope that I can focus the attention of the Congress on the need to lift the incomes of the American people, which means that if we're going to have a tax cut it ought to be for middle-class people to raise their children and educate themselves and their children, because that will raise incomes over the long run. And I hope I'll be able to persuade the Congress to raise the minimum wage. So I think I'll be involved in this debate with Congress.

Meanwhile, we're going to be pursuing our efforts to reform Government that we can do through the executive branch and our efforts to expand the American economy and our efforts to make the American people more secure. We will be pursuing those things just as we always have. And it will be a very exciting time.

I'm enjoying this, but I'm determined to see that the American people come out the winner. I do not want us to go back to trickle-down economics and to go back to the old debate, which is we should spend more on everything or less on everything. The less-on-everything crowd now has a majority in the Congress. What we should do is spend less on some things and more on some things and invest in things that will grow our economy and raise our incomes.

So I'm looking forward to being part of this debate. And I'm determined to see that it's a positive thing for the American people.

One more question from an Egyptian.

Antiterrorism Efforts

Q. Mr. President, Egypt has been—has a very good record combating and containing terrorism inside the country. What could the neighbors of Egypt in North Africa and the Middle East learn from the Egyptian experience?

President Mubarak. This question to me?

Q. Yes.

President Mubarak. Each country has its own tradition, its own way of living, its own way of dealing with the problems. We could manage to put down all the terroristic action to a great extent by law. We are not violating the law. Our neighbors, they have different characters, different situation, and they have their own idea that could make a good estimation of a situation to adopt what decision which could suit them

to put an end to terrorism that's completely different from ours.

President Clinton. Thank you.

NOTE: The President's 91st news conference began at 2:44 p.m. in the East Room at the White House. During the news conference, the following persons were referred to: Minister of Foreign Affairs Amre Mahmoud Moussa of Egypt, Foreign Minister Shimon Peres of Israel, Palestine Liberation Organization Chairman Yasser Arafat, Prime Minister Yitzhak Rabin of Israel, and President Hafiz al-Asad of Syria.

Memorandum on the Special Adviser on Assistance to the New Independent States of the Former Soviet Union
April 4, 1995

Memorandum for the Heads of Executive Departments and Agencies

Subject: Charter for Special Adviser to the President and to the Secretary of State on Assistance to the New Independent States (NIS) of the Former Soviet Union and Coordinator of NIS Assistance

The United States has a vital stake in the success of reform in the New Independent States (NIS) of the former Soviet Union. Ensuring effective support for the transformation underway in the NIS remains among the highest foreign policy priorities of my Administration. Over the past two years, bilateral assistance programs under the FREEDOM Support Act have played an important role in promoting democratic and economic reforms in the NIS, while projects funded through the Cooperative Threat Reduction (Nunn-Lugar) Act have promoted our denuclearization and nonproliferation policies. Despite remarkable progress, however, the success of reforms across the former Soviet Union is by no means assured. This fact, combined with budget realities that constrain the level of our financial aid to the region, make it imperative that our assistance be as targeted, relevant, and efficient as possible.

To assure maximum coordination of efforts to promote such reforms and policies within the Executive branch, I hereby designate Richard L. Morningstar as Special Adviser to the Presi-

dent and to the Secretary of State on Assistance to the New Independent States of the former Soviet Union and Coordinator of U.S. Assistance to the NIS in accordance with Section 102 of the FREEDOM Support Act. Mr. Morningstar will also act as Chairman of the previously established interagency NIS Assistance Coordination Group. In fulfilling these duties, Mr. Morningstar will preside over the allocation of U.S. assistance resources and direct and coordinate the interagency process on the development, funding, and implementation of all U.S. Government bilateral assistance and trade and investment programs related to the NIS.

To ensure that Mr. Morningstar will be able to carry out his responsibilities effectively, the Departments of Defense, Treasury, Justice, Commerce, Agriculture, Health and Human Services, and Energy, the Agency for International Development, United States Information Agency, Peace Corps, Environmental Protection Agency, National Aeronautics and Space Administration, Nuclear Regulatory Commission, Overseas Private Investment Corporation, Trade and Development Agency, and Export-Import Bank, and any other Executive departments and agencies with activities related to NIS bilateral assistance and export and investment activities are directed, to the extent permitted by law, to bring all programs and budget plans for such assistance and activities to Mr. Morningstar for review before submission to the Office of Management and Budget and before implementation. Mr. Morningstar shall be responsible for ensuring that all such plans are consistent with Administration priorities and policies. Heads of such entities shall designate an official at the level of Assistant Secretary or its equivalent to assist Mr. Morningstar in accomplishing the objectives of this mandate.

Mr. Morningstar will work with the U.S. Ambassadors to the NIS to strengthen coordination mechanisms in the field and increase the effectiveness of our assistance and export and investment programs on the ground. Assistance activities in the field will be coordinated by Ambassadors or their designates.

Mr. Morningstar will serve as a member of and consult with the Gore-Chernomyrdin Commission and the Policy Steering Group for the New Independent States to ensure that U.S. assistance and related activities are consistent with and support broader foreign policy objectives.

In carrying out these duties, Mr. Morningstar will report to me through the Assistant to the President for National Security Affairs and the Secretary of State, with policy guidance from the Policy Steering Group on the New Independent States.

WILLIAM J. CLINTON

NOTE: This memorandum was released by the Office of the Press Secretary on April 6.

Statement on Intent To Sign Self-Employed Health Insurance Tax Deduction Legislation
April 6, 1995

I intend to sign H.R. 831 because it reinstates and expands a much needed law that allows 3.2 million self-employed Americans and their families to deduct 25 percent of the cost of their health insurance, increasing to 30 percent in 1995.

This legislation is good for the country. I included it as part of my health reform bill last year because it restores fairness and security to an important group of Americans who work hard and play by the rules. Absent my approval of this legislation, almost 3.2 million self-employed workers—doctors, lawyers, farmers, artists, accountants—would not be able to claim this deduction for health insurance premiums on their 1994 income tax returns. By making this deduction permanent, we are treating them more like other businesses, and we are making them more competitive. And by making health care more affordable, we are shrinking the ranks of the uninsured and expanding coverage for more middle class Americans.

Because this health care benefit is so important, I will sign this legislation. But I am troubled by the fact that the conference committee took out a provision of law that simply would have required billionaires who made their money in this country to pay the taxes they owe. Instead, they decided to let them evade American income taxes by giving up their American citizenship. This is wrong. Billionaires who make their fortunes in this country ought to pay taxes here like everyone else. I am going to work to change this law in the future.

In addition, this bill carves out a special exception for one pending deal. This is the kind of dealing that goes on all the time in Washington.

That's why we need a line-item veto that covers both spending and special tax provisions. When I get it I can assure you I will use it to weed out special interest loopholes like the one in this bill.

But because of the important benefits of this legislation to our Nation's self-employed and their families, I could not justify a veto. The economic and health care interests of 3.2 million Americans and their families are too important to be held hostage.

Message to the Congress on Environmental Policy
April 6, 1995

To the Congress of the United States:

The United States has always been blessed with an abundance of natural resources. Together with the ingenuity and determination of the American people, these resources have formed the basis of our prosperity. They have given us the opportunity to feed our people, power our industry, create our medicines, and defend our borders—and we have a responsibility to be good stewards of our heritage. In recent decades, however, rapid technological advances and population growth have greatly enhanced our ability to have an impact on our surroundings—and we do not always pause to contemplate the consequences of our actions. Far too often, our short-sighted decisions cause the greatest harm to the very people who are least able to influence them—future generations.

We have a moral obligation to represent the interests of those who have no voice in today's decisions—our children and grandchildren. We have a responsibility to see that they inherit a productive and livable world that allows their families to enjoy the same or greater opportunities than we ourselves have enjoyed. Those of us who still believe in the American Dream will settle for no less. Those who say that we cannot afford both a strong economy and a healthy environment are ignoring the fact that the two are inextricably linked. Our economy will not remain strong for long if we continue to consume renewable resources faster than they can be replenished, or nonrenewable resources faster than we can develop substitutes; America's fishing and timber-dependent communities will not survive for long if we destroy our fisheries and our forests. Whether the subject is deficit spending or the stewardship of our fisheries, the issue is the same: we should not pursue a strategy of short-term gain that will harm future generations.

Senators Henry Jackson and Ed Muskie, and Congressman John Dingell understood this back in 1969 when they joined together to work for passage of the National Environmental Policy Act. At its heart, the National Environmental Policy Act is about our relationship with the natural world, and about our relationship with future generations. For the first time, the National Environmental Policy Act made explicit the widely-held public sentiment that we should live in harmony with nature and make decisions that account for future generations as well as for today. It declared that the Federal Government should work in concert with State and local governments and the citizens of this great Nation "to create and maintain conditions under which man and nature can exist in productive harmony, and fulfill the social, economic, and other requirements of present and future generations of Americans."

Over the past 25 years, America has made great progress in protecting the environment. The air is cleaner in many places than it was, and we no longer have rivers that catch on fire. And yet, this year in Milwaukee, more than 100 people died from drinking contaminated water, and many of our surface waters are still not fit for fishing and swimming. One in four Americans still lives near a toxic dump and almost as many breathe air that is unhealthy.

In order to continue the progress that we have made and adequately provide for future generations, my Administration is ushering in a new era of common sense reforms. We are bringing together Americans from all walks of life to find new solutions to protect our health, improve our Nation's stewardship of natural resources, and provide lasting economic opportunities for ourselves and for our children. We are reinventing environmental programs to make them work better and cost less.

My Administration is ushering in a new era of environmental reforms in many ways. Following is a description of a few of these reforms, grouped into three clusters: first, stronger and smarter health protection programs such as my proposed Superfund reforms and EPA's new common sense approach to regulation; second, new approaches to resource management, such as our Northwest forest plan, that provide better stewardship of our natural resources and sustained economic opportunity; and third, the promotion of innovative environmental technologies, for healthier air and water as well as stronger economic growth now and in the future.

Stronger and Smarter Health Protection Programs. Throughout my Administration, we have been refining Government, striving to make it work better and cost less. One of the best places to apply this principle in the environmental arena is the Superfund program. For far too long, far too many Superfund dollars have been spent on lawyers and not nearly enough have been spent on clean-up. I've directed my Administration to reform this program by cutting legal costs, increasing community involvement, and cleaning up toxic dumps more quickly. The reformed Superfund program will be faster, fairer, and more efficient—and it will put more land back into productive community use.

Similarly, EPA is embarking on a new strategy to make environmental and health regulation work better and cost less. This new common sense approach has the potential to revolutionize the way we write environmental regulations. First, EPA will not seek to adopt environmental standards in a vacuum. Instead, all the affected stakeholders—representatives of industry, labor, State governments, and the environmental community—will be involved from the beginning. Second, we will replace one-size-fits-all regulations with a focus on results achieved with flexible means. And at last, we're taking a consistent, comprehensive approach. With the old piece-meal approach, the water rules were written in isolation of the air rules and the waste rules, and too often led to results that merely shuffled and shifted pollutants—results that had too little health protection at too great a cost. With its new common sense approach, EPA will address the full range of environmental and health impacts of a given industry—steel or electronics for example—to get cleaner, faster, and cheaper results.

Better Stewardship of our Natural Resources. Just as representative of our new approach to the environment—and just as grounded in common sense—is the Administration's commitment to ecosystems management of the Nation's natural resources. For decades ecologists have known that what we do with one resource affects the others. For instance, the way we manage a forest has very real consequences for the quality of the rivers that run through the forest, very real consequences for the fishermen who depend on that water for their livelihood, and very real consequences for the health of the community downstream. But until recently, government operations failed to account adequately for such interaction. In many cases, several Federal agencies operated independently in the same area

under different rules. In many cases, no one paused to ponder the negative consequences of their actions until it was too late.

Often, these consequences were catastrophic, leading to ecological and economic train wrecks such as the collapse of fisheries along the coasts, or the conflict over timber cutting in the Pacific Northwest. When I convened the Forest Conference earlier this year I saw the devastating effects of the Federal Government's lack of foresight and failure to provide leadership. Here, perhaps more than anywhere else, is a case study in how a failure to anticipate the consequences of our actions on the natural environment can be devastating to our livelihoods in the years ahead. Our forest plan is a balanced and comprehensive program to put people back to work and protect ancient forests for future generations. It will not solve all of the region's problems but it is a strong first step at restoring both the long-term health of the region's ecosystem and the region's economy.

Innovative Environmental Technologies. Environmental and health reforms such as EPA's common sense strategy and natural resource reforms such as the forest plan provide an opportunity, and an obligation, to make good decisions for today that continue to pay off for generations to come. In much the same way, sound investments in environmental technology can ensure that we leave to future generations a productive, livable world. Every innovation in environmental technology opens up a new expanse of economic and environmental possibilities, making it possible to accomplish goals that have eluded us in the past. From the very beginning, I have promoted innovative environmental technologies as a top priority. We've launched a series of environmental technology initiatives, issued a number of Executive orders to help spur the application of these technologies, and taken concrete steps to promote their export. Experts say the world market for environmental technology is nearly $300 billion today and that it may double by the year 2000. Every dollar we invest in environmental technology will pay off in a healthier environment worldwide, in greater market share for U.S. companies, and in more jobs for American workers.

Innovations in environmental technology can be the bridge that carries us from the threat of greater health crises and ecological destruction toward the promise of greater economic prosperity and social well-being. Innovation by innovation, we can build a world transformed by human ingenuity and creativity—a world in which economic activity and the natural environment support and sustain one another.

This is the vision that Jackson, Muskie, and Dingell articulated more than two decades ago when they wrote in the National Environmental Policy Act that we should strive to live in productive harmony with nature and seek to fulfill the social and economic needs of future generations. We share a common responsibility to see beyond the urgent pressures of today and think of the future. We share a common responsibility

to speak for our children, so that they inherit a world filled with the same opportunity that we had. This is the vision for which we work today and the guiding principle behind my Administration's environmental policies.

WILLIAM J. CLINTON

The White House,
April 6, 1995.

NOTE: This message was released by the Office of the Press Secretary on April 7.

Remarks and a Question-and-Answer Session With the American Society of Newspaper Editors in Dallas, Texas
April 7, 1995

The President. Thank you very much. Thank you. "Fishbait" Favre. It's got kind of a nice ring, doesn't it? [*Laughter*] I knew he was born in New Orleans before he ever said it. I love to listen to people from New Orleans talk.

I thank you for that kind introduction. Your convention program chair, Bob Haiman, and your incoming president, Bill Ketter, ladies and gentlemen, I'm very glad to be here.

I thought that in addition to me you were going to hear from three people who had run, are running, and were about to run for President. But only Bill Weld showed up. I hope he stays in the "about to run." He and Steve Merrill are very impressive men, and I'm glad that they came here and gave the Republican point of view.

It's a privilege to be here. I'd like to begin by saying that I am very proud, and I know you are, for the work that the Inter American Press Association has done in its Declaration of Chapultepec. I know that you and the Newspaper Association of America have worked tirelessly for press freedoms all throughout the Americas. And just before I came out here I was proud to sign a Charter of Endorsement for the Declaration of Chapultepec. And I thank you for giving me that opportunity and for what you have done to advance the cause of a free press.

I was talking to a friend of mine the other day who said, "Well, in the '94 election we

discovered the limits of liberalism, and now we're about to discover the limits of conservatism." And it put me in mind of a story I once heard about the—and actually, I thought about it because I met Mr. Favre—about the late Huey Long, who, when he was Governor and he was preaching his share-the-wealth plan, was out in the country one day at a little country crossroads. And he had all the people gathered up. And he was going on about how the people were being plundered by the organized wealthy interests in Louisiana.

And he saw a guy out in the crowd that he knew and he said, "Brother Jones, if you had three Cadillacs, wouldn't you give up one of them so we could gather up the kids and take them to school during the week and take them to church on the weekend?" He said, "Sure, I would." He said, "And if you had $3 million, wouldn't you give up just a million of it so we could put a roof over everybody's head and make sure everybody had food to eat?" He said, "Well, of course I would." He said, "And if you had three hogs—" He said, "Wait a minute, Governor, I've got three hogs." [*Laughter*]

Anyway, that's the limits of liberalism. Now we're about to discover the limits of conservatism.

Ladies and gentlemen, we are at a historic moment in our country's history: on the verge of a new century, living in a very different kind of economy with a bewildering array of challenges and opportunities. In 1992 and in 1994, the voters spoke out and demanded bold changes in the way we govern and the policies we pursue. They know better than anyone else that they are living in a time with new challenges that demand new answers.

In the last 2 years, my administration has begun to meet those challenges. I ran for President because I felt we were being victimized by 12 years of gridlock in which the deficit had gone up, the wealthiest Americans had done quite well, the middle class had stagnated, and the poor were in trouble, in which the American dream was really at risk because half of the American people were working for the same or lower wages that they had made 15 years earlier.

I had a clear mission. I wanted to grow the middle class, shrink the under class, and speed up the opportunities for entrepreneurs. I wanted to promote the mainstream values of responsibility and work, family and community. I wanted to reform the Government so that we could enhance opportunity, shrink bureaucracy, increase our security, and most important of all, empower people through education to make the most of their own lives.

In the first 2 years we've made good progress. The economy is up, and the deficit is down. We've expanded educational opportunities from Head Start through more college loans that are more affordable. The American people are marching toward more security because there are no Russian missiles pointed at the children of our country for the first time since the dawn of the nuclear age, because we passed a serious crime bill that will lower the crime rate in many of our communities throughout the country, and because we've begun to address some of the problems of family security with the Family and Medical Leave Act. And certainly, we have done a lot to shrink and to reform the Government's bureaucracy.

But it is not enough. Too many Americans don't yet feel any of those benefits. Too many still feel uncertain about their own future, and too many people are overwhelmingly concerned about the social and the underlying moral problems of our society. And so in 1994, they voted to give the Republicans a chance to run the Congress.

In the last 100 days, the House of Representatives has passed a series of bold initiatives. We

will soon begin the second 100 days of this Congress. In the first 100 days, the mission of the House Republicans was to suggest ways in which we should change our Government and our society. In the second 100 days and beyond, our mission together must be to decide which of these House proposals should be adopted, which should be modified, and which should be stopped.

In the first 100 days, it fell to the House of Representatives to propose. In the next 100 days and beyond, the President has to lead the quiet, reasoned forces of both parties in both Houses to sift through the rhetoric and decide what is really best for America. In making these decisions, it is absolutely vital that we keep alive the spirit and the momentum of change. But the momentum must not carry us so far that we betray our legacy of compassion, decency, and common sense.

We have entered a new era. For years, out here in the country, the old political categories have basically been defunct, and a new political discussion has been begging to be born. It must be now so in Washington, as well. The old labels of liberal and conservative, spender and cutter, even Democrat and Republican, are not what matter most anymore. What matters most is finding practical, pragmatic solutions based on what we know works in our lives and our shared experiences so that we can go forward together as a nation. Ideological purity is for partisan extremists. Practical solution, based on real experience, hard evidence, and common sense, that's what this country needs.

We've been saddled too long with a political debate that doesn't tell us what we ought to do, just who we ought to blame. And we have got to stop pointing fingers at each other so that we can join hands.

You know, our country has often moved forward spurred on by purists, reformists, populist agendas which articulated grievances and proposed radical departures. But if you think about our most successful periods of reform, these initiatives have been shaped by Presidents who incorporated what was good, smoothed out what was rough, and discarded what would hurt. That was the role of Theodore Roosevelt and Woodrow Wilson in the aftermath of the populist era. That was the role of Franklin Roosevelt in the aftermath of the La Follette progressive movement. And that is my job in the next 100 days and for all the days I serve as President.

We stand at a crossroads. In one direction lies confrontation and gridlock; in the other lies achievement and progress. I was not elected President to pile up a stack of vetoes. I was elected President to change the direction of America. That's what I have spent the last 2 years doing and that's what I want to spend the next 100 days and beyond doing. Whether we can do that depends upon what all of us in Washington do from here on out.

So I appeal today to Republicans and to Democrats alike to get together, to keep the momentum for change going, not to allow the energy and longing for change now to be dissipated amid a partisan clutter of accusations. After all, we share much common ground.

For example, in 1992, I was elected to end welfare as we know it. That was part of my New Covenant of opportunity and responsibility. In 1994, the Republicans made the same demand with their contract. In the last 2 years, I have already given 25 States, one-half of the country, the opportunity to do just that on their own. And I introduced the most sweeping welfare reform the country had ever seen. I want to work with the Congress to get real welfare reform.

In 1992, I was elected to slash the deficit. That also was part of my New Covenant. In 1994, the Republican contract called for a continuing deficit reduction and movement toward a balanced budget. Well, I cut the deficit by $600 billion, cut 300 programs; I proposed to consolidate or eliminate 400 more. I want to cut the deficit. Except for the interest run up between 1981 and 1992, our budget would be in balance today. My administration is the only one in 30 years to run an operating surplus. I will work with the Republicans to reduce the deficit.

In 1992, I was elected to shrink the size of the Federal Government, which I have done. That, too, was a part of my New Covenant. In 1994, the Republican contract said we should shrink the Government. I have already cut 100,000 bureaucratic positions, and we are on the way under budgets already passed to reducing the Government by 270,000, to its smallest size since President Kennedy occupied this office. I want to work with Congress to reduce the size of Government.

We both want tax cuts, less intrusive Government regulations, the line-item veto, the toughest possible fight against crime. These were a part of the New Covenant and a part of the Republican contract. In 2 years, we have made real progress on all these fronts, but we can, and we should do more.

We are near many breakthroughs. The real issue is whether we will have the wisdom and the courage to see our common ground and walk on it. To do that, we must abandon extreme positions and work together. This is no time for ideological extremism. Good-faith compromising, negotiating our differences, actually listening to one another for a change, these are the currency of a healthy democracy.

In that spirit, I come here today to outline where I stand on the remaining items in the Republican contract and the unfinished business of my New Covenant.

Let's begin with taxes. In 1993, I made a down payment on the middle-class tax cut I advocated when I ran for President. We cut taxes for 15 million working families. What that means on average is that this year a family of four with an income of $25,000 a year or less will have about $1,000 in lower tax bills. We did this to ensure that nobody who works full-time and has children should live in poverty. If you want to reform the welfare system, you must reward work and parenting.

So I want a tax cut to expand, to include more members of the middle class. Why? Because half the American people are working for the same or lower incomes they were making 15 years ago. And we've had a recovery that's produced 6.3 million new jobs, the lowest combined rates of unemployment and inflation in 25 years, and we need to spread the benefits of the recovery.

But this $200 billion tax cut, which is really more than 3 times that if you look at it over a 10 year period, is a fantasy. It's too much. It's not going to happen. We can't afford it. A realistic cut would be somewhere around a third of that. That's something we can afford. In the world we're living in up there, if we go beyond that, what you're going to see is no success at deficit reduction or horrible injustice to the most vulnerable people in our country. So we can't pass that. Let's get over it and talk about what we can pass and work on doing it. Let's target a tax cut to the right people and for the right purpose.

We have to choose: Do you want a tax cut for the wealthy or for the middle class? The Republican plan gives half of the benefits to the 10 percent of the people who are best off, and most importantly, to the 10 percent of our people who have done very, very well in the last 15 years. Twenty percent of the benefits go to the top one percent of our people. They have done very well in the new global economy. The middle class has suffered the stagnant incomes. Let's direct the tax benefits to those people.

But we also have to choose what kind of tax break. Shall we just put money in people's pockets? Or shouldn't we do something that will strengthen families and increase the whole wealth and success of the United States over the long run? Let's help our people get the education and job training they need.

The technology revolution, the global economy, these are dividing opportunity at home and abroad. The middle class is splitting apart. And the fault line is education. Those who have it do well; those who don't are in trouble. So let's use the tax cut as I propose in the middle class bill of rights as sort of a scholarship given by America to people for their cost of education after high school. And let's provide for an IRA that people can withdraw from, tax-free, to meet the exigencies that their families face: college education, health care costs, first-time home, care of an elderly parent. These things will strengthen our country and we can afford it.

Let's take welfare reform. As I said, both of us, both the Republican contract and my New Covenant, have focused heavily on welfare reform. What do we agree on? That there ought to be a limit to welfare; that there ought to be flexibility for the States; that we ought to have the toughest possible child support enforcement; and that people have to take more responsibility for their own lives and for the children they bring into this world.

But the current House bill focuses primarily on cutting costs. It's weak on work and tough on kids. It punishes young people for past mistakes. We must require them, instead, to look to the future and in the future to be responsible parents, to be responsible workers, to be responsible students, and then give them the opportunity to do that.

The House bill also punishes young children for the sins of their parents. I think that's wrong. Rich or poor, black, white, or brown, in or out of wedlock, a baby is a baby, a child is a child. It's part of our future, and we have an obligation

to those children not to punish them for something over which they had absolutely no control.

Now, that's where I disagree. But look what we agree on. We are near historic change. We can do this. We can make a difference. We can break the culture of welfare, and we can do something good for our country to support the values we all believe in. And we can give these children a better future. But to do it, we're going to have to talk through our differences and get beyond the rhetoric to how these real lives work and not stand on the sidelines posturing for political gain.

Let's take cutting the deficit. The balanced budget amendment is dead. But now we have to get specific. How are we going to cut the deficit and move this budget toward balance? If we can focus on cuts, not making partisan points, that's the first step. There are cuts I can't live with. There are cuts the Republicans can't live with. Let's avoid them and make cuts we can all live with.

We shouldn't cut help for our children. That builds our future. We shouldn't cut their education, their immunization, their school lunches, the infant formulas, or the nutrition programs. There's no need to cut them. So far, based on the action they've taken, the Republicans want the poor in this country to bear the burden of two-thirds of their proposed cuts and only get 5 percent of the benefit of the tax cuts. It is not right. It is wrong. But that doesn't mean we don't have to cut the budget and reduce the deficit.

The rescission package that passed the Senate last night gives us a model about how we should proceed. The House passed a rescission package with completely unacceptable cuts in education, child nutrition, environment, housing, and national service. The Senate Republicans, to their credit, restored several of these cuts. I insisted on restoring even more and replacing them with better cuts. And almost every one of the Democrats in the Senate agreed.

So yesterday, over the course of the debate, they worked that out. Those cuts were restored as well. There will still be a $16 billion reduction in the deficit this year. The bill passed 99–0 in the Senate, and I will sign the Senate bill if the House and the Senate will send it to me. That's how we should be doing the business of America.

Let's talk about the line-item veto. As I said before, that was in the Republican contract, and

I campaigned for President on it in 1992. I appeal to Congress to pass it in its strongest form. I appeal to members of my own party who have reservations about it to support it as well. The line-item veto has now passed both the Senate and the House.

If you look at how it passed the Senate, that's an example of how we can make this system work. I strongly supported it. I campaigned to Democratic Senators and asked them to support it. They worked out their differences, and it passed overwhelmingly in the Senate.

The President and the Congress both need the power to cut spending. If you doubt it, if you doubt it, look at the bill that Congress recently passed to restore to 3.2 million self-employed Americans, farmers, small businesspeople, professionals, and all their family members, the 25 percent deduction for the cost of their health insurance. That was a part of my health care plan. I desperately want to do that. We ought to do more. They ought to be treated just like corporations. It is imperative to sign it. But hidden in that bill was a special tax break for people who did not need it. If I had the Senate version of the line-item veto, I could sign the bill and help the people who are entitled to it, and veto the special break. This is the kind of thing that's been hidden in bills of Congress forever. We can now do something about it, and we ought to do it.

Political reform, something that was also in the Republican contract: Two of the ten items in the Republican contract have actually become law. And two, term limits and the balanced budget amendment, have been defeated. Of the two that have become law, they were both about political reform, and they were also both part of my 1992 commitments to the American people. One applies to Congress the laws they impose on the private sector. The other limits the ability of Congress to impose unfunded mandates on State and local government. I was proud to sign them both. They will advance the cause of responsible Government in this country.

But political reform means more. It must include, I believe, both lobbying reform and campaign finance reform. If you doubt how much we need lobby reform, just go back and refer to the story that was rightly printed just a few days ago about how in this session of Congress you have lobbyists actually sitting at the table with Congressmen, writing bills for them and then explaining to them what the bills mean. It seems to me that since these bills help the people the lobbyists represent, but drastically restrict the ability of the Government to act in the areas of the environment, in protecting our people, we need some significant reform in our lobbying laws. So I don't think we should stop there.

Regulatory reform, another big item in the Republican contract: There are lots of horror stories. Every one of you probably knows a story that shows where a bureaucrat overreached or there were too many regulations or there was too little common sense. I am committed to changing the culture of regulation that has dominated our country for a long time. I have gone around espousing to everybody that they ought to read Mr. Howard's book "The Death of Common Sense."

But for 2 years, we have been working through the reinventing Government initiative that the Vice President has headed to change the culture of regulation. We deregulated banking. We deregulated intrastate trucking. We have reformed the procedures of the SBA. We scrapped the 10,000-page Federal personnel manual. We have dramatically changed the way the General Services Administration operates in ways that have saved hundreds of millions of dollars for the taxpayers and put more competition into the process, thanks to the GSA Director, Roger Johnson, who happens to be here with me today. We are working on these things to move forward.

But we must do more. And yet, surely, the answer is not to stop the Government from regulating what it needs to regulate. If the Republicans send me a bill that would let unsafe planes fly or contaminated meat be sold or contaminated water continue to find itself into city water systems, I will veto it. I will veto it. But if Congress will just sit down with me and work out a reasonable solution for more flexible regulatory reform, we can create an historic achievement.

I agree that Congress has a role to play. I agree that Congress sometimes hears things about the way regulations work that people in the executive branch don't. Congresswoman Johnson and Congressman Bryant and Congressman Geren flew down here with me today. They're out there all the time talking to their members. They may hear things we don't. That's why I approve of the Senate's 45-day override legislation. But I will veto any bill that lets a bunch of lawyers tie up regulation for years. We've got too much of that as it is.

So I say, flexibility, yes; reform, yes; but paralysis and straightjacketing, no.

Let's talk about legal reform. Are there too many lawsuits? Of course, there are. Do jury awards once in a while get out of hand? Yes, they do. Does this affect the insurance system in the country? It has an impact on it. But at a time when we're giving more and more responsibility to the States in which one of the signal ideas of the Republican contract that I largely agree with is that the State and local governments should have more responsibility, do we really want to take the entire civil justice system away from the States for the first time in 200 years? I don't think so.

Let me give you a couple of examples. Should we put justice out of the reach of ordinary people with a "loser pay" rule? No. Think about it this way: "Loser pays" will keep ordinary citizens from exercising their rights in court just as a poll tax used to keep ordinary people of color and poverty from exercising their right to vote. I will veto any bill with a "loser pay" requirement such as that that was in the House bill. I don't think it's right.

Punitive damages: they could stand some reform but not artificial ceilings. Punitive damages are designed to deter bad future conduct. Now, if you have a national ceiling of $250,000 think what that means—$250,000 may be too burdensome for a small-business person who loses a lawsuit. You don't want to put them out of business unless they're malicious. But does anybody seriously believe that $250,000 will have any kind of significant deterrent impact on a giant multinational corporation? So let's negotiate realistic reforms that improve the system, but don't wreck it.

Crime: Crime was a big part of the New Covenant, a big part of why I ran for President. The personal security of the American people should be our first concern. And we delivered. After 6 years we broke gridlock, and I signed a crime bill that was endorsed by all the major law enforcement organizations in the country, the cities, the counties, the prosecutors, the attorneys general, everybody. And it had bipartisan support, too, until we got close to the last election; Republicans and Democrats cosponsoring all major provisions.

What was in the crime bill? It had more punishment, "three strikes and you're out," expansion of capital punishment. It had more police, 100,000 police on our street. And I might say that over half of the communities in this country have already received grants under the police program just since last October. We're ahead of schedule and under budget. There are already about 17,000 police officers authorized and funded to be hired. It had more prisons, something the Republicans very much wanted, as long as the States agreed to change their sentencing procedures. And it had more prevention programs, something the police demanded. The police said, "You cannot police and punish and imprison your way out of the crime crisis. You have got to give these children in our country something to say yes to. You've got to give them a reason to stay off drugs, a reason to stay in school, a reason to believe they can have a future." So it had all those things.

Now, if the Republicans wish to continue to try to repeal the commitment to 100,000 police or to repeal the assault weapons ban, they have a perfect right to do it. But if they send me those provisions, I will veto them. On the other hand, while the rest of their crime bill needs some work and I disagree with some provisions of it, it has some good points. If we can build on the '94 crime bill instead of tear it down, we can continue our efforts to make the American people more secure. So let's do that. Let's pass a crime bill we can be proud of, that builds the country up and makes our citizens safer.

The environmental protection area: A big part of my New Covenant was protecting our environment and promoting our natural resources. It's something we can all give to our children whether we die rich or poor. And it is our obligation to our future economic health, because no nation over the long run succeeds economically unless you preserve your environment.

I just got back from Haiti, and I can tell you one of the biggest obstacles to the survival of democracy in that country is they have ripped all the trees off every hill in the country, and we need to plant tens of millions of trees. We could put half the young people in the country to work for a year just trying to undo the environmental devastation. And unless we do it, they're not going to be able to regain their economic footing.

I cannot and I will not compromise any clean water, any clean air, any protection against toxic waste. The environment cannot protect itself. And if it requires a Presidential veto to protect it, then that's what I'll provide.

I will also veto the House-passed requirement that Government pay property owners billions of dollars every time we act to defend our national heritage of seashores or wetlands or open spaces. If that law were on the books in every State in the country today, then local governments would completely have to give up zoning or be bankrupt every time they try to change a zoning law. That is why every time it's been on the ballot in a State—and it's been on the ballot 20 times, including in conservative, Republican States—it has been defeated. The people of Arizona voted against it by a 20-point margin last November.

Well, the people do not have to vote—do not have a vote on this issue in Congress. But I do, and I'll use it. This is not a good law.

Peacekeeping: Decades from now when we have our next Republican President—[laughter]—he or she will be very grateful that I refused to approve the so-called peacekeeping legislation passed by the House. The United Nations and the world community did not struggle through 45 years of stagnation because of Soviet vetoes to have to deal with a new stagnation because of an American congressional veto.

The United Nations is 50 years old this year. But it's only 4 or 5 years old as a real force for international stability and security as it was imagined by Woodrow Wilson and Franklin Roosevelt and Dwight Eisenhower and Arthur Vandenberg, responsible Republicans and Democrats. So let us learn from the United Nations mistakes in Somalia and the United Nations successes in Haiti and throughout the world, about how we can best keep the peace in partnership with our neighbors throughout the world.

In Haiti there were almost 30 countries in there with us and the multinational force, and under the U.N. mission there now, well over 30 countries, people who came from a long way away because they know the world must work together to promote humanity and peace and democracy and decency. Let us not walk away from the United Nations and isolate America from the world.

There's some other things I want to talk about. Those are the items in the Republican contract, many of which were also in my New Covenant and where I stand on them. But I want to talk about some other items as well, the unfinished business of the agenda that I ran for President on.

I was elected to fix a broken Government, to relight the dormant fires of the economy, to make sure that working families reap the just reward of their effort and are able to pass their children the same dream they had, and to end the sort of something-for-nothing mentality that had crept into our country by restoring the values of responsibility and work and family and community.

The Republican contract, even where I agree with it, does not deal with much of what is really at the heart of America's challenges today, opportunity and security for working Americans. So let me talk about these issues.

Health care: In the State of the Union I said I had learned that I bit off more than I could chew last year, and we have to reform health care a step at a time. But I haven't forgotten the need to reform health care. Everybody knows we still have problems. It costs too much. There are a lot of people who have inadequate coverage. There are a lot of people who have no coverage at all, and there are millions of Americans who could lose their coverage at any time. So I call on Republicans to join me in taking this one step at a time, beginning with things the majority of them have long endorsed:

First, making benefits portable so you don't lose your health care when you change jobs.

Second, requiring coverage for families with a preexisting condition so the whole family doesn't lose health care just because there's been one sick child. I saw a couple from Delaware on the street in Washington a couple of months ago when I was taking my jog, the best-looking family you ever saw. The young man and woman looked to be in their late thirties. They had five children. Their fourth child had a birth defect. And he was a small businessman. None of them had any health insurance. That's an intolerable situation in this country, and we shouldn't put up with it.

The third thing we ought to do is to establish voluntary pools, such as those established in Florida and many other States, which allow small businesses and self-employed people to buy health care on the same terms as those of us who work for Government or big corporations can buy it, to put some competitive power behind their need.

The fourth thing we should do is to expand home care for the elderly, so that families who are struggling to keep their elderly parents and grandparents at home in a more independent living setting have some alternative before putting them into a nursing home when it will almost certainly cost the Government much, much more money.

And finally, we ought to do our best in the way of coverage to help families keep their coverage when they're unemployed for an extended period of time. And we should do all this within the context of a determination to hold down the costs of health care, still the biggest problem for most Americans. We can do this without a tax increase and while working to bring the deficit down. We have been working very hard on this. The numbers clearly make that apparent.

The second issue I want to raise on our unfinished agenda is the minimum wage. The minimum wage is the key, first, to welfare reform. Unless work pays, why will people do it? There is some evidence that not only will the minimum wage increase I proposed not cost jobs, it might actually increase employment by drawing people into the ranks of the employed who are hanging out now. Not only that, working people simply cannot live and raise kids on $8,500 a year.

Now, the Republicans want—and they've wanted for a long time—they want to index tax rates against inflation, which has now been done. Now they want to index capital gains against inflation. They want to guard the defense budget against inflation. But they're willing to let minimum wage workers fall to their lowest real incomes in 40 years? That's what will happen if we don't raise the minimum wage. The lowest real incomes in 40 years, is that your idea of the legacy for working people in the aftermath of the cold war, in the information age, leading America into a bright, new time?

The minimum wage, again, has always before been a bipartisan issue. The last time we raised the minimum wage, it got an enormous vote in the Congress from Republicans and Democrats. Let's make the minimum wage a bipartisan issue again and raise it to a decent level, so that working people and their children will not have to worry about being punished for doing the right thing.

The last issue I want to talk about is education and training. I've already said most of what I want to say about it. The Secretary of Education is here with me today, along with many other people in the White House, my Chief of Staff, Mr. Panetta, and others. We've all worked very hard on education. Why? Because I believe that the most important job of Government today is to give people the tools they need to succeed in the global economy.

With all these changes that are going on, everybody knows the Government can't guarantee everybody a job. We haven't been able to do it in a long time, and our ability to guarantee the same job for a career is less than ever before. I can work to create healthy conditions in which large numbers of jobs will be created, but guaranteeing a particular job to a particular person for a lifetime, it is out. It's not possible.

The only thing we can do is to make sure that for a whole lifetime people will always be able to get the skills they need, beginning at the earliest possible time with good education. That means that as we cut the deficit and cut the budget, we must not cut education. We shouldn't cut Head Start. We shouldn't cut aid to public schools to meet national standards of excellence. We shouldn't cut apprenticeships to help young people who don't go on to college get good training so they can get a job with a growing income, not a shrinking income.

We sure shouldn't cut and make more expensive the college loan program when we need more people going to college and the cost of going is higher than ever before. And we should not cut our national service program, AmeriCorps, which lets people earn college money through community service. Cutting education in the face of global economic competition, as I have said repeatedly, would be just like cutting the defense budget at the height of the cold war. It undermines our security as a people, and we shouldn't do it.

I advocated in the middle class bill of rights a deduction for the cost of all education after high school; the ability to withdraw tax-free from an IRA to pay for the cost of education after high school; and a "GI bill" for America's workers that would collapse literally dozens of these Federal programs that are here, there, and yonder in job training into one block grant, and not give it to the States, give it to the people. Let Americans who are unemployed or grossly unemployed have a voucher for cash money which they can use at any education or training facility of their choice as long as it's decent and meets good standards, so that we can have a continuous, seamless web of lifetime of education and training opportunities for the people of the United States.

Well, there it is. That's what I'm for and what I'm against. I do not want a pile of vetoes. I want a pile of bills that will move this country into the future. I don't want to see a big fight between the Republicans and the Democrats. I want us to surprise everybody in America by rolling up our sleeves and joining hands and working together. I believe this is a time of such profound change that we need a dynamic center that is not in the middle of what is left and right but is way beyond it. That's what I want, and that's what I'm working for.

If you want to know how I'm going to make other decisions—if I left one out—I would refer you to what I said in my address to the Nation on December 15th. My test is: Does an idea expand middle class incomes and opportunities? Does it promote values like family, work, responsibility, and community? Does it strengthen the hand of America's working families in a global economy? If it does, I'll be for it, no matter who proposes it. And if it doesn't, I will oppose it.

The future I want for America is like the one I imagined I had when I was the age of these children that are here in this audience. We can give this to our children. In fact, we can give a bigger future to our children. I am absolutely convinced that if we are tough enough and wise enough and unpolitical enough to put the interests of ordinary Americans first, and to really focus on the future, that our best days are before us, better than we can even imagine. But it all depends on what we do at this crossroads. Let's get busy.

Thank you very much.

[At this point, the President took questions from newspaper editors.]

Newspaper Role in Community Dialog

Q. Mr. President, you talk about a civilized conversation in this country leading towards a new common ground. How would you challenge American newspapers to forward that conversation, doing things that we aren't doing now?

The President. Well, I don't know what each of you are doing or not doing now. But I will give you some examples. I'll give you three examples. I think you should try to replicate in your communities the kind of conversation that

Newsweek reprinted based on questions they asked Speaker Gingrich and me about what the role of Government is and what it should be. I don't think that we—I think both of us are a little bit frustrated about it, because we didn't know—we just answered questions, and then they had to turn it into an article, but it was the beginning of an interesting conversation about what the role of Government ought to be.

The second thing I would advise is to take each one of these issues—I saw in the, I think it was in the Dallas Morning News, one of the papers today I saw, that I read had a portrait of a family on welfare. Take each of these big issues and try to figure out how to go from rhetoric to reality so that people can understand what all these labels mean. Because if all you hear about these debates is what sort of pierces through in 10 or 15 seconds on the evening news, chances are your opinion will be more dominated by the rhetoric. And if it happens to comport with the facts, that's fine, but if it doesn't, that's not so good. Newspapers can do that. Newspapers can analyze in depth real, hard evidence on various problems.

And the third thing I think maybe you ought to consider doing is sponsoring conversations within your community of people of different political and racial and other stripes—just people who are different. Because we are running the risk—interestingly enough, we have more information than ever before, but the way we get it may divide us from one another instead of unite us.

And I think it might be really interesting if all the newspapers in the country sponsored community discussions. I don't mean bring people like me or people who want to be President, or even maybe people from Congress in from outside, but I mean the people in your local community who would represent different political points of view and live in different neighborhoods and are from different racial backgrounds and have an agenda of common topics that are being discussed all around the country, and let people listen to each other and talk to each other.

My experience has always been that the differences among us, except on a few issues, are not nearly as profound as we think they are. And then report that to your readers, because we have to establish some sense of common ground. If all of our public discourse is about segmenting the electorate and then trying to make sure that by election day you've got the biggest segment, and there's never an opportunity to redefine where we are in common, that may work okay in a stable time because the policies are more or less set, the direction is more or less set; nobody's going to veer too much one way or the other anyway. But in a time of real profound change where the information revolution has made all of us actors, it is important that we try to establish more common ground. So those would be my three suggestions.

V–J Day 50th Anniversary

Q. Mr. President, we're coming upon the ceremonies to commemorate the 50th anniversary of V–J Day. And someone suggested that it's time to try to heal the wounds of that war, and that the United States should take the first step by apologizing for dropping a bomb on Hiroshima and Nagasaki. Should we apologize? And did President Harry Truman make the right decision in dropping the bomb?

The President. No. And based on the facts he had before him, yes.

Cuban Refugees

Q. Mr. President, last week you went to Haiti, where the military operation of our troops and other nations really helped restore order and to stop the refugees from coming to our State and to our country. Several miles away, there are several thousand Cubans trying to flee that oppressive regime who are now being detained indefinitely in Guantanamo. What's the way out for our policy and for those Cubans?

The President. First, we are doing our best to deal with the situation at Guantanamo, which is a very difficult one, for reasons because of where you're from you understand as well as I do. We have moved quickly, or as quickly as we could to review the cases of the children and the elderly people who are there, and we have moved quite a lot of people into the United States. We are now having detailed discussions about what we should do about the remainder of the people who are there at Guantanamo. Meanwhile, we've done what we could to make their conditions as livable, as bearable as possible.

As to our policy, even though I recognize most countries disagree with it, I think being firm has been the proper policy. And I do not

believe we should change it except within the confines of the Cuban Democracy Act. I would remind everyone here who's interested in this that the Cuban Democracy Act, while it stiffened sanctions against Cuba, also for the first time explicitly laid out in legislative language the conditions under which the United States might change various actions toward Cuba in return for actions by the Cubans.

Let me give you just one example. We have established, for the first time, direct phone service into Cuba. And the lines are quite jammed, as I understand it. It's cut the cost of calling home and calling relatives for Cuban-Americans. And it's enabled the Cuban Government to earn some money, because in all direct telephone conversations internationally, countries—at least, many countries—put a fee on such conversations. We did that because we thought it was the appropriate thing to do given the state of our relations and because of some things that had changed. Cuba is now establishing a more genuine farmers market that shows some movement in that area.

But the Cuban Democracy Act gives us a framework for future movement, and I—and also a firmness in our policy. And I think we should stay with both, both the firmness and the framework of the act.

Multiracial Families

Q. We have heard from several people here that there ought to be a multiracial box on the U.S. census forms so that people with parents of two races wouldn't have to deny one of them. What do you think should happen here?

The President. I wouldn't be opposed to that. That's the first time I ever heard it, but it makes sense. It's interesting that you raised that because of a related debate that's going on in Washington today, which is whether we should pass a Federal law which makes it clear that we should not discriminate against parents of one race in their attempts to adopt a child of another race. And I personally strongly support that position. And we've been trying to work through it to make—I though we had adopted that position last year at the end of the year. We did in large measure. We're talking about whether we need any other legal changes to achieve that.

But I—we are clearly going to have more and more multiracial, multiethnic children and families in this country. You're the first person who ever asked me that question. But I think it ought to be done. I can't see any reason not to do it.

Telecommunications Legislation

Q. One of the issues we've been examining at this convention, Mr. President, is the new information age and our own role in it. And one of the issues that's likely to come up in the next 100 days to which you referred is a broad reform of telecommunications policy. Do you think that a pragmatic, practical compromise solution in this area, which affects how people get their dial tones and what is on the dial tone, is likely to come out of these discussions?

The President. I do. I think it is likely. Let me say that I very much wanted to pass a telecommunications act in the last session of Congress. And we came within a hair's breadth of being able to do it. Some rather—to me anyway—rather minor problems hung it up in the Senate. And as you know, it's not difficult to hang a bill up in the Senate. And so it got hung. If we can pass the right kind of telecommunications act, it can be good for American consumers and it can pump billions of more dollars into this economy and create a very large number of jobs.

It's interesting that you would ask me this. The Vice President and I had lunch yesterday, our weekly lunch, and we talked about this for quite some time. My concern about the bill in its present form in the Senate is that I believe, as written, it would lead to a rather rapid increase and a rather substantial increase in both telephone and cable rates in ways that I do not believe are necessary to get the benefits that the telecommunications bill seeks to achieve. So I would like to see some provisions in there which deal with that.

I can also tell you that the Antitrust Division of the Justice Department has some fairly serious reservations about how far it goes. Now I have in several areas been willing to see, because of the globalization of the economy, some modifications in our antitrust laws. But I'm concerned—and I think they're warranted. But I think that this may go too far. But the most important concern I have is, are we going to have a very large and unnecessary increase in cable and phone rates immediately if the bill, as passed, is adopted? That is my major concern. But I think we can get one, and we certainly need to get one.

First Lady's Role

Q. Mr. President, yesterday on the front page of the New York Times was this headline, "Hillary Clinton a Traditional First Lady Now." Could you tell us, was there a point where you sat down with the First Lady to discuss her role for the remainder of your term? [*Laughter*]

The President. No.

Q. And if so, what was the content of that discussion and what prompted it? [*Laughter*]

The President. I was trying to think of something really funny to say, but it would be a polite way of saying I don't discuss my private conversations with my wife. [*Laughter*]

Actually, while I was very pleased with the First Lady's trip and with the way my wife and daughter were treated and what they learned, and very, very pleased with the coverage, I don't really agree with that. I mean, I think that I very much wanted her to go to India, to Pakistan, to Bangladesh, Nepal, to Sri Lanka because that part of the world is a very important part of the world to us. And for various reasons, we have not been as closely involved, even with the democracies there, as we might have been, largely as a legacy of the cold war.

But one of the biggest obstacles to the modernization of those countries and to the vitality and preservation of democracy are the challenges faced by women and children there. I did not consider the trip either too traditional or unimportant. I thought what they were doing—what Hillary was doing was profoundly important. And after getting a blow-by-blow description of the trip for a good long while yesterday from both my wife and daughter, I still feel that way.

So I—when my wife was an unconventional First Lady of Arkansas and working full-time and, as she told that lady in the Bangladesh village, making more money than her husband—[*laughter*]—still her first concern was always for the welfare of mothers, children, and families. She founded an organization called the Advocates for Families and Children in our State. She was on the board of the Children's Hospital. We built an intensive care nursery there, the first time the State had ever been involved. This is a 25-year concern of hers, and I wouldn't over-read the significance of it.

I also wouldn't underestimate the significance of having a First Lady who can galvanize a global discussion about the role of women and young girls on our planet and for our future.

Electronic Information Regulation

Q. You alluded to our being in the information age. Many of us in this room are investigating and developing ways of disseminating information electronically. There are thousands outside this room who are doing the same. What role, if any, does the Federal Government have in censoring or regulating that information and news?

The President. Let me begin by saying I support what you're doing, and I've tried to bring the White House up to date electronically. You know, we have a pretty sophisticated E-mail operation. And now you can take a tour of the White House and all the Federal agencies on the Internet and find out more than you ever wanted to know. So we're trying to be there for you in virtual reality land.

I guess you're asking me about the bill that Senator Exon introduced on trying to regulate obscenity through the E-mail system, or through the electronic superhighway. To be perfectly honest with you, I have not read the bill. I am not familiar with its contents, and I don't know what I think. I do believe—about this specific bill. [*Laughter*] I'll tell you what I think about the issue.

I believe that insofar as that Governments have the legal right to regulate obscenity that has not been classified as speech under the First Amendment, and insofar as the American public widely supports, for example, limiting access of children to pornographic magazines, I think it

is folly to think that we should sit idly by when a child who is a computer whiz may be exposed to things on that computer which in some ways are more powerful, more raw, and more inappropriate than those things from which we protect them when they walk in a 7-Eleven.

So as a matter of principle, I am not opposed to it. I just can't comment on the details of the bill, because I do not know enough about it. And I do not believe in any way shape or form that we should be able to do on E-mail, or through the electronic superhighway, in terms of Government regulation of speech, anything beyond what we could elsewhere. I think the First Amendment has to be uniform in its application.

So I'm not calling for a dilution of the First Amendment. But if you just imagine, those of us who have children and who think about this, you just think about what's the difference in going in the 7-Eleven and hooking up to the computer. I think that we have to find some resolution of this. And within the Supreme Court's standards, which are very strict, I am not philosophically opposed to some action.

Thank you very much.

NOTE: The President spoke at 11:55 a.m. at the Loews Anatole Hotel. In his remarks, he referred to Gregory Favre, outgoing president, Robert J. Haiman, board of directors, and William B. Ketter, incoming president, American Society of Newspaper Editors; Gov. William F. Weld of Massachusetts; and Gov. Stephen Merrill of New Hampshire.

Remarks to AmeriCorps Volunteers in Dallas
April 7, 1995

Thank you. Let's give Alexis another hand. [*Applause*] Was she great, or what? I don't think there is much more for me to say. [*Laughter*] She said it all, and she said it well. Congratulations. Thank you for your example. I want to say, also, a special word of welcome and thanks to your Congresswoman, Eddie Bernice Johnson. We have been friends now for over 20 years. And I'm sure that when we first met, well, I thought she might be in Congress some day, but I'm sure she never thought I'd be

President. [*Laughter*] I want to thank all your— the local leaders for being here. We have people from the city council and from the county commission and from the State legislature. And we have Mrs. Rouse, who's on the State commission for AmeriCorps.

And Texas has been so supportive of AmeriCorps. The Dallas Youth Service Corps is doing a great job here with the Greater Dallas Community Services Community of Churches and other AmeriCorps programs. But I want to tell you something you may not know. Texas has the largest number of AmeriCorps volunteers of any State in the country. You have people who are walking a police beat, teaching kids, building homes, helping seniors, cleaning up litter, immunizing children, doing all kinds of things to make this State and these communities and our children stronger and better for the future and earning money for education as well.

I want to say a special word about this group. I didn't have a chance to ask everybody their story, but I can tell you just from the biographies I got walking down the block here, this is what I had in mind when we started AmeriCorps. I have met one person here who got off welfare to work in AmeriCorps and got a GED, and several others said they had gotten their GED. I met one person here who's done part of a college education and is going to use the AmeriCorps money to help pay for those college loans to get the college education. I met one person here who was born to a mother on welfare and was a Head Start child, who is a college graduate, who came all the way to Texas to help people who were like her when she was a little girl.

When I started this national service program with the idea of giving our young people a chance to serve in a domestic Peace Corps, just like the Peace Corps was when I was a young man, except I wanted it to also be like the GI bill. My idea was that we needed more people to go to college, but we needed more people to relate to each other across racial and income and political lines. And if we had a national service project where people could do whatever folks in the community needed done, not what some bureaucrat in Washington would decide but what people in the community needed done, and if they could do it without regard to their race, their income, their background, just if they were willing to serve and they wanted to earn some money to pay for college education or to pay for their further education, then we had a chance to get the American people together.

Everywhere else, the American people—somebody's always trying to divide us from one another. They're always trying to get us to fight. They're always publicizing our fights. AmeriCorps is about getting people together, doing grassroots work, earning money for education by serving your community. And all of you are doing it. I am very, very, very proud of you.

As you know, and as Alexis said, there's been some controversy about the AmeriCorps program. And there are some people who say, "Well, we have to cut the deficit and we have to cut some spending, so we ought to cut that because it's new, or we ought to cut that because it's inefficient." Well, it's not inefficient. You've got 20,000 young people out here working all across America for a minimum wage, working like crazy, and earning some money to go to college just like they would if they were serving in the military. The people who are serving in the military earn the GI bill. They're eligible for up to $30,000 in benefits. But letting people earn enough for 2 years' worth of benefits at about $4,700 a year, that's not too much to pay to give young people the privilege of service and the energy and the opportunity to work with other people in other ways.

There are people who say that any national program is too bureaucratic. There is no bureaucracy here. These programs in Texas were funded by competition. People have to compete for these projects and compete for these slots. And nobody gets it unless they're doing a good job.

Then there are people who say that if we actually give young people the opportunity to work full-time in volunteer work and pay them a minimum wage and then let them earn some money to go to college, somehow that will discourage all the other volunteers. Well, look around here. I don't think that's a very good argument. All you've got to do is look around to see that that is not true.

There is plenty of work to be done in this country, folks. And the Government cannot do it all, and it cannot be all paid for. It's got to be done by community service groups. And you're a part of that.

And there are people in our country who have dreams and aspirations and who have personal problems, and they can't be solved by some high-flown program. They have to be solved by people who make a decision to change their lives, just like all these young people behind me and all of you out there with your AmeriCorps T-shirts. But it helps to change your life if you know there's somebody pulling for you, somebody giving you a chance to serve and somebody giving you a chance to get a good education so you can have a good future. That's what AmeriCorps is all about. We ought to keep it. We ought to stand behind it, and we ought to keep going.

You will find this hard to believe, I bet, but when I was your age—most of you—when I got out of high school, our country had a lot of problems. The racial problems were more severe than they are now. And we were involved in a cold war with what was then the Soviet Union. And we didn't know for sure that there would never be a nuclear war. And now, for the first time since atomic bombs have been made, there are no nuclear weapons pointed at the American people by the Russian people. I am proud of that.

But this age and time has its own problems. If anybody had ever told me that we'd have as many children born out of wedlock, I wouldn't have believed that. If anybody had ever told me we'd have as many single mothers raising little children in poverty, I would not have believed that. We have new problems and new challenges. And the only answer to it is for people in the community to take responsibility for themselves and for each other and to have the chance to pull themselves up and work their way out. What did you say? That you wanted a hand up, not a handout. That's as good a way to say it as I can imagine. That's what AmeriCorps is all about.

This is a very great country, and there is nothing we face that we cannot do. But we're going up or down together. And if we're going up together, we're going to have to make sure everybody, everybody has a chance to get a good education, because in a world economy, what you can learn determines what you can earn. And we're going to have to remember that whatever we do and however busy we are and whatever else we've got on our mind, we need to take some time out to serve, to be citizens, to work together to solve our common problems.

Don't you feel better at the end of every day, after you work and you do something for somebody else? When you go home at night, aren't you proud of it? And aren't you making friends with people who are different from you that you would never have known otherwise? And don't you think that will stay with you all your life?

I just want you to make the most of your life that you can, solve as many problems in this community as you can, get that education, and stay with AmeriCorps. I'll stay with you, and together we can save it.

God bless you. Thank you.

NOTE: The President spoke at 3:15 p.m. at Fair Park. In his remarks, he referred to Alexis Brisby, AmeriCorps volunteer, and Eloise Medows Rouse, board member, Texas Commission for National and Community Service.

Remarks on Arrival at McClellan Air Force Base in Sacramento, California
April 7, 1995

Thank you very much. Thank you, Congressman Fazio, Congressman Matsui, General Yates. General Phillips, thanks for having me back. You'll have to start charging me rent if I don't quit coming out here. [*Laughter*] Lieutenant Governor Davis, Mayor Serna, Supervisor Dickinson, Mr. Sherman, to all the others who are here: Let me say, I love coming here. I've been in this hangar before, but I've never had so many young people and students here. I'm delighted to see all of you. Thank you for coming. I'm glad to see the college students, the ROTC students, the City Year students here, the elementary school students. I'd also like to say it is quite wonderful to come to California when there is no flood, no fire, no earthquake. I just want to be here. I just wanted to come. And when I was here not very long ago, I went out to Roseville, and I had a meeting in a home that had been totally destroyed. And the people who hosted me are here, and I understand they're rebuilding their home. I'd like to ask them to be recognized; they're brave people, Rick Merenda and his wife. Stand up there, and let's give them a hand. [*Applause*]

That was really ungracious of Congressman Fazio to mention the basketball game. [*Laughter*] But since he brought it up, I don't think I'm so brave for coming out. If we had won, it would really take courage for me to show up here. [*Laughter*]

I am delighted to be here at McClellan. Vic said this is my west coast home. We couldn't very well close this Air Force base; I wouldn't have anyplace to park when I fly out. I don't know what I would do.

I'm delighted to be joined here by the wonderful Secretary of Education, Richard Riley. I thank him for coming out West with me. And I have a lot of Californians on my staff, and a bunch of them came back with me: my Chief of Staff, Leon Panetta, who in his former life, or as he likes to say, back when he had a life, was a Congressman from northern California; and of course, Doris Matsui—Congressman Matsui in our White House is known as Doris' husband because she's a valuable member of our staff; and many others. We have tried to be closely in touch with California.

For the benefit of the Air Force base, I want to make one announcement today. I'm happy to report that Congress has passed my requested defense supplemental appropriations bill which will give us the funds we need to make sure we are adequately training and preparing our personnel in all the armed services. And I know that McClellan and its families are happy about the passage of the defense appropriations bill.

With all these young people here, I want to take just a few moments to talk about their future and ours and how they are bound up together. I ran for President in 1992 because I strongly felt that our National Government was not doing enough to invest in our future and to strengthen the future prospects of America's working families and our children. I believed then—and I still believe it was right—that we were exploding our deficit but reducing our investment in our people. I believed then and I believe more strongly today that the global economy in a technological information age will reward what we know and what we are capable of learning and, conversely, will punish us for what we refuse to learn and for the people whose skills and abilities we refuse to develop.

Now, there is a great debate going on today about what our mission should be as a Nation in the aftermath of the cold war and what the role of the National Government should be in that mission. But to me, it is crystal clear. Our mission should be to ensure that the American

dream is alive and well for every child in this country and every child in this hangar well into the next century.

Our mission should be that we maintain our position as the world's strongest nation and greatest force for peace and freedom and democracy and that we use that to help our own people develop their human capacities. And the role of the National Government, it seems to me, is clear. We must first strengthen our security around the world and here at home. That's why I have worked so hard to reduce the threat of nuclear weapons, to be a force for peace from the Middle East to Northern Ireland to Southern Africa but also to pass a crime bill here that will stiffen sentences, put more police on the street, have more prevention funds, and do everything we can to bring down the crime rate and make our streets and our neighborhoods and our schools safer places.

The role of the Government should be to change the Government. It should be smaller and less bureaucratic and less cumbersome and burdensome and more efficient and more flexible for the information age. We have done that. The Congress in the last 2 years has voted for budgets that will reduce the size of the Government by 272,000, to its smallest size since President Kennedy was in office; to deregulate great portions of activity the Federal Government used to do, to give more responsibilities back to the States. We are giving the American people a Government that is less bureaucratic.

But the last two things in some ways are the most important of all. Government's role is also to create economic opportunity and to help people who, through no fault of their own, have sustained economic burdens.

The recommendation from the Secretary of Defense for McClellan is that the airbase should stay open because of the important mission you are pursuing. But you know that California has been very hard-hit by base closings in the aftermath of the cold war's end. I took the position, which I here reaffirm today, that when the United States asked the people of California and the people of the United States all across this country to host our bases, to host our military families, to play a role in winning the cold war— if we have to downsize the military, we have an affirmative obligation to help the communities and the people rebuild their lives and to have prosperity and strength in the future. That is a part of building economic opportunity.

That's why I fought so hard to have conversion funds, to help people move from a defense-based to a civilian-based economy, and why I have supported bases like McClellan which have used their military technology for civilian purposes to help to strengthen us in the years ahead. That's what the general was talking about when he mentioned the intelligent tutor program—military technology being made available to school districts all across America to teach children as people in the military are taught to develop their skills more rapidly and more deeply than ever before. That is part of our obligation, to give people a chance to make the most of their God-given abilities by creating economic opportunity.

If you look—you have an example right here in Sacramento. Look at what happened with the Army depot and Packard Bell. The world's third largest computer manufacturer has moved onto large portions of the closed base and plans to employ more than 3,000 Californians.

There are many other things we have worked to do, to sell more of your high-tech products abroad, to sell your agriculture products abroad, to open up the California economy in a positive way. And the unemployment rate has dropped almost 2 percent in the last 2 years. We have a long way to go, but we are moving in the right direction. It is the affirmative responsibility of the United States Government to do everything we can in partnership with people to create those kinds of economic opportunities. If everybody has a good job and a bright future, this country's future as a whole will be more secure.

Now, the last thing that I want to say is perhaps the most important of all. I believe it is our responsibility to do everything we can through education to give the people of this country, and especially the young people of this country, the knowledge and the skills they need to compete and win in a tough global economy. We cannot guarantee people a job for life, but we can guarantee them access to education for life. And we ought to do it. Nothing is more important.

When I ran for President, I thought there were too many people in Washington who had rhetorical debates and didn't work on the real people's problems. I thought to myself, if I were living out in Sacramento, for example, and I

listened to what I see on television at night, I might wonder if those folks were really talking about me and my family and my children.

You know, we had trickle-down economics and tax-and-spend economics, and what we really needed was invest-and-grow economics. We once had people who thought the answer to our public's problems was to spend more money on everything. Now we have people who think the answer is to spend less money on everything. The answer is to spend less money on the wrong things and more money on the right things. And the most important right thing is education for our young people and for our adults.

You know, I am very proud of the fact that these Members of Congress behind me have been part of a group of people who supported my initiatives to expand educational opportunities, from Head Start for preschoolers to more investment so our schools could meet national standards of excellence, to apprenticeship programs for young people who don't go on to college, more affordable college loans for young people on better repayment terms, to lifetime training for adult workers. That must be our mission. We must make it clear that in the United States we will tolerate nothing less than the most excellent educational opportunities and the highest standards for all of our people for a lifetime.

You know, I see these young AmeriCorps people behind me who are cheering when I called their name. There are some people who believe we ought to get rid of AmeriCorps. They say it costs a lot of money, and besides that, why pay people to volunteer? Let me tell you what these young people do if you don't know. They can earn minimum wage and work for 1 or 2 years, and for each year they work they can earn money for their college education. They don't work in big national bureaucracies. They work in community service projects. They work side by side with other people. They help in floods and fires. They help to rebuild homes. They help to immunize children. They work with police on the beat. They do a lot of different things all across the country, not based on what someone in Washington tells them to do but based on what community leaders say they should do. And in so doing, they earn money and help build up their communities.

I just came from Dallas, Texas, where I met with an AmeriCorps volunteer who was 52 years old, who was going back working in the community to earn money to go to her local community college to get a degree in college. I met a young woman who got off welfare because they gave her a chance to work in AmeriCorps. And she got her GED, and now she's going to use the money to go to college. I met a young woman who was a graduate of one of our finest State universities. But she was born to a mother on welfare, and she thought she owed it to her country, since she had moved from welfare to a university degree, to give up a couple years of her life working in the community to help lift the prospects of other people. That is what AmeriCorps is all about. It is working to educate America.

The other day I was in Florida talking to people about college education. Many of you who have sent or are preparing to send a child to college know that it can be a pretty expensive proposition and that it's gone up quite a lot. There are some in Congress who believe that the way to reduce the deficit is to increase the cost of the student loans. I disagree with that. I don't think we ought to increase the cost of student loans at a time when we want more people to go to college.

Our proposal is different. Our proposal is to let more people borrow money on better repayment terms but to have tougher requirements to repay the loans. If everybody who borrowed money repaid it, we wouldn't have a budgetary problem with the student loan program. So what have we done? We've loaned money to more people at lower interest rates, but we're making more people repay the loans. That's the way to save money in the student loan program, not to cut the program, get the loans repaid.

And finally, to all of you let me say this: There is a lot of talk in Washington about cutting taxes. Now, nothing is more popular. But I would remind you of this: number one, we still have a sizable deficit, even though I have cut it by $600 billion, and we now have a Government that, except for the interest on the debt that was piled up in previous years, your Government has an operating surplus for the first time in 30 years. We do that.

But our interest payments on our debt are so great we have to keep bringing this deficit down. That limits the size of any tax cut. We have to continue to finance a strong national defense. That limits the size of any tax cut. We have to continue to invest in education. That will limit the size of a tax cut. So we have to ask ourselves, what kind of tax cut do we need, and who ought to get it?

My view is we shouldn't give a tax cut to people like me, in upper income groups, who did just fine in the eighties and the nineties. We ought to give it to middle class people whose incomes stagnated in the eighties and nineties who need the money. That's who ought to get it. And we ought to give it to people and not just give them a check that they can spend and then the money's gone; the money should be devoted to helping strengthen our families and to support education so that we raise people's income in the short run with a tax cut and in the long run by improving their earning skills. That's why I think the best tax cut would be giving the American people a tax deduction for the cost of themselves and their children for all education after high school. That is the best investment in our future.

Now, I also believe that we ought to have the individual retirement accounts, the IRA's, available to more Americans, and people ought to be able to withdraw from them tax-free to use money for education or for health care emergencies or for a first home or for the care of an elderly parent. That's the sort of tax cut we ought to have.

Now, believe me, my fellow Americans, we can afford that and still reduce the deficit, still increase our investment in education, and still have a strong defense. That is a responsible approach.

So I say to you without regard to your political party, this is a time of great change in our country. I want to work with this new Congress. I agree with them about a lot of things they want to do. But we can't go too far. We can't say that there's no difference in Government spending. Education is different. National defense is different. Things are different. Some things matter more than others. We can't say that everything the Government does is bad and everything that happens in the private sector is good. We need a partnership. And we know if California's economy is going to come back we ought to invest in defense conversion. We ought to do what we can to help the people in this State who have great talents and great resources, who can no longer use them in the defense plants but can use them in the economy of tomorrow.

And most importantly of all, we ought to look around at all these young people and say they deserve to believe in the American dream, in the promise of tomorrow. They deserve to be able to do whatever their God-given capacities and their willingness to work will let them do. Nothing, nothing, nothing is more important than that.

So, to all of you who have been at this base, who have worn the uniform of our country, who have stood up for the security of the United States, what did you do it for? So that freedom and opportunity might be passed on forever in this country. This is a very great country. There is nothing we cannot do if we do the best we can to do right by the young people who are here and all over America. That must be our mission. It is mine, and I believe it is yours.

Thank you, and God bless you all.

NOTE: The President spoke at 5:50 p.m. In his remarks, he referred to Gen. Ronald W. Yates, Commander, Air Force Materiel Command; Gen. John F. Phillips, Commander, Sacramento Air Logistics Center; Lt. Gov. Gray Davis of California; Mayor Joseph Serna, Jr., of Sacramento, CA; Sacramento County Supervisor Roger Dickinson; and Brad Sherman, chairman, California State Board of Equalization.

Statement on the National Railroad Passenger Corporation (Amtrak)
April 7, 1995

The service reductions announced by Amtrak are tough but necessary choices in the face of stark fiscal realities and, along with the adjustments Amtrak announced last December, represent an urgent attempt to move the passenger railroad toward a stable economic future.

This administration remains committed to the future of rail passenger service in this country and has included significant capital support for Amtrak in its 1996 budget.

To address the pressures Amtrak faces and to promote a more businesslike approach, the Department of Transportation today transmitted to Congress the "Amtrak Restructuring Act of 1995."

I encourage rail labor, Congress, Governors, mayors, and other constituents to continue to work closely with Amtrak as it works to develop rail passenger service for the 21st century. We look to our partners in Congress to support the "Amtrak Restructuring Act of 1995" and for continued financial support of rail passenger service.

Statement on the Nomination of Dennis J. Reimer To Be Chief of Staff of the United States Army
April 7, 1995

I am pleased to announce my intention to nominate General Dennis J. Reimer, U.S. Army, as Chief of Staff, United States Army, succeeding General Gordon R. Sullivan, who is retiring.

General Reimer currently serves as the Commanding General, U.S. Army Forces Command. In this capacity, he is responsible for over 60 percent of America's Army including Active, Reserve and National Guard units. During his distinguished career, General Reimer served two tours in Vietnam, was the Army's Deputy Chief of Staff for Operations during Desert Storm, and played a key role in the transformation of the cold-war Army to today's power projection Army. He brings to the job of Chief of Staff a clear vision of the national security environment the United States will face through the remainder of this decade and into the next century. This insight will enable him to address the full range of challenges confronting the U.S. Army, including readiness challenges, the impact of emerging technology, expanded mission requirements, and improving the quality of life for our soldiers and their families.

General Reimer takes over as Chief of Staff during one of the most important and demanding periods in the rich history of the U.S. Army. I know that I can count on him to continue the outstanding leadership demonstrated by General Sullivan and to maintain his high standards of stewardship to ensure that the U.S. Army remains fully ready and able to accomplish its important responsibilities under our national security strategy.

The President's Radio Address
April 8, 1995

Good morning. I ran for President because I believed the American dream was at risk for millions of our fellow citizens. I wanted to grow the middle class, shrink the under class, create more opportunities for entrepreneurs to succeed, so that our economy would produce the American dream. I wanted to promote mainstream values of responsibility, work, family, and community. And I wanted to reform Government to make it smaller, less bureaucratic, put it back on the side of ordinary Americans.

We're working at making progress on all these fronts—unemployment down, jobs up—real progress in giving people in the under class a chance to work their way into the middle class. But there's still a lot of challenges we face. There's no greater gap between mainstream American values and Government than the failed welfare system.

Last night the Speaker of the House, Newt Gingrich, spoke eloquently about the need to reform the welfare system. And I ran for President saying that I would work to end welfare as we know it. This has been a big issue for me for long time. I've worked to move people from welfare to work for 15 years now. So the Speaker and I have a lot in common. We both want bold welfare reform. We both think that we need to make people leave welfare after a specific number of years. We both want to require welfare recipients to work to get benefits. We both want States to have a lot of flexibility to adopt their own programs.

I've gone a long way toward doing that by letting 25 States adopt bold new reforms for their own welfare systems. And we both want tough steps to enforce child support. The welfare reform plan I sent to Congress last year included the toughest possible child support enforcement. And now the Speaker and his colleagues in the House have taken our child enforcement measures and put it into their bill, including our plan to ask States to deny driver's licenses and professional licenses to deadbeat parents.

In spite of these similarities, we still have two key differences I want to talk to you about. They relate to work and to children. First, cutting costs is the primary goal of the Republican welfare bill. By arbitrarily cutting future welfare costs the Republicans get money to pay for their tax cuts. Well, I agree we need to cut costs, but we also have to be sure that when people leave welfare they have the education, training, and skills they need to get jobs, not simply to be off welfare and turn to lives of crime or to remain in poverty.

If we cut child care, how can we expect mothers to go to work? If we cut job training, how will people learn to work? If we cut job programs and these people can't find jobs in the private sector, how can we require them to work?

My top priority is to get people off welfare and into jobs. I want to replace welfare with work, so people earn a paycheck, not a welfare check. To do that, we have to take some of the money we save and plow it into job training, education, and child care.

I want tough welfare reform, but we've got to be practical. If we're going to make people on welfare work, we have to make it possible for them to work. If we're going to make people self-reliant, we have to make it possible for them to support themselves. We can be tough, but we've got to be practical.

I want welfare reform that moves people from dependence to independence, from welfare to work. So my proposal is a welfare-to-work plan, not just a welfare plan that cuts welfare. So that's the first change I want to make in the Republican welfare proposal. Before I'll sign it into law, it's got to have a stronger work component.

Second, the House bill is too tough on children. It cuts off aid to children who are on welfare just because their mothers are young and unmarried. These children didn't choose to be born to single mothers; they didn't choose to be born on welfare; they didn't choose to be born to women who are teenagers. We ought to remember that a child is a child, a baby is a baby. Whether they're white, black, or brown, whether they're born in or out of wedlock, anybody anywhere is entitled to a chance, and innocence, if it's a baby. We simply shouldn't punish babies and children for their parents' mistakes.

So we can be good to our children and give them a chance to have a better life because we've got a stake in that. Just think about it. Every child born in America, whether they're born to a welfare family or to a middle class family or to a wealthy family, is going to grow up and be a part of our future. The child may grow up to be in a university or be in jail or somewhere in between. But the chances are awful good that what happens to the child will be influenced by what happens to the babies in their earliest days and months and years.

So let's don't punish these babies and children for their parents' errors. Instead, let's give them a chance to grow up with a good education and a head start, so they'll be independent, working citizens.

So I say to Speaker Gingrich and to the leaders of the Senate and the House in both parties, let's work together to get this job done. Let's prove to the American people that we can reform welfare, really reform it, without letting this issue divide us. It is time to end welfare as we know it, to put people to work without punishing children.

Thanks for listening.

NOTE: The address was recorded at 8 p.m. on April 7 in the Hilton Inn in Sacramento, CA, for broadcast at 10:06 a.m. on April 8.

Remarks to the California Democratic Party in Sacramento
April 8, 1995

The President. Thank you very much. Thank you for the wonderful, wonderful welcome. And thank you for the wonderful film. It's nice to see the record out there in a compelling way. Thank you, and bless you.

I guess you all know that this is Bill Press' birthday. We threw him a good party, didn't we? Happy birthday.

I'm delighted to be here with all the officers of the Democratic Party, with Arlene Holt and of course with our chair, Don Fowler. I thank him for this remarks. Wasn't Barbara Boxer wonderful this morning? I'll tell you, you have no idea what a joy it is to see her in Washington, with all those other politicians kind of tippy-toeing around and trying to be just careful, you know. And there's Barbara every day just right there through the door, the same way every day. I want to thank the members of the California delegation who are here, Norm Mineta, Bob Matsui, Vic Fazio, Maxine Waters, Walter Tucker. They have been our friends and our partners. They have worked hard to turn this country around and move it forward and to help California. I thank them. I'm glad to be here with Willie Brown. I was watching him on the television back there, and he was smiling, you know. And I thought, I hope I look half that good when I'm his age. The truth is he already looks younger than me, and I resent it. [*Laughter*] Senator Lockyer, I'm glad to be here with you. And Mayor Serna, thank you for hosting us. I'm glad to be here with your State controller, Kathleen Connell; your superintendent of education, Delane Eastin; and of course, I love hearing Gray Davis talk. It's nice to know that you're always going to have a Governor, no matter what, and a good one on occasion.

I'm delighted to be here with a number of my California staffers, of course, led by my Chief of Staff, Leon Panetta. I know a lot of you used to be represented by him, and you're glad to see him. And you all give him a good hand. He doesn't get much of this in Washington, so he needs it. I mean, he needs it. Give him really more. Give him a little more. [*Ap-*

plause] Don't overdo it; he might quit and come home. [*Laughter*] That was just about right. Thank you.

I want to also tell you that after we leave here we're going down to Los Angeles, and we're going to have an event with the National Education Association on school violence. So we have representatives here from the national NEA, and our wonderful Secretary of Education, Dick Riley, is also here with me today. And I'd like for you to welcome him.

I was looking at that film, and I don't know how many of you know this, but there was only one moment in that film when I got kind of a twinge and I sort of had to control myself, when that picture of me in the academic robe and the tassel—that was at UCLA. [*Laughter*] Well, they won it fair and square, and they deserved it.

I am delighted to be here. You know, you folks believed in the campaign I ran in 1992 well enough to go out and work your hearts out to try to turn the direction of the country and the direction of California around. And we carried this State for the first time a Democratic President had carried it since 1964, and I thank you for that.

I also want to thank you for all of the applause that came out of this audience when the picture of Hillary appeared on the screen. Thank you for that. Hillary and Chelsea have just come home, you know, from a very long trip. They went to India, to Pakistan, to Bangladesh, to Nepal, to Sri Lanka, always looking at the condition of women and young girls in these countries, in that very important part of the world. You know this in California because you have so many people living here who come from those places, but the future of the globe will be determined in no insignificant measure by what happens in those nations. And the ability to preserve democracy and hope and freedom in those nations depends in no small measure on how women and girls are treated and whether they have the opportunity to live up to their God-given capacities.

My fellow Americans, we are at an historic moment and an interesting time in our history. You know because of what was on that film that I have kept the commitments I've made to the people of California and the people of the United States in the campaign of 1992.

I ran for President because I was deeply concerned about the lives of ordinary Americans, because half of our people were working harder for the same or lower wages than they were making 15 years before; because people were working harder, sleeping less, spending less time with their children; because we had profound problems in the fabric of our society, pressures on the family unit, more and more of our children being born out of wedlock, high rates of crime and violence and drugs, the absence of hope for so many of our people who felt isolated and abandoned; because the Government seemed to me to be caught in a gridlock where one side could blame the other, but the facts were that we had 12 years of trickle-down economics in which the deficit exploded, investment in our people went down, and nobody was really willing to take on the serious problems of the country, so that most people in their ordinary lives just felt left out. The National Government became less and less and less relevant to their lives, except at tax time when it was a burden. And so I thought we could change that.

I ran for President because I thought our country had three great tasks: First, we needed to begin once again to reestablish the American economic dreams, to grow the middle class, shrink the under class, and create more opportunities for entrepreneurs to live out their dreams. Second, because I thought we needed to reassert the fundamental values that made this country great, responsibility, responsibility in our individual lives, in our work lives, in our family lives, and in our communities, taking responsibility one for another, understanding that we are going up or down together in this country whether we like it or not, so we had better make the most of it. And thirdly, because I thought we ought to reform Government, to make it more relevant and more effective to our daily lives, to do four things: to create more economic opportunity; to shrink the bureaucracy; to make our people more secure, not only around the world but here at home on our streets and in our schools and in our homes; and most important of all, to empower people through education to make the most of their own lives in the global economy.

Now, in the first 2 years, we have gone a long way toward keeping all those commitments. The economy is up; the deficit is down. We have the lowest combined rates of unemployment and inflation this country's had in 25 years in spite of the economic problems that continue to endure in this State, and I'm proud of that.

In California, which was hit hardest by the 1989–90 recession and hit by far harder than any other State by the defense cutbacks, the unemployment rate has now dropped about 2 percent. So we are moving in the right direction in terms of the economy. We're trying to help places that have been left behind with empowerment zones and extra investments in cities that need it.

We are trying to establish community development banks in cities that will loan money to people who previously could never get any money, so we can bring free enterprise into poor areas and give people the promise that they can get a bank loan and start a business and hire their friends and neighbors and get something to happen.

We have plainly shrunk the bureaucracy, something they never thought the Democrats would do. The Democrats reduced the deficit, and the Democrats shrunk the Government bureaucracy by 100,000 in 2 years and put it all into paying for safety on our streets. That's something the Democratic Party did.

My friends, when you go back out of this room and you see people you know who don't belong to the Democratic Party, you just remind them of this: that this Government is the first Government in 30 years that is running an operating surplus, that is, except for the interest on the debt run up between 1981 and 1982, before our administration took over, our budget would be in balance today. And don't you forget it. And you ought to be proud of that.

The third thing we have done is to make this country more secure. For the first time since the dawn of the nuclear age, there are no Russian missiles pointed at the children of the United States of America. And we have taken on a lot of tough issues to make our world more secure, from North Korea to Northern Ireland to Haiti to Mexico. I've done a lot of things that weren't popular, but they were right, to make this country more secure, to have this country have a better future.

And perhaps most important of all, we really have moved on the education agenda I promised in 1992. We expanded Head Start. We have given more money to our schools to meet high standards. We have supported apprenticeship programs for young people who don't go to college but do want to have good education. We have made over 1.5 million people right here in California alone eligible for lower cost college

loans and better repayment terms, so that everybody can go to college who wants to go. And here and throughout the country, our national service program has given 20,000 young people a chance to earn their way to college by serving their communities at the grassroots level in the best, old-fashioned, American tradition. And there are some of them right there.

Now, let's talk about where we are today. You might say, well, if we've got 6.3 million new jobs in the country; the lowest combined rates of unemployment and inflation in 25 years; we're making progress in terms of our national security abroad and here at home with the crime bill, the Brady bill, the assault weapons ban, 100,000 more police on our streets; if we have shrunk the size of the Federal Government; and if we are doing more for education and that's the central problem of our time, how come they won the last election?

Well, let's talk about it. One reason is we spent too much time working and too little time talking about it. And they're better talkers, and we're better workers. And we ought to give them credit for that. They're great; they say one thing one day and another thing the next, and it doesn't bother them. And they sometimes get rewarded for that. So you can say that's what happened. But that's not really what happened.

What really happened is that this country's economic problems have been building for 20 years, and our country's social problems, tearing at the fabric of orderly life, have been developing for 30 years. And they are clashing against one another in place after place after place. And Government's irresponsibility has been there for more than a decade. And in this new age, a lot of what we do in Washington to help the economy, whether it's bringing the deficit down to get interest rates down so people invest and create jobs or expanding trade so we get more high-wage jobs, those things have an indirect effect on people, not a direct effect on people.

So a lot of people's lives haven't changed. There may be more jobs, but most people haven't gotten a raise. There may be more jobs, but a lot of big companies are still downsizing and making people feel insecure. And a lot of the things that we have done that are good have an indirect effect on people. So in 1994, the people said, "We still feel insecure; we still feel uncertain. We want more done. We want it to happen faster." And they gave the Republicans a chance to control the Congress.

Well, in the last 100 days, the House of Representatives has certainly passed a series of bold initiatives. Of the 10 items on their contract, they passed all but one, term limits, which they didn't really want to pass anyway, now that they're in control. [*Laughter*] And then, in the Senate, one has been defeated, the balanced budget amendment. Two items [*applause*]—two items I was proud to sign into law, because I also campaigned on them in 1992, and I'll talk about that more in a minute.

So here we are now at the beginning of the second 100 days. Now, one of the things we ought to do is to reaffirm what we are as Democrats. Barbara Boxer did that; you cheered; that's good. Don't forget. Don't forget. But we also ought to say, what are we going to do in the next 100 days and beyond? What do you want us to do in Washington, what do we believe we must do, and what should you be doing out here in the country?

Keep in mind—keep in mind the object of this for you is to remind the American people that we've been up there fighting for them and that a lot of these items don't have much to do with their welfare. They won't raise their incomes; they won't educate their kids; they won't create any more jobs; they won't help to bring us together. That is not what is going on here. They basically amount to an attack on Government and an assertion that the private market is always better than anything done by Government.

Now, that is plainly not so. But let me go through these things with you item by item and tell you what I'm going to do on them. And let me remind you that we have an unfinished agenda. We have not yet done everything we pledged to do in 1992. I believe what the country wants us to do is to get up there and try to do something that makes sense that helps ordinary people improve their lives. That's what I think the country wants us to do.

When I ran for President, I wanted to do things to change your life for the better. I did not imagine that I would go there to try to make political points by piling up a stack of vetoes. I still don't want to do that, but I will if I have to. What I want to do is to do what is best for the country.

Now therefore, we have to look at where we are. So let's just go through the items, one by one, on their agenda and on our agenda. Taxes: In 1993, I made a commitment to try to give some tax relief to the middle class. In 1993, the Congress passed our economic plan which ended trickle-down economics, cut the deficit, and invested more in education and economic growth. What happened? We made a down payment on the middle class tax cut. In California today, when people file their taxes, the average tax cut for families of four with incomes of $25,000 a year or less in this State will be $1,000 because of what we did in 1993. We concentrated on that group of people. Why? Because people with modest incomes who work full-time and raise children should not be in poverty. You want welfare reform? Make work pay. Reward people who work.

So I do believe in this recovery. Since most people have not gotten a raise, we ought to have tax relief for people in the middle class so they can feel what is going on in the economy. But this $200 billion tax cut that was passed by the House is a fantasy. We can't afford it; it's not fair. It will be paid for by cutting programs for poor people and for children, and we shouldn't do it. That won't happen. So the question is, what will happen?

It's also important to remind you that we have to keep bringing that deficit down because that gets interest rates down. That means more money for more people in California to expand the economy, to buy homes, to do the things that have to be done to put this country back together.

So what should we do? First, we ought to target the tax cut to the right people. Give the tax cut to middle class people who are working hard and haven't gotten a raise. Don't give it to people who have done very well in the eighties and the nineties. Their tax bill gives half the aid, half, to the top 10 percent of our people and 20 percent of the aid to the top 1 percent. All of those folks have done real well in the eighties and the nineties. They do not need it. Middle class people whose incomes have been stagnant or declining need help. That's where the tax relief should go.

Second question: What should the money be for? Should we just give people a check and say go blow it? No. We should target the money to things that will grow our economy over the long run and lift people's earnings in the short run and the long run. If you get a tax cut, your income goes up. But will your income go up in the long run? It depends on what the tax cut is for. So I say, target the tax cut to the work that is being done in America that is most important. Target it to raising children and target it to education. Give a tax cut for the cost of education after high school to the American people.

I'll say more about this in a moment, but what is giving rise to all this anxiety behind the affirmative action debate? Because—I'll tell you what it is. The middle class is splitting apart in America. The middle class is splitting apart. This is a big, new development. From the year I was born at the end of World War II until the year I was first elected Governor of my State in 1978, all of us as Americans rose together economically. The income of all groups of Americans roughly doubled from 1950 to 1978, except for people in the lowest group, the lowest 20 percent. And theirs went up even more. So we were going up together, and we were coming together.

What's happened since then? We are splitting apart. Even within the great American middle class, we are splitting apart. Why? In a global economy the fault line is education. Those who have it do well; those who don't get punished. Give a tax break for education, so we can lift the country and put it back together again.

Let's talk about welfare reform. Yesterday the Speaker said he passionately wanted welfare reform. Well, so do I. In 1992, I ran for President with a commitment to end the present welfare system as we know it. In 1994, they put it in their contract. What happened in between? I have given 25 States, half of this country, permission to pursue welfare reform on their own initiatives. And I gave Congress the most comprehensive welfare reform ever presented.

What do I want to do? I want to promote work and responsible parenting and tough child support enforcement. That's what I want to promote. I want these young parents who made a mistake to have a chance to put their lives back on track. And I want these children to have a better future. Now, that's what's really important.

So I take up that challenge. Let's go do welfare reform. But look what's in the House bill. I agree that there should be time limits, if there's a job at the end of the road. I agree we should let the States have more flexibility, because the problems are different from State to State. And I am gratified that the House

took all of our tough child support enforcement provisions, including yanking driver's licenses and professional licenses from people who owe money for their kids and they won't pay.

But I do not agree with the rest of the bill because primarily it is designed to save money to pay for the tax cuts by cutting aid to welfare. We should cut aid to welfare by genuinely, honestly reducing the welfare rolls by putting people to work, so they can be good parents and good workers. That's the way to cut the welfare budget.

As compared with our support, theirs is weak on work and tough on kids. It ought to be the reverse. That's what ought to happen. Let me give you an example. Their bill says, no welfare if someone has a child before the age of 18 for the mother or the child at least until they become 18. If the State doesn't want to give them any money ever, that's fine. I just think that's wrong. Why punish the child for the sins of the parents?

You know, you look across this State or Nation, a baby is a baby. You know, in my little Baptist Sunday school class we used to sing a song, "Yellow, brown, black, or white, they are precious in His sight." In or out of wedlock, those kids are going to grow up someday. They're going to be in Stanford, Berkeley, or San Quentin, or someplace in between. You think about it. They're going to be in Stanford, Berkeley, San Quentin, or someplace in between. They're going to be in prison; they're going to be in university; they're going to be someplace in between. And whether they are or not is due in part to what we do and how we behave. Let us not punish the children and cut off our own nose to spite our face in this welfare reform. [*Applause*] Thank you.

And as to the parents, think of this. What good does it do to punish somebody for a mistake they have already made? If you have a child, better to say to the child, "Now things will change. You must be a responsible parent. You must be a student. You must be a worker. You must become independent. We want you to succeed as a citizen, as a worker, as a parent." So I don't have any problem at all with having tough requirements on children. But the tough requirements should be designed to give the child a chance to grow into responsible adulthood, to be a productive citizen. So let's be tough, but let's be smart. Let's do something that makes sense.

Senator Boxer talked about cutting the deficit. I'm glad they want to cut the deficit. We cut it $600 billion in the first 2 years without a lick of help from them, so I'd be glad to have some help.

When we did the deficit cutting before, they were AWOL. I was told the first week I became President by their leader in the Senate, "There will be no votes, none, for your deficit reduction package, none. We'll give you not one. We don't believe in imposing any tax increases on the wealthiest Americans, and we just want you to be out there. And if it succeeds, you can get credit, but we'll blame you anyway and call it a tax bill." That's the first week I was President, that's what they told me.

Well, we did it anyway, because it was right for the country. We—[*inaudible*]—some political heat because it was right for the country, and that's why we have 6.3 million jobs today. And you ought to go out of this hall and remind people that that's what we did and that's what we're going to do in the future.

But nonetheless, we're here where we are today, and the country would be better off if we could figure out a humane and smart way to reduce the deficit. So I say to the Republicans: Let's work on making sensible cuts, not partisan cuts. Let's don't do something that's really foolish. I don't think it helps us to cut our children. I don't want to cut immunizations or school lunches or infant formulas or nutrition programs. I can't imagine what good that will do.

In their budget, two-thirds of the cuts come out of the poorest people in the country who get only 5 percent of the benefit of their proposed tax cuts. You don't have to be a genius to figure out what happens to the fabric in America and our need to give everybody a chance at a fair shot at the American dream. It is not fair, and it is not in our interest to do that. So let us not make those cuts. That is wrong, it is unfair, it is unnecessary.

And let me give you an example. I want to compliment Senator Boxer and Senator Feinstein. We just had a big debate in Washington on the so-called rescission bill. Now, the rescission bill is a bill that cuts the present budget, the one that we adopted last year, to get savings to pay for our California earthquake aid and our California flood aid and to pay for some other investments we have to make and to reduce the deficit a little more. I was open to

that. But the House-passed bill had terrible cuts in it. They cut education. They cut child nutrition. They cut the environment. They cut housing. They gutted the national service program. A lot of it was politics and ideology. It was extremist.

I insisted on restoring some more cuts. The Senate Republicans were even embarrassed by some of the things they did, and they put some back in. And then we said, "Put the other cuts back for the kids. Restore them. We'll give you some better cuts." And Senator Boxer and every Democrat in the Senate refused to let the bill come for a vote until they did it. They did it. It was sensible. It passed 99–0 because of Barbara Boxer and the other Senate Democrats, 99–0. So I can tell you that it would work. It would work.

Political reform. The two bills I've signed are political reform bills. One applies to Congress the laws they put on the private sector; I'm for that. The other limits the ability of Congress to impose on State and local governments mandates they don't help pay for; I'm for that, and I'll bet your legislators are, too. But there's more to political reform than that. We need campaign finance reform, and we sure need lobby reform.

I'll guarantee you—you heard Barbara Boxer talk about this, when the Congress takes out a bill that will raise $3.2 billion over 10 years simply by telling billionaires, "Look, if you make a lot of money in our country as Americans, you can't get out of paying the tax that you owe on the money you made as an American by renouncing your citizenship before the tax bills are due." And it was put in, and then they took it out. Now believe me, that was not an act of total charity. Somebody lobbied for that, hard, carefully, secretly. And I think the American people are entitled to know. I think the American people are entitled to know.

So I applaud them for what they've done, but let's go the rest of the way. Let's give the American people what they really need, which is lobby reform, campaign finance reform, and an even shot in every election to have the will of the people manifested.

Let's talk about regulations. You know, they cuss regulations. Well, all of you can cuss regulations. I bet there's not a soul here that can't think of one stupid thing that was at least done to you at one time by the State, the Federal, or a local government. Everybody can tell a story that would make you believe the Government would mess up a one-car parade. That's the staple of American life. But the answer is to fix it, not to stop Government from regulating what it ought to.

We have done what we could to fix it. Let me give you an example. Our Environmental Protection Agency Director, Carol Browner, has set up a compliance center. If you're a small business person and you're worried, "Am I out of compliance with the environmental laws," if you call and ask for help in good faith, you cannot be fined for 6 months, because we know that you're trying to do better.

We now give our people the right to waive fines for any first-time violators if they're doing it in good faith. We now give our people the right to tell people, instead of being fined, why don't you keep this money if you will spend it to fix the problem that you've got in the first place, clean the environment.

So we're going to cut 20 million hours of paperwork burden out of the American people's time next year in dealing with the EPA. That's fine. But if they send me a bill that lets unsafe planes fly or contaminated meat be sold or contaminated water get into the city water systems, I will veto it, because we need to do that. [*Applause*] Thank you.

Look at this—let me give you some other examples. Look at the crime bill. Everybody is against crime. Anybody who is for crime, please stand up. [*Laughter*] And it's a very serious issue. It's a very serious issue. I never will forget when I was doing one of my town meetings in northern California, looking at that young man who changed schools with his brother because they were so terrified at the school they were in. And when they were standing in line to register at the new school, a crazy gunman walked in the school and shot his brother standing in line—somebody he didn't even know.

This is a big deal. And it's part of the volatility in our country today. People feel if we can't even be safe, is there no discipline, is there no control, is there no direction in our society? This is an important thing.

Well, after 6 years of political posturing, we passed the crime bill last year. All the law enforcement agencies in the country supported it. It had stronger punishments, including a "three strikes and you're out" law. It had more money for prisons if States had strong sentencing provisions. But it also had money for 100,000 police, for community policing of the kind that we have

seen actually lowers the crime rate, because, after all, that's our objective, isn't it? We want a safer society. We want to lower the crime rate. And it had money for prevention, to give our young people something to say yes to as well as no to. It was a balanced, balanced bill. And it was a joy to sign.

Now, they say they want their crime bill and they want to be even tougher on crime. Well, I say if they send me a bill that repeals 100,000 police or repeals the assault weapons ban, I will veto that bill because that is wrong. But if they have some good ideas that will allow us to build on last year's crime bill to be more effective in making people safer, we would be wrong to turn away from it. We would be wrong to turn away from it.

Crime should not be a Republican or Democratic issue. It was not a partisan issue last year until we got right up to the campaign and they saw that they could twist it around and turn it into a pork argument. They had been supporting the effort all along. And we should not do to the American people what they did to the American people to get a few votes in last November's election. This should not be a partisan issue. When somebody gets killed or robbed or raped, I don't care what their political party is, it is wrong. And all of us should say, "We don't want this to be a political issue. We'll work with you, but don't tear down what we've done."

Let's talk about environmental protection. I've already said I want to ease the burden of foolish regulation. But I do not want and I will not tolerate the compromise of any effort to clean our water or our air or to clean up our toxic waste dumps. That, too, would be wrong. The environment cannot protect itself. It requires effort. The California Desert Protection Act was a good example of the effort. In implementing environmental protection it requires sensible compromise.

I'm proud of the fact that previous administrations just let everybody fight, but we hammered out a compromise dealing with the old-growth timber in the Pacific Northwest. We handed out a compromise that we hammered out dealing with the farmers and the environmentalists over the use of water here in California. We've been able to work out some compromises dealing with the Endangered Species Act so that responsible developers can do their work in California. We should not be immune to compromise. A lot of these acts can be implemented in a way that defies common sense. But we should not, we should not sit on the sidelines and watch the work that has been done by Republicans and Democrats together for 25 years to protect the environment of America, be wiped away with some ill-advised laws overnight.

Let me give you one example. If that law, which was passed by the House, the so-called takings bill, which would require the Government to pay property owners billions of dollars every time we act to defend our natural heritage of seashores and wetlands and open spaces, were to pass, it would either tie our hands in the environment or bankrupt the budget. If that is the law in States throughout the country, what it means is that local Governments have to give up zoning altogether. This same provision has been on the ballot in 20 States and has been defeated every time, even in conservative Republican States. In Arizona, the bill the House just passed was on the ballot last November in Arizona, hardly a bastion of the Democratic Party, and it was defeated 60–40. Now, that's how extremist this legislation is. Now, the people don't have a vote on this bill, but I do, and I say no, it will not become the law of the land.

Let me say something else that most Americans don't care much about today, but I want you to think about it, and that's our foreign policy. The House passed a so-called peacekeeping bill that would restrict the ability of the United States to cooperate with the United Nations in solving the problems of this old world. Well, the U.N. is 50 years old this year, and it's going to be a big celebration out here of that. But it's only 4 or 5 years old in terms of a real force for peacekeeping, because the cold war and Soviet vetoes kept it from being what it could have been for a long time. Roosevelt and Woodrow Wilson, Dwight Eisenhower and Senator Vandenberg, Republicans and Democrats alike, always believed the United Nations could be a force for peace and that the United States would be a partner in that.

Now there are those who say that we're oppressed, we're mistreated in the U.N., everything's terrible, we should just walk away. Folks, they're wrong. They're just wrong. What we did in Haiti was a noble thing and a good thing. But for all of our frustrations in Bosnia, the United Nations troops on the ground there—none of them American—are risking their lives

to minimize the slaughter. They're doing it; they don't ask us for our troops. All we do is to supply them food and medicine, and our ships are there, our planes are there to help them in case they get in trouble. It would be wrong for us not to support them when they are there, putting their lives on the line, trying to keep people alive.

I know at a time when we have so many problems here at home it is easy to say let's just walk away from this. But we are a great country, and the world looks to us for leadership. We must not let this kind of thing stand.

So these are the things that are in the contract. I will work on welfare reform. I will work on crime. I will work on regulatory reform. I will work on tax cuts. I will work on deficit reduction with the Republicans. But my idea of cutting spending in the Agriculture Department is to close 1,200 offices—that's what we did—not to cut the School Lunch Program.

So I say to you, when you leave here and you see people you know who aren't ardent Democrats like us, say to them, "We're not against deficit reduction; we're not against tax cuts; we're not against welfare reform. We want America to be a safer place. We want our streets and our schools and our own homes to be safer, but let's don't go too far. Let's don't be extreme. Let's remember that we've got to put the American people first; we've got to put the future of this country first. And we've gotten past the first 100 days; now, let's roll up our sleeves and do something that makes sense. Otherwise, we'll have to say no. Better to say yes to our future, but better to say no than to go to an extreme which we will regret for the rest of our lives."

Now, I also ask for your support for three other things. They are unfinished agenda from the New Covenant that I ran on. One is, we've got to do something about health care. Now, I am well aware that by the time the interest groups and our political adversaries got through spending $300 billion to tell the American people how lousy my ideas were, reverse plastic surgery had been performed on them. [*Laughter*] And I am well aware of the fact that the American people believe that I bit off more than I could chew in the bill I sent to Congress last year.

But I also have not forgotten the fact that we got over 1 million letters, Hillary and I did, from people who had heartbreaking problems, that there are people every year who have to give up more and more coverage because of the cost of health care, that there are millions of people who don't have any health insurance, that we are the only wealthy country in the entire world where there's a smaller percentage of people today with health insurance than people who had it 10 years ago. Nobody else has this problem, only us, because we refuse to deal with it.

So let's take it one step at a time. Let's say, you cannot lose your health insurance when you change jobs. Let's make the benefits portable. Let's say that a family ought to be able to get health insurance even if somebody in the family has been sick. Preexisting conditions preventing people from getting health insurance is wrong. Let's say that every State ought to have a huge pool where all small business people and farmers and self-employed people can buy health insurance for the same price as those of us who work for government or big corporations can buy it. And let's expand home care for the elderly and the disabled, so that they don't have to spend themselves into poverty and go into a nursing home to get any decent care. We can afford to do this.

My fellow Americans, we can afford to do this without raising taxes and without expanding the deficit, while lowering the deficit. We can do these things. So let's ask them to do it. And let's do two more things. Let's ask the Republicans to start acting like Republicans used to act and join with us as Democrats and raise the minimum wage.

They say they want to index tax rates to protect against inflation, so we did that. Now they want to index capital gains to protect against inflation, which mostly helps the wealthiest people. And they want to guard the defense budget against inflation, and I respect that. The only people they don't want to protect against inflation are the people that are getting hurt worst by it.

You know, you cannot raise a child on $8,500 a year anymore. You just can't do it. And if we don't raise the minimum wage this year, next year the minimum wage will be at its lowest value in 40 years. Now, we're going around telling everybody, "Get off welfare; go to work." We're going to extol the work ethic; we're creating 6 million new jobs. Is your version of post-cold-war America, is your version of a high-technology information age one in which mini-

mum wage workers make their lowest income in 40 years? Not mine. Let's raise it, and let's ask them to help us.

Finally, let's ask them to reduce the deficit without cutting education. Let's say instead we should increase education. We should increase education. Do you really seriously believe that California is going to be stronger 10 years from now because of all the hits education has taken out here in the last few years?

Audience members. No-o-o!

The President. Nobody does. Nobody does. You know, they used to attack us and say, "Oh, the Democrats are indiscriminate. They just want to spend more money on everything." Well, that's not true anymore. We cut 300 programs. I've asked the Congress to cut 400 more or consolidate them. I don't want to spend more money on everything. I want to spend more money on the right things. They want to spend less money on everything. Neither extreme is right. The right thing to do is to say education is the fault line in the modern world; if you want the American dream, if you want the middle class to grow, if you want us to go up and down together, we had better get every last person in this country a decent education. And we had better not walk away from it.

You imagine this, imagine what California would have been like when all these layoffs started occurring if we had had the "GI bill" for America's workers that I proposed. Take all these Federal training programs, put them in a block of money, and send a check to the unemployed worker for 2 years, say, "Go out and get your training. Do not sit where you are. We will help you pay for 2 years of education for a lifetime." We're going to have to do this if we want America to grow. We're going to have to do it.

Let me close with a few words on this affirmative action issue and know where we are as Democrats.

Audience members. [*Inaudible*]

The President. Let me speak. Don't scream; let's talk. That's just what they want us to do. They want to get this country into a screaming match. They win the screaming matches; we win the conversations.

You already heard what Barbara Boxer said about the incomes. We know that. We know there's still disparity in incomes. I'm really proud of the fact that under my administration the African-American unemployment rate is below 10 percent for the first time in 20 years. But there's still a big disparity. But there's still a disparity, right? So we know that.

Let me tell you something else. There are still things in the human heart in this country that we're not totally aware of that affect our decisions. I'm old enough to remember that when I was still a young man first starting to vote, there were county courthouses on courthouse squares in my part of the country and in my State that still had restrooms marked "white" and "colored," in my lifetime, when I was as old as those young people out there.

Now, we have made great progress in the last 30 years. But we still don't all, any of us, understand fully what is in all of our hearts about all these complex issues of gender and race. Let me say something for all the people that are pushing for this. This is psychologically a difficult time for a lot of white males. Why? Because those who don't have great educations and who aren't in jobs which are growing, even though they may have started out ahead of those of you who are female and of different races, most of them are working harder for less money than they were making 15 years ago.

Imagine what it's like for them, just for a moment, to go home at night when they're my age, and they're nearly 50, and they think, "Gosh, when I was 20 I thought the whole world was before me. I thought by the time I was 50 I'd have three or four kids, I'd be sending them all to college, my retirement would be secure, we'd have a good life." Now they've been working for 15 years without a raise, and they think they could be fired at any time. And they go home to dinner, and they look across the table at their families, and they think they've let them down. They think somehow, "What did I do wrong?"

It's pretty easy for people like that to be told by somebody else in the middle of a political campaign with a hot 30-second ad, "You didn't do anything wrong; they did it to you." But what I want you to understand is, that doesn't make their feelings any less real. You may be aggrieved. Somebody may have been discriminatory against you, but that doesn't make their feelings any less real, either.

I got a letter the other day from a guy I went to grade school with. He was a very poor boy. He grew up and became an engineer. He worked over 20 years for a Fortune 500 com-

pany. They had a good year last year; they made a bunch of money. They laid off three of their engineers, gave their work to two others who were younger and less well-paid, and they trumpeted the fact that one of the other people was a minority. This guy wrote me a letter saying, "Mr. President, I'm glad you ordered a review of those programs, and I'm glad you didn't abandon them." But he said, "You have to understand what a lot of people are feeling out here is what I'm feeling. Three of us who are 50-year-old white males got fired. Now, they got rid of us because they wanted to cut their salary costs and cut their future health care and retirement costs. And the fact that we'd given over 20 years to our company didn't mean anything. There was no affirmative action reason they got rid of us, but it's easy for people like us to believe that's why it happened, because people then say, well, look at us, we're doing better on another front."

What I'm telling you, folks, is that what we have done to give more opportunities to women and minorities is a very good thing. And we should not stop doing that. But—and I'll give you three examples that I talk about all across the country that I'm proud of that prove that what we're doing is right.

If you look at the United States military, the United States Army not only produced General Powell, it produced a lot of other African-American generals and a lot of Hispanic generals. I was with a retired African-American general in Dallas yesterday who is phenomenally successful in business now and leading the fight to preserve the national service movement in Texas because he sees it as giving young people the kind of opportunity that he got in the Army. And nobody in America thinks that's a bad thing.

But they do make a special effort to make sure every time there's a promotion pool that it reflects the racial and gender makeup of the people in the rank just below. No unqualified person ever gets promoted, but they do really work hard to make sure that people's innate abilities get developed and that they're there and they get a chance. And it's made a difference.

I'll give you another example. The Small Business Administration under my administration last year increased loans to minorities by over two-thirds, to women by over 80 percent, but didn't increase loans to white men. And we didn't make a single loan to an unqualified person. We gave people who never had a chance before a chance to get in business. I'm proud of that. We didn't hurt anybody.

Look at the appointments our administration has made to Federal judgeships. Look at them. We have appointed more women and minorities to the Federal bench than the past three Presidents, one Democrat and two Republicans, combined. But you know what I'm really proud of? We have by far the largest percentage of judges rated well-qualified by the American Bar Association. We did the right thing giving people a chance.

So we have to keep working on this, but we have to realize that there is a real problem out there in this country. We can't deny that. There are a lot of people who go home every night and look across the table at their families and think that either they have failed or they have been stuck by somebody treating them unfairly. That is what we must respond to.

What the people who want to use this issue out here for political gain hope is that we will get in a big old shouting match with them, and they'll have more people on their side of the shouting match than we will, and it'll be a wedge, and they will drive it right through the stake of progressive efforts in the State and in this Nation.

And what we need here is what I've tried to do in Washington. We need to evaluate all these programs, we need to defend without any apology whatever anything we're doing that is right and decent and just that lifts people up, that lifts people up.

But we do not—we do not need to say that we're insensitive to what's going on in these other people's lives. We do not need to say that we are for people who are unqualified getting Government-mandated benefits over people who are. And we do not need to shrink as Democrats when we think there has been a case, however rare, of reverse discrimination. We entered a lawsuit, our Justice Department did, on behalf of a young, white man at Southern Illinois University who was told he couldn't even apply for a public job because he was the wrong gender and the wrong race. Now, that's clearly wrong.

So what we need to do is to say to these people—and what you ought to do in California—you can do it—you need to say, look, look around this room here. We're living in a global

society. Does anybody seriously believe that we'd be better off if we were divided by race and gender? Look at this room. California, when you get through this terrible downturn caused by the military cutbacks, is once again going to become the engine of America's economy in large measure because of your diversity. Because of your diversity. And everything we do to empower people, everything we do to empower people to contribute—when you empower people with disabilities to work and to be self-sufficient, you strengthen the rest of us. When we empower Native Americans through letting them have more economic power, more say over their own tribal affairs, that helps the rest of us because more people live up to their God-given capacity. That's important. When we find every person we can—however poor, however different, wherever they are—and give them a chance to become what they ought to be, we're all better off.

So we can use this occasion for a great national conversation. We don't have to retreat from these affirmative action programs that have done great things for the American people and haven't hurt other people. We don't. But we do have to ask ourselves, are they all working? Are they all fair? Has there been any kind of reverse discrimination? And more importantly, what we really ought to ask ourselves is, what are we going to do about all these folks that are out there working hard and never getting ahead. That's what the middle class tax cut is all about.

What are we going to do? What are we going to do about all these people who are being RIF'd by these big companies and by the Federal Government—although our severance package is much more humane—what are we going to do about these people in middle age who are being told, "Thank you very much for the last 25 years, but goodbye, goodbye before your full pension vests, goodbye 15 years before you can draw your pension. Goodbye to your nice health care package for yourself and your family. Goodbye to your future raises." What are we going to do for them?

Use this opportunity to tell people that we have to do this together. I'm pleading with you, stand up for the affirmative action programs that are good, that work, that bring us together, but don't do it in a way that gives them a cheap political victory. Do it in a way that reaches out and brings people in and says we care about you, too. Don't do it in a way that gives them a cheap political victory.

Now, I want to read you something. I want to read you something, and then I'm done. I got a letter—I got a great little poster. I had two posters greeting me when I came in from my morning run, one from a local kindergarten and one from the Bowling Green Charter School Number 8, Sacramento, California. And these children had written in their little hand-prints the virtues they were being taught in school. I want you to listen to these. These are what we are teaching our children: cooperation, respect, patience, caring, sense of humor, common sense, friendship, responsibility, flexibility, effort, creativity, initiative, communication, problem-solving, integrity, perseverance.

You know what? No place in there, this list of what we are teaching our children about how they ought to live, is demonize people that aren't like you, look for ways to divide people one from another, take a quick victory if you can by making people angry at one another. We do not practice our lives as citizens the way we teach our children to live, the way we try to run our families, the way we try to run our workplaces.

Now, that's what I'm asking you to do. Go out of here and engage these people and say, "Listen, we are moving this economy, we're moving on the problems of the country, we're changing the way the Government works, but we had better behave as citizens the way we try to teach our children to behave as human beings and the way we try to run the rest of our lives." You do that, and the Democrats are coming back.

Thank you, and God bless you.

NOTE: The President spoke at 10:22 a.m. at the Convention Center. In his remarks, he referred to Don Fowler, chairman, Democratic National Committee; Bill Press, chairman, and Arlene Holt, first vice chair, California Democratic Party; Willie L. Brown, Jr., California State Assembly speaker; and Bill Lockyer, California State Senate president pro tempore.

Remarks at the National Education Association School Safety Summit in Los Angeles, California
April 8, 1995

Thank you. Thank you for your welcome. Thank you for your work. Thank you for that very moving film. Thank you, Keith Geiger, for your introduction and for your outstanding leadership of this organization. You know, Keith Geiger is quite a gardener, and it's quite a beautiful day. It shows you how devoted he is that he's even inside, much less giving a speech. [*Laughter*] Thank you, Dick Riley, for such a wonderful job as Secretary of Education and for those fine remarks. Senator Carol Moseley-Braun, I'm delighted to see you. We're a little out of place here today. It's actually a pretty good time to be in Washington, DC. The cherry blossoms are out, and so is Congress. It's a pretty good time to be there. [*Laughter*] I know there are a lot of Los Angeles county supervisors and city council members here today, and I see your distinguished police chief—I know there are other—and I thank you for being here, sir.

I also know that this is not just a gathering of teachers. There are a lot of school support folks here and parents and police officers and concerned citizens about a subject that I care a great deal about, as you could see from the film that was put together by the NEA.

Shortly before the New Hampshire primary in 1992, I was walking in a hotel one night in New York, and some of you may remember, since you helped me, that I was not doing very well then, and my political obituary was being written over and over again. [*Laughter*] "Will he fall into single digits in New Hampshire, or will he hang on at 11 percent?" And I was feeling pretty sorry for myself. And we were having this big fundraiser in New York, and for all I knew, there wouldn't be three people there. And they took me in the back way, you know, and I walked through the kitchen, totally preoccupied with my own problems.

And all of a sudden this gentleman who was working in the hotel came up to me and said, "Governor, my boy, who is 10, he studies politics in the school, and he says I should vote for you. So," he says, "I'm going to vote for you. But" he said, "I want you to do something for me." I said, "What is it?" He said, "I want you to make my boy free." I said, "Well, what do you mean?" He said, "Well, I came here from another country, and we were very poor there, but at least we were free." He said, "Now we live in a place where we have a park across the street, but my boy can't go to the park unless I go with him to protect him. We have a neighborhood school that's just down the street, but my boy can't go to school unless I walk with him. If my boy is not safe, he is not free. So, if I vote for you as he asks, will you make my boy free?"

And the first thing I felt, frankly, was shame that I was preoccupied with my own problems. And the second thing I thought was, you know, how can we have learning in this country until our children are free?

Now we're having this huge debate in Washington about what the role of Government ought to be. Yesterday at the American Newspaper Editors Association in Dallas, I had a chance to say where I stood on the issues remaining both in the Republican contract and in the New Covenant that I ran on in 1992.

We know that we have a lot of economic challenges, that we have to grow the middle class and shrink the under class and make America a good place for a new generation of entrepreneurs. We know that the Government is not well-organized for the information age and it needs to be less bureaucratic and more flexible.

But we also know, I take it, that there are two great obligations that we must, we must pursue as a people, and they are related and they come together here. The first is that we have to enhance the security of our people, not only beyond our borders but here at home as well. And the second is that we have to empower them all through education to succeed in a world where education, more than ever before, is the key, not only to whether a society succeeds but whether individuals can live up to their own dreams.

Today you are coming to talk about both things. You can't succeed in school if you're not secure when you're there, and we can't expect our schools to be safe unless we do more

to make our communities safe and our homes safe. So you are dealing with two of the great questions of this time. I applaud you for doing it. This is a very impressive program, and I wish you well.

Last year I fought hard to pass that crime bill because it was comprehensive, because it did have tougher punishment and more prisons, but it also put another 100,000 police on our street in community settings so we could lower crime and make people safer, because it had provisions for making our schools safer, because it had a domestic violence component for violence against women and children.

And the Secretary and I fought very hard for the safe and drug-free schools act which would provide funds to over 90 percent in our school districts to help to keep the schools safe, whether it would be in the form of security officers or security equipment or other things designed to make our schools safer and more free of drugs.

As we debate all these issues, it's important not to forget that the first mission of Government is to keep its citizens safe within rules of law, and our second mission is to meet the challenges of the time. The challenges of this time are the challenges of education. And we cannot do one without the other.

One of the most disturbing things in America today is the fact that there's so much social tension growing directly out of the fact that most wages for most middle class people have been stagnant for more than 10 years. More than half the American people today are working a longer workweek for the same or lower wages they were making 15 years ago. When you think about every political issue that's being faced in this country that is divisive, if you just imagine that fact, it explains a lot. It explains a lot about the anxiety, the resentment, the frustrations that people have in this country.

But whatever the debates are, we have to say, let's don't do stupid things. Let's invest more time, effort, resources, organization, and passion into making our people safer and educating our people better.

I want to cut spending. Senator Carol Moseley-Braun could tell you the story. We just had—I was just with Senator Boxer up at the California Democratic Convention, and she was talking about this. We had a big debate about how we could lower the spending in this year's budget more, in the so-called rescission bill, to pay for the California earthquake costs and some other expenses we had and reduce the deficit a little more. And we got this bill originally from the House that was going to cut all kinds of education funding and cut funding for safe and drug-free schools, at a time when drug use is going back up among young people who have forgotten that is not only illegal, it is dangerous and stupid, and violence is a real problem.

So we worked and worked and worked. When the bill got over to the Senate, the Senate Republicans put some money back in, and then we insisted, if you're one of the Democrats, to let it come to a vote they'd have to put some more money—put the money back. So the money got put back.

But my point is that in Washington, where we're so far away from these problems—you heard—I can't remember whether it was Keith or whoever said it out here, that a lot of people who might pontificate about schools never have been in a classroom. Well, I have been. I dare say I've probably spent more hours in more classrooms in more States than any person who ever had the privilege of holding this office. And it is so easy to see where people in Washington—they get on a tear—that judgment goes out the window.

The Republicans used to attack the Democrats because they said they never met a program they didn't like. They were great at starting programs, but they couldn't stop them. Their solution to everything was to spend more money on it. Well, now the rage is, we never met a program we did like, and their solution to everything is spend less money on it. What we need is judgment. What we need is judgment. We need to reduce the deficit, but we need to invest more in education and we need to invest more in security because those two things together will determine our future.

I think you had somebody from the Centers of Disease Control in Atlanta earlier today. They are releasing today their preliminary report on school-related violent deaths. They have identified 105 violent school-related deaths in just the last 2 years. And they've shown that violence threatens schools and communities of all shapes and sizes. We know there are common elements to violent deaths among young people. The victim and the assailant usually know each other, they are usually the same race, and they're usually male. The incident starts as an argument, and there's usually a firearm involved.

Schoolyard fights have been around as long as schoolyards. But it used to be, when I got in them at least, that when kids got in fights, they fought with their fists and adults broke them up.

Today, there are guns on the playground, guns in the classroom, guns on the bus. And as was pointed out in the film, 7 times more often, there are knives there. So as a result, serious injury and death and terror are far more likely to occur.

You know, the thing about being young is you think you're going to live forever. Whatever is inside you working around is rushing at high tide, and the future is what happens 5 minutes from now. That's why our job is to calm people down and make them think about what happens 5 years and 10 years and 15 years from now. And we all have a fair chance to do it, unless they can do unlimited damage in the 5 seconds between when they start and when somebody else can get there. With a knife or a gun you can do unlimited damage.

I'll never forget when I was running for President, I gave a speech in New York City at a school. And I was talking about Martin Luther King, and everybody seemed so moved. And 2 weeks later, a kid got killed right in the same place I was standing.

I met a young man in northern California who had changed schools because his school was so violent, with his brother. And they were standing in line to register for class in the other school, and his brother got shot, this time by a stranger, just some nut walked in and got in a fight. His brother happened to be standing in the way.

The CDC found that in 1990, one in 24 students carried a gun to school in the 30 days before their study. In 1991, one in 18 carried a gun. Last week, the CDC reported that in 1993, one in 12 students carried a gun. That's more people than are packing a gun on the street. That's a higher percentage.

This is a national crisis. It requires a national response. It requires all kinds of people to be involved. Guns have no place in our schools and have no place in the hands of our children. If we don't stop this, we can't make the schools safe. We've always had bipartisan support for zero tolerance of guns in our schools. We ought to keep it that way. In 1990, a Democratic Congress passed a law creating gun-free zones around our schools, and President Bush signed it. At this moment, my administration is supporting that law all the way to the Supreme Court.

The crime bill we passed last year makes it a Federal crime for a young person to carry a handgun except when supervised by an adult. Last fall, we passed a law requiring States to adopt a simple but powerful rule: If somebody brings a gun to school, they'll be expelled for a year, no excuses. Senator Feinstein sponsored that law. Zero tolerance works. In 1993 in San Diego, the first year of the policy, the number of guns in schools was cut in half. This school year, authorities have found only five guns in the entire school system. It works.

That's why I directed Secretary Riley to enforce one rule for the whole country. If a State doesn't comply with zero tolerance, it won't get certain important Federal educational funds, period. I have been very strong in giving more flexibility to schools, more flexibility to school districts, more flexibility to States, and more flexibility to State governments in a whole wide range of areas. I've given 25 States permission to pursue welfare reform, 7 States permission to pursue big health care reform. And the education legislation we adopted last year, while enshrining then national education goals, gave local schools more flexibility in deciding how to educate their children than ever before. But this problem deserves and, indeed, requires a national response. Zero tolerance: There is no other rational option.

I also want to say something on behalf of the principals and the teachers who are here and even their security forces and their metal detectors. This is not just a school problem, this is a social problem. That's why we have to support the efforts of our police chiefs, our sheriffs, and our others to adopt policies that will lower the crime rate throughout our communities and throughout our country. That's why it is important to support the work that was done in the crime bill last year. That's why it's important to support the work of people struggling to reduce domestic violence throughout our country. The schools will have violence and weapons and trouble as long as our society has them.

We can do better in the schools. To be sure, we can do better. But we have to recognize it will never be a problem that is gone until we do better beyond the schoolhouse door. Parents have to teach their children right from wrong. Parents have to get involved, and community leaders have to get involved. We cannot expect the schools to do it all.

In the end, this country has got to get mobilized around this issue. I just studied about a year ago—I sat down one day and really looked at the differences between the 1980 and the 1990 census. And if you can bear to look at all of those numbers, you can see a lot about what's going on in your country. It is perfectly clear that the middle class in America is splitting apart. And that is what is giving rise to all of these social tensions.

From the year I was born until 1978 or so, we all rose together; in all income groups we rose together. We just about doubled our income, no matter whether we were in the top 20 percent, the bottom 20 percent, or someplace in between, except the bottom 20 percent increased almost time and a half what they had been earlier. So we were going up and going together.

Then, in 1978 or thereabouts, an amazing thing started to happen. Income stagnation among a lot of working people meant that for the first time since the end of the Second World War, the middle class started to split apart, so that this idea of the American dream began to be thwarted in family after family after family after family. Don't kid yourselves, that's really behind all this tension on affirmative action. That's really behind a lot of this tension and anxiety on immigration. It's behind a lot of this. There are too many families out here headed by people who think they have done everything they're supposed to do, who are living on the same or lower wages with a high level of job insecurity who don't believe they can do right by their children. Now, that's what's going on.

But the fault line dividing the middle class in the global economy is education. It's education. The only way we can offer hope to people of a successful life in the face of all these changes, the only way we can tell people you can seize all these wonderful things about the global economy is if we can educate everybody. And the only way we can do that is if we can make our schools safe and give childhood back to our children.

If there ever was an example of what I have been trying to preach for 3 or 4 years now, that we need a New Covenant among our people of opportunity and responsibility, this is it. Education is an opportunity. Lawfulness is a responsibility. And you cannot have one without the other. I will do everything I can to support you. I ask that you do only this, whether you are a Republican or a Democrat or an independent, ask our Congress to work with me to find ways to cut this deficit without under-mining our investment in either education or security. We must go forward together.

Thank you, and God bless you.

NOTE: The President spoke at 2:24 p.m. at the Century Plaza Hotel and Towers.

Remarks at the United Jewish Fund Luncheon in Los Angeles
April 9, 1995

Thank you very much, Peter, for your very fine introduction. To you and Gloria; to Irwin and Helgar Field; to our good friends Senator Boxer and Congressman Berman and his wife, Janice; Lew and Edie Wasserman; and Barbra Streisand and all the others who have come here to be with us today and mostly to all of you for inviting Hillary and me to share this moment with you, I thank you.

The terrible incident of violence upon the people of Israel, which reached today also to some Americans who were also affected, gives me a way of beginning what I came here to say to you. I offer my condolences and the condolences of the American people to the people of Israel and the Government of Israel as well as to the American citizens and their families who were affected by this attack.

Once more, the enemies of peace have sought to abuse the opportunity peace presents, to kill it, to kill hope, to kill all possibility of a normal life for the people of Israel, for the Palestinians who are struggling to do the right thing there, and for, indeed, people throughout the Middle East who can see a permanent and lasting peace within their grasp.

As we give our sympathies to those who have suffered and died and their families, let us stiffen our resolve to say to those who seek to abuse human life so that they can continue to kill and continue to keep peace from people who want it: You will not succeed. You must not succeed.

I ask you to think today for a few moments about the connection between what you hope will happen in the Middle East—what I have worked for as your President in terms of peace in the Middle East and Northern Ireland and South Africa and Haiti, worked for to reduce the nuclear threat in North Korea and to be able to say that this is the first time since the dawn of the nuclear age when no Russian missiles are pointed at the children of America—what is the connection between all of this and the work you have done here at home? The literally tens of millions of dollars that you have raised for any number of worthy public purposes and the partnerships that you have had with our Government, our National, State, and local governments, serving families, resettling refugees, helping the elderly and the sick, promoting education, and of course, as Mr. Gold said, dealing with the aftermath of the terrible earthquake; even the help you sent to the people of Rwanda and those who were affected by the Kobe earthquake—what is the connection between these two things?

You have a sense of mission and purpose. You know that it is for all of us to make the most of our God-given capacities, but that we can only do it if we work together with some common purpose. I believe that the role of our Government must be as a partner to people like you, people who are willing to give of your time and your money and your heart and soul to try to solve the problems of other people because you think your life will be richer and stronger as well, not—to use your phrase, sir—not because it's a matter of charity but because it's a matter of justice.

I have done what I could to be a good partner, and I thank you for what you said about the earthquake. We worked hard there. And we continue to work hard to make sure that all the consequences of the quake will be overcome and that the future will be bright.

What I want to say to you today is that if you look at the economic problems and the social problems tearing America apart, if you look at the level of violence and gangs and drugs among our children, the number of children who are born out of wedlock, if you look at the problems we have with stagnant incomes, and then you look on the other side of the ledger at the fact that we are creating new businesses at a record rate, we are creating new millionaires at a record rate, our country has the lowest combined rate of unemployment and inflation that we've had in 25 years, you might ask yourself, how can this global economy, how can the end of the cold war, how can the transfer from the industrial age to the information age bring us so much good and leave so many problems in its wake?

If you look at the Middle East, you see that the very act of making peace has made it possible to have more violence. Look at what happened in Gaza. If peace is made and the PLO has a government there and the borders are open and the people are more integrated, then the incomes of the Palestinians go up, prosperity increases, the love of peace deepens. But if the borders are open, then that means there is also a greater possibility for terrorism, violence, murder, and killing the peace.

I want to make this common point. I believe the greatest challenge to civilization at the end of this century, with the globalization of the economy and the revolution of information and technology we're seeing, is that all of the forces of integration, which give us the hope of building people up and having untold dreams fulfilled, seem to be accompanied by seeds of disintegration, which threaten our most basic human decency. And our job as citizens of our country and as human beings is to try to stabilize and shape and humanize those forces so that we can allow all the wonderful things of this new age to lift our people up and, at the same time, beat back the demons that would destroy us.

Now, I could give you a lot of examples of that. The financial crisis in Mexico: We signed NAFTA; everything looked great. The world financial markets are integrated. Money rushes into Mexico. Mexico grows more rapidly than ever could have happened 15 years ago. Errors were made, and instead of a mid-course correction, there is a huge flow of capital out of Mexico. The same speed that brought the country up threatened to bring it down, which is why I moved in to try to stabilize the situation. Overreaction, integration, disintegration.

Japan becomes a great industrial power by developing an incredible ability to fill different little market niches and do specific things, smaller and smaller things with bigger and bigger impacts. And the miniaturization and openness and rapid moving of that society also makes it possible for a religious fanatic to walk into a subway with a little piece of poison gas in a little vial and kill 60 people and hospitalize hundreds more.

Russia throws off the shackles of communism, gets rid of totalitarianism. No more oppression. Free enterprise banks. The first thing you know, the biggest problem is organized crime taking over the banks.

In the Baltics—Hillary and I went to the Baltics, and people were cheering us on, saying the United States got Russian troops out of the Baltics for the first time since before World War II, thank you very much. We had this moving ceremony. Everybody was in tears. We walked into a room to have a private meeting, and the first thing the leader of the country asked me for was an FBI office, because now that they were free they were going to be vulnerable to organized crime and drug transit.

Closer to home, the more free and open we are, the more the free markets can lift us up, the more people who have great skills will be rewarded. That's why education is more important than ever before. But things are happening so fast, people who are willing to work hard but don't know a lot and can't learn a lot or don't have access to learning are going to be far more punished than they have been in the past; which is why, in the last 15 years, you see a dramatic departure from all previous years before World War II, when the middle class is splitting apart. The forces of integration are giving people who can triumph in the information age untold opportunities in America, but there are forces of disintegration for those who don't have them. They're not as obvious and tangible as the disintegration that comes from an earthquake, but they are happening nonetheless.

And you have stepped into the breach. The generosity you have shown by raising this money and working in partnership with public agencies and dealing with all these problems is of more historic importance than at ever before, at least in the latter half of the 20th century. Because we have to find a way to push for peace in the Middle East and not let the forces of disintegration destroy it. We have to find a way to help people overcome the horrible legacy of totalitarianism and build the institutions of freedom and not let them be destroyed by people who abuse freedom.

We have to find a way in this country to lift up all people in the technological and information revolution, which gives us the potential of liberating poor people at a more rapid rate than ever before, without instead creating a huge class of new poor who are working all the time and cannot get ahead. That is what is fueling all the cauldron of feelings around immigration. It's what's fueling all the cauldron of feelings around the affirmative action debate in this State. It is the force of integration running smack dab against the force of economic disintegration.

And because you have a social conscience, because you understand that as a country and as a community we must go up or down together, because you know that our diversity, our freedom, our openness will ensure America's greatness indefinitely if we can solve this problem, you are critical to our future.

Now, in Washington today, we are having an unprecedented debate about what the role of the Government should be in this time. And it is fashionable now, as it once was fashionable to say that there were people in Washington who never met a Government program they didn't like, now you see people who never met one they did like. Where once the problem was people who wanted to spend more money on everything, today the problem is people want to spend less money on everything, who make no distinctions.

We cannot live without a public purpose and institutions to bring us together in public endeavors so that the forces of integration can triumph over the forces of disintegration, so that the people who are lifting us up can prevail.

I believe in the forces of the free market. I have done everything I could to unshackle them from destructive Government interference. I have done everything I could to expand trading opportunities for the American private sector. But the market alone, in a time when the forces of disintegration are powerful, will not solve all of our problems.

And so you must work with us to define the mission of your Government and the level of partnership we will have as we move toward the end of this century and into the next. But

as you go home today, I want you to think about it. Think about the terrible burden that the people of Israel bear. The more risks they take for peace, the more at risk they are from openness.

And the same is true of the Palestinians proceeding in good faith. They never had to run a police force before. They never had to turn the lights on before or run the water systems or make the trains run on time, to use the American slogan. They don't have the infrastructure to deal with this. And so their enemies say, "I liked it the other way. I could get plenty of money for making bombs. I could get plenty of ammunition for my uzi. I do not want to live in peace."

And peace requires openness and interchange so that the more risks you take, the more at risk you are because disintegration becomes an option as you try to integrate people and bring them together. In this kind of a world, we must have strong institutions devoted to preserving responsibility, family, work, community, to giving everybody a chance to imagine that their tomorrows can be better than their yesterdays.

Now, we could take every last issue being debated in Washington and every last issue being debated in the global community, and it all comes down to that. And I ask you not to forget that some of the forces who are arguing that we don't need any kind of Government are also arguing that we should withdraw from the United Nations, turn our back on peacekeeping, not be involved in the rest of the world. That would be a disaster for the future of our country and this globe. And we must not do it.

This is not a partisan issue. At the end of this century, at the dawn of the next, we must have public institutions working in partnership with public-spirited citizens to enhance our security, to enhance opportunity, to insist on more responsibility, and to empower people through continuous education to make the most of their own lives and to develop the self-confidence to believe that they can live good lives without hurting other people, that they don't have to define their success in life by someone else's failure. And that is the common element in all destructive behavior.

Why do people blow up buses in Israel? There are people who believe they can only be successful in life if someone else is dying. And in a much more pedestrian way, how many times do we see conflicts within our own borders from people who believe they can only be successful if someone else is failing?

You have believed, always, there was a public interest, there were shared values, there were common goals, we could go up together. That is what America needs now. We need it in thinking about our own problems. We need it in looking out to the world. We need to behave as citizens the way you behave as members of this organization. We need to give, because when we give, we get; because we're better off if we're all doing better. We dare not define our success in life by someone else's failure.

So I say to you, keep doing what you're doing. But when you go home and when you continue this conversation, think about how many examples there are of the point I have made to you today. And think about all the wonderful opportunities the world affords us. I believe

America's best days are still ahead. We have only to figure out how to get the benefits of these fantastic new changes without bearing the burdens of the forces of disintegration. It will not happen unless we believe in the public interest, unless we believe in the human ties that bind us, and unless we join hands to work together. That is the wisdom you have to give to the rest of America, and I ask you to do your very best to impart it.

Thank you, and God bless you all.

NOTE: The President spoke at 12:10 p.m. at the Beverly Wilshire Regent. In his remarks, he referred to Peter Gold, 1995 Jewish Federation campaign chairman, and his wife, Gloria; Irwin Field, Jewish Federation president, and his wife, Helgar; Lew Wasserman, chairman and CEO, MCA, Inc., and his wife, Edie; and entertainer Barbra Streisand.

Remarks to Working Women
April 10, 1995

Thank you, Marina. Thank you for having the courage to come up here and give that speech. For those of us who do it every day it may seem normal, but I couldn't help realizing what a brave thing it was for her to come up here and just stand in front of all of you and speak so eloquently and powerfully. And I know a lot of you who are out here representing working women in so many different walks of life identified with everything she had to say, so maybe you ought to give her another hand. [*Applause*]

Thank you, Karen Nussbaum, for the outstanding job you do. And thank you, Secretary Reich, for being the conscience of all working Americans in this administration. And thank you, Hillary, for being a good symbol of that.

This is an issue that's very important to me personally. My grandmother was a working woman from the 1930's on. My mother was a working woman from the 1940's on. It never occurred to me from the first day I met Hillary that we would not have a two-worker home. And as she told those village women—even in Bangladesh, now they know that, until I became

President, she always made more money than I did. [*Laughter*]

The interesting thing to me about this issue is that it really reflects the larger dilemmas of our society today. We want to have opportunities open for women to work and to fulfill their own dreams, and surely that is one of the things that drives women into the work force. But it's also true that a lot of women work even under the most difficult circumstances simply because they have to. And in either case, what we should want for women is to be able to be successful in the workplace and successful in the home.

This afternoon—as you heard, I got all these letters from all across the country; I want to read you just a couple. A working mother from Milwaukee said, "Between balancing home and working a job, you always feel like you're doing four things at once. You're doing your job, but you're thinking about what you're going to cook for supper and who's going to pick up the kids." A 34-year-old woman put it this way: "Being a working woman is like having two full-time jobs. We're expected to be perfect in both career and taking care of the home, but without adequate compensation for either." [*Laughter*]

As the son, as I said, the grandson, and the husband of working women, I hear these voices. I hear you. The 60 million American women who work do deserve a better deal. The recommendations that I have received we are committed to putting into action.

If you think about the great challenges facing America today, resolving the dilemmas of working women are critical to our meeting them. Women want to be treated as assets to be developed in the workplace, not costs to be cut. They deserve to work in an environment that treats them with dignity, respects the value of their families, and invests in their skills and their future. This is not just the fair and decent thing to do, it is the smart thing to do for America.

More and more as I serve in this office, it becomes clearer to me that the decent thing to do is the smart thing to do; that over and over and over again, all the new opportunities that this age offers us require us to fight against the temptation to take the shortcut, to take the easy way out, to hold the wages down, to deny the benefits, to deny the importance of raising children while being in the workplace. What is in our interest over the long run is to take advantage of all these rapid changes which are going on in our society and still allow people to have some stability, some order, some pace in their lives so that they can raise their children and honor their marriages and grow as people at work and after work. That, it seems to me, is a fundamental mission that this society—not this administration, this society—should be pursuing.

My mother worked for over 30 years, and she was always proud of what she did. And because we had two workers in the family, we always did pretty well. There are a lot of women out their now raising their children alone, and a lot of others in two-worker families where one or the other seems to be always out of a job because of all the changes that are going on today.

Then there are a lot of people who just have circumstances that are downright almost unimaginable. I never will forget the last race I made for Governor of my State. I always made a habit of going to a factory in the northern part of Arkansas, because they had the earliest factory gate in the State; everybody had to show up between 4 and a quarter to 5, everybody. And I was there at 4:30 one morning, and a pickup truck pulled up. And in this pickup truck

with one seat, there was a husband, a wife, and three little kids. And I saw the mother get out, and go to work at 4:30 in the morning. And I asked the father—I went over to the father, and I said, "How do you deal with this?" He said, "Well, I don't have to be at work until 6:30. But," he said, "my kids can't go to school until 7:30 or even to day care. So I had to find someone else to take my kids between 6 in the morning when I have to leave and the rest of the time. And we have to get them all up every day so we can drop their mother off, because we can't have anybody coming to our house."

This sounds like an extreme example, but a lot of you sitting in this audience have other examples that are just as difficult. This is the fact of life in America today.

Recently in Atlanta, I was down there for an economic conference, and I met a woman who ran a day care center who told me about all of the problems that the children were having from time to time. And she told me that she had a young boy who one day at lunchtime missed his mother so much, and she could not get off of work and come see him at the day care center. And he was crying and crying. So she suggested that he should draw a picture of his mother, and that would make him miss his mother less. So the boy drew a picture of his mother, but then he taped it to the chair next to his, and he wouldn't let anybody else sit in the chair all day long. [*Laughter*] He sat with his mother all day long at the day care center.

I know that if we lived in other countries we would have other problems. I know that America still has more opportunities for women than most societies. And I know that most of us are doing the best we can and most of you will do very well and your children will grow up fine. But I also know that we cannot become the society we want to be as we move into the next century unless we address the problems that came out of what these 250,000 women said to me when we asked all of you what the state of life was like in America today. Working women must count.

You know, we've already made a down payment. The First Lady mentioned the family and medical leave law. When I went home to Arkansas about a week ago and I went to my church—and the first person I met at my church was a woman I didn't know. She came out, and she said, "If you hadn't signed that family leave law, my family would have been ruined, because I got sick. And my husband and I were able to deal with that, and he could take some time off to deal with me, and neither one of us lost our jobs." It has made a difference. And I'd like to say to all those who said it was a terrible thing, it would bring down the job growth of the American economy and ruin small business: You were wrong. This was the right thing to do.

Our efforts to immunize all of the children in this country, to expand Head Start, to do what we can to expand child care, to strengthen child support enforcement, all these things are important to help you succeed, as people, as workers, as parents. But there is more that we should do. I have heard the recommendations. We cannot be satisfied until every person in this country has a chance to make the most of her God-given abilities.

You recommended and I have proposed giving a tax deduction for all expenses for education after high school. That's very important. You know, most adults have to change jobs now during a lifetime, and many can be out of work for a long time, and many will not be able to get jobs paying what their old jobs paid unless they can get more education. This is a terribly important thing. I've said this over and over again, but the community colleges in our country may be the most important institutions in America today as we try to get into the 21st century, because they're handy, they're flexible, they change, they're driven by the local markets, and they're open to everybody. And we have to do what we can to increase the availability of education, not simply for working people to be able to provide it for their children but to be able to have it for themselves as well.

You recommended and I also support streamlining the Federal job training programs. Now, there are 60 or 70 different job training programs, and I'm sure there was some reason that they were all passed separately. But today, most of you know where you need to go to get better training and education. So we want to collapse those, put them into a big pool, and let them become vouchers for unemployed people or very low-wage workers, so you can just use the money where you see fit, for a year and sometimes for 2 years, if you need it to get further education and training.

You recommended and I support expanding more affordable loans for college students through the direct loan program. This will be very important to a lot of you and to a lot of your children. If a person borrows money to go to college, they ought never to be discouraged from going or from staying because of the burden of the loan. Under our proposal, you not only can get the loan at a more affordable rate but you can pay it back as a percentage of your income, so you'll never go broke trying to pay your college loan back. That's an important thing to America's women.

Finally, you recommended and I support raising the minimum wage. I am very tired of hearing people say the only people on minimum wage are upper class college students who live with their wealthy parents and they don't need it. The other day on one of the local news programs, I was doing my little channel surfing and I saw they were doing a series on the minimum wage. And they went down to some town, I think it was in Virginia, and they interviewed a lady working for the minimum wage. She looked to be about my age. And the television reporter says, "Well, ma'am, they say here in your factory that if the minimum wage is raised, that there will be fewer jobs. You might lose your job." She looked at the television reporter, and she said, "Honey, I'll take my chances." [*Laughter*]

I don't believe you can support yourself and raise a child or more than a child on $8,500 a year. And we now have a—several years ago, we indexed the income taxes of the country so people weren't punished for making higher incomes with higher taxes. Now people in the Congress want to index the capital gains tax to protect the capital gains against inflation, and they want to index the defense budget to protect that against inflation. Why in the wide world wouldn't we want to protect against inflation the people who are working harder for the lowest money with kids to raise and a country to build? We ought to do this. It is time to do this.

So, we've got a lot to do. You've given us some good recommendations. I also want to say that there are a lot of people who would like to be working women who aren't—people on welfare. There's a lot of talk in this town now about reforming the welfare system, and I am for it. I was pleased to hear the Speaker last

Friday say that he really wanted to get welfare reform out.

But let us recognize what real welfare reform would be. It would be turning people who are permanently dependent into permanently successful workers who also are successful parents. That should be the goal of welfare reform. We should not punish people for the sins they committed in the past. Instead, we should say, we will help you if you will behave responsibly in the future as parents, as students, and as workers. If that is the focus of this welfare reform, believe me, there's a lot of reform that needs to be done.

Everybody in this society, we ought to have the same goal for. And someday we ought to be able to have a meeting like this where men and women all have exactly the same problems and exactly the same opportunities, because what our goal should be is that all of us should be able to live up to our God-given capacities, to follow our dreams, and to succeed as citizens, as parents, and as workers. And unless we can

do that, the American dream will not mean the same thing in the 21st century as it does today.

For all the wonderful things that are going on, all the millions of jobs we have created, the fact that now we have more new businesses created every year than before, we've got more new millionaires every year than before, that's a good thing. But the world is changing so fast, there are a lot of people that are getting caught at the breaking points, and we've got to have an institutional response to give people the sense that they can preserve their families and preserve some order and stability in their lives, even as they are changing.

Every one of you is entitled to that. That's what you are entitled to. And if you really count, that's what your country will give you.

Thank you very much.

NOTE: The President spoke at 1:14 p.m. in Room 450 of the Old Executive Office Building. In his remarks, he referred to working mother Marina Foley and Karen Nussbaum, Director of the Women's Bureau at the Department of Labor.

Message on the Observance of Passover, 1995
April 10, 1995

Warm greetings to all who are observing Passover.

A celebration of both liberation and spring, Passover is a special opportunity to give thanks for the blessings of freedom and to remember the faith that sustains us in our bleakest hours. During this holiday, millions of Jews around the world draw inspiration from the example of the Israelites, who preserved their beliefs, their culture, and their dignity throughout the brutal

winter of slavery. When the warm spring of freedom finally came, the Jewish people rebuilt their community and thrived, ultimately infusing every corner of the earth with a powerful commitment to faith and family.

This year, let the Passover holiday remind us of the hope that can sustain us as a people. Hillary joins me in extending best wishes to all for a meaningful Passover.

BILL CLINTON

Message on the Observance of Easter, 1995
April 10, 1995

Warmest greetings to everyone observing Easter Sunday.

On this day of great hope and promise, Christians the world over celebrate God's redemptive grace as manifested in the life and teachings

of Jesus of Nazareth. This day symbolizes the victory of good over evil, hope over despair, and life over death. Rejoicing in the miracle of Easter, we pledge anew to hold in our hearts Christ's message of peace and joy.

As springtime returns to our corner of the earth, we are reminded of the beauty of new beginnings. Our faith in God lifts our spirits, and many Americans step back from the concerns of daily life to reflect on the power of our religious traditions and on the values they teach us. During this time of renewal, let us all thank God for the countless wonders of creation and rededicate ourselves to the common ideals that have made ours a land of infinite blessings.

Hillary joins me in extending best wishes to all for a joyous Easter celebration.

BILL CLINTON

Statement on Signing the Emergency Supplemental Appropriations and Rescissions for the Department of Defense to Preserve and Enhance Military Readiness Act of 1995
April 10, 1995

Today I have signed into law H.R. 889, an Act "Making emergency supplemental appropriations and rescissions to preserve and enhance the military readiness of the Department of Defense for the fiscal year ending September 30, 1995, and for other purposes."

I commend the Congress for its action on my request to replenish the Department of Defense for funds used to perform contingency operations in the Persian Gulf, Somalia, Rwanda, Haiti, and elsewhere. These funds are required to ensure that our forces are provided the resources they need to continue their superb performance.

I also commend the Congress for recognizing that to maintain peace in today's world, we must continue our investments in a number of key nonmilitary programs. I commend the Congress for making certain that the United States is able to fulfill its promise to the Russians that is linked to their removal of troops from the Baltics. The Nunn-Lugar program was also spared from reductions that would seriously impair its effectiveness. In addition to enabling continued progress in dismantling the weapons of mass destruction in the former Soviet Union, the Nunn-Lugar program helps ensure that personnel in the strategic rocket forces of the former Soviet Union do not become a source of instability.

Although funding for debt forgiveness linked to the historic peace agreement between Jordan and Israel was removed from this bill, it remains urgent that the Congress pass debt relief for Jordan as part of legislation that can be signed into law. This agreement has improved prospects for overall peace in the region markedly, and I urge the Congress to support this American promise.

Regrettably, rescissions will reduce some of my Administration's technology priorities, which serve as a foundation for America's future competitiveness and national security. Nevertheless, reductions in this Act are less than those in earlier versions of the bill. The Technology Reinvestment Project (TRP), Advanced Technology Program (ATP), and National Information Infrastructure grants program will remain vital components of my Administration's technology-related initiatives.

Despite my Administration's objections, the Act contains a provision that will rescind $1.5 million for listing threatened and endangered species and determining critical habitats needed for the recovery of such species, while imposing a moratorium until the end of this fiscal year on the remaining funds. As a result, these provisions will impair the Administration's ability to proceed on its recently announced package of reform principles and consequently, our ability to respond to the needs and concerns of private landowners.

WILLIAM J. CLINTON

The White House,
April 10, 1995.

NOTE: H.R. 889, approved April 10, was assigned Public Law No. 104-6.

Letter to Congressional Leaders Transmitting a Report on Haiti
April 10, 1995

Dear Mr. Speaker: *(Dear Mr. President:)*

Attached, pursuant to section 3 of Public Law 103–423, is the sixth monthly report on the situation in Haiti.

Sincerely,

WILLIAM J. CLINTON

NOTE: Identical letters were sent to Newt Gingrich, Speaker of the House of Representatives, and Strom Thurmond, President pro tempore of the Senate.

The President's News Conference With Prime Minister Benazir Bhutto of Pakistan
April 11, 1995

The President. Please be seated. Good afternoon. It's a great pleasure for me to welcome Prime Minister Bhutto to the White House. I'm especially pleased to host her today because of the tremendous hospitality that the Prime Minister and the Pakistani people showed to the First Lady and to Chelsea on their recent trip.

I've heard a great deal about the visit, about the people they met, their warm welcome at the Prime Minister's home, about the dinner the Prime Minister gave in their honor. The food was marvelous, they said, but it was the thousands of tiny oil lamps that lit the paths outside the Red Fort in Lahore that really gave the evening its magical air. I regret that here at the White House I can only match that with the magic of the bright television lights. [*Laughter*]

Today's meeting reaffirms the longstanding friendship between Pakistan and the United States. It goes back to Pakistan's independence. At the time, Pakistan was an experiment in blending the ideals of a young democracy with the traditions of Islam. In the words of Pakistan's first President, Mohammed Ali Jinnah, "Islam and its idealism have taught us democracy. It has taught us the equality of man, justice, the fair play to everybody. We are the inheritors of the glorious traditions and are fully alive to our responsibilities and obligations." Today, Pakistan is pursuing these goals of combining the practice of Islam with the realities of democratic ideals, moderation, and tolerance.

At our meetings today, the Prime Minister and I focused on security issues that affect Pakistan, its neighbor India, and the entire South Asian region. The United States recognizes and respects Pakistan's security concerns. Our close relationships with Pakistan are matched with growing ties with India. Both countries are friends of the United States, and contrary to some views, I believe it is possible for the United States to maintain close relations with both countries.

I told the Prime Minister that if asked, we will do what we can to help these two important nations work together to resolve the dispute in Kashmir and other issues that separate them. We will also continue to urge both Pakistan and India to cap and reduce and finally eliminate their nuclear and missile capabilities. As Secretary Perry stressed during his visit to Pakistan earlier this year, we believe that such weapons are a source of instability rather than a means to greater security. I plan to work with Congress to find ways to prevent the spread of nuclear weapons and to preserve the aims of the Pressler amendment, while building a stronger relationship with a secure, more prosperous Pakistan. Our two nations' defense consultative group will meet later this spring.

In our talks the Prime Minister and I also discussed issues of global concern, including peacekeeping and the fight against terrorism and narcotics trafficking. I want to thank Prime Minister Bhutto and the Pakistani officers and soldiers who have worked so closely with us in many peacekeeping operations around the globe, most recently in Haiti, where more than 800 Pakistanis are taking part in the United Nations operation.

On the issue of terrorism, I thank the Prime Minister for working with us to capture Ramzi Yusuf, one of the key suspects in the bombing in the World Trade Center. We also reviewed our joint efforts to bring to justice the cowardly terrorist who murdered two fine Americans in Karachi last month. I thanked the Prime Minister for Pakistan's effort in recent months to eradicate opium poppy cultivation, to destroy heroin laboratories, and just last week, to extradite two major traffickers to the United States. We would like this trend to continue.

Finally, the Prime Minister and I discussed the ambitious economic reform and privatization programs she has said will determine the well-being of the citizens of Pakistan and other Moslem nations. Last year, at my request, our Energy Secretary, Hazel O'Leary, led a mission to Pakistan which opened doors for many U.S. firms who want to do business there. Encouraged by economic growth that is generating real dividends for the Pakistani people, the United States and other foreign firms are beginning to commit significant investments, especially in the energy sector. I'm convinced that in the coming years, the economic ties between our peoples will grow closer, creating opportunities, jobs and profits for Pakistanis and Americans alike.

Before our meetings today, I was reminded that the Prime Minister first visited the White House in 1989 during her first term. She left office in 1990, but then was returned as Prime Minister in free and fair elections in 1993. Her presence here today testifies to her strong abilities and to Pakistan's resilient democracy. It's no wonder she was elected to lead a nation that aims to combine the best of the traditions of Islam with modern democratic ideals. America is proud to claim Pakistan among her closest friends.

Madam Prime Minister.

Prime Minister Bhutto. Mr. President, ladies and gentlemen: I'd like to begin by thanking the President for his kind words of support and encouragement.

Since 1989, my last visit to Washington, both the world and Pak-U.S. relations have undergone far-reaching changes. The post-cold-war era has brought into sharp focus the positive role that Pakistan, as a moderate, democratic,

Islamic country of 130 million people, can play, and the fact that it is strategically located at the tri-junction of South Asia, Central Asia, and the Gulf, a region of both political volatility and economic opportunity.

Globally, Pakistan is active in U.N. peacekeeping operations. We are on the forefront of the fight against international terrorism, narcotics, illegal immigration, and counterfeit currency. We remain committed to the control and elimination of weapons of mass destruction as well as the delivery systems on a regional, equitable, and nondiscriminatory basis.

Since 1993, concerted efforts by Pakistan and the United States to broaden the base of bilateral relations have resulted in steady progress. In September 1994, in a symbolic gesture, the United States granted Pakistan about $10 million in support for population planning. This was announced by the Vice President at the Cairo summit on population planning. This was followed by the Presidential mission led by Energy Secretary Hazel O'Leary, which resulted in agreement worth $4.6 billion being signed. And now, during my visit here, we are grateful to the administration and the Cabinet Secretaries for having helped us sign $6 billion more of agreements between Pakistan and the United States.

During the Defense Secretary's visit to Pakistan in January 1995, our countries decided to revive the Pakistan-United States Defense Consultative Group. And more recently, we had the First Lady and the First Daughter visit Pakistan, and we had an opportunity to discuss women's issues and children's issues with the First Lady. And we found the First Daughter very knowledgeable. We found Chelsea very knowledgeable on Islamic issues. I'm delighted to learn from the President that Chelsea is studying Islamic history and has also actually read our holy book, the Koran Shariah.

I'm delighted to have accepted President Clinton's invitation to Washington. This is the first visit by a Pakistani Chief Executive in 6 years. President Clinton and I covered a wide range of subjects, including Kashmir, Afghanistan, Central Asia, Gulf, Pakistan-India relations, nuclear proliferation, U.N. peacekeeping, terrorism, and narcotics.

I briefed him about corporate America's interest in Pakistan, which has resulted in the signing of $12 billion worth of MOU's in the last 17 months since our government took office. I urged an early resolution of the core issue of Kashmir, which poses a great threat to peace and security in our region. It has retarded progress on all issues, including nuclear and missile proliferation. A just and durable solution is the need of the hour, based on the wishes of the Kashmiri people, as envisaged in the Security Council resolutions. Pakistan remains committed to engage in a substantive dialog with India to resolve this dispute but not in a charade that can be used by our neighbor to mislead the international community. I am happy to note that the United States recognizes Kashmir as disputed territory and maintains that a durable solution can only be based on the will of the Kashmiri people.

Pakistan asked for a reassessment of the Pressler amendment, which places discriminatory sanctions on Pakistan. In our view, this amendment has been a disincentive for a regional solution to the proliferation issue. Pakistan has requested the President and the administration to resolve the problem of our equipment, worth $1.4 billion, which is held up. I am encouraged by my discussions with the President this morning and the understanding that he has shown for Pakistan's position. I welcome the Clinton administration's decision to work with Congress to revise the Pressler amendment.

Thank you, Mr. President,

The President. Thank you.

Terry [Terence Hunt, Associated Press].

Pressler Amendment

Q. Mr. President, you both mentioned the Pressler amendment, but I'm not sure what you intend to do. Will you press Congress to allow Pakistan to receive the planes that it paid for or to get its money back?

The President. Let me tell you what I intend to do. First of all, I intend to ask Congress to show some flexibility in the Pressler amendment so that we can have some economic and military cooperation. Secondly, I intend to consult with them about what we ought to do about the airplane sale.

As you know, under the law as it now exists, we cannot release the equipment. It wasn't just airplanes; it was more than that. We cannot release the equipment. However, Pakistan made payment. The sellers of the equipment gave up title and received the money, and now it's in storage. I don't think what happened was fair to Pakistan in terms of the money. Now under

the law, we can't give up the equipment. The law is clear. So I intend to consult with the Congress on that and see what we can do.

I think you know that our administration cares very deeply about nonproliferation. We have worked very hard on it. We have lobbied the entire world community for an indefinite extension of the NPT. We have worked very hard to reduce the nuclear arsenals of ourselves and Russia and the other countries of the former Soviet Union. We are working for a comprehensive test ban treaty. We are working to limit fissile material production. We are working across the whole range of issues on nonproliferation. But I believe that the way this thing was left in 1990 and the way I found it when I took office requires some modification, and I'm going to work with the Congress to see what progress we can make.

Kashmir

Q. Mr. President, what was your response to Pakistan's suggestion that the United States would play an active role in the solution of the Kashmir issue?

The President. The United States is willing to do that, but can, as a practical matter, only do that if both sides are willing to have us play a leading role. A mediator can only mediate if those who are being mediated want it. We are more than willing to do what we can to try to be helpful here.

And of course, the Indians now are talking about elections. It will be interesting to see who is eligible to vote, what the conditions of the elections are, whether it really is a free referendum of the people's will there. And we have encouraged a resolution of this. When Prime Minister Rao was here, I talked about this extensively with him. We are willing to do our part, but we can only do that if both sides are willing to have us play a part.

Helen [Helen Thomas, United Press International].

Nuclear Nonproliferation

Q. Madam Prime Minister, why do you need nuclear weapons? And Mr. President, don't you weaken your case to denuclearize the world when you keep making exceptions?

Prime Minister Bhutto. We don't have nuclear weapons. I'd like to clarify that, that we have no nuclear weapons. And this is our decision to demonstrate our commitment to——

Q. But you are developing them?

Prime Minister Bhutto. No. We have enough knowledge and capability to make and assemble a nuclear weapon, but we have voluntarily chosen not to either assemble a nuclear weapon, to detonate a nuclear weapon, or to export technology. When a country doesn't have the knowledge and says it believes in nonproliferation, I take that with a pinch of salt. But when a country has that knowledge—and the United States and other countries of the world agree that Pakistan has that knowledge—and that country does not use that knowledge to actually put together or assemble a device, I think that that country should be recognized as a responsible international player which has demonstrated restraint and not taken any action to accelerate our common goals of nonproliferation.

The President. On your question about making an exception, I don't favor making an exception in our policy for anyone. But I think it's important to point out that the impact of the Pressler amendment is directed only against Pakistan. And instead, we believe that in the end we're going to have to work for a nuclear-free subcontinent, a nuclear-free region, a region free of all proliferation of weapons of mass destruction. And the import of the amendment basically was rooted in the fact that Pakistan would have to bring into its country, would have to import the means to engage in an arms race, whereas India could develop such matters within its own borders.

The real question is, what is the best way to pursue nonproliferation? This administration has an aggressive, consistent, unbroken record of leading the world in the area of nonproliferation. We will not shirk from that. But we ought to do it in a way that is most likely to achieve the desired results. And at any rate, that is somewhat different from the question of the catch-22 that Pakistan has found itself in now for 5 years, where it paid for certain military equipment we could not, under the law, give it after the previous administration made a determination that the Pressler amendment covered the transaction, but the money was received, given to the sellers, and has long since been spent.

Q. But will you get a commitment from them to sign the Non-Proliferation Treaty?

The President. I will say again, I am convinced we're going to have to have a regional solution

there, and we are working for that. But we are not making exceptions.

Let me also make another point or two. We are not dealing with a country that has manifested aggression toward the United States in this area. We're dealing with a country that just extradited a terrorist or a suspected terrorist in the World Trade Center bombing; a country that has taken dramatic moves in improving its efforts against terrorism, against narcotics, that has just deported two traffickers—or extradited two traffickers to the United States; a country that has cooperated with us in peacekeeping in Somalia, in Haiti, and other places.

We are trying to find ways to fulfill our obligations, our legal obligations under the Pressler amendment, and our obligation to ourselves and to the world to promote nonproliferation and improve our relationships across the whole broad range of areas where I think it is appropriate.

Prime Minister Bhutto. May I just add that as far as we in Pakistan are concerned, we have welcomed all proposals made by the United States in connection with the regional solution to nonproliferation, and we have given our own proposals for a South Asia free of nuclear weapons and for a zero missile regime. So we have been willing to play ball on a regional level. Unfortunately, it's India that has not played ball. And what we are asking for is a leveling of the playing field so that we can attain our common goals of nonproliferation of weapons of mass destruction.

Kashmir

Q. Mr. President, why has the United States toned down its criticism of India's human rights violations in Kashmir—why has the United States toned down its criticism of India's human rights violations in Kashmir?

The President. I'm sorry, sir. I'm hard of hearing. Could you——

Q. Why has the United States toned down criticism of India's human rights violations in Kashmir?

The President. There's been no change in our policy there. We are still trying to play a constructive role to resolve this whole matter. That is what we want. We stand for human rights. We'd like to see this matter resolved. We are willing to play a mediating role. We can only do it if both parties will agree. And we would like very much to see this resolved.

Obviously, if the issue of Kashmir were resolved, a lot of these other issues we've been discussing here today would resolve themselves. At least, I believe that to be the case. And so, we want to do whatever the United States can do to help to resolve these matters because so much else depends on it, as we have already seen.

Self-Employed Health Insurance Legislation

Q. Mr. President, a domestic question on the bill you signed today for health insurance for the self-employed. Other provisions in that bill send a so-called wrong message on issues like affirmative action, a wrong message on wealthy taxpayers. Why then did you sign it as opposed to sending it back? Were you given any kind of signal that this was the best you'd get out of conference?

The President. Well, no. I signed the bill because—first of all, I do not agree with the exception that was made in the bill. I accept the fact that the funding mechanism that's in there is the one that's in there, and I think it's an acceptable funding mechanism. I don't agree with the exception that was made in the bill. And it's a good argument for a line-item veto that applies to special tax preferences as well as to special spending bills. If we had the line-item veto, it would have been a different story.

But I wanted this provision passed last year, and the Congress didn't do it. I think it's a downpayment on how we ought to treat the self-employed in our country. Why should corporations get a 100 percent deductibility and self-employed people get nothing or even 25 percent or 30 percent? I did it because tax day is April 17th, and these people are getting their records ready, and there are millions of them, and they are entitled to this deduction. It was wrong for it ever to expire in the first place.

Now, I also think it was a terrible mistake for Congress to take the provision out of the bill which allows—which would have required billionaires to pay taxes on income earned as American citizens and not to give up their citizenship just to avoid our income tax. But that can be put on any bill in the future. It's hardly a justification to veto a bill that something unrelated to the main subject was not in the bill. It is paid for.

This definitely ought to be done. It was a bad mistake by Congress. But that is not a jus-

tification to deprive over 3 million American business people and farmers and all of their families the benefit of this more affordable health care through this tax break.

Pakistan-U.S. Relations

Q. Mr. President, don't you think that the United States is giving wrong signals to its allies by dumping Pakistan, who has been an ally for half a century, in the cold after the Iran war?

The President. First of all, sir, I have no intention of dumping Pakistan. Since I've been President, we have done everything we could to broaden our ties with Pakistan, to deepen our commercial relationships, our political relationships, and our cooperation. The present problem we have with the fact that the Pressler amendment was invoked for the first—passed in 1985, invoked for the first time in 1990, and put Pakistan in a no-man's land where you didn't have the equipment and you'd given up the money. That is what I found when I became President. And I would very much like to find a resolution of it.

Under the amendment, I cannot—I will say again—under the law, I cannot simply release the equipment. I cannot do that lawfully. Therefore, we are exploring what else we can do to try to resolve this in a way that is fair to Pakistan. I have already made it clear to you— and I don't think any American President has ever said this before—I don't think it's right for us to keep the money and the equipment. That is not right. And I am going to try to find a resolution to it. I don't like this.

Your country has been a good partner, and more importantly, has stood for democracy and opportunity and moderation. And the future of the entire part of the world where Pakistan is depends in some large measure on Pakistan's success. So we want to make progress on this. But the United States (a) has a law and (b) has large international responsibilities in the area of nonproliferation which we must fulfill.

So I'm going to do the very best I can to work this out, but I will not abandon Pakistan. I'm trying to bring the United States closer to Pakistan, and that's why I am elated that the Prime Minister is here today.

Prime Minister Bhutto. And I'd like to say that we are deeply encouraged by the understanding that President Clinton has shown of the Pakistan situation vis-a-vis the equipment and vis-a-vis the security needs arising out of the Kashmir dispute and also that Pakistan is willing to play ball in terms of any regional situation.

We welcome American mediation to help resolve the Kashmir dispute. We are very pleased to note that the United States is willing to do so, if India responds positively. And when my President goes to New Delhi next month, this is an issue which he can take up with the Prime Minister of India. But let's get down to the business of settling the core dispute of Kashmir so that our two countries can work together with the rest of the world for the common purpose of peace and stability.

The President. Thank you.

NOTE: The President's 92d news conference began at 1:50 p.m. in the Cross Hall at the White House. In his remarks, he referred to Prime Minister P.V. Narasimha Rao of India.

Statement on Signing Self-Employed Health Insurance Legislation
April 11, 1995

Today I have signed into law H.R. 831, the "Self-Employed Health Insurance Act," that extends permanently the tax deductibility of health insurance premiums for the self-employed and their dependents.

The Tax Reform Act of 1986 (Public Law 99–514) provided a 25 percent tax deduction for health insurance premiums for the self-employed and their dependents. However, this deduction expired on December 31, 1993. This Act reinstates the 25 percent tax deduction for health insurance premiums for 1994 and permanently increases that deduction to 30 percent beginning in 1995.

I strongly support the permanent extension of this deduction. This Act will permit 3.2 million self-employed individuals to claim this deduction for health insurance premiums on their income tax returns, beginning with returns filed for 1994. By making this deduction permanent, we are treating the self-employed more like other employers—as they should be.

The increase in the deduction to 30 percent is a step in the right direction. In 1993, in the Health Security Act, I proposed an increase in the deduction to 100 percent. Increasing the amount of the deduction will make health insurance more affordable for self-employed small business people who are today paying some of the highest insurance premiums in the Nation.

In approving H.R. 831, however, I must note my regret that the bill contains a provision that repeals, as of January 17, 1995, the current tax treatment for the sale or exchange of radio and television broadcast facilities and cable television systems to minority-owned businesses (so-called "section 1071 benefits").

My Administration has undertaken a comprehensive review of affirmative action programs, including certain aspects of the section 1071 benefits. The Act has unfortunately preempted the Administration's ability to examine section 1071 in the context of this comprehensive review.

I am also concerned that, in repealing section 1071 benefits, a highly objectionable provision was added to H.R. 831 in conference. This provision will permit certain pending applicants to receive section 1071 benefits, while denying them to other pending applicants. This is a perfect example of where a President could use line-item veto authority to weed out objectionable special interest provisions. I urge the Congress to appoint conferees and move forward expeditiously with line-item veto legislation that provides authority—this year—to eliminate special interest tax and spending provisions.

Finally, I regret that the conferees on the part of the House of Representatives objected to including in H.R. 831 a provision that would have closed a tax loophole for the wealthy. This provision, which was in the Senate-passed version of the bill, closely resembled a provision I proposed in my FY 1996 Budget. The provision would have prevented wealthy Americans from avoiding their U.S. tax obligations by renouncing their citizenship.

Despite these concerns, I am signing H.R. 831 because of the very important benefits this legislation will provide to our Nation's self-employed and their families.

WILLIAM J. CLINTON

The White House,

April 11, 1995.

NOTE: H.R. 831, approved April 11, was assigned Public Law No. 104–7.

Remarks on Arrival at Fort Benning, Georgia
April 12, 1995

Thank you very much, Senator Nunn, General Hendrix, Congressman Bishop, Congressman Collins, Mayor Peters, distinguished Georgia State officials and members of the legislature and local and county officials here. I am glad to be back in Georgia. If I had known that there had been no President here since 1977, I would have come to Fort Benning earlier. I'm glad to be here a little late.

You know, when Senator Nunn was reeling off all of the awards won by all the bases in Georgia, I thought to myself, well, that's why Georgia never suffered from any of the base closings. It had nothing to do with Sam Nunn's influence; it was all on the merits that you did so well. [*Laughter*]

I do want to say a special word of thanks to Senator Nunn for his leadership over so many years in behalf of a strong American military and especially for his counsel and advice to me after I became President. Having been a Governor, having never served in the Congress before, it was especially invaluable to have the counsel of Sam Nunn about matters of national security.

As I have said many times all across this country, the mission we face today as a people is to move into the 21st century, now just 5 years away, still the strongest country in the world, the world's greatest force for peace and freedom and democracy and still the country with the American dream alive, the dream that if you work hard and make the most of your own life, you can live up to your God-given capacities.

I believe that in this challenging but hopeful time we have to do a number of very important tasks. We are up there now trying to change the way Government works. We've been working on that for 2 years, to make it smaller and less bureaucratic but still able to do the work of the people. We have to create more economic opportunities for our people, and we are working on that—over 6 million new jobs in the last 2 years.

We have to invest in the education and training of our people. Much as the military has done, we must do for all Americans, and not just when they're young but throughout their work lives, to enable people to make the most of their own lives. We know clearly that in the 21st century, what you earn will depend upon what you can learn. And we know that the great divide in our country today between those that are doing well and those that are struggling is often defined by how much education they have and what they still can learn.

And finally and still critically, we have to strengthen our security at home and around the world. At Fort Benning, you have done a magnificent job of achieving that last goal. You are fulfilling the mission that President Roosevelt left to us. In his last speech, which he did not live to deliver, Franklin Roosevelt wrote these words, "We have learned in the agony of war that great power involves great responsibility. We as Americans do not choose to deny our responsibility." I thank you, America's soldiers, for upholding FDR's last commitment.

General Hendrix gave me a brief rundown of the commands based here, and I know that you are all proud of your work. But let me say a special word of thanks to those of you who served in Somalia, to those of you who went to Rwanda and saved so many lives there, to those of you who responded so quickly when Iraq made a move last fall toward Kuwait's border. When we sent you to the Persian Gulf, Iraq withdrew. And I thank you for that, and so do the people of Kuwait.

I have recently returned from Haiti, and I want to say a special word of thanks to the MP's, the engineers, the medics, the army civil-

bove left: Jogging with Special
lympians at Hains Point, June 29.
bove: Discussing welfare reform
th Cabinet members, Members
Congress, Governors, and State
d local officials at Blair House,
nuary 28.
ft: Meeting with search and
scue teams at the State Fair
ounds Arena in the aftermath
the bombing of the Alfred P.
urrah Federal Building in
klahoma City, OK, April 23.
ght: Accepting a ceremonial
eck representing the proceeds
a National Performance Review
tiative from the Vice President
d Federal Communications
mmission Chairman Reed
ndt at the Old Post Office,
arch 27.

March 27, 1995

PAY TO THE ORDER OF **The American Taxpayer** $ 7,736,020,384

Seven billion seven hundred thirty-six million twenty thousand three hundred eighty-four DOLLARS

For the Opportunity to Compete   *Personal Communications Services Industry*

Above: Greeting United Nations and U.S. troops at Warrior Base i Port-au-Prince, Haiti, March 31.
Left: Discussing agricultural issues with farmers in Billings, M June 1.
Right: Conferring with the Vice President in the Oval Office, March 8.
Overleaf: Finding time for Sock outside the White House, March

ians from this base who helped to give the people of Haiti a second chance. Ten days ago I saw dozens of hand-painted signs all across Port-au-Prince with three simple words, "Thank you, America." They were thanking you, Fort Benning. You did something remarkable, something astonishing, and something for which those people and our people should all be very grateful.

I also want to congratulate you on repeating your award, the Commander in Chief's Army Community of Excellence Award. I was kind of hoping my basketball team would do that this year. [*Laughter*] And I know just how hard it is to do. Are any of you planning on going for a "three-peat," I wonder? What do you think? [*Applause*]

I want to say, I know you won the last two awards with the help of someone who won't be around, and I'd like to especially acknowledge Sergeant Major Acebes, who is retiring tomorrow after 30 years. Could you stand up, sir? [*Applause*] I know a lot about him. A Ranger, a Special Forces soldier, a master parachutist, he's done it all. He's also reputed to be the best listener in the Army. He let his bulldog, Sister, even chew his ear off at one time. See, the President finds out things. [*Laughter*]

Ladies and gentlemen, even though we have downsized the military dramatically, and many of you have helped in that process and it has been somewhat traumatic, I think it is fair to say that no major organization in the history of the United States has ever gone through so much change so rapidly, with such a high level of professionalism and commitment and ultimate success. We still have the best trained, best equipped, most highly motivated, most effective military in the world.

It is now important that we do whatever we can and whatever we must to maintain that strength. On Monday, I was pleased to sign the defense supplemental appropriations bill, which will give us more funds in this fiscal year to maintain the readiness of our forces.

Even as you have served as such a valuable force for America's security interests around the world, I would like to close by thanking you for being a valuable force for our long-term security here at home. For so many of you are

role models to our young people, role models to those who are discouraged, who may want to quit, who may think that they can't make the most of their lives, who understand that they may have personal problems or be living in a country with big economic problems that they don't feel they can overcome. All of you can make a difference.

And our security involves what we do here at home as well as what we do beyond our borders. We spent a lot of effort, the Congress and I have, in the last 2 years, making sure that we could reduce the Federal Government dramatically and give that money back to our local communities to hire more police officers and to take other steps to make our streets safer. That's a part of our security, giving our people reward for work, permitting them to take a little time off without losing their jobs or giving them help in providing health care. That's a part of our security.

But doing something about the crime and the violence and the still-rampant abuse of drugs and alcohol among our young people, that is also a part of our security. And I cannot tell you how many places I go around this country where young people who are despairing, who are confused, who don't know what they're going to do with their lives at least look at you and know that if they live by old-fashioned values and they support the American way, they can succeed. You are that to them.

So I ask you, never forget that your mission in improving, enhancing, and protecting our security not only involves what you may be called upon to do in distant places around the world but what you may do every day just walking down a street or speaking to a child or standing tall so that people can see that in this country if you do the right thing, you can live a good life and be a great American.

Thank you, and God bless you all.

NOTE: The President spoke at noon at Lawson Army Air Field. In his remarks, he referred to Maj. Gen. John W. Hendrix, Commanding General, and Sgt. Maj. William Acebes, Command Sergeant Major, U.S. Army Infantry Center, Fort Benning; and Mayor Bobby Peters of Columbus, GA.

Remarks at the Franklin D. Roosevelt 50th Anniversary Commemoration in Warm Springs, Georgia
April 12, 1995

Thank you very much. Governor Miller, President Carter, other distinguished honorees, Commissioner Tanner, Mr. Barrett, Anne Roosevelt, and members of your family: Thank you so much for your wonderful remarks. And Arthur Schlesinger, thank you for yours. After the last three speakers, I see I don't have to worry about whether what I am about to say would be considered too political on this occasion. [*Laughter*] I am delighted to be joined here by two Members of Congress, Congressman Collins and Congressman Bishop; many State officials; and appropriately for this day, the Social Security Administrator, Shirley Chater. I thank the Morehouse Glee Club. I couldn't help thinking when I walked up here and heard them singing that President Roosevelt would have been happy to have had the opportunity to walk down these lanes and hear those melodic voices.

In the 50 years since Franklin Roosevelt died in this house behind me, many things have happened to our country. Many wonderful things have changed life forever for Americans and have enabled Americans to change life forever for people all across our planet. This is a time when we no longer think in the terms that people thought in then and perhaps a time when we cannot feel about each other or our leaders the way people felt then.

But I think it's important just to take a moment to remember that even though Franklin Roosevelt was the architect of grand designs, he touched Americans, tens of millions of them, in a very personal way. They felt they knew him as their friend, their father, their uncle. They felt that he was doing all the things he was doing in Washington to help them. He wanted them to keep their farms and have their jobs, have the power line run out by the house. He wanted them to be able to have some security in their old age and see their children come home in peace from war.

In my home State of Arkansas, the per capita income of the people was barely half the national average when Franklin Roosevelt began his work. And when he came there during the Depression, people were so poor that when they were preparing for him to come, there was lit-

erally not enough paint to paint the houses along his route. And so they all split the paint and painted the fronts of their homes so at least the President could see the effort they made. That's the way people felt.

My grandfather, who helped to raise me, was a man with a grade school education in a tiny southern hamlet who worked as a dirt farmer, a small storekeeper, and for an icehouse back before we had refrigerators and there really were iceboxes. He really thought Franklin Roosevelt cared about whether he had a job. And I never will forget the story he told me during the Depression when he came home—the only time in his life when he was unable to buy my mother a new dress for Easter, and he wept because he did not have $2. He thought Franklin Roosevelt cared whether people like him could buy their children Easter outfits. That is the way people felt. And even into the 1960's, when as a young man I began to go from town to town working for other people who sought public office, there were people in the sixties who had pictures of President Roosevelt, in modest homes in tiny, remote towns, on their mantels or hanging on the wall because they thought he cared about them.

Like our greatest Presidents, he showed us how to be a nation in time of great stress. He taught us again and again that our Government could be an instrument of democratic destiny, that it could help our children to do better. He taught us that patriotism was really about pulling together, working together, and bringing out the best in each other, not about looking down our nose at one another and claiming to be more patriotic than our fellow countrymen and women.

Above all, he taught us about the human spirit. In the face of fear and doubt and weariness, he showed we could literally will ourselves to overcome, as he had done—and as has been already said so powerfully—in his own life. He led us from the depths of economic despair, through a depression, to victory in the war, to the threshold of the promise of the post-war America he unfortunately never lived to see.

He did all these things and so many more to change America and the world, a lot of things we just take for granted today, that even today nobody's tried to do away with, like the Securities and Exchange Commission, which safeguards our financial markets, or the Tennessee Valley Authority or the very emblem of the New Deal, Social Security.

He and his remarkable wife, Eleanor, whom we remembered together and who we must remember today, did a lot of things just to bring out both the problems and the potential of Americans. And he also changed America with a brilliant team. I saw here today Mr. Schlesinger, I was looking at Mr. Galbraith sitting out there, wondering how many of you were going back over your lives and remembering what you were doing then. I'm very honored to have as my Deputy Chief of Staff here Harold Ickes, whose father was President Roosevelt's Secretary of the Interior. Like me, this is his first visit to Warm Springs. But he has lived with the honor of that legacy for his entire life.

I think it's also important that we remember today that President Roosevelt helped to found the March of Dimes, and today marks the 40th anniversary of Dr. Salk's discovery of the polio vaccine, developed because of the work of the March of Dimes, which continues to the present day.

If I might pick up on something that Arthur Schlesinger and that Anne said, I think if President Roosevelt were here, he would be asking us, "Well, this is all very nice, and I appreciate the honor, but what are you doing today? What are you doing today?"

At the end of the war, he left us what may be his most enduring legacy, a generation prepared to meet the future—a vision most clearly embodied in the GI bill, which passed Congress in June of 1944 just a few days after D-Day but before the end of the war in Europe and in Asia. He wanted to give returning GI's a hand up. He really captured the essence of America's social compact. Those people that served, they had been responsible, and they were entitled to opportunity.

The GI bill gave generations of veterans a chance to get an education, to build strong families and good lives, and to build the Nation's strongest economy ever, to change the face of America, and with it, to enable us to change the face of the world. The GI bill helped to unleash a prosperity never before known.

In the fifties, the sixties, and the seventies, all kinds of Americans benefited from the economy educated veterans and their fellow Americans built. And we grew, and we grew together. Nothing like it had ever been seen before. Every income group in America, every racial group, all were improving their standing and growing together, not growing apart.

Somewhere around 20 years ago, that began to change, not because of anything that was wrong with the GI bill or wrong with the institutions we had put in place but because the world changed. The economy became more global. Our financial markets became more global. There was an information and a technological revolution which exploded the unity of America's economic progress. And all of a sudden, we began to grow apart, not together, even when the economy was growing. We divided growth from equality for the first time since Franklin Roosevelt became President, and it has caused a terrible slew of troubles for the American people over the last 15 to 20 years.

In the 1980's, our response—since Arthur Schlesinger said that President Roosevelt was for democratic capitalism, I think you could say that the response in the 1980's was conservative Keynesianism. That is, blame the Government and blame the past, but deficit spend under the title of tax cuts and tilt the tax cuts to the wealthiest Americans because it is their investment that creates jobs.

Well, the massive deficits did spur growth, but it gave us the first permanent Government deficit in the entire history of the United States. And the inequality among working people did not go away; instead, it got worse. Meanwhile, our investment in our people—the thing Franklin Roosevelt believed most in—began to slow down, even in education and training, because we decided that there was something wrong with public activity.

The result: We intensified the splits in our economy. We divided even the great American middle class as incomes stagnated, as people worked longer hours and slept less and spent less time with their children and still felt less secure. And at the same time, many good things were happening, but only to those who were prepared to seize the changes that we live with.

It is amazing that in America we could have more than half the people today living on the same or lower incomes than they were enjoying 15 years ago and still creating the largest number of new jobs and having the largest numbers of millionaires coming out of our economy than we have ever known, these two things existing side by side, the good and the bad.

If President Roosevelt were here, what would he see today? He would see a country leading the world's economy, producing millions of jobs with people literally afraid that their lives are moving away from them. He would see a world of turbo-charged capitalism in which it is possible to succeed economically, but millions of Americans don't know if they can hold their families and their communities and the disciplined rhythms of life together. He would see people who are confused, saying, "Well, if there is an economic recovery, why haven't I felt it? He would see people angry, saying, "I've worked hard all my life; why was I let go at the age of 50, and how am I supposed to send my kids to college?"

He would see people who are cynical, a luxury no one could afford when one in four Americans were out of work or when our very existence was at stake in the Second World War. Now we can afford the luxury, and we have it in abundance, saying, "Well, it doesn't make any difference, nothing we do makes any difference. If I hear good news, I know they're lying."

He would see, indeed, a country encrusted with cynicism. He would see an insensitivity on the part of some people who say, "Well, I made it, and why should I help anyone else? If you help someone, all you make is an ingrate." He would also see a profound sense of division in the American psyche, people who really do believe that if someone else does well, that's why I'm not doing so well, and in order for me to do well, someone else must not do that well. That was not Franklin Roosevelt. He was not cynical. He was not angry. He was not insensitive. He did not believe in division. And he certainly was not confused.

He believed that we had to pull together and move forward. He believed we always had to keep the American dream alive. Langston Hughes once said, "What happens to a dream deferred? Does it shrivel like a raisin in the sun, or does it explode?" For Franklin Roosevelt, it was neither.

My fellow Americans, there is a great debate going on today about the role of Government, and well there ought to be. F.D.R. would have loved this debate. He wouldn't be here defending everything he did 50 years ago. He wouldn't be here denying the existence of the information age. Should we reexamine the role of Government? Of course we should. Do we need big, centralized bureaucracies in the computer age? Often we don't. Should we reassert the importance of the values of self-reliance and independence? You bet we should. He never meant for anybody, anybody, to become totally dependent on the Government when they could do things for themselves.

But should we abandon the notion that everybody counts and that we're going up or down together? Should we abandon the idea that the best thing we can do is to give each other a hand up, not a handout? Should we walk away from the idea that America has important responsibilities at home and abroad and we walk away from them at our peril? The answer would be, from him, a resounding no.

My fellow Americans, Franklin Roosevelt's first job was to put America back to work. Our big problem today is, Americans are back to work, but they feel insecure. They don't feel their work will be rewarded or valued. And we have to find a way to raise America's incomes by making Americans more productive and making this economy work in the way that President Roosevelt dreamed it would.

Everybody knows we have a Government deficit. I'm proud of the fact that we brought it down 3 years in a row for the first time since Mr. Truman was President. Everybody knows that, but let's not forget that we also have an educational deficit. Education is the fault line in America today. Those who have it are doing well in the global economy; those who don't are not doing well. We cannot walk away from this fundamental fact. The American dream will succeed or fail in the 21st century in direct proportion to our commitment to educate every person in the United States of America.

And so I believe if President Roosevelt were here, he would say, "Let's have a great old-fashioned debate about the role of Government, and let's make it less bureaucratic and more flexible. And those people in Washington don't know everything that should be done in Warm Springs." And he would say, "Let's put a sense of independence back into our welfare system." But he would also say, "Let's not forget that what really works in life is when people get a hand up, not a handout, when Americans go up or down together."

If you look at this great debate we're having in Washington with our twin deficits, the budget deficit and the education deficit, I say to you, we try to solve one without the other at our peril. We have brought the deficit down, and we will work to do it more. Congress and I, we will fight about what kinds of cuts we ought to have, but we'll get there and we'll bring it down some more. We already are running the first operating surplus in nearly 30 years, except for interest on the debt. And we will do better. But we cannot do it at the expense of education. We cannot do it at the expense of education.

There's a lot of talk about tax cuts. I say this, we have to worry about how much and who gets it and what for. We should not do it if we have to cut education. We should not do it if we have to explode the deficit. And if we're going to have a tax cut, we should do it in ways that lift the American people's income over the long run as well as the short run. We have to have—we have to have a sense that our future depends upon the development of our people. That's why I say, if we're going to have a tax cut, we must give people some tax relief for the cost of education. That is the most important tax cut we can have, and I will insist upon it and will not support a legislative bill that does not have it.

You know, everybody wants to have more disposable income, but what we don't want to have is disposable futures. So let us not sacrifice the future to the present. And let us not have a false choice between a budget deficit and an education deficit. We can have both.

I wish President Roosevelt were here. I wish he were just sort of on our shoulder to deride those who are cynical, those who are skeptical, those who are negative, and most of all, those who seek to play on fears to divide us. This country did not get here by permitting itself to be divided at critical times by race, by religion, by region, by income, you name it.

And just remember this: President Roosevelt died here, and they took his body on the train out, and America began to grieve. Imagine what the people looked like by the sides of the railroad track. Imagine the voices that were singing in the churches. They were all ages, men and women, rich and poor, black, white, Hispanic, and whoever else was living here then. And they were all doing it because they thought he cared about them and that their future mattered in common. They were Americans first. They were Americans first. That was his contract with America. Let it be ours.

Thank you, and God bless you.

NOTE: The President spoke at 1:14 p.m. at the "Remembering Franklin D. Roosevelt" 50th anniversary commemorative service at the Little White House. In his remarks, he referred to Gov. Zell Miller of Georgia; Joe Tanner, commissioner, Georgia Department of Natural Resources; Lonice C. Barrett, director, Georgia State Parks and Historic Sites; Anne Roosevelt, granddaughter of Franklin D. Roosevelt; Arthur M. Schlesinger, Roosevelt biographer; and John Kenneth Galbraith, author and economist.

Interview With Wolf Blitzer and Judy Woodruff of CNN
April 13, 1995

Ms. Woodruff. Mr. President, thank you for being with us.

The President. Glad to do it, Judy.

President's Goals and Republican Agenda

Ms. Woodruff. You are now well over 2 years into your Presidency. The common, increasingly common, perception out there is that because of the successes of the center-stage role that Newt Gingrich and the House Republicans have played, that your Presidency has been somehow diminished, made less relevant because of all the activity and the agenda-setting that they've been doing.

The President. Well, they had an exciting 100 days, and they dealt with a lot of issues that were in their contract. But let's look at what happens now. The bills all go to the United States Senate, where they have to pass, and then I have to decide whether to sign or veto them.

So now you will see the process unfolding. And I will have my opportunity to say where I stand on these bills and what I intend to do with the rest of our agenda. I have enjoyed watching this last 100 days, and have enjoyed giving them the chance to do what they were elected to do. And also I made it clear what I would not go along with.

Last Friday at the newspaper editors meeting, I went through item by item what's left on the Republican agenda that has not either been defeated or passed, and also the unfinished items on my agenda that will create more opportunity and more responsibility in this country.

Ms. Woodruff. But it's the Republican agenda. And I think it—isn't it the case that throughout American political history, the party that is controlling the agenda is dominating the American political scene?

The President. Well, I don't necessarily agree that it's the Republican agenda. You know, I brought up welfare reform before they did. I started reducing the deficit long before they did and without any help from them. We reduced the size of Government before they did. We reduced the burden of regulation before they did. We gave relief to the States from Federal rules before they did.

This can be an American agenda. And in addition to that, I have tried to make it absolutely clear that I believe that we must continue to press ahead nationally with the cause of education and training and that any tax relief must be geared to helping middle class people and to helping people educate themselves.

So I just simply disagree that it's an entirely Republican agenda. It's an American agenda. And there are a lot of things that are still unfinished on our agenda, but these things were started—many of the things that they talk about that will actually affect real people in their lives were begun under our administration.

Ms. Woodruff. But, Mr. President, again, the perception is Newt Gingrich has been out there on the news every day, the Republicans have been out there with headlines in the newspapers. How——

The President. Well, I'm not responsible—I can't control the perception. All I can do is show up for work every day. But I'll tell you this: our administration is the first administration in almost 30 years to run an operating surplus, that is, without interest on the debt. We have reduced the size of Government. We have done a lot of these things that they talk about. But more importantly, we've focused on creating opportunity for the American people.

Now, they are capturing the headlines now. They had their 100 days. Now the bills go to the Senate and the moderate Democrats, the moderate Republicans, and the President will have a huge say on what becomes law. I will have my say as the bills are debated in the Senate, and I'll decide whether to sign or veto them. So there will be more parity here as the American constitutional system unfolds.

And there are other items on our agenda that I want to see dealt with. I want them to raise the minimum wage. I want them to do something for education in the tax cut. I want them to deal with health care in a piece-by-piece basis. The American people thought I bit off too much at one time, so let's deal with it on a piece-by-piece basis. I've given them several elements that Republicans in the past have said they have supported.

I think the American people want us to work together. But meanwhile, look at where we are now compared with where we were 2 years ago. There are more jobs. There is more trade. There is a smaller Government, and we are moving in the right direction. That's all I can do. That's my agenda. If they are part of that— the American people can later sort out who gets credit for it when the elections get underway.

Taxes

Mr. Blitzer. Mr. President, Bob Dole, who is the Republican frontrunner right now for the Presidential nomination, has taken—accepted the pledge that he rejected in 1988, no more new taxes. Are you prepared to accept that pledge in New Hampshire as well, that you will not go forward with any new taxes?

The President. As a matter of principle, I think it's wrong for a President to do that. But look at our record. I told the American people exactly what I would do. I said the first time, when I go in I'm going to ask the wealthiest Americans to pay more, not because I'm for class warfare but because they can afford to. We'll cut spending, raise taxes on the wealthiest Americans, and bring the deficit down. We did that.

Now, what else did we do? We cut taxes on 15 million families with incomes of $25,000 a year or less an average of $1,000 a year. We made 90 percent of the small businesses eligible for a tax cut. We established a capital gains tax for investment, long-term and new businesses. We just—I just signed a bill passed by this Congress which I tried to pass last time which provides a tax cut for self-employed people for the cost of their health insurance. I have proposed a middle class tax cut in connection with continued deficit reduction and tied to education. That is my record.

I'm not out there raising taxes. I'm trying to lower the deficit and lower taxes. That is my record. That is my program for this Congress. That is the future. But on principle, I think a President runs the risk of breeding cynicism to sign that kind of pledge when you have no idea what will come forward.

Let me give you an example. I strongly believe that the Congress made a terrible mistake. The only tax break they've given anybody new this time is to reject my proposal to ask billionaires who gave up their American citizenship to get out of American taxes on money they made as Americans to pay their fair share. And for reasons I do not understand, the Republican Congress, in conference, in secret, after being lobbied by a former Republican Congressman and a former Republican Senator, let the billionaires off scot-free.

So if we sign that, am I raising taxes? I would sign that in a heartbeat. People ought to pay what they owe—they shouldn't be able to give up their citizenship—pay what they owe.

Mr. Blitzer. But you would have then signed that into law after they included it in the different package, the billionaires loophole.

The President. They didn't include the loophole, they refused to impose the tax. So what I think they ought to do is close the loophole. What I did was to give the small-business people and the farmers and the professionals whose families are unfairly denied a tax deduction for their health care costs that tax deduction so they could get it by tax day, which is next Monday. I had to do that. But they ought to put that back in. This is an unconscionable thing which has been done.

But would it violate the pledge, or not? That's the problem I have with the question you asked.

Mr. Blitzer. Let me ask you one more question on taxes. The flat tax: The Republicans have now authorized this commission that Jack Kemp will head to see if there's a possibility of going forward with a flat tax, a simple flat tax. Is this something that you think you would support?

The President. I'm for tax simplification. Anything we can do to simplify the Tax Code, con-

sistent with fairness and not exploding the deficit, we ought to do. The first time I heard about a flat tax I thought it sounded like a pretty good idea. But if you look at it, every analysis that I have seen done indicates that the flat tax proposals that are out there now will increase the deficit and increase taxes on all Americans with incomes of under $200,000 a year. So my answer is, I'm going to put a pencil to a piece of paper and figure out how it works. And my suggestion to the American people is that they should put a pencil to a piece of paper and see how it works.

We must not explode the deficit. And we must not have a big tax shift from people making over $200,000 to all people making under $200,000. That's not the fair thing to do.

President's Leadership

Ms. Woodruff. Well, in connection with that, Mr. President, you are the first President in something like I think it's 140 years to go this far in his Presidency without a single veto. Now, you've made some threats and you specifically made some at the end of last week. But House majority leader Dick Armey is out there, is just flatly saying that he thinks you're going to sign any tax cut bill, any tax bill that they send you. In other words, they're not taking you seriously.

The President. He's wrong. Keep in mind, why didn't I—I didn't have to veto anything in the last 2 years because it was only the third Congress since World War II, only the third Congress since World War II when a President passed more than 80 percent of its programs in the Congress. That's only happened—President Eisenhower did it, President Johnson did it, and I did it. The Congress did not send me anything they knew I was going to veto. So there was no need to veto.

Secondly, the abuse of the filibuster—and I say that advisedly, there has been an abuse of the filibuster, which means that one more than 40 Senators can hold up any bill—reduces the number of bills coming to the President's desk——

Ms. Woodruff. On which side are you talking?

The President. Well, in the last 2 years it worked for the Republicans. It may work for the Democrats this time. But the point is that the sheer number of bills coming to the President are now smaller than they used to be. Now, if I get the line-item veto—the line-item veto has passed the Senate; a line-item veto has passed the House. I worked very hard to get it through the Senate and to get the Democrats to go along with it, and they did. If they'll reconcile the differences, you will see a lot of vetoes under the line-item veto.

Ms. Woodruff. Well, again, on the veto point, I mean, you were just in Warm Springs yesterday honoring Franklin Delano Roosevelt. We looked into his record; over 13 years of his Presidency he had over 700 vetoes. And Arthur Schlesinger, the historian, was there at the ceremony. He was telling a reporter—he said Franklin Roosevelt loved a fight, and he said President Clinton would prefer to accommodate. Is that an accurate perception?

The President. No, I like to fight. That's how I got elected President. That's how I passed an economic program that broke the back of deficit spending and bipartisan irresponsibility. The Republicans and the Democrats sat up here for 12 years and told the American people what they wanted to hear. The Republican Presidents blamed the Democratic Congress. The Democratic Congress blamed the Republican Presidents. And they quadrupled the debt of this country when I got here.

What I did was to fight my battles in the Congress and by one vote in both Houses won a budget bill that reduced this deficit. I fought for a trade bill that gave us more trade. I fought to get a crime bill that would reduce the threat of violence on our streets. I've got things done that I wanted to signed. If they send me bad bills, I'll be happy to veto them. I think that the untold story of the last 2 years is how much we got done. I had no occasion to veto a bill. I have no doubt that I will have occasions to veto bills now.

Ms. Woodruff. But just quickly, Mr. President, again, maybe we're talking perceptions again, but the perception is that you are a President who will bend, who will not stick with what you originally said you were for. Hence, you've got people out there like Arthur Schlesinger saying he thinks you're an accommodator. I mean——

The President. Well, let me ask all those people then, if that's so true, why did I break the back of trickle-down economics? Why did I break the back of 12 years of Democratic and Republican irresponsibility in Washington, to reduce the deficit 3 years in a row for the first time since Mr. Truman was President? If that's so true, why were we able to pass the NAFTA,

which was deader than a doornail when I took office? If that's so true, why did we pass the crime bill with the assault weapons ban in it, which had been dead for 6 years? Why did we pass the Brady bill, dead for 7 years? Why did we pass family leave for working families, dead for 6 years? Because we got things done out of conviction and hard work.

Sometimes, it's more important what you do than what you don't do. Now, vetoes make a big splash. If they'll just simply send me some bad bills, I'll be more than happy to veto them. What we should be doing here is focusing on what we did to break gridlock, make this Government more responsible, and get things done. It was tough. It required hard fights. They were bitter, tough battles that we won. When you win, you don't have to veto. I like to win, and we won. And the American people are better off. But all this talk is, "Well, let's see some vetoes." Send me a bad bill, I'll be happy to veto it.

I have had three bills since this Congress started 100 days ago, three bills. They were all three bills I campaigned for President on: a bill to make Congress live under the laws it imposes on the private sector, a bill to reduce the burden of Federal action on State and local government, and a bill to provide a tax break to self-employed people for the health insurance costs they have. Those were things I ran for President on. How can I veto bills that I support? I support those bills.

Just because the Republican Congress passed them—I did not run for office to sign a pack of vetoes or to worry about my perception. I ran for office to turn this country around. This is a time of enormous change and uncertainty. Anytime a President takes on tough battles, gets things done, but tries to work through things in a spirit of good faith, you have to run the risk of changing perceptions.

It happened to Harry Truman. He barely had one in four people for it. And he was—until the last year of his campaign in 1948, he was regularly attacked not for being too decisive, too tough, too straightforward but for being too accommodationist—what did he stand for, where was he. These are—it's just part of the times. I can't worry about the perception. I have to be tough in fighting for what's right for the American people. That's what I have done. That's what I will do. I did it by passing bills the last 2 years. I'd like to do it by passing bills now, but that's up to the Congress. I told them Friday what I'd sign and what I'd veto. Let's see what they do.

Welfare Reform

Mr. Blitzer. Well, let's talk welfare reform, which, of course, is an issue very close to your heart. You have said you want to end welfare as we know it. The House version is apparently unacceptable to you, the Republican version passed in the House.

The President. Do you want to see a veto? If the Senate passes the House bill, I'd be happy to veto.

Mr. Blitzer. Well, the Senate looks like the Republicans are now suggesting they would take out some of the more—what you would consider onerous provisions of the House bill but still give the States block grants to reform welfare as the States, the Governors, want to do it— the Republican Governors, that is. Is that something you would accept?

The President. No, but I think that they deserve credit for making some progress. You know, the Catholic Bishops basically pointed out that the House bill could actually be a pro-abortion bill, could encourage abortion, it was so hard on children, and it was so weak on work. Now, the provisions proposed by these three Republican Governors that the Senate is looking at gets out a lot of the stuff that is tough on children and unfair to them. And that's good, and they deserve credit for that. It's still weak on work, and it's still unfair to the States that have huge growing populations of young children.

So this block grant proposal as it is written would put unbearable burdens on States, not necessarily—this is not a partisan issue, but the block grant proposal as written I think would be unfair to States like Texas and Florida, for example, and maybe very beneficial to States with static or declining welfare rolls.

Mr. Blitzer. Just to nail it down—so this Republican version in the Senate that is now being discussed, you would veto that?

The President. All we know about it is what we see in the papers. I believe that it is an improvement over the House bill. But it's got a long way to go. We need to be—what the American people want is to see people who are on welfare going to work and succeeding as workers and parents.

Now, what they've done that's good is they've adopted all my tough child support enforcement provisions. And I applauded the House for doing it. Line for line, they did it. I appreciate that, and it's good. The Senate now says, "Well, we're not going to be tough on children, we're not going to be—in effect, having a pro-abortion policy or at least a brutal-to-children policy." That's good. They deserve credit.

Now let's work on the work, and let's don't be fairer to the States that have bigger problems than some other States. The States—this proposal—I am for much, much, much more flexibility to the States. Keep in mind, it was our administration, not the two previous administrations but ours, that has given half the States the freedom to get out from under the Federal rules to do what they want on welfare. But we have to do it in a way that is fair to all the States. So my concern about the block grants is that it won't be fair to all the States.

Abortion

Mr. Blitzer. Just wrapping up this segment— on abortion, an issue you just raised, you have said repeatedly you would like to see abortion safe, legal, and rare. What have you done to make it rare?

The President. One of the things I've done to make it rare is to push very strongly for more adoptions and for cross-racial adoptions. One of the things that the Republicans and I agree on, although we may have some minor differences about how to do it, is that we should not hang adoptions up for years and years and years when there are cross-racial adoptions involved. If parents of one race want to adopt a child of another, they shouldn't be delayed and hung up by a lot of bureaucratic redtape. I think that is very important.

The other thing I think we have to do is to make it clear to people that if they have children, they will be able to raise them in dignity. I have tried to improve the lives of women and little children and support people who do bring children into this world, to say, "Okay, if you've got a child, even if you bore the child out of wedlock, you ought to have access to education and child care and medical care. And then you ought to get off welfare and go to work." I think if people see that they can bear children and still succeed in life, and if they understand that if they want to give the children up for adoption, that they can do that and know it would be done in a ready and proper way, I think those two things can really work to reduce abortions.

The other thing I think we have to do to reduce abortion is to keep campaigning against teen pregnancy. And we have worked very aggressively in this administration on anti-teen pregnancy campaigns. So those are three things we've done to try to make abortion more rare.

Russia

Ms. Woodruff. Mr. President, let's move to a somewhat different area, international relations. You're going to Russia in about a month, a little less than a month from now, to celebrate V–E Day, to meet with Boris Yeltsin. You are going despite the fact that the Russians have refused, so far, U.S. pleas that they not sell nuclear technology to Iran. And the question is, I mean, even setting Chechnya aside and what they've done there, given the fact that this whole question of nuclear proliferation poses such a dangerous specter—creates such a dangerous specter for the entire world, will the Russians pay no price for this policy of selling this technology to Iran?

The President. Well, first of all, let me explain why I'm going to Russia, and let's look at this issue in the larger context. We are still negotiating with the Russians on this issue. We do not want them to sell this technology to Iran. It is true what the Russians say, that it's light-water technology, it's the sort of thing North Korea is going to get as a part of denuclearizing North Korea. We don't want Iran to have anything, anything, that could enable it to move toward developing nuclear capacity, so that we do not support this. And we are continuing to work to try to dissuade them.

But look at our relationships with Russia in the broader context. First of all, I think it very important that the rest of the world continue to support democracy, economic reform, and nonaggression in Russia. If you look at where we are now compared to where we were 2 years ago, Russian reform, economically, is still in place, the democratic system is still in place in Russia, the elections system and the constitutional system is still functioning. They have come a long way.

They made this agreement with Iran before I became President. The question is, are they going to follow through on it or back off of it? But you have to see it in the larger context.

I am going, I might add, along with every other leader of a World War II country, to Russia because the Russians lost 20 million people in World War II, far more than any other country did. Their price was great. And part of their alienation from the rest of the world, and the West in particular, has been rooted in their collective consciousness that we never understood why they were more, we thought, paranoid, at least more isolated than the rest of us because of that cost. So I think I'm doing the right thing to go. I will continue to work on the Iranian thing, but I do not believe that disengaging with Russia and refusing to go and participate in this ceremony is the right way to do it.

Ms. Woodruff. Well, I understand what you're saying about history and about their sacrifice. And I think most Americans, no doubt, appreciate that point. But given the fact that the greatest danger out there facing this entire globe is nuclear proliferation, where is the United States prepared to draw the line?

The President. But what interest would it serve—if they can legally do this under international law, what interest would it serve for me to stay home when by going there and continuing to engage the Russians we might make progress?

Let me remind you of what has happened in Russia since I've been President. They have withdrawn all of their troops from the Baltics, for the first time since before World War II. We have completed START I. They are rapidly dismantling nuclear weapons. We have succeeded in getting all of the other former Soviet states to be nonnuclear states. So in the context of nonproliferation, we have made huge, huge progress in the last 2 years.

This is an area of disagreement. I intend to take it up with them. But I think engaging them, going at them, going right at them, and working through this is the way to do it.

Ms. Woodruff. Will they ultimately pay a price one way or another?

The President. Well, let's see what they do. Obviously, if they don't—obviously, if they do this, it will affect our relationships with them, just as all the positive things they've done have affected our relationships with them. The United States has been a very strong supporter of Russian reform. We have done everything we could to help them succeed, and we have gotten a lot for that. We have gotten a lot for that.

They are rapidly destroying their own nuclear missiles. We are moving in the right direction.

This is one area of disagreement, but it pales in comparison to all the progress we've made to lower the nuclear threat in the world in our other agreements with Russia.

Iran

Mr. Blitzer. Mr. President, you've had this dual containment policy towards Iran and Iraq. Yet, U.S. oil companies still are the biggest buyers of Iranian oil, and they sell it around the world except in the United States. There is some talk that you're thinking about strengthening the U.S. sanctions against Iran. Can you tell us where you stand on that?

The President. We're looking at what all of our options are. I think we need to be as firm as we can be. Our administration stepped in when Conoco signed that agreement, and they backed off of it. That was a good thing. And we are looking at what else we can do.

Mr. Blitzer. Well, you could pass proposed legislation or just take Executive orders to force U.S. companies to no longer purchase Iranian oil.

The President. We are looking at all of our options, and I'm going to get a report pretty soon on what I can do by Executive order, what I might ask the Congress to do. The Congress is also looking at this.

Every country that we speak with, every world leader I talk to in the region and beyond still believes that Iran is the biggest cause of instability and the biggest potential threat to the future. And they have chosen not to change their conduct, so we are forced to continue to look at our options.

American Prisoners in Iraq

Mr. Blitzer. How far are you willing to go in terms of Iraq in winning the release of the two American prisoners who are being held in Baghdad?

The President. I'm not prepared to make any concessions on the United Nations resolutions. The resolutions speak for themselves. Mr. Ekeus just issued his report in which he raised questions about what they might be doing on biological warfare. We saw in the horrible incident in the Japanese subway the potential of biological and chemical weapons in small vials, small amounts. So we have to separate the United Nations resolutions and the sanctions against

Iraq from this incident. I want those two Americans home; the government should give them clemency. They did not—clearly, they did not go across the border with any intent to do anything wrong. The United Nations has now taken responsibility for the mistake they made in letting them through the checkpoint. They should simply be released. It is the decent thing to do. But the United States cannot make any concessions on the sanctions issue to get their release. That would be wrong.

Cuba

Mr. Blitzer. One final loose end on an international issue, Cuba: Jesse Helms has a resolution, as you know, pending that would prevent the U.S. from dealing with companies in Europe or Canada or Japan that deal with Cuba, and this has caused an uproar around the world. You haven't taken a position on this Helms amendment yet. Are you prepared to say you support it or oppose it?

The President. I support the Cuban Democracy Act, which was passed in 1992 and which we have implemented faithfully. The Cuban Democracy Act gives us the leeway to turn up both the heat on the Cuban Government and to make certain changes in policy in return for changes that they make. It is a carefully calibrated, disciplined, progressive approach. I believe it will work. I do not—I don't know why we need any more legal authority than we already have.

I would be, obviously, as I have been in the past, interested in knowing the views of Senator Graham on this because I trust his judgment. He's been an expert in this area and he's worked hard and was a sponsor, along with Mr. Torricelli, of the last Cuban Democracy Act. But we have been very firm. Our administration's position has been much tougher than previous administrations, but we've also operated under the Cuban Democracy Act to restore, for example, direct telephone communications, which has been a good thing for the Cubans and a good thing for the United States.

So I like the way the act is now. I think we should continue to operate under it. I know of no reason why we need further action.

Ms. Woodruff. And just in connection with the Cuba question, Mr. President, your Secretary of State and National Security Adviser have been talking a little more lately about some diplomatic opening, further diplomatic opening to Cuba. Is there something you're considering of that nature?

The President. There is nothing specific. What I want us to emphasize is the Cuban Democracy Act was a very carefully drawn bill of balance, of sticks and carrots—not carrots and sticks, sticks and carrots. It toughened the sanctions on the front end but provided for the United States to take appropriate, carefully calibrated actions in return for things that might be done within Cuba to open the country politically and economically.

But I have been given no specific recommendations by them, and I certainly have not approved any.

Value of the Dollar

Ms. Woodruff. International economic question: It's 50 years after World War II. The German mark and the Japanese yen are doing a whole lot better, a whole lot better, than the American dollar out there. And as you know, critics are pointing to your administration, to U.S. policy, and saying the dollar is falling because the policies of this administration and this government have contributed, have been wrong. What's going on?

The President. The economic condition of the American people is a whole lot better than the economy of Japan and Germany right now, although the German economy is coming back. We have lower unemployment; we've produced more jobs; we have low inflation.

Now, when—I would remind you that when I was in charge of economic policy and the Congress was supporting it—I'm still in charge of economic policy; the question is, what's the Congress going to do—we had lower deficits, low inflation, high growth, and a dollar that was stronger. I have no idea what is happening in the markets with the dollar, and neither does anybody else entirely. You ask them, a lot of people who make a living doing this think it's maybe speculation. But I tell you this: We do have to reduce the deficit further.

But I would just like to point out that if you look at the total Government deficit in the United States on an annual basis today, it is tied with Japan for the lowest deficit in the world. It is lower than Germany's. It is lower than any other European country. What is going on here? If they're saying something about the deficit, it's not because of the way we've managed the last 2 years, it's because of the massive

accumulated debt of the previous 12 years which requires a lot of borrowing to finance.

So what does that mean? That means we have to do more deficit reduction. What does that mean? It means it's unwise to be out here talking about tax cuts until you explain how you're going to reduce the deficit. Deficit reduction and appropriate, targeted, modest tax cuts, that's my policy.

The world markets may not know it yet, but that's going to be the policy of the United States. The United States will continue to reduce the deficit. We'll reduce it more. We will have a responsible policy, and the dollar will respond accordingly.

Jonathan Pollard Espionage Case

Mr. Blitzer. Mr. President, I want to talk U.S. politics in a second, but one loose end. There's story out today that you're thinking about a swap that would free Jonathan Pollard, the U.S. naval intelligence analyst who was convicted of espionage for Israel, as part of a three-way deal with Israel, Russia, and the U.S. First of all, is that true? And second of all, do you think that— he's now served 10 years—is that long enough for the crime that he committed?

The President. No one has said anything to me about that, nothing.

Mr. Blitzer. On the swap, you mean?

The President. Nothing.

Mr. Blitzer. Okay.

The President. And on Pollard, I'm going to handle his case the way I handle anybody else's. I get recommendations when people apply for clemency from the Justice Department, I review them, and I make a judgment on them.

1996 Presidential Election

Mr. Blitzer. Let's talk U.S. politics for a few moments. Bob Dole is the frontrunner, but there are a lot of other Republicans out there. How do you assess the political scene right now in terms of the challenges, not only from the Republican side but potentially a Democratic challenger like former Governor Casey of Pennsylvania trying to come into this race as well?

The President. Well, on the Republican side, I don't know how to assess it because it depends, obviously, as any primary battle does, on how they distinguish themselves from each other and who votes in the primary and how the various States view it. And I simply don't know enough about their primary electorate to do that. I'm going to let them decide who they want to put up, and they'll do that in due course.

Bob Casey is a man I served with as Governor. I have a high regard for him, and I have a lot of respect for him. And I kept in pretty close touch with him and his family when he went through his medical problems. And I think he's a remarkable, resilient person. He is a committed anti-abortion, anti-choice person who has served with distinction in government. We agree on many, many issues. I believe you can be pro-choice and anti-abortion; he doesn't believe that. And he believes that the Democratic Party has been badly hurt by the abortion issue and that it's more important than any other issue. And he believes that with a real depth of conviction. And he will have to do whatever he thinks is right, and he will do that. I am sure he will do whatever he thinks is right.

I think when you look at the alternatives between the Democrats and the Republicans and the fact that the Republicans seem to like to—it's hard to know where they really stand on that issue; they talk one way and act another. I would hope that he would think about that and think about what would happen in the event of a campaign. But that's his decision, and whatever he does, I will respect.

Mr. Blitzer. Still on politics, Mr. President, some of your political aides talk about you as the "43 percent President," referring to the percentage of the vote you got in '92. Is it the operating assumption around here and with you that there will be a third candidate in the general election, that there will be a Democrat—you, a Republican, and someone else?

The President. I have no earthly idea. And you know—let me just say how I am doing this. Sometimes you talk to people who work around here about this stuff more than I do. I try to minimize that kind of speculation. We have no control over that.

After the November election, when the people decided to give the Republicans control of Congress, I made a decision which I am adhering to, which is that I would do the very best I could to do exactly what I thought was right, that I would not worry about the monthly fluctuation in the polls, that if anything, worry about it even less than I had in the 2 previous years when I had taken a lot of unpopular positions. And I'm going to do more of what I did down in Dallas on Friday where I just took an outline

of the positions that I feel and I just get up there and say what I think and let the American people digest it and deal with it the best way they can.

Ms. Woodruff. So you mean while there's all this wild political speculation out there about what's going to go on, you're able to ignore that? Is that what you are saying?

The President. I don't think about it much. Of course, I don't ignore it, but I don't spend a lot of time worrying about it. The one thing I think every President owes the American people is to focus on what the American people need, to do what he thinks is right and best, and to realize that you waste a huge amount of energy focusing on things over which you have no control. I have no control over who seeks the Republican nomination, whether anybody seeks the Democratic nomination, and I certainly have no control over whether there's a third-party candidate. That is irrelevant. So I can't worry about it. It's a waste of time.

Political Change in Southern States

Ms. Woodruff. Well, let me ask you about something over which you may have some control, and that is these defections of Democrats to the Republican Party. We had Congressman Deal, Senator Shelby, Senator Campbell. Just looking at the South alone, I mean, the trend is all in the Republican direction. Are we now in a situation where you've got an all solid Republican South where we used to have a solid Democratic South, and is there anything you can do to stop that?

The President. Well, the solid Democratic South in Presidential elections has been breaking up since 1948. Harry Truman stood up for civil rights, and he lost four States to Strom Thurmond.

Ms. Woodruff. So you are saying there is nothing you can do?

The President. Well, no, I think there is. I think what we have to do—first of all, we have to get down there and make our case at election time. You know, when I spoke to the Florida Legislature, for example, I noticed after it was over a lot of the Florida Democrats came up to me and said there were Florida Republicans who said they agreed with what I said. They did not know what the position of the administration was, and they felt reassured by it.

The South cares about education. The South cares about welfare reform. The South cares about a strong stance against crime. The South has done very, very well economically under our policies, changing trickle-down economics, not going back to tax and spend but working on the invest and growth strategy that I ran for President on.

Ms. Woodruff. But they are voting for Republicans?

The President. They are, but I think they will be fair-minded when there's an honest debate. I don't think that the—in many cases they've gotten the other side of the coin. If you look at Florida, for example, or in Georgia where you have two seasoned Democratic Governors that survived the biggest Republican tidal wave in decades, they did it because they were strong and tough and they stood up for what they believed in and they did not apologize or pussyfoot around. They just said, "Here's what I did, here's why I did it, and here's where I stand." And not only that, they talked about what they were going to do to in the future. And they survived the tidal wave. I think that the Democrats will do well by following the examples of Lawton Chiles and Zell Miller.

The Presidency

Mr. Blitzer. Mr. President, if you step back a little bit and look over the span of your Presidency, what has been the most exhilarating moment in your Presidency, and what has been the most depressing moment for you since becoming President?

The President. I've had a lot of exhilarating moments, but I think that in terms of what's happening for Americans, I was exhilarated when the economic plan passed by only a vote because I knew it was the beginning of turning the country around. And I knew that if we got the deficit down, if we gave lower income working people a break, if we made college loans more affordable, if we expanded Head Start— that is, if we offered more opportunity and demanded more responsibility; all that was in that economic plan—that we could get this economy going again and we could offer some opportunity. So that was a great moment for me.

On a purely personal basis, I think the passage of the national service bill and seeing all those young people come up here and seeing them go out across our country and sort of cut through all the rhetoric and bureaucracy and everything and just start changing America from the grassroots up and earning their way

into college has been the most personally rewarding thing for me.

Mr. Blitzer. And depressing?

The President. The most depressing moment, I think, for me was when our young men were killed in Somalia, because they went there to save the lives of the Somali people. They did a magnificent job, and it was a very sad thing. And I think we learned some valuable lessons from it, and the lesson is not to withdraw from the world, not to walk away. What we did in Rwanda, what we did in Haiti, especially, shows that there is a good way and a right way to do these things. But that was a very—personally, it was the most personally depressing moment to me.

Entertainment Industry Values

Ms. Woodruff. Mr. President, Bob Dole said this week, 2 days ago, that the entertainment industry in this country, television, movies, advertising, is poisoning the minds of American young people. He said Hollywood ought to be shamed into improving all of these things. You've gotten a lot of money from Hollywood interests and political contributions. Do you think Hollywood—should you be holding Hollywood more accountable for these sorts of things?

The President. Well, I would remind you that long before Senator Dole said anything about it, I actually went to Hollywood and challenged them to deglorify violence, to deglorify sexual misconduct, to deglorify drug use, to deglorify destructive behaviors, and to try to help to build this country up. I also said the same thing in the State of the Union Address. And if you'll remember, it got as strong a response as anything that we had done. I think there——

Ms. Woodruff. And you're still saying that?

The President. Absolutely. And I think there has to be—I think what we need is—nobody wants to abolish the first amendment, but people who can shape our culture have a responsibility to try to help build it up. And when they show things that are destructive, they need to be shown in a destructive light, not in a glorified light.

So if I might give you two examples, I think that one reason people liked "Forrest Gump" is they thought it reasserted American values. And it didn't hide the problems of the sixties, seventies, and eighties; in fact, it explored them, but it showed them in a sad and tragic light.

The movie "Boyz N the Hood" was a violent movie, but it deglorified, it demystified gang life. No one could watch that movie and walk away from it with anything other than that children should not do these things. So there is a way for these subjects to be dealt with and to be commercially successful and still send cultural messages that bring us together and make us stronger.

Ms. Woodruff. All right, Mr. President, thank you for joining us.

The President. Thank you.

NOTE: The interview began at 11:40 a.m. in the Roosevelt Room at the White House. In his remarks, he referred to Rolf Ekeus, chairman, United Nations Special Commission (Iraqi Weapons), and Americans David Daliberti and William Barloon, who were arrested for illegally crossing the Iraqi border on March 13.

The President's Radio Address
April 15, 1995

Good morning. This weekend, all across our country, Christians and Jews are gathered with their families to celebrate Easter and Passover. For them and for every American, Hillary and I wish that this season of faith and renewal will also be a time of hope.

In a few weeks, Congress will return from their own Easter recess and begin to sift through all the bills passed by the House and, in some cases, those passed by the Senate, too. A lot of that work is good. A lot of it I campaigned on in 1992: spending cuts, the line-item veto, paperwork reduction, tougher criminal sentences, and greater flexibility for the police to do their jobs. These things are also consistent with actions already taken by our administration to cut the deficit, the size of Government, the burden of regulation; to tighten enforcement on child support and college loan repayments; and to give more support to Head Start and affordable college loans, national service, and family leave.

But a lot of these proposals, these new ones, go too far: cuts in education and job training, undermining environmental protections, undermining our efforts to put 100,000 new police on our streets, legislation to permit the sale of assault weapons, and penalties for going into court to assert your rights as a citizen. I'm concerned that important issues will be lost in all the welter of detailed legislative proposals Congress has to consider. So I want to tell Congress and the American people what my priorities are.

There are three areas that I assign the highest priority. They're my "must" list. First is welfare reform. We must pass a bill that reforms the welfare system and restores mainstream values of work and family, responsibility and community. We must demand work and responsibility by setting definite time limits for welfare recipients and enforcing strict work requirements. We must promote family and responsibility by passing the toughest possible child support enforcement, including our plan to deny driver's licenses to parents who refuse to pay their child support.

We must also give the States more flexibility, building on the work I've already done by giving States freedom, 25 of them, from Federal rules so they can find new ways to move people from welfare to work. At the same time, we have to uphold our values of community and responsibility by avoiding proposals that punish children for their parents' mistakes.

Recent proposals by a number of Senators for welfare reform that don't penalize children born to teenage mothers are certainly a step in the right direction. And the House of Representatives has adopted all my proposals for tougher child support enforcement. I appreciate these efforts. We have to keep on working, however. All the proposals are still too weak on work and on helping people to move from welfare to work. We can and must work together to pass a welfare reform bill that I can sign into law this year. Delaying reform any further would be a betrayal of what the American people want.

Second on my "must" list are tax and spending cuts, the right kind in the right amount for the right people. These tax cuts must be directed at the right people, that is, the middle class Americans who need them to help them build a successful future. And they must be fully paid for by spending cuts. Tax cuts must include a deduction for the cost of college or other education after high school.

Then Congress and I need to work together to go beyond the $600 billion of deficit reduction we've already enacted. And I've already proposed another $80 billion in cuts on top of paying for all the tax cuts that I have proposed for the cost of education after high school for helping people with raising children and for an IRA which can be withdrawn from, tax-free, for the cost of education or health care, first-time home buying or caring for an elderly parent.

We've also worked with Congress on $15 billion of further cuts. And I am ready to do more. But we have to focus on our twin deficits— we have a budget deficit and an education deficit. And we cannot cut one at the expense of the other.

The third thing I want to do is to build on last year's crime bill, not tear it down. We should all be open to new proposals for tougher penalties and more support for our police, but they must not be a cover for cutting back on our commitment for 100,000 new police officers on our street or for repealing the assault weapons ban that would put our police and our citizens more at risk. If that happens, I'll veto it.

More police on the street is the single most effective crime-fighting tool we know of. And assault weapons have no place on our streets. Last year's bill did ban assault weapons in the future, 19 of them, whose only purpose is to kill people. But it also for the first time gave legal protection from Government meddling to over 650 kinds of hunting and sporting weapons.

Congress must send me a bill that doesn't scale back or repeal the efforts so I can sign it and it can become law. There is too much to do in crime to play politics with it or to go back.

Real welfare reform, tax and spending cuts that reduce both the budget deficit and the education deficit, and more steps to fight crime, not to back up on the fight: those are my top priorities. The first 100 days of this Congress produced a blizzard of ideas and proposals. The next 100 days must get down to the hard task of passing bills that command majorities in both Houses, bills that will help to build a stronger America, bills that I can sign into law.

In the coming months, we have an historic chance to make progress on the issues of great concern to all Americans. Let's get on with it.

Thanks for listening.

NOTE: The address was recorded at 4 p.m. on April 13 in the Roosevelt Room at the White House for broadcast at 10:06 a.m. on April 15.

Remarks at the White House Easter Egg Roll
April 17, 1995

The President. Thank you. First let me welcome all the children here and all the people like me who feel like children when they're at the Egg Roll.

I want to thank all of you who helped to make this event possible and remind you that this has been going on here at the White House now for more than 115 years. This is one of the most important traditions we have at the White House. It's really a day for children; it's a day for joy; it's a day for gratitude. And we're all very, very happy and proud to have you here.

Now, I don't want to delay the roll any further, so I think—Bernie is supposed to come up and give me the whistle after the rabbit gives me the jellybean carrot. [*Laughter*] I want you kids to eat your real carrots, too. [*Laughter*]

This is—this gentleman that's giving me the whistle, he's been doing this for 9 years now. Let's give him a big hand. This is Bernie Fairbanks. [*Applause*]

Where are they? Down there? Can you hear? Are you ready? You count to 3 for me.

Audience members. One, two, three!

NOTE: The President spoke at approximately 9:45 a.m. on the South Lawn at the White House. Prior to his remarks, Hillary Clinton welcomed the participants and introduced the President.

Remarks on Signing the District of Columbia Financial Responsibility and Management Assistance Act of 1995
April 17, 1995

Thank you very much. Thank you, Alice Rivlin, for your hard work on this issue and for being such a devoted resident of the District of Columbia. I told somebody in the Oval Office before we came out here that, unlike a lot of us who are transients, Alice Rivlin's not going anywhere. [*Laughter*] And she desperately wanted this to be done well.

Congressman Davis, Congressman Clinger, Congresswoman Morella, Congresswoman Norton, Mayor Barry, President Clarke, members of the City Council, and other friends of the District of Columbia, this is a very important day and a very important piece of legislation for all of us who care about our country's Capital and for all of us who love Washington as a city. I have lived here not only as President but also as a college student. I know this to be a city not only of our national monuments and political centers but also a city of neighborhoods, of Shaw and Anacostia and Cleveland Park and Adams Morgan and so many others.

So this is a very important day for a city, a city and thousands and thousands of people who live in it, who love it, who care about it, who have lives, many of them who have nothing to do with the politics of the Nation's Capital but who deserve to live in a city that works, that functions, and that also can symbolize the very best in America.

The health of the city and the security of its citizens have been threatened by the financial crisis. And I applaud all those who have come together to work together to begin the road back.

The purpose of the bill I am signing today is just that; it is a road back. The Financial Responsibility and Management Assistance Act will speed the District's recovery and return to fiscal health and will help over the long run to improve the delivery of services to its citizens.

For the past 2 years, I've worked hard to turn the economy of our country around. And we've seen dramatic improvements in the deficit, in the ability of this country to create jobs, and having a Government that is both smaller and more efficient.

But none of that means very much to people whose own lives are troubled with insecurity. And the citizens of the District of Columbia need to know that security, stability, growth, and opportunity will be the hallmarks of their living in our Nation's Capital.

This effort, as Alice Rivlin has said, is proof of what we can accomplish when we work together, when we put the interests of real people first, when we ignore partisan politics, and when we get on with the job at hand.

I want to thank Alice Rivlin, as I said, for all the work that she has been doing. I want to thank the Members of the Congress here present. Congressman Davis, I think, when he came to the Congress, never could have imagined that this would be his first big assignment. [*Laughter*] He is now, I guess, an honorary citizen of Washington, DC. Eleanor Holmes Norton, when she ran for Congress, probably never imagined that this would be one of the most important pieces of legislation which she would have to undertake. But they have worked together in good spirit, in good faith. And I thank them, along with the other Members who are present and Congressman Walsh and others, and also the Members of the Senate who worked so expeditiously on this legislation.

The legislation calls for the creation of the Financial Responsibility and Management Assistance Authority to monitor and certify District budgets and borrowing, to get the city back on solid financial footing. I expect to appoint the five members of this Authority very soon. All of them will have a commitment to this city, and all of them will either live or work here.

Our goals are clear. There are tough choices in the short term, but I am confident that this legislation will lead to better services, a more responsive government, to safer streets, and to a stronger city for the citizens of this District. All of them deserve that, and America needs that.

Thank you very much.

NOTE: The President spoke at 12:35 p.m. in the Roosevelt Room at the White House. In his remarks, he referred to Mayor Marion Barry of the District of Columbia and David Clarke, District of Columbia Council president. H.R. 1345, approved April 17, was assigned Public Law No. 104–8.

Statement on Signing the Executive Order on Classified National Security Information
April 17, 1995

Today I have signed an Executive order reforming the Government's system of secrecy. The order will lift the veil on millions of existing documents, keep a great many future documents from ever being classified, and still maintain necessary controls over information that legitimately needs to be guarded in the interests of national security.

In issuing this order, I am seeking to bring the system for classifying, safeguarding, and declassifying national security information into line with our vision of American democracy in the post-Cold War world.

This order strikes an appropriate balance. On the one hand, it will sharply reduce the permitted level of secrecy within our Government, making available to the American people and posterity most documents of permanent historical value that were maintained in secrecy until now.

On the other, the order enables us to safeguard the information that we must hold in confidence to protect our Nation and our citizens. We must continue to protect information that is critical to the pursuit of our national security interests. There are some categories of information—for example, the war plans we may employ or the identities of clandestine human assets—that must remain protected.

This order also will reduce the sizable costs of secrecy—the tangible costs of needlessly guarding documents and the intangible costs of depriving ourselves of the fullest possible flow of information.

This order establishes many firsts: Classifiers will have to justify what they classify; employees will be encouraged and expected to challenge improper classification and protected from ret-

ribution for doing so; and large-scale declassification won't be dependent on the availability of individuals to conduct a line-by-line review. Rather, we will automatically declassify hundreds of millions of pages of information that were classified in the past 50 years.

Similarly, we will no longer tolerate the excesses of the current system. For example, we will resolve doubtful calls about classification in favor of keeping the information unclassified. We will not permit the reclassification of information after it has been declassified and disclosed under proper authority. We will authorize agency heads to balance the public interest in disclosure against the national security interest in making declassification decisions. And, we will no longer presumptively classify certain categories of information, whether or not the specific information otherwise meets the strict standards for classification. At the same time, however, we will maintain every necessary safeguard and procedure to assure that appropriately classified information is fully protected.

Taken together, these reforms will greatly reduce the amount of information that we classify in the first place and the amount that remains classified. Perhaps most important, the reforms will create a classification system that Americans can trust to protect our national security in a reasonable, limited, and cost-effective manner.

In keeping with my goals and commitments, this order was drafted in an unprecedented environment of openness. We held open hearings and benefitted from the recommendations of interested Committees of Congress and nongovernmental organizations, groups, businesses, and individuals. The order I have signed today is stronger because of the advice we received from so many sources. I thank all those who have helped to establish this new system as a model for protecting our national security within the framework of a Government of, by, and for the people.

WILLIAM J. CLINTON

The White House,

April 17, 1995.

NOTE: The Executive order is listed in Appendix D at the end of this volume.

Statement on the Crash of an Air Force C–21 in Alabama
April 18, 1995

Hillary and I were very saddened to learn of the crash of an Air Force C–21 aircraft near Alexander City, Alabama, last night, with the loss of eight lives. The death of these individuals is a tragic loss for the U.S. Air Force and the Nation. Their death reminds us all how much we are indebted to those military and civilian personnel who serve in the defense of our Nation. Our hearts and our prayers go out to the families and friends of those who were killed.

The President's News Conference
April 18, 1995

The President. Good evening. Ladies and gentlemen, before we begin the press conference, I want to express on behalf of Hillary and myself our profoundest condolences to the families and to the loved ones of the eight Americans who were killed in the crash of the Air Force plane in Alabama last night.

Tonight I want to talk about welfare reform. But before I do, I'd like to take just a minute to put welfare reform into the context of what is going on now in the United States Congress. Before the Easter break, the House of Representatives produced a flurry of ideas and proposals. Some of them were good. Some need work. Some should be rejected. My job is to work with people of good faith in both parties, in both Houses, to do what is best for America.

I was not elected to produce a pile of vetoes. And the Congress was not elected to produce a pile of political issues for the next election. My philosophy is that we have to go beyond this kind of politics-as-usual, the old debate about whether there should be more Government or less Government. I think we need a better and different Government that helps people who are helping themselves, one that offers opportunity but demands responsibility.

I have some common goals with the new Republican majority in the Congress. They say they want to reduce the deficit and the size of Government. I support that. My administration has reduced the deficit by $600 billion and is reducing the size of Government by over 250,000 people. In fact, if it were not for the interest we have to pay on the debt run up between 1981 and 1992, our Government's budget would be in balance today. Let me say that again, because I don't think the American people know that. If it were not for the interest we have to pay this year on the debt run up between 1981 and 1992, our Government's budget would be in balance today.

The Republicans say that they want to be tough on crime. Our crime bill is tough on crime, and I want to work with them to build on that. The Republicans are supporting the line-item veto, and so am I. I worked hard to get a version of the line-item veto passed through the Senate, and I look forward to working with them, actually getting agreement in both Houses and having a line-item veto come into law.

As we look ahead, the issue is, what are we going to do on the outstanding matters? I have commented at length on them before the newspaper editors, but let me say again, I want us to show responsibility and common sense and decency. Do we need to cut regulation, as they say? Of course, we do. But we don't need to undermine our commitment to the safety of our skies or the purity of our water and air or the sanctity of our long-term commitment to the environment. Do we need to be tough on crime? Of course, we do, but we don't need to repeal the commitment to 100,000 police officers or the assault weapons ban. Do we need to cut taxes? I believe we do, but not as much as the House bill provides. I think the tax cuts should be targeted to the middle class and to education so we raise incomes and growth for America over the long run.

Now let's talk a little about welfare. That's an issue that the Republicans and I, and the congressional Democrats should be able to agree on. They say we should end welfare as we know it. That's a commitment I made in 1992 and again in 1993 and 1994. Welfare reform is surely an example where all the people ought to be able to get together in the Congress to have reform.

We all know what we need. We need time limits for welfare recipients. We need strict work requirements. We need very tough child support enforcement. We need more flexibility for the States. That's what our administration has been working on for more than 2 years now. We already have freed 25 States from cumbersome Federal rules and regulations so they can pursue welfare reform on their own. Tonight we're cutting redtape for two more States, for Montana and Missouri, one State with a Republican Governor, one State with a Democratic Governor, both committed to require people on welfare to go to work within 2 years. That's the same time limit I called for when I ran for President and that I called for last year.

Most people are in agreement on this. The question is, what are we going to do about it in Washington. In 1994, I introduced the most sweeping welfare reform ever presented to Congress. In 1994, Senator Dole, Senator Gramm, Senator Brown, and Senator Packwood cosponsored a pretty good bill. In 1994, Speaker, then-Congressman, Gingrich and 162 of the 175 House Republicans sponsored a bill that was an awful lot like mine. All of these bills were based on the same idea: The fundamental goal of welfare reform is to move people into the work force and to make them independent.

But the bill that passed the House of Representatives, supported by the House Republicans, in my opinion, is too weak on work and too tough on children. It saves a lot of money in the short run but at great damage to our long run interests, promoting responsible parenting and working to promote independence.

The only way to save money over the long run is to move people from welfare to work and to ensure that they have the skills to keep jobs and to stay independent. And it's wrong to cut children off just because their mothers are minor. After all, a child is a child, a baby is a baby. Whether they're white or black or brown, whether they're born in or out of wedlock, every child deserves a chance to make a good life.

Surely we should not punish children for the mistakes of their parents. Instead, we ought to give them a chance to become independent, full participating citizens, not part of the welfare population.

Let me say again, this does not have to be a partisan issue. I know that there are some here in Washington, for example, who want to fold this whole welfare reform issue into the broader budget debate. If you put it into the budget process, as those of you who live here know, it can be buried in a pile of other issues. And then there will be no need for a bipartisan consensus on welfare reform. But welfare reform is too important for that kind of Washington game. It should be open. It should be bipartisan. And we should get on with it right away.

I want to challenge Congress to pass a bipartisan welfare reform bill and put it on my desk by July the 4th, so that we can celebrate Independence Day by giving Americans on welfare the chance, the opportunity, the responsibility, to move to independence.

Surgeon General Nominee Henry Foster

Helen [Helen Thomas, United Press International].

Q. Mr. President, Senator Dole has threatened to block Dr. Foster's nomination as Surgeon General from reaching a vote or going to the Senate floor. I have a two-part question. Are you going to the mat to fight for it? Are you going to withdraw it? And do you think that abortion, which is still lawful in this country, will be a litmus test in Presidential politics?

The President. Yes, I'm going to the mat for the nomination. Whether abortion is a litmus test in Presidential politics is up to the voters. Dr. Foster is a good man with a good record as a family doctor, as someone who has helped thousands of mothers to give birth to their children, and as an academic and as someone who has supported policies that are pro-family and pro-child. He is qualified. He should be confirmed. He should not be caught up in any kind of politics, Presidential or otherwise.

Terry [Terence Hunt, Associated Press].

Russia-Iran Nuclear Cooperation

Q. Mr. President, two countries with which the United States has important relationships, Russia and China, want to sell nuclear technology to Iran over your objections. Can you explain why Russia, in particular, would want to give this technology to a neighboring country that intelligence agencies say is determined to acquire nuclear weapons? And do you think that when you go to Moscow that you will be able to persuade Mr. Yeltsin to cancel the sale?

The President. Well, as you know, I cannot explain why Russia would do it since I don't believe that it's in their interest to do it. I don't think it's right, and I don't think it's in their interest. If you ask them, I think they would say that they had a prior contractual obligation to do it, and they believe that the level of nuclear technology in the powerplants is so low that it won't lead to the development of a nuclear weapon. I believe that's what they would say. I think that's what the Chinese would say. But I disagree with them, and we're continuing to work with them.

The United States and our people have benefited greatly from this new engagement we've had with Russia and for our attempts to promote the nonproliferation agenda. There are nuclear weapons, large numbers of them now, being destroyed in Russia, weapons from Russia and the states of the former Soviet Union that had them before. And we are destroying weapons. For the first time, there are no Russian nuclear missiles pointed at the United States. So we are moving ahead in our nonproliferation agenda. I do not believe it's in their interest to do this. I understand what they say, but I disagree with them. And I hope I'll be able to prevail. I intend to continue to be quite aggressive on it.

Yes, Rita [Rita Braver, CBS News].

"The Tragedy and Lessons of Vietnam"

Q. Mr. President, you've been quoted as saying that you believe that Robert McNamara's new book, in which he essentially says that the U.S. had no underlying basis for the war in Vietnam, vindicates your own opposition to the war. I wonder if we could hear you talk about that and also if, in this time of reflection, you feel vindicated about your handling of your own draft status?

The President. On the second matter, I've said all I have to say about it.

On the first, I believed our policy was incorrect. I think the book supports that conclusion. But I do not believe that the book should be used as yet another opportunity to divide the United States over that. We should learn about what happened, resolve not to repeat our mistakes, honor the service of Americans, and go forward together. That's what we should be doing.

Japan-U.S. Trade

Q. The Japanese are threatening to pull out of auto talks unless U.S. negotiators stop threatening sanctions. Are you willing to do that? Are we at risk of a trade war?

The President. Well, we should not be at risk of a trade war, but I would remind you that we have been very patient as a country for a very long time in this area. And our major trade deficit in the world, except for our oil imports, has been with Japan and, of course, now with China and other countries in Asia combined. But Japan is a country that is a wealthy country, almost as wealthy as we are when you compare purchasing power parity, where consumer prices within the country of Japan are much, much higher than they are in the United States and could be maintained at that high level only by a sophisticated system of direct and indirect protectionism, which is most manifest in this area. We have strong differences. We have worked hard to resolve our trade differences with Japan. We have made some significant progress in other areas. And I'm going to let Ambassador Kantor continue to pursue this one in the way that we have agreed upon. I think that he is proceeding in good faith.

Political Division and Dialog

Q. Mr. President, when a politician starts talking about the irrelevancy or inadequacy of terms such as liberal and conservative, and even adds, as you did in Dallas, Democrat and Republican, usually they're in trouble or see a bad patch coming down the road. Is that the case with you, or why did you bring the issue up again?

The President. First of all, that's what I said when I ran for President, that's what I said when I was head of the Democratic Leadership Council, that's what I said when I was the Governor of my State, that we were going into a new era when a lot of the old divisions and old labels didn't mean the same thing. We have to redefine them. And I have sought to redefine them from the beginning of my campaign for President and indeed before. And I still find it very frustrating from time to time when I am not successful in redefining it, because I think the American people—to the American people, a lot of what they hear and see and read up here, is a real turn-off because it seems that these categories of debate are extreme on both sides and don't fit with their experience and their concerns for the future.

Q. Do you think you failed in that regard?

The President. No, I think that—I think that we're in a process in which a new political dialog and a new understanding is struggling to be born. I think that in the last election, if you say, you choose more government or less, less wins; you choose more taxes or less, less wins. But everybody instinctively knows that's not the real choice. The real choice is, does it makes sense to cut Head Start? Does it makes sense to cut immunizations for kids or college loans? No. Does it make sense to cut bureaucracy? Yes. So the real question is, how do we have a language that reflects what people know is the right thing for the country to do. And I'm doing my best to help the country develop the language and the debate.

Family Values and Moral Virtue

Q. Mr. President, I'd like to ask you a philosophical question tonight. A number of the Nation's social critics have been saying lately that America is what they call a morally bewildered society. And they cite as evidence the fact that much of the Nation's political discourse and its public debate centers on the subject of family values. These critics say that family values is really a fig leaf or a euphemism to cover up the Nation's moral relativism.

I'd like to know if you think that the distinction between moral virtue—in the ancient Roman or old Victorian sense—the distinction between that and family values is a valid and legitimate one? And if you do, do you think that you and the other candidates in the '96 Presidential contest should debate the Nation's social compact on the basis of instilling moral virtue rather than family values?

The President. Well, I think family values require moral virtue. I mean, family values mean to me that people make common sacrifices to stay together, to work together, to put primacy on the family unit and the rearing of children and to put their children first. I think that that has been at the bedrock of our success as a country and as a bedrock of other successful civilizations. And I think when people cease to put the interest of their children and the future ahead of their interest of themselves in the short run, we get in trouble.

I believe that if you look at the successes in this country, both the individual successes and the places where there are broad success, there are strong support for families, and families are generally successful. I also believe that America worries so much about moral relativism because we are the least relativistic of all the big countries. We are the most religious. We are the most likely to believe not only in God but in absolute rules of right and wrong here on Earth. And I think the fact that we worry about it shows that we have problems in our country which are inconsistent with our beliefs, and we know that we can't solve our problems purely by some common social action. We also require personal changes to solve those problems. I think that is a broadly held belief in the United States, and I certainly believe that. And my experience is consistent with that.

Yes, Mara [Mara Liasson, National Public Radio].

Affirmative Action

Q. Mr. President, in California recently you urged Democrats who are grappling with the issue of affirmative action to be sensitive to the feelings of angry white males. And if you were addressing a group of so-called angry white males tonight, how would you convince them that Federal programs that have goals of giving a certain percentage of contracts or jobs to minorities are good and fair for everyone, including white males?

The President. Well, first of all I don't want to prejudge the review of all the Federal programs that I'm going through. So I wouldn't—

I don't want to answer that question. But I would say first of all to them—I will answer the question when I complete the review, which won't be long. But I don't want to do—I would say, though, the earnings of male workers, including white male workers, have been declining when measured against inflation, for years now. So people are working harder—these male workers are working harder for lower wages, unless they have good educations or are in a section of the economy that's growing very rapidly. I would say to them, your problem is the problem of what's happening to wages and rising inequality in the United States. And it was caused primarily by foreign competition, technology, the weakening of organized labor, the collapse of the minimum wage, and according to the study which was in the paper today, the tax and budgetary policies of the last 12 years before I became President which aggravated inequality.

And what I am trying to do is, number one, give you equality again with better jobs, more jobs, a higher minimum wage, a tax cut for workers with modest incomes and children in the home, about $1,000 a year for incomes under $25,000 this year; and that on affirmative action, your principle should be, we're all better off if everybody's got an even chance, if there's no discrimination, if people have the opportunity to live up to the fullest of their ability, but the Government should never give someone who is unqualified anything over someone who is qualified.

Robert G. Torricelli Investigation

Q. Congressman Torricelli of New Jersey is embroiled in a controversy over the revelations he made about the CIA and its apparent involvement in murders in Guatemala. You have indicated your concerns about the CIA's conduct. I want to know what your thoughts are about Congressman Torricelli's conduct. Should he have revealed that information or not? And if he should not have, should he be disciplined?

The President. Well, what should happen to him depends on, number one, what the facts are and, number two, what the House decides to do with it. And they have to do their investigation, and they have to make their determination.

What I do believe is that the United States owes the American people a thorough investigation of the allegations of what went on. And

it may take a little time because these are things which occurred by and large before I became President. But I've asked the Intelligence Oversight Board to look into it. I expect them to do a thorough and deep job, and I expect to have the truth, and I expect us to take the appropriate action. That is exactly what we will do. But it is not for me to judge Congressman Torricelli.

Q. Are you concerned at all about the information coming out, as the person ultimately responsible as the guardian of American intelligence?

The President. I am concerned about the information coming out, but in the end, I think that it is unlikely, given the facts of this case, that certain information would not have come out.

Yes, Peter [Peter Maer, Westwood One Radio], and then Sarah [Sarah McClendon, McClendon News].

Middle East Peace Process

Q. Mr. President, outward appearances would indicate that one of your key foreign policy goals, a comprehensive Middle East peace, is deadlocked, especially on the Israeli-Syrian track. Is there a stalemate? And especially in light of the recent terrorist incidents and word today that Syria wants to get land to the Sea of Galilee?

The President. Well, I won't comment on the details of the negotiations between them because that would only complicate matters. It is difficult. We knew it would be difficult. I do believe that both Prime Minister Rabin and President Asad want to make a comprehensive peace. I do believe that both of them understand they don't have unlimited time. I do believe that the United States still has the trust of both parties in working to help them reach an agreement. And as concerned as I am about it, I am more hopeful today than I was, let's say, 45 days ago. We just have to keep at it.

Q. Sir, I want to ask you——

Q. [*Inaudible*]—stalemate incorrect then?

The President. I think the correct perception is that we're not on the edge of a breakthrough. But that does not mean that there is no ongoing work on this, and that does not mean that the parties have basically hardened their hearts and minds and decided that there will not be a resolution of this in the fairly near-term.

Central Intelligence Agency

Q. Sir, there's something funny going on out at the CIA. I wonder just how many times you have looked into it and had a really good, honest briefing on it. But today we have found out that they are taking their classified documents and sending them by mail to retired former CIA people. This gets them out of the records, out of the storehouse out there, and gets them into a private home where nobody could ever find them if they conducted a congressional investigation of CIA reports. Some of these are classified and some are not, but they have the names on them of the officers who worked on them, and they have mailed them back to the officers who worked on them. Why they are doing this I don't know, but it sounds like they are trying to keep us from getting a chance at the records.

The President. Let me make two comments quickly on that. First of all, I have made it clear to the Intelligence Oversight Board that I want a thorough investigation of all these matters—and clear to the CIA leadership there, including the Acting Director, that I want the records, the relevant records, secured and accounted for.

Secondly, I think this reinforces the need for the United States Senate to hold quick confirmation hearings and have a prompt vote on John Deutch to be the new Director. Let's get him out there so we can get on with the business of doing what we need to do.

1996 Presidential Election

Q. Sir, I know you've said that you'd like to put politics aside for a certain period, but last week you opened—you formally opened your campaign office for reelection in town here. And I was wondering if you might take a minute to say—to fill in the blank and say, "I believe I should be reelected President in 1996 because—" and take it from there.

The President. I believe I should be reelected—[*laughter*]—because I have done what I said I would do, because we have got good results, and because the policies that I now advocate, most importantly, will address the outstanding problems of the country.

If you look at this problem of inequality, if you look at the economic problems, what is the response? The response is to invest more in education, to raise the minimum wage, to expand trade in high wage products in the United States to generate more jobs.

If you look at the problems of the social fabric that you asked about, what is the answer? The answer is to tell people the truth about things they have to do to make things better, to assume more responsibility, to do the right things but to have policies, from welfare reform to supporting children, to doing things to make adoptions easier and more preferable to other alternatives, which we're working on now, that build up families and build up communities.

We are moving the country in the right direction. We are doing what we said we would do. We are getting results. This country is in a stronger position today than it was 2 years ago.

Taxes

Q. Mr. President, the idea of a flat tax is more and more popular with a lot of people. In your mind, what would be wrong with a flat tax? And more fundamentally, for lack of a more elegant term, what's wrong with blowing up the present tax structure as it is?

The President. Well, I tell you what, after I just went over my tax returns last week, that has more appeal than it did a week ago. [*Laughter*] And I think a lot of Americans feel that way.

On the flat tax. What we have to do is to put a pencil to a piece of paper and see how it works. All the studies I have seen say that all the proposals out there now will raise taxes for people with incomes under $200,000 and lower taxes for people with incomes over $200,000, like my wife and myself, which would be unfair, and that if they don't do that, they explode the deficit. So the question is, we can't explode the deficit, and we can't be unfair. Can we simplify the tax system without being unfair or increasing the deficit? And if we can do it, then I am open to it. But the studies are not promising on the proposals that are out there now.

Value of the Dollar

Q. Mr. President, both you and your Treasury Secretary have said repeatedly that a strong dollar is in America's interest. But some people don't believe you because they don't see you taking any specific steps to try to make that happen. Can you tell the American people why this would be in America's interest, particularly since a weak dollar encourages export sales, and since the inflation it might cause seems nowhere on the horizon? And if you do want a strong dollar, what can you do or what are you willing to do to achieve it?

The President. In the present climate, the ability of governments to affect the strength of their currency or in the case of Japan, as you see, that would like a weaker yen, the ability of governments that have strong currencies to get a weaker one, in the short run, may be limited, as we have seen in countless examples over the last several years. So what you have to do is work over the long run.

The United States does want a strong dollar. We believe in the importance of fundamentals in our economy. We believe in getting the deficit down, getting jobs up and pursuing a responsible course. I have done that for 2 years. I will continue to do that.

Yes, Judy [Judy Keen, USA Today].

Q. Can you tell us, sir—to follow up—what a strong dollar would do for the economy?

The President. Well, the point is that a weak dollar, eventually, over a long period of time, will weaken the economy, either by bringing inflation into it or by upsetting the whole complex international fabric of business relationships that are carried on in dollars. So we do have an interest over the long run in a strong currency. But we have to look at it—but for Government—Government actions need to be directed toward long-term fundamentals, sound economic policies, sound growth policies, sound investment policies.

Yes, Judy.

President's Leadership Role

Q. President Clinton, Republicans have dominated political debate in this country since they took over Congress in January. And even tonight, two of the major television networks declined to broadcast this event live. Do you worry about making sure that your voice is heard in the coming months?

The President. No. I would remind you, I had at least one press conference during the previous 2 years when I had it at night, but only one of the networks covered it, as I remember. But the important thing is for me to do these press conferences on a regular basis, and every 3 or 4 months, to do it at night so that anyone who wants to cover it can.

The Constitution gives me relevance. The power of our ideas gives me relevance. The

record we have built up over the last 2 years and the things we're trying to do to implement it give it relevance. The President is relevant here, especially an activist President. And the fact that I am willing to work with the Republicans. The question is, are they willing to work with me? I have shown good faith. That's how we got two of those bills in the contract that I supported in 1992 signed into law. That's how we got a strong showing among Senate Democrats for the line-item veto. I have shown good faith. The question is, what happens now?

Surgeon General Nominee Foster

Q. Mr. President, as a followup to Helen's question about the Foster nomination, it is now at the whim not only of Majority Leader Dole but three other Presidential candidates who are in the Senate, and then when the going gets tough, there are some Democrats who may very well run for cover. I'm wondering if you can tell us if Dr. Foster knows himself the difficult period that lies ahead if, as you say, you are going to the mat with this and whether—and the possible or probable outcome.

The President. I think he knows that it will be difficult. I think that he has been warned repeatedly, not by me but by reading it in the press or seeing it, that Presidential politics seems to have found its way into his nomination. But you know, sometimes the American system works the way it's supposed to, and sometimes the right thing has been done.

I will say again: He is a distinguished physician. He is a good man. He has a good record. He should be confirmed.

"Enola Gay" Exhibit Controversy

Q. Can you explain why you supported the veterans' effort to end the Smithsonian's exhibit of the *Enola Gay*, which was seen by many as an effort to educate the public on the pros and cons of the nuclear bomb? Is this subject taboo in the United States?

The President. No, I don't think the subject is taboo. I don't think the subject is taboo. But my simple position is, as I said to the newspaper editors, that painful though it is, even after 50 years, that President Truman did the right thing. And I do not believe that on the celebration of the end of the war and the service and the sacrifice of our people, that that is the appropriate time to be asking about or launching a major reexamination of that issue. Anyone who wants to write a book about it, express a contrary opinion, is perfectly free to do so, but I don't think that the policy of my administration or the United States should be to say that's the way to celebrate the 50th anniversary of the end of World War II. I disagree with that. I don't think it's right.

Yes, Jill [Jill Dougherty, CNN].

Russia and NATO

Q. Mr. President, in terms of your upcoming trip to Russia, in spite of what your administration has said numerous times to Russia about NATO expansion, the Russian—the Yeltsin government either does not understand or will not understand that that is not a threat to them. And in fact, some people in Russia are now talking about rearming in a nuclear fashion to allay some—any type of attack from the West.

When you meet with Boris Yeltsin, what will you say to him to convince him that it is not a threat?

The President. I will say what I have always said, that NATO is not an offensive alliance; it is a defensive alliance, a security alliance; that NATO has worked with Russia and Bosnia; that NATO has invited Russia to be a part of the Partnership For Peace and has not excluded anybody from potential NATO membership; that Russia, in terms of its security interest, has nothing to fear from a NATO which expands in a gradual, open, straightforward way and, at the same time, is deepening its relationship with Russia.

Q. Why does Mr. Yeltsin not understand that? He's said it numerous times.

The President. That is something you'll have to ask them. I understand they're—you know, they have the same sort of domestic political pressures that every country has and misunderstandings, but I think the United States has shown its good faith in our dealings with Russia. The United States did not move aggressively to help Russia overcome the burden of decades of Communist economics and other problems that were left when the cold war was over and the Soviet Union collapsed to turn around and make Russia an enemy. That is not why we did all that work to help rebuild their economy, to support their movement to democracy, to support their integration and their work with the G–7 and all these other countries. We have shown our good faith. But we cannot and we should not give any nation a veto over the expansion of NATO when it is otherwise appropriate to do so.

International Financial Reform

Q. Mr. President, concerning—to follow up on the question about the dollar, there is growing concern that there is instability within the international financial system as a whole. There are some proposals, like I know the Japanese Finance Minister put out a proposal regarding international financial reform, reform of the international system. How do you view this situation? And what would be your primary concerns in such a reform of the international financial system?

The President. First, let me say that this is an issue which needs to be addressed, but it needs to be addressed in a very thoughtful way so as not to further aggravate whatever conditions exist there. It is obvious that the integration of the global financial markets have—that that has many advantages—that you can get money to places in a hurry, that places that have been underdeveloped can develop more quickly, that you can develop the sophisticated trading relationships more rapidly, and that this is all a positive.

It is also obvious that as with almost every other element in the modern society that we live in, every force of integration carries within it the seeds of potential disintegration, of rapid unraveling. So last year that's why I asked the heads of the other G–7 countries, the other major economies, to devote a discussion this summer when we meet in Canada to this subject. We have been working on it; the Japanese have been working on it; the Canadians have been working on it; the Europeans have been working on it. And we will have a long talk about it this summer. We will do our very best to come up with sensible statements about where we go from here.

George [George Condon, Copley News Service].

Japan-U.S. Relations

Q. Mr. President, to follow up on the answer you gave a moment ago, when you spoke last week about President Truman's decision to drop the atomic bomb, Americans overwhelmingly thought you were right not to apologize. The Japanese overwhelmingly thought you were insensitive. Were you surprised that 50 years after the event there is still that wide divergence of opinion? And do you see any chance of that gulf ever being bridged?

The President. The way to bridge the gulf is to talk about the friendship that we have now, the respect and regard that we have now, the common interests that we have now. I did not say that to hurt anyone's feelings or to be insensitive to anyone in Japan. I know what a terrible, terrible loss of life there was, how many scarred families there were, how difficult it was. It was hard in World War II. Twenty million Russians lost their lives in World War II. No one can fail to be sensitive to the loss.

Do I wish none of it had happened? Of course, I do. But that does not mean that President Truman, in the moment of decision, made the wrong decision or that the United States can now apologize for a decision that we did not believe then and I do not believe now was the wrong one. That has nothing to do with my feelings for the Japanese people, my profound sorrow at the suffering and the agony that they went through.

But we have recovered from that. We have gone on from that. We have one of the world's most important bilateral relationships. The thing we need to do now is to join together and look to the future. We're up to our ears in challenges today. Let's get on with dealing with them in mutual respect and support. And that's the way to get this behind us.

Thank you very much.

NOTE: The President's 93d news conference began at 9:01 p.m. in the East Room at the White House. In his remarks, he referred to Prime Minister Yitzhak Rabin of Israel and President Hafiz al-Asad of Syria.

Exchange With Reporters Prior to Discussions With Prime Minister Tansu Ciller of Turkey
April 19, 1995

Turkey-U.S. Relations

The President. Let me say that, as always, it's good to have Prime Minister Ciller back in Washington. I welcome her here. Turkey is a valued, important ally of the United States, and our relationship will become even more important in the years ahead.

We're about to go into a meeting where we will discuss a number of issues, her programs for democratization and for economic reform, the Turkish operation in Northern Iraq, which obviously, the United States hopes will be limited in duration and scope. We'll talk about Cyprus and a number of other issues—whatever the Prime Minister wants to discuss. But I'm looking forward to the conversation, and I'm glad she's here.

Turkish Operations in Iraq

Q. Do you expect her to set a date for the evacuation from Iraq? And is Iraq supporting her drive against the Kurds?

The President. Why don't you ask her those questions?

Q. I will. Do you plan to set a date for withdrawal from Iraq? And is Iraq supporting this drive against the Kurds? Are there good Kurds and bad Kurds?

Prime Minister Ciller. As you know, we were together in the fight against Iraq in the Gulf crisis, and then we were together again with the United States in Provide Comfort to protect the Kurdish people in Northern Iraq against Saddam's regime. And it so happened, however, that Turkey was probably the only ally which paid—who paid very high costs because we happen to have a border with Iraq. And Northern Iraq, in time, became a no-man's land.

And this was not a decision that I enjoyed taking, but it so happened that the terrorists simply settled in Northern Iraq and planned to have operations within my country passing the borders. Any Western country in my position would have to have—would take the same kind of decision that I did. And we are there only for a limited time. We have gotten hold of the bases that we wanted to do. The majority of the job is done and over with. The withdrawal will be very soon, as I have said from the beginning.

The reason that I cannot announce a date is because it would not be fair for those people up on the mountains, 1,500 feet from the ground—meters from the ground, not feet—in the caves, in the snow, and they are approaching our borders. What they are doing is searching the caves up on the mountains for the guns and the ammunitions that would have been used to kill the innocent people in my country.

So I have to say that I'm very grateful to President Clinton for his support and for the fact that they knew about what was happening in Northern Iraq, that this became a no-man's land without authority, and it's not our making. It is not only our responsibility either. We have to think of a way to handle this. Otherwise, Turkey always ends up being the only ally to continually pay for this operation and the end result of this operation.

Q. Are you adamantly against the establishment of a state of Kurdistan? Isn't this the motive of the rebels?

Prime Minister Ciller. We are very friendly towards the Kurdish people in Northern Iraq. We have nothing against it. In fact, the Kurdish people in Northern Iraq were quite happy to see us come in because what had happened is that the Kurdish elements had been pushed towards south and had to evacuate Northern Iraq because of the terrorists. Now that the terrorists have simply run away, there is the possibility of these Kurdish elements coming back to Northern Iraq and settling.

We had, as you know, opened up our borders to the Kurdish people in Northern Iraq. Close to a million people came over after the Gulf crisis, and we sheltered them and we fed them. And last year only, we paid $13.5 million in foodstuff to the Kurdish people living in Northern Iraq. And every year, we supply the electricity and basic needs. So this has nothing to do with the Kurdish people.

Turkey

Q. Prime Minister, today in Turkey, 21 people have been arrested on allegations of trying to assassinate you. I wondered how you felt about your own security, if you were worried about the stability of your government.

Prime Minister Ciller. Well, I am not worried about the security of my country or myself. I have a mission, and that mission is a peace mission for the area. And that's what I'm going to discuss with President Clinton. And Turkey's actual acceptance into the European Community and Customs Union, I think, is a historic kind

of a turnaround. And I have to thank again the President's administration and to President Clinton for the very historic support they have given on the issue, because had Turkey been separated from Europe, it would have meant that fundamentalism would have moved up to the borders of Europe. And Turkey, in the area, is the only stable ally from Korea to the Gulf crisis.

We are—look at where we are stationed. North of us is the Soviet Union, having disintegrated. The new countries that have emerged have their own problems. East to us is Middle East. We are very friendly towards Israel—and I was the first Prime Minister to go to Israel—and friendly to the Arab world at the same time. And we have good relations with the Caspian Sea—new nations that have emerged, such as Azerbaijan and Armenia and——

Cyprus

Q. How about Greece? Cyprus?

Prime Minister Ciller. Oh, yes. The whole problem—that's why the Customs Union is so important because once—if and when Turkey is accepted as a full member into the European Union, as Greece is and as Cyprus will, together with the Turkish and the Greek side, the problem will be resolved in a very comprehensive way because then we won't have anything to fight about, such as migration or migration of labor or some of the basic problems that had continued for almost centuries now, as far as I'm concerned.

President's News Conference

Q. [*Inaudible*]

The President. I thought it was good, the press conference. There were a lot of questions. There were a broad range of questions. They were interesting questions, and I gave straightforward answers, and they were brief. So I thought it was good.

Debt Limit and Budget Legislation

Q. Mr. President, one thing you didn't get to answer last night is that Speaker Gingrich has threatened to put all sorts of legislation that you oppose onto the debt ceiling bill and in effect threaten you to veto the bill and shut the Government down. Would you do that if there was legislation on there you didn't like?

The President. No President of the United States can ever be, in effect, blackmailed by that sort of thing. I'm going to do what I think is right for the people of this country. And again—I will say again what I said last night, the only thing that's relevant to the American people in this whole process is what we do here to affect their lives, and their future, and their children's future.

I have demonstrated my commitment to working through this process. We've already signed two good bills. We're working on this line-item veto together. We can do a lot of work. We can have a lot of good ceremonies out there in the Rose Garden, or we can have the kind of conflict that could arise unless there is a real attempt to work these things out.

And I have been very, very clear and forthright about my position about these things all along and will continue to be. But a strategy to sort of put me in a box would be an error because I will still exercise the power of the Presidency in the interest of the American people.

[*At this point, one group of reporters left the room, and another group entered.*]

The President. Nice to see you all.

Turkish Operations in Iraq

Q. Mr. President, your administration has certainly shown a certain degree of understanding of Turkey's incursion in Northern Iraq. How willing are you to cooperate in possible secret arrangements for—[*inaudible*]—incursion in this region?

The President. Well, we're going to discuss that in our meetings. And I don't think I should say anything about it until we have meetings. But you know, the United States has had a strong relationship with Turkey. And I think it's very important that we continue that relationship into the future. And in order to do it, we're going to have to understand each other's position, each other's problems, each other's potential to work together. And I've tried to do that, and I've had a good relationship with the Prime Minister. She has been very forceful in coming to the United States and stating the interest of the Turkish people. And this is one of many things that we will discuss. But I look forward

to continuing to make progress on all these issues.

Turkey

Q. Will human rights and democratization be on the agenda?

The President. Sure. And the Prime Minister's talked about democratization. And I think—you know, for the Europeans, as you move toward the Customs Union and other things, these issues are quite important. And they're very important to the United States. But I have tried to also view them in the context of the imperative to fight terrorism and to promote human rights. And I think you have to do both. Preserving a democracy in which people have human freedom is a delicate operation. And it requires not only a lot of sensitivity and understanding, it requires a lot of discipline and respect for other people's rights as well. And the biggest threat to human rights all over the world today, after the—in the aftermath of the cold war when people now know that dictatorial political systems don't work, that totalitarian systems don't work, the biggest threat to human rights is the reaction caused by terrorism everywhere. And that is something we have to be sensitive to, whether it's a car bomb blowing up in the Middle East or a religious fanatic taking a vial of sarin into the subway in Japan. All these things threaten the fabric of human rights. So we have to continue to push governments all over the world to be more open to human rights and combat terrorism at the same time.

Q. Do you have any solution about—[*inaudible*]—administration?

The President. We're going to talk about it today. You know, the United States has expressed an understanding of what Turkey did, along with the hope that civilian casualties could be strictly limited, and that the operation would be limited in time and scope. But we're going to talk about it. The Prime Minister has probably got some good ideas, and we'll discuss it.

NOTE: The President spoke at 10:25 a.m. in the Oval Office at the White House. A tape was not available for verification of the content of this exchange.

Remarks on the Bombing of the Alfred P. Murrah Federal Building in Oklahoma City, Oklahoma
April 19, 1995

The bombing in Oklahoma City was an attack on innocent children and defenseless citizens. It was an act of cowardice, and it was evil. The United States will not tolerate it. And I will not allow the people of this country to be intimidated by evil cowards.

I have met with our team, which we assembled to deal with this bombing. And I have determined to take the following steps to assure the strongest response to this situation:

First, I have deployed a crisis management team under the leadership of the FBI, working with the Department of Justice, the Bureau of Alcohol, Tobacco and Firearms, military and local authorities. We are sending the world's finest investigators to solve these murders.

Second, I have declared an emergency in Oklahoma City. And at my direction, James Lee Witt, the Director of the Federal Emergency Management Agency, is now on his way there to make sure we do everything we can to help the people of Oklahoma deal with the tragedy.

Third, we are taking every precaution to reassure and to protect people who work in or live near other Federal facilities.

Let there be no room for doubt: We will find the people who did this. When we do, justice will be swift, certain, and severe. These people are killers, and they must be treated like killers.

Finally, let me say that I ask all Americans tonight to pray—to pray for the people who have lost their lives, to pray for the families and the friends of the dead and the wounded, to pray for the people of Oklahoma City. May God's grace be with them.

Meanwhile, we will be about our work.

Thank you.

NOTE: The President spoke at 5:30 p.m. in the Briefing Room at the White House. The related proclamations of April 20 and April 21 are listed in Appendix D at the end of this volume.

Letter to Governor Frank Keating on Disaster Assistance to Oklahoma City
April 19, 1995

Dear Governor Keating:

I have declared an emergency under the Robert T. Stafford Disaster Relief and Emergency Assistance Act (the Stafford Act) for the city of Oklahoma City in the State of Oklahoma due to the explosion at the Federal courthouse in Oklahoma City on April 19, 1995 in the State of Oklahoma. I have authorized Federal relief and emergency assistance in the affected area.

Emergency assistance under Title V of the Stafford Act will be provided. Assistance under this emergency declaration will be provided at 100 percent Federal funding.

The Federal Emergency Management Agency (FEMA) will coordinate Federal assistance efforts and designate specific areas eligible for such assistance. The Federal Coordinating Officer will be Mr. Dell Greer of FEMA. He will consult with you and assist in the execution of the FEMA-State Agreement governing the expenditure of Federal funds.

Sincerely,

BILL CLINTON

NOTE: This letter was attached to a statement by Press Secretary Mike McCurry announcing disaster assistance to Oklahoma City, OK.

Letter to Federal Emergency Management Agency Director James Lee Witt on Disaster Assistance to Oklahoma City
April 19, 1995

Dear Mr. Witt:

I have determined that the explosion at the Federal courthouse in Oklahoma City, on April 19, 1995, in the State of Oklahoma is of sufficient severity and magnitude to warrant an emergency declaration under subsection 501(b) of the Robert T. Stafford Disaster Relief and Emergency Assistance Act (the Stafford Act). My decision to make this declaration pursuant to subsection 501(b) of the Stafford Act is based upon the fact that the explosion occurred at a Federally-owned courthouse. I, therefore, declare that such an emergency exists in the city of Oklahoma City in the State of Oklahoma.

In order to provide Federal assistance, you are hereby authorized to coordinate and direct other Federal agencies and fund activities not authorized under other Federal statutes and allocate from funds available for these purposes, such amounts as you find necessary for Federal emergency assistance and administrative expenses.

Pursuant to this emergency declaration, you are authorized to provide emergency assistance as you deem appropriate under Title V of the Stafford Act at 100 percent Federal funding.

Sincerely,

BILL CLINTON

NOTE: This letter was attached to a statement by Press Secretary Mike McCurry announcing disaster assistance to Oklahoma City, OK.

Statement on Reform of Regulations Implementing the Community Reinvestment Act
April 19, 1995

Today I am pleased to announce completion of a commitment I made to reform the regulations implementing the Community Reinvestment Act. These reforms help fulfill two important promises I made to the American people: to increase access to credit for all Americans and to decrease Federal regulatory burdens.

Combined with my administration's community development banks and financial institutions initiative, the Empowerment Zone/Enterprise Community program, an expanded earned-income tax credit, and our continuing effort to strengthen the economy, the reformed Community Reinvestment Act regulations will give many more Americans a chance to realize the American dream by greatly expanding individual opportunity—empowering every American to improve their own lives.

At a time when funding from all levels of government is scarcer and scarcer, the ability of our communities to help themselves takes on special importance. That's what the Community Reinvestment Act is all about.

With the new regulations in place, the statute will increasingly have a positive impact on the lives of countless Americans who work and play by the rules. Many more financial institutions will discover new, profitable lines of business. And it doesn't cost taxpayers a dime. It can create miracles in small towns and big cities from coast to coast, miracles like mortgage or business loans for people who never thought they could own a house or business, multifamily housing loans, and commercial development loans in low to moderate income communities.

To maximize the benefits that can accrue to both banks and consumers, the final regulation issued today by the Office of the Comptroller of the Currency, the Office of Thrift Supervision, the Board of Governors of the Federal Reserve, and the Federal Deposit Insurance Corporation will place emphasis on performance, not paperwork. The new regulations will make the act easier for banks to implement and will result in more consistent evaluation of their performance. With these improved regulations in place, the statute can reach its full potential to help our communities help themselves. Now is the time to end uncertainty and get on with business, not to tinker with the statute.

Producing this final regulation has taken a lot of effort on the part of the regulators and has involved excellent input from financial institutions and community groups throughout the country. I want to congratulate and thank everybody who participated in this process.

Remarks Welcoming President Fernando Cardoso of Brazil
April 20, 1995

President Cardoso and Mrs. Cardoso, distinguished guests. I am pleased to welcome to Washington a good friend of the United States and one of our hemisphere's most dynamic leaders.

Mr. President, let me begin by expressing my appreciation and the appreciation of the American people for the call and the message you sent to us yesterday in the wake of the terrible incident in Oklahoma City. Let me say again, those responsible will be brought to justice. They will be tried, convicted, and punished. We will never let the forces of inhumanity prevail in the United States.

At this moment, the rescue efforts in Oklahoma City continue. And we hold out hope that more survivors will be found. To all those carrying on this dangerous work, to the families and loved ones of those still missing, our prayers are with you. And to all those here watching and those who are watching us through the airwaves, I have ordered all our flags today throughout the United States to be flown at half-mast. And I ask you now to join with me in a moment of silence for the victims.

[*At this point, a moment of silence was observed.*]

May God's grace be with them.

Mr. President, as the largest democracies in the Americas, our countries have a special responsibility to work together, to support the extraordinary trend toward democracies and open markets throughout our region. Today we will pursue that joint action. We both know it is needed to manage our common problems and to seize our shared opportunities.

Mr. President, your own life embodies the resilience of the democratic spirit of the Americas. Thirty years ago, you were forced into exile by the enemies of democracy. But instead of giving in to bitterness, you carried on the struggle for freedom with reason and reconciliation as your only weapons. And you prevailed.

Now you lead a nation that has remained at peace with its neighbors for more than a century. That strong tradition of peaceful relations and your personal commitment to democracy give Brazil a vital role to play in strengthening cooperation among the nations and deepening the roots of civil society throughout our hemispheres. The United States welcomes the opportunity to work with you in this noble cause.

We must also work to further the goal we set at the Summit of the Americas, to create a free trade area of the Americas by the year 2005. The building blocks of free trade, the North American Free Trade Agreement and MerCoSur, are in place. Now let us move forward to transform our vision of a commercially integrated hemisphere into concrete reality.

The emerging partnership between our two countries extends beyond supporting democracy in emerging markets. We are also joining forces to stop the proliferation of weapons of mass destruction, to protect the environment, to fight against drug smuggling, and to keep peace in countries that are threatened by ethnic conflict and civil war. The United States is counting on Brazil's continued leadership in meeting these major challenges of our time.

Mr. President, you represent a vibrant people whose pride in the past is matched only by their hope for the future. Your own efforts to bring economic stability and social justice to Brazil are responsible for much of that promise of tomorrow. On this solid foundation and under your leadership, Brazil is poised to take its rightful place as a shining example for all the Americas and all the world.

Mr. President, we are honored to have you here. Welcome to the White House. Welcome to the United States.

NOTE: The President spoke at 10:42 a.m. on the South Lawn at the White House. In his remarks,

he referred to Ruth Cardoso, wife of President Cardoso. The proclamation commemorating the victims of the Oklahoma City bombing is listed in Appendix D at the end of this volume.

The President's News Conference With President Fernando Cardoso of Brazil
April 20, 1995

President Clinton. Good afternoon. Please be seated.

I am delighted to welcome President Cardoso to the White House. For many years he has been one of the great leaders of the Americas. Although he was only inaugurated in January, President Cardoso has been a fighter for democracy throughout his life. He opposed the forces of authoritarianism at great personal risk to himself. More recently, he led the battle for economic reform during his years as Finance Minister, to reduce inflation, establish growth, and help Brazil fulfill the tremendous promise of its people and its land.

Today the President told me about his economic and constitution reform efforts, which are essential to placing Brazil on the path of sustainable development. I have every confidence in the President's ability to strengthen Brazilian democracy and to advance the visionary economic reforms he began as Finance Minister.

Brazil played a key role in forging the historic agreement at last year's Summit of the Americas. Today President Cardoso and I discussed how we could build on that success. We also discussed bilateral trade issues, and we reaffirmed our commitments to open our markets to each other's products. With 160 million consumers, Brazil is one of today's biggest emerging markets, and it offers great opportunity for Americans.

We know that one of the ways we will do this is to realize our common commitment to achieve a free trade area of the Americas by the year 2005. We have instructed Ambassador Kantor and Foreign Minister Lampreia to review trade relations between our nations, as well as those between the NAFTA and the MerCoSur countries, to consider ways to expand

the flow of goods and capital between our nations. One step will be the first meeting this June of the United States-Brazil Business Development Council, which will bring together private sector leaders to increase investment and trade in both our nations.

On security issues, we had a very good discussion about the need to stand firm together against terrorism. We reviewed the effort by the Rio Protocol Guarantors to find a lasting solution to the conflict between Peru and Ecuador over their borders. Progress has been made in implementing a cease-fire, now we must find an enduring settlement. I congratulate, again, President Cardoso on his outstanding leadership in helping to resolve this conflict. And the United States has been proud to have Americans working with Brazilians there to try to make sure we bring the conflict to a satisfactory conclusion.

Let me say that, finally, we also reviewed our common efforts against narcotics and money laundering. We agreed to begin a dialog on protecting the environment. U.S. aid funds will be increased this year to try to assist that effort in Brazil. And our governments will exchange ideas on reforming international financial institutions to meet the challenges of the 21st century.

I must say, I was especially impressed by the ideas that President Cardoso and the members of his administration have shared with us on the changes we need to make in the international institutions so that we can get the benefit of the globally integrated markets that we all want to benefit from without having too much instability undermine the march to progress.

With our two great nations cooperating as never before, we stand at a moment of unparalleled opportunity. We must now seize it, and we will seize it. We will promote democracy. We will advance prosperity. We will do it together. In the months and years ahead, I look forward to working with President Cardoso to forge an even stronger partnership between our nations and our peoples. We should do it. It is in our interest to do it, and it is the right thing for our hemisphere and for the world to do it.

Thank you, Mr. President.

President Cardoso. Mr. President, ladies and gentlemen, it was a great honor to be received by President Bill Clinton today. I know that this is a day of grief for this country, and I take this opportunity to extend to all Americans the solidarity of the Brazilian people. To you, President Clinton, I convey a personal message of support and encouragement. Mr. President, I will repeat what I said this morning: In my view, this terrorist act affects not only America, it affects all of us who believe in peace and democracy and in freedom for all.

During our meeting, I had a chance to express to you my personal friendship and the admiration that Brazil has for his permanent commitment to the cause of peace, prosperity, and democracy.

I had the privilege of meeting President Clinton during the Miami summit, as initiative that revealed his statesmanship and his vision of a better future for the Americas. Today, as we discussed the prospects for our hemisphere, I had the chance to assure him that the same spirit of cooperation that guided my country during the works of the summit will keep guiding us in implementing of its results.

I had also the chance to bring to the American people the message of a country that went through deep transformations and that today presents itself to the world as a solid democracy, a strong economy, and a vigorous and free society. This new country is a natural partner of the U.S., and I stressed to President Clinton that the time is right for the design of a new affirmative agenda that will bring our two countries even closer together.

And I must say that it was really highly impressive by the kind words by President Clinton and by the spirit in our discussions. We have so many values in common. We have a similar political will. We have the support of our people to work together in reaffirming our commitment

to reforms, to bring to our countries better conditions of life, and to go ahead with democracy.

I would like to add, Mr. President, that Brazil will support also the effort under the umbrella of the Organization of American States toward democracy and the specific program you referred to, and that Brazil will be always open in discussing the international financial issues, and Brazil is ready to assume more responsibilities at the world level in order to go ahead with the programs of peacekeeping and to do the best of our effort to really keep a world of peace.

Already in this context of this new agenda, Ambassador Lampreia, as you said, and Ambassador Kantor are being instructed to prepare a study of trade relations between Brazil and the United States with the objective of improving the flow of goods, services, and capital between our countries. In this same area, we agreed that the first meeting of the Brazil-U.S. Business Development Council shall take place in Denver this June, cochaired by Ambassador Lampreia and by Secretary Brown, in bringing together private sector representatives. I am confident that this first meeting will be a very important opportunity to increase even further the economic relations between our two countries.

In the discussion of the main themes of the international agenda, I expressed to President Clinton my view that the same democratic values that had proven its strength with the end of cold war should now guide us in the effort of building a new international order. Democracy should be the cornerstone, not only inside each society but also among nations. This is the guideline that Brazil will follow in the meetings in which the revision of the San Francisco Charter will be discussed.

I also had the chance to express to President Clinton our long-standing commitment to the cause of nonproliferation and peace. This commitment has a very concrete translation in our decision to ratify and fully implement the Tlatelolco Agreement and also in the creation of the Brazilian Space Agency, in our commitment by the executive branch to abide by the MTCR guidelines in the approval of the Quadripartite Nuclear Safeguards Agreement.

The very positive working meeting that I had the privilege to hold this morning with President Clinton is only a first step taken toward the strengthening of a new relationship that, built upon a solid base of shared values, will be decisive to make real the dream of a prosperous, fair, and free hemisphere for all of us.

Thank you very much.

President Clinton. Thank you.

Terry [Terence Hunt, Associated Press].

Oklahoma City Bombing

Q. Mr. President, the bombing in Oklahoma City has left many Americans wondering, if it can happen in the Nation's heartland, can it happen in their hometown? What can you say to calm these fears? And in particular, what can you say to the Nation's children, who have been terrified by seeing other children killed?

President Clinton. I would say, first of all, that we are working very hard to strengthen the ability of the United States to resist acts of terror. We have increased our efforts in law enforcement, through the FBI and the CIA. We have increased our ability to cut off money used for such purposes. We have increased our capacity to track the materials that can be used to destroy people. I have sent legislation to the Congress, as you know, that would increase this capacity even further. I have done everything I could and our administration has to bring home suspected terrorists for trial from Pakistan, from Egypt, from the Philippines, from elsewhere. We are moving aggressively. Today I have ordered new steps to be taken to secure Federal facilities throughout the United States.

I would say to the children of this country, what happened was a bad thing, an evil thing, but we will find the people who did it, and we will bring them to justice. This is a law-abiding country. And neither the leaders nor the citizens of this country will permit it to be paralyzed by this kind of behavior.

Mexican Financial Crisis

Q. I'd like to address this question to both President Cardoso and President Clinton. You both mentioned today the spirit of Miami, the economic integration of the Americas. Do you believe it's still possible after the collapse of Mexico?

President Cardoso. Should I answer in Portuguese or English? I will answer in Portuguese because it could be immediately transmitted to Brazil.

[*At this point, President Cardoso answered the question in Portuguese, and a translation was not provided.*]

If you would like, I can make a very brief summary. I said that I believe that what happened with Mexico is not an obstacle to go ahead with the Miami spirit. The Miami spirit was a result of a long history of good relationship among our peoples. And we believe that the immediate reaction patronized by President Clinton and then the international support to Mexico was a good example of the necessity of still more alive spirit like the Miami summit did in order to solve problems and crises which can occur from time to time, but together we will solve all these crises much more rapidly and much more energetically than alone.

President Clinton. I agree with that. I believe that, first of all, that the problem in Mexico has caused severe problems for the people of Mexico. It has also presented challenges to Brazil, to Argentina, indeed, to the United States. But look at the long run. The countries of our hemisphere are moving toward democracy, toward openness, toward free competition. The more we work together, the less likely it is that we will have future problems like we had in Mexico.

So, if anything, if there is any lesson to be drawn here, it is that we must work more urgently in these directions and more urgently to be strong together so that these events will not have the kind of shocking impact they had in Mexico.

Helen [Helen Thomas, United Press International].

Oklahoma City Bombing

Q. Mr. President, despite the horror of it all and the assumptions that may or may not be true, don't you think that it's time now to warn against hatred and violence against Middle Eastern stereotypes, just in case, since we do have strong laws in this country, I believe, against terrorism?

President Clinton. I would like to make, if I might, two comments with regard to that. Number one, I ask the American people not to jump to any conclusions. We have two missions now. One is search and rescue, search and rescue. We had a miraculous recovery of a teenage girl just hours ago, and we have six special teams from FEMA that will be on the ground today to continue this. The second is investigate. We have 200, 200 FBI agents on the scene and hundreds of other people all across America putting their best efforts behind this. Let us not jump to conclusions.

Then I would say, in response to your question, there were three Arab-American organizations which today condemned what was done. This is not a question of anybody's country of origin. This is not a question of anybody's religion. This was murder. This was evil. This was wrong. Human beings everywhere, all over the world, will condemn this out of their own religious convictions. And we should not stereotype anybody.

What we need to do is to find out who did this and punish them harshly. That's what we need to do. The American people should know that the best investigators in the world are working to find the truth. Let us support search and rescue and investigation and deal with the facts as we find them.

International Financial Institutions

Q. I'd like to direct my question to both Presidents. After the Mexican crisis, both governments, Brazil and the United States, talked about the need for equipping international financial institutions of means to react in those circumstances. I would like to know what you have discussed in that regard. And to President Clinton, since the United States and the G–7 countries seems to continue to be in no position to increase of capital of the IMF, how can the G–7 countries achieve that objective without providing the money to the institution?

President Cardoso. Well, in fact—have discussed a little, that point, and it seems to us, I would say, that the time is coming to take some important decision in that area. It's not easy. You know, the Bretton Woods institutions are now approaching the 50th anniversary. So it's time to implement some changes. We are discussing these changes. I had some ideas. I presented to President Clinton these ideas which are not, you know, unexpected ideas. Everybody knows that it is important to—maybe to give more leverage to the IMF to act more promptly and to solve these emergency problems. I'm convinced that the G–7 will take the issue, and I am waiting for additional initiatives, and Brazil is—will be ready to cooperate in these kind of initiatives.

President Clinton. Let me say, I strongly believe that there must be some changes. And I urged the G–7 countries last year, when we met in Italy, to devote this year's meeting to

reviewing the adequacy of the international financial institutions to meet the challenges of the present global economy.

Furthermore, if we expect the IMF and the World Bank to tell countries, "Look you must reform your economy; you must even be prepared to have the hard times that discipline sometimes brings in the short run to help prosperity in the long run," then surely we must have some capacity to cushion the same countries that are prepared to make those sacrifices against unforeseen and dramatic adverse changes that the underlying economic circumstances do not warrant. So we are looking into that.

But I think that it is important for me as President of the United States not to commit myself at this early juncture to specific reforms until after I have a chance to consult with all the other countries with whom we should work, not just the G–7 countries but the emerging economies, the powerful countries of the future, like Brazil, who lived through this system and have very good ideas about how to change it.

Yes, Brit [Brit Hume, ABC News].

Oklahoma City Bombing

Q. Two things, sir. First, how concerned are you that this incident in Oklahoma will be seen by those who feel that the United States should not have the kind of far-flung diplomatic and military undertakings that it does, that this is the kind of thing that happens when a nation, as some would say, meddles in the affairs of others? And second, if you know anything about it, sir, there's a wire service report that the British Interior Ministry says that a possible suspect in this case is—is being, or has been returned to the United States.

Thank you.

President Clinton. First, let me say, I would hope the American people would draw exactly the opposite conclusion from this. Our future lies in an open society, a free economy, and the free interchange of people of ideas and goods. In that kind of world, we cannot withdraw from the world, nor can we hide.

Look what happened in Argentina. No one thinks the Argentines are out there meddling in the affairs of people throughout the world. No great country can hide. We have to stand up, fight this kind of madness, and take appropriate steps.

Moreover, I will say again, we do not know who the perpetrator is. Technology gives power to people to do this sort of thing. Look at what happened in Japan, where there was no outside influence but a radical group within Japan able to take a little vial of gas and kill large numbers of people, this having happened twice now.

So the lesson for my fellow citizens should be, we're going to stand with freedom-loving people throughout the world, like President Cardoso, who despise this sort of evil, and we're going to stamp it out. And we're going to protect our people.

Now as to the second question. Let me say again, I was briefed last night at midnight; I was briefed this morning, early in the morning. I know what the status of our efforts are. They are intense, and they are comprehensive. But I do not believe we should be commenting on an ongoing investigation. And at the appropriate time, the Justice Department will say whatever it is that should be said.

I can tell the American people, they would be very proud of the efforts which have been made in this area since it occurred yesterday morning. They have been awesome, intense, comprehensive, and dogged. But I will not comment on the specific aspects of the investigation until the Justice Department determines it's appropriate to do.

Brazilian Patent Legislation

Q. I would like to direct the question to both Presidents. If the Brazilian Congress does not approve the intellectual property bill before the deadline for the USTR to start a new phase of investigation on Brazil, what course of action does each of you intend to take?

President Cardoso. Well, you know, the Brazilian Congress is a sovereign Congress. It can take the time it believes is necessary to discuss a bill. As you know, Brazilians know, the Brazilian Government has a clear idea and is exposing its own ideas to the Congress, is insisting on the necessity of a bill to protect intellectual rights. Also for Brazilians—at that point in time, there are many Brazilians who are urging, you know, the approval of this bill because they need to have their patents recognized across the world. And they have no possibility to ask the Brazilian Bureau to do it, because we don't have yet a law.

So I am convinced that the Congress will approve the bill as soon as possible. I'm expecting for this semester the last vote in the Senate, and then back to the House, but the House

has only one choice: assume that the Congress—that Senate added good things and then approve the amendments made by the Senate, or approve the law which has been already approved by the House.

So it's a matter of some—a couple of weeks or months. And this is important for Brazil; it is not for United States. It is important for Brazil because we are integrating at the global level the economy, and we need to protect our own interests through this bill.

President Clinton. Well, as you know, we have certain laws in this country we have to follow. But I am absolutely convinced after this meeting today that the President wants to pass that legislation. And I agree with him that the main beneficiary of that legislation would not be the United States or other nations trading with Brazil. It would be Brazil.

It is important that everyone in Brazil understands you are rapidly becoming not only a very great economy but a very sophisticated one. A product manufactured by Brazil is now going to be part of the space shuttle. You need— if you're going to be a high-tech producer of sophisticated and diverse products, you must have a strong patent law. Yes, it will protect our intellectual property, but more importantly, it will enable you to continue to grow your economy.

Rita [Rita Braver, CBS News].

Oklahoma City Bombing

Q. I know we're quite early on in the investigation on Oklahoma City, but Janet Reno has already said that the U.S. would seek the death penalty. I wondered if she did that with your concurrence. And also, if the United States should find that another country was behind this, should we expect military retaliation?

President Clinton. I must not and I must urge you not to speculate on who is guilty yet or what their connections are. That cannot help the course of the investigation. Let us wait and see what the facts are.

In response to your first question, she did say that with my knowledge and support. Just a few—oh, maybe in a couple of hours after this incident occurred, after we reviewed all the things that we could do to work on the search and rescue mission, I asked specifically whether the crime bill we passed provided for capital punishment in cases like this. If this isn't an appropriate case for it, I don't think there ever would be one. And I strongly support what she said.

We'll take—take one last question—

[*At this point, a question was asked in Portuguese, and a translation was not provided.*]

Brazilian Infrastructure

President Cardoso. OK. OK, the point raised is that Brazil needs something like $70 billion in the coming 4 years just to enlarge its infrastructure, and we have passed a bill on public services concessions. By the way, I was the author of the bill when I was Senator. It took 4 years to approve the bill. And now what is required is a set of rules by the executive branch in order to clarify how to do it. This is—at this point in time, we have a draft for this Executive order, and it is a matter of weeks and the Brazilian Government will approve these rules.

And of course, the Brazilian economy is open to foreign investors through this mechanism of concessions, public service concessions law, but also we are going ahead with our privatization program. As I said yesterday at the Brazilian-American Chamber of Commerce, we are ready to ask for more foreign capital in several areas.

It depends in some areas yet from our constitutional reform, and we are moving fast in that direction. I expect for the next months the approval of the constitutional amendments as sent to the Congress regarding economic order. As you know, President Clinton, constitutional amendments requires enormous debate at the Congress, and it takes time. To my view, what is going now on in Brazil is the Congress is reacting very quickly because they are about

to vote the first one of these amendments in a matter of maybe some days, and this will be a record. I am absolutely confident that the Brazilian Congress will approve what is needed for the Brazilian economic improvement.

That's all.

Oklahoma City Bombing

President Clinton. I agree with that.

Let me—we have to conclude. I want to make sure that I have been very clear on the question, Rita, that you asked. You asked, well, what if we find out someone did it affiliated with another country. I don't want anyone to assume that we are accusing anybody or anything today. We do not know.

On the other hand, let me reiterate what I said yesterday. Whoever did it, we will find out, and there will be justice that will be swift and certain and severe. And there is no place to hide. Nobody can hide any place in this country, nobody can hide any place in this world from the terrible consequences of what has been done. This was an attack on innocent children, on innocent victims, on the people there in Oklahoma City. But make no mistake about it, this was an attack on the United States, our way of life, and everything we believe in. So whoever did it, we will get to the bottom of it, and then we'll take the appropriate action.

Thank you very much.

NOTE: The President's 94th news conference began at 12:52 p.m. in the Rose Garden at the White House. In his remarks, he referred to Foreign Minister Luiz Felipe Lampreia of Brazil.

Memorandum on Employees Affected by the Oklahoma City Bombing
April 20, 1995

Memorandum for the Heads of Executive Departments and Agencies

Subject: Excused Absence for Employees Affected by the Bombing of the Federal Building in Oklahoma City

I am deeply saddened by the loss of life and suffering caused by the bombing of the Alfred P. Murrah Federal Building in Oklahoma City.

I convey my deepest sympathy and heartfelt sorrow to our fellow Americans and their families who have been affected by this senseless act of violence. Many parts of the Federal Government have been mobilized to respond to this tragedy.

As part of this effort, I ask the heads of executive departments and agencies having Federal civilian employees in the Oklahoma City area to excuse from duty, without charge to leave or loss of pay, any such employee who is prevented from reporting to work or faced with a personal emergency because of the bombing and who can be spared from his or her usual responsibilities. This policy should also be applied to any employee who is needed for emergency law enforcement, relief, or recovery efforts authorized by Federal, State, or local officials having jurisdiction.

Workers' compensation benefits are available in the case of Federal employees who were injured or killed in the bombing. The Department of Labor has sent a team of workers' compensation specialists to Oklahoma City to provide direct assistance to affected employees and their families.

WILLIAM J. CLINTON

Remarks at the State Dinner for President Fernando Cardoso of Brazil
April 20, 1995

Mr. President, Mrs. Cardoso, members of the Brazilian delegation, to all of our distinguished guests, Hillary and I are delighted to welcome you to the White House this evening.

Mr. President, I learned many things about you today. But one thing sort of surprised me: I learned that as a young man you were drawn to a life of the cloth. The reason I learned that and found it surprising was my grandmother told me that I would make a good minister if I were just a little better boy—[*laughter*]— and failing that, that I should go into politics. [*Laughter*]

But I think for a long time your family and friends believed you were more likely to wear a Cardinal's red hat than a President's sash. Well, you embraced politics, and now you lead your great nation. But I can't help wondering whether after 4 months in office, after spending 2,880 hours dealing with Congress and fielding questions from the media, whether you ever wonder if you made the right choice. [*Laughter*]

Let me say from the point of view of the people of the United States, you clearly made the right choice. And it is obvious to all of us that your faith has remained a powerful part of your life. Otherwise, it would be difficult to explain how you have endured arrest, blacklisting, and exile without giving in to despair; difficult to explain that although the enemies of democracy forced you to listen to your friends being tortured and later bombed the office where you worked, you never wavered from the ideals of tolerance and openness.

Those ideals animate your leadership in Brazil today and your quest for social justice for all

the people whom you proudly represent. And you have added to them an academic's expertise in policy and economics, which I am pleased to note, you have refined by teaching at some of our finest universities. We have all been impressed by the results you have achieved, especially the success of your "Real Plan."

Mr. President, I have been very pleased for the opportunity to continue the personal conversation we began in Miami last year at the Summit of the Americas. The warm and productive relationship that we have established mirrors the relationship that is growing closer every day between our two countries. We have common interests, bringing free trade to the Americas, promoting sustainable development throughout our hemisphere, keeping peace around the world. And that relationship is more important than ever.

I know from our discussions that we both believe Brazil and the United States have an opportunity, indeed an obligation, to be partners for progress in the Americas for all the years ahead. Today we have taken that partnership to a new level.

Let me also say, Mr. President, you know that you have come here, along with your wife and your fine delegation, at a very difficult time for our country. And all the American people have been profoundly impressed and grateful by your expressions of condolence and sympathy and your assertion that we are all partners in the struggle against evil and inhumanity. For that we are especially grateful, and we will never forget it.

So I ask all of you to stand and raise your glasses in a toast to President and Mrs. Cardoso and to the people of Brazil.

NOTE: The President spoke at 8:25 p.m. in the State Dining Room at the White House.

Remarks and an Exchange With Reporters on the Oklahoma City Bombing
April 21, 1995

The President. I wanted to make a couple of points. First of all, I was briefed late last evening by the Attorney General on the status of the investigation, and I am well satisfied with the efforts that are being made, the progress that's being made. I would just ask that you and the American people not rush to any conclusions unsupported by known evidence and that we give the investigators the space they need to do their job. They are working hard; they are moving ahead.

The second thing I'd like to say is that Hillary and I have decided to go to Oklahoma City on Sunday to be a part of the memorial service and to be with the families of the victims and the people of Oklahoma City. I think all America will be there in spirit and is there today, and I have determined that I should also declare Sunday a national day of mourning for the victims there and to ask people in their places of worship and in their homes all across America to pray for the people there and for the community.

The final thing I'd like to say is just a brief message to the children of this country. I have been very concerned with how the children in Oklahoma City and, indeed, the children throughout America must be reacting to a horror of this magnitude. And my message to the children is that this was an evil thing and the

people who did it were terribly, horribly wrong. We will catch them, and we will punish them.

But the children of America need to know that almost all the adults in this country are good people who love their children and love other children, and we're going to get through this. We're going to get through this. I don't want our children to believe something terrible about life and the future and grownups in general because of this awful thing. Most adults are good people who want to protect our children in their childhood, and we are going to get through this.

Q. Mr. President, do you know of any progress in the investigation?

The President. You know I'm not going to comment. I'm letting the Justice Department announce progress. I don't think that it's appropriate for me to say anything, except I can tell you that I know what they've done and the American people would be very pleased and very impressed by the work they are doing. But this is a big issue, and we don't want to undermine their ability to work by anything that is said or by jumping to unwarranted conclusions.

NOTE: The President spoke at 10 a.m. on the South Lawn at the White House, prior to his departure for Havre de Grace, MD. The proclamation declaring a national day of mourning is listed in Appendix D at the end of this volume.

Remarks on the 25th Observance of Earth Day in Havre de Grace, Maryland
April 21, 1995

Thank you so much. First let me say to all of you how glad we are to be here. I know a lot of you have been here since very early this morning, and you've had a little rain coming

out of the sky. You might have gotten a little more of the environment than you bargained for today. [*Laughter*] But I'm glad to see you all here bright-eyed, clear-eyed, and committed to preserving America's natural environment.

I want to thank Governor Glendening and Senators Mikulski and Sarbanes, Congressman Gilchrest, and the other State officials who are here, your mayor, and so many others for everything that they have done. I'd like to say a special word of appreciation to the man who was responsible for this wonderful walkway we came down, Bob Lee, and all the rest of you who worked on that. It's a great thing. I also want to thank the AmeriCorps volunteers who have done so much, who have done so much to help to keep the Chesapeake clean. And finally let me say a special word of thanks to Mary Rosso—didn't she do a good job up here—just like she was—[*applause*]—not only for the speech that she gave but for the work that she did that brought her to this place today.

Ladies and gentlemen, I want to do one other thing before I get into the remarks that I came to make today. You know that this is the 25th anniversary of Earth Day. Twenty-five years ago, Earth Day was an American celebration: Americans of both political parties; Americans of all races and ethnic backgrounds, Americans from all regions of the country; Americans who were rich, poor, and middle class; Americans just got together to reaffirm their commitment to preserving our natural environment; Americans who lived in the city and were worried about city environmental problems; and Americans who lived in places like this—people like me—who were interested in going to places like the Duck Decoy Museum, knew that if they wanted the ducks to fly in Arkansas and Maryland in duck season, we'd better clean the environment up. It was an American experience. We joined together to save the natural beauty and all the resources that God has given us and to pass it on to our children and grandchildren.

For a quarter of a century now, Americans have stood as one to say no to dirty air, toxic food, poison water, and yes to leaving a land to our children as unspoiled as their hopes. This Earth Day may be the most important Earth Day since the beginning because there is such a great debate going on now that threatens to break apart the bipartisan alliance to save this country.

And before I get into that, I want to ask a man to come up here who was mentioned by Vice President Gore, who started this whole Earth Day, and who sponsored a lot of the most important environmental legislation of our time, Senator Gaylord Nelson of Wisconsin. I'd like to ask him to come here. After—give him a hand. [*Applause*]

After Gaylord Nelson left the United States Senate, he went on to a distinguished career as head of the Wilderness Society and devoted the rest of his working life directly to our environment. And today on this 25th anniversary of Earth Day, I decided the best way I could celebrate this and try again to call forth this American spirit of dedication to our environment is to award to Gaylord Nelson our Nation's highest civilian honor, the Presidential Medal of Freedom.

I can't help noting that in 1789 the Continental Congress almost made Havre de Grace our Nation's capital. Now that I'm here, I see why it was a contender. And on the bad days in Washington, if it's all the same to you, I may just come back here and set up shop.

Ladies and gentlemen, if you ever doubt what we can do together to preserve our heritage, all you have to do is look at this bay. The beauty you see is God-given, but it was defended and rescued by human beings. Not long ago the Chesapeake was a mess. Garbage floated on it; shellfish were unsafe to eat. Now, I know there's still a lot more to do, but you know the bay is coming back because people overcame all that divided them to save their common heritage. People from Maryland, Virginia, Pennsylvania, the District of Columbia all joined together—with a Federal effort as well—citizens of all kinds, from both political parties, watermen, farmers, business people, environmental groups. They couldn't have done it without the bipartisan lines of defense sparked by the first Earth Day: the Environmental Protection Agency, the Clean Air Act, the Endangered Species Act, the Clean Water Act, all forged by Democrats and Republicans, by Presidents and Congresses working together.

Twenty-five years ago and more, we once had a river catch on fire. Lead was released into the air without a second thought. Our national bird was on the verge of extinction. Today we don't routinely dump sewage in our water anymore. We know better. Our children aren't dying from lead poisoning, and the bald eagle soars again all across America.

But what we're doing is more than about natural beauty. It also affects our health as well. A recent study by the Harvard School of Public

Health found that air pollution raised the risk of premature death by 15 or more percent.

Now, in this atmosphere of debate over environmental issues today, we all know that the particular solutions that were adopted 25 years ago aren't necessarily the right detailed program for today or for the next 25 years. But the old habit of putting American progress against nature is as outdated as the old belief that heavy top-down Government can solve all of our problems.

So as we say, well, should we reform the way we do things, let's not forget there is a right way and a wrong way to reform our approach to preserving our environment and protecting the public health. It would be crazy to throw the gains we have made in health and safety away, or to forget the lessons of the last 25 years. But that is just exactly what some of the proposed legislation in the United States Congress would do, and you must be clear about it.

Can this new Congress with these proposed bills prove that our air will be clean under the laws that have been proposed? Can they prove our water will be free of deadly bacteria? Can they prove our meat will be untainted? Bills passed in the House effectively hold up all regulations for 2 years. Should we wait that long for fresher air, purer water, safer food?

Instead of success stories like the Chesapeake, what if we face what happened in Milwaukee? In April of 1993, the citizens of Milwaukee drank the city's water not knowing it had been contaminated by a deadly bacteria. A hundred people died. Hundreds more fell ill—thousands more fell ill. The last casualty of that incident occurred just a few days ago when a child died from an infection, just a few days ago.

For more than a week, the people of Milwaukee were terrified to brush their teeth, make coffee, use ice cubes, even wash their clothes in the city's water supply. If you want to know how bad it was, you can ask Robert and Astrid Morris, who are here, or Susan Mudd, who along with her husband, Mayor John Norquist of Milwaukee, dealt with the terrible problems that faced all people of that city and reached into their own family. They were all in Milwaukee. Their loved ones suffered. They are here today. I'd like them to be recognized. They're over there. Raise your hands, and let's give them a hand. [*Applause*]

That's just one example of our continuing challenge on the health front. Two years ago, more than 400 people got horribly sick from eating hamburgers that contained the deadly *E. coli* bacteria. Children died. How could it happen? Well, at the time, inspectors from the Department of Agriculture merely looked, touched, and smelled meat and poultry to determine whether it was contaminated. Under the leadership of our then-Secretary of Agriculture, Mike Espy, we moved aggressively to step up inspections, and we proposed new regulations to use high-tech devices to really check the meat for its purity so that we'll be able to stop diseases that can infect our food.

But listen to this: The House of Representatives passed legislation that would handcuff our ability to address these two problems and many others as well. The House bill would hold up for a year regulations to protect people from the *E. coli* bacteria or from the microbial in the Milwaukee water. In fact, there were specific, separate votes on both those things where our people said, "Well, at least let's protect Milwaukee and that problem." "Well, at least let's deal with the *E. coli* problem. Surely we don't need to wait this long to put in these standards." And they said, "No, we don't need to do this."

Now, folks, in the politically attractive name of deregulation—who can be against that?—they have proposed a moratorium on all efforts to protect public health and safety, even these efforts, when we know there is a danger and we know what to do about it. This would stop good regulations, bad regulations, all regulations. They would block the safeguards that we have proposed to see that Milwaukee never happens again. They would block our efforts to make sure we don't expose anymore children anywhere by accident to the tainted meat with *E. coli* bacteria. We must not let this happen. And I will not let it happen.

Let me give you another example of what's going on. Should Government examine the cost and benefits of what it does before it moves? Of course. Don't you do that in your own life? Of course, you do. And I would support a reasonable bipartisan bill that says we ought to pay more careful attention to the cost and benefits of what we do. But under the so-called "risk legislation" pending in the Congress, every agency of our Government would have to go through an expensive and time-consuming process every time they want to move a muscle.

One line in this bill—I want to say this again—one line in this proposed legislation overrides every health and safety standards on the books. It says rather than our children's health, money will always be the bottom line.

This bill would let lawyers and special interests tie up the Government forever in lawsuits and petitions. The people proposing this bill, after railing for years and years and years about how we have too many lawsuits and too much bureaucracy, have constructed a bill designed to give relief to every lawyer in the country that wants to get into a mindless legal challenge and designed to construct gridlock and to make sure it gets into the court and lasts forever as long as it's about an environmental regulation. It would literally give polluters control over the regulations that affect them. It would lead to more bureaucracy, more lawsuits, but a whole lot less protection of the public health. And it should be defeated.

There is another bill in the House—it passed the House—called the so-called takings bill. And it has a very politically attractive purpose, to prevent the Government from taking property away from citizens without paying them for it. Well, that's already provided for in the Constitution. But it sure sounds good, doesn't it? You wouldn't like it if the Government showed up tomorrow on your front step and took your home away. And you'd expect even if it were an emergency and had to be done, to be paid for it. That's not what this is about. You're protected from that already. This is about making taxpayers pay polluters not to pollute. This is about making the Government pay out billions of dollars every time it acts to protect the public. It would bust the budget and benefit wealthy landowners at the expense of ordinary Americans.

This so-called takings bill has been on the ballot in 20 States. And every place it's been on the ballot, including some very conservative Republican States, the voters have voted against it. Well, the voters don't get to vote on the takings legislation, so the President will vote for them, and the President will vote no.

Ladies and gentlemen, you might wonder who thought up these bills. Well, the lobbyists for the big companies thought up these bills. And they were actually invited to sit down at the table and draft the bills and then explain them to the Congressmen who were supposed to be writing them.

Now, you know, lobbyists have always had an important role in the legislative process, and they always will. And all of us could be lobbyists at one time or another if something were going on in Congress or in the State legislature we didn't like or that we did like. But in my lifetime, nothing like this has ever happened. I mean, they're having meetings in which the lobbyists are writing the bills and explaining them to the Congressmen, who are then supposed to go explain why they're for them.

The lobbyists were given a room off the House floor to write speeches for the Congressmen explaining why they were supporting the bills that the lobbyists had written for them. When some Senators held a briefing on one of these bills recently, they invited the lobbyists to explain what they were for, since they had written it and the Senators hadn't quite got it down yet. [*Laughter*]

Now, I don't think that any party has a lock on purity, and I think that all politics is about compromise. But there has never in my lifetime been an example like this. And I don't think whether you're a Republican or a Democrat or a liberal or a conservative, I don't think you believe that that's the way your Federal Government ought to work when it comes to matters affecting the health and welfare of your children and the environmental future of the United States and, indeed, our entire planet. I don't believe you believe that.

On this Earth Day, let me pledge we will not allow lobbyists to rewrite our environmental laws in ways that benefit polluters and hurt our families, our children, and our future. Reform? Yes. Modernize? You bet. But roll back health and safety? No. Let DDT into our food again? Not on your life. Create more tainted water or toxic waste, the kind Mary Rosso and Angela Pool from Gary, Indiana, who is also with us here today, the kind of things they are fighting? Never. No. Say no, folks. Say no. Just say no to what they are doing.

I will support the right kind of change. I have spent 2 years working with the Vice President to do things people said couldn't be done. We have tried to improve the environment and advance the economy. He has proved with his reinventing Government initiative that you could reduce bureaucracy, shrink the size of the Federal Government, and improve the performance of the Federal Government so that people get more for their tax dollars. I support a bill in the Senate that is bipartisan that would give Congress 45 days to consider new regulations before they take effect. That is not an unreasonable amount of time. Government bureaucracies do make mistakes. Everybody can come up with some horror story they've had in their life. Do something reasonable like this. But to paralyze the ability of the Government of the United States to protect children from more Milwaukees and more *E. coli* hamburgers? No, no, no. Let's adopt a reasonable bipartisan bill.

Let me tell you something else we did that I hope you will support. Until recently, we discovered that many small businesses were literally afraid to come to the Environmental Protection Agency for help in cleaning up a problem because they thought they would be fined. They thought they'd go through a bureaucratic nightmare, and so they didn't come. And so under the leadership of Carol Browner, the EPA has changed its policy. Now, if a small business comes to the EPA in good faith for advice on an environmental problem, they will be given 180 days, 6 months, to fight it with—to solve it without being fined. That way they can spend the money repairing their businesses and repairing the Earth, not fighting with regulators.

The Vice President also said that the EPA was going to cut its paperwork burdens on Americans by 25 percent. Twenty million hours a year will be given by the Government back to the private citizens of the United States to do what they want. That's more important to a lot of people than money. We are giving 20 million hours from the Government back to the people of the United States to do what they want. I am all for making Government less burdensome. It shouldn't take a forest full of paper to protect the environment. No telling how many trees we're going to keep up by cutting the paperwork burden of the EPA. But to cut the mission of the EPA to protect the environment and the future? No. Let's change in the right way, not the wrong way.

My fellow Americans, in the next 10 years as we move toward the 21st century, indeed, in the lives of all the children here present throughout their lives, I predict to you we will become more concerned with environmental issues, not less concerned. We will have to deal with the shortage of clean water, with global climate change, with the unfair environmental burdens that are placed on poor communities

in America, with the political problems of uncontrollable immigration that are sparked all around the world in part because of environmental degradation.

Do you remember how just a few months ago the waters were full of Haitian boat people trying to get to the United States because of political oppression? One reason is nobody can make a living down there because they have ripped every tree off every spot of ground in the whole country. It is an environmental crisis as well as an economic crisis. So as we restore democracy, we know democracy will not prevail, we know that the Haitian people will not be able to live in Haiti and raise their children there and make money there and not seek to come to the United States or somewhere else unless we can rebuild the environment.

My fellow Americans, we must be more concerned with these issues, not less concerned with these issues. We cannot disarm our ability to deal with them. Our natural security must be seen as part of our national security.

Take a last look at this beautiful bay behind me. I'll never forget the first time I saw the Chesapeake, about 30 years ago now—a little more, actually. Will your children's children see what we see now and what I saw then? Will there be water clean enough to swim in? Will there be a strong economy that is sustained by a sound environment? Believe me, if we degrade our American environment, we will depress our economy and lower our incomes and shrink our opportunities, not increase them.

It is our landscape, our culture, and our values together that make us Americans. Stewardship of our land is a major part of the stewardship of the American dream since the dream grew out of this very soil. Robert Frost wrote, "The land was ours before we were the land." This continent is our home, and we must preserve it for our children, their children, and all generations beyond.

Thank you, and God bless you.

NOTE: The President spoke at 11:46 a.m. in the Park at Concord Lighthouse. In his remarks, he referred to Gov. Parris Glendening of Maryland; Mayor Gunther Hirsh of Havre de Grace; Charles Lee (Bob Lee) Geddes, management assistant, Harford County Department of Parks and Recreation; and Mary Rosso, founder, Maryland Waste Coalition.

Statement Announcing the Award of the Presidential Medal of Freedom to Gaylord Nelson
April 21, 1995

I am pleased to announce my intention to award the Presidential Medal of Freedom to former Senator Gaylord Nelson, who as State Legislator, Governor, and Senator championed the protection of our natural resources. As we commemorate the 25th anniversary of Earth Day, his creation, it is fitting that we honor this great American's lifetime of public service.

In establishing Earth Day, Gaylord Nelson helped us to recognize that our fragile environment was increasingly at peril and that each of us could make a difference. His work has inspired all Americans to take responsibility for the planet's well-being and for our children's future.

I look forward to presenting the Medal to Senator Nelson.

WILLIAM J. CLINTON

The White House,
April 21, 1995.

NOTE: An original was not available for verification of the content of this statement.

Remarks and an Exchange With Reporters on the Oklahoma City Bombing
April 21, 1995

The President. Good afternoon. First let me say how very proud I am of the swift and decisive and determined work of law enforcement officials on this case throughout the country. I know every American is proud of them, too. Their continued vigilance makes me sure that we will solve this crime in its entirety and that justice will prevail.

Today I want to say a special word of thanks to the Justice Department, under the able leadership of the Attorney General, to Director Freeh and all the hundreds of people in the FBI who have worked on this case, to the men and women of the Bureau of Alcohol, Tobacco and Firearms, to all the Federal authorities, and to all the State and local enforcement officials, especially those in Oklahoma who have been working on this case. And of course, I'd like to say a personal thanks, as I know all Americans would, to the Oklahoma lawman whose vigilance led to the initial arrest of the suspect.

As I said on Wednesday, justice for these killers will be certain, swift, and severe. We will find them. We will convict them. And we will seek the death penalty for them.

Finally, I know I speak for all Americans when once again I extend our deepest thanks to the brave men and women who are still involved in the rescue teams. Let us not forget them. There is a lot of work for them still to do. It is difficult, and it is often heartbreaking now.

Our thoughts and prayers continue to be with the people in Oklahoma City. And let me say again: You will overcome this moment of grief and horror. You will rebuild. And we will be there to work with you until the work is done.

Q. Mr. President, is there a sense now, sir, that this was not a foreign threat, that this was something from within our own borders?

The President. Let me say that I have never and the Justice Department has never said that it was a foreign threat. But the most important thing that you understand is that even though this is a positive development, this investigation has a lot of work still to be done in it, and therefore it would be—it would be wrong to draw any conclusions. There have been lots of twists and turns in this investigation. But I would say to the American people, we should not assume, as I said yesterday, that we should not assume that any people from beyond our borders are involved in it. We should not assume anything, except what we know.

Q. Any idea about motive, Mr. President? Anything in terms of the one suspect who's been arrested, any feeling about what—where he was or who he was or what he was up to?

The President. I would defer, with the same comment that the Attorney General and Director Freeh had on that, that we simply must not speculate on that at this time.

Q. Mr. President, will this prompt the United States—or the Government to take a new and a tougher look at the white supremacist groups, the hate groups, the militias? Is this going to trigger any kind of crackdown?

The President. Let me say that we need to finish this investigation now. We need to focus on this investigation. We need to finish this investigation. We need to finish the rescue. We then need to obviously examine anew, as we will over the next few days, the sufficiency of our efforts in the whole area of terrorism.

Maybe it would be helpful—let me just take a few moments to talk about what we have been doing for the last couple of years before the Oklahoma City incident, because I think it is apparent to any observant person that all civilized societies have to be on their guard against terrorism.

We have increased the counterterrorism budgets and resources of the FBI and the CIA. We arrested a major terrorist ring in New York before they could consummate their plans to blow up the U.N. and tunnels in New York City. We've retrieved terrorists who have fled abroad, as I said yesterday, from Pakistan, the Philippines, from Egypt, and elsewhere. We broke up a major terrorist ring before they could consummate their plans to blow up airplanes flying over the Pacific. We brought together all the various agencies of the Federal Government that would be involved in rescue and in response to a terrorist action and did a comprehensive practice earlier. And some of that work, I think, was seen in the very efficient way that they carried out their work at Oklahoma City.

And finally, let me say, there's been a lot of activity that the public does not see, most of which I should not comment on. But let me give you one example. There was one recent incident of which I was—or with which I was intimately familiar, which involved a quick and secret deployment of a major United States effort of FBI and FEMA and Public Health Service and Army personnel because we had a tip of a possible terrorist incident, which, thank goodness, did not materialize. But we went to the place, and we were ready. We were ready to try to prevent it. And if it occurred, we were ready to respond.

So we have been on top of this from the beginning. Finally, let me say, I issued the Executive order which gives us the ability to try to control funding more strictly. And I have sent counterterrorism legislation to the Hill, which I hope will be acted upon quickly when they return.

Rita [Rita Braver, CBS News].

Q. Mr. President, does the way this is coming down give Americans any reason to feel a little bit more secure that this particular group is not going to carry out something else, or do you just not know yet?

The President. I think Americans can be secure that our country has able law enforcement officials, that we work together well, that we have prevented terrorist activities from occurring, that, obviously, every civilized society is at risk of this sort of thing. I cannot, I must not comment on any of the specific people involved in this investigation at this time.

Wolf [Wolf Blitzer, CNN].

Q. Mr. President, is there anything that has come across your desk so far to suggest that this bombing in Oklahoma City could have been prevented, as other terrorist incidents that you were referring to were prevented? Was there a failure somewhere down the chain of command, someplace that a tip, a clue, a source, could have provided information leading to this explosion?

The President. I have no evidence to that effect at this time.

Gene [Gene Gibbons, Reuters].

Q. Mr. President, there has been a loud, constant drumbeat in this country in recent years: The Government is the enemy; the Government is bad. Given the way this case seems to be pointing, do you think that in any way contributed to what happened in Oklahoma City on Wednesday?

The President. I think it's important that we not speculate about the motives, the atmosphere, or anything else until this investigation is complete. It can only—anything I say could only undermine the successful conclusion of this.

Q. Mr. President, you have been cautious about warning us and all Americans not to draw any conclusions over the past several days. Can you rule out a foreign tie to a domestic group, and can you in any way blame this incident on any kind of climate presently in this country?

The President. I cannot rule in or rule out anything. It would be inappropriate. The investigation has not been completed. And again, that's a variation of the question that was just asked. I cannot and I should not characterize this in terms of the climate or anything else at this time.

Let us do this investigation. Let the people get the work done. Let us follow every lead, pursue every alley. Let's wrap this up so we can see it whole, and then there will be time for this kind of analysis. I understand why you want to do it. It's perfectly understandable and appropriate, but it's not ripe yet. We have to solve the heinous crime first.

Thank you.

NOTE: The President spoke at 4:05 p.m. in the Briefing Room at the White House. The Executive order of January 23 prohibiting transactions with terrorists is listed in Appendix D at the end of this volume.

Statement on Senator David Pryor's Decision Not To Seek Reelection
April 21, 1995

Throughout his career, David Pryor has been a champion of America's finest values. He is a fierce advocate for our children and the elderly and a ready voice for the cause of reason. From the State legislature and the Governor's office in Arkansas to the U.S. Congress, he has served our country from the bottom of his heart and in the best possible way. His retirement from the Senate will be a loss felt by us all.

I know I can continue to count on David's exceptional counsel, both as a valued adviser and a trusted friend. I look forward to his continued active involvement in the business of our Nation.

Remarks by the President and Hillary Clinton to Children on the Oklahoma City Bombing
April 22, 1995

The President. Today I've been joined by the First Lady and by children of people who work for our Federal Government, because we are especially concerned about how the children of America are reacting to the terrible events in Oklahoma City. Our family has been struggling to make sense of this tragedy, and I know that families all over America have as well.

We know that what happened in Oklahoma is very frightening, and we want children to know that it's okay to be frightened by something as bad as this. Your parents understand it. Your teachers understand it. And we're all there for you, and we're working hard to make sure that this makes sense to you and that you can overcome your fears and go on with your lives.

The First Lady has been very worried about all the children of our country in the aftermath of this tragedy, and she wants to talk with you, too, today.

Mrs. Clinton. I'm very happy to have this chance to talk with children here in the White House and children who maybe have been watching cartoons or just getting up around the country and turning on the television set. I know that many children around the country have been very frightened by what they have seen and heard, particularly on television, in the last few days. And I'm sure that you, like many of the children I've already talked to, are really concerned because they don't know how something so terrible could have happened here in our country.

But you know, whenever you feel scared or worried, I want you to remember that your parents and your friends and your family members all love you and are going to do everything they can to take care of you and to protect you. That's really important for each of you to know.

I also want you to know that there are many more good people in the world than bad and evil people. Just think of what we have seen in the last few days. Think of all the police officers and the firefighters, the doctors and the nurses, all of the neighbors and the rescue workers, all of the people who have come to help all of those who were hurt in Oklahoma. Think about the people around the country who are sending presents and writing letters. Good people live everywhere in our country, in every town and every city, and there are many, many of them.

Like many of the families in America, our family has spent a lot of time in the last few days talking about what happened in Oklahoma, sharing our own feelings, our anger, our tears, our sorrow. All of that has been very good for us. And I hope you are doing it at home as well.

I want all of the children to talk to people. Talk to your parents. Talk to your grandparents. Talk to your teachers. Talk to those grownups who are around about how you are feeling inside, how this makes you feel about yourself, so that they can give you the kind of reassurance, the hugs, the other ways of showing you that you can feel better about this because they love you and care about you very much.

And finally, I want children to think about ways that all of you can help. Sometimes writing a letter or drawing a picture when you're sad or unhappy can make you feel better. Perhaps you could even send those pictures and letters to children in Oklahoma City. Maybe you could send a toy or a present. Maybe you can also just be nicer to your own friends at school and to help take care of each other better. I think that's one thing that all of us can do.

Thankfully, we're going to be able to help the people there, and we're going to pray very hard for everybody who was injured and everyone who died. But let's also try to help each other. And there are many ways we can do that. And if we remember that, then I think all of us can get over being afraid and scared.

The President. I'd like to take a moment to say a few words about this whole thing to the parents of America. I know it always—or, at least, it's often difficult to talk to children about things that are this painful. But at times like this, nothing is more important for parents to

do than to simply explain what has happened to the children and then to reassure your own children about their future.

Experts agree on a number of steps. First of all, you should encourage your children to talk about what they're feeling. If your children are watching news about the bombing, watch it with them. If they have questions, first listen carefully to what they're asking, and then answer the questions honestly and forthrightly. But then reassure them. Tell them there are a lot of people in this country in law enforcement who are working hard to protect them and to keep things like this from happening. Tell them that they are safe, that their own school or day care center is a safe place, and that it has been checked and that you know it's safe.

And make sure to tell them without any hesitation that the evil people who committed this crime are going to be found and punished. Tell them that I have promised every child, every parent, every person in America that when we catch the people who did this, we will make sure that they can never hurt another child again, ever.

Finally, and most important of all, in the next several days, go out of your way to tell your children how much you love them. Tell them how much you care about them. Be extra sensitive to whether they need a hug or just to be held. This is a frightening and troubling time.

But we cannot let the terrible actions of a few terrible people frighten us any more than they already have. So reach out to one another and come together. We will triumph over those who would divide us. And we will overcome them by doing it together, putting our children first.

God bless you all, and thanks for listening.

[*At this point, the address ended, and the President and Hillary Clinton invited comments from the children.*]

The President. What about all of you, how do you feel about this? You got anything you want to say about what happened at the bombing? What?

Q. It was mean.

The President. It was mean, wasn't it? What did you think when you heard about it the first time?

Q. I didn't like it.

Mrs. Clinton. It was very mean.

Q. I thought those people that did it should be punished very badly—to hurt the children.

Mrs. Clinton. That's right, and they will be.

The President. They should be punished, and they will be.

Q. I feel sorry for the people that died.

The President. You feel sorry for the people that died. Good for you.

Q. When I first heard about it, I thought, who would want to do that to kids who had never done anything to them?

Mrs. Clinton. It's hard to imagine, isn't it?

The President. That's very hard to imagine. There are some people who get this idea in their minds that there are people who have done something to them when they haven't done anything to them and who are told over and over again that it's okay to hate, it's okay to hate, it's okay to lash out, even at people they don't even know. And that's a wrong idea.

That's the other thing I want to say to you. We need to—we need to all respect each other and treat each other with respect and be tolerant of our differences so that we don't have other people developing this crazy attitude that it's okay to hurt people you never even knew. Good for you.

Q. I feel really bad for the people that died and the people that are in the hospital, especially for the parents because it's really hard to lose a child.

The President. It's so hard.

Mrs. Clinton. And I think all of us have to do everything we can to help the people who were hurt and to make sure they get everything they need, not only in the hospital but after that because they'll need people to talk to as well. And we have to be to help the people who lost family members, like you said. It's going to take a very long time.

The President. And we have to feel bad for their parents, too. You know how much your parents love you, and can you imagine how they would feel? So we've got to feel bad for their parents, too, and give them a lot of support.

Q. I think the bomber should be in jail.

Mrs. Clinton. You are right. You are right. There are many, many people working hard all over the country to find out who did this. And they're actually making some progress in finding out who did it, and they will keep doing that until the people are caught——

Q. [*Inaudible*]—newspaper.

Mrs. Clinton. Yes, that's right. And they'll be caught, and then they'll be punished.

The President. Anybody else want to say anything?

Mrs. Clinton. What do you think you can do here, which is far away from where it happened, that could help other people and to do things that would be nice and, you know, as a way of helping?

Q. To send money to—[*inaudible*]——

Mrs. Clinton. That's a good idea.

Q. Send cards and presents.

The President. To Oklahoma City.

Mrs. Clinton. I think sending something—that would be good.

Q. Like, send some of your old clothes and everything.

Mrs. Clinton. Whatever they need, right? If somebody needs that, we should do that.

Q. Like, we can bring them flowers sometimes.

Mrs. Clinton. Bringing flowers to somebody is a really nice thing to do. Do you ever bring flowers to your mom or to a friend just because you love them? It's a good thing to do.

Q. At my brother's day care when my school was closed, we planted trees to remember the kids that got hurt.

Mrs. Clinton. That is a wonderful idea. Did you all hear what she said? They planted trees to remember the kids who got hurt. That's something that schools and day care centers could do all over the country.

The President. I think something should be done so that all of us remember those children in Oklahoma City, don't you? And all those people.

Q. We can write notes——

Q. You can pray for the family members and the rescue workers who have been helping people throughout this terrible incident and for the family members who lost their employees and children.

The President. That's right. That's something every one of you can do. You could say a prayer for them. It's a gift you can give them. It's very important. Thank you for saying that.

Q. We can write letters and notes and let them know that we understand how they're feeling.

The President. I think that's important, too.

Yes. Do you want to say something? You want to say something? Anybody else like to say anything? You got any other ideas of things we can do?

How many of you have really thought about this a lot in the last couple of days? Have you thought about it? You feel a little better now than you did a couple of days ago?

Q. Yes.

The President. Have you talked about it in your home? What about at school? Have they talked about it at school a lot? I think it's really important.

One more thing you can do is, to go back to what the First Lady said earlier, is when you see people at your school, if they're getting angry or they're getting mad or they say something bad about somebody just because of— because they're different than them, you ought to speak out against that. You ought to say, "Look, we're all Americans; we're all here. We have to treat each other with respect. We're all equal in the eyes of God." And we cannot, we cannot permit people to have the kind of hatred that the evil people had who bombed that building in Oklahoma City. That is a—it's an awful thing. And every one of you, every day, can be a force against that kind of thing. You can change the country with your prayers and with your voice and by reaching out in all the ways you said.

Thank you all very much.

Mrs. Clinton. I'm so glad you could be here.

Q. Mr. President?

The President. Yes.

Q. I'd like to thank you for having us here today and speaking to all the children.

Mrs. Clinton. Thank you.

The President. Thank you, Colonel. And I want to thank all the parents who are here. And I want to thank you for your service to our country and for working for our Government and assure you that most Americans, millions of them, the huge majority, really respect all of you. And all Americans are horrified by what has happened. And we thank you for being here, and we thank you for being good parents as well as serving our country and our Government.

Goodbye.

Mrs. Clinton. Thank you all.

The President. And bless you.

Q. Mr. President? President Clinton, there have been increasing reports about these so-called militia groups. Do you feel that the general atmosphere of antigovernment statements has contributed to the growth of groups like this?

The President. Let me say that first of all, that this is coming on us in a couple of waves. When I was Governor of my State in the early eighties, we dealt with a number of these people and groups at home. That's one reason I felt such a horrible pang when I saw what happened in Oklahoma, you know, because it's just next door to Arkansas. And we had two incidences near the Oklahoma border in the early eighties.

And in—as you probably know, there was just an execution in Arkansas a couple of days ago of a man who killed a State trooper and who was a friend of mine and a businessman in southwest Arkansas, who was part of this whole movement. And there were other instances as well.

And then it went down a while, you know, the sort of the venom, the hatred; the atmosphere got better, and the American people rose up against that kind of thing.

I think that we should wait until this whole matter is thoroughly investigated and until we know the facts to draw final conclusions.

But I will say that—that all of us, just as I told these children, all of us need to be more sensitive, to treat each other with tolerance, and not to demonize any group of people and certainly not these fine people who work for the Nation's Government. They are, after all, our friends and neighbors. We go to school with their children. We go to church with them. We go to civic clubs with them. This is—this is not necessary, and it is wrong.

But I will have some more to say about this whole matter as we know more facts about this case and about where we're going in the future.

Thank you.

NOTE: The President spoke at 10:06 a.m. from the Oval Office at the White House. These remarks were broadcast live on radio and television.

Remarks at a Memorial Service for the Bombing Victims in Oklahoma City, Oklahoma
April 23, 1995

Thank you very much. Governor Keating and Mrs. Keating, Reverend Graham, to the families of those who have been lost and wounded, to the people of Oklahoma City who have endured so much, and the people of this wonderful State, to all of you who are here as our fellow Americans: I am honored to be here today to represent the American people. But I have to tell you that Hillary and I also come as parents, as husband and wife, as people who were your neighbors for some of the best years of our lives.

Today our Nation joins with you in grief. We mourn with you. We share your hope against hope that some may still survive. We thank all those who have worked so heroically to save lives and to solve this crime, those here in Oklahoma and those who are all across this great land and many who left their own lives to come here to work hand in hand with you.

We pledge to do all we can to help you heal the injured, to rebuild this city, and to bring to justice those who did this evil.

This terrible sin took the lives of our American family: innocent children, in that building only because their parents were trying to be good parents as well as good workers; citizens in the building going about their daily business; and many there who served the rest of us, who worked to help the elderly and the disabled, who worked to support our farmers and our veterans, who worked to enforce our laws and to protect us. Let us say clearly, they served us well, and we are grateful. But for so many of you they were also neighbors and friends. You saw them at church or the PTA meetings, at the civic clubs, at the ball park. You know them in ways that all the rest of America could not.

And to all the members of the families here present who have suffered loss, though we share your grief, your pain is unimaginable, and we know that. We cannot undo it. That is God's work.

Our words seem small beside the loss you have endured. But I found a few I wanted to share today. I've received a lot of letters in these last terrible days. One stood out because it came from a young widow and a mother of three whose own husband was murdered with over 200 other Americans when Pan Am 103 was shot down. Here is what that woman said I should say to you today: "The anger you feel is valid, but you must not allow yourselves to be consumed by it. The hurt you feel must not be allowed to turn into hate but instead into the search for justice. The loss you feel must not paralyze your own lives. Instead, you must try to pay tribute to your loved ones by continuing to do all the things they left undone, thus ensuring they did not die in vain." Wise words from one who also knows.

You have lost too much, but you have not lost everything. And you have certainly not lost America, for we will stand with you for as many tomorrows as it takes.

If ever we needed evidence of that, I could only recall the words of Governor and Mrs. Keating. If anybody thinks that Americans are mostly mean and selfish, they ought to come to Oklahoma. If anybody thinks Americans have lost the capacity for love and caring and courage, they ought to come to Oklahoma.

To all my fellow Americans beyond this hall, I say, one thing we owe those who have sacrificed is the duty to purge ourselves of the dark forces which gave rise to this evil. They are forces that threaten our common peace, our freedom, our way of life.

Let us teach our children that the God of comfort is also the God of righteousness. Those who trouble their own house will inherit the wind. Justice will prevail.

Let us let our own children know that we will stand against the forces of fear. When there is talk of hatred, let us stand up and talk against it. When there is talk of violence, let us stand up and talk against it. In the face of death, let us honor life. As St. Paul admonished us, let us not be overcome by evil but overcome evil with good.

Yesterday Hillary and I had the privilege of speaking with some children of other Federal employees, children like those who were lost here. And one little girl said something we will never forget. She said we should all plant a tree in memory of the children. So this morning before we got on the plane to come here, at the White House, we planted that tree in honor of the children of Oklahoma. It was a dogwood with its wonderful spring flower and its deep, enduring roots. It embodies the lesson of the Psalms that the life of a good person is like a tree whose leaf does not wither.

My fellow Americans, a tree takes a long time to grow, and wounds take a long time to heal. But we must begin. Those who are lost now belong to God. Some day we will be with them. But until that happens, their legacy must be our lives.

Thank you all, and God bless you.

NOTE: The President spoke at 3:32 p.m. at the Oklahoma State Fair Arena. In his remarks, he referred to Gov. Frank Keating and his wife, Cathy, and evangelist Billy Graham.

Interview on CBS' "60 Minutes"
April 23, 1995

Oklahoma City Bombing

Steve Kroft. Thank you, Mike. Mr. President, you said this afternoon that our one duty to the victims and to their families is "to purge ourselves of the dark forces which gave rise to this evil." Can you bring the country up to date on the status of the investigation?

The President. Well, as you know, another person was arrested today, and the investigation is proceeding aggressively. I have always tried to be very careful not to reveal any evidence and to let the Justice Department, the Attorney General, and the FBI Director decide what should be released when. But I can tell the American people we have hundreds of people working on this. They are working night and day. They are doing very well. We are making progress.

Response to Terrorism

Mr. Kroft. You said immediately after the attack that we will find the people who did this, and justice will be swift, certain, and severe. If it had turned out that this had been an act of foreign-sponsored terrorism, you would have had some limited but very clear options. You could have ordered bombing attacks. You could have ordered trade embargoes. You could have done a lot of things. But it seems almost certain now that this is home-grown terrorism, that the enemy is in fact within. How do we respond to that?

The President. Well, we have to arrest the people who did it. We have to put them on trial. We have to convict them. Then we have to punish them. I certainly believe that they should be executed. And in the crime bill, which the Congress passed last year, we had an expansion of capital punishment for purposes such as this. If this is not a crime for which capital punishment is called, I don't know what is.

Capital Punishment

Ed Bradley. Mr. President, this is Ed Bradley in New York. There are many people who would question our system of criminal justice today in the United States—in fact, many people who have lost faith in our criminal justice system. With so many people languishing on death row today for so many years, how can you say with such assurance that justice will be certain, swift, and severe?

The President. Well let me say first of all, it's been a long time since there has been a capital case carried through at the national level. But our new crime bill permits that. Now, when I was Governor, I carried out our capital punishment laws at the State level. We just pursued the appeals vigorously. I do believe the habeas corpus provisions of the Federal law, which permit these appeals sometimes to be delayed 7, 8, 9 years, should be changed. I have advocated that. I tried to pass it last year. I hope the Congress will pass a review and a reform of the habeas corpus provisions, because it should not take 8 or 9 years and three trips to the Supreme Court to finalize whether a person, in fact, was properly convicted or not.

Mr. Bradley. But without a change in the law, you think that is what will happen?

The President. It may not happen. We can still have fairly rapid appeals processes. But the Congress has the opportunity this year to reform the habeas corpus proceedings, and I hope that they will do so.

Response to Terrorism

Mike Wallace. Mr. President, Mike Wallace. Are we Americans going to have to give up some of our liberties in order better to combat terrorism, both from overseas and here?

The President. Mike, I don't think we have to give up our liberties, but I do think we have to have more discipline and we have to be willing to see serious threats to our liberties properly investigated. I have sent a counterterrorism—a piece of legislation to Capitol Hill which I hope Congress will pass. And after consultation with the Attorney General, the FBI Director, and others, I'm going to send some more legislation to Congress to ask them to give the FBI and others more power to crack these terrorist networks, both domestic and foreign.

We still will have freedom of speech. We'll have freedom of association. We'll have freedom of movement. But we may have to have some discipline in doing it so we can go after people who want to destroy our very way of life.

You know, we accepted a minor infringement on our freedom, I guess, when the airport metal detectors were put up, but they went a long way to stop airplane hijackings and the explosion of planes and the murdering of innocent people. We're going to have to be very, very tough and firm in dealing with this. We cannot allow our country to be subject to the kinds of things these poor people in Oklahoma City have been through in the last few days.

White House Security

Mr. Wallace. People are wondering, Mr. President, if you're going to close down Pennsylvania Avenue in front of the White House to regular traffic. There are barriers there, of course, all the time. But there are those who suggest, particularly because of the man who tried to shoot up the White House, that maybe Pennsylvania Avenue itself should be shut down.

The President. Well, I hope that they won't have to do that. I hope that ways can be found to make the front of the White House secure without doing that, because millions of Americans go by Pennsylvania Avenue every year and see the White House and the overwhelming number of them are law-abiding, good American citizens, and I hope they won't have to do that.

1993 Tragedy in Waco, Texas

Mr. Wallace. Lesley Stahl has been out in Michigan with the Michigan militia for the past 24 hours. Lesley.

Lesley Stahl. Mike. Mr. President, what I kept hearing from the militia men there—and I gather this is true among all these so-called patriots—is the Waco incident. It seems to be their battle cry. It's their cause. They say that the Feds went into a religious compound to take people's guns away. They say no Federal official was ever punished, no one was ever brought to trial. I'm just wondering if you have any second thoughts about the way that raid was carried out?

The President. Let me remind you what happened at Waco and before that raid was carried out. Before that raid was carried out, those people murdered a bunch of innocent law enforcement officials who worked for the Federal Government. Before there was any raid, there were dead Federal law enforcement officials on the ground. And when that raid occurred, it was the people who ran their cult compound at Waco who murdered their own children, not the Federal officials. They made the decision to destroy all those children that were there.

And I think that to make those people heroes after what they did, killing our innocent Federal officials and then killing their own children, is evidence of what is wrong. People should not be able to violate the law and then say if Federal law enforcement officials come on my land to arrest me for violating the law or because I'm suspected of a crime, I have the right to kill them and then turn around and kill the people who live there. I cannot believe that any serious patriotic American believes that the conduct of those people at Waco justifies the kind of outrageous behavior we've seen here at Oklahoma City or the kind of inflammatory rhetoric that we're hearing all across this country today. It's wrong.

Ms. Stahl. But, Mr. President, there are tens, maybe more—tens of thousands of men and women dressing up on weekends in military garb going off for training because they're upset about Waco. Just what—despite what you say, we're talking about thousands and thousands of people in this country who are furious at the Federal Government for what you say is irrational, but they believe it.

The President. Well, they have a right to believe whatever they want. They have a right to say whatever they want. They have a right to keep and bear arms. They have a right to put on uniforms and go out on the weekends. They do not have the right to kill innocent Americans. They do not have the right to violate the law. And they do not have the right to take the position that if somebody comes to arrest them for violating the law, they're perfectly justified in killing them. They are wrong in that.

This is a freedom-loving democracy because the rule of law has reigned for over 200 years now, not because vigilantes took the law into their own hands. And they're just not right about that.

Response to Terrorism

Mr. Kroft. Mr. President, you have some personal history yourself——

The President. I do.

Mr. Kroft. ——with right-wing paramilitary groups when you were Governor of Arkansas. You considered proposing a law that would have outlawed paramilitary operations. Do you still feel that way? And what's your—what, if anything should be done? Do we have the tools? What should be done to counteract this threat?

The President. Well, let me say, first of all, what I have done today. I've renewed my call in the Congress to pass the antiterrorism legislation that's up there, that I've sent. I have determined to send some more legislation to the Hill that will strengthen the hand of the FBI and other law enforcement officers in cracking terrorist networks, both domestic and foreign. I have instructed the Federal Government to do a preventive effort on all Federal buildings that we have today. And we're going to rebuild Oklahoma City.

Now, over and above that, I have asked the Attorney General, the FBI Director, and the National Security Adviser to give me a set of things, which would go into a directive, about what else we should do. I don't want to prejudge this issue.

When I was Governor of Arkansas, this is over 10 years ago now, we became sort of a campground for some people who had pretty extreme views. One of them was a tax resister who had killed people in another State, who subsequently killed a sheriff who was a friend of mine and was himself killed. One was the

man, Mr. Snell, who was just executed a couple of days ago, who killed a State trooper in cold blood who was a friend of mine and servant of our State and got the death penalty when I was Governor. One was a group of people who had among them women and children but also two men wanted on murder warrants. And thank God we were able to quarantine their compound. And that was all resolved peacefully.

But I have dealt with this extensively. And I know the potential problems that are there. I don't want to interfere with anybody's constitutional rights. But people do not have a right to violate the law and do not have a right to encourage people to kill law enforcement officials and do not have a right to take the position that if a law enforcement officer simply tries to see them about whether they've violated the law or not, they can blow him to kingdom come. That is wrong.

Mr. Kroft. One of the things, or one of the most frightening things about this whole business, has been the fact that most of the materials that this bomb was made from are readily available. Great Britain, for example, has placed some controls over the concentrations of certain chemicals and explosives in fertilizer, for example. Are there things that can be done to eliminate availability and the accessibility of ingredients that can turn deadly?

The President. There may be some things that we can do both to eliminate them or to make it more difficult to aggregate them or to make sure that the elements will be identified in some way if they're ever used in a bomb so people know they're far more likely to get caught. All these things are being discussed now, and that's what I've asked the Attorney General, the FBI Director, and the National Security Adviser to make recommendations to me on.

Members of Congress have various ideas and have made suggestions. Law enforcement people and other concerned folks around the country have. They're going to gather up the best ideas and make these recommendations to me in fairly short order.

Oklahoma City Bombing

Mr. Bradley. Mr. President, do you think that what happened in Oklahoma City is an isolated incident carried out by a handful of people or is part of a larger, more coordinated effort involving a larger network of these groups?

The President. I don't think the evidence that we have at the present time supports the latter conclusion. And I think we should stick to the evidence. Just as I cautioned the American people earlier not to stereotype any people from other countries or of different ethnic groups as being potentially responsible for this, I don't want to castigate or categorize any groups here in America and accuse them of doing something that we don't have any evidence that they have done.

I do want to say to the American people, though, we should all be careful about the kind of language we use and the kind of incendiary talk we have. We never know who's listening or what impact it might have. So we need to show some restraint and discipline here because of all the people in this country that might be on edge and might be capable of doing something like this horrible thing in Oklahoma City.

Response to Terrorism

Mr. Wallace. To follow on Steve's question, Mr. President, no longer does terrorism have to be state-supported. There's terror on the cheap now. It cost the World Trade Center bomber, we understand, conceivably $3,000, $4,000 for all of what was involved, including the rental of the van. And today, I learned, that it's about $1,000 worth for the explosives and the van and so forth in the Oklahoma City bombing. What do you do about terror on the cheap?

The President. Well, you're right about that. And of course, the same thing could be true of the terrible things they've been going through in Japan. But the nations of this world are going to have to get together, bring our best minds together, and figure out what to do about this.

We have been working hard to try to get the legal support we need to move against terrorism, to try to make sure that we can find out who's doing these kind of things before they strike. But I do think there are some other things that we can do.

At one point people thought we couldn't do anything about airplanes, but we made some progress, significant progress, because of things like airport metal detectors and other sophisticated devices. And we'll tackle this. We'll make progress on this. We'll unravel it. But it is true that in a free society that is very open, where technological changes bring great opportunity,

they also make it possible to do destructive things on the cheap—to use your phrase.

So we're going to have to double up, redouble up our efforts and then figure out what to do about this. But we'll move on it, and I am confident that I'll have some further recommendations in the near future.

Oklahoma City Bombing

Mr. Wallace. CBS News has a report—or had a report, late this afternoon; I don't know whether you're familiar with it—about a man by the name of Mark Koernke, from the Michigan Militia, who apparently sent a fax, a memo, to Congressman Steve Stockman of Texas, who held onto it for awhile, and finally sent it to the NRA. And then the NRA held it—and it was important information, apparently—held it for 24 hours before they sent it on to the FBI. Can you shed any light on that?

The President. No. I can't shed any light on that. I don't want to do or say anything that would impair our investigation in this case. And I have urged other Americans to show that kind of restraint, and I must do so as well.

Violence in American Culture

Mr. Kroft. Mr. President, do you think that we are a violent nation, that violence is part of the American way of life?

The President. Well, we've always had a fair amount of violence. But organized, systematic, political violence that leads to large numbers of deaths has not been very much in evidence in American history except from time to time. That is, we're a nation—we're still a kind of a frontier nation. We're a nation that believes, indeed, enshrines in our Constitution the right to keep and bear arms. A lot of us, including the President, like to hunt and fish and do things like that. And then, of course, the number of guns in our country is far greater than any other, and a lot of them are misused in crimes and a lot of them lead to deaths. And there are a lot of knives and other weapons that don't have anything to do with guns that lead to death.

So we've had a lot of crime and violence in our country, but not this sort of organized, political mass killing. And we have got to take steps aggressively to shut it down. And I'm going to do everything in my power to do just that.

Mr. Wallace. You asked—I'm sure you asked yourself—we ask, why did—why did these people do it? The director of the Terrorism Studies Center over at the University of St. Andrew in Scotland says that these attacks, he expects, are going to be increasingly brutal, more ruthless, less idealistic. For some, he says, violence becomes an end in itself, a cathartic release, a self-satisfying blow against the hated system. Little that can be done about that, if indeed the man's right.

The President. Well, I think two things that could be done—these are things that you could help on. For all those people who think that they are going to have a self-satisfying blow against the system, I wish they could have seen that young woman that I stood by today who showed me the picture of her two young boys that are dead now, or those three children that I saw today whose mother died last year of an illness who lost their father—he still has not been found. I wish they could see the faces of these people. There is no such thing as a self-satisfying blow against the system. These are human beings, and there are consequences to this kind of behavior.

The other thing I think we could do, in addition to showing those people, is to ask the American people who are out there just trying to keep everybody torn up and upset all the time, purveying hate and implying at least with words that violence is all right, to consider the implications of their words and to call them on it.

We do have free speech in this country, and we have very broad free speech, and I support that. But I think that free speech runs two ways. And when people are irresponsible with their liberties, they ought to be called up short, and they ought to be talked down by other Americans. And we need to expose these people for what they're doing. This is wrong. This is wrong. You never know whether there's some fragile person who's out there about to tip over the edge thinking they can make some statement against the system and all of a sudden there's a bunch of innocent babies in a day care center dead.

And so I say to you, in America, we can be better than that. The predictions of the expert in Scotland don't have to be right for America. But we're going to have to examine ourselves, our souls, and our conduct if we want it to be different.

Mr. Wallace. Final question: Do we see too much violence in movies and television in the United States?

The President. Well, I have said before, I said in my State of the Union Address, that I think we see it sometimes when it's disembodied and romanticized, when you don't deal with the consequences of it. I think—when a movie shows violence, if it's honest and it's horrible and it's ugly and there are human consequences, then maybe that's a realistic and a decent thing to do. That movie "Boyz N the Hood," I thought, did a good job of that.

But when a movie—when movie after movie after movie after movie sort of romanticizes violence and killing and you don't see the human consequences, you don't see the faces of the mothers and the children that I saw today, the husbands and the wives, then I think too much of it can deaden the senses of a lot of Americans. And we need to be aware of that.

But it's not just the movies showing violence. It's the words spouting violence, giving sanction to violence, telling people how to practice violence that are sweeping all across the country. People should examine the consequences of what they say and the kind of emotions they are trying to inflame.

NOTE: The interview began at 6:03 p.m. The President spoke from the Oklahoma State Fair Arena in Oklahoma City. The interviewers were CBS correspondents Steve Kroft, Ed Bradley, Mike Wallace, and Lesley Stahl.

Statement on the 80th Anniversary of the Armenian Massacres
April 23, 1995

On this solemn day, I join with Armenians throughout the United States, in Armenia, and around the world in remembering the 80th anniversary of the Armenians who perished, victims of massacres in the last years of the Ottoman

Empire. Their loss is our loss, their courage a testament to mankind's indomitable spirit.

It is this spirit that kept the hope of Armenians alive through the centuries of persecution. It is this spirit that lives today in the hearts of all Armenians, in their church, in their language, in their culture. And it is this spirit that underpins the remarkable resilience and courage of Armenians around the world. The Armenian-American community, now nearly one million strong, has made enormous contributions to America. Now, with the emergence of an independent Armenia, the Armenian people are bringing the same determination to building democracy and a modern economy in their native land.

Even as we commemorate the past—which we must never forget—we commit ourselves today to Armenia's future as an independent and prosperous nation, at peace with its neighbors and with close ties to the West. That is why the United States has provided more than $445 million in assistance to alleviate humanitarian needs and support democratic and economic reform. I will do everything in my power to preserve assistance levels for Armenia.

I continue to be deeply concerned about the conflict in the region surrounding Armenia. The terrible effects of this war have been felt throughout the Caucasus: tens of thousands have died, more than a million have been displaced, economies have been shattered, and security threatened. The United States is committed to working with the Organization on Security and Cooperation in Europe (OSCE) to encourage Armenia and Azerbaijan to move beyond their cease-fire to a lasting political settlement. I plan to nominate a Special Negotiator for Nagorno-Karabakh at the rank of Ambassador to advance those negotiations. And I pledge United States support of OSCE efforts to back that settlement with a peacekeeping force.

The U.S. also seeks to encourage the regional cooperation that will build prosperity and reinforce peace. I commend the recent decision of the Government of Turkey to open air corridors to Armenia, which will make assistance delivery faster, cheaper, and more reliable. We had urged that it do so and hope this is a first step toward lifting other blockades in the region, initially for humanitarian deliveries and then overall. Open borders would help create the conditions needed for economic recovery and development, including construction of a Caspian oil pipeline through the Caucasus to Turkey, which is a key to long-term prosperity in the region.

The administration's efforts, assistance in support of reform, reinforced efforts toward peace settlement, building broad regional cooperation and encouraging the development of a Caspian oil pipeline through the Caucasus to Turkey, represent the key building blocks of U.S. policy to support the development of an independent and prosperous Armenia.

On this 80th anniversary of the Armenian massacres, I call upon all people to work to prevent future acts of such inhumanity. And as we remember the past, let us also rededicate ourselves to building a democratic Armenia of prosperity and lasting peace.

Remarks to the American Association of Community Colleges in Minneapolis, Minnesota
April 24, 1995

Thank you very much. Secretary Riley, thank you for your introduction. If I were you, I would go bowling. [*Laughter*] We're going to save your job. [*Laughter*] Thank you, Secretary Reich, for your enthusiasm, for being enthusiastic about the right things. In your heart alone you have enough domestic content to be the Secretary of Labor. Thank you, Jacquelyn Belcher and David Pierce. I also want to say how very glad I am to be joined here by the distinguished United States Senator from Minnesota, Senator Paul Wellstone, and his wife, Sheila, who's here; two of our colleagues in the House of Representatives, Congressman Bruce Vento and Congressman Bill Luther, also back there. Thank you for being here.

I want to say a special word of congratulations to the 20 students who were named to the 1995

All-USA Academic Team. I want to thank those who are watching us via satellite. And I also want to say a special word about some fine students and advocates I met just before I came in here. I met two students who have benefited from our direct loan program—I'll talk more about them in a moment; two students who are critically interested in public assistance to education, because without that they would not have been able to go to school; and I met a gentleman who is devoting his time to organizing people against the attempt in Washington to start charging interest on student loans while students are still in college. Sandra Tinsley, Jessica Aviles, Jeffrey Lanes, Robbie Dalton-Kirtley, who is also one of the academic team all-Americans, and Dave Dahlgren, I thank all of them for meeting with me, and they're here somewhere. If they are, they ought to wave or stand up—there's Jeffrey. Thank you. Thank you very much.

Before I begin today to talk about education and training, I'd like to say just a word or two if I might, before this audience of educators and people who believe in and appreciate the value of free speech, about where we are in the aftermath of the Oklahoma bombing and what we are going to do about the kind of America our children will inherit.

Yesterday Hillary and I joined tens of thousands of people in Oklahoma City, and of course millions of you all across the country, to witness the end result of abject hatred. I was there, as President, to represent all of you in the mourning. But also I felt that we were there, Hillary and I, as ordinary American citizens as well, as husband and wife, as parents, as neighbors of those people.

No words can do justice to how moving it was to be there yesterday. No words can do justice to the courage of those who worked in the rescue operation around the clock. And one person has already given her life in that endeavor. No words can do justice to the small acts of kindness and generosity, all the people in Oklahoma who won't take money at the gas station or the local coffee shop or the barber shop or even at the airline ticket terminal for people who are there working to try to help them put their lives together.

But I will never forget, more than anything else, the faces and the stories of the family members of the victims. I was walking through the room shaking hands with them, and I saw a lady with her children who had been in the Oval Office just a few weeks ago as her husband left my Secret Service detail to go to what seemed to be a less hectic pace of duty in Oklahoma City. I saw the children of a man who was a football hero at the University of Arkansas when so many people who are now on the White House staff were friends of his. The young Air Force sergeant took out two pictures his wife had taken of me just 3 weeks ago when I visited our troops in Haiti. And she was one of those troops, but she came home because we wound down our mission there. And she married her fiance, and 3 days later she went to the Federal building to change her name. And so he had to give me the pictures his wife took. I saw three children, teenage children, with a woman and another child taking care of them. One of them had one of my Inaugural buttons on. Their mother died last year of an illness. Their father went to our Inaugural, and they asked me to sign the pin to their father who is still missing—three teenagers losing both parents.

I could go on and on and on. I say to all of you, first we must complete the rescue effort and the recovery effort. Of course, we must help that community rebuild. We must arrest, convict, and punish the people who committed this terrible, terrible deed, but our responsibility does not end there.

In this country we cherish and guard the right of free speech. We know we love it when we put up with people saying things we absolutely deplore. And we must always be willing to defend their right to say things we deplore to the ultimate degree. But we hear so many loud and angry voices in America today whose sole goal seems to be to try to keep some people as paranoid as possible and the rest of us all torn up and upset with each other. They spread hate. They leave the impression that, by their very words, that violence is acceptable. You ought to see—I'm sure you are now seeing the reports of some things that are regularly said over the airwaves in America today.

Well, people like that who want to share our freedoms must know that their bitter words can have consequences and that freedom has endured in this country for more than two centuries because it was coupled with an enormous sense of responsibility on the part of the American people.

If we are to have freedom to speak, freedom to assemble, and, yes, the freedom to bear arms, we must have responsibility as well. And to those of us who do not agree with the purveyors of hatred and division, with the promoters of paranoia, I remind you that we have freedom of speech, too, and we have responsibilities, too. And some of us have not discharged our responsibilities. It is time we all stood up and spoke against that kind of reckless speech and behavior.

If they insist on being irresponsible with our common liberties, then we must be all the more responsible with our liberties. When they talk of hatred, we must stand against them. When they talk of violence, we must stand against them. When they say things that are irresponsible, that may have egregious consequences, we must call them on it. The exercise of their freedom of speech makes our silence all the more unforgivable. So exercise yours, my fellow Americans. Our country, our future, our way of life is at stake. I never want to look into the faces of another set of family members like I saw yesterday, and you can help to stop it.

Our democracy has endured a lot over these last 200 years, and we are strong enough today to sort out and work through all these angry voices. But we owe it to our children to do our part. Billy Graham got a standing ovation yesterday when he said, "The spirit of our Nation will not be defeated." I can tell by your response that that is true. But you must begin today.

The little girl who read the poem yesterday at our service said, "Remember the trust of the children. Darkness will not have its day." The trust of the children is what we are here to talk about.

This whole community college movement has made as big a contribution to the future of America as any institutional change in the United States in decades. All of you live every day with the future. You have important work to do. I ask you only to think of how different what you do is from what you have been hearing from the voices of division.

Why do community colleges work? Well, first of all, they're not encumbered by old-fashioned bureaucracies. By and large, they are highly entrepreneurial. They are highly flexible. They are really democratic—small "d"—they're open to everybody, right?—in the best sense. They are open to everybody. And people work together.

And when something doesn't work, they go do something else. That's what you do. You do it in a spirit of cooperation. You are remarkably unpolitical in that sense.

In other words, every experience you have—and you see people of all ages coming through your doors, walking out your doors, going on to better, more fulfilling, more satisfying lives, able to help themselves and strengthen America in the process. It is the direct antithesis of the kind of paranoia and division and hatred that we hear spewed out at us all over this country, day-in and day-out, by people exercising their free speech to make the rest of us miserable. And it contradicts the experience of what works in America.

So today that is why I have asked you to do this. I also want to talk to you a little bit about what I hope we can do in education. You want Americans to be more hopeful, you want this to be a more positive place, you want people to be rewarded for their labors—strengthen education in America. Build the community colleges; open the doors to all. That's the way to build the future of this country, not by dividing us and bringing us down but by uniting us, building us up, and pointing us toward the future.

You know, I have seen the faces of America's future. I met a 46-year-old former welfare mother at San Bernardino Community College, full of enthusiasm and hope for the future. I met a 73-year-old Holocaust survivor in Kutztown, Pennsylvania, who built a successful business and is now committed to investing in the education and training of his employees using his local educational institution. I met a 52-year-old woman at Galesburg Community College in Illinois, laid off from a factory job after 20 years but building a better future.

Today I met some impressive people. I met this fine young man down here, Jeffrey Lanes, who had an injury but didn't let it defeat him. Instead, he went back to school with the help of public assistance to make a new and better life for himself. But we are better off that he is going to have a better life. He is giving us a better America, and we thank him for it. And we ought to support opportunities for other people just like him.

I mentioned her before, but when I met Robbie Dalton-Kirtley, who's part of the All-USA Academic Team—she's one of these nontraditional students. She waited until her youngest child was in kindergarten, and she went back to school. She's from Flat Rock, North Carolina. But she is building a future that will strengthen not only Flat Rock, North Carolina, and her family but all the rest of us as well. So I thank you for what you are doing. And I ask you how we can do more of it, and what should we be doing in Government?

Well, when I ran for President, I ran with a heavy bias toward education. I look out on this crowd today, and I see a lot of people from our community colleges in Arkansas. I'm proud of the fact that when I was Governor we built more of them, we helped to strengthen the ones that were there, we helped some of the vocational schools to either convert or merge or to become more like, by diversifying their curriculum, the community colleges.

In fact, I was looking at a couple of people out there; I was at their places so often they probably wanted me to leave so they could get some work done when I was a Governor. [*Laughter*]

I ran for President in large measure because I felt that the work of America that was being done out in the grassroots, the work of creating opportunity and demanding responsibility and rewarding it, was not being done in Washington, that we were increasing our Government's debt at a rapid rate and unbelievably reducing our investment in our future. I believed then and I believe more strongly now that this country has two deficits. We've got a budget deficit, but we've got an education deficit as well. And we have to cure them both.

We are still living with the legacy of the explosive debts of the last 12 years. The budget cuts we have made already and the taxes we have asked the top one and a half percent of our people to pay—listen to this—would balance the budget to today. Today we would have a balanced budget except for the interest we owe on the debt run up between 1981 and the end of 1992. So we are bringing the deficit down. We are committed to that, but we have to remember we have more than one deficit.

You heard the Secretary of Labor talking about this, but I have been obsessed since the late 1980's with the increasing inequality in America. You know, when I was born at the end of World War II, I grew up in the American dream. And the great domestic crisis we had was a civil rights crisis. And we thought if we could just get over racial prejudice, that our

economy was so strong, our society was so powerful, that the American dream could just be opened up for everyone.

And from the end of the Second World War until the late seventies, that is pretty much what happened. All income groups increased together. And in fact, the poorest 20 percent of our people did slightly better than the rest of us in terms of where they started. We were growing together and going forward.

Today, we are going forward. Our economy has produced over 6 million new jobs. You heard what the Secretary of Labor said: We had the lowest combined rate of unemployment and inflation in 25 years, but we are not growing together. And that is why so many Americans say they do not feel more secure, even though we're having an economic recovery. They say, "Yeah, I read that in the papers, but it's not affecting my life. I haven't gotten a raise."

Sixty percent of our people are living on the same or lower wages than they were making 10 years ago, working a longer work week. Why? Because of the combined impact of the global economy, the technology revolution, the lack of a Government response to it. In fact, the Government response made it worse.

The minimum wage next year—if we don't raise it this year—the minimum wage next year will be at its lowest level in 40 years. That is not my idea of how to get to the 21st century. So we have these—[*applause*] Thank you.

So we basically are splitting apart economically. If you look at it, it is clear that the fault line is education. Earnings for high school dropouts have dropped at a breath-taking rate in the last 15 years. Earnings for high school graduates have dropped at a less dramatic rate.

The only group for which earnings have increased steadily are earnings for people who have at least 2 years of post-high school education and training. You, you are at the fault line in America. The fault line of American society is education. Those who have it are doing well. Those who don't are paying. And the future offers more of the same at a faster rate.

Therefore, it is clear that our common mission, if we want to help people help themselves and strengthen this country, must be focused on a relentless determination to see that every American lives up to the fullest of his or her capacities. It is in our common interest.

So all these wonderful stories you can tell about your community colleges, all these touching individual triumphs, are also the story of America's rebirth at the dawn of the 21st century. Make no mistake about it, you are doing more than helping individual Americans live out their dreams; you are creating the system in which we can keep the American dream alive for our country and the American idea alive for all the world in the 21st century. If you succeed, we will. You must succeed, and the rest of us must make sure we do what we can to help you do it.

I want to make some brief points today about what we are trying to achieve in this Congress and what we are trying to stop from being achieved in this Congress. And I want to ask for your help.

In the last 2 years, we had broad bipartisan support for the most substantial increased effort by the National Government to support education in a generation: big increases in Head Start; world-class standards for our schools and more flexibility for our teachers, our parents, our administrations, and our students to meet them; school-to-work programs so our young people who don't go on to 4-year colleges would have the opportunity to move into the workplace with the kind of training and skills that would give them jobs that would raise their incomes, not drive them down; tech-prep programs as a part of school to work. A lot of you are involved in the tech-prep issue, and it's something I know a lot about from my personal experience, enabling high school students to get work experience and to go straight to community colleges. We created AmeriCorps, our national service initiative. And more than 30 community colleges and this association are participating in AmeriCorps. We've got people doing everything from helping the elderly in Kentucky to tutoring kids in inner-city Chicago to helping with community policing in Rochester, New York, thanks to the community colleges. And I thank you very much for your endeavors.

Now, what should we do? Number one, do no harm. Don't undo what we just did. Number one, do no harm. Number two, yes, we need to reduce the deficit, but we should increase the Pell grant program as we have proposed, not reduce it, as some have proposed. Yes, we should cut the deficit, but one way to cut the deficit that is absolutely wrong is to start charging interest on student loans while the students are still in school.

There is an answer, you know, in education to the budget conundrum. Almost unbelievably, there is an answer. It is our direct student loan program. We want to make it available for anyone who wants to finance assistance to college.

The student loan program, the direct loan program, started when I became President because I wanted to find a way to cut the cost of college loans, to cut the unbelievable bureaucratic paperwork headache, and to give students more options about how to repay loans, because I began to see students in our State who were dropping out of college because they were terrified that they would never be able to repay their loans, especially students who were going to do things that were important to our society but didn't pay a lot, students who wanted to be teachers, students who wanted to be nurses, students who wanted to be police officers, students who wanted to serve the public and knew that they would have big loans and modest salaries to repay them with. So we began to look around for ways to do this. And we settled on, and the Congress adopted, the direct college loan program.

When I took office, everybody in the country was complaining about the way the student loan program worked. Students complained that they couldn't get loans or if they did it took them too long and it was an absolute nightmare to fool with the paperwork. Colleges complained that the paperwork was driving them crazy. And everybody was worried about the nature of the repayment terms and the fact that there weren't enough options. There was also, I might add, an unconscionable amount of loan default, people who would not pay their loans back, costing the taxpayers $2.8 billion a year. And the banks didn't have much incentive to help, because they had a 90 percent guarantee. So by the time—if they brought some sort of action, they'd spend the 10 percent trying to collect the rest, so why not just take a check from the Government?

Well, the direct loan program addresses all those problems. It lowers costs for students. It allows borrowers to choose flexible repayment arrangements, including a pay-as-you-earn option. Therefore, it doesn't doom anyone to a crushing debt burden. It's also, believe it or not, helping us to save billions of dollars of taxpayers' money. That plus Secretary Riley's more vigilant enforcement of the loan program have cut your losses as taxpayers from $2.8 billion a year to $1 billion a year, a reduction of almost two-thirds.

But get this—what are we going to do now? In the first year, we had 104 schools with over 252,000 students in the program. In the second year, we'll have more than 1,400 schools, representing 37 percent of all loans, committed to enrolling. Today I am proud to announce that in our third year, beginning July 1996, 450 new schools will join the program, which will mean 45 percent of all student loans will be administered through this program.

Now, that's the good news. You don't have to take my word for it. You can look at the students that I just mentioned, Jessica Aviles or Sandra Tinsley, they're both here. Go ask them about it. Listen to them talk about how much quicker they got the loan and what a joy it was not to have to go through the hassle and the delay and the uncertainty.

But here's the good news. If we keep going until we make the student loan program available to all the schools on a voluntary basis, it will save the taxpayers $12 billion over 5 years or about the same amount of money that would be saved if we started charging interest on student loans while the students are in college.

So if we want to reduce the deficit, let's reduce the deficit by increasing education, not by reducing it. That's the message that I want you to take out there.

The second thing I want to say to you is that we have a lot of Americans who are unemployed or underemployed who want more training and education. And a lot of them now only have access to certain highly specified and difficult-to-understand-and-access Government programs. There are dozens of Federal training programs, most of them enacted with the best of intention by Congress.

What we propose to do is to put the American people who need training in control of their own destiny with these programs, instead of just shifting the power from a Federal bureaucracy even to a State one. What we propose to do is to consolidate all these training programs and create a skill grant, essentially a training voucher to people who are unemployed or underemployed or qualified for Federal help, let them get the voucher and take it to their local community college and have access to the programs you offer for up to 2 years to get the training necessary for the future.

That is a much better expenditure of that money than to continue in these programs which may or may not be easily accessible and which require a whole lot of paperwork and are very confusing. We want to consolidate the money, give it directly to the people who are entitled to it in the form of a voucher, and let them take it to you to get the education you need. I hope you will help us pass that as well in this Congress.

Finally, let me talk about the tax cut issue. Everybody is for a tax cut. Who could be against it? Sounds great. But I would remind you that this is a serious issue, this deficit issue. We have worked very hard to reduce it by $600 billion. When we brought the deficit down, that's what drove interest rates down in 1993. That's what gave us our economic recovery. That's what unleashed the engine of American enterprise. And the uncertainty that hangs now around whether we continue to show discipline in our budget is causing difficulties for our economy.

We cannot afford a $200 billion tax cut and continue to reduce the deficit and meet our responsibilities to education and our future. We cannot afford to tilt most of the benefits of the tax cut to upper income people. They are doing very well in the economy as it is. They are doing very well. And this is not a statement of class warfare. I want to create more millionaires. I am proud of the fact that a lot of people have become millionaires since I have been President. But what will do that is a strong economy, a healthy economy in which everybody has the opportunity to succeed. That's what will create more successful entrepreneurs. If we have a system that grows the middle class and shrinks the under class and keeps this economy strong, the entrepreneurs will do well.

So what we should do is have a much smaller tax cut. It should be targeted sharply to people who need it, middle class people. And in my judgment it should be targeted to education. People should get a deduction for the cost of education after high school, because that will raise their incomes over the long run as well as over the short run. They will more than pay it back to the Treasury in future years because we will be accelerating the number and the intensity and the pace of those getting an education in America. That's the kind of tax cut we need: less, targeted to middle class, and focused like a laser beam on education. We need an education tax cut. That's all we need for this country.

Let me close by asking you once again to make your voice heard in another way. The community colleges of America look like America. If you go to a board meeting of a community college and hear people talk about what programs they're going to have and what projects they're going to have and what partnerships they're going to create, chances are a hundred to one you can't tell whether there's a Republican or a Democrat talking at the board meeting.

Community colleges are open to people of all races and backgrounds and religious faiths and views. They bring people together. They are America at its best. We need more of that in Washington. So if you believe that we shouldn't start charging interest on the loans, especially since there's a better way to reduce the deficit; if you believe we should increase the Pell grants, not decrease them; if you believe we should keep expanding the direct loan program on a purely voluntary basis and see if our program is as good as I think it is and people keep using it; if you believe we should have this training voucher instead of this complicated welter of Federal programs; if you believe it's important to cure the education deficit and the budget deficit and therefore we should

focus on a tightly targeted education-related tax cut, then go back home and ask the students and the faculty members and the board members to sign petitions that you can send to your local Members of Congress and your Senators, without regard to party.

We dare not let education become a political partisan issue in America. It was not in the last 2 years; it should not be in 1995 and 1996. Every American has a vested interest in seeing that we all go forward in education. Every single, solitary bit of evidence shows us it is the fault line standing between us and a future in which the American dream is alive for everyone. If you want to reward hard work in America, that work must be smart work. Our future is on the line.

So I implore you, when you go home, make your voices heard. Say it is not a partisan issue, it is not a political issue, it is a question of keeping the American dream alive into the 21st century.

Thank you, and God bless you all.

NOTE: The President spoke at 11:46 a.m. in the Grand Ballroom at the Minnesota Convention Center. In his remarks, he referred to Jacquelyn Belcher, chair, and David Pierce, president, American Association of Community Colleges.

Remarks on Departure From Minneapolis
April 24, 1995

Thank you. I'm so glad to see you all. As you can see, I'm here with Senator and Mrs. Wellstone and Congressman Vento and Congressman Luther and Attorney General Humphrey. And I'm glad to be here with all of them, and I'm glad to be with you.

I also want to tell you, I'm glad I've got this big wind because I just had lunch downtown at a place called Peter's Grill, and I'm so full, I need a nap. [*Laughter*]

Let me thank you for coming out today and tell you that I have had a wonderful trip to Minnesota. I want to thank the people here at the airbase for making me feel welcome, as they always do, and the Air Force reservists for their service. And I want to thank the young

AmeriCorps members who are here today for their service.

The men and women here at this Air Reserve unit have gone all across the globe to preserve our freedom and to fight for the freedom of others. They served in Operations Desert Shield and Desert Storm. They delivered food and supplies to people in Bosnia to help them survive. That's the longest airlift in history, thanks to the United States Armed Forces and the people here. And people here have even helped to fight the fires in California. We're grateful to all of them for all those services.

I want to say something about the AmeriCorps volunteers here. In Minnesota alone, in this first year for AmeriCorps, they're making 200 houses or apartments into real homes for working families. And that is a noble thing to do. You're teaching more than a thousand children who might not make it without you, and I hope you'll keep working with them, because they need you. They need you as role models and mentors. And in their work, they are also piling up some credits for themselves to help them pay for the cost of going to college. They represent the tradition of American service at its best, and we thank all these young people for their service. Thank you very much.

You know, this coming week is our National Volunteer Week, and tomorrow is a national day of service when a million Americans will join with many of you in special service all across America. It is fitting that National Volunteer Week should come now because volunteering is one of the best ways that Americans, and especially those fine people in Oklahoma, can deal with their grief and their pain and their loss.

I must tell you that yesterday when I saw them and I realized what they had been through and how so many of them had continued to work to help their friends and neighbors and loved ones—some of them haven't slept in days—it reminded me once again that service is the greatest gift of citizenship in this country.

And for all of you who are giving your service, whether here in the Reserve unit, or in AmeriCorps, or in some other way through your churches and synagogues or clubs or schools, I thank you, because the real heart of America is not in the Nation's Capital; it's out here with all of you and what you do every day to make your lives and this country's life better.

Thank you, and God bless you all.

NOTE: The President spoke at 3:15 p.m. at the Minneapolis-St. Paul International Airport. In his remarks, he referred to Hubert H. Humphrey III, Minnesota attorney general. The National Volunteer Week proclamation of April 21 is listed in Appendix D at the end of this volume. The National Youth Service Day proclamation of April 19, 1994, was published in the *Federal Register* at 59 F.R. 19123.

Remarks on Arrival in Des Moines, Iowa
April 24, 1995

Thank you very much. Thank you very much, Senator Harkin, and thank you, ladies and gentlemen, for that wonderful welcome. It's great to be back in Iowa when it's dry. [*Laughter*] I am glad to be here.

I want to thank the State officials who came here to greet me at the plane. Standing behind me, your attorney general, Tom Miller; your secretary of state, Paul Pate; your State treasurer, Mike Fitzgerald; your State auditor, Richard Johnson; and your secretary of agriculture, Dale Cochran, I thank them all for coming. I am also glad to see some old friends here. Your former Congressman, Neal Smith, who's been a great friend of mine, I'm glad to see him.

I'm glad to see all those folks from the United Rubber Workers Union, Local 310 here. Good luck to you. And I want to say a special word of welcome and thanks to the young national service AmeriCorps volunteers for their work. Thank you. I'd like to thank the base commander here, General Don Armington, for welcoming me and for making available this facility.

And as Tom Harkin said, I'm here for the National Rural Conference. I want to say to all of you before I begin that, how much I appreciate what Senator Harkin said and the response that you had to the terrible tragedy that the people of Oklahoma City have been through and that our entire Nation has been through. You, I know, are very proud of them for the way they have responded, the work they have done, and the courage they have shown. It was a very profoundly moving day yesterday.

Today and in all the days ahead, as we help them to rebuild and as we continue to search for total justice in that case, which we will see carried out, I ask all of you to remember what I said yesterday. This is a country where we fight and where people have died to preserve everyone's right to free speech, indeed, to all the freedoms of the Bill of Rights, the freedom of speech, the freedom to associate with whomever we please, the right to keep and bear arms, the right to be treated fairly and without arbitrary action by your Government, all those freedoms.

But we're around here after 200 years because of people like the people in Iowa, because we know that with all freedom comes responsibility. And the freer you are, the more responsible you have to be. We are the freest Nation on Earth after over 200 years because over time we have always been the most responsible Nation on Earth.

So when you hear people say things that they are legally entitled to say, if you think they're outrageous, if you think they either explicitly or implicitly encourage violence and division and things that would undermine our freedoms in America, then your free speech and your responsibility requires you to speak up against it and say, "That's not the America I'm trying to build for my children and my grandchildren. That's not what we want."

You know, the America we're trying to build is an old-fashioned America of common sense where hard work is rewarded, where families can be strong, where people can live in the way they want to live if they work hard and play by the rules.

I got tickled when Tom Harkin said, reminded me—I'd forgotten this—that Harry Truman said no one ought to be President who doesn't know anything about hogs. [*Laughter*] And I thought, now, how many hogs jokes do I know that I can actually tell in front of this crowd? [*Laughter*] One of the things that you have to know is how far you can go if you live on the farm and when you're going too far. I'll tell you one hog story about that.

When the famous, or infamous, Huey Long was Governor of Louisiana and the country was in a depression, Huey was trying to convince everybody that the answer was to just take the wealth away from everybody who had it and give it to people who didn't. And President Roosevelt was following a much more moderate but commonsense course to try to put the people back to work again.

So Huey Long was out on a country crossroads saying—he was giving his speech about how we ought to share the wealth, and he saw this fellow out in the crowd he recognized, and he said, "Brother Jones, if you had three Cadillacs, wouldn't you give up one of them so we could go 'round to all these places and gath-

er up the little children and take them to school during the week and to church on Sunday?" And the guy said, "Well, of course I would." And he said, "Brother Jones, if you had $3 million, wouldn't you give up a million dollars just so all these people around here could have a decent roof over their head and good food to eat?" He said, "Well, of course I would." And he said, "And Brother Jones, if you had three hogs—" And he said, "Now, wait a minute, Governor. I've got three hogs." [*Laughter*] So one of the things that you learn in a sensible rural environment is when not to go too far.

I wanted to have this rural conference here, and we'd indeed planned to have it a few months earlier, but as Senator Harkin knows, along toward the end of last year we had a very important vote on the GATT trade treaty and whether we would be able to open more markets to American farm products and whether we'd be able to require our trading partners and competitors in Europe to reduce their farm subsidies to levels that are fair with us. And so because we were fighting that battle, a battle important to you, we had to put off the rural conference.

But we're back here, and we're back here for a very clear reason. We know that in spite of the fact that the overall statistics for the American economy look good, there are still profound challenges in the American economy. And I'll just give you a few.

We have the lowest combined rates of unemployment and inflation we've had in 25 years. That's the good news, and it's something we can be proud of.

But in spite of that, we know that we're continuing to have problems. I'll just give you two studies that have come out in the last month, one showing that in spite of all this economic growth, in spite of over 6.3 million new jobs in the last 2 years, inequality is increasing in America among working people. Why is that? Because we've got a global economy and a technological revolution that have driven down wages for people with relatively low skills, because a smaller percentage of our work force is unionized today, because we have not let the minimum wage keep up with inflation, and because we have not invested in the continued education and training and skills of our people. The second study shows that this is more pronounced in rural America, where the population is likely to be older with a lower income because more and more young people are having a hard time making it.

I just left Senator Harkin's colleague, Senator Paul Wellstone, who told me that—he and Mrs. Wellstone told me that they have a child who is married, about to have a baby, living on a dairy farm, trying to make a living as dairy farmers. And that's the hardest work in the world, you know. It's 7 days a week, 24 hours a day; somebody's got to be there all the time. The milk doesn't quit coming just because you want to go to church or a basketball game on the weekend. But they were talking about how at a hard time they were making it. So this inequality, this wage stagnation we're seeing in America is much more severe in rural America. Part of it is a farm problem, but it goes beyond that. Most Americans, most Iowans who live in rural America do not live on the farm.

And so we have great challenges today: How can we keep the economic recovery going? How can we work together to do that, but how can we overcome this inequality by getting wages up again? And how can we overcome the difference in opportunity between rural and urban America? Because I think we all know that a lot of the problems that urban America has would be smaller if more people could make a good living in small towns and rural areas, that a lot of the aggravated problems of the urban life in the United States, and I might add, throughout the world, are as difficult as they are because it's harder and harder and harder for people to make a living and raise families and have a stable life in rural areas.

So we thought we ought to come to Iowa to talk about these things. Yes, a lot of the conversation tomorrow will be about the new farm bill, and there will be a lot of talk about—there's been a lot of talk about it. And I don't want to get into all the details today except to tell you this: I did not work for 2 years to get our competitors to lower their farm subsidies to a rate that would make it possible for us to compete with them, to turn around and one more time on our own destroy all the farm supports in this country, so once again we give our competitors the advantage. I don't think that's how we should proceed.

I believe the American farmers that I know would gladly give up all their Government support if they thought all their competitors would. But we are in a global economic environment, trying to preserve the quality of rural life, and

this is very important. So we need to talk about that.

We also need to talk about education. We need to talk about technology. We need to talk about crime. We need to talk about health care. We have a lot of things we need to talk about.

And what we're going to try to do is to create an environment in which we can build a bipartisan consensus for a strategy for rural America that will be part of the farm bill, yes, but also part of everything else that unfolds in Washington over the next 2 years. That is my goal.

In times past, these issues have not necessarily been partisan issues. I am doing my best to reach out the hand of good faith, cooperation with the Congress. I hope that we can achieve it in many areas: in reducing the deficit, in giving more responsibility back to the States, while preserving the national obligation to support our children and to support education, in trying to work toward having a safer and more secure country—I know that all of you care about that—and in trying to have a balanced view toward the things that we all have to support, including the quality of life in our rural States and our rural areas.

So I'm really looking forward to tomorrow. I'm glad we're going to do it here. I think the people of Iowa know that our administration has worked hard to try to support the interests of rural America. After all, even with Senator Harkin, we needed Vice President Gore to break the tie so that we could support our ethanol position. And I'm glad he could do that.

I ask all of you to remember now that here's where we are in America. You look at these fellows with their caps on; you look at all these children out here; you look at these young people who are going to work in their communities so they can earn some money to further their own education. There is a fault line in America today, and it basically is determined by education, along with where you live and what sector of the economy you work in. We have to preserve the American dream for all of these kids who are here, going into the 21st century. All these children, we have to hand it back to them.

And we have literally been in the first economic recovery since World War II where jobs went up, the economy seemed to be growing, inflation was down, but over half of the ordinary Americans did not feel any personal improvement in either their job security or their personal income. So the challenge today is for us to figure out how to keep the deficit coming down, how to keep the economy growing and producing jobs, how to keep inflation down, but how to do those things that we know we have to do to raise incomes and to bring this country back together again.

We have to believe that we are coming together when we work hard and we play by the rules. That is my goal and that will be the heart and soul of what is at stake tomorrow in this National Rural Conference which ought to be here in Iowa.

Thank you, and God bless you all.

NOTE: The President spoke at 3:50 p.m. in the National Guard hangar at Des Moines International Airport.

Message to the Senate Transmitting a Protocol to the Canada-United States Taxation Convention
April 24, 1995

To the Senate of the United States:

I transmit herewith for Senate advice and consent to ratification, a revised Protocol Amending the Convention Between the United States of America and Canada with Respect to Taxes on Income and on Capital Signed at Washington on September 26, 1980, as Amended by the Protocols Signed on June 14, 1983, and March 28, 1984. This revised Protocol was signed at Washington on March 17, 1995. Also transmitted for the information of the Senate is the report of the Department of State with respect to the revised Protocol. The principal provisions of the Protocol, as well as the reasons for the technical amendments made in the revised Protocol, are explained in that document.

It is my desire that the revised Protocol transmitted herewith be considered in place of the Protocol to the Income Tax Convention with Canada signed at Washington on August 31, 1994, which was transmitted to the Senate with my message dated September 14, 1994, and which is now pending in the Committee on Foreign Relations. I desire, therefore, to withdraw from the Senate the Protocol signed in August 1994.

I recommend that the Senate give early and favorable consideration to the revised Protocol and give its advice and consent to ratification.

WILLIAM J. CLINTON

The White House,
April 24, 1995.

Message to the Senate Transmitting the Jordan-United States Extradition Treaty
April 24, 1995

To the Senate of the United States:

With a view to receiving the advice and consent of the Senate to ratification, I transmit herewith the Extradition Treaty between the Government of the United States of America and the Government of the Hashemite Kingdom of Jordan, signed at Washington on March 28, 1995. Also transmitted for the information of the Senate is the report of the Department of State with respect to this Treaty.

The Treaty establishes the conditions and procedures for extradition between the United States and Jordan. It also provides a legal basis for temporarily surrendering prisoners to stand trial for crimes against the laws of the Requesting State.

The Treaty further represents an important step in combatting terrorism by excluding from the scope of the political offense exception serious offenses typically committed by terrorists, e.g., crimes against a Head of State or first

589

family member of either Party, aircraft hijacking, aircraft sabotage, crimes against internationally protected persons, including diplomats, hostage-taking, narcotics trafficking, and other offenses for which the United States and Jordan have an obligation to extradite or submit to prosecution by reason of a multilateral international agreement or treaty.

The provisions in this Treaty follow generally the form and content of extradition treaties recently concluded by the United States.

This Treaty will make a significant contribution to international cooperation in law enforcement. I recommend that the Senate give early and favorable consideration to the Treaty and give its advice and consent to ratification.

WILLIAM J. CLINTON

The White House,

April 24, 1995.

Remarks at the National Rural Conference Opening Session in Ames, Iowa
April 25, 1995

Thank you very much, Mr. Vice President. And thank you, ladies and gentlemen for that warm welcome.

The Vice President could have been—you know, that blue-ribbon remark at the Iowa Fair, he could have stuck it in a little more. He could have said that he still lives on his farm and I haven't lived on a farm in 40 years. As a matter of fact, I lived on a farm so long ago we had sheep and cattle at the same place. [*Laughter*] I got off because—that's true—and I got off because one of the rams nearly killed me one day, and because I didn't want to work that hard anymore. But I am delighted to be here.

I want to thank all of the people here at Iowa State who have done such a wonderful job to make us feel welcome and all the work they have done on this. I thank Congressman Durbin, who is here from Illinois, one of our conference's chief sponsors, and also a man who is not here, Senator Byron Dorgan from North Dakota, who was an originator of this conference.

I want to say I'm looking forward to working with Governor Branstad and his colleague from Nebraska, Governor Ben Nelson, as we work up to the farm bill, because they are head of the Governors' Committee on Agriculture and Rural Development. And we're looking forward to that.

I don't want to give a long talk. I came here to hear from you today. I will say, you've been given some materials for this conference. If you want to know what our record is in agriculture,

you can read it. We wrote it up for you, but I don't think I ought to waste any of your time on it today.

I want us to think about the present and the future. And I want to make just a couple of brief remarks. There are a lot of paradoxes in the American economy, and they are clearly evident in rural America today. We have in the last 2 years over 6 million new jobs, the lowest combined rates of unemployment and inflation in 25 years. In Iowa, the unemployment rate is about 3.3 percent, I think, which the economists say is statistically zero. And yet—I just got the report this morning—in the last 3 months, compensation for working people in America, all across America, increased at a lower rate than it has in any 3-month period in 15 years, totally against all common sense.

The good news is we have low inflation. The bad news is nobody's getting any more money for working. And it is more pronounced in the rural areas of America, where incomes have stagnated.

Now, we know something about the dividing lines of this. We know that education is a big dividing line. We know that people who have at least 2 years of education after high school tend to do well in this global economy wherever they live and people who don't tend to have more trouble. We know also, unfortunately, that rural areas are not doing as well as urban areas. But we know that, in a way, technology gives us a way out of this because there are a lot of things that rural areas have that urban areas would like to have, affordable housing, clean air, lower crime rates. And we know that technology permits us, if we are wise enough, to bring economic opportunity to places where it hasn't been before.

So what I want us to focus on today is, yes, agriculture specifically and the farm bill, but beyond that, what about rural America? What is our strategy to make rural America stronger economically, to reward the good values that reside there, to help to make it an important part of America's life in the 21st century, to help to make it a place where people will want to come back to and provide some balance in this country that we so desperately need?

I'd just like to mention just three examples, if I might, one in agriculture specifically. When this farm bill comes up, there's going to be a lot of people saying, "Well, we ought to just get rid of the whole program or cut it way, way back because we've got a deficit." Well, we do have a deficit, but I would remind you that the farm bill was—the subsidies programs were cut in '85. They were cut in '90. We had a modest reduction in '93. We finally—we worked for years and years and our administration worked for nearly 2 years to bring the Europeans to the table in the GATT agreement, to cut the subsidies in Europe. And finally we're on an even footing, and I don't believe that we ought to destroy the farm support program if we want to keep the family farm and give up the competitive advantage we won at the bargaining table in GATT.

We have a $20 billion surplus in agricultural trade. We've got a big trade deficit in everything else. I don't think we ought to give it up. Should we modify it? Can we improve it? I'm sure we can. Should we emphasize other things? Of course we should, but our first rule should be: Do no harm.

The second point I want to make is, I don't think we have done enough in some areas that relate to both agriculture and generally to rural development, especially in research. And Senator Harkin and Governor Branstad were talking to the Vice President and me before we came out here about the pork research project that was funded here at this school last year, that was targeted for deletion in the House's so-called rescission bill. The rescission bill is a bill designed to cut some spending so we can pay for what we have to pay for, for the California earthquake and to cut the deficit more. But

we need to know what we should cut and what we shouldn't.

We need more agricultural research, not less. If you want to—for example, I know it's a big controversy here in Iowa, and I don't pretend to know what the answer is, but I know this: I know if you want to have the kind of position you've got in pork production, if you want to keep having $3 billion a year income in hogs, you've got to find a way to preserve the environment. And if you want family farmers to be able to do it, you have to figure out a way to work the economics out. Laws will never replace economics. And therefore we should not back up on research. We should intensify research. As we give more responsibilities back to State and local governments, more responsibilities back to the private sector, the National Government still has a commitment, it seems to me, and an obligation to support adequate research.

The third thing I would like to say is, it seems to me that we need a much more serious national effort to focus on what our responsibilities are in the area of rural development in general. I have spent nearly 10 years seriously working on this issue. A long time before I ever thought about running for President, I was worried about the broader issues of rural development. I headed a commission called the Lower Mississippi Delta Rural Development Commission several years ago. And I have worked on this for a long time. I am convinced there are things we can do nationally that don't cost a lot of money that can help to support a real revolution in the economic opportunities and the social stability of rural America.

So I hope if you have ideas on that, you will bring them out, because even in Iowa, only one in five rural residents lives on a farm. We have to think about everyone else. And we'll have more people living on a farm and being able to sustain living on a farm if there is a more balanced economic environment throughout rural America.

So these are the things that we're interested in. I'm looking forward to this very much. I'd like to ask the president of this fine institution to come up and offer a few words, and then I would invite Governor Branstad and Senator Harkin up here. And then I'd like for our Secretary of Agriculture, Dan Glickman, to tell you about the hearings, the town hall meetings he had leading up to this conference, and then we'll get right into the first panel.

Thank you very much.

NOTE: The President spoke at 9:13 a.m. in the Great Hall of the Memorial Union at Iowa State University. In his remarks, he referred to Gov. Terry E. Branstad of Iowa and Martin C. Jischke, president of the university.

Remarks at the National Rural Conference Closing Session in Ames
April 25, 1995

First of all, let's give all the panelists a big hand for all the work they've done. [*Applause*]

I would like again to congratulate the Secretary of Agriculture and the Deputy Secretary and others on the fine work they did here. I want to thank the president of this fine university and all the people who have worked so hard to make this a success.

I want to remind all of you—I think you can see today that we care a lot about these issues and we're committed to doing something about them. So if you had ideas that were not expressed, fill out those forms and give them to us. They will not just be thrown away.

Finally, let me thank the State of Iowa, Senator Harkin, the Governor who is not here anymore but spent some time with us. Attorney General Miller was here, and we have the State treasurer, Mike Fitzgerald, and the State agriculture commissioner, Dale Cochran. Thank you all for being here.

Let me close by leaving you with this thought: The balance of power, political power, in this country has shifted. Never mind whether you think it's Republican, Democrat, liberal, or conservative. It's basically shifted to a suburban base. And most of those folks in the suburbs either once lived in a city or once lived in the country. But most—a lot of them are doing reasonably well in the global economy. And if they aren't, the only thing they may think they need from the Government is help with a student loan for their kids. And otherwise they may view anything any public entity does as doing more harm than good.

What we have seen today on this panel—and I know, and most of you don't, but I know that we had people up here who are Republicans and people who were Democrats. And I'll guarantee you, listening to this conversation,

you couldn't tell one from another. Why? Because what works is practical commitment to partnerships and to solving problems each as they come up, to developing the capacities of people, to dealing with the options that are there, and to going forward.

So we have two problems today in coming up with good legislation in the farm bill and in coming up with other approaches that are appropriate. One is that Washington tends to be much more ideological and partisan than Main Street America, particularly rural America. And we need more of Main Street up there, not more of what's up there down here.

The other is that demographically our country's political center has shifted away from the urban areas and the rural areas into the suburbs, and a lot of the people who have to make decisions on these matters, without regard to their party or their philosophy, have no direct experience or direct lobbying in the best sense on these issues.

Therefore, I think what we need—I cannot tell you how strongly I feel this—is for, in States like Iowa and every other State here represented, we need for people of good will to try to get together at the community level, across party lines, and come up with positions on these matters that can be communicated to the Congress, because Dick Durbin and Tom Harkin and Senator Grassley and others on the Republican side will be trying to craft legislation that makes sense in some way that will be much more difficult unless your voice is heard in partnership, not partisanship, and the voice from the rural heartland. I implore you to do that.

Meanwhile, I pledge to you that your day here has not been wasted. I have learned a lot, and we will act on what we have learned.

Thank you so very much.

NOTE: The President spoke at 2:47 p.m. in the Memorial Union at Iowa State University.

Remarks to Students at Iowa State University in Ames
April 25, 1995

Thank you so much. Thank you, Mr. Vice President, for your stirring speech. He tells all those jokes, and then he goes about disproving them with his speech. [*Laughter*] Thank you for your service to America. When the history of our administration is written, there may be differing opinions about the quality of the decisions that I have made, but no one will doubt that the right thing was done in naming Albert Gore Vice President and then providing him the opportunity to be the most influential Vice President in American history.

I also want to thank my friend Tom Harkin for being here with me and for what he said and for his heroic efforts in the United States Senate on behalf of the people of Iowa and the people of this country. Whether they are farmers or people in rural areas, students, or the disabled, he is always there. I'd also like to say that I know Tom lived here for a while with his wonderful wife, Ruth, who was once the county attorney here in this county. She is now the head of the Overseas Private Investment Corporation. And she has done more to create American jobs by financing international trade than any person who ever held her position. And you can be proud of her as well.

I want to thank Mayor Curtis for welcoming me here to Ames. I was looking forward to meeting Mayor Curtis, but to be fair, I'm such a big basketball fan, I was hoping to meet the other "Mayor" here as well. If I could shoot like that, I'd still be in the NBA; I wouldn't be up here today. [*Laughter*] And thank you, President Jischke and all of you at Iowa State, for making us feel so welcome. I thank the band for playing. And I'm glad they provided seats for you to see the event. When I used to play at things like this, they never gave us a seat, so I'm glad to see your smiling faces. And thank you, singers, for singing and for looking so wonderful up there.

Ladies and gentlemen, we had a wonderful rural meeting today, and I want to talk a little bit about that. But before I do, I want to thank all of you who have come up to me already today and expressed your sympathy with and support for the people in Oklahoma City. There was a sign over there—show me that sign you all waved. I want everyone to see that. It says, "Oklahoma City, Iowa Cares."

You may know that this is national service week in the United States, and today is our first annual National Day of Service. That's why I'm so glad to see all the young AmeriCorps members here doing their work.

I know that all of you are thinking about how we can serve and help the people of Oklahoma City as they work through the next stages of their tragedy. I can tell you that when Hillary and I were there on Sunday, we saw people who had not slept, who were working heroically, some at considerable risk to themselves, to try to clean out the last measure of the wreckage and to try to find those who are still unaccounted for, working in the hospitals, working on the streets. The police and firemen—many of them had not seen their families for days.

The response of our country to this bombing shows what a strong country we are when we pull together. I saw it when you had the 500-year flood here and I thought all the topsoil was going to be somewhere in the Gulf of Mexico before it got through raining. But I really saw it down there in the face of this terrible madness that those fine people have endured.

We must take away from this experience a lot of things. But we must never forget that it was a terrible thing. I will do all I can to make sure that we see the wheels of justice grind rapidly, certainly, fairly, but severely. But we must take away from this incident a renewed determination to stand up for the fundamental constitutional rights of Americans, including the right to freedom of speech. We have to remember that freedom of speech has endured in our country for over two centuries. The first amendment, with its freedom of speech and freedom of assembly and freedom of religion, is in many ways the most important part of what makes us Americans. But we have endured because we have exercised that freedom with responsibility and discipline.

That is what we celebrate when people come to the rural heart of America and talk about what can be done to develop it. And every speaker says, what a shame it would be if we continue to allow economic decline in rural America, where the values of work and family and community and mutual responsibility are alive and well.

I ask you on this National Day of Service to think of a personal service you can all render. Yes, stand up for freedom of speech. Yes, stand up for all of our freedoms, the freedom of assembly, the freedom to bear arms, all the freedoms we have. But remember this: With freedom—if the country is to survive and do well—comes responsibility. And that means even as others discharge their freedom of speech, if we think they are being irresponsible, then we have the duty to stand up and say so to protect our own freedom of speech. That is our responsibility.

Words have consequences. To pretend that they do not is idle. Did Patrick Henry stand up and say, "Give me liberty or give me death," expecting it to fall on deaf ears and impact no one? Did Thomas Jefferson write, "We hold these truths to be self-evident, that all men are created equal, . . . endowed by their Creator with certain unalienable rights, . . . among these are life, liberty, and the pursuit of happiness," did he say that thinking the words would vanish in thin air and have no consequences? Of course not. Are you here in this great university because you think the words you stay up late at night reading, studying, have no consequence? Of course not.

We know that words have consequences. And so I say to you, even as we defend the right of people to speak freely and to say things with which we devoutly disagree, we must stand up and speak against reckless speech that can push fragile people over the edge, beyond the boundaries of civilized conduct, to take this country into a dark place.

I say that, no matter where it comes from, people are encouraging violence and lawlessness and hatred. If people are encouraging conduct that will undermine the fabric of this country, it should be spoken against whether it comes from the left or the right, whether it comes on radio, television, or in the movies, whether it comes in the schoolyard or, yes, even on the college campus. The answer to hateful speech is to speak out against it in the American spirit, to speak up for freedom and responsibility.

That is so important to me, especially for all of you young people. I was so pleased to see at the National Rural Conference today so many young people, people who want to make their lives in rural America, people who want to believe that we can make economic opportunity come alive in rural America, that people can actually work and raise their families and children there and make a living and be good, fulfilled citizens there.

I was encouraged by that. After all, most of us in this country who make the speeches and make the decisions have lived most of our lives. We have already lived the American dream. We are here in positions—your university president, your Senator, the Vice President, and I—we're here because of what America has already given us. If they took it all away from us tomorrow, we would have had more than 99.999 percent of the people who ever lived in all of human history. It is for those of you who still have your lives before you that we must most urgently work to keep the American dream alive.

When I assumed this office, I told the American people that I thought we had two great responsibilities standing on the verge of a new century. One was to keep the American dream alive for all of our people, that if you work hard and play by the rules you should have a chance to live up to the fullest of your God-given capacities. And the second was to make sure that our country remained the world's strongest force for peace and freedom and democracy, so that we could operate in a world where people competed based on what was in their minds and their spirit and what they did with their hands and not what they did with their weapons. And we have pursued those courses with a vengeance.

If you look at where we are now after 2 years in terms of our objectives, to restore economic growth, to grow the middle class and shrink the under class, to help to rebuild the bonds of society by strengthening work and family and the sense of security the American people have, to give us a Government that costs less but works better, and to help people do more to help themselves, it is clear that much has been done but much, much more is still there to do.

The deficit is down. Trade has been expanded. We have the lowest unemployment and inflation rates combined in 25 years. We are moving ahead in so many ways to make our people more secure, more police on our street in rural areas and in cities and no Russian missiles pointed at the people of the United States for the first time since the dawn of the nuclear age.

But make no mistake about it, my fellow Americans, this is an unusual time, different from past times. The global economy, the revolution in technology, the changing patterns of work, all of these things, all of these things have created a situation in which we are able to create large numbers of jobs in the United States—in Iowa the unemployment rate the last time I checked was 3.3 percent—large numbers of jobs where people do not have an increase in their income or increase in their sense of job security.

So you have this unusual circumstance today with the economy growing, the deficit going down, all the indicators seeming to point us in the right direction, and more than half of the adults in America are working harder for the same or lower wages they were making 10 years ago.

That is the challenge to America today. It is a challenge faced by every advanced country faced with foreign competition, faced with technology, faced with all the changes you know well about. But it is a special challenge in America because there is more inequality here than in most other wealthy countries, and yet, we are the country that values the American dream. Whoever you are, wherever you're from, if you work hard and do your best to develop your ability, you will be rewarded. And so I say to you: That is our challenge, to reward people who make the effort you are making by being here today in this great university and all others in America who are willing to work.

So I ask you to think of just this point— there are so many issues to discuss and we talked about a lot of them today—but here I ask you to think of only this: What is the role of education? The middle class in America, my fellow Americans, is splitting apart today, something we have not known since the end of the Second World War, where inequality is increasing among Americans with jobs. It is splitting

apart, and the fault line is education. Why? Because in a global economy, where new technologies are always changing the nature of work, what we can earn depends on what we can learn. More than ever before, the prospects of people all across our country are determined by whether they have enough education to learn and learn and learn and whether there is available to them a system to keep learning for a lifetime.

Therefore, I say to you, as you hear the debates that are about to resume in the Congress about the Government deficit—yes, we have a deficit; it's a lot smaller than it was when we showed up 2 years ago, and it's going down some more, but it's still there. But the budget deficit is not the only deficit we have. We also have an education deficit, and you have millions and millions and millions of Americans who go home every night and sit down across the table and look at their wives or their husbands and their children and wonder whether they have failed, because as hard as they work, they cannot make it in the modern economy. And I tell you, the only way to turn that around is to revolutionize the availability and the quality of education to all of our people, without regard to their race, their income, their region, or their age. This should lead us to a clear conclusion: With a budget deficit and an education deficit, we cannot solve one at the expense of the other without hurting our country for a long time to come. We cannot back off of our commitment to education.

There are proposals in the Congress today to require students to begin paying interest on their student loans while they're still in school. That will increase the cost of education, reduce the number of people who would take student loans. Over the long run, it would reduce the number of people successfully completing their education. We ought to be cutting the cost of education to our young people, not increasing it, to get more people in and through college.

There are proposals to limit, and some even want to outright eliminate, the national service program. They say, "Oh, well, it's not necessary." Look at what is going on in rural Iowa. Look at what these young people are doing. Yes, they're earning money for a college education, but they're also doing things all across America to immunize children, to build housing for the elderly, to walk streets and keep them safer for all of our people, hundreds and hundreds and hundreds of things to build community in America. We should not eliminate it; we should have more young people getting their education through the national service program.

So our program is very different. We say, yes, reduce the deficit, but increase Head Start. Give our public schools more funds to meet national standards of excellence, to have computers in every rural school, to do the things that are necessary to open up educational opportunities to all of our children. We say, invest the small amount of money it would take to enable every State in the country to have apprenticeship programs to help the young people who don't go to college but do want to get some education and training after high school so they could be in good jobs, not dead-end jobs. We say, make available to every university and college in America the direct student loan program which is now available here at Iowa State, which cuts the cost of lending to the students, which cuts the bureaucratic hassle to the colleges and to the students, and which saves the taxpayers money.

If the Congress wants to know how to reduce the deficit and increase education, the answer is, don't give in to the special interest lobby seeking to limit the availability of direct loans. Let every school in the country have the option to do what we've done here. Let these young people get lower cost loans with better repayment terms direct from the Government. Cut out the middleman. You will reduce the deficit, increase the number of college loans, increase the number of students, and move this country into the future. That is the right answer for this problem.

And finally, let me say, with all this talk of tax cuts, remember we have two deficits. There should be no tax cut if it's going to increase the deficit. No tax cut should be adopted except in the context of reducing the deficit. It should be modest. It should be targeted to middle class people who need it. And I believe it should be targeted to education—a deduction for the cost of education after high school to Americans all across this country. That is the right kind of tax cut.

One of your distinguished alumni, George Washington Carver, said it best when he said, "Education is the key to unlock the golden door of freedom." Well, when he said it, he was thinking of personal freedom, personal opportunity, individual opportunity. But those of us

who are here, your president, your Senator, the Vice President, and I, we benefited from a new insight about education because we were raised in the aftermath of World War II. We were raised by a generation of people who in return for their service in the war were given the benefits of the GI bill. And guess what? It didn't just give individual opportunity and personal freedom to all those people, it exploded the possibilities of America. And we grew up in the most prosperous country the world had ever known because of millions and millions and millions of people getting individual opportunity.

Now, I can tell you with absolute certainty, even in the face of all the difficulties and complexities of the modern world, that education is more important to the future of all of us as Americans today than it was to America at the end of the Second World War when the GI bill was adopted.

So yes, let us continue to fight to tame the beast of the Government deficit. You should know the budget would be balanced today were it not for the interest we have to pay on the debt run up between 1981 and 1992. But we have to do better. We have to do better.

But as we do it, let us do it in a way that increases our commitment to and our investment in education, because that is the selfish thing to do as well as the selfless thing to do. Believe me, folks, if I could wave a magic wand and do two things to ensure the future of America so that I would know it wouldn't matter who was elected to any office, it would be these things: I would give every child a childhood in a stable family and guarantee every American a good education. That should be our mission. There would be no poverty, great hope, and an unlimited future if that could be done.

Lastly, let me say this: In Washington, the rhetoric often becomes too political and extremely partisan. What we heard today at this rural conference, we heard from Republicans and Democrats and independents. We heard people talking about the real problems of real people: How can a family make a living on the farm? What should be in the new farm bill to allow people to have other kinds of economic development in rural areas? How can we relieve the stress on families where, between the mother and father together, they may have three or four jobs and not enough time to be with the children? How can we guarantee the benefits of technology, access to health care, transportation for the elderly, decent middle class housing in rural areas?

And these things were discussed in practical, commonsense, old-fashioned American language so that at the end of the day, no one knew, having heard it all, what they heard from a Republican, what they heard from a Democrat, who these people voted for in the last election. Why? Because they were talking about the real stuff of life, not words used to divide people.

So I ask you to remember this: We'll always have our fair share of politics in the Nation's Capital, and the further away you get from the real lives of real people, the more partisan the rhetoric tends to become. But you, you in this great university and in this community, can have a huge influence in saying, "Put one thing beyond politics. Do not sacrifice the future of our education on the altar of indiscriminate budget cutting. Reduce the deficit in the budget. Reduce the deficit in education. Give the next generation of Americans the American dream."

Thank you, and God bless you all.

NOTE: The President spoke at 4:10 p.m. at the Hilton Coliseum. In his remarks, he referred to Mayor Larry R. Curtis of Ames, IA, and Fred (The Mayor) Hoiberg, Iowa State University basketball player.

Remarks to the Iowa State Legislature in Des Moines
April 25, 1995

Thank you very much, Mr. President, Mr. Speaker, Governor Branstad, Mr. Chief Justice and members of the supreme court, distinguished Iowa State officials. And former Congressman Neal Smith, my good friend, and Mrs. Smith, thank you for being here. To all of you who are members of the Iowa Legislature, House and Senate, Republican and Democrat, it is a great honor for me to be here today.

I feel that I'm back home again. When I met the legislative leadership on the way in and we shared a few words and then they left to come in here, and I was standing around with my crowd, I said, "You know, I really miss State government." [*Laughter*] I'll say more about why in a moment.

I'd like to, if I might, recognize one of your members to thank him for agreeing to join my team: Representative Richard Running will now be the Secretary of Labor's representative. Would you stand up, please? Thank you. [*Applause*] Representative Running is going to be the representative of the Secretary of Labor for region 7, Iowa, Nebraska, Missouri, and Kansas. And if you will finish your business here pretty soon, he can actually go to Kansas City and get to work—[*laughter*]—which I would appreciate.

I'm delighted to be back in Iowa. I had a wonderful day here, and it was good to be here when it was dry—[*laughter*]—although a little rain doesn't do any harm.

We had a wonderful meeting today at Iowa State University, with which I'm sure all of you are familiar, this National Rural Conference we had, designed to lay the groundwork for a strategy for rural America to include not only the farm bill but also a rural development strategy and a strategy generally to deal with the problems of rural America, with the income disparities with the rest of America, the age disparities with the rest of America, and the problems of getting services and maintaining the quality of life in rural America.

I want to thank Governor Branstad for his outstanding presentation and the information he gave us about the efforts being made in Iowa in developing your fiber optic network and developing the health care reform initiatives for rural Iowans and many other areas. I want to thank Senator Harkin for his presentation, particularly involving the development of alternative agricultural products as a way to boost income in rural America. And I want to say a special word of thanks to the people at Iowa State. They did a magnificent job there, and I know you are all very proud of that institution. And you would have been very, very proud of them today for the way they performed.

I'm also just glad to be back here in the setting of State government. You know, Governor Branstad and I were once the youngest Governors in America, but time took care of it. [*Laughter*] And now that he's been reelected, he will actually serve more years than I did. I ran for a fifth term as Governor. We used to have 2-year terms, and then we switched to 4-year terms. And only one person in the history of our State had ever served more than 8 years, and only one person had ever served more than—two people had ever served more than two terms, but those were 2-year terms—in the whole history of the State. So I was—I had served 10 years. I'd served three 2-year terms and one 4-year term, and I was attempting to be reelected. And I had a high job approval rating, but people were reluctant to vote for me because in my State people are very suspicious of too much political power, you know. And I thought I was still pretty young and healthy, but half of them wanted to give me a gold watch, you know, and send me home. [*Laughter*]

And I never will forget one day when I was running for my fifth term, I was out at the State fair doing Governor's day at the State fair, which I always did, and I would just sit there and anybody that wanted to talk to me could up and say whatever was on their mind, which was, for me, a hazardous undertaking from time to time—[*laughter*]—since they invariably would do exactly that. And I stayed there all day long, and I talked about everything under the Moon and Sun with the people who came up. And, long about the end of the day, this elderly fellow in overalls came up to me, and he said, "Bill, you going to run for Governor again?" And I hadn't announced yet. I said, "I don't know. If I do, will you vote for me?" He said, "Yes, I always have. I guess I will again." And I said, "Well, aren't you sick of me after all these years?" He said, "No, but everybody else I know is." [*Laughter*]

But he went on to say—and that's the point I want to make about State government—he said, "People get tired of it because all you do is nag us. You nag us to modernize the economy; you nag us to improve the schools; you just nag, nag, nag." But he said, "I think it's beginning to work." And what I have seen in State after State after State over the last 15 years, as we have gone through these wrenching economic and social changes in America and as we face challenge after challenge after challenge, is people able consistently

to come together to overcome their differences, to focus on what it will take to build a State and to move forward. And we need more of that in America.

In Iowa, you do embody our best values. People are independent but committed to one another. They work hard and play by the rules, but they work together. Those of us who come from small towns understand that everybody counts. We don't have a person to waste. And the fact that Iowa has done such a good job in developing all of your people is one of the reasons that you are so strong in every single national indicator of success that I know of. And you should be very, very proud of what, together, you have done.

I saw some of that American spirit in a very painful way in Oklahoma City this week, and all of you saw it as well. I know you share the grief of the people there. But you must also share the pride of all Americans in seeing the enormity of the effort which is being exerted there by firemen and police officers and nurses, by rescue workers, by people who have come from all over America and given up their lives to try to help Oklahoma City and the people there who have suffered so much loss, rebuild.

I want to say again what I have tried to say for the last 3 days to the American people. On this National Day of Service, there is a service we can do to ensure that we build on and learn from this experience.

We must always fight for the freedom of speech. The first amendment, with its freedom of speech, freedom of assembly, and freedom of worship, is the essence of what it means to be an American. And I dare say every elected official in this room would give his or her life to preserve that right for our children and our grandchildren down to the end of time.

But we have to remember that that freedom has endured in our Nation for over 200 years because we practiced it with such responsibility; because we had discipline; because we understood from the Founding Fathers forward that you could not have very, very wide latitude in personal freedom until you also had—or unless you also had great discipline in the exercise of that freedom.

So while I would defend to the death anyone's right to the broadest freedom of speech, I think we should all remember that words have consequences. And freedom should be exercised with responsibility. And when we think that others are exercising their freedom in an irresponsible way, it is our job to stand up and say that is wrong, we disagree. This is not a matter of partisan politics. It is not a matter of political philosophy. If we see the freedom of expression and speech abused in this country, whether it comes from the right or the left, from the media or from people just speaking on their own, we should stand up and say no, we don't believe in preaching violence; we don't believe in preaching hatred; we don't believe in preaching discord. Words have consequences.

If words did not have consequences, we wouldn't be here today. We're here today because Patrick Henry's words had consequences, because Thomas Jefferson's words had consequences, because Abraham Lincoln's words had consequences. And these words we hear today have consequences, the good ones and the bad ones, the ones that bring us together and the ones that drive a wedge through our heart.

We never know in this society today who is out there dealing with all kinds of inner turmoil, vulnerable to being pushed over the edge if all they hear is a relentless clamor of hatred and division. So let us preserve free speech, but let those of us who want to fight to preserve free speech forever in America say, we must be responsible, and we will be.

My fellow Americans, I come here tonight, as I went recently to the State legislature in Florida, to discuss the condition of our country, where we're going in the future, and your role in that. We know we are in a new and different world—the end of the cold war, a new and less organized world we're living in but one still not free of threats. We know we have come to the end of an industrial age and we're in an information age which is less bureaucratic, more open, more dependent on technology, more full of opportunity, but still full of its own problems, than the age that most of us were raised in.

We know that we no longer need the same sort of bureaucratic, top-down, service-delivering, rulemaking, centralized Government in Washington that served us so well during the industrial age, because times have changed. We know that with all the problems we have and all the opportunities we have, we have to think anew about what the responsibilities of our Government in Washington should be, what your responsibility should be here at the State level

and through you to the local level, and what should be done more by private citizens on their own with no involvement from the Government.

We know now what the central challenge of this time is, and you can see it in Iowa. You could see it today with the testimony we heard at the rural conference. We are at a 25-year low in the combined rates of unemployment and inflation. Our economy has produced over 6 million new jobs. But paradoxically, even in Iowa where the unemployment rate has dropped under 3.5 percent, most Americans are working harder today for the same or lower incomes that they were making 10 years ago. And many Americans feel less job security even as the recovery continues. That is largely a function of the global economic competition; the fact that technology raises productivity at an almost unbelievable rate so fewer and fewer people can do more and more work, and that depresses wages; the fact that unless we raise it in Washington next year, the minimum wage will reach a 40-year low.

There are a lot of these things that are related one to the other. But it is perfectly clear that the economics are changing the face of American society. You can see it in the difference in income in rural America and urban America. You can see it in the difference—the aging process in rural America as compared with urban America. And if we want to preserve the American dream, we have got to find a way to solve this riddle.

I was born in the year after World War II at the dawn of the greatest explosion of opportunity in American history and in world history. For 30 years after that, the American people, without regard to their income or region, grew and grew together. That is, each income group over the next 30 years roughly doubled their income, except the poorest 20 percent of us that had an almost 2½ times increase in their income. So we were growing and growing together.

For about the last 15 or 20 years, half of us have been stuck, so that our country is growing, but we are growing apart even within the middle class. When you put that beside the fact that we have more and more poor people who are not elderly, which was the case when I was little, but now are largely young women and their little children, often where there was either no marriage or the marriage is broken up so there is not a stable home and there is not an adequate level of education to ensure an income, you have increasing poverty and increasing splits within the middle class. That is the fundamental cause, I believe, of a lot of the problems that we face in America and a lot of the anxiety and frustration we see in this country.

Every rich country faces this problem. But in the United States it is a particular problem, both because the inequality is greater and because it violates the American dream. I mean, this is a country where if you work hard and you play by the rules, you obey the law, you raise your children, you do your best to do everything you're supposed to do, you ought to have an opportunity for the free enterprise system to work for you.

And so we face this challenge. I have to tell you that I believe two things: One, the future is far more hopeful than worrisome. If you look at the resources of this country, the assets of this country, and you compare them with any other country in the world and you imagine what the world will be like 20 or 30 years from now, you'd have to be strongly bullish on America. You have to believe in our promise. Secondly, I am convinced we cannot get there unless we develop a new way of talking about these issues, a new political discourse, unless we move beyond the labeling that so often characterizes and, in fact, mischaracterizes the debate in Washington, DC.

Now, we are having this debate in ways that affect you, so you have to be a part of it, because one of the biggest parts of the debate is, how are we going to keep the American dream alive? How are we going to keep America the world's strongest force for freedom and democracy into the next century and change the way the Government works?

There is broad consensus that the Government in Washington should be less bureaucratic, less oriented toward rulemaking, smaller, more flexible, that more decisions should be devolved to the State and local government level and, where possible, more decisions should be given to private citizens themselves. There is a broad agreement on that.

The question is, what are the details? What does that mean? What should we do? What should you do? That's what I want to talk to you about. There are clearly some national responsibilities, clearly some that would be better served here at your level.

The main reason I ran for President is, it seemed to me that we were seeing a National Government in bipartisan gridlock, where we'd had 12 years in which we exploded the deficit, reduced our investment in people, and undermined our ability to compete and win in the world. And I wanted very badly to end the kind of gridlock we'd had and to see some real concrete action taken to go forward, because of my experience doing what you're doing now.

My basic belief is that the Government ought to do more to help people help themselves, to reward responsibility with more opportunity and not to give anybody opportunity without demanding responsibility. That's basically what I think our job is. I think we can be less bureaucratic. We have to enhance security at home and abroad. But the most important thing we have to do is to empower people to make the most of their own lives.

Now, we have made a good beginning at that. As I said, we've been able to get the deficit down. You know here in Iowa, because you're a farming State, that we've had the biggest expansion of trade in the last 2 years we've seen in a generation. We now have a $20 billion surplus in agricultural products for the first time ever. This means more to me than you, but we're selling rice to the Japanese, something that my farmers never thought that we'd ever do. We're selling apples in Asia. We are doing our best in Washington, some of us are, to get the ethanol program up and going. This administration is for it, and I hope you will help us with that.

And we're making modest efforts which ought to be increased to work with the private sector to develop alternative agricultural products. Today I saw corn-based windshield wiper fluid and, something that I think is important, biodegradable, agriculturally rooted golf tees— [*laughter*]—and a lot of other things that I think will be the hallmark of our future. We have only scratched the surface of what we can do to produce products from the land, from our food and fiber, and we must do more.

In education we are beginning to see the outlines of what I hope will be a genuine bipartisan national partnership in education. In the last 2 years, we increased Head Start. We reduced the rules and regulations the Federal Government imposes on local school systems but gave them more funds and flexibility to meet national standards of education. We helped States all over the country to develop comprehensive systems of apprenticeships for young people who get out of high school and don't want to go to college but don't want to be in dead-end jobs. We are doing more to try to make our job training programs relevant.

And we have made literally millions of Americans eligible for lower cost, better repayment college loans under our direct loan program, including over 350,000 students and former students in Iowa, including all those who are at Iowa State University. Now, if you borrow money under that program, you get it quicker with less paperwork at lower cost, and you can pay it back in one of four different ways based on the income you're going to earn when you get out of college. Believe it or not, it lowers costs to the taxpayers.

And we have demanded responsibility. We've taken the loan default costs to the taxpayers from $2.8 billion a year down to $1 billion a year. That is the direction we ought to be going in.

We've worked hard to increase our security at home and abroad. The crime bill, which was passed last year by the Congress after 6 years of endless debate, provides for 100,000 more police officers on our street. We have already—over the next 5 years—we've already awarded over 17,000 police officers to over half the police departments in America, including 158 communities here in Iowa. It strengthens punishment under Federal law.

The "three strikes and you're out" law in the crime bill is now the law of the land. The first person to be prosecuted under this law was a convicted murderer accused of an armed robbery in Waterloo last November. If he's convicted, he will go to jail for the rest of his life.

The capital punishment provisions of the crime bill will cover the incident in Oklahoma City, something that is terribly important, in my view, not only to bring justice in this case but to send a clear signal that the United States does not intend to be dominated and paralyzed by terrorists from at home or abroad, not now, not ever. We cannot ever tolerate that.

We are also more secure from beyond our borders. For the first time since the dawn of the nuclear age, there are no Russian missiles pointed at America's children. And those nuclear weapons are being destroyed every day.

We have reduced the size of the Federal Government by more than 100,000. We are taking it down by more than a quarter of a million. We have eliminated or reduced 300 programs, and I have asked Congress to eliminate or consolidate 400 more. We have tried to give more flexibility to States; several States have gotten broad freedom from Federal rules to implement health care reform. And we have now freed 27 States from cumbersome Federal rules to try to help them end welfare as we know it.

In the almost 2 years since Iowa received only the second welfare waiver our administration issued, the number of welfare recipients in Iowa who hold jobs has almost doubled from 18 to 33 percent. You are doing it without punishing children for the mistakes of their parents, and I want to say more on that later, but you are doing it. And that is clear evidence that we should give the States the right to pursue welfare reform. They know how to get the job done better than the Federal Government has done in the past. We should give you all more responsibility for moving people from welfare to work.

Now, here's where you come in, because I want to talk in very short order, one right after the other, about the decisions we still have to make in Washington. Do we still have to cut the Federal deficit more? Yes, we do. We've taken it down by $600 billion. The budget, in fact, would be balanced today if it weren't for the interest we have to pay on the debt run up between 1981 and 1992.

But it's still a problem, and you need to understand why it's a problem. It's a problem because a lot of people who used to give us money to finance our Government deficit and our trade deficit need their money at home now. That's really what's happening in Japan. They need their money at home now.

We must continue—we must say to the world, to the financial markets: We will not cut taxes except in the context of reducing the deficit. America is committed. Both parties are committed. Americans are committed to getting rid of this terrible burden on our future. We must continue to do it.

Now, the question is, how are we going to do that? Should we cut unnecessary spending? Of course we should. How do you define it? Should there be more power to State and local governments and to the private sector? You bet. But what are the details?

In other words, what we've got to do in Washington now is what you do all the time. We've got to move beyond our rhetoric to reality. And I think it would be helpful for you because we need your voice to be heard. And at least my experience in the Governors' Association was, or working in my own legislature, was that on these issues we could get Republicans and Democrats together. So let me go through what we've done and what's still to be done.

First of all, I agree with this new Congress on three issues that were in the Republican contract, and two of them are already law. Number one, Congress should apply to itself all the laws it puts on the private sector. We should know when we make laws in Washington what we're doing to other people by experiencing it ourselves. That was a good thing.

Number two, I signed the unfunded mandates legislation to make it harder, but not impossible when it's important, but much harder, for Congress to put on you and your taxpayers unfunded mandates from the Federal Government where we make you pay for something that we in Washington want to do. I strongly support that, and I think all of you do, as well.

The third thing we are doing that we have not finished yet, although both Houses have approved a version of it, is the line-item veto. Almost every Governor has it. I don't want to embarrass anybody here, but I don't know how many times I had a legislature say, "Now, Governor, I'm going to slip this in this bill because I've got to do it, and then you can scratch it out for me." [*Laughter*] And it was fine. We did it. Now if they slip it in a bill, I have to decide what to do or not. I have to decide. When the farmers in Iowa desperately needed the restoration of the tax deduction for health insurance, the 25 percent tax deduction that self-employed farmers and others get for health insurance, there was a provision of that bill I didn't like very much. I had to decide, am I going to give this back to 3.3 million self-employed Americans and their families, to lower the cost of health care by tax day, or not? But when we have the line-item veto, it won't be that way. And we need it.

Here are the hard ones: number one, the farm bill. Should we reduce farm supports? Yes, we should, as required by GATT. I worked hard to get the Europeans to the table in agriculture in this trade agreement. A lot of you understand that. The deal was, they would reduce their subsidies more than we would reduce ours, so we would at least move toward some parity, so that our farmers would get a fair break for a change. Now some say, let's just get rid of all these farm support programs.

Well, if we do it now, we give our competitors the advantage we worked for 8 years to take away. We put family farms more at risk. Now, if anybody's got better ideas about what should be in the farm bill, that's fine. If anybody's got a better idea about how to save the family farmers, let's do it. If anybody has new ideas about what should be put in for rural development, fine. But let us do no harm. Let us not labor under the illusion that having fought so hard to have a competitive agricultural playing field throughout the world, having achieved a $20 billion surplus in agriculture, we can turn and walk away from the farmers of the country in the name of cutting spending. That is not the way to cut the Federal deficit.

I'll give you another example. Some believe that we should flat-fund the School Lunch Program. And then there's a big argument in Washington; is it a cut or not? Let me tell you something, all these block grants are designed not only to give you more flexibility but to save the Federal Government money. Now, it may be a good deal, or it may not. You have to decide. But when we wanted to cut the Agriculture Department budget—we're closing nearly 1,200 offices, we're reducing employment by 13,000, we eliminated 14 divisions in the Department of Agriculture—my own view is, that is better than putting an arbitrary cap on the School Lunch Program, which will be terribly unfair to the number—to the numerous school districts in this country that have increasing burdens from low income children. There are a lot of kids in this country, a lot of kids, the only decent meal they get every day is the meal they get at school. This program works. If it's not broke, we shouldn't fix it. So I don't agree with that. But you have to decide.

Welfare reform. I've already said, we have now given more welfare reform waivers to States to get out from under the Federal Government than were given in the last 12 years put together. In 2 years, we've given more than 12 years. I am for you figuring out how you want to run your welfare system and move people from welfare to work. I am for that.

But here are the questions. Number one, should we have cumbersome Federal rules that say you have to penalize teenage girls who give birth to children and cut them off? I don't think so. We should never punish children for the mistakes of their parents. And these children who become parents prematurely, we should say, "You made a mistake, you shouldn't do that; no child should do that. But what we're going to do is to impose responsibilities on you for the future to make you a responsible parent, a responsible student, a responsible worker." That's what your program does. Why should the Federal Government tell you that you have to punish children, when what you really want to do is move people from welfare to work so that more people are good parents and good workers? You should decide that. We do not need to be giving you lectures about how you have to punish the kids of this country. We need a welfare bill that is tough on work and compassionate toward children, not a welfare bill that is weak on work and tough on children. I feel that that should be a bipartisan principle that all of us should be able to embrace.

Now, the second issue in welfare reform is whether we should give you a block grant. Instead of having the welfare being an individual entitlement to every poor person on welfare, should we just give you whatever money we gave you last year or over the last 3 years and let you spend it however you want? There are two issues here that I ask you to think about, not only from your perspective but from the perspective of every other State.

In Florida, the Republicans in the legislature I spoke with were not for this, and here's why. The whole purpose of the block grant is twofold. One is, we give you more flexibility. The second is, we say in return for more flexibility, you ought to be able to do the job for less money, so we won't increase the money you're getting over the next 5 years, which means we'll get to save money and lower the deficit. If it works for everybody concerned, it's a good deal.

But what are the States—there are two problems with a block grant in this area, and I want you to help me work through it, because I am for more flexibility for the States. I would give every State every waiver that I have given to any State. I want you to decide what to do with this; I want you to be out there creating innovative ways to break the cycle of welfare dependency. But there are two problems with this. Number one, if you have a State with a very large number of children eligible for public

assistance and they're growing rapidly, it's very hard to devise any formula that keeps you from getting hurt in the block grants over a 5-year period. And some States have rapidly growing populations, Florida, Texas, probably California.

Number two, a total block grant relieves the State of any responsibility to put up the match that is now required for you to participate in the program. Now, you may say, "Well, we would do that anyway. We have a tradition in Iowa of taking care of our own." But what if you lived in a State with a booming population growth, with wildly competing demands for dollars? And what about when the next recession comes? Keep in mind, we're making all these decisions today in the second year in which every State economy is growing. That has not happened in a very long time.

Will that really be fair? How do you know that there won't be insurmountable pressure in some States just to say, "Well, we can't take care of these children anymore; we've got to give the money to our schoolteachers; we've got to give the money to our road program; we've got to give the money to economic development; we've got environmental problems." So I ask you to think about those things. We can find a way to let you control the welfare system and move people from welfare to work, but there are two substantive problems with the block grant program that I want to see overcome before I sign off on it, because there is a national responsibility to care for the children of the country, to make sure a minimal standard of care is given. [*Applause*] Thank you.

In the crime bill, there is a proposal to take what we did last time, which was to divide the money between police, prisons, and prevention and basically give you a block grant in prevention, and instead create two separate block grants, one for prisons and one for police and prevention, in which you would reduce the amount of money for police and prevention and increase the amount of money for prisons, but you could only get it if you decided—a mandate, but a funded one—if you decided to make all people who committed serious crimes serve 85 percent of their sentences.

So Washington is telling you how you have to sentence people but offering you money to build prisons. The practical impact means that a lot of that money won't be taken care of, and we will reduce the amount of money we're spending for police and for prevention programs. I think that's a mistake.

I'm more than happy for you to have block grants for prevention programs. You know more about what keeps kids out of jail and off the streets and from committing crime in Des Moines or Cedar Rapids or Ames or anyplace else than I would ever know. But we do know that the violent crime rate has tripled in the last 30 years and the number of police on our street has only gone up by 10 percent. And we know there is city after city after city in America where the crime rate has gone down a lot, a lot, when police have been put on the street in community policing roles.

So I say, let's keep the 100,000 police program. It is totally nonbureaucratic. Small towns in Iowa can get it by filling out a one-page, 8-question form. There is no hassle. And we should do this because we know it works. There is a national interest in safer streets, and it's all paid for by reducing the Federal bureaucracy. So my view is, keep the 100,000 police. Give the States flexibility on prevention. And I hope that you will agree with that. That, at any rate, is my strong feeling.

Lastly, let me say on education, I simply don't believe that we should be cutting education to reduce the deficit or to pay for tax cuts. I don't believe that. I just don't believe that.

So my view, my view on this is that the way to save money is to give every university in the country and every college in the country the right to do what Iowa State has done: go to the direct loan program, cut out the middleman, lower the cost of loans, save the taxpayer money. I am strongly opposed to charging the students interest on their student loans while they're in college. That will add 18 to 20 percent to the cost of education for a lot of our young people. We'll have fewer people going to school. We want more people going to school. I think that is a mistake.

I believe if we're going to have a tax cut, it should be targeted to middle class people and to educational needs. I believe strongly we should do two things more than anything else: Number one, give more people the advantage of an IRA, which they can put money into and save and then withdraw to pay for education

or health care costs, purchase of a first-time home, or care of an elderly parent tax-free; number two, allow the deduction of the cost of education after high school to all American middle class families. Now, that, I think, will make a difference.

This is very important for you because, remember, if we have a smaller total tax cut, if we target it to the middle class, we can have deficit reduction without cutting education, we can have deficit reduction without having severe cuts in Medicare. Governor Branstad said today, one of our biggest problems is the unfairness of the distribution of Medicare funds. You are right. It's not fair to rural America. But there's a lot more coming and more than you need to have if we have an excessive tax cut that is not targeted to education and to the middle class.

So that, in brief, is the laundry list of the new federalism, the things you need to decide on. I do not believe these issues I have spoken with you about have a partisan tinge in Des Moines. They need not have one in Washington.

But I invite you, go back home—this is being televised tonight—go back home and talk to the people you represent and ask them what they want you to say to your Members of Congress about what we do in Washington, what you do in Des Moines, what we do in our private lives, what should be spent to reduce the deficit, what should be spent on a tax cut, what should be in a block grant, and where should we stand up and say we've got to protect the children of the country. These are great and exciting issues.

Believe me, if we make the right decisions, if we make the right decisions, the 21st century will still be the American century.

Thank you all, and God bless you.

NOTE: The President spoke at 7:32 p.m. in the Senate Chamber at the State Capital. In his remarks, he referred to Leonard Boswell, president, Iowa State Senate; Ron Corbett, speaker, Iowa State House; Gov. Terry E. Branstad of Iowa; Arthur McGiverin, chief justice, Iowa Supreme Court; and former Representative Neal Smith and his wife, Bea.

Statement on the Death of Naomi Nover
April 25, 1995

Hillary and I were so saddened to learn of the death of Naomi Nover. Naomi's years of dedication to her craft and her efforts to cover events here at the White House up until just a few months before her death were a lesson to us all in hard work and the persistence of the human spirit. She will be missed greatly, and our thoughts are with her sisters and the rest of her family at this difficult time.

Letter to Congressional Leaders Transmitting a Report on Cyprus
April 25, 1995

Dear Mr. Speaker: (Dear Mr. Chairman:)

In accordance with Public Law 95–384 (22 U.S.C. 2373(c)), I submit to you this report on progress toward a negotiated settlement of the Cyprus question. The previous report covered progress through January 31, 1995. The current report covers the period from February 1, 1995, through March 31, 1995.

During this period my Special Emissary for Cyprus, Richard I. Beattie, and the State Department's Special Cyprus Coordinator, James A. Williams, visited Turkey and met with Turkish leaders. Constructive discussions were held on how best to move the process forward after the elections in northern Cyprus in April. Prime Minister Ciller expressed her willingness to assist in finding a solution during her recent visit and restated Ankara's commitment to work with the United Nations in producing an overall solution to the Cyprus problem.

On March 6, the European Union agreed to begin accession negotiations with Cyprus after the conclusion of the 1996 Intergovernmental Conference. On the same date, the European Union concluded a customs union agreement with Turkey. I believe talks on membership in the EU for the entire island of Cyprus, together with Turkey's integration into Europe, will serve as a catalyst to the search for an overall solution on Cyprus.

Sincerely,

WILLIAM J. CLINTON

NOTE: Identical letters were sent to Newt Gingrich, Speaker of the House of Representatives, and Jesse Helms, chairman, Senate Committee on Foreign Relations.

Remarks on Counterterrorism Initiatives and an Exchange With Reporters
April 26, 1995

The President. I asked the leaders of Congress from both parties to come to the White House today because I know that we have a shared commitment to do everything we possibly can to stamp out the kind of vicious behavior we saw in Oklahoma City. Everyone here is determined to do that, and I want us to work together to get the job done.

On Sunday, I announced the first series of steps we must take to combat terrorism in America. Today I'm announcing further measures, grounded in common sense and steeled with force. These measures will strengthen law enforcement and sharpen their ability to crack down on terrorists wherever they're from, be it at home or abroad. This will arm them with investigative tools, increased enforcement, and tougher penalties.

I say, again: Justice in this case must be swift, certain, and severe. And for anyone who dares to sow terror on American land, justice must be swift, certain, and severe. We must move on with law enforcement measures quickly. We must move so that we can prevent this kind of thing from happening again. We cannot allow our entire country to be subjected to the horror that the people of Oklahoma City endured. We can prevent it and must do everything we can to prevent it. I know that we would do this together without regard to party, and I'm looking forward to this discussion of it.

Q. Civil libertarians are worried there may be some ability by law enforcement agencies to abuse the power that you may be given.

The President. I think we can strike the right balance. We've got to do more to protect the American people.

NOTE: The President spoke at 5:09 p.m. in the Cabinet Room at the White House, prior to a meeting with congressional leaders. A tape was not available for verification of the content of these remarks.

Remarks on Presenting the President's Service Awards
April 27, 1995

Thank you very much, Eli Segal, for your words of introduction and for your outstanding leadership of our national service efforts. And thank you, Marlee Matlin, for your leadership in a volunteer capacity of the most important volunteer efforts in our country.

Just over a week ago we were reminded that there are those who want to see our Nation torn apart. But amid the grief and the destruction we have also seen how quickly the overwhelming majority of Americans come together to help each other to rebuild and to make this country stronger.

When Hillary and I were in Oklahoma City last Sunday, we saw a community working around the clock to rebuild itself. Compassion and assistance flowed in from all over the United States. Americans were united in a spirit of service. It is that spirit which we honor today.

It gives me tremendous pleasure to be here with all of you to celebrate National Volunteer Week and to honor the recipients of the President's Service Awards for 1995. Today we'll hear stories of ordinary Americans doing extraordinary things, teachers and homemakers, carpenters and business leaders, people from small neighborhood organizations and large corporations. Our honorees comfort the sick and fight illiteracy. They repair our parks and keep our young people out of gangs. They come from all corners of the Nation. They are diverse in age and background. Yet they are united by something larger than all of us, the simple desire to fulfill the promise of American life.

A couple of days ago I was in Iowa for our rural conference. Those of us who come from small towns know that we don't have a person to waste in our communities or in our country. Large or small, our communities have never been built with bricks and mortar alone. They are sustained by the faith that there will always be people there to lend a hand.

That's why more than 90 million Americans lend a hand every year, 90 million. At a time when the American people are working harder and longer than they have been in the last 10 years at their own jobs, they still find time to volunteer to help others. Americans know we can never be fulfilled as a country unless we are prepared to take responsibility for each other.

I'm proud that we're joined to honor this year's award recipients by two young members of AmeriCorps, Brent Bloom and Izabel De Araugo. They and their fellow corps members are showing that we gain when we give. In return for help with college, they're helping others. AmeriCorps efforts go hand in hand with the voluntarism we celebrate today. It is a great partnership.

I want to say a special word of appreciation for Brent Bloom. He lives in Oklahoma City, where he works in a homeless shelter while studying for a pre-med degree at Oklahoma University. A little more than a week ago, Brent heard the explosion that was felt all around America. He went straight to the Federal building, told the first police officer he saw that he knew emergency first aid, and then spent the rest of the day and well into the night sorting through the wreckage and saving lives. [*Applause*]

In the weeks since, he has been working with Feed the Children, helping children, families, and the extraordinary rescue teams. He deserves our gratitude and the applause you just gave him. He and countless others who are working to heal the wounds from last week's bombing are living proof that we are truly a nation of volunteers. They show us once again that altruism will always triumph over the forces of divisiveness.

Let me say, too, if I might, a word of appreciation to another volunteer who is not here today. When the explosion occurred in Oklahoma City, a nurse named Rebecca Anderson rushed to the bombed Federal building as well to help. She was hit by some falling debris in the building, suffered a hemorrhage, and later died. She left behind four children. But even in death, she continued to serve, for she donated her heart for a heart transplant which occurred yesterday and saved the life of one more person. That is the real America, and no matter what else happens, we should never forget it.

You know, "voluntary" derives from a Latin word which means both "wish" and "will." I cannot imagine a more accurate combination for what we celebrate today: uniting the wish for a better world with the will to make it happen, neighbor to neighbor, community to community. Each act of service pulls us together and pushes us forward. Let's keep it up.

Thank you very much.

NOTE: The President spoke at 12:54 p.m. in the Rose Garden at the White House.

Statement on the Observance of Freedom Day in South Africa
April 27, 1995

A full year has passed since South Africa embarked on a bold course to build nonracial democracy. Americans vividly remember watching inspiring scenes of the people of South Africa standing patiently in long lines to cast their first votes together. Their work for a democratic future still touches us all.

Under President Mandela's wise leadership, South Africa has taken the road of reconciliation and consensus building. The United States remains determined to assist South Africa in these efforts, through our assistance program, the U.S.-South African Binational Commission launched in March, and a wide array of public and private sector initiatives to support the rebuilding of South Africa.

South Africans are charting a course to meet the country's pressing economic and social needs. The Government of National Unity has promoted sound economic policies. The American private sector—business, private voluntary organizations, and academic institutions—has joined efforts to nurture and sustain democracy and economic growth in South Africa. Over 300 American companies have returned since apartheid ended.

On this Freedom Day, April 27, I congratulate the people of South Africa on their progress and courage. They stand as a symbol of hope in a strife-torn world. The American people wish them every success.

Remarks on Presenting the Teacher of the Year Award
April 28, 1995

Thank you very much, Secretary Riley, Governor Knowles, to our distinguished Teacher of the Year. We're fortunate to be joined here by many friends of education. I cannot mention them all, but I would like to mention a few: First, my longtime friend Gordon Ambach, the

607

executive director of the Council of Chief State School Officers; Scholastic, Inc., CEO and president Dick Robinson and senior vice president Ernie Fleishman; president of the AFT Al Shanker; and I know that Keith Geiger, the president of the NEA, was on his way here— I don't know if he's here yet; Assistant Secretary of Education Tom Payzant, I'd like to thank him for his work and for coming here from a school district to make sure we keep grounded in the real world. I want to say a special word of welcome to all these fine teachers here who represent, along with our Teacher of the Year, 46 of the total honorees throughout the United States. We're very, very glad to have all them here, and I think we should give them a hand this morning and a welcome. [*Applause*]

Before I make my remarks about the Teacher of the Year and the importance of education today, I want to say one word about our ongoing efforts to protect the American people from ever again having to endure what the American people have endured in Oklahoma City.

Sunday I announced the first in a series of new steps to combat terrorism in America, whatever its source. Wednesday I invited Republican and Democratic leaders from the Congress to the White House to do more. I announced at that time I would send to Congress new legislation designed to crack down on terrorism. These new measures will give law enforcement expanded investigative powers, increased enforcement capacities, and tougher penalties to use against those who commit terrorist acts.

I'm encouraged so far by the response from Members of Congress in both parties. And I say again, Congress must move quickly to pass this legislation. The American people want us to stop terrorism. They want us to put away anyone involved in it. We must not allow politics to drag us into endless quibbling over an important national item. We must not delay the work we have to do to keep the American people safe and to try to prevent further acts of this kind. We must allow the American people to get on with their lives, and all of that is caught up in this measure. I have put tough legislation on the table. It reassures the American people that we are doing all we can to protect them and, most importantly, their children. We must not dawdle or delay. Congress must act and act promptly.

All Americans have responded with great spirit to this awful tragedy. Law enforcement has

been swift and sure. The rescue efforts have been truly heroic and not without their own sacrifices. Communities have come together as we reach out to support the people who have endured so much. Now, working together, we are going to do more.

The thing that I notice most, perhaps, about the Oklahoma City tragedy was how moved all Americans were by the plight of innocent children. It is hard to think of anything good coming out of something so horrible. But if anything, I think the American people have reaffirmed our commitment to putting the interests of our children and their future first in our lives.

In the brief time since he took office, the Governor of Alaska, Tony Knowles, who is sitting here behind me, has already worked to do that in Alaska. Alaska, as you know, is vast and faces unique problems and challenges. Those challenges are being met through satellite technology the Healthy Start program which ensures that children start school well-nourished and ready to learn. That is a sort of commitment that all of us now must take into our lives, into our States, into our schools, into our communities.

I ran for President to make sure that the American dream would be available to all of our children well into the next century. I wanted to make sure that we could deal with the challenges of today and tomorrow presented by the global economy, presented by the revolutions in technology in ways that gave everybody a chance to live up to the fullest of his or her God-given capacities. We know that more than anything else today, that requires a good education.

We know that the technological revolution and the global economy, with all of its pressures, have begun in every wealthy nation to put unbelievable strains on the social contract, to split apart the middle class. That is happening more in the United States than any other country, and the fault line is education. If you look at what is happening to adults, working people and their families, in their workplaces all across this country, those who are well-educated are doing very well in this global economy, and those who lack an education are having a very difficult time.

We owe it to the children of this country to make sure that every one of them has the best possible education. And in doing that, we are being a little bit selfish because this country itself will not be strong into the next century unless we dramatically improve the reach and depth of our common efforts to educate all of our people.

As I have said many times in many places, we face two great deficits in this country, a budget deficit that is the product of too many years of taking the easy way out and an education deficit that is the product of too many years of ignoring the obvious. We have worked hard to try to address both over the last 2 years, reducing our deficit by $600 billion over a 5-year period and increasing our commitment to education.

We must do more on both, but we dare not sacrifice one at the expense of the other. The answer to the budget deficit is not to reverse the gains we have made by expanding Head Start, by expanding opportunities for young people who don't go to college to move from school to work with good jobs and good futures, by expanding our commitment to childhood nutrition and the health of our children, by expanding our efforts to give people the chance to go to college through more affordable college loans and the AmeriCorps national service program. We cannot cure one deficit at the expense of the other.

And indeed, in some areas we should plainly be doing more. The Goals 2000 legislation for the first time set America on a course of national excellence in education, while giving teachers like the ones we celebrate here today more opportunities working with their principals to have flexibility from cumbersome Federal rules and regulations to do what they know best in educating their children. We should be putting more money into our schools with less rules and regulations, but higher standards, higher expectations, and honest measurement of educational progress.

We should be doing more of what we've been doing in the last 2 years, not less. And we can do it and bring the deficit down. We must attack both deficits at once and not sacrifice education on the altar of deficit reduction.

We must also realize that the work of America is a work that is not done by government alone or even primarily by government. As I used to say over and over again when I was a Governor and much closer to the schools of our country, nothing we do in government will matter at all unless there are people like the teachers who are being honored here today. What we do in Washington only empowers people to do better by our children in every school in the country. What happens in the home and what happens in the school and how they relate to and reinforce one another will have the deciding influence on the quality of education in the United States and the future of this country as we move into this new and exciting age.

Many of you remember Jesse Stuart, who taught in a one-room schoolhouse in the rural South and wrote a wonderful book called "The Thread That Runs So True," in which he said, "A teacher lives on and on through his students. Good teaching is forever, and the teacher is immortal." Well, just like Jesse Stuart, the 1995 National Teacher of the Year has taught in a one-room schoolhouse, but hers is in rural Alaska, where it's a little colder in the wintertime.

Elaine Griffin's work at the Kodiak Island schools of Akhioc and Chiniak over the past 20 years has significantly expanded the educational, social, and cultural environments for the students in her K-through-12 classroom. With her husband, Ned, she brings in members of the community to share their talents with the students. And as the students learn about their own history, they are also being taught to understand distant lands. Many of the students have participated in foreign exchange programs. And I must say that Elaine and Ned have created their own cultural exchange with their three remarkable children, whom I just had the privilege of meeting in the Oval Office, whom I know that she will introduce in a moment.

College attendance has increased significantly among their students. In Akhioc, a remote village where teen pregnancy, alcoholism and suicide were common, Elaine expanded the K-through-8 program so that it included high school. Today, 90 percent of the children in that remote village graduate from high school. And America is better for it.

Elaine, it is my pleasure to present the 1995 Apple Award honoring you as the National Teacher of the Year and to thank you on behalf of all the American people for your dedication to your students and to the best in this country. You are truly a model for all the teachers of this country but for all the citizens as well.

Congratulations, and God bless you.

NOTE: The President spoke at 12:05 p.m. in the Rose Garden at the White House.

Message on Public Service Recognition Week, 1995
April 28, 1995

Greetings to everyone celebrating Public Service Recognition Week, 1995.

Our nation's government has tremendous potential for good when it works in partnership with citizens to expand opportunity. With the assistance of dedicated public employees, our government has helped to advance civil rights, defend freedom, protect our environment, and uplift the lives of countless Americans. All those who serve the people of the United States can be proud of their contributions to this important legacy.

As our Administration continues its efforts to make government work better and cost less, this week offers Americans a special opportunity to learn more about the importance of public service. Every citizen has a solemn responsibility to understand and become involved in ensuring our country's success. I encourage all of you to discover the many ways in which our government is changing to keep pace with the times. Your participation can help to ensure a brighter future for you and your family and for communities throughout the land.

Best wishes for a most successful week.

BILL CLINTON

NOTE: Public Service Recognition Week was observed May 1–7.

The President's Radio Address
April 29, 1995

Good morning. America has been through a lot in the last week. But if anything good can come out of something as horrible as the Oklahoma City tragedy, it is that the American people have reaffirmed our commitment to putting our children, their well-being and their future, first in our lives.

In that light, I was terribly disappointed that this week the Supreme Court struck down a law passed by Congress under President Bush and sponsored by Senator Herb Kohl of Wisconsin to keep guns away from schools. The law was a bipartisan approach to school safety based on common sense. Simply said, it was illegal to have a gun within 1,000 feet of a school.

We all know that guns simply don't belong in school. So Members of Congress of both parties passed the law. Unfortunately, the Supreme Court struck down the specific law. They said the Federal Government couldn't regulate that activity because it didn't have enough to do with interstate commerce.

Well, this Supreme Court decision could condemn more of our children to going to schools where there are guns. And our job is to help our children learn everything they need to get ahead, in safety, not to send them to school and put them in harm's way. I am determined to keep guns out of our schools. That's what the American people want, and it's the right thing to do.

Last year, I persuaded Congress to require States to pass a law that any student who brought a gun to school would be expelled for a year—no excuses, zero tolerance for guns in schools. But after Congress passed the law, I was worried that it would be hard to enforce. So I directed the Secretary of Education, Dick Riley, to withhold Federal aid from any State that did not comply with the law.

The Supreme Court has now ruled we can't directly ban guns around the school. Therefore, today I am directing the Attorney General to come back to me within a week with what action

I can take to keep guns away from schools. I want the action to be constitutional, but I am determined to keep guns away from schools. For example, Congress could encourage States to ban guns from school zones by linking Federal funds to enactment of school zone gun bans. At least we could tie the money we have for safe schools to such a ban. At any rate, I am confident that the Attorney General will give me advice about what action I can take. We must reverse the practical impact of the Court's decision. If young people can't learn in safety, they can't learn at all.

Now, according to the Center for Disease Control in Atlanta, violence threatens schools in communities of all shapes and sizes. They've identified 105 violent school-related deaths in just the last 2 years. And we know there are common elements to violent deaths among young people. Usually, the victim and the assailant know each other, the incident starts as an argument, and usually there is a firearm present.

Schoolyard fights have been around as long as schoolyards. But it used to be that when kids got in fights, they fought with their fists, adults broke them up, and the kids got punished. Today, there are guns on the playground, guns in the classrooms, guns on the bus. In 1990, the CDC found that 1 in 24 students carried a gun in a 30-day period. By 1993, it was down to 1 in 12. The number of high school students carrying a gun doubled in only 3 years.

This is certainly a national crisis, and we must have a national effort to fight it. We need a seamless web of safety that keeps guns out of the hands of our children and out of our schools. That's why we fought for the provision in last year's crime bill which now makes it a Federal crime for a young person to carry a handgun, except when supervised by an adult. And that's why we must make sure that anyone who does bring a gun to school is severely disciplined. And that's why we're going to find a way to ban guns inside or near our schools.

I'm committed to doing everything in my power to make schools places where young people can be safe, where they can learn, where parents can be confident that discipline is enforced.

We all know that we have to work together to get this done. Principals and teachers must take the lead for safe schools and teaching good citizenship and good values. And parents have to recognize that discipline begins at home. The responsibility to raise children and to make them good citizens rests first on the shoulders of their parents, who must teach the children right from wrong and must get involved and stay involved in their children's education.

I pledge that we'll do our part to help make our schools safe and the neighborhoods around them safe. But in the end, we'll only succeed if we all work together.

Thanks for listening.

NOTE: The address was recorded at 2:48 p.m. on April 28 in the Roosevelt Room at the White House for broadcast at 10:06 a.m. on April 29.

Remarks at the White House Correspondents' Association Dinner
April 29, 1995

Thank you very much, Ken. To all the members of the White House press who are here; to all the members of the White House staff and the administration who are here and who have to endure this every year with me. [*Laughter*] Let me say I have had a wonderful time tonight. I kind of hate to come up here; I'd rather listen to Conan talk to that worthless redneck on the screen—[*laughter*]—for another half an hour.

I identify with Conan O'Brien. Like me, he's a young man who came from obscurity—[*laugh-ter*]—and chose a sidekick with more inside experience. And despite his many accomplishments, 250 million Americans never get to see him in prime time. [*Laughter*]

I feel your pain. [*Laughter*]

Speaking of young people, it was announced tonight, you know, that my Press Secretary, Mike McCurry, and his wife, Debra, just had their third child, Christopher. I want to make another announcement: Before my term is over, Christopher will become the youngest member of the White House Press Office—[*laughter*]—

just barely younger than the rest who work there. [*Laughter*]

You know, I practiced for this night. I had all this humor and everything, but—and I really believe that you could tell I—I really liked that—whoever that awful person is that played me. [*Laughter*] I thought it was wonderful.

The Book of Proverbs says, "A happy heart doeth good like medicine, and a broken spirit drieth the bones." And I believe that. But I think you will all understand that—and I hope my wonderful comedy writers will understand— if I take a few moments tonight not to be too funny here at the end because of the tragedy in Oklahoma City, which has captured us all and which still is the focus of our efforts, for understandable reasons tonight, as the rescue workers are still laboring and as the law enforcement officers are still working.

Tonight, as Ken and I were sitting here, and he let me read his latest essay about the heroism of the people in Oklahoma City. And I want to say something personal to all of you. I know that for virtually everybody in the press in this room, this has been a very painful experience for all of you, too, who have covered it, and to have been Americans, to have been parents and children and brothers and sisters, and to have identified with the human tragedy on such a massive scale.

And what I want to do tonight is to tell you that I really appreciate the way this incident has been presented to the American people. I think you have made an extraordinary effort to capture both the horror and the humanity of the situation, to somehow grasp and communicate to your fellow citizens the incredible honor with which so many people have performed in these last difficult days.

Most of you were able, and I think it was difficult, to show commendable restraint in not jumping to any conclusions about who did this terrible thing. And most of you have really done a great deal to help the American people find some renewed strength and energy. And I thank you for that. And I hope in the days ahead you will be able to continue it.

As this story unfolds, I would ask you to continue to return to Oklahoma City, to update our country on how the families who have suffered so much are rebuilding their lives, and to remind us about the countless heroes we have all seen there. The terrible people who did this thing do not deserve to be celebrities,

although they will become famous. But the victims and their families and the people who have labored, they don't deserve to be forgotten.

The heroes of this tragedy embody the unbreakable spirit of our Nation. They should always be remembered, the hundreds of rescue workers who defied the rain, the cold, the heartache, and a very real risk to their own lives. People like Rebecca Anderson, a nurse with four children, whose parents still live in my home State, who was hit by a piece of concrete and later died trying to help others. Even in death, she continued to serve the living by giving her heart to save the life of a man from Oklahoma and one of her kidneys to save the life of a woman from New Mexico.

Now, folks, that is the real America. Sometimes all of us forget it a little bit. Sometimes all of us are too bound up in what we are doing. But this country is bound together in a way that the people like those who committed those crimes in Oklahoma can never understand. And I know our Government is not perfect, and I know it makes mistakes. But this is a very free country and a very great country. And a lot of the people who are out there complaining about it today would not even be able to do what they do in the way they do it in most of the other democracies in the world today. And we should never forget it.

I say this tonight not to pour cold water on this wonderful evening and not because I haven't enjoyed it—I think I laughed harder tonight than anybody else here—but because as long as this work is going on, I think I owe it to you to tell you for all of our sometimes conflicting interests, I am really proud of the work the American press corps did in bringing this to the American people. And the work is not over. The understanding is not over.

We have a lot of difficult decisions to make in the weeks and months ahead. As you know, I feel very strongly that the country should adopt stronger measures against terrorism. It will be debated in the Congress. Some of the measures are complex. You will have to explain them to the American people. I ask only that in all of this, you never forget the human dimension that you have so skillfully and heroically brought home to all the people of this country.

We are going to get through this, and when we do, we'll be even stronger. We've been around here now for more than 200 years because almost all the time more than half of us wind up somehow doing the right thing. And we will do the right thing again.

I'd like to close with words written by the wonderful poet W.H. Auden over 50 years ago: "In the deserts of the heart, let the healing fountain start. In the prison of his days, teach the free man how to praise."

We praise America tonight, and we thank you for bringing it home to us in such a powerful way in these last days.

Good night, and God bless you all.

NOTE: The President spoke at 10:47 p.m. at the Washington Hilton. In his remarks, he referred to Ken Walsh, outgoing president, White House Correspondents' Association, and entertainer Conan O'Brien.

Remarks to the American Gathering of Jewish Holocaust Survivors in New York City
April 30, 1995

Foreign Minister Peres, thank you for your powerful words, the example of your life, and your tireless work for peace. Rabbi Lau, Governor Pataki, Senator Moynihan, Senator D'Amato, members of the New York congressional delegation, Speaker Silver, Ambassador Rabinovich and members of the Diplomatic Corps, Mr. Mayor, and of course, my friend Benjamin Meed. I thank you and your wife for joining us and helping Hillary and me and, through us, the entire United States last year to understand the deepest and profoundest meaning of the Warsaw Uprising.

This year we mark the 50th anniversary of the end of the Holocaust. Since Biblical times, 50th anniversaries have had special meanings. Our English word "jubilee" comes to us from the Hebrew word for that anniversary. And the Scripture tells us that every 50th year is to be holy and the land should be left fallow and slaves freed upon the blowing of a shofar. It was a year in the Scriptures that closed an era and began another.

We think of such things here on the end of this century and the beginning of a new millennium, but in profound ways there can be no such closure for the half-century after the Holocaust. For all of those who lived through it and all of us who came after, the Holocaust redefined our understanding of the human capacity for evil. Anyone who has stood in that tower of photographs in the Holocaust Memorial Museum in Washington, who has seen those unforgettable, warm, expressive faces from that small Lithuanian town, anyone who has seen

the horror even in pictures knows that we must now and never allow the memory of those events to fade.

The Bible also made the link between memory and deed, enjoining us so often to remember the years of slavery in Egypt and the acts of the wicked and then to act morally. Today we must remember those years of radical evil as though it were a commandment to do so because, as we have seen, hatred still flourishes where it has a chance. Intolerance still lurks, waiting to spread. Racist violence still threatens abroad and at home.

We are taught in our faith that as much as we might regret it, deep within the human spirit there is, and will always remain until the end of time, the capacity for evil. It must be remembered, and it must be opposed.

The commandment to remember is especially great now because, as the Foreign Minister said, this has been a very bloody century. And soon, the living memory of the Holocaust will pass. Those of us, then, who were born after the war will then have to shoulder the responsibility that the survivors have carried for so long: to fight all forms of racism, to combat those who distort the past and peddle hate in the present, to stand against the new forms of organized evil and counter their determination to use and to abuse the modern miracles of technology and openness and possibility that offer us the opportunity to build for our children the most remarkable world ever known but still carry, within these forces, the seeds of further destruction.

I have hope for the future because our Americans are embracing the responsibility of memory. In the 2 years since the Holocaust Memorial Museum opened, more than 4 million people—more, many more than were expected—have visited that remarkable place. The daily number of visitors is still increasing, and about 8 of every 10 Americans who visit are not Jews. Twenty thousand school groups have been there already, and with the help of the museum, some 40,000 teachers around our country now teach about the Holocaust in their classes. Perhaps those children one day will be the kind of adults who would stop and ask why and do more if someone ever came to take a friend or a neighbor away.

If so, we will have been true to the memory of the victims of the Holocaust, and we will have pressed the cause of decency and human dignity yet one more step forward. This is our task: making memory real and making memory a guide for our own actions.

I am reminded of the extraordinary visit I had last year to the Old Jewish Cemetery in Prague, that great forest of stones. As you know, everyone who visits there, or any Jewish cemetery, puts a stone on a grave, adding to memory, never subtracting from it. For me, someone new

to the experience, it was an overwhelming symbol of how we all ought to think and live.

Over the centuries, memory has been built there in Prague in a very deep and profound way, in the city that Hitler wanted to turn into a museum for what he hoped would be an extinct people. We, too, now must add to those stones, stones of remembrance, like this daylong gathering, stones that add to the memory of the victims and to our knowledge of the barbarism that claimed them.

Ultimately, I wanted to be here today, after all our country has been through in these last days, because you have taught me that the vigilance of memory is our greatest defense, and I thank you all for that.

NOTE: The President spoke at 2:35 p.m. at Madison Square Garden. In his remarks, he referred to Foreign Minister Shimon Peres of Israel; Rabbi Yisrael Meir Lau, chief Rabbi of the Ashkenazic Jews of Israel; Gov. George E. Pataki of New York; Sheldon Silver, New York State House speaker; Mayor Rudolph Giuliani of New York City; and Benjamin Meed, president, American Gathering of Jewish Holocaust Survivors, and his wife, Vladka.

Remarks at the World Jewish Congress Dinner in New York City
April 30, 1995

Thank you very much. Thank you, Edgar. Foreign Minister Peres, thank you for being here, for your visionary leadership, your wise words. To all of the friends of Edgar Bronfman who are here from Canada and from around the world, I am profoundly honored to be with you this evening and to receive this wonderful Nahum Goldmann Award.

I know he was the president of the World Jewish Congress, the World Zionist Organization, the Jewish Agency, Conference of Presidents of Major Jewish Organizations. Every group I can think of associated with Edgar Bronfman, except the Seagram's Group—[*laughter*]—we would all like to be president of that, thanks to the work he has done. I would remind you, Edgar, that I'm a relatively young man without a great deal of job security. I hope

you will keep me in mind in the future. [*Laughter*]

We gather—I wish you wouldn't laugh quite so much at that. [*Laughter*] We gather tonight to celebrate the accomplishments of an extraordinary man. For all of you, your presence here is testimony to your shared values, your shared goals, and to the countless lives that Edgar Bronfman has touched. In these years of great change and opportunity and of great anxiety and even fear, in years of too much cynicism, the Jewish community has found in Edgar Bronfman the rarest of combination, a leader armed with passion for his people's cause and endowed with the strength to act on that passion. As president of the World Jewish Congress and a citizen of the world, Edgar Bronfman has given life to

Emerson's observation that an institution is the length and shadow of one man.

In the long years when the Soviet Union imprisoned Jews within its borders, many raised their voices in anger, but Edgar journeyed to Moscow to win their release. When millions in Russia and all across Eastern Europe won their freedom from tyranny's grip, many rejoiced, but Edgar took the lead in helping Jewish communities reclaim their proud spiritual and physical heritage that many feared had been lost forever. And as a new era of peace dawns in the Middle East, many celebrate, but Edgar works every day to reconcile the people of Israel and the Palestinians and to bring new life to ancient lands. Wherever Jews dream of a better life and wherever those dreams are threatened, Edgar Bronfman is sure to be found.

A week ago today, Hillary and I went to Oklahoma City to mourn with and pay our respects to the victims and families of the terrible bombing there. Last summer, Edgar undertook a similar journey of his own when he flew to Argentina just hours after hearing of the bombing of the Jewish community center in Buenos Aires. There in the midst of the rubble and the ruins, he called on leaders, visited the injured, spoke to the children, told them to stand firm against those who traffic in fear, to hope and not hate, but to work every day to turn that hope into reality. In these times, that is a lesson every citizen of every continent should learn and take to heart. It echoes loudest in the ears of those who have known so much terror and so much sorrow.

As was said earlier today by my friend Benjamin Meed, we mark the time when half a century ago the most terrible chapter in the history of the Jewish people was brought to a close. Unfortunately, 50 years later, merchants of hate still live among us here at home and around the world. Of course, we cannot compare their actions or their capabilities to the horrors that were visited upon the Jewish people, but they do practice and they do preach violence against those who are of a different color, a different background, or who worship a different God. They do feed on fear and uncertainty. They do promote paranoia. In the name of freedom of speech, they have abandoned the responsibility that democratic freedoms impose on all of us.

In this freest of nations, it must strike all of you as ironic that many of these people attack our Government and the citizens who work for it, who actually guarantee the freedoms that they abuse. In the name of building a better future, they would relive the most destructive chapters of evil. So while we cannot compare what they are saying and doing to what the Jewish people suffered decades ago, we dare not underestimate the dangers they pose. They can certainly snuff out innocent lives and sow fear in our hearts. They are indifferent to the slaughter of children. They threaten our freedoms and our way of life, and we must stop them.

Our early patriot Samuel Adams once said, "If we suffer tamely a lawless attack upon our liberty, we encourage it and involve others in our doom." Here in America it is not only our right, it is our duty to stop the terror, to bring to justice the guilty, and to stand against the hatred, and to help others in other lands to do the same.

Since the beginning of our administration we have taken broad and swift measures to fight terrorism here and abroad. We have brought to trial the alleged bombers of the World Trade Center, who struck at the heart of this city. We have actively pursued those who crossed the line into illegal and violent activity. We have taken strong actions against nations who harbor terrorists or support their bloody trade. We have worked to prevent acts of terror, sometimes with remarkable success. And in a world where open borders and new technologies make our job harder, we have worked closer and closer with other nations to unravel the networks of terror and hunt down those who threaten our people.

But the tragedy of Oklahoma City and its aftermath have made it clear that we must take stronger steps. This week I asked Congress to approve my antiterrorism initiatives: the power to hire 1,000 new Federal officials in law enforcement and support to create a new counterterrorism center under the direction of the FBI; to authorize the military to use its special capabilities in incidents involving chemical, biological, and nuclear weapons of terror in our country. Our proposals would also allow us to tag materials used to make bombs so that suspects could be more easily traced.

Although no one can guarantee freedom from terror, at least these common sense steps will help to make our people safer. So tonight I appeal again to Congress to pass these measures without delay.

While we take these actions at home, we must also continue and strengthen our fight against terror around the world. Tonight I want to speak to you about terrorism in the Middle East, about rogue nations who sponsor death in order to kill peace and what we can do further to contain them.

From the beginning of my Presidency, our policy in the Middle East has run on two tracks. Support for the peace process that reconciles Israel and her neighbors: I have been honored to work with Prime Minister Rabin and Foreign Minister Peres and their government and the people of Israel in that regard. And the policy of the United States has been the correct one, that we would never seek to impose a peace on Israel and her neighbors, but if Israel takes risks for peace we will be there to minimize those risks and maximize the chances of success. And we are ahead of where we were 2 years ago, and by God's grace, we will continue to make progress in the years ahead. I am especially proud of this work that we have all been able to do and particularly proud of the work of Secretary Christopher in this regard.

But the second part of our policy in the Middle East is also important: opposition to all those who would derail the peace process, promote terrorism, or develop weapons of mass destruction. The dangers remain great. The closer we come to achieving peace and normalcy in the region, the more desperate become the enemies of peace. On buses and along busy streets, terrorist attacks have claimed innocent lives, and we grieve with the families of the victims.

We have strengthened our efforts to act against groups like Hamas and Hezbollah, and we are encouraging Chairman Arafat in his efforts to crack down on arrests and prosecute those extremists who resort to violence. But individuals and extremist groups are not the only threat. Israel shares the lands of the Middle East with nations who still seek to destroy the peace, nations like Iran and Iraq and Libya. They aim to destabilize the region. They harbor terrorists within their borders. They establish and support terrorist base camps in other lands. They hunger for nuclear and other weapons of mass destruction. Every day, they put innocent civilians in danger and stir up discord among nations. Our policy toward these rogue states is simple: They must be contained.

Iran has presented a particular problem to the peace process of the peoples of the Middle East. From the beginning of our administration, we have moved to counter Iran's support of international terrorism and in particular its backing for violent opponents of peace in the Middle East.

At the same time, we have tried to stop its quest to acquire weapons of mass destruction, which would make it a threat not only to its neighbors but to the entire region and the world. Our policy has helped to make Iran pay a price for its actions. The nation has effectively been cut off from receiving credit from international financial institutions.

The United States and our allies in the G–7 have stopped Iranian purchases of weapons from our nations. We have refused to cooperate with Iran on sensitive matters such as nuclear energy and have tightened trade restrictions on items that might be used to build weapons.

We have not always been successful, as all of you know. The most recent reports of Russia's agreement to sell gas centrifuge equipment to the Iranians and to train nuclear technicians from Tehran are disturbing to me. Because Iran has more than enough oil to supply its energy needs, we must assume that it seeks this technology in order to develop its capacity to build nuclear weapons.

The United States has an overwhelming interest in fighting the spread of these weapons. And Russia, as a neighbor of Iran, has a particular interest in the same goal. If Russia goes forward with the sale of nuclear reactors, it will only undermine that objective. We have strenuously urged the Russians to reverse these decisions, and I will make that case directly to President Yeltsin when I visit Moscow in just a few days.

My fellow Americans, I speak especially to you when I say that many people have argued passionately that the best route to change Iranian behavior is by engaging the country. Unfortunately, there is no evidence to support that argument. Indeed, the evidence of the last 2 years suggest exactly the reverse. Iran's appetite for acquiring and developing nuclear weapons and the missiles to deliver them has only grown larger. Even as prospects for the peace in the Middle East have grown, Iran has broadened its role as an inspiration and paymaster to terrorists. And there is nothing to suggest that further engagement will alter that course.

That is why last month, after the Conoco Company announced a $1 billion contract to help Iran develop its oil reserves, I was prepared to stop the project by signing an Executive order banning any United States firms from financing, supervising, or managing Iranian oil reserves. But Conoco ultimately decided to abandon the deal. And let me add that one of the most effective opponents of that was Edgar Bronfman. As a major shareholder in Conoco, he would have gained financially from that. But he put the public interest above his self-interest, as he has so often throughout his life.

I did not reach my decision in that case lightly. One of the major hallmarks of our administration's foreign policy has been opening new markets abroad and aggressively helping our firms to compete, to create jobs for Americans here at home. But there are times when important economic interests must give way to even more important security interests. And this is one of those times.

So tonight, in this great dinner in honor of this champion of freedom, I am formally announcing my intention to cut off all trade and investment with Iran and to suspend nearly all other economic activity between our nations. This is not a step I take lightly, but I am convinced that instituting a trade embargo with Iran is the most effective way our Nation can help to curb that nation's drive to acquire devastating weapons and its continued support for terrorism.

The Executive order I plan to sign next week will cover not only the energy sector but all United States exports to Iran and all investments by American firms and the branches they own or control. We estimate that the embargo will have a limited effect on our companies and our workers. But after reviewing all the options, I have determined that if we are to succeed in getting other nations to make sacrifices in order to change Iran's conduct, we, too, must be willing to sacrifice and lead the way. In my discussions with President Yeltsin and with the G–7 leaders in Halifax in June, I will urge other countries to take similar or parallel actions.

I do want you to know that I do oppose the suggestion some have made that we impose a secondary boycott and prohibit foreign firms doing business with Iran from doing business with the United States. I don't agree with that. I think that decision would cause unnecessary strain with our allies at a time when we need our friends' cooperations. My decision to impose this embargo should make clear to Iran and to the whole world the unrelenting determina-

tion of the United States to do all we can to arrest the behavior and ambitions of that nation.

It would be wrong to do nothing. It would be wrong to do nothing as Iran continues its pursuit of nuclear weapons. It would be wrong to stand pat in the face of overwhelming evidence of Tehran's support for terrorists that would threaten the dawn of peace.

Securing a lasting and comprehensive peace must be our urgent priority. The heart of our efforts, of course, is the continuing strong relationship between the United States and Israel. But we must make it work by standing against those who would wreck the peace and destroy the future even if peace is made.

Let me say to you tonight, the strategy we have pursued is working. Never before have Arabs and Israelis met so frequently, traveled so freely, understood so well that their common destiny in peace and prosperity is urgent for all. When they are ready to turn a page on the path, the United States will work with them to shape a future of hope. And we will not stop working until the circle of peace is complete.

Six months ago, when I had the great honor to visit Jerusalem after we signed the peace treaty between Jordan and Israel, I said to the members of the Knesset that the enemies of peace will not succeed because they are the past, not the future. We must work to make that statement true.

Foreign Minister Peres said that he felt sorry for me because we had lost our enemy. And we all laughed a little bit uncomfortably because we knew there was a grain of truth in what he said. Oh, we knew so clearly when we had the Soviet Union, the cold war, and the massive nuclear threat. Today, no Soviet Union, no cold war, and for the first time since the dawn of the nuclear age, no Russian missiles are pointed at the children of the United States. That is a cause for celebration, and we should be happy about it.

But I will tell you what I think the threat to the 21st century will be, and you can see its outlines all over the world today. The threat to the 21st century is simply this: These children who are here tonight should grow up in the most exciting, most prosperous, most diverse world in the entire history of humanity, but all the forces that are lifting us up and bringing us together contain a dark underside of possibility for evil, so that the forces of integration that are lifting the world up and bringing the world together carry within them the seeds of disintegration. And the great challenge for the 21st century will be how to see the opportunities presented by technology, by free movement of people, by the openness of society, by the shrinking of the borders between nations without being absolutely consumed by the dangers and threats that those same forces present.

That is the challenge of the 21st century because evil has not been uprooted from human nature, and the more open and the more flexible we are, the more vulnerable we are to the forces of organized evil. That is what you saw in Oklahoma City. That is what you saw in the terrible incident with the religious fanatic taking a little vial of poison gas in the subway in Japan. That is what I see when I go to Russia and what they really want from me now is an FBI office because organized crime is taking over their banks. Or when I went to the Baltics, and in Riga what they really want is some law enforcement help because now that the totalitarian regime has been stripped away from the Baltics, they are worried that their port will become a conduit for drugs and other instruments of destruction.

And that is what you see in the Middle East. Why do the terrorists seek to blow up innocent people in Israel? Because the only way to make the peace work between the Israelis and the Palestinians is to have free movement between the two. And if free movement between the two means that innocent people are killed, then the Government of Israel, because the people demand it, must erect barriers. And then when the barriers are erected, the income goes down in the Palestinian area, making the peace a failure. The openness makes the peace possible to succeed and provides the threat to its undoing. That is a microcosm of the challenge of the 21st century.

If you go home tonight and think about it, nearly every modern problem can be explained in those terms. The forces of progress and opportunity and integration all carry within them the seeds of abuse by organized evil. And we must stand up against it.

In Proverbs, the Scriptures say that there will someday come a time when the wicked are overthrown and there are no more, but the house of righteousness will stand. Now in my Baptist upbringing, all the preachers used to tell us that that would only happen when the end of human time had come and we were all lifted to the hereafter. No one knows that, but I will say this: Edgar Bronfman has worked to hasten the day when the house of righteousness will stand, and so must we.

This can be a great time for human history, and our children and grandchildren can have a great future because of the lives of people like Edgar Bronfman. But the challenge is clear: Can we make the forces of terror the past? Yes, we can, but we have to work at it.

Thank you, and God bless you all.

NOTE: The President spoke at 9:34 p.m. in the Grand Ballroom at the Waldorf-Astoria Hotel. The Executive order of May 6 prohibiting certain transactions with respect to Iran is listed in Appendix D at the end of this volume.

Remarks at the Women Voters Project Kickoff Luncheon
May 1, 1995

That may be the best introduction I ever received, and if I had really good judgment, I'd just sit down. [*Laughter*]

Thank you, Ellen Malcolm, Senator Mikulski, and Congresswoman Sheila Jackson-Lee, and to the Members of Congress who are out in the audience, my longtime friend Ann Richards. I met Ann Richards over 20 years ago. And I think she was living in a place called Lacy Lake View. And it was easy for me to see even then, and even by Texas standards, she was a little bit larger than life. [*Laughter*] Humor and empathy, grit and grace, courage and decency, I respect her, and I envy her. Her jokes are always better than mine. [*Laughter*] And you'll all remember that she delivered one of the best political lines ever. It perfectly captured the mood of America. Do you remember? "Pass the Doritos, Mario." Didn't you always want to do one of those commercials? I did. [*Laughter*]

I'm also indebted to Ann Richards for another reason. She and Hillary went out to dinner last night, and by apparent happenstance, Julia Child was eating at the same restaurant. So the people who were running the show decided that they should have everything Julia was having, plus whatever they ordered. According to my wife, anyway, they had a 10-course, 4-hour meal, after which they were wheeled out on gurneys. [*Laughter*] The good news is, I got home from New York last night about 1:30 a.m., and it was perfectly easy to get Hillary up to talk with me. [*Laughter*]

I want to say a special word of appreciation to Ellen Malcolm, for her vision and her work, her phenomenal energy have played an immeasurable role in electing more women to high public office in this country than would have been conceivable before she began her important work.

I thank her for her recitation of the work that our administration has done. We have tried to involve women at an unprecedented level. I noticed when I started this administration, people were, even in some of the great establishment newspapers, they were always criticizing me for trying to have a diverse administration, as if there were something wrong with it. Well, I never had any quotas, and evidence of that is, we still only have only 44 percent of my appointees are women, but that's about twice as good as anybody else ever did, and I'm proud of that.

But I have always believed we could achieve excellence with outreach and effort, without quotas, and I always thought we had kind of a stupid quota system before. It was just never stated. There were just some things that weren't women's work. Now, that's a quota system, and we paid for it. And our country's better off now that we're scrapping it.

In the beginning, they used to criticize the judicial appointments process. But after 2 years, mercy, they looked up, and we'd named more judges in that time period than previous administrations and more women and minorities than the three previous Presidents, Democratic and Republican, combined. But the thing that was interesting and important to me is, we had the highest percentage of people rated well-qualified by the American Bar Association of any administration since they'd been keeping records.

Under the leadership of Erskine Bowles, who is now my Deputy Chief of Staff, the Small Business Administration increased loans to women businesses by over 80 percent in one year. And they did it without reducing the number of loans to white males, and they did it without making a single unqualified loan.

We can do this, folks. The old system was the quota system. We need a system where everybody in America has a chance to serve and live up to the fullest of their God-given abilities.

Women's health is a terribly important issue to me. Ellen talked about it. My grandmother and my mother were working women and nurses. And this morning Hillary kicked off a new chapter in our campaign against breast cancer. The most important issue in women's health this week is the need to raise our voices in support of Dr. Henry Foster to be our Surgeon General.

He is a good man. He is a good doctor. He has spent his entire life delivering babies, bringing health care to people who wouldn't otherwise have it, training doctors to go out and help give health care to people who otherwise wouldn't have it, and spearheading a nationally televised—nationally recognized program to reduce teenage pregnancy. It received one of President Bush's Point of Light awards. Henry Foster is a pro-life, pro-choice doctor who deserves to be confirmed as Surgeon General. Henry Foster's record should be seen in the lives of thousands of babies that he has helped come into this world in a healthy way and the people he has tried to educate and the people he has tried to help. And he deserves to be more than a political football in the emerging politics of this season.

We are on the verge of a new century and a difficult and different time when everything is changing and everything, including our politics, is somewhat unpredictable. As we look into the next century, there's a lot to be happy about: the end of the cold war, the receding of the conventional nuclear threat, the emergence of the information age, and all the exciting possibilities of the global economy. But the great challenge of this age and the great challenge I predict to you of the next 50 is that all the forces that are lifting us up and opening unlimited possibilities to our children and our grandchildren, all the forces that are driving us toward a more integrated and cooperative world have a dark underside of disintegration. Because of so many of the things that are happening, we are lifting people up and seeing people beat down at the same time.

There is great economic division in all the advanced countries. Why? Because more than ever before, education determines income and future prospects. So there is a great fault line in the great American middle class today which is responsible for a lot of the anxieties and a lot of the political issues and a lot of the divisiveness in our country. Those that have a good education are being lifted up; those that don't are being left behind.

More than half—more than half—of the male workers in this country are working a longer work week for a lower wage than they were making 10 years ago. That is a phenomenally important fact, not just economically but psychologically. All over America, men come home from work at night and sit down across the table with their families and know they're working as hard as they can, and they feel less secure, and they wonder if they've let their families down.

We have to do things that will change that. We have to bridge the economic divide and unleash the potential of all of our people. And the key issue there is education, constant, unrelenting dedication to excellence in education for a lifetime. It is necessary if we're going to bring this country back together.

We have these profound social divisions in our country. We have so much diversity now it is really a—it's a gold mine for us. Ann Richards took the lead in trying to get the Congress to ratify the NAFTA agreement because she knew that we had to be more closely connected with other countries in the world and that our ethnic and racial diversity is a gold mine. But when people are frightened, it's easy to focus that fright on people who look different than we do or who think differently than we do about certain things. So there is this great social division: Will our diversity become a source of unity and strength, or will it be a source of our undoing?

And then there are deeper moral divisions that I want to talk about today which are most clearly manifested in the varying attitudes in this country toward violence. And it's something we're all living with in a very personal and human way because of the way we have shared the grief and outrage of Oklahoma City.

The condition of women in all three of these areas is profoundly important. And the response

of women to all of these changes is important. As Ellen said, we've made a good beginning to try to help deal with these problems, to strengthen families and support incomes with the Family and Medical Leave Act. The earned-income credit this year will give the average family of four with an income of under $25,000 an average tax cut of $1,000. We have set in motion a plan under the leadership of Secretary Shalala to immunize all the kids in this country under the age of 2 by 1996. Those are important things.

This Congress of the last 2 years voted virtually to fully fund the Women, Infants and Children program to make sure that child nutrition and care for pregnant women was on the front burner. We have had dramatic expansion in our education efforts, from Head Start to apprenticeships for young people who don't go to college but want good jobs, to more affordable college loans for millions of people, to the national service program which has enabled young people to serve their communities and earn money to go to college. All these things are terribly important.

We have a future economic agenda and a families agenda that involves raising the minimum wage, which I hope you will all support. Two-thirds of all the beneficiaries of an increase in the minimum wage will be working women, working women.

There was a remarkable show on one of our television stations up here the other night, a news program on a little town south of here that had a lot of minimum wage workers. And they went and interviewed a woman working in a factory. And the news reporter said, "Now, you know, your employer says that if the minimum wage goes up, that they'll either have to put more money in machines or they'll lose business. In any case, you might lose your job if the minimum wage is raised." And she looked at him and said, "Honey, I'll take my chances"— [*laughter*]—which I thought was the best one-line response I've seen on the news in a long time. If we don't raise the minimum wage, next year it will be at a 40-year low. That is not my idea of what America should look like as we move into the global economy.

We ought to have welfare reform, but it ought to be the right kind of welfare reform. We shouldn't be punishing people for mistakes in the past. We should be giving them opportunity and imposing responsibility as they move into the future so people can succeed as successful workers and successful parents. It ought to be a work-based, parent-based strong program that lifts people up, not puts them down basically just as a guise to save money. That is very important. You should be involved in the welfare reform effort.

And we should continue to invest more in education, not less. I say to the Congress over and over, we have two deficits, not one. Yeah, we've got a budget deficit, but we've also got an education deficit. And if we try to solve the budget deficit at the expense of the education deficit, we will be cutting off our nose to spite our face, because we will lower the incomes of America and their capacity to pay taxes. So there are things we can do to deal with the economic divide where the fault line is education. And we are working to do things that will bring us together and to lessen these social tensions by lifting up everybody in their work and in their family life.

But we have to say that America has special problems which we have all begun to think more about because of the heartbreak of Oklahoma City, and that is violence. It has many forms. We live with it in our streets and our schools and our homes, where we work, where we live, where we play. Yes, we see it visibly if there is an action against a clinic where legal abortions are performed. But we also see it in some of our churches and synagogues. I never will forget being in Brooklyn one day with Congressman Schumer and driving by a synagogue with a big swastika on it—in the United States in 1992.

We also see it, unfortunately, in our families. Violence can do a lot of damage in a country and it certainly has here. In Oklahoma City, we suffered a terrible wound because it was an act of terrorism. And as we mourn the dead and heal the injured, console the grieving and begin the rebuilding, we must also spare no effort to bring to justice those responsible. We must also understand that even punishing the guilty will not be enough if we cannot protect the innocent in the future. So I say to you my fellow Americans: I take a back seat to no one in my devotion to the Constitution. But we can protect the Constitution and our freedom and be tougher on terrorism in America, and we must.

I have sent to Congress a large number of suggestions that will strengthen our hand in dealing with this issue. And again, I urged them to act on it and act on it without delay. The stories you do not read in the newspaper are those that are most important—the bombs that don't go off, the schemes that are thwarted before they succeed—and we must be better and better and better at that. Whether terrorism is hatched abroad or within our borders, we must be better.

But we must also stand up against those who say that somehow this is all right, this is somehow a political act, people who say, "I love my country, but I hate my Government." These people, who do they think they are, saying that their Government has stamped out human freedom?

I don't know if there's another country in the world that would, by law, protect the right of a lot of these groups to say what they want to say to each other over the shortwave radio or however else they want to say it, to assemble over the weekend and do whatever they want to do, and to bear arms, which today means more than the right to keep and bear arms, it may mean the right to keep and bear an arsenal of artillery. Is there a—who are they to say they have no freedom in this country? Other countries do not permit that.

I plead with you, do not lose your concentration on this issue. This is a big issue. Remember what I said earlier: The forces that are lifting up the world have a dark underside. What makes the global society work? What makes the information age work? Openness. Free movement. Low barriers to the transfer of people, ideas, and information. What does that mean? You can have a terrorist network on the Internet exchanging information about building bombs. What does that mean? You can build the bomb in one State and get in your truck and drive somewhere else freely and without being interrupted. What does it mean? It's easier to get into other countries where you want to make mischief. The open society is at more risk to the forces of organized evil.

Don't forget about the people in Oklahoma City. Don't forget about their families. Don't forget about what they need to rebuild, and don't forget about what we need to try to prevent future incidents of this kind. Do not lose your interest in this issue as it fades into the past. We have a lot of work to do.

Let me also say that I hope that this incident will focus us a little more on the general problem of the extraordinary level of violence in our society, to find its common roots as well as to understand the differences in the different kinds of violence we have. I have to say this, and maybe it's an old-fashioned view, but I believe that it is innate in human nature that there is the capacity to do wrong and to harm others. And we are all balanced in different ways, subject to different forces. There are always excuses or reasons that can be given. I'm sorry for whatever terrible thing happened to the suspect in the Oklahoma City bombing case, but we have to stop making excuses and start thinking about what we can do to build a responsible, nonviolent society.

There is a lot of good news out there. I was in New York yesterday, where the crime rate has been going down for several years and where this year the murder rate is so far—knock on wood—more than a third below what it was last year. And this is happening all over the country. But violent crime is much higher today than it was a generation ago. There's been rising incidence of sexual assaults, muggings, homicides, some of it caused by street gangs which themselves systematically terrorize law-abiding citizens in their area of operation, first in our inner cities and now spreading more and more to suburbs and to small towns.

Increasingly, the victims of crime and the culprits alike are young people, even children. Today, believe it or not, there are thousands of children who stay home from school every day in America because they're afraid that violence will await them there. And even more children go and learn about fear in their classrooms and hallways.

Sometimes the sole motivation for crime is hate or racial prejudice or extreme ideology. We've seen people killed and others wounded only because they were working at clinics. In the last decades we've been forced to acknowledge the full extent of reality about which we had long remained in denial which may not be able to be explained in terms of hate, racial prejudice, or extremist ideology, and that is the epidemic violence visited on women and children, often in the home.

I have known about this problem for a long time. I understand how it rips up family. Hillary and I were regular visitors at a shelter for battered women and their children when we lived at home. I have talked with abused children. I know that this problem of domestic violence is a difficult one. We have begun to be aggressive with it. America must be aggressive with it.

We see how much of crime among our young people is still due to drugs. And it's shocking to me that, for reasons that are not entirely understandable, as the economy has gotten better but some places have been left behind, casual drug use among some of our young people is going up again. This is a bad thing. We must speak against it. It will lead to more violence.

If you look at the profile of every penitentiary in the country, every Governor in America, including Ann Richards and Bill Clinton, every Governor in the country in the last 15 years has given speech after speech after speech about how tough we were on crime and how many prison cells we've built. If you go behind those bars, you'll see them just full of people who basically had two problems: They had no education, and they were either addicted to drugs or alcohol. And so we continue to pay the price in violence and wrecked lives.

All of you have cared a great deal about making democracy work for all Americans. And you've done a good thing. And when we change our economic policy, when we broaden the doors of opportunities for people and permit more women and others who have been traditionally denied a chance to live up to their fullest capacities a chance to do it, we're all better off, and we're all strengthened. But when this country has the plague of violence we endure in so many ways, we are all weakened.

The most tragic thing outside the human loss in Oklahoma City itself to me was seeing the absolute terror that inflicted the lives of millions of American children who felt vulnerable, who felt that they somehow no longer understood what the rules were, didn't know if their parents could protect them, didn't know if right and wrong would reign in America.

So I say to you, we need to take a serious look at this whole issue of violence. We tried to address it in the crime bill last year with more police on the street because we know that that prevents crime, with the assault weapons ban and the Brady bill, with stronger sentences and prevention programs for our young people, and programs for drug education and prevention and treatment.

We also understand that poverty breeds crime. That's why I worked so hard on the earned-income tax credit, to say that if you do work you shouldn't be still in poverty. We ought to reward work. The real heroes in this country today are people who are being pounded by this global economy, who are living in neighborhoods that are difficult, and still get up every day and go to work and raise their children the best they can, obey the law, pay their taxes, and try to make things work. They deserve economic policies and security policies that give them a chance to be honored for their work.

I do want to say again, though, we have to try to look deeper at the cause of the violence. Ellen mentioned that I recently appointed Bonnie Campbell, of Iowa, to direct our Office of Violence Against Women. And one of her most important jobs will be simply to educate the American people about the scope of this problem and what should be done and how to root it out. But our goal must be not just to punish people who do this but to stop it from happening in the first place, to change the spirit and the culture of America.

Yesterday—or, excuse me, late last week, I met with Eileen Adams, another distinguished appointee at the Justice Department, who runs our Office of Victims Rights. And we honored people who spend all their time working with victims of crime. I met mothers who'd lost their children. I met a woman who had been victimized by a repeat sex offender who was released on parole, who molested her, poured gasoline over her body, set her afire, and left her to die. And this young girl—having literally had her body burned beyond recognition—and her brave mother have worked for more than a decade, after this child was maimed and blinded and burned almost beyond recognition, to put her life back together physically and spiritually. And now the mother and the daughter spend all their time trying to help victims of crime.

We must address what is causing the United States to commit the whole range of violence that we see. And none of us can escape our responsibility. We have to say: What do we expect from individuals? And we're not going to tolerate the defense that somebody else made me do it. What will families have to do? What will community organizations have to do? What must the churches do? What must the Government do? Where have we been wrong? What must the media do? And what must the culture do, the influence centers in our culture, the entertainment industry, the sports industry?

There have now been—the Vice President told me this morning before I left to come over

here, there have now been 3,000 studies on the relationship between violent behavior and exposure to violence through entertainment in ways that desensitize people to it, and they all show that there is a connection.

Now, that doesn't mean that we should have all movies and books without violence. This is a violent country. It's a part of real life. It doesn't mean they can't be exciting. But it does mean when we desensitize and deaden people to the reality of violence, we cannot be surprised when our children, who do not know right from wrong and are not as well developed as those of us who are older, have a desensitized reaction to their own conduct. So we must all say: What is our responsibility? We must all accept the fact that our words do have consequences. We must accept that.

We must ask, without pointing the finger of blame necessarily, we say: Do you say things or do things that either reinforce violent behavior, encourage violent behavior, act as if at least it doesn't matter to you, or numb people to what it's really like? And what could we do to deal with this in a comprehensive way? We don't need to make this a political issue. We must not make it a partisan issue. But neither can anybody run and hide under the sheet and say, well, I didn't do this, that, or the other thing; therefore, what I did do was fine.

This horrible thing that has happened to us in Oklahoma at least imposes on us a responsibility to all examine the roots of violence in this country. We need not be more violent than other countries. We need not abuse our freedom so cavalierly. We need not snuff out more lives. But above all, if we do this, we can't be selective. We can't condemn one act of violence and condone another. That would be like trying to put out a fire by just watering one room and leaving the others to burn.

For too long, people, I think, have taken the easy way out and blamed violence only on the environment in which a person grows up. Well, that's, doubtless, true. But if that's true, why do most people who grow up in horrible environments turn out to be law-abiding citizens? Why do some people succeed against all the odds? Other people, because it lets them off the hook, just want to blame the individual and ignore the root causes. Well, if that's true, why are some groups of people so much more law abiding than others and so much less violent than others? We've got to set aside our preconceptions and our ideological baggage. And I say again, we don't need partisanship here; we need to look at violence with new and fresh eyes.

My administration has worked to make our country safer. It's worked to give more people the liberation of education. It's worked to make the economy stronger. And we can do more on all these fronts. But the thing that is driving violence in America is deeper than that, deeper than all these things.

So I ask you to work on this, to work on this with me. Yes, continue your passion for the cause of violence against women and children. Yes, continue your passion for the proposition that people who only perform legally under the law should not have their places of business bombed.

But be concerned about the political violence that makes people believe that they can literally claim to be political prisoners when they murder innocent children. And be concerned about the violence that grows out of our total insensitivity to the welfare of all these children who are growing up on the meanest streets in America. Be concerned about the violence that may at least be legitimized by the cultural forces and the daily words that all of us endure and sometimes enjoy.

We all have a role in this. This is a big issue. It will not be solved overnight. But it will be hard enough, I will tell you again, it will be hard enough for us to combat the forces of disintegration and organized evil into the 21st century if we are at our best. If we are at our best, it will be hard enough. If we continue to be insensitive to the role all the forces in our society play to the environment in which we operate, it may be a battle we can't win.

I honestly believe that the years ahead of us will be the most exciting, most productive, most rewarding years in all of human history, especially for people who historically have not been able to live up to the fullest of their capacity. But to do that, we must—we must—root out this scourge of darkness within our country, and we can do it.

Thank you, and God bless you all.

NOTE: The President spoke at 1:02 p.m. in the Grand Ballroom at the Washington Hilton at the EMILY's List 10th anniversary celebration. In his remarks, he referred to Ellen Malcolm, founder and president, EMILY's List, and Ann Richards, former Governor of Texas.

Remarks to "I Have A Future" Program Participants
May 1, 1995

Dr. Foster, Dr. Peters, Jason and LaShonda, the "I Have A Future" teens and parents, and the national community leaders that are here. I have received, in this room named for Presidents Theodore and Franklin Roosevelt, Kings and Queens, Prime Ministers and Presidents, Senators and Congressmen and Governors, Nobel Prize-winning scientists, world-famous citizens. I have never been prouder to receive people in this room than I am to have you here today. LaShonda and Jason have said everything that needs to be said about this, about Henry Foster and about the "I Have A Future" program.

For a very long time, I have been concerned about how many of our young people we are losing because of teen pregnancy or drugs or violence or just giving up on school. This pro-gram, which combats teen pregnancy through abstinence and hope, which keeps people in school and off drugs and away from violence, is what America ought to be about. We have people here every day making speeches about all this. You have actually done something about it.

We have people here every day rushing to define people that they're opposed to in little cardboard cut-out terms, so that it will fit in 15 or 20 seconds that shoots across the airways at night on the evening news. Now you know, because you know Dr. Foster, how easy it is to make something big little, something little big, something straight twisted, something good look wrong.

Henry Foster has been a teacher and a doctor. He has done everything he could to promote life's best values. He has spent a lifetime addressing the problems that are now engulfing our country. If we can't save you kids, we can't save America. If we can't convince you that violence is wrong, that drugs are wrong, that teen pregnancy is wrong, that you've got to live for yourself and make the most of your life, we can't save America. Most folks get so cynical and skeptical, they think nothing good can happen. Well, here it is, something good happening, something wonderful happening, something that is changing lives and it is bringing people together, something that there is no partisan politics in, something that is just good, rooted in old-fashioned, good, decent American values.

Everybody that looks at it has reached the same conclusion. My predecessor, President Bush, honored the success of this program by naming it one of the 1,000 Points of Light. President Bush's Secretary of Health and Human Services, Dr. Lou Sullivan, said that "I Have A Future" is the kind of program this country needs because it turns young people's lives around. I didn't say that, though I sure believe it. They said that.

So I say to you, I'm glad you came up here to fight for Henry Foster, and I'm glad you came up here to fight against people who are compelled, for political reasons, to label Americans and put them in little boxes and turn them into something they're not.

I'm glad you came up here to tell the Members of Congress, "If you want me to grow up to be a good citizen, if you want me to believe in the American way of life, then you had better honor it in the decisions you make." If we can't confirm Henry Foster to be the Surgeon General of the United States, what kind of person can we confirm? He deserves it, and America needs the kinds of thing that you have shown us here today.

When you go home, you remember what I told you: In this room, Kings and Queens, Presidents and Prime Ministers, Senators and Congressmen and Governors, Nobel Prize winners, world-famous people, but you are carrying the future of America in your soul, in your spirit, in what you believe in, and in what you do. And America has a future if you have a future.

Tomorrow, you show that to the Congress, and you show that to America, and you say, "We're not going to let this good man be put in a little box for somebody's political objectives. The future of the children of this country is more important than that."

Thank you, and God bless you.

NOTE: The President spoke at 2:45 p.m. in the Roosevelt Room at the White House. In his remarks, he referred to Surgeon General nominee Henry Foster; Dr. Sheila Peters, coordinator of community services, "I Have A Future" Adolescent Health Promotion Program; and program participants Jason Gordon and LaShonda Maryland.

Remarks on Presenting the 1994 Commander in Chief Trophy to the United States Air Force Academy Football Team
May 1, 1995

Please be seated. I'm delighted to see all of you here: Senator Burns; Secretary Widnall; to our distinguished military leaders who are here, General Shalikashvili, General Fogelman, General Stein; members of the Board of Visitors of the Air Force Academy; Coach DeBerry; and the seniors of the Falcons football team. I want to congratulate the Air Force Academy on winning the Commander in Chief trophy now for the 6th year in a row.

When I presented the Air Force Academy the Commander in Chief trophy 2 years ago, I had just become President, and I didn't understand that the idea of a traveling trophy meant that it was supposed to go back and forth between Colorado and Washington—[*laughter*]—once a year. I now understand what this traveling trophy is, and I think I will be far more comfortable in doing my duty today.

I was impressed with the Air Force Academy's ferocious defense. We could use some of your coaching up here from time to time, Coach. Sacking the opposing quarterback a record 48 times; 2 straight games holding your opponents to minus 4 yards rushing; and after years of a wishbone offense, which I have followed closely, you pass more, over 1,500 yards this year. I think it's more appropriate for the Air Force Academy to have a big air attack. [*Laughter*]

More importantly, you've won this trophy 6 years in a row, and you won this year because the young men who play football have embraced the lessons that Coach DeBerry has taught. The values of discipline, teamwork, and faith produce success not only on the field but also in the Air Force and in life.

I look forward to seeing all of you again on May 31st, when I will have the honor of speaking at your commencement. And I am very proud that in 30 days all the young men behind me will be commissioned as second lieutenants in the United States Air Force.

Having said that, I am very pleased now to present the Commander in Chief trophy to Coach DeBerry and the Air Force Academy Falcons, and to invite the coach up here to make whatever remarks he'd like to make.

Congratulations.

NOTE: The President spoke at 6:44 p.m. in the Roosevelt Room at the White House. In his remarks, he referred to Lt. Gen. Paul Stein, USAF, Superintendent, and Fisher DeBerry, football coach, U.S. Air Force Academy.

Message on the Observance of Cinco de Mayo, 1995
May 1, 1995

Warm greetings to everyone celebrating Cinco de Mayo.

The Fifth of May offers all of us a chance to celebrate the cultural diversity that helps to make our nation great. The vibrant Mexican culture, based on faith, family, and patriotism, has added a wealth of tradition to this country. Cinco de Mayo is an important part of this legacy, reminding us of the courage and commitment that can sustain the forces of freedom even when they are confronted with overwhelming opposition.

The liberty won by the outnumbered Mexican army more than a century ago lives on today as a part of the rich heritage of the Mexican people. Each time we remember the victory at the Battle of Puebla, we rejoice in the triumph of freedom and the blessings of tradition.

Hillary and I are pleased to extend best wishes for a most memorable and enjoyable holiday.

BILL CLINTON

Message to the Congress Reporting Budget Rescissions
May 2, 1995

To the Congress of the United States:

In accordance with the Congressional Budget and Impoundment Control Act of 1974, I herewith report three rescission proposals, totaling $132.0 million.

The proposed rescissions affect the Departments of Justice and Transportation, and the National Aeronautics and Space Administration.

WILLIAM J. CLINTON

The White House,

May 2, 1995.

NOTE: The report detailing the proposed rescissions was published in the *Federal Register* on May 9.

Remarks to the White House Conference on Aging
May 3, 1995

Thank you so much. Thank you, Mr. Vice President. Thank you for your remarks, and thank you for doing such a good job for America. Thank you, Secretary Shalala, Secretary Brown, Mr. Flemming, Mr. Blancato, Fernando Torres-Gil. Hugh Downs, thank you for being master of ceremonies. I wish I could sit here and watch you work the whole time. I'm delighted to see you. To Congressman Martinez and Congresswoman Morella; the former Members of Congress who are here; the Senators who have gone because they have to vote. I want to say a special word of thanks to the Conference Chair and one of the best friends I ever had in my life, David Pryor. I think he is a wonderful man.

As all of you know, Senator Pryor is now retiring from the Senate. I can remember when, as a young Congressman, he once volunteered as an orderly in Washington area nursing homes to document the conditions under which seniors were then living. And when he couldn't get the Members of Congress to listen, he conducted hearings out of a trailer in a parking lot. The trailer led to the creation of Claude Pepper's House Aging Committee. And as chairman of the Senate's Special Committee on Aging, David Pryor has led fight after fight after fight for the interests of the seniors in this country, especially in his efforts to expand the availability and limit the cost of prescription drugs. We will miss him, and we should be grateful to him.

I'm glad to see all of you in such good spirits. I hope you will stay that way. [*Laughter*] I hope you'll stay that way because I am identifying more and more with you and—[*laughter*]—and I understand Secretary Shalala read the letter we got from the child that said old people are smart and Bill Clinton is old. [*Laughter*]

I remember very clearly about 6 or 7 years ago when I had 2 events occur within 2 days, when I knew I was getting older. My hair had begun to gray, but I thought I was still in reasonably good shape. I felt fairly chipper. And I was making the rounds in my State, and this beautiful young girl, whose parents were very close friends of mine, and therefore I felt that I'd almost had a hand in her upbringing from the time she was born—she was 18 or 19 years old and she was nearly 6 feet tall. And she was just beautiful. And she came up to me— I was so pleased to see her—she came up to me and threw her arm around me, looked me straight in the eye, and she said, "Governor, you look so good for a man your age." [*Laughter*]

And then, the very next day I was in a different part of the State, and I saw this wonderful retired schoolteacher, who was then 80 years old, who had worked in every single campaign I had ever run. And I was so happy to see her. And she said, "Governor, I'm so glad to see you. You're aging gracefully." [*Laughter*]

But I think the right thing about this, you know, is to have a good attitude about it. All of you have a good attitude. That's a big part of this.

I just want to tell you one more story that illustrates the right attitude. It's a true story. We had a man in north Arkansas in a little rural county who ran a tiny phone company back when there were lots of these little phone companies. And he was about 92 years old. And they decided to give—actually, he was 96. And the people in the town decided they'd give him a banquet. And everybody got up and said nice things about him, you know, and the time came for him to speak. And he said, "The very first thing I want to do is to thank my secretary." And he introduced her, and she was 72. He introduced her and said, "I want to thank my secretary. She has been with me for 40 years. She has been wonderful. I don't know what I'm going to do when she passes on." [*Laughter*] So you've got to have the right attitude. Now, if you're all in the right attitude, let's get after it.

I am proud to convene this 1995 White House Conference on Aging. This is the fourth of these Conferences in the history of our country, the first to be held since 1981, the last of the 20th century. I thank the Members of Congress and the citizens of this country from both parties who have supported this endeavor. These Conferences have a productive history, from the establishment of Medicare, Medicaid, and the Older Americans Act, as a result of the 1961 Conference, to the creation of the House Select Committee on Aging, coming out of the 1971 Conference.

But this Conference must be about looking forward, not looking back. All across our country we have seen a dramatic reversal in the way we think about older Americans. We have, after all, twice as many older Americans as we had 30 years ago. And 30 years from now, we'll have twice as many again. People over 55 are younger, healthier, better educated than ever before, and beginning entirely new careers and endeavors in life as they grow older.

Your job here, more than anything else, is to help determine how to use the accumulated experience and judgment of older Americans to make all of our country stronger in the future. That is the purpose of our National Senior Corps, which works with AmeriCorps, our national service initiative in which—[applause]—thank you. The Ameri- Corps program is a national service program in which young people earn money for their education by doing community service. And not all of them are young. I've met retired naval officers in Texas doing work in AmeriCorps and intending to go back to college.

But the Senior Corps, like the AmeriCorps volunteers, are a new source of energy for American social problems and challenges. And they make sure that, as the poet said, the best is yet to be. Your conference agenda confirms your concern with the future. Issues such as crime, ethics, and ways to inspire a renewed sense of community affect all Americans, regardless of their age. To be honest, seniors are in a better position than ever before to help us address these concerns.

I want to mention just a couple of things that have happened since 1981 that are very important with reference to your agenda. First, briefly, since 1981, you and your generation won the cold war and the battle against communism, and you can be very proud of that. And we are now trying to finish that work so that for the first time since the dawn of the nuclear age there are no Russian missiles pointing at the American people.

But we know there are still threats to our security, and we were reminded of it very painfully in the last few days. So I ask all of you as you focus on crime to remember that we need to continue the fight to lower the crime rate. And with a strategy of punishment, police,

and prevention, we can do that. But we must focus on the special problems of terrorism to which all open societies are vulnerable. I have sent legislation to the Congress to address this terrorism problem. It has broad bipartisan support. The leaders of the Congress are working with me on it. We must pass it and pass it this month. And I urge you to take a stand for that on behalf of all Americans.

The other truly remarkable thing that's happened since 1981 affects you particularly. Just one year after the last Conference in 1982, for the first time in the history of the United States, older Americans were less likely to be poor than Americans under 65. In the full span of our country's history, that is a stunning change and a remarkable achievement. We have seen it happening over the course of the past several decades. Since 1960, the poverty rate among elderly people has declined by 65 percent. It did not happen by accident. It happened because the American people kept faith with the social compact first forged 60 years ago when President Roosevelt signed the Social Security Act.

That compact has then been strengthened over the last three decades with Medicare, with Medicaid, with the cost-of-living adjustments to Social Security, with community-based services under the Older Americans Act like Meals on Wheels, transportation, and with efforts to prevent abuse of the elderly. This is a remarkable record, and you should be proud of it. It happened because people understood that their Government could be made to work for them in a positive and strong way. And it is something our country should be very proud of.

Now, our administration is committed to continuing that work—first, to the core principles that have made Social Security work. America has a solemn commitment to every person still working, no matter what their age, that Social Security will be there for them and their families when they need it.

We have also worked to strengthen retirement and to make it safer through strengthening private pensions. The Retirement Protection Act signed late last year reformed the Pension Benefit Guaranty Corporation and secured 8½ million pensions that were at risk in this country, stabilizing 40 million others. It was a remarkable bipartisan achievement.

So every American should be proud that we have completely altered the way our people live their lives as they grow older, providing new hope for an entire lifetime of purpose and dignity. But we must remember that with this kind of opportunity in a democracy goes continued responsibility. Our job today is to preserve this progress not only for you during your lifetimes but for all generations of Americans to come.

You are here to look ahead to the next 10 years and beyond, and not just to the past or to your personal concerns. We know that with regard to seniors, our country has been moving in the right direction. But the truth is, we know that too many younger Americans are not. We have to think about this: How are we going to pass along the next century with the American dream alive and well for our children and grandchildren?

From the year I was born, right after the war, well into the seventies, almost to the end of the decade, people at all levels of our country grew economically, and they grew together. Prosperity was unprecedented. Without regard to income groups, people's incomes rose. Today, we have to face the hard fact that 60 percent of working Americans today are working for the same or lower wages than they were making 15 years ago, while working, on average, a longer work week.

We also have a new class of poor people, mostly unmarried, uneducated young women and their little children. We must do more to discourage the things that create poverty, especially teen pregnancy, and to require more education and efforts to enter the work force for those who are dependent upon welfare.

But the real problem facing this country is the problem of the middle class and stagnant earnings, and the insecurity of the American dream that so many people feel, and the gnawing worry so many working people have when they come home at night that they won't be able to give their children a better life than they enjoyed.

The new split in the middle class is caused by the global economy and the technology revolution. And it is rooted, more than anything else, in one word: education. We know that those who have it and continue to get it and learn for a lifetime do well, and those who don't, tend not to do very well.

So as we look ahead to the next 10 years, the question is: How can we preserve the gains and enhance the quality of life further and enhance opportunities to serve and to live and to grow and to thrive for seniors, while reversing the economic fortunes of those who are stuck and being driven away from the American dream, who are younger, and dealing with the fundamental problems of this country, which include the education deficit and also the budget deficit? It exploded in the 12 years before I became President. It too is undermining our ability to give your children a better future and to build opportunity.

For the past 2 years, our administration has made great strides in dealing with that deficit. We've passed two budgets—[*applause*]—we've passed two budgets that cut it by $600 billion over 5 years. I want you to hear this very carefully. When you hear that we have not cut spending, that we have not reduced the deficit, we have reduced the deficit by $600 billion over 5 years. And this is the more important fact: If it were not for the interest we must pay this year on the debt run up between 1981 and the end of 1992, the budget would be in balance today.

We have also worked to strengthen the Medicare trust fund. It still has problems, but it's stronger than it was on the day I became President.

Despite all that, we know we have to do more. I have been consistently saying for 3 years, beginning with my first address to the Congress and, indeed, all during my campaign in 1992, that we will never fundamentally solve the deficit problem and have the funds we need to invest in education and the future growth in earnings of our people until we are able to moderate the growth of health care spending.

Ask any Member of Congress here present today. All defense and domestic spending are either frozen or declining. Social Security and other retirement income is increasing, but only at the rate of inflation. We have to pay interest on the debt, and we're driving that down, but that changes as interest rates change. The only thing that is going up by more than the rate of inflation and the increased population growth in the programs are the health care programs. Over the next 5 years alone, almost 40 percent of the growth in Federal spending will come from the rise in Federal health care costs— more than our economy is growing, more than inflation is going up, faster than other items of Government spending.

So let us not pretend that there is not a challenge here for us to face, and let us face the challenge with good spirits. You and I know that there is a right way to face this challenge and a wrong way to face the challenge. But not facing the challenge is not an option.

I believe it is wrong simply to slash Medicare and Medicaid to pay for tax cuts for people who are well-off. Beyond that, reducing the deficit is terribly important. But it is also important that Congress protect programs for seniors like Medicare. We must have a sense of what our obligations are. Some proposals would increase the out-of-pocket costs on Medicare by up to $3,500 for our seniors.

I also think it's wrong to cut Medicaid over $150 billion in ways that threaten long-term care for seniors. Let me just say in parentheses here, I hope that if nothing else comes out of this Conference, the American people will come to understand that Medicaid is not simply a program for poor people. Yes, it provides health coverage to people on welfare and their children. But two-thirds of the Medicaid budget goes to care for the seniors and the disabled in this country, two thirds of the Medicaid budget. To give you a stark example, if Medicaid were not there, middle class people all across this country struggling to raise and educate their children would face nursing home bills for their parents that would average $38,000 a year. Medicaid is primarily a program for the elderly and the disabled.

It is wrong in my judgment to reduce coverage under the Medicare program, or to undermine health services in rural and urban areas that are already underserved, or to make changes that just simply coerce beneficiaries into managed care. We can't save Medicare and Medicaid by using savings to fund tax cuts for people who are already well-off or other purposes. That is the wrong way to approach this problem. But we must approach the problem. The right way is to start from the perspective of the people the system is intended to serve, to ask, what does it take to preserve and strengthen it, and what is fair to expect of everyone to do that, to preserve and strengthen it.

For 3 years I have said that the right way is to strengthen Medicare and Medicaid by containing costs as part of a sensible overall health care reform proposal that works for everyone.

If you want to hold down costs, expand coverage, and reduce the deficit, you must reform the health care system. You have to expand long-term care, for example, in terms of the options for seniors, not restrict it. Look at the

growth in the population. Look at what's going to happen in the next 30 years. If you don't provide for people to get more long-term care in their homes and in other less expensive settings, if you don't provide—[*applause*]—thank you. If you don't provide for alternatives to more expensive hospital care, if you don't provide, in other words, for the problem in the least costly way, given what you know is going to happen to our population, then we will have greater costs, not lower costs.

So let's look at this in the right way. I do want to work with the Congress. But we must do it in the right way. I have said all along that I will evaluate proposals to change Medicare and Medicaid based on the issues of coverage, choice, quality, affordability, and costs.

We ought to have some simple tests. For example, does a proposed change reduce health care coverage by eliminating services or by charging seniors with modest incomes more than they can possibly be expected to pay? Does it deal with this long-term care problem in a way that will lower costs per person in long-term care but recognize that we have to have more options? Does it restrict choice by forcing seniors to give up their doctors and enter into managed care programs whether they're good ones or not? Or does it instead increase choice by giving people incentives and options to enter into managed care programs and other less costly options that might be made more attractive to them? Does it reform Medicare and Medicaid to lower the rate of cost increases without threatening the quality of care? Does it keep health care affordable for seniors, and does it help to control costs for the Government?

Many people say, well, all these things are mutually inconsistent. But that cannot be. We are spending over 14 percent of our income as Americans on health care. No other country is over 10 percent. We know that there are changes that we can make that will improve coverage, broaden services, control costs, and help us with the deficit. But we can only do it if we start from the point of view of what it takes to have a health care system with integrity that can be fairly paid for, in a fair manner.

So, while I will not support proposals to slash these programs, to undermine their integrity, to pay for tax cuts for people who are well-off or to pay for—all by themselves to pay for these kinds of arbitrary targets on the budget, I cannot support the status quo. And neither can you.

We must find a way to make this system work better that deals with the internal issues of the system, your health care issues and those that are coming behind you, and that deals with the genuine problems the Congress faces with our budgetary situation. That's why I have said repeatedly that when the Republicans present their budget as required by law, we will evaluate where they are in terms of their commitments and what they want to do, where we are, and then we will do our best to work through this. I will not walk away from this issue.

I watched from afar, when I was a Governor and a citizen, for 12 years while people here walked away from problem after problem. And I sustained, as President, an agonizing experience when large numbers of people walked away from problems that I asked them to face for short-term political gain. I will not do that. The status quo is not an option.

But in order for us to have discussions, we have to know where everyone stands. I have presented a budget. I have said for 3 years where I stand. As soon as we see the budget that is legally mandated from the Members of Congress who are in the majority, we will then talk about where we go from there and what we can do, so that I can make sure that your interests and the interests of people coming behind you are protected but that no one pretends that the status quo is an option. We can pursue both those goals and do it in the right way.

Now, let me also say there are other right ways to address this problem that we in the executive branch can be doing right now. You know, waste, fraud, and abuse has become a tired phrase in politics. But the truth is there's a lot of it in the health care system, and you know it as well as I do. With all the problems we have today with income for citizens and with the budget for the Government, people who rip this system off jeopardize the health of beneficiaries and the stability of our Government and our economy.

Since the beginning of this administration, Secretary Shalala and Attorney General Reno have worked hard to crack down on fraud and abuse. And I am pleased to announce today that, as a part of phase two of the Vice President's outstanding reinventing Government initiative, we are taking an additional strong measure. We are forming a multistate effort to identify, prosecute, and punish those who willingly defraud the Government and who victimize the public.

In five States, with nearly 40 percent of all the Medicare and Medicaid beneficiaries—New York, Florida, Illinois, Texas, and California—we will have an unprecedented partnership of Federal, State, and private agencies. For every dollar we spend, we will save you $6 to $8 in the Government's health care programs to stabilize what we need to be doing. This is a win-win situation for everybody except the perpetrators of fraud. And it's about time they lost one.

Let me close with this thought. This should be an exciting time for you. You should welcome this challenge. You should know that I will be there, with you and for you, to protect the legitimate interests of the senior citizens of this country and not to see us trade the long-term welfare and health of the American people for anybody's short-term gain. But you should also know that we need you to be here for us. We need for you to say, "These are changes that make sense. These are changes that don't. These are things that will make us all stronger. These are things that will help you guarantee higher incomes and better wages and a better future for our children and our grandchildren. These are things that will bring us together." This country is always strongest when we are together.

We are always strongest when we are together. I'll bet you more than half of the people in this room wept in the aftermath of that terrible tragedy in Oklahoma City. We were for a moment once again one family, outraged and heartbroken. And you saw what happened when people gave up their lives and came from all over the country to go there to help with the rescue effort, to help to deal with the families who are grieving, to help with all the efforts that were going on. That's when we're strong.

The theme of this conference is "Generations Aging Together." You know when we're together we're strong. And so many forces in America today are trying to turn us all into consumers of goods or politics or other things, so that we're all divided up in little markets and segmented and we fight with each other all the time. And the people that provoke the fights make a lot of money or votes or whatever out of us when we do that. But that's not when we're strong.

I saw the end of the film, when you quoted my speech at Normandy. I don't know that I have ever or ever will have a greater honor than to go and honor the generation of my parents for winning the Second World War. We were one, because of what you did, because of your sacrifice.

And I just want to say to you today, we can win the challenges of today and tomorrow. We can make the 21st century an American century. We can continue the progress in expanding the quality of life for our seniors. We can solve the health care crisis. We can do it if we will do it together. Lead us there. Help us there. And I will stay with you.

Thank you, and God bless you all.

NOTE: The President spoke at 11:52 a.m. at the Washington Hilton. In his remarks, he referred to Arthur Flemming, Chairman, and Robert B. Blancato, Executive Director, White House Conference on Aging; and Hugh Downs, co-anchor, ABC News' television program "20/20."

Statement on Initiatives To Combat Medicare and Medicaid Fraud
May 3, 1995

These initiatives are the right way to control health care costs and protect Medicare for our senior citizens. They will help ensure that Medicare dollars, on which so many of our seniors rely, go to the people who deserve them.

NOTE: This statement was included in a White House statement announcing a crackdown on fraud and abuse in Medicare and Medicaid as an outgrowth of the effort to reinvent Government.

Message to the Congress Transmitting Proposed Legislation To Improve Immigration Enforcement
May 3, 1995

To the Congress of the United States:

I am pleased to transmit today for your immediate consideration and enactment the "Immigration Enforcement Improvements Act of 1995." This legislative proposal builds on the Administration's FY 1996 Budget initiatives and complements the Presidential Memorandum I signed on February 7, 1995, which directs heads of executive departments and agencies to strengthen control of our borders, increase worksite enforcement, improve employment authorization verification, and expand the capability of the Immigration and Naturalization Service (INS) to identify criminal aliens and remove them from the United States. Also transmitted is a section-by-section analysis.

Some of the most significant provisions of this proposal will:

• Authorize the Attorney General to increase the Border Patrol by no fewer than 700 agents and add sufficient personnel to support those agents for fiscal years 1996, 1997, and 1998.

• Authorize the Attorney General to increase the number of border inspectors to a level adequate to assure full staffing.

• Authorize an Employment Verification Pilot Program to conduct tests of various methods of verifying work authorization status, including using the Social Security Administration and INS databases. The Pilot Program will determine the most cost-effective, fraud-resistant, and nondiscriminatory means of removing a significant incentive to illegal immigration—employment in the United States.

• Reduce the number of documents that may be used for employment authorization.

• Increase substantially the penalties for alien smuggling, illegal reentry, failure to depart, employer violations, and immigration document fraud.

• Streamline deportation and exclusion procedures so that the INS can expeditiously remove more criminal aliens from the United States.

• Allow aliens to be excluded from entering the United States during extraordinary migration situations or when the aliens are arriving on board smuggling vessels. Persons with a credible fear of persecution in their countries of nationality would be allowed to enter the United States to apply for asylum.

• Expand the use of the Racketeer Influenced and Corrupt Organizations (RICO) statute to authorize its use to pursue alien smuggling organizations; permit the INS, with judicial authorization, to intercept wire, electronic, and oral communications of persons involved in alien smuggling operations; and make subject to forfeiture all property, both real and personal, used or intended to be used to smuggle aliens.

• Authorize Federal courts to require criminal aliens to consent to their deportation as a condition of probation.

• Permit new sanctions to be imposed against countries that refuse to accept the deportation of their nationals from the United States. The proposal will allow the Secretary of State to refuse issuance of all visas to nationals of those countries.

• Authorize a Border Services User Fee to help add additional inspectors at high volume ports-of-entry. The new inspectors will facilitate legal crossings; prevent entry by illegal aliens; and stop cross-border drug smuggling. (Border States, working with local communities, would decide whether the fee should be imposed in order to improve infrastructure.)

This legislative proposal, together with my FY 1996 Budget and the February 7th Presidential Memorandum, will continue this Administration's unprecedented actions to combat illegal immigration while facilitating legal immigration. Our comprehensive strategy will protect the integrity of our borders and laws without dulling the luster of our Nation's proud immigrant heritage.

I urge the prompt and favorable consideration of this legislative proposal by the Congress.

WILLIAM J. CLINTON

The White House,
May 3, 1995.

Message to the Congress Transmitting Proposed Legislation To Combat Terrorism
May 3, 1995

To the Congress of the United States:

Today I am transmitting for your immediate consideration and enactment the "Antiterrorism Amendments Act of 1995." This comprehensive Act, together with the "Omnibus Counterterrorism Act of 1995," which I transmitted to the Congress on February 9, 1995, are critically important components of my Administration's effort to combat domestic and international terrorism.

The tragic bombing of the Murrah Federal Building in Oklahoma City on April 19th stands as a challenge to all Americans to preserve a safe society. In the wake of this cowardly attack on innocent men, women, and children, following other terrorist incidents at home and abroad over the past several years, we must ensure that law enforcement authorities have the legal tools and resources they need to fight terrorism. The Antiterrorism Amendments Act of 1995 will help us to prevent terrorism through vigorous and effective investigation and prosecution. Major provisions of this Act would:

• Permit law enforcement agencies to gain access to financial and credit reports in antiterrorism cases, as is currently permitted with bank records. This would allow such agencies to track the source and use of funds by suspected terrorists.

• Apply the same legal standard in national security cases that is currently used in other criminal cases for obtaining permission to track telephone traffic with "pen registers" and "trap and trace" devices.

• Enable law enforcement agencies to utilize the national security letter process to obtain records critical to terrorism investigations from hotels, motels, common carriers, storage facilities, and vehicle rental facilities.

• Expand the authority of law enforcement agencies to conduct electronic surveillance, within constitutional safeguards. Examples of this increased authority include additions to the list of felonies that can be used as the basis for a surveillance order, and enhancement of law enforcement's ability to keep pace with telecommunications technology by obtaining multiple point wiretaps where it is impractical to specify the number of the phone to be tapped (such as the use of a series of cellular phones).

• Require the Department of the Treasury's Bureau of Alcohol, Tobacco, and Firearms to study the inclusion of taggants (microscopic particles) in standard explosive device raw materials to permit tracing the source of those materials after an explosion; whether common chemicals used to manufacture explosives can be rendered inert; and whether controls can be imposed on certain basic chemicals used to manufacture other explosives.

• Require the inclusion of taggants in standard explosive device raw materials after the publication of implementing regulations by the Secretary of the Treasury.

• Enable law enforcement agencies to call on the special expertise of the Department of Defense in addressing offenses involving chemical and biological weapons.

• Make mandatory at least a 10-year penalty for transferring firearms or explosives with knowledge that they will be used to commit a crime of violence and criminalize the possession of stolen explosives.

• Impose enhanced penalties for terrorist attacks against current and former Federal employees, and their families, when the crime is committed because of the employee's official duties.

• Provide a source of funds for the digital telephony bill, which I signed into law last year, ensuring court-authorized law enforcement access to electronic surveillance of digitized communications.

These proposals are described in more detail in the enclosed section-by-section analysis.

The Administration is prepared to work immediately with the Congress to enact antiterrorism legislation. My legislation will provide an effective and comprehensive response to the threat of terrorism, while also protecting our precious civil liberties. I urge the prompt and favorable consideration of the Administration's legislative proposals by the Congress.

WILLIAM J. CLINTON

The White House,
May 3, 1995.

Interview With Laurie Montgomery of the Detroit Free Press and Angie Cannon of Knight-Ridder Newspapers
May 4, 1995

The President. Hello.

Ms. Cannon. Good morning, Mr. President.

The President. Good morning. How are you?

Ms. Cannon. Good, how are you doing?

The President. Great.

Ms. Montgomery. Good morning, Mr. President. My name is Laurie Montgomery. I'm a reporter with the Detroit Free Press. And I'm going to be asking you most of the questions this morning. I have some that I think are real important to Michigan right now. Could I go ahead?

The President. Sure, have at it.

Ms. Montgomery. All right. I've got three related to the Oklahoma City tragedy, and one about trade talks with Japan. And then we've got a few other ones if there's time.

The President. Okay.

Militia Groups

Ms. Montgomery. So, first, in the wake of the bombing, you've proposed to expand the FBI's power to investigate terrorist groups by using standards that determine when a group or individual becomes an appropriate target for surveillance. Tomorrow you're heading to Michigan, home of the Michigan Militia. I was wondering how dangerous you consider the militia movement. And from what you know now, does it currently present an appropriate target for FBI surveillance?

The President. Well, first of all, I think it's important not to generalize. I think it's important not to generalize. We need to look at the facts of each one. But let me tell you, when I was the Governor of my State, as you know, for 12 years before I became President, and in the early eighties, we had the first wave of these groups coming to Arkansas. And I will give you three examples of what happened, where I judged each on the facts.

First, we had the tax resister Gordon Kahl, who killed two people in North Dakota and wounded three others and took the position that he had a right to live in this country and not pay taxes. And he killed the sheriff, who was a very good friend of mine in Arkansas, when they tried to arrest him. He presented a threat to the United States. And he—of course, he was subsequently killed there in a shoot-out.

Secondly—let me just lay the predicate here—secondly, we had a man that expressed these same views but took the law into his own hands, named Snell, who killed a State trooper who was black and killed a pawnshop owner that he thought was Jewish. He was executed in Arkansas a few days ago. But he was arrested and convicted and sentenced to death when I was Governor. He presented a threat by his conduct. He took his words into action.

Then we had a group of about 200 people that occupied an armed compound in north Arkansas, and they had two people who were wanted for murder. There were murder warrants out on them. And they refused to give them up, but we basically had a coordinated effort, and we in effect declared—we had an embargo, or we cordoned off their area, a blockade, and eventually the women and children came out, and eventually the men gave up. Those that were subject to indictment were treated appropriately; the others went right on with their lives. So they handled it in the appropriate way.

So this country allows people broader personal freedoms than almost any democracy in the world, particularly with regard to the right to keep and bear arms.

Ms. Montgomery. And I guess my question is, absent the sort of action that you described, murdering a sheriff——

The President. It depends on—but here's the deal. The FBI needs to be in a position, without abusing people's freedoms, to try to prevent things like Oklahoma City from happening.

Ms. Montgomery. And should they do that by beginning surveillance of some of the religious groups?

The President. We have to be able to gather intelligence from people if we have reason to believe that they are threatening to use violence.

That's the issue. The question is, is there reason to believe that these people are likely, that any groups are likely to use violence? And I think what our bill does is to give the FBI the means, in a high-tech world with a lot of high-tech criminals, to use high technology within appropriate safeguards to try to prevent the Oklahoma Cities, to try to prevent these things from happening in the first place.

Ms. Montgomery. And I guess what I'm asking is, from what you know now, would some of these militias currently present an appropriate target for the use of that sort of surveillance?

The President. From what I know now, the FBI would have to consider that based on the rhetoric and the conduct and make a judgment based on the facts of each group. I don't want to jump the gun here. I think it's important—what I'm asking for is to give us the tools we need to combat terrorism.

I know—for example, if you look at Israel, for all the terrible incidents they have endured, well over half of the planned terrorist incidents in Israel never occur because they have the capacity to defang them. We have endured this awful bombing in Oklahoma City and the World Trade Center bombing, which came from a group outside this country that infiltrated here. We also—our Federal authorities have been successful in heading off at least two other incidents of terrorism that we know about that they were able to stop from occurring.

We just believe—I cannot tell you how strongly I believe that this is the major threat to the security of Americans looking toward the 21st century, that the fundamental problem—it's not just in America. It's the same thing with that group of religious fanatics where the guy broke the vial of sarin gas in the Japanese subway. It's exactly the same thing. The things which will make life exciting for all of our young college graduates—high technology society, free flow of people, goods, technology, and information, a highly open world society—make people very, very vulnerable to the forces of organized evil.

Ms. Montgomery. I guess I'm asking, you know, just in case there are any Michigan Militia members in the audience in Spartan Stadium tomorrow, you know, do you think that they are——

The President. Well, that's not my—I'm not going to make that judgment. I'm not the person to make that judgment. What I believe is the

FBI, if they have reason to be concerned about it, should have the ability to look into any group where they think there is a likelihood that they might break the law in a violent way against citizens of the United States. That's what I believe.

Ms. Montgomery. You've been pretty tough specifically on some of these militia groups. What do you think motivates them?

The President. Well, I think a lot of them have had experiences in their life which profoundly alienate them from the American Government. And I would remind you that suspicion of government and the desire to limit government power is at the core of what created the United States in the first place. The whole Constitution is written to limit the power of government. The Bill of Rights limits the power of the Federal Government to move against individuals. The separation of powers limits the power of any branch of Government. They check each other, the executive, legislative, and judicial. The division of authority between the Federal and the State and local governments limits the power of government in that way.

Our whole system was set up basically to try to guard against the abuses of government power which the original Americans have lived under, under monarchies. And we know that there—that we have—from time to time, governments make mistakes. And our government, not only at the Federal level but State government and local government, does occasionally abuse its authority. We know that. People are people everywhere. And people in government authority make mistakes. Every one of us, including the President, can cite an example where he or she believes the Government oversteps its bounds, from something as innocent as being rude to a citizen in a Social Security line or who's trying to get information about taxes or trying to deal with an EPA regulation, to something as terrible as an unjustified arrest or an unjustified prosecution. Everybody can cite an example. There are no perfect people in the world.

But we have a Constitution and a system that gives people the right of redress. And what I think about those folks is, I don't know what at all their life experiences have been; I know that in our country they have more freedom to speak, to organize, and to bear arms, and especially to bear arms, than they would have

in virtually any other democracy on the face of the Earth.

So I would say to them that you have these freedoms. And if you don't like the way things are going, you can participate in elections. You can call in on talk shows. You can be part of forums. You can file lawsuits. You can do all kinds of things that are perfectly legal. You also have the right in our country to go meet on the weekend and talk about your feelings and express your feelings and do target practice and all these other things. But you do not have the right to break the law. And you certainly do not have the right to commit violence. There is a line over which people shouldn't step, and we have to draw the line clear and bright.

Ms. Montgomery. Do you have the right to say you're willing to use violence if you feel threatened by your Government?

The President. What I think is you have a right—there's all kinds of free speech rights. All they have to do is—you know, the Supreme Court has outlined the parameters of free speech. And the line, basically, in threatening other people is like the guy that cries fire in the crowded theater. That's the classic example. So what I think is that the closer you come to advocating violence, the more, at least, our law enforcement officials have to have the ability to at least look into whether they believe an incident is about to occur and whether they can head it off. I think the American people are entitled to that amount of protection.

Ms. Montgomery. Your discussion of the Constitution sort of goes to the heart of what these really extreme versions of these militia groups would say is what they're afraid of, that the Federal Government is not adhering to the Constitution. And that's the paranoid extreme. What I want to ask you about is that you can make the argument that that is a very extreme version of some fairly popular views.

You know, we've seen since the bombing that there are thousands of ordinary people who are just stunningly distrustful of their Government, who don't pay taxes and reject driver's licenses. Even when Malcolm X's daughter was charged, a lot of people said, "Oh, that's the FBI just coming after us, making things up." Do you think Americans are more suspicious of their Government than they should be? Why, and what do you think, if anything, you can do about it?

The President. Well, first of all let me say again, our country was founded on suspicion of government. But our country was founded on the belief that you could have a decent government, and that societies have to have government to do certain limited functions that will not be done in other ways. And over 200 years, we have defined and redefined over and over again what those powers were.

In times of great national duress, the Government has taken powers to itself that we would never tolerate in ordinary times. Look at what Abraham Lincoln did, for example, during the Civil War just to try to hold the country together. So, that has ebbed and flowed. We all, all of us as Americans, part of your birthright as an American is to have a healthy suspicion of the Government.

Ms. Montgomery. So you don't think it's particularly strong right now or——

The President. No, no, I do. I think it is stronger now. We're going through a period now when it is much stronger among certain groups than it has historically been. Sometimes it's because of their personal experience; sometimes it's because the anti-government voices are louder and better organized. But the point—and my own view is that the suspicion of the Government prevents people from making good—if it's blanket and if it's extreme, it keeps you from making good judgments about whether particular actions are right or wrong and keeps us from seeing what our challenges are and which challenges we have to meet through government and which challenges we have to meet as private citizens.

But that is not the important thing. My view of that is irrelevant. The first amendment gives people the right to say what they want to say, to believe what they want to believe, and to organize. But there is a bright, clear line against violation of the law and taking force and violence into your own hands. That is the bright, clear line.

Ms. Montgomery. Sure. I was talking on more of a philosophical level, actually, in the sense that, you know——

The President. What I think we ought to do about that is, yes, I think that the sort of generic antigovernment feelings are keeping people from evaluating whether specific—whether it's my administration or the Congress or a particular bill pending, if you have a generally negative view of what is a very great country that is

doing very well today compared to what other countries are doing, but which has some serious challenges which have to be met, some of which require Government response and some of which don't, it's hard to think about those things with a clear head if you're negative almost to the point of being paranoid, if you don't believe anything good can ever happen.

You know, if it's like—but that is not what I am concerned with now. I mean, I worry about that, and I think what I'd like to see is a sort of a discussion about that. One of the things I think in the wake of the American people's wonderful concern for the victims in Oklahoma, and they're seeing these Federal employees there and their children who were killed as real citizens, as people, as the people with whom they go to church and go to the ball park and eat lunch at the civic club once a week with and do all those things—I think it would be a good thing. And this is something that could occur basically on the radio shows all over the country, where people are invited to call in.

We ought to ask ourselves, you know, to think of something—what do they do that is right; what do they do that is good; what matters that is a positive force; what do we think ought to be changed? In other words, we ought to have a balanced debate here, and it ought to be a grassroots debate. And my sense is that there's a lot of energy out there in our people for this kind of conversation, and we need to give it outlets.

Ms. Montgomery. Is there anything more you can do to encourage that, to help people feel more comfortable?

The President. Well, I intend to do—I'm going to continue to try to talk about these things and talk about it more and encourage others to do that as well.

Freedom of Speech

Ms. Cannon. So, in other words, Mr. President, what you're suggesting is, instead of some of the talk radio shows being purveyors of paranoia or just constant sneering, just sort of——

The President. Now, those are your words, not mine.

Ms. Cannon. Okay. [*Laughter*]

The President. [*Inaudible*]—always try to get me into a discussion that I don't want to have instead of the one I do want to have.

Ms. Cannon. No, but I mean to try to turn the content of those shows over into something a little bit more constructive.

The President. Well, let me say this. This is a general observation. I think, insofar as talk radio is giving our country a sort of a set of townhall meetings that are constant and give even people who are too shy ever to have their pictures on television the opportunity to call in and express their views and engage in a conversation, I think that's a very positive thing in the country. And I don't think it matters whether the talk radio shows or the talk shows are themselves conservative or liberal or what else, wherever they exist.

What I'm suggesting, though, is that we ought to use these forums now to try to reopen this conversation and really talk these things through. Now, I think some speech is wrong. I cannot defend some of the things that Gordon Liddy has said. I cannot defend some of the things some of these more extreme talk show hosts have said, even more extreme than that in these little shortwave programs that plainly are encouraging violence. I think that people should just speak out against that.

But what I would like to see is more of the people who consider themselves moderate to liberal calling the conservative talk shows and people who consider themselves conservatives calling the liberal talk shows. And I think the American people—we forget that we are strongest when we are united and that 90 percent of the times, our differences are nowhere near as important as the things which bring us together. And we forget that we have challenges today that are profound and that provoke a lot of anxiety in our country. You know, more than half our people are working harder for lower wages than they were making 15 years ago. I understand that. I'm doing my best to do something about it.

But instead of having this sort of undifferentiated anxiety and lashing out, what we need to be talking about is, every generation of Americans has had their own set of challenges and problems. We are no different from any other. There is no reason to believe, if you go back through all of human history, that there will ever be a time without problems. And this is the set of problems we face today. We have a lot of problems. But we also have vast opportunities. And if you look at where our country is, compared with so many others in the world,

most of us would not trade places with people in any other country in the world. I know I wouldn't, and I wouldn't want my child to be growing up in any other country besides America now, and I think most people feel that way.

So, I'm hoping that we can draw the lines of things that we think are unacceptable that are just purely fostering hatred, division and encouraging violence and still have a conversation with differences of opinion. I think—and I also would tell you that my job as President is not to try to silence people with whom I disagree, no matter how bitterly I disagree. My job is to try to see that the Constitution is protected and that the laws are upheld, that the American people are safe and secure to lead whatever lives they want to lead, to do whatever they want to do, and to express whatever political views they have.

Director of Media Affairs Lorrie McHugh. Angie, Laurie, we have to wrap this up.

Japan-U.S. Trade

Ms. Montgomery. Okay, one last question. Speaking of trading places, a question about the trade talks this week with Japan: There have been some reports of disagreement within your administration about taking firm action against Japan. Are you personally committed to proposing formal sanctions if the Japanese do not make sufficient concessions on autos, and by what date?

The President. First of all, I am committed to taking a strong line here. I have worked for over 2 years on this. I have done everything I could to open American markets, to expand trade. I supported NAFTA. I supported GATT. I have tried to be very strongly supportive of the American automobile industry and their trade interests. And this administration has been a good friend of the auto industry in many, many ways as you—and we have worked hard, and we are proud of the success that they're now enjoying.

But the one thorny problem that never seems to get solved is the inaccessibility of the Japanese markets, not only to autos but also to auto parts—in some ways, an even bigger problem for us in the near term. And we have taken a very strong line here because we've tried all those other things and they have not worked. So we are going to have to be very strong, and to be strong you have to be prepared to take strong action if your words fail.

Ms. Montgomery. So thumbs up on sanctions?

The President. So thumbs up on very strong responses, but my trade negotiator, Mickey Kantor, is in the middle of these negotiations—and he has done a great job. I think he is the best Trade Ambassador we have ever had, at least in the last 20 years. He has been very tough. He's opened more markets, taken more actions, succeeded in doing things that had never been done before. We're even selling rice in Japan, something we never thought we could do.

The last big trade hurdle we have is the auto markets and the auto parts markets in Japan. And I do not want to say anything in this interview that complicates his life. I can just tell you, the United States is committed to taking strong action. We are taking a tough position. It doesn't matter what anybody says in my administration; I support the line that Ambassador Kantor has taken. It is my line. It is my conviction. We have done everything we could do, and it is not in the interest of the Japanese Government or people to be in the position they're in now.

NOTE: The interview began at 11:25 a.m. The President spoke by telephone from the Oval Office at the White House.

Statement on Proposed Legal Reform Legislation
May 4, 1995

The Senate is engaged in the laudable goal of seeking to reform our legal system. Yesterday they went much too far by adopting an amendment to cap punitive damages in all civil lawsuits. In its present form the Senate bill sharply limits the damages paid by many classes of offenders who deserve to pay much more to their victims for the harm they have inflicted upon them.

The bill now before the Senate might be called the "Drunk Drivers Protection Act of 1995," for what it does is insulate drunk drivers and other offenders from paying appropriate amounts of punitive damages justified by their deeds. I insist that we hold drunk drivers fully responsible. When they cause injury and death to innocent adults and children, we should throw the book at them, not give them a legal limit on damages to hide behind.

The Senate should reconsider its position. At the least, it should remove damage caps on lawsuits involving drunk drivers, murderers, rapists, and abusers of women and children, despoilers of our environment like the *Exxon Valdez*, and perpetrators of terrorist acts and hate crimes.

All of these receive undeserved protection from the present bill. The Senate should reserve its compassion for the people who deserve it. If this bill comes to my desk as it is now written I will veto it, and therefore I encourage the Senate not to vote to limit debate on the bill at this time.

The administration supports the enactment of limited, but meaningful, product liability reform at the Federal level. Any legislation must fairly balance the interests of consumers with those of manufacturers and sellers.

Message on the Observance of the 50th Anniversary of the Allies' Victory in Europe: V-E Day, 1995
May 4, 1995

As we commemorate the fiftieth anniversary of V-E Day, a grateful nation remembers all of the brave Americans who served in World War II.

In the spring of 1945, after almost six years of fighting, the war in Europe came to a dramatic close. As word of German General Jodl's surrender in Reims spread around the globe, celebrations broke out from New York and London to Paris and Moscow. Still, celebrations were tempered as President Truman reminded a worldwide radio audience that the war was not yet won. Many thousands more were yet to die fighting for the principles we hold so dear.

Half a century later, as Americans gather to mark the triumph over fascism and tyranny in Europe, we remember all those who fought to preserve our liberty. We honor our distinguished veterans—those who came home and those who did not return. We also honor their families—those who contributed to the battlefield victory through their efforts and prayers on the home front. These valiant men and women toiled to support and defend the cause of freedom fifty years ago, and they succeeded in preserving its blessings for generations to come. On behalf of Americans everywhere, I salute these heroes. They have our eternal gratitude.

Best wishes to all for a memorable observance.

BILL CLINTON

Remarks to the American Jewish Committee
May 4, 1995

Thank you very much, Mr. Rifkind. Justice Ginsburg—this was one of my better moves, don't you think? [*Laughter*] Another one of my better moves, Secretary and Mrs. Riley and distinguished members of the diplomatic corps and my fellow Americans.

I can't speak long because I don't want to have a controversy with Senator Dole. I would never take his time knowingly. [*Laughter*] I sort of hate to do this to the American Jewish Committee, taking Alan Moses away. I can't think of any better person to serve as our Ambassador to Romania, but I hate to do it for you, and I really hate to do it for me. At least you've got a good successor, but I do not want to establish the principle in this town that 4 years is enough for anyone to serve as President. [*Laughter*] Alan, I thank you for your willingness to serve, and I am delighted to see you're here with your wife and also with your mother. It's wonderful to see her. Welcome, and thank you.

Let me briefly say in response to the introduction that I have worked hard, as all of you know, on a two-track policy in the Middle East. First, to try to make peace, not to impose peace but to try to help the parties in the Middle East to make peace. In my first meeting with Prime Minister Rabin, whom I look forward to seeing again in the next several days, I said, "If you are prepared to take risks for peace, it is the obligation of the United States to minimize those risks." That is what we have tried to do. We have worked together. We have worked with the parties in the Middle East who are interested in peace. We are working even as we speak to make further progress.

Second thing we have sought to do is to contain those who would upset the balance of forces for peace in the Middle East. We have taken strong stands against Iraq, we have demanded that Libya give up the people that are accused of downing Pan Am 103, and we have taken strong stands against Iran. For 2 years I hoped against hope that Iran would be persuaded to stop trying to develop weapons of mass destruction and supporting terrorist groups. It became clear to me that that would not happen, and therefore I have imposed the embargo which was announced last Sunday, which I thank you for your support on. I hope that we will be able to persuade others that terrorism and the proliferation of weapons of mass destruction have no place in the modern world.

Let me close by asking you to think of this: The 21st century should and I believe will be the most exciting time in all of human history, the time that is most full of human potential. It can be a very great time for America if we face our problems at home first and if we make sure that all of our people can compete, which means more than anything else we must solve the education deficit in the United States and create a system of lifetime learning that all people can access.

But I believe that the great threats to security in the 21st century will be very different from those of the 20th century. The history of this century is littered with the blood of millions and millions and millions of people who were killed either because two different countries were fighting with each other over land or an oppressive government was prepared to kill millions of its citizens to maintain its power. The realities of the global economy, the explosion of the information age make those things less likely to occur. We'll always have to fight abuse of power at home and abroad, wherever it occurs, but that is less likely to mark the 21st century.

In the 21st century, which will be characterized, as we already know, by lightning flashes of exchange of information and money and technology and great mobility of people, all of the forces that are bringing us to a more integrated world and making people see that it makes sense to stop killing each other and to make peace, whether it be in the Middle East or Northern Ireland or any other place in the world, all those forces of integration have a dark underside of disintegration and make us very, very vulnerable, the more open we are, to the forces of organized evil.

That is what we lived through in Oklahoma City. That is what we endured at the World Trade Center. That is what the Japanese people suffered in the subway when a religious fanatic could walk in with a little vial of sarin gas and break it open and kill 60 people. And make no mistake about it, that is why innocent Israelis are still being killed by car bombs in the Middle East. Why? Because the only way peace in the Middle East can work is if the Palestinians and the Israelis stay integrated. And if the Israeli people can be rendered insecure so that the Israeli Government has to raise the border again, so that the Palestinians can't come to Israel and their incomes drop, then they won't believe in the peace anymore, and the enemies of peace will win.

So all through the next decades you and I will be involved in a constant struggle, with our friends from the diplomatic corps—and there are countries that are here present—to try to get the benefits of all these forces that are bringing us together without being undermined by the forces of disintegration that move into open societies and open interchanges between countries and choke the life out of hope.

That is the challenge of the 21st century. That is why I've asked the Congress to pass this antiterrorism legislation. And before he gets here, I thank Senator Dole for committing to pass that bill and put it on my desk by the end of the month. It was a good and noble thing and a great gesture. I thank him for that.

These are the things we often work together on. There is no room for partisanship here. Nor should there be differences of religion or culture or nationality across international borders. All of us that want ordered societies where human potential can be expressed and peace can be achieved must stand against the forces of organized evil that cross national borders and kill without a second thought, whether they are paranoid forces rising up from within or people flying in from without. That is our challenge.

So now the challenge in the Middle East is the challenge at home. Let us keep working for peace, and let us determine to defend ourselves against those that would undermine the glorious potential of the century upon which we are about to enter.

Thank you, and God bless you all.

NOTE: The President spoke at 7:30 p.m. at the Grand Hyatt Hotel. In his remarks, he referred to Robert S. Rifkind, president, American Jewish Committee.

Remarks at the Michigan State University Commencement Ceremony in East Lansing, Michigan
May 5, 1995

President McPherson, Governor Engler, Ambassador Blanchard, distinguished Members of Congress and State officials, members of the board of trustees, distinguished faculty, honored guests, family members, and most importantly, members of the class of 1995, I'm honored to be your speaker today and to be back on this wonderful campus, the site of one of the great Presidential debates in 1992.

I have fond memories of Michigan State. And I was sitting there thinking of all the uses to which I might put my honorary degree. Maybe I will get more respect in Washington now. [*Laughter*] Regardless, now I know who I'm supposed to root for in the Big 10.

Speaking of sports, I want to take a moment of personal privilege to offer my very best wishes on his retirement to your distinguished basketball coach, Judd Heathcote.

And as a person who never, ever, would have had an opportunity to be here today doing what I am doing, I want to thank President McPherson, the present and past Governors of Michigan, and all others who have supported the remarkable set of educational opportunities for young people in Michigan, especially in higher education. The tuition guarantee program to keep tuition increases here to the rate of inflation for 5 years is a standard I wish other universities all across America would follow.

I also hope that other States will follow the example of the Michigan Education Trust and of Michigan State in entering into the direct loan program, which will lower the cost of college loans for young people and improve their repayment options so more people can afford to go to college and stay there until they get their degrees.

I also want to say that I am deeply honored to be joined today by another Michigan State alumnus who spoke from this platform last year, my friend and fellow Arkansan Ernest Green. He was one of the Little Rock Nine, a brave group of Americans who staked their lives for the cause of school integration and equal opportunity in education in my State almost 40 years ago. He made the right choice at the right moment in his life. He is a good model for you, and I hope you will do the same.

As I was reminded by your president and others when we gathered just a few moments ago, the last sitting President to address this assembly was Theodore Roosevelt in 1907. There were fewer than 100 graduates in the senior class then. But it was a time not unlike this time. We are on the edge of a new century; they had just begun a new century. We are on the edge of a new era; they had just begun the dawn of the industrial age. Like us now, they had many, many opportunities but pro-

found problems. And people were full of hope mixed with fear.

But President Roosevelt and his generation of Americans were optimistic, aggressive in facing the challenges of the day, and determined to solve the problems before them. They launched the Progressive Era, using the power of Government to free the market forces of our country from the heavy hand of monopoly, beginning to protect our environment for future generations, to keep our children out of sweatshops, to stand strong for America's role in the world.

Theodore Roosevelt and the Americans of his generation made the right choices at the right moment. They met the challenges of the present, paved the way for a better future, and redeemed the promise of America.

Our journey as a nation has never been an automatic march to freedom and opportunity. In every generation there has come a point of challenge in change when critical decisions are made by our people to go forward or turn back, to reach out or turn inward, to unify or divide, to believe or doubt.

Today, we stand at the end of the cold war and the industrial age, at the onset of the global economy and the information age. Throughout all 219 years of our Republic, times of great change like this have unleashed forces of promise and threat, forces that uplift us and unsettle us.

This time is not different. You are walking into a future of unlimited possibilities. But more than half your fellow citizens are working harder, spending less time with their children, and earning about the same they did 15 years ago. You can look forward to bringing your children into an exciting world, freer of the dangers of war and nuclear annihilation, but the dangers here at home are still profound. Too many of our children are not born into stable families. Our streets are still too violent. And new forces threaten the order and security which free people everywhere cherish.

And so, my fellow Americans, it falls to your generation to make your historic choices for America. This is a very new and different time. But the basic question before us is as old as our country: Will we face up to the problems and seize our opportunities with confidence and courage? It is our responsibility to make that choice again.

Because you have a fine education, with all its power and potential, when you leave this stadium your responsibility to your families, your community, and your country will be greater than ever before. With your lives fully before you, you too must once again redeem the promise of America.

On the homefront, there is reason for optimism. Though income stagnation and economic uncertainty plague too many of our people, unemployment is down, inflation is low, our deficit is declining, trade is up, and most importantly of all, educational opportunities are increasing. Though crime and violence, drug abuse and welfare dependency, and out-of-wedlock pregnancies are still too high and threaten our social fabric, we are making a serious assault on all of them, and we can make progress on all of them. Though Government is still too cumbersome and outdated, it is growing smaller, more flexible, less wasteful, and more effective. In all these endeavors, you must demand higher standards and more personal responsibility. But you must know that progress is possible.

Beyond our borders there is also reason for hope. Since the end of the cold war, the bonds among nations and the forces of commerce have grown stronger. There is now a greater understanding of our world's environmental challenges and a willingness to do something about them. Freedom, democracy, and free enterprise are on the march. Large countries are much less likely to go to war with one another. I am very proud to say that for the first time since the dawn of the nuclear age, no Russian missiles are pointed at the people of the United States. And I am equally proud to say that next week I will become the first American President in nearly 40 years to visit Russia when no American missiles are pointed at the people of Russia.

Therefore, you who graduate today will have the chance to live in the most exciting, the most prosperous, the most diverse and interesting world in the entire history of humanity. Still, you must face the fact that no time is free of problems, and we have new and grave security challenges.

In this, the 20th century, millions of lives were lost in wars between nations and in efforts by totalitarian dictatorships to stamp out the light of liberty among their subjects. In the 21st century, bloody wars of ethnic and tribal hatred will be fought still in some parts of the world. But with freedom and democracy advancing, the real threat to our security will be rooted in the fact that all the forces that are lifting us up and opening unparalleled opportunity for us contain a dark underside. For open societies are characterized by free and rapid movements of people and technology and information, and that very wonder makes them very, very vulnerable to the forces of organized destruction and evil. So the great security challenge for your future in the 21st century will be to determine how to beat back the dangers while keeping the benefits of this new time.

The dark possibilities of our age are visible now in the smoke, the horror, and the heartbreak of Oklahoma City. As the long and painful search and rescue effort comes to an end with 165 dead, 467 injured, and 2 still unaccounted for, our prayers are with those who lost their loved ones and with the brave and good people of Oklahoma City, who have moved with such strength and character to deal with this tragedy.

But that threat is not isolated. And you must not believe it is. We see that threat again in the bombing of the World Trade Center in New York, in the nerve gas attack in the Tokyo subway, in the terrorist assault on innocent civilians in the Middle East, in the organized crime plaguing the former Soviet Union now that the heavy hand of communism has been lifted. We see it even on the Internet, where people exchange information about bombs and terrorism, even as children learn from sources all around the world.

My fellow Americans, we must respond to this threat in ways that preserve both our security and our freedoms. Appeasement of organized evil is not an option for the next century any more than it was in this century. Like the vigilant generations that brought us victory in World War II and the cold war, we must stand our ground. In this high-tech world, we must make sure that we have the high-tech tools to confront the high-tech forces of destruction and evil.

That is why I have insisted that Congress pass strong antiterrorism legislation immediately, to provide for more than 1,000 new law enforcement personnel solely to fight terrorism, to create a domestic antiterrorism center, to make available the most up-to-date technology to trace the source of any bomb that goes off, and to provide tough new punishment for carrying stolen explosives, selling those explosives for use in a violent crime, and for attacking members of the Uniformed Services or Federal workers.

To their credit, the leaders of Congress have promised to put a bill on my desk by Memorial Day. I applaud them for that. This is not and must never be a partisan issue. This is about America's future. It is about your future.

We can do this without undermining our constitutional rights. In fact, the failure to act will undermine those rights. For no one is free in America where parents have to worry when they drop off their children for day care or when you are the target of assassination simply because you work for our Government. No one is free in America when large numbers of our fellow citizens must always be looking over their shoulders.

It is with this in mind that I would like to say something to the paramilitary groups and to others who believe the greatest threat to America comes not from terrorists from within our country or beyond our borders but from our own Government.

I want to say this to the militias and to others who believe this, to those nearby and those far away: I am well aware that most of you have never violated the law of the land. I welcome the comments that some of you have made recently condemning the bombing in Oklahoma City. I believe you have every right, indeed you have the responsibility, to question our Government when you disagree with its policies. And I will do everything in my power to protect your right to do so.

But I also know there have been lawbreakers among those who espouse your philosophy. I know from painful personal experience as a Governor of a State who lived through the cold-blooded killing of a young sheriff and a young African-American State trooper who were friends of mine by people who espoused the view that the Government was the biggest problem in America and that people had a right to take violence into their own hands.

So I ask you to hear me now. It is one thing to believe that the Federal Government has too much power and to work within the law to reduce it. It is quite another to break the law of the land and threaten to shoot officers of the law if all they do is their duty to uphold it. It is one thing to believe we are taxed too much and work to reduce the tax burden. It is quite another to refuse to pay your taxes, though your neighbor pays his. It is one thing

to believe we are over-regulated and to work to lessen the burden of regulation. It is quite another to slander our dedicated public servants, our brave police officers, even our rescue workers, who have been called a hostile army of occupation.

This is a very free country. Those of you in the militia movements have broader rights here than you would in any other country in the entire world.

Do people who work for the Government sometimes make mistakes? Of course they do. They are human. Almost every American has some experience with this, a rude tax collector, an arbitrary regulator, an insensitive social worker, an abusive law officer. As long as human beings make up our Government, there will be mistakes. But our Constitution was established by Americans determined to limit those abuses. And think of the limits: the Bill of Rights, the separation of powers, access to the courts, the right to take your case to the country through the media, and the right to vote people in or out of office on a regular basis.

But there is no right to resort to violence when you don't get your way. There is no right to kill people. There is no right to kill people who are doing their duty or minding their own business or children who are innocent in every way. Those are the people who perished in Oklahoma City. And those who claim such rights are wrong and un-American.

Whenever in our history people have believed that violence is a legitimate extension of politics, they have been wrong. In the 1960's, as your distinguished alumni said, many good things happened, and there was much turmoil. But the Weathermen of the radical left who resorted to violence in the 1960's were wrong. Today, the gang members who use life on the mean streets of America, as terrible as it is, to justify taking the law into their own hands and taking innocent life are wrong. The people who came to the United States to bomb the World Trade Center were wrong.

Freedom of political speech will never justify violence—never. Our Founding Fathers created a system of laws in which reason could prevail over fear. Without respect for this law, there is no freedom.

So I say this to the militias and all others who believe that the greatest threat to freedom comes from the Government instead of from those who would take away our freedom: If you say violence is an acceptable way to make change, you are wrong. If you say that Government is in a conspiracy to take your freedom away, you are just plain wrong. If you treat law enforcement officers who put their lives on the line for your safety every day like some kind of enemy army to be suspected, derided, and if they should enforce the law against you, to be shot, you are wrong. If you appropriate our sacred symbols for paranoid purposes and compare yourselves to colonial militias who fought for the democracy you now rail against, you are wrong. How dare you suggest that we in the freest nation on Earth live in tyranny! How dare you call yourselves patriots and heroes!

I say to you, all of you, the members of the Class of 1995, there is nothing patriotic about hating your country or pretending that you can love your country but despise your Government. There is nothing heroic about turning your back on America or ignoring your own responsibilities. If you want to preserve your own freedom, you must stand up for the freedom of others with whom you disagree. But you also must stand up for the rule of law. You cannot have one without the other.

The real American heroes today are the citizens who get up every morning and have the courage to work hard and play by the rules: the mother who stays up the extra half hour after a long day's work to read her child a story; the rescue worker who digs with his hands in the rubble as the building crumbles about him; the neighbor who lives side-by-side with people different from himself; the Government worker who quietly and efficiently labors to see to it that the programs we depend on are honestly and properly carried out; most of all, the parent who works long years for modest pay and sacrifices so that his or her children can have the education that you have had and the chances you are going to have. I ask you never to forget that.

And I would like to say one word to the people of the United States. I know you have heard a lot of publicity in recent days about Michigan and militias. But what you have seen and heard is not the real Michigan. This is the

real Michigan. This is the real Michigan in this stadium today. The real Michigan is Michigan State. It's the astonishing revival of the automobile industry, with the remarkable partnership between the autoworkers and the management. Real Michigan is Kellogg's Corn Flakes and the best cherries in the world. The real Michigan is the Great Lakes and the UP. And most of all, the real Michigan was presented to me when I got off the plane and one of your local officials told me that here in mid-Michigan in only 5 days, the people of this area raised $70,000 to pay for the help that people need in Oklahoma City. And that money is now on its way to Oklahoma City in a 27-car caravan, led by members of 27 different law enforcement agencies from this part of your wonderful State. That is what I want America to know about the real Michigan.

So, my fellow Americans and members of the class of 1995, let me close by reminding you once again that you live in a very great country. When we are united by our humanity and our civic virtue, nothing can stop us. Let me remind you once again that our best days as a nation still lie before us. But we must not give in to fear or use the frustrations of the moment as an excuse to walk away from the obligations of citizenship.

Remember what our Founding Fathers built. Remember the victories won for us in the cold war and in World War II, 50 years ago next week. Remember the blood and sweat and triumph that enabled us to come to this, the greatest moment of possibility in our history.

Go out and make the most of the potential God has given you. Make the most of the opportunities and freedoms America has given to you. Be optimistic; be strong. Make the choices that Theodore Roosevelt made, that Ernest Green made. Seize your moment. Build a better future. And redeem once again the promise of America.

Thank you, and God bless you all.

NOTE: The President spoke at 1:30 p.m. in Spartan Stadium. In his remarks, he referred to Peter McPherson, president, Michigan State University; Gov. John Engler of Michigan; and James J. Blanchard, U.S. Ambassador to Canada.

Statement on Gun-Free School Zones
May 5, 1995

In my radio address last week, I asked the Attorney General to recommend what constitutional steps I could take to ensure that guns are kept away from our children's schools. The Attorney General has responded to my request, and next week I will submit legislation to Congress that will put the gun-free school zones act on firm constitutional ground. This legislation is the most straightforward option available and must be acted on immediately. I am determined to keep guns away from schools and am committed to working with the Congress to make our schools safe havens where young people can learn and grow free from harm.

Statement on the Death of Lewis Preston
May 5, 1995

Hillary and I were deeply saddened to learn today of the death of Lewis Preston.

As President, Lewis Preston brought strong management to the World Bank. During a time of monumental change in the international arena, including the entry of the former Soviet Union into the free market and the emergence of a democratic South Africa, Lewis Preston provided steady leadership and helped to make the World Bank a more open and effective institution.

Our thoughts and prayers are with his family and friends.

Nomination for Archivist of the United States
May 5, 1995

The President today announced his nomination of former Kansas Governor John Carlin as the Archivist of the United States at the National Archives and Records Administration.

"John Carlin will provide necessary leadership in terms of managing the institution, providing fiscal responsibility, and performing the important cultural and historical responsibilities," the President said. "He is an experienced leader with proven commitment to preservation, access, and use of Government records. I am confident his sharp communication skills as well as his experience working with Congress and balancing budgets will provide the skilled management the Archives needs during these challenging times."

NOTE: A biography of the nominee was made available by the Office of the Press Secretary.

The President's Radio Address
May 6, 1995

Good morning. This morning I want to talk with you about the problem of illegal immigration. It's a problem our administration inherited, and it's a very serious one. It costs the taxpayers of the United States a lot of money, and it's unfair to Americans who are working every day to pay their own bills. It's also unfair to a lot of people who have waited in line for years and years in other countries to be legal immigrants.

Our Nation was built by immigrants. People from every region of the world have made lasting and important contributions to our society. We support legal immigration. In fact, we're doing what we can to speed up the process for people who do apply for citizenship when they're here legally. But we won't tolerate immigration by people whose first act is to break the law as they enter our country. We must continue to do everything we can to strengthen our borders, enforce our laws, and remove illegal aliens from our country.

As I said in my State of the Union Address, we are a nation of immigrants, but we're also a nation of laws. And it is wrong and ultimately self-defeating for a nation of immigrants to permit the kind of abuse of our immigration laws we have seen in recent years.

This week, I sent strong legislation to Congress to try to stop those abuses, to secure our borders in the future, and to speed up deportation of illegal immigrants.

Our immigration policy is focused in four areas: first, strengthening border control; second, protecting American jobs by enforcing laws against illegal immigrants at the workplace; third, deporting criminal and deportable aliens; fourth, giving assistance to States who need it and denying illegal aliens benefits for public services or welfare.

Let me talk a little bit about two or three of these issues. First of all, on strengthening border control: For 2 years, we've been working very, very hard to strengthen our borders. We've put the best American technology to work at our borders. We've added a lot of Border Patrol agents, 350 last year, 700 this year. We're going to add at least another 700 next year.

In El Paso, our border guards stand so close together they can actually see each other. They maintain a sealed border in what used to be the biggest route into America for illegal aliens. We're extending this coverage to other sectors of the borders. We'll increase border control by 51 percent this year over 1993 and by 60 percent along the southwest border. That's pretty good for just 3 years.

We're also helping States to remove illegal aliens who are criminals, and I want to talk more about that in a moment. But focus on this: Right now we're deporting 110 illegal aliens everyday. That's almost 40,000 a year. And we're going to do even better.

Now, let me talk a little bit about increasing deportations. Our plan will triple the number of criminal and other deportable aliens deported since 1993. We want to focus on the criminal population or on those who are charged with crimes but who are here illegally. Every day, illegal aliens show up in court who are charged. Some are guilty, and surely, some are innocent. Some go to jail, and some don't. But they're all illegal aliens, and whether they're innocent or guilty of the crime they're charged with in court, they're still here illegally and they should be sent out of the country.

If they're sentenced to jail, they should go to jail. But then after their term is over, they should be removed from the United States. And when there is a plea bargain, I want deportation to be part of the deal. We've been doing this now in southern California, and just in southern California, under this provision, we're going to send out 800 to 1,000 illegal immigrants this year. It simply doesn't make any sense for us to have illegal aliens in our custody, in our courts, and then let them go back to living here illegally. That's wrong, and we should stop it.

Now, in addition to strengthening the Border Patrol, deporting more aliens who are part of our court system, and really cracking down on inspection at the work site in America, we have to face the fact that we've got another big problem, and that is the backlog. There is actually a backlog in the deportation of illegal aliens of over 100,000. That's 100,000 people we have identified who are still awaiting the completion of their deportation hearings. I have instructed the Justice Department to get rid of this backlog. If it takes extra judges, we'll ask Congress for the money to get them. We cannot justify continuing to have this large number of illegal aliens in our country simply because our court system won't process them.

We also have hundreds of thousands of people who have been ordered to leave our country, who then disappear back into the population. I have instructed the Justice Department, and particularly the Immigration and Naturalization Service, to come up with a plan in which we can cooperate with the States to identify these people and move them out as well.

Our country was built by immigrants, but it was built also by people who obeyed the law. We must be able to control our borders; we must uphold respect for our laws. We're cracking down on this huge problem we found when

I got here, and we're going to keep working at it until we do much, much better.

Thanks for listening.

NOTE: The President spoke at 10:06 a.m. from the Map Room at the White House.

Remarks to the American Israel Public Affairs Committee Policy Conference
May 7, 1995

Thank you. If I had really good judgment, I would stop now while I'm ahead. [*Laughter*] You're not supposed to clap for that. [*Laughter*]

Thank you, Steve, for that wonderful introduction and for your leadership. Mr. Prime Minister, Ambassador Rabinovich, the Israeli Minister of Health, Larry Weinberg and Lester Pollack and Neal Sher and members of our administration who are here, Mr. Lake and Ambassador Indyk, Secretary Glickman. I can't help pointing out that we have been a country now for a very long time, and the Jewish people have a special relationship with the soil; Dan Glickman is the first Jewish-American Secretary of Agriculture in the history of the Republic. I'm also delighted to see one of the best friends Israel has in the United States, Senator Frank Lautenberg, out there in the audience. It's good to see you, Senator.

I'm delighted to be here tonight among so many familiar faces and to have Steve remind me of that remarkable occasion I had to meet with this group in 1989. I first spoke with an AIPAC group in my home State, in Arkansas, 5 years before that. I thank so many of you here for your support and your counsel. And I am deeply honored to be the first sitting President ever to address this conference.

There are many things for which I could express my thanks to AIPAC. I would like to begin by thanking you for having all these students here tonight. I think that's a wonderful—[*applause*]—thank you. Thank you. I must say, when we came out to such a nice, enthusiastic reception, and the Prime Minister and I were standing here and they started shouting, "Four more years," Steve whispered in my ear. He said, "Do you think they're talking about you or Prime Minister Rabin?" [*Laughter*] And it wasn't so many years ago when we could have voted the students in both places in my home

State, but we've changed that now, so you'll have to decide. But I'm glad to have you here.

I want to thank you for helping to make the partnership between the United States and Israel what it is today. I want to thank you for understanding, by the enormous response you gave to the Prime Minister, the incredibly pivotal role he has played in making that partnership what it is by having the courage to take the risks he has taken to make a lasting peace. Few individuals that I have ever met have risen to the challenge of history as he has.

He could well have been content simply to be a member of the heroic generation that defended Israel at its birth and then to have risen to lead the Israeli military in preserving its strength against all odds. But instead, he has shepherded the Jewish state into a new era. And I am persuaded that no matter what happens in the days and weeks and months ahead, there will be no turning back, thanks in large measure to Prime Minister Rabin.

He has sacrificed many things large and small to make this relationship work and to pursue the peace. He has, for example, endured the ban on smoking at the White House. [*Laughter*] But I want you to know something else. When we first met, as I have said over and over again, he was looking at me and I was looking at him, and he was sort of sizing me up, and I already knew he was bigger than life. [*Laughter*] I said, "If you will take risks for peace, my job is not to tell you what to do, how to do it, or when to do it, it is to minimize those risks." That is what I have tried to do.

I can tell you something, my fellow Americans: If they were easy, somebody would have done it before. Anytime a leader takes on an issue this fraught with difficulty, this full of emotion, where every day and every way even the leader must sometimes have mixed feelings about the decisions that have to be made, that requires a level of fortitude and vision most people in any elected democracy cannot muster. You have to be willing to watch your poll ratings go up and down like a bouncing ball. You have to be willing to be misunderstood. You have to be willing to know that no matter what you do, if it is all right, things beyond your control could still make it turn out all wrong. And if you do it anyway because you know that it is the only honorable course for the long-term interests of your people, that is true statesmanship. And that is what the Prime Minister has done.

I would like to ask your leave for a moment to discuss one other issue before I return to the Middle East. This weekend I have been working on two major areas of foreign policy: first of all, preparing for the very good meeting I just finished with the Prime Minister and, secondly, getting ready for the upcoming trip I will take to Moscow and Kiev. Tomorrow marks the 50th anniversary of the victory of the Allied forces in World War II in Europe. We will mark that day here in a very moving and wonderful ceremony. Then I will get on the plane and travel to Moscow and then to Kiev to honor the sacrifices in that war of the peoples of Russia and the Newly Independent States.

Five decades ago, the people of the United States and the then Soviet Union joined together to oppose an evil unmatched in our history. In that conflict, 27 million Russians lost their lives—or members of the Soviet republic. They were soldiers and citizens; there were untold tens of thousands of women and children; they were Russians and Belarussians, Uzbeks and Jews, Ukrainians, Armenians, and more. Death touched every family. The siege of one city took a million lives in 900 days. This week we will honor that almost unimaginable sacrifice.

But the trip also gives us a chance to look forward. Just as we fought five decades ago for our common security against the common evil, today we can fight for our common security by striving for common good. Fundamentally, this trip is about making the American people more secure and giving them a better future.

We've always based our policies from the beginning of our administration on a sober assessment of the challenges faced by these nations and a conviction that cooperation was in our best interests. We supported the forces of openness, democracy, and reform in Russia for one

reason above all: It is good for the American people and good for the rest of the world.

In the last 2 years, that policy has made every American safer. It's helped Russia become a partner for trade, investment, and cooperation and to assume its rightful place among the nations of the world. We've got some concrete benefits to show for it. Some of you may not know this, but because of the agreement made last year between the United States and Russia, for the first time since the dawn of the nuclear age, there are no Russian missiles pointed at the citizens of the United States.

We're destroying thousands of nuclear weapons at a faster rate than our treaties require. We have removed nuclear weapons from Kazakhstan, and Ukraine and Belarus soon will follow. We're cooperating with the Russians to prevent nuclear weapons and bomb-making materials from falling into the hands of terrorists and smugglers. We're working together to extend indefinitely the Nuclear Non-Proliferation Treaty. For the first time in half a century, there are no Russian troops in Central Europe or the Baltics. Almost 60 percent of the Russian economy is now in private hands, and the elements of a free society—elections, open debate, and a strong, independent media, whether the politicians like it or not—are beginning to take root.

Compared with only a few years ago, when severe disagreements with Moscow paralyzed our relations and threatened nuclear confrontation, we live in safer, more hopeful times because of this extraordinary opening to new freedom in Russia.

Of course, ultimately, the fate of this country, like every other, lies in the hands of its own people. And there is still a struggle between the proponents of reform and the forces of reaction. Peaceful, democratic change is not inevitable, and the forces of reform will suffer setbacks. But after all, that's no different from what happens in any democracy. The forces of hope and fear are not always in the proper balance.

Nonetheless, in the struggle for freedom, the engagement and support of the West, and especially the United States, can make an important difference. So more than ever, we have to engage and not withdraw. We will have our differences with Russia, but even our differences today occur in a different context. The movement of the relationship is plainly toward increasing democracy and increasing security. The interests of our people are clearly best supported by supporting that transition in Russia to a more free and open society. When we have similar goals, we'll cooperate. When we disagree, as we do and we will, we must manage those differences openly, constructively, and resolutely.

The war in Chechnya, where continued fighting can only spill more blood and further erode international support for Russian reform, is a case in point. And Russia's cooperation with Iran is another.

All of you know that Iran, a country with more than enough oil to meet its energy needs, wants to buy reactors and other nuclear technology from Russia. This fact, together with other evidence about Iran's nuclear program, supports only one conclusion: Iran is bent on building nuclear weapons.

I believe Russia has a powerful interest in preventing a neighbor, especially one with Iran's track record, from possessing these weapons. Therefore, if this sale does go forward, Russian national security can only be weakened in the long term. The specter of an Iran armed with weapons of mass destruction and the missiles to deliver them haunts not only Israel but the entire Middle East and, ultimately, all the rest of us as well.

The United States, and I believe all the Western nations, have an overriding interest in containing the threat posed by Iran. Today Iran is the principal sponsor of global terrorism, as the Prime Minister has said. It seeks to undermine the West and its values by supporting the murderous attacks of the Islamic Jihad, Hezbollah, and other terrorist groups. It aims to destroy the Middle East peace process.

You know the need for firm action here as well as I do. And I thank you for your long history of calling attention to Iran's campaign of terror. I thank you for urging a decisive response, and I thank you for supporting the action we have taken. We have worked to counter Iran's sponsorship of terrorism, its efforts to acquire nuclear weapons. We led our G–7 allies to ban weapons sales, tightening trade restrictions on dual-use technology, and in preventing Iran from obtaining credit from international financial institutions. But more has to be done. That's why I ordered an end to all U.S. trade and investment with Iran.

I understand this will mean some sacrifice for American companies and our workers. But the United States has to lead the way. Only

by leading can we convince other nations to join us. I hope you will help us convince other nations to join us.

Let me mention two other nations. We have also taken a strong stand against Libya. We remain determined to bring those responsible for the bombing of Pan Am 103 to trial. And make no mistake about it, though U.N. sanctions have weakened Saddam Hussein, he remains an aggressive, dangerous force. He showed that last October, menacing Kuwait until our Armed Forces' swift and skillful deployment forced him to back down. As long as he refuses to account for Iraqi weapons programs, past and present, as long as he refuses to comply with all relevant Security Council resolutions, we cannot agree and we will not agree to lift the sanctions against Iraq. We will not compromise on this issue, and we value the support we have received from the Prime Minister and the State of Israel.

Our measures to contain these rogue nations are part of a larger effort to combat all those who oppose peace, because even as we achieve great strides in resolving the age-old conflict between Arabs and Israelis, there remains a struggle between those searching for peace and those determined to deny it, between those who want a better future and those who seek a return to the bloody past in the Middle East. No one should doubt the determination of the United States. We will oppose the enemies of peace as relentlessly as we support those who take risks for peace.

Now I want to go over some of the things that the Prime Minister has said because it is important that we be seen as one voice on these issues. As Steve said, before I was elected to office I vowed to be an unshakable supporter of Israel. I have kept that commitment. We have maintained current levels of security and economic assistance. We've made clear to all that our commitment to the security and well-being of the Jewish state is absolutely unwavering and will continue to be. In any agreement, in any agreement Israel concludes with Syria, it will have the means to defend itself by itself. And no child in Kiryat Shemona or Metulla will go to bed afraid for his or her safety.

Today, Israel's military edge is greater than ever because the United States has kept its word. We approved the purchase of F–15–I's for the Israeli Air Force because Israel should have the world's best long-range, multiple-role fighter. We have continued the transfer of 200 fighter aircraft and attack helicopters that began after the Gulf war. We are committing over $350 million, the major share of development costs, for the Arrow missile system to assure that Israel never again is left defenseless in the face of a missile attack.

We delivered the most advanced multiple-launch rocket system in the world to give Israeli defense forces the firepower they need. And to help enhance Israel's high-tech capabilities, we approved the sale of supercomputers, and we allowed access for the first time to the American space launch vehicle markets.

As you and AIPAC have argued for a decade, this is a two-way relationship that has real benefits for both our nations. Our strategic and intelligence cooperation is now deeper than ever. This year we conducted the largest ever joint military exercise with the IDF. We are pre-positioning more military hardware in Israel. And the Pentagon has signed contracts worth more than $3 billion to purchase high-quality military products from Israeli companies.

The landmark events of the last 2 years were, in part, possible because the United States worked to ensure Israel's strength, because we helped to give Israel the confidence to make peace by minimizing those risks, because we built a relationship of trust, and because we made it clear that no one could drive a wedge between us. And, Mr. Prime Minister, as long as I'm here, no one will ever drive a wedge between us.

But we have a new problem here at home to which others have alluded. Here in the United States and in positions of authority, there are those who claim to be friends of Israel and supporters of peace and people who believe they are friends of Israel and supporters of peace, whose efforts would make Israel less safe and peace less likely. Under the cover of budget cutting, back-door isolationists on the left and the right want to cut the legs off of our leadership in the Middle East and around the world. They want to deny the United States the resources we need to support allies who take risks for peace.

Legislation being prepared in Congress could reduce by as much as 25 percent our foreign policy spending, which is now just a little over one percent of the Federal budget and is clearly, as a percentage of our income, by far the smallest of any advanced nation in the world. We did not win the cold war to walk away and blow the peace on foolish, penny-wise, pound-foolish budgeting.

Consider this: Everybody is happy that we're helping Ukraine, Belarus, and Kazakhstan get rid of nuclear weapons on their territory. That makes us safer. But we can't do it for free. We're helping to build democracy in Central and Eastern Europe, but we can't do that for free. We're combating the international flow of drugs that plagues our communities, but we can't do that for free.

All over the world, in countries that are desperately poor, people are trying to learn how to support themselves and to sustain their environment so that they can have orderly societies and be part of peaceful cooperation and not be consumed by the radical currents sweeping across the world. And for a pittance, by American standards, we can make all the difference in the world. But we cannot do it for free.

More than any audience in this country, perhaps, you understand that. You understand the importance of our leadership and the reasonable price we must pay to sustain it. If we have to abandon that role simply because we are denied the tools of foreign aid and security assistance, one of the first to be affected is Israel, because Israel is on the frontline of the battle of freedom and peace, and Israel's strength is backed by America's strength and our global leadership.

There may be some who say, "Well, I'm going to cut all this, but I'll protect bilateral assistance to Israel." Ask the Prime Minister. Even if that is done, other budget cuts would threaten our efforts to help Israel reach a lasting peace with its neighbors, because those efforts depend upon our ability to support everybody who takes risks for peace. If we renege on our commitments to Egypt, to Jordan, to the Palestinians, we will never convince anybody else that we will stand behind our commitments. We cannot do it. We must not do it.

I thank you for your vision in supporting debt relief for Jordan. We need that kind of support to help the risk takers, including the Palestinian Authority, demonstrate to their people that peace does bring benefits, that it promises a better life for themselves and for their children. The price we pay for these programs, I say again, is small compared to their benefits.

So I ask you to help me to win bipartisan support to preserve American leadership, to prevent the isolationists from risking all that was achieved in the cold war and its aftermath. And I ask you to do something else when you go home. Survey after survey after survey show that if you ask the American people what are we spending on foreign aid and welfare, poll after poll after poll says we're spending somewhere between 40 and 50 percent of our budget on foreign aid and welfare. The truth is, we're spending a nickel of our budget on foreign aid and welfare—all of our foreign assistance programs probably define a little over 2 cents in the budget; our direct welfare programs, about 3 cents. If the American people knew the facts, they would support these endeavors. If they understood that of the 22 wealthiest countries in the world, we are dead last in the percentage of our income and the percentage of our national budget going to these programs, they would not walk away from this.

So when you go home, don't just lobby Congress. Write your folks in the local newspaper, call in to some of those talk radio shows from time to time, and tell the American people the truth.

Let me say just a few words about where we are now in the Middle East. The conflict of decades will not end with the stroke of a pen, or even two pens, but consider how far we have come. No one who was there will ever forget that brilliant day on the White House lawn when Prime Minister Rabin and Chairman Arafat resolved to end their conflict. No one who was there will ever forget the magnificent ceremony in the Araba on the ground at the Patriarch's Walk when Israel and Jordan made peace after 46 years. Those were two of my proudest moments as President. They should be two of every American's proudest moments for our country in the last 2 years.

There is a constituency for peace in the Middle East growing stronger and stronger. Thanks in large measure to the tireless efforts of Secretary Christopher, Israel and Syria are engaged in serious, substantive negotiations on the terms of a treaty which can both secure another of Israel's borders and put an end to the entire conflict. A number of Arab countries, Morocco, Tunisia, Oman, Qatar, have begun to normalize relations with Israel. We have begun to dismantle the Arab boycott, and I think we'll see its end before too long. I will not rest until we do see the end of the boycott. It is high time, and it should be ended.

I think all of you know that peace requires more than treaties. It surely requires economic progress. We are moving aggressively on this front. We're continuing to provide the $10 billion in loan guarantees so Israel can absorb the 600,000 emigrants from the former Soviet Union and finance the investment and infrastructure it needs for a growing economy. We are cooperating to turn cutting-edge technologies into new products and to create new jobs for our nations, working to create a Middle East development bank, encouraging development in Israel and Jordan that will generate good new jobs, starting to attack the economic discontent of Egypt's young where extremism has its roots.

After all these efforts, and for all the energy the Israelis, Arabs, and Americans have devoted to the cause, the circle of peace is not yet closed. And the dream of the day when all Israelis are truly secure in their homes and free from fear is not yet fulfilled. The closer we come to achieving that peace, the more desperate and fanatical become the enemies of peace.

In the wake of the tragedy in Oklahoma City, about which the Prime Minister spoke so eloquently, I think our Americans now feel more strongly than ever and understand more clearly than ever the sense of horror and outrage at terrorism, at the bus bombings, the attacks on soldiers, the killings in the streets of Jerusalem. The cost of all this inhumanity and cowardice has been appalling. We grieve with the families of the victims. We thank the Prime Minister for going to see the family of Alicia Flatow, and we honor the memories of Alicia and Corporal Waxman and so many others.

We are encouraging Chairman Arafat to continue and to intensify his efforts to crack down on extremists. He is now taking concrete steps to prosecute those who plan and carry out acts of violence. These measures and others to confront terror and establish the rule of law must be continued. The peace will never succeed without them.

As I said in the Knesset last fall, the enemies of peace will not succeed, because they are the past, not the future. We will continue to do everything in our power to make that statement true.

But we face today in the Middle East, in Russia, and throughout the world a whole set of new challenges in a new era. The global economy, the explosion of information, the incredible advance of technology, the rapid movement of information, and people, all these forces are bringing us into a more integrated world. They prod people, on the one hand, to realize that it makes sense to stop killing each other and to make peace and to start working together, whether that's in the Middle East or Northern Ireland or Southern Africa. That means that the next century can be the most exciting time, the time most full of human possibility in all history.

But we also know that all these forces of integration have a dark side as well, for they make us vulnerable in new ways to organized destruction and evil, in terrorism terms and in terms of proliferating weapons of mass destruction. We see that not only at the terrible tragedy in Oklahoma City or the World Trade Center or the streets of Israel, we also see it in the subway stations of Japan. The more open and flexible our people become, the more we move around and relate to each other, the more vulnerable we will be, and the more vigilant we must become.

In the Middle East, as nowhere else, these two forces of integration and disintegration are locked in a deadly struggle: a strong Israel, backed by a strong America, building peace with its neighbors, a new openness in the region, but on the other side, these continuing desperate attempts of fanatics eager to keep old and bloody conflicts alive.

We can beat them. We must beat them. But we are going to have to work at it. We cannot grow weak. We cannot grow weary. And we cannot lose our self-confidence. If we give up on the peace, if we give up on our freedoms, if we walk away from what we are and what we can become, in the United States, Japan, the former Soviet Union, but most of all in the Middle East, then they will have won, even if we defeat them.

So I ask you in closing, stand for the forces of the future. Stand with this brave man in his attempts to make peace. And let's don't stop until the job is done.

Thank you, and God bless you.

NOTE: The President spoke at 10 p.m. at the Sheraton Washington. In his remarks, he referred to Steve Grossman, president, Larry Weinberg, chairman emeritus, and Neal Sher, executive director, American Israel Public Affairs Committee; Prime Minister Yitzhak Rabin and Health Minister Efraim Sneh of Israel; Itamar Rabinovich, Israeli Ambassador to the United States; Lester Pollack, chairman, Conference of Presidents of Major American Jewish Organizations; Martin Indyk, U.S. Ambassador to Israel; and Hamas kidnaping victim Cpl. Nahshon Waxman.

Letter to Congressional Leaders on Additional Economic Sanctions Against Iran
May 6, 1995

Dear Mr. Speaker: (*Dear Mr. President:*)

On March 15, 1995, I reported to the Congress that, pursuant to section 204(b) of the International Emergency Economic Powers Act (50 U.S.C. 1703(b)), and section 301 of the National Emergencies Act (50 U.S.C. 1631), I exercised my statutory authority to declare a national emergency to respond to the actions and policies of the Government of Iran and to issue an Executive order that prohibited United States persons from entering into contracts for the financing or the overall management or supervision of the development of petroleum resources located in Iran or over which Iran claims jurisdiction.

Following the imposition of these restrictions with regard to the development of Iranian petroleum resources, Iran has continued to engage in activities that represent a threat to the peace and security of all nations. I have now taken additional measures to respond to Iran's continuing support for international terrorism, including support for acts that undermine the Middle East peace process, as well as its intensified efforts to acquire weapons of mass destruction. I have issued a new Executive order and hereby report to the Congress pursuant to the above authorities and section 505(c) of the International Security and Development Cooperation Act of 1985 (22 U.S.C. 2349aa–9(c)).

The new order I have issued with respect to Iran:

—Prohibits exportation from the United States to Iran or to the Government of Iran of goods, technology or services, including trade financing by U.S. banks;

—Prohibits the reexportation of certain U.S. goods and technology to Iran from third countries;

—Prohibits transactions such as brokering and other dealing by United States persons in Iranian goods and services;

—Prohibits new investments by United States persons in Iran or in property owned or controlled by the Government of Iran;

—Prohibits U.S. companies from approving or facilitating their subsidiaries' performance of transactions that they themselves are prohibited from performing;

—Continues the 1987 prohibition on the importation into the United States of goods and services of Iranian origin; and

—Allows U.S. companies a 30-day period in which to perform trade transactions pursuant to contracts predating this order that are now prohibited.

With the exception of the trade noted above, all prohibitions contained in the Executive order are effective as of 12:01 a.m., eastern daylight time, on May 7, 1995.

This new order provides that the Secretary of the Treasury, in consultation with the Secretary of State, is authorized to take such actions, including the promulgation of rules and regulations, as may be necessary to carry out the purposes of the order. The order also authorizes the Secretary of the Treasury to require reports, including reports on foreign affiliates' oil trading with Iran. There are certain transactions subject to the prohibitions contained in the Executive order that I have directed the Secretary of the Treasury to authorize through licensing, including transactions by United States persons related to the Iran-United States Claims Tribunal in The Hague, established pursuant to the Algiers Accords, and other international obligations and United States Government functions. Such transactions also include the export of agricultural commodities consistent with section 5712(c) of title 7, United States Code. In addition, United States persons may be licensed to participate in market-based swaps of crude oil from the Caspian Sea area for Iranian crude oil in support of energy projects in Azerbaijan, Turkmenistan, and Kazakhstan.

This order revokes sections 1 and 2 of Executive Order No. 12613 of October 29, 1987, and sections 1 and 2 of Executive Order No. 12957 of March 15, 1995, to the extent they are inconsistent with this order. The declaration of national emergency made by Executive Order No. 12957 remains in effect and is not affected by this order.

Sincerely,

WILLIAM J. CLINTON

NOTE: Identical letters were sent to Newt Gingrich, Speaker of the House of Representatives, and Albert Gore, Jr., President of the Senate. This letter was released by the Office of the Press Secretary on May 8. The Executive order of May 6 is listed in Appendix D at the end of this volume.

Remarks on the 50th Anniversary of V-E Day in Arlington, Virginia
May 8, 1995

Thank you, Colonel McIntosh, for those remarkable words and your remarkable service. General Shalikashvili, Secretary Perry, Secretary Brown, Father Sampson, Members of Congress, members of the Armed Forces, distinguished guests, American veterans all, and especially to our most honored guests, the veterans of the Second World War:

Fifty years ago on this day the guns of war in Europe fell silent. A long shadow that had been cast on the entire Continent was lifted. Freedom's warriors rejoiced. We come today, 50 years later, to recall their triumph, to remember their sacrifice, and to rededicate ourselves to the ideals for which they fought and for which so many of them died.

By Victory Day in Europe, from the beaches of Normandy to the gates of Moscow, some 40 million people lost their lives in World War II. These enormous but faceless numbers hid millions upon millions of personal tragedies: soldiers shot and shattered by weapons of war, prisoners cut down by disease and starvation, children buried in the rubble of bombed-out buildings, and entire families exterminated solely because of the blood that ran in their veins. And for every death, so many more fell wounded, physically and emotionally. They would survive, but their lives would be changed forever.

At war's end, an 8-year-old boy, already a veteran of air raids and bomb shelters, was asked what he wanted to be when he grew up. He answered with one word, "Alive."

The American people, secure on our continent, sobered by memories of the last war, were not eager to enter into the struggle. But they were stirred by the extraordinary courage of the British, all alone and carrying liberty's flickering torch into Europe's darkening night. Pushed by their passion for freedom, prodded by the wise leadership of President Roosevelt, and provoked finally by the infamy at Pearl Harbor, Americans went to war.

It became an all-consuming effort. Millions were heroes here on the homefront. They built the planes, the ships, the tanks, the trucks that carried the Allied armies into battle. They bought victory bonds to pay for the war. They collected scrap metal for weapons, worn-out rubber for tires, left-over fat for explosives. And they planted 20 million victory gardens to help feed the Nation.

With good cheer they sacrificed, rationing food and clothing, holding themselves to 3 gallons of gas a week. And President Roosevelt willed them onward. "There is one front and one battle," he said, "where everyone in the United States, every man, woman, and child, is in action. That front is right here at home."

Across the ocean, their fathers and brothers, sisters and mothers, friends and neighbors gave the best years of their lives to the terrible business of war. Some of them were among the greatest leaders our country and the world have ever known: Eisenhower, Marshall, Bradley, Patton. But no matter their rank, every soldier, airman, marine, sailor, every merchant marine, every nurse, every doctor was a hero who carried the banner of justice into the battle for freedom.

Some of them are here with us today. The gentleman who introduced me, Frederick McIntosh, was then an Air Force lieutenant. He flew, as has been said, 104 missions. His daring dive-bomb raids on D-Day helped clear the way for the Allied landing. Another veteran behind me, Robert Katayama, a private with the Japanese-American 442d Regimental Combat Team that finally broke through the formidable Gothic line in Italy after 5 months of ferocious assault; another, Anna Connelly Wilson, a nurse who tended American soldiers moving gasoline and munitions across the deserts of Iran into the hands of our Russian allies; another, Abben MaGuire, a Navy demolition expert who landed on Omaha Beach ahead of the Allied assault, clearing mines, barbed wire, and booby traps under heavy fire from the enemy; another, George Ellers, a seaman on Coast Guard boats, charged with protecting the merchant marine armadas that ferried food and supplies from America to Europe and beyond; Joseph Kahoe, a lieutenant with the all-African-American 761st Tank Battalion, who braved the deadening cold of the Ardennes and the brutal Nazi counterattacks to help win the Battle of the Bulge; and Father Francis Sampson, an Army chaplain who parachuted into Normandy, then into Holland, was wounded, captured, but managed to escape.

In their bravery, and that of all their brothers and sisters in arms, America found the will to defeat the forces of fascism. And today we, the sons and daughters of their sacrifice, say thank you, and well done.

I ask all the veterans of World War II now to stand and be recognized. [*Applause*]

During the war's final weeks, America's fighting forces thundered across Europe, liberating small villages and great cities from a long nightmare. Many witnessed an outpouring of love and gratitude they would remember for the rest of their lives.

Deep in the Bavarian countryside, Corporal Bill Ellington piloted his armored vehicle into a battle against retreating enemy troops. As a firefight raged, a rail-thin teenage boy ran, shouting toward the tank. He was a young Polish Jew, Samuel Pisar, who had survived 4 years at Auschwitz and other concentration camps, but along the way had lost his entire family. Samuel Pisar had seen the tank and its glorious 5-point white star from his hideaway in a barn.

As Ellington looked down at him, the boy dropped to his knees and repeated over and over the few words of English his mother had taught him: "God bless America. God bless America." And Ellington, the son of a slave, lifted the boy through the hatch and into the warm embrace of freedom.

Bill Ellington died a few years ago. But Samuel Pisar, now an American citizen, is here with us today. And I'd like to ask him to stand as a reminder of what that war was all about. [*Applause*]

The saga of hope emerged from the ashes of a horror that defies comprehension still: the Nazi death camps. In the gas chambers and crematoriums was proof of man's infinite capacity for evil. In the empty eyes of the skeletal survivors was a question that to this day has never been answered: How could this happen?

But at 2:40 a.m. on May 7th, in a small redbrick schoolhouse in France, the Germans signed their unconditional surrender. The armistice took effect the next day, this day 50 years ago.

News of the victory spread and grew from a ripple of excitement to a river of joy. The liberated capitals of Western Europe were awash in relief and jubilation. The boulevards burst with flag-waving, teary-eyed thanksgiving celebrants. Everywhere people tore down their blackout curtains and let the light of peace shine out.

In the sky over Moscow, gigantic white rays of light from huge projectors slashed the darkness of night, and a 1,000-gun salute shook the city. There, too, millions teemed into the street. But their joy was dulled by the pain of their nation's unique sacrifice, for one out of every eight Soviet citizens was killed in World War II, 27 million people. At almost every table in every home there was an empty place.

In London, where a brave and defiant people had stood alone through the war's darkest hours, great bonfires ringed the city. And on the balcony of Buckingham Palace, Prime Minister Churchill stilled the delirious crowd with his own silence. Then he took one, deep, all-embracing bow, and the crowd exploded into a roar of triumph. "This is your victory," Churchill declared. And the people of the United Kingdom answered back as one: "No, it is yours." Of course, both were right.

Here at home, the Washington Monument, the Capitol Dome, the Statute of Liberty were bathed in floodlights for the very first time since Pearl Harbor. New York was New Year's Day and the Fourth of July rolled into one. Millions cheered, shouted, sang, danced in the streets. And in an image that traveled all around the world, a sailor took a nurse in his arms and kissed her, with all the pent-up youthful enthusiasm of a people forgetting for an instant the new burdens of adulthood.

Less than a month in office, President Truman addressed the Nation and said, "This is a solemn but glorious hour. I only wish FDR had lived to witness this day." Millions of Americans shared that conviction, for in their darkest hour, President Roosevelt refused to let us give up in despair. He rallied the Americans to defeat depression and triumph in war. And so it was his victory, too.

It was America's victory, but the job for us was not yet complete. In the Pacific, war raged on. During the 3 months between V-E and V-J Day, many thousands more of our fighting men and women would lose their lives. After Japan surrendered, who could have blamed the American people for wanting to turn from the front lines abroad to the homefront? But after winning the most difficult and crucial victory in our Nation's history, our leaders were determined not to repeat the mistakes of the past.

Instead, they took to new challenges with a newfound confidence. And this remarkable generation of Americans then, through NATO, the United Nations, and the Marshall plan, created the institutions and provided the resources and the vision that brought half a century of security and prosperity to the West and brought our former enemies back to life and to true partnership with us. And their special resolve and military strength held totalitarianism in check until the power of democracy, the failure of communism, and the heroic determination of people to be free prevailed in the cold war.

Today we must draw inspiration from the extraordinary generation we come here to honor, a generation that won the war and then made sure we would not lose the peace, a generation that understood our destiny is inexorably linked to that of other nations, a generation that believed that with our great wealth, great power, and great blessings of democratic freedom come great responsibilities to stand for and work for the common good.

So let me say again to the generation that won the Second World War, on this 50th anniversary, on behalf of the American people, we say thank you. Thank you, and God bless you. Because of all you did, we live in a moment of hope, in a Nation at peace. For the first time since the dawn of the nuclear age, no

Russian missiles are pointed at our children. Our economy is sound. And because free markets and democracy now are on the march throughout the world, more people than ever before have the opportunity to reach their God-given potential. All because of what you did 50 years ago.

But there is one thing that even you could not do, that no generation can ever do. You could not banish the forces of darkness from the future. We confront them now in different forms all around the world and, painfully, here at home. But you taught us the most important lesson: that we can prevail over the forces of darkness, that we must prevail. That is what we owe to you and the incomparable legacy you have given us and what we all owe to the generations of remarkable Americans yet to come.

Thank you for teaching us that lesson. God bless you, and God bless America.

NOTE: The President spoke at 11:35 a.m. at Fort Myer.

Remarks on Antiterrorism Legislation
May 8, 1995

Before I leave on this trip, I want to say a word about the antiterrorism legislation that I have sent to the Congress.

I sent that bill to Congress because it will strengthen our ability to investigate and prosecute and to deter—to deter the kinds of problems we saw and the kind of horror we endured at Oklahoma City and of course at the World Trade Center.

I applaud the fact that the leadership in Congress has said that they will have that bill on my desk by Memorial Day. That is only 3 weeks away. And so, before I leave, I want to urge Congress again to pass this legislation and to do it without delay.

Nothing can justify turning this bill into a political football. We have kept politics completely out of our fight against terrorism. We kept it out of our mourning. We kept it out of our law enforcement efforts. We're going to keep it out of the rebuilding efforts in Oklahoma. And we must keep it out of this legislative effort.

The Government needs the ability to deal with the technological challenges presented by terrorism in the modern age. This legislation does it, and there is simply no reason to delay it. Nothing can justify it. And it needs to pass and pass now.

Thank you.

NOTE: The President spoke at 1:05 p.m. at Andrews Air Force Base, prior to his departure for Moscow, Russia.

Statement on Welfare Reform Initiatives in Delaware
May 8, 1995

Today my administration has approved a bold plan for welfare reform in Delaware that promotes work, requires parental responsibility, and protects children. Delaware is the 28th State welfare reform experiment to be freed from Federal rules and regulations under this administration. Under Governor Tom Carper's leadership, Delaware will impose a time limit on benefits, provide job training opportunities, increase child support enforcement, and require teenage mothers to live at home and stay in school.

In particular, I am pleased that Delaware joins 14 other States in requiring welfare recipients to sign personal responsibility agreements, which is a contract for work, in order to receive assistance. These contracts were an important part of the welfare reform legislation I sent Congress last year and are essential to real reform that moves people from welfare to work. Personal responsibility is at the heart of welfare reform, and personal responsibility contracts must be part of any national welfare reform plan.

I will continue to work with Congress to enact welfare reform legislation that includes real work requirements and the incentives and resources for States to move people from welfare to work. Welfare reform must be tough on work and on parents who walk away from their responsibilities, not tough on children.

Message to the Senate Transmitting the Hungary-United States Extradition Treaty
May 8, 1995

To the Senate of the United States:

With a view to receiving the advice and consent of the Senate to ratification, I transmit herewith the Treaty Between the Government of the United States of America and the Government of the Republic of Hungary on Extradition, signed at Budapest on December 1, 1994. Also transmitted for the information of the Senate is the report of the Department of State with respect to this Treaty.

The Treaty is designed to update and standardize the conditions and procedures for extradition between the United States and Hungary. Most significantly, it substitutes a dual-criminality clause for the current list of extraditable offenses, thereby expanding the number of crimes for which extradition can be granted. The Treaty also provides a legal basis for temporarily surrendering prisoners to stand trial for crimes against the laws of the Requesting State.

The Treaty further represents an important step in combatting terrorism by excluding from the scope of the political offense exception serious offenses typically committed by terrorists, e.g., crimes against a Head of State or first family member of either Party, aircraft hijacking, aircraft sabotage, crimes against internationally protected persons, including diplomats, hostage-taking, narcotics-trafficking, and other offenses for which the United States and Hungary have an obligation to extradite or submit to prosecution by reason of a multilateral treaty, convention, or other international agreement. The United States and Hungary also agree to exclude from the political offense exception major common crimes, such as murder, kidnapping, and placing or using explosive devices.

The provisions in this Treaty follow generally the form and content or extradition treaties recently concluded by the United States. Upon entry into force, it will supersede the Convention for the Mutual Delivery of Criminals, Fugitives from Justice, in Certain Cases Between the Government of the United States of America and the Austro-Hungarian Empire, signed at Washington, July 3, 1856, with certain exceptions.

This Treaty will make a significant contribution to international cooperation in law enforcement. I recommend that the Senate give early and favorable consideration to the Treaty and give its advice and consent to ratification.

WILLIAM J. CLINTON

The White House,
May 8, 1995.

Remarks at the Dedication of the Central Museum for the Great Patriotic War in Moscow, Russia
May 9, 1995

President Yeltsin, Mr. Prime Minister, Prime Minister Major—[*inaudible*]—Shevardnadze, Mr. Mayor—[*inaudible*]—the veterans of the Great Patriotic War. We come together today as friends to celebrate our shared victory over fascism, to remember the sacrifice of those of you who made it possible, and to fulfill the promise of an enduring peace that shown so brightly, but all too briefly, 50 years ago today.

Brave men and women from our nations fought a common enemy with uncommon valor. Theirs was a partnership forged in battle, strengthened by sacrifice, cemented by blood. Their extraordinary effort speaks to us still of all that is possible when our people are joined in a just cause.

With me today is an American veteran of the Great War, Lieutenant William Robertson. As the war entered its final days, Lieutenant Robertson's patrol sighted troops led by Lieutenant Aleksander Sylvashko across the Elbe River. Crawling toward each other on the girders of a wrecked bridge, these two officers met at the midpoint and embraced in triumph. They exchanged photographs of wives, children, loved ones, whose freedom they had defended, whose future they would secure. The Americans did not speak Russian, and the Russians did not speak English, but they shared a language of joy.

The Americans at the Elbe remember how their new Russian friends danced that night, but how their jubilation turned solemn, because each of them had lost someone, a family member, a loved one, a friend. One out of every eight Soviet citizens was killed, soldiers in battle; prisoners, by disease or starvation; innocent children who could find no refuge. In all of the 27 million people who lost their lives to the war, there were Russians and Belarussians, Uzbekhs and Jews, Ukrainians, Armenians, Georgians, and more. These numbers numb the mind and defy comprehension.

I say to you, President Yeltsin, and to all the people of Russia and the other republics of the former Soviet Union, the cold war obscured our ability to fully appreciate what your people had suffered and how your extraordinary courage helped to hasten the victory we all celebrate today. Now we must all say, you wrote some of the greatest chapters in the history of heroism, at Leningrad, in the battle for Moscow, in the defense of Stalingrad, and in the assault on Berlin, where your country lost 300,000 casualties in only 14 days.

I have come here today on behalf of all the people of the United States to express our deep gratitude for all that you gave and all that you lost to defeat the forces of fascism. In victory's afterglow, the dream of peace soon gave way to the reality of the cold war, but now Russia has opened itself to new freedoms. We have an opportunity and an obligation to rededicate ourselves today to the promise of that moment 50 years ago when Europe's guns fell silent.

Just as Russians and Americans fought together 50 years ago against the common evil, so today we must fight for the common good. We must work for an end to the awful savagery of war and the senseless violence of terrorism. We must work for the creation of a united, prosperous Europe. We must work for the freedom of all of our people to live up to their God-given potential. These are our most sacred tasks and our most solemn obligations.

This is what we owe to the brave veterans who brought tears to our eyes when they marched together with such pride and courage in Red Square today. And this is what we owe to the generations of our children still to be born. Let us do our duty, as the veterans of World War II did theirs.

Thank you.

NOTE: The President spoke at 1:55 p.m. at the Poklonnaya Gora Monument. In his remarks, he referred to President Boris Yeltsin of Russia, Prime Minister John Major of the United Kingdom, Chairman Eduard Shevardnadze of the Republic of Georgia, and Mayor Uri Luzhkov of Moscow.

Statement on Senate Confirmation of John Deutch as Director of Central Intelligence
May 9, 1995

I am very pleased with the Senate's overwhelming 98–0 vote to confirm John Deutch as Director of Central Intelligence. The Senate's action is further affirmation of the outstanding leadership and management skills John Deutch will bring to the intelligence community and the CIA. I have the greatest confidence that he will bring a renewed sense of purpose, direction, and spirit to the CIA and the intelligence community.

Remarks at a State Dinner in Moscow
May 9, 1995

President Yeltsin, President Mitterrand, Prime Minister Major, Chancellor Kohl, Mr. Secretary-General, ladies and gentlemen:

Tonight we gather to recall one victory and the countless millions of sacrifices that produced it. It is fitting for all of us that we recall that day here in Russia, where virtually every family had a loss to mourn and a hero to remember.

A crowded 50 years separates us today from that moment. Yet it is still near in so many ways, woven with the entire war into the living memory of our civilization. Each of us has been touched by that war, even those who were born after its end.

World War II left us lessons, not for an evening but for a lifetime. We would be remiss not to mention two of them tonight. The first is the extraordinary power of men and women who joined together to fight for a just cause. The heroism of those who confronted and defeated tyranny, the alliance of Soviets, British, French, Chinese, Canadians, Yugoslavs, Poles, Americans, and so many more will forever remind people of the strength that is found in common purpose.

It inspires us here today. One-time opponents are now valued and trusting friends. And with Russia's turn to democracy, the alliance for freedom stands on the verge of great new possibility. Together we can face vistas of promise which separately we could never even imagine. And together we can face the challenges to our humanity in this age: terrorism, the proliferation of weapons of mass destruction, and the continued lust for killing based on ethnic, religious, or tribal differences.

As we look to new horizons in the new century, let us remember also another lesson of the Great War, the resilience of hope. Our nations prevailed because they never lost hope. It is the touchstone of our humanity.

Let us renew that hope tonight. And let us remember the words of Olga Berggolts, the poet of the awful siege of Leningrad. She said, "Again from the black dust, from the place of death and ashes, will arise the garden as before. So it will be. I firmly believe in miracles." The resolve of her city, the perseverance of its people in the face of unspeakable horror, gave her that belief in miracles. Fortified by the wonders we have seen in just the last 6 years, that belief surely lives on with us today.

And so, ladies and gentlemen, I propose a toast tonight to the heroism of 50 years ago; to the honor of the Russian people and the other Soviet peoples in the awful losses they suffered and what they gave to us; and most of all, to the hope that will carry us onward to miraculous new days ahead.

Thank you very much.

NOTE: The President spoke at 7:31 p.m. in the Palace of Congresses at the Kremlin. In his remarks, he referred to United Nations Secretary-General Boutros Boutros-Ghali.

Exchange With Reporters Following Discussions With President Boris Yeltsin of Russia in Moscow
May 10, 1995

Q. Mr. President, have you reached any agreements?

President Clinton. We're not finished with our conversations, and we'll have a statement later. We're having a good meeting, and I would just say again what I have said repeatedly—President Yeltsin and I have worked hard for more than 2 years to improve the safety and security of the people of Russia and the people of the United States. We are dismantling nuclear weapons at a more rapid rate than our treaties require. And we are working hard to improve the securities of our people. And that's what we've been doing here this morning. We've had a very good meeting, and we'll have more to say about the conversations we've had and will continue to have when we do our press statement.

Q. [*Inaudible*]—solve—[*inaudible*]—problems—[*inaudible*]—any of the problems? Iran?

The President. No one will ever solve all the problems, but—[*inaudible*].

NOTE. The exchange began at approximately 11:30 a.m. at the Kremlin. A tape was not available for verification of the content of this exchange.

The President's News Conference With President Boris Yeltsin of Russia in Moscow
May 10, 1995

President Yeltsin. Mr. President, ladies and gentlemen, journalists: This is the seventh meeting of the Presidents of the U.S. and Russia. This visit by Bill Clinton to Russia is of particular importance. The participation of such a high guest in the 9th of May celebration is seen by us as a tribute to the people killed in our common struggle against fascism.

Before each Russian-U.S. summit, there is no shortage of all kinds of speculations about Russian and U.S. contradictions. Sometimes they even refer to crises in our relations. The results of the Moscow talks have yet again denied these speculations.

Of course, even after the summit, differences to a number of issues have not disappeared. The important thing is that we seek to address these problems while maintaining a balance of interests and without prejudice to each other's interests but, on the contrary, in assisting each other.

The agenda of this meeting was very busy and comprehensive. We addressed the key issues of international life, issues which are of top priority for both countries. I'm referring, above all, to the evolution of the European security structures, the START treaty and the ABM Treaty, strengthening the nonproliferation regime, economic cooperation, and terrorism.

It is of fundamental importance that the discussion which we had about the model for European security proceed at taking into account the new role of the Organization on Security and Cooperation in Europe. Today, this organization is beginning to play a central role in maintaining stability on the European Continent.

We exchanged views on NATO issues. Today we better understand the interests and concerns of each other, and yet we still don't have answers to a number of questions. Our positions even remain unchanged.

I hope that our joint statement on matters related to strengthening European security will provide a starting point for further efforts because it provides for cooperation in the establishment of a single indivisible Europe looking into the future.

A serious document has been agreed on the problem of the ABM. We adopted a joint statement on the nonproliferation of nuclear weapons. I believe that that agreement will mark a major contribution to the adoption at the New York conference of a decision on an indefinite and unconditional extension of the NPT treaty. The conference will probably end tomorrow.

At the negotiations, the question was raised about future Russian supplies of equipment to Iran. That is, of course, not a simple question, and of course, you are going to ask that question, and both Presidents will answer that question.

We discussed in detail the implementation of the economic charter we signed last year. As a result, we adopted a statement on the question of economic reform, trade, and investment. The U.S. President expressed his support for our reforms. We agreed to speed up the process of Russia's entry to the system of international economic institutions, above all, the COCOM.

Of course, we discussed the Chechen issue. This is an internal matter for Russia, but I also believe it does have an international aspect. Russia has accepted the presence at Grozny of the OSCE assistance group.

Terrorism knows no borders. Unfortunately, U.S. citizens recently were confronted with that barbarous phenomenon. I believe that everybody would agree that we should fight this evil jointly, and we have agreed upon that.

During the talks, we had a fruitful exchange of views on the meeting of the political eight in Halifax, and not of the political but also of the economic eight. We also discussed a number of other international issues.

Now I am ready to answer your questions. I give the floor to the President of the United States of America, Mr. William Clinton.

President Clinton. First of all, I'd like to thank President Yeltsin and the Russian people for making me and the rest of our American delegation and the others who came here for the celebration of the 50th anniversary of the end of World War II feel so welcome. I was honored to play a part in that, and I think it was a very important day for our country and for our relationship.

Today we focused on the future. And if you ask me to summarize in a word or two what happened today, I would say that we advanced the security interests of the people of the United States and the people of Russia. We increased the safety of the future of our peoples, and we proved once again that this regular, disciplined, working relationship that we have established, rooted in Russia's commitment to democracy and in a mature and balanced dialog and a commitment to continue to work on the

differences between us in the areas of common opportunity, we proved that this is a good relationship and that it is worth the investment and that we are approaching it in the proper way.

I characterize this as a success from a security point of view for several reasons. First of all, with regard to European security, while there was not an agreement between us on the details on the question of the expansion of NATO, Russia did agree to enter into the Partnership For Peace. And I committed myself in return at the meeting at the end of this month to encourage the beginning of the NATO-Russia dialog, which I think is very important. There must be a special relationship between NATO and Russia.

We agreed to continue to discuss this at Halifax, and again at the end of the year when we see each other. And I made it clear that I thought that anything done with NATO had to meet two criteria: Number one, it must advance the interests of all the Partners For Peace, the security interests of all of them, including Russia, and number two, it must advance the long-term goal of the United States, which I have articulated from the beginning of my Presidency, of an integrated Europe, which I believe is very important. And I think Russia shares both of those objectives.

Secondly, with regard to the nuclear sales to Iran, as you know, the United States opposes the sale of the reactor and the centrifuge. I want to say that I was deeply impressed that President Yeltsin told me that he had decided, in the interest of nonproliferation, not to supply the centrifuge and related equipment to Iran. I shared with him some of the intelligence from the United States on the question of whether Iran is trying to become a nuclear power. And we agreed in light of the questions of facts that need to be determined here and Russia's strong support for nonproliferation, to refer the question of the reactor itself to the Gore-Chernomyrdin commission for further work on resolution.

I was very pleased today that we were able to make progress on the outstanding issues relating to weapon sales which will permit Russia to be a founding member of the post-COCOM regime, something, again, which will make the world a safer place.

Fourthly, we agreed that both of us would work as hard as we could to get START II ratified this year, and then to go beyond that to talk about what we could do further to support the denuclearization of the world and of our two arsenals.

Fifthly, we agreed that we should step up our efforts in combating terrorism and organized crime, a problem that affects not only our two nations but also many others in the world, as we have sadly seen. And we discussed some fairly specific things that we might do together to intensify our efforts.

As President Yeltsin said, we reaffirmed today in specific actions our support for the Non-Proliferation Treaty, and we look forward to its permanent extension. And we hope that the indefinite—excuse me, the indefinite extension will be adopted soon.

And finally, we were able to reach agreement on the ABM theater missile defenses issue, which is a very important one, and many of the Americans here know, important for our attempts to go forward on START II and other things back home.

We talked about our economic cooperation. We talked about the progress Russia is making. I expressed again the strong concern of the United States that the violence in Chechnya should be brought to an end. I urged the permanent extension of the cease-fire. I was encouraged that President Yeltsin, I believe, understands the gravity of this matter and also wants it concluded as quickly as possible.

So we are, I think, in a better position in our two countries today, and our people will be safer as a result of this meeting. It was an advance for security. There was significant progress made. And we still have work to do.

Press Secretary Sergey Medvedev. Now, dear colleagues, you have an opportunity to ask questions. I wish to remind you that we will give you the floor in sequence with my colleague, the Press Secretary of the U.S. President, Mr. McCurry.

The first question, please.

NATO Expansion and Russian Security

Q. Russian Public Television. Boris Nikolayevich, before the negotiations began, both sides were quite categoric on questions at issue. Are any concessions possible today on the NATO problem? Are there any linkages possible? I know that President Clinton insists on flank restrictions in the south of Russia. Well, if both sides do not concede, what will President Clinton bring back to the United States?

President Yeltsin. Well, I must tell you that we didn't have such a trading system in our talks. On the contrary, on the question of flank restrictions, Bill was the first to bring this matter up. And he said that he will surely support us on this difficult issue because it is true we are sort of in a trap with that issue.

Now, about NATO, we should look at this question in broader terms. What about general European security and NATO? I cannot say that after protracted discussions today on this subject—and by the way, we even had to change the schedule—we, in fact, had a never-ending meeting, and we were not able to dot the i's and cross all the t's. And we decided, first, if it is so difficult, let us not hurry, and then let us continue our consultations when we meet in Canada in Halifax.

We also believe that it may be we won't be able to agree in Halifax either. And we may need another meeting in November when the United Nations marks its 50th anniversary. We will meet in New York once again, and maybe at that time we may come to some final agreement.

President Clinton. I think this meeting was a win-win meeting. That is, I do not—I believe that both our countries advanced our interests and the interests of our people.

With regard to European security, the important thing for me was—not that Russia and the United States would agree today on the details of NATO expansion—indeed, it's important for all of you to understand, NATO has not agreed on that. NATO has not agreed on that.

This whole year, 1995, was to be devoted for the rationale for expanding NATO and then determining how it might be done, with no consideration whatever of who would be in the included membership and when that would be done. That was the plan. So not only has there—have we not agreed on that, as far as I know, there may be significant differences among the NATO partners themselves.

The important thing for me was that the President and I would agree that European unity, integration, is still our goal—we don't want a differently divided Europe—and that our NATO expansion plans should enhance the interests, the security interests of all of our partners, including Russia. Now, for my part, I haven't changed my position from the beginning on how this should be done.

The second thing I want to say is, the most important thing to me is that Russia has now agreed to proceed with participation in the Partnership For Peace, which is becoming very, very important in its own right and a significant force in increasing a sense of trust and understanding and working together in security within Europe.

With regard to the flank issue you mentioned, we have not worked out all the details of that. We've agreed to continue working on it. The problem is, of course, that the treaty becomes effective at a certain date. Its terms were negotiated in a previous time. Then there is a lag time for modifications of the treaty. We believe some modifications are in order. We are supporting the Russian position there. What we want to do is to figure out a way for us to preserve the integrity of the treaty and compliance with it, but, in the end respond to the legitimate security interests of Russia. And I believe we can get there.

Russia-Iran Nuclear Cooperation

Q. Mr. President, you made clear in advance on the Iran nuclear deal that you wouldn't be satisfied with anything short of an outright cancellation of that sale. Today you said that it's going to be referred to a lower level, that you weren't able to solve this question. I want to know, are there any repercussions? Are you disappointed that you weren't able to get this sale closed? And will you resist Republican threats to cut off foreign aid to Russia?

President Clinton. Well, first of all, this sale was in the pipeline, announced, and is legal under international law. I believe it is unwise. I think it should not go forward. We actually got more done today than I thought we would do, and we are ahead of where I thought we would be.

As I said, President Yeltsin made it clear to me that even though it would be some financial sacrifice to Russia, he did not believe they should proceed with the centrifuge and the related portions of the sale that could have a much more direct and immediate impact on weapons production. I gave him some of our intelligence and made the best arguments I could about why I thought the whole sale should not go forward. And we agreed that since some of this involves an evaluation of technical matters, it would be appropriate to refer to the Gore-Chernomyrdin commission where we have gotten a lot of useful work done between our two

countries. So we are actually further down the road on that issue than I thought we would be.

Now, with response to the particular arguments about the cutoff of aid, I think what we should do is to look at the progress we have made today, look at the progress we have made in the last 2 years, ask ourselves whether the United States is safer and more secure as a result of these efforts. I think the answer is yes. We should keep working. We should treat this like a business relationship that is furthering the security of both countries, and we should do whatever is in our interest. And I believe that the programs that we presently have underway are clearly in our interest.

President Yeltsin. I would like to add to what President Bill Clinton just said. The point is that the contract was concluded legitimately and in accordance with international law, and no international treaties were violated in the process. But it is true that the contract do contain components of peaceful and military nuclear energy. Now we have agreed to separate those two.

Inasmuch as they relate to the military component and the possibility, the potential for creating weapons-grade fuel and other matters, the centrifuge, the construction of silos, and so on—we have decided to exclude those aspects from the contract, and the military component falls away, and what remains is just a peaceful nuclear power station on light water reactors, which is designed to provide heat and energy.

Any more questions?

Please, colleagues, it's our task.

Q. Boris Nikolayevich, could you clarify, if possible, the mechanism for decisionmaking regarding the Iranian contract? According to President Clinton, the materials will be referred to the Gore-Chernomyrdin commission; who will then decide? Will they report to the heads of state, or will some other mechanism be worked out?

President Yeltsin. After this question has been comprehensively considered by the Gore-Chernomyrdin commission, we, the two Presidents, will receive all the material and we will make the final decision.

Chechnya

Q. [*Inaudible*]—seem ironical to you that you have just celebrated the end of World War II and the killing goes on in Chechnya? And it really has appalled the world, the killing of civilians. So what are you going to do about it, and how can you stop it?

President Yeltsin. Well, first, there are no hostilities underway in Chechnya right now. Therefore, that is—there is no irony there. Furthermore, the armed forces are not involved there. Today, the Ministry of the Interior simply seizes the weapons which are still in possession of some small armed criminal gangs. But most importantly, we are doing some creative work there. We are rehabilitating buildings, utilities, trade, we ensure the necessary financing.

The Chechen government has been set up, and it is headed by a Chechen, and it operates in accordance with the Russian Constitution. The dates for parliamentary elections are now being discussed. Therefore, creative work is being done, and I believe that soon we will have a normal situation there, the situation of a democratic republic, with all the ensuing rights for the citizens living in Chechnya.

Terrorism

Q. [*Inaudible*]—radio station. I have the following question: The people are very impressed with incidents of brutal terrorism. Boris Nikolayevich, you said that you discussed this and you agreed on some common actions. Could you elaborate on that? And I would be grateful if both Presidents could at least briefly address this question.

President Yeltsin. Well, first we convinced each other that without joint efforts, we will not be able to cope with this evil in the world. What we really need is joint efforts—joint efforts, not talk, not conferences, not meetings but actions. And as regards actions, of course we did not discuss the matter specifically, but we have instructed our governments to work out those actions and to proceed without delay to taking those actions.

President Clinton. He asked for an answer, I'd like—we talked; we did not agree on a number of specific actions, but we discussed some. And I think it might be helpful.

First of all, President Yeltsin and I and the leaders of many other countries in the world are quite concerned that the great security threat of the 21st century might not be all those we had been discussing, either explicitly or by implication here in the last few moments. They instead might be coming from often nongovernmental sources in terms of terrorism and orga-

nized crime and the proliferation of weapons of mass destruction, getting into the hands of terrorists and organized criminals. So we discussed how we could cooperate more with law enforcement and intelligence. I think you know that the Federal Bureau of Investigation is opening an office here in Moscow, and we have been working with Russia for sometime now.

We discussed how we could make sure we each were as technologically advanced as possible, because many of the adversaries we face are very advanced. And we discussed how we might work together to try to limit the destructive capacity of terrorists and organized criminals and limit their ability to proliferate the weapons, particularly in the biological and chemical area. It's a great concern to me, and both Russia and the United States probably have some resources there that we can bring to bear.

And I think in light of what happened in Japan, all advanced countries should be very, very concerned about the prospect of the merger of terrorism with weapons of mass destruction, biological, chemical, and small-scale nuclear weapons.

Chechnya

Q. President Clinton, you've just heard President Yeltsin describe the situation in Chechnya in a way that may be at odds with news dispatches coming from the part of the country describing a massacre. And I wondered if—what your reaction is to his description, whether you accept it, if not why not, and what impact these reports of terrible things there may be having on the countries eager to join NATO, and what you would have to say to him about that?

President Clinton. Well, I will say to you what I said to him personally already, and I think what he knows and Chancellor Kohl and other friends of Russia have said: The civilian casualties and the prolongation of the fighting have troubled the rest of the world greatly and have had an impact in Europe on the attitudes of many countries about what is going on here and about future relationships. I don't think anyone is unaware of that.

What I have urged President Yeltsin to do is to try to make a permanent cease-fire, to try to move rapidly with the cooperation of the OSCE to get a democratic government there and to bring this to a speedy resolution, because I do believe it is something that is very troubling to the world, particularly in the dimensions of civilian casualties.

And I'm sure all the American journalists here know that we have a missing relief worker there ourselves. And I asked the President to help me find whatever could be found about Mr. Cuny, and he said that he would direct the Russian authorities there to try to help us. But this is a troubling thing for the world, and it's been a difficult thing for them as well.

President Yeltsin. Looking at my watch, shall we agree, Mr. McCurry, just one question on each side?

Economic Reform in Russia and Ukraine

Q. Boris Nikolayevich, we will have a meeting at Halifax with the eight. Do you intend to improve on the results of the similar meeting in Naples? Did you discuss anything like that this time with Bill Clinton? Did you agree that Bill Clinton will help you somewhere in some of Russia's aspirations?

And the question for the U.S. President— this is also a question from Ukraine—what are you bringing to Ukraine?

President Yeltsin. Whoever I met during these celebration days, of course, with everybody we discussed Halifax. I and Russia are, of course, concerned about our role in the G–7 or in the G–8. That is why this morning, at 9 a.m., I had a meeting with the Prime Minister of Canada, Mr. Chrétien, who will act as cochairman. We discussed the U.N. views—we discussed his views on the problem. I discussed this with Bill Clinton, with Helmut Kohl, with François Mitterrand.

Well, generally speaking, everybody is optimistic on this subject, and they wish to support Russia. To give you an example, Mr. Chrétien this morning said that Russia in Halifax will have 3 times more opportunities than last year in Naples. Well, that's not bad. The minimum we count on is as follows: The political eight, we believe, has now asserted itself; it is a fact of life; we are part of the political eight.

Now about economic matters. At Halifax, first they will address the economic matters of the G–7 and then they will address international matters pertinent to the whole world. As regards their internal business, well, we have no claims to that. They discuss specific issues and important issues related to trade and other economic matters. But as regards global strategic matters of importance to the entire world, Russia should

participate in such discussions fully. So I think we can call this seven and a half.

President Clinton. [*Inaudible*]—specific questions. The United States, since I have been President, has supported two major aid packages to Russia to support the conversion to a market economy and to try to assist in developing all of the institutions necessary to make that successful, as well as to support our denuclearization efforts under the so-called Nunn-Lugar funds.

We were also very strongly supportive of the recent $6.8 billion standby loan that the International Monetary Fund granted to Russia as a result of the economic reforms initiated under President Yeltsin. So I think that your country has a great deal to be proud of in the economic progress that has been made.

I know you still are dealing with a lot of economic difficulties; all market economies do. And the markets don't solve all problems. So you have to work on trying to deal with those. But I believe that our partnership has been a good investment for the United States because we have a stronger, more democratic, more open, more free Russia, and we will continue to support that direction.

With Ukraine, I must say, they've made a remarkable amount of progress in the last year or so, and I think President Yeltsin feels the same way. I am encouraged by the balance and discipline coming out of the government in Ukraine, and I will continue to support the process of reform there.

Russia-Iran Nuclear Cooperation

Q. President Yeltsin, several U.S. officials, including the Secretary of State, have suggested that if you go along with the sale of the nuclear reactors to Iran, this would endanger Russia's becoming a full member of the G–7 and other international institutions. And several Republican leaders in the U.S. Congress have warned that if you go ahead with this sale, it would endanger continued U.S. assistance to Russia. Are these kinds of threats persuasive, or was the intelligence information that President Clinton showed you today of Iran's nuclear ambitions, was that the convincing element to you? Or are you still basically at a disagreement with the United States over Iran's nuclear ambitions?

President Yeltsin. We're not afraid of threats. We never react to threats. But as for your question, we have already told you, with the President, that technically we need to sort the question out. We need to sort out what relates to peaceful and to military purposes. And this has been entrusted to the Gore-Chernomyrdin commission. Once we get to signatures—once we get a document signed by two, we the Presidents will make the final decision.

President Clinton. This may be a fitting question to close this press conference.

I think it is important that the people of the United States and the people of Russia understand that from time to time, as with any sort of relationship, there will be differences of opinion. Occasionally, there will even be occasions where our interests are different. What we have been working on for over 2 years now are areas where our interests are not different, working through areas where our opinions might be.

Now, in the case of this Iranian matter, just to take one example, if the United States is right and Iran is attempting to develop the capacity to build nuclear weapons, that would be more of an immediate security threat to Russia than to the United States, because you are closer to the country.

So we don't really have different interests here. Both our countries are committed to the fight against terrorism. Both our countries are committed to the Nuclear Non-Proliferation Treaty and its indefinite extension. Both our countries are dismantling our own nuclear arsenals at a more rapid rate than our treaties require.

Now, in playing this relationship out, there will come times when there will be differences.

If we ultimately differ on something, I think that we all know there may be consequences to having different positions and different actions. But I think we should be quite careful in using the language of threats in a relationship that in the last 2 years has made the world a much safer place. We have seen Russia's democracy strengthened. We have seen Russia's transition toward a private economy go more rapidly than all experts predicted. We have seen discipline asserted in this economy to a greater degree than most experts predicted. And we have seen more progress on thorny difficulties, complex matters, than most experts predicted.

As a result, the people of the United States, the people of Russia, and the people of the world are safer today than they were 2 years ago and than they were before this last meeting between us occurred. That is the fundamental story. We will have differences. They will have consequences. But we should stay away from big words like "threats" when we're managing matters which can be managed in a relationship that is quite good for the world and that has made us all safer.

Thank you.

NOTE: The President's 95th news conference began at 2:40 p.m. in the Press Conference Hall in the Kremlin. In his remarks, he referred to Frederick Cuny, an American relief worker in Chechnya who disappeared in April. President Yeltsin spoke in Russian, and his remarks were translated by an interpreter.

Russia-United States Joint Statement on Missile Systems
May 10, 1995

The President of the United States of America and the President of the Russian Federation, taking into account the threat posed by worldwide proliferation of missiles and missile technology and the necessity of counteracting this threat, agreed on the following basic principles to serve as a basis for further discussions in order to reach agreement in the field of demarcation between ABM systems and theater missile defense systems.

The United States and Russia are each committed to the ABM Treaty, a cornerstone of strategic stability.

Both sides must have the option to establish and to deploy effective theater missile defense systems. Such activity must not lead to violation or circumvention of the ABM Treaty.

Theater missile defense systems may be deployed by each side which (1) will not pose a realistic threat to the strategic nuclear force of the other side and (2) will not be tested to give such systems that capability.

Theater missile defense systems will not be deployed by the sides for use against each other.

The scale of deployment—in number and geographic scope—of theater missile defense systems by either side will be consistent with theater ballistic missile programs confronting that side.

In the spirit of partnership, the Presidents undertook to promote reciprocal openness in activities of the sides in theater missile defense systems and in the exchange of corresponding information.

NOTE: An original was not available for verification of the content of this joint statement.

Joint Statement on European Security
May 10, 1995

Presidents Clinton and Yeltsin conducted a thorough review of progress toward their shared goal of a stable, secure, integrated and undivided democratic Europe. They agreed that the end of military confrontation, ideological conflict, and division of the Euro-Atlantic region into opposing blocs has created an historic opportunity for all of its peoples. They emphasized their determination to cooperate closely to ensure that in the future, all peoples of the Euro-Atlantic region shall enjoy the benefits of a stable, just and peaceful order.

The Presidents note that the task of strengthening Euro-Atlantic security now requires dealing with challenges very different from those of the Cold War era. Aggressive nationalism, proliferation of weapons of mass destruction, unresolved territorial disputes, and violations in the area of human rights present serious threats to stability, peace and prosperity. The Presidents agree that the effort to deal with these challenges must be based on respect for the principles and commitments of the OSCE, particularly concerning democracy, political pluralism, respect for human rights and civil liberties, free market economies and strict respect for sovereignty, territorial integrity, and self-determination.

The Presidents reviewed prospects for Euro-Atlantic structures in response to the opportunities and challenges posed by the new era. They agreed that the central element of a lasting peace must be the integration of all of Europe into a series of mutually supporting institutions and relationships which ensure that there will be no return to division or confrontation. The evolution of European structures should be directed toward the overall goal of integration. President Clinton stressed that the process should be transparent, inclusive and based on an integral relationship between the security of Europe and that of North America.

The Presidents note the historic task of working closely together toward fuller participation of democratic Russia and the United States of America in the range of worldwide political, economic, and security institutions of the 21st Century. It was in this spirit that the two Presidents reviewed steps in the evolution of the Euro-Atlantic security system through the further development of relevant organizations and bilateral and regional cooperation. This includes the decision of Russia to proceed with its individual Partnership Program for the Partnership for Peace and with the document on a broad, enhanced Russia-NATO dialogue and cooperation.

President Clinton supported Russia's efforts to develop further its partnership and cooperation with the EU. He stressed U.S. support for Russia's participation in the WTO, GATT and other institutions important to European and global economic and security architecture, as appropriate.

The Presidents agree that the OSCE's commitments in the areas of human rights, economics, and security provide a foundation for their effort to build a stable and integrated Europe. In this regard, special attention should be devoted to strengthening the peacekeeping capabilities of the OSCE and to its potential in the sphere of preventive diplomacy and the peaceful settlement of disputes.

The Presidents recalled the decision of the December 1994 OSCE Summit in Budapest to develop a model for ensuring comprehensive security for Europe in the 21st Century. The United States and Russia believe that such a model should aim to build an undivided Europe, a common space of security and stability, and a system that ensures the widest cooperation and coordination among all countries of the Euro-Atlantic region. In this system, all states will have, as stated in Budapest, the inherent right of all states freely to choose or change their security arrangements, including treaties of alliance, as they evolve.

NOTE: An original was not available for verification of the content of this joint statement.

Joint Statement on Nonproliferation
May 10, 1995

The President of the United States of America, William J. Clinton, and the President of the Russian Federation, B.N. Yeltsin, at their meeting in Moscow May 9–10, 1995, expressed the strong view that the Nonproliferation Treaty (NPT) Review and Extension Conference underway in New York should decide to make the Treaty permanent. The two leaders pledged that the United States and Russia will continue to work to ensure the full implementation of the Treaty. In particular, they reaffirmed the commitments by the United States of America and the Russian Federation, under Article VI of the NPT, to pursue negotiations in good faith on effective measures relating to nuclear disarmament, which remains their ultimate goal.

The two Presidents also reaffirmed that the United States and the Russian Federation will continue to work together closely to promote broad nonproliferation goals. They agreed that, in the newly-established bilateral working group on nonproliferation, the two sides would consult in a timely manner on issues of mutual concern, including how best to fulfill their responsibility to cooperate with other NPT parties in the peaceful uses of nuclear energy, while at the same time fulfilling their responsibility to avoid risks of proliferation. The leaders recognized the importance of a responsible approach to the transfer of nuclear-related material, equipment, and technology and to nuclear-related training. In this connection, they reaffirmed their commitments to the NPT and to the Nuclear Suppliers Group Guidelines, and in particular to the principles that nuclear transfers should take place only under full-scope International Atomic Energy Agency (IAEA) safeguards and only when a supplier is satisfied that such transfers to any non-nuclear weapon state would not contribute to the proliferation of nuclear weapons.

The leaders directed the working group on nonproliferation to prepare assessments of proliferation threats in various regions of the world, to consider practical means of addressing those threats, to assess evidence regarding possible noncompliance with nonproliferation commitments, and to report to them periodically on its progress.

The two Presidents strongly supported the concrete progress recently made in their two countries' cooperation in ensuring the security of nuclear weapons and nuclear materials that can be used in such weapons. They reiterated their call for broad and expanded cooperation on a bilateral and multilateral basis, consistent with their international obligations, to strengthen national and international regimes of control, accounting, and physical protection of nuclear materials, and to prevent illegal traffic in nuclear materials. They directed all relevant agencies and organizations in their respective countries to facilitate in a coordinated manner, effective cooperation to this end.

They directed that the Gore-Chernomyrdin Commission prepare a joint report on steps that have been accomplished and additional steps that should be taken to ensure the security of nuclear materials.

The leaders reaffirmed their strong support for the IAEA and reiterated their view that its safeguards program plays a fundamental role in the global nuclear nonproliferation regime. They stressed the importance of enhancing the IAEA's ability to detect diversions of nuclear material and to provide increased assurance of the absence of undeclared nuclear activities, in particular through the effort currently underway to strengthen the effectiveness and improve the efficiency of the safeguards system.

The Presidents agreed that the formal participation of the Russian Federation in the multilateral nonproliferation export control regimes would significantly strengthen those regimes as well as broaden the basis for cooperation between the two countries on nonproliferation.

They agreed to direct officials in their respective governments to address expeditiously the issues affecting Russian membership in the various regimes, with a view to ensuring active U.S. support for Russian admission to each of the regimes at the earliest possible date.

NOTE: An original was not available for verification of the content of this joint statement.

Joint Statement on Economic Reform, Trade, and Investment
May 10, 1995

The President of the United States of America and the President of the Russian Federation welcomed the significant progress made in Russian economic reforms and bilateral trade and investment since their last meeting in Washington in September 1994. They underlined their support for full and early realization of the bilateral economic partnership described in their September 1994 Washington Summit Joint Statement on "Partnership for Economic Progress."

Economic Reform

The President of the Russian Federation reaffirmed Russia's determination to implement firmly its 1995 economic reform program, including reduction of government deficits and other anti-inflationary measures, privatization, comprehensive tax reform, strengthening of the free market and integration into the world economy. The President of the United States of America welcomed these policies and pledged continued strong U.S. support for their complete implementation.

The President of the United States of America and the President of the Russian Federation commended the deepening interaction between Russia and the leading industrial countries and the formation of the "Political-8," and expressed their hope for fruitful cooperation during the forthcoming Halifax Summit in June 1995.

Trade

The President of the United States of America expressed strong U.S. support for Russian accession to the World Trade Organization (WTO), and both Presidents agreed to cooperate on accomplishing this objective.

The President of the United States of America and the President of the Russian Federation welcomed the doubling of bilateral trade between 1992 and 1994 to a level of $5.8 billion. They pledged that as trade continues to expand both countries would work together to resolve trade frictions when arise in a mature trade relationship. They also agreed that bilateral trade and foreign and domestic investment would benefit from stricter enforcement of intellectual property rights and they agreed that both governments would engage in broader cooperation in this area. The President of the United States of America reiterated his government's recognition that Russia is an economy in transition to a free market.

Investment

The President of the Russian Federation informed the President of the United States of America that his government has issued a decree permitting full implementation of the Oil and Gas Framework Agreement, under which the U.S. Export-Import Bank can proceed with $1.3 billion in approved loans and authorize $700 million in requested loans for the important oil and gas sector. The two Presidents also undertook to accelerate implementation of the $750 million Eximbank-Gazprom financing facility.

The President of the Russian Federation noted the importance of the IL–96M project to civil aviation cooperation between the two countries and the President of the United States of America confirmed that the U.S. Export-Import Bank is reviewing a financing application for this project.

The two Presidents welcomed progress made in negotiations between American and Russian companies on production sharing agreements and look forward to the signing of these agreements within the next few months, as well as the passage of the Law on Production Sharing and the ratification of the Bilateral Investment Treaty.

The President of the United States of America and the President of the Russian Federation welcomed the commitments of the Overseas Private Investment Corporation of over $2 billion in loan guarantees, insurance and investment funds, and of the U.S. Trade and Development Agency of over $35 million for feasibility studies on 87 separate projects in the Russian Federation. They looked forward to the opening in Moscow in June of a new Russian Business Information Service for trade with America, with assistance from the U.S. Government.

Future Mandate

The President of the United States of America and the President of the Russian Federation commended the achievements of the Joint Commission for Technological and Economic Cooperation (the Gore-Chernomyrdin Commission) and, stressing their commitment to a strategic economic partnership, requested recommenda-tions from the Joint Commission on further moves to strengthen and expand bilateral trade and investment and market access, and cooperation in the areas of energy, space, science and technology, health and agriculture and conversion of defense production facilities.

Noting the importance of regional development, the two Presidents announced the inaugural meeting in Seattle this June of the working group between the private and public sector leaders of the Russian Far East and the U.S. west coast, based on the initiative of the President of the Russian Federation in Seattle in September 1994.

The President of the United States of America and the President of the Russian Federation noted that a strong basis for economic, commercial and technological cooperation between the two countries has been created, which is aimed at supporting the transformation of the Russian economy and Russia's full integration into the world economy. The two Presidents expressed strong support for these historic goals.

NOTE: An original was not available for verification of the content of this joint statement.

Joint Statement on the Transparency and Irreversibility of the Process of Reducing Nuclear Weapons
May 10, 1995

The President of the United States of America and the President of the Russian Federation,

After examining the exchange of views which took place during the December 1994 meeting of the Gore-Chernomyrdin Commission in regard to the aggregate stockpiles of nuclear warheads, stocks of fissile materials, and their safety and security, as well as a discussion of the Joint Working Group on Nuclear Safeguards, Transparency and Irreversibility of further measures to improve confidence in and increase the transparency and irreversibility of the process of reducing nuclear weapons,

Reaffirm the commitment of the United States of America and the Russian Federation to the goal of nuclear disarmament and their desire to pursue further measures to improve confidence in and increase the transparency and irreversibility of the process of nuclear arms reduction, as they agreed in January and September 1994;

Reaffirm the desire of the United States of America and the Russian Federation to exchange detailed information on aggregate stockpiles of nuclear warheads, on stocks of fissile materials and on their safety and security and to develop a process for exchange of this information on a regular basis; and

Express the desire of the United States of America and the Russian Federation to establish as soon as possible concrete arrangements for enhancing transparency and irreversibility of the process of nuclear arms reduction.

Taking into account the proposal by President B.N. Yeltsin for a treaty on nuclear safety and strategic stability among the five nuclear powers, they declare that:

—Fissile materials removed from nuclear weapons being eliminated and excess to national security requirements will not be used to manufacture nuclear weapons;

—No newly produced fissile materials will be used in nuclear weapons; and

—Fissile materials from or within civil nuclear programs will not be used to manufacture nuclear weapons.

The United States of America and the Russian Federation will negotiate agreements to increase the transparency and irreversibility of nuclear arms reduction that, *inter alia*, establish:

—An exchange on a regular basis of detailed information on aggregate stockpiles of nuclear warheads, on stocks of fissile materials and on their safety and security;

—A cooperative arrangements for reciprocal monitoring at storage facilities of fissile materials removed from nuclear warheads and declared to be excess to national security requirements to help confirm the irreversibility of the process of reducing nuclear weapons, recognizing that progress in this area is linked to progress in implementing the joint U.S.-Russian program for the fissile material storage facility at Mayak; and

—Other cooperative measures, as necessary to enhance confidence in the reciprocal declarations of fissile material stockpiles.

The United States of America and the Russian Federation will strive to conclude as soon as possible agreements which are based on these principles.

The United States of America and the Russian Federation will also examine and seek to define further measures to increase the transparency and irreversibility of the process of reducing nuclear weapons, including intergovernmental arrangements to extend cooperation to further phases of the process of eliminating nuclear weapons declared excess to national security requirements as a result of nuclear arms reduction.

The Presidents urged progress in implementing current agreements affecting the irreversibility of the process of reducing nuclear weapons such as the June 23, 1994, agreement concerning the shutdown of plutonium production reactors and the cessation of use of newly produced plutonium for nuclear weapons, in all its interrelated provisions, including, *inter alia*, cooperation in creation of alternative energy sources, shutdown of plutonium production reactors mentioned above, and development of respective compliance procedures.

The United States of America and the Russian Federation will seek to conclude in the shortest possible time an agreement for cooperation between their governments enabling the exchange of information as necessary to implement the arrangements called for above, by providing for the protection of that information. No information will be exchanged until the respective arrangements enter into force.

NOTE: An original was not available for verification of the content of this joint statement.

Remarks to Students at Moscow State University
May 10, 1995

Thank you very much, Rector Sadovnichy, Mrs. Sadovnichy. To the faculty and, most of all, to the students of Moscow State University, I am deeply honored to be here and to be here just a few years after my predecessor President Reagan also spoke to the students.

I can think of no better place than a great seat of learning like Moscow State University to speak about the past and future of Russia. In this spirit, Mikhail Lomonosov lives on, for just as he modernized your ancient language

for the Russian people two centuries ago, today you must take the lead in shaping a new language, a language of democracy that will help all Russia to chart a new course for your ancient land. Here, you openly debate the pressing issues of the day. And though you can only hear echoes of your nation's history, you are living it and making it as you ponder and prepare for what is yet to come.

Yesterday all of Russia and much of the entire world paused to remember the end of World

War II and the terrible, almost unimaginable price the peoples of the Soviet Union paid for survival and for victory. Because our alliance with you was shattered at the war's end by the onset of the cold war, Americans never fully appreciated, until yesterday, the true extent of your sacrifice and its contribution to our common victory. And the Russian people were denied the full promise of that victory in World War II, a victory that bought the West five decades of freedom and prosperity.

Now the cold war is over. Democracy has triumphed through decades of Western resolve, but that victory was also yours, through the determination of the peoples of Russia, the other former Soviet republics, and the countries of Central and Eastern Europe to be free and to move into the 21st century as a part of, not apart from, the global movement toward greater democracy, prosperity, and common security.

Your decision for democracy and cooperation has given us the opportunity to work together to fulfill the promise of our common victory over forces of fascism 50 years ago. I know that it was not an easy decision to make and that it is not always an easy decision to stay with. I know that you in Russia will have to chart your own democratic course based on your own traditions and culture, as well as on the common challenges we face.

We Americans have now spent over 200 years setting our own course. Along the way we have endured deep divisions and one Civil War. We have made mistakes at home and in our relations with other people. At times we have fallen short of our own ideals. Our system can sometimes seem unnecessarily burdened by divisions and constraint. But as Winston Churchill once said, "Democracy is the worst system of government, except for all the others." It has produced more prosperity, more security, and more opportunity for self-fulfillment than all of its competitors in the entire world in the last 200 years.

The United States supports the forces of democracy and reform here in Russia because it is in our national interest to do so. I have worked hard to make this post-cold-war world a safer and more hopeful place for the American people. As President, that is my job. That is every President's job. But I have had the opportunity, unlike my recent predecessors, to work with Russia instead of being in opposition to Russia. And I want to keep it that way.

I am proud that for the first time since the dawn of the nuclear age, no Russian missiles are pointed at the children of America. And now that I am here, I might paraphrase what your Foreign Minister told me in Washington last month: I am also proud that no American missiles are pointed at you or me for the first time since the dawn of the nuclear age.

Both our nations are destroying thousands of nuclear weapons at a faster rate than our treaties require. We have removed the last nuclear weapons from Kazakhstan, and Ukraine and Belarus will soon follow. We are cooperating with you to prevent nuclear weapons and bomb-making materials from falling into the hands of terrorists and smugglers. We are working together to extend indefinitely the Nuclear Non-Proliferation Treaty, the cornerstone of our efforts to stop the spread of nuclear weapons.

Your progress on the economic front is also important. I have seen reports that more than 60 percent of your economy is now in private hands. Inflation is dropping, and your government is taking sensible steps to control its budget deficit. Managers work to satisfy customers and to make profits. Employees, more and more, search for the best jobs at the highest wages. And every day, despite hardship and uncertainty, more and more Russian people are able to make decisions in free markets rather than having their choices dictated to them.

We have supported these reforms. They are good for you, but they are also good for the United States and for the rest of the world, for they bring us together and move us forward.

I know there are severe problems. There are severe problems in your transition to a market economy. I know, too, that in anywhere free markets exist, they do not solve all social problems. They require policies that can ensure economic fairness and basic human decency to those who need and deserve help.

Finally, I know that all democracies, the United States included, face new challenges from the emergence of the global economy and the information age, as well as from the threats posed by the proliferation of weapons of mass destruction, by organized crime, and by terrorism. But the answer is not to back away from democracy or to go back to isolation. The answer is not to go back to defining your national interest in terms that make others less secure. The answer is to stay on this course, to reap the full benefits of democracy, and to work on these problems with those of us who have a stake in your success, because your success makes us safer and more prosperous as well.

That success, I believe, depends upon three things: first, continuing to strengthen your democracy; second, improving your economy and reducing social and economic problems; and third, establishing your role in the world in a way that enhances your economic and national security interests, not at the expense of your friends and neighbors but in cooperation with them.

First, the work of building democracy never ends. The democratic system can never be perfected, because human beings are not perfect. In America today, we are engaged in a renewed debate over which decisions should be made by our National Government and which ones should be made locally or by private citizens on their own, unimpeded by Government. We argue today over the proper roles of the different branches of Government, and we argue over how we can be strengthened, not weakened, by the great diversity in our society. These are enduring challenges that all democracies face.

But no element among them is more fundamental than the holding of free elections. In our meetings today, President Yeltsin once again pledged to keep on schedule both a new round of parliamentary elections in December and the Presidential election next June. He has shown that he understands what has often been said about a new democracy: The second elections are even more important than the first, for the second elections establish a pattern of peaceful transition of power.

Therefore, I urge all Russians who have the right to vote to exercise that vote this year and next year. Many people sacrificed so that you could have this power. I address that plea especially to the young people in this room and throughout your great nation. Your future is fully before you. And these elections will shape that future. Do not fall into the trap that I hear even in my own country of believing that your vote does not count. It does count. It will count if you cast it. And if you do not cast it, that will count for something, too. So I urge you to exercise the vote.

But the heart of a democracy does not lie in the ballot box alone. That is why it is also important that your generation continue to demand and support a free and independent press.

Again, this can be a difficult, even dangerous process, as the people in your press know all too well. Dmitriy Kholodov and Vladislav Listyev were murdered in pursuit of the truth, victims of their vigorous belief in the public's right to know. You must not allow those assassins who targeted them to steal from your people one of the essential freedoms of democracy, the freedom of the press.

There is another challenge, a challenge of building tolerance, for tolerance, too, lies at the heart of any democracy. Few nations on Earth can rival Russia's vast human and natural resources or her diversity. Within your borders live more than 100 different ethnic groups. Scores of literary, cultural, and artistic traditions thrive among your people. And in the last few years, millions have returned to their faiths, seeking refuge in their stability and finding hope in their teachings. These are vital signs of democracy taking root.

Given your nation's great diversity, it would have been easy along this path to surrender to the cries of extremists who in the name of patriotism have tried to rally support by stirring up fear among different peoples. But you have embraced, instead, the cause of tolerance. The vast majority of Russians have rejected those poisonous arguments and bolstered your young, fragile democracy.

When Americans and others in the West look back on the events of the last 4 years, we are struck by the remarkably peaceful nature of your revolutionary transition. Your accomplishment, to go through a massive social and political upheaval and the breakup of an empire with so little brutality and bloodshed, has few precedents in history. Your restraint was a critical factor in paving the way for Russia to take its place in the global community, a modern state at peace with itself and its neighbors.

Now, it is against this backdrop, this great achievement, that we Americans have viewed the tragedy in Chechnya. As I told President Yeltsin earlier today, this terrible tragedy must be brought to a rapid and peaceful conclusion. Continued fighting in that region can only spill more blood and further erode support for Russia among her neighbors around the world.

Holding free elections, ensuring a free and independent press, promoting tolerance of diversity, these are some of the difficult tasks of building a democracy. They are all important.

But these efforts also depend upon your economic reforms. Your efforts on the political front will benefit from efforts on the economic front that generate prosperity and give people a greater stake in a democratic future.

To too many people in this country I know that economic reform has come to mean hardship, uncertainty, crime, and corruption. Profitable enterprises once owned by the state have been moved into private hands, sometimes under allegedly questionable circumstances. The demands of extortionists have stopped some would-be entrepreneurs from even going into business. And when the heavy hand of totalitarianism was lifted from your society, many structures necessary for a free market to take shape were not there, and organized crime was able to move into the vacuum.

These are real and urgent concerns. They demand an all-out battle to create a market based on law, not lawlessness, a market that rewards merit, not malice. Economic reform must not be an excuse for the privileged and the strong to prey upon the weak.

To help your government break the power of those criminals, our Federal Bureau of Investigation has opened an office here in Moscow. And we are cooperating with your government's attempts to strengthen the integrity of your markets.

Pressures in the market economy are also leaving some people behind, people whose needs are not being met and who are not able to compete and win, while some of the richest are said to pay no taxes at all. Those Russians who lose their jobs or who live in poverty deserve an economic and social safety net that is strong enough to break their fall and keep them going until they can get back on their feet.

Finally, market economies require discipline. Cutting inflation helps families struggling to become members of the new Russian middle class so they need not fear the future. Continuing your country's recent record of more realistic budgets is vital to achieving long-term economic stability. I say this from experience. From the beginning of my administration I have pursued these goals, because even though they require some sacrifice in the short term, they promise lasting economic growth that will benefit all of our people and yours as well.

The transition to a more honest and open market economy requires time. New problems will appear as your economy gains ground. But in the midst of the pain, I would urge you also to see the promise. Countries that were in economic ruin at the end of World War II today rank among the world's most dynamic nations because they have made a market economy and democracy work.

Finally, Russia's success at political and economic reform at home requires an approach to the world that reinforces your progress and enhances your security. Russia and the United States must work together in this regard. We must work for our common security. More than anything else, that is what my meeting with President Yeltsin today was all about, and we made progress in many areas. I would like to report them to you.

First, Russia agreed to implement its Partnership For Peace with NATO. And I agreed now to press NATO to begin talks on a special relationship with Russia.

The United States has made it clear that we favor a strong continuing NATO, that any admission of new members be based on the principles we have articulated along with our partners. It must be gradual and deliberate and open and consistent with the security interests of all of our partners for peace, including Russia.

My goal since I became President has been to use the fact that the cold war is over to unify Europe for the first time in its history. And that is what we must all be working for. President Yeltsin's decision to join the Partnership For Peace will support that move toward security and unity.

Second, the United States strongly believes that there should be no future nuclear cooperation with Iran. We believe that is in Russia's interest. Today President Yeltsin said that Russia would not sell enrichment technology or training to Iran because that could clearly be used to develop a nuclear capacity. And that should be more important to you than to us because you are closer to Iran than we are. I gave President Yeltsin some intelligence that the United States Government has that we believe supports the proposition that no nuclear cooperation in the future, not even the light water reactors, should proceed. And the two of us agreed to ask the special commission headed by Prime Minister Chernomyrdin and Vice President Gore to look into this matter further.

On the outstanding issues of arms sales to Iran, we reached agreement with Russia which will now permit Russia, your country, to be one of the founding members of the so-called post-COCOM regime, an agreement among nations to limit the sales of all dangerous weapons around the world in ways that will increase your security and ours.

Next, we agreed to immediately work to see if we could get our respective parliamentary bodies to ratify the START II treaty this year so that we could continue to reduce our nuclear arsenals and, after START II is ratified, to consider further reductions in the nuclear arsenals of the United States and Russia to make your future safer. We also agreed to a statement of principles on one of the most difficult issues in our security relationship, how we define so-called theater missile defenses in the context of our Antiballistic Missile Treaty—designed, again, to make us both safer.

Next, we agreed to begin visits to our biological weapons installations this August as part of our continued commitment to reduce the threat of biological and chemical weapons proliferation throughout the world. And if you consider what recently happened, the terrible incident in the subway in Japan, our future security and your future security is threatened not only by nuclear weapons but by the potential of biological and chemical weapons falling into the wrong hands as well.

And finally, in the wake of all those incidents, the problems in Russia with organized crime, and the awful tragedy that we had in our country in Oklahoma City, the United States and Russia agreed that we must work much harder in sharing information, sharing technology, sharing research in the areas of combating terrorism and organized crime.

This meeting was a success because every one of those decisions will give you and your counterparts in the United States a safer future. And we need to do more of this kind of work together.

As we close the door on this 20th century, the bloodiest century in the history of the world, I am convinced that the next century and your most productive years will be the most exciting time, the time most full of possibility in all history. The global economy, the explosion of information, the incredible advances in technology, the ability of people to move rapidly across large spaces, all of these trends are bringing us into a more integrated world. But we must all realize that these forces of integration have a dark underside.

In the 21st century, we will face new and different security threats. In the 21st century, I predict to you, there will be no world war to write about between nations fighting over territory. I predict to you that there will not be a new great colossus killing tens of millions of its own citizens to maintain control. I believe the battles of the 21st century will be against the organized forces of destruction that can cross national lines or threaten us from within our borders. We see these forces in the bombing of the World Trade Center, in the terrible tragedy in Oklahoma City in the United States. We see it in the bombings on the streets in Israel, designed to kill the peace process in the Middle East. We see it in that terrible gas attack in the Tokyo subway. We see it in the problems that you and so many other nations have with organized crime.

The more open and flexible our societies are, the more our people are able to move freely without restraint, the greater we are exposed to those kinds of threats. And so we must become more and more vigilant. We must work together to defeat these new security threats, for in this new century, the world wants and needs strong democratic countries where people are truly free and secure. And this world needs a strong and democratic Russia to help meet these challenges.

It is in that context that I have pledged to President Yeltsin we will continue to work on all the issues between us. And it is in that context that I urged the President to have no future nuclear cooperation with Iran.

Think about the future that we have together. We have already witnessed what Russia can do on the world stage when it is completely engaged and committed to democracy. From the Near East to as far away as El Salvador, America and the world have been made more secure by Russian leadership and cooperation. As Russia takes her rightful place, we believe that the trends toward democracy and economic freedom and tolerance must and will continue.

Yesterday your nation looked back at 50 years and paid homage to the heroes of World War II. Today let us look ahead 50 years to the next century when your children and your grandchildren will recall those who stood against the coups, who voted in free elections, who claimed their basic human rights and liberties which had been so long denied, those who made Russia a full partner in the global march toward freedom and prosperity and security. They will look back, and they will be grateful.

I know there are some in this country who do not favor this course. And believe me, there are some people in my country who do not believe that you will follow this course. They predict that, instead, you will repeat the patterns of the past. Well, of course the outcome is not assured; nothing in human affairs is certain. But I believe those negative voices are mistaken.

All sensible people understand the enormous challenges you face, but if there is one constant element in your history, it is the strength and resilience of the Russian people. You have survived in this century devastating losses in two World Wars that would have broken weaker spirits. You succeeded in bringing an end to a communist system and to a cold war that had dominated human affairs for decades. You have ushered in a new era of freedom. And you can go the rest of the way.

In the future, your progress may well be measured not by glorious victories but by gradual improvements. And therefore, in your efforts you will need time and patience, two virtues that Leo Tolstoy called the strongest of all warriors.

You must know in this endeavor that you will not be alone, for Russians and Americans share this bond. We both must learn from our past, and we both must find the courage to change to make the future that our children deserve. For the sake of your generation and generations to come, I believe we will all rise to the challenge.

Thank you very much.

NOTE: The President spoke at 6:12 p.m. in the Main Hall at the university. In his remarks, he referred to Viktor Antonovich Sadovnichy, rector of the university; Foreign Minister Andrey Kozyrev of Russia; and journalist Dmitriy Kholodov and television personality Vladislav Listyev, who were assassinated in Russia. A tape was not available for verification of the content of these remarks.

Statement on Trade With Japan
May 10, 1995

For more than 2 years, I have committed my administration to a bipartisan effort to open world markets. I have done this because where markets are open, Americans compete and win, and that means more high-paying U.S. jobs.

Over the past 20 months, my administration has made every effort through negotiations to remove obstacles to Japan's auto and auto parts market. Unfortunately, those negotiations have not produced meaningful results. Today we announced U.S. action in response to the continued discrimination against U.S. and foreign competitive autos and auto parts in Japan. I want to underscore my strong support for these actions.

At my direction, my administration will finalize a preliminary list of Japanese goods for retaliation. I also have directed Ambassador Kantor to send a pre-filing notification to the Director General of the WTO, indicating our intent to pursue a WTO case against Japan's unfair trading practices in the auto and auto parts sector.

Japan is a valued friend and ally. Our political and strategic relations are strong. Even in trade, we have worked together to promote successes in the Asia-Pacific Economic Cooperation forum (APEC) and the Uruguay round of the GATT. It is in the context of this overall strong relationship that we must directly address our differences.

Message to the Congress Transmitting Proposed Legislation To Amend the Gun-Free School Zones Act of 1990
May 10, 1995

To the Congress of the United States:

Today I am transmitting for your immediate consideration and passage the "Gun-Free School Zones Amendments Act of 1995." This Act will provide the jurisdictional element for the Gun-Free School Zones Act of 1990 required by the Supreme Court's recent decision in *United States* v. *Lopez.*

In a 5–4 decision, the Court in *Lopez* held that the Congress had exceeded its authority under the Commerce Clause by enacting the Gun-Free School Zones Act of 1990, codified at 18 U.S.C. 922(q). The Court found that this Act did not contain the jurisdictional element that would ensure that the firearms possession in question has the requisite nexus with interstate commerce.

In the wake of that decision, I directed Attorney General Reno to present to me an analysis of *Lopez* and to recommend a legislative solution to the problem identified by that decision. Her legislative recommendation is presented in this proposal.

The legislative proposal would amend the Gun-Free School Zones Act by adding the requirement that the Government prove that the firearm has "moved in or the possession of such firearm otherwise affects interstate or foreign commerce."

The addition of this jurisdictional element would limit the Act's "reach to a discrete set of firearm possessions that additionally have an explicit connection with or effect on interstate commerce," as the Court stated in *Lopez*, and thereby bring it within the Congress' Commerce Clause authority.

The Attorney General reported to me that this proposal would have little, if any, impact on the ability of prosecutors to charge this offense, for the vast majority of firearms have "moved in . . . commerce" before reaching their eventual possessor.

Furthermore, by also including the possibility of proving the offense by showing that the possession of the firearm "otherwise affects interstate or foreign commerce," this proposal would leave open the possibility of showing, under the facts of a particular case, that although the firearm itself may not have "moved in . . . interstate or foreign commerce," its possession nonetheless has a sufficient nexus to commerce.

The Attorney General has advised that this proposal does not require the Government to prove that a defendant had knowledge that the firearm " has moved in or the possession of such firearm otherwise affects interstate or foreign commerce." The defendant must know only that he or she possesses the firearm.

I am committed to doing everything in my power to make schools places where young people can be secure, where they can learn, and where parents can be confident that discipline is enforced.

I pledge that the Administration will do our part to help make our schools safe and the neighborhoods around them safe. We are prepared to work immediately with the Congress to enact this legislation. I urge the prompt and favorable consideration of this legislative proposal by the Congress.

WILLIAM J. CLINTON

The White House,

May 10, 1995.

Exchange With Reporters Prior to a Meeting With Opposition Leaders in Moscow
May 11, 1995

Q. Good morning, Mr. President.

The President. Good morning. How are you?

Q. Very good, sir. Does President Yeltsin have any reason to be upset at this meeting you're having this morning?

The President. I don't think so. I'm looking forward to this breakfast. I want to have this opportunity mostly just to listen to all these leaders talk about the conditions here in Russia, what the people are going through. It's an opportunity for me to learn and to reemphasize that I came on this trip because, first, I wanted to express the feelings of the United States on the 50th anniversary of the end of World War II and to finally acknowledge the enormous sacrifice of the Russian people and, secondly, because I am trying to increase the security of the people of America and the people of Russia in this partnership. So I'm glad to have a chance to have this meeting.

Q. What are you going to tell them?

The President. Just what I told you just now. I'm going to listen. I'm going to listen.

Q. Do you think you have—you've been emphasizing the security aspect of your trip. Do you think you've succeeded?

The President. Yes. We're in better shape than we were before I got here. It was a good trip.

[*At this point, one group of reporters left the room, and another group entered.*]

Q. [*Inaudible*]—did you run today, Mr. President? Did you run today?

The President. I didn't. I ran yesterday, and I was——

Q. What about today?

The President. ——in the gym this morning. I ran away from the weather. I worked out in the gymnasium at the hotel. I was weak today. I gave in to the weather.

NOTE: The exchange began at 8:45 a.m. at Spaso House. A tape was not available for verification of the content of this exchange.

Remarks on Arrival in Kiev, Ukraine
May 11, 1995

President Kuchma, Mrs. Kuchma, distinguished members of the government: It is a great honor for me and for our party to be in one of Europe's oldest nations and youngest democracies.

This trip, which follows my stopover here in January of 1994 and President Kuchma's trip to Washington last fall, will give us an opportunity to continue the tremendous progress we have made in building strong and productive ties between our countries.

This week in Washington, Moscow, and now Kiev, we celebrated an alliance that turned back the forces of fascism 50 years ago. Our victory was shared. But its cost to the people of the former Soviet Union was unique. On this land alone, more than 5 million Ukrainians lost their lives to the war.

Now, the tremendous will the Ukrainian people brought to the war effort is building a great future for this nation. The United States has an important stake in that future. A secure, stable, and prosperous Ukraine can become a hub of democracy for Central Europe and an important political and economic partner for the United States.

Already, we have seen what such a partnership can accomplish. Ukraine chose to give up nuclear weapons when the former Soviet Union dissolved. Your decision has made the Ukrainian people, the American people, and the entire world much safer and more secure. On behalf of the United States, I want to thank you for that brave and wise decision.

We have also been heartened by the bold steps Ukraine has taken over the past several months to foster free markets. Those were the right steps, and the international community has given the right response, large-scale assistance to help Ukraine stay on the path of reform. I want President Kuchma and the Ukrainian people to know that the United States and the West will stay the course with you.

I look forward to discussing the potential for strengthening the economic ties between our two nations. The private sector can be the engine of economic growth for Ukraine. And as prosperity takes hold, 52 million Ukrainians can become major consumers of our goods and services. That will produce more jobs, at better wages, in both our countries.

The United States admires the extraordinary progress Ukraine has made in such a short time. Building democracy and a successful market economy takes time and patience. Ukrainian people are demonstrating an abundance of both, and I am here to reaffirm our country's strong support for your courage and vision.

Thank you very much.

NOTE: The President spoke at approximately 3:25 p.m. in the Mariinsky Palace Courtyard. In his remarks, he referred to President Leonid Kuchma of Ukraine and his wife, Lyudmyla Niaolayivna Kuchma.

Statement on Extension of the Nuclear Non-Proliferation Treaty
May 11, 1995

Today in New York the nations of the world made history. The decision by consensus to extend indefinitely the Nuclear Non-Proliferation Treaty without conditions is a critical step in making the American people—and people throughout the world—more safe and secure. It will build a better future for our children and the generations to come.

Indefinite extension of the NPT has been a central priority of my Administration—the primary item on the most ambitious arms control agenda since the dawn of the nuclear age. For 25 years, the NPT has been the cornerstone of global efforts to reduce the danger of nuclear weapons. Today's overwhelming consensus in favor of making the treaty permanent testifies to a deep and abiding international commitment to confront the danger posed by nuclear weapons.

It is fitting that we should do this today. This week, all the world's peoples have joined together to commemorate the events of 50 years ago, when the Allied forces defeated fascism but much of the world lay shattered by war and shrouded by the dawn of the atomic age. After five decades of cold war competition and the specter of nuclear holocaust between East and West, the decision to make the Non-Proliferation Treaty permanent opens a new and more hopeful chapter in our history.

The nuclear danger has not ended. The capability to build nuclear weapons cannot be unlearned, nor will evil ambition disappear. But the overwhelming consensus in favor of the Treaty and its future attests to a deep and abiding international commitment to confront the nuclear danger by rejecting nuclear proliferation. This decision says to our children and all who follow: The community of nations will remain steadfast in opposing the dangerous spread of nuclear weapons.

I am especially pleased to receive this news in Kiev, for Ukraine's adherence to the NPT as a nonnuclear weapons state and its action to bring START I into force were major contributions to the effort to achieve indefinite extension of the Treaty. I want once more to thank President Kuchma for these important and positive steps.

This moment also owes much to the progress made by the United States and Russia in reducing and dismantling strategic nuclear arsenals. As one of the three depositaries of the NPT, Russia has worked closely with us and others to bring about the Treaty's indefinite extension.

This event is a victory for all. I want to express my appreciation to all of the countries who worked hard to achieve a successful outcome to the NPT Extension Conference, and who have made a decision that strengthens the security of every nation and of all people.

Message to the Senate Transmitting the Convention on Nuclear Safety
May 11, 1995

To the Senate of the United States:

I transmit herewith, for Senate advice and consent to ratification, the Convention on Nuclear Safety done at Vienna on September 20, 1994. This Convention was adopted by a Diplomatic Conference convened by the International Atomic Energy Agency (IAEA) in June 1994 and was opened for signature in Vienna on September 20, 1994, during the IAEA General Conference. Secretary of Energy O'Leary signed the Convention for the United States on that date. Also transmitted for the information of the Senate is the report of the Department of State concerning the Convention.

At the September 1991 General Conference of the IAEA, a resolution was adopted, with U.S. support, calling for the IAEA secretariat to develop elements for a possible International Convention on Nuclear Safety. From 1992 to 1994, the IAEA convened seven expert working group meetings, in which the United States participated. The IAEA Board of Governors approved a draft text at its meeting in February 1994, after which the IAEA convened a Diplomatic Conference attended by representatives of more than 80 countries in June 1994. The final text of the Convention resulted from that Conference.

The Convention establishes a legal obligation on the part of Parties to apply certain general safety principles to the construction, operation, and regulation of land-based civilian nuclear power plants under their jurisdiction. Parties to the Convention also agree to submit periodic reports on the steps they are taking to implement the obligations of the Convention. These reports will be reviewed and discussed at review meetings of the Parties, at which each Party will have an opportunity to discuss and seek clarification of reports submitted by other Parties.

The United States has initiated many steps to deal with nuclear safety, and has supported the effort to develop this Convention. With its obligatory reporting and review procedures, requiring Parties to demonstrate in international meetings how they are complying with safety principles, the Convention should encourage countries to improve nuclear safety domestically and thus result in an increase in nuclear safety worldwide. I urge the Senate to act expeditiously in giving its advice and consent to ratification.

WILLIAM J. CLINTON

The White House,
May 11, 1995.

Letter to Congressional Leaders Transmitting a Report on Democracy Promotion Programs
May 11, 1995

Dear Mr. Chairman:

I am pleased to transmit herewith a report on the democracy promotion programs funded by the United States Government. The report is required by section 534 of the Foreign Relations Authorization Act for Fiscal Years 1994 and 1995 (Public Law 103–236).

The report reviews the current status of U.S.-sponsored programs to promote democracy. As part of the Vice President's National Performance Review, agencies will be seeking ways to further streamline these programs in the coming months.

Sincerely,

WILLIAM J. CLINTON

NOTE: Identical letters were sent to Jesse Helms, chairman, Senate Committee on Foreign Relations, and Benjamin A. Gilman, chairman, House Committee on International Relations.

Remarks at a State Dinner in Kiev
May 11, 1995

President and Mrs. Kuchma, to all of our hosts, on behalf of all the Americans here, let me say that we are glad to be here and we thank you, Mr. President, for your warm remarks.

Mr. President, on my first trip to the Ukraine, I only visited the lounge at Boryspil Airport, and you promised me when we met in November that the hospitality would be even better in Kiev. Thank you for keeping your word and for this wonderful welcome.

Mr. President and distinguished guests, we had a very good meeting here today, but perhaps the most important thing which happened today, which both of us worked on, occurred in New York where the nations of the world made history. By indefinitely extending the Nuclear Non-Proliferation Treaty, we have taken a critical step in making the American people, Ukrainian people, and the people of the world more secure. More important, this action will build a better future for our children, for future generations.

For 25 years, the NPT has been the cornerstone of global efforts to reduce the dangers of nuclear weapons. Making the treaty permanent opens a new and more hopeful chapter in our history, a time when all nations will be more secure. We owe a great debt of thanks to the men and women who've worked so hard to make this possible.

This achievement was key goal of our foreign policy in the United States this year. And I want to say a special word of thanks to the representatives of my Government who worked so hard for this day.

It is especially fitting that we celebrate this event in Kiev, for Ukraine has been at the forefront of those nations that have been striving to reduce the threat posed by nuclear weapons. By your decision to eliminate the nuclear arsenal on your territory, to bring the START I agreement into force, and to adhere to the NPT, Ukrainian people have made a major contribution to reducing the nuclear dangers in Europe and throughout the world.

I once again want to thank President Kuchma for his brave and wise leadership. Over the last few days, we have spoken a great deal about the hardship and the heroism in the Great War of 50 years ago. This evening I would like to pay tribute to the courage and endurance of the Ukrainian people today. After a century of totalitarian rule, famine, and war, you have emerged to freedom and independence and set for yourselves the highest goals. In the face of a difficult, often wrenching transition, you have persevered and added honor to your nation.

I salute you, Mr. President, because you have played such an important role in maintaining the resolve of your people. Every democratically elected leader knows it is difficult to pursue a course that causes pain in the short run, even if it is best for the people in the long run. Mr. President, you have carried forth without wavering. An American President can look back on the experience of his predecessors over more than 200 years and know that others have walked this path before. But you are forging a new democratic tradition, untested and unknown but based on your judgment and your convictions. You have written a record of achievement and shown a determination that will be remembered long into the future.

This record should not and will not go unanswered. You have challenged us, and we are responding with strong support for Ukrainian reform. And we will continue to stand by you and work with Ukraine to fulfill its ambitions to become a prosperous democracy. Our legacy will not only be Government-to-Government programs but a genuine partnership between Ukrainian and American citizens, equal to the challenges of the coming century.

Ladies and gentlemen, let us raise a glass to the health and happiness of President and Mrs. Kuchma and to Ukraine, where one of Europe's oldest nations is building a vibrant new democracy, and to the growing friendship between our peoples.

NOTE: The President spoke at approximately 8:15 p.m. at Mariinsky Palace.

Remarks at the Menorah Memorial at Babi Yar in Kiev
May 12, 1995

Thank you, Rabbi, to the people of Ukraine, and especially to the veterans of World War II and the children who are here.

Here on the edge of this wooded ravine, we bear witness eternally to the consequences of evil. Here at Babi Yar, almost 54 years ago, more than 30,000 men, women, and children were slaughtered in the first 3 days alone. They died for no other reason than the blood that ran through their veins. We remember their sacrifice, and we vow never to forget.

In late September 1941, the Nazi occupying army ordered the Jewish population of Kiev together, with their valuables and belongings. "We thought we were being sent on a journey," one survivor recalled. But instead they were being herded to the ravine, stripped, and shot down. By year's end, more than 100,000 Jews, 10,000 Ukrainian nationalists, Soviet prisoners of war, and gypsies had been exterminated here.

The writer Anatoly Kuznietzov was a child in Kiev during the war. He remembers the day the deportations began. "My grandfather stood in the middle of the courtyard straining to hear something. He raised his finger. 'Do you know what?' he said with horror in his voice. 'They're not deporting them. They're shooting them.'"

Years later, Kuznietzov brought the poet Yevgeny Yevtushenko to Babi Yar. And that night, Yevtushenko wrote one of his most celebrated poems:

> Over Babi Yar there are no memorials. The steep hillside, like a rough inscription. I am frightened. Today I am as old as the Jewish race. I seem to myself a Jew at this moment.

These words speak to us across the generations, a reminder of the past, a warning for the future.

In the quiet of this place, the victims of Babi Yar cry out to us still. Never forget, they tell us, that humanity is capable of the worst, just as it is capable of the best. Never forget that the forces of darkness cannot be defeated with silence or indifference. Never forget that we are all Jews and gypsies and Slavs. Never forget.

May God bless this holy place.

NOTE: The President spoke at 12:12 p.m.

Remarks at Schevchenko University in Kiev
May 12, 1995

Thank you very much.

I first would thank Olexiy Meleshchuk for that fine introduction. I thank Olena Sheveliova for her fine remarks and for representing the university students here. I thank the rector, Viktor Skopenko, for his remarks and for the honorary degree, which I will treasure and display in the White House.

I am delighted to be joined here by my wife and by ministers and other important members of our administration, by the mayor of Kiev and members of your National Government, and by former President Kravchuk. I am glad to see them all here, and I thank them for being here with me today. I am deeply honored to be the first American President to appear before the people of a free and independent Ukraine.

Today we celebrate the alliance of our peoples, who defeated fascism 50 years ago. We shared victory then, but the cost to your people of that victory was almost unimaginable. More than 5 million Ukrainians died in the conflict. I am pleased that now after all these years we can pay tribute to the extraordinary sacrifice here in the Ukrainian homeland.

It is fitting that we are meeting at this institution, named for Taras Schevchenko. More than 30 years ago, America recognized his passion for freedom by erecting a statue of Schevchenko in the heart of our Nation's Capital. Now, at last, America also honors this great champion of liberty in the heart of Ukraine's capital.

I am also glad that we are meeting here at this university because so much of your nation's future depends upon this place of learning and others like it throughout your land. Here, the knowledge that Ukraine needs to build itself will be found. Here, the dreams of a new Ukraine will be dreamed.

I would like to say a special word to the students and scholars here. I know the times are difficult now, and I commend you for taking the hard road, for putting the needs of your future and your nation above immediate personal concerns. Your efforts will be repaid, for your independent country has a better chance to create freedom and prosperity than it has had in centuries, and to do it in a way that is uniquely your own as one of Europe's oldest peoples forging one of its newest democracies.

Ukraine is rising to the historic challenge of its reemergence as a nation on the world's stage. Already your nation can claim responsibility for a major contribution to global peace. Your wise decision to eliminate nuclear weapons on your territory has earned your nation respect and gratitude everywhere in the world.

Your accession to the Nuclear Non-Proliferation Treaty has sent an unmistakable message for peace and against weapons of mass destruction. Without those farsighted acts, the historic vote yesterday by the world's nations to extend the Non-Proliferation Treaty indefinitely and unconditionally would not have been possible. This will make the people of the world for generations to come safer and more secure.

For 25 years, this treaty has been the cornerstone of the world's efforts to reduce the dangers of nuclear weapons. I am proud of the leadership of the United States in securing the extension of the treaty. But I am also proud of the role that Ukraine played, and you should be proud as well. In the short period of your independence, you have helped make the world a safer, more hopeful place, and I thank you for that. [*Applause*] Thank you.

A few moments ago Rector Skopenko quoted Taras Schevchenko's question, "When will we receive our Washington with a new and righteous law?" The answer is now, because so many Ukrainians are striving to build a nation ruled by law and governed by the will of the people. Holding free, fair, and frequent elections, protecting the rights of minorities, building bridges to other democracies, these mark the way to a "new birth of freedom," in the phrase of our great President Abraham Lincoln.

Already you have held a landmark election that produced the first transfer of power from one democratic government to another in any of the nations that emerged after the collapse of the Soviet Union. You have put tolerance at the heart of your law and law at the heart of your state. You have claimed your place in the ranks of the world's great democracies, as demonstrated by the sight of your flag flying next to the American flag at the White House during President Kuchma's historic visit last November.

You have earned the admiration of the free world by setting on a course of economic reform and staying on that course despite the pain of adjustment. President Kuchma's decision to launch ambitious economic reforms and to press ahead with them was truly bold. We know that after so many decades of a command-and-control economy, reform carries real human cost in the short term in lost jobs, lower wages, lost personal security.

But your efforts will not be in vain, because the course is right, even if the path is difficult. The toil is bitter, but the harvest is sweet, as the old proverb says. In time, your transformation will deliver better, more prosperous lives and the chance for you and your children to realize your God-given potential. You and your children will reap the harvest of today's sacrifices.

In the pursuit of peace and prosperity, you have been well served by President Kuchma and his government's bold and farsighted leadership. You should know this: As you build your future, the United States will stand with you.

For America, support for an independent Ukraine secure in its recognized borders is not only a matter of sympathy, it is a matter of our national interest as well. We look to the day when a democratic and prosperous Ukraine is America's full political and economic partner in a bulwark of stability in Europe.

Fifty years ago, Americans and Ukrainians engaged in a common struggle against fascism, and together we won. When U.S. troops met a Soviet force at the Elbe for the first time and made that legendary handshake across a liberated Europe, the unit they met was the First Ukrainian Army.

Cruel events made that embrace brief. During the decades of East-West separation, it was left to a million Ukrainian-Americans to keep alive the ties between our people. They fought hard to ensure that the hope for freedom for you never died out. Today, their dreams are being fulfilled by you. And on behalf of all Ukrainian-Americans, I rejoice in standing here with you.

In the months and years ahead, our partnership will grow stronger. Together we will help design the architecture of security in an undivided Europe so that Ukraine's security is strengthened. We will increase defense contacts between our nations, consult with one another as NATO prepares to expand, and foster ties between Ukraine and the West. Ukraine has already taken a strong leadership role in forming the Partnership For Peace, which is uniting Europe's democracies in military cooperation and creating a more secure future.

We will work with one another as Ukraine becomes a full partner in the new Europe, and we will deepen the friendship between our peoples in concrete economic ways.

The United States has shown its support for Ukraine in deeds, not just words: in the commitment of more than a billion dollars in assistance over 3½ years for political and economic reform, another $350 million to help eliminate nuclear weapons, in leading the world's financial institutions to commit $2.7 billion for Ukraine's future and urging our partners in the G–7 to do even more. We will continue to work to assist you to build a brighter future.

Our nations have established vigorous trade and investment ties, and a group of American and Ukrainian business people are promoting these ties here in Ukraine this year and next year in their meeting in the United States. Together we will enter into exciting new ventures, such as a commercial space launch cooperation.

All these efforts will help to build a Ukraine that is sovereign and democratic, confident and successful, a Ukraine that will fulfill the hopes of your 52 million citizens and provide an essential anchor of stability and freedom in a part of the world still reeling from rapid change, still finding its way toward the 21st century.

Of course, in the end it is you who will make your own future. The people of Ukraine have it in their power to fulfill their oldest wishes and shape a very new destiny. To live up to that promise, to make the most of your role in this global economy in the information age, your ability to learn and learn and learn will be essential. And so I urge you to take to heart the words of Schevchenko: "Study, my brothers, study and read, learn of foreign things, but don't forget that which is yours."

Our two nations are bound together by a common vision of freedom and prosperity. Together we shall make that vision real.

As the great poet of our democracy, Walt Whitman, wrote a century ago, "The strongest and sweetest songs yet remain to be sung." Those strong, sweet songs are of free people fulfilling their hopes and dreams; they are the songs of Ukraine's tomorrows.

God bless America. *Slava Ukrainiy.*

NOTE: The President spoke at 11 a.m. at the Volodomyrs'ka Street Plaza. In his remarks, he referred to student speakers Olexiy Meleshchuk, Kyiv-Mohyla Academy University, and Olena Sheveliova, Schevchenko University; Viktor Skopenko, rector, Schevchenko University; and Mayor Leonid Kosakivsky of Kiev.

Message to the Congress Transmitting the District of Columbia Supplemental Budget and Rescissions
May 12, 1995

To the Congress of the United States:

In accordance with section 446 of the District of Columbia Self-Government and Governmental Reorganization Act, I am transmitting the District of Columbia's 1995 Supplemental Budget and Rescissions of Authority Request Act of 1995. This transmittal does not represent an endorsement of the contents of the District's budget.

WILLIAM J. CLINTON

The White House,
May 12, 1995.

The President's Radio Address
May 13, 1995

Good morning. It's good to be back home after my trip this week to Russia and Ukraine. I went there to join with two of our brave allies in World War II to commemorate the 50th anniversary of our victory over fascism in Europe.

Just as we did here at home this week, people all over the world remembered the sacrifices that protected our freedom and made our world more secure. But I also went on this trip to make Americans more secure in the future.

I want to take a moment to report on some of the highlights of my meeting with Russian President Yeltsin that will increase our security.

First, he agreed to move ahead with Russia's participation in the Partnership For Peace. That's the military cooperation program between NATO and other European democracies who all pledge to respect each other's borders and to work together to strengthen collective security in Europe.

Second, President Yeltsin agreed to cancel the sale of nuclear enrichment technology to Iran, which clearly could be used to develop nuclear weapons.

Third, we agreed to ask the special commission headed by Vice President Gore and Russian Prime Minister Chernomyrdin to look into whether Russia's sale of nuclear reactors to Iran could help to produce nuclear weapons.

Fourth, we resolved outstanding issues that will help lead Russia to close down conventional arms sales to Iran.

Fifth, we agreed to begin visits to biological weapons factories this August as a part of our common efforts to reduce the threat of biological and chemical weapons proliferation. This has particular importance to us now in the wake of the use of poison gas by a radical group in Japan's subways and indications that such groups all over the world are working to get access to chemical and biological weapons.

And sixth, in light of the tragedies in Oklahoma City and Russia's plague of organized crime, we agreed to share technology and information and law enforcement resources in increasing our common efforts to combat terrorism and organized crime.

One other important decision this week will also help to make this a much safer world for many years to come. The United Nations agreed to make the Nuclear Non-Proliferation Treaty permanent. This Treaty has been our main weapon in limiting the spread of nuclear weapons for 25 years, and now it will be in effect indefinitely. This was not an easy fight to win, and I am very proud that the United States led the effort to extend this essential and powerful tool in our common efforts to make all Americans and all people throughout the world more secure.

This week, besides working for a more secure world for Americans, we've also worked to open economic opportunities for our people throughout the world. The United States is deeply committed to open and fair trade among the nations of the world. That's why I have fought so hard in the last 2 years for the largest market opening initiatives in over a generation: NAFTA, the North American Free Trade Agreement; the GATT world trade agreement. I've worked to get our partners through the Asia-Pacific region and here in our own hemisphere to commit to free and fair trade by certain dates. And that's why I have fought to eliminate Japanese trade barriers that shut out competitive American products made by skilled American workers.

We've concluded 14 results-oriented agreements in 27 months to open Japan to everything from our apples to our rice, our telecommunications equipment to our construction services. And these agreements are beginning to pay off in terms of jobs and profits here in America.

But when it comes to selling cars and auto parts to Japan, we are still hitting a brick wall. Foreigners have about 30 percent of our market but only 4 percent of Japan's market, both for cars and for car parts. We've been hitting that brick wall long enough. Now we must act to protect and create American jobs.

In the United States, auto and auto parts industries employ nearly 2.5 million Americans and account directly for 5 percent of our total economy. But because of all the other products purchased by automakers, when we sell more cars, it has a positive ripple effect throughout our economy. Our efforts to open Japan's markets as wide as ours is good for American workers and American companies. It's also good for Japanese consumers, who today pay much higher prices because of their trade barriers.

Opening Japan's markets is a win-win situation for everyone. But old habits and entrenched interests die hard. For more than 20 years, every American President has wrestled with this problem. Our administration has talked with Japan for 20 months now. But there's a big difference between talk and results. I am determined to open Japan's auto market. That's why I've asked my administration to draw up a list of potential sanctions to impose against Japanese imports. We are prepared to act, and we will act soon if we must.

We don't want a trade conflict with Japan, but we won't hesitate to fight for a fair shake for American products. And I want to emphasize

two things: We seek no special preference for American cars and auto products over those of others. We want all, all countries to have equal access to Japanese markets. We'll always take our chances with fair competition.

I also want to emphasize that Japan is a valued friend and partner. We cooperate on many important issues, including efforts to open trade in other areas and to advance our common security interests. Japan should join us again. Together we must make sure that the future is not only safer and more secure but also prosperous, more prosperous for the American people and for people throughout the world.

Thanks for listening.

NOTE: The address was recorded at 8:50 p.m. on May 12 in the Map Room at the White House for broadcast at 10:06 a.m. on May 13.

Statement Honoring Law Enforcement Officers
May 13, 1995

You are gathered here tonight to honor the memory of 298 of your fellow law enforcement officers who laid down their lives to make our society more lawful and our lives more secure. In the finest tradition of America's law enforcement, every day these officers took to the streets and put the safety and well-being of other Americans above their own. By giving their lives to uphold the rule of law, these officers made the ultimate sacrifice to preserve our freedom. They are American heroes, and I thank them and their families on behalf of a grateful nation.

Tonight then, as you add the names of these brave men and women to the many thousands

of fallen officers whose names already adorn the walls of this great memorial, let us honor the memory of all of these officers by rededicating ourselves to restoring the line between right and wrong and purging our society of the dark forces that threaten our common peace, our freedom, and our way of life.

NOTE: Attorney General Janet Reno read the statement to participants assembled at the National Law Enforcement Officers' Memorial for the seventh annual candlelight vigil.

Remarks at the Peace Officers Memorial Service
May 15, 1995

Thank you very much. Thank you, Dewey Stokes, for your kind introduction, for your stirring call to continued vigilance in the cause of law enforcement, and for your 8 years of fine leadership of the FOP. I have enjoyed working

with you, and I know that I speak for all law enforcement, and indeed, all Americans who know anything about what has been done in this town in the last 8 years to fight for more sensible and more peaceful laws for our people, when I thank you for 8 years of service and congratulate you on what you have done. Thank you, Karen Lippe, for what you said. Attorney General Reno; Secretary Rubin; Senator Biden; Congressman Lightfoot; I see Senator Thurmond and Congressman Ramstad out in the audience—there may be others; members of the law enforcement community in the United States and their family members; and most especially to the fine families whom we honor here today for the awful losses they have sustained.

I am proud to be with you here today to honor the 157 men and women who died for their country, for law, for order, for peace and freedom last year. They will long be remembered for their service to our communities, to their families, and to the Nation. They were in every sense American heroes.

Just before I came out here I had the privilege of meeting with the family of Hank Daly, who was gunned down in Washington last November by a man who brought an assault weapon to the station house. To the Daly family and to all the families who are here, I say a profound thank you.

Today we pay tribute not only to those who died but to the families and friends who lost them and to the fellow officers who carry on the work that they did. We are here as well to carry on that work, to ensure that we live in a nation that is safe, just, and free.

Freedom has endured in this country for more than 200 years now because we have always recognized that we cannot have liberty without responsibility. If we are going to preserve the enormous freedom we have in America, the freedom to speak, the freedom to assemble, the freedom to bear arms, then all Americans must join in and join you and recognize that we cannot preserve the freedoms without responsibility.

If we aren't safe in our homes at night, if our children aren't safe as they go to and from school, if our parents and grandparents are afraid to leave their apartments, if our shopkeepers are afraid to go to work and stay there, if our police officers have to live in mortal fear every single day, then to that extent, my fellow Americans, we are not free. And it is not enough for citizens to say, "Fighting crime is the Government's job, and as long as I'm not violating the law, I have utterly no responsibility to help. I'll oppose any reasonable law enforcement measure I don't like. I will go about my business. I have no responsibility." Neither is it enough for people in Government to say, "We've gone so far; we can't go any further. Until our people, our culture, our values change, we'll just be too lawless and too violent."

My friends, violence in America cannot pose a choice between individual responsibility and social responsibility. The level of violence and crime, the death we mourn and honor today demands more of both.

Government's first responsibility is law and order, to prevent crime, to punish criminals, to give you in law enforcement the tools you need to do both. That is why I was proud to stand shoulder to shoulder with you last year to pass the crime bill and the Brady bill before it. The FOP and every major organization of law enforcement in our country supported and fought for those measures.

The crime bill, as Dewey said, will put 100,000 more police officers on our streets, prevent crime, and toughen sentences. And it will make clear, as Dewey called for, that anyone who murders a law enforcement officer from now on will face the death penalty.

Police officers like you engaged in community policing are the single best way to fight crime and to prevent it. I will not stand for any attempt to undermine our common efforts to put 100,000 more police officers on the street. I will not allow you to be outnumbered or to be outgunned. The Brady bill was the right thing to do. And it is saving lives in America today. The people who are against you and would not support you were wrong. We have evidence you were right, and we must stand with you.

And you asked us to ban deadly assault weapons for a reason. You were tired of seeing criminals like drug dealers use weapons of war to gun down police officers on our streets. We did that in a bill which also protected hundreds of sporting and hunting weapons. And because of the ban on assault weapons, every year from now on there will be fewer names on the memorial not far from here.

We have also done a great deal to increase the partnership between national law enforcement and those at the State and local level. For that I thank the Attorney General and the Secretary of the Treasury. I thank the Directors of the Secret Service and Alcohol, Tobacco and Firearms who are here and the FBI Director and all who have worked so hard so that we could do our part to help you to keep America safer.

But the guts of what we did was in the crime bill, the Brady bill, and the assault weapons ban. So when the NRA holds its annual meeting later this week, I want them to know they can pressure Congress all they want to try to repeal the assault weapons ban, but as long as I am President that ban will be the law of our land.

I also agree with the fine letter that President Bush wrote just a few days ago. Law enforcement officers in this country deserve our respect and support. No one has the right to run them down or to suggest that somehow it is all right for them to be put in harm's way. That is not the American way, and anybody who does it ought to be ashamed of themselves.

You never walk away from your responsibility. And your country is not about to walk away from you. If you're going to do your job on the streets, we all have to do a better job, not just here in Government but as citizens and parents. We have to do a better job knowing that we are raising children who understand that actions have consequences, who know the difference between right and wrong, who understand that they need to be part of a country and a community that looks out for them and gives them people to look up to, like all of you and all the men and women we honor today.

The tragic bombing in Oklahoma City last month first unmasked the evil that humans are capable of. But the incredible response of the brave people of Oklahoma City and those who came from all over America to lend a hand also shows us that in this country of ours, in the end, good can prevail.

Eight Federal law enforcement officials died in the line of duty in the Oklahoma City bombing. One of them, Al Whicher, a Secret Service agent who served on my security detail and President Bush's, had just recently moved to Oklahoma City, where we all thought he and his family would have a more regular and more relaxed life.

I will never forget the look I saw this morning in Mrs. Daly's face when she said, "I knew my husband was going to be in law enforcement, and I was proud of that. But I never expected this to happen to us." As I look across this sea of people wearing their corsages today, I'm sure that you never expected it to happen to you.

Let me say, first of all to you, that I know this is a painful day for you. And I applaud your personal courage in enduring the pain to be here. But you have set an example for your country by being willing to be here. You have let America see you. And as long as America sees you, we will not be able to forget what our duty is to those whom you loved and all others who do that work. Thank you for your courage for being here.

Here in Washington our duty is to bring the terrorists who committed the horrible act in Oklahoma City to justice. And we will do that. And we must do everything in our power to make sure such a tragedy never happens again. Because open societies all over the world are now more vulnerable to the organized forces of destruction and evil, whether they rise up from within our country or come here from without, we must do what we can to ensure that law enforcement has the tools to deal with this profound threat to our security and our way of life. I have sent Congress legislation that will do exactly that.

Last month, in the wake of the Oklahoma City tragedy, congressional leaders promised that I would have the antiterrorism legislation on my desk by Memorial Day. Since then we have seen disturbing signs of the old politics of diversion and delay. This plays into the hands of those who would blame the law enforcement officers who keep the law, rather than the criminals who break it. We make a grave mistake in this country, my fellow Americans, when we confuse responsibility in that way. And we must not tolerate it.

Come Friday, a month will have passed since the Oklahoma City bombing. Congress must act and act quickly. It would be a good way to honor the victims of Oklahoma City and the police officers we honor today if the Congress would say, "This is not a political issue; this is an American issue. We're going into the next century with the tools to fight the kind of outrage we endured in Oklahoma City. And we are going to do it without delay."

My fellow Americans, we can win the fight against terrorism, and we can lower the crime rate in America. We can reduce the number of law enforcement officers we have to honor here every year. And we can reduce the number of innocent citizens who are killed, the number of innocent children who are deprived of the chance even to grow up. We can do this if we will stand shoulder to shoulder, citizens and law enforcement, and do what we know works to lower the crime rate, catch criminals, and punish them appropriately. If every law-abiding citizen will raise a voice against crime and violence, that is the beginning of wisdom and progress.

So I ask you all today, never forget that the overwhelming majority of people in this country honor you, value you, care for your welfare and the welfare of your families. But never forget, until our job is done we must live with the burning reminder of the heartbreak of the families here today, and we must do our duty. No turning back. And we must not let any group in this country say that they don't have responsibility for improved law enforcement and a lower crime rate, that they don't have a responsibility to help, that they can ignore what you know works to save lives and build a better future.

You can be very proud of the progress which has been made in the last couple of years, not just here in Washington with the crime bill, the assault weapons ban, and the Brady law but on your streets, on your streets where in place after place the crime rate is declining. But we are a long way from home.

The happiest day in the lives of people in law enforcement will be the day when we can come here and have not one single solitary heartbroken family to honor.

Thank you, and God bless you all.

NOTE: The President spoke at 12:49 p.m. at the West Front of the Capitol. In his remarks, he referred to Dewey Stokes, national president, Fraternal Order of Police, and Karen Lippe, president, Fraternal Order of Police Grand Lodge Auxiliary. The related proclamation designating Peace Officers Memorial Day and National Police Week is listed in Appendix D at the end of this volume.

Remarks on Budget Proposals and an Exchange With Reporters
May 16, 1995

The President. First of all, I want to welcome the Members here for this meeting. And as you know, we're going to be discussing the budget. And we'll just make a couple of observations.

I have just returned, as you know, from my trip, and I look forward to having the opportunity to study in detail the budget resolutions passed by the Senate and the House—or offered by the Republicans in the Senate and the House.

Obviously, I believe that deficit reduction is good for our economy. It lowers interest rates. It promotes growth if it's done in the right way. We're using 7-year figures now. The last Congress reduced the deficit about a trillion dollars over 7 years, or about as much as the Republican proposals recommend.

I am concerned, as I have said repeatedly for months now, about three things. I do not believe that we should cut Medicare deeply, cut long-term care for the elderly deeply to pay for tax cuts for upper income citizens. I believe that we have to slow the growth of Medicare. I am glad to hear the majority in Congress acknowledging that, after 2 years of denying that

there is a crisis in Medicare; I agree that there is. But the proper way to do it is within the context of health care reform so that we can consider the implications on the health of our people, the welfare of our people, as we do this.

And the third thing I would say is that we have two deficits in the country that are hurting us badly. One is the budget deficit; the other is the education deficit. The most significant thing about America in the last 15 years is the stagnant wages of working people and the growing inequality among middle class people because they do not have the skills they need to compete in the global economy. So I don't think we should cure the budget deficit by enlarging the education deficit.

Those are my three preliminary observations. And I look forward to having the chance to study this and to work with them and with the Democrats in the Congress to continue to bring this deficit down. We must do that. We all agree with that. But there's a right way and a wrong way to do it, and we're going to be discussing that in greater detail today.

Budget Proposals

Q. Senator Dodd says it may be time to drop all proposals for a tax cut right now and to focus instead on deficit reduction. Are you willing to drop your middle class tax cut proposal if the Republicans drop theirs?

The President. Well, first of all, I believe that we can pay for something in the range that I have proposed with a dramatic—*[inaudible]*—deficit reduction. I think you could—I think we can achieve that. But I—I want to—that's my position, but I want to have a chance to meet with these folks today and hear from all of them, and we'll be talking more about this.

I believe that what I recommended is the right course. I'm prepared to hear from anybody else who's got any other ideas. My concern is, I don't want to see us just jump off the deep end on Medicare cuts without understanding what the implications are to pay for huge tax cuts which we plainly can't afford and which mostly go to upper income people. I do not believe that we can fix Medicare unless we have some idea of how the system is going to be reformed and what the consequences will be. And I don't believe that we should be eviscerating the education budget and making it harder for people to go to college and stay there, for example.

Now, other details and other issues—I'm going to review their proposals and evaluate them, and then we'll be glad to work with them and go forward.

Japan-U.S. Trade

Q. *[Inaudible]*—go in effect today. *[Inaudible]*—when you meet with Prime Minister Murayama you'll be able to resolve this matter and avoid a trade war with Japan that could affect security and other strategic interests as well?

The President. I certainly hope that we'll be able to resolve this. And as you know, we—the way this issue works—the Trade Ambassador, Mr. Kantor, will announce the details of what we propose. They won't actually go into effect if we can avert the disagreement with the Japanese. But if you look at the special problem of autos and auto parts and how long we have labored over them and how reasonable the United States has been for years, even for more than a decade, I believe that this is something we have to go forward on. The Japanese Government has acknowledged that we have important security interests and other interests in common and that we cannot let our entire relationship be left by this. That is a welcome observation by them, and I agree with them. But we can't anymore deny this or sweep it under the rug. We've got to go forward; we're going to do that.

NOTE: The President spoke at 9:04 a.m. in the Cabinet Room at the White House, prior to a meeting with congressional leaders. A tape was not available for verification of the content of these remarks.

Remarks on the National Performance Review
May 16, 1995

Thank you very much, Mr. Vice President, Secretary Reich, Mr. Dear, to our friends from Maine, all of them, for the fine work they have done. Congresswoman Norton and members of the DC City Council and others who are here, we're glad to be in the District of Columbia and in one of the most interesting workplaces I've been in in a while. I want to thank the folks who work here for making us feel welcome and for taking a little time off from work to let us come in and interrupt the flow of events. I'm sure that's not a terrible burden. [*Laughter*] I want to thank Mr. Gawne for having us here.

Mr. and Mrs. Gawne made us feel very welcome when we came in, and they didn't waste much time in establishing the productivity of their leadership by pointing out that they have 6 children and 14 grandchildren, and most of them are here today. [*Laughter*] I'd also like to say a special word of appreciation to the Vice President's reinventing Government team who worked so hard on this. Elaine Kamarck is here and many others who worked so hard on it; I thank all of them.

We have taken this business of trying to make the Government work and make sense very seriously. We have worked at it steadily now for a good long while. We think it's one of the most important things we can do to make the American people believe, first of all, that their tax dollars are not being squandered but instead are being well spent and, secondly, to fulfill some important public objectives.

Protecting the health and safety of our country's workers is an important national value. It's something we should all share. From the Triangle Shirtwaist fire back in 1911, which galvanized the conscience of our Nation, to the fire in Hamlet, North Carolina, in 1991—which I remember so very well because 25 poultry workers were killed there and thousands and thousands of people work in the poultry industry in my home State—we have recognized that we have a special responsibility as a people to ensure that workers are not put in undue jeopardy. We don't believe that anyone should have to endanger their personal health or their very lives to make a living for their families, to live a life of dignity.

But still, in spite of all the progress that has been made, over 6,000 Americans every year die at work. That's 17 a day. And about 50,000 more people die each year from exposure to chemicals and other hazards in the workplace. Six million Americans are injured, and the injuries alone cost our economy over $100 billion a year. So it is obvious that we still have work to do and that to whatever extent we can reduce death and injuries in the workplace, we will not only improve the quality of life in this country, we will also reduce the cost of these terrible tragedies in ways that strengthen our economy.

The Occupational Safety and Health Administration has been at work in this cause since it was created with bipartisan support in 1970. Since that time, workplace deaths have been cut in half. Cotton dust standard has virtually eliminated brown lung disease. Deaths of construction workers from collapsing trenches has been cut by a third. There have been many achievements that all Americans can be proud of. And today, we should reaffirm that commitment.

But we also have to recognize that like other Government regulatory agencies, OSHA can and must change to keep up with the changes and the times. We also recognize that any organization that is established and gets going in a certain direction, if it's not careful, whether it's in the public or the private sector, can wind up pursuing prerogatives that strengthen its organization rather than fulfill its fundamental mission.

That was the brilliance of the story that the Vice President told about what the Maine OSHA people did and how they changed, not only replacing yesterday's Government with a new Government that fits the needs of an information age that is less bureaucratic and that recognizes that the way we protected workers' safety in the last 25 years may not be the best way to do it in the next 25 years but also recognizing that, frankly, sometimes the rules have simply become too complex, too specific for even the most diligent employer to follow and that if the Government rewards inspections for writing citations and levying fines more than ensuring safety, there's a chance you could get more citations, more fines, more hassle, and no more safety.

So we believe that in this, as in every other area, we have to constantly innovate. And we're announcing these initiatives today.

Let me say to you that of all the things we've done in reinventing Government, this one has a particular personal meaning to me because of the experience I had for so many years as the Governor of my State. We were one of 29 States, first of all, that had a partnership with OSHA. And we worked hard to help implement the worker standards that the National Government set with State people who worked in partnership with manufacturers, because in the 1980's, when manufacturing was going downhill in America, we were increasing manufacturing employment in my State, partly because we had that kind of partnership.

I was interested in it from a human perspective because I spent so many hours, countless hours, in literally hundreds of factories in my State talking to the people who worked in the factories, watching what they did. And finally, I became personally acquainted with it because for several months in one year I was Governor, I took a day off a month to work in manufacturing operations. That will give you a clear perspective about wanting to be safe in the workplace. I worked in a food processing plant. I worked in a joist manufacturing operation. I helped to make refrigerators from 3 p.m. to midnight one night on a Friday night. And I even worked in an oil refinery. And it gave me a keen appreciation, first of all, for the need of people who are operating these things to be treated in a fair and sensible way by the Government so people could make a living and they could make a profit; and, second, for the absolute imperative for people to be able to work in a safe and secure environment.

Unless you've ever seen one of those huge metal stamping machines come down on a piece of sheet metal, you can't imagine what it was like to think about the days when people had to put their hands under those machines with no guards, knowing one mistake would be the hand would be gone forever. Unless you've actually seen things like that, it is hard to visualize what is at stake here.

We believe in this country that you can do the right thing and do well. We believe that is a general principle that we have to have throughout the economy. Mr. Correll, here from Georgia Pacific—I've been in every single one of his operations in our home State. And they have done some remarkable things. I believe you can do the right thing and do well. And we have to see day-in and day-out that we have a Government that makes sure we're all trying to do the right thing and that we can do well at the same time.

That is what we are trying to do today, saying to businesses, you have choice. You can put in place a health and safety program that involves your workers and that tries to find and fix hazards before an accident happens, and OSHA will be a partner. There will be reduced penalties or, in some cases, no penalties at all. You will be inspected rarely, if ever. You will get help when you want to comply. But if a business chooses not to act responsibly and puts its workers at risk, then there must be vigorous enforcement and consequences that are serious when violations are serious.

This new approach is not an abstract one. We have seen it. It works in Maine. If it worked in Maine, it will work everywhere else. To borrow a phrase from politics: I hope when it comes to worker safety, as Maine goes, so goes the Nation.

Secondly, we need to make sure that worker safety rules are as simple and sensible and flexible as they can be. You've already heard the Vice President say that OSHA will now allow plastic gas cans on construction sites. That may not sound like a big deal, but it's absolutely maddening if you're on the other side of a dumb regulation like that. Until now, OSHA required that work site first aid kits be approved by a

doctor. That doesn't make a lot of sense, So, from now on, you can buy one at the drugstore.

This is just a downpayment on the things that we intend to do. As part of the page-by-page regulatory review I ordered earlier this year, on June 1st, I expect to see dozens and dozens more rules on my desk ready to be discarded or fixed, including hundreds of pages of detailed standards that have literally been on the books unchanged since the early 1970's.

The third thing we intend to do is to extend our reinvention to the way men and women on the frontlines work with employees and businesses to promote safety. I'm interested in results, not redtape. The Vice President says that all the time. We're determined to make that the rule of the land in worker safety, in the environment, in every other area that we can possibly extend it to.

We're interested in prevention, not punishment. It would suit me if we had a year in this country where OSHA did not levy a single fine, because if that happened, we'd have safer workplaces, more productive businesses, we'd be making more money with happier people going to work every day.

We are going to redesign OSHA's offices, five of them every quarter, to produce safety, not just citations. We're cutting the time between the complaint by a worker and the resolution of a problem in half. We're focusing inspections on the gravest hazards. Already if a construction site has a strong health and safety program, inspectors are limited to the biggest hazards, lasting a few hours, not a few days. Now we'll expand that to other industries as well.

We want to use common sense and market incentives to save lives. Last year, the OSHA office in Parsippany, New Jersey, had an idea: Rather than finding a hazard, writing a citation, fighting for months about it, why not give the employer a financial incentive to simply fix it on the spot? That leads to more safety and much less hassle. Lives are already being saved there, too. And today, we are determined to expand this so-called quick fix program nationwide. There really are some quick fixes when you're dealing with stale bureaucracy, and we intend to find them all and put them into effect. Giving employers a choice, commonsense regulation, commonsense enforcement: that will be the new OSHA, the right way to protect the safety of people in the American workplace.

But even as we take these steps, we have to recognize that there is a very different approach at work here in Washington. The leadership of the new Congress is mounting an assault on our ability to protect people in the workplace at all. Responding to the entreaties of powerful interests, they are ready to throw the baby out with the bathwater and, in so doing, to put at risk the health and safety of millions of ordinary American workers. They're not trying to reform the system of worker protection as we are but instead to dismantle it and, therefore, to destroy our ability to pursue its fundamental purpose.

The budget proposed in the Senate would cut in half the funding for worker health and safety, decimating enforcement, research, and even compliance assistance, something that I've found in my own personal experience to be the most important thing of all with employers of good will. The House budget would even eliminate outright the National Institute of Occupational Safety and Health. They say they don't want redtape, but this is an agency with no inspectors, the National Institute of Occupational Safety and Health. They say we should be guided by better scientific evidence in our work, and I agree. This agency exists solely to give us better evidence to guide our work. The Safety and Health Institute does important work, it doesn't cost a lot of money, and we ought to preserve it.

The regulatory legislation moving through Congress, which was literally written by lobbyists who then wrote speeches for the Members to explain what it is they were introducing and supporting, would tie worker protection efforts up in knots. It would override every health and safety standard on the books and let special interests dictate the regulatory process. They have proposed freezing all Federal regulations and have gone after the worker protection standards with a little bit of extra gusto. They don't want rigorous reform. It looks to me like they want rigor mortis. [*Laughter*]

Now, I am the last person in the world to stand up here and defend some dumb rule, regulation, or practice or people who say that people who are elected come and go; we'll be here in this agency forever; you do it our way or not at all. But we have proved, we have proved that most Federal employees want to do the right thing, that they want the American people to do right and to do well. We have proved that we can change the culture of bureaucracy. And we're going to do more of it.

So we should reform. We absolutely should. But we should not roll back our commitment to worker safety. Remember, there's still a lot of folks out there working in situations that are dangerous. And not every workplace can be made 100 percent safe. I know that. And workers have a responsibility to take care of their own safety and to be careful and to be diligent. I know that. But we have a public responsibility that all of us share as Americans to work for safer workplaces.

If we take that seriously and we apply ourselves to the task in the way the Vice President and the Secretary of Labor have outlined today, if we follow the example of the fine OSHA leaders, business leaders, union leaders like those we recognized in Maine today, we can do what we need to do. We can do what we need to do and still pursue the public interest.

We do not have to grow the American economy by going back to the time when we acted as if worker safety doesn't matter. It does matter. It matters a lot to people. And just because the Government has been slow on the uptake in the past, and every now and then somebody makes a mistake and overreaches, doesn't mean we can walk away from our fundamental public duty.

So let's continue on this path. Let's change this thing. Let's make it work. Let's lift unnecessary burdens and keep making sure we're committed to the health and welfare of the American workers so we can do right and do well.

Thank you very much.

NOTE: The President spoke at 12:48 p.m. at the Stromberg Sheet Metal Works, Inc. In his remarks, he referred to Joseph Dear, Assistant Secretary of Labor for Occupational Safety and Health; Robert Gawne, CEO, Stromberg Sheet Metal Works, Inc., and his wife, Patricia; Elaine Kamarck, Senior Policy Adviser for the Vice President; and A.D. (Pete) Correll, chairman and CEO, Georgia-Pacific Corp.

Remarks on the First Anniversary of the School-To-Work Opportunities Act of 1994 in White Plains, Maryland
May 17, 1995

Well, Nancy, you may not be famous yet, but you're a lot more famous than you were 5 minutes ago. [*Laughter*] I wish I had thought of that Michael Jordan line; I'd throw the whole speech away. [*Laughter*]

I want to thank Nancy and Lorrie and the other students who showed me around this fine place and showed me what they do here. I thank you for that. I thank Secretary Reich and Secretary Riley for the work they have done to put this school-to-work partnership together with the Education Department and the Labor Department. I thank Senator Kennedy for his sponsorship of this legislation and your Congressman, Steny Hoyer, for the work he did to pass it. I'm glad to see Mr. Pastillo here, and I thank him and all those who have worked so hard on this. I'll never forget the conversation I had with the Ford CEO, Alex Trotman, about this issue in the White House not all that long ago, in urging more corporate involvement in business sponsorship of the school-to-work concept. President Sine, I thank you for being here and for the work that all the community education institutions in America are doing to help prepare young Americans to succeed in the global economy. They may be the most important institutions in the United States today, and I thank you for that. I want to thank all the State and local officials from Maryland who are here. Lieutenant Governor Kathleen Kennedy Townsend and Senator Miller, I'm glad to see you. And I know that, Governor McKernan, you shouldn't feel alone, there are lots of Republicans here today—[*laughter*]—county commissioners, members of the House of Delegates, county officials here, the sheriff, and others.

This ought not to be a partisan issue. And I thank you, sir, for your leadership. He wrote a fine book about it, which Mr. Pastillo referenced in his introduction. And Governor McKernan sent me a copy of it, autographed it, and I read it. And I thought if my dear mother were still living, she would wonder which of us were more successful, because she always thought whether you wrote books or not was a real standard of whether you'd done anything in life. [*Laughter*] So according to my mother's life, you've done something very important. And we are very grateful to you, sir, for the leadership you have given this movement all across America. The United States needs desperately for every young person in this country to have the opportunity that these young people have had. And thanks to you and your efforts, more will have that chance. I thank you.

I would also like to thank our host here, Automated Graphics. Thank you very much for having us here. We are grateful, and we appreciate it.

I want to say a little about this in a larger context. What we are doing here today to celebrate the one-year anniversary of the school-to-work program is really adapting to the information age in the 21st century one of the oldest traditions in the United States. Just imagine, for example—here we are in Maryland—what if we were here 200 years ago? You would be a young person living in a settlement in Maryland called Port Tobacco, which was then a big town around these parts. You'd be in a promising new country. George Washington would be your President. John Adams would be your Vice President. Pretty good lineup. [*Laughter*] And everybody would be optimistic. And most people would be like Nancy, they'd get up at 5 a.m. or 5:30 a.m. every morning and go to work. If you wanted a better job, you'd probably leave the country and come into town, where you would walk down a main street and you would look at the people who were working. Two hundred years ago, you'd see a blacksmith, a carpenter, and of course, a printer. If you wanted to learn how to do those jobs, you'd simply knock on one of the doors and hope that in return for hard work, you could get a craftsman to teach you those skills. That's the way it was done 200 years ago.

And for a long time, that's the way it was done, as one generation kept faith with the next. Well, we know that we can't exactly do it that way anymore, but if you think about it, that's what the school-to-work program is all about in modern terms for the modern economy. And it's very, very important.

This year, we are seeing grants that involve over 100,000 students nationwide, over 40,000 employers, including very large and very powerful employers in this country but also some very, very small ones. And there are over 2,500 schools all across America involved in this program. The act was a genuine partnership. It set up no bureaucracy whatever. It simply made grants to local partnerships, many of them in poor areas, and gave students the chance to show what their hard work could do.

This year, we are doubling the school-to-work funding for the eight pioneer States that already have programs. Seed grants will go out to 20 new States so that all 50 States will have some participation in the school-to-work program. By 1997, every State in America will have a school-to-work program up and running.

One thing that I want to emphasize that is very important is that the school-to-work program rests on a few very big ideas. One of the ones that's most important to me is that there is no choice to be made between practical workplace skills and academic knowledge, that the two reinforce each other and go hand in hand. When I was growing up, there was always this bright line between what was a vocational practical skill and what was an academic skill. It was probably a mistake then; it is certainly a mistake now. We have to abolish that line.

School-to-work is for all kinds of students. After high school, some will go straight to a job. Some will go on to a community college. Others may go to a 4-year college. Some who hadn't planned on getting more education will get more education because they were in the school-to-work program and because they see it will help them in their work lives.

Our country has enormous potential and a few very large problems. You know what they are as well as I do. You know we have too much crime and violence. You know we have major pressures on the family and the community in our country. What you may or may not know is that underlying a lot of this is the fact that more than half the people in this country today are working a longer work week than they were 10 years ago for the same or lower wages. And the reason is we have not created in this country the kind of education and training programs we need to adapt to a global economy, where everybody's earnings are to some extent conditioned on the pressures being put on us from around the world and where everybody's

earnings more and more depend upon not only what they know, but what they are capable of learning.

In the last 15 years, for example, earnings for high school dropouts in the work force have dropped at breathtaking rates. They're about 25 percent lower than they were 15 years ago. Earnings for high school graduates are not down that much, but they're also down significantly.

The only people for whom earnings have increased in the last 15 years are people who get out of high school with usable skills and have at least some kind of education and training for about 2 years after high school. It can be in the workplace; it could be in the service; it can be in a community college; it can be in a college. But you have to create this sense of ongoing upgrading of the skills if we're going to grow the middle class and shrink the under class in this country. If we could do that, a lot of our other problems would be smaller.

I want to emphasize again that this has been a bipartisan effort, which perhaps ought more properly to be a nonpartisan effort. After all, in the post-cold-war era, there are certain things that are critical to the American dream; growing the middle class and shrinking the under class and giving people the chance to help themselves is clearly that. We ought to have partisan differences over how best to achieve that goal, but we ought to be committed to that goal. And if you're committed to a goal, very often you wind up agreeing on the details.

For example, there's been a remarkable amount of bipartisan support in the United States Congress and in the administration on what the defense budget ought to be at the end of the cold war. Everybody knows it has to go down, and everybody knows it shouldn't go down too much because every time in our history we've taken it down too much, we have wound up getting ourselves in trouble, and we have to build it up all over again. Better to spend enough money to maintain the strongest military in the world to prevent bad things from happening. So we argue a little bit around the edges, but more or less we are moving in the same direction, because we understand that's important to our security. The same thing could be said today about the other problems we have.

We have two big deficits in America today. We've got a huge Government deficit, a budget deficit. But we also have an education and training deficit. And we can't solve one without the other. We ought to bring both into balance. We ought to get rid of both deficits. And I think we can.

In the last 2 years, we've made a remarkable amount of progress. Over a 7-year period, the budgets that were adopted in the last couple of years reduced the deficit by $1 trillion. Your budget deficit would be gone today, we would be in balance today, were it not for the interest we have to pay on the debt we ran up in just the 12 years before I took office. So this is a—what I want to say to you is that this idea of having a big structural deficit in America with our budget is a new idea, but it didn't happen overnight. And we can't solve it overnight, but we have to solve it. And we are moving on it, and we will continue to do so.

We also see in the last 2 years, thanks to Senator Kennedy and others, a remarkable bipartisan assault on the education deficit: big increase in Head Start, the Goals 2000 initiative, which is designed to see that more of our schools meet really high standards and that we measure them and tell people the truth about how our schools are doing, but that we help our schools to achieve those standards through grassroots reforms. We've reformed the student loan program, to lower the cost of college loans, make the repayment terms easier but be tougher on collecting the bills so that the defaults have gone from $2.8 billion a year down to $1 billion a year, but we're making more loans to more young people at lower costs. Those are the kinds of things that we did, all in a bipartisan manner.

Now we've asked the Congress to collapse a lot of these training programs into a big voucher so that when someone loses a job or if someone's working for a very low wage and they need to go back to the community college or participate in a program like this, they can just get a voucher from the Government and use it for 2 years to get training throughout a lifetime. Because all of you who are in this program, you'll have to continue to upgrade your skills over the course of your working life if the objective is to have good jobs, good jobs, good jobs. These are all things that we have been doing together, and we need to continue to do it.

There is this bill that I have spoken about, this rescission bill. I want to tell you about it. A rescission bill is a bill that cuts the budget in the year where you're in right now. That's what this rescission bill—the rescission bill proposes cuts to the present budget year. I believe we ought to make some more cuts. We've got to keep bringing the deficit down. The problem I have with the rescission bill that was reported out of the conference committee between the Senate and the House is that it makes the education deficit worse. And it doesn't even make the education deficit worse to reduce the budget deficit; it makes it worse to increase pork barrel spending.

Earlier this year, I worked with the United States Senate on a rescission bill which would cut exactly the same amount in Federal spending as this bill does and provide needed funds to the Federal Emergency Management Agency to deal with the horrible problem in Oklahoma City, to help to finish the work of rebuilding California after the earthquake, to help us to fight domestic terrorism, to do things that really need to be done and still reduce the deficit.

But there's a right way and wrong way to do it. I think you have to cut pork barrel projects before you cut people. Unfortunately in this conference committee, what was, I think, a pretty good bill became a bad bill. It cuts our efforts to help people and puts pork back in the bill.

I want more than $16 billion in spending cuts, but there's a wrong way and right way to do it. This bill that came out of the committee cuts our efforts to make sure our schools are safe, drug-free, which is a big deal in a lot of places in America. It cuts our efforts to help our schools meet new higher standards through innovative reforms, cuts our efforts to provide college aid to young people who will work in community service projects in AmeriCorps, the national service program, and, yes, it also cuts the school-to-work programs.

Now, in this bill, they found a way to pay for $1.5 billion worth of courthouses and special-interest highway projects and other low-priority spending. They kept in the law an unforgivable tax loophole which lets billionaires beat their U.S. taxes by giving up their citizenship after they've earned the money as American citizens. But they cut more from education, away from the Senate bill that I had already agreed to.

Now, I believe a bill that cuts education to put in pork is the wrong way to balance the budget, and I will veto it. We should be cutting pork to give more people like these young people standing behind me a chance to be at school-to-work.

I want to make it very clear: I am not against cutting spending. I have a bill right here which will cut out their pork, restore education, and reduce the deficit by more than the bill they're sending to my desk. So, yes, I'm going to veto that bill, but I want them to pass this bill. Let's cut the deficit and put education back.

I want to say this again: I have no problem with cutting spending. I've been doing it for 2 years. We've got to keep doing it. This proposal cuts the pork, restores education, and reduces the deficit by more than they propose to do it. So, yes, I will veto the rescission bill, but I want to cut the spending. And I will send this to Congress immediately. We shouldn't—we shouldn't be cutting education to build courthouses. We should be cutting courthouses to build education. That is the right way to do it.

Let me also say that in the bill that went into this conference committee between the House and the Senate there was a so-called lockbox, which I supported, which basically said, if we're going to cut this spending, let's reduce the deficit. Let's don't spend—let's don't take these cuts and put them into paying for tax cuts when we've still got a big budget deficit. The lockbox was taken out in the conference, too, and I think that was a big mistake.

You know, we cut some other things that weren't all that easy to cut because we thought we had to bring the deficit down. I don't think we should start by getting our priorities reversed.

And finally, let me just mention, I was with Congressman Hoyer on Earth Day not very long ago, and I was in Maryland. We talked about the environment. There's another thing which is in this bill which I really object to, which would basically direct us to make timber sales to large companies, subsidized by the taxpayers, mostly in the Pacific Northwest, that will essentially throw out all of our environmental laws and the protections that we have that surround such timber sales. It will also put us back into the courts. So it would seem to allow to cut more timber, but actually it means lawsuits and threats to the environment.

I don't want to spend too much of your time on it, but this kept our country tied up in court for years and years. We finally got out of court with a plan that would cut trees, save the environment, and help communities in logging areas to go through economic transformation to diversify their economy. That is the right way to do this.

So let's go back and make this bill what it ought to be, a deficit reduction bill that also takes care of Oklahoma City, the California earthquake, the terrorism threat, and reduces the deficit and keeps programs like school-to-work in place. That is the proper way to do it.

Remember, we have two great deficits. It is true that for the first time in our history we let the budget deficit get out of hand. That is true. We are bringing it down. We've got to bring the budget to balance. That is true. But you cannot do it by ignoring the fact that one of the reasons that we're hurting is that people aren't making enough money. And when they don't make much money, they don't pay much taxes, and that also increases government deficits not just in Washington but at the Statehouse in Maryland, in the local school districts, in the local communities, in the local counties.

We have to attach both of these deficits together. And we can do it. This is a very great country, and this is not the biggest problem in the world. This is not the Second World War; this is not the Great Depression; this is not the Civil War. We do not need to throw up our hands. We do not need to get into a shouting match about it. And we ought to be able to agree, just as we agreed on the goal of national security to win the cold war, that we are going to win the war for the American dream in the 21st century by getting rid of both of these deficits, the budget deficit and the education deficit. You have helped us by being here today.

Thank you, and God bless you all.

NOTE: The President spoke at 12:28 p.m. at Automated Graphics Systems, Inc. In his remarks, he referred to school-to-work students Nancyann Kesting and Lorrie Long; Peter J. Pastillo, executive vice president, Ford Motor Co.; John Sine, president, Charles County Community College; and former Maine Governor John McKernan, Jr., chairman, Jobs for America's Graduates.

Statement on Secretary of Commerce Ronald H. Brown
May 17, 1995

Secretary Brown's success as Secretary of Commerce is unparalleled. Through his service, the Department has expanded opportunities for American businesses in this country and abroad. I know him to be a dedicated public servant. The Attorney General has determined that the facts warrant the appointment of an independent

counsel. As I have noted in the past, the legal standard for such an appointment is low. I am confident at the conclusion of the process, the independent counsel will find no wrongdoing by Secretary Brown. In the interim, I value his continued service on behalf of this country.

Letter to Congressional Leaders Reporting on Iraq's Compliance With United Nations Security Council Resolutions
May 17, 1995

Dear Mr. Speaker: (Dear Mr. President:)

Consistent with the Authorization for Use of Military Force Against Iraq Resolution (Public Law 102–1), and as part of my effort to keep the Congress fully informed, I am reporting on the status of efforts to obtain Iraq's compliance with the resolutions adopted by the U.N. Security Council.

Since its recognition of Kuwait last November, Iraq has done little to comply with its numerous remaining obligations under Council resolutions. At its bimonthly review of Iraq sanctions in March, the Security Council voted unanimously to maintain the sanctions regime on Iraq without change. We shall continue to insist that the sanctions be maintained until Iraq complies with all relevant provisions of U.N. Security Council resolutions. Ambassador Albright's trip to several Security Council capitals in late February solidified the support of a majority of Council members for the U.S. position.

According to the April report to the Council by UNSCOM Chairman Ekeus, Iraq remains out of compliance with its obligations regarding weapons of mass destruction (WMD). While UNSCOM reports that the elements of its regime to monitor Iraq's capability to produce weapons of mass destruction are in place, continued Iraqi failure to provide complete information about its past weapons programs means UNSCOM cannot be assured that its monitoring regime is comprehensive. Of greatest concern is Iraq's refusal to account for 17 tons of biological growth media which could be used to

produce biological weapons. According to UNSCOM, ". . . the only conclusion that can be drawn is that there is a high risk that they (the media) had been purchased and in part used for proscribed purposes—the production of agents for biological weapons." Iraq disingenuously continues to claim that it has never had a biological weapons program.

At the same time, the International Atomic Energy Agency (IAEA), continues to investigate reports that Iraq has restarted its nuclear weapons program. According to press reports, a dissident Iraqi nuclear scientist passed documents to the IAEA which suggest Iraq has restarted its prohibited research into nuclear weapons production. This information is very preliminary; the IAEA's investigation continues.

In addition to failing to comply with the WMD provisions of Security Council resolutions, the regime remains in violation of numerous other Security Council requirements. The regime has failed to be forthcoming with information on hundreds of Kuwaitis and third-country nationals missing since the Iraqi occupation. As I previously reported, the Kuwaiti government submitted to the Secretary General a list of the military equipment looted from Kuwait during the war. Iraq has still not taken steps to return this or other Kuwaiti property stolen during the occupation, with the exception of one Kuwaiti C–130 and a small number of military vehicles, all in derelict condition. Ambassador Albright has presented to the Council evidence acquired during Iraq's troop movements last October that proves that hundreds of pieces of Kuwaiti military hardware remain in the arsenals of Saddam Hussein's Republican Guard.

The Council on April 14 unanimously adopted Resolution 986, an effective means to provide relief for the hardship that ordinary Iraqis are suffering as a result of Saddam's failure to comply with Council requirements. The resolution was a collaborative effort of a number of Council members, including co-sponsors Oman, Argentina, Great Britain, Rwanda and the U.S., all of whom share a deep concern for the humanitarian situation in Iraq. Resolution 986 addresses all arguments made previously by the Government of Iraq to justify its failure to implement Security Council Resolutions 706/712, an earlier proposal to permit Iraq to sell oil to purchase humanitarian goods. Saddam Hussein's government immediately denounced the new Resolution and the rubber-stamp Iraqi National Assembly rejected it by unanimous vote on April 25.

The sanctions regime does not prevent the shipment of food or medicine to Iraq. However, Saddam has chosen to squander Iraq's resources on his repressive security apparatus and personal palaces, while using the suffering of ordinary Iraqis as a propaganda tool to press for the lifting of sanctions. Resolution 986 undermines his self-serving excuses for neglecting the legitimate needs of the Iraqi people.

The no-fly zones over northern and southern Iraq continue to deter Iraq from using its aircraft against its population. However, the Iraqi government persists in its brutal campaign against its perceived enemies throughout the country. Iraqi forces periodically shell villages in the south and the north with artillery. In the south, Iraq's repression of the Shi'a population, and specifically the Marsh Arabs, continues, as does a policy of deliberate environmental devastation. The threat to the traditional way of life of Iraqis Marsh Arabs remains critical. In the last few years, the population of the marsh region has fallen sharply as Iraqi military operations have forcibly dispersed residents to other areas and thousands of Shi'a refugees have sought refuge in Iran.

The Special Rapporteur of the U.N. Commission on Human Rights (UNHRC), Max van der Stoel, continues to report on the human rights situation in Iraq, including the Iraqi military's repression against civilian populations. His work has also reported on the phenomena of political killings, mass executions, and state-sponsored terrorism. Clearly, the Government of Iraq has not complied with the provisions of UNSC Resolution 688 demanding that it cease repression of its own people.

The Special Rapporteur has asserted that the Government of Iraq has engaged in war crimes and crimes against humanity, and may have committed violations of the 1948 Genocide Convention. The Special Rapporteur continues to call on the Government of Iraq to permit the stationing of human rights monitors inside Iraq to improve the flow of information and to provide independent verification of reports of human rights abuses. We continue to support Mr. van der Stoel's work and his call for monitors.

Baghdad's attempts to violate the U.N. sanctions continue unabated. Since October 1994, 12 maritime vessels have been intercepted and diverted to Gulf ports for attempting to smuggle commodities from Iraq in violation of sanctions. Gulf states have cooperated with the Multinational Interception Force in accepting diverted ships and in taking action against cargoes in accordance with relevant U.N. Security Council resolutions, including Resolutions 665 and 778.

For more than three years, the story has not changed; the Baghdad regime flouts the sanctions, demonstrates disdain for the United Nations and engages in actions that we believe constitute continuing violations of Security Council Resolutions 686, 687 and 688.

We are monitoring closely the plight of the civilian population throughout Iraq. Our bilateral assistance program in the north will continue, to the extent possible. We also will continue to make every effort, given the practical constraints, to assist the populations in southern and central Iraq through support for the continuation of U.N. humanitarian programs. Finally, we will continue to explore with our allies and Security Council partners means to compel Iraq to cooperate on humanitarian and human rights issues.

Security Council Resolution 687 affirmed that Iraq is liable under international law for compensating the victims of its unlawful invasion and occupation of Kuwait. The U.N. Compensation Commission (UNCC) has received about 2.6 million claims worldwide, with an asserted value of approximately $176 billion. The United

States has submitted approximately 3,300 claims, with an asserted value of about $1.8 billion.

To date, the UNCC Governing Council has approved some 220,000 individual awards, worth about $870 million. About 580 awards totaling almost $11.7 million have been issued to U.S. claimants.

The UNCC has been able to pay only the first small awards for serious personal injury or death ($2.7 million). Unfortunately, the remainder of the awards cannot be paid at this time, because the U.N. Compensation Fund lacks sufficient funding. The awards are supposed to be financed by a deduction from the proceeds of future Iraqi oil sales, once such sales are permitted to resume. However, Iraq's refusal to meet the Security Council's terms for a resumption of oil sales has left the UNCC without adequate financial resources to pay the awards. Iraq's intransigence means that the victims of its aggression remain uncompensated for their losses four years after the end of the Gulf War.

In sum, Iraq is still a threat to regional peace and security. Thus, I continue to be determined to see Iraq comply fully with all its obligations under the UNSC resolutions. I will oppose any relaxation of sanctions until Iraq demonstrates its overall compliance with the relevant resolutions.

As I have made clear before, Iraq may rejoin the community of civilized nations by adopting democratic processes, respecting human rights, treating its people equitably, and adhering to basic norms of international behavior. The umbrella opposition organization Iraqi National Congress espouses these goals, the fulfillment of which would make Iraq a stabilizing force in the Gulf region.

I appreciate the support of the Congress for our efforts, and will continue to keep the Congress informed about this important issue.

Sincerely,

WILLIAM J. CLINTON

NOTE: Identical letters were sent to Newt Gingrich, Speaker of the House of Representatives, and Strom Thurmond, President pro tempore of the Senate.

Remarks at WETA's "Women of Country: In Performance at the White House"
May 17, 1995

The President. Thank you very much. Where I was raised we didn't know it was country; we thought it was the only music there was. [*Laughter*]

Ladies and gentlemen, country music vividly demonstrates America's fundamental ability to adapt and to change, to innovate, while never forgetting the best of our past in the mountains of Appalachia, in the hills and fields of the South, in the plains and deserts of the cowboy West. We took ancient folk ballads, we mixed in blues and gospel and came up with a whole new kind of song. As an American and as a southerner, I take special pride in seeing our country music now spreading all across the planet. And I'm very proud that our theme this evening is the women of country.

Our host has a well-earned reputation for nurturing and encouraging country talent, and for a little country homespun wisdom. He's worked with everybody from Hank Williams, Dottie West, and Elvis, to Dolly Parton and Paul McCartney. He's probably the best known guitarist in the world. Please welcome Mr. Chet Atkins.

[*At this point, the performances proceeded.*]

The President. Thank you so much. I want to thank Suzy Bogguss, Alison Krauss, Kathy Mattea. Thank you all, and thank all the wonderful musicians who played with you. Thank you, Kathy, for singing the song for me and the Secretary of Education that we love so much.

Thank you, Chet Atkins, for bringing so much alive to all of us. Thank you for bringing my old friend Randy Goodrun back. He's playing with a lot higher class musicians than he did 30 years ago when we started. [*Laughter*]

Ladies and gentlemen, in country music we truly hear America singing. It's the honest sound of our day-to-day triumphs and our heartbreaks, our joy, our sorrow, our love, and our hope. These women of country are using their power and their skill and their heart to make this music even richer and more compassionate and more wonderful.

Thank you, and good night.

NOTE: The President spoke at 7:44 p.m. on the South Lawn at the White House.

Remarks on Budget Proposals and an Exchange With Reporters
May 18, 1995

The President. I want to say something about the discussions now going on about the rescission bill. First of all, for me, this is not a partisan issue at all. This is about pork. And in this pork battle, Democrats aren't blameless either. This is about pork over people.

Now, let's look at what happened. I worked hard with the Senate to get a big deficit reduction bill that would protect people and education and our efforts to raise the incomes of the American people as much as possible. Then they went into conference behind closed doors and took out a lot of the people programs that will raise incomes and increase security to put in pork.

There's one congressional district with nine road projects in it. One courthouse cost over $100 million. And those two things alone will take over $200 million away from our efforts to make sure our children go to safe schools, to make sure that we can fund our national service program to let young people do community service work and earn money to go to college. There is even a project in there that gives a million dollars to a city street. Now, what's the Federal Government got to do in that?

You know, if we're going to bring this budget into balance, we're going to have to make a lot of tough decisions. We're going to have to have a lot of serious cuts. And we have to change the way we do things here, and we have to be very careful about how we spend the money we do spend. We've got to spend it on things that matter like education and training and building up the American people.

So, that's my position. If they'll get rid of the pork, we can have a bill.

Budget Proposals

Q. Mr. President, your administration isn't blameless, either, though, is it? These aren't pro-

grams that were just put in. These are programs that were put in the budget that you signed off on and Democrats approved. If it's pork, wasn't it pork then? Why did you approve it?

The President. Because we're going to cut $16 billion out. Because a $100 million courthouse is not as important to raising incomes as the school-to-work program to give young people who don't go to 4-year universities a chance to get good training, or as a program for women and infants to make sure they're properly nourished, or as a program to let our young people work in their communities and earn money to go to college. It just doesn't compute.

There's nowhere near—you know, special interest road projects, nine in one congressional district, are not as important as giving our teachers the training they need to make sure our students reach world-class standards in education. The judgments are wrong. If we're going to get serious about continuing the spending cuts and continuing the cuts in the deficit, moving this thing to balance, we cannot afford to choose pork over people.

It is a very simple choice, and it has nothing to do with partisan politics. And if they will fix it, we can have a bill.

Q. If they will put the AmeriCorps program back in and fully fund that, would that be enough for you? Would you then let the rescission bill go through?

The President. For one thing, on AmeriCorps, I didn't ask for AmeriCorps to be fully funded at the level that we funded it in our budget. I only asked that it be funded at the level that the Senate—the United States Senate passed a rescission bill with a bipartisan vote. And all I asked the conference to do was to leave the people programs, the education programs in at the Senate level. I asked the conference also to take out some very harmful language on the environment dealing with the forests in the Pacific Northwest which will cause us all kinds of legal problems and headaches. I hope that can be modified as well.

But I accepted some cuts in every—I think we're going to have to look at everything for cuts, but what I asked was that we not cut below what the Senate did. And what happened was, they cut below what the Senate did to stick in a bunch of pork projects. And that wasn't right.

And I want to say this: To the people of Oklahoma and California and Louisiana and the other States who need the emergency aid, they can get that aid today, they can get that aid tomorrow with more deficit reduction than is in this bill that came out of the conference

if the Congress will just take out the pork and put back the people.

Secretary of Commerce Ronald H. Brown

Q. Can I ask you one question on Secretary Brown? Are you concerned, sir, that the investigation of Secretary Brown and other Cabinet officials is giving at least a perception they haven't lived up to——

The President. Read what the Attorney General's referral said, and I think you will see why I asked him to stay on.

NOTE: The President spoke at 2:22 p.m. in the Oval Office at the White House, prior to a meeting with congressional leaders. A tape was not available for verification of the content of these remarks.

Message to the Congress Reporting on the National Emergency With Respect to Iran
May 18, 1995

To the Congress of the United States:

I hereby report to the Congress on developments since the last Presidential report on November 18, 1994, concerning the national emergency with respect to Iran that was declared in Executive Order No. 12170 of November 14, 1979, and matters relating to Executive Order No. 12613 of October 29, 1987. This report is submitted pursuant to section 204(c) of the International Emergency Economic Powers Act, 50 U.S.C. 1703(c), and section 505(c) of the International Security and Development Cooperation Act of 1985, 22 U.S.C. 2349aa–9(c). This report covers events through April 18, 1995. It discusses only matters concerning the national emergency with respect to Iran that was declared in Executive Order No. 12170 and matters relating to Executive Order No. 12613. Matters relating to the March 15, 1995, Executive Order regarding a ban on investment in the petroleum sector, and the May 6, 1995, Executive Order regarding new trade sanctions, will be covered in separate reports. My last report, dated November 18, 1994, covered events through October 18, 1994.

1. There have been no amendments to the Iranian Transactions Regulations, 31 CFR Part

560, or to the Iranian Assets Control Regulations, 31 CFR Part 535, since the last report.

2. The Office of Foreign Assets Control ("OFAC") of the Department of the Treasury continues to process applications for import licenses under the Iranian Transactions Regulations. However, a substantial majority of such applications are determined to be ineligible for licensing and, consequently, are denied.

During the reporting period, the U.S. Customs Service has continued to effect numerous seizures of Iranian-origin merchandise, primarily carpets, for violation of the import prohibitions of the Iranian Transactions Regulations. OFAC and Customs Service investigations of these violations have resulted in forfeiture actions and the imposition of civil monetary penalties. Additional forfeiture and civil penalty actions are under review.

3. The Iran-United States Claims Tribunal (the "Tribunal"), established at The Hague pursuant to the Algiers Accords, continues to make progress in arbitrating the claims before it. However, since my last report, the Tribunal has not rendered any awards although payments were received by claimants in late November for awards rendered during the prior reporting pe-

riod. Thus, the total number of awards remains at 557. Of this total, 373 have been awards in favor of American claimants. Two hundred twenty-five (225) of these were awards on agreed terms, authorizing and approving payment of settlements negotiated by the parties, and 150 were decisions adjudicated on the merits. The Tribunal has issued 38 decisions dismissing claims on the merits and 85 decisions dismissing claims for jurisdictional reasons. Of the 59 remaining awards, three approved the withdrawal of cases and 56 were in favor of Iranian claimants. As of April 18, 1995, the Federal Reserve Bank of New York reported that the value of awards to successful American claimants from the Security Account held by the NV Settlement Bank stood at $2,365,160,410.39.

Iran has not replenished the Security Account since October 8, 1992, and the Account has remained continuously below the balance of $500 million required by the Algiers Accords since November 5, 1992. As of April 10, 1995, the total amount in the Security Account was $191,219,759.23, and the total amount in the Interest Account was $24,959,218.79.

The United States continues to pursue Case A/28, filed in September 1993, to require Iran to meet its obligations under the Algiers Accords to replenish the Security Account. Iran has yet to file its Statement of Defense in that case.

4. The Department of State continues to present United States Government claims against Iran, in coordination with concerned government agencies, and to respond to claims brought against the United States by Iran.

On April 18, 1995, the United States filed the first of two parts of its consolidated submission on the merits in Case B/61. Case B/61 involves a claim by Iran for compensation with respect to primarily military equipment that Iran alleges it did not receive. The equipment was purchased pursuant to commercial contracts with more than 50 private American companies. Iran alleges that it suffered direct losses and consequential damages in excess of $2 billion in total because of the U.S. Government's refusal to allow the export of the equipment after January 19, 1981, in alleged contravention of the Algiers Accords. As directed by the Tribunal, the United States' submission addresses Iran's claims regarding both liability and compensation and damages.

5. The Foreign Claims Settlement Commission ("FSCS") on February 24, 1995, successfully completed its case-by-case review of the more than 3,000 so-called "small claims" against Iran arising out of the 1979 Islamic revolution. These "small claims" (of $250,000 or less each) were originally filed before the Iran-United States Claims Tribunal, but were transferred to the FCSC pursuant to the May 13, 1990 Settlement Agreement between Iran and the United States.

The FCSC issued decisions on 3,066 claims for total awards of $86,555,795. Of that amount, $41,570,936 represented awards of principal and $44,984,859 represented awards of interest. Although originally only $50 million were available to pay these awards, the funds earned approximately $9 million in interest over time, for a total settlement fund of more than $59 million. Thus, all awardees will receive full payment on the principal amounts of their awards, with interest awards paid on a pro rata basis.

The FCSC's awards to individuals and corporations covered claims for both real and personal property seized by Iran. In addition, many claims arose out of commercial transactions, including contracts for the sale of goods and contracts for the supply of services such as teaching, medical treatment, data processing, and shipping. The FCSC is now working with the Department of the Treasury to facilitate final payment on all FCSC awards.

6. The situation reviewed above continues to implicate important diplomatic, financial, and legal interests of the United States and its nationals and presents an unusual challenge to the national security and foreign policy of the United States. The Iranian Assets Control Regulations issued pursuant to Executive order No. 12170 continue to play an important role in structuring our relationship with Iran and in enabling the United States to implement properly the Algiers Accords. Similarly, the Iranian Transactions Regulations issued pursuant to Executive Order No. 12613 continue to advance important objectives in combating international terrorism. I shall continue to exercise the powers at my disposal to deal with these problems and will continue to report periodically to the Congress on significant developments.

WILLIAM J. CLINTON

The White House,
May 18, 1995.

Message to the Congress Reporting on the National Emergency With Respect to Proliferation of Weapons of Mass Destruction
May 18, 1995

To the Congress of the United States:

On November 14, 1994, in light of the dangers of the proliferation of nuclear, biological, and chemical weapons and their means of delivery ("weapons of mass destruction"), I issued Executive Order No. 12938 and declared a national emergency under the International Emergency Economic Powers Act (50 U.S.C. 1701 *et seq.*).

As I described in the report transmitting Executive Order No. 12938, the new Executive order consolidated the functions of and revoked Executive Order No. 12735 of November 16, 1990, which declared a national emergency with respect to the proliferation of chemical and biological weapons, and Executive Order No. 12930 of September 29, 1994, which declared a national emergency with respect to nuclear, biological, and chemical weapons, and their means of delivery. The new Executive order also expanded certain existing authorities in order to strengthen the U.S. ability to respond to proliferation problems.

The following report is made pursuant to section 204 of the International Emergency Economic Powers Act and section 401(c) of the National Emergencies Act regarding activities taken and money spent pursuant to the emergency declaration. Additional information on nuclear, missile, and/or chemical and biological weapons (CBW) nonproliferation efforts is contained in the annual report on the proliferation of missiles and essential components of nuclear, biological, and chemical weapons, provided to the Congress pursuant to section 1097 of the National Defense Authorization Act for Fiscal Years 1992 and 1993 (Public Law 102–190), also known as the "Nonproliferation Report," and the annual report provided to the Congress pursuant to section 308 of the Chemical and Biological Weapons Control and Warfare Elimination Act of 1991 (Public Law 102–182).

The three export control regulations issued under the Enhanced Proliferation Control Initiative (EPCI) are fully in force and continue to be used to control the export of items with potential use in chemical or biological weapons or unmanned delivery systems for weapons of mass destruction.

In the 6 months since I issued Executive Order No. 12938, the number of countries that have ratified the Chemical Weapons Convention (CWC) has reached 27 (out of 159 signatory countries). I am urging the Senate to give its advice and consent to ratification as soon as possible. The CWC is a critical element of U.S. nonproliferation policy that will significantly enhance our security and that of our friends and allies. I believe that U.S. ratification will help to encourage the ratification process in other countries and, ultimately, the CWC's entry into force.

The United States actively participates in the CWC Preparatory Commission in The Hague, the deliberative body drafting administrative and implementing procedures for the CWC. Last month, this body accepted the U.S. offer of an information management system for the future Organization for the Prohibition of Chemical Weapons that will implement the CWC. The United States also is playing a leading role in developing a training program for international inspectors.

The United States strongly supports international efforts to strengthen the 1972 Biological and Toxin Weapons Convention (BWC). In January 1995, the Ad Hoc Group mandated by the September 1994 BWC Special Conference to draft a legally binding instrument to strengthen the effectiveness and improve the implementation of the BWC held its first meeting. The Group agreed on a program of work and schedule of substantive meetings, the first of which will occur in July 1995. The United States is pressing for completion of the Ad Hoc Group's work and consideration of the legally binding instrument by the next BWC Review Conference in 1996.

The United States maintained its active participation in the 29-member Australia Group (AG), which now includes the Czech Republic, Poland, Slovakia, and Romania. The AG reaffirmed in December the member's collective belief that full adherence to the CWC and the BWC provides the only means to achieve a permanent global ban on CBW, and that all states adhering to these Conventions have an obligation to ensure that their national activities support these goals.

The AG also reiterated its conviction that harmonized AG export licensing measures are consistent with, and indeed actively support, the requirement under Article I of the CWC that States Parties never assist, in any way, the manufacture of chemical weapons. These measures also are consistent with the undertaking in Article XI of the CWC to facilitate the fullest possible exchange of chemical materials and related information for purposes not prohibited by the Convention, as they focus solely on preventing assistance to activities banned under the CWC. Similarly, such efforts also support existing nonproliferation obligations under the BWC.

The United States Government determined that three foreign nationals (Luciano Moscatelli, Manfred Felber, and Gerhard Merz) had engaged in chemical weapons proliferation activities that required the imposition of sanctions against them, effective on November 19, 1994. Similar determinations were made against three foreign companies (Asian Ways Limited, Mainway International, and Worldco) effective on February 18, 1995, and imposed sanctions against them. Additional information on these determinations is contained in a classified report to the Congress, provided pursuant to the Chemical and Biological Weapons Control and Warfare Elimination Act of 1991. The United States Government continues to monitor closely activities that may be subject to CBW sanctions provisions.

The United States continued to control vigilantly U.S. exports that could make a contribution to unmanned delivery systems for weapons of mass destruction, exercising restraint in considering all such transfers consistent with the Guidelines of the Missile Technology Control Regime (MTCR). The MTCR Partners shared information not only with each other but with other possible supplier, consumer, and transshipment states about proliferation problems and also stressed the importance of implementing effective export control systems.

The United States initiated unilateral efforts and coordinated with MTCR Partners in multilateral efforts, aimed at combatting missile proliferation by nonmembers and at encouraging nonmembers to adopt responsible export behav-

ior and to adhere to the MTCR Guidelines. On October 4, 1994, the United States and China signed a Joint Statement on Missile Nonproliferation in which China reiterated its 1992 commitment to the MTCR Guidelines and agreed to ban the export of ground-to-ground MTCR-class missiles. In 1995, the United States met bilaterally with Ukraine in January, and with Russia in April, to discuss missile nonproliferation and the implementation of the MTCR Guidelines. In May 1995, the United States will participate with other MTCR Partners in a regime approach to Ukraine to discuss missile nonproliferation and to share information about the MTCR.

The United States actively encouraged its MTCR Partners and fellow AG participants to adopt "catch-all" provisions, similar to that of the United States and EPCI, for items not subject to specific export controls. Austria, Germany, Norway, and the United Kingdom actually have such provisions in place. The European Union (EU) issued a directive in 1994 calling on member countries to adopt "catch-all" controls. These controls will be implemented July 1, 1995. In line with this harmonization move, several countries, including European States that are not actually member of the EU, have adopted or are considering putting similar provisions in place.

The United States has continued to pursue this Administration's nuclear nonproliferation goals. More than 170 nations joined in the indefinite, unconditional extension of the Nuclear Non-Proliferation Treaty (NPT) on May 11, 1995. This historic decision strengthens the security of all countries, nuclear weapons states and nonweapons states alike.

South Africa joined the Nuclear Suppliers Group (NSG), increasing NSG membership to 31 countries. The NSG held a plenary in Helsinki, April 5–7, 1995, which focused on membership issues and the NSG's relationship to the NPT Conference. A separate, dual-use consultation meeting agreed upon 32 changes to the dual-use list.

Pursuant to section 401(c) of the National Emergencies Act, I report that there were no expenses directly attributable to the exercise of authorities conferred by the declaration of the national emergency in Executive Order No.

12938 during the period from November 14, 1994, through May 14, 1995.

WILLIAM J. CLINTON

The White House,
May 18, 1995.

Remarks at the Congressional Asian Pacific American Caucus Institute Dinner
May 18, 1995

Thank you, Admiral, for that introduction, and thank you, ladies and gentlemen, for that rousing welcome. Can we do this again tomorrow night?

Thank you, Admiral. Thank you, Gloria Caoile. To all the Members of Congress who are here—I thought I had a list of all of them, but I can look outside there and see I don't. I have seen Congressman Mineta, Congressman Matsui, Congressman Underwood, Congressman Kim, Congressman Faleomavaega. I see Congressman McDermott out there—your Medicare hearing was great—[*laughter*]—I watched you on C-Span—all the Members of Congress. I want to know I'm watching you all the time on C-Span. [*Laughter*] I see Senator Inouye and Senator Robb, and there may be others here. And if I have not mentioned you, I am sorry, I apologize.

I'm delighted to see your co-emcees here. First, Ming-Na Wen, whom I first saw in the wonderful movie "Joy Luck Club" when Amy Tan came to the White House and showed it, and then my daughter makes me watch "ER" whenever I can. [*Laughter*] I was tired when I got here, and then I shook hands with her and my blood started pumping, so I feel so good. [*Laughter*] I'm especially glad to see George Takei, because I came here to talk about how we're going to take America into the 21st century, and he's already been there. [*Laughter*] This may be largely an academic exercise to him.

I'm glad to be joined by Secretary of Transportation Federico Peña and by Phil Lader, the SBA Administrator, and many others whom I will mention in a moment who are here tonight. And I also—I met the board members, or at least several of them, on the way in tonight. I want to thank all of you for serving and for constituting this organization.

Hillary and our daughter, Chelsea, just got back from a remarkable trip to Southern Asia. They went to India, to Pakistan, to Bangladesh, to Nepal, and to Sri Lanka. I got a few shirts and a lot of pictures out of it—[*laughter*]—and a world of education, because I watched several hours of rough film footage of their trip. And I must tell you that it was an immensely rewarding thing for them and for us, and I hope and believe it was good for the United States.

We are at an extraordinary moment in our Nation's history, not only for the Asian Pacific American community but for all of our people who understand that we're going through profound changes, economic and social changes, that we have great problems and great challenges but, frankly, more opportunities than any other country if we understand what an incredible resource our people are and how fortunate we are, on the verge of a totally globalized economy, to have perhaps the most diversified citizenry anywhere in the world.

If we understand that we don't have a person to waste and that we have to face our challenges together, there is no stopping the United States. I have been particularly gratified to have the services of so many people from the Asian Pacific American community in our administration. Many of you out here, I see, have accepted various appointments to boards and commissions, and many of you work full-time for the White House or the administration, including Doris Matsui in Public Liaison. [*Applause*] Listen, she gets a hand when I'm in the non-Asian crowds. I think she must be the best politician in the White House, certainly the best politician in the Matsui family.

I see Congressman Pastor out there, an Hispanic/Asian American Congressman; Maria Haley with the Export-Import Bank; Ginger Lew at the Commerce Department; Denny Hiyashi of HHS; Debra Shon with the Trade

707

Representative's Office; Paul Igasaki of the EEOC; and Edward Chow of Veterans Affairs. And tomorrow I will get a list of everyone in my administration I have omitted to mention tonight, and I will eat a lot of crow.

We are a nation of immigrants. Not very many of us can trace our lineage back originally to this continent. It is a good thing to recognize and celebrate that fact. That was the purpose behind Congressman Horton's tireless efforts to have the month of May designated as Asian/Pacific American Heritage Month.

I want to add my sincere congratulations to the well-deserved recognition Congressman Horton is receiving tonight. He did America a great service with this action. Thank you, sir. Stand up. Thank you. [*Applause*]

The month of May has great significance in Asian Pacific American history. The first week of May in 1843, the first Japanese arrived in America. On May 10th, 1869, Golden Spike Day, the Transcontinental Railroad, built in large measure with Chinese labor, was completed. Today, more than 150 years later, nearly 8 million Asian Pacific Americans can trace their roots to Asia and the islands of the Pacific.

As we face the challenges of the global economy in the information age, we turn to you for hope and inspiration. You know well about overcoming barriers and embracing change. You know well about the importance of preserving the traditional values of family and hard work, and sacrifice today for a better future tomorrow. And yet, you have shown the most remarkable ability to adapt to changing circumstances of perhaps any group of your fellow Americans.

Some of you are fifth generation citizens; others are the first in your families to call yourselves Americans. But all of you are willing to work hard to overcome obstacles to pursue the American dream. As immigrants and the descendants of legal immigrants, you understand, perhaps more than most, what it means to take on the responsibility of facing up to building a new life in a difficult and new circumstance.

As we debate immigration policy in this country—and we should, and we all know that we have a problem of illegal immigration which undermines the support that has traditionally existed in America for legal immigration, at least in modern times—we should all remember something that President Kennedy once said in describing the value of immigration, and I'd like

to quote: "Immigration gave every old American a standard by which to judge how far he had come, and every new American a realization of how far he might go." It reminded every American, old and new, that change is the essence of life and that American society is a process, not a conclusion. Let us remember that today in this time. We welcome your creativity, your contributions, and your criticisms as we struggle to prepare all Americans for the coming century.

For the past 2 years I have been focused—some would say obsessed—with getting our people to do the things that I believe we must do to move into the next century. I think that what we have to do does not fall easily into the categories of established political debate or even into the established agendas of the political parties. The future should not belong to Republicans or Democrats; it should belong to all Americans who are willing to do what has to be done to keep the American dream alive.

In the next century, we have to face the fact that we will have more opportunities than ever before but that there will be challenges that are different than we have faced before. We will have to face the fact that wealth and success will not only depend upon hard work, it will require more smart work. We will have to face some new and different challenges to our security, for the information age requires us to be more open, more flexible, more mobile, to be able to get more information more quickly, to democratize access to all kinds of facts that previously were the province of the privileged few.

But we know that as we do that, we give rise to new security challenges, for the open and flexible and fast-moving society is very vulnerable to the forces of organized destruction. We saw that most heartbreakingly recently in Oklahoma City. We live with the bitter aftertaste of the World Trade Center. And our hearts ache with the Japanese people when they endured the ability of one fanatic to go into the subway and break open a vial of poison gas and kill several people and hospitalize hundreds of others. All this is a reminder that in the 21st century we may be beyond the cold war, we may succeed—and that's what my recent trip to Russia was partly about—in completely removing the burden of the nuclear terror from our children and our grandchildren. But we cannot avoid organized, destructive, evil ,forces that will come at us in different ways, with the proliferation of biological and chemical and perhaps even small-scale nuclear weapons. That is what we must fight against. We must fight to protect the benefits of the open society with genuine security for all of our people.

I think you could argue that the last 2 years have been a good downpayment on the future we are trying to build. Our economy has produced 6.3 million new jobs. Finally, after years of stagnation, we're beginning to produce high-wage jobs in the economy again. Our deficit is down by over $600 billion over a 5-year period. Today, our Government's budget would be balanced—today—but for the interest payments we are required to make this year on the debt run up between 1981 and the end of 1992. So we are moving in the right direction.

We are shrinking the size of the Federal Government. It's over 100,000 people smaller than it was when I came here, and we're going to shrink it by much, much more. But I would say to you again, in the wake of what we have seen in terms of expressed animosity toward our Government, the people that are working for our Government, therefore, are doing more work with fewer people. They, too, are being more and more productive, and they are entitled to our respect, not our condemnation. They are Americans too.

The Small Business Administration, for example—its Administrator is here, Mr. Lader—is having a huge reduction in its budget, but they've increased their loan volume by 40 percent. That is the kind of thing we see going on all over the Government. We have done what we could to support small business. It is really the engine of opportunity, historically, for the Asian Pacific American community. In the budget in 1993, we increased the expensing provisions for small business by 70 percent and adopted for the first time a capital gains tax for people who really invest long-term in businesses, who hold the investment for 5 years or longer.

Now, the SBA loan application has gone from an inch thick to a page long, and you can get an answer in a week instead of 2 or 3 months. We know that these are the kinds of things that we ought to be doing throughout the Government to create opportunity.

Perhaps more importantly because so many of you will make the most of it, we saw in the last 2 years the biggest expansion of trade opportunities in a generation in America, with the passage of NAFTA and GATT and with the Asian-Pacific Economic Cooperation group really getting organized for opening trade and tearing down trade barriers first in Seattle and then in Jakarta, where some of you were as we committed ourselves to an open trading system by the year 2010 for all the Asian-Pacific countries, including the United States of America.

We have done what we could to make it easier for working families to deal with this world of new challenges and changes, with dramatic increases in education and training opportunities, with the Family and Medical Leave Act, with tax reductions for working families with incomes of under $28,000 a year, so anybody that works full-time and has children in the home should not live in poverty. If we want to reward work and family in this country, we ought to reward work and family. We shouldn't just talk about it. We ought to do it. And if you work full-time, you ought not to be in poverty if you have to go home at night to children who deserve a decent future.

As well as anyone else, you know that we must do more in education to raise the quality as well as the quantity of education in America, and so we have tried to do that. We've expanded educational opportunity, everything from more people in Head Start to lower cost college loans for young people who go to college, better repayment terms. But we also have begun to give funds to States for the first time to really raise the standards of excellence in education, let people decide at the local level how to achieve these new standards, but to finally, finally, fully measure our children by global standards of excellence, so that we will know whether our schools are doing the job. And if they aren't, we will know what we have to do about it. This is an investment we must continue to make, even as we downsize the Government. We have to continue to invest in the education of our people. That is our future.

Indeed, if you ask me what the greatest threat to the preservation of the American dream in the next century is, I would have to say it is that the middle class is splitting apart instead of swelling and coming together. From the end of the Second World War until about 15, 16 years ago, American incomes grew together, without regard to income group, and we also were coming together. That is, incomes were going up, and the poorest people's incomes were going up a little faster than middle class people and the wealthiest people's incomes were. So, we were increasing equality and increasing growth at the same time. For the last 15 years, that has all changed, partly as a result of our going into a global economy, partly as a result of the dramatic explosion in technology putting higher and higher premiums on high skill levels and the ability to learn for a lifetime.

We see now, today, that slightly more than half of our people are working harder for the same or lower wages they were making 10 years ago. So that, while in the last 2 years we've had more small businesses formed than in any period in history, we've seen more new millionaires in America than at any time in history—a cause for celebration—we see more and more and more people going home at night after a hard day's work, sitting down with their families, wondering if they'll be able to guarantee their children a better opportunity, wondering if, as hard as they've worked, somehow they've done something wrong and failed. They haven't failed. What we have done is failed to keep up with the changes in the global economy which require every advanced country to have a system of lifetime education and training available to all people so they can move into higher paying jobs.

The dispute we are having today, which I hope will be very short-lived, over the so-called rescission bill in the Congress, which I have said I will have to veto if it comes to me in the present form, is not a partisan dispute. I say it is not a partisan dispute; there were members of both parties in that conference committee that produced this final bill.

It is a dispute about yesterday's politics and tomorrow's politics. For I believe we, whether we're Democrats or Republicans, have to keep bringing the deficit down and we have to be prepared to make tough, sometimes unpopular budget cuts to liberate the American economy from the crushing burden of debt we have sustained in the last 12 years. We cannot continue this way. We've brought it down a lot; we have to continue until this budget is brought into balance. We must all do that. But in a time when we are cutting spending, we have to be more careful with the dollars of yours that we do spend than ever before. If we are going to spend less and cut the deficit, what we have to spend must be spent with even greater care.

And my dispute with the bill produced by the conference committee is not how much money was cut. In fact, I have offered even greater cuts. We have to start now to cut more spending. My problem is when the bill moved from a public process to a private process, over $1 billion in educational opportunities were taken out of the bill and $1 billion-plus of pork was put back into the bill, everything from a special Federal grant to a city street, to nine specific road projects in a single congressional district, to $100 million for one courthouse in return for cutting out over $200 million to make our schools safe and drug-free, cutting out funds to give our children a chance to work in community service and earn college education, cutting out funds to train our teachers to meet international standards of excellence instead of just to continue to do what's being done in schools when it's not good enough. And I could go on and on.

So the issue is not cutting spending. I am for that. And it is not a partisan issue. Both parties were represented in the conference committee. It is about the old politics against the new politics. If we're going to have the courage to cut this deficit and to make unpopular spending cut decisions, then every dollar we do spend should be spent to take us into the 21st century, to raise incomes, to increase jobs, to give us a better future. That is what is at stake here, and we must fix it.

And let me say one other thing that we must focus on and that I hope you will all be thinking about and celebrating tonight. As we define our security as a people and our strength as a people, we have to protect ourselves against destruction from within and without. That's what the crime bill is all about, putting more police on the street, having more prisons, having more prevention programs. It's what the antiterrorism legislation I sent to the Congress is all about. But let us never forget the real security we have as Americans comes from the positive things about this country. The real security we have as Americans comes from the fact that almost all of us are devoted to our families, raise our children as best we can, put in a full day's work every day, pay our taxes as best we can legally, and otherwise obey the law and respect the differences in this country.

Now, we have free speech and free association. And we are proud of our differences. I am proud of the fact that you live in a country which encourages you to gather here because you share a common ethnic and geographic heritage. I am proud of that.

I am proud of the fact that Hispanics and African-Americans and Polish-Americans and other Americans have that same opportunity. I am proud of the fact that people who have different religious convictions that lead them to different political conclusions have the freedom to organize and speak their mind even if they think I am wrong on everything. I am proud of that. That's what America is all about. I am proud of that.

But every group should remember one thing: There are very few countries in the world where you have as much freedom to do as many different things as you do in this country. There are very few places in the world that are blessed with respecting diversity as we do in this country. And so there should be a limit on the extent to which we go beyond celebrating our diversity to glorifying division. There should be a limit to the extent to which we go beyond disagreeing with our opponents to demonizing them.

You know, I'll just give you one example from my own experience. There's not a politician in this audience, I don't believe, including me— so I will only criticize myself, I have done this— there is no telling how many times in my life, just since I've been President, I have been so proud of being able to get the Congress to pass budgets that reduce the size of the Federal Government by 270,000 while we're taking on a higher work load. And I go around and brag about it, and I don't know how many times I have used the term "Government bureaucrat." And you will never find a politician using that term that doesn't have some slightly pejorative connotation. That is, we know taxpayers resent the money they have to pay to the Government, and so we try to get credit by saying we're being hard on bureaucrats or reducing bureaucrats.

After what we have been through in this last month, after what I have seen in the eyes of the children of those Government bureaucrats that were serving us on that fateful day in Oklahoma City, or in their parents' eyes who were serving us when their children were in that daycare center, I will never use that phrase again.

I had to face the fact that I was out there trying to get some political credit from my fellow citizens by implying that people who are in a certain category were taking their money for no good reason. Well, we have to downsize the Government. We have to have early retirement programs. We have to stop spending on some of the things we're spending on. And the Democrats and Republicans both have to get on that program, and we have to work together on it. But we should never—and everybody has got one story where some person working for the Federal Government or a State or a local government has been unreasonable in pursuit of a regulation or unreasonable in enforcement of the law or just not polite to someone when they came in.

But remember, most of those people are just like most of you: They love their children. They get up every day and go to work. They do the very best they can. They try to do honor to this country. And they take those jobs knowing they will never be rich, but drawing some fulfillment from the fact that they are serving the public. And that's just one example. All of us should now begin to think about this again, about the way that this country works and that we can celebrate our diversity and our differences, but we have to be connected in a seamless web of commitment to common values with a common vision of the future.

Yes, we've got a lot of problems. But we've had worse problems in the past. Yes, we have problems of getting along together, but nothing compared to the shame of what happened to Japanese Americans during the Second World War.

There is nothing wrong with this country that we can't fix if we have the right attitude and enough courage and vision and willingness to think in new terms about a new future rooted in old values. That is what Asian Pacific Americans are most famous for among your fellow citizens. And so I ask you to help lead us into that future.

Thank you, and God bless you.

NOTE: The President spoke at 7:37 p.m. at the Hyatt Regency. In his remarks, he referred to Adm. Ming Chang, USN, Ret., acting chairman, Congressional Asian Pacific American Caucus Institute; Gloria T. Caoile, dinner chair; actors Ming-Na Wen and George Takei; and author Amy Tan.

Remarks Prior to a Meeting With Law Enforcement Leaders and an Exchange With Reporters
May 19, 1995

The President. I asked the heads of all of these major law enforcement organizations to come and meet with me in the White House today for two reasons. First, some of our work to enhance the safety of America's police officers and America's citizens and to better protect the police officers, to help them protect us, a lot of that work is under attack.

Some in Congress want to undermine our efforts to put 100,000 police officers on the street. Some want to repeal the Brady bill, even though it's stopped over 40,000 fugitives and felons from purchasing weapons last year alone. And some want to repeal the ban on deadly assault weapons, even though it is helping to protect the lives of innocent police officers and children on our streets.

I want to enlist these leaders' continued support in fighting these misguided attempts to roll back the clock in the fight against crime. And I want to make it clear that if Congress gives in to the political pressure to do this and repeals any of these measures, I will veto them in a heartbeat. In any fight between our country's law enforcement and the Washington gun lobby, I will side with law enforcement.

Secondly, I want to discuss the attempts by a vocal minority to run down our police officers for their own benefit. The people who tried to make police officers the enemy when we were having a lot of controversy in this country back in the 1960's were wrong, and the people who are trying to do it today are wrong.

I don't care if you want less Government or more Government. I don't care if you favor repeal or retention of the assault weapons ban. Whatever you believe, no one has a right to attack those who uphold the law. Police officers risk their lives to protect our lives. They're on our side. I hope anyone who thinks otherwise has learned a valuable lesson in the debate in this country in the last couple of weeks.

I hope the NRA knows by now that anyone who pretends that police officers are the enemy is only giving aid and comfort to criminals, who are really the enemy. I am glad the NRA apologized for the cruel attack on law enforcement officers in their fundraising letter on Wednes-

day. However, I note today that yesterday they seemed to be bragging about how much money they made from the fundraising letter in which they attacked police officers as "jackbooted thugs."

Now, if the NRA's apology is sincere, what they ought to do is put their money where their mouth is. They ought to give up the ill-gotten gains from their bogus fundraising letter, for which they have already apologized and acknowledged as inappropriate. They ought to turn that money over to the organization that helps the families of police officers who died in the line of duty. They made the money by attacking the police. They admitted they did the wrong thing. They ought to give the money up. That would show true good faith and would set the basis for an honest and open dialog in this country about issues that ought not to divide us by party, by region, by ideology, or in any other way. They ought to give the money back.

Thank you.

National Rifle Association

Q. Do you think they will?

The President. I don't know.

Dewey Stokes. I think they rescinded their statement the other day in the paper at home. One of the NRA members said in our local newspaper that they didn't mean that apology.

Q. Have they said it to you? Have they said it formally at all, except in——

Mr. Stokes. They said it in the newspaper the other day. They did not accept—they did not think that apology reached out to law enforcement.

Q. Well, are any of your people across the board resigning from the NRA?

Mr. Stokes. I've had some calls from—some of our members have resigned from the NRA, yes, in the last—since their letter came out about a week ago.

Budget Resolution

Q. Mr. President, do you have any words for the Senate as they're starting to debate the budget resolution today?

The President. Just what I've said all along. First of all, let me say again, I hope very much that we can—ultimately, we'll wind up agreeing on a rescission package to start cutting spending more right now. I want to cut spending by more than the House and Senate agreed in their committee to cut it, but I think it's cut in the wrong way. We shouldn't put pork back in the budget and cut education. I have said what I think about this. I think we have to continue to work for a balanced budget. I think we can achieve a balanced budget. I do not believe that the right way to do it is by making severe cuts in Medicare and Medicaid, the health care of our seniors and disabled population, and using that money to pay for tax cuts for upper income people. I do not believe that it's right to make it more expensive to go on to college. I don't think we ought to raise taxes on our lowest income working families with children. Those are the three things that I think are wrong.

I think there is a lot to commend the efforts that have been made by the Republicans in Congress. I think that, you know, they have shown that it is arithmetically possible to reach a balanced budget. And I believe that if we continue to work on a lot of the things that we're doing constructively in health care and other areas, we can achieve this. But I don't believe that we can do it with those three big, big problems out there. And I hope that we can work those out in the weeks and months ahead.

Q. How do you think you're going to——

Q. Senator Gramm just charged that you are committed to protecting the Government that you know and love and programs that have failed for the last 40 years.

The President. [*Inaudible*]—Senator Gramm— let me just say this: I don't want to get in a fight with Senator Gramm, but look at the record. He was here during the Reagan years and the Bush years when they quadrupled the Government deficit. And I would just point out

that the administrations that he supported always sent budgets to Congress that were in excess of the ones Congress approved. I would point out that if it weren't for the interest run up before I ever showed up here, if it weren't for the interest run up between 1981 and the end of 1992, we would have a budget that is in balance today. And I have already cut or eliminated some 300 programs, and we propose, in this new budget, to cut or eliminate some 400 more.

We have done more to challenge and change the status quo in 2 years than the previous administrations did in the last 12, perhaps the last 20. Furthermore, I don't see Senator Gramm out there campaigning for lobby reform, campaign finance reform. I don't even know what's happened to the line-item veto. If they're worried—if they want me to show them how to end the status quo, send me the line-item veto. Where is it?

If I had the line-item veto, we wouldn't be having this argument about the rescission bill. I could just get rid of it. All the things that— Senator Gramm is defending this rescission bill—$1 million for a city street, nine highway projects in one congressional district, $100 million for a courthouse—when we're cutting education? It seems to me that he's on the side of the status quo. I want to cut spending, but I want to change the way the Government works here. And I would urge him to stop protecting the Republican pork, just as I'm willing to scrap the Democratic pork, and let's put partisan politics behind us and get on with moving the country forward.

NOTE: The President spoke at 10:25 a.m. in the Cabinet Room at the White House. Dewey Stokes was national president of the Fraternal Order of Police. A tape was not available for verification of the content of these remarks.

Interview With Peter Malof of New Hampshire Public Radio
May 19, 1995

Mr. Malof. Well, I sure appreciate you joining us.

The President. Glad to do it.

Federal Budget

Mr. Malof. I guess you folks down in Washington are officially in the thick of the budget battle. Your reaction to the rescission package just passed by the House was that it favors pork over people, and you promised a veto. Republicans are saying they're outraged. How comfortable are you with the prospect that your role may be shaping up more and more to be a blocker of action rather than an initiator?

The President. Well, I don't want to block action. I have offered even more spending cuts than is in their bill. This is not about cutting spending, and they know it. I worked in good faith with the Republican majority in the Senate to shape a rescission bill that would be better for the American people and would still cut spending. For example, I worked with the Senate to add back some of the money in the LIHEAP program, which goes to States like New Hampshire to help older people with their utility bills, but we cut spending somewhere else.

So we had an agreement that I would go along with this bill, and we worked in good faith. Then the Senate and the House Members went behind closed doors when nobody was looking and—remember, this is not a partisan issue—members of both parties put a lot of pork in the bill and took a billion and a half dollars in education funding out.

Mr. Malof. Now, correct——

The President. And so—let me just finish—so all I told them was, I am all for it, cutting this much spending. Indeed, I think we should cut a little more spending. I offered another $100 million in spending cuts. But I don't believe—if we're going to balance this budget and cut back on Government spending, then we need to be very careful about how we spend the money we do spend. We ought to target it to education. We ought to target it to things that will raise incomes and grow jobs in America and improve the security of the American people.

Instead, they took out money to make our schools safer and more drug-free. They took out money to fund college educations for young people who are working in their community in the national service program that's received broad bipartisan support in New Hampshire.

They—instead, they put in $100 million for a courthouse. They put in even more road projects into a Congressman's district who now has nine special-purpose road projects in his district. They even put in a million dolllars for a city street in a State in the Midwest where the mayor didn't ask for the money. Now, that's what was done behind closed doors. That's the old politics.

If we're going to change things around here, we've got to move away from the old politics, cut unnecessary spending, and then when we do spend money, the money ought to be well spent. We shouldn't be trading in pork for people, behind closed doors. That's what we did, and it was wrong. And I want to change that. But I'm all for the spending cuts.

Mr. Malof. Now, it's my impression that the only new spending in the House bill is disaster relief, antiterrorism laws, and Oklahoma City aid. You originally signed on to items that you're now calling pork, such as the highway construction and——

The President. That's right. That's when we had a—that's right. But that's when we were spending more money. But let's just—let's look at the real facts.

If we're going to cut $16 billion worth of spending, and I signed—let me remind you that I signed on to it because the Congress has the ability to put these special projects in there and because I don't have the line-item veto, which the Republicans say they are for and which I have agreed with the Republicans for. Now, they passed the line-item veto in the House, they passed one in the Senate, but they're different. If they had—they still have not appointed the conferees to resolve the difference between the House and the Senate. If they had sent me the line-item veto, we wouldn't be having this discussion today.

But if you say—if they say we want to cut $16 billion and I say we want to cut $16 billion and then we reach an agreement—I reached a good-faith agreement with the Senate, and then they go behind closed doors and they say, "No, no, no, we don't want to do all this education business; we want some of our pork-barrel projects. So we'll cut education a billion and a half and put pork in." Now, that's what happened.

If you're going to cut spending, you have to make choices, what you cut and what you keep. If you're going to spend more money, you can spend more money on different things.

But I will say again, I think they're wrong to put in pork-barrel projects and cut education. And I don't think they can defend it. And they're not trying to defend it very hard; they're just talking about process.

Mr. Malof. Obviously, nobody's saying we don't need deficit reduction. The question seems to be how, and how fast? Do you consider yourself at odds with those who are determined to actually balance the budget by the year 2002?

The President. Well, I'm—first of all, I'm not—certainly not at odds with those who are determined to balance the budget by a date certain. And I invited the Congress to do what the law required them to do and submit a budget and then to work it through. They're now in the process of working through that budget. I want to evaluate it, and then I would—including the date. But I think we have to balance the budget. I think we have to do it by a date certain, and I agree with that. And I think we ought to do it in a bipartisan fashion. And I will support them.

They haven't had—let me just point out—I am prepared to work with them to reduce the deficit and to bring the budget into balance. For 2 years, for 2 years, they said no to all my efforts to get them to work with me. So we reduced the deficit 3 years in a row for the first time since Harry Truman, with nobody helping us in the other party, none of them.

And they were all saying we were going to have a big recession, and it would wreck the economy. A lot of those people who are up there in New Hampshire running for President said, "If President Clinton's budget passes, it will wreck the economy." Well, New Hampshire had a 7.6 percent unemployment rate when I became President, and it's 4½ percent today. You've got almost 40,000 new jobs, and in the previous 4 years you lost over 40,000 jobs. So they were wrong.

So now they believe in deficit reduction. And I say, welcome to the party, I'm glad to have you here, and I will work with you on it. But there is a right way and a wrong way to do it. And if we're going to cut spending more quickly, I will support that. But that means that the money that is left, the money we do spend, has to be spent even more carefully. I think people in New Hampshire will really identify with that. If you're going to spend—if you spent $10 yesterday and you're going to spend $8 today, then you've got to be more careful about how you spend the $8. That's my argument over this rescission package.

If they'll take the pork out and put the people back, I will sign even more deficit reduction than they have.

Middle Class Tax Cut

Mr. Malof. I understand.

Finally, Granite Staters are by no stretch of the imagination a tax-friendly bunch. But according to surveys, we're in step with the rest of the country in preferring deficit reduction to tax cuts. Are you determined to stick to fulfilling your long-delayed promise to cut taxes on the middle class even though it would set back the pace of deficit reduction? Because I would think if you back away from tax cuts, you'd be opening yourself up to more attacks that once again you haven't done what you'd say you would.

The President. Well, first of all, let's look at what I did do, before we get all carried away here. Let's look at what we—let's look at what we did do. In 1993, we cut taxes for lower middle income working families with children an average, this year, of $1,000 a family, for working people with incomes of $27,000 a year or less. We've already done that. We also cut taxes for 90 percent of the small businesses in America that increased their investments in their own business. So we did do that while reducing the deficit.

Do I believe that we can bring the budget into balance within the next few years and still have a tax cut? I do, but not one the size that the House of Representatives has adopted. You can't, you can't cut taxes as much as the House has and balance the budget. It won't happen. And it's not right, frankly, to cut taxes in ways that largely benefit upper income people and to pay for it by cutting Medicare and Medicaid to the elderly and disabled. When I was in New Hampshire 4 years ago, I met people who were already making a decision every week between buying drugs and paying for food. We don't want to make that worse.

So my answer to you is, if we have a targeted tax cut that focuses on the middle class and rewards education and childrearing, we can do that and we can afford to do that in the context of deficit reduction. But we cannot afford a big, broad-based, huge tax cut in the magnitude that the House passed and balance this budget without doing severe damage to the elderly of this country, including the elderly people in New Hampshire.

Federal Budget

Mr. Malof. And do I understand you correctly that you are not prepared at this point to set a date for balancing the budget, a year?

The President. No, but I can say this. I think it can be done——

Mr. Malof. [*Inaudible*]

The President. Well, it can—first of all, it can be done in 7 years. The question is, what is the penalty, and what are the tradeoffs? I think it clearly can be done in less than 10 years. I think we can get there by a date certain.

But I want to evaluate the actual budget that the Republicans finally agree on. That is, the Senate has to adopt their budget proposal. Then they'll get together and reconcile the differences. Then I have to do what I promised them I did; I promised them that if they would adopt a budget, that I would negotiate with them in good faith and that I would propose a counter-budget. That's what I—I gave them my word I'd do it, and I will do it. I owe that to them, and I owe it to the American people.

Look, I believed in deficit reduction before they did. My budgets, adopted in the last 2 years, are giving us 3 years of deficit reduction for the first time since Mr. Truman was President. And had it not been for the debts run—the interest we have to pay on the debt run up in the 12 years before I came to town, we would have a balanced budget today. That is, the only reason for the deficit today is the interest we are paying on the debt run up between 1981 and the end of 1992. And both parties bear responsibility for that because in every year but one, the Congress, then in the hands of the Democrats, actually adopted less spending than the White House, then in the hands of the Republicans, asked for.

So this is not a partisan issue with me. America has a vested interest in the future in bringing this deficit down and bringing the budget into balance. And I will work with them to do it. And yes, it can be done, and it can be done by a date certain.

Mr. Malof. Okay. Mr. President, thank you very much for taking the time to talk with us.

The President. Thank you.

NOTE: The interview began at 12:26 p.m. The President spoke by telephone from the Oval Office at the White House. The interview was broadcast live on WEVO, Concord, NH; WEVH, Hanover, NH; and WEVN, Keene, NH.

Remarks at the Women's Bureau Reception
May 19, 1995

Thank you very much. I was sitting here listening to my marvelous wife speak, and I was thinking, you know, I've been seeing her lately long distance, on Oprah Winfrey and on the "Morning Show" this morning, and I thought, boy, I'm glad she lives here. [*Laughter*]

I want to thank Secretary Reich and the Women's Bureau Director, Karen Nussbaum. She has done a wonderful job. I am very grateful to her and to him. I want to say a special word of appreciation to the people who sponsored this event today: from American Home Products, the senior vice president, Fred Hassan, and the corporate secretary, Carol Emerling. Let's give them a hand for what they did. [*Applause*] There are many distinguished women leaders here today, but I do want to recognize one person who has been a friend of mine for more than 20 years now, Congresswoman Eddie Bernice Johnson, from Texas. We're glad to see you. Thank you very much for being here.

You know, the concerns of working women are one of the few subjects that I didn't have to be educated about—[*laughter*]—because I grew up with them. I lived with my grandparents till I was 4, and my grandmother was a working woman from the 1930's on. In the little town where I was born, an awful lot of the women, both white and black, who lived in poor families or near-poor families worked as a matter of course. No one gave much thought to it one way or the other. My mother was a working woman from the 1940's on, beginning shortly after I was old enough to at least crawl around on my own. And it certainly never occurred to me from the first day that I met Hillary that she would do anything other than pursue her career. [*Laughter*] As a matter of fact, I spent the first 2 or 3 years of our relationship trying to talk her out of it because I thought it would be bad for her career. But it's worked out all right for her, I think. [*Laughter*]

You know, 75 years ago a reception like this would not have taken place. In 1920, women had less than one in five jobs in this economy and, as Hillary said, were only then gaining the right to vote. When she said, "In 25 years from now, the President and her husband would open the time capsule," I looked at Karen and Bob and said, "If the demographic trends continue, the percentages will almost mandate a woman President." [*Laughter*] Karen said, "Yes, if they vote their own interests." [*Laughter*] To which I replied, "We should give them every opportunity." [*Laughter*]

When the Women's Bureau was born, it was designed then to improve the lot of women in the work force by fighting for fair wages and expanding opportunities for education and training and protecting women physically at work.

Those folks 75 years ago, I think, would be surprised at how far we've come. Hundreds of women here celebrate the progress that we have made in all walks of American life. I'm proud that in this administration we have six women Cabinet Secretaries, twice as many as has ever served in any Cabinet of the President before. Over 40 percent of our appointees have been women, and a far higher percentage of women have been appointed to the bench and to major Federal positions than previous administrations. Two of these appointees are former Directors of the Women's Bureau: Esther Peterson, the U.S. Representative to the U.N. General Assembly, and the Assistant to the President for Public Liaison, Alexis Herman, who is here with six other Directors of the Women's Bureau. Let's give them all a hand here. [*Applause*]

All of you represent women across this country who work long hours, do your best to raise your families, and contribute to your communities. Extraordinary working women today are doing their best to hold our country together, our communities together, and frankly, our hard-pressed middle class together. They de-

serve our admiration, our respect, and most importantly, our support.

I ran for office in large measure because I was afraid that having won the cold war, we might squander the peace and the victory; that having struggled so hard to make the American dream available to other people around the world, we might lose it for large numbers of our people here at home as we move into the 21st century and the global economy, the technological revolution opening all of us to unbelievable pressures and changes which can be good or difficult.

I believe that my job is, first, to provide for the security of the American people; secondly, to give people the tools they need to help themselves live up to their God-given potential; and thirdly, to try to create as many opportunities as I possibly can.

In a way, the first major piece of legislation I signed as President, which had been bouncing around here for 7 years and had suffered through two vetoes, was emblematic of all three of those objectives. It was the family and medical leave law.

Not very long ago, I was home for a couple of days and I went back to my old church, and a lady I didn't know came up to me and said, "I really want to thank you. I know we're not supposed to talk about politics at church, but I don't really think this is politics. I got cancer, and I had to take some time off and deal with it, and my husband had to take some time off and work with me. And neither one of us lost our jobs, and we're both back working now. And it wouldn't have happened if it hadn't been for the family and medical leave law."

I am proud of the fact that we have moved aggressively to immunize all of our children under the age of 2; to enroll every pregnant woman and infant in the country who needs it in the Women, Infants and Children Program for nutrition; to expand Head Start and lift the standards in our schools and expand apprenticeship programs for young people who don't go on to universities; and something which will make a big difference in the lives of young women in the future, to dramatically expand and make more affordable loans to go to college.

But there is much, much more to be done. I am proud of the fact that last year the Small Business Administration cut its budget but expanded loans to women entrepreneurs by 85 percent in one year—I might add, without reducing loans to qualified males. [*Laughter*] We expanded for everybody.

But I think it's important that we recognize that women in the workplace are caught in a lot of cross-currents today, because all American workers, or at least more than half of us, are working longer hours for the same or lower pay that we were making 10 years ago. And therefore, more and more parents are working harder for the same or less and spending less time with their children. Women feel this pressure very deeply insofar as they have either sole, primary, or even just half of the responsibility for taking care of their children as well as earning a living. Because male workers over the age of 45, on average, have lost 14 percent of their earning power in the last 10 years, women in the work force and in the home feel the anxiety of their husband's sense of loss and insecurity and frustration and anger.

What is causing all this, and what are we to do about it? Well, what is causing it all is the impact of the global economy and the dramatic revolution in technology on our society, opening up all kinds of new changes in ways that are perfectly wonderful if you can access them but terrifying if you cannot. For example—we don't have the figures yet on '94, but I think '94 will confirm '93's trend—in 1993 we had the largest number of new businesses started in America in any year in history and the largest number of new millionaires in America in any year in history. And that is a good thing. That is a good thing. And that is happening because so many of us are now able to access the world of the future. Many of you in this room are part of the trend toward a brighter, bigger, broader tomorrow.

But there is also a fault line in our society that is splitting the middle class apart, putting unbearable pressures on families, making them less secure and making them less able to live up to the fullest of their abilities. You know it, and I know it.

That's why the family and medical leave law was important. If people are going to be working for smaller companies, not bigger ones, and moving around, at least they ought to know they can take some time off without losing a job if there's someone sick in their family or if a baby is born or some other emergency arises. That's why it was important.

That's why the efforts of the Secretary of Labor and the Secretary of Education to create a fabric, a seamless fabric, of lifelong learning, whenever people lose their jobs or feel that they're underemployed, it's terribly important.

And that's why I believe it is especially important to women that we raise the minimum wage this year. Women represent three out of five minimum wage workers but only half the work force.

I have done everything I could to create a climate in which people are encouraged to choose work over welfare, in which people are encouraged to be successful parents and successful workers. I believe that. That's what the earned-income tax credit was all about in 1993. Let me tell you what that meant: That meant this year that the average family of four with an income under $27,000 got a $1,000 tax cut below what they paid before this administration came into office. And it means 3 years from now, if the Congress will stick with it and not repeal it, we will be able to say that no one who works full-time and has children at home, when they go home from work, will live below the poverty line. That is the best war against welfare we could wage.

But it isn't enough. If we do not raise the minimum wage this year, next year it will be, in real dollar terms, the lowest it has been in 40 years. Now that is not my idea of what the 21st century American economy is all about. I want a smart-work, high-wage economy, not a hard-work, low-wage economy. And the working women of America and their children and their husbands deserve it as well.

You know, I don't get to watch a lot of kind of extra television, but the other night, just by accident, I was watching a news program where a special was being done on the minimum wage. And I don't even know if it was a national program or one of the State networks around here, but they went down South to a town that had a lot of minimum wage workers. And they went in this plant to interview a remarkable woman who worked in this plant at a minimum wage. And they said to this lady, "You know, your employer says, if we raise the minimum wage, that they'll either have to lay people off or put more money into machinery and reduce their employment long-term. What do you say to that?" I could not have written the script. [*Laughter*] This lady sort of threw her shoulders back and looked into the eyes of the television reporter and said, "Honey, I'll take my chances." [*Laughter*]

If we are going to bring our budget deficit into balance, which will be good for all of us, if we are going to have to over a period of years cut back on expenditures that the Government used to make, that makes it even more important for people who do go out into the private sector and work full-time, play by the rules, and want to make their own way without public assistance, to be rewarded for that work. This is a huge issue.

One other thing I want to say that must be done this year: The Secretary of Labor has taken the initiative in trying to consolidate a lot of these various job-training programs into a fund from which you can get a check or a voucher, if you're unemployed or underemployed, to take to the local community college or the training institution of your choice to get permanent reeducation opportunities for a lifetime. And we ought to do that.

I'd like to close by introducing someone who was a working woman, who was a particular influence in my life at an early time. The people who sponsored this event invited me to pick someone to participate, and so I picked this person. Lonnie Luebben was my 11th grade honors English teacher. And I believe that I was in the first class she taught, but anyway, she looked awful young at the time—[laughter]—and she still does. She had a remarkable way of making literature come to life. And one of the most memorable trips I ever took in my life—I still remember—it was the first time I ever went to the wild mountains of the Ozarks in north Arkansas, along the river that was the

first river Congress, over 20 years ago, set aside in the national wild rivers act. They thought it was the wildest of all the rivers in the United States. [*Laughter*] And we explored caves that still had ammunition stored from the Civil War. We talked to mountain people who had never been more than 20 miles away from home. It was one of the most remarkable experiences I have ever had. She taught me a great deal about American folklore and literature and life. And just before we walked out here, she gave me a contribution for the time capsule, the textbook with which she taught our class so many years ago.

So if you will forgive me, I would like to close this event by asking my teacher to come up here and accept my thanks for being a working woman over 30 years ago. Thank you very much.

Again, let me thank American Home Products. Let me thank all of you for coming. Let me thank Congresswoman Eddie Bernice Johnson. And I've just been told that Congresswoman Lynn Woolsey is also here somewhere; thank you. There she is, the heroine of the State of the Union Address.

I thank you all. Please stay around. Have a good time. We're delighted to see you. Goodbye. Thank you.

NOTE: The President spoke at 5:38 p.m. on the South Lawn at the White House, at a 75th anniversary celebration of the Department of Labor's Women's Bureau.

Message on the Observance of Armed Forces Day, 1995
May 19, 1995

Every year on this day our citizens join in honoring you, the men and women who wear our nation's uniform. You risk your very lives to defend the liberties we hold dear. Americans everywhere recognize your dedication and professionalism, and all of us feel profound respect, pride, and appreciation for our Armed Forces.

As we commemorate the fiftieth anniversary of the Allied victory in World War II, everyone on Earth should pause to express heartfelt gratitude to those who fought and sacrificed in that

awful conflict. We do no greater honor to the memory of those lost in World War II than to continue their fight against tyranny and oppression everywhere.

Each of you has stood to carry on that fight in this past year. You have been called to serve in lands far from home. You have brought freedom and security to our friends and allies and humanitarian aid to those in need. In Haiti, you helped restore democracy; in the Persian Gulf, you faced down the forces of aggression;

and in central Africa, you delivered lifesaving food, water, and medicine. Throughout the year, you maintained the security of our country at home and at posts around the world.

Whether you serve in the Army, the Navy, the Air Force, the Marine Corps, or the Coast Guard, your standards of excellence and your selfless service are models for all Americans. I am proud to salute you for your many extraordinary accomplishments.

BILL CLINTON

NOTE: Armed Forces Day was observed on May 20.

The President's Radio Address
May 20, 1995

Good morning. Today the Secretary of the Treasury, who oversees the Secret Service, will announce that from now on the two blocks of Pennsylvania Avenue in front of the White House will be closed to motor vehicle traffic.

Pennsylvania Avenue has been routinely open to traffic for the entire history of our Republic. Through four Presidential assassinations and eight unsuccessful attempts on the lives of Presidents, it's been open. Through a civil war, two world wars, and the Gulf war, it was open. But now it must be closed. This decision follows a lengthy review by the Treasury Department, the Secret Service, and independent experts, including distinguished Americans who served in past administrations of both Democratic and Republican Presidents.

This step is necessary in the view of the Director of the Secret Service and the panel of experts to protect the President and his family, the White House itself, all the staff and others who work here, and the visitors and distinguished foreign and domestic guests who come here every day.

The Secret Service risk their lives to protect the President and his family. For 130 years, they have stood watch over the people and the institutions of our democracy. They are the best in the world at what they do. Though I am reluctant to accept any decision that might inconvenience the people who work or visit our Nation's Capital, I believe it would be irresponsible to ignore their considered opinion or to obstruct their decisions about the safety of our public officials, especially given the strong supporting voice of the expert panel.

Clearly, this closing is necessary because of the changing nature and scope of the threat of terrorist actions. It should be seen as a responsible security step necessary to preserve our freedom, not part of a long-term restriction of our freedom.

First, let me make it clear that I will not in any way allow the fight against domestic and foreign terrorism to build a wall between me and the American people. I will be every bit as active and in touch with ordinary American citizens as I have been since I took office. Pennsylvania Avenue may be closed to cars and trucks, but it will remain open to the people of America. If you want to visit the White House, you can still do that just as you always could, and I hope you will. If you want to have your picture taken out in front of the White House, please do so. If you want to come here and protest our country's policies, you are still welcome to do that as well. And now you will be more secure in all these activities because it will be less likely that you could become an innocent victim of those who would do violence against symbols of our democracy.

Closing Pennsylvania Avenue to motor vehicles is a practical step to protect against the kind of attack we saw in Oklahoma City, but I won't allow the people's access to the White House and their President to be curtailed. The two blocks of Pennsylvania Avenue in front of the White House will be converted into a pedestrian mall. Free and public tours will continue as they always have. For most Americans, this won't change much beyond the traffic patterns here in Washington. For people who work in Washington, DC, we will work hard to reroute the traffic in cooperation with local officials in the least burdensome way possible.

Now let's think for a minute about what this action says about the danger terrorism poses to the openness of our society or to any free society. The fact that the Secret Service feels compelled to close Pennsylvania Avenue is an important reminder that we have to come together as a people and hold fast against the divisive tactics of violent extremists.

We saw in the awful tragedy of Oklahoma City and the bombing of the World Trade Center that America, as an open and free society, is not immune from terrorists from within and beyond our borders who believe they have a right to kill innocent civilians to pursue their own political ends or to protest other policies. Such people seek to instill fear in our citizens, in our whole people. But when we are all afraid to get on a bus or drive to work or open an envelope or send our children off to school, when our children are fixated on the possibility of terrorist action against them or other innocent children, we give terrorists a victory. That kind of corrosive fear could rust our national spirit, drain our will, and wear away our freedom.

These are the true stakes in our war against terrorism. We cannot allow ourselves to be frightened or intimidated into a bunker mentality. We cannot allow our sacred freedoms to wither or diminish. We cannot allow the paranoia and conspiracy theories of extreme militants to dominate our society.

What we do today is a practical step to preserve freedom and peace of mind. It should be seen as a step in a long line of efforts to improve security in the modern world that began with the installation of airport metal detectors. I remember when that started, and a lot of people thought that it might be seen as a restriction on our freedom. But most of us take it for granted now, and, after all, hijackings have gone way down. The airport metal detectors increased the freedom of the American people, and so can this.

But more must be done to reduce the threat of terrorism, to deter terrorism. First, Congress must pass my antiterrorism legislation. We mustn't let our country fight the war against terrorism ill-armed or ill-prepared. I want us to be armed with 1,000 more FBI agents. I want the ability to monitor high-tech communications among far-flung terrorists. I want to be able to have our people learn their plans before they strike. That's the key. Congress can give us these tools by passing the antiterrorism bill before them. And they should do it now. Congressional leaders pledged to pass this bill by Memorial Day, in the wake of the terrible bombing in Oklahoma City. This is a commitment Congress must keep.

On a deeper level, we must all fight terrorism by fighting the fear that terrorists sow. Today the Secret Service is taking a necessary precaution, but let no one mistake: We will not relinquish our fundamental freedoms. We will secure the personal safety of all Americans to live and move about as they please, to think and to speak as they please, to follow their beliefs and their conscience, as our Founding Fathers intended.

Thanks for listening.

NOTE: The address was recorded at 9:28 a.m. in the Oval Office at the White House for broadcast at 10:06 a.m.

Remarks at the White House Conference on Character Building for a Civil and Democratic Society
May 20, 1995

Thank you very much. Thank you very much, Dr. Etzioni. Thank you for that introduction and for the inspiration that your work has given to me and to so many others, for your wonderful book, "The Spirit of Community," and for working on this as hard as you have. I'd like to say a special word of thanks to one of the cofounders of this network—he's been a member of the White House staff since I became President—Bill Galston, for his constant inspiration and prodding to me. I'd like to thank the Secretary of Education and Tom Payzant, the Assistant Secretary for Elementary and Secondary Education, for what they have done to try to promote character education as a part of the larger strategy toward a new communitarian vision for our country.

You know, from the time I began thinking about how we would get into the 21st century, and long before I even thought of running for President, it seemed to me that the—there were three words which were inextricably linked, as if you think about America moving into the future: opportunity, responsibility, and community. Those were the three words that basically were at the heart of my campaign for President and have been at the heart of what I have tried to do as President. I also believe that Government cannot do these things for America. I believe that we have to have, in a complicated, open, pluralistic society like this one, a great network of people working together in every major important center of our society. And that's what I want to talk to you about today.

I'd like to begin with a few comments about the most obvious recent event that, in terms of your Government's action, that you must have noticed when you came in today, which is that I have approved of the Secretary of the Treasury's decision to close the two blocks of Pennsylvania Avenue just here in front of the White House to vehicular traffic.

I did this reluctantly. Pennsylvania Avenue has been open to ordinary traffic since the beginning of our Republic. I did it after an extensive review by the Secret Service, the Treasury Department officials, and a distinguished independent panel of American experts who have served in administrations of both the Democratic and Republican Presidents, all recommending that this be done. They believe it is necessary to protect the President and his family, the structure of the White House, the hundreds of people who work there, and the people who come and visit there, both on official business and as ordinary citizens. They believe it is necessary to protect the White House against the kind of attacks that were sustained in Oklahoma City.

Now, I want to emphasize a couple of things about this. First of all, access to the White House itself will not be limited. The area will be converted into a pedestrian mall, and people will be able to visit as they always have. They'll be able to have their picture taken out front with cardboard figures as they always have. [*Laughter*] They'll able to go to Lafayette Park and protest against the President as they always have. And indeed, they will be able to do that more protected themselves from becoming innocent victims of those who would seek to destroy the symbols of our freedom. We also will be working with the local officials here to make every effort to reroute the traffic in a way that minimizes inconvenience and disruption to the lives of those who live in or work in Washington, DC.

Our society, as an open society, is, as we saw with Japan and the terrible incident in the Japanese subway, vulnerable to the forces of organized destruction from within and beyond our borders. And we must take reasonable precautions against them, not to restrict our freedom but to secure it. And as technology changes the opportunity for organized destruction, we have to respond to that.

I think the American people should see this in the same context that they viewed metal detectors in airports. Do you remember when they started? There were those who say "Oh, this is a big infringement on our freedom." But most of us now are only too happy to go through those metal detectors because we see that there are a lot fewer hijackings. And so it is a way of preserving our freedom by changing to meet the changing realities that technology and time give for the expression of organized destruction. And we should view it in that way.

But we should also recognize that our job is to minimize the fear that can seep into a society. That's one of the reasons that Hillary and I wanted to have the program we had with the children after Oklahoma City, because we were worried about children all across America and especially, of course, children in Oklahoma being literally fixated on these events and their vulnerability to such things.

So, it's important to put them in a larger context. And in that sense, it's also important to prevent such things from happening whenever we can. This is a preventive action we're taking today.

I have asked Congress to pass this anti-terrorism legislation to give me both people and technological tools—not to me but to me being the United States, to us—to deal with the technological and organizational realities of the modern terrorist threat so that we can prevent these things from happening more and more and more. And the leaders of Congress have pledged to pass that legislation by Memorial Day. It is a commitment I hope they will keep because we need the legislation in preventive ways.

Now, what's that got to do with what we're doing here today? The strength of our society is far more than our ability to stop bad things from happening and to punish wrongdoers when they do such things. This country is still around today after more than 200 years as the most successful, vibrant democracy in all of human history, not because we could stop bad things from happening, although that was important. If the Civil War had turned out differently, we wouldn't be here today as a country. If Hitler had been allowed to prevail in Europe, it would be a very different world today. So stopping bad things from happening is quite important; it shouldn't be minimized.

But the fundamental strength of America, and the real reason we're here after more than 200 years, is not our capacity to stop bad things from happening but our ability to do good and, indeed, our ability to be good. De Tocqueville said, "America is great because America is good."

So, the truly great things about our country involve the literally billions of actions that are now taken by our 250 plus million citizens every day of the world. They get up, they go about their business, and most of them do the very best they can to be responsible, first of all, as individuals and then to be responsible for their families, to be responsible at work, to be successful members of their community, to be good citizens.

Most of our fellow citizens do everything they're supposed to do pretty much when they're supposed to do it, even things they find most distasteful, like paying their taxes. It has long been observed by—I know that when I was a young law student taking tax law—and it gave me a headache. I just couldn't stand it. I hated the course, all those rules and regulations. When it was all said and done—the professor said at the beginning, in the middle, and at the end of the course, "Now, remember, in spite of all these rules and regulations that no one can keep up with and hardly anyone understands, the real thing that makes this work is that you live in a good country where most people just get up and, on their own, do the right thing because they think this is part of the obligation of citizenship." It made a deep impression on me.

So, I think that when we view the problems of America today, and there are plenty of them—the intolerance, the increasing divisiveness of political forces, the seeming two-edged sword of the information revolution where more and more information seems to be organized

to harm instead of to enlighten, to divide instead of unite—when we look at all of this, we have to see it against the background of the fundamental fact that this is a very great country full of very good people and almost all of us get up every day and do what we're supposed to do as best we can; that there are new and different challenges we face today that put extreme pressure on us in trying to do good and be good, pressure in the family, pressure in the workplace, pressure in the community and in the larger society; that we are trying to cope with economic and social stresses and with the exposure to all kinds of forces in a complex modern world that we often were not exposed to in the past and that none of—some of us had never been exposed to before.

And I think that the real trick is how we can keep the basic values that have made our country great and take advantage of the modern world with all the things that are different. That has always been the genius of America, to preserve what is right there in the Constitution and to take it throughout history. We know that we are capable of doing it unanimously. What we're really all afraid of is that somehow we'll be undone either by some small minority of us who do wrong and force all the rest of us into a way of living that is so radically different from what's been before that we don't preserve what's uniquely American, or we're afraid that all these forces will upset the internal balance in so many of us that we will lose our way.

And yet, we know that fundamentally we shouldn't be pessimistic about it, and we're reminded of it every time something bad happens in America. When we had a 500-year flood in the Middle West or that massive earthquake in California or the World Trade Center bombing or the horrible, horrible tragedy of Oklahoma City, you see not only the loss and the evil and the darkness, you also see the fundamental goodness of the American people. These people everywhere just stop what they're doing and show up to help.

I remember when they had that awful hurricane in Florida and I went down there, the first guy I met was an independent trucker from Michigan who literally canceled all of his runs, stopped all of his business, and filled his one big semi truck and brought it all the way to Florida—stopped his whole life. And he was just a single business person who was not like me, an employee of the Federal Government who could maybe get time off. [*Laughter*] He risked everything just because it was the right thing to do. Here was this guy showing up and happy as a clam, didn't have any idea what was going to happen when he went back to Michigan, how he was going to put it back together. He was happy doing something for other people, consistent with his personal values and what he had learned in his family and church and what he had imparted to his children.

Now, the question is, how can we preserve the traditional values and how can we find at least a measure of the fulfillment in doing right and good things in ordinary life that we find when disaster strikes? Is there something endemic to the modern world or human nature that says that we can't do that? I don't think so. But we plainly live in a world that is changing so fast, where people are exposed to so many forces, that the ties that bind us are stretched more than there were in the world in which I grew up. I don't think there's any question about that. The opportunities for individuals to have their internal equilibrium upset are far greater today than they were a generation ago.

It's important not to romanticize the past, however. Remember what Will Rogers said about that? "Don't tell me about the good ol' days; they never was." It's important not to romanticize the past. While I grew up in a society which was much more stable and where I didn't have anything like the kind of forces bearing down on me that teenagers do today, when I was a child I also lived in a segregated society in which a huge number of people my age were never going to be given any opportunities that I took for granted. So it is important for us not to overly romanticize the past but also to recognize that the present is changing so fast and people are exposed to so many different things that it is very, very difficult to build the kind of coherent, character-based society that builds both individual and social responsibility and gives people the necessary balance between stability and change that allows you to live the fullest possible, most rewarding life and to have a society that is both growing and vibrant and stable. I think we all recognize that as a sort of central challenge of this time.

And I think what happens when a big disaster occurs, everybody throws off all the things that are bothering them and gets back to basics. People stop looking at each other as people of different races or religions or philosophical positions or political parties and realize that there is a common humanity there after all. The trick will be to manage our differences on a daily basis in a way that recognizes our common humanity and to find organized ways to stamp out the social evils that are consuming us, without doing away with our personal freedoms. And I believe that we can do these things. I believe that sometimes we throw up our hands too much in the face of all the difficulties that we have. But we have to identify what the problems are and move on them.

I also believe that the central insight of what Dr. Etzioni has done is important to emphasize here. Everyone has a role to play. And we can solve this in a free and open society, not by any Governmental policy but by Government, like every other part of society, playing its own role.

If we could start with some of the problems that are disintegrating forces in our society, I would like to focus on some that we don't often focus on, and those are the economic ones. We all know we have too much crime and violence and drugs and family breakdown. And I don't mean to minimize those things; they are profoundly important. But we are aware and sensitive to those things. I want you also to think about things that may be more pedestrian but also are reinforcing the problem that we come here to talk about.

The average American today is working a longer work week and spending fewer hours with his or her children than they were 25 years ago, for the same or lower wages they were making 15 years ago. Literally 60 percent of the American work force is making the same or less, when you adjust for inflation, than they were making 15 years ago and working harder and spending less time with their children than they were 25 years ago. Family income has gone up in many places only because there are now two workers in the family.

There is also in our country a feeling that there is much less security because more and more people are changing their jobs. The census tells us that there's been about a 14 percent decline in earnings for men between the ages of 55 and 65—excuse me, 45 and 55. It could have something to do with the so-called angry white male phenomenon. So that when people reach the peak of what they thought was going to be their—not only their earning capacity but their ability to have a profound and positive impact on their families and on their society, their communities, many of them now are at a vulnerable period when they're having to deal with changes that they took for granted when they were in their twenties but never expected to have to face all over again in their forties or early fifties. This is a profound thing.

So that we at least thought when we started out in life, we'd have different kinds of things to feel anxieties about as we got older. I mean, just getting older is bad enough. [*Laughter*] And now, we're having to feel anxieties about things that we thought would be behind us as a people into our 40's and 50's. This is a profound thing. No one has really studied the implications this has for citizenship and why more and more people may be vulnerable to siren songs of resentment that divide us instead of unite us.

I'm telling you, there are millions of people that go home every night and sit down at the dinner table and look across the table at their families and wonder whether they have failed them, when all they ever did was show up for work, because of the way the global economy has impacted on them in this society. This is a significant thing.

And when you combine that with the fact that there is so much mobility in this society, much more than ever before, it is more difficult for many of these people to get the kind of support networks they need in their communities because a lot of folks live in communities where neighbors don't know their neighbors anymore. And if there's a high crime rate in the community, they don't have any way to get to know them.

So that all these things need to be seen in that context. There is a great deal of uncertainty out there, which makes people yearn for certainty but also makes them vulnerable to the wrong kind of certainty, certainty that pits people against one another instead of gives them a way to say, "Here are my problems; what are your problems? Let's get together and figure out how to solve them."

So I think that the sense of, literally, physical instability so many adults feel make it more difficult to hold our society together and make it more difficult to impart the fundamental character strengths and traits, and the accompanying security of knowing that you're in the right place in your life, that are essential to a strong society—not an excuse for not doing it, but it's

important to understand the context in which we operate here.

Now, one of the things that we have thought about in our administration is that in this environment, when so many of our children are in families that are at least not traditional families, when their parents are working, working harder and maybe spending less time with them, and when their neighborhoods may be less settled and in many cases less safe, it is more important than it has been perhaps in immediately previous years to reemphasize the role of character education in our schools—something which once was taken for granted as a part of education, sort of faded away, and we believe should be brought back. We know it has to be a supplement for the work that families and communities do, not a replacement. We know there's no substitute for the character lessons that are imparted to people by their parents and grandparents or for the guidance that a father or mother can bring or, maybe even more importantly, for the sense of security and rootedness that the right kind of relationships within families give us all. But still, I think it's important to recognize that all of our children show up for school sooner or later, and character education can be a vital part of building the kind of society that recognizes responsibilities and has a sense of community.

This is an issue I've been involved with for years. Several years ago in the mid-eighties, I served on the Carnegie commission for middle school education. There were two Governors on that commission; I had the privilege of being one. The other was the distinguished Republican Governor of New Jersey, Tom Kean. And one of the recommendations we made was that we should teach our children in middle school with specific objectives to, quote, "behave ethically and assume the responsibilities of citizenship in a pluralistic society," and that we had to connect our schools to our communities, which together share responsibility for each student's success.

When I became President, we started to work on this through the Department of Education. Secretary Riley has helped us to go a good ways toward the right kind of introduction of values into our schools. Everybody knows that education is about more than intellect. Everybody knows, as my mother used to say, there's a lot of smart fools running around in this old world. [*Laughter*] And what we want to do is to build good citizens as well as intelligent people.

We need to learn what it takes to build up and not tear down a society over the long run. So we've worked hard on that. Most of you know that the Elementary and Secondary Education Act contained new authority for programs that foster character education, for us to support them. And in partnership with local communities, we are now making States eligible to compete for grants to help to support the institution of character education programs in local school districts all across the country. I personally long for the day when this is once again a regular part of the curriculum of every school district in the United States. I think it is very, very important.

The safe and drug-free school program, which is one of the things I've been fighting for in this little rescission battle we've got going on here in Washington today, also has specific, explicit efforts in it to create an environment in which children are able to learn and in which we not only make schools safe and drug-free by negative actions like security devices but in which we change the attitudes of children about what is acceptable within the schools, what is acceptable conduct within the schools.

All of you know that there is some evidence out there already that these character education programs really work to lower the drop out rate, to increase educational performance, and to increase good citizenship. It is elementary. It is simple. But I think it is profoundly important that young people be taught that it's important to tell the truth, that it's important to be trustworthy and for people to be able to rely on you, that it's important not to abuse the freedom you have by undermining other people's ability to exercise their freedom. They need to be taught certain basic things in the context of the school environment, which is, after all, for many of them, the first diverse community they will ever be a part of. So I feel very strongly that this is part of what we ought to be doing, but not all.

I think that, as I said, the fundamental insight that I have gotten about how to do this from Dr. Etzioni is that we have to build networks. And this, as you know, is the second conference on character building we've had where we've welcomed people to the White House. I would very much like to see this institutionalized as an annual event that goes way beyond my administration, that encompasses Republicans and

Democrats, and that has nothing to do with politics.

Indeed, I think we should view this effort in our country not as bipartisan but as nonpartisan. And we need to think about ways that we can continue to build networks that work together for a generation, because a lot of our problems were a generation in coming and they're going to be a generation in going, and because there is nothing we can do that will stop the world from changing as quickly as it is, so we're going to have to work harder and harder to think of ways that keep the ties that bind. Therefore, I believe this should become a permanent fixture of our national dialog.

I would like to also, from my point of view, take this up a notch in the present time because of the dimensions of our challenges. On June 21st, I'm going to invite leaders to come here from all around the country to listen to each other, to open a dialog, to try to find common ground on our great social challenges of the day, and to talk about what it would take to build not only good character but good citizenship from people individually and in groups, and to see whether or not we can accelerate this dialog throughout the country. I am going to ask academic and business leaders, religious leaders, media people, people from the sports community, people from other aspects of the private sector, and of course, Government folks to try to build the kind of partnership that I think is necessary.

James Madison once said that all governments required virtue of their citizens, but democracies needed it more than other kinds of government. And I believe that. Some of you may know that Hillary is now working on a book about the responsibilities we owe to our children. The title will come from that old African proverb, it takes a whole village to raise a child.

Now, I ask you to think about this—and I would like to make some closing remarks about where I'm going with this June 21st conference and invite you to give me your ideas about it. I think that in the world we are living in, it will take a lot of people, and not just Government programs, to keep our children off the streets and in school. It will take every parent, teacher, friend, and loved one we can find to teach children, given all their different circumstances in America today, the differences between right and wrong and to give them the kind of self-esteem they need to do well in a troubled world, to say no to the right things but also to figure out what to say yes to, which in the end is the basis of the quality of life we all live.

And I am absolutely convinced, as I have watched the patterns of life in our society, that as people go through different stages in their lives or they're in different places in society, most of them are not most influenced by Government, there are other forces which are influencing them, and that we all have to pull together if we're going to have any hope of succeeding in this enterprise.

If you look at business, for example—I mentioned the economic changes—I had to fight like crazy for the family and medical leave law. It had already been passed by Congress twice and vetoed twice by well-meaning people who thought that—business people said, "Oh, the world will come to an end if the family medical leave law passes." But it cannot be, if you think about it, first and foremost, it cannot be that a society where the economic forces require most adults to work—women and men, even parents of very young children—it cannot be that a good society can be built unless people can succeed as both workers and parents. If we cannot succeed as workers, then our standard of living will fall and everything that we think about America will begin to be eroded. But if we don't succeed as parents, then we'll have a lot of people with money and miserable lives. And we have too many people in this country today, not only poor people but people who aren't poor, who have miserable lives.

So, the first and most fundamental thing we have to say is, how are people going to succeed as workers and as parents? The Government can do the family and medical leave law, but that's just the first step. How can you justify the fact that most people are working harder for less money when business profits are up and corporations are up? We had record numbers of new millionaires last year. I like that, by the way. I don't think wealth formation is bad. I think it's good. But the thing that holds a democratic society together is that everybody gets their fair share.

In the 12 years before I became President— this has nothing to do with Government policies, nearly as I can determine—executive salaries went up 4 times as much as workers' salaries went up in major American corporations and 3 times as much as corporate profits went up.

And you can say, "Well, labor's not worth as much as it used to be because technology means fewer people can do more with less." That may be, but all those people are still people. They have children to raise. They have mortgages to pay. They have problems to confront.

One of the companies that I really admire in this country today has set up a system in which both the workers and the executives get paid based on the performance of the company, so that when the company does well, the workers have just a big a gain as the executives. And if the company has a bad turn, the executives have to take an even bigger hit percentagewise than the workers. Now, that's the kind—they also have as part of their bonus program a $2,000-a-year grant to every child of every employee in the company that goes to college. They have one person that sent 11 kids to college working for that company. The only reason I'm not telling you who the company is, is I don't want every person with six or more children in America to go apply for work there. [*Laughter*]

But don't you see? Here is a company that says, "Okay, we want to make money. We want to do well. We think we can do right and do well. We want a—we believe we'll make more money if the people working for us know they can make more money if the company does well." This is part of citizenship. I'm not suggesting the Government should mandate this. I'm talking about partnerships, networking, community, open and honest discussion. But first and foremost, most of the work of building character in America is going to be done in the family, and you must make it possible for people to succeed as parents and workers. So, that should be a part of this debate.

Now, the media has a responsibility here. We have tough choices to make as a country. People need to know the facts that will shape their future—important for adults, important for children. Let me give you an example: Weekly Reader is launching a new project to teach the value of citizenship to young children through stories. That's a good thing. That's the sort of thing the media can do. I'm not suggesting the Government should mandate it, but we should talk about it. Nobody should feel threatened or feel like we're trying to encroach on the first amendment by discussing the power on social behavior that the media has. We should be able to discuss it without anybody being defensive about it.

Here in Washington, we are facing difficult but important issues of public policy. We have two huge deficits from a public policy point of view. We've got a Government budget deficit, which is much lower than it was when I became President, but it's too big. And we do need, in a global economy, a balanced budget because we don't want to be more dependent than we have to be on outside forces and we want to be able to invest in our future. But we also have a big education deficit and training deficit compared to many other countries and compared to what we need for America to be the strongest and greatest economy in the world in the 21st century.

So, we've got a big, tough decision here. How are we going to solve one without undermining the other? Can we do both at the same time? If so, how? Now, this can immediately dissolve into a huge political screaming match in which one party sticks up for one, the other sticks up for the other, everybody gets reelected at election time, and nobody gets anything done. That would not be good. What we need to do is to figure out how we can reach across the divides to a common consensus that will permit us to pursue both these objectives at the same time.

The American people are ready for some tough decisions and difficult medicine, but they want to know that it's fair and sensible and what's down there at the end of the road. And to do it, we need to get information in a way that is not designed to divide us but is designed to shed more light than heat. And it is a very difficult thing, but very important.

Religious and community institutions have an important role to play. You know, if every church in America, every church in America had not only a vigorous program for its own members and the people it's recruiting but also an outreach to a fixed number of families and children to fight the problems of out-of-wedlock birth, teen pregnancy, drug addiction, school dropout—if every single church had just a fixed and reasonable number of kids it was targeting, it might have more impact than all the Government programs we could ever devise.

This is the most religious country in the world. We have the largest number of churches, the most diverse group of people worshiping in different kinds of religions. And again, it's not for the Government to require this, but it's worth talking about. Because there is a great debate today in the religious community about whether the best thing you can do for society to make it better is go out and try to actually work with people who are in trouble and make them better individually, or to simply make political prescriptions that everyone else should follow and if they do, fine, and if they don't, we'll wait for the next election.

So, I think this is a debate we ought to have. Because—I have no objection, by the way, to the political debate, and I have encouraged the people of faith who come to different political conclusions than I have to be a part of the debate. I don't think that's bad. But I think we are not purely either political animals, people who go to work, or churchgoers. We also have community responsibilities and opportunities. And the organized churches of this country can have a big impact on changing the lives of people and improving the character of people and the prospects of people today in the country. And many do, many do. If all did, it would make a big difference in our ability to move forward on common ground.

If you think about—let me mention the entertainment industry. There's been a lot said about that, and I got a big standing ovation at the State of the Union from both Republican and Democratic Members of Congress when I talked about the damage that comes to our society from incessant, repetitive, mindless violence coming through entertainment. There are lots of studies showing that young people tend to get numbed to violence and to the consequences of it from constant overexposure to it. And I say this not to point the finger at anybody. I have enjoyed more than my fair share of what I would call cheap thrills movies in my time, so I am not being sanctimonious about this. I'm just saying it is an established fact that if children from very early ages are exposed to huge volumes of a certain kind of entertainment, it desensitizes them to the same sort of conduct in the real world. There's lots of evidence about that.

And that's why, frankly, I welcome the networks' recent efforts to reduce prime-time violence and why I would applaud the decision that Time-Warner announced this week to set standards for controversial music and to balance creative expression with corporate responsibility. And I applaud the efforts of Bill Bennett, who was here yesterday, to get that done. The country owes him a debt of gratitude, and we should applaud Time-Warner as well.

The children's educational television act—television education act was passed back in 1990. I think there is more to do here. We need—the broadcasters need to read that act again and adhere to its spirit as well as to its letters. We should be thinking twice before movies and rap music that celebrate violence against women or law enforcement officers are put out there in huge volume, in piling one on top of one another. There is a connection, in this sense, between words and deeds. We do get dulled of that to which we are overexposed in a banalizing way.

Let me finally say that I think politicians have a responsibility here. And instead of criticizing others, let me start with myself. If you want to be an elected official in a democracy you must, first of all, get people to identify with you more than your opponent. And you must say, "Here are the differences between us, and here's what I stand for. Here are the choices we face, and here are the decisions I would make. And here is why I would make those decisions." So in that sense, conflict and difference and dividing up the electorate are the essence of politics.

But there is a big difference between division and difference of opinion and destruction and demonization. And there is a big difference between difference and dehumanization. Let me just begin—let me just—I'll start with me, because this is something I've been through in the last few weeks.

I know that I—I don't know of a politician that hasn't done this that's been around very long, but I don't know how many times that I have made references to Government bureaucrats, right? Because when a politician stands up and says something about Government bureaucrats, 99 times out of 100, the word is used in a pejorative sense, right? And it's used to remind you of the fact that the person you've elected is not really a part of the Government, he's a part of you, that he's more like a tax payer than a tax consumer. And we know you resent paying your taxes, and we know you think a lot of it is wasted. And so, if we who are elected talk about Government bureaucrats, you'll know we're still on your side, even though we're living over here on the other side.

You know what I'm talking about. Now, almost—first of all, there is some individual truth to all this. That is, there is hardly an American living who hasn't had some encounter with the Government that was distasteful, right? [*Laughter*] Because as long as people are running the Government, they will be like people running churches, people running businesses, people running whatever it is you do: People are imperfect, and they'll mess up, and when they do, they drive other people up the wall.

But the Government has a special relationship to people because it has the power of law behind it. So, almost everybody can remember someone who was at least rude or perhaps a law enforcement official that abused authority on occasion or a tax person who was really unfair or a regulator who was overbearing. Almost everybody has had some experience because we live in a society of human beings where people mess up. So there is some truth to that.

It is also true that at this time, the Government tends to lag the private sector in changes. Sometimes that's good; sometimes that's bad. But it does because the environment in which the Government operates is not as competitive. But that is, we normally have—we have more of a monopoly on income and customers, so it lags. On the other hand, that's not all bad because it helps to be a force of stability too, sometimes, in times of great change. But the Government, in the end, must follow the great trends of the day.

So, must the Government become less bureaucratic, more flexible, more open? Will it be smaller? Will fewer people do more with less? Absolutely. All that will happen. We had to take the size of the Government down. It's already over 100,000 smaller than it was when I became President. We had to get rid of hundreds of programs that just didn't make any sense any more. We have to do these things. And we have to take it down more. We have to continue to reduce unnecessary spending. And we'll have to have more people take these early retirement packages and all that. That's all true.

But that's different from saying "Government bureaucrats" in a demeaning way. Let me tell you something—you think about this. The children who died in that child care center in Oklahoma City were the children of Government bureaucrats. The people who were carried out of that building from the Agriculture Department, from the Veterans Affairs Administration, from the Housing and Urban Development Department, and from all of our law enforcement agencies, the Secret Service, the ATF, all of them, they were all Government bureaucrats. And I will never, knowingly, use that term again.

So we've all got to start with each other here. I don't know that that's a very good character example. I don't know that that does much to build good character, when you identify a group as a group and pretend that as a group there's something wrong with them.

So I would say to you, to all of you, I am basically very optimistic about the future of this country. I know we're more violent than we need to be, but we always have been. We always have been, and we need—we've got to get a hold of it. And I know we have too many out-of-wedlock births, but it's a trend that is gripping an awful lot of Western countries. And people have forgotten, in my judgment, the profound emotional consequences to the children who grow up in unstable and inadequately supported environments. So we're not alone in that. We have way too much drug addiction, and we are really almost alone in that. Hardly any other advanced country has anything approaching the levels of violence and drug addiction we do. So we do have profound problems.

Our political debate is too polarized. And we have a lot of people who talk a lot about what's wrong with everybody else and don't do very much to change it. There are all kinds of problems. But look, this is not the Great Depression; this is not World War II; this is not the Civil War; we are not starting from scratch like the Founders did.

We know what to do. We know the difference between right and wrong. We know how to do this. And we can do what we have to do. We can do this. This is not a cause for wringing

of hands. It is difficult. It is a new challenge to figure out how we all work together and still leave room for our differences, how we identify the specific roles of the various influence centers in our society to reinstill character and give a good life to our people. But the fundamental fact is that this is a very great country, and nearly everybody is still getting up every day and doing the very best they can to do what is right. Nearly everybody desperately wants to have children who have good character and who do good and who are good, nearly everybody.

So I think what you are here about is profoundly important. But what I want to say to you is, do not be discouraged. In the light of the whole history of our Republic, this is our job at this time. It is not an undoable job. It is profoundly important. It will be difficult because of all the forces working on people's state of mind that undermine what we have to do. Because it's so much easier in the world today to identify what we're against instead of what we're for. It's so much easier in the world today not to look at the problems within our own hearts and minds because we can always find somebody we think is worse. So it is so much easier to put this off and delay it. And there are no institutions really for bringing us all together, across all the lines that divide us, in our common cause of building what is good about America and building up what is good within the character of our people. But we can do it. And I believe we will.

Thank you very much.

NOTE: The President spoke at 10:30 a.m. in Room 450 of the Old Executive Office Building. In his remarks, he referred to Amitai Etzioni, founder and chair, Communitarian Network.

Statement on the Hospitalization of Les Aspin
May 20, 1995

I was saddened to hear that former Defense Secretary Les Aspin was hospitalized earlier today. Hillary and I wish him a speedy recovery.

Our prayers are with him and his family at this time.

Statement on the Second Anniversary of the National Voter Registration Act of 1993
May 20, 1995

Two years ago today, I signed into law the National Voter Registration Act, better known as "motor-voter." This commonsense law is making it easier for all Americans to register to vote. Motor-voter promised to open up the democratic process, and I am pleased to report that it is delivering on that promise.

Across America, nearly 2 million citizens have registered to vote in the 5 months since the law went into effect. In Georgia, 180,000 people registered in the first 3 months of this year, compared to only 85,000 all last year. In North Carolina, 30,000 citizens are registering per month, up from 6,000 a month in 1991. And in Alabama, 43,000 people registered in the first 3 months of this year, compared to only 23,000 in the same period last year.

Motor-voter is working because it makes sense. The Act simply requires States to make registration easier by making more forms available, at motor vehicle offices, social agencies, and through the mail. It is that simple.

Motor-voter is the latest step in our Nation's efforts to enfranchise all our citizens, giving them the power to affect their own destiny and our common destiny by participating fully in our democracy. I am proud to see it working so well.

Remarks at the White House Photographers Association Dinner
May 20, 1995

I want to gets lots of records of you clapping for me. [*Laughter*] Well, ladies and gentlemen, tonight I feel your pain. [*Laughter*] Is there a courier around here anywhere? [*Laughter*] I hate these name tags. [*Laughter*]

I just wanted you to see what it feels like to have your picture taken when you're eating. [*Laughter*]

I am here tonight to address a very relevant issue: The President is funny. The power of the Presidency makes me funny. [*Laughter*] If you don't believe me, don't laugh at these jokes, have a nice audit. [*Laughter*]

You know, I used to complain about how all of you were trying to get my attention, you know, for photos—"Over here!" "Over here!" "Over here!" "Over here!" "Just one more!" "Just one more!"—and I didn't like the way you tried to get my attention until I heard about how the Russian police tried to get Jeremy Gaines' attention last week. [*Laughter*] Now you can "just one more" me from now to kingdom come, and I won't bite. [*Laughter*]

You know, I thought Mike McCurry was a model Press Secretary, even before I saw this month's Esquire. Did you see him, with his model picture from the 1970's? This man used to be a model. This goes to show you that not all plastic surgery works. [*Laughter*] If you like the outfit he's wearing tonight, however, you can order it from the White House spring catalog. [*Laughter*]

You know, I'm sorry I've never been here before. I really do like all of you very much. But it wasn't until a few days ago that I found out that this is the only place I could be with you and you wouldn't have all those question-askers around with you. [*Laughter*]

One of the things I want to do is to compliment Mike McCurry's policy of having the Press Office staff in the White House send him a note each day to show what good deeds they've done for the press corps or kick a dollar into the pizza fund. This, of course, was an expansion, an improvement on my original idea in which everybody at the White House kicks in a dollar anyway and we just order pizza. [*Laughter*]

Tonight I want to share with you some of the notes Mike has received from the staff:

To Mike from McNeely: "Yesterday I performed my annual ritual of getting out of the shot." Think about that. [*Laughter*]

To Mike from Josh: "I held Paul Hosefros of the New York Times by the feet and suspended him from the ceiling so the New York Times could run one more bizarre angle of the President's picture." [*Laughter*]

To Mike from Ralph: "I gave Ira Wyman CPR after he jogged with the President." [*Laughter*]

To Mike from Sharon: "I helped Ken Lambert prepare for his interview with Jesse Helms regarding his pending NEA grant." [*Laughter*]

Now, not everybody could meet Mike's challenge, so the pizza fund only had about 20 bucks in it. So I decided the First Lady should manage the fund. [*Laughter*] And she has invested it so wisely—[*laughter*]—that beginning Monday morning, daily, the Four Seasons will be catering filet mignon in the Press Office. [*Laughter*]

I had a wonderful time tonight being on the other end of the camera.

I want to congratulate the award winners and to say to all of you, the photographers, editors, engineers, producers, and cameramen and women with whom I've shared these extraordinary past couple of years, I watch your work with great appreciation. You have transmitted images that no one who was there could never forget. I know I'll never forget, from the DMZ in Korea to the swollen banks of the Mississippi River to the beaches of Normandy, the NCAA championship—the one I liked—[*laughter*]—this remarkable picture on the cover of your program, which hangs in my private office in the White House because I liked it so much.

And like the priest who gave us the wonderful invocation, I want to say a special word of thanks for the work all of you did to make Oklahoma City real to us, both the agony and America at its best.

The great photojournalists, the men and women who are carrying on the great tradition of Mathew Brady, from the Civil War to Robert Capa's D-Day photography to Joe Rosenthal's remarkable memory of Iwo Jima, I salute you all.

I thank you for what you have done. And I hope that as we continue our journey together, me in the limo and you guys 20 cars behind—[*laughter*]—you will every now and then cut me a little slack for being nearly 50 and a bit on the heavy side. [*Laughter*]

Now before I leave tonight, I want to make one very important policy announcement. I will not jog in the morning. In fact, I will do nothing until 10:45 a.m., so the pool call time is 10:30 a.m., not 6:45 a.m. [*Applause*]

Now I'm going to go so you can enjoy the rest of the evening. Now, I'll start late so you can have a good night's sleep. The pool has to go with me, and the rest of you can stay. [*Laughter*] Ralph, you can stay, too. [*Laughter*]

Good night, and God bless you all. Thank you.

NOTE: The President spoke at 8:10 p.m. at the Washington Hilton. In his remarks, he referred to Robert W. McNeely, Director, White House Photographic Services; Joshua A. King, Director of Production for Presidential Events; and official White House photographers Ralph Alswang and Sharon C. Farmer.

Statement on the Death of Les Aspin
May 21, 1995

I speak for millions of Americans when mourning the death today of Les Aspin and join many others in saying that he was my friend.

As a Member of the House of Representatives for 22 years, chairman of the House Armed Services Committee for 8, Secretary of Defense, and Chairman of the President's Foreign Intelligence Advisory Board, Les rendered our Nation extraordinary, selfless service.

Les Aspin accomplished greatly because he cared greatly. He brought the same commitment to his most recent assignment that he brought to Washington as a young congressional aide, staff assistant at the Council of Economic Advisers, and Defense Department official in the 1960's.

No one knew better than he how Washington works, but he never thought of it as a game for its own sake. He was here to make a difference. And he did. He probed and helped shape a generation of American defense policies and budgets, culminating in the decisive bottom-up review of our military strategy, which he conducted as Secretary of Defense.

Les Aspin was unique. He brought the light of his joy in living and the heat of his intellect to every occasion. He never met a person who didn't like him. And we all will miss him.

Remarks on Signing the Paperwork Reduction Act of 1995
May 22, 1995

Thank you very much. Mr. Bersoff, thank you for your comments and for the outstanding example of the family business you have built to such a remarkable extent. Thank you, Sally Katzen.

Before I begin, as a matter of personal privilege, I would just like to say a brief word about the death of my good friend Les Aspin. Hillary and I grieve his loss, and along with all other Americans, we thank him for the remarkable service he rendered to our country as a distinguished Congressman from Wisconsin, as the chairman of the Armed Services Committee of the House, as Secretary of Defense, and as head of the President's Foreign Intelligence Advisory Board. He did a lot of work to keep us safe through a turbulent time, and we are all very, very much in his debt.

Let me thank the Members of Congress who are here. You know, I've got to say, I was sitting here listening to Mr. Bersoff talk, and I thought, it'll be a miracle if we get this on the news tonight, because this is something we did without anybody fighting. [*Laughter*] And the real reason this languished around for 5 years was because nobody was fighting anybody else about it. And after I got here, I discovered some of the best ideas in Washington were not being implemented simply because there was no anger attached to them. It's a sad thing to say, but it's absolutely right.

And so, sometimes energy is not behind things that hang around here for years, because there's no real brutal conflict. And in that context, I want to thank the Members of Congress who are here for overcoming all the inertia against consensus—[*laughter*]—and actually passing a bill that everybody was for. And I thank you. I thank Senators Nunn, Roth, and Glenn; Representatives Meyers, Sisisky, Peterson, and Davis, all of whom are here; and of course, former Congressman Horton and former

Senator, now Governor, Lawton Chiles for the work that they have done.

This is a remarkable bill, and I want to talk about what it does. But first, let me say that for a bill in which there was not a lot of opposition, there was an awful lot of support and input about exactly how to do this. People all over our country, big and small businesses, organizations from the National Governors' Association to the National Association of Towns and Townships to librarians actually testified in favor of this bill—what we ought to do and how it ought to be done.

The legislation recognizes that the private sector is the engine of our prosperity, that when we act to protect the environment or the health of our people, we ought to do it without unnecessary paperwork, maddening redtape, or irrational rules.

We have to reform our regulatory system in ways that protects the larger public interest without strangling business. These changes reflect the right way to reform Government. It is very consistent with the things that I believe need to be done. In the last 2 years, we have already reduced the size of the Federal bureaucracy by more than 100,000 employees, going down under existing budgets to a reduction of more than 272,000. And if the last few weeks are any indication, we're about to reduce the Government some more.

This Paperwork Reduction Act helps us to conquer a mountain of paperwork that is crushing our people and wasting a lot of time and resources and which actually accumulated not because anybody wanted to harm the private sector but because we tend to think of good ideas in serial form without thinking of how the overall impact of them impacts a system that is very dynamic and very sensitive to emerging technologies but which Government does not always respond to in the same way.

I want to say again how much I appreciate the work that Sally Katzen and her shop have done. And I want to thank the Congress for enabling them to continue on the job.

In recent months, some others have made similar announcements. Carol Browner, at the EPA, announced that she would cut the paperwork requirements of the EPA on the private sector by 25 percent. To give you an idea of what that means, that is 20 million hours of labor a year.

We often debate here what we can give the American people. We're about to have a debate: Should we give the American people more funds for education, more funds for Medicare, or more money back in a tax cut? But nothing is more precious, I see as I get older, than your own time. And for a Government to give the American people back, at no cost to the public interest, 20 million hours, is an extraordinary gift and worth a great deal of money and additions to the quality of life.

The FDA is going to dramatically speed approvals of many different kinds of medical devices. The SBA has reduced the inch-thick loan form applications to one page.

Here are some other places we will cut. The Department of Agriculture so far has eliminated the need for more than 3 million pages of Government forms from a quarter million farmers. The Department of Energy took these 3 big binders here, filled with reporting requirements, and sliced them to 11 pages—11 pages from those 3 big binders. That saved $48 million a year, but it also gave the gift of time back to the people who were subject to it.

The Department of Education required both parents to sign a student loan and other financial aid forms. This is impossible in some cases when the noncustodial parent is not available. In lots of homes today, it's hard for both parents to be in the same place at the same time anyway. Now, one parent's signature is all that's required.

So far, we have eliminated the forms represented in this large stack of papers here on the table. When you count all the people and all the businesses that have to fill out the forms already eliminated, in one year, we've eliminated paper that would stretch end to end from Washington, DC, to San Francisco, California.

To further reduce these burdens, I have directed our agencies to continue to review their regulations, to eliminate the outdated and streamline the bloated. I have also directed them, whenever possible, to cut in half the frequency of reports they require from citizens. For example, if they ask for quarterly reports, why don't we just have them twice a year instead?

As we reform, we need not compromise the quality of life or the needed oversight from the Government. But the truth is, we can actually improve the system by making it less hidebound and by innovating as Americans are innovating.

Today I want to add another dimension to this effort: From this point forward, I want all of our agencies to provide for the electronic submission of every new Government form or demonstrate to OMB why it cannot be done that way. The old way will still be available, but I think once people see how fast and efficient electronic filing can be, we'll see less paperwork and more of these. So, we're trying to do our part to act in good faith the way these Members of Congress intended the executive branch to act.

As you know, these little things store incredible volumes of information—incredible. My daughter knows more about it than I do, but I'm learning myself, just in the things that we do, incredibly how much more we can do and at a tiny fraction of the space involved, not to mention the speed. So the more we use electronic transmissions, the more we'll all be working quicker and smarter, giving better service to the American public, a more efficient Government, and far, far less paperwork.

I want to say again, the remarkable thing about this effort was that at the time we actually got it through the Congress, there was not a single dissenting vote. But very often the things we do not do in life are the things we all know we should do. That is a principle that extends beyond this bill.

And we owe a great debt of gratitude to the Members of Congress, especially those here present, who exercised the leadership to get this done, as well as to Governor Chiles and former Congressman Horton for the work they did to pave the way. So I would like to ask the Members to come up while we sign the bill, and Congressman Horton and Governor Chiles to come up as well. Please come up, and we'll do it.

Thank you very much.

[At this point, the President signed the bill.]

Thank you very much. We're adjourned. Thank you.

NOTE: The President spoke at 2:18 p.m. in Room 450 of the Old Executive Office Building. In his remarks, he referred to Ed Bersoff, president and chief executive officer, BTG, Inc. S. 244, approved May 22, was assigned Public Law No. 104–13.

Message to the Congress Transmitting a Report on Trade With Romania
May 19, 1995

To the Congress of the United States:

I hereby transmit a report concerning emigration laws and policies of the Republic of Romania as required by subsections 402(b) and 409(b) of Title IV of the Trade Act of 1974, as amended ("the Act"). I have determined that Romania is in full compliance with the criteria in subsections 402(a) and 409(a) of the Act. As required by Title IV, I will provide the Congress with periodic reports regarding Romania's compliance with these emigration standards.

WILLIAM J. CLINTON

The White House,
May 19, 1995.

NOTE: This message was released by the Office of the Press Secretary on May 23. The related memorandum is listed in Appendix D at the end of this volume.

The President's News Conference
May 23, 1995

The President. Good afternoon. I want to speak with you today about legislation that Congress is considering which would place new restrictions on how America conducts its foreign policy and slash our budget in foreign affairs. I believe these bills threaten our ability to preserve America's global leadership and to safeguard the security and prosperity of the American people in the post-cold-war world. The world is still full of dangers but more full of opportunities, and the United States must be able to act aggressively to combat foreign threats and to make commitments and then to keep those commitments. These bills would deprive us of both those capabilities.

Supporters of the bills call them necessary cost-cutting measures. But in reality, they are the most isolationist proposals to come before the United States Congress in the last 50 years. They are the product of those who argue passionately that America must be strong and then turn around and refuse to pay the price of that strength or to give the Presidency the means to assert that strength.

The price of conducting our foreign policy is, after all, not very high. Today, it's slightly more than one percent of the budget. Let me say that again: slightly more than one percent of the budget. That's about one-fifteenth of what Americans think it is, according to the most recent surveys. And it's only one-fifth of what Americans believe would be about the right amount to spend.

In other words, we don't spend 15 percent of the budget on foreign policy, or even 5 percent, but just a little over one percent. And that one percent, which includes our contributions to the multilateral development banks, helps to dismantle nuclear weapons, saves lives by preventing famines, immunizing children, and combating terrorists and drug-traffickers. Bills in both the House and the Senate place new restrictions on our ability to meet these dangers as well as to take advantage of all the opportunities that are out there for the United States.

For example, one bill, "The American Overseas Interests Act," which is being debated on the House floor just this week, would compromise our efforts to stop North Korea's nuclear program, impose conditions that could derail our support for democratic reform in Russia, and restrict the President's ability to prevent illegal immigration. The bill would also mandate an ill-conceived restructuring of agencies responsible for our foreign affairs.

Taken together, these constraints represent nothing less than a frontal assault on the authority of the President to conduct the foreign policy of the United States and on our Nation's ability to respond rapidly and effectively to threats to our security.

Repeatedly, I have said there are right ways and wrong ways to cut the deficit. This legislation is the wrong way. We did not win the cold war to walk away and blow the opportunities of the peace on shortsighted, scattershotted budget cuts and attempts to micromanage the United States foreign policy.

That's why Secretaries Christopher, Perry, and Rubin and Ambassador Albright have recommended that I veto this bill being considered by the House this week. But it is not too late to reconsider. These are dangerous proposals. Our administration is ready to work with Congress, and I remain hopeful that the long tradition of bipartisanship in foreign affairs, which I have appreciated and been a part of, will continue throughout this session of Congress.

I urge Congress to send me a bill that protects the fundamental interests of the American people, a bill that I can sign.

Budget Proposals

Q. Leon Panetta said that trying to balance the budget in 7 years would be nuts. Laura Tyson said it would be bad for the American economy. And over the weekend, you said it could be done and that after the Republicans propose and dispose of the budget they're dealing with now, you would offer your own plan to do so. Can you tell us why the disagreement within your administration, and what exactly you do intend to propose?

The President. Well, it can be done, but it is not good policy to do it. Those things are not inconsistent. It is mathematically possible to do it, but having analyzed the alternatives for doing it, we believe that it cannot be done

consistent with the interests of the American economy.

Now—in other words, I believe that all Americans should be committed to bringing our budget into balance within a reasonable amount of time that we can determine. And I believe we should be committed to working together toward that end. But I do not believe it is good policy, based on my understanding of this budget, which is pretty good now, to do it in 7 years.

Keep in mind—let's back up a minute. What is the fundamental problem with the American economy? Is it the deficit? I have worked hard to reduce the deficit. But what happened when we reduced the deficit—the Republicans now use 7-year terms, so let's talk about 7 years. In 1993, the deficit reduction plan we adopted reduced the deficit by $1 trillion over 7 years. And even though not a single one of them voted for it and never engaged us in any kind of cooperative effort, they obviously like building on it, and it makes it possible for them to argue that now the budget can be brought into balance.

What did we get out of it? We got declining interest rates and a growing income for the economy, 6.3 million new jobs. What is the problem now with the American economy? The incomes of the American people are not going up in the global economy. If you reduce the deficit to zero, if you balance the budget in 7 years, with the evidence we now have, that would either require massive tax increases or massive budget cuts, which would be unfair to our long-term objective to stabilize the incomes and the way of living of the American people. If you ignore it, the same thing would happen. So that's the point that we made. I don't think the two things are inconsistent at all.

Q. What are you going to do? What are you going to do, sir?

The President. I'm going—well, for one thing, the Republicans have to resolve the differences between themselves. They have to produce a budget resolution. The President has no role in the budget resolution and cannot veto it; it's a guidance. Then the budget process will begin. That's the reconciliation process, and that process the President has a role in, because I have a veto. I have shown—if you look at the debate in the rescissions bill, you see that I have shown good faith. I will not do what they did 2 years ago. I will not walk away from this process.

Look at the rescission bill. At the appropriate time, I sat down with the Republicans in the Senate, who made it clear that they wanted us to do that; we worked out an agreement for big spending cuts. Then, when it was changed behind closed doors, I offered an alternative budget in the rescission context—what I have done today. It was a responsible thing to do. I still want deficit reduction in the rescission bill. I still want to work with the Congress, and I will do so.

And if you look at how I handled the rescission business, we put people first, we put investment first, but we reached agreement on how much we should cut, spending and rescissions. We can do the same thing here.

Q. [Inaudible]—your own counterbudget and to get the budget into balance in less than 10 years. Could you share with us some ideas about how you would do that?

The President. Well, we've already made clear—I've already made clear what my problems are and where we need to start. First of all, I told everybody, including the White House Conference on Aging, that we were going to have to make some changes. But let's deal with what I think the problems are.

Both of the Republican budget proposals propose big cuts in Medicare outside the context of health care reform. When I presented my initial budget to the Congress, I said we can cut the deficit much more, but we have to do it in the context of health care reform. Otherwise, you're going to have a lot of hardship on elderly people and others. Secondly, the tax cut is way, way too big, and it is essentially paying for tax cuts to people who are not needy and who are doing well in this economy by cutting Medicare. Thirdly, the education cuts are too deep. And fourthly, the Senate proposal cuts—raises taxes on working Americans with children with incomes under $28,000 and lowers taxes on people with incomes over $200,000. That's the reverse of what we ought to be about. And finally, the 7-year period is an arbitrary period not dominated by an analysis of economic policy and what's good to raise incomes but basically just a figure picked out of the air. So that's where I think we ought to begin.

Helen [Helen Thomas, United Press International].

Foreign Affairs Legislation

Q. Mr. President, are you going to veto the foreign affairs bill on the recommendation of your Cabinet if the changes you asked for are not made?

The President. I can't conceive of permitting it to become law, because it is an assault on the ability of the President to protect the interests of the American people and to pursue the foreign policy of the country.

And let me say that, again, I have worked with Congressman Gilman, with Chairman Gilman, for 2 years on many issues. I have worked with Republicans in both the House and the Senate. I have appreciated the support, even on controversial issues, given to me by the leadership of the House and the Senate when we were dealing with the very difficult issue of Mexico, for example.

So I do not want to jumpstart what has been—an unusual partisan split over foreign affairs. But while I hope it doesn't happen anytime soon, someday there'll be a Republican President here again. And this is about the Presidency. The Presidency cannot be hamstrung. We must allow the President to conduct the foreign policy of the United States in ways that make us safer, more secure, and more prosperous. This bill will undermine that objectives.

And again, I'd say, the one good thing that could come out of this great debate is, every single survey shows that the American people think we're spending 15 to 20 percent of their tax money on foreign aid. When you ask them what the right amount would be, they say, "Oh, about 5 percent." What would be too little? "Under 3 percent." But we're just spending a little more than one percent. We're spending about what the American people think—maybe they think we should spend more. We should not destroy the foreign aid budget.

But, furthermore, we should not handcuff the President. That is not the way to conduct the foreign affairs of this country. You cannot micromanage foreign policy.

Q. So is the answer, you will veto it?

The President. If this bill passes in its present form, I will veto it, yes.

Northern Ireland Peace Process

Q. Mr. President, the Irish economic conference is taking place here this week. I wonder if you could tell us if the tragedy, the terrible tragedy in Oklahoma City, has in any way altered your attitude toward the Sinn Fein party in Northern Ireland or towards Mr. Gerry Adams, who has defended terrorist actions in Britain?

The President. As long as he continues to renounce terrorism and as long as they continue on the progress that they—the path that they have set, including the willingness to talk about weapons decommissioning, then I think we're doing the right thing. We are supporting an end to terrorism and the beginning of peace and, I hope, more prosperity in Northern Ireland. That is consistent with our position here. And I think that's the right thing to do.

We're supporting an end to the kind of agonies that the people in Northern Ireland and Great Britain generally have suffered in the last 25 years and that the American people suffered most significantly in Oklahoma City but also at the World Trade Center.

Budget Proposals

Q. If the Republicans don't make a move on the budget in the areas you've asked them to, on Medicare in the context of health care reform and so on, will you still lay out a counterproposal that gets to balance?

The President. Well, when we get into the— when we get into the reconciliation process— I don't believe in idle exercises. When we got into the—look what we did in the rescission bill. I was very specific in dealing with the rescission bill. First of all, I sat down and tried to have a good-faith negotiation at the first opportunity. The first opportunity I had to negotiate in good faith with the Republican majority in Congress was in the United States Senate, and we did it in good faith and in great detail. And we did it in the context of agreeing to meet a target of significant deficit reduction.

Then, when the House and Senate went behind closed doors and put all that pork in the bill and took the education out of it and took the investments in environmental protection out of it, I said we had to make some changes, and I offered a specific alternative in the context of a decisionmaking process where I could have an impact. That is the procedure I will follow in dealing with the larger budget.

If you look at the rescission bill, you will see the way I am prepared to go forward. I will bargain and negotiate and deal in good faith, because I believe in deficit reduction. I believe in a balanced budget. But I also know we've got to invest in the people of this country if we're going to raise their incomes.

Bosnia

Q. You spoke earlier about keeping foreign commitments and why you thought that was important. Two years ago in this room, Secretary of State Warren Christopher said the clock is ticking on Serb aggression. The blockade of Sarajevo has been tightened; the snipers are back at work. Apparently you're the only person in the world who can stop this. Are you prepared to do more?

The President. Well, I do not—let me just say this: From the beginning of my campaign for President, I said that the one thing I did not think we should do is to send American troops into combat into Bosnia, nor did I believe we could be part of a United Nations mission in Bosnia with the kind of conditions on involvement that have been imposed on the UNPROFOR forces. I do not apologize for that. I think I was right then. I think that has still been the right case, right decision.

Every effort to be more aggressive in promoting peace and fighting aggression in Bosnia that has been made in the last 2 years has been made at the initiative of the United States. I thought for sure after the events of a few days ago, once again NATO airpower would be called into action. And I strongly supported it, and I was very surprised after the commanders on the ground asked for it that the United Nations stopped it.

But I believe that we are doing, at the moment, all we can do. We do not want to collapse the U.N. mission. And I believe the United Nations made a mistake in not calling NATO airpower in when the commanders asked for it. We are still doing the airlift there, now the biggest one in the history of the United States, the biggest one in world history. And we are prepared to do more. But I do not believe the United States has any business sending ground troops there. Yes?

Aircraft Contract With Saudi Arabia

Q. Mr. President, there were talks over the weekend between American industry and Saudi officials to try to expedite the transaction you brokered for Saudi Arabia to buy Boeing and McDonnell-Douglas commercial transports. Do you know what the outcome of those talks were? And do you know if there's going to be further delay in consummating the transaction, or is there a fixed date to close on it?

The President. I'm sorry, I do not know. I have done what I could to make sure that the contract stayed on track, but I do not know.

Thank you very much.

NOTE: The President's 96th news conference began at 2:24 p.m. in the Rose Garden at the White House.

Remarks at the Democratic Congressional Dinner
May 23, 1995

Thank you, Senator Daschle, for your leadership and your stirring introduction and your wise predictions. [*Laughter*] Thank you, Congressman Gephardt, for your leadership and your steadfastness. Congressman Matsui, Senator Dorgan, Senator Kerrey, and Congressman Frost, thank you for taking on the burden of our campaign committees and the hard work of recruiting our candidates and raising our funds and rebuilding our majorities. And thank you, ladies and gentlemen, for being here.

I thank all the Democratic Senators and Members of the House who are here, and many Members of Congress who are former Members of Congress who are here. If you will forgive me, I'd like to ask for a moment of applause for the memory of a former Member of Congress who is not here, Les Aspin, one of the finest people I ever knew. [*Applause*]

This has certainly been an interesting time, hasn't it? [*Laughter*] What's that old adage that we should—somebody should spare us from living in interesting times. It is a great honor and a great obligation for us to have the chance to serve in an interesting and profoundly important time, a time of great change, great opportunity, great dislocation, great difficulty, and great challenge for the people of this country and, therefore, those of us who wish to serve them.

At a time when many are so preoccupied with their own difficulties, it is difficult to sort through the blizzard of information and disinformation they get, even to understand what it is we are trying to do, much less to grasp how it will affect them. But I think, more and more, as time goes on now, the choices before the American people are becoming clearer, and I trust the direction we must take is as well.

We now hear the folks in the other party claiming great high ground for wanting to reduce the deficit and asking us to help. You remember how much help we got from them in the last 2 years? And I would remind you, those of you who voted for that, to remember that by their new 7-year calculations the 1993 budget plan that the Democrats adopted, without any help or even so much as serious discussion, cut the deficit a trillion dollars. They predicted the world would come to an end. Instead, the recession came to an end, and we had lower unemployment, low inflation, a booming stock market; first time in 20 years we've had unemployment among African-Americans below 10 percent; highest number of high-wage jobs in 6 years; a real sense of change in the economy, according to all the numbers.

But that hasn't filtered down to a lot of Americans yet. And that's what I want to talk to you about tonight. What are we doing here? Why are we Democrats? What do we hope to achieve? How do we communicate with the American people? And what does it all mean?

Well, the first thing I want to say is that we should just be grateful that we've had the chance in the last 2 years to do the right things. And we should understand if we failed, either through our own limitations or because of the circumstances of the time, to communicate what we had done to the people of this country, the fact is that in the light of history, the last 2 years will be viewed as a time when we got the deficit down, regained control of our economic destiny, actually invested more in our people and in their education and in their future, and made a serious effort to have the American people move into the 21st century with the American dream alive and well and with our security better protected at home and abroad.

In the last 2 years, we had the most productive time in terms of a partnership between the President and Congress in the last 30 years. And what was done in the crime bill, in the trade legislation, in the family and medical leave law, in act after act after act, was good for the American people. And we should be proud of that, and we should talk about it. And we should move forward.

We should also say to our friends in the other party, we do not intend to do you the way you did us, even though you were richly rewarded for doing it—[*laughter*]—because, unlike you in the last 2 years, we care so much about this country, we'll work with you. But you have to remember what we stand for, and you have to be willing to deal with what we stand for.

They are learning a little lesson now with their budget proposals and the real meaning of their contract on America, of what all people in public life learn, and that is that there are limits to calls for sacrifice. [*Laughter*]

My senior Senator, Dale Bumpers, he loves to tell a story about Huey Long being out on a country cross—is he here? I heard somebody clapping; I thought he was clapping. [*Laughter*] He loves to tell a story about Huey Long being out on a country crossroads speaking to a group of people about—in the Depression—about how we needed to share the wealth. And he spotted a farmer he knew, and he said, "Now, Brother Jones, as hard as times are, if you have three Cadillacs, wouldn't you give one of them up so we could go around and take up all the little kids in the country and take them to school during the week and to church on Sunday?" And he said, "Sure, I'd do that." And he said, "If you had $3 million, wouldn't you give up a million dollars so we could feed all the people in this county and put a roof over their head?" He said, "Of course I would." He said, "And if you had three hogs—" He said, "Now, wait a minute, I've got three hogs." [*Laughter*]

You think about that. We might have had some difficult cases to make in the last 2 years, but we never had to try to argue with a straight face why we ought to cut Medicare and Medicaid for elderly people in nursing homes to pay for a tax cut for people who have done very, very well in the 1980's and 1990's, and will do well in the 21st century. At least we didn't have to make that case.

On the other hand, it is important for us to participate and to be a part of changing this country for the better. The Democrats are a positive party. We win by promoting hope over fear, by promoting unity over division, by promoting progress over the status quo. And fundamentally, the difference between our party and the other party is still that we believe in the potential of every human being, and we believe that every person has a right to be protected from oppressive forces that would weigh him or her down, and every person has the right to be empowered to make the most of their own lives.

We believe in "cut and invest," not "slash and burn." We believe not in trickle-down, but in growing the middle class and shrinking the under class. We believe not in cutting people loose in a market-only world that is a cold and hard world but in having a partnership between the people and their Government and the private sector that grows the economy, creates jobs, and also makes sure everybody has a chance to stake out their piece of the American dream. We believe that the power of the Government ought to be used to elevate people. We believe that we should have a partnership with business that challenges them to train their workers and treat them right but challenges us here in Government to create policies that will enable us to succeed at home and abroad. And we have done that. And we will continue to do that.

Now, what are some examples of that? Well, the Commerce Department is one. Sometimes I think the reason our friends on the other side of the aisle are so anxious to eliminate the Department of Commerce is they are absolutely livid that a Democratic Secretary of Commerce has gotten more jobs for Americans abroad than all the Republicans in the last several decades.

We believe you can cut Government and make it work better for people. What are some examples of that? The Small Business Administration has lowered its budget and dramatically increased its loan volumes to women, to minorities, and to white males all at the same time, and nobody unqualified got a loan. And America is stronger as a result of that kind of effort.

We believe America has more than one kind of deficit. Yes, there is a budget deficit. We know all about it. It's a lot lower than it was before we went to work on it. And yes, we want to bring it down again. If, in fact, by bringing it down we could lower interest rates, put money into the pockets of ordinary Americans in the business sector, and invest and grow and get more jobs in this economy, that's what we ought to do. But let's not pretend that nothing we do here is worthwhile. We also have an education deficit in this country, and we have to address that as well.

And it isn't popular to say anymore because there is this sense that all of the money we spent on poor people is wasted, but that's just not true. And whether we like it or not, an increasing percentage of the babies that are born in this old world, in this country, are poor. And they need food to eat, and they need medical care and medicine for their bodies, and they need an opportunity to get off to a good start in life. And if we don't give it to them, we may balance the budget for the next 5 years, but in 15 years we'll have the awfullest deficit you ever saw, and we'll be spending it all on prisons and drug rehab programs instead of education and training and job creation.

Something else that isn't popular to say—today it's all the rage, if you ask any American what should you do to balance the budget, they'll say, "Cut foreign aid." But a recent poll has done us a great service. It's told us what the American people really mean. They were asked, "Well, how much money is in foreign aid?" The American people say, "Fifteen percent of the budget." "How much is too much?" They say, "Ten percent is way too much." "What's about right?" "Five percent." "What's too little?" "Under 3 percent." How much do we really spend? Just a little over one percent. [*Laughter*]

So this matters, folks. It matters to our ability to grow in the 21st century whether these countries that have embraced democracy and free markets are going to be given a little bit of help now, most of which immediately benefits us, by the way, to have their people get a good education and a good job and encourage American investment and become people who can buy our products and our services in the 21st century.

The Democrats believe, in short, that we have a budget deficit and an education deficit, that we need a thriving free market that is vigorous and competitive, but that the Government has a role to play in partnership with that market to help us abroad and to strengthen us at home, and that if we can grow the middle class and shrink the under class and keep a healthy economic environment, the rest of us will do very well indeed.

I am proud of the fact that in the last 2 years we've had more new businesses and more new millionaires created in the United States than at any comparable time in the history of our Republic. I am proud of that. But let's not kid ourselves. One of the reasons that we had difficulty in 1994, having both the White House and the Congress, is that millions and millions of Americans are out there working harder today than they were 10 years ago for less money. Millions of Americans go home every night from work and sit across the table from their children and their spouses and wonder if somehow they have failed. They hear all this stuff about the glories of the global economy and all these things about the glories of the market. And they read all these things that I say about how we've gotten the deficit down and got the jobs up. And all they know is, they're in a tight, and they're scared, and they're concerned about the future. And they wonder if anybody's still on their side. They wonder if anybody really cares about them.

Did you see the story of the young woman who brought her sister and her mother to see me, whose husband was—her father, the young girl's father, was on the picket line at the Bridgestone strike? And because her father was on strike and because they'd been replaced, this family had to pick up their own health insurance, as the law now provides. And so she missed out on her trip to Washington until Jesse Jackson ran into this young girl and paid to bring her family up here, because this girl and her sister were diabetics. And they were paying $600 a month for health insurance while they were unemployed. That's true all over America today.

There are people out there who just want to know that we are on their side, that we are still fighting for them, that we still believe in them, and that we're going to make America work for them. And they're entitled to know that.

I'm very proud of the fact that the crime rate has come down in this country now in both years I've been President. I am proud of that. And we've worked on that. But before we get carried away, let me remind you that the rate of violent, arbitrary crime by teenagers against teenagers is still going up because we've got all these kids out there who are disconnected. And they need to know somebody cares about them, and they need to know that they don't have to resort to violence, they don't have to resort to a gang, they don't have to leave school and do something terrible to feel like they're a part of something that will get them through to tomorrow.

This is not all that complicated. Oh, I know we're living in a new and different and exciting time, and I'm the biggest policy wonk in town. [*Laughter*] But when you strip it all away, we, the Democrats, have got to be there to say you can have economic growth and social justice. In fact, you cannot have economic growth over the long run without justice.

Do we want to make folks on welfare go to work when they can? You bet we do. Do we want to be able to reexamine our programs? Of course, we do. Do we want to be able to shed unnecessary bureaucracy? Yes, we do. Our administration has shrunk the Federal Government more than the folks that were here before us, and we will do more. We will do that. But let's not forget: Why are we doing all of this? Why are we here? Because we believe we can make a difference to the future of this country. And there is no other reason.

So I say to you, you should be of good cheer. We have a lot of things to do. We've taken a licking, and we're—as Mark Twain said, the reports of our demise are entirely premature. [*Laughter*] But the most important thing is, we have a chance tomorrow to go out and do something good for America. And we're going to do it. We're going to do it.

We're going to prove that you can reduce the deficit, that we can bring this budget into balance over a period of time without ignoring the investment deficit in our people, without gutting the environment, without destroying our future, without forgetting our obligation to grow the middle class, to shrink the under class, and to give our people some hope and decency and dignity in life. We're going to prove that you can do that. We are. They are. The Members here are. We're going to do that for America, and we can.

So you go home tonight, you just remember, one of the biggest problems with Washington is, most of our headlines and most of our conversation is consumed by process and conflict within the Beltway. And when we talk about people beyond the Beltway, we're normally talking about them in terms of the latest poll numbers: Who are they for this week? What are they saying this week? The fundamental reality of those people's lives has not changed all that much yet. And we have to give them a strong economy, a decent sense to empower themselves through education, a real commitment to a Government that serves everybody and not just the special interests, and does not forget the poor, because the children are the poor in this country, the children are the new poor in America, and they will be not children before you know it.

And we have got to find a way to solve all these problems together. The biggest problem we face today, I sometimes think, is that there aren't any simple answers to complex challenges. But there are answers. There are answers. And I have the privilege to go all over the world in your behalf. And I can tell you that nearly anybody would gladly trade places with where we are now at this point in our history.

So I say again, be of good cheer, but don't forget why you're here. Yes, we want to win elections, but we want to win elections for a purpose, because we believe you can attack the budget deficit and the investment deficit, the education deficit; because we believe we can make more millionaires and grow the middle class and stop this awful two decades of stagnant and declining incomes and increasing inequality; because we believe most poor people will go to work and do the right thing, given the opportunity and the responsibility to do so; because we believe we have a responsibility to the national security of this country in terms of making our streets safer at home and America safer abroad. And we are making progress on all those fronts.

So I say to our friends across the aisle: We will be your partner. We will not walk away from you in spite of our experience in the last 2 years. But we will come on our own terms with our own values, putting the American people first.

Thank you, God bless you, and good night.

NOTE: The President spoke at 9:25 p.m. at the Washington Hilton.

Message on the Observance of National Missing Children's Day, 1995
May 24, 1995

Greetings to everyone observing National Missing Children's Day, 1995. I am pleased that so many Americans are joining together to improve safety and reduce crime in communities across the country.

In the wake of the tragedy in Oklahoma City, we have drawn strength from reaffirming our commitment to protecting our children—making their well-being and security our highest national priority. Until we have done everything in our power to help young people lead happy, productive lives, we cannot say that our country is prepared for the great challenges that lie ahead.

The devastating effects of child abduction threaten our hopes for a brighter future. It is a tragedy that occurs daily and causes untold anguish to the families and children involved. I commend the many caring organizations who have dedicated their resources to raising public awareness of child abduction and to protecting young people from victimization. Your efforts are serving to return many children, safe and sound, to their families and homes.

Hillary and I join you in offering our prayers for all missing children and their families, and we wish you the best for a memorable day.

BILL CLINTON

NOTE: National Missing Children's Day was observed on May 25.

Message to the Congress Transmitting a Report on Aeronautics and Space
May 24, 1995

To the Congress of the United States:

I am pleased to transmit this report on the Nation's achievements in aeronautics and space during fiscal year 1994, as required under section 206 of the National Aeronautics and Space Act of 1958, as amended (42 U.S.C. 2476). Aeronautics and space activities involve 15 contributing departments and agencies of the Federal Government, as this report reflects, and the results of their ongoing research and development affect the Nation as a whole in a variety of ways.

Fiscal year 1994 featured many important developments and changes in U.S. aeronautics and space efforts. It included 7 Space Shuttle missions successfully completed, 15 Government launches of Expendable Launch Vehicles (ELVs), and 4 commercial launches from Government facilities. Among notable developments in the ELV area were the launch of the Deep Space probe, Clementine, initial use of the Titan IV Centaur upper stage, and the first launch of the Taurus launch vehicle. Highlights of the Shuttle missions included the highly successful servicing mission for the Hubble Space Telescope (HST), which replaced several faulty parts and installed a sophisticated package of correc-

tive optics to compensate for the spherical aberration in HST's primary mirror. Also, the flight of the Space Radar Laboratory began to provide information on environmental change, and a mission with a Russian astronaut, Sergei Krikalev, as a member of the crew signalled the beginning of a three-phased cooperative program in space between Russia and the United States.

In a year of tremendous accomplishments for the international Space Station, National Aeronautics and Space Administration (NASA) developed an initial set of specifications that included Russian elements as part of the design. Russia's agreeing to join the 12 original participating nations as a partner resulted in the expansion of the existing Shuttle/Mir program into Phase I of the international Space Station program, which officially began with Sergei Krikalev's flight on the Shuttle. All of the partners held a successful systems design review in Texas in March, and in June Russia and the United States signed an interim agreement on the Space Station and a $400 million contract for Russian space hardware, services, and data. In August, the program completed a vehicle architecture review and in September, the Space Station

743

Control Board ratified the recommendations it included. The redesigned Space Station costs $5 billion less than Space Station Freedom and still offers increased research capability and user flexibility.

In aeronautics, activities included development of technologies to improve performance, increase safety, reduce engine noise and other environmental degradation, improve air traffic management, lower costs, and help American industry to be more competitive in the world market. For example, high-speed research continued during fiscal year 1994 to focus on resolving critical environmental issues and laying the technological foundation for an economical, next generation, High Speed Civil Transport (HSCT). In this connection, the United States reached agreement with Russia to use the Tu-144 supersonic transport as a testbed for HSCT development. In addition, efforts in advanced subsonics focused on reducing aircraft and engine noise levels, on development of wind shear sensing devices, and on creating technologies that will improve general aviation aircraft.

In space science, astronomers using HST's revitalized optics discovered disks of protoplanetary dust orbiting stars in the Orion Nebula, suggesting that the formation of planets in the Milky Way and elsewhere may be relatively common. Also, HST's revelation of helium in distant constellations provides valuable information about the conditions in the universe during its initial evolution. The Spacelab Life Sciences–2, U.S. Microgravity Payload–2, and International Microgravity Laboratory–2 greatly increased our understanding of the role of gravity on biological, physical, and chemical processes. In biology, we learned that gravity affects the function of the neural connections between brain cells; this can have profound implications for rebuilding damaged brain cells due to strokes and disease. In Earth science, the Space Radar Laboratories–1 and –2, plus the Lidar

In-Space Technology Experiment payload, used powerful radar and laser technology to penetrate cloud cover and map critical factors on a global scale. Also, the highly successful launch of the Clementine Deep Space Probe tested 23 advanced technologies for high-tech, lightweight missile defense. The relatively inexpensive, rapidly-built spacecraft constituted a major revolution in spacecraft management and design; it also contributed significantly to lunar studies by photographing 1.8 million images of the surface of the Moon.

Additionally, on May 5, 1994, the White House announced that the National Oceanic and Atmospheric Administration (NOAA), the Department of Defense, and NASA were establishing a joint program to effect the convergence of civil and military polar-orbiting operational environmental satellite systems into a single operational program. Other White House announcements during the year included a policy for licensing U.S. firms by the Secretary of Commerce to operate private remote sensing systems and sell their images to domestic and foreign entities and a national space transportation policy that will sustain and revitalize U.S. space transportation capabilities by providing a coherent strategy for supporting and strengthening U.S. space launch capabilities to meet the growing needs of the civilian and national security sectors.

Thus, Fiscal Year 1994 was a highly successful one for the U.S. aeronautics and space programs. Efforts in both areas have contributed significantly to furthering the Nation's scientific and technical knowledge, international cooperation, a healthier environment, and a more competitive economy.

WILLIAM J. CLINTON

The White House,
May 24, 1995.

Letter to Congressional Leaders Reporting on Bosnia-Herzegovina
May 24, 1995

Dear Mr. Speaker: (Dear Mr. President:)
In my report to the Congress of November 22, 1994, I provided further information on the

deployment of U.S. combat-equipped aircraft to support efforts of the United Nations and the North Atlantic Treaty Organization (NATO) to achieve peace and stability in Bosnia-Herzegovina. On December 22, 1994, I also provided my fourth report on the continuing deployment of a U.S. Army peacekeeping contingent as part of the U.N. peacekeeping mission in the Former Yugoslav Republic of Macedonia. I am now providing this follow-up report, consistent with the War Powers Resolution, to ensure that the Congress is kept informed about important U.S. contributions in support of multilateral efforts in the former Yugoslavia.

U.S. combat-equipped fighter aircraft and other support aircraft continue to contribute to NATO's enforcement of the no-fly zone in the airspace over Bosnia-Herzegovina. In accordance with U.N. Security Council Resolutions 781, 786 and 816, this operation has since April 1993, enforced a ban on flights not authorized by the United Nations Protection Force (UNPROFOR). Enforcement of the no-fly zone, has resulted in the almost complete elimination of fixed-wing air to ground bombing and other air combat activity within the zone thereby greatly limiting the scope of the conflict in the region. Military personnel from 11 other NATO member nations have joined us in this effort, which has involved almost 60,000 sorties since the operation began. U.S. forces currently assigned to this operation consist of approximately 100 tactical aircraft as well as supporting tanker and other support aircraft.

The U.N. Security Council has established safe areas in Bosnia-Herzegovina and has authorized Member States and regional organizations, in close coordination with the United Nations, to take all necessary measures, through the use of air power, to support UNPROFOR in its mandate related to the safe areas. The Council has also authorized Member States and regional organizations, in close coordination with the United Nations, to take all necessary measures to extend close air support to protect U.N. forces in Croatia. More than 70 U.S. aircraft, including those identified above, are available for participation in authorized NATO missions for these purposes.

On March 31, 1995, the Security Council separated UNPROFOR into three operations: The United Nations Confidence Restoration Operation in Croatia (UNCRO); The United Nations Preventive Deployment Force (UNPREDEP) in the former Yugoslav Republic of Macedonia; and UNPROFOR in Bosnia-Herzegovina. A U.S. Army contingent remains deployed as part of UNPREDEP. Through observation and monitoring along the Serbian border, UNPREDEP continued to be effective in preventing the Balkan conflict from spreading and thereby contributes to the stability of the region. The approximately 500 U.S. soldiers contributing to this mission are assigned to the 3rd Battalion, 12th Infantry, 1st Armored Division, Baumholder, Germany.

In addition to these operations, U.S. forces have conducted more than 4,300 missions in support of the U.N. High Commissioner for Refugees airlift to Sarajevo. U.S. medical and other support personnel continue to provide critical services in support of UNPROFOR and UNCRO. U.S. naval forces are also continuing to assist in enforcing U.N. sanctions, subject to the restrictions of the Nunn-Mitchell Amendment, as part of NATO's participation in Operation SHARP GUARD.

The United States strongly favors a continued U.N. peacekeeping presence in the former Yugoslavia and a continuation of negotiations through the Contact Group. However, given the increase in fighting in Bosnia-Herzegovina and Croatia, it may become necessary for NATO to assist in the withdrawal of peacekeepers from these areas. Because of the significant period of time needed to prepare and deploy the necessary forces to support such a withdrawal, our senior military commanders recommended that we take certain steps now to preposition the necessary communications network in order to be prepared to meet this contingency. Accordingly, on April 6, 1995, the North Atlantic Council authorized the Supreme Allied Commander for Europe to assemble, train and deploy into Croatia 80 communications personnel. Twenty U.S. soldiers are participating in this operation.

These continuing efforts are being taken in conjunction with our allies to implement the decisions of the U.N. Security Council and the North Atlantic Council and to assist the parties to reach a negotiated settlement to the conflict. I have directed the participation of U.S. Armed Forces in these operations pursuant to my constitutional authority to conduct U.S. foreign relations and as Commander in Chief, and in accordance with various statutory authorities.

I am providing this report as part of my efforts to keep the Congress fully informed, consistent with the War Powers Resolution. I am grateful for the continuing support that the Congress has provided, and I look forward to continued cooperation with you in this endeavor. I shall communicate with you further regarding our efforts to foster peace and stability in the former Yugoslavia.

Sincerely,

WILLIAM J. CLINTON

NOTE: Identical letters were sent to Newt Gingrich, Speaker of the House of Representatives, and Strom Thurmond, President pro tempore of the Senate.

Remarks Following a Meeting With Surgeon General Nominee Henry Foster and an Exchange With Reporters
May 25, 1995

The President. Good morning, ladies and gentlemen. Dr. Foster and I have just had coffee. We discussed some of the issues we always discuss in terms of the health challenges our country faces. And of course, we discussed the upcoming vote in the Senate committee on the question of his confirmation. I want to say again, he has my strong support. I believe that he should be voted out of the committee and he certainly should be confirmed by the United States Senate.

In the hearings, he clearly demonstrated his qualifications to be America's doctor. And as I have said repeatedly, I hope the American people will never forget the group of young people who came up from his home State and his home town to talk about the work he had personally done to urge them to live upright and healthy and productive lives and the work that he had done to rescue them from difficult circumstances. If he is not qualified to be America's doctor, it's hard to imagine who would be.

There have been a lot of politics and a lot of talk back and forth on this nomination, but now the time has come to do the right thing. And I trust that the committee and, ultimately, the Senate will do the right thing and confirm Dr. Foster as Surgeon General.

Surgeon General Nominee Foster

Q. Do you think they will, the committee and the Senate?

The President. I believe they will.

Q. What do you base your optimism on?

The President. Well, I base my optimism on the fact that usually in this country right prevails over political pressure over the long run. They have—we have dragged this thing out. You known, Dr. Foster was never a political football

before; President Bush thought enough of him to make him one of the Points of Light. And because we had a hearing, and he demonstrated in the hearing why he should be a Surgeon General, and he answered all the questions.

Q. Do you think you can overcome the filibuster, sir?

The President. Let's get out of committee first. I think you've got to get out of the committee, and then I think he certainly should be. We'll have lots of arguments to make about that in the appropriate time. I think, if the majority of the United States Senate is for him, he should certainly be confirmed.

Budget Proposals

Q. Mr. President, it looks like the rescission bill is going to pass today. Do you still intend to veto it? And what happens next?

The President. Well, the answer to your question is yes, if it passes in this form.

I want to emphasize, first of all, I am for a rescission bill that cuts this much spending. I have sent a bill to the Congress that cuts even more from the deficit. I have been very specific about it.

My objection is that having—after I negotiated with the Senate on spending reductions, we got politics as usual. Congress went behind closed doors and cut a lot of education and training out and put some pork in the bill for specific Congressmen and specific congressional districts and States. That's the old politics. What we're doing here now is new and different, and we can't continue to do it.

So if the bill comes to me in the same form, without the restoration of the education and training, yes, I will veto it. Well, what happens next? Then—well, they have a bill right now which they could vote on today and send to me before they go on recess, which would cut the spending, restore the education by not protecting the pork. Now, that's my position. And that's what I think should be done.

If instead I get the bill and there's a veto and they go home for their break, then when they come back, we ought to get together and restore the education and the training funds, reduce the deficit by as much or even more than is in this present bill, and then let them send it to me, and I will sign it. I am for making a downpayment on the deficit reduction in this rescission bill.

I certainly want to get the money out to Oklahoma City, to finish our obligations in the California earthquake, to deal with the floods in the South, and of course we've got some other problems in other parts of the country, to fulfill the commitment of the United States on the Jordan issue as part of our Middle East peace process. I want to do all of that, to cut the spending and to get that money out there. But if we're going to be cutting around here, we cannot afford pork protection, politics as usual. We have to do what we're going to do in the open, not go behind closed doors and change all the priorities. We need to do this in a disciplined, good way.

So that is my position. It is very clear, and it has nothing to do with deficit reduction. I am for as much—I will support more spending reduction, but not in this form.

Bosnia

Q. Do you support, sir—do you support NATO air strikes around Sarajevo today?

The President. Well, my position is that NATO should be prepared to react when our commanders on the ground need them. And you know, I've been—of all of our NATO allies, the United States has been the most vigorous proponent of the use of NATO airstrikes in all appropriate circumstances. And we've laid those out repeatedly.

Thank you.

White House Security

Q. Mr. President, after still one more attack on the White House, are you starting to think, "Why me?"

The President. No. [*Laughter*] I do think—first of all, the American people should know that the system here worked and the Secret Service did a terrific job. And the two agents in question immediately put themselves in harm's way to do their job. And the system worked exactly as it is supposed to work. And the whole rest of the system worked. It was amazing. It worked. It worked quickly. And it's something that every citizen of this country can be very proud of.

I—to answer your other question, I don't, no. I just think that in a couple of cases, we've had people who for their own personal reasons have seen this as a symbol of something that they could attach themselves to in some way or another.

I do—I will say again that in our country today, we all need to try to reach out to each other and to talk and to reach across our divides when a lot of people out there may be like this gentleman, in trouble, and maybe can be brought back just by people reaching out to them and by trying to avoid letting things get to that point. And certainly I think that about the political rhetoric and dialog.

So I hope that we'll take another opportunity to reexamine, all of us, how we might make this country work better and have more thoughtful words and try to keep people from getting to extreme positions in their lives. But in this case, I don't feel badly at all. The Secret Service did a terrific job, and I'm very proud of them.

Thank you.

Q. So you have no fears?

The President. No.

NOTE: The President spoke at 8:54 a.m. in the Rose Garden at the White House.

Remarks to the White House Conference on Trade and Investment in Ireland
May 25, 1995

Thank you very much. Secretary Christopher, Secretary Brown, Senator Mitchell, Deputy Prime Minister Spring, Sir Patrick Mayhew, Mr. Ambassador, ladies and gentlemen, to all of you of Irish, British, and American heritage from the business communities of these great nations, I thank you for being here. I have looked forward to this day for a long time, to having people like you here who see the opportunities for trade and investment that come from peace and the opportunities for trade and investment to support peace. I'm especially delighted that so many are here from Ireland and the United Kingdom. And to all of our friends from Northern Ireland, your attendance here shows your dedication to a future of cooperation and prosperity, and we're particularly glad to have you.

Let me say a special word of thanks to George Mitchell for the tremendous work he has done in organizing this conference. His devotion to the cause of nurturing peace and growth in Northern Ireland and the Republic's border counties has played a central part in the progress that we celebrate here today. I'm delighted that he will lead another mission to Ireland this summer and even more pleased that he's agreed to continue his work in overseeing our economic initiatives through the end of this year.

Ireland is lucky to have George Mitchell on its side, even if it has to put up with the envy of the United States Senate, the Supreme Court, and Major League Baseball. [*Laughter*] You know, George is Irish and Lebanese. Maybe when we succeed in Ireland, if the Secretary of State is not finished, he'll volunteer for other duty. [*Laughter*]

As all of you know, the United States has a keen interest in a stable and democratic and prosperous Europe, but that interest is particularly strong when it comes to Ireland. Our strong bonds of kinship, culture, and history shared with the peoples of the United Kingdom in Ireland are well-known.

This is a moment of historic opportunity for you and historic interest for the United States. For my own part, people ask me from time to time why this is a matter of such deep personal interest to me. It goes beyond my Irish roots. I wish I could just say that's all there was to it. But an important part of our mission at this moment in time as Americans is to help reconcile the divisions which keep people apart and lead them sometimes to violence both within our own country and around the world.

If you look into the next century, you could thank the good Lord that we may, we may succeed in removing the nuclear threat from the children of the 21st century. But we still see these ancient impulses that keep people apart based on religious or racial or ethnic differences. I tell my fellow Americans all the time that the great genius of our country in the next century may be our ability to exalt the greatest amount of diversity of any large country in the world. But it is still a challenge for us here. You see it all the time. And we can think of no greater mission in our quest to reconcile diversity than trying to help peace and prosperity succeed in Northern Ireland and in Ireland in general.

This is, as I'm sure you know, an extraordinary gathering of which you are a part. Never before have representatives of all the political parties in Northern Ireland, officials from the United Kingdom and Ireland, and so many business leaders joined to help us to build a better tomorrow. The conference shows anew the historic progress that has been made toward a just and lasting settlement and toward a peace that respects the rights and traditions of both communities.

In the last few months, thanks to the ceasefire and the momentum of the negotiations, a powerful transformation has begun. Peace is closer than it's been in a generation. For the first time in decades, children can walk to school without worrying. Families that have endured so much violence with so much dignity can now enjoy the blessings of days without violence and nights without fear. The roads between north and south are more open than they have been in 25 years. And citizens of the Republic are visiting the north in even greater numbers. In Belfast, the army patrols have ended; the body armor and helmets are gone; hundreds of troops are now going home.

These landmark achievements would not have been possible without the leadership and courage of Prime Minister Major, Prime Minister Bruton, and before him, Prime Minister Reynolds. With the Joint Framework Document, they are paving the way for a new and hopeful era of reconciliation. All true friends of Ireland are grateful to them and to the parties that have risen to their challenge. I salute them, and I salute others who work for peace, individuals such as Foreign Minister Spring, Sir Patrick Mayhew, and that tireless advocate of peace, our friend John Hume.

We pay tribute as well to the brave people of Northern Ireland whose courage has brought them to this point. The United States is proud to have helped them and all peacemakers, and today I renew my pledge to do everything in my power to support their efforts. I know—[*applause*]—thank you. I know I speak for all Americans when I say that people who take risks for peace, here and anywhere else in the world, will always be welcome in the White House, in Washington, and throughout our country.

This momentum must be maintained. The ministerial-level talks represent a step of tremendous promise. I hope the parties can soon sit down together to discuss the future and their differences. That is the best guarantee of a permanent peace.

But there must be progress as well outside the conference rooms. Violence is diminished, but it has not disappeared. I call on all those who continue to employ violence to end the punishment beatings and the intimidation. And to all who are observing the cease-fire, I appeal to you to take the next step and begin to discuss serious decommissioning of weapons. Paramilitaries on both sides must get rid of their bombs and guns for good. And the specter of violence that has haunted Ireland must be banished, once and for all.

It is also time to begin healing the wounds of a generation. Many innocents disappeared during the Troubles. Others were banished from their homes. Today, there are families that have still not had the chance to grieve in peace, to visit the graves of their loved ones, to reunite after years of separation. It is time to allow families to be whole again.

As everyone knows, peace is more than cease-fires and formal agreements. It demands real hope and progress in the hearts of people. It demands common striving for the common good. It is time for those who have been most affected by the fighting to feel this kind of hope and this sense of progress. As Yeats wrote, "Too long a sacrifice can make a stone of the heart." There must be a peace dividend in Northern Ireland and the border counties so that everyone is convinced that the future belongs to those who build, not those who destroy, so that the majority that supports peace is strengthened, so that there is no slipping back into the violence that frustration breeds.

That is why this conference is so important. It underscores that all sides have an interest in investing in the future of Northern Ireland and that all sides will benefit from the peace. Our own experience here in America shows what a difference that kind of progress and benefit can bring. More than a century ago, our great sage Ralph Waldo Emerson said that trade was the principle of liberty, that it made peace and keeps peace. That is what we wish for Ireland, and now it is time to realize that wish. The end of organized violence makes that possible.

So I urge American businesses and all others to consider investing in Northern Ireland and the border counties. The opportunities are excellent. The work force is well-educated and well-motivated. The productivity levels are high. The unit labor costs are low. The labor relations are good. The infrastructure, the communications, the access to the European market are fine. With the prospect of an enduring settlement on the horizon, business confidence is rising fast. Experts predict investment booms on both sides of the border and an increase in tourism in the north that could exceed 100 percent.

Already, the United States is the number one investor in both Northern Ireland and the Republic. American companies employ nearly 10 percent of all the workers in Northern Ireland's manufacturing sector. And Ireland imports almost $3 billion worth of American goods. The firms that we have in these markets are increasing their investments, strengthening their positions in Europe, building businesses that create jobs on both sides of the Atlantic. By doing well, these companies are also doing good.

More investment in Northern Ireland promises to lift the region out of the cycle of despair that leads to violence. It will reduce the chronic unemployment than runs around 50 percent in some urban areas and has deadened the dreams of so many. If growth is accompanied by an end to discrimination, by fair and nonsectarian employment practices, and encouraging investment in areas in greatest need, then both Catholics and Protestants will feel that they have a stake in their society and its peaceful future. When both communities feel the benefits of peace and see that they are distributed fairly, despair will lose its hold, and all will have the chance they deserve to fulfill their God-given potential.

"Peace," Yeats said, "comes dropping slow." The past will not be overcome in a day, but the perception of change provides the kindling for hope, and the opportunities for positive, powerful, profitable change clearly are now present in Northern Ireland.

As long as I am President, the United States will continue to encourage that change. I am proud of all that Secretary Brown has done in achieving—on his mission to Ireland last December. I'm proud of the many efforts of the Department of Commerce, USAID, USIA, and other Government agencies to support reconciliation in Ireland. I am proud of the work of the State Department, and I want to say a special word of thanks to our Ambassadors in the area, Ambassador Crowe and Ambassador Jean Kennedy Smith, for the outstanding work that they have both done. Thank you.

Ours is the first administration ever to include appropriations for the International Fund for Ireland. The IFI have lived up to our hopes for it. The fund supports over 3,000 economic development projects and has created some 23,000 jobs in areas that were recruiting grounds for the paramilitaries. It is promoting cooperation across the border and between communities.

The record challenges us to go even further. So we have increased our funding request for the IFI to almost $60 million over the next 2 years. And we are working to build more bridges across the ocean through exchange programs for managers, students, agricultural experts, artists, and scholars, programs that establish bonds of friendship, while transporting ideas and information, benefiting people on both sides of the ocean.

There are some in Washington who would like to cut our funding for these and other programs that support peace in Ireland and throughout the world. That would be a grave error. The United States has an abiding interest in creating peace and the opportunities it brings. We must have the resources to foster peace and stand by those who take the hard risks for peace. We have seen time and again that our investments in peace, whether in the Middle East, southern Africa, Haiti, or Ireland, have always yielded great benefits for the American people in growing markets, great stability, increased security.

I hope all those who want to see peace in Northern Ireland will keep that in mind. Peace has a price, but it is a small one compared to the alternative, and it is a price very much worth paying.

I'm also glad we've been able to help the cause of peace through this conference and other economic initiatives, because Ireland has given us so much. The two communities that today are coming together in cooperation have each given America a rich legacy. In our Nation, Catholic and Protestants have been intertwined, and together they have contributed immensely to the greatness of our people and the success of America. There is evidence all around us. In places like New York, Pennsylvania, and Ohio, counties, cities, and towns with names like Londonderry, Ulster, and Antrim dot the map. Often these places mark the frontier in the 18th century when Ulster Protestants, some of them my ancestors, pushed west to build new lives and a new nation. These settlers were the forebears of nearly a dozen American Presidents, including Andrew Jackson, William McKinley, and Woodrow Wilson.

Irish Catholics contributed just as much to our country's rise, whether in building railroads or institutions. A visiting journalist in the last century took the measure of that effort when he said that in America you could see water power, steam power, horse power, and Irish power. [*Laughter*] And he concluded, "The last works hardest of all." [*Laughter*] In this half of our century, the names John F. Kennedy, Justice William Brennan, Speaker Tip O'Neill only began to tell the story of Irish Catholics' contribution to all the branches of American democracy.

These true traditions, harnessed together in the New World for common goals, has been America's great fortune. Time and again, we have seen peoples of different backgrounds and ancestries put freedom over faction, the goals of the community over the interests of its separate parts. Of the gifts we can give to Ireland, this example of people joining together for the common good clearly is the greatest. The challenges of the coming century demand that we keep in mind the example of those who went before us, who built bridges across their differences and found the strength to pull together.

We now face a whole new set of challenges in this new era. The global economy, the explosion of information, the advance of technology, the growing mobility of people, all these forces are bringing us into a more integrated world, more full of possibilities than ever before. The next century can be the most exciting time in all human history because of the opportunities for human possibilities.

But we have to recognize that all these forces of integration have a darker side as well. If we do not rise to the challenges they present, we become vulnerable to the organized forces of destruction and evil, for the modern world requires us to be open in order to take advantage of all the forces of integration. And as we become more open, we become more vulnerable to those who would hate and those who would destroy.

As the people of Northern Ireland are showing, we can seize the moment. We can turn away from terror. We can turn away from de-

struction. We can turn toward peace and unity and possibility. But to keep this process going, to lock in the accomplishments, we must make hope real. To grasp the opportunity, we must build stronger businesses and communities and families. We must have more and better jobs. We must strengthen the prospects of a better tomorrow.

That is the way to preempt fanaticism. That is the way to close the book on old and bloody conflicts. That is the way to give our children the future they all deserve. The chance is there. It is here. It is now. We have it in our power to make all the difference. Let us do it.

Thank you, and bless you all.

NOTE: The President spoke at 10:48 a.m. at the Sheraton Washington Hotel. In his remarks, he referred to George Mitchell, Special Adviser for Economic Initiatives in Ireland; Deputy Prime Minister Richard Spring, Prime Minister John Bruton, and former Prime Minister Albert Reynolds of Ireland; Secretary of State for Northern Ireland Sir Patrick Mayhew and Prime Minister John Major of the United Kingdom; Ambassadors to the U.S. Sir Robin William Renwick of the United Kingdom and Dermot Gallagher of Ireland; John Hume, leader, Northern Ireland Social Democratic and Labor Party; U.S. Ambassador to the United Kingdom William J. Crowe; and U.S. Ambassador to Ireland Jean Kennedy Smith.

Statement on the United Nations/NATO Decision To Launch Airstrikes in Bosnia-Herzegovina
May 25, 1995

I welcome the decision of the U.N. and NATO to launch airstrikes today against a Bosnian-Serb ammunition site following the violence of the past several days in and around Sarajevo. This action was taken in response to Bosnian-Serb defiance of yesterday's UNPROFOR demand for the return of heavy weapons to designated weapons collection points in accord with existing agreements.

This action should help NATO and the U.N. sustain their ability to ease suffering in the re-

gion. I hope that today's airstrikes will convince the Bosnian-Serb leadership to end their violations of the exclusion zone and comply with their other agreements with the U.N.

I appreciate the courage and dedication of the U.N. forces on the ground in the former Yugoslavia and trust that this evidence of U.N. and NATO determination will serve to enhance the ability of these forces to remain and perform their missions.

Message to the Congress on Small Business
May 25, 1995

To the Congress of the United States:

I am pleased to forward my second annual report on the state of small business, and to report that small businesses are doing exceptionally well. Business starts and incorporations were up in 1993, the year covered in this report. Failures and bankruptcies were down. Six times as many jobs were created as in the previous year, primarily in industries historically dominated by small businesses.

Small businesses are a critical part of our economy. They employ almost 60 percent of the work force, contribute 54 percent of sales, account for roughly 40 percent of gross domestic product, and are responsible for 50 percent of private sector output. More than 600,000 new firms have been created annually over the past decade, and over much of this period, small firms generated many of the Nation's new jobs. As this report documents, entrepreneurial small businesses are also strong innovators, producing twice as many significant innovations as their larger counterparts.

In short, a great deal of our Nation's economic activity comes from the record number of entrepreneurs living the American Dream. Our job in Government is to make sure that conditions are right for that dynamic activity to continue and to grow.

And we are taking important steps. Maintaining a strong economy while continuing to lower the Federal budget deficit may be the most important step we in Government can take. A lower deficit means that more savings can go into new plant and equipment and that interest rates will be lower. It means that more small businesses can get the financing they need to get started.

We are finally bringing the Federal deficit under control. In 1992 the deficit was $290 billion. By 1994, the deficit was $203 billion; we project that it will fall to $193 billion in 1995.

Deficit reduction matters. We have been enjoying the lowest combined rate of unemployment and inflation in 25 years. Gross domestic product has increased, as having housing starts. New business incorporations continue to climb. We want to continue bringing the deficit down in a way that protects our economic recovery, pays attention to the needs of people, and empowers small business men and women.

Capital Formation

One area on which we have focused attention is increasing the availability of capital to new and small enterprises, especially the dynamic firms that keep us competitive and contribute so much to economic growth.

Bank regulatory policies are being revised to encourage lending to small firms. Included in the Credit Availability Program that we introduced in 1993 are revised banking regulatory policies concerning some small business loans and permission for financial institutions to create "character loans."

New legislation supported by my Administration and enacted in September 1994, the Reigle Community Development and Regulatory Improvement Act of 1994, establishes a Community Development Financial Institutions Fund for community development banks, amends banking and securities laws to encourage the creation of a secondary market for small business loans, and reduces the regulatory burden for financial institutions by changing or eliminating 50 banking regulations.

Under the Small Business Administration Reauthorization and Amendments Act of 1994, the Small Business Administration (SBA) is authorized to increase the number of guaranteed small business loans for the next 3 years. The budget proposed for the SBA will encourage private funds to be directed to the small businesses that most need access to capital. While continuing cost-cutting efforts, the plan proposes to fund new loan and venture capital authority for SBA's credit and investment programs. Changes in the SBA's 7(a) guaranteed loan program will increase the amount of private sector lending leveraged for every dollar of taxpayer funds invested in the program.

Through the Small Business Investment Company (SBIC) program, a group of new venture capital firms are expected to make available several billion dollars in equity financing for startups and growing firms. The SBIC program will continue to grow as regulations promulgated in the past year facilitate financing with a newly created participating equity security instrument.

And the Securities and Exchange Commission's simplified filing and registration requirements for small firm securities have helped encourage new entries by small firms into capital markets.

We are recommending other changes that will help make more capital available to small firms. In reauthorizing Superfund, my Administration seeks to limit lender liability for Superfund remediation costs, which have had an adverse effect on lending to small businesses. Interagency teams have been examining additional cost-effective ways to expand the availability of small business financing, such as new options for expanding equity investments in small firms and improvements to existing microlending efforts.

We've also recognized that we can help small business people increase their available capital through tax reductions and incentives. We increased by 75 percent, from $10,000 to $17,500, the amount a small business can deduct as expenses for equipment purchases. Tax incentives in the 1993 Budget Reconciliation Act are having their effect, encouraging long-term investment in small firms. And the empowerment zone program offers significant tax incentives—a 20 percent wage credit, $20,000 in expensing, and tax-exempt facility bonds—for firms within the zones.

Regulation and Paperwork

But increasing the availability of capital to small firms is only part of the battle. We also have to make sure that Government doesn't get in the way. And we're making progress in our efforts to create a smaller, smarter, less costly and more effective Government that is closer to home—closer to the small businesses and citizens it serves.

In the first round of our reinventing Government initiative—the National Performance Review—we asked Government professionals for their best ideas on how to create a better Government with less red tape. One recommendation was that Federal agency compliance with the Regulatory Flexibility Act—that requires agencies to examine proposed and existing regulations for their effects on small entities—be subject to judicial review. In other words, they said we need to put teeth in the legislation requiring Federal agencies to pay attention to small business concerns when they write regulations. That proposal has been under debate in the Congress.

Federal agencies are already considering and implementing specific ways to streamline regulations and make paperwork easier for small businesses to manage. For example, the Environmental Protection Agency (EPA) responded to small business owners and advocates who said that the agency's toxic release inventory rule was especially costly and burdensome. In November 1994, the EPA announced a final rule that will make it easier for small businesses to report small amounts of toxic releases.

And SBA has slashed the small business loan form for loans under $100,000 from an inch-thick stack to a single page. The SBA is also piloting a new electronic loan application that will involve no paperwork, but will allow business owners to concentrate on the business at hand—building a successful operation.

When businesses are unable to succeed, no one is served by a process that entangles small business owners in an endless jumble of paperwork. Sweeping changes made to bankruptcy laws in the past year will help small businesses reorganize. Small firms with less than $2.5 million in debt may utilize a streamlined reorganization process that is less expensive and more timely.

My Executive order on Regulatory Review provides a process for more rational regulation, and we've been listening to the concerns of small firms through a Regulatory Reform Forum for Small Business. Five sector-specific groups have made specific proposals for regulatory relief. These groups have said that a comprehensive, multiagency strategy, with better public involvement, is probably the most cost-effective way to improve both the quality of regulations and compliance with them. The key is to make sure that Government serves small business and the American people, not the other way around.

Electronic Commerce and Government Procurement

The reinventing Government initiative also called for expanded use of electronic marketing and commerce, and we have made great strides in providing information about Government programs electronically. These methods will increase small business access to markets.

Another area that has been sorely in need of reform is the Government procurement process. In October 1994, I signed into law the Federal Acquisition Streamlining Act, which will change the way the Government does business.

The law modifies more than 225 provisions of procurement law to reduce paperwork burdens, improve efficiency, save the taxpayers money, establish a Federal acquisition computer network, increase opportunities for women-owned and small disadvantaged businesses, and generally make Government acquisition of commercial products easier. This report documents how small businesses are doing under the old system; my hope is that opportunities for small business success will be even greater once these reforms are in effect.

Human Resources

Beyond encouraging an economic environment that supports small business success, opening doors to capital resources, buying more of our goods and services from small firms, and getting out of small business' way, I believe we in Government have a responsibility to ask whether we are doing enough to ensure a healthy and adequately prepared work force.

I remain committed to seeking a way to provide health insurance coverage for all Americans. As this report clearly shows, the number of uninsured Americans is too high—and it's growing. Millions of those citizens are in working families. And the sad fact is that many of those workers are in small businesses, which have seen their premiums and deductibles soar. We must make sure that self-employed people and small businesses can buy insurance at more affordable rates—whether through voluntary purchasing pools or some other mechanism.

We also ought to be able to ensure that our citizens are adequately provided for when they reach the end of their working years. Here too, small firms have been at a disadvantage. Our proposed pension legislation exempted most small plans from compliance and reporting increases.

And while our industries restructure and move from an age of heavy industry to an information age that demands new skills and new flexibility, we need to make sure that our work force has the skills and tools to compete. That is why I proposed the Middle Class Bill of Rights, which would provide a tax deduction for all education and training after high school; foster more saving and personal responsibility by permitting people to establish an individual retirement account and withdraw from it tax-free for the cost of education, health care, first-time house buying, or the care of a parent; and offer to those laid off or working for a very low wage, a voucher worth $2,000 a year to get the skills they need to improve their lives.

International Trade

We also want to empower small businesses to succeed in a global economy. One of the greatest challenges in the next century will be our international competition. Ninety-six percent of all exporting firms are small firms with fewer than 500 employees, but only 10 percent of small firms export; therefore the potential for increasing small firm exports is significant. I believe the North American Free Trade Agreement and the General Agreement on Tariffs and Trade will benefit small firms interested in expanding into international markets in this hemisphere and beyond.

Lending to small exporters is being eased through reforms in the Export-Import Bank's Working Capital Guarantee Program. New one-stop export shops are moving in the right direction to assist small firms by providing access to export programs of the Department of Commerce, Export-Import Bank, and Small Business Administration all under one roof.

Hearing from Small Business

Small businesses are too important to our economy for their concerns not to be heard. That is why I have given the SBA a seat on the National Economic Council and invited the SBA Administrator in to Cabinet meetings.

Over the past 2 years, my Administration has been asking questions of small business owners and listening to the answers—seeking advice and guidance from a diverse audience of business leaders to determine the most critical problems and devise solutions that work.

This year presents a special opportunity for small business persons to make their concerns known at the White House Conference on Small Business, set to convene in Washington in June 1995. In State conferences leading up to the national conference, small business owners have been frank about their concerns. I look forward to hearing their small business action agenda.

I firmly believe that we need to keep looking to our citizens and small businesses for innovative solutions. They have shown they have the ingenuity and creative power to make our economy grow; we just need to let them do it.

WILLIAM J. CLINTON

The White House,

May 25, 1995.

Remarks at the White House Conference on Trade and Investment in Ireland Reception
May 25, 1995

Thank you very much. Let me welcome all of you again and say a special word of welcome to Deputy Prime Minister Spring, Sir Patrick Mayhew, Ambassador Gallagher, Ambassador Renwick, Ambassador Crowe, Ambassador Smith, to Senator Mitchell, to the people who are here from the International Fund for Ireland. Let me say a special word of thanks to the Chairman, Willie McCarter, and to my good friend and appointee Jim Lyons. And let me remind all of you that, appropriately enough, the band that just entertained us is known as Celtic Thunder. We arranged the Irish weather here tonight—[*laughter*]—to remind you that we are all here under a very large tent in more ways than one.

If yesterday and today all of us have done what we set out to do, then we will all be sharing the same hopes and joining the same work for the future of Northern Ireland and the border counties of Ireland. We are especially committed to the economic revival of the people who live there, all of the people who live there.

We know that many people will be skeptical about the possibilities of peace and others will be skeptical about the possibilities of economic progress. George Bernard Shaw once recognized that skepticism about economic matters dies hard, and since he had a foot in Ireland and a foot in England, I thought I would remind you of what he said. He said, "If you lined up end to end all the economists in the world, you still would not reach a conclusion." [*Laughter*] I think today even Mr. Shaw would share our optimism.

I hope that this conference stirred your thoughts and your imagination for the future, that you have had an opportunity to exchange ideas and plans, that you will act on the things that you have thought about and dreamed about here. The people who are gathered here have the opportunity to make all your ideals real.

We in government can make a difference in political negotiations as the first bridge between groups that history has separated. We can be a catalyst for change. But sustained progress will require more. It demands the engagements of all the major groups within society, the companies that provide the economic lifeblood, the churches, the political parties, the civic associations.

Already there has been tremendous progress. We can see that in the desire for peace that runs throughout Northern Ireland and—let me emphasize this—in the work of the 200 community and civic leaders who traveled here at their own great expense to advance the cause of reconciliation. We thank them especially for being here. These men and women are on the frontlines bringing down the barricades, bringing together the people of the Shankill and the people of the Falls.

I want to thank, as well, the Irish-American community, the business community, and the nongovernmental organizations. You have risen to the task. Now let me say that, as I thank you—is the sound off? That's good, because I'm almost through. [*Laughter*]

I asked you here tonight mostly to celebrate and not to hear another speech. I ask you to remember that the United States is always with you.

Just behind me here, through the—you can almost see them, even through the plastic cover—are the two oldest trees at the White House, two grand magnolias planted over 165 years ago by Andrew Jackson, the son of an immigrant farmer from the Carrickfergus in County Antrim. Every day I look at those two old trees and think about our Nation's past and our Nation's future. Today I will look at them with fresh eyes to think about Ireland's past and Ireland's future, the future of the people of Northern Ireland and the people of Ireland.

755

Thank you all. Good luck. God bless you.

NOTE: The President spoke at 6:19 p.m. on the South Grounds at the White House.

Remarks at a Meeting With Surgeon General Nominee Henry Foster and an Exchange With Reporters
May 26, 1995

The President. I want to thank the Senate Labor and Human Resources Committee for endorsing the nomination of Dr. Foster to be Surgeon General and for doing it in a bipartisan fashion. I'd also like to say a special word of appreciation to the people of Tennessee who stood with him and especially to the young children in the "I Have A Future" program who came up here and talked about how he helped to turn their lives around, helped to convince them to stay in school, to keep working, to turn away from drugs, from teen pregnancy, from the other problems that bother so many of our children.

This is a good day for the United States, and I look forward to going on to the next stage and to working right through until we get Dr. Foster confirmed.

Q. Mr. President, what are you going to do if the——

The President. I would like for Dr. Foster to say something, too.

Dr. Foster. I, too, would like to thank the Senate Labor and Human Resources Committee for a fair hearing and for moving this forward to the full Senate. I also particularly want to thank the person on that committee who knew me best, Senator William Frist, for supporting my nomination. And lastly, I want to thank the President, his administration, congressional Members, and my family for supporting me so stoutly during these times.

Bosnia

Q. Mr. President, what are you going to do if the U.N. peacekeepers are harmed in Bosnia by the Serbs? They have threatened to retaliate on the bombing.

The President. We'll have to examine their actions as they take them. The United States is in a—I want to make clear the position we're in here. We, as a part of and a leader of NATO, responded to the request of the United Nations,

which I thought was very appropriate, to deal with the shelling of Sarajevo and the shelling of civilians by the Bosnian Serbs, in clear violation of the understandings that have been in place for quite some time now. And we did that in an appropriate way against military targets, so that the taking of hostages as well as the killing of civilians by them is totally wrong and inappropriate, and it should stop.

The United Nations, the forces on the ground and the United Nations Command obviously will have to analyze these circumstances on a daily basis. We will work with them, and we'll do whatever is appropriate. And I still believe that the action we took was appropriate. It was in response to the request from the U.N., and it certainly was provoked by the inappropriate shelling of civilians by the Bosnian Serbs.

Q. Do you have a backup plan if something happens? You're sending an aircraft carrier to the Adriatic. Does that have a——

The President. I can't comment any further on what's going on now. I think it's important for the United Nations, who have the forces on the ground, to be able to deal with this situation. And as the events unfold, I'll be happy to comment.

China

Q. Mr. President, why are you giving China MFN again, sir?

The President. Well, I haven't made a decision on that yet. But as you know, I said last year—and I believe—that we should continue to press China on the human rights issues, but I don't believe that singling China out on the MFN is necessarily the best way to do it. There are other countries with whom we have human rights differences as well. And we have certainly pressed our differences with China, not only person-to-person, face-to-face with the Chinese but also in the appropriate international forum, and we will continue to do that.

And we also have other differences with them. I agreed to let President Li from Taiwan come here. I thought that was the appropriate thing to do. We won't always agree with the Chinese, but I think it's important that when we disagree, we do it in the right way, aggressively and forthrightly, but in the proper forum.

Bosnia

Q. President Yeltsin has called Mr. Major and Mr. Kohl complaining about the—*[inaudible]*—has he tried to reach you, and what would you tell him?

The President. Not yet, no. If he did, I would tell him just what I told you, that the United Nations asked for this; they certainly weren't put up to it, that the Bosnian Serbs went way beyond the bounds of acceptable conduct. There have been clear restrictions on bombing civilians and shelling those areas for a long time now. I would ask him to call the Serbs and tell them to quit it and tell them to behave themselves and that this would not happen.

Surgeon General Nominee Foster

Q. Are the Democrats ready to overcome a filibuster on the Foster nomination if it happens?

The President. The Democrats are not numerous enough to overcome a filibuster. But Senator Frist and Senator Jeffords put their country above their party today and did what they thought was right, and I think there will be others. There may even be some who may not think they should vote for him, Dr. Foster, who believe that it's wrong to filibuster a nomination of this kind.

In the past, when the Democrats were in the majority in the Senate, they often did that as well. They often gave Republican Presidents votes on their nominees, even if they didn't agree with them. This—it would be unusual and unwarranted if this fine man were denied his day in court in the Senate, and I don't believe the American people want that to happen, and I don't believe that a majority of the Senate wants that to happen.

Q. What are you doing for the rest of the day?

The President. Working. *[Laughter]*

NOTE: The President spoke at 12:33 p.m. in the Oval Office at the White House. During the exchange, a questioner referred to President Boris Yeltsin of Russia, Prime Minister John Major of the United Kingdom, and Chancellor Helmut Kohl of Germany. A tape was not available for verification of the content of these remarks.

The President's Radio Address
May 27, 1995

Good morning. It has now been over 5 weeks since the tragic bombing in Oklahoma City. In the days immediately after that tragedy, congressional leaders pledged to have the legislation I proposed to crack down on terrorism on my desk by Memorial Day. The Senate is now considering the antiterrorism bill. I'm glad they're working on it. At the same time, I disagree with the position of some Senators from both parties that three crucial weapons in the fight against terrorism should be stripped from the bill.

The first concerns my proposal to expand the wiretap capabilities of Federal investigators. Terrorists move around. They don't want to be caught. They go from State to State, from motel to motel, from pay phone to pay phone. We need the power to move our taps and surveillance as fast as the terrorist moves his base of operations. But those who want to weaken my antiterrorism bill want law enforcement to go back to court for a new wiretap order each and every time a terrorist moves, unless we can specifically show that he's trying to evade our surveillance.

We should protect citizens' privacy rights. But we shouldn't force law enforcement to lose valuable time by making them get a court to agree that a terrorist is trying to knowingly evade us. Have you ever heard of a terrorist who wasn't trying to evade the police? I don't care whether a terrorist is trying to knowingly evade the police. I care that he or she may be trying to plan another Oklahoma City bombing. And I want the police to stop those people cold.

The restrictive view taken by some people in Congress would handicap our ability to track terrorists down, follow them when they move, and prevent their attacks on innocent people.

The second disagreement I have is about my request that we should be able to use the full resources of the military to combat terrorists who are contemplating the use of biological or chemical weapons. In general, the military should not be involved in domestic law enforcement in any way. That's why it's against the law. But there is a limited exception to this authority, granting the authority to cooperate with law enforcement to the military where nuclear weapons are involved. There's a good reason for this. The military has the unique technical expertise, sophisticated equipment, and highly specialized personnel to fight a nuclear threat. Well, the same is true for biological and chemical weapons, which seem even more likely to be used in terrorist attacks in the future, as we saw recently in the terrible incident in the Japanese subway.

Therefore, I can't understand how some Senators could actually suggest that it's okay to use the military for nuclear terrorism but not to use them for chemical and biological terrorism. We need their unique knowledge in all instances. I want law enforcement to have the authority to call in the military to deal with these chemical or biological weapons threats when they lack that expertise, equipment, or personnel. There's simply no reason why we should use anything less than the very best we have to fight and stop the extraordinary threat now posed by chemical and biological terrorism all around the world.

Finally, I strongly disagree with Senators who want to remove a provision of my bill that will help us track down terrorists by marking the explosive materials they use to build their weapons. It would be a relatively simple matter to include something called a taggant in materials used to build explosive devices. That way, law enforcement could track bomb materials back to their source and dramatically increase their ability to find and apprehend terrorists.

There is no reason to delay enactment of a law that would require taggants in explosive materials. Every day that goes by without a law like that is another day a terrorist can walk into a store and buy material that is virtually untraceable. As long as the basic building blocks of bombs are sold without taggants, we can only hope they're not being bought by terrorists.

The Senators who want to oppose my bill on these points simply argue that these provisions will open the door to an overly broad domestic use of military troops, to overly invasive wiretapping, or to an erosion of the constitutional rights of those who buy explosives. I disagree. Constitutional protections and legal restrictions are not being repealed. We are simply giving law enforcement agencies who are committed to fighting terrorists for us the tools they need to succeed in the modern world.

I want to work with Congress to resolve these differences and to make my antiterrorism bill the law as soon as possible.

On this Memorial Day weekend, we honor those who fought and died in our Nation's wars to keep America free. In the 21st century, the security of the American people will require us to fight terrorism all around the world and, unfortunately, here at home. It's a fight we have to be able to win.

Thanks for listening.

NOTE: The address was recorded at 2:22 p.m. on May 26 in the Oval Office at the White House for broadcast at 10:06 a.m. on May 27.

Remarks at the POW/MIA Postage Stamp Unveiling Ceremony
May 29, 1995

Thank you very much, Secretary Brown, for your remarks and for your service. Postmaster General Runyon, Senator Simpson, Congressman Bishop, Secretary and Mrs. West, General and Mrs. Shalikashvili, to the distinguished service chiefs who are here, members of the Armed Forces, and especially to our veterans on this Memorial Day: We are proud to have you all here at the White House and honored to have the opportunity to unveil this stamp, which honors the extraordinary sacrifice of American prisoners of war and the memory of all those who never came home. It will help to ensure that all these Americans who gave so much to our freedom are never forgotten.

We are especially fortunate to have a number of former prisoners of war joining us here today. They represent a half-century of commitment to the principles that our Nation has stood for throughout the world. They embody a level of devotion and service almost unimaginable. And I am proud to recognize several of them who are here today.

Lieutenant Colonel Charles Prigmore was a young bombardier during World War II. On his 14th mission over Germany, his plane was shot down, and he spent a year as a POW. Today, he is the national commander of the American Ex-Prisoners of War. Colonel Prigmore, would you be recognized, please? [*Applause*] Thank you.

Infantryman Bill Rolen fought at Anzio Beach and helped to liberate Rome. During the invasion of southern France he was captured and forced to spend the rest of the war in a slave labor camp. Mr. Rolen, welcome. [*Applause*] Thank you.

When the Philippines were attacked in 1941, Ruby Bradley had already been an Army nurse for 7 years. She was captured just days after Christmas, and her internment lasted until 1945. Ms. Bradley. [*Applause*] Thank you.

Robert Fletcher was serving in Korea in 1950 when he was captured. He spent nearly 3 years as a prisoner of the North Korean and Chinese forces before he finally could return home. Mr. Fletcher. [*Applause*] Thank you.

Captain Isaac Camacho, a green beret, was captured outside Saigon when his camp was overrun in 1963. He endured the jungle prisons of the Viet Cong for nearly 2 years and was one of the very few to escape and to survive. It is especially appropriate to have him here today because he is still a servant of our country; he is the U.S. Postal Service station master in El Paso, Texas. Captain Camacho. [*Applause*] Thank you, sir.

And finally, Lieutenant Colonel Rhonda Cornum is a flight surgeon who served in Operation Desert Storm. On a rescue mission in Iraq, her helicopter was shot down. She was badly injured, with broken arms and a gunshot wound,

captured by Iraqi forces, and held until the end of the fighting. Colonel Cornum. [*Applause*] Thank you.

Ladies and gentlemen, these and the others who have suffered similar fates are American heroes, among the finest and bravest individuals our Nation has ever produced. They had to bear hardships, but never faltered. They inspire us still, and will for generations to come. I am pleased now that millions of Americans will be reminded every day of the extraordinary service they rendered, and all others like them rendered, by this new stamp.

On this Memorial Day, as every year, we also remember those who answered the call but never came home. Their loss is the greatest cost our Nation has paid for freedom. We can only imagine the pain their families have experienced, the grief that comes with uncertainty, the grief that comes with being denied a proper and clear grave. We know very well our obligation to them and their families to leave no stone unturned as we try to account for their fate and, if possible, to bring them home.

We have worked hard and made good progress. We have put the issue of MIA cases ahead of all others in our dealings with Vietnam. And today I am proud to say that we are receiving more cooperation from Hanoi than ever before.

A Presidential delegation headed by the Veterans Department Deputy Secretary, Hershel Gober, has just returned from Vietnam and Laos, and we believe that cooperation with both these nations will continue. Our joint investigations are moving forward, and the Vietnamese are turning over essential documents. More than 200 sets of remains have been returned since I became President. Of the nearly 200 so-called discrepancy cases, we have confirmed the fate of all but 55. And we will not stop until we have taken every possible step for every MIA and every MIA family.

I want to say a special word of appreciation to all those who have participated in this remarkable effort. There is nothing like it in all the history of warfare. Never has so much been done to get this kind of accounting. I thank the families involved, the veterans groups involved, those who have served in the active duty military as a part of this, and others who have played critical roles.

I also thank the Americans who have worked to help the Vietnamese to identify their MIA's as well. That, too, is an astonishing development in the history of warfare. And the American people are indebted to all of you who have played a role in this remarkable endeavor.

Thanks to our new relationship with Russia, we're also making progress on the MIA cases from World War II, the Korean War, Vietnam, and a number of cold war incidents. The U.S.-Russia Joint Commission on POW-MIA's has gained access to thousands of pages of once-classified documents, conducted hundreds of interviews in Russia and in the other New Independent States, received important information about the fate of American service personnel.

Those missing from the war in Korea, along with the MIA's from all our Nation's conflicts, will not be forgotten in the heart of America. Our work will go forward until we have done all there is to do. We owe it to them, to their families, and to our country to work on this until the job is done.

And we must remain true to our entire commitment to stand by all those who stood watch for freedom. Whether it is protecting benefits that veterans have earned or improving health care or breaking the cycle of despair for homeless veterans or confronting the legacy of Agent Orange or getting to the bottom of Gulf war-related illnesses, we must uphold our solemn obligation to our veterans, not for a few months or for a few years but for the entire lifetime of this Nation.

And we owe it to the legacy of our veterans to protect the national security in the future. We are working hard to end the legacy of the cold war. The United States and Russia are destroying nuclear arsenals. And I am proud that for the first time since the dawn of the nuclear age, there are no nuclear weapons pointed at the children of the United States of America. I am proud that the United States and Russia joined together to secure the indefinite extension of the Non-Proliferation Treaty, so that more and more nations will be making and keeping a promise not to develop nuclear weapons.

But we know that we have challenges from other weapons as well, from biological and chemical weapons. We must work to contain them. And we know that we have the challenge not only of nations that still seek to do us and other freedom-loving peoples harm but also from terrorists around the world and here at home who would threaten our security and our way of life.

We must stand up to all these security threats as a way of honoring those who have sacrificed and served our country. They brought us to this point, and we owe it to them to give our children the opportunities we have all enjoyed.

So on this Memorial Day, I say to all of you, we honor the sacrifices of those who never came home, the sacrifices of those who were imprisoned but came home, the sacrifices of all who gave and all who serve. God bless you all, and God bless America.

And now, for the proper unveiling of this much-deserved stamp, let me introduce our very fine Postmaster General, Mr. Marvin Runyon, and thank him again for the outstanding job he has done.

Mr. Runyon.

NOTE: The President spoke at 9:15 a.m. on the South Lawn at the White House.

Remarks at a Memorial Day Ceremony in Arlington, Virginia
May 29, 1995

Thank you very much, Secretary Perry, Secretary Brown, Major General Gorden, Chaplain Cottingham, General and Mrs. Shalikashvili, and to the other members of the Joint Chiefs of Staff and their wives, to all the members of the Armed Forces who are here, and the veterans, especially to the POW's and their family members and the family members of MIA's whose sacrifice and service we honored today just a few moments ago with the unveiling of the special stamp in honor of POW's and MIA's, and of course, to Sergeant Major Rodriguez and Mrs. Rodriguez.

Sergeant Major, if you had known 50 years ago you were going to be here today and had 50 years to get ready, you could not have done any better job than you did, and we thank you. This fine American was decorated by President Roosevelt with the Purple Heart for his action in combat on Iwo Jima. He later led an honor guard for President Truman. He represents the vital ties to the past that inspires us today, and we thank him and all others for their service.

Today we feel close to that past and to all those who stood fast when our freedom was in peril 50 years ago. We remember the valiant individuals from all of our wars who fell while defending our Nation. They fought so that we might have the freedom which too many of us take for granted but, at least on this day, we know is still our greatest blessing.

At this sacred moment, we put aside all that might otherwise divide us to recall the honor that these men and women brought to their families and their communities and the glory they bestowed upon our beloved Nation. All across our great country today, in cities and towns great and small, wreaths and flags adorn our cemeteries. Friends and family members and those who simply are grateful for their liberties will gather for a parade or visit the graves of some of these heroes, tell a new generation the stories of how America was kept free and strong. We must remember to do justice to their memories. We must remember that so we can go forward.

Especially in this last year, the 50th since World War II, we Americans have remembered and paid homage to the generation that fought that great struggle in ceremonies in Normandy, at Nettuno Beach in Italy, at Cambridge Cemetery in England, the Manila Cemetery in the Philippines, the Iwo Jima Memorial here in Arlington, and in Moscow.

As we look across the gulf of time and look at the veterans of that conflict who still are among us, we continue to draw strength from their marvelous achievement. We remember anew the indomitable power of free men and women united by a just cause.

Fifty years ago today, the war in Europe was over. American armed forces worked to restore order to a wrecked continent, taking charge of shattered communities, tending to the survivors of the awful concentration camps. But the celebration of victory was short because our battle-weary Nation was shifting troops and energies from one theater to another. Little was certain. Virtually every household still had someone in

uniform, and no one could say even then who would survive.

In the Pacific war, fighting raged on in the Philippines. Okinawa, the bloodiest battle in the Far East, was already almost 2 months old and far, far from over. By the time it ended on June 22, that small island would claim the lives of more than 12,000 Americans.

Still, our forces never faltered. Half a world away from their homes, far from their families, they fought for their country, their loved ones, and for the ideals that have kept this country going now for more than 200 years. They knew their mission was unparalleled in human history: to fight for freedom, for democracy, and for human dignity all the world over. In those distant places and harrowing times, ordinary people performed extraordinary deeds.

Many who fell there are now here in Arlington, in this hallowed ground. We come here to honor their sacrifice, to give them thanks for safeguarding our homes and our liberties and for giving us another 50 years of freedom. But we also come here because we understand what they fought for. Here, among the dead, in the perfect rows of stone, we see the life of America for which they sacrificed so much.

Four graves around here today tell a good story. Right over there, down Grant Drive, is the grave of Colonel Justice Chambers of the United States Marine Corps Reserve. For his extraordinary courage in taking vital high ground during the landing on Iwo Jima, he was awarded the Congressional Medal of Honor. Just next to him lies Lieutenant Commander Barbara Allen Rainey. She was the mother of two daughters and the Navy's first female aviator. She died in a plane crash in 1982. Further down the walk lies the grave of Rear Admiral Richard E. Byrd, Jr., known throughout the world as the first person ever to fly over the North Pole. And next to him lies General Daniel "Chappie" James, a Tuskegee Airman who flew nearly 200 combat missions, a pilot in Korea and Vietnam as well. He rose through the ranks to become the first African-American four-star general.

These four were very different in race and gender, service and generation. But they were united in their service to America. Together, their lives are proof of perhaps our greatest American truth: that a nation of many really can be brought forth as one. Together, they show the tremendous strength that not only our Armed Forces but our entire Nation has drawn from our remarkable diversity. They remind us of the riches our democracy creates by bringing the benefits of liberty to all Americans, regardless of their race or gender or station in life. They remind us of why so many have sacrificed so much for the American idea.

Today, more than ever, we rededicate ourselves to the vision for which they live. Generations before ours met challenges to democracy and freedom, defeated the threats of fascism and communism, and now it is for us to rise to the new challenges posed by the forces of darkness and disintegration in this age at home and abroad.

In an uncertain world, we still know we must maintain armed forces that are the best-trained, best-equipped, and best-prepared in the world. That is the surest guarantee of our security and the surest guarantee that we will not repeat the mistakes of the past, when America disarmed encouraged people to abuse the decent liberties we all are willing to fight for.

Now, we must finish the security work of the last 50 years by ending the nuclear threat once and for all. I am very proud of the fact, and I know all of you are, that today, we and the Russians are destroying the weapons of our nuclear arsenal and that for the first time since the dawn of the nuclear age, no Russian missiles are pointed at the people of the United States of America. I am proud of the fact that the nations of the world recently voted to extend indefinitely the Non-Proliferation Treaty and that Russia and the other states of the former

Soviet Union and the United States were on the same side, asking countries to forswear ever developing nuclear weapons.

I know we have more to do in trying to stem the proliferation of biological and chemical weapons and to defeat the forces of terrorism around the world. No free country is immune from them. But we can do this, and we must.

In honor of all those who have fallen, from the dawn of our Nation to this moment, we resolve to uphold not only their memories but their ideals: the vision of America, free and strong, conferring the benefits of our beloved land on all our citizens. They sacrificed so that we could do this.

Our debt is, therefore, to continue freedom's never-ending work, to build a Nation worthy of all those who fell for it, to pass to coming generations all that we have inherited and enjoyed. This must be our common purpose: to make sure all Americans are able to make the most of their freedoms and their God-given abilities and still, still, to reaffirm our conviction that we are, from many, one.

And so we go forth from this place today, remembering the lives of people like Chambers, Rainey, Byrd, and James. From their example, let us carry forth that passion and let us strengthen our national unity.

God bless you all, and God bless America.

NOTE: The President spoke at 11:32 a.m. at Arlington National Cemetery.

Remarks on Clean Water Legislation
May 30, 1995

Thank you very much. This country would be better off if we had a few more little old ladies in tennis shoes, don't you think, like Minny Pohlmann? [*Applause*] Thank you, Minny, for your introduction, and more importantly, thank you for the many years of work you have done to clean up the Potomac and to set an example about responsible environmentalism.

Secretary Babbitt; Administrator Browner; to the CEQ Chairman, Katie McGinty; George Frampton; Bob Stanton; Mike Brown; to Neal

Fitzpatrick, the conservation director of the Audubon Naturalist Society; and the two young people who came up with me, Hannah and Michael—where are they, where are the young people who were with me? Thank you very much. And to all the schoolchildren who are here—I wish you could have heard what they were saying over there as I was looking at some of the species that live in this water, because it is still not as pure as it ought to be, and reading the sign over there. Have you all read the sign on the creek? "Fish from these waters contain PCB's. Do not eat catfish, carp, or eel from these waters. You may eat a half a pound per month of largemouth bass or a half a pound per week of sunfish or other fish. Choose to eat younger and smaller fish of legal size. Always skin the fish, trim away the fat, and cook so that it drains away. The practice of catch and release is encouraged. Swimming is prohibited still due to high levels of bacteria."

To those who say we have nothing more to do to clean up America's waterways, I urge them to come here to Pierce Mill and read the sign. We still have a lot of work to do on this, the most simple necessity of our lives, water.

Pierce Mill and this part of Rock Creek Park are very important in the history of our country. Teddy Roosevelt used to come here to walk and to look at the creek, to get a little exercise. I admire Teddy Roosevelt for many reasons, but one of the most important is that he taught us the necessity of preserving our natural resources and protecting our natural world. He established the National Wildlife Refuges. The Forest Service grew in size and vision under his leadership. His actions led to the creation of the National Park Service, which takes care of this very park. This great Republican President taught us that it would be foolhardy and spendthrift to try to play politics with our environmental treasures. Caring for our land wasn't just for Democrats or just for Republicans, it was an American cause and just plain common sense. That was true at the beginning of this century when Teddy Roosevelt was President; it's even more true at the end of this century as we look toward a new millennium.

Roosevelt's legacy of nonpartisanship on the environment extended throughout most of this century. It was under another Republican President, Richard Nixon, that we created the Environmental Protection Agency, passed the Clean Water Act, and created the White House Council on Environmental Quality.

For a long time, therefore, Americans have stood as one in saying no to things like dirty water and yes to giving our children an environment as unspoiled as their hopes and dreams. It is because of this commitment on the part of millions of Americans of both parties and all races and ethnic backgrounds, people from every region of our country and all walks of economic life, that last week you were able to take your children—last weekend—to a beach that was clean or a lake that was full of fish

or a river that was safe to swim in. And that's why I want to talk to you about some of the things that are going on now that present a threat to that way of life.

Some Members of the new Congress, operating with major industry lobbyists, have come up with a bill that would roll back a quarter-century of bipartisan progress in public health and environmental protection. The bill would let polluted water back into our lives. It would increase the threat of improperly treated sewage being released into our waters. The sewage could then wash up on our beaches, maybe on the very beach where you taught your children to swim.

Members of Congress who support this legislation actually have the nerve to call their bill the "Clean Water Act." And the House of Representatives actually passed it just before the Memorial Day weekend. But newspapers all over America are calling it the dirty water act. And it won't get past my desk.

We have worked as one people for 25 years—as one people for 25 years—across party lines to make our environment safer and cleaner. We cannot turn away from it now. There is still more to be done, not less.

Let me tell you about the true Clean Water Act, the one we have in place now, the one I'm going to use the power of the Presidency to protect. Every year the real Clean Water Act cleans more than a billion pounds of toxic pollutants from our water. Every year it keeps 900 million tons of sewage out of our rivers, lakes, and streams. In human terms, it keeps poisons out of your child's evening bath and bedtime glass of water.

Once a river of ours was so polluted that it actually caught fire. Thanks to that act, that doesn't happen anymore. The story used to be that if you fell into the Potomac, which this stream runs into, you had to go to a doctor and get shots to protect yourself from disease. Because of the genuine Clean Water Act, that's on its way to being a dark and distant memory. Today, the Potomac has rebounded, and many parts of it are safe for fishing and swimming.

Under the new bill in Congress all this could change. Instead of getting progressively cleaner, our water quality would go straight down the drain. We've heard all about beaches that have had to be shut down because of water waste and syringes on the sand. Some of us have been unlucky enough to have that experience first-hand.

The House bill would only increase this risk. Under its provisions, many coastal cities would be able to dump inadequately treated sewage and industrial waste into the ocean, increasing your family's chances of finding waste in the water when you're swimming or boating.

But this fight isn't just about how clean the water is when you're on vacation. It's also about the water that you drink every day, the water that you bathe in, the water that you use at home, the water that keeps you and your children and all of us alive.

Americans have a right to expect that our water will be the cleanest in the world. Clean water is essential to the security our people deserve, the safety that comes from knowing that the environment we live in won't make us sick. With all the other changes and challenges that the American people have to confront in the world today, they sure should not have to worry about the quality of their water. That is one uncertainty that even in this rapidly changing world we ought to be able to remove from every family in the United States of America.

This House bill would put the cleanliness and safety of our water at risk. Industries in our country use roughly 70,000 pollutants, chemicals, and other material that can poison water if they're not controlled properly. This bill would make it easier for those poisons to find their way into our water.

Current law requires that we use the best achievable technology to keep our water clean and safe. Amazingly, the House bill actually says we don't need to bother with the best technology; it says that second or even third best is good enough. That's crazy. There's no reason on Earth why Americans should have to settle for anything less than the best when it comes to keeping our water safe and pure.

Now, here's the part that really gets to me. This bill would also postpone, perhaps indefinitely, action against some of the suspected sources of cryptosporidium in drinking water. Now, we all remember what that is. That's the deadly bacteria that contaminated Milwaukee's water supply just 2 years ago. One hundred people died from drinking it; thousands more fell ill. For more than a week, the people of Milwaukee were terrified to brush their teeth, make coffee, use ice cubes, even wash their clothes in their own city's water supply. If you can believe it, this bill that passed the House would prevent us from doing everything in our power to make sure that this never happens again.

Who could possibly think up such a bill? Well, the lawyers and the lobbyists who represent the polluters who wrote the bill. They were invited into the back rooms of what once was your Congress to write a bill that provides loopholes for their industries. They want to make it possible for their companies to get around the standards that are designed to protect us all. If the bill becomes law, that's exactly what will happen.

But it won't. It won't. I am encouraged that some people in the Senate on both sides of the political aisle have expressed the gravest of reservations about this House bill. But if the special interests should get it through the Senate as well in the way that the House passed it, I will certainly have no choice but to veto it. And I will do it happily and gladly for the quality of water in this country.

A big part of the American dream goes way beyond economics and has to do with the preservation of our liberties and the stewardship of our land. This is a part of the American dream. The stories these children told me this morning about the dreams they have for clean water and a clean environment and growing up in an America where they'll be able to take their children to places like Pierce Mill, that's a big part of the American dream. A lot of people sacrificed to give us this dream. And we shouldn't squander it in a momentary lunge away from common sense and the common direction the American people have been taking for a generation now.

Teddy Roosevelt said the Nation behaves well if it treats the natural resources as assets which it must turn over to the next generation, increased and not impaired in value.

Now, let's get away even from the beauties of the stream. Look at this—every time I give a talk they give me one of these—[*laughter*]—because they're afraid I'll get hoarse or need it otherwise. We take this for granted. It's clean. It's safe. It's available to everyone. It won't make us sick. We have to have it to survive. Our lives depend on it. Why in the world would we do anything, anything at all, which would take away the simple security of the safety of this water from our children, ourselves, and our future?

Ladies and gentlemen, this does not have to be a political issue. For 25 years, it has not been a partisan issue. We are seeing in this area a dramatic, unusual, unwarranted departure from the commonsense course that has kept America moving toward a cleaner environment and a better tomorrow. Let's get back on course. That's the real progressive future.

Thank you, and God bless you all.

NOTE: The President spoke at 10:37 a.m. at Pierce Mill in Rock Creek Park. In his remarks, he referred to Robert Stanton, Regional Director, National Capital Region, National Park Service; and Michael Brown, Assistant Superintendent, Rock Creek Park.

Remarks at the United States Air Force Academy Commencement Ceremony in Colorado Springs, Colorado
May 31, 1995

The President. Thank you very much, General Stein.

Audience member. Soo-o-o-ey! [*Laughter*]

The President. That's my home State cheer, for those of you unused to foreign languages being spoken here in Falcon Stadium. [*Laughter*] Thank you very much.

General Stein, thank you. Secretary Widnall, General Fogleman, Governor Romer, Congressman Ramstad; to the distinguished faculty and staff; to the proud parents, family, and friends; to the members of the Cadet Wing: We gather here to celebrate this very important moment in your life and in the life of our Nation. Gentlemen and gentleladies of this class, the pride of '95, this is your day. And you are only one speech, one pretty short speech—[*laughter*]—away from being second lieutenants.

I am honored to share this day with some exceptionally accomplished alumni of the Air Force Academy: General Fogleman, the first of your graduates to be the Air Force Chief of Staff; General Hopper, the first African-American graduate of the Academy to serve as the Commandant of Cadets; and a member of my staff, Robert Bell, who is the first graduate of the Air Force Academy to be the Senior Director for Defense Policy and Arms Control at the National Security Council. As I look out at all of you, I imagine it won't be too long before there's a graduate of the Air Force Academy in the Oval Office. If it's all the same to you, I'd like to delay it for just a few years. [*Laughter*]

I also want to congratulate the Air Force Academy on extending its lock on the Commander in Chief's trophy here that—I'm in your

stadium, I think I ought to mention that your winning squad came to see me in the White House not very long ago, and I said that before I became President I didn't understand that when I heard that the Commander in Chief's trophy was a traveling trophy, that meant it was supposed to go back and forth between Washington and Colorado Springs every year.

I want to do my part in another longstanding tradition. By the power vested in me as Commander in Chief, I hereby grant amnesty to cadets who are marching tours or serving restrictions or confinements for minor misconduct. Now, General Stein, I have to leave it to you to define which offenses are minor, but on this day, even in this conservative age, I trust you will be fairly liberal in your interpretation of the term. [*Laughter*]

Members of the class of 1995, you are about to become officers in the United States Air Force. You should be very proud of what you have already accomplished. But you should be sobered by the important responsibilities you are about to assume. From this day forward, every day you must defend our Nation, protect the lives of the men and women under your command, and represent the best of America.

I want to say here as an aside, I have seen something of the debate in the last few days on the question of whether, in this time of necessity to cut budgets, we ought to close one of the service academies. And I just want to say I think that's one of the worst ideas I ever heard of.

It was General Eisenhower who as President, along with the Congress, so long ago now recognized that national defense required a national commitment to education. But our commitment through the service academies to the education and preparation of the finest military officers in the world must never wane. And I hope your commitment to the cause of education as an important element in what makes our country great and strong and safe will never wane.

As President, my first responsibility is to protect and enhance the safety of the American people and to strengthen our country. It is a responsibility that you now have chosen to share. So today, I thought what we ought to do is talk about the steps that we will have to take together to make the world safer for America in the 21st century.

Our security objectives over the last 50 years have been dictated by straightforward events often beyond our control. But at least they were straightforward and clear. In World War II, the objective was simple: Win the war. In the cold war, the objective was clear: Contain communism and prevent nuclear war. In the post-cold-war world, the objectives are often more complex, and it is clear that American security in the 21st century will be determined by forces that are operating both beyond and within our own borders.

While the world you will face is far from free of danger, you must know that you are entering active service in a moment of enormous hope. We are dramatically reducing the nuclear threat. For the first time since the dawn of the nuclear age, there are no Russian missiles pointed at the people of the United States.

From the Middle East to South Africa to Northern Ireland, Americans are helping former adversaries turn from conflict to cooperation. We are supporting democracies and market economies, like Haiti and Mexico in our own region and others throughout the world. We are expanding trade. We are working for a Europe allied with the United States, but unified economically and politically for the first time since nation-states appeared on the European Continent. Just yesterday, Russia's decision to actively participate in NATO's Partnership For Peace helped to lay the groundwork for yet another important step in establishing a secure, stable, and unified European Continent for the next century.

Clearly there are powerful historical forces pulling us together: a worldwide thirst for freedom and democracy; a growing commitment to market economics; a technological revolution that moves information, ideas, money, and people around the globe at record speed. All these things are bringing us together and helping to make our future more secure.

But these same forces have a dark underside which can also lead to more insecurity. We understand now that the openness and freedom of society make us even more vulnerable to the organized forces of destruction, the forces of terror and organized crime and drug trafficking. The technological revolution that is bringing our world closer together can also bring more and more problems to our shores. The end of communism has opened the door to the spread of weapons of mass destruction and lifted the lid on age-old conflicts rooted in ethnic, racial, and religious hatreds. These forces can be all the more destructive today because they have access to modern technology.

Nowhere are the forces of disintegration more obvious today than in Bosnia. For the past 2½ years, the United States has sought to contain and end the conflict, to help to preserve the Bosnian nation as a multistate entity, multiethnic entity, to keep faith with our NATO allies, and to relieve human suffering.

To these ends, we have led the NATO military responses to calls by the United Nations for assistance in the protection of its forces and safe areas for the people of Bosnia, led efforts to achieve a negotiated settlement, deployed peacekeeping troops to the Former Yugoslav Republic of Macedonia to contain the conflict within the present borders of Bosnia, and conducted the longest humanitarian airlift to the people there in history.

Two weeks ago, the Bosnian Serbs unleashed 1,400 shells on the civilians of Sarajevo. The United Nations called this attack a return to medieval barbarism. They asked for a NATO air response, which we supported. Now we have joined our allies to develop a coordinated response to the Serbs' continued refusal to make peace and their illegal capturing of United Nations personnel as hostages.

We believe still that a strengthened United Nations operation is the best insurance against an even worse humanitarian disaster should they leave. We have a longstanding commitment to help our NATO allies, some of whom have troops in the U.N. operation in Bosnia, to take part in a NATO operation to assist them in a withdrawal if that should ever become necessary. And so, if necessary, and after consultation with Congress, I believe we should be prepared to assist NATO if it decides to meet a request from the United Nations troops for help in a withdrawal or a reconfiguration and a strengthening of its forces.

We have received no such request for any such assistance, and we have made no such decision. But in any event, we must know that we must continue to work for peace there. And I still believe that we have made the right decision in not committing our own troops to become embroiled in this conflict in Europe nor to join the United Nations operations.

I want to say to you, we have obligations to our NATO allies, and I do not believe we can leave them in the lurch. So I must carefully review any requests for an operation involving a temporary use of our ground forces. But we have made the right decision in what we have done and what we have not done in Bosnia.

I believe we must look at all of these problems and all these opportunities in new and different ways. For example, we see today that the clear boundaries between threats to our Nation's security from beyond our borders and the challenges to our security from within our borders are being blurred. One once was clearly the province of the armed services, the other clearly the province of local law enforcement. Today, we see people from overseas coming to our country for terrorist purposes, blurring what is our national security. We must see the threats for what they are and fashion our response based on their true nature, not just where they occur.

In these new and different times, we must pursue three priorities to enhance our security. First, we have to combat those who would destroy democratic societies, including ours, through terrorism, organized crime, and drug trafficking. Secondly, we have to reduce the threat of weapons of mass destruction, whether they're nuclear, chemical, or biological. Third, we have to provide our military, you and people like you, with the resources, training, and strategic direction necessary to protect the American people and our interests around the world.

The struggle against the forces of terror, organized crime, and drug trafficking is now uppermost on our minds because of what we have endured as a nation, the World Trade Center bombing, the terrible incident in Oklahoma City, and what we have seen elsewhere, the nerve gas attack in Tokyo, the slaughter of innocent civilians by those who would destroy the peace in the Middle East, the organized crime now plaguing the former Soviet Union—so much that one of the first requests we get in every one of those countries is "Send in the FBI; we need help"—the drug cartels in Latin America and Asia that threaten the open societies and the fragile democracies there. All these things we know can emerge from without our borders and from within our borders. Free and open societies are inherently more vulnerable to these kinds of forces. Therefore, we must remain vigilant, reduce our vulnerability, and constantly renew our efforts to defeat them.

We work closely with foreign governments. We share intelligence. We provide military support. We initiate anticorruption and money-laundering programs to stop drug trafficking at its source. We've opened an FBI office in Moscow, a training center in Hungary to help combat international organized crime. Over the past 2 years, we've waged a tough counterterrorism campaign, strengthening our laws, increasing manpower and training for the CIA and the FBI, imposing sanctions on states that sponsor terrorism.

Many of these efforts have paid off. We were able to arrest and quickly convict those responsible for the World Trade Center bombing, to stop another terrible planned attack in New York as well as a plan to blow up American civilian airliners over the Pacific, and help to bring to justice terrorists around the world.

In the aftermath of Oklahoma City, our top law enforcement officers told us they needed new tools to fight terrorism, and I proposed legislation to provide those tools: more than 1,000 new law enforcement personnel solely working on terrorism; a domestic antiterrorism center; tough new punishment for trafficking in stolen explosives, for attacking members of the Uniformed Services or Federal workers; the enabling of law enforcement officials to mark explosive materials so they can be more easily traced; the empowering of law enforcement officials with authority to move legal, and I emphasize legal, wiretaps when terrorists quickly move their bases of operation without having to go back for a new court order; and finally, in a very limited way, the authority to use the unique capacity of our military where chemical or biological weapons are involved here at home, just as we now can call on those capabilities to fight nuclear threats.

I'm sure every graduate of this Academy knows of the posse comitatus rule, the clear line that says members of the uniformed military will not be involved in domestic law enforcement. That is a good rule. We should honor that rule. The only narrow exception for it that I know of today is the ability of law enforcement in America to call upon the unique expertise of the military when there is a potential threat of a nuclear weapon in the hands of the wrong people. All we are asking for in the aftermath of the terrible incident in the Tokyo subway is the same access to the same expertise should chemical and biological weapons be involved.

The congressional leadership pledged its best efforts to put this bill on my desk by Memorial Day. But Memorial Day has come and gone, and only the Senate has taken the bill up. And even there, in my judgment, there are too many amendments that threaten too much delay.

Congress has a full agenda of important issues, including passing a responsible budget. But all this will take time. When it comes to terrorism, time is a luxury we don't have. Some are even now saying we should just go slow on this legislation. Well, Congress has a right to review this legislation to make sure the civil liberties of American citizens are not infringed, and I encourage them to do that. But they should not go slow. Terrorists do not go slow, my fellow Americans. Their agenda is death and destruction on their own timetable. And we need to make sure that we can do everything possible to stop them from succeeding.

Six weeks after Oklahoma City, months after the first antiterrorism legislation was sent by the White House to Congress, there is no further excuse for delay. Fighting terrorism is a big part of our national security today, and it will be well into the 21st century. And I ask Congress to act and act now.

Our obligations to fight these forces of terror is closely related to our efforts to reduce the threat of weapons of mass destruction. All of us, I'm sure, ached and wept with the people of Japan when we saw what a small vial of chemical gas could do when unleashed in the subway station. And we breathed a sigh of relief when the alert officers there prevented the two chemicals from uniting and forming poison which could have killed hundreds and hundreds of people just a few days after that. The breakup of the Soviet Union left nuclear material scattered throughout the Newly Independent States

and increased the potential for the theft of those materials and for organized criminals to enter the nuclear smuggling business. As horrible as the tragedies in Oklahoma City and the World Trade Center were, imagine the destruction that could have resulted had there been a small-scale nuclear device exploded there.

The United States will retain as long as necessary an arsenal of nuclear forces to deter any future hostile action by any regime that has nuclear weapons. But I will also continue to pursue the most ambitious agenda to dismantle and fight the proliferation of nuclear weapons and other weapons of mass destruction since the dawn of the nuclear age.

This effort is succeeding, and we should support it. No Russian missiles are pointed at America. No American missiles are aimed at Russia. Because we put the START I treaty into force, Russia is helping us and joining us in dismantling thousands of nuclear weapons. Our patient, determined diplomacy convinced Ukraine, Kazakhstan, and Belarus to give up their weapons when the Soviet Union fell apart. We are cooperating with these nations and others to safeguard nuclear materials and stop their spread.

And just last month, we got the indefinite and unconditional extension of the Non-Proliferation Treaty, which will benefit not only this generation of Americans but future generations as well by preventing scores of countries from developing and acquiring nuclear weapons. More than 170 nations have signed on to this treaty. They vow they will either never acquire nuclear weapons or, if they have them, that they won't help others obtain them, and they will pursue arms control and disarmament.

We have to now go even further. There is no excuse for the Senate to go slow on approving two other vital measures, the START II treaty and the Chemical Weapons Convention. START II will enable us to reduce by two-thirds the number of strategic warheads deployed at the height of the cold war. The Chemical Weapons Convention requires the destruction of chemical weapon stockpiles around the world and provides severe penalties for those who sell materials to build these weapons to terrorists or to criminals. It would make a chemical terror, like the tragic attack in the Tokyo subway, much, much more difficult. Both START II and the Chemical Weapons Convention will make every American safer, and we need them now.

There is more to do. We are working to complete negotiations on a comprehensive test ban treaty, to implement the agreement we reached with North Korea to freeze and dismantle that country's nuclear program, to strengthen the Biological Weapons Convention. It is an ambitious agenda, but it is worthy of this moment, and it will make your future as officers in the United States Air Force, American citizens, and when you're parents and grandparents more secure.

Finally, let me say that none of this will work unless we also are faithful to our obligation to support a strong and adaptable military for the 21st century. The men and women of our Armed Forces remain the foundation, the fundamental foundation of our security. You put the steel into our diplomacy. You get the job done when all means short of force have been tried and failed.

We saw your strength on display in Haiti, where a brutal military regime agreed to step down peacefully only, and I emphasize only, when it learned that more than 60 C–130's and C–140's loaded with paratroopers were in the air and on the way. Now the Haitian people have a second chance to rebuild their nation.

We then saw your speed in the Persian Gulf, when Iraq massed its troops on the Kuwaiti border and threatened regional instability. I ordered our planes, ships, and troops into the Gulf. You got there in such a hurry that Iraq got out of the way in a hurry.

We saw your compassion in Rwanda, where you flew tons of supplies, medicines, and foods into a nation torn apart by violence and saved countless lives.

All over the world, you have met your responsibilities with skill and professionalism, keeping peace, making peace, saving lives, protecting American interests. In turn, your country has a responsibility to make sure you have the resources, the flexibility, the tools you need to do the job. We have sought to make good on that obligation by crafting a defense strategy for our time.

And I'd like to say here today that one of the principal architects of that strategy was our recently deceased former Defense Secretary, Les Aspin. During his many years in the Congress as head of the Armed Services Committee, as Secretary of Defense, and as head of the President's Foreign Intelligence Advisory Board,

he devoted a lifetime to this country's defense. And we will miss him terribly. And we are very grateful for the legacy he left: a blueprint for reshaping our military to the demands of the 21st century, a blueprint that calls on us to make sure that any force reductions we began at the end of the cold war do not jeopardize our strength over the long run, that calls on us to provide you with the resources you need to meet the challenges of a world plagued by ancient conflicts and new instabilities.

All of you know here that after World War II a major drawdown left us at a major disadvantage when war broke out in Korea. And just 5 years after the post-Vietnam drawdown, in 1980, the Army Chief of Staff declared that we had a hollow Army, a view shared by most experts. We have been determined not to repeat those mistakes.

Even as we draw down troops, we know we have to be prepared to engage and prevail in two nearly simultaneous major regional conflicts. Some argued that this scenario was unrealistic and excessively demanding. Recent events have proved that they were wrong and shown that we are pursuing the right strategy and the right force levels for these times.

Last summer, just before the North Koreans finally agreed to dismantle their nuclear program, we were poised to send substantial air, naval, and ground reinforcements to defend South Korea. Just a few months later, we deployed tens of thousands of troops to the Gulf and placed thousands more on alert. And in between those crises, I gave the go-ahead to the 25,000 troops engaged in Operation Uphold Democracy in Haiti.

In Haiti, the operation was especially historic because it was the most fully integrated military plan ever carried out in our history. The four services worked together, drawing on each other's special abilities more than ever before. And for the first time, we were ready to launch Army infantry and an air assault from a Navy aircraft carrier. When we decided to send our troops in peacefully, we did it in hours, not days. That kind of innovation and the ability to do that is what your country owes you as you walk out of this stadium today as officers in the United States Air Force.

This then will be our common security mission, yours and mine and all Americans': to take on terrorism, organized crime, and drug trafficking; to reduce the nuclear threat and the threat of biological and chemical weapons; to keep our military flexible and strong. These must be the cornerstones of our program to build a safer America at a time when threats to our security have no respect for boundaries and when the boundaries between those threats are disappearing.

Abroad, as at home, we must measure the success of our efforts by one simple standard: Have we made the lives of the American people safer? Have we made the future for our children more secure?

Let me say to this class, I know that the rewards of serving on the front lines of our foreign policy may seem distant and uncertain at times. Thirty-four years ago, President Kennedy said, "When there is a visible enemy to fight, the tide of patriotism runs high. But when there is a long, slow struggle with no immediate visible foe, your choice will seem hard indeed." Your choice, your choice, ladies and gentlemen, to take on the problems and possibilities of this time, to engage the world, not to run from it, is the right choice.

As you have learned here at the Academy, it demands sacrifice. In the years ahead, you will be asked to travel a long way from home, to be away from your loved ones for long stretches of time, to face dangers we perhaps cannot yet even imagine. These are the burdens you have willingly agreed to bear for your country, its safety, and its long-term security.

Go forth, knowing that the American people support you, that they admire your dedication. They are grateful for your service. They are counting on you, the class of '95, to lead us into the 21st century, and they believe you truly do represent the best of America.

Good luck, and Godspeed.

NOTE: The President spoke at 11:13 a.m. at Falcon Stadium. In his remarks, he referred to Lt. Gen. Paul Stein, USAF, Superintendent, and Brig. Gen. John D. Hopper, Jr., USAF, Commandant of Cadets, U.S. Air Force Academy; Gen. Ronald R. Fogleman, USAF, Air Force Chief of Staff; and Gov. Roy Romer of Colorado.

Interview With the United States Air Force News in Colorado Springs
May 31, 1995

Q. Sir, thanks for letting us have the interview, first. Could you give me just your impressions after giving the speech at the Air Force Academy? What are your thoughts about our next generation of military leaders?

The President. Well, I was terribly impressed with them. You know, I stood up there and shook hands with every one of those young people when they came across to get their diplomas. I talked to many of them, and I looked them all over pretty good, and I feel a lot better about my country. I think every American would feel an enormous sense of pride and confidence in our future if our people, if all of our people could have seen what I saw today.

Q. Quality of life is a major concern in the military today. Military members spend a lot of time away from their families. Housing is a problem. Depending on who you talk to, you get different quotes of how far the military trails their civilian counterparts. What can you do to assure the military people that the military is a good career? What incentives can you offer?

The President. Let's talk about the quality of life issues, apart from pay, just for a moment. One of the things that I have done since I have been President is to go back to Congress on a couple of occasions to try to get more funds to fund quality of life improvements, to improve the housing, to improve family supports like child care centers, to do the kinds of things that would make the military more attractive to stay in, and to make it more family-friendly, because you know a majority of our enlisted personnel now are married. And I think that's very important.

I am, frankly, reassured that the new Congress, even though we're going to have to cut a lot of spending, has committed to maintain the defense budget that I have laid out and also continue to support my request for extra funds for quality of life improvements.

I visit a large number of bases every year, and whenever I have time, I try to talk to not only our uniformed personnel but some of the spouses, and when possible, even some of the children, about what the quality of life is like and how we're doing. So I can tell you that I think the Congress, and I know the President, we are committed to trying to address these issues and improve them. In the years when the drawdown was so quick, from '87 forward, I think some of the quality of life issues did suffer, the quality of housing and some of the other supports. But we're going to have an opportunity to try to address that, and I'm committed to doing it.

Q. You touched on the increased OPS tempo, and we will get to the pay, but is the drawdown over? I mean, can we say that the drawdown is——

The President. Yes, it's leveling out. And the other thing I wanted to say about the quality of life is that so many people are being asked to do so many more missions away from home and more different things. That is inevitable; that's part of the changing nature of our security mission in the world. But we are looking at using more reserves, more guardsmen to help us.

I just got back from Haiti not very long ago, and I was quite encouraged by the success of the reservists and the guardsmen in Haiti, how happy they seemed to be to be there and how it helps to alleviate overly stringing out our full-time personnel. So that's another thing we're going to look at.

We've got a real problem with AWACS teams with that, as you probably know. And we're going to look at that as well as the possibility of using some reservists in fulfilling our AWACS missions.

Q. The drawdown, are we at——

The President. The drawdown, we're about done. We're leveling out now. And we're going to be able to—we're going to have to manage it very carefully from here on out, because we are committed still to maintaining throughout this century a level of force in Europe somewhere around 75,000 to 100,000. We have obligations in Korea which we certainly can't shrink from now, particularly as we're trying to work through this difficult issue of the North Korean nuclear capacity. And we're also heavily committed in other parts of Asia in ways that I think would be a mistake to walk away from.

And then, of course, a lot of our forces that are based here in the United States are being used all around the world in different ways. We have obligations in the Atlantic and in the Adriatic related to Bosnia and NATO generally, and we have to be available to do the kinds of things that we had to do in Haiti, the kind of things we did in Rwanda.

So I believe we're just about leveled out. And I think it's important that we not go too low. We don't want to repeat the mistake that we've made after every single conflict in the 20th century. We went down too fast. We did it after World War I; we did it after World War II; we did it after Korea; we did it after Vietnam. And we went down too far.

I think that the length of the cold war has given—and the experiences, the bitter experience of trying to rebuild after Vietnam has given our current crop of military leaders and our political leadership a little better historic memory. And I think there's a real sense of pride that the United States clearly has the finest military in the world, the most well-motivated, the most—the best trained, the best equipped, and in many ways the most talented. And I don't think anybody wants to do anything to undermine that. So—and I think all of us who know anything about it know that we have stretched you about as thin as we can.

Q. How do you attract the kind of people that it takes to maintain that best equipped, best Air Force, especially with the gap in the pay?

The President. Well, I think the—I think— first of all, let's talk about the pay. We now have the funds from Congress to now resume pay increases and to keep it up at whatever the legal level is. And if Congress chooses to raise the legal level—that is, they choose to let us do a little more percentage-wise per year— we'll even be able to keep up with that as long as it's not too much. But now we at least know we can fund pay increases every year up to the legally authorized limit, which is a good thing.

And I think what—most people that join the military know they'll never get rich, but they want to know that they're not going to be impoverished, and they want to have a predictable income. So my goal here is to have a predictable income that goes up on a regular basis so that if you join or if you reenlist, you'll know what the 5-year trend is going to be, for example.

In addition to that, I think it's important to maintain the educational benefits, both the

Montgomery GI bill benefits and to emphasize what I think a lot of people get out of the military, which is that they can do exciting and interesting things and they're almost continually being educated and trained. I mean, if every major company worked on developing the capacity of its people the way our armed services do, we would be even more powerful economically than we are.

So I think that—I think the mission is what really attracts people, and knowing that if they join the United States military forces, they'll be the absolute best in the world at what they do and they'll be doing something wonderful for their country.

But I believe that maintaining the quality of life issues and keeping the training and readiness up and making sure that people have the chance to be continuously retrained for different things, those issues—based on what the service personnel I have visited with in Europe and Asia, in the Pacific, and all over the continental United States, based on what all those folks have told me, I would say those are the major issues.

Q. Mission: what is the mission, do you see, in the future for the military? Are we going to be a security force for the world, or do you see it turning more to looking inside our own borders? Or is it going to be a happy medium of that?

The President. Well, I think that we will do more and more things in cooperation with others, just by the nature of it. I think we will be working with the United Nations; we'll be working with NATO; we'll be working with the Partnership For Peace. I think we'll be called upon in small numbers to—just because our prestige means so much—to help do things. We had 10 personnel, I think only 10, that were involved in trying to help resolve the border conflict between Ecuador and Peru. But it made a huge difference that a small number of American military personnel were willing to be part of a bigger unit. And we felt comfortable that our people were not going to be put in harm's way by doing that.

So I think we'll be doing a wide variety of things. But our fundamental mission will be, first and foremost, as long as there is a threat to the United States from nuclear powers, we will be arrayed so that we can protect against that threat. Secondly, we will be deployed so that we can protect our treaty alliances, the peo-

ple to whom we have sworn mutual security commitments. And we have those obligations, and we will honor them. Thirdly, we will try to use our military resources so that we can reduce the threat of the proliferation of weapons of mass destruction and the threat of terrorism to our people and the threat of disruptions in other countries which could affect our security. That's what we did in Haiti, for example, where we were able to restore democracy there. And then when we can perform a humanitarian mission with an acceptable limitation on the mission, an acceptable level of risk, and we have enough control over the circumstances that we have to be involved in, as we did in Rwanda, I think we still should be prepared to do that.

I think that we did a lot of good in Somalia. We had the most painful experience that I've had personally as Commander in Chief there. But our people did a lot of good. They saved hundreds of thousands of lives. But because of the relationship between the United States and the United Nations, we were in an untenable position there for a period of months, and we paid a terrible price for it. But we learned from it. And in Rwanda, we went in under different circumstances and again saved countless thousands of lives, in ways that again helped the security of the United States because of what it did for our relationship to all the African countries.

So there will be a lot of things we have to do. But we have these core security missions that I mentioned first and foremost that we must continue to maintain.

Q. Finally, sir, you've basically got the attention of the entire Air Force. Is there anything you would like to pass along, add, that we didn't cover today?

The President. I would like to say, first of all, a simple thank-you to the members of the Air Force for their service and for their dedication. I realize that these last few years have been very difficult for people who have been through them with downsizing. There's never been anything like it, as far as I know, in the public or the private sector, for a successful enterprise to come out on its feet the way our military has. And I'm very grateful, not only as President but as an American citizen.

Secondly, I would like to say that I and my entire administration are committed to trying to improve the quality of life, to trying to keep the pay coming, to trying to make the circumstances as good as they possibly can be, that the future will be more exciting, more diverse, and therefore a little more strenuous in some ways than perhaps the past has been, but we will do our best to make the Air Force an attractive career for dedicated, committed American patriots. And as long as the people out there are doing their best, we owe it to all of them to do our best. And that's what I'm committed to doing.

NOTE: The interview began at 2:25 p.m. in the Tea House at the U.S. Air Force Academy.

Remarks to the Community at Peterson Air Force Base in Colorado Springs
May 31, 1995

Thank you very much. It's wonderful to see all of you, all of the service personnel, all of your families, all the kids who are here. I thank you for coming. And I just want you to know I kept the rain away. They thanked me at the Air Force Academy, and I said, "You know, when you're President, you get blamed for so many things you didn't do; it's okay to take credit for a thing or two you didn't do, either." [*Laughter*] But I'm very, very glad to be here, glad to see all of you. I want to thank Chief Master Sergeant Sue Turner for her introduction. If she were running for office, she'd get a lot of votes just on being brief, I think. [*Laughter*] And I thank her for what she said. I'm glad to be here with your Governor, Roy Romer, General Ashy, and others.

Earlier this month—I want to say something serious, if I might, for a moment—our Nation lost six patriotic reservists of the 302d Airlift Wing based here at Peterson. Today, I, as their President, just want to remember them with my respects, my gratitude, my thanks. And I'd like to ask if we could all just have a brief moment of silence in their memory, please.

[*At this point, a moment of silence was observed.*]

Thank you very much.

Like the Rockies, the men and women here of Peterson stand tall and strong and proud. You're always ready. You are the sentinels of our air sovereignty. You're the home base for our Space Command and for NORAD. You are our eyes in space.

I did a couple of interviews yesterday with some Colorado newspapers, and one of them asked me if we still needed eyes in space since the cold war was over. And I said, the last time I checked we had more stuff up in space every day; I thought we needed more eyes, not fewer. I thank you for what you're doing.

You have made America safer. You have made the world safer. And as we face the new challenges of the 21st century, you know as well as I do that the American military will continue to play a vital role, not only in the defense of our freedom and our security but also in advancing the cause of democracy and freedom throughout the world.

We have seen painfully in the United States in the last several months, first at the World Trade Center and then at the awful incident at Oklahoma City, that our security can be threatened in a global economy with open borders and lots of personal freedom here at home as well as beyond our borders. We had those two terrorist incidents: One of them occurred from people I believe were deeply disturbed and way off track within our country; another occurred because this is a free country and people can come and go here, and people who bore us ill will and wanted to destroy a symbol of American democracy came into this country and set that bomb at the World Trade Center.

I'm also happy to tell you that other sentinels of freedom working to thwart terrorism stopped two terrible incidents that were planned, one to blow up another bomb in New York and another that was designed to take some aircraft out of the air, flying out of the West Coast going over the Pacific.

But we now know that the security threats we'll face in the future, rooted in terrorism and organized crime and drug trafficking, are closely tied to things the military has had to work on for years, trying to stem the proliferation of weapons of mass destruction, stand up to rogue states, and protect our security interests around the world. We're going to have to fight on all these fronts, and you're going to have to continue to be the best trained, best equipped, best motivated, most flexible military in the world for us to succeed.

I am committed to making sure that you always are that and to doing whatever we have to do to improve the quality of life and the conditions of living, so that the best people in America want to be in the military and want to stay in the military.

Since I have been President, I have twice had to go back to Congress to ask for large appropriations totaling over $35 billion to help to maintain our training, our readiness, and our quality of life. And this year I asked the Congress for a supplemental appropriation to cover contingencies in the Defense Department so we could fund a pay increase at the maximum legal level allowable and continue to make improvements in readiness and the quality of life. We are going to continue to do that. If you're com-

mitted to serving America, the people who make the decisions about investments in your future should be committed to making sure that you can serve and succeed, that you can have good families and a good life in the United States military. And we are very grateful to you for that.

Let me say, what I most wanted to do was to have a chance to say thank you personally and to go down the row and shake hands with the children. And while I am very good at stopping the rain, I am not good at keeping it away forever. So I'm going to terminate my remarks with a heartfelt thank-you to all of you for your service to the United States.

God bless you all, and thank you. Thank you very much.

NOTE: The President spoke at 3:50 p.m. on the flight line. In his remarks, he referred to Gen. Joseph W. Ashy, commander in chief, North American Aerospace Defense Command, commander in chief, U.S. Space Command, and commander, Air Force Space Command.

Interview With Jim Gransbery of the Billings Gazette in Billings, Montana
May 31, 1995

[*The interview is joined in progress.*]

Farm Bill

Mr. Gransbery. ——envision sharp reductions in both mandatory and discretionary spending for farm programs and research. To what extent are you willing to go, a veto or whatever, to get a farm bill that adequately meets your funding requirements to protect farmers' income and future research?

The President. I'm willing to go quite a long way. You know, I went to Ames, Iowa, a couple of weeks ago to hold a rural conference to give agricultural interests from around the Middle West a chance to come in and testify on a strictly nonpartisan basis just to say what they thought ought to be done in the farm bill. And I pointed out that we had already put in our budget certain reductions in agricultural supports that were consistent with the GATT agreement we made with Europe and the others,

other countries, to try to get everybody to reduce their agricultural supports.

Now, the—and I think the numbers that are in the marks, in the Republican marks, are excessive. You know, we might be able to cut some more, but there's a limit to how much we can cut and still be competitive. Up here, you know, you've got special problems. I worked for a very long time to get this agreement last year with the Canadians on wheat to limit imports and then to set up this commission to try to resolve that problem.

But I think that it's a great mistake to look at these farm subsidies just as sort of special Government spending programs instead of looking at them in the context of how we do in international markets. If everybody did away with their protectionism, we wouldn't have to spend a plug nickel on agriculture in America. Our people would do just fine.

And so, I think the proper way to do this is through negotiations with our competitors and to keep driving the subsidies down in a way that opens up markets to our farmers and tries to keep—therefore, have some reasonable relationship of the competitiveness of American agriculture to the incomes people can earn.

If we cut excessively, one or two things, or both, will happen: You will either have substantial losses of American markets—markets for American farmers, or you'll have a lot of individual farmers go under and corporate farms take them over, or both.

So I think it's very important—and Secretary Glickman, the new Agriculture Secretary, as I'm sure you know, was a Congressman from Kansas for 18 years, knows a lot about agriculture. He's out and around the country now talking to farmers, trying to continue to get more ideas about what we can do to put some more flexibility in the farm program that the farmers have asked us for, what we can do to help make more farm income from within the United States by diversifying products and building on the base farm production to develop new products and a lot of that.

But we are still going to have to be very careful, not only about how much farm prices—farm programs are cut but how they're cut. It's not just important to the dollar, but it's also important what form they take if your goal is to preserve productive, competitive family farms. And that's my goal. That's what I think our interest should be. We can't be in the business of propping up somebody that can't do it, but everybody knows that's generally not the problem with American agriculture.

So, that's where we are. And I intend to make a hard fight out of it. And we have some allies in the Congress among the Republicans and the Democrats. I know that the urban Democrats and the suburban Republicans are the majority, but there are some that are sensitive to these issues. And of course, we have some—in the agriculture committees themselves, we've got some folks in both parties that understand these issues. And so I think we'll be able to make some progress there.

Militia Groups

Mr. Gransbery. Sir, are you here in Montana to take on the ideology of the so-called militia and similar anti-Government groups? How serious a threat do you think they really are?

The President. Well, the first answer to your question is no, I'm not here in Montana to do that, although if—that presumably will be a part of my townhall meeting because you've got a strong militia presence here. I'm here because I think it's important that the President explicitly acknowledge and listen to all the concerns that the Mountain West has about—have about the Federal Government. All these concerns have to be listened to.

Now, on the militia movement, I think that the answer is—how much of a threat? It just depends on who you're talking about, what the group is and what they've said and what they're prepared to do. I had a lot of experience with the militia movement 10, 11 years ago in a different incarnation when I was Governor, groups that were—they were then calling themselves survivalists. And we had a tax protester from North Dakota or South Dakota, Gordon Kahl, killed in Arkansas.

Mr. Gransbery. I remember that, yes.

The President. We had another guy, Snell, just executed in Arkansas, who killed a pawn shop owner he thought was Jewish and then killed a black State policeman who was a good friend of mine, shot him down in cold blood.

And we had a group called the Covenant of the Sword and the Arm of the Lord that had 200 people in an armed encampment in north Arkansas that we were able to seal off and persuade them to voluntarily evacuate and give up a major, major arsenal. And then those that were wanted—there were two who were wanted on murder warrants there—they were arrested. And everybody else that wasn't one was let go, and they didn't come back. So I went through that, through the difficult times of the early eighties.

I do not—my view is that all these groups and individuals have to be viewed based on the facts, you know. What are they doing and what are they saying? But I don't believe that anybody has a right to violate the law or take the law into their own hands against Federal officials who are just doing their job. I don't believe that.

Bosnia

Mr. Gransbery. If U.S. combat ground troops are sent to Bosnia, what are the rules of engagement? Will they be there to secure the safety of the U.N. peacekeepers, or will they be asked to neutralize the Bosnian Serbs as well?

The President. Well, the answer is that, first of all, they have not been asked for, and no decision has been made to send them. But going back to a time before I became President, there was a general commitment made by the United States that if our NATO allies who were part of the U.N. force in Bosnia got in trouble and needed our help to evacuate them, that we would do that, because we have air and naval presence in the area and we can move manpower off of our naval presence into the area.

As you know, our role in Bosnia has been to try to confine the conflict to Bosnia. Our troops are in the Former Yugoslav Republic of Macedonia. We have also supported certain efforts in Croatia to try to confine the conflict. And then we had played a major role in the airlift, which is now the longest humanitarian airlift in history.

Now the question has arisen, if these people, if the U.N. forces want to stay in Bosnia but have to relocate so they can concentrate themselves in more secure areas, if they needed help from us, would we be willing to give it? My instinct is, as long as the mission was strictly limited for a very narrow purpose and it was something that we could do for them that they couldn't do for themselves, upon proper consultation with Congress, I would be inclined to do that. But they would not be going there to get involved in war or to be part of the U.N. mission.

The United States—first of all, Europe wanted to take the lead here. It was the right thing to do. And we had no business involved in ground war in Bosnia.

Natural Resources Policy

Mr. Gransbery. Natural resource issues, grazing, mining, lumbering, wools, are all flash points in the West. Your administration appears to have antagonized just about every one on all sides of these issues. In view of the fact that you captured electoral votes in the West in 1992, what policies can you establish now to regain your political support, especially in the Rocky Mountain West?

The President. Well, let's just take them one at a time. On the grazing issues, which I think gave the Republicans their little opening to claim we were waging war on the West, the administration—the Interior Department made a mistake. They just made a mistake. They proposed as a negotiating strategy raising the grazing fees too high in 1993. It was wrong. But after strenuous objection by a number of people, led by Senator Baucus, we immediately dropped it, immediately. That should have been evidence that we weren't trying to wage war on anybody out here. Since then, what we've been trying to do is to develop a responsible way of managing the federally owned lands that permit people to continue to graze them in a responsible manner. And I've been trying to follow the model that was developed down in Colorado to use more local input.

On the mining, I just simply believe that the mining law of 1872 needs to be modernized. I don't think that it's served the public interest very well, but I don't think we should do it to the extent that we put people out of business.

On the timber, the truth is that the timber people ought to be for me. The previous——

Mr. Gransbery. I beg your pardon?

The President. The timber people ought to support what I've done. If you look at where we were before, look at the fact that the old growth forests were tied up in court for years and years and there were no contracts let—that's mostly, you know, Washington, Oregon, Northern California. That's where the big controversy was on the timber. The previous administration, President Bush's White House, they complained about it, but they didn't get their Government in line. They had six Government agencies that had five different legal positions in the cases in court.

So I got all of our people together. I said, we've got to come out with a position that will get this case out of court so we can do what we can to preserve the forest but so we can get people logging again. And that is what we did. We did something the previous administration couldn't do. And I have been—we are letting contracts there now. We are giving landowners, especially small landowners, more flexibility over their land. We have just released a contract, the U.S. Forest Service has, for a half a billion board feet of salvaged timber in Idaho, primarily in Idaho.

The only difference now is whether we should have a law which basically says that no one can file a suit on any timber contract for 30 months. You know, I think that goes too far. But I am trying to get it where these folks can log again. I have worked hard on that, and I think that, frankly, that's just a bum rap. That's what I believe.

You know, I come from a State that has a lot of national forest land and that has a lot of logging. And I have really worked hard to make that one go. So one of the things that I hope to do when I get out of here is get a better sense of how people perceive what our administration is doing and how—you know, if there are problems between my office and the White House and what's actually happening out here on the ground, I want to get a sense of what they are and move through them.

But you know, if I had been trying to wage war on the West, I don't think the West would have done as well as it has in the last 10½ years. The economy out here is booming because I followed good economic policies. And I really have tried to be sensitive to all the incredibly conflicting interests. And you pointed it out—I may ask people on both sides—you know, most of the environmental groups don't think I've been—[*inaudible*]——

Mr. Gransbery. That's true.

The President. ——enough. I mean, I think it's a mistake to take an extremist position on one side or the other. If you look at Montana, for example, you have got a huge stake in preserving the environment and permitting people to grow wheat and raise cattle and do whatever else they're trying to do. And what we've got to do is to try to work it out.

What I generally try to do is try to push as many of these decisions as I can down to representative local groups so that people don't feel that alienated bureaucrats in Washington are shoving them around. I don't want them to feel that way.

NOTE: The interview began at approximately 6:45 p.m. in the President's limousine en route to Montana State University. The press release issued by the Office of the Press Secretary did not include the complete opening portion of the interview. A tape was not available for verification of the content of this interview.

Remarks to the Community in Billings
May 31, 1995

Thank you very much. Thank you for that wonderful, wonderful welcome. It is great to be back in Montana and great to have that kind of reception. I know it's hot, and I was thinking you might just feel the need to stand up and down now and then to keep cool. [*Laughter*]

I want to thank the Billings High School Band. Didn't they do a good job on "Hail to the Chief"? Thank you, Chancellor Sexton, for making me feel at home. Thank you, Governor Racicot, for coming out here and meeting me at the airport and coming over to be with us here. You know, I was a Governor for 12 years, and I served with 150 other Governors. Most of my friends in Arkansas thought that I just couldn't get another job. [*Laughter*] But in a lot of ways, it was the best job I ever had. At least you could know people, and they knew you, and—because I come from a State that's a little bigger than Montana but not much, more populous but smaller. And I always loved being Governor. Three people I served with are also here today, and I'd like to introduce them: the Governor of Colorado, Roy Romer; the former

Governor of Wyoming, Mike Sullivan; and your former Governor, Ted Schwinden. They're all over here with me. I hate to tell Governor Racicot this, but when we started, Governor Romer and Governor Schwinden and I didn't have any gray hair, and Governor Sullivan had lots of hair. [*Laughter*]

Congressman Williams, thank you for your wonderful introduction and for your incredible enthusiasm and for occasionally playing golf with me. [*Laughter*] I'd also like to say a special word of appreciation to Senator Baucus, who is not here but who has given me a lot of good advice over time, and I've been better off when I've taken it than when I've ignored it. [*Laughter*]

I also want to tell you, I'm glad to be here at this campus. You know, the last time I was here, I appeared at the other college, so this is sort of equal time. And I thank you for giving me a chance to give you equal time.

I feel very much at home here. I was saying before, before I became President, for 12 years I was Governor of Arkansas. And I knew everybody and everybody knew me, and they called me by my first name. And even my enemies smiled when they saw me. And if people were mad at me, they told me to my face, but they didn't have to hear it indirectly from somebody else; we all really knew what was going on.

And one of the most frustrating things about being President is, with 260 million people in this country and so many intermediaries between you and the White House and the people out where they live, it's hard to know sometimes—I mean, look, half the time when I see the evening news, I wouldn't be for me, either. [*Laughter*] So I'm glad to be back at a place where we can be directly involved and know the truth, right?

I'd also like to thank my friends from the American Indian tribes from Montana for coming today. Thank you very much. I'm glad to see you.

I see another person from Montana back in Washington from time to time that some of you know and all of you must admire very greatly, Senator Mike Mansfield. You know, he's 90-some-odd now, and he still gets out and walks every day, and he's still just as blunt and straightforward as he ever was. About a year and a half ago, we had a ceremony in the Rose Garden at the White House, naming former Vice President Mondale to be the Ambassador to Japan. And Mike Mansfield showed up because they had served together in the Senate. I saw him back there, and I thought, well, I'll just mention that Mike's here, and he's probably gone out and had his walk for the day, and he'll like that. So I said, "And I see Senator and former Ambassador to Japan Mike Mansfield in the back, and I'll bet he's already walked his 5 miles today," And there was total quiet before they started applauding, and he said, "Seven." [*Laughter*]

When I was a young man in college in Washington, I worked for my Senator, Senator Fulbright, who served with Mike Mansfield and who just died at the age of 90, just before his 90th birthday. And when I showed up in Washington, he was 87. And the day before he had lunch with me, he'd had lunch with Mike Mansfield. And Mike Mansfield said, "Now, Bill, how old are you again?" And he said, "I'm 87." And Senator Mansfield said, "Oh, to be 87 again." [*Laughter*] I say that to tell you he's still in real good shape, and you can still be very proud of him.

Ted Schwinden and I were laughing as I was coming in here today. Ten years ago this summer, my family and I came here to Montana and spent the night in the Governor's Mansion and got up the next morning about 4:30 and piled into a helicopter to explore the wildlife of the Missouri River area where you have the wildlife refuge. Then we got on a rail line and went from Cutback all the way to Whitefish, except we weren't in a railcar, we were in one of those Blazers that has the attachments to the rails. Now, I thought I had been in remote circumstances and rough conditions—[*laughter*]—but we went over a gorge that was about 300 feet high in a Blazer on a narrow set of railroad tracks, and I wasn't nearly as courageous as I thought I was. But I still remember how beautiful it was all the way down in that gorge and how well I could see it. We went to Glacier National Park. We stayed on a little lake in a lodge I think that's now closed. It was one of the great experiences that our family has had together, ever, in our whole life, and I'm always grateful for that.

Tomorrow I'm going to have a townhall meeting here, and we're going to bring in all kinds of people with things they want to say about what they think the National Government should be doing. And a bunch of them are going to say things they think we ought to stop doing. And I'm just going to listen and then try to respond.

Tonight what I'd like to do is to tell you a little bit about why I ran for President and what I've tried to do, where we are now, and some things that are going on in Washington that I think very much affect you and your future. And I want you to think about it and then just tell your elected representatives what you think about it. I wish it were possible for this kind of atmosphere to be recreated all across America and for people to see and feel the kind of informal communication and openness that I feel here.

I ran for this job because, frankly, I was worried about the direction of our country. And in 1992, we were in a recession. We'd had the lowest job growth rate since the Depression. We'd had almost 15 years then—actually more—of stagnant incomes for most Americans. I can now tell you that for the last 15 years, 60 percent of the American people are working longer every week for the same or lower incomes they were making 15 years ago. And we kept piling up a big national debt and at the same time reducing our investments in the things that make us richer and stronger, like education and technology and things that grow the economy and finding a way to preserve the environment and still permit economic opportunity to flourish.

And I went to Washington with some pretty simple goals. I wanted to get our economic house in order so we could grow the middle class and shrink the under class. I wanted to see us face problems that had been long ignored, like the deficit problem and the crime problem in many of our high crime areas. I wanted to find a way to promote environmental protection and economic growth. I wanted to give the American people a system of education and human investment that would permit people to make the most of their own lives, whether they were moving from welfare to work or we were just giving everybody a better chance to go on to college or providing apprenticeship programs for young people who didn't go to 4-year schools but did want to have good jobs. And I wanted to shrink and reorganize the Federal Government so we could give more decisions back to State and local governments and private citizens but so that we could do what we have to do in Washington well and give you greater confidence in doing it. That's why I went there.

In the last 2 years, we have made, I think, some remarkable progress in changing the circumstances in Washington, less progress in changing the circumstances in people's lives in America because when a country gets going in one direction for 10 or 20 years, it's hard to turn it on a dime. But let me just give you a little bit of a progress report.

To use the 7-year figure now favored by the Republican majority in Congress, the budgets we adopted in 1993 and '94 reduced the deficit by $1 trillion over 7 years, 3 years in a row, for the first time since Harry Truman was President. So much so—I want you to understand, we've still got a big deficit problem, but the Federal budget would be in balance today—today—but for the interest we have to pay on the debt that was run up in the 12 years before I moved to Washington. So we've made a good beginning on the deficit.

We expanded trade in ways that really help agriculture, and we fought for fair trade. We've been able to sell things from the West that

I never thought we'd sell in Japan, like apples and other kinds of fruit. We got a deal with Canada on wheat at least for a year and set up a joint commission to try to get wheat farmers here in the northern part of our country a fair deal in growing and selling their wheat. We have taken some very strong action, as you know, in Japan with regard to their trade practices on automobiles and auto parts. But we've also been able to sign over 80 trade agreements with various countries, including Japan, in the last 2 years. And as a result of that, the economy is healthier.

We've had over 6.3 million new jobs. The unemployment rate in virtually every State in the country is substantially lower than it was 2 years ago. And we're in the second year in a row when the economies of all 50 States are growing. It's been a long time since that happened, and I'm proud of that.

We were also able to cut Federal programs, many of them, eliminate a lot of them, and focus more money on things that I thought would matter. We increased funding for Head Start. We increased funding to make sure everybody could get immunized, all parents could immunize their children under the age of 2 by the year 2000. We put more money into child nutrition, and we put lots more money into various education programs, especially programs to increase access to higher education.

We reformed the student loan program to lower the cost of student loans, make the repayment easier, but collect more of the loans. It's an unbelievable story, what has been done there. It may not be popular to say at a student audience, but I went through college and law school on student loans, and it really burned me up that we were spending nearly $3 billion a year of taxpayers' money covering for the loans of people who took out student loans and wouldn't repay them. I don't think that's right. And we cut that by two-thirds in 2 years. So we had more investment in education but also more accountability. We made progress there.

We shrunk the size of the Government. Forget about the budget that's being debated in Washington now. If not one more thing were done, the size of the Federal Government would shrink by 270,000 people over 5 years, to its smallest size since John Kennedy came here to Billings, Montana, in 1963—if nothing else were done.

We also did something I'm very proud of, and there's some people in the audience that are the beneficiaries of it. We created a national service program to promote community service and give people education credits. If they would work in their community, they could earn money to go to college. And I know we've got some national service people from Montana here, and I thank you for your service. Up there they are.

There were a lot of difficult and controversial issues that the Congress had to face in the last session. One of them was the crime bill, which split the country over the issue of gun control, I think largely because of the rhetoric as opposed to the reality. I supported and signed the crime bill that put another 100,000 police out in our country. It put police, I think, in some 40 communities here in Montana—already have received funds to hire more police officers here—perhaps more. It increased the application of capital punishment to about 60 new offenses. It provided for more funds for States that have to build prisons. It provided some funds for prevention programs to give young people in trouble something to say yes to as well as something to say no to. You know, if every kid in the inner cities in this country belonged to the 4–H, we wouldn't have much of a crime problem, but they don't have that option here, and a lot of you know that.

And it had the infamous assault weapons ban, which some people I hear have characterized as "my war on guns." Now, I want to say something about that. Senator Howell Heflin from Alabama, a great friend of mine, 73 years old, got up in the Senate, and he gave—this is almost verbatim, the brief speech he gave on this. He said, "I have never been for gun control, but," he said, "I read this list of 19 assault weapons, and," he said, "I have never seen an Alabama hunter with one of these guns." [*Laughter*] He said, "But I read the other list in this bill everybody talks about. There are 650 weapons in this bill that now can't be regulated by the Government, that are protected from Government regulation, and every weapon I have ever seen in the hands of an Alabama hunter is on that list. So I'm going to vote for this, because I think the bill does more good than harm."

Now, I say that to make this point. Whether you're for or against that, we have made a big mistake in this country, with all the tough issues we've got, to let an issue like that become more symbol than substance. So we've got a tough problem in a lot of cities in this country. I've gone to hospitals and met with emergency room personnel who tell me that in some of our urban areas, the mortality rate from gunshot wounds is 3 times as high today as it was 15 years ago because people are more likely to have more bullets in their bodies when they're hauled in.

Now, that may be very foreign to you here. But the Congress and the President sometimes have to make legislation that applies to the whole country and that deals with the problems of America, and we try to do it in the fairest way we can. That doesn't say that we never make a mistake. I think we did the right thing there, because I got tired of hearing police officers tell me that they were scared to put on their badge and go outside and go to work every day. And I got tired of reading about little kids who were honor students in their inner-city schools being shot at bus stops because they got caught in crossfires. And I decided that we should take a chance to try to make a difference. This is a terrible, terrible problem. I say that to make this point in general—[*applause*]—thank you.

I say that what we need in this country desperately today is more meetings like this. And I wish we could stay all night, and you could just ask questions, and I'd answer them, and I'd ask you questions, you'd answer them. That's what I'm going to try to do tomorrow night. I'm going to go out tomorrow and meet with some farmers, and we're going to do that and talk about the farm bill, because I think that's a big part of it.

But we have got to stop looking for simple answers to complicated problems, and we have got to stop demonizing each other as Americans. And just let me give you an example. Let's look at what we're facing now; all these things affect you. Should we—let's just look at all the issues we're facing.

We've got to pass a budget now, and we have to continue to bring the deficit down, and we ought to be able to tell you that we're going to balance the budget. That's true. Why? Because in a global economy, if you run a big debt all the time and you have to keep borrowing money from other people, they have too much control over your economic well-being, and because if you have to keep spending tax money paying off yesterday's deficit and today's deficit, you don't have the money you need to invest in education. And sooner or later, all the money you take in in taxes, you're paying out in interest. So that's a good thing to do. But the reason it is a good thing to do is, it will contribute to raising the living standards and increasing the security of the people of our country. Therefore, it ought to be done in a way that raises the living standards and increases the security of the people of our country, which is why I say we should not cut education to do it, we should find a way to do it and increase our investment in education.

We all know that we have to slow the rate of growth of the Government's medical programs, Medicare and Medicaid. They've been growing at about 9, 10 percent a year, when inflation's about 3 percent a year and health care inflation generally was 4.5 percent last year. We know we've got to slow the rate of growth of that. But we don't want to do it in a way that closes a bunch of rural hospitals that are the only access to health care people in places like rural Arkansas and rural Montana have. Does that mean we can walk away from the problem? No, it just means we need to have our head on straight when we're dealing with it. We need to do what's practical and understand how it will work.

We all know that the Government can overreach in its regulatory authority. Does that mean there should be no national standards on clean water or clean air or safe drinking water, after what happened to those poor folks in Milwaukee? I don't think so. So we've got to find a way to make the bureaucracy more flexible.

The Environmental Protection Agency, under our administration, is going to cut paperwork burdens by 25 percent in one year next year. The Occupational Safety and Health Administration is going to dramatically slash regulations on businesses that will work with them to be in compliance with safety rules. The Small Business Administration has cut their budget and increased their loan volume by 40 percent. There is a right way and a wrong way to do this. And the only way we can do it in the right way is if we stop looking for simple answers to complicated problems and talk common sense to one another, if we stop treating each other like enemies and start treating each other like we're all friends, we're all Americans, we're all part of a big American family.

I believe that if we'll keep our eye on the prize—what is the prize? We have to increase the incomes and the security of the American people. We have to protect what is good about our country and what works and change what doesn't and get ourselves into the next century with the American dream alive and well for our children.

I'll just give you one last example: You look at this farm bill. Most Democrats and Republicans in the Congress are from urban or suburban areas. Most of them want to do the right thing. Most of them think we spend too much money on farm programs. Well, the farmers in the audience know we have already substantially cut farm subsidies in the last 5 or 6 years, substantially. I've fought like crazy to get the Europeans to make a deal on agriculture so we could cut agricultural subsidies some more. I don't know a farmer in my home State that wouldn't give up every lick of Government support if every other country would give up all theirs and we just had a fair chance to compete in a global marketplace.

So, do we need to deal with this agricultural issue? Yes, we do. But if you just blow off all these supports and everybody else keeps doing it, what's going to happen? One of two things: We either lose markets, or we'll lose all the family farmers, and big corporations will be running all the farms in the country, or a little bit of both.

So let's do this in a sensible way, and let's listen to one another. You'd be amazed how many of these hot-button issues we have in Washington are basically more rural-urban issues, more regional issues than they are partisan issues. And I'm telling you, a lot of these things have a commonsense, sensible resolution if we will simply work on it.

Now, this is a great country. And if you look at where we are, going into the next century, I'm telling you, I have had the privilege of representing you all over the world. And no American who understood the facts of the 21st century would trade places with anybody in any other country, because of what we have here.

But what we have to realize is, the thing that gives us all this juice for this global economy in this information age—where people in Montana can hook in on the Internet and find out things that are in a library in Australia and do all kinds of things that I can't even figure out how to do but my child, because she grew up in the computer age, understands—the reason we are in this kind of position is because of everything we have in this country, because of the natural resources and the phenomenal beauty and the massive space, because of the ethnic diversity, because of the strength in the cities as well as in the rural areas, because of all these entrepreneurs, these high-tech people, in these burgeoning suburban areas. But the thing that makes it work is that we've got all this stuff in one place, one country, but we are all so different.

So we have to have some common values, some common allegiance to the law of the land, and some way of working out our differences. But instead of thinking our differences ought to make us put our head in the hole and try to tell everybody else to go home and leave us alone, or just vote against anybody that we think disagrees with us or comes from some different place, we should learn to resolve these differences in a humane and decent way, because it is the differences in America that are our meal ticket as a whole country to the 21st century and the American dream.

I'll tell you something: One of the reasons I wanted to come here to have this townhall meeting, apart from the fact that I have such wonderful memories about this State and I'm grateful to you for voting for me last time, but the other reason is that out here in Billings, Montana, a while back when a group of skinheads threw a bottle and a brick into homes of two Jewish families displaying menorahs, you didn't throw up your hands and sit around and just take sides. You said that this was a community issue. Your police chief—your former police chief—said hate crimes are not a police problem, they're a community problem. And I guess that's what I want to tell you about the political divisions in this country today. They're not just a political problem, they're a community problem.

The publisher of the Billings Gazette, Wayne Shile, published a full-page drawing of a menorah. And I want to tell you something: In the orthodox Jewish communities in New York City, they knew about Billings, Montana, and they felt more like Americans because you did that. Ten thousand families pasted these drawings in their windows. That's what we need to do in other areas as well.

I spoke at the Air Force Academy commencement today down in Colorado Springs. There were 11 foreign students graduating from the Air Force Academy. All of our service academies take a limited number of students every year from other countries. And it's a great thing for our country. They go back home; they do very well; it builds a lot of good will. The number one student this year was from Singapore. And when he stood up to be recognized, all those red-blooded American kids that he scored higher than clapped for him and were proud of him. That is the American way. They did not feel threatened by that.

I stood there and shook hands with nearly a thousand of those graduates, the finest looking young men and women you can possibly imagine, from every State in this country, from all kind of backgrounds, all different racial and ethnic groups. They were all Americans. And they learned to live with each other and to work out their differences there.

And I'm telling you, if I could wave a magic wand and do one thing for this country, just one thing—it would be more important than who the President is, how the Congress votes on a particular bill—it would be to try to get us out of this way we are communicating with one another so that every time we have a difference, we turn it into a wedge and a divide and we try to beat each other to death with it. That's not right. It's not the American way.

Look, we got a lot of complicated problems. And we are a very different, divergent country. But it's our meal ticket to the future. It's what makes us the most relevant place in the world in the 21st century.

Why do all these people want to come here? Why do they ask us for help everywhere? Because they think, with all of our problems, we've got our act together. And we ought to have it together.

So I say to you, my fellow Americans, whatever your party, whatever your views on any particular issue, this country is slowly turning, and we are moving toward the 21st century. And what we don't want to do is take a position on a complicated issue that starts throwing the babies out with the bath water.

What makes us great is our people, our land, our vision, our system of opportunity. And we have the opportunity now to tackle some long-delayed problems, like the budget deficit, and some long-ignored needs, like competing with other countries in our investment deficit so that we invest in our people's education; we invest in the technology and the research and the things that will generate high-wage jobs; so that we show prudence in the budget, but we still figure out how we're going to keep a viable agricultural sector, for example, into the 21st century; and so that we face up to the fact that a whole lot of people's anxieties are because of all these changes that we haven't adjusted to. We can't keep the American dream alive if 15 years from now 60 percent of the people are still working harder for less money.

So let's talk about what's really eating us. Let's deal with each other as neighbors. And let's make ourselves a promise that as we go through these next 6 or 7 months, that we won't take the easy way out. We will bring the budget into balance, while investing in our future. We will make the Government less bureaucratic, but we will protect our environment. We will find a way to give local control to people, but we will still do the right thing.

When it's all said and done, we'll still have heated disagreements—nobody will know if they're right, and nobody will be right about everything—but at least we can recreate a process, an environment, a spirit of community that will permit us to go on. We cannot get from here to where we need to go if everything we do is dictated by the most emotional, highly charged 15-second sound bites we can think of to send our opponents up the flagpole. We cannot get there.

And let me just close with a story, a true story, that will show you my bias in all this. In 1989 I was the Governor, and I was trying to decide whether I should run for a fifth term. And everybody in my State believed in term limits, but they sort of liked me. And they couldn't figure out what to do about it, and neither could I, frankly, because I had this big education program I wanted to get through the legislature before I left office.

And I went out to the State fair one day, and I visited all the, you know, the livestock barns and saw all that, and then I came into this hall where I always had a Governor's Day every day. And anybody in the State could come up and talk to me and say whatever they wanted, which was hazardous sometimes for me. [*Laughter*]

And along toward the end of the day, this old boy came in in overalls. He was somewhere in his mid-seventies. And he put his hands in his overalls, and he said, "Bill, you going to run again?" I said, "I don't know. If I do, will you vote for me?" He said, "Yeah, I guess so. I always have." And I said, well—I'd been Governor 10 years by then—I said, "Aren't you sick of me after all this time?" He said, "No, but everybody else I know is." [*Laughter*] He said, "I'm going to vote for you because of the way you nag us all the time. All you talk about is education and the economy and forcing everybody to work together and making things better." And he said, "You're just a nag." But he said, "Frankly, I think it's finally beginning to work." And my State had an unemployment rate above the national average in every year I was Governor until the year I ran for President, when we led the country in job growth.

It takes a long time to turn and to face things. But this country is still around here after 200 years because we found a way to disagree in a way that permitted us to work together and move forward. And we can win the struggle for the American dream in the 21st century if we will find that way now.

Thank you, and God bless you all.

NOTE: The President spoke at 7 p.m. in the Alterowitz Gymnasium. In his remarks, he referred to Ronald Sexton, chancellor, Montana State University, Billings.

Remarks in a Roundtable Discussion With Farmers and Agricultural Leaders in Broadview, Montana
June 1, 1995

The President. Thank you very much. I want to mostly just listen to you, but I thought that it might be helpful for me to talk for a minute or two about the kinds of decisions that are coming before our country in the next year, on the farm bill and other things.

I want to thank Senator Baucus and I want to thank Congressman Williams for always making sure that the White House and the President know about the concerns and the interests of the people of this State. They have never been bashful about doing that, and they've done a pretty good job of it. And I thank them for that.

I have been concerned about the interest and welfare of agriculture and rural America generally for a long time and a long time before I became President. A lot of you know that the State where I lived, Arkansas, where I was Governor for 12 years, is a big agricultural State. And it's a different kind of agriculture, by and large. I had Les take me out in the field and explain how you bring in the wheat crop, when you do it, and how you decide what land to lay out. But my State is principally rice, soybeans, and then wheat, and chicken and also a lot of—there's a big hog-growing operation and a sizable cattle operation there.

And I've been through a lot of things with farmer friends of mine. I was Governor all during the 1980's when we lost a lot of our farmers, and a lot of my friends went down. And we were struggling even to keep our rural banks alive and keep them in a position where they could finance farms. We changed all of our State laws to try to do that. So I've seen the worst times of agriculture.

I think the '90 farm bill in many ways has worked reasonably well, although I think there are some problems with it. Since I have been President, I have worked very hard on an overall economic strategy for our country which kept in mind the important role of agriculture. We have fought like crazy to have more trade and fairer trade for American agriculture.

We were able to get the GATT world trade agreement because, after years and years of fighting, we were able to persuade the Europeans to agree to reduce their agriculture subsidies so that they wouldn't be pushing us out of markets because they were subsidizing to a greater extent than we were.

We were able to begin to export some things to Japan and China and the Far East that we'd never been able to export before, principally rice, apples, and other fruit products.

We negotiated, as Max said, this one-year agreement with Canada and set up this commission to try to resolve this problem that they have. And as you know, they—you understand this far better than I do—but there were some things which happened in the original trade negotiations with Canada, and there are some things that are basically endemic to the way they organize their agriculture which make it almost impossible for us to get a fair deal unless we have a specific bilateral agreement on it. So we've been working very hard on that.

A few weeks ago, I went to Ames, Iowa, to Iowa State University, and had a National Rural Conference and talked to farmers from all over the country about some other problems we've got, specific problems like the beef problem with Korea. And we also talked about the need to continue in this new farm bill a decent level of support for agricultural research, a decent level of effort and a greater effort for the development of alternative products out of the farming now done in America.

We had farmers from the Middle West bring some very impressive things that they had made from their sort of side businesses in agriculture, including windshield wiper fluid. And they even gave me some golf tees, which I used. They're biodegradable, and that's important because I break one every time I swing a club. [*Laughter*]

I think it's very important that as we look ahead, that we deal with not only the question of how much we're going to spend on agricultural supports but what these programs are going to look like. Are we going to have, for example, a greater effort to help young farmers get into farming, when the average age of farmers keeps going up and up and up? Are we—if we want to get the prices up and have a long-term responsible program for the environment, shouldn't we preserve the conservation reserve program, or something awful much like it, no matter what we do to the rest of the farm supports?

And then there's this larger question of what the overall role of agriculture is to America. Yes, we do spend a substantial amount of money on farm supports. But as all of you know, we spend dramatically less than we did 10 years ago. The supports were cut a lot in '85; they were cut a lot in '90 and '93. And then again in this '96 budget, we proposed some modest cuts, mostly to tighten up the income eligibility.

But my belief is that since agriculture is producing this year over $50 billion worth of farm exports, the largest dollar value of exports in our history—we're going to have more than a $20 billion trade surplus in agriculture. And to give you some idea of the figures, roughly, we'll have a trade deficit maybe of something over $100 billion, and 60 percent of it is in automobiles from Japan and auto parts, and the rest of it's in oil. And otherwise we're pretty much in balance, thanks almost entirely to the massive surplus we enjoy in agriculture and in the sale of airplanes and airplane parts. And otherwise, we're more or less in balance.

So to me this is a very big thing. And I know—I imagine people in Montana are pretty much like people in Arkansas; everybody wants to see the budget brought into balance. Everybody knows that things got haywire in the last 12 years. You need to know that the budgets that Max and Pat voted for would have the Federal Government in balance today. We would have a balanced budget today but for the interest we have to pay on the debt run up between 1981 and the day I became President.

So we turned this deficit thing around. We need to keep bringing it down, but we need to look at the agricultural issue in light of how you live here and the importance to the United States of this massive economic strength we have in American agriculture, which means every person in the country has benefited by what you do, by having the cheapest, best food in the world and also by having an enormous economic weapon in a global economy.

So that's kind of the perspective I'm looking for. We're going to have to make some changes in the farm program, but I want to get your feedback on your lives, your work, your experiences, and what you think we should be thinking about as we—number one, we're coming up to the end of the one-year deal on the Canadian agreement, as Max said, but we're also going to have to rewrite the farm bill. We do it every 5 years, and this year it coincides with this effort that is being made to balance the budget.

So we need to really think this through. And that's why I wanted to be here. And I'm not going to say any more. I want to listen to you now.

Senator Max Baucus. Thank you very much, Mr. President. Anybody who wants to—Diana or Steve?

Export Enhancement Program

[*At this point, Steve Heiken asked about congressional appropriations for the Export Enhancement Program.*]

The President. Well, I like that program. I've used it quite a lot, the Export Enhancement Program. And if they refuse to appropriate any money for it, then I will try to offset the impact of that by two things. One is trying to get our Trade Ambassador, Mr. Kantor, to go back and do even more than he's already done. I think he's the best trade person we've had in many, many years, but there may be some things he can do. And secondly, there may be some other ways that we can help other countries to finance agricultural purchases through other instruments of other financial institutions.

I think it would be a mistake to do away with the EEP completely, given the way the world works now. You know as much or more about it than I do, but I think we ought to maintain the program.

Regulatory Reform

[*Citing his own farm as an example, Les Auer asked if farmers could be better stewards of the land without excessive Government regulation.*]

The President. In general, I think the answer to that is yes. I think the trick is, from my point of view, is how to get the best environmental results and have some standard that will also deal with the people that might abuse their privileges, and how to do it with fewer regulations. And I think there are ways to do it.

Let me just say, for example, in the Agriculture Department, Secretary Glickman is in the process of cutting the regulations of the Ag Department. And the target is to save the farming population of our country and others regulated by the Ag Department 2.5 million hours a year and $4 billion a year by reductions. The EPA is cutting their paperwork burden by 25 percent in one year.

And basically what we're trying to do is to go to a system in which we can go to people and say, "Look, here are the general standards in the law and the things that are necessary to preserve the land, water, and air over the next generation. But this rulebook is not necessary if you can meet the standards however you please, if you can find some other way to do it." We're now doing that through the EPA. We're going to have 50 experimental projects where we just go to people and say, "Can you meet the standards? And if you do, you can get rid of the rulebook." And so that way we'll have the benefit of a common standard and a common commitment to environmental protection without having the cost and burdens of excessive regulation.

I think that the regulatory system in America has basically built up over the last 35 years under Democrats and Republicans alike. And partly it has come about because of the abuses that are there. But believe it or not, sometimes even the people who are being regulated wanted us to be more specific and more detailed because they thought that would protect them in other ways.

The problem is there's no way to write rules and regulations that cover every commonsense occurrence that will happen in the life of a farmer or a businessperson. You just can't do it. We were talking about it last night at dinner. So anyway, we're trying to move to a different regulatory system which would keep our commitment, our common commitment, to a clean environment or to a safe workplace but would give the people who have previously been overregulated far more freedom in deciding how to meet those objectives. And I think that's the right way to compromise this out.

Ethanol

[*Mary Schuler asked about efforts to increase ethanol use, in view of the court ruling against the 30 percent mandate.*]

The President. Well, as you know, I'm a strong supporter of that program. We prevailed by one vote because the Vice President had to go over to the Senate and vote for it. Remember that? One of Al Gore's best lines is, every time he votes we win. [*Laughter*] But we won that day. And then they took us to court, and we lost.

We're looking at the case now, reviewing it, to see whether or not we think we've got any chance at all to prevail on appeal. And if we think we've got any chance at all, we're going to appeal the thing. But we're reading it now and trying to reach a judgment about that.

And I would be interested in knowing from you whether there are some other things we can do to increase the use of ethanol, because I think that's good environmental policy as well as good farm policy. And again, it adds to the value of the farm dollar in America. And to whatever extent we can add to the value of the farm dollar in America, we are thereby less vulnerable to the vagaries of the global economy, to what happens in the weather or the

politics or the finances of some other country. We'll be a lot better off.

So if you have any specific ideas or you or any of your organizations want to give me any more ideas about what else I can do to promote ethanol use, I will, because I'm strongly in favor of it. I think it's good economics. It's good environmental policy. And it helps us to become more independent.

Mary Schuler. There is legislation, isn't there, that the Government vehicles are to use ethanol? Is that being——

The President. Yes, that's a possibility. One of the things we're trying to do is to see to what extent the Government can be a leader in all these areas, because we're trying to get the Government to—we could use more ethanol; we could use more natural gas in vehicles. There are lots of things we can do that would strengthen our energy independence, and that's one option.

I don't know that the volumes will be enough to make a significant difference in your price in Montana, but it's something we could begin to do. The Government has the capacity to create certain markets, and at least to demonstrate to others that they work. So that's something maybe we ought to look at. We might be able to do that without legislation. I'll look at it.

Extension Program

[*Kelly Raths, 4-H representative, expressed support for full funding of the agricultural extension program.*]

The President. When I was at Montana State yesterday, I said if every kid in America were in 4-H, we'd have about half of the problems we've got. I believe that.

Kelly Raths. That's right.

The President. Let me explain how this budget works. The Senate and the House pass a budget resolution, and basically, what they do is to make certain commitments on deficit reduction in general terms and in categories. The actual budgeting, then, passes over—as soon as the Senate and the House resolve their disagreements because their budgets are different, principally, in the volume of the tax cuts and who gets them and when they would come and all that—when they resolve that, then the appropriations committees go to work, so that while these budget resolutions may not have suggested any cuts in any particular programs or may have suggested drastic cuts in other programs, the appropriations committees may differ entirely, and the only thing they'll have to do is to meet a certain level of cut for all the things that are within each subcommittee of the appropriations committee.

So it's not clear which programs will be cut and which programs will be exempted from this resolution. Those are just suggestions from the committee, but these budget committees set the outline. Then the appropriations committee have to really make the budget decisions.

But essentially, I agree with you. The programs are good. I think they're of modest cost, and they benefit huge numbers of people, and they're the kind of—if you will, the kind of preventive character-building programs that I've tried to support in the crime bill, and I'm having a harder time getting protected there.

Conservation Reserve Program

[*Bud Daniels expressed support for the conservation reserve program as an environmentally beneficial alternative to unnecessary increases in production of grain or livestock.*]

The President. Cattle prices don't need to go in that direction.

Bud Daniels. No, they don't.

The President. Well, the honest answer to your question is—first of all, let me point out, just going back to what Les said, the conservation reserve is a classic example of the kind of environmentalism we ought to be practicing in this country. Instead of beating somebody over the head with a stick and giving them a rulebook 9 inches thick, here is an incentive to basically restore wildlife and biodiversity. And it's been, I think, a resounding success.

Now, it's like everything else. People can show you where there's been something or other they don't like about it, but it's basically worked. It's done what it was intended to do, in my opinion.

The answer to your question, whether it will survive or not, depends upon, in large measure, upon you and the other people in agriculture throughout the country and on the decisions that we all have to make once we decide how much overall agriculture has to be cut.

The thing that I don't like about the way that this budget process is unfolding is, if you decide—it's kind of backward—if you decide, well, you're going to have to balance the budget

in 7 years instead of 9 or 10 or some other time, and you decide that you're going to have to set aside a certain amount of money for a tax cut, then you wind up being very arbitrary in how much you're going to cut various things.

And what we really ought to say is, go back to what Max said—I believe most farmers in America would gladly give up all of their Government subsidies—we might still want a conservation reserve for environmental reasons—but would gladly give up all of their Government subsidies if all of our competitors would. So this is, as I keep hammering this issue, this is a question of our standing in the global economy. We worked like crazy to pass the GATT so we could reduce some of our subsidies but so that competitors of ours that subsidize more would have to reduce more.

So the simple answer to your question is—let's just say—I proposed, because of the GATT, another $1.5 billion in reductions in agricultural subsidies. They propose, I think, $8 billion or $9 billion. I think that's an excessive number over a 7-year period. But let's say that the $8 billion number passes, or it's a $5 billion number, whatever it finally is, then you've got to—then you, the agricultural community, have to figure out what is the most sensible way to allocate that cut. And if you want to keep the conservation reserve, then you've got to give up more of something else. And if you want to modify it, then you maybe make it less costly, and you do something else.

These are decisions we're all going to have to make together. I guess that's the one thing that I want to impress upon you today, is that I have a Secretary of Agriculture from Kansas who served for 18 years in the Congress, I care about this issue, and whatever level of funding we wind up with, we need to make the best decisions. If the farm supports are cut, are they going to still be the way they are now? Are we going to give farmers more flexibility within the support framework to decide what they plant? Is that a good or a bad idea? These are things that we need input from the agriculture community on.

But this is not a done deal yet. No one knows what the final number is going to be and what the final form is going to be. And I think you ought to be able to shape it, looking at what has worked fundamentally in the 1990 farm bill and what the continuing problems are.

Livestock Industry

[Gary Ruff asked if the Justice Department could investigate possible antitrust violations in the cattle market.]

The President. I mean, do you think that the market may be so concentrated that it violates the antitrust laws?

Gary Ruff. I do.

The President. Well, I think that ought to be explored. If you think there's a credible case for that, we'll look into it.

Mr. Ruff. Well, the Packers and Stockyards Commission is doing some looking into it, but I really feel that the Justice Department——

The President. But the Antitrust Division needs to look into it as well.

Family Farms

[Keith Schott described his situation as a young family farmer and asked about expectations for his future.]

The President. Well, before this last round of discussion on agriculture, I really believed that we had bottomed out in the shrinking of the farm sector. That's what I believe. And I believe that because even though productivity will doubtless continue to improve in agriculture, we have been moving to a system where we could fairly compete around the world so that I thought that we would be able to essentially continue the structure of family farming that we now have. And it's dramatically lower, obviously, than it was a generation ago, and that was inevitable because of the increasing productivity of agriculture. It's true everywhere. There are not nearly as many people in farming anywhere as there used to be. But I really thought we had pretty much bottomed out.

And I think, as you know, there are basically two purposes for all these farm programs, if you really look at it. One is to allow us to be competitive with people around the world. The other is to try to deal with the fact that farming has become more and more capital-intensive. And if you want family farmers to farm, you have to have some system which rides them through the tough times. Otherwise, the economics will turn all the farms over to big corporations who can finance their own tough times.

I mean, if you basically think about it, that's—in a lot of our States where large corporate farms exist, they don't need the support programs because the good years overweigh the bad years and they don't have to worry about the bank loans.

Now, one of the things that we have ignored in this whole system is that the barriers to entry have gotten higher and higher. So most of the young farmers that are in farming today are people that got their farms from their parents, because the barriers to entry are so high.

And what I was hoping would happen is that, even though we might have to cut the support program some more, that we would have no backing off of agricultural research, no backing off of the development of alternative agricultural endeavors in this country like the ethanol program, and that we might be able to develop some sort of first-time farmer financing system that would help to lower the barriers to entry. Because I think we are in a position now just—if you project—if you look at world population growth, if you look at the fact that we are pretty much now committed to sustaining our own capacity to produce food in an environmentally responsible way, it is now—I think that it is more likely than not that for the next generation, anyway, we could keep the present structure of family farms, that you wouldn't have to see the continuing collapse if we could work the economics out on the barriers to entry.

Now, if you have an excessive reduction in the farm support programs, one of two things or both will happen: You will either give up market share overseas, or you will create such difficulties from year to year for family farmers that there will be an increase in concentration in ownership.

So again, I would say to you that the big picture looks better for you and for people like you coming forward, because I think that we are going to be able to maintain the present level of production and the present level of acreage for quite a long while now because of how we're positioned in the global economy and what's happened with population growth in other parts of the world.

But I am very concerned that—again, I am all for cutting the deficit—the Republicans are now using 7-year numbers, the Congress is. Under those 7-year numbers, the budgets that we passed cut the deficit a trillion dollars over 7 years. I'm all for that. But I think we have to say, why are we doing that? Because we want to take the burden of debt off our children, because we want to get interest rates down, because we want to be freer of the flows of foreign money. In other words, we want to raise incomes and strengthen the economy. That means that the deficit reduction has to be pursued in the context of raising the incomes of the American people, growing the middle class, shrinking the under class, pursuing these goals in a consistent way. That's what I believe.

So you know what I'd do. What I'd do is have a more moderate agricultural cut. And what I would try to do is to preserve the things that support family farms, diversify farm income, diversify production of different products in America, and try to get some way to ease the barrier of entry to first-time farmers. That's what I would do if I could design this program for the next 5 years all by myself.

Senator Baucus. Mr. President, I think we have time for one more question before we go have dinner here pretty quickly.

The President. Yes, all those folks are starving to death and getting nothing out of it.

Vocational Education

[*Jason Noyes, second vice president, Montana Future Farmers of America, asked about funding for vocational and agricultural education.*]

The President. I have tried to do two things on the vocational education issue, generally. One is, along with all the other education programs, to argue that we ought to look at our situation in America as having both a budget deficit and an educational deficit. If you look at—there's a bigger difference in the incomes of people by virtue of how much education they have in this country than ever before, the biggest difference ever since we've been keeping these statistics. And it's because more and more people's incomes, not just farmers but other people's incomes, are now set in a global economy, which means that you have to address the education deficit as well as the budget deficit. And that means that there has to be an appropriate level of investment for things that we want to produce.

If you look at vocational training generally, one of the things that I'm proudest of that our administration has done is that we have worked very hard to help every State that wanted to participate set up a system of moving young people from high schools who don't go to 4-year institutions—may go to community colleges or vocational schools but don't go to 4-year institutions—into an educational program that would also be a vocational program where they would be working and learning at the same time.

And I believe very strongly that we have to abolish what I think is an artificial distinction between academic education and vocational education. For a long time, people kind of put down vocational education. But if you look at it, there's now a lot of evidence that a lot of people learn better when they're doing, plus which a lot of these vocational programs, including agriculture, now require higher levels of knowledge of computers, for example, than a lot of traditional academic courses do.

So I think we have an idea battle we have to fight, which is to raise the status of vocational education generally and abolish, just erase, the line between what's vocational and academic; and secondly, to keep our levels of investment in all kinds of education that we need for the future high enough to raise incomes.

The biggest problem in America today, economic problem, is that more than half the people are working harder than they were 15 years ago for the same or lower incomes, not just farmers, wage-earning, hourly wage-earning Americans. That is the biggest problem we've got.

The American dream requires a growing middle class and a shrinking under class, and requires a system—and I think the principal role of Government today in the economy should be to help people help themselves. And if you've got people who are out there working hard and they're productive, or they're prepared to be, that's what I think we ought to be doing.

The Government—we don't have the money or the independence from other countries to do what we did in the Great Depression, just to try to create jobs for everybody and do those kind of things. We don't have the money or the position in the world economy. But we do have the capacity to help our people help themselves. And I think we ought to be doing more of it, not less of it. And I think you can do that. If you look at what a small percentage of the Federal budget this is, it is wrong to say that you cannot do that and drastically reduce this deficit, move it into balance.

[*Senator Baucus thanked the President and suggested continuing the discussion over lunch.*]

The President. I just want to say this one more time. This farm bill is not written. And there's two issues. One is how much we're going to cut spending. We're all going to cut spending, I'm telling you. And we'll probably wind up cutting it a little more than you want, but I hope we're going to cut it substantially less than they want right now. But the issue is not only how much are we going to spend but how are we going to spend it.

And Montana is a place where the family farm is alive and well. I think that's an important value in America. So I would just implore you, through all your organizations, to look at this and give us some guidance about how it ought to be spent: How should the support programs be structured? How should we maintain the Conservation Reserve? Should there be an entry-level program for new farmers? These are things that are terribly important. It's not just the amount of money; it is how we spend it.

And as I—I'm having a different argument up there in Washington now, but the more you cut, the more important it is how you spend what's left. It's more important now how we spend what's left. So I want to ask everybody here to be active in how this thing is structured, because we've got an opportunity, I believe, to preserve the structure of our agriculture we've got in America today and see it grow economically if we don't blow it.

Thank you.

NOTE: The President spoke at 12:25 p.m. at the Leslie Auer farm.

Remarks at a Town Meeting in Billings, Montana
June 1, 1995

Gus Koernig. Anything you'd like to say, Mr. President, or you just want to jump in?

The President. I think we ought to jump in. I had a wonderful stay in Montana. I had a great opportunity to speak to a large number of Montanans at Montana State University last night. I've had a great day today, as you know. And these folks have brought their questions; I think we should begin.

Gun Control Legislation

Mr. Koernig. Okay. I'm told I get to start. So, as you're probably aware, sport hunting is very popular in Montana. More than 60 percent of the men in this State, more than 30 percent of the women purchase game hunting licenses every year. There is a lot of concern here on the parts of people that legislation such as the Brady law and the assault weapons ban are a sign of more things to come, and there is a lot of concern and more than a little fear and uneasiness about this. What can you say to these folks here in our audience to address that?

The President. Well, first of all, let me tell you where I'm coming from on this. For 12 years, before I became President, I was the Governor of Arkansas, a State where more than half the people have a hunting or a fishing license or both. I would never knowingly do anything to undermine the ability of people to hunt, to engage in recreational shooting, to do anything else that is legal with appropriate firearms.

I strongly supported the Brady bill for a clear reason: We knew it would work to keep a significant number of people from getting guns who either had past criminal records or had mental health histories that made them unfit to be gun owners. And it has, in fact, done that.

I supported the assault weapons ban for a simple reason: because the death rate from gunshot wounds in a lot of our cities where the crime rate is high has gone up. I went to emergency rooms where hospital personnel pleaded with me to do something about this problem, because the average gunshot wound victim they were seeing had more bullets in them than just a few years ago because of the widespread use of these assault weapons by gang members. I saw a lot of children who were innocently caught in crossfires in this kind of thing. All the law enforcement agencies in the country asked for help on the assault weapons ban. So I supported it. But the bill that I passed also contained a list of 650 sporting weapons that could not be in any way infringed by Federal action, that were protected. There were 19 assault weapons and their copycats that were prohibited. I still believe it was the right thing to do. I strongly believe it was the right thing to do.

Now, we can differ about that, but I just want to make two points in closing. As President, I have to make laws that fit not only my folks back home in Arkansas and the people in Montana but the whole of this country. And the great thing about this country is its diversity, its differences, and trying to harmonize those is our great challenge.

I did this because I thought it would give our law enforcement officers a better chance to stay alive and to keep other people alive. That's why I did it. I did it because it has clear protections for hunting and sporting weapons. And I think, frankly, that the NRA has done the country a disservice by trying to raise members and raise money by making extremist claims for this. I mean, they put out a letter in which they called Federal officials "jackbooted thugs," as you know, but the other part of the letter accused me of encouraging Federal officials to commit murder. And I just think that's wrong.

You know, one of the problems we've got in this country is, everybody wants simple answers to complicated questions, and so we all start screaming at each other before we listen and talk. That's one reason I'm here tonight.

So I did it; I think it's the right thing to do. But I do not plan to do anything which would undermine the ability of people in Montana or any other State in this country to lawfully use their weapons.

Mr. Koernig. We promise not to scream tonight. Our first question.

The President. You can if you want.

Bosnia

[A 14-year-old exchange student from Serbian-occupied territory asked about efforts to bring peace to her country and to encourage more student exchanges in the meantime.]

The President. Thank you very much. Let me answer the second question first, because it's an easier answer. The answer to your second question is yes, I want to see young people come over here and live in America and have the experiences you're having. And I think it would be very beneficial for Americans to have people from your country who have been

through what you have been through and your family has been through come here and talk about it. So, yes.

The first question is, can I do anything to bring an easier end to the fighting, or a quicker end to the fighting? We are doing what we can. Let me tell you what we're doing. First of all, we are leading the largest humanitarian airlift in human history now into Bosnia, trying to make sure we get as much food and medicine in there. Secondly, I have, near where you're from in the Former Yugoslav Republic of Macedonia, stationed some American troops to try to make sure that the conflict can't spread beyond Bosnia and that no one believes they can in—sort of start a whole regional war. The third thing we've tried to do through NATO is to support the British, the French, the Canadian, and the other European troops that are in Bosnia in their peacekeeping efforts. We have tried to make sure that we created safe areas in the eastern enclaves and around Sarajevo, that we tried to collect all the heavy weapons that the Serbs have which give them such an enormous advantage on the battlefield. And that's what caused this latest trouble we had over there, because they broke the agreement they made and they put 1,400 shells into Sarajevo.

Now, I have to tell you, though, I think in the end this war will only end when the parties are willing to negotiate a peace, in peace, just the way we're bringing an end to the war in the Middle East, the way we're bringing an end to the conflicts in Northern Ireland. I do not believe there is a military settlement that the United States can enforce. And I do not favor sending our troops into combat there to try to assure victory or to force through military means an end to the fighting. All it would do is get a lot of Americans killed and not achieve the objective. So I don't think we should do that. But we should do everything we can short of that.

Welfare, Regulations, and Taxes

[A participant asked about combating the negativism expressed by coworkers leaning toward a militia mentality.]

The President. Well, first of all, I think one of the things that has happened is that increasingly in this information age, with all this explosion of access to information, one of the things that's happening that's not good is that people are more and more and more listening to people who tell them just what they want to hear or play on their own fears. And that's isolating us. One reason I like this is that there are a lot of people here of different points of view. So I think—I would urge you to urge them to open their ears and eyes to different points of view. Now, let me just deal with the three issues you mentioned. You mentioned welfare; you mentioned Government regulation; you mentioned taxes.

On the welfare issue, most Americans believe, I learned from a recent poll, that we're spending 45 percent of your money on foreign aid and welfare. In fact, we're spending about a nickel of your money on foreign aid and welfare, your tax money. For the last 2 years, 2½ years, I have done everything I could to convince the Congress to pass a welfare reform bill which would invest more in work and require people on welfare to move to work and would give people who are parents of small children the ability to work and still see that their kids are taken care of. When that has not happened, I have given 29 States now the permission to get out from under all these Federal rules and regulations and adopt their own plans to move people from welfare to work.

On the regulation issue, we have reduced more regulations than the two previous administrations. We're going to cut enough paperwork this year to stretch page by page from New York to San Francisco. So if you want me to defend Government regulation, you're talking to the wrong person. I can't even defend everything that's been done since I've been here, because I believe we do have to change the way the Government works. But the final thing I would tell you is, I do not believe that we should abandon our commitment to a clean environment and to the quality of life that makes everybody in the world want to live in a place like Montana. But I think we have to change the way we regulate and do it better.

On the tax issue, the American tax burden is about the same as it is in Japan and, on average, about 50 percent lower than it is in the European countries. And I have done what I could to bring it down for middle class people who are overtaxed. Today, families of four with incomes of $28,000 a year or less this year paid $1,000 less than they would have before I became President, because of taxes we cut in '93.

And I want to provide further tax relief to middle class Americans to educate their children, to raise their children, and to help to save to pay for health insurance or care for their parents.

So we're working on all these things. The answer is not to join the militia and opt out. The answer is to come in here and opt in and be a vigorous voice of citizen responsibility.

Federal Employee Safety

[*The daughter of a Bureau of Land Management employee expressed concern for her father's safety.*]

The President. First of all, I want to thank your father for serving his country by working for the Federal Government. Maybe the most important thing I can do is to remind the American people that the people who work for the Federal Government are citizens and human beings too. And I think the one thing that happened in Oklahoma City is a lot of people realized all of a sudden that all of these people we deride all the time for working for the Federal Government are people that go to church with us, that send their kids to our schools and show up at the softball parks and the bowling alleys and contribute to the United Way.

And I think that if you want to disagree with the policy of the Government, disagree with it. If there is a single Federal official—there's nobody, including me, who has never felt that they were mistreated by somebody working for the Government. So if somebody believes someone who is working for the Government has mistreated them, take it to the appropriate authority, make it public if you want to, but be specific. But do not condemn people who work for the Government. That's the kind of mentality that produced Oklahoma City.

And all these people out here in these various groups that are sending faxes around trying to tell people, you know, how they can get ready to assault Federal officials who are doing their jobs, trying to justify taking violent action, I don't think they understand how many people there are out there that are in an unstable frame of mind that might take them seriously and actually kill or take other violent action against Federal authorities. It is awful. Just a couple of days ago, we lost another FBI agent in Washington, DC, and I talked to that man's widow today. He has four children; he has a grandchild.

He was a human being. He was an American. And apparently, the person who shot him had a vendetta against all law enforcement officials. Now, we cannot have that kind of climate in this country.

And I think the most important thing we can do to make your father safer is to have everybody in this room, whatever their political party or their view, stand up and say it is wrong to condemn people who are out there doing their job and wrong to threaten them. And when you hear somebody doing it, you ought to stand up and double up your fist and stick it in the sky and shout them down. That is wrong. It is wrong.

And I hope everybody in this State heard what you said today. And I hope you feel better in school next week—although I guess you're out for the summer. [*Laughter*] Thank you.

The Environment

[*A participant asked about enforcement of air quality standards in Billings.*]

The President. All I can tell you is, I'll be glad to look into it. I tried to prepare for this, and I tried to think of every issue I might be asked about. I don't know the answer to it, but I will get back to you with an answer. I will look into it, and I'll get back to you with an answer.

Let me just make a general comment, and you may have other questions about this. There are problems in the application of all of our environmental laws because people are applying them and because we have followed a regulatory model that might have made sense 20 years ago that I don't think makes as much sense anymore. So nearly everybody maybe could cite his case where we have—you don't think we've gone far enough; somebody else thinks we've gone way too far with it, whether it's clean air, clean water, the Endangered Species Act, you name it.

But I would remind you, just running through the question you asked me, the thing we have to do for Montana is to permit people to make a living and preserve the quality of life, because that's why people want to live here and that's why people pour in here by the millions every year, to see what you've got they don't have. And that's why we have to try to do that for everybody in America, and we've got to try to find the right way to do it. But you made the

point. I'll look into it. I can't answer the question specifically.

[*A participant asked about protection of Yellowstone National Park in view of a proposed gold mine 2½ miles from the park.*]

The President. Well, first of all, let me thank you for the question. I'm very worried about it because of the site. I know it's on private land, but it's only a couple of miles from Yellowstone and from Clark Fork. I spoke with Senator Baucus today at some length about this. I asked him to take a car ride with me for about 15 minutes so he could walk me through this and all of his concerns.

What I believe we have to do now is, you know, they—there has to be an environmental impact statement filed on this. And Senator Baucus has set out five very specific extra high standards he thinks ought to have to be met before they get approval under any environmental impact statement. And I guess I would have to tell you that's the way I feel.

I think that the people of Montana are entitled to know that we have gone the extra mile because of the unique place where this site is. And I don't want to prejudge the environmental impact statement; I believe most of these decisions should be made on the merits. But it just stands to reason, given the tailings and the other dimensions of the mining project, that it's going to have to meet a very high standard before you can be absolutely certain you're not doing anything to Clark Fork or to Yellowstone. And no amount of gain that could come from it could possibly offset any permanent damage to Yellowstone.

So you just need to be sure and you need to watch this, and I will watch it. I assure you I will, and I know that Senator Baucus and others will.

Agriculture Policy

[*A farmer asked about the 1995 farm bill and farm loan rates.*]

The President. First of all, since I've been President we've raised the loan rate once, as you probably know. I have also tried to do two other things for farmers, particularly farmers in this part of our country. One is to find more markets to sell products and to use things like the Export Enhancement Program, the EEP program, to help to facilitate those sales. The other is to try to give you some protection from unfair competition. You know, our administration moved to get that moratorium on increased imports from Canada, and we set up that commission to work on that problem, on the wheat issue. So I have tried to be responsive to the problems here. It is going to be difficult to get a big increase in the loan rate because of the budgetary situation we're in.

I don't agree that the trade deals are necessarily bad. There are some—the Senators from North Dakota think that the agreement the United States made with Canada before NAFTA and before I became President had something to do with what you're dealing with, with the wheat now. I wasn't there. I can't comment on it; I don't know. But our agricultural exports this year will be the largest they've ever been. We'll have a trade surplus of over $20 billion in agriculture.

What I am worried about is the last point you made. It used to be when agricultural exports went up, farm income went up. It doesn't necessarily happen anymore. It used to be if you could get more jobs into the American economy, people's wages would rise. If you'd told me 2½ years ago that I could get the Congress to lower the deficit 3 years in a row for the first time since Mr. Truman was President and increase investment in education and technology and expand trade for American products and create 6.3 million new jobs, but the incomes of most working Americans wouldn't go up, I wouldn't have believed that. That's what the global economy has done, and that's our big problem.

Now, here's what's going to happen in agriculture in this farm debate, and I'll tell you what I'm going to try to do. The Congress has said we ought to cut another $8 billion or $9 billion out of farm supports. Farm supports were cut in '85; they were cut in '90; they were cut modestly in '93. They've been cut modestly in '95 by me because the Europeans are having to cut more under the GATT deal we made. If we cut $8 billion or $9 billion in farm supports, in my opinion, two things are going to happen. Number one, we're going to produce less and lose markets overseas, and number two, more family farmers will go out and corporate farmers will come in.

There are two reasons for the farm price supports. One is to enable us to compete with people around the world. The other is to enable

efficient family farmers to ride through the hard years. Corporations don't need that; they can either borrow the money or have cash reserves to ride through the hard years. So I'm going to be pushing for changes in this farm bill which help preserve family farmers instead of changes which undermine them. And I told a bunch of farmers I met with today near here at the Les Auer's farm, I said, you know, what we need to do is not only look at how much this budget's going to be cut but how this farm program is going to be structured, because if we don't do it, family farmers, without regard to their politics, are going to be in trouble.

Racism and Native Americans

[*After the station took a commercial break, a consultant and lobbyist for Native American organizations asked about efforts to combat racism.*]

The President. Well, let me tell you one thing I'm doing specifically. Late next month—this month, it's June 1st, isn't it—this month, I'm going to have a meeting in Washington, bringing in people from all sectors of our society to talk about what we can do to recreate a sense of good citizenship in America and of respecting our diversity. That doesn't mean we ought to agree. We're always going to have disagreements. We ought to have disagreements. That's why we've got a first amendment, so we can all disagree and fight like cats and dogs. But we've reached a point in this country now when too many of us are looking at each other as enemies.

And I cannot tell you—you know, I've had the privilege of representing you around the world and trying to end the nuclear threat and expand opportunities for Americans and make peace elsewhere. This country's meal ticket to the 21st century is our diversity. But it's a headache, right? Look at—even in Montana, with the relatively small population you have, you have a lot of people with different views on every issue. But I'm telling you, it's our meal ticket to the global economy. And we have got to find a way, in a community setting like this, to stop looking at each other as enemies and start looking at each other as friends and neighbors even when we have differences and try to find a way to resolve the differences, instead of drive wedges into the differences, make them bigger, so we can belong to organizations that will hate each other more than we did before and we give all our money to keep driving ourselves apart instead of spending our money to bring ourselves together. I believe that's very important.

And for the Native Americans, it's terribly important. You know, I have supported legislation to give Native American tribes more autonomy, to respect their religious and other cultural traditions. And I am now doing things to try to build economic development opportunities in all rural areas of the country, including for American Indians who live on reservations. None of this is going to work unless all of us figure we got a vested interest in everybody else doing well.

So, you know, most Americans get up every day and go to work and pay their taxes and obey the law and raise their kids the best they can, and they're pretty fine people. And we don't deserve to be wasting our energy hating each other. And it's a bad mistake. And to go back to what that lady said, part of it is the flip side of the technology and information revolution. You can talk to people on the Internet now who have all the same fears you do, and you never have to fool with anybody, or even look them in the face, that disagrees with you.

But what's—our bread and butter is that we're different. So anyway, starting at the end of this month we're going to see if there's some disciplined, organized way we can take this message across America and involve people of different parties, different perspectives, radically different political views on issues in the idea of recreating a sense that we're all neighbors. [*Applause*] Thanks.

Social Security

[*A participant suggested that the Social Security Trust Fund be removed from congressional control and put into a private trust with a private board of directors.*]

The President. Well, first of all, yes, it would be possible to do that. Let me say with regard to your assertion about mismanagement, I don't necessarily agree with that. It is true that the Congress raised the Social Security tax back in 1983 because the Social Security Trust Fund was in trouble, because the American people kept demanding opportunities for people to retire at younger ages while we were living to be older and older. So they decided to gradually,

a month a year, over a period of several years, raise the retirement age to 67. They funded the thing better, and then they essentially used the Social Security tax to downplay the deficit, which meant that most of the Social Security money was being invested in Government bonds.

Now, they are good. That's money in the bank; that money will go back there. And there are those who argue that, well, if it were invested in other things it could have earned a higher rate of return, and therefore, we wouldn't—we'd have a more stable Social Security System for a longer term. That may be true, but we'd have to be willing to assume a higher rate of risk as well. And that's one of the things we're debating now.

But I can tell you right now the Social Security Trust Fund is solvent, and it's solid. There will be financial problems in the Social Security Trust Fund in the second decade of the next century because my crowd will reach retirement age. I'm the oldest of the baby boomers, and the people born between 1946 and 1964 are the largest single group of Americans ever born. So when we start to work less and play more golf and go hunting and fishing, it's going to be a real burden on everybody still working unless we have some reforms. And I think we ought to—that's one of the things we ought to look at.

We did take one step last year: We made the Social Security program and agency totally independent of any other arm of the Federal Government. And there is a report coming out sometime in the next couple of weeks about what else we ought to do to make it stable into the next century. We have a solemn obligation to do it, and as long as I'm there, I'm going to do everything I can to make sure that the money is there for you and everybody else who paid into it.

AIDS

[*A participant questioned administration policy and efforts regarding AIDS.*]

The President. First of all, it's not true that I have made no major speeches about AIDS. I appointed the first AIDS czar the country ever had. I got the Ryan White Act fully funded. We increased funding for AIDS research and AIDS care by 3 times or more the amount that the rest of the budget was going up, and then we did it—when we were cutting almost everything else, we were spending much more money on AIDS. This administration has done far more on research and care and raising the visibility of the issue than anyone ever has.

I don't mind you being frustrated, because it's frustrating until we find a cure. We are finding ways, by the way, to keep people alive more and more, and we're also finding ways that children who are born HIV-positive can get through it in a hurry and maybe even have totally normal life expectancy.

All I can tell you is what my commitment is. My commitment is, during these budget wars, to see that medical research in general and AIDS research in particular are continued to be increased—it's a very small part of the overall budget, but it's a big part of our future—and to try to make sure that we have adequate levels of care.

Now, let me say one final thing. The health care reforms that I proposed last year did not pass. But there are two things that I think we ought to do that would make a huge difference to people with HIV and all of their family members and friends. The most important is to try to provide some alternatives to either no care or nursing home care in the home or in boarding homes, some other options for long-term care for families. That's also a big deal for people with disabled relatives and people with parents that maybe don't need to be in a nursing home but need some help. I believe that that ought to be part of all these arguments about cutting Medicare and Medicaid. It ought to be done in the context of health care reform, and we ought to push for that again. And I will do that. The other thing I think we have to do is to make it possible for more Americans to buy into health insurance pools that they can afford.

So I am going to work on that with this Congress and, believe it or not, in spite of all the things you hear now, I think we've got a reasonable chance to achieve both of those goals. And I think if you and people like you will lobby on the care issue, the Ryan White issue, I think we have a chance to get that carved out from the cuts. And I hope you will do that.

I can tell you, too—I've said this elsewhere—it would be a lot easier if they didn't have just an arbitrary date for balancing the budget and then have to churn everything else in there. If you'd say, "What do we have to do? How

much does it cost to do it? How are we going to cut? How long will it take to do it?" it would lead you to a conclusion that you could do it but you'd have to take a few more years.

Prisons

[*A participant questioned increased spending for prisons and suggested changes in the Federal sentencing guidelines for nonviolent offenders.*]

The President. The Attorney General is reviewing that, and there is a commission, you know, that's supposed to make recommendations on it. I have to tell you, all of you folks, that the Federal Government adopted these sentencing guidelines to get out of the feeling a lot of Americans had that the sentence a person got and the time a person did was totally arbitrary, that it varied so dramatically from judge to judge and State to State that it was hard to believe that justice was ever being done. And some people, it would seem, would do something terrible and not do any time at all. So we went to the sentencing guidelines.

Most people who practice law and who deal with the sentencing guidelines now believe just what this gentleman said, that it requires people to serve too much time in prison for relevantly minor offenses and lets serious offenders off for doing too little time, costing the Federal taxpayers more.

I don't think you should assume that nothing's going to be done on that. I'll be honest with you, the Members of Congress and the people in the Justice Department and everybody else is reluctant to touch them for fear that if you change anything, they will be excoriated by somebody saying, "Well, here's one case, and this guy is doing one day less," and how terrible it is. Again, we live in an age where there are a lot of complicated problems that don't have simple answers, but those 30-second bullets that come screaming over the air waves like—seem to have a simple answer. But I think that we need to have a careful review of them and see if we can't reach a sense in the country that they could be modified in ways that would actually make the American people safer.

We can't totally jail our way out of this crime problem, folks. Russia is the only country in the world with the same percentage of people behind bars as America has. South Africa has—is the only country in the world that has about half the percentage of people behind bars. Nobody else is above 20 percent of percentage of people in prison that we have.

So, I know a lot of people think that the courts are lenient and the prisons are weak. But the truth is, we send more people to jail and keep them longer there than any other country does. And I'm all for it if they're the right people, if they're the dangerous people that shouldn't be let out, that ought to be kept behind bars. But right now, prison expansion is normally the biggest item in every State government's budget today. In California, they're building more prisons and spending less on education, thereby ensuring they'll have to build more prisons and spend less on education—you see what I mean.

So I agree it ought to be looked at. But to do it, we need people who are out here in the country who would foster a non-demagoguing debate about it, because every time the Justice Department even seeks to raise it, you have all of the things you can imagine being said about it.

Health Care Reform

[A participant praised Hillary Clinton's efforts on health care reform and asked if the President would continue to pursue it.]

The President. I'm trying to think of all of the things I want to say to you. When I was a boy, I lived on a farm in Arkansas that had sheep and goats and cattle, and I nearly got killed by a ram; so I'm glad that your sheep are well-behaved. I don't have that—I've still got a scar up here that I got when I was 6 years old.

Two things happened on the health care reform. Somewhere between $200 and $300 million was spent to advertise to convince the American people we were trying to have the Government take over health care. And the American people basically wound up believing it, so that Congress could get off by just walking away from it. That's essentially what happened. I don't think it was true.

On the other hand, the second thing that happened was, I have to take responsibility—not my wife, not anybody else, me, because I've been in this business a long time—for biting off more than we could chew at once. Health care is one-seventh of our economy. It's the number one concern for a lot of people when they get sick. And there is only so much change

you can accommodate at one time. I think that I have to take responsibility for making our plan vulnerable to being both distorted but also to failing, and I regret that very much.

So what are we going to do now? Because every year, more and more working people don't have health insurance. Every year, more and more people who are self-employed or farmers or people in small businesses can't afford to buy insurance or have to pay more for less coverage. And every year, more and more cost gets either put off onto the Government or onto people that do have good insurance policies. Now, if we cut Medicare and Medicaid and take that money away from hospitals in Montana and Arkansas and other places and New York City, that will put even more pressure on either closing hospitals or raising insurance rates for people that have good insurance. So this is a very complicated thing.

My answer to you is twofold. Number one, if it is appropriate, that is, depending on what we do this year, I'll certainly intend to discuss the health care in the context of the campaign in 1996. But, number two, remember I have said to the American people all along Medicare and Medicaid are going up too fast; I agree with the Republican majority in Congress on that. We won't have any money for anything else if we continue to have to spend 10 percent, 11 percent more every year for Medicare and Medicaid. That's the only—look, under my budgets, everything else is virtually flat or declining. On the other hand, you can't just cut it without trying to reform the system. And I believe there are some important medical reforms that can be done this year that would make health care more available and more affordable to people and would reduce some of the disruption that's otherwise going to come if you just have huge cuts in Medicare and Medicaid.

So I'm not giving up on getting something done this year. And there are a lot of people in both parties in Congress who are prepared to talk about some step-by-step reforms that would make a difference.

Cooperation With Congress

[A participant asked why the President had not cooperated with the Republicans after their election victory.]

The President. I think the American people do want it. And I have tried to cooperate. Let me just give you three—a couple of examples and remind you that cooperation means just that. It requires two people to cooperate, two sides.

Example number one: I signed and strongly supported a bill, the first bill the Republican Congress passed, to apply to Congress all the laws they put on the private sector, because I figure that'll make them think twice before they ask private employers to go out and do a lot of things that they don't have to do—the first thing we did.

The second bill we did was a bill sponsored by Senator Kempthorne in Idaho to limit the ability of Federal Government to impose unfunded mandates on State and local government. I was strongly for that. I signed it.

The third thing I did was to help them break a filibuster and get strong support among Democrats in the Senate for the line-item veto, which they all said they wanted. You remember the House passed a line-item veto on President Reagan's birthday as a present for him; that was weeks ago, right? The line-item veto—one of the things the Republican Congress said that was essential to cut spending—I said, "Give it to me. I'll cut it." Do you know—so we had a line-item veto pass the House, a line-item veto pass the Senate, and I am still waiting for a conference committee to be appointed. And one of the Republican Senators said last week, "Oh, we're not going to give President Clinton the line-item veto. We may not like the cuts he makes in spending." So here I am, all dressed up and ready to cooperate. [*Laughter*]

Now, on the—let me give you one other example. They wanted to cut some money out of this year's budget to make a downpayment on balancing the budget. That's what this so-called rescission bill is. They wanted to do it so they would raise money to pay for Oklahoma City, the California earthquake, and the floods that are now going on in the Middle West and still have some money to bring the deficit down starting this year even more. And I said, fine. They said $16 billion; I said, fine. I met with the Republican Senators, and we worked out an agreement. And then all the Democratic Senators, just about, voted for it. It was a great deal, right? So then they go behind closed doors, and they take a billion four that we agreed on

and spending on education and health care and veterans and a bunch of other stuff out and put in a billion four worth of courthouses and special street and road projects and some other things.

Now—and so I said, "Look, I want to sign this bill; I want to cooperate. But I made a deal. Then you guys went behind closed doors. You took people out; you took pork in." We've got to raise incomes of Americans. We shouldn't be cutting education. We shouldn't be cutting those opportunities. I do not want to have a pile of vetoes, but I am not going to sign a bill that gets changed behind closed doors after the cooperation we had agreed on produced this bill.

So, I still want to cooperate with them. I'll help them balance the budget, too, but not if it collapses the American economy or wrecks Medicare or closes every country hospital in Montana and my home State. I want to cooperate, but it takes two to tango.

Power Marketing Administrations

[*After the station took a commercial break, a participant questioned the proposed sale of Energy Department power marketing administrations to private interests.*]

The President. Well, the argument is, let me just say—let me put it in a larger context. The Office of Management and Budget, under my administration and under the previous Republican administrations, has always routinely tried to put something on this in the budget. The Congress now has voted to do it at least one time, but it has to go through another committee, so it might be able to be headed off.

When they brought it to me, I said I don't necessarily believe this is going to save money. This is a one-time savings, all right, and you can argue that the power is subsidized, but I will approve this only if you do two things, in our proposal. One is you have to put a lid on how much rates can go up, and two—which makes it less attractive, obviously, to private utilities. And two is there has to be an extraordinary effort to let public power authorities buy the capacity first, which would, in effect—since they're getting it, since the power marketing authorities primarily sell to public power authorities, as you know—which would essentially be a change of assets; you could take it off the government's books, it would look like you lowered the deficit, but it wouldn't lead to a rate increase because you'd have the same integrated network.

So that is what I am trying to do with this proposal. That's what I believe should be done. I do not believe we should sell it and get a one-time gain out of it if it's going to explode electric rates in Montana or in any other State.

There may be a way to do it that would increase the cash flow of the Government and help the Congress and the President to bring the deficit down, but it should only be done if it can be managed without a big hit on the electric rate payers. And I think the way I suggested is a possible way to do it. And if it doesn't work out, then, in my opinion, it shouldn't pass at all.

Government Response to Protest

[*A participant asked about the contrast between antigovernment protest in the 1960's and 1970's and in the present.*]

The President. Well, first of all, there were some people in the '60s and '70s who went beyond their first amendment rights and advocated violence. And they were wrong then, and this crowd is wrong now.

And it's very interesting to me to see that there are some public officials in our country who are only too happy to criticize the culture of violence being promoted by the media in our country or the rap lyrics that are coming out in some of our recordings—which I have also criticized before they did, by and large— but are stone-cold silent when these other folks are talking and making violence seem like it's okay.

And I believe, again, if we're going to create an American community where we can disagree, vote differently, work through our differences, but all think we're friends and neighbors and get closer together, we have to have a uniform standard that says violence is wrong, illegal conduct is wrong, and people that are out there encouraging people and explicitly tell them when it's okay for them to take the law into their own hands and be violent, they're wrong.

And people who are out there demeaning and dehumanizing people just because they work for the Federal Government are wrong. I am not defending every person who ever did anything for the Federal Government, including me. I make mistakes. Everybody who works for the

Government makes mistakes. They're human. When somebody does something wrong, it ought to be zeroed in on, targeted, and talked about. You can do that without dehumanizing people.

I'll tell you, I've been guilty of it. Every politician I've ever known, including me, will sometimes give a speech to people like you and talk about Federal bureaucrats. We've reduced the number of Federal bureaucrats, by the way, by over 100,000, and we're going down to 270,000 in the budgets we've already adopted, to the smallest Government since President Kennedy came here in 1963.

But I realized after Oklahoma City that every time I did that, I did that to try to make those of you who are taxpayers think that I was identifying with you more than them. And that is wrong. That is dehumanizing. That young girl's father is an American citizen who made a deliberate decision that he would never be a rich person because he wanted to serve the United States in a Federal agency. And I've been guilty of it, too.

We all have to realize that we have to change the way we talk and the way we think about this. We don't have to quit disagreeing. We don't have to quit arguing. But this whole climate is bad. It's good for their politics. It helps them raise a lot of money and generate—you know, if you keep people torn up and upset, fear may be a stronger force than hope. But it's not good for America. And we're better than that, all of us are.

Canada-U.S. Trade

[*A participant asked about the trade imbalance with Canada in regard to cattle and grain.*]

The President. Well, first of all, we were the first administration that ever did anything. We got—we had a one-year agreement to limit Canadian imports of wheat, to set up a joint commission to try to deal with this and to try to work it out, because the Canadian wheat problem is somewhat analogous to the Japanese automobile problem that you know I'm also involved with now. And that is that they have a system which does not fall into the category of tariff— right?—which is a tax on imports, or protectionism, which is a legally explicit barrier to imports. It is the way their economic system is organized, works de facto to give them an unfair advantage, in both cases. And these things are not—they're very difficult to take care of in trade laws, which is why you have to take them one by one and take a lot of heat when you're doing it.

So all I can tell you, sir, is that I am doing my best to deal with the situation I found when I became President 2½ years ago. And we have not solved the problem but at least we've put it on hold, and we've done more than has been done in the past. And I will continue to do my best to work on it.

Town Meetings

Mr. Koernig. We are unfortunately, Mr. President, and everybody here, just about out of time. I have one final question.

The President. It seems like we just got here.

Mr. Koernig. I know, it does. I have one final question for you. This is the first townhall meeting you've done in over a year. You did quite a few of them, and then you stopped. Why did you stop, and why are you starting again?

The President. I don't really know why I stopped. One of the things that frustrates me—the young gentleman was asking me about cooperating with Congress, and during the break I said, you know, when we do things, it's not news; it's only news when we're fighting. And one of the things that I noticed is I'd go out and do these townhall meetings, and we'd have, you know, 30, 40 questions, and there would be one where there would be a little—sparks would fly, and that would be the only thing that would get any kind of real legs out of it, so that if the American people drew any conclusion, they would think that I was here making the problem I'm trying to combat worse.

And that may be a reason we kind of stopped doing them, but I think it was a mistake. I think these things are good, because first of all, it's easy for the President to become isolated, particularly in this security environment we live in today. And I think people who have questions should be able to confront their elected officials face to face, personally. And I think it's good to create this.

I look kind of hypocritical going around saying we ought to all start treating each other like friends and neighbors if I'm holed up someplace or I only talk when I'm giving a speech to people who can't respond. So I'm glad to be here.

Mr. Koernig. We're glad you're here too. We're glad that you chose Billings as the place to start doing townhall meetings again. I know that I speak for everyone in Montana and people of northern Wyoming in thanking you very much for being with us tonight, sir.

The President. Thank all of you very much. I can't believe it's 8 o'clock.

Mr. Koernig. I'm Gus Koernig at KTVQ in Billings. I'm told you have some closing comments to make.

The President. No, I'm fine. I'll tell you what I'll do. Does anybody have a question that could be answered yes or no? [*Laughter*] Yes, no, maybe—what—quick.

Anticrime Efforts

Q. Mr. President, as the costs of incarcerating criminals continues to rise, will you take actions to support early intervention and educational programs that will help children not to become criminals but to become successful members of our society?

The President. Absolutely. It was a big part of the crime bill last year. The crime bill had money for prisons, money for police, and money for prevention, and money for punishment. Some in Congress want to take the prevention money out; I want to keep it in.

Anybody else—yes, quick.

Education Funding

Q. Mr. President, will you veto the rescission bill if they do not put education back into the proposed cuts?

The President. Yes, I will. But I want to sign a rescission bill. They're right, the Congress is right to cut that spending, but they shouldn't have done what was done in the conference committee. If they will fix the education, I'll sign it. We ought to have one. It's the right thing to do, but we've got to establish some standards. When you cut spending, what you do spend becomes even more important.

The Environment

Q. Mr. President, if the Republicans rewrite the Endangered Species Act or the Clean Air and Water Acts, will you veto that revision?

The President. Well, it depends on what they do. If this bill the House passed on clean water passes, I'll veto that. But I do believe that there are Republicans and Democrats in the Senate who will try to work together to give us some responsible revisions. And we're trying to revise the way the Endangered Species Act is administered, and all these things trying to push more down to the local level. But we can't abandon them. There is a reason that we have an Endangered Species Act. We brought the eagle back, we're bringing the grizzly bear back, and if we can preserve diversity, it will be good for the environment. But we've got to do it with common sense, and we can do that.

Native American Issues

Q. I want to know if you'd fully fund the tribally controlled community colleges?

The President. Well, we've got some—you know, we did some things for the tribal community colleges that had not done before and made them eligible for certain streams of Federal money. I can't promise to fully fund anything in this budgetary environment; I wish I could, but I can't.

Q. Dave Henry, a Federal whistle-blower of the Bureau of Indian Affairs, formerly. The Indian trust accounts are short between $1 billion and $2 billion—that's with a "b," not an "m"—billion dollars Federal—Indian personal money gone. Could you please ask the Bureau of Indian Affairs to reform the system accounting for Indian trust funds?

The President. I will look into that. That's the second question I don't know the answer to tonight, but I'll look into it.

Any real quick yes or no's?

Campaign Finance Reform

Q. Will you support any change in procedures which would eliminate the soft money in political campaigns which is allowing wealthy individuals in corporations to give very large amounts to the political campaigns?

The President. Yes, I will. I think that the Democratic majority in Congress last time made a mistake not to pass campaign finance reform. I think the lobby reform bill ought to pass as well, which would ban the giving of gifts and

require disclosure of lobbying activities. Those two things would do a lot to straighten up politics in Washington. Yes, I will—both of them, strongly.

Mr. Koernig. Mr. President, this is absolutely the last question.

The President. Okay.

The Environment

Q. Can we do anything to save the endangered species that are out there that people are killing and that we can try to set laws so they will be free to roam and so their population can grow?

The President. That's what the Endangered Species Act is supposed to do. And the people who don't like it believe that we try to save endangered species that aren't important and hurt people a lot economically. And here's what we've got to do. What we've got to do is to find a way to make sure that we don't hurt people so much economically but we do save the species. And in a way, they're all important because it's the whole web of our country, all the biological species, that give us what we know of as Montana or my home State. So I'm going to do what I can to save the Endangered Species Act and to implement it in a way that makes good sense, so all the people who don't like it will dislike it less and we'll save the species.

Mr. Koernig. Mr. President, thank you again. That was a terrific encore.

The President. Thank you.

Mr. Koernig. Thank you folks, and good night.

The President. They were good, weren't they? Thank you.

NOTE: The town meeting began at 7 p.m. in the KTVQ television studio.

Remarks on the Downing of a United States Aircraft in Bosnia
June 2, 1995

Good afternoon. I am very concerned about the loss of our F–16 over Bosnia and the fate of the American pilot, and we are following that situation closely.

I have spoken today with President Chirac about the situation in Bosnia and about the

meetings that Secretary Perry and General Shalikashvili will be attending. I've spoken with Secretary Perry and will meet with him and General Shali later today. We've also been in touch with the NATO commanders and with other governments.

I want to reiterate and make absolutely clear that our policy on Bosnia remains firm. For reasons that I think are obvious, I will have no further comments on this situation today. Thank you very much.

NOTE: The President spoke at 2:20 p.m. in the Rose Garden at the White House. In his remarks, he referred to Capt. Scott F. O'Grady, USAF, and President Jacques Chirac of the European Council.

Remarks to the NCAA Men's and Women's Basketball Champions
June 2, 1995

The President. Thank you very much. Ladies and gentlemen, I'm sorry that other events dictated that we started a little late today, but I want to welcome all of you to the White House and all the people who have come from California and Connecticut: Senator Lieberman, Congresswoman Kennelly, Congresswoman DeLauro, Congressman Gejdenson; and from California, the president of—the chancellor of UCLA, Chancellor Young; and the officers of UConn, the chairman of the board, Lew Rome, and the president, Harry Hartley. I am delighted to welcome all of you back to the White House who have been here before and those who are coming for the first time, to welcome you here.

You know, we ought to get something obvious out of the way. These championships were hard on the Vice President and me. I mean, we just have to hope our ticket does a little better in '96. [*Laughter*]

But some of you know, I am a near-fanatic basketball fan, and I think that any serious student of basketball would have to say that this year in the championship, not only the teams with the best records but the best teams in the United States won the championships and deserve—[*inaudible*].

I remember vividly when Tyus Edney came out of the final game with his wrist injury, and all the people were saying, "Well, this may be the undoing of UCLA." And I was sitting there looking at the team and I said, "I don't think so." [*Laughter*] I remember people—the discussions that I've heard, year-in and year-out, about how you have to have 10 players to win the final. And in the final, when you see the really great players with their adrenalin pumping, I don't think so.

And so, I want to congratulate again Coach Harrick and the Bruins on reviving UCLA's magnificent tradition, winning their 11th national title, and I think that they've got a great future. I also want to congratulate Ed O'Bannon on being selected the most outstanding player of the tournament and the NCAA player of the year for his fantastic season.

I do want to say one thing. I had the privilege of coming to UCLA and giving the commencement address and being with Chancellor Young a couple of years ago. I have to chide you on one thing: I've been very proud of the very outspoken and courageous stance you've taken in favor of continuing affirmative action programs, so we can—[*applause*]—but if you had really believed in spreading opportunity around, you would not have permitted both the O'Bannon brothers to be on your team. [*Laughter*] Nonetheless, I forgive you for that minor lapse. [*Laughter*]

I also want to say a special word of appreciation to Coach Geno Auriemma and the Connecticut Huskies for establishing the most outstanding winning record in the history of college basketball, men or women's basketball. I want to congratulate Rebecca Lobo, who couldn't be here today. We're all sorry about that. But she's representing the U.S. national team in games in Europe. She once wrote to the president of the Celtics, saying that she'd be the first woman to play for their team. All I can say is that may or may not happen. But the Connecticut Huskies did more to make the rest of America appreciate women's basketball than any team has ever done. And they made millions of fans that will help other university teams all across this country for years and years and years in the future, and we thank you for that.

So let me say I'm glad you're here. I also want to say to the coach, this team came to the White House once before, and somebody messed it up, and they didn't get in, even the back door. Today they came in the front door with full honors, and I'd like to invite their coach to come up for a few words. Thank you, and congratulations.

[*At this point, University of Connecticut women's coach Geno Auriemma made brief remarks, and team captain Pam Webber presented gifts to the President. University of California, Los Angeles men's coach Jim Harrick then made brief remarks, and team captain Ed O'Bannon presented gifts to the President.*]

The President. Is that your dad? [*Laughter*] Stand up, Daddy. [*Laughter*]

Now, here's what we're going to do. I'm going to take a picture with each team, and then we're going to break up, take the ropes down, we'll all visit a little, okay?

But you know, every year this is so humbling for me. Most days I wake up and I'm 6 foot 2½ inches, and I'm halfway tall. This day I'm just another person looking up. [*Laughter*]

Thank you all for coming. It was a great day. Thanks.

NOTE: The President spoke at 2:30 p.m. in the East Room at the White House. In his remarks, he referred to Charles E. Young, chancellor, University of California, Los Angeles.

Letter to Congressional Leaders on Most-Favored-Nation Trade Status for Former Eastern Bloc States
June 2, 1995

Dear Mr. Speaker: (*Dear Mr. President:*)

I hereby transmit the document referred to in subsection 402(d)(1) of the Trade Act of 1974, as amended (the "Act"), with respect to a further 12-month extension of the authority to waive subsections (a) and (b) of section 402 of the Act. This document constitutes my recommendation to continue in effect this waiver authority for a further 12-month period, and includes my reasons for determining that continuation of the waiver authority and waivers currently in effect for Albania, Armenia, Azerbaijan, Belarus, Georgia, Kazakhstan,

Kyrgyzstan, Moldova, Mongolia, Tajikistan, Turkmenistan, Ukraine, and Uzbekistan will substantially promote the objectives of section 402 of the Act. I will submit a separate report with respect to the People's Republic of China.

Sincerely,

WILLIAM J. CLINTON

NOTE: Identical letters were set to Newt Gingrich, Speaker of the House of Representatives, and Albert Gore, Jr., President of the Senate. The related memorandum is listed in Appendix D at the end of this volume.

Letter to Congressional Leaders on Most-Favored-Nation Trade Status for China
June 2, 1995

Dear Mr. Speaker: (*Dear Mr. President:*)

I hereby transmit the document referred to in subsection 402(d)(1) of the Trade Act of 1974, as amended ("the Act"), with respect to the continuation of a waiver of application of subsections (a) and (b) of section 402 of the

Act to the People's Republic of China. This document constitutes my recommendation to continue in effect this waiver for a further 12-month period and includes my reasons for determining that continuation of the waiver currently in effect for the People's Republic of China will substantially promote the objectives of section 402 of the Act, and my determination to that effect.

Sincerely,

WILLIAM J. CLINTON

NOTE: Identical letters were sent to Newt Gingrich, Speaker of the House of Representatives, and Albert Gore, Jr., President of the Senate. The related memorandum is listed in Appendix D at the end of this volume.

The President's Radio Address
June 3, 1995

Good morning. I want to talk with you today about the conflict in Bosnia and the United States policy with regard to it for the last 2½ years since I've been President.

Let me begin by saying that I know all Americans join with me in sending their prayers to the family and loved ones of an American pilot who was shot down yesterday while doing his duty flying over Bosnia.

When I became President, we found a war going on in Bosnia that was fueled by ancient, bloody divisions between Bosnian Serbs, Muslims, and Croats. The United Nations had a mission there whose purpose was not to fight the war but to help prevent the slaughter of civilians, to deliver humanitarian assistance, and to try to limit that conflict as much as possible while the peace process moved forward to end the conflict diplomatically and to preserve the Bosnian state.

I determined that the role of the United States should be to vigorously support the diplomatic search for peace and that our vital interests were clear in limiting the spread of the conflict. Furthermore, our interests were in doing what we could, short of putting in ground forces, to help prevent the multiethnic Bosnian state from being destroyed and to minimize the loss of life and the ethnic cleansing.

I determined that we certainly should not have ground forces there, not as a part of the military conflict nor as a part of the United Nations peacekeeping mission, but that instead we should do everything we could to limit the conflict to its present parameters and to support our other objectives.

In our efforts to limit the conflict, we have stationed some troops in the former Yugoslav Republic of Macedonia to make sure that we don't have a Balkan-wide conflict. We must remember that the Balkans are a troubling area

and that it was trouble in the Balkans that sparked World War I.

Secondly, we have used our air power in three ways in Bosnia. First, we have conducted the longest lasting humanitarian airlift in all history, and we've saved a lot of lives doing it. Second, we have enforced the no-fly zone in order to stop the bombing campaign and at least take the war out of the air. That has saved a lot of lives, too, and that is what our brave young pilot was doing yesterday when his plane was shot down. And thirdly, with our NATO allies, we have made our air power available to maintain a fire-free zone around Sarajevo and other populated areas and to support the collection of heavy artillery. This, too, has largely been a successful effort, which has minimized the fighting and the killing and the dying.

This policy has not only worked to minimize the loss of life but also to maximize the chances for peace in a very troubling area. I know it's frustrating to everyone, as it is to me, that we can't completely solve all the world's problems and that more progress toward peace hasn't been made in Bosnia. Sometimes we have to do what is appropriate to minimize disasters that we confront, while we work over the long run on resolving them through diplomacy.

But let's look at what has been done. In 1992, the year before I became President, some 130,000 people were killed in the Bosnian conflict. In 1994, because of the policies that our allies and the United States have pursued together, including the presence of the United Nations troops in Bosnia, the casualties have dropped from 130,000 in 1992 to about 2,500 in 1994, still tragic but dramatically reduced. And all of this has been accomplished without any involvement of American ground forces in combat or peacekeeping missions. The British, the French, the Dutch, the Canadians, and others have carried that burden.

This has not been a perfect peace. Recently, after the peace in Sarajevo broke down and 1,000 or more shells were dropped on the city, the United Nations asked for air support, as they have in the past, with success. We gave it, and unfortunately, the Serbs captured U.N. personnel. I have made it very clear to the American people all along that actions like this could occur because of the vulnerability of the U.N. peacekeepers who are spread out in small numbers all across the country. Now we are doing everything we can to secure the release of the U.N. personnel.

But let's not forget this policy has saved a lot of lives. And in the end, the conflict will only be resolved by diplomacy. Now, the United Nations faces a choice: It can either get out, or it can strengthen its forces in order to fully support the mission.

If our allies decide to stay, we want to support them, but within the very careful limits I have outlined. I want to make it clear again what I have said about our ground forces. We will use them only if, first, if there is a genuine peace with no shooting and no fighting and the United States is part of policing that peace. That's exactly what we've been doing in the Middle East since the late 1970's without incident. It's worked so well that I imagine most Americans don't even recall that we still have forces there.

Second, if our allies decide they can no longer continue the U.N. mission and decide to withdraw, but they cannot withdraw in safety, we should help them to get out with our unique capacities. They have borne the risk for the world community of working for peace and minimizing the loss of life. And I think that's an appropriate thing for us to do.

The third issue is the remote, indeed highly unlikely event that Britain, France, and other countries, with their considerable military strength and expertise, become stranded and could not get out of a particular place in Bosnia. The question has been raised about whether we would help them to withdraw as a last resort. I have decided that if a U.N. unit needs an emergency extraction, we would assist after consulting with Congress. This would be a limited, temporary operation, and we have not been asked to do this. I think it is highly unlikely that we would be asked to do it. But I do believe that these people who have put themselves at risk are entitled to know that the U.S. will stand with them if they need help to move to safety.

Now, as this conflict continues and as the diplomatic efforts go on, we must remember that our policy in Bosnia has reduced the level of violence, has reduced the loss of life. In the last several days, our allies, in the face of their hostages being taken, have said that they expect those people to be released but that they do not want to give up their efforts to bring peace to Bosnia. They do not want us, they do not expect us to put American ground troops into Bosnia. But we do have an interest in doing what we can short of that to contain the conflict and minimize and eventually end the human suffering. I believe this is the appropriate, acceptable, proper policy for the United States.

Thanks for listening.

Note: The President spoke at 10:06 a.m. from the Oval Office at the White House. In his remarks, he referred to Capt. Scott F. O'Grady, USAF.

Remarks on the National Homeownership Strategy
June 5, 1995

Look at it this way, Jean, all your other speeches will be easier now. [*Laughter*] You did very well, and I thank you and Jim for coming.

Ladies and gentlemen, I have looked forward to this day for a long time, and I care a lot about this issue. I'm glad to see so many distinguished Americans here. I welcome Congress-man Bono, who was, before he became a Congressman, a mayor and therefore has an intimate personal experience with this whole issue. And I'm, of course, delighted to see my good friend Millard Fuller here, who has done as much to make the dream of homeownership a reality in our country and throughout the world as any living person. And we thank you, sir, for your work.

Before I get into my remarks, I think it's important for me to make a brief reference to another subject. Congress is coming back to work today after a break, and the anti-terrorism bill that I sent to Congress is being considered in the Senate. It will give law enforcement the tools it needs to crack down on terrorists that they, people in law enforcement, asked me to seek from Congress, first a couple of months before the Oklahoma City tragedy, to deal especially with the problems of international terrorism coming into the United States, and then some more things that were asked for in the wake of Oklahoma City.

This is very, very serious legislation. The Congress not only has the right, it has the responsibility to review the bill and to hear those who think that in some ways its law enforcement provisions are too tough. There ought to be a full debate. But we cannot afford to let scores of unnecessary amendments drag down this process. In that I agree with the statements made by the majority leader of the Senate, Senator Dole. So I call upon my fellow Democrats and Republicans to limit amendments, curb politics, ignore narrow interests, to agree to the simple pact that there should be no excuses, no games, no delays. The time is now to enact this important legislation.

You can be sure that terrorists around the world are not delaying their plans while we delay the passage of this bill. It is within our reach now to dramatically strengthen our law enforcement capabilities and to enhance the ability of people in law enforcement to protect all kinds of Americans. We have an obligation to do that. And so I would urge the Congress to take this bill up and to get on with it, to limit the number of amendments as soon as possible so that we can go forward.

Now, let me get back to the subject at hand. I am delighted to be here. You might ask, why do I care about home ownership? After all, I live in America's finest public housing. [*Laughter*] The answer is, I once had a life, and I hope to have one again some day. [*Laughter*] When I was 19, I built a home as part of what I did that summer.

When I was trying to coax my wife into marrying me, we were both living in Fayetteville, Arkansas, teaching at the University of Arkansas. And I had not gotten a definite answer;

I think that's the most delicate way I can put this. [*Laughter*] And Hillary had to go away to somewhere—I can't remember where she was going now, but anyway she was taking a trip on an airplane, so I was driving her to the airport. And we drove by this wonderful old house. It was an old, old, very small house, and she said, "Boy, that's a beautiful house." And I noticed that there was a little "For Sale" sign on it. So I took her to the airport, went back, and bought the house. And when she came home after the trip, I drove by the house. I said, "See that house you liked? I bought it while you were gone. Now you have to marry me." [*Laughter*] And it worked; 20 years ago this fall, it worked. Most people do it the other way around, but you know—[*laughter*]

I still remember that home cost $20,500. It had about 1,100 square feet. And I had about a $17,500 mortgage on it, and my payments were about $176 a month, as I remember, something like that. And that was 20 years ago this fall that I signed that fortuitous contract.

Those prices aren't very much available anymore, but the objective for young people, with their futures before them and their dreams fresh in their minds, starting out their families, to be able to own their home and to start a family in that way, that's a worthy objective—just as worthy today and, I would argue to you, more important today than it was 20 years ago, more important today than it was 20 years ago. We just had a report come out last week asserting that it may be that up to one-third of our children are now born out of wedlock. You want to reinforce family values in America, encourage two-parent households, get people to stay home? Make it easy for people to own their own homes and enjoy the rewards of family life and see their work rewarded. This is a big deal. This is about more than money and sticks and boards and windows. This is about the way we live as a people and what kind of society we're going to have.

And I cannot say enough in terms of my appreciation to Secretary Cisneros, who is a genuine visionary, to the Vice President for all the work he and the National Performance Review have done on this, and to all of our partners who are here, all the people in public and private life whose work is home ownership. Since the day I asked Secretary Cisneros to build this strategy, he has done about everything a human being could do. And I can say without knowing that I'm overstating it, that if we succeed in doing this, if we succeed in making that number happen, it will be one of the most important things that this administration has ever done, and we're going to do it without spending more tax money.

Two years ago, I met a couple having their own first home dream come true. They're here today. Patty and Matt Murray had just bought a home in Frederick, Maryland, where I was visiting, promoting my economic plan along with the realtors to bring down the deficit, to bring down interest rates, to bring down home mortgage rates so people can afford to buy their own home. Now they have a stake in a better life, and I'm glad that they're here today. I would like to ask them to stand. I would also like to ask now all the other young couples that came here—I just want you to see them. That's where I was 20 years ago. I want all of you to stand here, all these first-time homebuyers that we invited to come here. [*Applause*]

We have to remember that there are millions of people just like them who believe that home ownership is out of reach. They may be paying monthly rents that could cover a mortgage payment. They may scrape to save, but a downpayment is still out of reach. They are locked out by rigid restrictions or by a home-buying system just, as Jean said, too difficult or too frightening. And that is not right.

One of the great successes of the United States in this century has been the partnership forged by the National Government and the private sector to steadily expand the dream of home ownership to all Americans. In 1934, President Roosevelt created the Federal Housing Administration and made home ownership available to millions of Americans who couldn't afford it before that.

Fifty-one years ago just this month, Harry Truman rewarded service men and women with the GI bill of rights, which created the VA Home Loan Guarantee Program. That extended the dream of home ownership to a whole new generation of Americans. For four decades after that, in the greatest period of expansion of middle class dreams any country has ever seen anywhere in human history, home ownership expanded as incomes rose, jobs increased, the educational level of the American people improved.

But in the 1980's, as the Vice President said, that dream began to slip away. I ran for President in large measure because I wanted to restore that dream, to grow the middle class, shrink the under class, promote the mainstream values of work and responsibility, family and community, and reform Government in a way that would enhance opportunity and shrink bureaucracy.

We've made good progress, but we have to do a lot more. I ask all of you just one more time to look at that chart. And I wish I had a lot of other charts to show you that would reinforce that. Home ownership declines, then stabilizes at a lower level. At the same time, more and more American families working harder for the same or lower wages every year, under new and difficult stresses. It seems to me that we have a serious, serious unmet obligation to try to reverse these trends. As Secretary Cisneros says, this drop in home ownership means 1.5 million families who would now be in their own homes if the 46 years of home ownership expansion had not been reversed in the 1980's.

Now we have begun to expand it again. Since 1993, nearly 2.8 million new households have joined the ranks of America's homeowners, nearly twice as many as in the previous 2 years. But we have to do a lot better. The goal of this strategy, to boost home ownership to 67.5 percent by the year 2000, would take us to an all-time high, helping as many as 8 million American families across that threshold.

This is the new way home for the American middle class. We have got to raise incomes in this country. We have got to increase security for people who are doing the right thing, and we have got to make people believe that they can have some permanence and stability in their lives even as they deal with all the changing forces that are out there in this global economy.

No person, even the President, can look at these young people and say, I will guarantee you, no matter what happens in the global economy, you will always have the job you have today, and you'll make more money next year than you did this year. You know no one can guarantee that in the global economy. That's not the way the world works anymore.

But we can guarantee to people that we're going to empower them to help themselves. We'll make home ownership more accessible. We'll make lifetime education and training more accessible. We'll make the things that make life work for people who are trying to do the best they can for themselves there. We have to begin with the basic things that make it worth doing.

As the Vice President and I said in a book we put out in the election campaign in 1992, our economic strategy includes a commitment to work to provide decent, safe, affordable homes to all Americans and to do it with an alliance of the public and private sector.

I want to say this one more time, and I want to thank again all the people here from the private sector who have worked with Secretary Cisneros on this: Our home ownership strategy will not cost the taxpayers one extra cent. It will not require legislation. It will not add more Federal programs or grow Federal bureaucracy.

It's 100 specific actions that address the practical needs of people who are trying to build their own personal version of the American dream, to help moderate income families who pay high rents but haven't been able to save enough for a downpayment, to help lower income working families who are ready to assume the responsibilities of home ownership but held back by mortgage costs that are just out of reach, to help families who have historically been excluded from home ownership. Today, all across the country, I say to millions of young working couples who are just starting out: By the time your children are ready to start the first grade, we want you to be able to own your own home.

All of our country will reap enormous benefits if we achieve this goal. Home ownership encourages savings and investment. When a family buys a home, the ripple effect is enormous. It means new homeowner consumers. They need more durable goods, like washers and dryers, refrigerators and water heaters. And if more families could buy new homes or older homes, more hammers will be pounding, more saws will be buzzing. Homebuilders and home fixers will be put to work. When we boost the number of homeowners in our country, we strengthen our economy, create jobs, build up the middle class, and build better citizens.

I thank Millard Fuller especially for the work that Habitat for Humanity has done in building better citizens. I remember the day we dedicated the very first Habitat house built in my home State, that went to a woman who went to church with me and worked for the State government and still her income was so low she was eligible to be considered there. And I was so proud of her because she and her children, for the first time, felt that all these incredible years of sacrifice and labor she had endured were about to be rewarded. And it made her a better citizen, and it made everybody that put a hammer to a nail a better citizen, and it made all of us who saw it unfold better citizens.

H.L. Mencken once wrote that "A home is not a mere transient shelter, its essence lies in its permanence, in its quality of representing in all its details the personalities of the people who live in it."

What we are doing today will allow more homes to be blessed by more families. I hope it will start all these young people on a path that will take them to great joys in their personal lives, and perhaps to other homes, but something they will always know that their country wanted them to have because they were entitled to it as a part of the American dream.

Thank you very much.

NOTE: The President spoke at 11:50 a.m. in the East Room at the White House. In his remarks, he referred to new homeowners Jean Mikitz, who introduced the President, and her husband, Jim; and Millard Fuller, founder and president, Habitat for Humanity International.

Interview With Larry King
June 5, 1995

Vice President's Role

Mr. King. Good evening. We have checked all of our history books, and as best we can figure out, this is the first time ever a sitting President and Vice President have ever been on a program, radio or television, together while in office.

We'll be entertaining your calls later. Also, later in the program we'll be giving you a number for Save the Children. I'm wearing a Save the Children tie in conjunction with our 10th anniversary. We'll be associating Save the Children programs throughout the month, and we'll tell you later where you can order beautiful ties like this. The President and Vice President have them as well, but are not wearing them tonight. But they both have or are in possession of these ties.

We'll talk about lots of things, but the most obvious to me—if something, God forbid, happened to you, how long would it take to brief you?

The Vice President. Oh, that's not a hypothetical that I'm comfortable with, but there are procedures that are in place that we've discussed because it's our duty to the country and the Constitution.

Mr. King. Are you and—is he——

The President. I know what you're asking. The answer is, no time at all. I think it's clear that the Vice President is more closely involved with all the decisions of this administration than any of his predecessors. In the——

Mr. King. So you could take over——

The President. Absolutely. I think that we were very fortunate when Harry Truman became President—he'd just been in office a little while, and at that time Vice Presidents weren't as involved as they now are. But he turned out to be a great President. But we were lucky, because he wasn't in the loop on a lot of things. And then, of course, when President Johnson had to become President, he had been Senate majority leader and there was a little more of a—he had a more active role. But Presidents Carter, Reagan, and Bush, I think, all tended to give the Vice President a much larger role. And then, because of the relationship we have and because of my conviction about what the Constitution really requires me to do and because it's good for the American people, Vice President Gore is the most involved Vice President in the history of the country.

Mr. King. So you never feel, Mr. Vice President, out of the loop?

The Vice President. No, never. And it's been a great privilege, really.

Mr. King. Do you talk every day?

The Vice President. Every day, many, many times.

Mr. King. You're not—if you're in different parts of the world, you talk every day?

The Vice President. Just about. There are times when we don't, if he's on another con-

tinent than I am, but even then sometimes we do.

1996 Presidential Election

Mr. King. And are you two definitely running again as a ticket? I don't think we've officially——

The Vice President. He's not ready to make any announcements.

Mr. King. Oh, come on, make it. Everybody makes it here; make it. [*Laughter*]

The President. I haven't asked him yet, but if he's willing, that would be my intention.

Mr. King. Okay, your intention is to run again and ask him to serve again.

The President. Absolutely.

Mr. King. And would you serve again if asked?

The Vice President. Well, I enjoy this job a great deal, and I count it a privilege to have this learning experience and to be able to work for and with President Clinton. You shouldn't have any doubt about that. But we're waiting on any formal announcements.

Bosnia

Mr. King. I just wanted to know. Anything you can tell us about the pilot?

The President. No, except that we're working on it very hard.

Mr. King. Is he signaling? Is there a report of signals out of Bosnia?

The President. Well, you know what the news reports are, but I can tell you that I have been keeping on top of this ever since the first report of the missing plane. And we're doing everything we can, but it's best that we say as little as possible.

Mr. King. Is this, Mr. Vice President, as some diplomat called it today, "a great failure of Western diplomacy," all Western diplomacy?

The Vice President. Well, clearly, this is a tragedy that has been unfolding for a long time, some would say for 500 years. But certainly, it was a full-blown tragedy before we ever got here. But I think that it's important to realize that NATO, the most successful alliance in history, never really did that great a job when it was outside of the NATO area, dealing with a conflict between two countries neither of whom was a part of NATO. And that's the situation here.

They have done a great deal. And I think a lot of people have not paid much attention to the change that has come about since President Clinton's policy was put into place. Some of the numbers aren't very well known, but the change has been pretty significant.

The President. Let me just say this. First of all, I disagree with that.

Mr. King. You disagree with the Vice President?

The President. No, I agree with him, and I disagree with those who say——

Mr. King. Oh—it's failed.

The President. ——that the whole thing has been a great failure. It has not been a success. But remember, how long has this war been going on? Since 1991, in essence. That's 4 years. It's tragic; it's terrible. But their enmities go back 500 years, some would say almost a thousand years.

Now, what are our interests and what are our objectives there? First of all, we don't want the war to spread beyond Bosnia. Secondly, we want to alleviate the human suffering and reduce the killing. And thirdly, we want to support a diplomatic process for peace.

Now, let me just follow up on what the Vice President said. The war hasn't spread. We've worked hard on that. We've worked with our NATO allies and with the U.N. in the longest humanitarian airlift in history and to keep the skies free of bombers to take the war out of the air, which is what our brave pilot was doing when he was shot down. We have worked with the U.N. peacekeepers on the ground to try to establish safe havens through the use, again, of only of our air power; we have no ground forces there.

In 1992, the year we had our interview in Orlando, about 130,000 people were killed in Bosnia. Last year, 1994, less than 3,000 people were killed there. That's still tragic, but I hardly think that constitutes a colossal failure, especially—now, let me just say one other thing. Look at—you're going to go to the Middle East on Thursday with your interviews——

Mr. King. We're going to talk to all of them.

The President. We look at the progress in the Middle East. We look at progress in Northern Ireland. We look at the joy we have in the elections in South Africa. All those conflicts went on for a lot more than 4 years. And I'm proud of the role the United States is playing in the peace process in all those places, but it became possible when people decided they wanted to make peace and they wanted to stop

killing each other there. That's the point I want to make.

So, I'm not happy with everything that's happened in Bosnia. I wish there were some clear-cut answer. I don't think we should have ground troops there in combat or in the peacekeeping force.

Mr. King. At all?

The President. No. I've said where I think—if they make a peace, they stop fighting, they want us to help police it like we have in the Middle East since the late seventies, that's something that we would consider doing, after consultation with Congress. If our people—if the U.N. has to pull out, they're our NATO allies and they need us, I'd be inclined to help them. If they get stranded and they're in desperate conditions, I'd be inclined to help them. I think that's something we should look at. But we shouldn't be involved on the ground there. We have achieved these other objectives.

And if you go from 130,000 dead down to under 3,000 dead and you've still got a talk going, you've got a chance of a diplomatic solution, what is the difference in that and Northern Ireland, the Middle East, and these other places? It takes time.

Mr. King. If it spreads, do we have to go? Like to Macedonia, would we have to go?

The President. We have to do—we have troops in Macedonia because we are determined not to have a Balkan war. That, after all, is how World War I got started. We don't want this thing to spread across the Balkans, and I think all Americans would understand that.

Mr. King. Do we have a moral obligation, Mr. Vice President, to these people? Moral, if not strategic?

The Vice President. I think the world clearly has an interest in doing what is reasonable and necessary to stop an ethnically based conquering by one country of another. And our NATO allies have shown tremendous courage and fortitude in putting their troops there on the ground. We've chosen not to do that. They are closer to it. It is on the Continent of Europe. We've provided some support to them, but our allies are the ones that are there on the ground. And I think that that's the correct choice for them to make.

The President. But Larry, first of all, we've spent a great deal of money there, running this humanitarian airlift, giving air support, trying to create free-fire zones, if you will, around Sarajevo and the other populated eastern enclaves, in doing all the things we've done to support the no-fly zone and to support the British, the French, the Dutch, the Canadians, and others there on the ground. All of us have done this at a significant investment. And they are at some risk, as you see when several hundred of them got captured. If you reduce the casualties from 130,000 to under 3,000 and you at least have the possibility of cease-fires and ongoing negotiations and you continue humanitarian aid, it seems to me that that is fulfilling a moral obligation.

Do we have the capacity to impose a settlement on people who want to continue fighting? We couldn't do that in Northern Ireland. We couldn't do that in the Middle East. And I would submit, if you look at the population and the geography and the history of Bosnia, we cannot do that there. So I believe we're doing the right thing.

[At this point, the network took a commercial break.]

Mr. King. There's a lot of bases to cover. One more—are you now optimistic on Bosnia? Are you sounding like things are going to turn better?

The President. What I think is that we have to continue to pursue a strategy of diplomacy and keeping people alive and minimizing the brutality and trying to make the peacekeeping mission work. If it fails, then we'll have to consider what our options are then.

Mr. King. But no troops.

The Vice President. Anyone who is worried about the U.S. sending ground troops there should not be. That's not going to happen.

Middle East Peace Process

Mr. King. We have the Middle East program coming Thursday night with Hussein and Rabin and Arafat. You've been talking to people involved. How is it going? We've got a chance for Syria to get involved with the peace treaty.

The President. I think we've got a chance to make it this year. And I think that Mr. Arafat is trying to implement his part of the accords. I think he's making progress. Prime Minister Rabin has shown great courage. King Hussein has always wanted these days to come about, and he's working hard to work through the things that have to be done. President Mubarak

in Egypt has been a great support. And I think President Asad wants peace. We're——

Mr. King. You do?

The President. Yes, I do. I am convinced he does. Now, there are a lot of difficult stones in the road, and we may not make it, but I think we've got a chance.

The Vice President. Well, let me just recall for you, Larry, that a lot has happened since this President came into office. The state of war between Israel and Jordan, after 46 years, was ended, right out here on the South Lawn of the White House, with President Clinton presiding over it. The long period of estrangement and no even—not even any talking between the PLO and Israel was ended with the famous handshake, again presided over by President Clinton. He went to the signing of the agreement in the Middle East.

The dialog with Syria has now reached the point where people who follow this very, very closely, as we do, believe that there is the kind of movement that can really inspire a great deal of hope. This is a fundamental change. Now you have, on a regular basis, Arafat sitting down with Israeli leaders and beginning to work through all of the problems there. And all of the leaders there give President Clinton the credit for the progress.

The President. I would say this: In light of what we've been through in Oklahoma City and with the World Trade Center, if we could succeed in bringing a comprehensive peace to the Middle East and then we could bring the benefits of that peace to all the people who live there, I believe that that would help us to defeat terrorism in all continents in the next century. I think it's a huge deal for all the people of the world.

Japan-U.S. Trade

Mr. King. Quickly, on the Tokyo thing, are we going to settle that before the date of imposition of tariffs?

The Vice President. Well, that's up to Japan.

Mr. King. Strictly up to Japan, no more meetings?

The President. Well, we'll be—we're prepared to meet and talk, I think, but look——

Mr. King. What's the date, June what—24th?

The President. Let me say—I have worked with four Japanese governments. We have succeeded in pushing through a new world trade agreement. We have gotten, I think, 14 specific agreements with Japan, including agreements to import rice. But the real problem with the Japanese-American trade relationship, and with the Japanese trade relationship with many other countries, is autos and auto parts. It's 60 percent of our trade deficit with Japan. And we know we're competitive in price and quality. And we know there are indirect problems that are not covered by the specific letter of normal trade agreements. So we have to be firm here.

I have done everything I could for 2½ years to have a good, constructive, friendly relationship with Japan. We are allies, we are friends, but we must be firm on this.

The Vice President. I was watching television yesterday, and I saw an advertisement saying, "Free trade—these firm moves against Japan are a terrible mistake." And then at the end of the commercial, it said, "Paid for by Japanese Auto Association." And I would just say to them that if they, in any way, misjudge the strength and resolve of the President in pursuing this, they're making a serious mistake, because they're the ones that are acting contrary to what it would take to have more——

Mr. King. You're not going to give on this, is what you're saying.

The President. We want to open the market. We don't even—we just want to open the market. Let me say for the benefit of the Americans who are watching this, this is in Japan's interest as well. Japan has suffered from low growth. The Japanese people have apparently higher incomes than the American people, but their living standards are lower because they pay about 40 percent more for consumer products.

Mr. King. Are you saying their leaders are letting them down?

The President. I'm saying that their ingrained institutional resistance to change is not only hurting the American working people, it's hurting the Japanese people.

[*The network took a commercial break.*]

Closing of Pennsylvania Avenue

Mr. King. What you're looking at now is the front of the White House, which is becoming a mall or an esplanade. No cars anymore on Pennsylvania Avenue because of security threats. There are the barricades. You have to go in through the side; you can't go in through the front anymore. Tragedy?

The President. Well, I wish it hadn't been necessary. But the truth is that, so far, it's increasing public access to the White House, and it hasn't interrupted traffic too much. On the weekends now, the whole Pennsylvania Avenue is just flooded with people. They're riding bikes; they're skating; they're skateboarding; they're on rollerblades.

Mr. King. Is this going to be like an esplanade? It's going to be like——

The President. We want it to be a big public space. You know, in a time of less security consciousness back in the thirties, the back lawn of the White House, the large back lawn, used to be open every Sunday in the spring and summer for ordinary citizens to go and picnic and sort of be there in the atmosphere of it. Now we can do that in the front because of what's happened. I wish it hadn't been necessary, but we're going to make something good come of this.

The Vice President. There's a difference between access for people and access for cars and trucks. And actually, this space is more accessible to people now.

Antiterrorism Legislation

Mr. King. Where's your terrorism bill? Flying in the Senate, stopped in the House?

The Vice President. Well, the President's been working extremely hard on that, and I have to tell you—he won't say this the same way I do—I would personally like to say I'm very frustrated with what the House of Representatives is doing. The President's made it clear why this is necessary for our country, and it's not right for the House of Representatives to sit on this because some of the Members of Congress are scared that some of these antigovernment sentiments are so strong that they'll be expressed against them if they increase the ability of the Government to fight against lawbreakers.

The President. I'd like to say, though, that this is not just a—this is not necessarily a partisan deal. Senator Dole, so far as we speak tonight, has done what he's said he'd do. He asked me and the Democratic leadership to try to reduce the number of amendments offered by the Democrats. He said he'd try to reduce the number of amendments offered by Republicans. They did that today. They adopted a major amendment that I wanted to put taggants in illegal explosives, or explosives that could be held illegally, so we could trace them. They're moving that bill. And it seems to me that we're moving in the right direction in the Senate.

I was quite disturbed at the people in the House saying, "Well, maybe we ought to go slow on this." Look, I had an antiterrorism bill in the Congress 2 months before Oklahoma for foreign terrorists. Then the FBI and others said, "We'd like some changes to deal with domestic terrorism," and we presented that. The bill is moving in the Senate. It must move in the House. We can't go slow on it. We can't.

Mr. King. What's stopping you in the House?

The President. Well, we don't know. Nothing has happened yet. We hope, if we can get this bill out of the Senate, that the House will then move rapidly.

Mr. King. What has Mr. Gingrich said about it?

The Vice President. Well, he said that they might have to go slow. And the terrorists aren't going slow.

Mr. King. So you're saying tonight to the House, get a move on?

The President. Look, this is a big deal, and this should not be partisan. And I know that some of these groups that hate the Government think that their civil liberties may be infringed here. The Congress has the right, indeed, the responsibility, to review the provisions of this act, but not to go slow. The people who do this terrorist work, they operate on their own timetable; they don't sit around and wait for Congress to enact laws.

We know that we can do a better job in stopping things from happening. Let me say, in spite of the horror of Oklahoma City and the World Trade Center, our people stopped another planned bombing in New York, stopped a plan to explode some airplanes flying out of the West Coast airports over the Pacific. We can do more of this. In Israel now, with all of their problems with terrorism, they head off the vast majority of terrorist threats. We can prevent this, but we're not used to dealing with it. We need more tools. That's what this legislation is for, and we can't delay.

Oklahoma City Bombing

Mr. King. Are we still investigating Oklahoma City heavily?

The Vice President. Oh, yes. The President put together—let me just expand on that briefly. The President, immediately following the explosion in Oklahoma City, without a moment's delay, was on the telephone to the Attorney General, the FBI, and the law enforcement community. And from the first half-hour, you saw assembled the most impressive law enforcement team ever put together in the history of the United States of America. I was there last week, watching them comb through every piece of the rubble of that building, down to pieces this big, getting every scrap of evidence that they could possibly find. It is an incredibly impressive operation.

Mr. King. Do you believe it was just two people?

The President. I believe we should let the investigation unfold.

[*The network took a commercial break*]

Habeas Corpus Legislation

Mr. King. In this segment, concerning legislation, there's apparently a confusion over whether you're for or against an amendment regarding habeas corpus.

The President. Well, in addition to the antiterrorism legislation, we've been trying to pass, and I tried to pass last year and failed to do it, a bill which would reform the habeas corpus procedure, the criminal appeals procedure.

Mr. King. So?

The President. In death penalty cases, it normally takes 8 years to exhaust the appeals; it's ridiculous. And if you have multiple convictions, it could take even longer. So there is a strong sense in the Congress, I think among Members of both parties, that we need to get down to sort of one clear appeal, we need to cut the time delay on the appeals dramatically, and that it ought to be done in the context of this terrorism legislation so that it would apply to any prosecutions brought against anyone indicted in Oklahoma. And I think it ought to be done.

You know, we have some differences about exactly what the details are and what the best and fairest way to do—to apply to all criminal cases, but I think it definitely ought to be done. We have—for 15 years, I have been trying to get Congress to clarify this. And I have strongly believed it for a very long time, since I was an attorney general and a Governor and I had been on the receiving end of these interminable appeals.

Mr. King. Are there those in Congress who think you're against this?

The Vice President. There are some in both parties who, in good conscience, think it would cause problems for a criminal procedure.

Mr. King. Constitutionally.

The Vice President. Well, they're worried about it. But the President's for it. And if they want to put the right version of it on this bill, fine.

The President. There are some good and bad—we don't have time to get into all of the details of it. There are things that I like better in some versions than others.

Mr. King. But you're, in essence, for it?

The President. I'm not only for it, we need to do it. You can't justify this lengthy appeals process.

1993 Tragedy in Waco, Texas

Mr. King. Are we going to have the full Waco story come out?

The President. Yes, but I think we already have had it. I mean, after all, we had an independent panel review what the ATF people did there. We've already had 10 congressional hearings on Waco. And I think the American people should remember that. I'd just like to remind you of the facts. There was action taken based on mistakes made. There is new leadership at the ATF. The facts were made known of what they did and the FBI did and others did, and there were 10 congressional hearings last year.

If they want to have other hearings, fine. But let's not lose the forest for the trees here. All this renewed interest in Waco came up by people who were worried about the fact that there would be a renewed interest in exploring the kind of militant groups that the suspect in the Oklahoma City bombing was involved with. So if they want to look into Waco, fine, but let's not forget what the real problem is here. The real problem is what happened at Oklahoma City.

At Waco, whatever else the facts are, it's clear there was a valid warrant. The people in the cult shot first and killed innocent Federal law enforcement officials. When the FBI went after them, based on their best available intelligence at the time, they killed the children there—the people there, not the Federal officials—the people in the cult did. And when they finally had their place inspected, what did we find? We found illegal machine guns, illegal explosives, and the capacity to build another 100 high-caliber illegal machine guns. And Koresh shot his way into the leadership of the cult.

So there's a lot of historical revision going on here to take people's attention off Oklahoma City.

[The network took a commercial break.]

Violence in Entertainment

Mr. King. People often ask, what do you talk about during breaks? We were talking about movies. Now, normally that would be considered inconsequential, except movies are suddenly political.

Okay, what do you make of Bob Dole and the charges that—well, I'll tell you something he said yesterday. He said, "Mr. Clinton will not criticize the movies like I do because if he needs a million dollars, he has to go to Hollywood." And he said, "If he needs $2 million, he has to go see Barbra Streisand, and she has to put on a concert." She'll be here tomorrow night, so I mentioned that. Your thoughts on Mr. Dole.

The President. Well, first of all, if I had any criticism it would be that the whole thing has been politicized, like in those comments you made.

The truth is, I was talking about violence and—in rap music and movies in 1992, in 1993. I went to Hollywood and met with a bunch of the people in production and challenged them to reduce it. I met with people—the members of—the representatives of television networks and challenged them. And I talked about it—if you remember, I got a big standing ovation in the State of the Union Address, talking about it.

Mr. King. So you agree with Senator Dole?

The President. So I think it's an absolutely legitimate point for discussion. Tipper Gore, years ago, long before there was any politics in it, was talking about how we needed to take——

Mr. King. Labeling records.

The President. Yes, and to take—and to just—so that people could know whether these things were consistent with what you'd want young children to see and hear.

I don't believe in censorship, and I don't believe in singling Hollywood out. What I believe we need to do is to say to ourselves, what has happened to our ability to have an American community that raises good citizens with good values, who are—who grow up into good people? That these kids—how do we reduce the teen violence? How do we reduce——

Mr. King. They're saying that Hollywood contributes to it.

The President. Well, I think—and I think that's—I think excessive exposure to mind-numbing violence or crass abuse of people in sexual and other ways has a bad impact on young children, especially if they don't have the kind of structure and other leadership in their life that they need.

But what I would say is that we need to ask ourselves: What does the entertainment community need to do? What does the media need to do? What does the business community need to do? What does the religious community need to do? What do the politicians need to do? What's our contribution to all this? That is, my only quarrel with all this is I don't want to see it politicized. I agree with a lot of what Senator Dole said. I don't know about the specific movies; I hadn't seen most of the ones he mentioned. But I think that we need to do this in a spirit not of dividing each other but of asking everybody to come forward and be accountable.

Mr. King. Is the rap on Time-Warner fair?

The Vice President. Well, I think that they have put out a lot of material that they shouldn't have. And it's not true that this administration hasn't talked about it. In fact, there was a public back-and-forth when one of their properties had some inappropriate material on President Reagan's Alzheimer's disease, and we said, "Hey, wait a minute." And they pulled it back. And I give them credit for that. And there have been other examples.

And let me say this: My wife, Tipper, began working on this and talking about this 18 years ago. And a few years after that, she began to get criticized from all parts. Before they were in the White House, Bill and Hillary Clinton were among the few who stood up and said, "We support what Tipper Gore is saying about this." And it took some doing, but she succeeded in getting the voluntary system of labeling for records. But she's continued talking about it. And she and I have appreciated the fact that this is the first President to talk about this in the State of the Union Address, to go to Hollywood and make a speech about it, and to take on this phenomenon in a responsible way, not in a partisan way.

Mr. King. Are you also against violent movies that Mr. Dole didn't mention, like "True Lies," let's say, a Schwarzenegger movie that had a lot of violence?

The President. Well, let me say—I don't want to get into critiquing every movie. There have been about 3,000 studies of the impact of constant exposure to violence on children through television and through the movies. Almost all of them, not all but almost all of them, conclude that what is really bad is the aggregate impact of it, the total volume of it, plus the treatment of violence as something casual and crass.

Mr. King. Everyday——

The President. Like you and I were talking about "Braveheart." That's a violent movie, but it doesn't glorify violence. It's ugly, and it's awful.

Now, I feel that we ought to go after this in a responsible way. I was not upset when Senator Dole raised this issue. I just don't think any of us ought to be doing it as a way of sort of dividing the American people.

You know, we ought to get on this—a friend of mine said today, we need to get on the solution side of these problems. We need to challenge Hollywood. Most of these people, they're good people out there. They want to do the right thing. And we're not talking about censorship; we're talking about responsible, honest debate. We all have to say, what contribution are we making to creating an America that is too divided, that doesn't raise good children with strong values who are good, law-abiding citizens when they grow up?

Mr. King. We'll be back. We'll include some phone calls for the President and Vice President of the United States right after this.

[*The network took a commercial break.*]

Mr. King. Timeth flieth. We're moving along. Let's take a call. Jameson, Pennsylvania, for President Clinton and Vice President Gore. Hello.

Q. Hello. Good evening. Thank you, Larry, for the opportunity.

Mr. King. You're welcome.

Negative Criticism

Q. Good evening, President Clinton and Vice President Gore. This is indeed an honor. Like you, President Clinton, I saw President Kennedy when I was younger, and it has sparked my interest in studying the Presidency.

Mr. King. Ma'am, I wish you would get right to the question. I don't mean to interrupt, but we have long——

Q. My question is, I respect the Presidency of the United States, and I think it's an important job. How frustrating is it for you to try to get your message out to the people when it seems like the opposing party is criticizing you constantly?

Mr. King. What do you make of the daily hate? There is a lot of hate in America.

The President. There is, and I would say to her, I don't mind the daily criticism. What I don't like and don't agree with is the sort of atmosphere of negativism and cynicism. That is, I should be criticized by people who disagree with me; we should have an honest debate. That's really the way you make progress in this country. But we have gotten to be entirely too negative and cynical and divisive, and that's one of our country's big problems. We need to get out of being quite so partisan and quite so personal and quite so interested in the destruction of our opponents.

This country, with all of its problems, no other country would trade places with us as we get ready to go into this new century, because our productivity, the strength of our people, the wealth of our resources, the diversity of our population in a global economy—if we can just figure out a way to restore middle class dreams and middle class values and pull this country together, there's no stopping the United States.

So I say to the lady, it bothers me not to be criticized, but it bothers me that there is an atmosphere that is more negative than positive. America should be more positive than negative.

1996 Presidential Election

Mr. King. A couple of political things. Do you think Senator Dole will be your opponent?

The Vice President. I don't know. I don't know.

Mr. King. Do you think so?

The Vice President. It looks that way now, but it's impossible to tell. It's so far off.

The President. I don't know. One thing I've learned watching this for 30 years, is you can't tell now who will be there then.

Mr. King. Mr. Gingrich will be in New Hampshire all weekend; so will you. You'll be there for Dartmouth on Sunday. Do you think

he might enter the race? That's just a thought. You know, just three people talking.

The President. I don't know. You've got to ask him. I really don't know. I talk to him all the time, but not about this.

Mr. King. Would you regard it as a challenge if he did? Do you think he'll——

The President. Well, it would be interesting. Of course, he'd have to be nominated first. But it would be interesting.

Mr. King. Senator—Mr. Vice President? I'm so used to calling him——

The Vice President. I'm still in the——

Mr. King. I know, you're still in the Senate.

The Vice President. I'm still in the Senate. And you know, the experience of voting in the Senate's made me a more optimistic person, because I've noticed that every time I vote, we win. [*Laughter*]

Mr. King. Good line.

The Vice President. But to answer your question, I don't know. It sounds——

Mr. King. Would it be formidable?

The Vice President. You know, we're not going to rank any potential opponents for the President. Anybody who got the nomination would be, by definition, the nominee of the other party and formidable. But it sounds to me like he kind of wants to, but maybe I have it wrong, and I have no idea.

Mr. King. Mr. Perot has called a meeting in Dallas with his large group. He says every Republican candidate has agreed to go. Will you go?

The Vice President. I'm inclined not to go, because I have a lot of respect for the United We Stand group, and I hope that they will review my record in terms of what they said they wanted done in 1992, because I have done or advocated a vast majority of what they did. But I don't believe—I think the President's in a little different category. I don't think the President should start the politicking too soon. I've got a job; I'm supposed to be working for the American people. I'm trying to work with this new Republican Congress, and I want to diminish partisan politics and my personal politics for as long as I can.

Q. Therefore, you'll ask the Vice President not to go, either?

The President. We haven't even discussed it. I'm telling you what my instinct is.

The Vice President. I don't plan to go. I think that the party chair has already expressed his intention to go.

Mr. King. He will go?

The Vice President. Yes.

Surgeon General Nominee Henry Foster

Mr. King. Foster, is he going to go through?

The President. I think he will. I think we're very close to having the votes to break filibuster, and I think a filibuster would be wrong. He's a good man. He cleared the committee; he was treated fairly, in a bipartisan way. He had all those kids from Tennessee from those housing projects come up and say, "Here's a guy that told us to abstain from premature sex, to stay off drugs, to be good people." That's the message we need going out to America's children.

Mr. King. Is Senator Dole going to bring it to the floor?

The Vice President. I hope he will. Nobody in America is better qualified to lead a crusade against this epidemic of teen pregnancy.

Mr. King. And you think they'll override a Gramm filibuster if it comes to the floor?

The President. I don't see how a majority of the Senate, even 60 percent of them, could say this man's not entitled to a vote, up or down.

[The network took a commercial break.]

Balanced Budget

Mr. King. We're back. The Republican National Committee sent out a news release today, Haley Barbour talking about your appearance tonight on this program and saying, 3 years ago on this show you promised the American people you would offer a plan to balance the budget. Do you have such a plan?

The President. Well, as you know, I have said that I will work with the Republicans to balance the budget. And at the proper time, I will offer how I think the best way to do is.

But let's just point out, in 1994, the Republicans told the American people all I did was raise taxes. And they basically turned things upside down; they won the Congress. But what we did, in fact, was to use their 7-year number. We reduced the deficit by a trillion dollars 3 years in a row for the first time since Truman was President. They talked about how terrible it was, but it produced low interest rates, high growth, 6.3 million new jobs.

And I might say to the American people, the Republican plan does not repeal my plan, it builds on it. If they didn't take the deficit reduction we'd already achieved, they could never get to a balance in 7 years or any other figure.

Mr. King. So you say we're going to have something from you after——

The President. So I think—I'll be happy to work with them, but I want—I thought it was important, after they won the election on a set of specific promises, that they have a chance to go and say how they thought it should be done.

Now, you know what I think is wrong with their budget. I think that it cuts Medicare and other health programs to the elderly way too much. It cuts education too much. It uses those cuts to finance a tax cut that is entirely too large and tilted to upper income individuals who are doing very well in the present economy and who basically just want us to get the deficit down.

So, we need to do this, but there's a right way and a wrong way to do it. And at the proper time, I will say what I think the right way is.

Mr. King. And the proper time is imminent or not imminent?

The President. I will do it when I think the proper time is.

Mr. King. Dana Point, California, with Vice President Gore and President Clinton—hello.

Q. Hi, Larry. I enjoy your show. My name is Michelle Denise. Also, I'd like you to know I enjoy Jerry Spence.

Mr. King. Everybody does. He's an international hero, Jerry Spence.

Q. He is quite a character.

The President. He looks good in those jackets.

Mr. King. Doesn't he? Boy. This trial is going forever, right?

Okay.

Defense Base Closures

Q. This question is both for Mr. Clinton and Gore. Are we going to continue our military base closures in consideration that we might possibly be spreading ourselves too thin——

Mr. King. Any chance of that?

The Vice President. Well, the base closure procedure is locked into law. It's bipartisan in nature. It has caused a lot of difficulty. The President has directed his Cabinet to address the problems that have been created. There have been some very imaginative plans to try to use some of these facilities for other purposes and bring back employment and new opportunities in the community. But this was put into place long before we got here, and according to the law, it's going to continue for a while.

The President. But let me answer the security concern the lady raised. Defense spending peaked in about 1987 and since then has been cut about 40 percent. We have suggested that we add back a few billion dollars so we can get our training and our readiness up and support a good quality of life so we can keep first-rate people in the military, because it's the people that make it go.

The answer to your question, ma'am, is that we actually have more base capacity than the number of our men and women in uniform would justify. So we have to bring down the bases a little more so that they're basically in line with the size of our forces. The size of our forces now will enable to meet our security needs and meet our strategic objectives. But we can't cut it a lot more. We should stay about where we are.

Mr. King. Barbra Streisand is here tomorrow night. And are you both fans of hers? Do you like her speaking out on politics, by the way?

The President. I think she's—just as—if we have a right to speak out on entertainment, I think she has the right to speak out on politics. [*Laughter*] I think that she should do it.

Mr. King. David Letterman is here on Friday.

The Vice President. Tell him I said hello.

Mr. King. I will. Do you plan to return to that show?

The Vice President. I hope to sometime.

Mr. King. Would you recommend the President even appear with David?

The Vice President. I'm going to let him make that decision. [*Laughter*]

The President. But you know, since we got this procurement reform passed, there are no more of those $10 ashtrays and $500 hammers. So he's got no gig anymore. [*Laughter*]

Mr. King. Thanks, guys. You don't want to do a Brando close, do you? [*Laughter*]

The Vice President. Just a handshake. [*Laughter*]

Mr. King. Just a handshake.

The President. We've enjoyed doing the show.

Mr. King. Oh, let me—here—President Clinton does Brando. Do it once.

The Vice President. You missed it.

The President. It's been great being on your show, Larry.

Mr. King. Thank you.

The President. You're a good man; you've got a real future in this business. [*Laughter*]

Mr. King. Thank you. Thank you.

The President. Good night.

Mr. King. Good night.

The Vice President. Good night.

NOTE: The interview began at 9 p.m. in the Library at the White House.

Remarks to the National Governors' Association Summit on Young Children in Baltimore, Maryland
June 6, 1995

Thank you very much. To Governor Dean and Governor Leavitt and all of the Governors who are here, Governor Glendening and Mayor Schmoke and Congressman Cardin: I'm glad to be back in Baltimore. I'm going to have to register as a citizen and begin to pay taxes if I don't stay out of your State a little more, Governor.

I am delighted to be here in Baltimore because Baltimore was one of the six cities which won a highly contested race for the empowerment zones in our country. And I con-

gratulate Mayor Schmoke on that, and I look forward to his work, along with the Governor and others, in making Baltimore an even stronger and greater city as a result of that.

Governor Dean, I want to thank you for your leadership of the Governors' Association. I don't think I ever enjoyed any job more than being chairman of the Governors' Association, although it was not always easy to please all the Governors. I think it's still not always easy to please all of the Governors. [*Laughter*]

I'm delighted to see so many representatives of State government, county government, local government here. My good friend Representative Blue from North Carolina, it's nice to see you here; Representative Campbell; and Commissioner Franke, thank you for your work, sir.

I thank all of you for coming here to meet about the fate of our children. This has been a concern of mine, as the Governor said, for a long time and, of course, a profound concern for my wife. When I met her, she was spending an extra year in law school to do 4 years instead of 3, so that she could devote a year to the study of the laws that affected our children. And I might say she then predicted a lot of the more disturbing trends which we've seen unfold in our country over the last 20 years.

Hillary is working on a book now about children's issues and the responsibilities we owe to them, and she picked the title of the old African proverb, "It takes a village to raise a child." I want to come back to that a little bit during my remarks because I think there is a great difference of opinion about that in the United States today. I began with the premise that the first responsibility for children lies with their parents, but that since all our futures are bound up in theirs, the rest of us share a responsibility in the United States and in our States and in our communities for their welfare. I do believe, in other words, that it takes a village to raise a child, especially when you consider the facts of life that children face today.

I ran for this job because I wanted to ensure a better future for our children, to ensure that instead of losing so many of our children and seeing so many of them grow up with the American dream beyond their grasp, that they could be rewarded for their work and that the values that we all share of work and family and community would be stronger, not weaker, when they came of age.

I realized that people my daughter's age were in danger of growing up to be the first generation of Americans to do worse economically than their parents but, perhaps even more important, to live in a country that was less supportive of the kind and quality of life that most people in my generation took for granted.

The recent report of the Carnegie Corporation tends to corroborate a lot of those disturbing trends with statistics you all know well. In "The Quiet Crisis," they say that still, after years

of effort, compared to other industrialized countries, our infant mortality rates are higher, our low-birth-weight baby rates are higher, our teen pregnancy rates are much higher, our childhood immunization rates are lower, and of course, our children are subjected to far, far higher rates of violence in the United States than they would be in any other country in the world.

If we are going to rescue our children's future, we have to do a number of things. We have to grow the middle class and shrink the under class. We have to support policies that reinforce work and families and communities. We have to change the way the Government operates so that it promotes independence, not dependence, opportunity and not bureaucracy. We have to give our youngest children things that they can't guarantee for themselves.

If you believe it takes a whole village to raise a child, it means that the Government has a responsibility, working with people in the private sector, to guarantee children who can't get it for themselves health, safety, and education, and then when they get older, to empower them to make the most of their own lives. To do that, I believe we need not another ideological war but a passionate and practical commitment to what we know will work. The whole issue of welfare is at the core of that.

But let me just say for a moment, for the last 2½ years a great deal of what I have sought to do has been centered in that conviction, that we have to have a passionate and practical effort to go beyond ideological wars right to the heart of what will make life better for our children. We've worked hard to strengthen families and to give children a better start.

The earned-income credit will now provide a tax reduction for working families with children with incomes below $27,000 an average of $1,000 a year. That's a pro-family policy. We should continue that, not reverse it.

The family and medical leave law, more than anything I've done as President, has caused ordinary citizens to come up to me and say, "Thank you. I had a sick child. I had a sick spouse. My wife had a baby. We were able to continue to work and to provide for ourselves. We were able to be good parents and successful workers." That, it seem to me, is the kind of thing that we ought to do.

Secretary Shalala, who is here, has worked very hard to expand immunization so that all our children under the age of 2 will be properly immunized by the turn of the century. We have expanded Head Start dramatically. The Goals 2000 program in which many of you have participated—most of you have—emphasizes grassroots reforms to achieve national, indeed, international standards of excellence.

When children are more independent, we have given them access to lower cost, better repayment terms for college loans with tougher requirements to repay them. We've worked with you for more apprenticeship programs for the young people who don't go to 4-year colleges and universities, through the school-to-work program. And of course, many of you have been very active in the national service program, AmeriCorps, which gives our young people a chance to give something back to their communities and earn more funds to go on to school. And I want to say a special word of thanks to Senator Mikulski of Maryland for her work on national service.

The crime bill was an important part of this because it emphasized not simply more punishment and more prisons but also protecting children through 100,000 more police officers on the street and through prevention programs that give our young people something to say yes to as well as something to say no to.

We were able to do those things and still reduce the deficit. The new majority in Congress uses 7-year terms. We use—the deficit is going down by a trillion dollars over 7 years, thanks to the '93 and '94 budgets. More than 6.3 million new jobs came into our economy. But we did it while saying that it takes a whole village to raise a child; that children deserve education, health, and safety; that families should be strengthened and supported; that work should be exalted; and that parents have to be able to succeed in the world we are living in, both as parents and as workers.

One thing we did not do is to pass comprehensive welfare reform. And that is now what is before the Congress. And that, more than anything else in this debate, captures a lot of the philosophical arguments that are at the core of what is going on in our national discussion today.

I don't think there's any question that I believe we ought to reform the welfare system. I was proud to represent the Governors when the Family Support Act was written under President Reagan's administration with strong bipartisan support. I realize what the shortcomings of

it are, especially since it was never properly funded. And therefore, I have now given, the Secretary and I have, 29 of the 50 States exemptions from Federal rules and regulations to pursue your own path to welfare reform to move people to work. Nothing like that has ever been done before.

In Missouri, Vermont, and Wisconsin, Governors Carnahan, Dean, and Thompson are using their waivers to impose time limits and to require work. In Ohio and Oregon, Governors Voinovich and Kitzhaber are moving people to work by using money now spent on welfare and food stamps to subsidize private sector jobs. Others are doing other things that are very important. Every Governor I've ever spoken with, without regard to party, understands that welfare reform is important and must, first and foremost, be about work.

Unfortunately, to my mind, the welfare reform bill in Congress—or the debate—has not focused as much as it should have about work. And I believe that in important respects, the tenor of the debate not only in the House but also in the Senate puts both children and States at risk. The House bill, clearly, was too tough on children and too weak on work. Finally, after a lot of efforts, the House did agree to be tough on deadbeat parents, something that everyone among the Governors agreed it needed to be done. The Senate Finance Committee reported a bill out the other day that clearly is a step in the right direction in many areas but, I believe, still misses the point on work and on children.

According to the Congressional Budget Office, the current Senate Finance Committee bill will not succeed in moving people from welfare to work. The Congressional Budget Office—and the person who wrote the report was generally acknowledged to be one of the preeminent Republican experts on welfare reform—concluded that only six of our States would be able to fulfill the bill's work requirements in the year 2000 with the bill's funding provisions. Forty-four States will fail. Six out of fifty in baseball is a .120 batting average. You can't play for the Orioles with that batting average; you can't stay in the minor leagues. And you sure won't elevate children or end welfare as we know it.

The reason the Senate bill failed on the standard of work seems to me is clear. It takes away the tools that States now use to move people from welfare to work: child care, job training, greater incentives for job placement.

I very much want to work across party lines to solve this problem. But if we're going to end welfare as we know it, Congress must pass a bill that meets some basic principles. First, we have to require people who can work to go to work and make sure that they have the child care to do it so that they don't have to hurt their children to do the right thing as citizens. It defies common sense to insist that people go to work when they have very young children if doing so will actually cost them money.

Second, the legislation should have real work requirements, but it ought to be backed up with the resources necessary to get people into jobs and keep them there. According to the CBO, the Congressional Budget Office, it would cost you, the States, $10 billion a year by the year 2000 to meet these requirements just in the Senate bill. And yet, this bill asks you to meet these requirements with less money than you have now.

Now, I was a Governor long enough to remember what an unfunded mandate is. A lot of you—Governor Voinovich was in the Rose Garden celebrating when we signed the unfunded mandates bill; I strongly supported it. Just because this doesn't say it's one doesn't mean it isn't by another term. So I think we have to look at this forthrightly.

The third thing that I think is important is that welfare reform should have real incentives to reward the States who do succeed in putting people to work, not for cutting them off. The current bill gives States an incentive instead to save money simply by throwing people off the welfare roles. The House bill even gives States what the Catholic Church has called an illegitimacy bonus, an incentive for more people to have abortions. That is not welfare reform. If we're going to change the culture of welfare, we have got to reward success, we've got to depart from the status quo. I want a performance bonus but one that will force the welfare bureaucracy and the welfare recipients to focus on work.

The fourth thing I believe is that the legislation should protect States so they can continue to move people from welfare to work even when there is an economic downturn, extraordinary population growth, or unpredictable emergencies. In their current forms, these bills could really hurt the high-population States, the

growth States, like Florida and Utah and others, and could put every State at risk in the next recession or profound natural disaster.

Finally, let me say we ought to protect our children. If you believe it takes a whole village to raise a child, we should avoid mean-spirited restrictions on benefits to children. We should avoid cuts in child nutrition and adoption and child protective services. We should give States more flexibility, but we should also make sure States continue to fulfill their responsibilities. The proposed legislation contains no incentives or requirements for States to maintain their own funding for cash assistance or for child care or work supports.

Now, I know that if you believe in the pure theory of State experimentation—and you know that I believe a lot of that, because if you just look at what's in these 29 waivers, I have pretty much gone along with anything the States wanted to do to move people from welfare to work. So you might argue that, in theory, if we believe that States ought to have great flexibility, why don't we just give them a block grant without any requirement for local maintenance or anything of that kind? But the serious danger there is that this will become a race to the bottom. It's always cheaper to cut people off welfare than to move them to work. It will always be cheaper to lower benefits than to figure out how to reduce the caseload by moving them to work.

We already do less for young children than most of our major competitors—perhaps all of our major competitors—throughout the world. And I just believe that we cannot allow welfare reform to be a race to the bottom.

Let me say again, I know in theory it's right, but let me remind all of you, I served for 12 years as a Governor. I served in good times and bad times. I know that the last 2 years, this is the second year in a row when in all probability all 50 States will have economic growth. That is a highly unusual circumstance over the last two decades.

And I'm just telling you, I've been in enough State legislatures in my life, not just in my State but all around this country, to know what's going to happen. If you put this welfare reform block grant with less money and no local maintenance requirement up against the Medicaid cuts and the education cuts and the other things that are in this budget, you tell me how the poor children of your State are going to fare when they have to deal with the nursing home lobby. And I'm not complaining about the nursing home lobby; you just tell me how they're going to fare.

You know, everybody wants to cut Medicaid to shreds, because they say that's just a poor person's health care. You know as well as I do almost 70 percent of that money goes to the elderly and the disabled. And they're all coming to see you and your State legislators.

Now, how are they going to do? How are these poor children going to do? How are they going to do against some of my favorite lobbies—the education lobbies? How are they going to do? Not very well. How are they going to do against a lobby that no one can say no to, the prison lobby? The crime rate goes up, and your legislature stiffens sentences, and people don't want you paroling folks that have no business on the street. And the only way you can get this Federal money for prisons is if you promise to leave people in longer and ignore your own parole laws. When you have to match that money or build prisons on your own, how are you going to stand up and say, "Well, somehow we're going to keep doing what we used to do for poor children?"

And you can walk away and say, "Well, what we used to do doesn't work, so maybe we shouldn't do anything." But the truth is we do less—I will say it again—we do less for children than the countries with which we compete.

And this is not a partisan issue, at least it never has been before. Everything that happened in the last 2 years on Head Start, on every education initiative we did, on the family and medical leave, every single thing was a bipartisan issue, everything.

Now, I think there are two big debates that are undergirding this welfare debate, and I'd like to just put it out on the table today. One is the debate about what causes people to be on welfare. Is it economic and politics, or is it culture? That's really what's behind all this debate about what's in the movies and in the rap lyrics and all.

And by the way, I think it's a positive thing. You know, Mrs. Gore was talking 18 years ago about the dangers of destructive entertainment forces on children. I've been challenging Hollywood and the television networks to reduce violence for years. I don't mind this debate. I think this is a good debate.

But the truth is, it's not either/or. You see, there was one young girl interviewed in a movie line last week—asked her, what do you think about this debate in Washington about whether movies were causing the breakdown of families. And she said, "Well, my father's working three jobs. I'll tell you, that's not good for our family. I wish he'd just come home and spend some time with me."

On the other hand, people who deny that culture is a force are wrong. The States in this country with the lowest incarceration rates also have the highest high school graduation rates, and they often don't spend the most money. There are almost no poor children in families with two parents in the home. So if I could just wave a magic wand and make this problem go away, I would never have another kid in a home where there weren't two parents until the child reached a certain age so that then the child could take care of himself or herself. That would be a wonderful thing if that could be done. And in that sense, there is a cultural component to all this.

So the people that are out there exhorting parents to be more responsible, and especially male parents to be more responsible, people like this Promise Keepers group, they deserve our support. They deserve our support. There is a cultural element in all this. But to say that there is no national responsibility on the economic and political side, I think is just plain wrong and defies the experience of every, single, solitary country in the world. And I might add that all the people that are out there working in the private charities, go interview them and ask them if they think that we can just walk away from this.

So I would say, this cultural debate is a very good thing, and we ought to have it. But there is plainly a political and economic root to this. If you look at rising poverty and stagnating middle class incomes in this country, it is clearly the result of international economic trends sweeping all advanced countries and national economic policies. And all those things are reinforced, one with another.

We are on the verge of having a 40-year low in the minimum wage. Why would somebody who was on welfare who had two kids, who at least had health care from Medicaid and they've got food stamps, go to work if we won't even raise the minimum wage to keep it up to where it was 10 years ago—in fact, we're going to let it go to a 40-year low?

So I implore you, Governors are supposed to be the places where people look at the real world and they get away from all this theory and look at the practice. There's a political and an economic element to this problem, and there is a cultural element to the problem. That is one big deal. I think there is a public responsibility and there is a private responsibility, both, not either/or.

There's another debate going on here which is, what is the most important thing we can do to help grow the economy and stabilize the society? And on one side of that debate there are those who say the most important thing we can do is to reduce the deficit and shrink the Government, and nothing else really matters because the Federal Government would mess up a one-car parade.

And on the other side of that debate are not people who say we need a big Government, we need an expanded bureaucracy; that debate is not existent in Washington. You look at the record. We have reduced already, with the two budgets already adopted, the size of the Federal Government by 270,000. Congressman Cardin's already voted to do that, to bring the Federal Government to its smallest size since President Kennedy was President. We've had dramatic changes in regulation. The 29 States with the waivers from Federal rules on welfare is just one example. The deficit has been brought down three times in a row for the first time since Mr. Truman was here. Nobody is for a higher deficit. That is not the issue.

The issue is, are there any other responsibilities of the National Government? I believe there are some. I think we have to help people who cannot help themselves through no fault of their own, not because they're irresponsible but through no fault of their own, like little children who are poor. And I think we have to empower people to make the most of their own lives, because that way we'll all be better off. That's what I believe. Therefore, I don't think that you can sacrifice our responsibility to educate people and our responsibility for basic health and safety, security issues, on the altar of deficit reduction.

You know, sometimes I think my big problem is that I was for some of these things before they were popular, like deficit reduction.

Everybody's for it now. That doesn't mean we didn't do a lot of it in the last 2 years.

So we have to decide that. Now, don't kid yourself—from the point of view of the Congress, welfare reform has stopped being welfare reform primarily. Primarily welfare reform is a way to cut spending on the poor, so that we don't have to worry about it and we can balance the budget in 7 years and give a big tax cut, largely benefiting upper income people who have done pretty well in the 1980's. That's what this is about.

It is true that a lot of people genuinely believe the States ought to have more say over this. So do I. It is true that a lot of people believe the prior system didn't do much good for people who were permanently dependent on welfare. So do I, and I have for 15 years. But we should not confuse—if we really say it's more important to cut spending so that we can balance the budget in 7 years and still give a tax increase to upper income people, even if we're going to hurt poor children, people ought to just say that flat out because that's what's really underneath this.

So I ask you to think about it. What's it going to be like the next time the coasts are growing and the Middle West is in a depression, when the farmland goes to pieces? What's it going to be like the next time there's a high-tech collapse and the coasts are in trouble and only the heartland is doing well? What's it going to be like the next time we have a serious national recession if there is not even a maintenance-of-effort requirement, if there is no real effort to have work? You know what it's going to be like. You'll have less people moving from welfare to work, more people getting less money, and the most important thing is our children, our future, will be in more difficult circumstances.

You could not design a program that would be too tough on work for me. You could not design a program that would give the States any more flexibility than I want to give them as long as we recognize that we, our American village, have a responsibility to our children and that in the end, our political and economic policies must reinforce the culture we're trying to create. They ought to be pro-family and pro-work. But if we get in the fix in this country where people cannot succeed as parents without being derelict at work or they cannot succeed at work without being derelict to their children, which is exactly what exists for too many people in America today or that is their deep worry, then we are going to suffer. We are going to suffer economically, and we are going to suffer culturally.

Now, I think this is a huge opportunity. We can save some money and reduce the deficit in this welfare area. I have proposed that. I think we can. I don't believe every penny we're spending is sacrosanct, but I just would say to you we must not walk away, and you should not walk away, and you shouldn't want us to put you in a position to walk away from our fundamental responsibilities. Just imagine all the debates that are going to occur here. Children are not very well organized. Poor children are very poorly organized. They will not do well on balance in all the State legislatures of the country the next time things are really bad and, especially, after all the other budget cuts come down to all the other people who will also be on your doorstep.

We can have welfare reform. We can balance the budget. We can shrink the Government and still be faithful to our fundamental responsibilities to our children and our future. Let's don't make it either/or. Let's do it all, do it right, and take this country to the next century in good shape.

Thank you, and God bless you all.

NOTE: The President spoke at 1:38 p.m. at the Stouffer Renaissance Harbor Place. In his remarks, he referred to Governors Howard Dean of Vermont, Mike Leavitt of Utah, Parris N. Glendening of Maryland, Mel Carnahan of Missouri, Tommy G. Thompson of Wisconsin, George V. Voinovich of Ohio, and John A. Kitzhaber of Oregon; Mayor Kurt Schmoke of Baltimore; State legislators Daniel T. Blue of North Carolina and Jane L. Campbell of Ohio; and Randall Franke, president, National Association of Counties.

Letter to Congressional Leaders Transmitting a Report on Conflict Resolution in Africa
June 6, 1995

Dear Mr. Chairman:

Pursuant to Public Law 103–381, Sections 8 and 9, I hereby transmit the Inter-Agency Plan and Progress Report on Conflict Resolution in Africa.

Sincerely,

WILLIAM J. CLINTON

NOTE: Identical letters were sent to Jesse Helms, chairman, Senate Committee on Foreign Relations; Mark Hatfield, chairman, Senate Committee on Appropriations; Benjamin A. Gilman, chairman, House Committee on International Relations; and Bob Livingston, chairman, House Committee on Appropriations. This letter was released by the Office of the Press Secretary on June 7. An original was not available for verification of the content of this letter.

Remarks at the Safe and Drug-Free Schools Recognition Program
June 7, 1995

Jaime, I think I can speak for every adult in this audience today and say that there's not a person here who wouldn't be proud to be your parent when you graduate from high school tomorrow. Thank you, and God bless you for everything you've done and said. Thank you,

Marilyn, for being here. Thank you, Director Brown, and thank you, Secretary Riley.

Ladies and gentlemen, the statement you just heard from this fine young woman, about to begin her life after high school, is as clear an example as I could ever think of of what I think we ought to be doing as a country. You hear all these debates up here in Washington about whether the Government should do this, that, or the other thing, whether our problems are fundamentally to be addressed by political action, or whether all of our problems are just cultural and if people would just simply take responsibility for themselves and do the right thing we wouldn't have any problems, and therefore we should just ignore any spending call— nothing is really worth investing in, let's just make everybody do the right thing.

The truth is, in the real world we need to do both things. Parents have to set better examples; they have to teach their children. We need to tell young people at the earliest possible age, "There comes a time in life when you cannot blame other people for your own problems, and whatever your difficulties are, you have to behave and you have to take control of your own lives." But it's also true that, in the meanwhile, somebody has to pay to protect these children if they need protection to be safe in school, and somebody has to make provision to bring people into the schools who can do the kinds of things that Jaime talked about, who can be the role models, who can talk about how to diffuse conflict, who can talk about how to avoid violence, who can talk about the imperative of staying off of drugs, which is still, I would remind you, at the root of more than half of the problems that we're dealing with in this country today.

So this is one more time a phony, overly politicized debate here. It's not either/or; it is both. And we have responsibilities here, those of us who work here, to make sure that every single child in America has a chance to get out of school safe and educated and be the kind of person that was reflected in what Jaime said here today. We have a partnership obligation to do that for America.

That is at the heart of a lot of arguments we're having here in Washington. Last night I received Congress's rescission bill. The rescission bill cuts spending from this year's budget. I believe we ought to do that and make another downpayment on balancing our budget. I've done everything I could to cut this deficit. In 1993, unfortunately with only Democrats voting for it, we voted for a deficit-reduction program and passed it and I signed it, which reduced the deficit over the 7-year period now popularly discussed by $1 trillion. I believe in cutting the deficit.

We froze discretionary spending completely, which means every time we gave more money to education, we had to cut something else. And we did it gladly. We cut waste and duplication and bureaucracy and committed to reduce the size of the Federal Government by 270,000 people. But we increased investment in Head Start. We made college loans more available, more affordable. We supported schools with the Goals 2000 programs, which were not mandates from the Federal Government but were programs like the safe and drug-free school program, where we give money to local school districts and they decide how you can make the school safest, how you can make the schools the most drug-free, just the approach the leadership of this new Congress says they favor, let people at the local level make more of their decisions. But we thought we ought to be partners because not every local school district had the money to guarantee safety and the best possible efforts to make children safe, to make them learn how to avoid violence and to stay drug-free.

Now, after all this, I can tell you that the budget today would be in balance, today, but for the interest we'll have to pay this year on the debt that was run up in the 12 years before I became President. That is the problem. We took leave of our collective financial senses about a dozen years ago and began to put this country in the ditch. And we've got to take it out. But we cannot do it overnight. And we must recognize that the only deficit in this country is not the budget deficit, there's a deficit in this country in the number of drug-free children. There's a deficit in this country in the number of safe schools. There's an education deficit in this country. And we dare not ignore those problems. We can do both. That's the right way to approach this problem.

I worked in good faith with Members of the Congress to craft a rescission bill that would cut spending by a set amount and do it in the right way. I actually agreed with the spending cuts passed by the United States Senate with a bipartisan majority, an overwhelming bipartisan majority, because it protected programs like the drug-free school program, the national service program, the education programs that we're working so hard on. Unfortunately, what happened is after the Senate passed the bill, they went into a closed-door conference with Members of the House who had passed a bill that did cut all these things, and instead of cutting more spending, they took out a lot of education investment. They took out half the drug-free school money and substituted courthouses, highways, and city streets in selected States and congressional districts. In other words, they decided to cut school safety to increase pork.

The bill cuts, as Secretary Riley says, half of the safe and drug-free schools money this year in anticipation of eliminating it altogether next year. Now, I'm sure that all the people that voted to do it will tell you, "We favor these efforts; we just think people ought to do the right thing." Well, I think people ought to do the right thing, too. But if Jaime knows what she's talking about—and the chances are she knows a lot more about this than most people who live in Washington, DC, and work for the Federal Government in the Congress or the executive branch—in order to do that, we need a partnership. We need public action and personal responsibility.

I cannot in good conscience sign a bill that cuts education to save pet congressional projects. That is old politics; it is wrong. It wasn't a good policy when we were increasing spending on everything. It is a terrible policy if you're going to cut education to put pork back in. If we're going to cut spending to balance the budget, we must be even more careful about how we spend the money we do have. And we have to put education and our children and their future first.

So in just a few moments, I'm going to go over there and veto that bill. But I want to say this: I lived and worked here for 2 years with a crowd that had the "just say no" philosophy, and unfortunately it wasn't about drugs: Just say no, and then go out and tell the American people nothing is happening, even when it is. And a lot of people in our party think, "Well, that policy benefited them so much at the polls last November, why don't we do it? Why don't we just say no now? That seems to be what's popular." It may be popular in the short run, but it is wrong for America.

I do not want to just say no. I have not said no to this. I agreed to the spending cuts passed by the Senate by Republicans and Democrats. And so what I'm going to do, when I veto this, is to say yes. I'm going to send this bill right back. And this bill says, "Take out the pork; put back the education; send it on over. Let's cut spending and protect education and protect safe and drug-free schools."

I want to say one other thing, too. In this so-called spending cut bill, at the last moment there was also, I think, a very bad environmental provision added, which says that no environmental laws will apply for the next 3 years to any cutting of so-called salvage timber in our forests, and we'll just have the taxpayers pay for whatever damage occurs to the environment. Well, ladies and gentlemen, we're here on education, but the most pro-environment people in America are the children of America. And they know they've got the biggest dog in that hunt, as we say back home, because they're going to be around here longer and their children will be around here longer. Nobody has worked any harder than I have to start logging again in our country's forests in an appropriate way. Suspending all the environmental laws of the country for 3 years is not the appropriate way.

So what I want to do is to say to the Congress, "Look, just put the education back in; take the pork out." I'm for actually slightly more spending cuts than they are—that's their wind blowing, not mine. [*Laughter*] The nice thing is—now you'll all look at the chart. [*Laughter*] You can see I'm actually for slightly bigger spending cuts than they are. I just don't think we ought to use this spending bill to do something bad to the environment, and I certainly don't think we ought to use it to cut out half the safe and drug-free schools money to build courthouses and city streets and pet highway projects. That is not good judgment. We need a partnership here. This is the right thing we should be doing.

Let me just say one other thing about this cutting spending. I have now seen two separate news reports in which the majority in Congress, according to some of their members, say that they have decided not to pass the line-item veto after all, after campaigning on it for a dozen years now. This line-item veto is a tool that would permit the President to single out special pork projects, veto them, send them back to Congress, and Congress would be able to override the veto. But they would have to vote on these projects separately instead of burying them in big bills that a President cannot in good conscience veto.

Now, that line-item veto was part of their Contract With America and a part that I embraced. President Reagan was for it. President Bush was for it. The House passed it on President Reagan's birthday. They talked about what an urgent thing it was. Now they say they don't think they ought to give it to me this year because I might use it. [*Laughter*]

Well, today I am sending a letter to the Speaker of the House and the Senate Majority Leader, asking them once again to send me the line-item veto. They have said they were for it for a dozen years. They have portrayed it as the salvation of all of our problems. It's not the salvation, but it's an important part of it. And they say they're worried that I might line-item veto special tax breaks instead of special spending increases. It's six of one and half dozen of the other. But I'll make them a deal: If they'll send me the line-item veto this year, I will not line-item any tax cuts they sign. If they pass all these big tax cuts and wreck education and Medicare to cut taxes, I'll veto the whole thing. But I've already said that. But I will not—if they'll send it to me this year, I won't use it on any tax legislation. I will only use it on spending.

So I ask them again: Send me the bill. Send me the bill. Send me the line-item veto, and I will see whether America agrees that what we ought to do is to protect education, to protect things designed to enhance our security like safe and drug-free schools, to protect the welfare and the future of our children, and I will show you once again that there is nobody who wants to reduce the deficit and to balance the budget more than I do. I just want our incomes to go up and our future to be stronger and our kids to be healthier and better educated when we do it. Send it back here, let me sign it, and let's get to work and prove we're serious.

I want to say again that the primary purpose of this event is to honor all of you who have worked to make the safe and drug-free schools program work. I don't think I have had any more moving experiences than going into schools in this country over the last several years—and I began to do it not only when I was Governor in my own State but in other schools—see people succeeding against all the odds because their schools are safe and drug-free. I have been into schools in very high crime areas, where the children come to school every day and there are no weapons in the lockers and there are no drugs in use and children do not fight in the schools. I know this can be done.

I also know that this requires good management, good discipline, but also special skills and

sometimes extra resources in the poorer school districts of our country. And I know that we can't afford to be satisfied even with the stories that are here, the wonderful, good stories that we honor today. What we want is, next year, to have every school do as well as you have done. That's what you want, too, isn't it? And that's why we have to support programs like this.

As I said, we let the school districts decide how to spend the money, whether it's on metal detectors and increased security or drug education and gang prevention and violence prevention techniques.

Our children do need a constant drum beat to remind them that drugs are wrong, illegal, not safe, will put you in jail, and can cost you your life. I know that. I have had this scourge in my own family, and I know that no amount of help from anybody else will ever replace people taking responsibility for themselves and saying, "I will not be destroyed by my own behavior." But I also know that very few people make that decision once they're in trouble without a little help and support and discipline from people who understand how to deal with this problem. And I think you know that, as well.

I do not believe that our children are inherently violent, although violence is going up dramatically among young people even as the crime rate drops. And I do believe that there are some cultural reasons for it. I think we do get deadened to violence if we're over-exposed to it as children, collectively in show after show on television and movie after movie. I believe all that. But that's not an excuse to leave assault weapons on the street or keep police officers out of the school or not do what we can and we must to change that. So it's not either/or; it is both.

I am very pleased with the work that Secretary Riley, that Director Brown, that Attorney General Reno have done. We're working hard now to try to find a way to comply with the Supreme Court's decision saying that the present law making it illegal for anyone to have a gun within a thousand feet of a school is not constitutional and to try to find a way to make it constitutional so that all of our States will have this protection and not just some.

I also am proud of the fact that we fought last year for a law requiring States to expel students for a year if they bring guns to school, no excuses, zero tolerance. That's something the Government ought to stand for. If we're not for zero tolerance for guns in the schools, what are we for? There should be zero tolerance for guns and for drugs in our schools.

So let me say in closing, perhaps the most meaningful things said here today were said by Jaime. I want you all to think about her tomorrow when she graduates from high school. Then I want you to think about all the kids in this country that are in the grip of drugs and gangs and guns and violence. I want you to think about all the teachers who wonder every year whether they should continue to teach because they are having to deal with these problems and they don't feel that their schools are either organized to deal with it, supporting them in dealing with it, or bringing in the other people and resources who can deal with it. And I want you to ask yourself, is there a courthouse in America, is there a city street in America, is there a single solitary special highway project in America worth the price, worth the risk that we will not have more children like her? The answer is clearly no, no, no, no.

Now, I would like to ask Jaime Chambron to come up and receive her award; Marilyn Green, a wonderful teacher, to come up and receive her award; and John Torres, a D.A.R.E. officer who represents people who are literally beloved by schoolchildren all over America who changed their lives because of their role models, to come up here and receive his award.

Let me again say to all of you, I am profoundly grateful to you. I am asking for an end to the word wars and the artificial divisions here. You are being honored because you are making a difference in people's lives. That's what we got hired to do. And if we could get every American on the solution side of the problems, we'd be a lot better off. I hope this veto, plus this substitute, will be a good start in bringing all of us back to the solution side of the problems, beginning with education and safe and drug-free schools.

Thank you, and God bless you all.

[*At this point, the President presented the awards.*]

The President. Thank you for being here. Thank you, students, for being here. We're adjourned. Thank you very much.

NOTE: The President spoke at 1:49 p.m. in the Rose Garden at the White House. In his remarks, he referred to Jaime Chambron, Largo High School student, Largo, FL.

Message to the House of Representatives Returning Without Approval Legislation for Emergency Supplemental Appropriations and Rescissions for Fiscal Year 1995
June 7, 1995

To the House of Representatives:

I am returning herewith without my approval H.R. 1158, a bill providing for emergency supplemental appropriations and rescissions for fiscal year 1995.

This disagreement is about priorities, not deficit reduction. In fact, I want to increase the deficit reduction in this bill.

H.R. 1158 slashes needed investments for education, national service, and the environment, in order to avoid cutting wasteful projects and other unnecessary expenditures. There are billions of dollars in pork—unnecessary highway demonstration projects, courthouses, and other Federal buildings—that could have been cut instead of these critical investments. Indeed, the Senate bill made such cuts in order to maintain productive investments, but the House-Senate conference rejected those cuts.

For example, H.R. 1158 would deprive 15,000 young adults of the opportunity to serve their communities as AmeriCorps members.

It would deprive 2,000 schools in 47 States of funds to train teachers and devise comprehensive reforms to boost academic standards.

It would reduce or eliminate antiviolence and drug prevention programs serving nearly 20 million students.

It would prevent the creation and expansion of hundreds of community development banks and financial institutions that would spur job growth and leverage billions of dollars of capital in distressed communities across the country.

And it would seriously hamper the ability of States to maintain clean drinking water, thus jeopardizing the health of residents.

In the end, the Congress chose courthouses over education, pork barrel highway projects over national service, Government travel over clean water.

At my instruction, the Administration has provided alternatives to the Congress that would produce greater deficit reduction than H.R. 1158, cutting even more in fiscal year 1995 spending than is included in H.R 1158. But the spending reductions would come out of unnecessary projects and other spending, not investments in working families.

My position on this legislation has been made clear throughout the legislative process. The Administration strongly and consistently opposed the House version of the bill because it would have unnecessarily cut valuable, proven programs that educate our children, invest in our future, and protect the health and safety of the American people. We worked closely with the bipartisan leadership of the Senate to improve the bill, and I indicated my approval of those improvements. Regrettably, the conference went well beyond the spending reductions contained in the bipartisan compromise despite my Administration's consistent urging to adhere to the Senate bipartisan leadership amendment.

In addition, I continue to object to language that would override existing environmental laws in an effort to increase timber salvage. Increas-ing timber salvage and improving forest health are goals that my Administration shares with the Congress. Over the last 6 months, my Administration has put in motion administrative reforms that are speeding salvage timber sales in full compliance with existing environmental laws. It is not appropriate to use this legislation to overturn environmental laws. Therefore, I urge the Congress to delete this language and, separately, to work with my Administration on an initiative to increase timber salvage and improve forest health.

My Administration has provided the Congress with changes that would enable me to sign revised legislation. I urge the Congress to approve a bill that contains the supplemental funding included in H.R. 1158—for disaster relief activities of the Federal Emergency Management Agency, for the Federal response to the bombing in Oklahoma City, for increased antiterrorism efforts, and for providing debt relief to Jordan in order to contribute to further progress toward a Middle East peace settlement—along with my Administration's alternative restorations and offsets.

I will sign legislation that provides these needed supplemental appropriations and that reduces the deficit by at least as much as this bill. However, the legislation must reflect the priorities of the American people. H.R. 1158, as passed, clearly does not.

WILLIAM J. CLINTON

The White House,
June 7, 1995.

Letter to Congressional Leaders on Line-Item Veto Legislation
June 7, 1995

Dear Mr. Speaker: *(Dear Mr. Leader:)*

I am deeply alarmed by today's press report that some Republicans in the House and Senate want to continue to hold back the line-item veto so that I don't have it during this year's budget process. The line-item veto is a vital tool to cut pork from the budget. If this Congress is serious about deficit reduction, it must pass the strongest possible line-item veto immediately, and send it to my desk so I can sign it right away.

This is not a partisan issue. Presidents Reagan and Bush asked Congress for it time and again, and so have I. It was part of the Republican Contract with America. It has strong support from members of Congress in both parties and both houses. No matter what party the President belongs to or what party has a majority in Congress, the line-item veto would be good for America.

If Congress will send me the line-item veto immediately, I am willing to pledge that this year, I will use it only to cut spending, not on tax expenditures in this year's budget. I have already put you on notice that I will veto any budget that is loaded with excessive tax breaks for the wealthy. But I need the line-item veto now to hold the line against pork in every bill the Congress sends me.

The American people have waited long enough. Congress should give them and the Presidency the line-item veto without further delay.

Sincerely,

BILL CLINTON

NOTE: Identical letters were sent to Newt Gingrich, Speaker of the House of Representatives, and Bob Dole, Senate majority leader. This letter was made available by the Office of the Press Secretary but was not issued as a White House press release.

Statement on the Commission on Immigration Reform
June 7, 1995

Having met this morning with Chair Barbara Jordan, I want to congratulate the Commission on Immigration Reform for its recommendation on legal immigration. Consistent with my own views, the Commission's recommendations are pro-family, pro-work, pro-naturalization. As with the Commission's first report on illegal immigration, which we are now aggressively implementing, the Commission has again laid out a roadmap for the Congress to consider. It appears to reflect a balanced immigration policy that makes the most of our diversity while protecting the American workforce so that we can better compete in the emerging global economy. The administration looks forward to working with Congress on this issue.

Statement on Senate Passage of Antiterrorism Legislation
June 7, 1995

I am gratified that the Senate has passed a sweeping, bipartisan antiterrorism bill, as I called for in the wake of the bombing in Oklahoma City. This legislation will give law enforcement the tools it needs to do everything possible to prevent this kind of tragedy from happening again. It will also help us prosecute and punish terrorists more effectively. I urge the House to do its part and get a bill on my desk without delay.

Message on the Rescue of Captain Scott O'Grady
June 8, 1995

All Americans rejoice with me at the successful rescue of Captain Scott O'Grady tonight and join his parents in their relief after days of uncertainty and anguish. Captain O'Grady's bravery and skill are an inspiration. So are the bravery and skill of those who took part in the operation to rescue him. They are all American heroes. Please give them each—and all the men and women who supported them—our heartfelt thanks for a job done so very well. This is a moment that will long be remembered by a nation that is very proud of all her sons and daughters serving under your command.

NOTE: The message was sent to Gen. George Joulwan, Commander-in-Chief, U.S. European Command. An original was not available for verification of the content of this message.

Remarks at a Swearing-In Ceremony for Officers Hired Under Community Oriented Policing Grants
June 8, 1995

Thank you, Attorney General Reno, for your outstanding work. Thank you, Mayor Rendell, Senator Biden, Senator Kennedy, Senator Kerry, Congressman Foglietta, ladies and gentlemen from all across our country who are here today.

These 263 new police officers are living proof that our crime bill will help to make your communities safer and help to make America safer. I want to thank the Attorney General for the work she has done to cut through the redtape and the bureaucracy to turn the crime bill into a reality. The Congress passed it, and I did push hard for it. But in no small measure because of the Attorney General and the dedicated people at the Justice Department, we have already awarded almost 17,000 new police officers to over half the police departments in the United States. We are under budget and ahead of schedule.

And most important, I want to thank all of you who are with us today who are dedicating your lives to law enforcement. I know I speak for all Americans when I say thank you.

I want to take a moment, if I might, to speak about another person to whom we all want to say thank you today, an American hero who risked his life and service to our country. I know all of you and all of our fellow citizens join me in rejoicing at the rescue of Captain Scott O'Grady late last night. We share the relief of his family, his friends, and his loved ones that he is now safe and sound. I can tell you that he's now on a United States aircraft carrier, and we're looking forward to having him back home on American soil. His bravery in the face of great danger and uncertainty is an inspiration to all of us. I can tell you, having followed this almost hour by hour for the last 6 days, when he gets back here and tells the whole story, it will be an astonishing story, indeed. He was well-trained and well-prepared, but he also rose to an extraordinary challenge. I also want to say how very proud I am of the skill of all of those who took part in the operation to rescue him and those who supported them.

Yesterday evening, when it became clear that Captain O'Grady had been located in general and that a rescue operation was possible and we began to get regular reports and then it became obvious that he could be rescued but that the group could not get in and out before daylight in Bosnia, there was no doubt in the minds of either the commanders or our people in uniform that even though that entailed some increased risk, they had to go and get him out, that he had survived for 6 days, and 6 days was long enough. And they did their job.

And last night, when I talked to Captain O'Grady's parents after 1 o'clock in the morning, they and all of his siblings were full of joy and pride and gratitude. Let me tell you that they proved once again, all these people, that our country has the finest Armed Forces in the world. And we are very, very proud of them and ecstatically happy today.

I want to say to all of you here in uniform, you, too, are our country's heroes. Each and every one of you will make our streets a little safer, at more risk to yourselves. There is nothing more effective in the fight against crime than more police officers on the beat. This is not a partisan issue. This is an issue on which all Americans can be on the solution side.

We know that we owe it to our children to give them back the freedom to walk to school in safety. I have said this before, and I want to say it one more time: I intend to keep my promise to the American people to put 100,000 more of you on the streets. And I will fight and veto, if necessary, any attempt to stop us until there are 100,000 of you out there protecting the American people.

We need more police on the street. We need to get our children and our assault weapons off the streets. Our neighborhoods are not a place for military assault weapons, violent criminals, or gangs. In recent months, we have seen all too clearly that keeping our country safe and secure requires new efforts by both our Government and our people.

The crime bill provides law enforcement the tools they ask for. After the tragedy in Oklahoma City and what we endured in the World Trade Center, law enforcement needs additional tools to crack down on terrorists wherever they may come from, from within or beyond our borders.

I am very pleased that last night the Senate passed my antiterrorism legislation. I thank Senator Dole and the Republicans who voted for it. I thank Senator Daschle and the Democrats who voted for it. I thank them for working together. That's what America expects us to do, after all.

Now I want to urge the House of Representatives to act as quickly as possible. Some there have said maybe they ought to slow this up. Well, I assure you that the people who work in terrorism operate on their own timetable, and they will not pause for an extended debate in the United States Congress. So let this bill be reviewed. Let it be examined. That is the job of the legislative body. But let us act quickly. The safety and security of our people is not now and must never become a partisan issue.

Now, let me say one other thing. The budget passed in the House of Representatives, as distinct from the one passed in the Senate, reduces the crime bill by about $5 billion. We do need to cut spending further. We can move toward a balanced budget. But I don't think that is a good idea.

The crime bill was carefully balanced. It was worked on for 6 years. Senator Biden gave a major portion of his entire life's energy to it. And it was calibrated to fight crime in several ways: It had more police, more punishment, more prisons, and more prevention. And it had all those elements because the law enforcement community told us that we need to have those elements. I believe as strongly as I can say that we can continue to reduce the deficit, we can balance the budget without undermining the crime bill. And that is exactly what we ought to do.

In the next few months, as we get into this budget debate and we argue about what to cut and where to spend, how soon we need to balance the budget, and what other objectives we need to pursue, I want to tell you that underneath all this there will be a huge debate that

you will see played out in a lot of ways. And it's a debate that I strongly believe is a false one. Those who argue that we can cut anything except national defense, anything else at all to balance the budget as quickly as possible, basically believe that most of the problems of this country are cultural in nature, that if people would simply behave themselves and take responsibility for their own lives and tend to their families and show up for work everyday, we wouldn't have the problems we've got, and therefore it is not necessary to make these investments.

Others will argue that the first responsibility of Government is law and order, that another responsibility of our Government in this time, with this global economy just beating the living daylights out of working Americans so that they never get a pay raise even though they work harder—there is a responsibility to help people make more of their own lives, to get the education and training they need to compete and win in a global economy.

There are others who will argue that there are people who through no fault of their own, because they're very young children or elderly or disabled, cannot take care of themselves and deserve some support from our Government. And so you'll see this big argument, the cultural side and the economic and political side. I personally believe it's a phony argument.

Now, I know from my own family's experience—I had a brother who was addicted to drugs and who did time because of that—I know that there is no program in the world that can make people do the right thing if they're not prepared to take responsibility for themselves. I am well aware of that. I know that.

But I also know that unless we take responsibility collectively for doing what we can, we will have people killed on the streets that don't need to be killed. We will have young people who lose their futures who don't need to lose them. We will have people whose incomes never get better because we don't invest in them and give them a chance to succeed. We will hurt the elderly and the defenseless because we don't recognize our common responsibilities. We have cultural problems and economic and political challenges in this country, and we should not permit Washington to be divided over what is essentially a phony choice. Keep in mind, often when we talk about cultural problems up here, we're looking for an excuse not to do our part and assume our responsibility.

So let's say there are both kinds of challenges in America. Let's get everybody on the solution side of dealing with them. And don't you let for a minute anybody try to push you into one camp or another. Life is all about personal responsibility and our actions together as families, communities, and as a nation.

Captain O'Grady triumphed because he was personally responsible, personally able, personally courageous. He also got the finest military training in the world from the United States of America. You will do well as police officers if you are personally dedicated, not to abusing your authority but to using it to the maximum extent to protect people and to stop crimes from occurring and to punishing people when they do commit crimes. But it matters if you're well-trained. It matters if you're well-supported. It matters if you're properly funded.

Do not let America be divided over this debate. We have our responsibilities here in Washington. You have your responsibilities on the streets and in your own homes. If we all do our job, we can move America forward. If we get caught up in a bogus debate about whether our problems are cultural or economic and political, we will never get to the end of the road. They are both, and we must act that way.

Let me just say one thing in closing. The crime rate is going down all over America. In most major cities the crime rate has dropped substantially in the last couple of years. A lot of that is because of able and visionary mayors like the mayors that we honor here today, because of the reforms that have been undertaken in cities, like those that I saw when Mayor Rendell and I walked in his neighborhood streets in 1992 and as I have done since then in the city of Philadelphia.

But let's don't forget one thing: The crime rate, especially random violence among very young people, is still going up, which means that the long-run battle to recover our children and to turn them away from mindless violence and to protect those who are not violent from that is still hanging in the balance.

So I honor you today for your contribution. I tell you that for the next 10 years, you may be involved in the most important national security battle in the United States. And I ask you when you go home to ask every single citizen in your communities to help you win this fight. It is truly the fight for America's future.

Thank you, and God bless you all.

NOTE: The President spoke at 12:07 p.m. on the South Lawn at the White House. In his remarks, he referred to Mayor Edward Rendell of Philadelphia, PA.

Statement on House Action on Foreign Affairs Legislation
June 8, 1995

This bill (H.R. 1561) would take us in an isolationist direction at a time when America is ready to lead in the world. I am gratified that argument was persuasive to enough Members of the House to sustain a possible veto.

We are particularly concerned about the vote to lift unilaterally the arms embargo in Bosnia. As we have said, we believe this is counterproductive to our efforts to bring about a negotiated settlement.

Remarks to the Friends of Art and Preservation in Embassies
June 8, 1995

One of these days we're going to have an event where I have to be introduced by the First Lady when we've had one of those other days. [*Laughter*] Lord only knows what will happen—[*laughter*]—but it will be another adventure.

I am delighted to see all of you here. I'm glad to be here with our friend Lee Annenberg and with Ann Gund and with all of you who support this important work.

Let me say that this has been an interesting day at the White House. We swore in 263 police officers earlier today. We've had all kinds of people in here from all over America. But mostly we have been celebrating the liberation of that fine young Air Force captain from Bosnia.

Sometimes I read even in the American press from time to time that we don't seem to be doing anything in Bosnia and we don't seem to have exerted ourselves. You should know that we have over 1,000 American troops on the border of Bosnia in the Former Yugoslav Republic of Macedonia to make sure that conflict doesn't spread. We have 200 Americans in the hospital unit in Croatia. And we have flown the longest humanitarian airlift and the largest one in history, larger than the Berlin airlift, to guarantee food and medicine to people in the besieged areas of Bosnia. And perhaps most importantly of all, people like that fine young captain have been flying for a couple of years now to keep the war out of the air. And for all of our frustrations and feelings of anxiety and anger, in 1992 there were about 130,000 civilians killed, a staggering number, in that troubled land. Last year there were under 3,000.

So I ask you to remember as we celebrate this liberation that a lot of people stick their neck out every day, and the results have been important. If you look at Northern Ireland or South Africa or the Middle East, the lesson of this time is that it's very difficult to enforce peace on people that want to keep fighting with one another, but what you try to do is to keep it within some bounds of humanity, keep working on diplomacy until they spend their destructive energies and start trying to build again.

And once in a while the risk becomes apparent, as it was in the case of this brave pilot. And for 6 days he held out against a lot of attempts to find him and to shoot him and capture him. And he represented the best in our country. He told me today when we visited on the phone—I talked to his parents last night at 1:30 a.m., and they asked me if I was going to call him. I said, "No, you call him. I'm going to bed. I just wanted—[*laughter*]—I wanted you to know he was home safe." But he told me today that he was on the ground between 3 and 5 minutes before armed people made it to his parachute. He had 3 to 5 minutes to find a place to hide and begin this incredible odyssey that I'm sure some day will be a very great movie that all of us will think is suitable for everyone to see. [*Laughter*]

Let me say on behalf of all of our administration and especially the people who work in America's diplomatic efforts, we are profoundly grateful for what you do. By putting American art in our embassies around the world, you are part of our public diplomacy, you expose an important part of the essence of America to people all around the world. And it couldn't happen without you.

I also want to thank you because you have put, I think, now over 2,200 works of American art in more than 170 countries, raised over $7 million to fund projects at embassy residences in Beijing and Cairo and Rome and London, Singapore, Tokyo, and Warsaw. And I've been to a lot of those places, so I am one of the chief beneficiaries of your efforts. And I thank you for that.

You couldn't do it alone. The State Department couldn't do it alone. This represents one of those remarkable partnerships between the public and the private sector in America that almost nobody knows about but everyone takes for granted when they benefit from it.

We're having such a raging debate in this country today about whether public is bad and private is good, whether all of our efforts should be directed at correcting personal conduct or at changing economic or political direction. I think these debates make for very interesting print and maybe news coverage at night, but they don't conform to the real-world experience of most people.

Most of us, I think, all of our lives have felt that when people get together in some sort of constructive partnership, that's what works best. And I think one of the most frustrating things to me about going to work every day, in this otherwise exhilarating environment, is knowing that what comes across to the American people are these polarized choices and conflicts and rhetorical battles which don't reflect the way any sensible person would run his or her family or business or charitable organization or hospital or church or you name it.

You have done what I think is best about America. You have taken the world as you find it, worked together in a real spirit of partnership, recognized that there is a personal responsibility and opportunity and also a public responsibility in this area. I wish we had more of it, and I'm glad we've got you. Thank you very much.

I have a lot to be grateful to Lee Annenberg and her fine husband, Walter, for, but not so long ago we were here to announce that the Annenbergs had decided to donate a staggering sum for the purpose of trying to improve public education in this country. I think there is no more noble cause. And because of what they have done, all across America people are doing things differently, striving for global standards of excellence in grassroots community schools. And for that and for this and for so much else, the country owes a great debt of gratitude to Lee Annenberg, and I am very pleased to introduce her now.

Thank you.

NOTE: The President spoke at 6:17 p.m. in the East Room at the White House. In his remarks, he referred to Leonore Annenberg, chairperson, and Ann Gund, vice chairperson, Friends of Art and Preservation in Embassies.

Remarks on the National Performance Review
June 9, 1995

We brought Paul Condit up here as a part of the Vice President and my continuing cultural education of Secretary Rubin. We found out that even though he's very brilliant, there are serious gaps in his knowledge. When I met him, he didn't know who Aretha Franklin, B.B. King, or Rod Stewart was, and he had never met a redneck in his life. [*Laughter*] We are correcting that, part of our reinventing Government. [*Laughter*]

Do you know what Paul Condit was saying to me when the Vice President was talking? He said, "Mr. President, this stuff is great. But you need to reinvent communications; it ain't getting out." He said, "Nobody knows anything about this." I said, "Well, you'd have to be here awhile for me to explain it to you." [*Laughter*]

The greatest compliment I have received since I have been President was when we were in Montana the other day and—I didn't get it directly—you may have seen the—I went out to a farm to talk about agriculture because we have to rewrite the farm bill as we're trying to reduce spending. And I insisted that we go to a Republican farmer's farm and that we have equal numbers of Republicans and Democrats in the crowd. One of my staff members was standing next to one of these farmers, and we were talking about all this, you know, all this agriculture. And he asked the farmer, he said, "Well, what do you think about this?" And the farmer looked at him and said, "He ain't nothing like they make him out to be, is he?" [*Laughter*]

You learn to speak maybe in a way that people can understand if you spend more time on a John Deere tractor. And Paul Condit has, and we thank him for being here. I also thank the Vice President for the incredible job he has done on all these projects. And I thank Secretary Rubin and Commissioner Chater, Commissioner Richardson, Deputy Secretary Glynn, and all the people who have worked on this.

We do have an obligation to communicate what we're doing, but we also have an obligation to do the right things and to stop doing the wrong things. And our SBA Director, Phil Lader, is going to—we're going to have this White House Conference on Small Business next week. I'm very excited about it. I hope it is an opportunity to talk to the American people and to talk to the small business community about what we're trying to do. But I hope it's also a chance for us to continue to do more of the right things and to keep changing.

The truth is that—as the Vice President said, I could have listened to that story all day, analogizing what if the Federal Government was running a John Deere dealership. I wish I had thought of that myself. [*Laughter*] The truth is that one of our big problems is that almost everybody who works for the Federal Government is honest, hard-working, well-meaning, and really wants to serve. But we are trapped inside a system that there are some things we can't change, and one is we basically have guaranteed revenues and guaranteed customers, and that means that we change less quickly than the private sector that has neither. But if we don't change, then the voters eventually will try to find a way to get through the elected officials to the permanent Government. And in a way, people's perceptions are not all that specific even if they're generally accurate. We might wind up going from one extreme to the other.

So what we tried to do when we got here was to prove that it was actually possible for the institutional Government to change, something that most people simply didn't believe. Most people believed that politicians would come and go, but the Government would go on forever. And interestingly enough, in the last several years I have noticed politicians beginning to adopt the same rhetoric in an attempt to be popular with the people, so that people would be in control here for 7 or 8 years and still be cussing the Government as if, "What do you expect me to do? I'm just the President," or "I'm just the Secretary of the Treasury" or, you know, "What do you expect me to do?"

In the course of that I think that we have been less sensitive than we should have been, as I have said repeatedly—and I'm a guilty party—to treating Federal employees like people. And we must never contribute to this atmosphere of resentment of the people who work for the Federal Government, because most people who work for the Federal Government are like most people anywhere. Given the choice between productive or unproductive, most people would choose to be productive. Given the choice between being relevant or irrelevant, most people would gladly choose to be relevant. Given the choice between building and tearing down, most people would choose to build.

And what we have tried to do with this national performance review, which the Vice President has doggedly pursued—what we have tried to do, even though we couldn't get it out and we knew there was probably never any way to make it a popular, big headline-grabbing issue, is day by day, week by week, department by department, agency by agency, employee by employee, to chip away at the habits and institutional conduct of the Federal Government that is not good for America and not going to take us into the 21st century in good shape and to flip it around so that our public institutions could do the public's business in a way that maintained the trust of the people who are paying the bill.

And all of you who have been a part of that deserve a lot of credit for what you've done. And I just want to urge you to keep doing it. We'll keep trying to figure out how to get it out, to use Paul's expression. But the main thing we need to do is to keep doing what has been done.

Some of this involves changing laws. You know, I recently signed the Paperwork Reduction Act. Last Congress, we passed the procurement reform which the Vice President was able to popularize on the David Letterman show by trying—by breaking the ashtray. But that broken ashtray was a way of getting out the idea that we were wasting, at a minimum, hundreds of millions of dollars a year with antiquated procurement practices.

The Paperwork Reduction Act, when Paul waves that around, it's a way of illustrating the burden that is on us to make sure that we are not asking people to spend their time, their money, and their resources on fooling with us if they don't have to and if there is no public purpose served by it.

Now, that is one of the things, it seems to me, that if you talk to anybody about what they really resent about our Government, if they have any kind of success in life, they'll normally talk about regulation and paperwork, even before taxes. And we are trying to do something about that. Small businesses and big businesses, too, have been screaming at us for years to do something about it, and we are trying to do it.

Now, the Department of Treasury has taken the lead by spearheading the Simplified Tax and Wage Reporting System. Because of that, today we are announcing a plan that should lead to the elimination of the need to file W–2 forms in multiple places. You will only need to file once, and you will have a single point of contact for customer service. This will save time and hassle and about a billion dollars a year—which is real money even up here, Paul—a billion dollars a year. When we free people from the burden of paperwork so that they can create jobs, opportunity, services, and products for the American people, we have saved much more than that.

In addition, I am going to send legislation to Congress that will remove the legal barriers that keep Federal and State agencies from working together in commonsense ways to ease the paperwork burden on all taxpayers.

Most taxpayers currently have to fill out both a State and Federal income tax form. Depending on where you live and work, you might also have to do a local income tax form. Most of the information on the State and city forms is simply a repeat of what's on the Federal form. So with some teamwork and some modernization of the tax system, the Federal Government is now going to create partnerships with State and city governments to eliminate the need for duplicate filing.

Since we came into office, we have permitted 29 States to have systems in which taxpayers can satisfy both their Federal and State personal income tax filing requirements with a single electronic transmission. More than a million and a half returns were filed this way this year. Next year, 32 States are going to participate. You can imagine what will happen to the paperwork burden as more and more people file electronically, one time, both State and Federal. The IRS handles 2 billion pieces of paperwork a year.

So we are going to reduce regulation. We are going to speed transmission. We're going to make it easier for the taxpayers. And as an extra added bonus to the Vice President, we're going to save 14 to 15 more forests by the turn of the century by reducing this level of paperwork. This is a big deal. Now, what we have to do is make sure people know they can do it and more and more people do it.

We're going to clear away the barriers to full partnerships with State and local governments for employment as well as for personal tax information. We estimate that with a partnership with 20 percent of the States by the year 2000, we can reduce the burden to taxpayers just on this item alone by $1.5 billion and save the Government millions and millions of dollars in the process.

I invite Governors and mayors all across this country to join us in having businesses and taxpayers file their information just one time. This is the right way to fix the Government. There is no need for two or more filings. We are prepared to do our part in a technical way and in a legal way to make it possible for taxpayers all across America to have fewer piles like this.

This is the kind of service the American people are entitled to expect from a modernized tax system, and frankly, this is the kind of thing we're going to have to do to get the inordinate compliance costs with taxation systems in America down. This is what reinventing Government is all about.

I want to again say to all of you who worked on this project, I appreciate it very much. We now have to sign a memorandum of understanding which requires all these various agencies to work together. And we're going to sign that, and then I'm going to ask Paul Condit to sign it as a witness to make sure that he'll have something to get out when he goes home to Seminole, Texas. [*Laughter*]

So Secretary Rubin, Deputy Labor Secretary Glynn, Commissioner Chater, Commissioner Richardson, please come up here and sign the memorandum of understanding.

Thank you very much, ladies and gentlemen.

NOTE: The President spoke at 12:25 p.m. in the Cash Room at the Treasury Department. In his remarks, he referred to Paul Condit, president and general manager, Texas Equipment Co., Inc.; and entertainers Aretha Franklin, B.B. King, and Rod Stewart.

Remarks at the Faces of Hope Reunion Luncheon
June 9, 1995

Thank you very much. Congratulations, Leslie, that's a—[*laughter*]—Mr. Vice President, that may be your most memorable example of reinventing Government there. [*Laughter*] I promised you a personal service administration, and there's a living example of it.

Let me say, it is wonderful to be here with all of you today. I want to thank the people who have worked so hard to keep this group together and in contact with us. I appreciate Sue Hazzard and Ann Walker and all the rest of you who worked on this. Let me thank you, because these are really very disparate people, living very different lives all over the country and getting even further and further apart. One of you has since moved to Alaska since we've started—came back. I thank you for being here.

Before we start, I'd like to just say that four of the people who were our Faces of Hope in 1992 have since passed away. Josh Cox, who was mentioned earlier; Sheri Kohlenberg, who came to see me with her husband and her son, Sammy—they're here. And Sammy left me something I thought was a dinosaur. He said it just looks like one, but anyway it's still in the White House over there. Sarah Weber, whose mother and sister are here; and Michael Quercio, whose partner is here. And Michael and I jogged together right before I became President, and I got to see him when I dedicated the new Kennedy Library. I miss them all very much; I know all of you do. And I'd like to ask if we could just have a moment of silence for them.

[*At this point, a moment of silence was observed.*]

Amen.

You know, all of you, in various ways, inspired us in this—when we ran for President, but you have very different stories: Some of you struggled to overcome great personal adversity; some of you still struggle with it; some of you struggle with your children; some of you were people who led what looked on the outside to be ordinary lives, but performed extraordinary service for others; some of you achieved very great things in your own lives, but took time to do things for others. There are a lot of different kinds of stories here. But the one thing that struck me about all of you was that you fundamentally decided that you would take an affirmative view of your life and life in general, that you decided that you would try to look for what could be done tomorrow to make it better, instead of just wallowing in what didn't happen yesterday or things that were beyond your control. You decided that you would make a constructive contribution to your own life and to the lives of others. You lived with hope. And that is a very important thing. You had a lot of influence on this administration, as the Vice President said. I think of all of you every time when I go someplace out in the country and our national service AmeriCorps people are there, because that's what they do.

I was in Texas the other day with people who are in the AmeriCorps program, all doing national service, earning money to go to college. One of them was a woman who retired from the military, said she never had a chance to go to college—she had the GI bill, but she wanted to do this service in her community before she went back to college; with two young people who had babies out of wedlock, as teenagers were on welfare, got themselves off welfare, got high school diplomas, and were then contributing to AmeriCorps before going to college so they could help other people avoid the kind of problems they've had; and with one young girl who was a college graduate, who was raised the child of a mother on welfare, who decided after getting out of college she still ought to do the national service program because she ought to help other people.

Now, everything—and I kept asking myself today, you know, what has all this got—how does it tie together? And I think, for me, all of you represent people who try to make something good happen. You didn't just talk; you acted. You tried to get on the solution side of—what I call being on the solution side of whatever your problems or challenges were, whether it was in your own family or in your community.

And one of the biggest problems we have in Washington and one of the reasons politics is such a turn-off to people today is that it comes across to the American people over the air waves as being nothing but rhetoric and conflict and not being on the solution side. No one would run a family, a business, a charitable enterprise the way it appears that things here are run often. It would just run right off the tracks. You know that. You remind me here every day of what we should be doing.

And you had another influence that hasn't been mentioned yet that you ought to know. When I became President, I put a lot of time and effort into making sure we had good people who were well organized in our casework division, where we get letters from people just like you all over America just asking for help with a problem or advice. About once a week, I get letters that I personally sign from ordinary American citizens who wrote the White House and asked for some problem—everything is—you know, they have a sick child, they don't qualify for Government help, to "My father was supposed to get a medal in World War II, and he never got it," and all kinds of things in between. And I organized this because I made up my mind that I did not want to forget about people like you and the work that we do here.

Because of a lot of folks like you, we have managed so far—even in these difficult budgetary times when we have reduced the size of the Government by 100,000 and we have shrunk the deficit and we're going to have more cuts, we have increased our investment in education, medical research, and particularly, we have emphasized research and treatment for AIDS. And I'm not sure we would have been able to fight off all of those budget cuts if I hadn't actually met a lot of you and gotten to know you. Because of some of you here, when we passed the crime bill we were able to say, "Okay, you put more police on the street and have more punishment, but put some money into giving these kids something to say yes to." There were two former gang members here from L.A. who spend their lives trying to keep peace on the streets of Los Angeles; better we should support them, also cheaper for you.

These are the kinds of things that we have tried to do. Because of you, we fought for the family leave law, and we've tried to fight for programs that would not only protect the environment but would also help to provide for economic transition where people are dislocated. When we had to cut back on defense, we provided for economic transition so we wouldn't forget about the people who lost their jobs because we won the cold war and we had to cut back on defense—because of you and people like you. And that's very, very important.

We're having two big debates here in Washington today, and you put the lie to both of them. And so I want to talk about it. You'll hear it when we talk about what we're going to do to the budget. Debate number one is whether all of our problems are primarily personal and cultural, that is, if we'd all just behave and do the right thing there wouldn't be any problems—which is, at one level, plainly true, right—or whether our problems are political and economic, that is, we have an obligation to help each other make the most of our own lives and overcome our problems.

You put the lie to that debate. That is a bogus debate. Nothing I can do here in Washington will really solve your problems if you're not doing your part. On the other hand, if we don't do our part here, a lot of you still won't

be able to do what you can do to make the most of your lives and the people you're trying to help. So I hope that when people look at you and think about people like you, they will say, the answer to that is both. I'll do my part, but you guys do yours.

The second big debate is whether, even though we have to do things together, the Government is so clumsy, inefficient, and inept, we ought to throw it away and just tell everybody to behave right in their private charities: "Do good. Go forth and do good."

My answer to that is, that is also a bogus debate. It's interesting to me that all of the people who work in charitable work say they'd like the Government to be a partner, that we need more charitable contributions, we want people to give more, but we need to have a partnership.

We have other debates like that. Is it more important to balance the budget or to invest money in the education of our people so they raise their incomes and generate more tax revenues because we've got more people in higher efforts? My answer is, we have to find a way to do both. And what you do in your private lives is you balance—a lot of you balance all these conflicts all the time, these kinds of conflicts, and you go on and live your life. That's what we have to do here. And that's what you inspire me to do.

You know, I was so moved, for example, after the horrible tragedy in Oklahoma City, by how much work the private charities were also doing there and how they did things that we could not have done, but we did things that they needed us to do.

A lot of you, I have seen you in your literacy centers or your work to help kids, older kids. And you get funds from the private sector, but you also need us to do our part.

And you know, when we showed up here, we really tried to shrink the size of Government, to reduce bureaucracy, to bring the deficit down, and we've done that. But we also tried to invest more in helping people make the most of their own lives. And it seems to me, that is the fundamental responsibility we have, and that is what we're trying to do here.

There are 90 million Americans who volunteer. And some of you are some of them, and God bless them. We need more of it. But the main thing we need to do is to make practical decisions here that work right, not have a lot of theoretical debates that drive a stake through the heart of America's citizenry.

And you know, a lot of things are going on here I don't really understand. But I'm doing my best to remember you and every time I come up to one of these decisions to say, what is best for the American people? What is best for the American people?

And it's sometimes very hard and very frustrating, because we just came from an event where the Vice President had a John Deere dealer from West Texas talking about what we were going to do to reduce reporting requirements on the income tax system and how we'd reinvented Government. And the John Deere dealer whispered to me, he said, "You know, Mr. President, this all sounds real good, but you need to reinvent what you're saying to the people because it ain't getting out out there." It was funny.

The reason is, the way we talk up here doesn't really often square with the way you live out there. But let me just give you an example of what's going on. We have people here in Washington in important positions who say that we should drastically cut the amount of money we're investing in poor folks because we're just corrupting them and making them dependent. I haven't noticed anybody who really likes poverty very much, but that's what they're saying.

My belief is we have had some programs that made people dependent, and I want to change them. I want to change the welfare system and support people who are putting people to work. I don't think anybody wants to be on welfare, and if they do, they shouldn't. So I have no problem with tough requirements to get people into training programs, require them to work. I think that's good. But to say you can do it for free, I think, is wrong.

Then we have people, some of the same people who say we should cut back on the Government's investment in these kind of public endeavor, they say, "Well, the charities should do more. We should just give more money to charitable contributions." But now I wonder whether they really mean that.

I just want you to understand the difference between where you live and what's going on here. For example, last week I heard about this letter—listen to this—a letter that was sent to the chief executive officers of 82 of the biggest companies in this country. And it warned these chief executive officers that they were in serious

danger of giving money—the letter implied that they were sure these poor men were ignorant, maybe there were some women on the list, I haven't seen the whole list—maybe they were ignorant, but they were in serious danger of giving money to private organizations that were promoting the welfare state, undermining the free enterprise system, eroding the fabric of our country. I quote—the letter said, you are giving charitable contributions which, quote, "support the expansion of the welfare state."

Now, these are people that want the Government to give less, right? So I was surprised to find out this letter was not for some fringe group. Now, this was a letter signed by the majority leader of the House of Representatives on very official-looking stationery. So I couldn't wait to get my hands on a list of these subversive groups that were getting money from big American companies. Here are some of the groups that were on the list: The American Cancer Society, the American Heart Association, the American Lung Association—what do they have in common—the League of Women Voters, a dangerous outfit—[*laughter*]—the B'nai B'rith, the NAACP, the Nature Conservancy—they help States buy lands so people will be able to enjoy it forever, with enormous business support.

Now, I asked myself when I read about this, and I saw this letter, how can we have the Government give less money and then have a major leader of the Congress tell people that they ought to give less—big corporations ought to give less to groups dedicated to reducing disease, fighting racism, protecting the environment, and promoting jobs and encouraging Americans to vote? Why? Because there's probably some segment of the political base there that really likes that stuff and pumps a bunch of money into it, and because maybe these people are advocating things that some of the big organized power groups here don't like.

But don't you see, what I'm trying to say is, this doesn't have anything to do with the way you live. And we have got to get Washington, DC, back on the solution side of America's challenges to help people make the most of their own lives, to help people who through no fault of their own cannot care for themselves, to really support work and family and community instead of talking about it and then just keep trying to drive stake after stake after stake through the American people to divide us and disillusion us and convince each other that we're enemies.

At the end of the Civil War, just shortly before he was assassinated, Abraham Lincoln gave a speech in which he said—and we had had a pretty good fight then; we really were divided—he said, "We cannot be enemies. We must be friends." Now, that's the way you live, and you are entitled to a political system that

reflects the hope that you gave to the four of us. That's what we're trying to give you.

Thank you, and God bless you all.

NOTE: The President spoke at 2:15 p.m. on the State Floor at the White House. In his remarks, he referred to the upcoming wedding of Faces of Hope participant Leslie Williams.

Message to the Senate Transmitting the Belgium-United States Extradition Treaty
June 9, 1995

To the Senate of the United States:

With a view to receiving the advice and consent of the Senate to ratification, I transmit herewith the Extradition Treaty Between the United States of America and the Kingdom of Belgium signed at Brussels on April 27, 1987. Also transmitted for the information of the Senate is the report of the Department of State with respect to the Treaty.

This Treaty is designed to update and standardize the conditions and procedures for extradition between the United States and Belgium. Most significantly, it substitutes a dual-criminality clause for the current list of extraditable offenses, thereby expanding the number of crimes for which extradition can be granted. The Treaty also provides a legal basis for temporarily surrendering prisoners to stand trial for crimes against the laws of the Requesting State.

The provisions in this Treaty follow generally the form and content of extradition treaties re-

cently concluded by the United States. Upon entry into force, it will supersede the Treaty for the Mutual Extradition of Fugitives from Justice Between the United States and the Kingdom of Belgium, signed at Washington on October 26, 1901, and the Supplementary Extradition Conventions to the Extradition Convention of October 26, 1901, signed at Washington on June 20, 1935, and at Brussels on November 14, 1963.

This Treaty will make a significant contribution to international cooperation in law enforcement. I recommend that the Senate give early and favorable consideration to the Treaty and give its advice and consent to ratification.

WILLIAM J. CLINTON

The White House,

June 9, 1995.

Message to the Senate Transmitting the Belgium-United States Supplementary Extradition Treaty
June 9, 1995

To the Senate of the United States:

With a view to receiving the advice and consent of the Senate to ratification, I transmit herewith the Supplementary Treaty on Extradition Between the United States of America and the Kingdom of Belgium to Promote the Repression of Terrorism, signed at Brussels on

April 27, 1987 (the "Supplementary Treaty"). Also transmitted for the information of the Senate is the report of the Department of State with respect to the Supplementary Treaty.

This Supplementary Treaty is designed to facilitate the extradition of terrorists, and is similar to the protocols to extradition treaties currently in force with other countries, including Australia, Canada, Spain, the Federal Republic of Germany, and the United Kingdom. Upon entry into force, the Supplementary Treaty will amend the Treaty for the Mutual Extradition of Fugitives from Justice, signed at Washington on October 26, 1901, as amended by the Supplementary Conventions, signed at Washington on June 20, 1935, and at Brussels on November 14, 1963, if that Treaty is still in force, or the Extradition Treaty Between the United States and Belgium signed at Brussels on April 27, 1987.

I recommend that the Senate give early and favorable consideration to the Supplementary Treaty and give its advice and consent to ratification.

WILLIAM J. CLINTON

The White House,
June 9, 1995.

Message to the Senate Transmitting the Switzerland-United States Extradition Treaty
June 9, 1995

To the Senate of the United States:

With a view to receiving the advice and consent of the Senate to ratification, I transmit herewith the Extradition Treaty Between the Government of the United States of America and the Government of the Swiss Confederation, signed at Washington on November 14, 1990. Also transmitted for the information of the Senate is the report of the Department of State with respect to the Treaty.

The Treaty is designed to update and standardize the conditions and procedures for extradition between the United States and Switzerland. Most significantly, it substitutes a dual-criminality clause for a current list of extraditable offenses, so that the new Treaty will cover numerous offenses not now covered by our extradition treaty with Switzerland, including certain narcotics offenses, important forms of white collar crime, and parental child abduction. The Treaty also provides a legal basis for temporarily surrendering prisoners to stand trial for crimes against the laws of the Requesting State.

The Treaty further represents an important step in combatting terrorism by excluding from the scope of the political offense exception offenses typically committed by terrorists for which both the United States and Switzerland have an obligation under a multilateral international agreement to extradite or submit to their authorities for the purpose of prosecution. These offenses include aircraft hijacking, aircraft sabotage, crimes against internationally protected persons (including diplomats), and hostage-taking.

The provisions in this Treaty follow generally the form and content of extradition treaties recently concluded by the United States. Upon entry into force, it will supersede the Extradition Treaty of May 14, 1900, and the Supplementary Extradition Treaties of January 10, 1935, and January 31, 1940, Between the United States of America and the Swiss Confederation.

This Treaty will make a significant contribution to international cooperation in law enforcement. I recommend that the Senate give early and favorable consideration to the Treaty and give its advice and consent to ratification.

WILLIAM J. CLINTON

The White House,
June 9, 1995.

The President's Radio Address
June 10, 1995

Good morning. I know all Americans share my deep pride and joy in the safety of Captain Scott O'Grady. We're proud of his courage and his tenacity. And we are very grateful to our armed forces for his swift and brilliant rescue. I'm glad we have him back safe and secure.

Today I want to talk about a very real threat to the safety and security of young Americans here at home: drunk driving. Drunk driving, especially by young people, is one of the most serious and one of the most avoidable threats to public health in America. I'm joined in the White House by members of Mothers Against Drunk Driving, Students Against Drunk Driving, AAA, and the National Safety Council. In no small measure because of the determined work of private organizations like these, we have taken some very important steps over the last decade to reduce drunk driving.

Most of us who were Governors of our States during that period strengthened our own laws against drunk driving. In 1984, President Reagan signed a bill giving States a strong incentive to raise their drinking age to 21. Today, that is the law of the land in every State. As a result, teenagers can no longer drive to neighboring States with lower drinking ages. This happened all the time before we had a uniform drinking age, and all too often with tragic consequences.

The crime bill I signed into law last year puts tough new penalties on the books for people who drive drunk with children in their cars. It also makes it easier for States to prosecute anybody who drives under the influence of drugs or alcohol. And deaths due to drinking and driving have dropped as a result of the progress we've made, 30 percent in the last 12 years. The number of people under 21 killed because of drunk driving has dropped 50 percent since 1984.

This is good progress, and I expect the new penalties in the crime bill will help to improve things even more. But it's not good enough. Some 18,000 people will die this year because someone sat down at the wheel after sitting down at a bar. That's about one every 30 minutes. Well over a million people will be injured, one every 26 seconds.

This may sound unbelievable; it's certainly unacceptable. But over 40 percent of all Americans will be involved in an alcohol-related crash at some time in their lives. Twenty-two hundred people were killed last year because of young drivers who were drinking and driving. Of that group, 1,600 were young people themselves. There's something wrong in America when hundreds and hundreds of our young people are dying because hundreds and hundreds of our young people are drinking and driving.

In most States, drunk driving is defined as a blood alcohol content of .1 percent. When underage drinkers become underage drunk drivers, I believe we should go further. I want Congress to call on the States to adopt zero tolerance laws for teenage drinking and driving. A blood alcohol content of .02 percent, the equivalent of one beer, one wine cooler, or one shot of alcohol, should be enough to trigger the drunk driving penalties for people under 21. After all, if it's illegal for people under 21 to drink at all, it should certainly be illegal for them to drink and drive. That's a no-brainer.

Zero tolerance will save lives. It's already saving lives in 24 States, including my home State. Alcohol-related crashes are down 10 to 20 percent in those States overall. And in some States like Maine and New Mexico, all fatal crashes at night involving young people actually dropped by one-third after they adopted a zero tolerance law. Unfortunately, there are still 26 States, including large States like New York, Texas, and Florida, that draw thousands of vacationing teenagers every year, without these zero tolerance laws. It's time to have zero tolerance for underage drunk driving all across America, not just in some States.

As we redefine the relationships between States and the Federal Government, it is clear there are many things the States can do better than we can do in Washington. And I've done as much as I could to push more authority and decisionmaking back down to the States, to encourage innovation in important areas like welfare and health care reform. But there are other things that are so important to our safety, our security, to our children, and our future that the Federal Government has a responsibility to act.

I don't think there's any question that the fight against teenage drunk driving demands national action. Congress should make zero tolerance the law of the land. Drinking and driving don't mix for anyone. They certainly shouldn't be mixed by teenagers. The faster we act, the sooner the States will act and the more lives we'll save. Let's get to it.

Thanks for listening.

NOTE: The address was recorded at 11:07 a.m. on June 9 in the Roosevelt Room at the White House for broadcast at 10:06 a.m. on June 10. In his remarks, the President referred to Capt. Scott O'Grady, USAF, who was rescued after being shot down and stranded in western Bosnia.

Remarks at the Dartmouth College Commencement Ceremony in Hanover, New Hampshire
June 11, 1995

Thank you very much. President Freedman, Acting President Wright, Governor Merrill, thank you for your warm welcome. To my distinguished fellow honorees—I was thinking when they were all introduced, all the others who won this distinction of your honorary degrees, that if my blessed mother were still alive, she would be saying, "See, Bill, they accomplished something; you're just a politician." [*Laughter*] I am honored to be in their company, and I thank them all for the contribution they have made to the richness that is American life. To the board of trustees and especially to the parents and families and members of the class of 1995, let me begin on a very personal note. I always love coming to New Hampshire. I am delighted to be back at Dartmouth, but I am especially grateful to be here seeing my good friend President Jim Freedman looking so very well and back here at this graduation.

I also want to thank Dartmouth for something else, for contributing to my administration with the Secretary of Labor, Bob Reich, who came with me today. I understand that I have caused something of an inconvenience here—[*laughter*]—and that we are now breaking tradition here at Memorial Field, having left Baker Lawn. But I did a little historical inquiry and determined that when President Eisenhower came here in 1953, Baker Lawn replaced the Bema as the site of commencement. I am reliably informed, however, that the next time a President shows up, you will not have to move to the parking lot at the West Lebanon Shopping Center. [*Laughter*]

You know, when President Eisenhower came here, he said, "This is what a college is supposed to look like," And I have to tell you, even in the rain it looks very, very good to me.

I want to thank you, too, for honoring the class of 1945. See them there? They did not have a proper commencement because they left right away to finish the work of World War II. One of the greatest privileges of my Presidency has been to express over the last year the profound gratitude of the American people for the generation that won World War II. A year ago this past Tuesday, I stood on the bluffs of Normandy to say to the brave people who won a foothold for freedom there, we are the children of your sacrifice. I say again to the class of 1945: The class of 1995, the generation of your grandchildren, and all of us in between are the children of your sacrifice, and we thank you.

To those of you in this class, the 50 years that have elapsed since they sat where you sit today have been a very eventful time for this old world. It has seen the ultimate victory of freedom and democracy in the cold war, the dominance of market economics and the development of a truly global economy, a revolution in information telecommunications and technology which has changed the way we live and work and opened up vast new possibilities for good and for evil.

The challenge of your time will be to face these new realities and to make some sense out of them in a way that is consistent with our historic values and the things that will make your own lives richer. The challenge of your time, in short, will be to redeem the promise of this great country.

Now there are unparalleled opportunities for those of you with a wonderful education in this global economy and this information age. And you don't have to worry about things that your parents used to worry about all the time. I am very proud of the fact that in the last 2 years, for the first time since the dawn of the nuclear age, there are no Russian missiles pointed at the people of the United States of America. And I might add, there are no American missiles pointed at the people of Russia.

From the Middle East to Northern Ireland, from South Africa to Haiti, where, as the citation said, my friend Bill Gray did such great work to restore democracy, we see ancient conflicts giving way to peace and freedom and democracy in a genuine spirit of reconciliation. Hundreds of millions of people now breathe the air of freedom who, less than a decade ago, found it a distant dream. Every country in Latin America but one is now a democracy.

I am proud that our Nation could support these developments. But as all of you know, this new world is not free of difficulty, for the forces of opportunity contained within them seeds of destruction. The heavy hand of communism and dictatorships have given way to bloody conflicts rooted in primitive religious, ethnic, and racial hatreds from Europe to Africa. The mobility of money and people and the advance of technology have strengthened the hand of organized crime and drug traffickers from Latin America to Asia to the former Soviet Union. And we have all been reminded recently that none of us in this open, free-flowing world of ours are immune from the forces of organized evil and terrorism.

The possibilities of more rapid economic development have posed new threats to the global environment. Rapid changes in the world economy have brought vast new opportunities, but they have also brought uncertainty, stagnant incomes, and indeed, rapid insecurities, even in the wealthiest countries in the world. And we have seen it in ours.

Here at home, though we have made progress on our deficit and expanding our trade and taking serious action against crime and trying to increase the ability of our country to educate our people and to welcome those from around the world, as so many of you have come to

find your educational opportunity here, we know that for the first time since this generation left in World War II, Americans are worried that their children will not have a better life than they enjoyed. Half of all of our people are working harder for less than they were making 15 years ago, because the global economy punishes people who don't have the skills to learn to compete and to win in a world that is changing daily, indeed, hourly.

In our Nation, for the first time since World War II, we have watched, over the last decade and more, the great American middle class which is the core of our idea of America begin to split apart along the fault line of education. And of course, we all know that our social fabric today in this country is being rent apart by what is happening to our children. More and more of them are subject to violence and abuse. A higher and higher percentage of them are born into poverty. More and more of them are having children while they're still children. Even though the overall crime rate in this country has gone down, random violence among children is still increasing. More and more children are spending more of their lives with one-parent families, sometimes trapped on welfare, but more often, far more often, being raised by utterly exhausted parents who are working two or more jobs to give their children a chance, just a chance, at a good life.

Because in the 1980's we were unable to resolve these problems, because inequality and insecurity increased, because the realities of today and tomorrow were not addressed, the American people have continued to lose faith in the ability of their Government and sometimes, even more importantly, in the ability of our society to solve these problems. And perhaps the most important difficulty we face is the increasing cynicism of our own people.

Today in Washington we're having a great debate about what to do about all this, and that's a very good thing. On the one side, we have people who say that most of these problems are personal and cultural, and if all of us would just straighten up and fly right we wouldn't have these problems anymore. And of course, at a certain level that is self-evidently true. None of you would have a diploma today if you hadn't done the right thing to earn it. And nothing can be done for anyone to get out of a tight in life unless people are willing to do for themselves. But that ignores the other side of the debate, which is that there are plain economic and social factors that are not even common to the United States, putting pressure on people and taking away their hopes and threatening their dreams.

We have a great debate about what the most important thing for our Government to do is. On the one side are those who say that the Government can't really do anything to solve our problems anyway, so the most important thing is to balance the budget as quickly as possible without regard to the consequences. On the other hand, there are those who say we have a budget deficit and we ought to do something about it, but we have an education deficit as well. And when we have so many poor children, we need to invest in people to make sure they can live up to their God-given potential and that that is also important.

Today what I want to say to you is, wherever you come down in all these great debates, the most important thing is that you should be a part of the debate because your life will be far more affected by what happens in the next 2 years than my life. I have been given the opportunity of the American dream. I was the first person in my family ever to graduate from college. When I was a young boy growing up in Arkansas, one of our honorees President Overholser's father was the Presbyterian minister in my hometown. He raised one daughter to be the president of Duke, the other daughter to be the editor of the Des Moines Register. We came out of a place that, at the end of World War II, had an income barely over half the national average. But we were fortunate enough to live through a time when opportunity was expanding and when we were trying to come to grips with our racial and other problems in this country.

And what I wish to say to you is that you are going into the time of greatest human possibility in all history, but you must address the fact that all of our forces of opportunity have seeds of destruction. You must make sense and clarity out of complex problems. And I think you must do it with a much greater sense of optimism and hope than we are seeing in most debate today. There is nothing wrong with this country that cannot be solved by what is right with it, and you should never forget that.

We have a lot of things to do here in America. We have to grow our middle class again and shrink our under class and give our children

something to say yes to. We have to strengthen our families and our communities and make the idea of work more real to people for whom it has become unattainable. We have to preserve our environment and enhance our security at home and abroad. And I would argue that we must maintain the leadership of the United States in the world as a force for peace and freedom.

To all those who want to withdraw, who want to turn away, who want to abolish our foreign assistance programs, let me remind you: Look at the history of the 21st century. Every time America turned away from the world, we wound up with a war that we had to clean up and win at far greater costs than if we simply stayed involved in a responsible manner.

But our most important mission today, I would argue, is to help people make the most of their own lives. You can come down in many places on all these debates in Washington and around the country, but it is self-evident that unless people in this country, wherever they come from, whatever their race or economic standing or region, can make the most of their own lives, whatever is in there—the magic inside all of us—we will not fulfill our common destiny.

And today, more than ever before, it really does all begin with education, what we know and what we can learn. The class of 1945 saw the greatest explosion of economic opportunity in all human history after World War II, in no small measure because every one who participated was given the opportunity to get a higher education through the GI bill. And I am absolutely convinced that that was one of the two or three reasons that the United States of America developed the finest, largest, broadest, deepest system of higher learning in the entire world. And it is still the best system in the entire world because of what happened then.

When President Eisenhower faced the dilemma of the Soviets beating the United States into space and the fact that we had let a lot of our educational opportunities go downhill, he launched a great education initiative, giving loans to people all across the country and giving them good opportunities to pay them back. And they called it then the National Defense Education Act. The idea was that even in the late fifties, education was a part of our national security.

I tell you that that is more important today than it was in 1945 and more important today than it was in the late fifties. Men my age, between 45 and 55, grew up believing that when we reached this age, we'd have the security of knowing we could send our children to college, we'd have a decent retirement, we'd be living in our own homes, if illness came we'd be able to take care of it. We took these things for granted if we worked hard, obeyed the law, and paid our taxes. In the last 10 years, earnings of men between the ages of 45 and 55 have gone down 14 percent because in the global economy, if you live in a wealthy country and you don't have an education, you are in trouble. We cannot walk away from our obligation to invest in the education of every American at every age.

And to those who think there is no public role in that, I say: Just remember all of those who need those student loans, who need those Pell grants, all the universities who benefit from the research investments. There is a role for our Nation in the national education agenda of our future, and we should maintain it.

But let me make one other point as well. Education is about more than making money and mastering technology, even in the 21st century. It's about making connections and mastering the complexities of the world. It's about seeing the world as it is and advancing the cause of human dignity. Money without purpose leads to an empty life. Technology without compassion and wisdom and a devotion to truth can lead to nightmares. The sarin gas in the Japanese subway was a miracle of technology. The bomb that blew up the Federal building in Oklahoma City was a miracle of technology. We have got to use our knowledge to become wiser about the things which we do not understand and to find ways to use our knowledge to bring us together in ways that reinforce our common humanity.

I want to thank Governor Merrill for his support here in New Hampshire for our national service program, AmeriCorps, because I think it exemplifies that kind of objective. And I want to thank Dartmouth for participating in it.

The idea behind national service is to make a connection between ideas and the real world of need out there beyond the ivory towers of academia, to make a connection between earning an education and advancing the quality of life for others who may not have it, a connection

to be wanting to be respected for who you are and what you believe and not demeaning or demonizing those who are different.

I want to say a special word of thanks to the medical school for the partnership in health education project of the Koop Institute, which sends medical students into elementary schools up here in New Hampshire and in Vermont to help to promote health and prevent disease among young people. That also is a purpose of education, building connections, giving to others, helping to bind us together.

A society is not a collection of people pursuing their individual economic, material self-interests. It is a collection of people who believe that by working together they can raise better children, have stronger families, have more meaningful lives, and have something to pass on to the generation that comes behind. That also is the purpose of education, and we need it more than ever today.

And so, my fellow Americans, and those of you who will live and work here, you must decide: What is this new world going to be like? You can probably do fine, regardless. You have a world-class education at a wonderful institution. You have the luxury of deciding. Will you devote your lives and your compassion and your conviction to saying that everybody ought to have the opportunity that you had? Will you believe that there is a common good and it's worth investing a little of what you earned as a result of your education in? Will you believe that education is about more than economics, that it's also about civilization and character? You must decide. Will you work for more equality and more opportunity? Will the information superhighway be traveled by all, even poor kids in distant rural areas? Will they be connected to the rest of the world, or will the information superhighway simply give access on the Internet to paranoids who tell you how to make bombs? Will education lead you to lives of service and genuine citizenship or a politics of hollow, reactionary rhetoric where, in the name of reducing Government, we abandon the public interests to the private forces of short-term gain?

Just a few days ago, at Harvard, President Václav Havel of the Czech Republic said that our conscience must catch up with our reason or all is lost. I say to you today, we are having a great debate in the Nation's Capital, and we ought to have it. It can be a good and healthy thing. But some things must be beyond debate. We are all in this together.

A country at a crossroads has a chance always to redeem its promise. America is the longest lasting democracy in human history because at every crossroads we have redeemed that promise. And you must do it again today.

We've got a real chance to make a real life together, folks. Yes, there's more ethnic and racial diversity in this country than in any other large country. Yes, there's more income differential, and that's getting worse, and it's troubling. But this is still, for my money, the country that's the best bet to keep alive hope and decency and opportunity for all different kinds of people well into the next century.

I've had the privilege of representing you all over the world, and I think all the time, every day, about what it's going to be like in 20 or 30 or 40 or 50 years, when you come back here for that remarkable reunion that they're celebrating today. And I am telling you, if you will simply use what you have been given in your lives, from God and the people who have helped you along the way, to rebuild this country and to bring it back together and not to let us be divided by all these forces, to lift up these forces of opportunity and to stamp out the seeds of destruction, you still are at the moment of greatest possibility in all human history.

Your late president, John Kemeny, who came to this country after fleeing Hungary, told the last commencement he presided over in 1981, the following: "The most dangerous voice you'll ever hear is the evil voice of prejudice that divides black from white, man from woman, Jew from Gentile. Listen to the voice that says man can live in harmony. Use your very considerable talents to make the world better." Then he ended the speech with, as I understand, the words with which he ended every commencement: "Women and men of Dartmouth, all mankind is your brother. And you are your brother's keeper. Do not let people divide you one from another."

Do not let people make you cynical. And do not think for a minute that you can have a good, full life if you don't care about what happens to the other people who share this Nation and this planet with you.

Good luck, and God bless you.

NOTE: The President spoke at 11:44 a.m. on Memorial Field. In his remarks, he referred to James Freedman, president, and James Wright, acting president, Dartmouth College; Gov. Stephen Merrill of New Hampshire; and honorees William H. Gray III, Special Adviser on Haiti, and Nannerl Overholser Keohane, president, Duke University.

Remarks in a Town Meeting With Speaker of the House of Representatives Newt Gingrich in Claremont, New Hampshire
June 11, 1995

The President. Thank you very much. Thank you. Thank you very much, Lou. Mr. Speaker, Governor, Mayor Lizott, Congressman Bass, Mrs. Gingrich, Mrs. Zeliff, to Sandy Osgood, and to the Stevens High School Band, thank you very much for keeping everybody entertained while I got away from Dartmouth and got over here.

I am delighted to be back in Claremont again. I have spent some happy days here. And I was invited to come here, as you know, when you folks found out—I think it was actually Lou's idea; he found out I was going to be at Dartmouth giving the speech. And then I was inter-

viewed, and someone said, "Well, the Speaker is going to be here for the whole weekend. What advice would you give him?" And I said, "Well, I'd give him two pieces of advice. I think he ought to—if he's going to be in Concord, he ought to go down to Mary Hill's grocery store and talk to her because she's a wise woman. And he ought to do one of these little town meetings like I do from time to time." And so he called me, and he said, "I accept." [*Laughter*]

So that's how you became transformed into this. I'm going to talk for a couple of minutes; he's going to talk for a couple of minutes. Then we're going to spend most of our time just answering your questions. But let me be very brief and say that when I came here in 1992, I was running because I thought we ought to change the direction of the country. I thought that we were in danger of losing our standard of living and that we were coming apart when we ought to be coming together. I was worried about the decline in middle class incomes, the growth of the under class, the high unemployment rate at the time, an exploding deficit, a declining level of investment. I was also worried very much about the breakdown of our families, the number of children growing up in poverty, and the whole breakdown of a lot of the social factors that are very important to all of us and made us what we are.

I said then and I will reiterate today that I thought what we needed then—I still believe what we need is an economic strategy that focuses on creating jobs and raising incomes, a social strategy that rewards work and family, in terms of welfare reform and everything else we do, it reinforces responsible childrearing and responsible work, that we ought to do it in a way that reduced the size of the Government and reduced the bureaucratic burden of the Government but kept the Government on the side of ordinary Americans.

Now, what I tried to do is follow policies—whether it was reducing the deficit, expanding trade, increasing investment in education, promoting welfare reform—things that would help people to make the most of their own lives. I've also tried to do things I thought would increase security for American people, whether it was the Family and Medical Leave Act or the crime bill or the things we've tried to do in foreign policy or the antiterrorism legislation that the Speaker will take up when the Congress meets again starting tomorrow.

Now, we have a lot of differences, and perhaps these differences will come out. But we also have some areas in which we can work together. I think the most important thing is that we try to identify clearly the places where we disagree but then make our best effort, our dead-level best effort, to work together to move this country forward.

It seems to me that a lot of our problems are not particularly partisan in nature. We do have—for example, as I have said from the day I became President, we cannot afford not to do something about the fact that Medicare and

Medicaid costs have risen at much more rapid rates than Government revenues are going up, so that every year we spend more and more on Medicare and Medicaid, which means we have to either spend less on something else or explode the deficit. But I think how we do it and how long we take to do it and the manner in which we do it is critical.

So we need to discuss these things in an open way. And one of the things that I like about New Hampshire that I don't like about modern politics, generally, because it's so different, is that when I was running here in '92, I really felt that most people were making their decisions based on encounters like this rather than 30-second television ads or some blurb that comes across the airwaves where one politician is hitting another one and trying to use some emotional issue to divide the American people instead of to bring them together. I think that is what you have done for Presidential politics, which is why I hope you'll always be able to have this first-in-the-Nation primary for both parties, so we'll all have to go through this process of getting to know each other.

So having said that, I'd like to now bring the Speaker on, let him say a word or two, and then we'll get on with your questions.

Mr. Speaker.

Speaker Gingrich. Let me say—let me say, first of all, that I am delighted to be here, and I appreciate very, very much—I appreciate very much the opportunity to be here. And I want to thank both Lou Gendron and I want to thank the President for having been willing to allow me to come over.

[At this point, there was a disturbance in the audience.]

Speaker Gingrich. I think, despite this particular gentleman, I think that the tradition of New Hampshire for townhall meetings is exactly the right sort of thing to do.

Now, let me just say, if I might, that I am delighted to be here and that you ought to know this is a historic moment, the President visiting you, as we are told—the first time since, I believe, Calvin Coolidge came here in the 1920's that a President has visited, although of course many candidates have been here in the primaries. And I believe in all of American history there has never been a townhall meeting where a President and a Speaker have been there at the same time. So literally, the city of Claremont is setting history today.

Marianne and I are delighted to be here with Congressman Bass and Mrs. Zeliff and with Governor Merrill. But I wanted to say two things that have happened to me today that are classically New Hampshire. One I did on my own, and one the President recommended.

First of all, we got up very early this morning, and I want to report that we did see four moose, and one of them was a huge bull that stood in the middle of the road and stared until every single photographer who was with me could get their picture. [*Laughter*] The other was, I have to report, Mr. President, I broke down; we stopped at the Dunkin Donuts in Berlin this morning after seeing the moose, and this is why you've done better with your figure than I have with mine. [*Laughter*] I failed. But I followed his advice.

Let me say also to the band—I had a chance to listen a while ago—I thought you set exactly the right tone and exactly the right mood. I am grateful that you all would allow me to come and join the President. I hope today we can talk in a positive way about the positive things we Americans need to do.

And I agree with the President—the New Hampshire tradition of this kind of a discussion where we can sit, you can ask questions, we can both talk, and we're not in 9-second or 20-second or clever advertisements or any of that stuff. And I just want to say one thing about where we are that I think all of you can identify with. I called my mom a while ago, and I called my mother-in-law, and said, "Gee, I'm here now, and what should I do?" and all that. And I also talked to my two daughters. We have all three generations involved now in this discussion.

But let me tell you what I really honestly believe—and I think this is pretty close to the President's—most of you lived through the Depression, and it was hard. And you saved freedom in World War II. And you saved freedom in Korea. And you paid the taxes. And you worked at the jobs to help win the cold war. And you raised your children, and you wanted them to live in a better country. And now, you're helping raise your grandchildren.

And I believe all Americans can be told the truth and can actually watch their leaders have honest, open disagreements and can talk things out, and we can find common solutions. And

I believe this process, working with the President, with the House and the Senate, with the Governors, I believe we can get to a balanced budget in a positive way. I believe we can save Medicare, and it will not go broke, despite the trustees' report. I believe we can create a better future for our children and grandchildren. But it's got to be done exactly like here today.

So I hope with your permission, the President and I will now have a dialog with you, and maybe the country can learn a little bit about working together, not just buying commercials and attacking each other.

Thank you for letting me be here.

The President. Who would like to go first? Who's got a question? Yes, sir.

Lobby and Health Care Reform

[*A participant asked if a bipartisan commission could be formed to address lobby reform.*]

The President. Well, I would certainly be open to that. Let me back up and say one of the differences we have—let's talk about one of the differences we have about this. No one seriously believes that the budget can be balanced unless we can reduce the rate of increase in Medicare and Medicaid costs. We agree on that. We disagree on how much we have to reduce it and how it ought to be done.

I also believe that it would be far better if we could do it in the context of health care reform so that, for example, for seniors, we would provide some incentives for less expensive but more widely available long-term care short of nursing homes. We would have more emphasis on preventive care, because one of the big problems with Medicare is—there are three issues here: What is the medical rate of inflation, and can we get it down to the overall rate of inflation? You know, health care costs have been going up more than medical costs—regular costs. The second issue is how many new folks are coming on to Medicare every year. The third issue is how much more will the same people use the system because people are living longer and longer, and the longer you live, the more you need to use it.

And all these things are at the core of what we have to work out about how much we try to control the spending. It may be that the only way to do that is in the context of some sort of base closing commission, like you say. But I think we have to tell them what their mission is. That is, it seems to me that the mission can't just be to save money. It has to be not only to stabilize the Medicare fund over the long run but to do it in a way that doesn't force retirees without the means to do it to shoulder much bigger increases for their own health care or run the risk of having professionals jump out of the health care system.

Now, that is what my problem is. I just think that—we have to be very careful about this. We've worked hard to bring down the cost increases. But to get much—to go lower, we're going to have to have structural changes that provide for real options and quality of health care, in my opinion. Without health care reform, I don't think you can go dramatically lower.

Speaker Gingrich. Let me just ask first, I— [*applause*]—let me stop, and please applaud. I think this is—to have the President here is a good thing.

Let me—I think you were saying something a little different. I'll talk about Medicare in a second. But I think you were raising an issue that's very interesting. If I understood, sir, you're suggesting that when this whole issue of lobbyists and campaign finance and, you know, we have this whole issue about gifts in the Congress, which I'm, frankly, very uncomfortable with—I mean, I just—I don't know how all of you would feel, but when you come down to talking about yourself, it's very tricky sometimes. And I think you were suggesting—I've never heard this proposed before—that maybe if we had sort of a blue-ribbon commission of people that really had respect and integrity, that would look at the whole lobbying political process——

The President. Is that what you—I thought you were talking about health care reform.

Speaker Gingrich. No, no——

The President. You want to do it on lobby reform? In a heartbeat. I accept. Because, otherwise—otherwise, in this—we cannot pass lobby reform or campaign finance reform or anything else. I would love to have a bipartisan commission on it. It's our only chance to get anything passed. I accept.

Speaker Gingrich. Let's shake hands right here in front of everybody. How's that? Is that a pretty good deal?

The President. I accept.

Speaker Gingrich. I'll tell you, if every question is this productive—now, can I just take one minute, Mr. President, and talk about the Medicare thing? I do think the President put

his finger on something here where I think we analyze it slightly different, but we both have the same commitment. And let me say, because I did talk both to my mother-in-law and my mother today, I can report that I'm checking in pretty much with people who are immediately concerned about Medicare.

There are two differences. One is, I agree with the President that there are a number of things that have to be changed about health care in America. For example, I believe if you're in the insurance system, we ought to guarantee tomorrow morning that you have portability, that you can change insurance and change jobs and there are no preconditions. And I feel this personally because my older daughter has a precondition, and she's been through a period where she had to spend a whole year in vulnerability without any insurance.

So I think step by step—I think where we disagreed strategically is, I think you can do those one building block at a time and get them through and get them signed. I think it's very hard as a practical matter to get a big comprehensive bill through because it seems to break down of its own weight.

Now, specifically on Medicare, I hope this summer that we'll be able to work with the President and with his Cabinet. We're going to propose a plan in general terms that takes current spending, which is $4,800 a year per senior citizen, and moves it up over the 7 years of the budget to $6,400 per senior citizen. That takes into account additional people. But it will be a $1,600 or 33 percent increase. That's less than the current projections—I'm not going to try to kid anybody—but it is an increase.

And what we're trying to do right now is find a way, first of all, to guarantee that everyone who wants the current Medicare can keep it. And it may—you may have some increase in the amount you pay, much along the line you had in the last 6 or 7 years. But you can keep the current system. Nobody's going to be forced to change. Nobody has to leave.

But at the same time, I'm hoping that working with the President and his administration, we can find five or six additional options: Managed care for those who want it—in some counties, a lot do; in other counties, very few people do. Medical savings accounts, which is a new idea that lets people have savings which could then be applied to long-term care, for example. A voucher system, which some big companies are now using, which is very effective, where you can go to any doctor you want and we pay directly to the doctor of your choice, your control. And finally, something which I think we'll get overwhelming support for—if you look at your bills and you see waste or fraud, I'd like us to work in a system so if you spot it and you report it, you get a percentage of the savings, so every senior citizen in the country has a good, sound reason to check on waste and fraud to help us get that out of the system, because there's a General Accounting Office report that says there's about $44 billion a year in waste and fraud in both Medicare and Medicaid combined.

So I'm just suggesting, if we can work together and get the Senate with us, we can, by the end of the summer, keep the current system and offer four or five options and move towards a system where you become a customer and you're making the choice for you about which one you like. And if you prefer the current system, you get to keep it. That's your choice.

The President. Here's what my concerns are. Will I work with them and try to work this out? Absolutely. But here's what my concerns are. It sounds like a lot to increase something by one-third over 7 years. But that's about 4 percent a year. And this last year we had medical inflation at about 4½ percent, and that was good. We don't know whether it will stay that way, and the problem is that the Medicare population is going to get older and older. And as they get older, people use the system more. So I don't know that we can keep it to 4 percent a year.

The Republican in the Senate, Senator Packwood, with the major responsibility for this says that we can stabilize the financial fund of Medicare with savings at about half the level proposed in the Speaker's budget. It's not really his budget, but—well, it is now. They passed it. And I would prefer not to say right now we're going to cut at a level greater than I believe we have to in ways that I think will certainly require a lot of people who cannot afford it to pay more until we have explored all other alternatives, because I believe we can get there without doing this.

And as you know, I believe—let me say, there are going to have to be some changes. We cannot leave the system the way it is. We can't pretend that just because we're at a senior center that there will be no changes. There have

to be some changes. But I think these reductions from the projected levels of spending I think are too severe, and what I favor is having a smaller tax cut and a smaller Medicare reduction and Medicaid reduction. And then let's see how much we can save year by year, because we have not tried a lot of these things.

He and I both, for example—I really believe you ought to have incentives to join managed care plans. I don't think anybody ought to make you do it; I just think you ought to have incentives to do it. Out West, I know, there's one managed care plan for Medicare that offers people the right to get into Medicare for 95 percent of what the per-person cost is, and they give them a prescription drug benefit along with health care and still make money.

I think you should have the right—I think, you know, people ought to be able to try to talk you into doing that, that that ought to be an option, not a requirement. If you want to stay in the program, I think you ought to be able to stay in the program.

The way it works now is, you don't pay for part A, but you do pay more, as you said, by about the rate of inflation for the doctor bills and things like that. So that's where I would start these negotiations. I'd say, let's cut it as little as possible until we know how much we can save, because if we lock ourselves into a tax cut and we lock ourselves into other spending, then we'll wind up just not funding it, even if we wind up hurting people. And I don't think we ought to do that. I have no problem with all these experiments, but let's know what we're going to do.

Speaker Gingrich. Can I make one other comment? I'll just make one quick comment, and then we'll go back to a question here.

But let me just say, I think in spirit we're not that far apart. The thing that is driving us is that the trustees reported that Medicare will go broke by 2002. It starts to lose money next year and it literally runs—this is part A. This the hospital part. And all of you—folks who may be watching may not get it, but every person in this room understands part A, or every person in this plaza understands part A.

We start first with two big steps here. And then I think we can talk about exactly how we make the transition. One is, how do we save it for your generation? And that's very, very important. And we have to—and the earlier we can take some changes, the easier it's going to be to make that transition by 2002.

But I must tell you—I become 52 this coming week. And I'm older than he is, and you can see where the gray hair up here—but I started thinking about when the baby boomers start to retire, the weight of the current system financially is so enormous—and we've seen some numbers—$3,500,000,000,000 a year would be the cost of Medicare alone, not counting Social Security.

And so, part of what I hope we can do is set up a second commission—to go back to this gentleman's idea—and this would be a commission that would look out beyond saving Medicare in the short run and start to talk now about what do we need to do for the baby boomers in their retirement years and their health care. Because frankly, that makes everything we're worried about—the folks who replace us 20 years from now are going to have a much bigger challenge than we have in figuring out how the baby boomers retire and what happens with them.

But I think that's something we could probably work on in a positive way together.

The President. Let me just, again, reemphasize two or three points. I, in general, am going to agree with that. We need to focus on some things we know right now will work. We know we could save money long-term in the system if there were other options for long-term care in addition to nursing homes. There will always be people who need to be in nursing homes. But there should be other options. Today, there aren't any. And you've got all kinds of middle class families where the parents have to spend down all their assets to qualify for Medicaid to get into a nursing home because there's nothing else they can do. So we wind up cutting off our nose to spite our face, you know. In order to keep the family from going broke, the Government winds up paying more than might otherwise be necessary.

But to be fair, we don't know how to cost that out. We ought to get more people the option of going into a managed care program. If somebody says, "For the same price you're paying now we could also give you a prescription drug benefit, but you'd lose a few options on who your doctors were," then you should decide whether you want to do that or not. You could decide. We ought to do that. We ought to do more wellness and prevention planning.

My only fear is that we should be very careful about how we plan the budgets over the next 5 or 6 or 7 years. When I became President, the Medicare trust fund was projected to go broke in 1999. So we pushed it back to 2002. I think we have to push it back another 4 or 5 years. We've got to keep doing that. But I agree with—one thing the Speaker said I absolutely agree with—when you think about what the baby boomers require, which is, what, 2019 or 11 or whenever it was, I'm trying to push it—whenever I get that age—[laughter]—that's going to require a significant long-term structural adjustment. We'll have to look at what we can do there.

But the main thing we can't do—we can't have this thing go broke in the meanwhile. And I'm just telling you that less drastic procedures in my judgment can keep it from going broke if we make some other changes in our overall budgeting, without undermining our ability to balance the budget.

Who's got another question?

Congress

[*A participant asked Speaker Gingrich when Congress would stop playing special interest and partisan politics and start working together for the good of the country.*]

Speaker Gingrich. I think that's a very good question. It's partly, of course, answered by this gentleman, who I think has a great idea. You now have us publicly in front of you and all these reporters saying we're going to work together. And I hope we can develop a blue-ribbon commission pretty fast, because that's a part of it.

Part of it is why I said I was glad the President suggested this and then agreed to do it. I think just having your leaders chat rather than fight is a good thing. I think—it sets a different tone.

Now, I want to commend the President. He sent up some very important antiterrorism legislation. We had a meeting of all the Republican and Democratic leaders with him. We talked about it right after the Oklahoma City bombing. It then got bogged down in both Houses, frankly, more than it should have. Senator Dole then made an appeal to the President because the Senate has—see, in the House you have very strict rules, and you can get something through in a day if you work at it. In the Senate, if you have one or two Senators who don't like something, it takes forever.

Now, I don't think the Arkansas Legislature, back when the President was Governor, quite had a senate that had that kind of power. I think it was—you know, this filibuster—so Senator Dole appealed to the President, and the President, frankly, rose to the occasion, worked out a bipartisan agreement, and I think dramatically changed the tone of that antiterrorism debate and helped us get something through that was very, very positive.

So I think there are steps like this. I hope—I reacted positively the other day when the President said he was going to have a budget proposal. We're in conference now. But frankly, if they do submit something this week or next week, we're not—I mean, we're going to take—we're going to sit down and look at it all. I think this summer we ought to work on Medicare together. We shouldn't have a Republican plan and a Democratic plan.

In the House we've tried that. We had Mike Parker, who's a Democrat, who met with our budget committee members all through the budget. We had some Democrats, not a lot but some, who voted with us on the budget. In the Senate, Senator Kerrey from the entitlement commission and Senator Nunn and one other Senator voted for the budget.

But we ought to—when we can, we ought to pick up on what you said. It's very hard, though, for a practical reason. The Founding Fathers designed the Congress to be where everybody sends their representative. And it's the place where everybody shows up with their ideas. And I'll tell you, some days, even with the best of will—Congressman Gephardt, for example, and his wife, Jane, are good friends to Marianne and me—even with the best of will, you find yourself some days wondering how did you get into the particular mess you're in.

And the Founding Fathers wanted an arena in the House and Senate to fight out our passions instead of having a civil war. They wanted us to send everybody from every part of the country. And their idea was that they wanted a system so inefficient that no dictator could force it to work. Now, the problem with that is——

The President. They sure did that.

Speaker Gingrich. I was going to say, they succeeded. We can barely get it together voluntarily. So, Mr. President——

The President. Let me say, I think there are a couple of things we need to try to be candid about. One is my great frustrations since I've been President is that—I have a line that I sometimes say in speeches; I'll just tell you, I was in Montana the other day, and I said, "Shoot, if all I knew about me was what I saw on the evening news, I wouldn't be for me half the time either." [*Laughter*] I mean, the truth is that it is so difficult for us in Washington to communicate with people out in the country, with all of the layers between us, that what often is the only way to break through is some fairly extreme statement.

The Speaker is real good at that; he can break through like nobody I've seen in a long time. [*Laughter*] But it will get covered. He can break through.

The easy way for—let's take this Medicare debate. The easiest way for us to break through is for him to say, they want to fix the trust fund and the Democrats have no plan, and for me to say, he cuts Medicare too much and it will cost you a lot. Now, the truth is we both believe that, but it's more complicated than that. And the problem we have is that in a difficult time like this, where we're moving into a whole new era, there very often are not simple answers to complex problems; but simple answers very often move the electorate.

So if you don't want that, if you want a reasoned debate and you really want to say to the Republicans and Democrats, "Look, get together and do something that is good for the country and put party aside," then out here in the country, when the Congressmen and the Senators come home on the weekends, you need to tell them that. And you need to say it over and over and over again: "We will stay with you. We will not be spooked by this or that lunge in one direction or the other. We'll give you 4, 5, or 6 months to try to work through this budget, and that's what we expect you to do."

You have to send a different signal. You have to send a different signal. You have to make people believe they can take complicated positions, explain them to you, and if you think that makes sense, you'll stick with them. And if you do that, I think you can change the way politics work in America.

Speaker Gingrich. Can I make one quick story before I take another question, because it is so much what he just said, and I, actually, I wrote it it in a book, it was so vivid to me.

I'll get to—you're going to love this. No, you're going to love this.

The President. Senator Dole hasn't given me permission to read that book yet. [*Laughter*]

Speaker Gingrich. Well, I thought I'd get you a copy soon.

The President. That's good.

Speaker Gingrich. But let me tell you, because it was so vivid and it makes the President's point. We had a meeting, you'll remember well, where Dick Armey and I were down there and the whole brandnew leadership after the election. And obviously, the President wasn't all that thrilled to have the Republicans win the election. And we understood that, and heck, we wouldn't have been—you know, I wasn't all that thrilled, frankly, to have George Bush lose that last one, so we understood his feelings. We had a great meeting. It was a meeting that I almost could have been on C-Span because the country wouldn't have believed—we talked about line-item veto, which is currently a little bit bogged down, but we'll get to it.

The President. Give it back to me. [*Laughter*]

Speaker Gingrich. We talked about unfunded mandate reform, which he signed very early. We talked about passing the Shays act to apply the law to the Congress that applies to us, which he signed very early. We had things going on that were positive. Dick Armey and I walked out front—we're in the White House, in front of the White House drive there. We say to the White House press corps, "We had a great, positive meeting. We're going to be able to work a lot more than people think." And we began to list these things. The second question we were asked: "What do you think it will break down over?" And both of us got mad. He's right; I get too hot sometimes. So I just said to the reporter, I said, "You just heard the leaders of the Republican Party say that the Democratic President today had had a wonderful meeting on behalf of America; we're trying to work together. Couldn't you try for 24 hours to have a positive, optimistic message as though it might work?" It's a true story, and he did it. It was a great meeting that he called.

The President. The trick is, in a funny way, is not to hide the differences but to get them out in a way that—where those of us on opposite sides can understand the other's opinion. Like there's a way to make an argument to get the maximum amount of votes out of it in the shortest amount of time through emotion, and there's a way to make the same argument so that your opponent at least understands your position. And I bet it's the same way here around a gaming table or anything else. There's two ways to talk to people when you've got a difference of opinion.

More than half the time in this country—this is an interesting little historical fact—more than half of the Presidents who have served have had the Congress in the hands of the opposite party, at least one if not both Houses. Now, that's what—the voters seem to think that's a good idea, and they keep doing it. So we have to try to figure out how to make it work.

Who's got—yes. Mr. Peabody, you're looking good in your Navy cap.

United Nations Peacekeeping Role

[A veteran expressed concern that proposed legislation would adversely affect the United Nations and peacekeeping efforts.]

Speaker Gingrich. Let me say, first of all—and I appreciate very much your comment about the two of us being here. And I hope you're right.

Let me say, first of all, on a lot of foreign policy issues, we work very closely together. And we have tried very hard on Russia, on the Middle East, on a whole range of areas to be very supportive. The President and his senior advisers have always been open in briefing me and have always been open to my phone calls or my visits. We've tried in the House to stop some things that would have been very destructive. And I've tried in public, and I've learned a fair amount in the last 6 months, that a Speaker—it's very important for me to be careful and to be modulated on a number of foreign policy issues. And while we can tangle on domestic politics, there really is a great lesson to be learned from Arthur Vandenberg in World War II.

But let me tell you the two things I think where maybe you and I just disagree. And I hope you won't mind my being direct. First, I don't think the last 50 years the peace was kept by the United Nations. Over the last 50 years, the peace was kept because the United States of America spent a lot of money and sent its young men and women all over the planet. And we were the strongest military power in history. And we built an alliance called NATO. And we took enormous risks. And our children—my father fought in Korea and Vietnam. We're now risking our children in Bosnia, in Iraq, in a whole range of—in Haiti, where the President, frankly, has so far—and I hope it works out perfectly—has so far had a much better policy than I thought he would. It worked better than I thought it would. And he deserves to be commended for, I think, having taken some risk in Haiti.

But first, I will say to you—first, I believe we have to recognize that what won the cold war and what kept the peace was America's willingness to lead. And that nothing—you're wearing a Navy cap—if my choice is three U.N. Secretary-Generals or one aircraft carrier, I can tell you which one I prefer to keep the peace in a dangerous world.

But I want to say, secondly, about the U.N.—because I'm a big fan of Franklin Roosevelt's, I'm frankly a fan of Woodrow Wilson's, and I think what they were trying to accomplish was terribly important—I think we have to revisit the United Nations current structure. I mentioned this to the National Security Adviser the other day.

The U.N. current system of command and control is a nightmare. And anybody anywhere in the military—and the President knows this, because he gets briefed on it—any of our military who looks at what's been happening in Bosnia just wants to cry. You don't send in the military to be hostages; you send in the military to rescue hostages. And the U.N. system—I'm willing to take the U.N. system seriously enough to actually encourage our Government to take the lead in reforming the current peacekeeping system because if it's not reformed, it's going to collapse and become a joke, and you'll see NATO replace it in Bosnia in the not-very-distant future. And I take it very seriously.

Over the long run, Churchill once said, "Jaw, jaw, jaw is better than war, war, war." And I think Churchill was right. But to get there, we have to be strong, we have to lead our allies, and together I think we have to learn the lessons of what doesn't work in the U.N. And my hunch is, frankly, if this bill is going to ever become law, there's going to be some fairly intense negotiating between Senator Dole and myself and the President, because otherwise he's going to veto it, and we won't have the votes to override him. So I think we're not—you're not going to necessarily see exactly the bill that's currently there.

The President. Let me just say very briefly, I agree that the United Nations didn't keep all the peace in the last 50 years. What I think is that the end of the cold war gives us the opportunity to have the U.N. fulfill its promise. And the United States has had, before me and during my administration, serious disputes with the U.N. about the way it's managed and the way certain crises are handled.

Now having said that, I disagree with the foreign affairs bill going through because it ties the President's hands in too many ways. I disagree—I'll say something that's unpopular here—I disagree with all the cuts in foreign aid in the budget. Most people believe that we're spending 10, 15 percent of your tax money on foreign aid. We're actually spending about a penny and a half. We're spending a smaller percentage of our budget on foreign aid than any advanced country in the world. And yet, you'd be amazed how far a little bit of money from the United States goes in stabilizing democracy all over the world.

For the United Nations, a lot of—some of their peacekeeping has worked. It worked in—it made a real contribution in Cambodia. It's made a contribution elsewhere.

The problem in Bosnia—let's just talk about that—is that great countries, France, Britain, The Netherlands, Ukraine, sent their soldiers there to be the U.N. peacekeeping force under terms of engagement that the United States could never agree to because they basically agreed until just this last incident that they—the Serbs could, in effect, take them hostage and they wouldn't fight back. And we could never agree to that.

Now, having said that, it's still true that 130,000 people died in Bosnia, civilians, in 1992, and under 3,000 died there last year. And a lot of us made contributions to that. So sometimes, as bad and as ragged as it is, the U.N. is better than nothing. And I think it is our forum.

And a lot of good things have happened in the U.N. We have been able to pursue our nonproliferation agenda. We've been able to pursue our action to reinforce what we're trying to do with North Korea to keep them from becoming a nuclear power. We've been able to do a lot of good things.

And I think we should look for ways to strengthen the U.N., not weaken it, because I agree with him and what he said—if it is weak and if it fails, it will all come back on the shoulders of the United States. And another generation of young Americans will have their necks on the line if we fail to have an effective, strong United Nations, which is why I think we should support it and make it work.

Minimum Wage

[*A participant asked if a minimum wage rate of $4.50 would be too high.*]

The President. No, I'm for raising it. You know I am.

Speaker Gingrich. Let me say that I think that I'd like to see every American make as much as they can possibly make. But I also am concerned—no, I don't think it's too much. I'm very concerned, however—there's a disagreement among economists about this. I'm very concerned that if you raise the cost of the first job for the poorest person, for example, in the inner city, that what you tend to do is increase black, male, teenage unemployment, which is exactly the thing you don't want to do.

And so my goal is to have a rapidly growing economy where, frankly, wages keep going up because people are better educated, more productive, and can compete in the world market. And we've been telling the Russians and the Ukraines and the Poles and the Hungarians that the free market works and you've got to get out in a free market and you've got to compete in a world market.

And my concern is just that as you go through this transition that if we raise the minimum wage—and, again, you get economists on both sides of this argument. But the group we—we don't hurt anybody who's an industrial plant that's doing well. We don't hurt anybody who's already working for the Government. But if you are the marginal employee and you're out there, you are the first laid off. And that makes it harder for Hispanic and black teenagers to get decent jobs, and we already have too much unemployment and too much long-term lack of job skills among minority teenagers. But I think that's a legitimate disagreement probably between the two of us.

The President. Let me just tell you what the contrary view is, what my view is. And it is true that there are economic studies that say if you raise the minimum wage, you raise incomes for people who are at the minimum wage

and a little above it, too, who get bumped up, but it costs some jobs. There are other studies that say it doesn't cost any jobs because, for example, people on welfare or out of the work force will think it's more worth their while to come in and compete for those jobs and they'll want to work more.

The reason that I am for it is that I believe that—first of all, I know that a significant percentage of people on the minimum wage are women workers raising their kids on their own. And I just believe that we shouldn't allow— if we don't raise the minimum wage this year, then next year, after you adjust for inflation, it will be at a 40-year low. And my idea is that we ought to be trying to create a high-wage, high-growth economy and that is as little regulated as possible. But this is a minor amount of regulation on the bottom end.

And there are other ways to deal with this market problem. I know Barbara Jordan, a former colleague of yours, headed a commission for me on immigration. She's recommended a modest decline in the immigration quota every year. And I think Senator Simpson, the Republican Senator from Wyoming, has recommended the same thing. If you did that, you might have exactly—you might still, therefore, have exactly the same demands for low-skilled people who are already in the United States and you wouldn't, therefore, be any net out even if you did raise the minimum wage.

I just think it is—the people I guess I admire most in this country are the people that get up every day and work their—themselves to death for the minimum wage or just a little bit above it——

Speaker Gingrich. Note that editing, I might point out. That was very well done. [*Laughter*]

The President. Self-editing. And they come home and they're dog-tired at night, and they're raising their kids and they don't have enough money to live on. And they don't break the law. They don't cheat on their taxes. They don't do anything wrong, and it's all they can do to keep body and soul together. And I guess, my instinct is that you get way more good than harm out of it. And I believe, if you go back to when they did it when—the last time it was done was when, '89 or something—I think, on balance, we did fine as a result of doing it. And I think we should do it again.

Immigration and Welfare Reform

Speaker Gingrich. Can I add one more comment? Let me add one more comment because I think he's making a point here that's very important in thinking about the totality, when you mentioned immigration.

I think, in addition to the recommendations of the commission—which I think was a very important thing to do, and I think that Barbara Jordan was a superb person to head it up—I think we've got to look very seriously at illegal immigration because I can tell you, even in north Georgia, we now have a very large number of illegal immigrants working, for example, in the chicken industry. And it is on the verge of getting out of control all over this country. And so even if we were to close down legal immigration or slow it down, if the illegal immigration just keeps pouring in, the effect of driving out American workers is devastating.

Second, I think we have to have welfare reform that reemphasizes work, which is part of why we, frankly, want to get it back to the Governors and have Governor Merrill working on welfare reform, to reestablish work because if it costs you—in New York City, if you lose money going to work at minimum wage, then even when you raise the minimum wage, you can't afford to go to work.

And so—and the President, again—he campaigned on replacing welfare as you know it. And he's committed to welfare reform that gets us in that direction.

The last thing, I guess, I'd like to say—and I don't actually know where you are on this right now. I believe we both have to have much more adult education. I have suggested we tie, for example, unemployment compensation to training so that people, when they're not on a job, are learning. If we're giving them money, they're actually getting trained and learning, much more like the Swedish and German model.

And part of the reason we proposed the $500-per-child tax credit is because the day you go to work, you start paying Social Security FICA taxes. It is very regressive on the poorest workers. And the mothers that the President has just referred to who may have, say, two or three children, who are working at minimum wage, if they could get $1,000 or $1,500 back from their Government in a child tax credit, we think

that helps that mother take care of those children.

It's a different approach. But again, it's a way of trying to get more cash into those pockets. And I agree with the President. We have got a find a way to get—I think it's now 40 percent of our children are in poverty—we have got to find a way to raise our children and get those children out of poverty.

The President. On illegal immigration—we've increased by about 40 percent the number of border guards we've got, and we're sending illegal immigrants back more rapidly than ever before, especially if they come in contact with the criminal justice system. What we need—and maybe we can work together on this—is the capacity to go into more workplaces and find people who are taking jobs away from Americans illegally. And I think that's important.

On welfare reform—we don't have time to debate that today. We agree on the ends. We have big disagreements about the means. But I've given 29 of the 50 States permission to get out from under all the Federal rules and to do things like take food stamp and welfare checks and give it to employers as a wage supplement and let employers then hire somebody off welfare and use the welfare check to cut the employers' cost to put the people to work instead. And I think that's good.

AmeriCorps

[A former VISTA volunteer expressed support for the AmeriCorps program and asked the President and Speaker Gingrich to comment.]

Speaker Gingrich. Sure. Let me say this is an area where I think the President has a good idea, but we disagree, I think, about philosophy of Government and about setting priorities. But it's not a bad idea. I don't think AmeriCorps in any way is a bad thing. And in a minute, since I'm going to go first, I am confident that he will tell you vividly how good an idea it is.

But I have two concerns that I think are a different direction, philosophically. One is that I believe—and we have people like Congressman Kolbe and Congressman Knollenberg who are developing a bill that would give a every taxpayer a tax credit to give the money directly to charities so that charities could do it directly. I believe we want to have less Washington-based bureaucracy and fewer decisions made in Washington. And we want to strengthen the private charities.

So if you said to me tomorrow morning would I rather strengthen AmeriCorps or the Salvation Army, the truth is—and I happen to agree with a book by Marvin Elasky called "The Tragedy of American Compassion," where he argues that the kind of transformation that you can get from 100 Black Men or from Habitat for Humanity, whose pin I'm wearing—the kind of groups that aren't restricted by legitimate Government restrictions but are able to go in in a much more spiritual basis and a much more directed basis and help people change—you get a stronger, healthier society by getting it totally out of Government. That's a difference of philosophy about the size of Government.

There's a second difference. If we're going to balance the budget, I think this is a time to be very tough-minded about priorities. Now, the President lists this as one of his highest priorities and is fighting very ably for it and is going to, frankly, keep it. If we can get to a signable rescission bill, it's going to contain— it's going to keep AmeriCorps, and that's the power of the Presidency. I would just suggest that when you sit down and look at what it takes to balance the budget over 7 years or 10 years, it's hard. And if you're setting priorities about which programs to keep and which not, you can have a legitimate, honest debate about how many things you can afford to do in Washington and how many things you need to get back home to New Hampshire or you need to ask the private sector.

But it's an area where I—I don't fault his vision and his desire to recruit people at all, and I think it's, frankly, a program that's very defensible. It's just one—it's a question of philosophy and priorities.

The President. Let me give you my side of it. The reason I got the idea of doing AmeriCorps was, basically, I thought we ought to have more scholarship money available for young people that wanted to further their education or for even not so young people who wanted to do it. And I thought we needed to promote the idea of service here in this country among young people, at least in a symbolic way. If I could fund it all, if the Speaker would support me, I'd get up to a couple hundred thousand people in AmeriCorps in no time. But I wanted to do it especially as we bring down the size of the military, because a lot of young

people who otherwise would have gone into the military and gotten wonderful training and served their country in invaluable ways and changed their whole lives forever now won't be able to do it because we just have—we don't have a need for the same size military.

And this idea intrigued me. It was promoted by a lot of other people. I didn't come up with it; I just thought we ought to do it. And it is not organized—even though it's funded by Washington and there's a general policy group in Washington or a board—Governor Merrill can tell you from what they have here in New Hampshire—it is very—there is very little bureaucracy. People competed for the money. If your project got the money, you just kept it. There's almost—very few reporting requirements and no rules and regulations from the Federal Government. But with 20,000 people in AmeriCorps, which is what we had this year, we have more people doing that than were ever in the Peace Corps in any given year.

And the other day I was down in Dallas, just for example, where a retired African-American general supervises our AmeriCorps program. And I saw four volunteers: two girls who were teenage mothers and on welfare, who got themselves off welfare, got a high school equivalency, and were working to help other people get off and earning money for college; a woman who was retired from the Navy, believe it or not, who said, "I don't even know if I'll ever use this credit, I just wanted to serve my country again working in the neighborhoods"; and a young woman who had a degree from the University of Florida, whose mother was on welfare when she was born, and she had always done very well and she just wanted to go back and give something, try to change that neighborhood.

I think it's important for us to find some ways for people of different racial and income backgrounds and regional backgrounds to work together for the common good in a nonbureaucratic way. So I think it's a tiny cost for a big gain. And that's our difference.

Questions?

Lou Gendron. Mr. President, Mr. Speaker——

The President. Do you want to have one more question——

Mr. Gendron. Ladies and gentlemen, we have time for one more question.

Line-Item Veto

[*A participant asked if the line-item veto would lower the budget and help reduce the deficit.*]

Speaker Gingrich. The answer is yes, it would. And I support it. And I'm hoping we're going to be in conference this summer. And the line-item veto's aimed specifically at appropriations bills. And he's already indicated that's how he'd use it. And I hope we're going to be able to get it passed and to him this summer so he can actually use it. I strongly favor it. I think 43 of the Governors have it. I think you had it when you were Governor of Arkansas.

And I think—now, it's not going to be by itself a panacea, but it's going to cut a couple of billion dollars a year of pork out, maybe as much as $10 billion if we—under certain circumstances.

And I supported it when we had Ronald Reagan and George Bush. And just as the other night, frankly, we tried to repeal the War Powers Act to give the President back the right—the legitimate power of the Commander in Chief, I think that any President ought to have the line-item veto. And I support President Clinton getting it.

The President. I want to say, first of all, thank you very much for that. We have—some of the Republicans were worried because the line-item veto legislation might also permit the President to line-item-veto special tax, as opposed to general tax legislation, special tax legislation. I think it should include that.

But what I said—I sent a letter, or I sent a statement to the Speaker and to the majority leader of the Senate saying that I know that a lot of the Republicans may think they want to give tax cuts which they believe are good, which I don't agree with, so I would commit, that for the remainder of this budget cycle this year, if they would pass it this year, I would only use it on spending this year as a gesture of good faith so we could get it into the law and begin to see how it works.

Before we leave, I should have said one other thing on the U.N. thing that I didn't. With all the differences we've had, except for the United Nations and one or two other minor things, the Speaker has been very supportive of me on foreign policy. And one of the things we have to do together is to figure out how to make his party in the House somewhat less isolationist than it is. And I think they're only reflecting the views of their constituents. That is, people want us to tend to our problems here at home. They don't want us to waste any money overseas. Nothing is more unpopular than doing that now. But this is a very small world, and every time the United States walks away from problems around the world, we wind up paying 10 times the price in blood and money later on. So this is something we're going to have to work together on.

Speaker Gingrich. If I could—let me say thank you and goodbye first, and then let the President have the final say, as is appropriate.

Let me just say, first of all, I agree with what he said, although I can tell you in both parties the difficulties and the problems of carrying the burden of America——

The President. Same with the Democrats; it's not just the Republicans.

Speaker Gingrich. There's a real challenge for all of us to go back home and explain why America has to lead.

Let me finally say to Lou and to everybody here who invited us, I think this has been the best New Hampshire tradition, the best American tradition. I think it is fabulous that you have us come over and—are we all right still? And I just want to say thank you to all of you, and again, I want to thank the President. He didn't have to do this. It was his idea. I think it's good for America, and I'm grateful for the chance to be here.

The President. Let me close by thanking you. I've enjoyed this, and I expect you have, too. And most of all I want to thank all of you for having us here, for listening, for asking the questions.

Q. This man wants to say something, Mr. President.

The President. What? My chops are no good today. [*Laughter*] Well, I'll be over there in just a minute.

What I want to say is, when you all hear us debating these issues, I want you to think about some real big questions. And I want you to think about the things that affect you, of course. When you hear these numbers batted around, it won't mean anything. I want you to think about if we propose a change in Medicare, if he does, I do, what will—how will it affect you? I want you to think about that, because you should, and you should let us know.

I also want you to think about the big issues. What do you think the Federal Government ought to be doing? What is the role of the Federal Government as we move into the 21st century? How important is it to reduce the budget deficit as opposed to dealing with, let's say, the needs of our people for more investment in education and training, and do you want us to do both?

We have problems in America that are not just political and economic, they are also social, cultural, personal problems. Some people you can't help unless they also are willing to help themselves. On the other hand, you can't just go around and point the finger at people and tell them to help themselves if they need a little help to get down the road in life.

So these are big, fundamental, basic questions that are now being debated all over again in Washington, maybe for the first time in 50 years, where we're really going back to basics. And you need to be a part of that.

If you want us to work together, instead of figuring out who's got the best 30-second attack on the other, you need to really hammer that home. You need to tell the Congressmen. You need to tell the Governor. You need to tell all of us that—be clear about your difference, but don't divide the country. And let's try to do this.

Let me just close by saying this: I wouldn't trade places with anybody in any other country. I get to represent you around the world. And with all of our problems, the diversity of America, the power of our entrepreneurial system, the resources and resolve of our people, we're still in better shape for the next century than any other major country in the world. And don't you ever forget it.

And what we owe you is our best efforts not only to show you how we disagree in ways that make us look better than the other but to actually get things done that your lives and your children and your grandchildren. I'm going to do my best to do my part.

Thank you, and God bless you all.

NOTE: The President spoke at 4:45 p.m. at the Earl Bourdon Senior Centre. In his remarks, he referred to Louis Gendron, president, Claremont Senior Citizens Congress; Mayor Paul Lizott of Claremont, NH; and Sandy Osgood, director, Earl Bourdon Centre.

Remarks at a Fundraising Dinner for Senator John Kerry in Boston, Massachusetts
June 11, 1995

Thank you very much, Senator Kerry. Thank you for your remarks and for your example. Teresa, congratulations. I could listen to you talk all night long. Senator Kennedy got so wound up, you'd have thought he was on the ballot next week again. [*Laughter*] That's why he won. He believed in what he was doing, and that's why he won. Thank you for your spirit and your courage and your unflagging energy. Vicki, it's nice to see you. Senator Leahy, Congressman Kennedy, Congressman Markey, Congressman Meehan, my note says that Congressman Frank's here—he may not be or he may—are you here? Thank you. I want to tell you something: When nobody else will stand up, Barney will. He's got—where I come from—thank you—thank you very much. I was going to say, where I come from, that counts for something, and I've never forgotten it. Your State chair, Joan Menard, and your wonderful, wonderful mayor, Tom Menino, I thank him so much. President Bulger, it's always good to be here with you. I have kissed the Blarney Stone, paid homage, done everything I'm supposed to do here tonight. The mayor of Galway was—is he here still? Where is he at? Anyway, I think—you know, I have to go back to Ireland, and I was wondering if you would consent to be my tour guide if I go back, give me a little direction. Speaker Flaherty, the Secretary of State Galvin, Auditor DeNucci, and Elaine Schuster, thank you so much. You are indefatigable. I am so impressed by how you keep coming back and helping us in our need. And sometimes I think we take our friends for granted, folks, and we should never do that, and I thank you.

Somebody told me my friend Governor Dukakis is here. Is he here? Hello, Mike. Stand up. God bless you. Thank you.

I've had a rather interesting day, you know? [*Laughter*] I got up at 5:30 this morning, and it's been a hard week at the White House. We're dealing with—you know, I had to veto the rescission bill last week, and we were dealing with a lot of other things, but overarching everything, of course, was the fate of Captain O'Grady. And it was a few days before we even knew for sure he was alive. And the whole remarkable story is beginning to come out, and of course, we're going to receive him at the White House tomorrow, and I'm looking forward to that. I know all America will be rallied and full of joy and energy.

But anyway, I was pretty tired anyway, and I rolled out of bed at 5:30 this morning, and I hauled up to New Hampshire, and I spoke at the Dartmouth commencement and shook hands with about 1,600 students. And then I went to a reception and shook hands with a couple hundred more people. I went to Claremont, and Speaker Gingrich and I did our little town hall meeting. And I thought it was a good thing, good thing for America, and I hope you did, too. We didn't get into all of the issues, but we got into some of them. And we had a civilized way, I think, of explaining what the differences are.

What I'd like to talk about a little bit tonight is why I'm still here and why I'm glad you're here. I was looking at Ted Kennedy give his speech so brilliantly tonight and wanting to cheer every word, and then I watched Teresa speak and I watched John speak and I watched John's movie, and I'm feeling sort of mellow. I got to thinking, you know, it's a miracle any of us are still around, you know, the whole complex of circumstances that brings any person to any point in time, where you're in a position to do whatever it is we're trying to do now. It's a great privilege. It's an honor.

And so I was thinking to myself, in this time when our tide is supposed to be out and theirs is supposed to be in, why would I not leave my party? Why am I proud to be here with John Kerry? Why was I proud when Ted Kennedy fought back and won? And I'd like to tell you why I am, based on what I know and what I see as your President.

We are getting back to first principles today, really getting back to first principles. Sometimes I get in trouble in Washington when I'm in these arguments with—because I forget that things I assume everybody else agrees with, a bunch of folks in the Congress now don't agree with at all. But that's not all bad. We're going to have this huge debate.

For example, one of the issues that now is really open for debate is whether most of these social problems that Senator Kerry talked about are caused by economic and political and social factors or whether they're largely personal and cultural, that is, they can only be fixed by people just stopping doing what they're doing wrong and beginning to behave.

Now, there's some truth to that, isn't there? I mean, at one level that's just self-evident that people should behave, and if they don't do what they're supposed to do, nothing the rest of us can do will make anybody get an education or make anybody put a gun down or make anybody stay out of a gang. That is self-evident at one level.

But if you have the opportunity to do what I have done, which is to sit with Mayor Menino and his youth council, you know that it makes a whole lot of difference if somebody is trying to help these kids make the right decision. So I'm a Democrat because I believe the problems are personal and cultural, but not exclusively personal and cultural, and I think we're put on this Earth to try to help other people make the most of their lives, and we're better off when we do that, and I have learned that.

I hear these—there's a big debate in Washington about if the Government is not very good, what should we do, what is the most important thing? And some people think balancing the budget as quickly as possible is the most important thing, no matter what the consequences. I think it's an important thing; that's why we worked hard on our deficit reduction package. We got interest rates down. We got the economy coming back. We have over 6 million jobs to show for it. It is not an insignificant thing.

But it is not the only thing, because it's not as if this country's not worth anything, you know. When we invest in the education of our people, when we invest in medical research, when we invest in the things that make us richer and smarter and stronger, we have assets, and they bring us things.

And I would tell you we have a budget deficit, but we also have an education deficit in this country. It is not solely a money problem, but money is related to it. One of my rules of politics is, when somebody tells you it's not a money problem, you can bet your life they're talking about somebody else's problem. [*Laughter*] You think about that.

Yes, there is a budget deficit, but there is an investment deficit in people. And so, let us find a way to balance the budget and still invest in the education and training and empowerment of all of these people we expect to lead us into the 21st century. That's why I am a Democrat, and I'm glad to be one, because I believe that.

If you believe, as some say now, that the Government can't do anything right and always burdens the private sector, then obviously it makes logical sense to rewrite the environmental laws of the country by letting the people who are covered by those laws, who in the course of their economic activities damage our environment, rewrite the laws. Because if you have no faith in Government at all, then you're not doing anything wrong by letting the polluters rewrite the laws. Because Government is by definition bad, what is public is bad, what is private is good, if that's what you believe.

Senator Kerry sponsored, I think, two of the only environmental pieces, except the California desert bill, that passed the Congress last year, the Marine Mammal Protection Act and another piece of legislation. We thank you for that.

See, I just don't believe that. And Republicans used not to believe that. Richard Nixon signed the law creating the Environmental Protection Act. Richard Nixon signed the first Clean Water Act. Teddy Roosevelt was the first and perhaps still the greatest of all environmental Presidents. There were only 20 head of buffalo left in the entire United States when Teddy Roosevelt set aside the buffalo preserve out West. If you ever go out there, you ought to go see it. It's a big deal. And it's stood for all kinds of other values.

And when I was a boy growing up in the woods and in my little national park in my hometown, I was really grateful to Teddy Roosevelt. And I always thought that using the power of the Government to protect our natural heritage was not really a partisan deal, it was something we had all agreed upon that we had to do, because all of our short-term impulses sometimes have to be subordinated to the long-term good of the United States. All of them, all of them do. So that's why I'm still here.

If you believe that the market always solves all problems and therefore the Government messes it up, it's understandable why you'd be against raising the minimum wage. But to me, this country's done pretty well in the 20th century, raising the minimum wage on a pretty regular basis. And now if we don't raise it this year, it's going to be at the lowest level in 40 years next year. And I'm telling you—we always talk about how we want to reform welfare and people ought to go to work—let me tell you something, folks, there are thousands, tens of thousands of people that get up in this country every day—in fact, a few million—and go to work for the minimum wage. And a lot of them are the sole support of their children.

What kind of courage does that take? Who can live on that? And they get up, and they show up for work every day, and they work for their minimum wage. And they trudge home, and very often they live in a place that's hard to live in, and their kids are exposed to problems that most of our children aren't. And they always pay their taxes, and they never break the law, and they just do the best they can. They are real American heroes. I think we ought to raise the minimum wage. I think that's the right thing to do.

So that's why I'm proud to be a Democrat. We could lose every election in the country, and I'd still be right there, because I couldn't get over that. I could never get over that. And I say that not to be critical of other folks who really have different views but just to tell you that I feel very fortunate just to be able to stand here tonight. And I'm the first person in my family that ever got a college education. I had student loans, and I paid them back, but I needed them badly. And I always thought it was our job to go up or down together.

And one of the things that has struck me so much in the last 2 months—they've been pretty difficult, emotional months for America. And they're sort of bracketed, if I will just take the last 6 or 7 weeks, by our national heartbreak in Oklahoma City and our national exultation at this remarkable young Air Force captain who kept himself alive for 6 days, when people were all around him, and I mean literally all around him, with guns in their hand, wanting at least to imprison him and probably to kill him. And we get together at times like this and we feel, even in the midst of tragedy, better about our-selves because we are part of something bigger than ourselves. We really feel like we're Ameri-cans again. And I guess the reason I still belong to this party is, I think we ought to feel like we're Americans again every day. I think we ought to be working together every day.

And I want you to think about this one issue to illustrate it. It relates to Senator Kerry. There are a lot of things I like about John Kerry. I like the use—and I mean this is a positive way—I like the use that he has made of his experience in the war in Vietnam, which was the seminal experience of our generation. I like what it has done to his sense of conscience, his sense of responsibility, his sense of reaching out even to Vietnam. I like the fact that it has made him feel a much greater sense of accountability for power. Once you see power exercised in a way that you think is unaccount-able, that is erroneous, and you can't change it quick enough to save people that you're trying to save, it makes you interested in things like what we did with Mr. Noriega or what the BCCI issue was all about or what the S&L bailout turned out to be. It makes you interested in accountability, and I like that.

I like the fact that he's kind of like me, he's interested in all of these technology, future-ori-ented issues and basically has a rosy view of tomorrow. But the thing I really like is that he cares, still, as a United States Senator, about the issue that still has the capacity to tear the heart out of this country, which is the rising tide of violence among young people.

Let me tell you that the crime rate is going down in almost every major city in America. It's a cause for celebration. It's a tribute to enlightened leadership. It's a tribute to the po-lice forces of this country. It means that our crime bill strategy, which Senator Kennedy and Senator Kerry worked hard for, was the right one to put more police officers on the street and to emphasize prevention as well as punish-ment. It means all that.

But in spite of all of that, underneath all of those numbers, there is an almost astonishing rising tide of random violence among children. And I'll tell you this one story, from my home-town, Little Rock, Arkansas. Just a few days ago—I get the local hometown paper, and I try to read it; it kind of keeps me rooted. And there is this remarkable story, and I only saw the top—I saw this beautiful picture of this

schoolchild and these little questions this child had answered in the picture—big color pic-ture—"If I could do anything, I would have people be nice to each other." "I wish peo-ple"—blank, you know, it was one of those fill-in-the-blanks things. "I wish people wouldn't ever join gangs." "I want to live a long time." "When I grow up, I want to be a police officer."

I got to laughing, and then I looked at the headline and the whole thing. And this child whose picture was here in the corner with this—"This is what I want to do, and I want people to be nice and no gangs, no violence"—this child and a brother and a sister, the three of them, young children, 10, 12, and 14, as I re-member, were lined up and assassinated, assas-sinated by apparently three young men, only one of them using a weapon, because they had an older sister or half-sister who allegedly was involved in the death of one of these other people's siblings. So their idea of retribution was to go wipe these kids out.

And I'm not trying to get you down about this, but what I'm trying to do is to say to you that a lot of this political rhetoric that we engage in is very divorced from reality. And this country is in a strange position now, because I'm telling you, I still think we're in the best position for the future of any major country in the world: We have the strongest economy, the most vital business sector; we are well-con-nected with the rest of the world; we're the most ethnically diverse. Everything is great. But underneath this, we've got these kids that lit-erally are so disconnected, so numb, so unreached that they are killing each other al-most without remorse and really believing that nobody loves them and what difference does it make and if they live to be over 21, it will be more than they expect.

This Nation cannot tolerate that. And the only way we will ever turn it around is to reexamine every single thing we are doing, yes, and be willing to change it if necessary. But we also have to make a commitment that somehow we're going to do, on a national basis, what the mayor here is trying to do with this youth council. Because all these kids start out as good kids. You know, when they're 6 months old, they haven't decided that they're going to grow up and wipe somebody out. And things happen that make them unable to imagine the life that we take for granted.

You know that wonderful line from Yeats, "Too long a sacrifice can make a stone of the heart." We have a lot of kids whose hearts turned to stone. Now, I don't pretend for a moment that if John Kerry and I win reelection in 1996 that by 1998, on July 16th, every teenager in this country will all of a sudden turn into an Eagle Scout and no one will ever pick up a gun or a knife. But I do think it makes a difference. I do believe it makes a difference whether the people who hold public office imagine that they must make connections with people that are different from themselves and feel that we have a collective responsibility not only to seize our opportunities but also to beat back our problems.

I say this again not to depress you, because I believe that our Nation is in the best position of any country to seize the opportunities of the 21st century but only, only if we understand that every single opportunity in this chaotic and fast-changing world has within it the seeds of destruction.

And this is one example: Oh, it's wonderful if you can take advantage of the global economy, but if you can't you're going to be one of the 60 percent of American workers that are working harder today for less money than you were making 10 years ago. It's wonderful if you can hook into the Internet and you're a rural kid somewhere out in the Mountain West and find the whole world at your fingertips. But if you're a paranoid crazy, you can also learn how to make a bomb. It's wonderful that we can move around all over the world, but it also makes us more vulnerable to terrorism.

Every one of these leads us to the same conclusion. It is folly for us to believe that we can live and function and make the most of our own lives all by ourselves. Whether we like it or not, beyond our families, we have work, we have communities, we have States, and we are part of a country.

Near the end of the Civil War, Abraham Lincoln said, "We cannot be enemies, we must be friends." We conduct our national politics as if we are trying to segment each other into different groups of enemies and demonize our Government as the instrument of our common coming together.

You are here, every one of you, because you know better. So I will say to you in the end, the reason I hope you will work hard to reelect John Kerry is that his life is an example of understanding, down to the fiber of his being, that we must go forward together and that every time we lose a child, we lose a part of ourselves. And no, we're not making excuses for other people's irresponsible behavior. No, we're not taking onto ourselves things that we cannot achieve. But we do understand that in this imperfect world, the thing that makes America great is when America is together. We have been divided long enough. We have been distracted long enough. We have demonized each other long enough. There are children out there to be saved and a world to be made, and that is what we intend to do.

Thank you, and God bless you all.

NOTE: The President spoke at 9 p.m. at the Park Plaza Hotel. In his remarks, he referred to Senator Kerry's wife, Teresa Heinz; Senator Edward M. Kennedy's wife, Victoria; William Bulger, Massachusetts Senate president; Charles Flaherty, Massachusetts House speaker; William Galvin, Massachusetts secretary of the Commonwealth; Joe DeNucci, Massachusetts auditor; and Elaine Shuster, Democratic Party activist.

Remarks to the White House Conference on Small Business
June 12, 1995

The President. Thank you very much. Someone once told me that half of making a small business work was just consistent, unfailing enthusiasm. I think you have demonstrated that today. [*Laughter*] And I hope you never lose it.

Let me thank, first of all, my good friend Alan Patricof for the wonderful job that he has done in putting this whole conference together. I want to thank the other commissioners for the work they have done, the corporate sponsors, all the people, the staff people, who worked on our meetings out in the State and the regional meetings and made sure that we got the reports back here. I thank them all. I thank Phil Lader for the fine job that he has done.

And I want to say a few more words in a moment about the Vice President and the re-inventing Government group. But let me tell you, their—we tried to do something that's hard to do and may never register, but I noticed for years every President would come here and just continue to run against the Government. And it was always good politics, except the Government never changed because most people who worked here say, "Presidents come and go, but we'll be here when they're gone." [*Laughter*] And we decided that most of those people were pretty good people and that they didn't wake up every day wanting to make your life miserable and wanting to do things that were counterproductive and hurt the American economy.

And the Vice President and people with whom he has worked, Elaine Kamarck, Bob Stone, Sally Katzen, so many others, they actually decided to see if they couldn't get these folks involved in working with us to try to change the culture of Washington so that when we're gone, they'll be different. And that's never been done before in my lifetime. And I want to thank him and all of them for doing it. It's hard work. It's thankless work. It's hour after hour after hour of arguing and gaining ground inch by inch that no one will ever see. But I'm telling you, that is what we were hired to do. And that is what he has led the way in doing. And the country owes him a great debt of gratitude.

You know, there have only been three of these conferences held since our Nation was founded. This will be the last one in the 20th century. I also want to thank the Members of the Congress who made this possible, people in both parties who supported it. And I want to say a special word of thanks to all of you. Everybody here had to take precious time away from your business, and some of you had to close your businesses down and come here at great personal financial sacrifice to yourselves, and I want this to be worth your while. And I'm grateful to you for doing it, and I thank you.

You know, sometimes I think things are pretty rough around here, and I often think they're entirely too partisan. We—the Speaker of the House and I tried to change a little of that yesterday up in New Hampshire, and I think we did the right thing.

Just in case you think this is something new, let me tell you that in 1938, President Roosevelt invited small business people from around the country to gather over at the Commerce Department. Just after the morning session started, the participants became so argumentative that the Commerce Department guards had to be called in. [*Laughter*] An inventor from Philadelphia became so rowdy that the DC police had to take him out of the room—[*laughter*]—and I quote from the historical record, "put him in a hammerlock, give him a finger twist, and assign three officers just to keep him quiet." [*Laughter*] Well, it was 42 years before they held another White House Conference on Small Business. I hope you all make it to the lunch break today. [*Laughter*]

You know, the last couple of conferences have really produced some positive efforts, from the Paperwork Reduction Act of 1980 to the Regulatory Flexibility Act in 1980. This year is no different. This conference is going to produce some substantive changes, and it already has, because of the State and regional meetings. And I want to talk to you about them today, ideas that grow out of the recommendations that you and your colleagues all across America have made.

I ran for President with a pretty simple vision: I wanted to restore the American dream and bring the American people together in a period of rapid change here at home and around the world, an economy in which jobs and capital, technology and ideas flow across borders at lightning speed, with great opportunities but enormous challenges, an economy in which we were producing jobs and businesses at record rates but in which incomes were stagnant and insecurity was rising for people, especially in their middle-aged years when they needed to be thinking about whether they could guarantee their children a better shot than they had had.

My job as President is to do everything I can to see that our people and our businesses have the tools they need to meet the demands of the present age and seize the opportunities. We know that small business is the engine that will drive us into the 21st century. We know that big corporations get a lot of attention—[*applause*]—thank you—we know that the big companies get a lot of attention. And they should; they do important things for America. But you employ most of the people, create more than half of what we produce and sell, and create most of the new jobs, and we need to respond to that.

Small business is the American dream. We look around this room, we see, and you can hear when you share each other's stories, innovation and ingenuity and daring.

I'll never forget one thing that Hillary told me years ago. We were talking about all the jobs we had when we were kids and all the jobs we had going through college and law school and all of that. And she said that the most important job she ever had in her life she thought as a child was a job she had working in a small store in her hometown when she was in high school in the summertime, because this person just opened this new business to try to compete with the only other person doing the same thing in town. And she said for a couple of weeks nobody came in. And she realized, and I've heard her say it to me 50 times since she first said it, the extraordinary amount of personal courage it takes to start a new enterprise and risk yourselves in this environment. That is what made this country great. And we have to nourish it, support it, enhance it, not undermine it. That's why you're here.

When I came here 2½ years ago, the first thing we had to do is to try to generate a broad-base economic recovery because we were in a period of the slowest job growth since the Great Depression. And we were having serious problems. We had quadrupled our country's debt and tripled the annual deficit in only 12 years, while reducing our investment in the future in many important areas. We knew we had to get our fiscal house in order, bring that deficit down, and at the same time continue to invest in the skills of our people and the technologies of the future, to open markets, to create more jobs, and also, and quite importantly, to reinvent the way this Government works to make it relevant to the future toward which we're heading, not tied to the past which we have long since left.

Now this hard work is paying off. There's a lot of work still to do, but the facts speak for themselves: The economy is up; inflation is low; trade is expanding; interest rates and unemployment are down. The strategy is working. Over 6½ million new jobs have come into this economy in the last 2 years, almost all of them in the private sector, a far higher percentage of new jobs in the private sector as opposed to Government than in the previous decade. We have more than 80 new trade agreements covering everything from cellular telephones to rice from my home State and everything you can imagine in between. The deficit is being cut already by a trillion dollars over 7 years, and we are going to cut it more.

The deficit is now going down 3 years in a row under the budgets already passed for the first time since Mr. Truman was the President of the United States. And under the budgets already passed, thanks to the reinventing Government effort, we are going to reduce the size of the Federal Government by 270,000. It will make it the smallest it's been since President Kennedy was the President of the United States.

In 1993, more new businesses sprung up than in any previous year since World War II when we started keeping these statistics—and 1994 broke the record of 1993—and more and more importantly are staying alive. In the last 2 years, business failures and bankruptcies have plummeted. We wanted to keep it that way. We're doing everything we can to accelerate that trend.

In the 1993 economic program which was passed by the Congress, there was a 50 percent cut in capital gains for 5-year investments in new businesses capitalized at $50 million a year or less. I think that will increase access to capital for small businesses. We raised the amount that can be deducted for equipment expenses by 75 percent. We extended the research and experimentation tax credit. We have just extended the deduction for self-employed people for their health insurance premiums, and next year it will go up to 30 percent from 25 percent. We've also scrapped export controls and expanded export assistance to help not only big businesses but small businesses sell their products around the world.

When I came to this office, I had three basic goals for small business: I wanted to give new life to the Small Business Administration; I wanted to make it easier for you to get credit; and I wanted to cut Government regulations that didn't make any sense so you could grow faster. We've come a long way toward meeting these three objectives.

Under the extraordinary leadership of both Erskine Bowles and Phil Lader, two people who became heads of the SBA not because they happened to be involved in politics but because they knew something about small business, which seems to me that should be the basic criteria for anybody who ever gets that job in the future under any administration.

We have a leaner, more invigorated, more committed SBA than ever before. We've shrunk the applications for most common loans from over an inch thick to a page long, one single page. The SBA budget is now less than the taxes paid every year by three companies that received critical SBA help early in their careers—Intel, Apple, and Federal Express.

In the past year, more private capital was invested in SBA's venture capital program than in the previous 10 years combined. We have dramatically reduced the credit crunch in many parts of the country by revising banking regulations to encourage lending to smaller firms. And the SBA loans grew from 32,000 in 1992 to an estimated 67,000 this year. And though we more than doubled the number of loans, the cost to the taxpayers was reduced. We've expanded loans to women- and minority-owned businesses dramatically, dramatically, without— this is the important criteria—we have done it dramatically without lowering the volume of loans to other business or without lowering the credit standards one single bit.

The Vice President talked a little bit about the Herculean work that he and the others in our reinventing Government group have been doing to reduce regulations. Last Friday we announced an initiative that will allow you to report wage and tax information to one place. Instead of sending the same data to many different Federal and State organizations, you can now send it to one place, and we'll do the rest. Next year, in 32 States next year, people will be able to file their State and Federal income taxes together, electronically. Now, that will really save a lot of paperwork and problems.

Today I want to make two further announcements. First of all, we're committed to making the regulatory burden lighter, literally lighter, specifically 39 pounds lighter. [*Laughter*] As part of the review I ordered at the beginning of the year, we are taking 16,000 pages from the Government's Code of Federal Regulations. I thought you would like to see those pages. Could you bring them out, please?

These are our others.

Audience members. IRS! IRS! IRS!

The President. Hey, I'm working on that.

Now, if you place these end to end, they would stretch for 5 miles: 50 percent of the SBA regulations; 40 percent of the regulations of the Education Department—I want to compliment them; they're also trying to fulfill my mandate to have national standards of excellence and then support for grassroots education reform, not education reform right out of Washington—40 percent of the regulations; 25 percent of the reporting burden of the EPA. Now, let me give you an example of what this is.

Audience member. IRS! IRS! IRS!

The President. Do you want to give this talk? [*Laughter*] We're working on that. I already told you we dramatically cut the reporting requirements. We're working on the regs, too, on the IRS. If you knew how hard we had to work on all these, you'd come on up here and help us some more. [*Laughter*] That's why you're here. Give us a list of the other things you want cut. That's why you're here.

Audience member. IRS!

The President. If you give a list, you file your report—you know how this works. You've got to get your votes up and make your recommendations. But this will make a difference. This will make a difference.

Let me just give you one example of the kind of thing—if I were a betting person, and I could afford it—[*laughter*]—I would wage a considerable amount of money that no one will ever write me a letter complaining about the demise of these regulations. But I was being reasonably conscientious, like I am, I wanted to make sure we weren't getting rid of something terribly essential, and so I asked the reinventing Government folks to give me an example of the kind of things we're getting rid of that I could relate to from my Arkansas roots. And I hate to tell you this, folks, but we're about to lose the regulation that tells us how to test grits. [*Laughter*] Now—it's terrible.

Now, listen to this. I want you to ask yourself if you can do without this: "Grits, corn grits, hominy grits, is the food prepared by so grinding and sifting clean, white corn, with removal of corn bran and germ, that on a moisture-free basis, its crude fiber content is not more than 1.2 percent, and its fat content is not more than 2.25 percent." Here's the interesting part— [*laughter*]—"When tested by the method prescribed in paragraph (b)(2) of this section, not less than 95 percent passes through a #10 sieve"—[*laughter*]—"but not more than 20 percent through a #25 sieve." [*Laughter*] Now, here's (b)(2); it tells you how to get that done: "Attach bottom pan to #25 sieve. Fit the #10 sieve into the #25 sieve, pour 100 grams of sample into the #10 sieve, attach cover, and hold assembly in a slightly inclined position. Shake the sieves"—[*laughter*]—"by striking the sides against one hand with an upward stroke, at the rate of about 150 times a minute." If you've never been in a marching band, how do you know what 150 times a minute is? [*Laughter*] "Turn the sieves about ⅙ of a revolution each time in the same direction after each 25 strokes." [*Laughter*] "The percent of the sample passing through a #10 sieve shall be determined by subtracting from 100 percent the percent remaining in the #10 sieve. The percent of material in the pan shall be considered as a percent passing through a #25 sieve."

I don't know if we can do without that or not. What they ought to do is just have a designated taster like me in every State that knows what grits taste like. [*Laughter*]

Now, I have to tell you, there is some real sacrifice in this, though. We've all had a good laugh, but there's some real sacrifice. I personally am having to give up this 2,700-word regulation on french fries. [*Laughter*] Don't worry about it, folks; our health insurance plan has counseling for this sort of thing. I'll be all right. [*Laughter*]

Let me tell you that we've had a good laugh here today, but—and while a lot of this seems self-evident, it's not always easy to get rid of these things that are outdated and don't make any sense to us. But it's even harder to make regulations that need to be on the books but have become tangled up and senseless over the years untangled, sensible, and workable.

So we're also working to make another 31,000 pages of these Federal Government regulations simpler, clearer, and more relevant to your lives—things that most of you would admit ought to be done, but just don't make sense in the way they're being done—to bring common sense back into the way we do business.

Here is proof of the example. Today I want to announce a plan to reform the laws and regulations governing pension plans in our country. And almost every one of them came from you. That's why I am urging—that's why I said to the gentleman who mentioned the IRS and the others, this is what this conference is for. When you hear this, you may want to clap, but remember, it's happening because of you. And we can do more because of you.

But let me just go over this. You may recognize these ideas because we got them from you. The pension laws enacted over the last 20 years with the best of intentions are now so utterly complicated that you need a SWAT team of lawyers and accountants to help you fill out the forms and comply with the rules. Running pension plans takes so much time and costs so much money that only 15 percent of the small businesses in our country have them. Most of you just give up, and who could blame you?

Simple streamlined pension plans, however, are good for everyone, for small business because they boost morale and give people a stake in the company, for workers because they encourage savings, and we need to do everything we can to see that our people put away more money for the future.

So here's what we're going to propose: Start a simplified IRA-based pension plan for companies with 100 or fewer employees. Under this plan, if you guarantee your employees a certain contribution, you will be exempt from complex antidiscrimination rules.

Second—I don't know how many times I've heard this myself—second, fair treatment for families who work together. Get rid of the family aggregation rule. Get rid of the family aggregation rule, which treats family members as a single entity, dishonors the hard work of individuals, and is a drag on that great American institution, the family business.

Third, simplify. There is currently a seven-part test to determine whether or not someone is a, quote, "highly compensated employee." That is nuts. [*Laughter*] So, we believe that there ought not to be a seven-part test. We simply ought to have a simple guideline that will save all of us time and money.

Now, we can do all of these things without opening the system to abuses. Safeguards for fairplay are still in place. But we can do it, and we should. There is a lot more to do.

I want to make two points in closing. Number one, you can make progress on these problems. It's hard work. It's more difficult than giving speeches about how bad it all is, but it can be done.

The second point I want to make is, we know you made a sacrifice in time and money to come here. We know people like you made those sacrifices to come to the regional conferences and the State conferences. This is serious business. We did not ask you to do it just so we could cheer and have a good time, although that's important. We want your further ideas. We are doing these things because people like you all over America said they ought to be done.

Lastly, let me say that for all of the challenges and difficulties in this country, I wouldn't swap with any other country in the world as I look to the future and what it holds.

So, in a few moments, the Vice President and I are going back to the White House and we're going to welcome that fine young Air Force captain, Scott O'Grady, and his family there. And I want you to think about everything this country's got going for it.

First of all, and most important, it's got you and people like you, great entrepreneurs, great citizens, people who work hard, make the most of their lives, doing the best that they can with their families, contributing to their communities.

Secondly, we have more diversity in this country, more ethnic and cultural diversity, than any other advanced country. And that's a huge asset in a global economy. It's a huge asset.

Thirdly, we have a phenomenal set of assets and technology and research capability. And we have a Government that can change and can be a partner as we build the economy of the 21st century. We have profound challenges. But what I want you to believe from this experience today is that we can change, we can make it better, and that it comes from you. We will listen. That's why we wanted you to be here. I want you to be screaming and yelling and having a good time. I will not send the DC police after you—[*laughter*]—as long as you will send me some more good recommendations so we can do this again next year.

Thank you, and God bless you all.

NOTE: The President spoke at 10:40 a.m. at the Washington Hilton.

Remarks at a Ceremony Honoring Captain Scott O'Grady
June 12, 1995

Thank you very much, Mr. Secretary, General Shalikashvili, to all the members of the Armed Forces here, the distinguished Members of Congress, the members of the O'Grady and Scardapane families, to our distinguished guests.

I am tempted to say that we actually arranged this weather today so that Captain O'Grady would know for sure that he was not going to be left high and dry. [*Laughter*]

We are all here to thank our men and women in uniform for the rescue of Captain Scott O'Grady. Their mission made all Americans proud, just as Captain O'Grady's courage has made all Americans proud. We know that the skill and professionalism of our Armed Forces and the intelligence that backs them up are unmatched. We know that the months, the weeks, the years in training someday, somewhere will always have to be put into effect. And last week, those of you who brought life to that training and saved one brave man's life said more about what we stand for as a country, what our values are, and what our commitments are than any

words the rest of us could ever utter, and we thank you for it.

Consider this, that an F–16 pilot in Captain O'Grady's "Triple Nickel" squadron picks up a faint radio signal and relays it to an AWACS plane. Within minutes, the AWACS operators positively identify Captain O'Grady and pinpoint his location. Then just hours later, no less than 40 airplanes and helicopters are airborne, led by a combat search and rescue team from the 24th Marine Expeditionary Unit, commanded by Colonel Martin Berndt. The AWACS aircraft, a marvel of our technology, guide two Super Stallion helicopters to within 50 yards of Captain O'Grady. In 2 minutes, the marines secure the landing site and whisk the captain to safety under hostile conditions.

When I spoke to Captain O'Grady once he was on board the U.S.S. *Kearsarge*, he told me his rescuers were the real heroes. Well, it can't be done any better than they did it. They showed our Nation and the world the best of our teamwork. When we finished our conversation, Captain O'Grady remarked, "Mr. President, I just want to say one thing: The United States is the greatest country in the world. God bless America." The men and women of our Armed Forces also bless our America with your service and your skills. Because you do your job so well, our Nation will always be the land of the free and the home of the brave.

Now let me say it was a very great personal honor for me to host Captain O'Grady and all the fine members of his family, beginning with his grandparents and going down to his brother and sister and some of his friends, at the White House for lunch today. I can tell you that he

certifies he got a better meal today than he did in those 6 days in Bosnia. But he gave us something more precious than we can ever give him, a reminder of what is very best about our country.

And I'd like to now ask Captain O'Grady to come up here and say what's on his mind and heart to the people who gave him back his freedom.

Captain Scott O'Grady.

NOTE: The President spoke at 1:42 p.m. at the Pentagon.

Remarks to the United Auto Workers Convention
June 12, 1995

Thank you very much. Thank you, Owen, for that fine introduction, and thank you for your leadership over the years. I want to congratulate you and the other officers who are retiring. I want to say a special word of hello to all the brothers and sisters of the United Auto Workers throughout the country, especially those from my home State of Arkansas with whom I've worked over the years.

I'd like to say a word also to Dennis Fitting, the president of Local 455 out of Saginaw, who was with me last Friday at the White House for a reunion of a group of exceptional Americans whom I met along the campaign trail in 1992. We call this group the Faces of Hope, and I want to thank Dennis for being a member of the group and for his commitment to our efforts to move America forward.

All of you know better than anybody that Owen Bieber has dedicated his entire life to improving the lives of working families. He took over the UAW 12 years ago, during one of the toughest periods in your entire history. In all of the years, he has never wavered, even in the face of administrations here in Washington that were sure less than friendly. He's always stood strong not only for UAW workers and their families and their incomes and their future but for the kind of broad social progress that has been the hallmark of the UAW since its beginning in the 1930's. Whether it was in the fight for civil rights or the fight to end apartheid in South Africa, your solidarity with the Amer-

ican farm workers, the UAW has always been there for others as well as for your own interests.

Owen Bieber has truly carried on the legacy of Walter Reuther. And moreover, in a very difficult period in our country's history, he has set the stage for even greater strength for you in the 21st century. We all owe him our deepest gratitude and our best wishes. And I feel especially indebted to him for his advice, his counsel, and his ferocious support. Thank you very much, Owen. We all wish you well and Godspeed.

Now, I know you haven't elected your new officers yet, but I wanted to say that I personally would feel a whole lot better about my campaign if we could go into 1996 with poll numbers looking like Steve Yokich's do right now for you.

One of the most memorable moments in my 1992 campaign, and I had a lot of memorable moments with the UAW, but one of the most memorable was the opportunity I had to walk the picket line with Owen and the striking workers of Caterpillar in Peoria. I looked into the tired but determined faces of men and women on that picket line, and I realized how much was at stake for them and for all the rest of us as well.

I ran for President because I believed we had to do more to help those workers and millions of Americans just like them who had seen their stake in the American dream uprooted during the 1980's, people who were being abandoned by Washington, people who were working harder and harder for less and less. Their struggle showed me better than any report or any poll that the fight to save the American dream and the fight to save American families must begin with the fight to save America's workers and their incomes and their jobs. Of course, the struggle at Caterpillar is still not over, but my administration continues to walk the line with you, and we'll stay there.

I came to Washington to work with you and with all other Americans to turn these disturbing economic trends around. I wanted to shrink the under class and to grow the middle class. I wanted to rebuild a sense of hope and community. I wanted to help people to make the most of their own lives. I wanted to reward the values that have kept this country strong, the values of work and family and community. And so I've worked hard to develop an economic strategy that focuses on both creating jobs and raising incomes. And I've focused on a social strategy that would, instead of just talking about family values or work, would actually reward work and family and responsible parenting and good citizenship. And it's beginning to work.

In the past 2½ years, our economic strategy has added almost 7 million new jobs to our economy, and nearly all of them have been in the private sector. We're cutting the deficit by a trillion over 7 years, reducing it for 3 years in a row for the first time since Harry Truman was President. But we have been able to invest more in the education and training of our people and in the promotion of our children and strengthening our families.

We've been able to give a tax cut to 15 million working families through the earned-income tax credit. What that means in simple terms is that this year working families with two children with an income of under $28,000 will have a tax break of about $1,000.

We want to make it so that every family who works for a living will not live in poverty. We want parents who are willing to work full-time to be good parents and good workers at the same time. That's also why I worked so hard and you worked so hard for the passage of the Family and Medical Leave Act. It will make a real difference to working families in this country.

As you know, we're having a big debate now in Washington over balancing the budget. As I have said many times, I want to balance the

budget. It will help you if we do. It will lower interest rates. It will free up money to invest in the private sector and new jobs. It will mean that we can spend more of your tax money on things like the education of our children and less paying interest on the debt.

But we cannot balance the budget by giving a huge and untargeted tax cut that benefits mostly very wealthy people and paying for it by excessive cuts in the Medicare program. We can't do it by walking away from the fact that we have not only a budget deficit but an education investment. You know as well as anyone, from the increases in productivity the UAW has achieved in the last several years, that we have to have constant education and training if we're going to guarantee our young people the incomes and the security they need.

So I say, we all know that the countries that do the best job of educating all their people will be the real winners in the global economy. No one understands this more than you. You have led the way with your apprenticeship programs and your training programs. You have worked and worked and worked to support the kind of lifelong learning agenda that is central to my efforts to revitalize the American middle class.

And that's why, even though I agree we should balance the budget, we don't have to be targeted into an arbitrary timetable, funding excessive tax cuts to people who are doing well and don't need it, and having excessive cuts either in Medicare for our elderly or in the investments that make our country strong.

I'm fighting to preserve our investments, like the direct student loan initiative, which lowers the cost of college loans to your children, eases their repayment terms, and makes it possible for more of our young people to go and to stay in college; our innovative school-to-work apprenticeship efforts, which involves partnerships with unions and community colleges and employers all over the country; our successful national service initiative, AmeriCorps, which gives 20,000 young people college scholarship funds in return for community service work in their local community, helping people to help themselves.

We can't afford not to support something as important to our future as the education and training of all of our people. That's why I am also supporting a new "GI bill" for America's workers, to collapse about 70 smaller Government training programs into one big block and to give people a check or a voucher when they're unemployed or when they're underemployed so that they can take the money for up to 2 years to a local community college or to any other approved training program to get the kind of training they need. When people lose their jobs in this country today, too often people walk away from them. And it's wrong.

Let me take just a moment to talk about one other aspect of our strategy that is crucial to our future. As we enter the 21st century, trade is becoming more and more important to the long-term health of the American economy. We only have 4 percent of the world's population. Our success in the future rests heavily on being able to sell our goods and our services to the other 96 percent of the world.

When we open new markets, we find new consumers for our products. When we sell more products, we create more jobs. Every billion dollars in new exports creates 17,000 new American jobs. That's why I've done my dead-level best as President to open new markets around the world. The Congress has helped me, because it means so much to our economy and to our way of life. The fight for open trade should not be a partisan issue. Democrats and Republicans work together to put in place more than 80 trade agreements in just over 2 years.

I know you haven't always agreed with us, and I understand. I think I did the right thing, because we get the burdens of low wage countries shipping goods into this country and into our markets no matter what we do. The trade agreements we've reached aren't just pieces of paper; they're meaningful, concrete pacts that open up markets to us and create jobs that, on balance, pay above the national average.

Open trade is now expanding all around the world, everywhere, that is, but Japan. Of all the industrialized countries, Japan imports fewer manufacturing goods for their size than any other by a long shot. At times, some people said it was our fault that we didn't sell more there. They said our deficit was too high. They said our products were not competitive.

Well, we cut the deficit, and on an annual basis now, our deficit is as small a percentage of our income as that of any other advanced country in the world. And all of you and millions of American workers like you worked hard to make sure that our products could compete and win in terms of price and quality.

Now, in some areas we have made progress with Japan over the last 2½ years. We've concluded 14 results-oriented agreements. Believe it or not, they're now eating American rice in Tokyo. Japanese consumers are buying everything from our apples to our telecommunications equipment. But in many areas, Japan's market remains stubbornly closed. There's no question this is about artificial trade barriers, not the quality of American products.

By some estimates, if Japan had open markets, the increase in U.S. exports would create hundreds of thousands of American jobs. By the way, it would have been good for the Japanese, too, because their consumers pay almost 40 percent more than they should for the basic necessities and products of life.

Japan's trade barriers are most unfair, as you well know, when it comes to cars and car parts. In the last 25 years, we shipped 400,000 cars to Japan, and they shipped 40 million cars to us. That's a 100:1 ratio. Be sure and quote that number the next time somebody tells you there's not really a trade problem here.

Twenty-two years ago, in 1973, the Big Three had less than one percent of Japan's auto market. Every President since then has tried to fix this problem and open the Japanese market to American cars. You know what kind of success we've all had, what kind of market share the Big Three has today, after 22 years? A whopping 1.5 percent.

Now, you know how bad this problem is. Our auto industry accounts for about 5 percent of our gross domestic product directly. It employs 2½ million Americans. But when the auto industry does well, so do a lot of other people, the people who make iron and steel and aluminum and rubber and glass and semi-conductors, the things the auto industry needs. American auto parts are so good that we have an auto parts trade surplus of $5.1 billion around the world, because demanding companies like BMW and Mercedes use our auto parts all the time. But with Japan, we have $12.8 billion trade deficit.

My fellow Americans, this is a simple question of fairness. The American auto market is open to Japanese products, more open than the European market, more open than most markets in the world. The Japanese auto market, by contrast, is still closed to American products. We have tried and tried other means as long as we could. And we have tried long enough. Now we must act decisively to level the playing field and to protect American jobs.

I have ordered the U.S. Trade Representative to impose 100 percent tariffs on 13 Japanese-made luxury cars by June 28 unless Japan agrees to open its markets to cars and car parts before then. Now the ball is in their court. I hope Japan is ready to reach a serious agreement. But make no mistake, if we have not resolved this by June 28, these sanctions will go into effect.

I'm gratified that there's so much overwhelming bipartisan support for this policy in the Congress. It's time for the Japanese to play by the same rules the rest of us play by. If working Americans see us continue to put up with unfair deals, they'll lose their faith in open trade. And we can't afford that. We've made too much progress opening markets to risk letting this problem with Japan spin out of control. We can't hesitate to fight for our rights.

Japan is a valued friend and partner. We cooperate on a host of other issues. Our trade relationship must also reflect that kind of cooperation. It has to be a two-way street. That's all I'm working to do. Just as we must be good partners with the other nations of the world, we know that Japan must be a good partner with us.

Let me say again, this is not just in our interest; this is in their interest. Even though their incomes are high, they are paying almost 40 percent more for consumer products than they should. We'll all win if we have fair and open trade.

I also want to ask all of you to be partners in strengthening the economy. I believe good, strong unions and good faith collective bargaining are essential to helping us meet the challenges of the future. That's why one of the first things I did upon taking office was to rescind the anti-union Executive orders of the previous 12 years. And 3 months ago, I signed an Executive order that states loud and clear we will not allow companies that do business with the Government to permanently replace striking workers.

The right to strike is a fundamental American right. Anyone who tries to deny that right can expect a fight from this administration. Labor unions have worked too hard in the 1980's and the early nineties. They have made too many concessions. They have changed too many work rules. They have shown over and over and over

again the willingness to make changes to become more productive and more competitive. When they make those kind of changes and show that kind of flexibility and when they have the kind of results that have been achieved, they deserve to be respected. And the spirit as well as the letter of the law should be honored.

We will also fight any attempts by companies to dominate labor unions. I will veto any effort to weaken Section 8(a)(2) of the National Labor Relations Act. And I am fighting to preserve your hard-earned wage protections. The Davis-Bacon Act and the Service Contract Act are the foundations for decent living standards for many, many Americans. Some want to take that away, but I want to stand at your side to protect that standard of living that you have fought long and hard to maintain. I don't agree with those who criticize these acts as inefficient or excessive. I believe that the Davis-Bacon and Service Contract Act simply put the American Government on the side of favoring a high-wage, high-growth economy. I don't believe we should support policies that increase the inequality that has grown so much over previous years. I believe we should go up or down together. We should have shared sacrifice; we should have shared benefits. And I will veto any effort to repeal those laws.

I also believe, as you do, that collective bargaining is not a privilege but a right. Our appointments to the NLRB, Bill Gould, Peggy Browning, and the General Counsel, Fred Feinstein, are committed to preserving that right.

And so, together, we are all working here, fighting hard to help you hold onto what you've struggled to win over six decades. But after standing in your way for 12 years, there are those in Congress who now want you to believe they're on your side. Kind of reminds me of the words to a country and western song, "How can anything that sounds so good make me feel so bad?"

There are those who talk about the health and safety of working Americans that try to weaken, even to gut health and safety standards; those who say they support work over welfare but support a welfare reform bill that's weak on work and tough on children, one the Congressional Budget Office says is unworkable in 44 of our 50 States. They say that work should pay, but they oppose raising the minimum wage to make it a living wage. All of you know how important the minimum wage has been to making sure people have a decent standard of living in this country.

You know, I saw something recently that brings home the need for an increase in the minimum wage more than anything else that I've seen in recent months. I was watching a news special on television, and they went down South to a town that had a lot of minimum-wage workers. There they interviewed a remarkable woman in a local plant who was working for the minimum wage. They said to her, "You know, your employer says if we raise the minimum wage, then they'll either have to lay off people or put more money into machinery and reduce their employment long term, and you could be affected. What do you say to that?" And the woman just threw back her shoulders and smiled and said, "Honey, I'll take my chances."

There are a lot of women and no small number of men out there who are in that situation. Some of them are raising their kids on the minimum wage. The truth is we have looked at all the arguments, pro and con. There is really no evidence that a raise in the minimum wage will cost jobs, but we do know it will make more people want to move from welfare to work. We do know it will reward work. And we know if we don't raise the minimum wage, next year it will be at a 40-year low, once you adjust for inflation.

That's not my idea of the 21st century economy. My idea of the 21st century economy is

Americans working hard, working smart, well-trained, well-supported, competing and winning in the global economy, doing the kinds of things the UAW is doing today, not driving down the minimum wage so that more and more people work harder and harder just to fall into poverty. That's wrong, and we need to turn it around. We need to give everybody a fair shot at the American dream.

In closing, let me say that our work here requires a partnership with you, so that we'll be ready to compete and win in the 21st century, so that we don't raise the first generation of Americans to do worse than their parents, so that instead we begin to grow the middle class and shrink the under class again. The future of our Nation depends upon rewarding the efforts of workers like you. You and your families are the heart and soul of America, so we have to work together to preserve not only what has been won but to fight for the jobs, the incomes, the justice, the American dream of the future. We can do it. We can do it.

Thank you, and God bless you all.

NOTE: The President spoke by satellite at approximately 5:45 p.m. from Room 459 of the Old Executive Office Building to the UAW convention in Anaheim, CA. In his remarks, he referred to Owen Bieber, outgoing president, and Steve Yokich, incoming president, United Auto Workers.

Statement on the Retirement of Lane Kirkland
June 12, 1995

American workers and workers around the world owe a tremendous debt of gratitude to Lane Kirkland. For nearly five decades, he has been a catalyst for international democracy and a guiding force for workplace fairness, dignity, and innovation.

His record of achievement rivals the great labor leaders that came before him, and his ideas and accomplishments will benefit working

families for generations to come. He served with distinction during some of the toughest times for American workers and brought creativity, a laser-like determination, true grit, and an unparalleled intellect to his job as president of the AFL–CIO.

Hillary and I wish him the very best for the future and will always be grateful for his strong support, keen advice, and valued friendship.

Remarks at a Memorial Service for Les Aspin
June 13, 1995

I would like to begin by thanking all the people who have spoken before. Each of them has given us a little slice of the incredible, complex, rich person that Les was. I think he would have liked this service. I think somewhere he's saying, "Gee, I guess I did all right."

I always identified with Les Aspin. We were policy wonks. We sometimes worried more about our workload than our waistlines. And on occasion, we forgot that in this complicated world, how things appear are sometimes almost as important as how things are. But I will never forget that the essence of him was truly extraordinary. And I am in great debt to the contribution he made to my life and to the work of this administration.

One of my favorite pictures that has been in the press since I've been in office is one of Les and I walking across the White House lawn. I had my arm around him, and we looked like we were deep in thought. You know, what I was really telling him is, "You have to stop working so hard, lose some weight, loosen up." [*Laughter*] If the Presidency is preeminently a place of the power of persuasion, I failed on that occasion. [*Laughter*]

A friend once described Les' idea of a vacation as thinking about defense in a different setting. [*Laughter*] Once when he did take a few days off, he sent a postcard home to his staff. On the front, there was a picture of a beach; on the back he had scribbled, "Why are you wasting time reading postcards?"

Those of us who had the privilege of being close to Les Aspin know that he was not only exceptionally brilliant, he was iconoclastic in the best sense. That was a great benefit now as we go through this period of transition from the cold war into a new and exciting but still troubling world.

He was always questioning the conventional wisdom and always refusing to be bound by it. He was a good teacher. I learned a lot from him. I remember the first time I came to see him, I was the Governor of my home State and not a candidate for President, a curious person. And when I left his office after our first talk, I was utterly exhausted. I thought I had finally found somebody with 4 times the

energy I have. Through the years, I sought him out more and more. And in 1992, he, more than any other person, was responsible for the fact that in our campaign we determined that both parties would be strong on defense.

Les Aspin did a lot of different things in a lot of different ways. He showed sophistication, and then he showed the lack of it. But, as has been said in different ways today, everyone who really knew him never doubted one thing, that his first and foremost concern was to do whatever would make this country stronger and safer and better. That is what he cared about above all else.

As the cold war wound down, he played a critical role as chairman of the Armed Services Committee. But as my Secretary of Defense, he was finally able to put his remarkable knowledge and passion and vision for defense policy at work to reshape our forces to the demands of the 21st century. The blueprint he took the lead in drafting will guide us into that new world. It will guide us for decades to come. And all of us will be in his debt.

After he left the Defense Department, we continued to talk, and I continued to be amazed by his incredible openness to service, by his incredible passion for the issues with which we were all called upon to deal. And he answered the call to serve again as the head of our Foreign Intelligence Advisory Board, a post that is not much known outside of Washington but is of profound importance to the future of this country. Then he agreed to serve on the Armed Services Commission on Roles and Missions. He did all these things no matter what else was going on in his life, no matter what had happened to him, with incredible good humor and grace and passionate devotion.

It has been said that true patriotism is not short, frenzied outbursts of emotion but the steady dedication of a lifetime. By that standard, Les Aspin was a true and remarkable patriot who made a dramatic positive difference to the United States and all the people who live there.

We will miss him terribly, but as you heard today, his legacy remains all around us in the streets of Beloit, Racine, Kenosha, throughout southeast Wisconsin—how he loves that place.

It will be seen in the students and the graduates of Marquette University, in the men and women who wear our uniform around the world and do more good in conditions that are more safe and secure because of his labor.

It also lives on, as we heard today so movingly, in the memories of those of us who were lucky enough to have known and loved him. He left each of us our own stock of Les Aspin stories, guaranteed to bring a smile to our faces and warmth to our hearts as long as we remain on this Earth.

Well, Les is God's servant now. And finally, finally, he is with someone with sufficient energy to keep up. [*Laughter*]

NOTE: The President spoke at 3:18 p.m. at St. John's Church.

Statement on the Nuclear Agreement With North Korea
June 13, 1995

I welcome the agreement reached between the United States and the Democratic People's Republic of Korea in Kuala Lumpur on key issues related to implementation of the US–DPRK Agreed Framework. Achieved through close consultation with our friends and allies in the Republic of Korea and Japan, the agreement keeps North Korea's dangerous nuclear facilities frozen and confirms that the Korean Peninsula Energy Development Organization (KEDO) will select the reactor model and prime contractor for the light-water reactor project. At the same time, KEDO has confirmed that both the reactor model and prime contractor will be South Korean.

In addressing these and other issues, today's understandings are an important step on the road toward full implementation of the US–DPRK Agreed Framework, which provides the international community with assurance against a North Korean nuclear threat and North Korea with opportunity to rejoin the community of nations. We also continue to believe that the resumption of North-South dialog is essential not only to the full implementation of the Agreed Framework but also to the continuing effort to build lasting prosperity and a stable peace on the Korean Peninsula.

Statement on the Supreme Court Decision on Affirmative Action
June 13, 1995

The Supreme Court's decision sets a new legal standard for judging affirmative action, but it must not set us back in our fight to end discrimination and create equal opportunity for all.

Despite great progress, discrimination and exclusion on the basis of race and gender are still facts of life in America. I have always believed that affirmative action is needed to remedy discrimination and to create a more inclusive society that truly provides equal opportunity. But I have also said that affirmative action must be carefully justified and must be done the right way. The Court's opinion in *Adarand* is not inconsistent with that view.

It is regrettable that already, with the ink barely dry, many are using the Court's opinion as a reason to abandon that fight. Exaggerated claims about the end of affirmative action, whether in celebration or dismay, do not serve the interest all of us have in a responsible national conversation about how to move forward together and create equal opportunity.

The Supreme Court has raised the hurdle, but it is not insurmountable. Make no mistake: The Court has approved affirmative action that is narrowly tailored to achieve a compelling interest. The constitutional test is now tougher than it was, but I am confident that the test can be met in many cases. We know that from the experience of State and local governments, which have operated under the tougher standard for some years now.

Some weeks ago, I directed my staff conducting the review of Federal affirmative action programs to ask agencies a number of probing questions about programs that make race or sex a condition of eligibility for any kind of benefit. What, concretely, is the justification for this particular program? Have race and gender-neutral alternatives been considered? Is the program flexible? Does it avoid quotas, in theory and in practice? Is it transitional and temporary? Is it narrowly drawn? Is it balanced, so that it avoids concentrating its benefits and its costs? These are tough questions, but they are the right policy questions, and they need answers.

I have instructed the team conducting the administration's affirmative action review to include an analysis of the *Adarand* decision and its implications in their report.

Message to the Congress Transmitting the Report of the Department of Housing and Urban Development
June 13, 1995

To the Congress of the United States:

Pursuant to the requirements of 42 U.S.C. 3536, I transmit herewith the 29th Annual Report of the Department of Housing and Urban Development, which covers calendar year 1993.

WILLIAM J. CLINTON

The White House,
June 13, 1995.

Address to the Nation on the Plan To Balance the Budget
June 13, 1995

Good evening. Tonight I present to the American people a plan for a balanced Federal budget. My plan cuts spending by $1.1 trillion. It does not raise taxes. It won't be easy, but elected leaders of both parties agree with me that we must do this, and we will.

We're at the edge of a new century, living in a period of rapid and profound change. And we must do everything in our power to help our people build good and decent lives for themselves and their children.

These days, working people can't keep up. No matter how hard they work, one, two, even three jobs, without the education to get good jobs, they can't make it in today's America. I don't want my daughter's generation to be the first generation of Americans to do worse than their parents. Now, balancing our budget can help to change that if we do it in a way that reflects our values and what we care about the most: our children, our families, and what we leave to generations to come.

That's why my budget has five fundamental priorities: First, because our most important mission is to help people make the most of their own lives, don't cut education. Second, balance the budget by controlling health care costs, strengthening Medicare, and saving Medicaid, not by slashing health services for the elderly. Third, cut taxes for the middle class and not the wealthy. We shouldn't cut education or Medicare just to make room for a tax cut for people who don't really need it. Fourth, cut welfare, but save enough to protect children and move able-bodied people from welfare to work. Fifth, don't put the brakes on so fast that we risk our economic prosperity.

This can be a turning point for us. For 12 years our Government, Congress and the White House, ducked the deficit and pretended we could get something for nothing. In my first

2 years as President, we turned this around and cut the deficit by one-third. Now, let's eliminate it.

It's time to clean up this mess. Here's how: First, I propose to cut spending in discretionary areas other than defense by an average of 20 percent, except education. I want to increase education, not cut it. We'll continue to cut waste. Under Vice President Gore's leadership, we're already cutting hundreds of programs and thousands of regulations and 270,000 Federal positions. We'll still be able to protect the environment and invest in technology and medical research for things like breast cancer and AIDS. But make no mistake, in other areas there will be big cuts, and they'll hurt.

Second, we should limit tax cuts to middle income people, not upper income people, and target the tax cuts to help Americans pay for college, like we did with the GI bill after World War II. Let's help a whole new generation of Americans go to college. That's the way to make more Americans upper income people in the future.

Third, don't cut Medicare services to the elderly. Instead of cutting benefits, maintain them by lowering costs. Crack down on fraud and abuse, provide more home care, incentives for managed care, respite benefits for families of Alzheimer's patients, and free mammograms. For all Americans, I propose the freedom to take your insurance with you when you change jobs, to keep it longer after you lose a job; insurance coverage even if there are preexisting conditions in your family; and lower cost insurance for groups of self-employed and small business people. If we don't have tax cuts for upper income people, as congressional leaders have proposed, we won't need to make harsh cuts in health care or in education.

Finally, balance the budget in 10 years. It took decades to run up this deficit; it's going to take a decade to wipe it out. Now mind you, we could do it in 7 years, as congressional leaders propose. But the pain we'd inflict on our elderly, our students, and our economy just isn't worth it. My plan will cut the deficit year after year. It will balance the budget without hurting our future.

This budget proposal is very different from the two passed by the House and the Senate, and there are fundamental differences between Democrats and Republicans about how to balance the budget. But this debate must go beyond partisanship. It must be about what's good for America and which approach is more likely to bring prosperity and security to our people over the long run. We ought to approach it in the same spirit of openness and civility which we felt when the Speaker and I talked in New Hampshire last Sunday.

There are those who have suggested that it might actually benefit one side or the other politically if we had gridlock and ended this fiscal year without a budget. But that would be bad for our country, and we have to do everything we can to avoid it. If we'll just do what's best for our children, our future, and our Nation, and forget about who gets the political advantage, we won't go wrong.

Good night. Let's get to work.

NOTE: The President spoke at 9 p.m. from the Oval Office at the White House.

Remarks on Welfare Reform and an Exchange With Reporters
June 14, 1995

The President. I'd like to, if I might, just say a couple of words. First of all, I want to thank Senator Daschle, Senator Moynihan, Senator Breaux, Senator Mikulski for coming here today to discuss welfare with the Vice President and me and Governor Romer and Secretary Shalala.

Last night I laid before the Nation my plan to balance the budget in 10 years in a way that is consistent with the long-term prosperity of the American people and our fundamental interests. And one of the priorities I stated was pursuing the right kind of welfare reform. I still believe that the Republican bill is too tough on children and too weak on work and runs the risk of undermining our fundamental commitment to the welfare of children without moving people from welfare to work.

I want to endorse today the bill authored by Senators Daschle, Breaux, and Mikulski because it does meet those criteria. It is—it supports work. It supports doing the things that are necessary to get people into the work force and protecting children, especially dealing with the child care issues and requiring States to continue to support the children of the country who, through no fault of their own, are born into poor families.

So I believe this is the right kind of welfare reform. It also saves money. It will help us balance the budget, but it does it in the right way.

Federal Budget

Q. Mr. President, the Democratic reaction to your budget has been overwhelmingly negative. Do you have a revolt on your hands on Capitol Hill?

The President. Well, I think it's been sort of decidedly mixed, don't you? Senator Breaux was just telling me that he and Senator Lieberman endorsed it today.

Q. But a lot of people feel that you have let them down, you pulled the rug out from under them.

The President. Well, let me just say, a lot of people—I'm sympathetic with the Democratic position. The Democratic position is the Republicans won the Congress by just saying no. They voted against deficit reduction. They proposed health care plans and then walked away from them. They just said no, and somehow they were rewarded for that. And therefore, we should just say no, at least for a much longer time.

But I do not believe that's the appropriate position for the President even if it—the voters have a lot on their hands in their own lives. It's hard not to figure out what's going on in your own life today without trying to figure out what's going on here. And I don't believe it's right for the Democrats to kind of overreact to the last election.

Even though I don't think they were treated fairly—I don't think the last Congress got anything like the credit they deserved for reducing the deficit, bringing the economy back, and doing all the wonderful things that were done—

I still believe that the long-term best interests of the country are furthered by bringing the deficit down in a way that increases our investment in education, preserves our commitment to the historic commitments of the Democratic Party to helping those in need, permits us to protect the environment and have a strong defense and do the things the country needs.

So I believe I have done the right thing. I know there will be those who think that it's the wrong time or the wrong thing, and they are free to express their opinion. But I still feel very good about what I——

Q. Mr. President, much of that criticism appears to be directed at your proposal to cut the growth of Medicare.

The President. Well, I believe—if you look at what we've done—first of all, we've already cut the growth rate of Medicare. The inflation rate has been coming down. And we've done it without cutting services to the elderly.

Their proposal will provide for drastic cuts in services to the elderly. Our proposal will provide for some health care reform which expands health care coverage, including to the elderly, and cuts the rate of increase at a more moderate rate than the Republicans do and in a way that enables us to avoid cutting services to the elderly or charging low-income elderly people a couple of thousand more dollars for health care that they can't afford. We're not going to do that.

So if you look at the details of our proposal compared with theirs, I think ours is going to stand up very, very well. And that's why I have urged all the Members to look at the details, look at the facts before they reach a final judgment.

Q. Do you want to meet with Republicans as well?

Q. Where does it all go from here, Mr. President, a budget summit?

The President. [*Inaudible*]—the details, like welfare reform.

NOTE: The President spoke at 12:33 p.m. in the Oval Office at the White House, prior to a meeting with congressional leaders. A tape was not available for verification of the content of these remarks.

Exchange With Reporters Prior to Discussions With President Jacques Chirac of France
June 14, 1995

The President. Let me say that it's a great honor to have President Chirac here for he first time since his election, although he's been here before and we've had several good visits since I've been President. And I'm looking forward to the conversation. We have had no conversations yet, and we're going to have a press availability at the conclusion of our meetings.

French Nuclear Tests

Q. Have the French set back the world in terms of resuming their nuclear testing?

The President. I think I would—what we want to do is get a comprehensive nuclear test ban treaty. That's high on our agenda, and we have agreed not to test while we search for that. And I'll—if there are further questions on that, I will answer them at the——

Iraq

Q. Do you have any information about this happening in Iraq? Do you think it is a coup attempt against Saddam?

The President. I'd rather answer all these questions at the press availability.

[At this point, one group of reporters left the room, and another group entered.]

France-U.S. Relations

Q. Mr. President, can you say something about this visit of the French President, new-elected?

The President. First, let me say it's a great honor to have President Chirac here for his first visit as President. But we have known each other since I became President. And I think you met my wife before I was elected. I've had many good visits with him, and we've talked extensively by telephone since his election. But I look forward to this. And of course, after our meeting we will have a press availability, and we'll be able to answer questions about the subject of our talks at that time.

Q. How is the mood between France and the United States today with the new President here in Washington?

The President. I think it's very good. I know that I personally have a lot of confidence in President Chirac. I think he's entered office with a lot of energy and direction and conviction about the things that are good not only for France but for our alliance and our common search for security and for democracy and the world and for peace. And I'm looking forward to it. I think he's going to make an enormous contribution to our common causes.

NOTE: The President spoke at 1:48 p.m. in the Oval Office at the White House. A tape was not available for verification of the content of this exchange.

The President's News Conference With European Union Leaders
June 14, 1995

President Clinton. It's a great pleasure to welcome President Chirac and President Santer to the White House, the first visit for both leaders in their present positions to the Oval Office.

I begin with congratulations to President Chirac on his outstanding victory last month. From our many contacts with him throughout his long public service, the United States knows that he is a true and reliable friend, and he will be a strong and effective leader for France and for Europe. In his short time as President, he has already demonstrated this leadership. We applaud his determination to create jobs and economic growth for his own country, and with Jacques Chirac as President, we are sure that the French commitment to peace, stability, and progress is in excellent hands. France, as all of you know, was America's first ally. We know that our relationships will grow even stronger in the coming years.

It was a pleasure as well to meet President Santer, whose leadership in the cause of Europe follows in the great tradition that began with Jean Monnet. More than 30 years ago, President Kennedy spoke of a strong and united Europe as an equal partner with whom we face, and I quote, "the great and burdensome tasks of building and defending a community of free nations." This is more true than ever. And our summit today shows the United States partnership with Europe is a powerful, positive force.

The three of us reviewed a lot of economic and security issues: our efforts to help the countries of Central Europe and the former Soviet Union; we reaffirmed our commitment to strengthening NATO and proceeding with the steady process of enlarging the alliance; we agreed to continue liberalizing trade. We agreed that senior representatives of the U.S. and the EU will work together to develop a common agenda for the 21st century. Secretary Christopher has already provided a road map for this dialog in his recent speech in Madrid.

We discussed our efforts to strengthen the U.N. peacekeeping forces and to reduce the suffering in Bosnia. In the midst of the tragedy, we must not forget that the common efforts have already saved thousands of lives, and we must continue to work together.

We also explored a number of issues that the leaders of the G-7 will deal with in Halifax, and I'd like to mention a couple of them if I might. The Halifax conference marks another step in our effort to build the structures of the global economy for the 21st century. In the face of astonishing change, the growing economic ties between nations, the rapid movement of people and information, the miracles of technology, our prosperity depends upon preparing our people for the future and forging an international system that is strong enough and flexible enough to make the most of these opportunities.

At home we have been working hard to establish a steady record of growth, investment in our people, in bringing down our budget deficit. I am proud that our deficit today is now the lowest of all the G-7 countries. Our new budget proposal to balance the budget in 10 years will permit us to do this and continue to invest in the education and development of our people.

Abroad we have set out clear goals: to open world markets, to help the former Communist countries transform themselves into free market democracies, to promote economic reform in the developing world, to speed reforms in the international financial institutions. These efforts have yielded tremendous successes: NAFTA, GATT, agreements with the Asia-Pacific region and in our own hemisphere. We have supported the nations in Central Europe, the New Independent States, and the developing world in their historic turn toward free markets. Now we have a chance to reap enormous benefits in better jobs, greater opportunities, and growing prosperity.

We will build on our agreements last year in Naples when we meet in Halifax to focus on reforming the institutions of the international economy. The IMF, the World Bank, the regional banks have served us very well over the last half-century. And they have grown, taken on new missions as the times demand. But to deal with a new economy, we have to give them new guidance and new momentum.

First, we must work to identify and prevent financial problems like Mexico's before they become disasters and rock the global economy. And when crises occur, we must have efficient ways to mobilize the international community.

Second, we have to examine how best to adapt for a new era the multilateral development banks and the social and economic agencies of the U.N. These organizations have helped dozens of countries to build their economies and improve the lives of their people. We must not walk away from those banks and our obligations to the developing world. This is a point that President Chirac made to me in our meeting and one with which I strongly agree.

Finally, together with Russia, we will discuss a range of political issues that include Bosnia, Iran's nuclear ambitions, European security, and reform in Russia. We will consider new forms of cooperation to combat international crime, terrorism, and nuclear smuggling, because prosperity without security means little.

Also, I will be having some bilateral meetings, as all of you know, including a meeting with the Prime Minister of Japan, at which time we will review the position the United States has taken on our trade disputes with Japan regarding autos and auto parts. As you know, we are going to be meeting about that again shortly after the Halifax summit. My determination there remains as firm as ever. I believe we can reach a successful conclusion, and I intend to do everything I can to see that it is done.

Let me again thank President Chirac and President Santer and offer them the opportunity to make a couple of opening remarks.

Mr. President.

President Chirac. Mr. President, ladies and gentlemen. Mr. President, 40 years ago, when I was working as a soda jerk in the Howard Johnson restaurant—[*laughter*]—I didn't think that one day I would be in the White House beside the President of the United States for a press conference. And I appreciate it very much. It's rather moving for me. Since that time, I unfortunately forgot most of my English. [*Laughter*] That's why I'm going to speak French, if you don't mind—[*laughter*]—just to say a few words to start with.

Firstly, I would like to thank you very much for the welcome you have extended to me. I'd also like to tell you how pleased I am to see that on the main issues we are facing in the world today, and namely relations with France and with Europe, we have total convergence of views.

We're living in a world that is becoming increasingly disintegrated. We see a rising trend of selfishness and isolationism in many, many countries. And so, it is very reassuring indeed to see that the world's greatest nations realize how important it is to have solidarity amongst one another. This is true in politics. This is true in the social and economic areas. It's also true when we face challenges together throughout the world and crises together throughout the world. And this is why I said that we are in agreement on most of the points, even if on some issues we do have divergent views.

Mr. President, as the President of the European Union for a few more weeks, I would like to express my gratitude for the stance that you have taken on Bosnia, which is of great concern to me personally. I would like to say to you that we would like the entire Western world to be more attentive to the problems of the developing issues. And this is something that I will take up in Halifax. This is something that we must do something about. It's an ethical problem, a moral problem. It's also in our own interest, given the population growth that we see in many of these countries.

I think that we must also work more closely together when it comes to addressing regional crises. We've seen the eruption of regional crises in many different parts of the world, in Africa, in Europe, elsewhere. I think that we must, again, think more carefully about the main issues, the main challenges we are facing today, mainly employment. And this is why I am very pleased to make—that my request that a second G–7 meeting be held on employment and that you welcomed that. The first meeting was indeed a success.

I also think that we ought to undertake great efforts to fight against organized crime. In the United States some recent successes have been achieved in the fight against drugs. And I think that everything that deals with money laundering, fighting against drug trafficking, fighting against the spread of AIDS, again we must pool our efforts, enhance our efforts, and make sure that we work together in a complementary fashion. Now, in Halifax I will be touching on those points as well.

Now, we have an additional issue, monetary insecurity, currency fluctuations. This is something that is a worldwide problem and a European problem, in particular. So these are the issues that I, as President of the European Union, have raised in my conversations with the President of the United States and will also be discussed during our meeting in Halifax.

President Santer. Thank you, Mr. President. The wide range of issues we covered in our stimulating discussions today is testimony to the importance of our mutual relationship. Ours is undoubtedly the world's most important bilateral partnership. The regular six-monthly meetings between the United States and the European Union as such are catalysts for announcing our cooperation. The continued strengthening of the Union allows this cooperation to be balanced and effective.

Despite the excellence of our relations, there is no place for complacency. In a world searching for new equilibrium, every opportunity must be taken to broaden and deepen the relationship. This will provide the foundation for global stability and prosperity.

That is why I called at the beginning of this year for a review of the transatlantic partnership and launched the year with a transatlantic treaty. I am happy that since then, on both sides of the Atlantic, vivid debate is starting on the future of American and European relations. Today's meeting shows that there is a clear political will to explore the various means of structuring our relationship in view of the 21st century.

It is too early to commit ourselves to precise concepts. This will need more time. But what we must achieve is a formula which would integrate the political, economic, and security components of that relationship. A lot will obviously depend on the outcome of the 1996 intergovernmental conference which will define the future shape and role of the European Union itself. But it is not too early to immediately improve our consultation mechanism and to concentrate on concrete action, delivering tangible results in the short term. And that is what we have done today.

We have also discussed the idea of launching a new transatlantic initiative at our next meeting in Madrid in December. I very much welcome that, as I welcome the decision to charge a small group of senior-level representatives to examine ways of strengthening the European Union and the United States relationship and prepare the Madrid meeting.

Today's meeting has confirmed my belief that we are on the right track and that the transatlantic partnership will further prosper, to the benefit of our peoples and indeed of the whole world.

Thank you so much.

President Clinton. Helen [Helen Thomas, United Press International].

French Nuclear Tests

Q. President Chirac, your decision to resume nuclear testing has provoked worldwide consternation. Are you willing to reconsider? And also, President Clinton, has his decision handicapped the drive for a comprehensive test ban?

President Chirac. Well, obviously, the question that you've put to President Clinton is a question that he shall answer. But for me, I would say that no, I am not at all willing to go back on the decision that I've taken. But I would like to recall that we are talking about a very limited number of tests for a preestablished time frame, that is, from September to May 1996, and that France has made a commitment to sign without reservations once it is ready to do so, that is, in the autumn of 1996, we will then be in a position to sign the comprehensive test ban treaty.

Q. So the protests don't bother you? I mean, the fact that the rest of the world really is disarmed by your decision?

President Chirac. Well, unfortunately, I haven't really seen that the rest of the world is unarmed in this. [*Laughter*]

President Clinton. As you know, we regret the decision, and we have worked hard to try to stop the test as a way of setting up greater willingness to have a comprehensive test ban treaty. And we have forgone testing ourselves. But I do want to point out that the French have pledged before President Chirac came here—and he has reaffirmed that pledge, which you just heard—to achieve a comprehensive test ban treaty by next year. Also, France was very helpful in supporting the indefinite extension of the Nuclear Non-Proliferation Treaty.

So I believe on the larger goals that we still are united, and I believe we will achieve the success that we seek.

Mr. President, would you like to call on a French journalist?

President Chirac. A French journalist, is there a French journalist who would like to ask a question?

Iran

Q. A question to both Presidents: Concerning the way of dealing with Iran as a terrorist state, are both of the governments on the same wavelength, or is it still a bone of contention?

President Clinton. You think I should go first? [*Laughter*]

President Chirac. Yes, you are the host. [*Laughter*]

President Clinton. It's the least I can do as the host.

I don't know that we're on the same wavelength. As you know, many countries disagree with the position the United States has taken, but we believe the evidence is clear that Iran is a major sponsor of terrorism. And we believe the evidence is clear that they are attempting to develop the capacity for nuclear weapons. And we think that neither of those things should be supported and, in fact, should be opposed.

We also believe, regrettably, that the evidence is that a constructive engagement with the Iranians has at least so far failed to produce any positive results, failed to change the course of conduct of the country. And that is why we decided to take even stronger action recently and stop our direct and indirect trade with Iran. And I believe it is a proper course. I will attempt to persuade others that it is a proper course, at least insofar—certainly insofar as it affects sensitive things like technologies which can be used for military benefit and certainly to develop nuclear capacity.

Bosnia

Q. I'd like to ask President Clinton, thousands of government troops are converging on Sarajevo vowing to break the 3-year-old Serb stranglehold on the capital. Do you think that a military solution is possible there? And do you think that the U.N. peacekeepers should get out of the way and open the way for any attack?

President Clinton. Well, you really asked two different questions there. In the first—whether the road can be opened to Sarajevo militarily is not the same question as whether a military solution is possible in a larger sense. And my judgment is, and I think President Chirac agrees, that in the end a military solution is not available to the Bosnian Government. And I'm quite concerned about it.

And therefore, I believe that what we are trying to do in strengthening UNPROFOR—you know that President Chirac has taken the lead, and the United States certainly supports him in principle, in developing a rapid reaction force to try to strengthen the UNPROFOR troops there and to protect his own troops more. And we believe that that and a vigorous continued pursuit of diplomacy offers the best hope of saving the Bosnian state and minimizing casualties.

In terms of whether in this narrow moment such an action would succeed, I think our military leaders' judgment would be better than mine. But I think the larger point is that we have discouraged all the parties from continued violence. That's one of the reasons that we agreed with the U.N.'s request for a bombing support when Sarajevo was shelled by the Serbs recently. We think that the position of the United States should be to support our allies who are there on the ground, to support strengthening the U.N. mission, and to discourage all increases in violence, to try to keep the lid on the violence and put the pressure on all parties, including Serbia proper, to support those actions which would lead to a negotiated settlement. Would you like to comment on that?

President Chirac. On Bosnia, we share the same view. Firstly, the UNPROFOR soldiers have been scattered throughout the country as part of a humanitarian and peacekeeping policy. They have been spread out across a vast terri-

tory, which is, furthermore, occupied by terrorists and, in particular, Serbian terrorists.

Now, the inevitable happened, that is to say, availing themselves of the first pretext that came along, the Serbians took hostages, and the UNPROFOR soldiers on the ground were incapable of defending themselves. Now, a soldier ought to be able to defend himself at all times, especially if he is running a risk of physical danger or death. And in that kind of case, it is impossible to allow for him to be humiliated. But the soldiers of UNPROFOR have become increasingly humiliated. So it's a question of honor, and that called for a reaction.

And so, France and the United Kingdom, along with some Dutch reinforcements, we have decided to create a rapid reaction force. The objective of this is not to attack anyone. It is going to be part of the existing U.N. mission and will cooperate with NATO, of course. The mission here is to react, to react anytime U.N. soldiers are attacked, humiliated, or deprived of their freedom. In order to achieve this, we had to develop a force that has the means to react, namely artillery, helicopters, and tanks.

Now I have heard, in some quarters, from some political leaders who are wondering whether or not this Franco-British initiative is just a first step towards a withdrawal of UNPROFOR in Bosnia. Well, this is obviously absurd. If such a withdrawal were ever to take place—and I certainly hope that it does not—this is something that has already been planned for. We've already come up with contingency plans for a withdrawal.

So what I would—what we were trying to do with the creation—what we are trying to do with the creation of the rapid reaction force is to enhance the capability of the soldiers to carry out their mission. And the quicker we can do this, the quicker the Serbs themselves will realize that they can't get away with murder.

And this is why we require the general agreement of the Contact Group. And I can say that the Russians have agreed to this and almost all the countries we've consulted have agreed. Now, it is up to the United States Congress to give the green light to this initiative. And obviously, I hope that it will.

It's important to bear in mind that any delay shall be seen by the Serbs as a glimmer of hope. And they shall be banking on internal dissension within the Contact Group—shall give them more time. And they have to understand that time is running against them. So that is the rationale behind this rapid reaction force which is being set up and which is, for the most part, composed of French and British troops.

President Clinton. If I might just make one other response to the original question. You know that the sympathies of the United States and this administration are with the struggle of the Bosnian Government to preserve the territory, certainly the territory that has been agreed to in the Contact Group proposal, and to end the kind of behavior that we saw in the taking of the U.N. hostages.

The question here is, therefore, would this action, even if it could succeed, ultimately strengthen or weaken the efforts of UNPROFOR to strengthen itself. President Chirac is taking bold actions here to try to strengthen UNPROFOR. Would it increase or decrease the chances that ultimately these objectives that we all share would prevail? What other consequences could occur in other parts of the country as a result of this? All these things need to be taken into consideration, which is why the United States has taken the position that, for the time being, all the parties should take as much care as possible to avoid further actions, because we believe that we have the best chance now of strengthening UNPROFOR and getting some new energy behind a lot of these diplomatic initiatives. This had nothing to do with where our sympathies are in terms of whether that road ought to be opened.

Yes, it's time for a European journalist. Go ahead.

Algeria

Q. Did you talk about Algeria?

President Clinton. No, but we will tonight. Let me say I'm very interested in Algeria and the implications of what happens there for other countries. And President Chirac knows much more about it than I do. Your country has had a very long history there. And I look forward to a rather detailed discussion about it this evening.

Vietnam

Q. Mr. President, you're being urged by Members of Congress and by, we're told, officials of your own State Department to proceed with the establishment of full diplomatic relations with Vietnam. Do you think the time is

right for that? And in your view, does Vietnam now meet your criteria for the establishment of these relations?

President Clinton. I have discussed this issue with some Members of Congress; you're correct about that. I specifically have talked with Senator McCain and Senator John Kerry in my office, and I had a—and Senator Robb. I also had a passing conversation with Senator Bob Kerrey about it. And of course, I've talked with Herschel Gober, the Deputy Director of the Department of Veterans Affairs, who just went to Vietnam on a mission.

They brought back a number of documents, a significant number of documents which I am now having analyzed with a view toward trying to determine whether or not the standards that I have set forth have been met. When that analysis is complete, I will then reach a judgment and, of course, make it public. But I think I should await the analysis of the documents.

I will say that the Vietnamese have been quite forthcoming. They have worked with us. If you look at the extraordinary efforts the United States has made to determine the fate of POW's and MIA's and the level of success that has been achieved, even though, to be sure, there are still outstanding cases, there's nothing quite like it in the history of warfare. And I think that the American people should be very proud of the efforts particularly made by our military, our active duty military and those supporting them, to determine the fate of every possible POW and MIA.

But I cannot answer your question until the review of the documents has been completed.

Middle East Peace Process

Q. Mr. President Clinton, what are your thoughts about the July 1st deadline which was set between the Palestinians and the Israelis for implementing the second phase in the Oslo accords? And what are the economic incentives that you are envisioning to guard and promote the peace process in the Middle East?

And a question for President Chirac. What is the package, the economic package that the European Community is about to promote or to advance to strengthen the peace in the Middle East?

Thank you.

President Clinton. Well, we're working toward the deadline, and we're working closely with the Israelis and the Palestinians. As you know, we're in constant contact with both of them. And we're doing what we can to get other supporters involved in the process of rebuilding the Middle East. We support the establishment of a development bank, which we believe is the least costly and most effective way to leverage public capital with private investment to redevelop the region.

And I can tell you that today I feel pretty hopeful about where we are and where we're going there, both in terms of the relationships between Israel and the Palestinians and in terms of the larger issues of Middle East peace. I have been pleased by the courage and the vision shown by all the leaders there in achieving the progress that's been achieved thus far.

And of course, as you know, we still have two countries to go. We have to resolve the differences between Israel and Syria, which are difficult, but they are both working on them. And then, of course, we would then hopefully get an agreement with Lebanon and Israel.

So I feel hopeful about it, and we're prepared to invest quite a lot of money in it. And we believe that the institution of a development bank is not only that favored by the people in the Middle East but also is the most cost-effective way to leverage a large amount of private capital with public investment. We do have to show the Palestinian people some benefits of the peace. And we are committed to doing that.

President Chirac. Yes, I would just like to make a brief reply to that last question. Development in these countries is a categorical imperative. What do the Palestinians today need? They need a house, and they need a job. And for that, it takes money.

Let me just remind you that France is the largest financial contributor to the Palestinian Authority's budget. And France has every intention of participating in the development efforts, which to us seem to be exemplary. Now, we fully agree with the idea of setting up a financial system that would be as efficient as it is quick in bringing forward results.

Now obviously, none of this has been fully decided yet. Is it going to be a bank or is it going to be something that's easier to set up over the short run? I think that that is more a matter of technical detail. But France will be there, and we'll be participating.

President Clinton. [*Inaudible*]—point, and then I owe this journalist a question because she thought I was calling on her.

The other thing that I would emphasize in addition to investment is—to pick up on a point the President made in his opening remarks—is that we, all of us, have to be involved in a stronger effort to combat terrorism because insofar as the Israelis and others can succeed in combating terrorism, the relationships between Israel and the Palestinians can be more open. The biggest threat to the success of the peace has been closing up the borders as a necessity of dealing with the terror, so that it drives the income of the Palestinians down. So they will develop a lot of their own economic opportunities if we can permit them to do so in peace and openness. And we should work on it.

Bosnia

Q. Mr. President, is the United States prepared to pay its share of the creation of a rapid deployment force for Bosnia under the U.N.? And President Chirac, you have suggested that the time may have come for the United States to get tough on Bosnia. What did you mean by that remark, and what specifically are you asking the United States to do to help your troops on the ground?

President Clinton. The answer to your first question is that it depends upon whether the Congress is willing to participate as well. And so, I have received correspondence and contacts with Congress about this. I have begun opening discussions about it, and I am consulting with them. But that is up to the Congress as well as to the President. I support, in principle, this rapid reaction force, and I think it has a chance to really strengthen the U.N. mission there. To what extent we can contribute depends upon congressional consultations which have only just begun.

President Chirac. Well, perhaps I must have misspoken, even in French, because I never said that the United States had to take a tougher stand on Bosnia. I never even mentioned the idea that they ought to send ground troops. We have a convergent strategy for the time being, and I fully support the American stance. I hope that this time my point has been made understood.

NOTE: The President's 97th news conference began at 5:15 p.m. in the East Room at the White House, with President Jacques Chirac of France, in his capacity as President of the European Council, and Jacques Santer, President of the European Commission. President Chirac spoke in French, and his remarks were translated by an interpreter.

Remarks on Departure for the Group of Seven Summit
June 15, 1995

Good morning. As you know, I am leaving this morning for my third annual meeting with the leaders of the G–7 industrialized nations. This summit marks another concrete step in our efforts to advance the security and prosperity of the American people by seizing the opportunities of the global economy.

At home, we are working hard to put our economic house in order. We are creating millions of jobs, working for economic growth, and cutting the deficit, which is already the lowest of all the advanced countries in the world. With our new budget proposal we will wipe out the deficit in 10 years, while still making room for critical investments in education and training, which our future demands. Going into this meeting the United States is in a strong position to continue leading our allies in the fight for long term global prosperity.

From the beginning of our administration, we have led the international effort to expand trade on a free and fair basis. We helped to expand world markets with NAFTA and GATT and trade agreements with the Asian-Pacific countries and here with the nations of the Americas. We are helping the former Communist countries to convert to free market economies. In all these areas we have turned back the forces of isolation which tempt us to turn away from the challenges and opportunities of the world.

In Halifax, together with our partners, we will focus on continuing to reform the institutions of the international economy so that we can have more stable, reliable growth—the World Bank, the International Monetary Fund, and others. For a half century, they have been a sound investment, and we are committed to maintaining our support for them. But now we have to give them new guidance in this new economy so that they can continue to serve our national interests in a changing global economy.

One of the key issues we'll be addressing is creating ways to identify and prevent financial problems from exploding into crises, as they did in Mexico. We will embrace joint initiatives to contain and defuse any crisis that does develop, so that the United States is not the world's lender of last resort. And we'll continue to explore how international organizations, which have helped so many countries to improve the lives of their people, can better aid developing nations and expand the world's market economies.

Finally, together with Russia, we will examine the challenges to our safety and well-being that no country can resolve alone. We'll look at new ways we can work together to combat the scourges of terrorism, nuclear smuggling, drug trafficking, and organized crime. And of course, we will discuss a lot of the security issues that concern us all, including Bosnia and Iran's nuclear ambitions.

When I arrive in Halifax today, I'll be meeting with Prime Minister Murayama of Japan. Our relationship is strong, and we are cooperating on a broad variety of issues, including North Korea, which is terribly important to both of us, the environment, and the problems of terrorism which have visited both our nations recently. But I will also make it clear to the Prime Minister that I am determined to carry through on my effort to open Japan's auto markets. Millions of American exports and thousands of American jobs depend upon our success. And I will say again it is in the long term interest of both the Japanese people and the people of the United States that this trade effort succeed.

All around the world free markets, open trade, new technologies are bringing countries closer together. Every day they are producing untold new opportunities for our people; they also lead us into uncharted territory with new problems. I believe on balance the future is very bright if we have the discipline to face these issues as they arise.

As the world's leading industrialized democracies, those of us in the G–7 have a very special responsibility to address these forces of change. That's what we'll be doing at Halifax.

Thank you very much.

NOTE: The President spoke at 8:40 a.m. at Andrews Air Force Base in Camp Springs, MD. In his remarks, he referred to Prime Minister Tomiichi Murayama of Japan.

The President's News Conference With Prime Minister Tomiichi Murayama of Japan in Halifax, Canada
June 15, 1995

The President. Good afternoon. Before turning to my meeting with Prime Minister Murayama let me begin by thanking Prime Minister Chrétien and the people of Halifax for welcoming Hillary and me and our delegation to Canada. Even on our short boat ride across the harbor, we could see why this city and indeed all of Nova Scotia are favorite sights for so many American tourists. I hope the important business we do here won't prevent us from enjoying a little of this very beautiful place.

Our business began today with the meeting with Prime Minister Murayama, the third in the constructive dialog we began last November. Our discussion focused on the strength of the U.S.-Japan relationship, and we are determined to make it stronger still. Never have the ties between our nations been more important, and never have they been closer.

Our two great democracies are also the world's largest economies. Together we make up more than 30 percent of the world's gross domestic product. And trade between our people is growing rapidly.

Our security ties have never been closer. Friends and foes alike know the Japanese-American relationship is the most important force for peace and stability in the Asia-Pacific region. Every day our people work together on the vital challenges of our times, protecting the environment, responding to natural disasters, combating the deadly trade in illegal drugs, and fighting the terrorists who have threatened both our nations from abroad and from within.

No issue is more important to our nations than stopping the spread of nuclear weapons. Prime Minister Murayama and I, along with our South Korean allies, have worked tirelessly on our strategy to stop the development of North

Korea's nuclear program. We pledged to push forward with this week's important agreement to implement that strategy. Japan has agreed to make a significant contribution to the light-water reactors that will supply energy to the North Koreans without producing weapons-grade materials. And I thank the Prime Minister for Japan's ongoing commitment to the fight against weapons of mass destruction.

The Prime Minister briefed me on plans for the upcoming meeting of the Asian-Pacific Economic Cooperation forum. APEC, as all of you know, has become an essential part of America's strategy for regional prosperity. Japan and the United States will work together so that November's meeting in Osaka sustains the momentum toward free and open trade in the Asia-Pacific region, achieved in Seattle and Indonesia last year.

We also discussed our progress and our disagreements on trade. Fifteen times since the beginning of my administration, the United States and Japan have concluded agreements to open markets and increase trade across a wide variety of products and services. The latest, reached just this week, offers tax and financial incentives to Americans who want to establish on-the-ground operations in Japan. The Prime Minister and I also agreed to extend the 1993 framework on trade negotiations, and I am optimistic that that will advance both our interests in free and open trade. Once again, this proves that our countries can and do work together to solve our disputes and enable American companies to better compete in the Japanese market.

But we also, as all of you know, have real differences. The Prime Minister and I discussed the problem of access for U.S. airline cargo carriers to the Japanese market, for example. I again expressed to the Prime Minister my concern that Japan honor rights that our carriers now have guaranteed under existing civil aviation agreements.

On the difficult issue of autos and auto parts, we had a frank and open exchange of our views. We agreed that our negotiators should redouble their efforts to seek a solution to those differences when they meet in Geneva next week. But I made it clear that I am determined to carry through on my effort to open Japan's auto markets. Billions of dollars in American exports and thousands of American jobs are at stake. They depend upon our success.

Opening these markets, as I have said repeatedly, will benefit not only the United States but Japanese consumers as well. I have instructed our negotiators to pursue every possible avenue of resolution before the June 28 deadline, and I remain hopeful that an acceptable, meaningful agreement can be reached. But if a solution cannot be found by the deadline, I will impose sanctions, and the United States will also pursue a case before the World Trade Organization.

At times like these, it is tempting to focus only on the differences that bring our two nations to the negotiating table. But I ask you again not to lose sight of the broader truths of our relationship. Only decades after the end of the terrible war that pitted our people against each other, the United States and Japan are allies and share a profound commitment to democracy, security, and prosperity. Our common agenda embraces everything from the fight to preserve our global environment to the global fight against AIDS, promoting the cause of women in developing countries, now to working together on natural disasters like earthquakes and dealing with our common concerns after Oklahoma City and the terrible incident in the Japanese subway with terrorism and the proliferation of weapons of mass destruction.

In any relationship as broad and deep as ours, there will always be differences. But the United States and Japan agree, no one issue, no one difference, will allow us to undermine our alliance or stop us from pursuing our shared goal and our common interests. Our two great democracies will never rest in our pursuit of a better, a safer, and a more prosperous future for all of our people.

Mr. Prime Minister.

Prime Minister Murayama. In my meeting with President Clinton for a couple of hours, until a while ago, I engaged in a candid exchange of views on the present and future of Japan-U.S. relations and the stance that we'll take as we go to the G-7 summit meeting. And I think the meeting was very meaningful.

The Japan-U.S. relations have grown over the past 50 years, since the end of the Second World War, and are connected by a strong bond of cooperation and collaboration.

President Clinton and I confirmed that security dialog is progressing smoothly. Thanks to the President's cooperation, the issue of U.S. military bases in Okinawa has seen important progress. And the response to North Korea's nuclear development issue, which seemed to test our bilateral collaboration, has produced important results, thanks to the solidarity of our two countries and the Republic of Korea, and it is a matter that we expressed appreciation for.

Common agenda—that is to say, our cooperation from global perspectives—is a symbol of creative partnership between our two countries. We today received a joint report containing new areas of cooperation. And the President and I are of the view that such cooperation should be promoted further.

As was mentioned earlier by the President, we also discussed the auto issue as well as the civil aviation issue. While the two countries remain apart on these issues, the President and I see eye to eye that we both will do our utmost to settle the issue as early as possible through the consultations slated for next week in Geneva. By the way, since the President has alluded to this matter, I should like to say that I asked for expeditious removal of the unilateral measures since they violate the rules and spirit of the World Trade Organization.

Now, in connection with that, including the civil aviation issue, we both agree that Japan-U.S. relations are a bilateral relationship of vital importance, so much so that the auto issue and aviation issue should not be allowed to adversely affect the overall Japan-U.S. relations.

We'll welcome President and Mrs. Clinton as state guests in November. Today's meeting with the President took place at a midpoint between my visit to Washington, DC, earlier, in January, and his visit to Japan in November. I am determined to further strengthen our bilateral partnership in the run up to the President's visit and beyond into the future.

Lastly, I proposed to the President to hold a bilateral symposium of seismologists on earthquakes, in order to enable the peoples of our two countries who have experienced the great Hanshin earthquake and the Northridge earthquake, respectively, make the most of their experiences and the lessons. And the President has agreed to the proposal.

Thank you.

Japan-U.S. Trade

Q. Did you hear anything new today from Mr. Murayama to indicate a willingness to open Japan's auto markets, or was he inflexible? And also, was there anything that you heard from him that might lead you to extend the June 28th deadline?

The President. The answer to the second question is, no. The answer to the first question is, we did not negotiate here, and we should not have. We had many other matters to discuss. We are both very ably represented by Ambassador Kantor and Minister Hashimoto and others on our behalf, and we have scheduled resumption of talks on the 22d and 23d in Geneva. So we did not discuss the details. But I did not and I will not agree to extend the deadline.

North Korea

Q. On the North Korean issue, up to the U.S.-North Korean agreement in Malaysia, I think there was some awkwardness in relations amongst Japan, Korea, and the United States. I wonder how the collaborative relationship will be kept up in the future? And how will Japan cooperate with this issue, including Japan's financial cooperation, and if a substantial payout is made, when will that be?

Prime Minister Murayama. Well, on that question of North Korean nuclear development issue, as was mentioned, in fact, we did discuss a lot of things. The talks in Malaysia were a very difficult one, and the United States continued to negotiate tenaciously. And as a result, the U.S. and North Korea finally arrived at a joint press conference. And we very much—highly appreciate all those efforts and the result.

Now, there may have been some misunderstanding amongst the parties in the process, but after overcoming those misunderstandings, we have had very close contacts between Japan and the United States as well, and we arrived at this agreement. So we would like to actively promote the outcome.

What sort of burden shall we take? When will we come up with a conclusion? Those are matters that we'll have to work on and finalize in the days ahead. At any rate, on this matter, Japan and the United States at the end of the day will continue to maintain close cooperation and act in concert. There is an agreement on that.

Japan-U.S. Trade

Q. Mr. President, what if the June 28th action, the imposition of tariffs, were to ignite a trade war with Japan? Won't that do more to adversely impact the jobs and the exports that you're trying to protect in the first place, sir?

The President. Well, of course, we hope that won't happen. But we've already considered the alternatives, and I believe we're on the right course.

Q. Did you get any assurance from the Prime Minister as to what the Japanese response might be?

The President. We did not discuss the details of the trade issue, other than to talk about the firmness of the June 28th deadline and our common hope and our common pledge that we could have a satisfactory resolution on the 22d and the 23d when our negotiators meet. And of course, the Prime Minister very ably restated his position, as he did here.

Prime Minister Murayama. With regard to June 28th, we did hear remarks from the President, and so, in response, I said that the 28th of June, we understand, is a deadline set by Section 301, but that is a matter of U.S. domestic law. As far as Japan is concerned, the auto talks are not talks conducted under Section 301. That is the Japanese understanding, and I stated that clearly.

What is important is that we do not engage in talks with both of our fists raised but rather talk to each other in good faith and try to resolve the problem through talks and let us work on that. And fortunately, on the 22d and 23d of June, there will be some Cabinet level talks in Geneva. And through those talks, we hope that we'll be able to come up with a solution that will be convincing to the international public opinion as well. And so let us do our utmost.

Q. I'd like to ask the same question to both of you on the auto issue. Does that mean that each side will step one head ahead of the positions that you've stuck to so far? I wonder if you've engaged in discussions with that sort of feeling or intention to make a step forward.

Prime Minister Murayama. Well, these are talks, consultations. So if both sides remain stuck into their principles, there will be no talks. We certainly have to keep our eye on overall flows or developments and try to walk closer to each other. Otherwise, there will be no solution. So where we can yield, we should yield to each other, so that we should find out the ways that will lead us at the end of the day to a solution. And let us find a way to do that. That is something that we've agreed on.

The President. I have nothing to add to what the Prime Minister said. As you know, the objective of the United States is to open the market, to be free to compete. But it would have been inappropriate for us to engage in the details of the discussion. As I said before, we have both been very ably represented by people who have dealt with this issue for a long time. And so we reasserted the framework from which we are both proceeding, which I have stated and which he has stated. We did not negotiate the details of the agreement.

Q. Mr. President, you said in your opening statement that the security relationship between the United States and Japan has never been stronger. But administration officials have said that frictions on trade could eventually lead to a deterioration of that relationship. What is your read of that? If this isn't solved——

The President. That is exactly why both the Prime Minister and I today said that we have made a common commitment not to allow our entire relationship to be defined by a trade difference. Even in the area of trade, we've made 15 agreements in 2½ years. That's pretty impressive. Even though the autos and auto parts are a bigger part of our economy, a bigger part of their economy, and a bigger part of the trade imbalance than all these other things combined, they are still significant.

And in other areas—what Japan and South Korea and the United States are doing with the North Korean nuclear problem is a matter of profound importance to every Japanese citizen, every American citizen, and all the people who live in North Asia. The things that we can do together to deal with problems like biological and chemical weapons being used in terrorist attacks—we are both more vulnerable to that as we open our societies to the 21st century—to organized forces of destruction.

The responsibilities we both have to the rest of the world to try to lead in environmental protection, in the fight against AIDS, and many other areas, these matters make it imperative that we maintain the closeness of our relationship. And we have pledged to each other today that however difficult our differences get in one area or the other of this relationship, we will not let it destroy the bonds of friendship and common values that are imperative for not only the American and the Japanese people but for the entire world.

Prime Minister Murayama. The President has said it all, so I really don't have anything to add. But this cooperation based on Japan-U.S. relationship will contribute not only to the Asian economy but contributes very importantly to the world economy as well. So that is our common understanding. It is from that vantage point that we engage in cooperation on issues of global scale which we have referred to. So we both have reaffirmed that we will continue cooperation in those areas as well.

Q. Once again, on the auto issue, in the series of Japan-U.S. auto issues, you are far apart on one single issue, and that is whether the volunteer purchases should be increased or not. I wonder if the Clinton administration plans to continue to stick on that position, and would the Murayama administration continue to refuse? If so, I think agreement or compromise will be very difficult. I wonder how you intend to settle the problem, with emphasis on this one point of auto purchase plan?

Prime Minister Murayama. As the President mentioned earlier, in our talks today we did not go into details of those talks because, as the President mentioned, we have outstanding negotiators, and on the 22d and 23d, there will be further talks in Geneva on that issue. And including that aspect, I hope that there will be in-depth discussions in Geneva and somehow we'll be able to come up with a force that will lead us to the settlement of the issue through talks. So let us both make efforts to that end.

The President. You have identified by your question one of the very key issues in the negotiations. Any answer that we give will undermine the possibility that a successful negotiation can occur.

Thank you very much.

[At this point, the President was presented with a plaque from the children of the Kobe area

in Japan in appreciation of U.S. assistance after the Hanshin earthquake.]

The President. We'll hang this in the White House as a constant reminder about this.

NOTE: The President's 98th news conference began at 4:40 p.m. at Dalhousie University. Prime Minister Murayama spoke in Japanese, and his remarks were translated by an interpreter. In his remarks, the President referred to Minister of International Trade and Industry Ryutaro Hashimoto of Japan.

Statement on the Resignation of Admiral William O. Studeman as Deputy Director of Central Intelligence
June 15, 1995

With regret at his departure but gratitude for his 32 years of service to our country, I have today accepted the resignation of Admiral William O. Studeman as Deputy Director of Central Intelligence.

Throughout an extraordinary and exemplary career, Admiral Studeman has done honor to his uniform. He rose through the ranks of the Navy, serving as a career intelligence officer, Executive Assistant to the Vice Chief of Naval Operations, Director of Long Range Planning, and ultimately, the 53d Director of Naval Intelligence.

The practical and profound expertise Admiral Studeman developed in intelligence has served him and our Nation well in two critical assignments, Director of the National Security Agency and then Deputy Director of Central Intelligence. Within the intelligence community, in Congress, and throughout the executive branch, he earned a reputation for integrity, collegiality, and competence of the highest order.

As Deputy Director of Central Intelligence, Admiral Studeman served two Presidents and three Directors of Central Intelligence. On two extended occasions, he took on the responsibilities of Acting Director. I am especially grateful for the continuity and leadership he provided to the entire intelligence community in a time of great change. Admiral Studeman helped begin the difficult but vital task of transforming the community to meet the new challenges of the post-cold-war world. He led efforts to streamline our intelligence agencies while making sure that they maintained the unique information advantage the United States must have in meeting threats to our security and prosperity. The many initiatives he took and innovations he made have set a strong foundation for the intelligence community as we move into the 21st century.

Admiral Studeman has offered to stay on the job during the coming weeks pending his successor's confirmation, an offer I have gratefully accepted. In the years to come, I know and expect that Admiral Studeman will make his voice heard as we continue to adapt the intelligence community to the demands of a new era.

Bill Studeman has dedicated his professional life to making the American people safer and more secure. Today, on behalf of all Americans, I thank him.

The President's News Conference in Halifax
June 16, 1995

The President. I'd like to begin my statement with an American issue. I want to congratulate Salt Lake City on their successful pursuit of the Olympics in 2002. This will be an historic event for Salt Lake City—[*applause*]—there was good applause there, maybe a native or two back there. It's a great event for Salt Lake City. They sought the Olympics many times over the last several years, and I congratulate them. It's a great thing for the Western part of the United States and, indeed, for our whole country.

I want to particularly congratulate Governor Mike Leavitt; the mayor of Utah—of Salt Lake City, Dee Dee Corradini; and Tom Welsh, the president of the Salt Lake City Bid Committee, for their efforts and a job well done.

From the beginning of our administration I've worked hard to make the global economy work for the American people. We live and work in a global market. Our living standards depend upon our ability to compete and to keep one step ahead of economic change.

In the past 2½ years, we have fought at home for a comprehensive economic strategy that would create jobs and lift the incomes of our people, focusing on reducing the deficit but investing in our people, in their education and their future. My new budget proposal continues to reflect these priorities.

At the same time, we have worked to open more markets around the world to our products in free and fair competition from others, through NAFTA, GATT, our work with the Asian-Pacific countries and with the countries of the Americas. We've also worked hard to encourage the global trend toward market democracy in the former Communist countries.

I am pursuing this strategy, above all, for one reason: to renew the promise of America in the 21st century. But I also want to preserve the leadership of America as a force for peace and freedom, for democracy and prosperity.

This G–7 meeting has moved us a step closer to these goals. We've taken concrete steps to strengthen the international financial system, something we promised to do last year in Naples. And let me give you one and perhaps the most important example.

Earlier this year, we in the United States were confronted with a serious financial crisis in Mexico. It posed a risk to markets throughout the world, and it certainly threatened our own economic health as well as our long-term relationships with Mexico, involving a number of other issues. We led the effort to stabilize Mexico, and from all signs, it seems to be working. President Zedillo and his team have worked hard to live within the discipline the markets have imposed and to move Mexico to a brighter and better future.

But we learned two important lessons in dealing with the Mexican crisis. First, the world clearly needs better tools to identify problems like this so that they can be prevented, and second, the international system must have a stronger way of resolving these crises once they do occur.

We were fortunate in the Mexican instance that the United States had access to a fund which could permit us to make some guarantees and move to put together an international approach to this problem. But the U.S. will not be able to be the lender of last resort in other crises of this kind. So here in Halifax, we have begun to forge the tools to deal with these kinds of problems in the future.

We agreed to create an early warning system that will sound the alarm when nations begin to encounter real problems, before the severity of the Mexican crisis develops. We call for early and full disclosure of critical monetary and financial information. We'll establish tougher reporting standards for nations so that markets will react more quickly and nations will be pressed to implement sound policies in a timely manner. This may be the best discipline for preventing future crises.

When these problems do occur, we must respond decisively. And leaders of the G–7 have taken crucial steps toward that end. We've called upon the International Monetary Fund to establish a new mechanism to ensure that we can act swiftly when one nation's economic crisis threatens the world economy. We propose to double the funds available for this purpose to more than $50 billion from those nations with a stake in a stable international financial system. That will require loans from the United States which must be authorized by Congress. I know a lot of you are thinking about that, but they are scored as cost-free to the American taxpayers, because they're viewed as risk-free because they go to the international institutions.

The G–7 leaders have also agreed that the international financial institutions, the World Bank, the IMF, and the agencies of the United Nations, must continue on a path of reform. These institutions have served us well for half a century. We will continue to support them, but they must adapt for a new era. We put forward new principles that will focus their work on addressing vital human needs: the alleviation of poverty, supporting private sector development, promoting sustainable development, environmental protection alongside economic growth. The resulting economic growth will bolster democracy and stability in developing nations and, of course, create future markets for American exports.

The leaders at Halifax are also discussing new security threats that no nation should face alone. And we'll have more to say about that tomorrow. But let me say we have agreed that the G–7 must work together far more energetically and comprehensively to counter the growing dangers posed by terrorists, international criminals, nuclear smugglers, and drug traffickers. We must cooperate more closely to counter terrorism and criminal activities sponsored by states, groups, and individuals. These are among the foremost challenges of the post-cold-war world.

These are issues which affect the lives of the American people in a very direct way. How we deal with them, whether and how we strengthen the international financial system and reform its institutions and how we fight challenges like terrorism will in no small way determine our citizens' future prosperity and security, how they feel about themselves and the future their children will enjoy.

To create new high-wage jobs, to raise incomes, to expand economic opportunity, the United States must continue to lead, even as we work hard on these matters at home. We cannot—I will say again—we cannot walk away from our global leadership responsibilities. In Halifax we've taken another solid step along that road. It will make the economy work better for the American people, and I believe it will help us to prevent future Mexicos and to deal with those crises in a much more effective way when they do occur.

Bosnia

Q. Mr. President, the United States has told the United Nations that for budgetary reasons it could not be counted on to pay the lion's share for a rapid response force in Bosnia. My question is, can a rapid response force in Bosnia be effective without the major financial backing of the United States?

The President. Yes. I'd like to review for a moment how that decision was made, however. I want to begin by saying I strongly support the rapid reaction force. It will give some muscle, some support, some security to the United Nations troops there. It will be staffed primarily by the British and French, with contributions from other countries that are on the ground there. It will have the mission of preserving

the integrity of the U.N. force, being able to rush in and help to redeploy them when necessary, to support them in fulfilling their mission, and to take the necessary action if they are under threat. This offers the promise of making the U.N. mission more effective. I strongly support it.

Because the financing of this would have to be, obviously, approved by the Congress, I consulted with the Senate majority leader and with the Speaker of the House. And because President Chirac was in Washington, he went by to see them as well. They sent me a letter saying that they supported the concept of the rapid reaction force and they understood why President Chirac wanted a vote in the United Nations right now, because things are pretty tense in Bosnia and because he was coming here, and that they would certainly understand if I voted for the resolution in the United Nations but that in the absence of appropriate and thorough congressional consultations, they could not agree to pay for it through an assessment.

So Ambassador Albright last night was able to get a modification of the resolution which simply leaves open the method by which the rapid reaction force will be funded, either through assessments or through voluntary contributions. We and others have made several voluntary contributions to the United Nations in the past for other important missions.

I believe the United States should pay a share of this. I will support that, and I will do my dead-level best to argue that case in Congress. This rapid reaction force gives these countries the power that they have lacked to protect their troops and to preserve the honor of their country and to pursue the U.N. mission in a way they have not been able to since they have become more vulnerable to being taken as hostages.

Yes.

Q. Mr. President, how much are you hamstrung in the discussions on Bosnia here at the summit by the fact that you can't make a firm commitment on U.S. support for the rapid reaction force and the fact that the United States does not have troops on the ground in Bosnia?

The President. Well, I have made some firm commitments for support. We have promised some equipment. We have promised some strategic lifts. We have promised the kind of air cover which we have given to other U.N. missions.

The United States has spent a lot of money and provided a lot of support to the United Nations mission in Bosnia, through NATO, through participating in the humanitarian airlifts, which are now by far the largest humanitarian airlifts in history. I urge you to remember that not only has the death rate gone way, way down in the last 2 years, but there are now about 2.8 million Bosnians dependent upon the humanitarian aspect of this mission. Just because it hasn't succeeded in ending the war does not mean it has been a total failure in keeping people alive while we search for a political solution.

So I was able to make those commitments based on the resources we have now. And I have made it clear from the beginning that we would not be involved with ground troops in this U.N. mission. I have made it clear the circumstances under which we would help our NATO partners and our U.N. partners to withdraw or to help them if they were in a terrible emergency. And I think that everyone understands that and is more or less not only reconciled to it but supportive of it.

This is something that the Europeans wanted to take the lead on and decided to take the lead on before I became President. And we have taken, I think, a very vigorous and aggressive position through NATO. But I do not believe the United States should send ground forces into the U.N. mission as it is constituted, and I certainly don't believe we should send our ground forces into some sort of combat situation in Bosnia.

Our vital interests, I will reiterate, are in keeping the conflict from spreading. That's why we do have forces in the Former Yugoslav Republic of Macedonia. That's why we have worked very hard to see that Bosnia and Croatia have an agreement which has shut down a big part of the war. In minimizing the human loss, in supporting our NATO allies, and preserving the integrity of this operation, we have done everything we could to those ends. I do not believe that this is a situation which warrants the introduction of America's ground forces.

Federal Budget

Q. You mentioned your budget, and it has been out for a little while now. It seems to be garnering more support from Ross Perot than some of your fellow Democrats. What is going on?

The President. First of all, I think that—I think there are two things going on. First, I think the Democrats are still in the position where the Democrats in Congress do not have to offer an alternative. And a lot of them could not possibly have had the opportunity to study this budget resolution in any detail. And frankly, there are some political feelings among some of our Democrats which are entirely understandable. I mean, they're—so what some of them are saying is, "Look, the Republicans won the Congress with a 'just say no' position. They refused to participate in deficit reduction. They put forward a health care plan and then walked away from their own plan. And they were rewarded somehow as the party that was responsible on the economy and health care and other things with a 'just say no,' organized, heavily financed attack, attack, attack, attack position. Why shouldn't we do the same thing?"

My answer to them is we may have failed to communicate to the American people that what we did was good for the United States in the last 2 years, that we would have a balanced budget today were it not for the interest we have to pay on the debt run up in the 12 years before I showed up, but our job is to do what's right for America. And the President, particularly, is in a different position.

I thought that I owed it to the country and to the Republicans to give them the opportunity to make their budget proposal first. I always said to the American people that we could not balance the budget without reducing the rate of growth of health care expenditures, but we ought not to be cutting services to elderly people who needed it. What we ought to be doing is reforming health care. My proposal reflects that. I think I have done the responsible thing. And I hope, as time goes on, I'll be able to persuade more and more Democrats and Republicans that I did the right thing. And I thank Mr. Perot for his support.

Yes.

Bosnia

Q. Mr. President, back on Bosnia for a moment, sir. Despite your support for the peacekeeping forces, the U.N. peacekeeping forces in Bosnia, are you at all moved by the appeal made at the White House the other day by Bosnian President Haris Silajdzic, who called the arms embargo an instrument of genocide? How do you answer him when he asks, "Why won't the U.S. let the Bosnian Muslims defend themselves?"

The President. First of all, the arms embargo would be an instrument of genocide if the U.N. mission weren't keeping more people alive. In 1992, 130,000 civilians, more or less, died in Bosnia. In 1994, the best figures we have indicate that fewer than 3,000 people died.

When NATO was working with the U.N., we were able to create some safe areas around Sarajevo and the eastern enclaves which have since been eroded by the taking of U.N. hostages. But that's why the rapid reaction force is so important, to put some real steel back into the U.N. mission.

On principle, you know that the sympathies of the United States are with the Bosnian Government, and more strongly than some of our allies feel. But the question is, will this thing ever be settled on the battlefield? I think the answer to that is no. If that's true, shouldn't we support the Bosnian Government's position that it has accepted the Contact Group proposal, do everything we can to strengthen the U.N., keep as many people alive as possible, not allow an erosion of their territorial position insofar as we can prevent it, and keep pushing for a diplomatic settlement? That's what I believe is the best thing to do.

Lifting the arms embargo cannot be seen in an isolated circumstance. And I want you all to consider this. This is not an example where you can just kick the can down the road; this is the most complex problem in foreign policy today. If the United States—first of all, our European allies simply disagree with lifting the arms embargo. If we were to lift the arms embargo unilaterally, what would happen? The U.N. mission would immediately collapse and withdraw. We would have immediate responsibilities to send our people in to help them withdraw if they asked for it and needed it.

After that happened, then what happens? There are a lot of people in the United States, including many in Congress in both parties, who say, "That is no concern of ours; all they have asked us for is to lift the arms embargo and let the arms flow in there."

But I ask you: If the United States—if the United States cratered the U.N. mission by a unilateral lift of the arms embargo and then the lift of the arms embargo did not produce the military results on the ground that the Bosnian government hoped and if, instead, they

began to lose more territory and more and more people started to die because of our unilateral action ending the U.N. mission, what would we do then? The chances that we would be drawn in are far greater than that the United States could walk away from an even greater mess that we had created all by ourselves with our European allies pleading with us not to do it.

Therefore, I will say again, if the U.N. mission does fail, if our allies decide to leave, I would strongly support lifting the arms embargo. It's the best alternative at that moment. But I cannot in good conscience support a unilateral lift of the arms embargo when the British and the French and the others are willing to say, "We'll send more troops there; we'll stiffen our capacity to keep the peace and to work for the peace." I cannot do that.

Yes.

Q. Mr. President, how can you push for a diplomatic settlement if every proposal that's been made, including the U.S.-backed proposal to give half the country to the Serbs, is rejected by the Serbs? What ideas are out there? There's nothing going on; there's no diplomatic initiative in the air right now. So what do you mean when you say push for a diplomatic settlement?

The President. There's nothing—there will never—they will not make peace, sir, until they get tired of fighting each other. I agree with that. Now, that is also true of Northern Ireland. How long has this war been underway? Four years. How long has this peacekeeping initiative been underway? A little less time than that. How long did they fight in Northern Ireland before they began to do what they're doing now? Twenty-five years. How long have they been fighting in the Middle East? Over four decades before we made the progress we're making now. You cannot simply say, given—how deeply rooted are the conflicts between the Bosnians of—that are Serbian, Croatian, and Muslim? At least, at least going back to the 11th century?

So I say to you, there is nothing great going on right now. What is the answer? To do something else that might make it worse? Or to try to minimize human life, ensure that it doesn't—the loss of human life—ensure that it doesn't spread, and keep working for what I think is, based on the historical evidence, the only way fights of this kind ever get settled, which is when they—people decide that's it's better for them to make a deal than to keep killing each other.

Yes.

Q. Mr. President, it is the President of France who has pushed the hardest on the rapid reaction force, and he has described it in terms of, "We can't be humiliated." These terms sort of harken back to the Vietnam quagmire, if you'll forgive that word, and I was hoping that you could outline exactly what you think the mission is—would be of this force. Could you give it in the most specific terms possible? Because as many people have said, unless we know exactly what the mission is, there could be a disaster.

The President. Well, in fairness to the President of France, I thought that Americans might hear that in his rhetoric. But keep in mind, when the argument was made in Vietnam that we couldn't be humiliated, the argument was there that we had to do more to Americanize the war, that is, we were involved in Vietnam supporting the side of the South Vietnamese government in a conflict with the Vietcong and North Vietnam on the other side.

In this case, the French President is taking the position that the honor of the country is eroded when U.N. personnel in blue helmets can be taken prisoner at will and they have no capacity to defend themselves. So he is not suggesting that they should get involved in this conflict in a military way on one side or the other. He is suggesting, however, that they ought to be able to move on the roads at will, that they ought to be able to do what they're supposed to do under the U.N. mandate without being taken prisoner, being shot at, being victimized; and that the rapid reaction force is supposed to be able to get them out of tights if they get in it and to support them when they need the support. He is not suggesting that the rapid reaction force would increase the level of military conflict or that there would be any military initiative taken by that force.

Yes.

Q. The British have said that you here at this summit have committed the U.S. to paying its fair share of that rapid reaction force. Since the Republican leadership has said that they don't want Congress to pony up the money, just what options are available to you to come up with that money? And secondly, by the Republican leadership doing what they did in advance of the U.N. vote, does it unnecessarily tie your hands in the conduct of foreign policy?

The President. No, in this case, I think, what they did was to make it possible for me to vote for an initiative that they agreed with in principle but weren't prepared to say they would pay for. That is—let me back up and say—there are two issues here. One is, under our law, the President is plainly required to consult with the Congress before agreeing to a course of action that would require the expenditure of money. You don't have to agree with the Congress, but at least you have to consult with them.

President Chirac came in and said, "Look, timing is of the essence, and we need a vote on this, and we need it now." So I called Senator Dole and Speaker Gingrich, and I have no—we had a good conversation, and I have no quarrel with the letter they sent, because I said, "I don't have time to do the consultations if he is right and we need the vote now."

So the letter they sent to me said two things. But the most important thing, apropos of your point is, "You can do this, but our committee chairmen have very serious reservations about this mission, what its role is going to be, what its function will be, and whether we should pay for it. So if you do it, you have to know that we are not committing in advance to appropriate the money."

Now, what I told the British was, and what I told all of my colleagues last night, was that I would make my best efforts to secure funding for it because I believe it's the right thing to do.

Now, the second issue I want to say is, as you know, the leadership of the Republican Party disagrees with our policy. They favor a unilateral lift which would collapse the U.N. mission. That's what they think the right thing to do is. But they know that the President has to make foreign policy and that I have no intention of pursuing that for the reasons I have already explained.

Q. [*Inaudible*]—and funding——

Q. Mr. President——

The President. We're working on that.

Q. Since UNPROFOR is now unable to carry out its mission to deliver humanitarian relief to Sarajevo or to maintain the weapons exclusion zone around the city and Sarajevo is once again being strangled, why have you urged the

Bosnian government not to use force to defend itself?

The President. Well, first of all, my sympathies are with them. I agreed to the statement that we all signed off on last night because the French and the British are doing their best to get more troops there through the rapid reaction force, which would permit the U.N. to fulfill its mandate which includes opening Sarajevo, and because I believe that has the best chance of opening Sarajevo without other adverse consequences to the Bosnians.

In other words, I tried to make sure that resolution was carefully worded to say, right now don't increase hostilities, because I don't believe this is a good time to do that when we are trying to strengthen the rapid reaction force and when, if we are successful, they will be better able to guarantee the openness of Sarajevo.

My sympathies with them are complete. They have a right to want their city to be open. And the Serbs have been shelling it on and off for 4 years whenever they could get away with it. So I don't agree with what's going on. But if the rapid reaction force works and the U.N. mission can work again and Sarajevo can be protected again, then I believe we're better off, and I believe, more importantly, they're better off if it can be done that way. I think there will be fewer casualties, and I think their politi-

cal position will be stronger. That's why I agreed to support the settlement.

Q. [Inaudible]—lift the siege?

The President. I'm saying, no, that's not their job. Their job is to back up and protect the U.N. mission. But I think it will show that the U.N. mission will have a greater capacity to do what the U.N. has authorized it to do, which is to be able to get in and out of Sarajevo.

Now, that is not the same thing as saying they will take a unilateral military action to lift the siege, but then the Serbs and everybody else, for that matter, will have to think about the Blue Helmets in a little different way before they just say, "I'm sorry, you can't cross this road; I'm sorry, we're going to take you a prisoner; I'm sorry, we're going to treat you like dirt; I'm sorry, we're going to ignore the U.N."

That is what President Chirac and Prime Minister Major want to avoid having happen to their troops again. And if it is seen in that light, then I think at least we have to give them a chance to try to make the U.N. mandate work again.

Thank you very much.

NOTE: The President's 99th news conference began at 4:20 p.m. at Dalhousie University. In his remarks, he referred to President Jacques Chirac of France and U.S. Representative to the United Nations Madeleine K. Albright.

Memorandum on Supporting the Role of Fathers in Families
June 16, 1995

Memorandum for the Heads of Executive Departments and Agencies

Subject: Supporting the Role of Fathers in Families

I am firm in my belief that the future of our Republic depends on strong families and that committed fathers are essential to those families. I am also aware that strengthening fathers' involvement with their children cannot be accomplished by the Federal Government alone; the solutions lie in the hearts and consciences of individual fathers and the support of the families and communities in which they live. However, there are ways for a flexible, responsive

Government to help support men in their roles as fathers.

Therefore, today I am asking the Federal agencies to assist me in this effort. I direct all executive departments and agencies to review every program, policy, and initiative (hereinafter referred to collectively as "programs") that pertains to families to:

- ensure, where appropriate, and consistent with program objectives, that they seek to engage and meaningfully include fathers;
- proactively modify those programs that were designed to serve primarily mothers and children, where appropriate and consistent with program objectives, to explicitly

include fathers and strengthen their involvement with their children;

- include evidence of father involvement and participation, where appropriate, in measuring the success of the programs; and
- incorporate fathers, where appropriate, in government-initiated research regarding children and their families.

I ask the departments and agencies to provide an initial report on the results of the review to the Vice President through the National Per-

formance Review within 90 days of the date of this memorandum.

The information gained from this review will be combined with information gathered through the Vice President's "Father to Father" initiative and other father involvement programs to determine the direction of those programs for the future. The National Performance Review, together with the Domestic Policy Council, will recommend further action based on the results of this review.

WILLIAM J. CLINTON

Letter to the Speaker of the House of Representatives on a Bipartisan Commission on Political Reform
June 16, 1995

Dear Mr. Speaker:

I was delighted when you and I agreed to the suggestion of a citizen in New Hampshire that we create a bipartisan commission to address the issues of political reform. As you stated at the time, this proposal offers the best chance in a generation to break through the stalemate between the parties that has blocked progress for reform. As you know, the citizen stated that this commission should be modeled after the base closing commission; I agree. This is an idea with wide appeal: in addition to our agreement, this proposal has previously been endorsed by Senate Majority Leader Dole, and a similar proposal has been introduced by Representatives Maloney, Meehan, Johnson, and others. I am writing to set forth my views on the best way to write into legislation the agreement we reached in New Hampshire.

As you know, to succeed, such a panel must be distinguished and truly bipartisan; it must have a firm deadline for action; and it must have a mechanism for presenting its proposals to the President and the Congress in such a way that we will be forced to act on them in a timely and comprehensive manner. Several times in recent years, particularly thorny issues, including base closings and congressional and judicial pay, have been addressed in this fashion.

First, the commission should be bipartisan in nature. Under this model, it would be comprised of eight members, appointed by the President in consultation with the leaders of the Congress.

The President would make two appointments; two would be made in consultation with the Speaker of the House; two would be made in consultation with the Majority Leader of the Senate; one each would be made in consultation with the minority leaders of the House and Senate. No more than four commissioners could be members of any one political party. To ensure that the commissioners are independent, receive the trust of the people, and can take a fresh look at these issues, they should not be current Federal officials or Members of Congress, or officers of or counsel to the political parties. In this fashion, we have an opportunity to achieve consensus and balance that will produce a national consensus on reform.

Second, the commission should be given a firm deadline in which to act—by February 1, 1996. These issues, while difficult, are not new, and can be fruitfully addressed in that time. The American people want to know that we will act during this Congress, and I believe the best chance of that is before the electoral season begins in the summer of 1996. The commission would be charged with considering all the issues of political reform, including campaign finance reform and lobby reform. Let me be clear: I do not believe that this proposal for establishing a commission should deter or detract from previously scheduled Senate action on political reform (S. 101), a measure I strongly support. That would be contrary to the purpose of the entire enterprise—making progress on reforms that are stalled, not to delay action on measure that are moving forward. If the Congress has taken final action on any of these matters before the commission meets, the panel could choose not to address them altogether.

Third, its recommendations must be dealt with in an expedited and comprehensive manner, in the same fashion as the proposals of the base closing commission. They would be sent to the President, who would reject them or send them on to the Congress in their entirety. They should then be considered on the "fast track"—an up or down vote, with no amendments, within 30 days of the submission by the President. Only in this way can the American people be assured that narrow interests do not pick apart the coherent and comprehensive recommendations of the bipartisan commission. (As you know, the recommendations of the base closing commission take effect

unless they are rejected by the Congress, but in this instance I believe it is more appropriate to give the Congress the opportunity to vote up or down.)

Working together to follow up on our New Hampshire agreement, we have a rare opportunity for truly bipartisan cooperation on a matter of urgent concern to the American people. We have a chance to put aside partisan interests to work toward the national interest. I look forward to working with you toward this end, and to hearing your views on this proposal or others you might have for moving ahead, and I have directed my staff to meet with your staff on this matter. If we take these steps, we will set in motion a process that could truly transform American politics for the better.

Sincerely,

WILLIAM J. CLINTON

Remarks on the Unveiling of a Group of Seven Commemorative Plaque in Halifax
June 17, 1995

Ladies and gentlemen, I just wanted to say a few words—I'm sure I speak on behalf of all of us here—to thank the people of Halifax and Nova Scotia and the leaders for making us feel so welcome and to say a special word of appreciation for the leadership Prime Minister Chrétien has given to this conference. The people of Canada can be very, very proud of the direction and leadership that he gave this G–7 conference. It has been more businesslike, more informal, and more specific in its sugges-

tions for what we can do to improve the lives of our people than many of our previous meetings. And I think it is due to the leadership of the Prime Minister. And all of us wanted to express that to the people of Canada. We are very, very grateful for it.

Thank you.

NOTE: The President spoke at 10:05 a.m. at the Halifax Waterfront. A tape was not available for verification of the content of these remarks.

The President's Radio Address
June 17, 1995

Good morning. I'm speaking to you from Halifax, Canada, where I've been meeting with the leaders of the world's largest industrial democracies. We've taken concrete steps to strengthen the world economy. We've agreed on measures to anticipate and prevent future financial crises, like the one that happened ear-

lier this year in Mexico, and to promote economic growth in countries that will provide markets of tomorrow for our American exports.

The work we're doing here is part of my administration's strategy to create jobs and raise incomes and living standards for the American people. Our responsibility is to restore the

American dream, to give our children the chance that we've had to make America work well for all people who work hard.

To do that, one of the things we have to do is to reduce the deficit and balance the budget. Earlier this week, I outlined my plan to balance the budget in 10 years. This plan proves we can balance the budget while we continue to invest in the things that will keep America strong, things like education, health care, medical research, and technology. My plan will keep our economy strong as we eliminate the deficit. And unlike other plans, my plan protects the people in our country who have so much to give and who have given so much.

For example, my plan would avoid a number of cuts proposed by the Congress that would seriously hurt hundreds of thousands of American veterans. The House budget plan has proposed quadrupling the amount veterans pay for the prescription drugs they need, while cutting taxes a lot for upper income Americans who don't really need a tax cut.

Under my plan that wouldn't happen. We can balance the budget in 10 years without harming the people who protected our Nation and who now have to get by without much to live on.

The Senate budget plan has similar flaws. For example, it proposes to deny veterans benefits to anyone in the military who is injured unless that injury is directly connected to the performance of his or her duties. Now, think about what that means. A young Army sergeant stationed overseas is on his way home from the movie theater one night when he's off duty. He gets hit by a drunk driver, and he's paralyzed. The Senate budget says, "Tough luck, no veterans benefits to help you with the injury."

I think we've got a duty to help our veterans when they're sick or injured. But we also have a duty to balance the budget. What I want you to know is that we can do both. My plan cuts Federal spending by $1.1 trillion. It does not raise taxes. It is disciplined, comprehensive, and serious. It won't be easy, but we need to do it, and we can.

Let's keep in mind the purpose. The purpose is to renew the American dream, to grow the middle class in terms of jobs and incomes, and to give poor people the chance to work themselves into the middle class.

With that purpose in mind, my balanced budget has five basic priorities: First, help people make the most of their own lives. That means that while we cut the deficit, we have to increase investment in education, not cut education.

Second, we have to control health care costs, but do it by strengthening Medicare, saving Medicaid, not by slashing services for the elderly. We can maintain benefits by cutting costs through genuine reform, like more home care for the elderly so they can stay out of more expensive institutions, preventive mammograms, and respite care for people with Alzheimer's, and cracking down on fraud and abuse and giving people more incentives to go into managed care.

Third, cut taxes, but do it for the middle class, not the wealthy. We shouldn't cut education or Medicare just to give people money who don't really need it. Instead, let's help middle class Americans pay for college, like the GI bill did for veterans after World War II.

Fourth, save money by cutting welfare, but do it in a way that saves enough for investment to move people to work. Don't save money just by throwing people off the rolls or hurting their children, who are vulnerable through no fault of their own. The congressional proposals are tough on kids and weak on work. We need to be tough on work and supportive of children. The congressional approach will cost a lot more money down the road than it will ever save.

The fifth principle is, as I've said before, balance the budget in 10 years. We could do it in 7 years, as some in Congress want. But there's no reason to inflict the pain that would cause or to run the risk of a recession. Think about it like this: If you bought a home with a mortgage, you'd sure want to pay it off just as fast as you could without hurting your family. But if the choice was pay it off in 10 years and pay your medical bills and send your daughter to college, or pay it off in 7 and go without the best care and tell your daughter you're sorry but she'll have to fend for herself, I don't think you'd have a hard time making the right choice. We can have all the benefits of balancing the budget without a lot of the burdens if we'll do it in 10 instead of 7 years.

Now, don't let anybody fool you: balancing the budget is not going to be a walk in the park. It will require real cuts; it will cause real pain. But the difference between my plan and the congressional plans is the difference between necessary cuts and unacceptable pain. Remember the goals: Restore the American dream, promote jobs and higher incomes, reinforce families and communities.

This is a time when we must, more than ever before, join together to seize the opportunities before us, a moment of immense promise. We can renew the American dream, and we have to do it and do it right.

Thanks for listening.

NOTE: The address was recorded at approximately 5:30 p.m. on June 16 at the Chateau Halifax for broadcast at 10:06 a.m. on June 17.

Exchange With Reporters Prior to Discussions With President Boris Yeltsin of Russia in Halifax
June 17, 1995

Q. Mr. President, let me ask you a question. Are you now changing your mind as to the people against whom Mr. Yeltsin is waging a war when you learn what's going on in Budennovsk? That's Russian Television News question.

President Yeltsin. In the first place, I would like to say that my friend Bill has never wavered in his opinion. He has always supported and is supporting Russia and President Yeltsin.

I would like to say that the storming of the hospital is continuing, that we have liberated 200 hostages, and the operation is going on. I am in contact, in constant contact with our commanders who command our special forces who stormed the hospital, and I am in full control of the situation.

Taking this example, you should judge for yourselves that Chechnya today is the center of world terrorism, of bribery and corruption and mafia. We couldn't act otherwise. We had to destroy those terrorists and bandits.

Well, not all in the world understood this situation correctly, and perhaps not all of the mass media understood correctly. But I am very glad that my friend Bill understood me correctly and, nonetheless, always defended his position no matter what happened.

I just have to say that our state Dumas, as a matter of fact, today has made the decision to have the President go back, come back home and make a visit to Budennovsk. I think, therefore, that this is a bad mistake, a bad move on their part because now I, myself, become a hostage to these very same bandits by having to go back there.

And moreover, I have to say that after my discussion yesterday—and I once again reiterated that today to our partners in the G–7 and

told them what kind of people we're dealing with, what kind of horrible criminals with black bands on their foreheads—they now much better understand that this is really the only way that we can deal with these criminal elements. They really now understand much more.

Dear journalists, Bill and I accumulated a whole host of very important issues—global issues, not some internal Russian disputes and issues or internal American problems. These are really serious, overwhelming global issues. And therefore, I say, we've got to go.

Thank you, and goodbye.

Q. President Clinton, do you agree with what he said about your position?

President Clinton. Well, let me tell you what my position is. First of all, it is true that the United States has always said that Chechnya was a part of Russia and was ultimately a problem that had to be resolved by the people of your nation, consistent with your constitutional laws.

It is also true that we believe that terrorism everywhere is wrong, that terrorism in the Middle East is wrong, that people blowing up our Federal building in Oklahoma City is wrong, and people taking over a hospital in your country and killing innocent civilians is wrong, and has to be resisted strong.

But I also subscribe to the position taken by the G–7 that sooner or later—better sooner than later—the cycle of violence has to be broken. And ultimately, in any democracy, there has to be a political solution to people's differences. And so that is what we have urged.

President Yeltsin and I have had several conversations about this. When I was in Moscow, I said that I understood it was a terribly difficult situation for Russia but that the United States believed that ultimately in any democracy, all decisions were finally resolved in a political manner in a way that would permit the cycle of violence to be broken.

So that is our position. It is still our position. And we hope that it will become more possible now. But nothing—nothing—can justify this outrageous act at your hospital and innocent people being killed. It's just wrong.

I want to mention one other issue because it won't be in the headlines, but it's terribly important. When President Yeltsin and I were together in Moscow for the anniversary of the end of World War II, we talked about the problem of nuclear security. And I told him then I thought it was very important that we work closely together on the problem of nuclear security, not just in Russia but in other countries where this is an issue, and on the problem of nuclear smuggling, because with so many terrorist groups around the world, we don't want small-scale nuclear weapons being added to their already impressive arsenals.

So when he came to this meeting, President Yeltsin suggested that we have a summit next year in Moscow dealing with these issues and involving many, many countries that have this problem. And I think we all agree. We think it's a very constructive suggestion. And we believe that, together, by next year we can make some real progress in making the world more secure for this problem in reducing the likelihood of nuclear smuggling and, ultimately, the

likelihood of these small-scale weapons being used to further the cause of terrorism.

So that is one of the positive things that came out of this summit, from my point of view, along with the agreement we all made to work together more closely in fighting terrorism and the agreement we made to try to prevent further Mexican crisis and continued reform of the international financial institutions.

So from my point of view, this has been a very successful meeting. I know that the problem in Chechnya is occupying everyone's attention. The gripping scene at the hospital must have a hold on the imagination of the Russian people, very much like the explosion in Oklahoma City had on our people. And we join the Russian people in condemning terrorism in the strongest possible terms.

But we hope that in the end all the people of Russia, including the people in Chechnya, can be reconciled so that your democracy can flourish everywhere and the cycle of violence can be broken. And that is our prayer, and that is our policy.

Thank you very much.

NOTE: The exchange began at 2:49 p.m. in the Cavalier Room at the Citadel Hotel. President Yeltsin spoke in Russian, and his remarks were translated by an interpreter. A tape was not available for verification of the content of this exchange.

Teleconference Remarks With the U.S. Conference of Mayors
June 20, 1995

The President. Thank you. Thank you very much, Mayor Rice. And I want to begin by congratulating Mayor Ashe on a great year as president. I have enjoyed working with you very much. And I look forward to working with you, Norm, in the year ahead. I also want to say hello to some of my old friends in Miami. I see Mayor Daley and Mayor Clark are there. I understand that Secretary Brown and Secretary Cisneros are also both with you today.

Let me say before I go forward that I noticed in one of the previous sessions you had that it was suggested that we don't need the Depart-

ment of Housing and Urban Development anymore. Let me say that I think Henry Cisneros and his whole team have done a magnificent job, and I don't think we want to send Andrew Cuomo to the beach just yet. I hope you agree.

I also want to thank all of you for giving me this chance to speak with you today. I'm very proud that our administration has worked in an unprecedented partnership with our cities, our communities, and especially our mayors. You make real budgets. You deal with real problems. You know the real concerns of our people as we try to restore the American dream. I'm looking forward to our continued cooperation. And I want to keep focused on the real problems our country faces.

You have heard, in the previous speakers who have appeared before you, strands of the great debates now going on in Washington and throughout our country. There are those who say that our primary problems are personal and cultural, not economic and political. There are those who say that the biggest problems we face are due to the fact that the Federal Government has too much authority and more ought to be given to the State and local level.

Well, I have to say to you that I'm glad to have these debates. I was making these arguments long before this Presidential election season, indeed, long before I became a candidate for President in 1992, when I was a Governor, working on the values problems we face, like teen pregnancy and youth violence and all kinds of personal irresponsibility in our society. You and I know that unless people do the right things themselves, that we can't solve the problems of our society. And I was calling for a devolution of responsibility back to local and State governments long before I ever ran for President. So these are not just issues of a political season for me.

But let's keep our eyes on what we have to do in terms of the real problems that you deal with every day. We do have a values crisis in this country. We need to exalt responsibility and work and family and community. We need to be less violent, less irresponsible, and less divisive.

We do have an economic problem in this country. We've got years of stagnant wages and people who are working hard and being punished for it. We need to grow the middle class and shrink the under class and empower people to make the most of their own lives.

We've got a governmental problem in this country. We need a Government for the 21st century that is less bureaucratic and more entrepreneurial and more oriented toward partnerships where more is done at the grassroots level.

Now, I believe all that. But the question is, what are we going to do about it? And if we use a lot of rhetoric to divide the American people again and to divide the problems we face in terms of values as against economics and national as against local, instead of recognizing that what we need is to face these issues and all their aspects and we need a real hard-

nosed partnership, then we'll be in trouble. After all, the problems that you face every day are the very reasons I ran for President. I believed we had to empower our people and our communities to meet the demands of change at the grassroots level where people live.

Now, there are some in Washington who believe we can make Government work just by juggling programs from the Federal bureaucracies to the State bureaucracies. You and I know that the right way is to give local governments, community organizations, and individual citizens and their neighborhoods the tools they need, the resources they need to improve their own lives.

In 1992, I laid out an agenda to send power, capital, and, most important of all, hope to the people who are working hard to make the most of their communities and their own lives. We still have a good ways to go, but I am proud that we have kept that commitment.

Look at what we have already achieved together: We created the empowerment zones and the enterprise communities, awarding tax incentives and grants to spur economic growth in 105 communities that also supports good values. We're creating a network of community development banks and financial institutions to lend, invest, provide basic banking services in places that need the most to the people who can do the most to change the social conditions we all want to change. We passed final regulations for the Community Reinvestment Act to help our banks and thrifts make good loans and investments, to help people rebuild our troubled communities. The SBA established one-stop capital shops to distribute $3 billion in loans and investments for small and minority businesses over the next 5 years. We fought to save the community development block grants and our economic plan in the face of huge opposition.

Now, those are the things that we have done together—just some of the things we've done together. Now it's up to us to continue a partnership to create jobs, raise incomes, lift living standards, and improve the values and the strength of our communities. We can do that, and we have done that, working with the new Congress.

I have supported and signed into law, for example, the bill to minimize the unfunded mandates that tell you what to do without giving you the resources to do it. I was proud to do that. But I also want you to know that I vetoed the rescission bill in part because of the cuts that affect you directly. For example, the Congress in this rescission bill would cut grants to cities that have already been obligated to make our water safer. These grants were already committed; the letters had gone out. To cut them now would be worse than an unfunded mandate; it would be a defunded mandate. And I don't intend to let that happen.

Another reason I vetoed the rescission bill is because the Congress had cut the community development financial institutions and added language which made it almost impossible for them to operate. I am proud that we've already awarded one large bank in Los Angeles, and we've got more work to do on that front. We shouldn't turn back now from a proven commitment that will bring free enterprise to the most distressed areas of our country.

Now we have to approach a new budget. And as we do it, I want to continue to work together with you to seize this opportunity to build a stronger future for all of our people, to do it in a way that supports our economic interests and our values and works to reform the Government and give you more responsibility.

For the first time in a long, long time, the leaders of both political parties now share the will to balance the Federal budget. That's an important issue, and I want to talk about it just a moment. We know that that requires some tough calls. But if we can balance the budget, it will mean in the years ahead there'll be more money to invest in our people, in our cities, and in our future, and less money that has to be spent just paying interest on yesterday's debt. The difficult task ahead is for us to have the will necessary to do it and to cast partisanship aside so that we can get the job done in a way that helps instead of hurts the long-term prospects of our people. We need a budget that balances debts and credits but also keeps our values in balance. That's what our responsibility as leaders demands.

We faced that challenge together in the first 2 years of our administration when we cut the deficit by $1 trillion in 7 years and still were able to invest in the tools that our communities and our people have to have to compete and win in the global economy. The work now has to go on.

Now, with that in mind, last week I outlined my plan to eliminate the deficit in 10 years. My plan cuts Federal spending by $1.1 trillion,

on top of the $1 trillion in deficit reduction enacted in our '93 budget plan. This new budget does not raise taxes. It is disciplined, it is comprehensive, and it is serious. It won't be easy, but we need to do it, and we can. Our plan proves that you can balance the budget and still invest in things that will keep America strong and growing, like education, health care, research, and technology.

To accomplish these goals we have to focus on five basic priorities. First, we've got to help people make the most of their own lives. That means, while we cut the deficit, we should increase investment in education, not cut it.

Second, we have to control health care costs, but we should do it by strengthening Medicare, saving Medicaid, reforming them, not by slashing services for the elderly. We can maintain benefits by cutting costs through genuine reform, including cracking down on the substantial amount of Medicaid fraud and abuse and giving more incentives for more efficient and cost-effective ways of delivering care.

Third, we need to cut taxes, but for the middle class, not for the wealthiest Americans who don't really need it.

Fourth, we can save money by cutting welfare, but we have to do it in a way that saves enough for investment to move people to work. The congressional proposals are too tough on children and too weak on work. We need to be tough on work and supportive of children.

And in that regard, I want to thank all of you there who, in the spirit of bipartisanship, have come out in support of our efforts to achieve real welfare reform that moves people from welfare to work. The bill that was recently introduced in the Senate by Senators Daschle and others achieves that objective. And those of you who are supporting it, I am very grateful for that. We can save funds, but we have to save enough to invest in people, to empower them to end welfare as we know it, not just to cut people off and not worry about the consequence to the children.

The fifth principle is to balance the budget in 10 years, not 7. Now, we could do it in 7 as some in Congress want, but there's no reason to inflict the amount of pain that would cause or to run the risk of recession. A highly respected economic group out of the Wharton Business School recently estimated that one of the Republican budgets would actually cause a recession, driving unemployment to 8.6 percent and delaying balancing the budget by 2 years anyway.

Now in spite of all this, don't let anybody fool you. Balancing the budget in 10 years will require real cuts; it will cause real pain. We can and we should discuss where those savings should be found. We have to decide about whether the savings should come out of programs like the community development block grants, which I know are very important to you and which I have strongly supported. I still believe in them very strongly. But let me be straight with you. If we don't cut the community development block grant, then there will have to be some cuts in some other programs that you and I care about.

We have to do that if we're going to bring the budget into balance. But let me say again, we should do this. We should do this. We never had a huge structural deficit before the 12 years before I became President, before the years between 1981 and 1993. And I'll tell you how big the problem is. Right now, today, our budget would be in balance today if it were not for the interest we have to pay on the deficit run up between 1981 and 1993 in January. So we have got to turn this around. We cannot continue something that we only started 12 years ago.

But I want to remind you there is a big difference between my plan and the congressional plans. It's the difference between necessary cuts and unacceptable pain. It's the difference between a deficit reduction plan that goes to balance budgets and still invest in our future and one that cuts off our future. It's the difference between one that will reduce the deficit in ways that will promote long-term growth and one that will reduce the deficit in ways that risk a severe, near-term recession.

I am going to fight to avoid cutting education, hurting people on Medicare, undermining critical investments in our communities. It would be wrong to sacrifice those investments just to meet a 7-year deadline when we can get the job in 10 years. It would be wrong to cut in those areas that will help our people restore the American dream, raise our incomes, so that we can give a tax cut to people who don't really need it.

One of our most important challenges is to make sure that the American people feel more secure in their homes and neighborhoods as well. And therefore, I thank you again for joining me in the fight against crime and the fight for the crime bill last year. Without your support, we could not have possibly passed it, especially given the bitter opposition of some Members of Congress to the assault weapons ban and to giving cities the flexibility that you need in the prevention funds.

I know some of you had conflicting opinions and different needs when it came to our plan to provide 100,000 new police officers. But I believe we have a national crisis on crime because we don't have enough police officers on the street. Over 30 years we watched as the violent crime rate tripled and our police departments only increased by 10 percent. Now we've found the funds to pay for police in the right way. We cut unnecessary Government at the national level and sent the savings to our communities for more police officers. That is the kind of bargain the American people deserve. The philosophy behind that was to do what could be done to reduce crime.

But I would also remind you, under our plan, we gave localities enormous flexibility in spending the prevention funds because you know what works at the local level. It is ironic today that there are those who are trying to dismantle our national commitment to put 100,000 police on the street in the name of giving you more flexibility when less than a year ago they were saying that giving you more flexibility would lead to widespread abuse in the spending of Federal money.

The truth is that a lot of these programs to give you more flexibility, from welfare to crime, are really just ways to cut spending that invests in our future and our economy and our security. If we'll adopt my budget plan, we can give you more flexibility and still do those things and balance the budget. Behind all of these initiatives are not just shuffling from Federal to State bureaucracy, but trying to empower our people directly—is the philosophy that we are using to help our people meet the demands of the global economy in their own lives.

Some still say, as I said—let me just give you one example, finally—that we ought to trust the Federal Government to train our workers. We've got about 70 or 80 different training programs. Then there are some that say, "No, let's give all these programs to State government." But I say, we shouldn't empower one bureaucracy over another. In the future, in every one of your cities, the ability of the American people who live there to do well in the global economy will depend upon our ability to directly empower individual Americans, to directly empower them to make the most of their own lives, including having a lifetime right to constant reeducation and training.

So let me talk with you, finally, today about an effort that we're making now that would give people those most important tools they need to build better lives. It is central to the rebirth of your cities. If you have more people who can get good jobs and who can earn higher incomes, then so many of the problems that you face, so many of the problems you face will be lessened.

So here's how I want our people to get those jobs and to keep them in this global economy that is always demanding more and more of them. I want to do something that's modeled on the GI bill. Fifty years ago, as World War II was coming to an end, our country created the GI bill that gave a whole generation of Americans the education to create an unprecedented prosperity. What I have proposed today is a "GI bill" for America's workers, to help a whole new generation of Americans secure decent lives and decent incomes for themselves and their families.

The principle is simple: Education and training can no longer stop at high school. We've all got to keep on learning to keep pace with the dynamic global economy. And the best way to make it happen is to put the power directly in the hands of individual Americans who have to do the learning. Today there is a confusing maze of 70—at least 70—job training programs sponsored by the Federal Government. What we want to do is to consolidate them into a single grant, and that grant will have but one purpose, to put money directly into the hands of people who need it.

Through our school-to-work initiative, we'll continue to help high school students or graduates who want further training get that in order to compete. Through our skilled grants, we'll help the worker who has lost a job, who is grossly underpaid and underemployed to take the responsibility to get a new leg up in the global economy. We also want to make it easier and cheaper for workers to get loans to build on their education. That means expanding, not cutting, Pell grants and direct student loans. And it means the right kind of tax cuts, not tax cuts for people who don't need them but tax cuts for middle income Americans who can use the money to invest in their training and their children's education. We propose a tax cut for the cost of all post-high-school education.

Now, these things will make opportunity real for more Americans and make opportunity real for more of your cities. The "GI bill" for America's workers will make it possible for more and better jobs for people who live in your communities and will help attract jobs and expand your economic base.

You think about it: If everyone considering investing in your communities knew that every person who wanted a job could get the job training in a direct voucher from the Federal Government which could go to your community colleges, to get the kind of training they need, that would help us to do what you need to do. We want to make you a full partner in designing a system of adult education and job placement. That will mean that community colleges, which are the new lifeblood for so many of your citizens, will be even stronger and, more importantly, will mean that you will be able to use this as a tool to develop your own economies.

I believe this approach will play a major role in our goal, our common goal to restore the American dream. I'm pleased that this morning in the Los Angeles Times there was an article that I hope you've all had a chance to read, written by Al From, the president of the Democratic Leadership Council, a Democrat, and by Jack Kemp, the former Secretary of Housing and Urban Development, a Republican. Here's what they say about our "GI bill." They say, quote, it "offers an all-too-rare opportunity for Members of Congress of both parties to discard partisan squabbling and cooperate on a measure that can help hard-working Americans acquire the skills they need to lift their incomes. . . . The needs of this great country of ours demand that all of us, Democrats and Republicans alike, ask ourselves the question: 'Can we make it work?' The correct answer is: We must."

I could not have said it better. Al From and Jack Kemp, the Republicans and the Democratic mayors out there who are listening to me today, just remember, as we balance the Federal budget, as we help all Americans prepare for a bright future, we have got to seize this moment of great opportunity. We've got to put our national priorities above party politics and put the American people first. That's what I was trying to do when I had that conversation in New Hampshire with the Speaker of the House the other day.

This is a moment of immense promise. We can renew the American dream. But we have to work together, and we have to avoid trying to divide our people by false choices. Good economics, sound values, strong communities, a Government that works: That's what we really need, and I will work with you to achieve it.

Thank you very much.

[At this point, Mayor Norman Rice of Seattle, WA, president, U.S. Conference of Mayors, thanked the President and asked about welfare reform.]

The President. I think the prospects for real welfare reform really depend upon whether the Senate Republicans, or at least the block of moderate Republicans who understand these issues, will work with the Democrats on something like the Daschle bill.

You know, there is a hard core in the Senate who are demanding that there be no welfare reform bill unless all aid is cut off to unmarried mothers and their children born out of wedlock, even though the Catholic Church, the National Governors' Association, your group, everybody I know says that that would be unfair to children.

If the rest of the Republicans will leave that block and join with Senators Daschle and Breaux and Mikulski and the others who are on this bill, we could work out a bill that would make a real difference.

And let me say, one of the important things, I think, about the Daschle bill is that it really heavily emphasizes the importance of child care. As I look back over the time that has elapsed since, as a Governor, I worked on the welfare reform bill of 1988, if you ask me what its single biggest shortcoming was, I would say that we should have done more in child care.

And if we do what I have suggested here—and I think a lot of the Republicans want to do this—and we take all these various training programs and put them into a big block and let unemployed workers access them, then that could help to provide the training money for an awful lot of people on welfare who want to move to work, so that if the Daschle bill itself or any future amplification of it that could have bipartisan support in the Senate, could really focus on child care, I think we could

get a welfare reform bill that is tough on work and good for children, instead of the other way around.

So I would urge all of you—especially the Republican mayors; you have a lot of allies in the Republican Party in the Senate—welfare reform ought to be a bipartisan issue. If we could get a good bill out of the Senate, I feel confident that we could have a bipartisan majority in the House that would vote for it as well if we could get it out of the conference committee.

So that is what I would implore you all to do. This is a huge deal for the United States. And the Daschle bill is an opening, an outreach for a genuine bipartisan compromise that doesn't just dump a lot of money back on the States and localities—excuse me, a lot less than you used to have, in a way that would lead to people being cut off with nothing good happening.

[Mayor Richard M. Daley of Chicago, IL, vice president, U.S. Conference of Mayors, asked what the mayors could do to ensure continued funding for policing and other crime prevention efforts.]

The President. I think, Mayor, what you have to do is to, again, emphasize in the Senate where this is being debated and ultimately in the conference committee that we need to have more flexibility for the cities but that it is unacceptable, at least for me and I hope for many of you, to come off of our commitment on 100,000 police.

I have watched many panels, and I've seen a lot of your mayors on C-Span. You know, I actually get to watch you as well as you watching me, and I know that some of the mayors believe that we've been too firm on the police requirements, because some cities have already increased their police forces and can't take maximum advantage of this. But I have to tell you, I think there is a national interest in increasing the police forces of this country by about 20 percent. And after all, this crime bill was funded by a reduction in the national employment of people in the Federal Government.

On the other hand, I have been strongly in favor of absolutely maximum flexibility for you in other aspects of the crime bill and would be in favor of even more flexibility in other aspects of the crime bill as long as we don't undermine our commitment to 100,000 police. If we can get more flexibility in the other areas of prevention and imprisonment, I would be in favor of it. I will work with you to do anything I can in that regard.

Mayor Rice. Thank you, Mr. President. The next questioner is Paul Helmke, mayor of Fort Wayne.

Mayor Helmke. It's good to have the opportunity to talk to you again, Mr. President.

The President. Thank you.

[*Mayor Helmke, chair of the advisory board, U.S. Conference of Mayors, asked the President what could be done to ensure that Federal funds to cities remain flexible so mayors can meet the needs of their citizens.*]

The President. First of all, Paul, let me say that I think that we have to do this. I didn't give you any specific numbers in my remarks, but let me tell you that even with a 10-year balanced budget plan, if you don't cut education and if you have a tax cut much smaller than the ones contemplated by either the Senate or the House, it would still require about a 20-percent overall cut in other discretionary spending because we're all at about the same place on where we think defense ought to be.

Now, that's over a 10-year period—for my budget at least. What I think we need to do here is, before this budget is actually passed in the fall or in late summer, but probably be in the fall, we need to know before the budget is passed what the new arrangements with our cities will be.

Let me just give you one example. I would like to preserve the community development block grant program, if we can. I have proposed it to be continued at the present level of funding in 1996. The Senate budget resolution proposes to cut it in half. What I think we ought to do—and I know—by the way, I wanted to compliment Secretary Cisneros. He has been waging a very strong fight within our administration to try to make sure that the cuts come in other

areas and the community development block grant program is preserved at its present level. We could do that. You might argue that we could even increase it if some of the other categorical programs were folded into it so that if we are going to go forward here, maybe some new purposes should be added to it.

I am open to all that. I want to reduce regulation. I want to increase your flexibility, not just for the cities but for all local units. We just announced a 40-percent cut in the regulations of the Department of Education, for example. Most of you don't run your own school districts, but some of you do, and that will be important to you.

We are moving in the right direction here. But I think we have got to be willing, before this budget is passed, to sit down with the cities and, in fairness, also with the States and the counties, and try to design what the new agreement will be about this money and how it's going to be funded. And I think there are great opportunities for you to get some more flexibility and for you to determine how we ought to do it. And I am more than willing to go forward with you on that basis.

Mayor Rice. Mr. President, we thank you very much for giving us this opportunity, and we will take the challenge to respond and open up a dialog that really moves this country forward in the interest of cities and the people that we represent.

The President. Thank you. Mayor Rice, Mayor Daley, Mayor Helmke, thank you all. I appreciate your good work.

NOTE: The President spoke at 11:15 a.m. from Room 459 of the Old Executive Office Building to the meeting in Miami, FL. In his remarks, he referred to Mayor Victor Ashe of Knoxville, TN, immediate past president, U.S. Conference of Mayors, and Mayor Steve Clark of Miami, FL.

Statement on House Action To Lift the Moratorium on Oil and Gas Drilling on the Outer Continental Shelf
June 20, 1995

Today's vote by a House subcommittee to lift the moratorium on oil and gas drilling on the

Outer Continental Shelf would overturn a longtime bipartisan consensus on the need to protect the environment and economies of California, Florida, the Pacific Northwest, Alaska, and other coastal States.

This action is a mistake, and I will have no part of it. I will not allow oil and gas drilling off our Nation's most sensitive coastlines on my watch. America's coastlines are simply too important to our economy and our way of life.

This is yet another example of the zealous efforts of the Republican Congress to roll back environmental laws. Those laws serve the American people well, and I will fight to maintain them.

Message to the Congress Transmitting the Latvia-United States Fishery Agreement
June 20, 1995

To the Congress of the United States:

In accordance with the Magnuson Fishery Conservation and Management Act of 1976 (16 U.S.C. 1801 *et seq.*), I transmit herewith an Agreement Between the Government of the United States of America and the Government of the Republic of Latvia Extending the Agreement of April 8, 1993, Concerning Fisheries Off the Coasts of the United States. The Agreement, which was effected by an exchange of notes at Riga on March 28, 1995, and April 4, 1995, extends the 1993 Agreement to December 31, 1997.

In light of the importance of our fisheries relationship with the Republic of Latvia, I urge that the Congress give favorable consideration to this Agreement at an early date.

WILLIAM J. CLINTON

The White House,
June 20, 1995.

Remarks at the Congressional Picnic
June 20, 1995

Let me welcome you to the back lawn of the White House. I believe this is the first time in 3 years we've done this when we have not had a tent. And thank goodness the weather cooperated. But as a result of that, we all have a lot more room to get up and walk around. And I think it's a little cooler and breezier than it normally is. We're delighted to have you all here.

I want to thank the Marine Free Country Band that was playing a little bit before we came up. They did a great job. And I want to say a special thanks to David Sanborne and the Manhattan School of Music Orchestra who are about to entertain us and who are quite wonderful.

We're going to listen to them play a few songs, and then I want—Hillary and I want to get up and kind of wander around and say hello to all of you. I want to thank you again for coming and echo the Vice President's words—we really look forward to this every year, a time when Members of Congress can come and bring their families and just relax and have a good time and enjoy this wonderful place that is America's home. I think it puts us all in a little better frame of mind. And I know it always energizes me to get up in the morning and go to work with a more positive outlook.

We're delighted to see you. We welcome you. And let's get on with the show. Thank you very much.

NOTE: The President spoke at 7:58 p.m. on the South Lawn at the White House.

Remarks at the Presidential Scholars Awards Presentation Ceremony
June 21, 1995

Thank you. That was one of the more unusual introductions I've ever had. [*Laughter*] But I do have a lot more wrinkles inside and out than I had when I showed up here, grayer hair, and a few more scars, which are deeper wrinkles. But it has been a great joy, thanks in no small measure to people like those who have joined us here today.

I thank Secretary Riley and Secretary Kunin and all the fine people at the Education Department; the leaders of the education groups who are here; the members of the Commission for Presidential Scholars, Governor Sinner and others, who have served so well and who have selected all of you, so you know how wise they are. I thank them for their service to education, which is really service to our future.

I want to make a brief announcement before I make the comments I have to make to you about education. Most of the people my age who were drawn into public service—as I hope each of you in your own way will become a public servant, even as a private citizen—were attracted by the example set by President Kennedy and the people who came into his administration. Many people now know that when I was about your age I met President Kennedy here in the Rose Garden, 32 years ago next month. It inspired me and my entire generation to believe that we should ask not what our country could do for us but what we could do for our country, how we could serve.

And when I became President, I asked the American people to join me in a season of service. I asked the Congress to establish a national service corps, AmeriCorps, that would give our young people and sometimes people who aren't so young the opportunity to earn money for education but to do it by serving people here in our community, at the grassroots level, all across this country. That idea was inspired by the Peace Corps. And the Peace Corps continues the tradition of service that John Kennedy established to this day.

President Kennedy started the Peace Corps to help expand the circle of freedom and democracy when it was threatened by communism and by the cold war. But it has continued throughout all these years, in countries all across the globe, to help people solve real problems, to go beyond language and racial and ethnic and religious and the political differences to unite us at the most fundamental human level in fulfilling our potential. The Peace Corps is very, very important.

Just a few weeks ago, my Director of the Peace Corps, Carol Bellamy, had the great honor to be named the head of UNICEF on behalf of the United Nations. And now I have to replace her. And today I want to announce that the distinguished gentleman behind me, who has been my faithful friend and aide for many years and is now the White House Communications Director, Mark Gearan, will be the new Director of the Peace Corps.

Mark, please stand up. [*Applause*] Thank you.

I think it would be fair to say that if we had a secret ballot for who the most popular person working in the White House is, Mark Gearan would probably win it in a walk. He has the understanding and the ability to build bridges and the tenacity to cross them. I am proud to nominate him to lead our Peace Corps into the 21st century, to keep the vision and the spirit of John Kennedy alive and the dream of America alive all over the world.

Thank you. Thank you very much.

I am very proud that all of you are here today, and I hope while you're here you'll have a chance to look around this magnificent city. I recently represented all of you in Kiev in the Ukraine, commemorating the end of World War II and the 50th anniversary of that. And the mayor of Kiev proudly told me that Kiev, of all the capital cities in the world, had the second largest percentage of its land in parkland and forest, exceeded only by Washington, DC.

I think it is the most beautiful capital city in the world. It is also full of our common history. If you walk through the Capitol or look at the White House or go over to the Lincoln Memorial or go up the hill leading to the eternal flame on President Kennedy's grave at Arlington, you have to imagine all that has taken place here. The White House just behind me has, after all, been here now for almost 200 years; it was opened in 1800. Every President but

George Washington has lived here. And he, of course, was responsible for building it.

When you put your hand in the river of our history, you can't help being touched by it and being changed by it. You have to be reminded of all this country has stood for and what it has accomplished. You also have to be sobered by the fact that not so far from here there live a lot of other young people your age who are among the poorest young people in our country, who live in some of the highest crime areas in our land, and have some of the most limited futures facing them. I'm very proud of the fact that year before last my Secret Service detail gave to the First Lady and me, as a Christmas present, the adoption of one of those schools to try to help give those young people a better future as well.

Today, as every day, the fundamental purpose of America is to preserve our freedom, maintain our democracy, and do what is necessary to help the American people make the most of their own lives.

There is a great debate going on here in Washington today. Those who want to shrink our Government sometimes say that the real problems of America are not after all economic, political, or educational, they're just personal, moral, and if you will, cultural. Well, at one level they're obviously right. None of you was brought here today by a Government program. None of you was brought here today even by the teachers whom you brought with you. If you had not been willing to study, to work hard, to make the most of your own lives, you would not have won this award and you would not be going on to the rich and full lives that you will doubtless lead. But it is also true that none of us, none of us, from the President on down, comes here to this tent alone. And to believe that is folly. We do have an obligation to make our country stronger so that we can make individual Americans stronger. And we do it together.

I ran for this job because I was really worried that your generation could become the first generation of Americans not to do as well as your parents. I ran for this job because I was worried that the diversity we have in our country, the incredible racial and ethnic diversity we have, could become more divisive than uniting, at a time when we're moving into a global society.

And believe me, no country on the face of the Earth, no other great country has the asset America does in our diversity. Look around at you; look at each other. This is something that any intelligent nation would kill for, because in the global economy of the 21st century, how we relate to people who live beyond our borders, how we trade with them, how we learn with them, how we avoid conflict with them, how we work through our differences in honorable ways, how we bridge those cultural barriers will determine in no small measure what your future will be like. And America, because we are home to so many different people—one of our counties, Los Angeles County, has over 150 different racial and ethnic groups within one county. That is our meal ticket to the future. It is in so many ways the American dream. It must not be allowed to divide us. So I wanted us to have a better future and a more united future.

Now today, we are facing some stark choices. I've worked hard for the last 2½ years to try to get this economy going and to give our country a strategy that would deal with the problems of the moment but always keep our eyes on the long run. It is our responsibility here to always be thinking of the next generation, even when we have to make unpopular decisions to do it.

So we had this huge Government deficit, something we never had to worry about before about 12 years before I became President. And I did my best to try to bring it down. And we have reduced it dramatically in 2 years, but we did it in a way that allowed us to still increase our investment in education, increase our investment in technology, increase our investment in medical research, increase our investment in the future.

Now, make no mistake about it, it's very important to get rid of the deficit. Let me just give you two examples of how important it is. Our budget would be in balance today, and your generation would not have to worry about that, but for the interest we pay on the debt run up in the 12 years before I became President—never mind the previous 200, just in that 12—we would be in balance.

Our interest payments on the debt are so large that next year they will exceed our defense budget. Every year if we have to pay more and more and more on interest on the debt, it's less and less and less we can invest in education or technology or the care of poor young children or needy seniors. This is a big deal, and it matters.

But the question is, how can we do it in a way that is good for the long-run and the short-run futures of America? We're at an historic moment because for the first time leaders of both parties who conspired to increase the debt in the 1980's have now agreed that we should balance our budget. And that is a good thing.

We owe it to your generation to end the policy that is only—basically was 12 years old when I became President, that we should always, always run a deficit no matter what the condition of the economy is. But there is a very different approach, as the Secretary of Education has said, between what I think we ought to do and what the Congress believes we ought to do. And it will affect your future and the future of those who will be under this tent in the years ahead, when we are long gone from here.

Now we'll both, the Congress and I, have to agree that we have to make big budget cuts. And if we're going to reach an agreement, we're both going to have to agree to give up the chance to score small political points and instead score a big victory for all Americans. But there are real differences here. There's a big difference between necessary budget cuts and unnecessary pain. There's a real difference between creating a stronger economy with the right kind of balanced budget and actually driving the country into a recession with the wrong kind of balanced budget. And we have to recognize, as all of you know and you look out to the rest of the world, the budget deficit is not the only deficit we have. We still have some education deficits. We've still got a lot of poor children and some social deficits. We've still got some technology deficits we need to close. We have to make some investments even as we close the deficit.

Now, let me give you an idea of something you may already know but, just for example, so that nobody is under any illusion about what's going on, you probably all know that more than half the American people are working harder today for the same or lower incomes than they were making 15 years ago, when you take account of inflation. You may know that people my age, men between the ages of 45 and 55, after you adjust for inflation, are working harder and making on average 14 percent less than

they were 10 years ago. Many of you may come from families with hard-working parents who have lost their jobs and been unemployed for protracted period of times or not been able to find new jobs that pay the same as their old jobs or have the same level of benefits.

More than anything else, this is because more and more people in America are working in a global economy where their income and their support is determined by their level of education. Earnings for high school drop-outs have plummeted in the last 15 years; they've dropped by more than 25 percent. Earnings for people who just graduate from high school have dropped in the last 15 years. Earnings for people who get 2 or more years of college have gone up or at least held steady. Earnings for people who have a college degree have gone up. You may know young people who got out of college who are still having a hard time finding a job. I know there are some, and I'm very concerned about it. But still, playing the odds, education is more important to the economic future of individual Americans and our entire country than it has ever been.

Now, in this kind of circumstance, cutting education would be like cutting the defense budget at the height of the cold war. It will undermine our common security. And we can balance the budget without doing it, and that's exactly what we ought to do.

Let me just tell you, my proposal is to balance the budget in 10 years. We've taken—we've gotten rid of a third of the deficit in 2 years. So, over a 12 year period, we would go from a huge deficit to zero. This huge deficit was run up in 12 years; we can take it down in 12 years.

My proposal would not have big tax cuts for upper income people who are doing pretty well in our economy today and don't really need them. We would save that money and put it back into education and into medical care for the elderly and others who are in real need.

Those are the two principal differences. Those 3 years give you millions of dreams, millions of American dreams. Let me tell you what a difference those 3 years and the size of the tax cuts can make. Specifically, I propose in my balanced budget to increase overall investment in education and training by $40 billion in 7 years. The Congress proposes to reduce our investment in education and training by $43 billion over the same period.

I propose to increase Head Start funding by $1.5 billion by 2002, to reach another 50,000 children, for a total of 800,000. The House budget would cut up to 200,000 people from this year's Head Start rolls.

In the Goals 2000 program, which is a local reform, national standards program that promotes all kinds of grassroots reform, we propose to reach another 44 million children in 85,000 schools with Goals 2000, to support reforms that include things that people in Congress say they're for, like character education and charter schools and more public school choice. That's what we propose to do—44 million children getting help. Congress would kill support for Goals 2000. We want our kids to be thinking about learning, not about their safety, so we want to keep funding for safe and drug-free schools. Congress would cut the program by 30 percent and just give it to the States to figure out what to do with it.

I bet most of you are going to college, and I hope you are. For you and millions of other Americans, here is what is at stake. We want to increase the phase-in of our Federal direct loan program. That means we'll have more college loans at lower cost and better repayment terms. That means $25 billion in loans to 6 million students a year at lower cost to everyone. The House budget proposal would eliminate the in-school interest exemption. That doesn't make a lot of sense to you. Let me tell you what it means.

It could mean that students who get college loans would have to pay $3,000 more for their loan than under our plan. We want more people going to college, not less. I just gave you the economic statistics—the more college graduates we have, the higher incomes you have, the more people are paying taxes, the faster you bring the budget down. Isn't it better to bring the budget down with educated citizens than by cutting our nose off to spite our face by cutting education and cutting the college loans? That is a big, big mistake.

We want to increase the Pell grants to reach almost a million more students and raise the maximum award because there are a lot of poor young people out there that deserve a chance to go to college and need those Pell grants. The congressional budget would freeze this proposal for 7 years at the present level.

We want to expand the national service program to give a million people a chance to serve

their country and earn money for their education. The House of Representatives would eliminate it.

And we want to help adults as well. You know, when I was your age, over 80 percent of people who were laid off from their jobs were called back to the job they were laid off from. Now, over 80 percent of the people who are laid off from their jobs are not called back to the jobs from which they were laid off, and they have to try to find a new job. That is a stunning difference in a generation.

What does that mean? It means from the moment people are laid off they should be in a new training program if that's what they need. And we propose to collapse—the Department of Education, the Department of Labor are working on collapsing 70 different Government programs and adding more money into it to create a vast pool, kind of a scholarship pool for unemployed workers in America, so that they can apply and get a voucher or a chit worth $2,600 a year to take to their local community college for up to 2 years to get the training they need. Every unemployed person in America would have it from the day they were unemployed. It will make a big difference to the future of this country.

I am saying this to you because you are going to college in this time. Your lives will be lived in an environment created by the decisions we make today. We are not talking about luxuries; we are talking about the things that made this country great.

And I want to close by asking all of you— I know you were invited to bring a teacher with you, and I want to ask all the teachers to stand. But before I do, I want everybody to look at the teachers who stand up here and ask yourselves if we are really going to build a better tomorrow by taking $40 billion away from their ability to create more students like you. I think the answer is clear.

Would all the teachers here please stand today? Give them a hand. [*Applause*]

Congratulations again on your magnificent award. Good luck with your future. I wish you well. Remember this: One thing only you owe your country, your devotion to making sure that every other young person in this country will always have the opportunities that brought you to this day.

Thank you, and God bless you all.

NOTE: The President spoke at 12:10 p.m. on the South Lawn at the White House.

Remarks on Surgeon General Nominee Henry Foster
June 21, 1995

The President. Good afternoon. I'd like to begin by saying that I was quite pleased that 57 of the Members of the Senate today voted to allow a simple up or down, yes or no vote on the nomination of Dr. Foster. A strong majority, 57, voted to give him a fair chance and a full vote. But a small minority are using this nomination to dictate a litmus test to the rest of America.

That is wrong. And the American people are not going to understand it. The Senators who voted to deny Dr. Foster an up or down vote did a disservice to a good man. They also did a disservice to our whole system of democracy. And make no mistake about it, this was not a vote about the right of the President to choose a Surgeon General. This was really a vote about every American woman's right to choose.

Henry Foster is qualified to be our Surgeon General. He spent 38 years in medicine. He spent a lot of his time working to improve the health of women and children in poor and rural areas. He's delivered thousands of babies and trained hundreds of young doctors. His efforts to curb teen pregnancy have earned him high praise among Republicans and Democrats. He shares my view that abortion should be rare and safe and legal.

Don't you think it's interesting that we finally found a person in this country who's actually done something, actually done something to try to reduce teen pregnancy, actually done something to try to convince large numbers of young people that they should not have sex before they're married, who's actually done something to deal with this problem, but because he cannot pass the political litmus test that has a stranglehold on the other party, they cannot even allow a simple vote? Did the Democratic Senate deny a simple vote to their controversial nominees for the Supreme Court, a lifetime job? No.

This man got 57 votes—43 people say no because they are in the grip of people who don't question my right to choose him but question American women's right to choose. It is wrong. What's fair is fair, and he ought to get an up or down vote. He's actually done something about the problem they all claim to be concerned about, and he ought to be given a chance to do something about it for the whole country.

[*At this point, Dr. Foster made brief remarks.*]

The President. Let me just say one other thing. Let me remind you that the committee approved Dr. Foster's nomination. This should be about whether the President has a right to make this decision if the person is qualified. The committee ruled that he was. The only other question worth asking and answering right now is, are we going to try for another vote? Yes, we are. Do I know what the outcome will be? No, I don't. But I'm not through yet, and we're going to do our best to win it.

Thank you very much.

NOTE: The President spoke at 1:36 p.m. in the Rose Garden at the White House.

Letter to Senator Robert Byrd on Proposed Drunk Driving Legislation
June 21, 1995

Dear Robert:

Drinking and driving by young people is one of the nation's most serious threats to public health and public safety. I am deeply concerned about this ongoing tragedy that kills thousands of young people every year. It's against the law for young people to drink. It should be against the law for young people to drink and drive.

As you know, earlier this month, I called on Congress to make Zero Tolerance the law of the land. I support your amendment to the National Highway System Designation Act, which would achieve this goal.

A decade ago, we decided as a nation that the minimum drinking age should be 21. In 1984, President Reagan signed bipartisan legislation to achieve this goal, and today all 50 states have enacted such laws. Our efforts are paying off—drunk driving deaths among people under 21 have been cut in half since 1984.

But we must do more. Twenty-four states and the nation's capital have enacted Zero Tolerance laws that consider a driver under age 21 to be "driving while impaired" after just one full drink of alcohol. These laws work—alcohol-related crashes involving teenage drivers are down as much as 10–20 percent in those states. If all states had such laws, hundreds more lives could be saved and thousands of injuries could be prevented.

I commend your efforts today, and I urge the Senate to pass your amendment.

Sincerely,

BILL CLINTON

NOTE: This letter was made available by the Office of the Press Secretary but was not issued as a White House press release.

Remarks at the Groundbreaking Ceremony for the Women in the Military Service Memorial in Arlington, Virginia
June 22, 1995

Thank you very much. Thank you, General Mutter. Thank you to all the fine active duty and veteran women, servicepeople who have just speaken—spoken. Speaken! I can't even talk, I'm so excited. [*Laughter*]

I'll tell you, when our wonderful World War I veteran got through talking, I thought there's no point in my saying a word. It has all been said. I thank all the members of our military, beginning with the Secretary of Defense, the Service Secretaries, General Shalikashvili, the Joint Chiefs, those who preceded them—I see General Powell and others here—for their support of this endeavor. I thank the Members of Congress who are here. General Vaught, I thank you for your determination. I don't believe that anyone in the United States could have said no to you on any important matter; I know I couldn't. And I congratulate you on this triumph of your vision and will.

To all the remarkable servicewomen who surround me here, out in the audience and on the podium, let me say to all of you: Thank you for your service to America. We are all proud to be here to break ground on a memorial that will recognize a contribution that you have made far beyond the call of duty.

Women have been in our service, as has been said, since George Washington's troops fought for independence, clothing and feeding our troops and binding their wounds. They were in the struggle to preserve the Union as cooks and tailors, couriers and scouts, even as spies and saboteurs. Some were so determined to fight for what they believed that they masqueraded as men and took up arms.

Women were there during the two World Wars, and slowly, our military establishment that for decades had sought to limit women's roles brought them in to serve as WACS and WAVES, SPARS and WASPS and Women Marines. In our Nation's shipyards and factories, women helped to build democracy's arsenal. From the beaches of Normandy to the Pacific Islands, they endured bombs, torpedoes, disease, deprivation to support our fighting forces.

Despite this history of bravery and accomplishment, for very much too long women were treated as second class soldiers. They could give their lives for liberty, but they couldn't give orders to men. They could heal the wounded and hold the dying, but they could not dream of holding the highest ranks. They could take on the toughest assignments, but they could not take up arms. Still, they volunteered, fighting for freedom all around the world but also fighting for the right to serve to the fullest of their potential. And from conflict to conflict, from

Korea to Vietnam to the Persian Gulf, slowly, women have overcome the barriers to their full service to America.

The past few decades have witnessed a remarkable series of firsts: the first woman company commander, the first female service academy graduate, the first woman skipper, the first female fighter pilot, the firsts that are here with us today. Twenty-five years ago this month, Anna Mae McCabe Hays became the first woman promoted to general. Hazel Johnson-Brown was the first minority woman to reach that rank. And 2 years ago, it was my honor to nominate the Secretary of the Air Force, Sheila Widnall, to become the first woman to head one of our service branches. I am honored to be with all of them today.

But just as important as these firsts are those who have followed them, proving that they were not an accident or an aberration, for women today are test pilots and drill sergeants, squadron commanders and admirals, academy instructors and service recruiters. I am very proud of the fact that during our administration almost 260,000 new positions in the military have been opened to women who wish to serve.

And I might say that this is a tribute not only to the women in the service but to the men in leadership positions who had the wisdom and the understanding and the ability to proceed with this remarkable transformation and strengthening of our military in a climate of tolerance and teamwork and respect. I know of no other institution in our society which could have accomplished so much in such an incredibly efficient and humane and professional way. And so we should be proud of all who played a role in that.

And let me say, before I go further, our Nation, as you know, is involved now in a great debate over the subject of affirmative action. Before people rush to judgment, I would like to remind all Americans that the United States military is the strongest in the world because it has found a way to make the most of the talents of every American without regard to gender or race. And as a nation, we must continue to search for ways to make the most of the talents of every American without regard to gender or race.

There are so many individual stories, the stories that this memorial will tell. But in their detail and drama, they help us understand more of what has occurred than the speeches we can give. Some of these women are here today, and I would like to ask them to stand:

Women like June Wandrey Mann, who volunteered for the Army Nurse Corps in the Second World War, who served 2½ years overseas from primitive field hospitals in Tunisia and Italy to a center for concentration camp survivors outside of Munich. In her courage and caring, Lieutenant Wandrey represents the best of America. Would you please stand. [*Applause*] Thank you. And I might add, you still look terrific in your uniform.

Women like Charity Adams Earley, who was mentioned earlier, the Women Army Corps' first African-American officer. Along with thousands of other African-American veterans, both men and women, she helped our Nation act on a truth too long denied, that if people of different races could serve as brothers and sisters abroad, surely they could learn to live together as neighbors at home. Colonel, would you please stand. [*Applause.*] And I might add, she gives a resounding speech.

Women like U.S. Air Force Captain Teresa Allen Steith of the 60th Air Mobility Wing from Travis Air Force Base in California, who was among our first soldiers to set down in Haiti last year and who for 3 months helped planes and troops and cargo move in and out of the Port-au-Prince airport. Because she and the rest of our troops did their job so well, the people of Haiti now, remarkably, have a second chance at democracy. And this Sunday, this Sunday, they will be going to the polls to exercise their newfound rights for the first time in 5 years. And this time, they won't be stolen from them, thanks to people like you, Captain. Thank you very much, and God bless you.

Women like Barbara Allen Rainey, the mother of two daughters, the Navy's first female aviator, tragically the victim of a training crash. Her story reminds us that even in peacetime, those who wear the uniform face danger every day. Now she rests just behind me in the quiet of these sacred grounds.

This memorial will tell the stories of these women and hundreds of thousands more. It makes a long overdue downpayment on a debt that we will never fully repay, a debt we owe to generations of American women in uniform who gave and continue to give so much to our country and a debt we owe yet to future generations of women who will in the future dedicate their own lives to the defense of our freedom.

May this memorial say to each and every one of them: We cherish your devotion; we admire your courage; we thank you for your service. God bless you, and God bless America.

NOTE: The President spoke at 1:10 p.m. at Arlington Cemetery. In his remarks, he referred to Maj. Gen. Carol Mutter, USMC, Commander, Marine Corps Systems Command, and Brig. Gen. Wilma Vaught, USAF (ret.).

Remarks on Senate Action on the Nomination of Henry Foster To Be Surgeon General in Edison, New Jersey
June 22, 1995

Good afternoon. Today 43 Republicans in the Senate failed the fundamental test of fairness. By choosing to side with extremists who would do anything to block a woman's right to choose, those Senators have done a disservice to a good man, done a disservice to the nominating process, and sent a chilling message to the rest of the country.

The American people are smart enough to see through what just happened. They know this is not about my right to choose a Surgeon General; this is about the right of every woman to choose. The committee recommended Dr. Foster to the Senate. A clear and substantial majority of Senators were prepared to vote for his nomination. But a determined minority succumbed to political pressure and abused the filibuster rule.

It's wrong for a man as qualified and committed as Dr. Foster to be denied this chance to serve our country. He has gone where too few of us have ever dared to go. He has ridden the rickety elevators in high-rise projects to talk to young people about the importance of abstinence and avoiding teen pregnancy. He has traveled the backroads of rural Alabama, bringing health care and hope to women and children who would otherwise have never seen a doctor. He has been a father figure to many children who do not see their own fathers.

He has actually done something, in short, about the problems a lot of people in Washington just talk about. He's done something about teen pregnancy. He's done something to convince young people to abstain from sex. He's done something about women's health and crime prevention and giving young people hope for the future. One of his former patients even talked about how he talked her out of having an abortion.

Now, you would think that those who deplore teen pregnancy, advocate abstinence, and oppose abortion would want to support a man who has actually done something to advance the aims they say they share, instead of just use them as political weapons. But no, in their brave new world, raw political power and political correctness, pure political correctness, are all that matter. They are determined to call the tune to which the Republican Party in Congress and in their Presidential process march.

Well, they won a victory today, but America lost. And all those young people who came up here from Tennessee, what about them? What about those young people that came here believing in the congressional process and told the Members of Congress that Dr. Foster had encouraged them to avoid sex, to stay away from teen pregnancy, not to do drugs, to stay in school? They had a role model, and they saw their role model turned into a political football. In 1995, Henry Foster was denied even the right to vote.

A minority in the Senate may have denied him this job, but I am confident that he will go on to serve our country. I think more of Henry Foster today than the first day I met him. This is not a good day for the United States Senate. But it is a good day for Henry Foster. He didn't get what he deserved, but he is still deserving. Those who denied him the right to a vote, they may have pleased their political bosses, but they have shown a lack of leadership that will surely be remembered.

Thank you very much.

NOTE: The President spoke at approximately 3:45 p.m. at the landing area at the Ford Motor Co. plant.

Remarks to Ford Motor Company Employees in Edison
June 22, 1995

The President. Thank you very much. I like your spirit.

Audience member. Give 'em hell, Bill!

The President. You help, and I will. [*Laughter*]

I want to thank Denton and Earl and Peter for being here with me today. I want to say a special word of thanks to Ford Motor Company for being a good partner with the United States of America to build our economy and to get a fair trade policy and to do a lot of things we need to do in this country. Ford has been a good citizen of this Nation and has helped immeasurably to further the aims of this administration. I thank you, Peter, and I thank all of you for the contribution you have made to that.

Some of you may know that my main claim to your affection is that I own a car that's older than some of the people who work here. I own a 1967 Mustang, and Mustangs were made here in this plant from '65 to '70, here and in San Jose, California. And I own one of them. And I enjoy having it.

I want to talk to you today very briefly about two things: one of them has already been discussed, trade; the other is what we can do here at home to build up our economy and strengthen our people.

I ran for the job that I now hold because I was really concerned that we were going to raise the first generation of Americans who wouldn't do as well as their parents. It bothered me that more than half of our people were working a longer workweek for the same or lower wages they were making 15 years earlier. It bothered me that we were coming apart with all of the social problems and tensions we had in this country when we need to be working together.

You've proved in this plant that if you work together you can compete and win and do well. And that's what America has to do. And I have done everything I could for 2½ years to try to restore the American dream—not only to create jobs, but to raise incomes and to give working families some security, that if they do work hard and play by the rules they're going to be all right and our children are going to be all

right. That, it seems to me, is the most important thing we can do.

There are a lot of things we can talk about, but I just want to talk about two today that are very important. The first is, what do we do about the economy here at home? The second is, how do we relate to the rest of the world?

And let me talk a little about the economy here at home. When I became President, we had just finished 12 years in which we had quadrupled—increased by fourfold—the national debt—by fourfold. But we were reducing our commitment to the things that make us rich, to education, to technology, to building the skills and the technology and the kind of partnerships that really generate jobs and incomes in the world today. So what I tried to do was to flip that around. I tried to bring the deficit down but to increase our investment in education, technology, basic research and to form a real partnership with the private sector to help to sell American products.

Now, we have reduced the deficit by about $1 trillion over a 7-year period. We have increased our investments in education, research, and technology. We are working more closely with business than ever before. And we have to show for it a lower unemployment rate and over 6.7 million new jobs. I am proud of that. But we have to remember that we've been getting into the rut we've been in for 20 years. And I'll just give you two examples. We created 6.7 million new jobs, the unemployment rate went down, but the average income of the American people didn't go up. We have to keep working on that. People have to be rewarded for their work. We can't expect working people to make a profit for their companies unless they can also make a profit for themselves.

Now, you've got a unique situation in Washington where the leaders of Congress want to balance the budget, and that's a good thing. And I do, too, and that's a good thing. Why is that important? I'll tell you why it's important. Because if it were not for the interest we have to pay—I want you all to listen to this—if it weren't for the interest we have to pay on the debt this country ran up in just the 12 years before I became President—forget about the other 200 years—just those 12 years, our budget would be in balance today, and we would have more money to spend on your children's education, more money to spend on the health care of elderly people through Medicare and Medicaid, more money to spend on new technologies to guarantee Americans good jobs in the future. So we need to get rid of this deficit.

But the question is, how should we do it? Keep in mind, every day my objective is more jobs, higher income, more security for people who are working hard. That's what I go to work and try to guarantee. So there's a big difference between my budget and the one the leaders of Congress have proposed because I think mine will do more for jobs, incomes, and security of families.

Here's what the differences are. First, we cut spending, except for defense, Social Security, and medical costs, about 20 percent across the board, except for education; we increase spending on education. I think your children should be able to go to college. They should be able to get good training programs. They should be able to be in good preschool programs. I think that's important.

Second, we want to slow the rate of growth in the medical costs the Federal Government pays; that's Medicare and Medicaid, which is mostly for elderly people and disabled people. But I don't want to charge middle and lower middle income elderly people on Medicare more money for the same health care, and I don't want to see them have to give up their health care. So we cut medical costs less than the Congress does because I think it's important to protect Medicare and to protect the people who are on it who have paid into it and who don't have enough money to live on as it is.

Third, we have a much smaller tax cut than they do, and ours is targeted not to upper income people but to middle class people and focused on education and childrearing. I think everybody ought to get a tax deduction for the cost of sending their kids to college. I am for that.

The fourth thing we do is to save money on welfare spending. But I want to be honest with you, we don't save as much money as the Congress does because I think we should hold some money back to give to the purpose of education and training and child care for people on welfare so you can actually get them to work.

We don't want to cut these kids off and put them in the street. We want people to go to work and be good parents and good workers. So we ought to invest enough in child care and education to get that done. So we do that.

And the fifth thing that my plan does is to balance the budget over 10 years. They balance the budget over 7 years. If you go to 10 instead of 7, you can increase education, not cut it; you can protect elderly people on Medicare; you can invest enough in welfare to get real welfare reform to put people to work; and you don't have to risk a recession.

The Wharton Business School over in Philadelphia, not far from here, did an analysis of the congressional budget and estimated that they're cutting so much out of the economy so fast it would drive unemployment up and slow the economy down. We want to lower interest rates, free up money, balance the budget in ways that grow the economy.

So when you hear these debates—I want to work with the Congress. I don't want a partisan fight. I want to put America first. I want you to know, if somebody tells you that we don't need to balance the budget, that's not true, because every year we don't balance the budget, we're spending more and more of your tax money on interest payments and less money on things that we all want. We do need to do it, but the aim is your jobs, your incomes, your family security. And the test of every decision we make should be, is it going to increase those? And I think my budget does that.

Now, the second point I want to make is we can't grow the American economy alone if we don't have the right kind of relationship with the rest of the world. We know—you sell these trucks here all over the world, don't you? And we know that your earnings are above the national average, aren't they? And we know generally that jobs related to trade in America pay better than jobs that have no relationship to the global economy. We also know that because of all the changes you and others have been through, millions of people like you in America in the last 15 years, we are the high quality, low cost producer of many, many, many products that can be sold all over the world.

So I have done my best to negotiate agreements that would open markets around the world and make everybody else's market as open as ours. We're opening markets to the south of us in Latin America, and you're selling some trucks down there. We're opening markets with Europe and other countries. We have had all kinds of new trade agreements.

Even with Japan, we have had 15 new trade agreements, so that we're selling rice and apples and cellular telephones over there for the first time. This movement toward open trade now that America is competitive is a good thing for us. Why? Because we have open markets. So we can't stop some people from being at risk from low cost competition if it's generally low cost and good quality. We can't stop that. But if we don't get a fair deal going the other way, then we get it coming and going. We don't have a chance to create the high-wage jobs from trade to replace the low-wage jobs that we lose. And we don't have the chance to give people the security they deserve if they are competitive in the world market. That is what is at stake.

Now, here's the problem. Our relationship with Japan has simply been different than that with everybody else. And their system of protecting their products and their markets is different from the things you can normally reach with a trade agreement. They're not necessarily tariffs; they're not necessarily quotas. It's a highly complicated system of doing business that works to freeze us out.

You know, your leader has said he didn't know the exact numbers. I'll tell you what the exact numbers are over the last 20 years. Twenty years ago we had less than one percent of the Japanese market in automobiles. You know what it is today: 1.5 percent. Big deal. Since we have been trading cars both ways, we have shipped a total, cars and trucks, of 400,000 vehicles to them. They have shipped a total of 40 million to us.

Audience members. Boo-o-o!

The President. Now, that's a hundred to one. Now, if all this were fair and they didn't want to buy anything we had produced and we were buying what they had to produce, it would be fine. In auto parts—forget about what you do here; let's just talk about auto parts—with the whole rest of the world, we have a $5.8 billion surplus. That's a huge number of jobs. Every billion dollars is about 17,000 more jobs; it's a lot of jobs. With them, we have a deficit in auto parts of over $12 billion a year.

Now, you say, well, if it were fair it would be all right. These luxury cars that are at issue here in our trade dispute, you can buy some of them for $9,000—they're made in Japan,

right—you can buy some of them for $9,000 less here in America than they pay in Japan for them. A carburetor made in Japan costs 3 times as much there as it does here. I am for free trade, but I am for fair trade, and that's not fair. And you know it's not fair.

And guess what? It's not good for them. They're rolling in dough, but their economy is not growing. Their people look like they're making more money than you are, but they're paying 40 percent more for all of their consumer products. So the average working stiff in Japan is not doing much better than a lot of people in other countries, not doing as well as many American workers, and would be doing much better if they had free and open competition and it drove down the prices that their consumers are paying, because as you well know, when you pay the bills every month, every worker is also a consumer.

What I am trying to do is not just good for us; it's good for them. They're a great democracy. We work together on a lot of things. But you know we had to change; all of us did. A lot of you went through gut-wrenching changes in the last 20 years to make sure this plant would be recognized for its low error rate and its high quality production. We all have to change. Their system is not fair. And that is what we are trying to get done. We're trying to open it so that you will have free access to their markets like they have to ours. And it's a fight worth making.

Now today and tomorrow, in Switzerland, the representatives of our Government and the Japanese are talking, and they're trying to avoid what's going to happen next week. But on the 28th, if we don't have an agreement that will take us toward opening their markets and fair treatment for American products and American workers, then I have ordered the U.S. Trade Representative to put tariffs of 100 percent on 13 of their luxury cars.

I want to say again, I think you can compete with anybody where you get a fair shot. If people don't want what we produce, that's a different story. But I think it is wrong for America to be leading the way in opening our markets and putting our workers at risk in competition and not have the same rights in every other major market, in countries that are as rich as we are. That is not right. You deserve a fair chance.

So I want you to think about this. Every time you wonder what we're doing up there or you see a fight going on in Washington, you just remember my test is: Will it create jobs; will it raise incomes; will it make working people more secure if they're doing their part? That's what I think about every day. If everybody in this country had a job, if every job paid enough to support children, we wouldn't have a lot of the problems we have today.

You know, there's a lot of talk about how angry voters are—or angry men are. Well, you know, one reason is that 60 percent of the hourly wage earners in this country are working a longer workweek for about 15 percent less than they were making 10 years ago. If that wouldn't make you mad, I don't know what would.

Now, you can lead the way. The auto companies now can lead the world. And they can lead America back toward a high-wage, high-growth economy. I don't want any special breaks, but I do want a fair deal. If you get a fair deal, if you have a Government that works for you, that invests in your education, that gets rid of this deficit, that looks toward the future, I think you can take care of your families and your communities and the future of our country. But I'm going to be in there plugging for you. You stay with us, and we'll get the job done together.

Thank you very much.

NOTE: The President spoke at 4:19 p.m. In his remarks, he referred to Denton Grenke, plant manager, and Peter J. Pestillo, executive vice president, Ford Motor Co.; and Earl Nail, bargaining unit chairman, UAW Local 980.

Remarks at a Fundraising Dinner in Somerset, New Jersey
June 22, 1995

Thank you very much, ladies and gentlemen. Let me begin by joining with Al and Tipper and Hillary and thanking tonight's dinner chairs, Al Decotis, Lew Katz, Ray Lesniak, Jack Rosen, and Bob Raymar. They were terrific, and so were all of you. Thank you for your remarkable help.

I am also delighted to be here with two of my former colleagues, former Governor Brendan Byrne and former Governor Jim Florio. I thank them and their wonderful wives for coming tonight. I'm glad to see them.

I want to say something selfish. I think New Jersey did a good thing for New Jersey by re-electing Frank Lautenberg. But we needed him back, and I saw it today on the floor of the Senate. And this country needs Bill Bradley, and you must, you must send him back to the United States Senate and the United States.

I have always loved coming here. I have been, frankly, rather astonished from the beginning of my campaign that the State of New Jersey was so good to me, beginning way back in 1991 when I was a stranger from a small southern State, as my former adversary, Mr. Bush, used to say. And every time I came here I always felt at home. I felt that I understood the people. I felt a certain kinship.

And when we began our general election campaign here with the bus tour and then ended up in the Meadowlands and then New Jersey—I have heard it a thousand times—always closes Republican, but it didn't close enough to take the State away from the Clinton-Gore ticket—I was profoundly grateful.

And now I come to say to you, I thank you for this remarkably successful dinner. It will enable Terry McAuliffe and Laura Hartigan and all of our finance staff to continue on their goal of financing our campaign next year and this year so that I can devote my energies to being President and to running in a responsible way. And you have done a very great thing. But I also want to tell you that we need your help, beginning tomorrow morning, to talk to everyone you can about what is really at stake in this election.

I have to tell you that there are differences now in Washington more profound than the partisan differences even of the last few years and certainly of the last 50 years. There are also opportunities to work together. And which way we take in the next few months will be determined in part by what the American people say. And whether we keep going forward or take a huge lunge off center will be determined by how the American people vote in 1996.

I want to say to all of you that I never could have dreamed when I started this that our partnership, the one Hillary and I have enjoyed with Al and Tipper Gore, would have been as remarkable as it has been. I thank Tipper for her tireless advocacy for the interests of mental health and women and young girls and so many other things that she has fought for. And I have said this repeatedly, but I believe with all my heart that Al Gore will go down in American history as the most influential and productive Vice President in our country's history.

The other day we had the White House Conference on Small Business in Washington. There were 3,500 delegates there, and I think we had only appointed about 300; the rest were elected from their States, and well over half of them were Republican. And all they had been—a lot of them had just been fed this sort of propaganda, this steady stream of propaganda people put out. And the Vice President got up and introduced me, and we talked about our reinventing Government program.

We reminded them that we had increased their ability to write off their capital expenses by about 70 percent, that we had offered a capital gains tax for small businesses, and that we had reduced regulations dramatically and we were about to reduce 16,000 more—and we brought them out, the 16,000 regulations—including half of the paperwork regulations of the Small Business Administration. And these people, a lot of them were literally dumbfounded. They didn't know whether to believe it, because that's not what the propagandizers had been telling them for 2 years. But it was true. They liked it. And we ought to be the candidate of small businesses in 1996, thanks in large measure to Al Gore. And I thank him for that.

Hillary and I began this day publicly at Arlington National Cemetery, doing something else that is a symbol of what the choices in 1996 will be all about. We dedicated a memorial, the groundbreaking of a memorial to the 1.8 million American women who have served in our Armed Forces but have never been recognized before. In our administration, we have not only promoted things like family and medical leave and child care for people to move from welfare to work but greater investment

in medical research affecting women, greater access to mammograms, a greater commitment to the future of women's health. But I was able to announce today something I am very proud of: Since our administration has been in office we have opened 260,000 more positions and different roles for women in the United States military. I am proud of that, and I hope all of you are as well.

The Vice President gave you a summary of the record of our administration. It's led to lower inflation, lower unemployment, more jobs, and a better future. But this is still a troubled time for our country, and we are trying to decide which way to go, with all the challenges we face in a confusing time, that I believe has far more hope than fear ahead for America. I ran for President because I wanted to restore the American dream of opportunity for those who would behave responsibly and because I wanted to bring this country together. I was sick and tired of seeing politicians exploit the differences of race and religion and region and income and background among Americans, to drive wedges between us for their own personal benefit. And I still believe that's what we ought to be doing in your Nation's Capital.

Today, because of the November elections, you can ask Senator Lautenberg and Senator Bradley, we are back to debating first principles. Things that we used to take for granted are no longer taken for granted in the United States Congress. There are a whole group of people in this Congress who believe that all of the problems of America are personal and cultural, and if people would just get up every day and behave themselves there would be nothing wrong in this country, and therefore we don't even need a Government.

There are those of us who believe that some of these problems are economic and social and that of course they're personal and cultural— if people don't behave, there's nothing you can do for them—but that we are going up or down together, and we need a partnership in this country.

That is a fundamental debate. And if you want to know the difference between a Republican and Democrat in Washington today, it is largely around that issue. Are the problems just personal and cultural, or are they personal, cultural, and political and economic and social?

There are people today in Washington who believe that the Federal Government is absolutely worthless except for national security, and therefore, the most important thing to do is to balance the budget as quickly as possible; it doesn't matter what else you cut. Then there are those of us who honestly believe we should balance the budget but believe we have an education deficit as well and believe we have to do this in a way that will grow the economy, create jobs, raise incomes, and reinforce the partnership between business and Government that ought to exist.

There are people in Washington today who believe the environment is a nice thing and people who think right will protect it but that the Government should do nothing to protect it. You heard the Vice President say a committee of the House today voted to allow blanket offshore oil drilling all over the United States. You don't know the half of it. That is just scratching the surface. But they honestly believe the Government has no role in trying to protect our common natural resources. And then there are those of us who believe that we can find ways to protect the environment and grow the economy and that if we want this country to be around for our grandchildren and our grandchildren's grandchildren, we had better protect the environment while we are growing the economy.

There are people in Washington today who believe that the only answer to crime is to lock more people up for a longer period of time and that things like the Brady bill and the assault weapons ban are a ridiculous infringement on the right of everybody else to do whatever they want to do and that what we really should do is do nothing but take everybody we ever catch and lock them up, throw the key away, and forget about everything else. Then there are those of us who believe that fighting crime is a more complicated thing and that the best thing to do is to prevent it in the first place, like dealing with any other problem, and that we ought to listen to law enforcement and work with them.

And I'm telling you, folks, these are big, profound debates. And that's really what this election is all about. There are those of us who believe that you can be passionately in favor of life and still be for a woman's right to choose. And they don't believe that. So—and don't kid yourself, that's what this fight over Dr. Foster was all about. It was not about my right to choose a Surgeon General, it was about a wom-

an's right to choose. It was not about whether he was capable of being a powerful role model for young people. He's one of the few people in America, one of the very few people in America who enjoyed a prominent social and economic position, who gave years and years and years of his life to reaching out to poor children and telling them they should not have sex when they weren't married, they should not become pregnant as teenagers, they should not get on drugs, they should not be violent, they should stay in school.

He went into poor tenements in Nashville, he rode dusty country roads in Alabama to bring health care to women and children who did not have it and would never have seen a doctor. One of his patients said that he had personally talked her out of having an abortion. But because he had observed the constitutional right to choose, he wasn't pure enough, he wasn't politically correct enough for the people who are trying to create a brave new world in Washington with a stranglehold on the other party. And you better stand up against it and help us fight against it.

These are big choices. Now we both want to balance the budget. That's good. They want to do it in 7 years, with a huge tax increase. We say, if you do it in 10 years, have a smaller tax increase targeted to education, you can increase investment in education and medical research and technology and our economic partnerships; you don't have to cut Medicare so much that you really hurt older people who don't have enough to live on as it is. You can have a decent, humane budget and still balance it if you do it in the right way, not the wrong way. That's the difference between us.

They think the most important thing to do in the area of crime is to repeal the assault weapons ban. Jim Florio gave his governorship for it, and if I have to give the White House for it, I'll do it. It will be over my dead body if they do that. [*Applause*] Thank you.

Let me just say one thing in closing. We can do this one of two ways. We can fight, or we can work together in good faith. Something happened to our whole country when that bomb blew up in Oklahoma City. It was an awful, heartbreaking, wrenching event, and it shook this Nation to the core. And we lost some of the edge that we felt for those who were different from us and who disagreed with us.

We were all a little less willing to demonize people with whom we simply disagree.

And then something good happened to this country when that brave young Air Force pilot, Scott O'Grady, survived for 6 lonely days in Bosnia and was rescued. And we saw what was best about America. And nobody cared if he had an Irish or a Polish name or if his skin was black, brown, or white. He had done something very brave and profoundly good that didn't have much to do with the kind of partisanship that covers so much of what is done in Washington.

And it was in that honest spirit that I offered the Republicans a balanced budget that the Democrats and the rest of the country, in my judgment, can in good conscience support; that will grow and not shrink the economy, and build up, not tear down, the middle class; that will help people to move from welfare to work, not just throw innocent children off of welfare. That is the spirit that I am trying to capture.

It was in that spirit that I agreed to have that conversation with the Speaker of the House up in New Hampshire a few days ago. I tell you, my friends, I did not sign on to be President just to say no, just to divide the country, just to try to prove I can be more clever than they are in these political debates. But I will not back down from my commitment that we have to grow the economy, build the middle class, reach out a helping hand to the poor, be fair to those who through no fault of their own need some help, preserve our environment, and bring this country together. I am telling you, that is the most important thing we have to do.

You know, one of the greatest honors of being President is being able to represent you when I go to other countries. I just was in the Ukraine in the beautiful city of Kiev, and I spoke outdoors at the university. There were tens of thousands of people there. And all along the road, four and five deep, people were there waving their American flags, cheering as Hillary and I rode by. And you know, I looked at her and I said what I always say, "They're not cheering for me. They're cheering for America, for what we are, for what we represent, for the hope that they feel."

Many of you have supported our administration's efforts in trying to make peace in the Middle East. They haven't asked "me" to do that, they have asked "us" to do that. Many of you have been involved in our efforts to try to help support the peace process in Northern Ireland. They didn't ask "me" to do that, they asked "us" to do that. America—that's what they think "we" are—bringing people together, bridging differences, moving forward.

There is no country in this world better positioned for the 21st century, better positioned to hand down our dreams to our children than the United States. But now we are back to debating first principles in Washington. We thank you for your financial investment tonight, but we ask you for your voice. We ask you for your labors. We ask you for your passion. We ask you for your heart. We are going to have to fight and debate and struggle to make sure that in this season we make the right decisions.

Thank you, and God bless you all.

NOTE: The President spoke at 8:56 p.m. at the Garden State Convention Center.

Teleconference Remarks With Democratic Governors in Little Rock, Arkansas
June 23, 1995

The President. Hello, Governor Romer.

Gov. Roy Romer. Yes, Mr. President. I'm here, and also on the line are Howard Dean, Evan Bayh, and Bob Miller and Tom Carper.

The President. It's nice to hear your voices.

Governor Romer. Mel Carnahan would be here, but he's in Korea, Mr. President.

The President. I'm sorry he can't be here, but I hope he does well on his trip to Korea. And I want to thank him for his support as well. And I want to thank all of you for your letter in support of the budget plan that I have presented.

I know that all of you have experience in balancing budgets, and you know that it takes a combination of discipline and compassion and hard choices. And I believe that my budget meets the test that you try to meet every year.

As you know, the Congress yesterday, both Houses of Congress, the Republican majorities, have agreed now to reconcile the differences between their two. I am glad that both the President and the majority in Congress are committed to a balanced budget, and I believe most of the Democrats in Congress are as well. But I still disagree fundamentally with the way in which they propose to balance the budget. And I think it will complicate your lives as Governors considerably.

I believe that their plan is still too extreme, runs a significant risk of putting the economy into a recession and raising unemployment. It cuts education at a time we should be increasing it. It cuts Medicare beneficiaries in order to pay for large tax cuts that disproportionately go to the most well-off people in our country who don't really need them. And because the cuts are so severe in some areas, I believe they'll be very difficult for you to manage.

Our plan balances the budget over 10 years instead of 7, increases education along with inflation, from Head Start to our investments in college loans and scholarships. It preserves—while slowing the growth of Medicare and Medicaid, it preserves the integrity of the incomes of people on Medicare, so that these middle and lower middle income elderly people, who many of whom don't have enough to live on as it is, are not going to have to pay more for their medical benefits or give up a lot of medical care. It is a much more sensible approach to welfare, and the tax cuts are much, much smaller and targeted toward individuals and toward education and childrearing. So I believe that it's a better plan.

But now that the Senate and House have resolved their differences, we can proceed to what I hope will be an honest, open, and civil discussion with the American people about the agreements and the differences in our two plans. And I hope in the end we'll wind up doing a balanced budget in the right way that will grow the economy and that will support you and what you're trying to do at the State level. And I cannot tell you how much I appreciate your support. You may have some questions about what we're doing, and I'd like to hear from you now.

[Governor Romer of Colorado stated that all of the Democratic Governors favored the President's 10-year plan for balancing the Federal budget and asked what they could do to refocus the debate on the importance of investing in education.]

The President. Well, I think that's one of the things the Governors have to do, to help us on. And you have raised a point that has been almost completely absent from this debate in Washington because there's so much focus on the Federal investments and the Federal programs. The Republican alternative as compared to mine will have a bad effect on education in a direct way and in an indirect way. And I think most of the people covering this debate even have not thought about that.

Directly, it will obviously cut our ability to invest in everything from Head Start to the funds we give to you for Goals 2000 to help promote reforms, to the apprenticeship programs, to college loans.

But indirectly, you've made a very important point. Most of the funding for education in our country comes from the State and local level, and increasingly, States are playing a larger and larger role in school funding and in university funding. And if we cut Medicaid as severely as they propose to cut it—70 percent of that money goes to the elderly and the disabled—they will show up in the legislatures all across America. The pressures to avoid severe human hardship will be enormous, and therefore, the pressures on you to divert money that would otherwise go to education for the State level into nursing home care, into the care of the disabled, will be very, very great indeed. And there's been almost no discussion of this. So this could be a huge indirect cut in education as well.

And I think most Americans know we ought to be increasing our investment in education. In the global economy it's one thing we can do to ensure a good life with a secure income for our people. And I would urge the Governors to focus on the indirect impacts of this budget as well as the direct ones, because that's something our citizens will understand if it's explained to them. It's something the press corps will understand and report if it's explained to them. But it's been almost totally absent from the debate so far. And it's a huge factor that has to be considered.

[*Gov. Howard Dean of Vermont supported the President's plan for its approach in dealing with Medicaid costs and asked the President to comment on the impact of the Republican budget plan on Medicaid.*]

The President. Well, I would just make a couple of points. And Governor Miller may want to talk more about this in a moment because he comes from such a high-growth State, but I think two things are going to happen if the Medicare and Medicaid budgets that they advocate actually become law. One is that the reductions in spending are so significant that there's no way that the high-growth States won't be adversely affected. That is, you may be able to take account of inflation and the fact that people as they live longer will use more health services, but there won't be enough to guarantee that the States with fast-growing populations that depend upon Medicare and Medicaid will be taken care of. There just won't be enough.

The second thing is that the cuts are so significant that it will virtually end the ability of States to expand health care coverage to the working poor through the Medicaid program and through a lot of the self-initiated reforms at the State level.

You know, what we tried to do—Governor Dean just alluded to it—after the failure of the health care reform effort in Congress last year, we just tried to support States that were finding ways to expand coverage and increase health care security for their people. I think that it will be almost impossible for the States to do that if the Medicare and Medicaid funds are cut this much. In fact, I think you'll be in a position of either dramatically increasing the cost of health care beyond the ability of low-income people to pay it or cutting back on the services you provide to them. I think if you look at these numbers, it's very difficult to imagine how that won't happen in almost every State in the country.

[*Gov. Evan Bayh of Indiana endorsed the President's plan for avoiding the shift of health care costs from the Government to consumers and asked why Congress would not make this compromise.*]

The President. Well, let me answer your question and then comment on what you said earlier.

I think that what I'm hoping will happen is that now there will be a discussion out in the country and a lot of moderate Republicans as well as independents and Democrats will say that, in the interest of economic growth and in the interest of fairness and in the interest of the integrity of the operation of a lot of our common efforts like education and health care, we ought to move more toward the framework that I have outlined.

I think that—I'm very much hopeful that you'll be able to discuss this budget at some point with the Republican Governors, and they will at least be able to embrace part of it because we've got now a serious economic study which predicts that the Republican budget would cause a recession. We've got a lot of evidence that it will hurt the States. But on the other hand, they are trying to balance the budget and, I agree with you, that's a goal we all ought to embrace because—well, let me just give you—you've all seen how the Federal-State partnership has been eroded as we have to devote more and more of our resources to paying interest on the debt. The budget would be balanced today because of our previous deficit reduction efforts in the last 2 years but for the interest on the debt run up in the 12 years before I became President. That's how bad a problem it is recently. And next year we'll pay more interest on the debt than we will for defense.

So we've got to balance the budget. But I'm hoping what you can do is to help me reach responsible Republican State legislators, State office-holders, Governors, and thoughtful independents to say let's do it, but let's do it in the right way.

Let me make just one other comment. Roy Romer pointed out one of the possible indirect impacts of the Republican budget, which was to—if we cut health care too much here and you have to take up the slack at the State level, you'll invest less in education. So we'll be cutting education at the Federal and the State level because of this budget.

You have pointed out two other indirect impacts, which we have already seen over the last 10 years. On health care, if we don't cover the full cost of health care for those who are insured by the Government, then hospitals and doctors will simply shift that cost on to private citizens and on to their health insurance bills, which will put more and more pressure on more and more employers to either drop health insurance coverage altogether or to dramatically increase the cost of it. And if we cut taxes too much here in Washington and put you in a bind at the State level or people at the local level, there will be offsetting increases at the State and local level.

Now, we know what happened in the 1980's, the tax cuts in Washington mostly benefited upper income people. The tax increases at the State and local level, because they were concentrated on sales taxes and property taxes, mostly taxed middle income people. So again, I think we ought to think about protecting the middle class. Most American wage earners are working harder for the same or lower wages than they were making 10 years ago. We don't need to lower their incomes by these budget decisions.

So I would say anything you can do to tell the Democrats and others who aren't for a balanced budget they ought to be for a balanced budget—I appreciate what you said, Evan, about the Beltway, as opposed to the heartland; I think most Democrats out there in the country are with us; that's positive. But anything you can do, to go back to Governor Romer's point and your point, to try to help the American people and the press, who communicates to the American people, understand the indirect consequences of this budget, for education, for health care, and for taxes, I think will be very, very helpful, because there will be significant indirect consequences that ought to be taken into account.

[*Gov. Tom Carper of Delaware endorsed the President's plan. Gov. Bob Miller of Nevada pointed out that the congressional plan failed to consider the impact on States which faced rapid growth and asked if the President's plan addressed that concern.*]

The President. Yes. We maintain the present approach, for example, toward helping States fund welfare. And if you had a huge increase in the number of poor children, under our plan, there would be provisions for funneling more funds there in ways that would enable you to match them and go forward. Under their plan, they're going to cut it so much there's no way they can take account of growth. They try to on welfare for poor kids, but they just can't get there. There's no way, just because the size of the cut.

By the same token, with the medical programs, Medicare and Medicaid, with the size of the cuts that are coming in, they won't be able to take account of growth. And they will force States to either reduce medical coverage or try to get some cost out of people that we know are so poor they don't have the money in the first place.

Now, I would say those would be the two biggest areas where the high-growth States will be cut, in medical coverage and in the care for poor children.

[*Governor Romer said the conversation had been very helpful and again praised the President's budget plan.*]

The President. Thank you. Let's just keep talking about it. And let's use this debate. Now there's one alternative and not two, and we can use the debate. And again, I would say, let's try to get—let's try to go beyond partisanship as much as possible, look at the direct and the indirect impacts of both budget proposals. And we'll get to the end of the road in the right place.

Thank you very, very much.

NOTE: The President spoke at 11:15 a.m in a telephone conference call from the Excelsior Hotel in Little Rock.

Remarks at the America's Hope, Arkansas' Pride Luncheon in Little Rock, Arkansas
June 23, 1995

Thank you so much. Thank you for being here. Thank you for being in such a good frame of mind. And thank you for making Hillary and Al and Tipper and me feel so wonderful today.

You know, I've always kind of resented Al Gore for being a little smarter than I am and knowing a little more about various things. And now he's gotten funnier than I am. I really— [*laughter*].

I thank you, Maurice Mitchell and Skip Rutherford and Jay Dunn and Doug Hatterman and all the others who worked. I have to mention one person I know is not here and another person I have not yet seen. I know a lot of people worked hard on this, but I know that my longtime friend Merle Peterson, who's away, and Jimmy Red Jones sat in a room and called a lot of you and harassed you until you bought tickets to this. [*Laughter*] And I want to thank them and all the rest of the committee for the work that they did.

I would like to thank Mack McLarty and all those from Arkansas who work in the administration, as well as those who work here in the Arkansas office who've tried to give you a lifeline through the fog that Washington can become. I thank them for representing me. I want to say a special word of thanks to Mack for all the many things he's done over the last 2½ years. I got a vivid picture of one of them yesterday when we were in New Jersey at a Ford plant which doubtless had made various vehicles that the McLarty dealerships had sold over the years. But I couldn't help thinking, you know, Mack has basically become the country's point person in all of our developing economic and political relationships with Latin America, which have expanded by more in the last 2½ years than in any previous point in history. And this Ford plant in New Jersey was making trucks being sold in Latin America. And I never realized it before, but there was McLarty always thinking about what it's going to be like 20 years from now when he's running all those Ford dealerships again. [*Laughter*] You can be very proud of the leadership he has given to our country, and I thank him for his long friendship.

And Bruce Lindsey, Marsha Scott, all the other people from Arkansas, and the people who run this office, they have enabled me to try and stay in touch with you in times when it has not always been easy. And Carol Rasco is not here; she's getting ready for our economic conference in the Pacific Northwest. But I see some people here particularly involved in health care and social services I know call her. I thank them for the work they've done to make it possible for us to try to stay in touch with one another.

I also want to say a special word of thanks to Congresswoman Blanche Lambert Lincoln and Congressman Ray Thornton. And congratulations, Congressmen, to you and to our Senators and to our Governor on Red River. Nice work. Truman Arnold is very happy he can keep working for the—[*applause*]—Truman Arnold woke up this morning thinking he could keep working for our reelection and for our party now.

We wish you well, Congressman Thornton. I wish you weren't retiring, but whatever you decide to do, I imagine you will make a good show of it. You always have. And you've really served our State well, and you've served our Nation well, and we thank you for that.

I want to say, as Hillary did, a special word of thanks to Senator Bumpers and Senator Pryor. They have fulfilled a lot of roles that maybe on some occasions they would rather not have done in the last 2½ years. And we've had some rough spots in the road. We've had some ups and downs, but they have always, always, always been there. And in very personal ways that will probably never become fully known or appreciated, I can tell you that I am profoundly grateful to both of them.

I saw Dale on television the other night speaking to the Small Business Conference, talking about the importance of balancing the budget and doing it in a humane way and the right way. And a lot of those Republicans were really listening to him in ways that only he can communicate. I think of all the times when David has taken the floor of the Senate to try to restore just a little bit of humanity and sanity to a national political debate that has gotten way too out of hand too often in the last 2 years, and I thank him for that.

And let me also say I am especially glad to see Governor and Mrs. Tucker here today and especially grateful for the reception you gave them. As an Arkansan, I felt exactly the same way. And thank you, Governor, for being here. We're proud of you. Thank you.

I might also note that the last time I checked, the unemployment rate in Arkansas is down to 4.1 percent, which is—after what we suffered all those years, that's another reason to rejoice.

You know, I was listening to the Vice President go through that whole litany, and I have to say I'm also especially indebted to the people who have spoken here before me, to Tipper for all the work she's done in mental health and for the courageous and sometimes lonely battles she always wages within the administration to remind all of us that that's a very important part of health care, and to Tipper and to Hillary for the work they've done to try to make sure we increase our emphasis on women's health concerns.

And I was very proud of Hillary yesterday in particular. She took me along, and I spoke to a remarkable event in front of the Arlington Cemetery yesterday where we broke ground, long overdue, on America's first memorial for the 1.8 million women who have worn the uniform of our country in military service. One of the things that I am quite proud of that almost nobody knows—there are a lot of achievements of this administration that fall into that category—one of the things that I'm very proud of that almost nobody knows, that I think is part of the enduring influence of my wife and my wonderful departed mother, is that in the last 2½ years we have opened up to women in the services 260,000 positions previously denied them in the service of their country. And I'm very proud of it, and the military is very proud of it.

I said that last comment, and the Vice President was up here giving our record and it reminded me about a week ago, maybe 2 weeks ago now, we had an event at the Treasury Department. And we were announcing one of our continuing Al Gore genius moves to reinvent the Government and make it easier to deal with. And this one had to do with the fact that next year, in 32 States, people can file their taxes, State and Federal together, electronically, no paper, no hassle, file them both together. We'll distribute it, we'll do all the work. And we always try to have a real person like one of you at one of these announcements to explain how this will actually change people's lives.

So, it was just before the Small Business Conference started, and we got this John Deere dealer from west Texas come who happened to be a supporter of mine, probably the only person in the whole county—[*laughter*]—there he was. But anyway, he ran a good-sized John Deere dealership, and he got up there and he said—I got so tickled—he said—he brought all the paper that he'd been using on his taxes and he said, "I can throw all this away, and it's great." And he explained how much money

he was going to save, but he said, "You know," he said, "you fellows have been doing a great job of reinventing Government. What you need to do is reinvent communication because it ain't getting out to the rednecks that I sell John Deeres to." [*Laughter*]

You know, some nights I watch the news and I feel like that old country song "They Changed Everything About Me But My Name." [*Laughter*] That's beginning to change as well. I want to have—for just a moment I want to have a serious conversation. The Vice President has outlined a great deal of what we have done—and I use the word "we" in the largest sense. One of them, our proudest achievements, has very little to do with me except that I made it possible, and I think the history books will reflect that Al Gore was the most influential and effective Vice President of the United States in the history of our Republic through the 21st century.

We were at the Small Business Conference the other day; we hauled out 16,000 Federal regulations that we were getting rid of because of the reinventing Government task force: cutting half the regulations of the Small Business Administration, 40 percent of the regulations of the Department of Education, dramatically changing the way the Occupational Safety and Health Administration is going to work, reducing the paperwork burdens of the Environmental Protection Agency by 25 percent, setting up a hotline so that if a small business person calls the EPA now, that person cannot be fined if he or she is calling for help to try to figure out how to solve a problem.

These are important changes in the way our Government relates to people. But I have to tell you that what is going on in America today is more than just whether this administration is achieving things that are or are not known about. This is a period of deep and profound change in the whole world and in this country, the way we work, the way we live, the conditions in which we raise our children, the opportunities available to us, and the challenges confronting us. They're different. And all of us are the product of our own experiences. I tell everybody that works at the White House all the time, especially young people who see things they don't understand, I keep telling everybody we all see the world through the prism of our own experience. Even our imaginations are limited by what we have known and felt and seen.

And yet, all these things are happening around us, some utterly wonderful and some utterly horrible that go beyond our ability even to imagine a resolution of. A lot of good things, the end of the cold war, the growth of the information age, the fact that a kid in the most remote mountain school in Arkansas can now hook into an Internet which will pull information out of a library in Australia, just for example—now, these are wonderful things. And we see all these things, and it's just staggering, it's so wonderful. We see a lot of our old problems appear to be getting better. The crime rate as a whole is dropping in almost every major city in America. That's the good news. And I could give you 50 other examples of good news. We had the biggest expansion of trade opportunities in our country in the last 2 years that we have had in a generation, maybe ever.

But underneath that, it seems that every opportunity has within it the possibility of something new going wrong. Crime rate goes down, but the arbitrary rate of violence among teenagers goes up, giving us chilling feelings about what the crime rate might be like in 10 or 15 years. And more and more and more young kids are just being kind of left alone out there to raise themselves, struggling to figure out what to do, stuck in home environments, community environments, and school environments that aren't likely to help them to turn around the challenges they face.

All this wonderful technology and this easily accessible information has its dark underside. You can get on the Internet now and tap into one of these fanatic extremists, and they will explain to you how you too can make a bomb just like the one that blew up the Federal building in Oklahoma City. The explosion of technology means that a radical religious group in Japan can figure out how to get a little bitty vial of gas and walk into a subway and break it open and kill a bunch of totally innocent people and put hundreds of others in the hospital.

So you see the point I'm trying to make: There is so much good in the world, so much new possibility; but the Scripture tells us that the darkness that is in the human soul will be with us until the end of time, and those dark forces are finding new expressions as well. And we're all sitting around here trying to figure out how to make sense of this and what to do, so that what is really going on in Washington, which is confusing to people, is not much different than what's going on inside a lot of people's heads, which is confusing to people. And it's because it is really new.

I am proud of the fact that this administration negotiated agreements, which means that there are no nuclear weapons pointed at the children of Arkansas since the dawn of the nuclear age. I'm proud of that. But the paradox is—let me just give you the paradox—the paradox is a year or so ago, Hillary and I went to Riga, Latvia, to celebrate the withdrawal of Russian troops there for the first time since before World War II, tens of thousands of people in the street weeping with joy, loving America. A poll just came out and said that Bill Clinton was the most popular politician in Latvia. I'm trying to figure out how to get on the ballot there, give them some electoral votes. [*Laughter*]

But then we go into—it was a wonderful survey. It wasn't me; I was America. It didn't have anything to do with me; I was the United States. But then we go behind closed doors into a meeting, and the first thing they ask me for is an FBI office. Why? Because when you rip away the iron hand of communism and you take out the Russian army—there is this huge port, the largest city in Northern Europe that most people couldn't even find on a map here, that they're now terrified will become a great transit point for drug trafficking and organized crime of all kinds. The most popular thing we've done in Russia in the last year is not dismantling the nuclear weapons, it's opening an FBI office in Moscow. Why? Because they got rid of communism, and they didn't have things like the Federal Deposit Insurance Corporation or the Securities and Exchange Commission, so within no time at all, half of their financial institutions were controlled by organized crime.

I say this to make a point. We have to go back deep inside now to our basic values and our basic institutions. And the debates we are having in Washington now are over fundamental things that we used to take for granted.

When I was Governor here, in all the years until the last year when I ran for President, we only had an unemployment rate below the national average one month, one month. A lot of my legislators are out there. They remember how we struggled with that, but we had a consensus. We disagreed on the details, and we fought at election time, but there was a general consensus that if we made our State more attractive economically and that if we continued to invest in the skills of our people, that in the end that strategy would be rewarded. And it might take a decade to turn it around, but it would be rewarded.

And I'm convinced that everybody in this room, in addition to the great leadership we have in our State today, played a role in the fact that we have an unemployment rate below the national average today. It did not happen overnight. It's all of you who are entrepreneurs, all of you who built your own companies, all of you who came in here and invested in our State from beyond our State's borders, sometimes from beyond our Nation's borders. It happened—being driven in a direction.

But we basically accepted fundamental assumptions. A lot of that is out the window now. And I want you to try to understand what we're going through and why sometimes it doesn't seem to make sense when you see it over the airwaves. We are debating now really first principles in Washington. For example, there's a significant number of people in Congress who believe all of our problems are personal and cultural in nature, and if everybody would just wake up tomorrow and behave themselves, we wouldn't have any problems, and therefore, we don't need the Government to do anything, whatever the Government does will only make it worse. And if we just give you the money back, everything would be fine, because all of our problems are personal and cultural.

Now, at a certain level that is true, isn't it? I mean, no matter what we do with the government in Arkansas or Washington, if people won't behave themselves and do right and make the most of their own lives, nobody can do that for you. That's something you have to do for yourselves. At some point, no matter how much adversity people face, some people make it, and some don't. And it's their responsibility. On the other hand, if you play the odds, you know that really successful communities, States, and nations do the best they can to make sure that everybody has the best chance to make the most of their own lives.

I don't see it that way; I don't think that it's either—that it's an either/or thing, that all of our problems are personal or cultural on the one hand or political or economic on the other. I think the answer is both. But because things are changing and people are confused, the extreme sides of the debate are really being argued out all over again, just as they were literally decades ago at the beginning of this century when the excesses of the industrial revolution were being felt.

Let me give you another example leading from that. A debate—we never had that debate in Arkansas. We never saw any inconsistency between fighting teenage pregnancy on the one hand and trying to get more responsibility and investing more money in preschool education on the other. The idea was both, right?

Give you another example—a lot of people feel, flowing from the first debate, that since the Government only messes things up, the fundamental responsibility of the Government is to maintain national defense, cut taxes, and balance the budget as quickly as possible without regard to the other consequences of what's being done. They honestly believe this. This is not a—I'm being, I think, fair and accurate.

Then there are others who feel that the budget deficit is a terrible thing but not the only deficit the country has; and that if we don't educate our kids and if we don't at least take care of our fundamental obligations to the elderly people on Medicare who don't have enough money to live on as it is, that the country will come apart at the seams more; and that we have certain common responsibilities. And some people think that if we never balance the budget, it's better to keep investing that money.

But I don't see it that way. I think that we ought to balance the budget, because we never had a permanent deficit before 12 years ago— I mean, 12 years before I took office—we haven't had a balanced budget since '69. But in the seventies, all of you will remember we had all that stagflation. Oil prices were going crazy, and the reasons for the deficits were largely localized and—we never had a built-in deficit every year, year-in and year-out, in this country's history until 1981. And we've taken it down by a trillion dollars over a 7-year period since I've been in office.

We ought to balance the budget. Next year— we'll be seeing more money on interest on the debt next year than we will spend on national defense. The budget would be balanced this year, right now, because of the cuts we've already made, were it not for the interest we have to pay just in the 12 years before I showed up up there. That's how big a problem it is. It erodes our competitive position in world markets. It drives our incomes down. And it undermines our ability to borrow to invest in the future.

You know, there's a difference between borrowing money to build a business or buy a house and borrowing money to go out to eat tonight. There's a big difference. And we've got it all mixed up. You can't tell what we're doing now. So we need to do that.

But we also have to realize—I think that we do have more than one deficit. And at the end—in this information age and this global economy, for us to be cutting education is like cutting defense at the height of the cold war. I don't think it makes any sense.

But there is this ideological debate over—and the third big debate, maybe the most important one of all, is the one that—there are people who honestly believe that if you think all of our problems are personal and cultural and moral, if you believe the Government can't do anything right but mess up a one-car parade, the only thing it's supposed to do is national defense, cut taxes, and balance the budget, then a lot of the same people believe that anyone who disagrees with them are intrinsically a threat to the Republic and anything you do to beat them or put them in a bad light is all right, so that the politics of demonization, the meanness quotient of our politics, the distortion level of it has increased quite a bit in recent years.

Now, I think it's good to fight and argue, but I think we're around here after way over 200 years because, no matter how the arguments came out, we kept this thing going in the middle of the road and going forward, not too far left, not too far right, but always forward. And that's why we're still around.

But I'm just telling you these are fundamental debates that are going on so that it's no longer the kind of normal debate you see in Washington. Instead of the range of difference being like this, it's more like this now. And it's because of all these changes that are going on in the country and in the world.

Let me just give you some specific examples because I think it's a phony debate. I think we need to worry about going forward, now how far we can get out on these extremes. I think we need to return to our basic values. You know, go back and read the Constitution, the Declaration of Independence. We got together as a Nation because we thought it was self-evident that all people were endowed by

God with certain inalienable rights, among them life, liberty, and the pursuit of happiness and that it was necessary to form governments to pursue these ends.

And our Constitution was created with the flexibility to enable us to change to meet the challenges of new times and with the iron-clad guarantees of the Bill of Rights that there were limits beyond which Government could not go in infringing upon the freedoms of individuals. And all of our debates, if we'll get back to those basic things and the facts, will lead us to a practical solution that will push us ahead. But I'll just give you some examples.

The family leave law: There were people who were ideologically opposed to the family leave law because they said Government shouldn't tell business anything. But the truth is that most parents are also workers today. Whether you think it's a good idea or a bad idea, whether it's a single-parent household or a two-parent household, most parents are also workers. If you believe that the family is the most important institution in our society, on the one hand, and you also believe that if we're not competitive globally, on the other, we're in deep trouble, then this country has no more important objective than enabling people to not have to make a false choice. We must enable people to be successful parents and successful workers. That's why I was for the family leave law.

But not everybody feels this way. That's big debate up there. And when you hear this rhetoric you have to understand that. There are a lot of people—there are honest people who honestly believe that it was a wrong thing to do.

It sure didn't hurt the economy. We've had 6.7 million new jobs since it passed, record numbers of new business formations in 1993 and 1994. So all those predictions that it was going to hurt the economy or be burdensome were wrong. It's an ideological debate.

Second, the environment: Most people, I believe, here think that we have to be able to grow the economy in a way that preserves the environment so our grandchildren and our grandchildren's grandchildren will still have Arkansas to live in. And a big part of what we define of Arkansas is that. And most of the time when we fought about the environment when we were—when I was Governor, we fought over how to achieve that goal and whether the Government was going too far, the regulations should be done in a certain way or another way. But we were fighting over how to achieve that goal.

That is not the debate up there anymore. The debate is far more fundamental. There are people who believe, "Well, it's a nice thing to preserve the environment, but in the end nobody will ever really let it go down the tubes. And the Government will mess it up. Get the Government out of it. And if the environment is abused in the short run, so what. Somehow the planet will regenerate itself."

Let me tell you—a committee of Congress just the other day voted to eliminate all controls on offshore oil drilling in the United States, all of them, everywhere, without regard to any evidence of how much oil is there or whether it's worth the risk or whether there's any evidence of safe drilling or what the differences in the areas are or what would happen to tourism or what would happen to retirement or what would happen to anything. Why? Because they're ideologically opposed to the Government having any kind of partnership at all with the private sector on this.

And that's just one example. But I'm telling you, folks, it is an economic as well as an environmental issue. We're on our way to Portland, Oregon, the Vice President and I are, when we leave you. And we're dealing with a terrible set of problems up there, where a lot of the timber people want to cut more timber in the forest, and because the waters have been more polluted they're losing the salmon. And that's just one example.

I believe we've got to find a way to do both. Our State has used the Nature Conservancy more than any State in the country, I think, to buy land to set aside, because, as Will Rogers said, "They ain't making no more of it." And the people who supported it were the business people in our State. This is a fundamental debate.

I'll give you a third example: Dr. Foster. Al Gore alluded to him. Dr. Foster. There are people in Washington, and they were—they had enough influence to keep his nomination from coming to a vote—who believe that he is unfit for any public office ever because he performed a few legal abortions, and therefore, he should never be considered for any public service and if the people who wanted to be President in the other party knew what was good for them, they would vote no. And since we had enough

votes to confirm him, they could not even let him come to a vote.

Now, here's a guy, unlike the rest of—most of the rest of us—who's actually done something to try to reduce teen pregnancy, to try to reduce the number of abortions, and to try to tell kids on a consistent, disciplined way, who don't have other role models to tell them, that they should not have sex before they're married. Here's a guy who's actually gone out and organized a program that was recognized not by me but by my predecessor, President Bush, in an organized, disciplined fashion to tell young people, "I don't care what kind of problems you've got, I don't care what your peer pressures are. I don't care what you're going through. You have no business having sex. You cannot promote teen pregnancy, and you ought not to do it to your life. You ought to stay off drugs, stay in school, and do a good job with your life." Here's a guy who's ridden country dusty roads in Alabama and brought health care to people that they never could have gotten otherwise. Here's a man who's delivered thousands of babies, and had at least one of his former patients stand up and publicly say, "I was going to have an abortion, and he talked me out of it. He talked me out of it."

In other words, here's a guy who has actually lived what other folks say they believe in. But in this sort of new world that's taken hold up here, he wasn't politically correct and pure enough to serve as Surgeon General, even though he had actually done the things they say they wish to do. This is a profound debate. And so they were even willing to abuse the filibuster process.

Clarence Thomas could have been kept off the Supreme Court if the Democrats had said, "Well, we don't have enough votes to beat him, but we sure got enough votes to keep him from coming to a vote." But they said, "No, that would be morally wrong. The President has a right to make an appointment. The committee has a right to make the recommendation. And the Senate ought to vote." But not in this new world. In this new world that are no rules except winning and losing, because one side is all good and the other side is all bad. If we had had that attitude for the last 219 years, we wouldn't be here today. We wouldn't be here today.

So what is to become of us as a people? I ran for this job because I wanted to do two things, two big things: I wanted to restore the

American dream; I wanted to get the economy going; I wanted to lift stagnant wages and get the jobs coming back into the economy and fix the education system so people could actually get out of this awful two-decade slump we've been in where even when the economic numbers get better, nobody ever gets a raise. But I also wanted to bring the country together.

Now, the second issue is even more important than the first. And it can be a very good thing that we are having these big debates over fundamental questions. But I want you to understand just how deep and fundamental these debates are.

If you look at the budget debate here, I applaud the Republicans for being for a balanced budget, and I hope all the Democrats will be, for the reasons I just explained. It is not right for our country to have a permanent deficit. I wasn't for the amendment because we ought to have the right to borrow when we need to. But we shouldn't be in a system of permanent deficits.

But my budget reflects what I just talked to you about. My budget reflects the idea that we need to keep going forward. So I believe that I'm right. I think we should balance the budget but increase our investment in education. I think we have to cut the rate at which we're increasing health expenditures but not so much that we're going to close down rural hospitals or urban hospitals and not so much that we're going to burden elderly people who don't have enough to live on as it is and can't afford to pay a whole lot more for their health care and shouldn't be asked to give up health care. I believe that we ought to cut spending on welfare but not so much that we don't invest in child care and basic training so we can actually move people from welfare to work instead of just throwing poor kids in the street. The objective of welfare reform should be to help people, again, become good workers and good parents, not just to save money.

I believe any tax cut we have should be so small it doesn't require us to cut these other things and should be focused on the people who need it to help them raise their kids and educate them. That's why I proposed a tax deduction for the cost of education after high school. I think that's important.

And I know if you cut the tax cut back and focus it on education and childrearing and take 10 years instead of 7 to balance the budget,

then you don't have to cut education, and you don't have to imperil Medicare and Medicaid and you don't have to go from a welfare reform plan that should be tough on work but good to children to one that doesn't have any work and sticks it to kids. It moves us ahead. But it's not an ideologically extreme position. It says we have two things we want to do: balance the budget and bring our country together and raise incomes and move forward. And we can do them both. And that's what's going on up there now. These are big, fundamental questions.

I just want to say, in closing, that a lot of what's happened to you here, a lot of the outrageous, outrageous things that have been said about our State and a lot of the licking that you've taken is a product of the confusion and the disorientation of the times and the idea that there are no rules and people just sort of flailing around trying to win another one to get to tomorrow. That is not what made this country great. That is not what made this country great, and it's not what you taught me to do here.

And I just want you to know, the greatest thing that ever happens to me is when I get to be all of you. Hillary and I were in Ukraine for the 50th anniversary of the end of World War II. And I gave a speech at the university there, and there were, I don't know, 60,000 people or something in the streets. And then everywhere we drove, they were four or five deep waving American flags. And I met all these old veterans from World War II who fought with the Americans then, telling me everything they did and showing me all their medals, you know. They weren't waving at me, they were waving at America. They were waving at America.

You know, everything the Vice President said—I'm glad I have a chance to play a major role in what we're doing in the Middle East and what we're doing in Northern Ireland and what's happening in Haiti and the deneutralization of the world—I'm glad about all that. But the only reason I had that chance is because for a little while in our country's history I get to become all of us, the United States. And I am telling you I've been there.

There is no country in the world as well positioned as we are for the next century. There is no country—*[applause]*—because we do have a limited Government that allows the private sector to flourish and entrepreneurs to do well, but we have enough ability to work together to solve common problems that we can do that. We have the potential for the right balance and the right flexibility.

There is no country that is any better positioned because of our terrific geographic and economic and racial, ethnic and religious diversity. But unless we learn to how to recover both the sense of personal responsibility and a sense of appreciation for people who are different from us, unless we learn how to resolve our differences without demonizing people and how to look toward the long run, we could squander the most colossal opportunity our country has ever had.

Because of the way technology works in the 21st century, Arkansas can not only have a lower unemployment rate than the rest of the country, our people can actually enjoy a standard of living equal to that of any people in the world. And that can happen everywhere. But it depends upon whether we can go back to these first principles and go forward with a sense of balance and mutual respect.

At the end of the Civil War, Abraham Lincoln said, "We cannot be enemies. We must be friends." That is what I say to you. And when you get angry about things you think are happening and when things happen you don't understand, just remember, this is still the greatest country in the world. It is still the greatest country in the world.

Stand up and fight for what you believe in. But fight against people who want to throw this country way off the track. And fight for the idea that we can pull together. After that Oklahoma City bombing, America was shaken to its very core. But it threw some of the meanness out of all of us. And it made all of us reexamine

where we are. And our sort of heart and our common sense were reasserted. After that wonderful young Air Force Captain Scott O'Grady survived 6 hideous days in Bosnia and was rescued by a brilliant American operation, we were all exhilarated, and that put some of the energy back in all of us.

What I want you to know is to get to tomorrow, we have to have the heart and the openness to other people that we found in the tragedy of Oklahoma City and the self-confidence and energy that we had when that boy came home. And if we do that, we're going to be just fine.

That is the issue in 1996. That is what you're investing in. It's my last election. I'll never run for anything else. [*Laughter*] You'll never have to come to one of these again. You'll never be dunned again. [*Laughter*] You'll never have to stand in line again if you don't want to. But just know this time, this time, the stakes are the highest they have ever been, higher than they were in '92 because of where we have moved and where we can go. It is worth the fight. And I can't make it without you, but together I think we will.

God bless you, and thank you.

NOTE: The President spoke at 1:35 p.m. in the William J. Clinton Ballroom at the Excelsior Hotel. In his remarks, he referred to Maurice Mitchell, legal counsel, Arkansas Democratic Party; luncheon organizers James L. "Skip" Rutherford, Jay Dunn, Doug Hatterman, Merle Peterson, and Jimmy Red Jones; Truman Arnold, acting national finance chair, Democratic National Committee; and Gov. Jim Guy Tucker of Arkansas and his wife, Betty.

Statement on Guestworker Legislation
June 23, 1995

I oppose efforts in the Congress to institute a new guestworker or *bracero* program that seeks to bring thousands of foreign workers into the United States to provide temporary farm labor.

In its most recent report, the bipartisan Commission on Immigration Reform chaired by Bar-

bara Jordan unanimously concluded that a large-scale guestworker program would be a "grievous mistake." We have worked hard to reduce illegal immigration and have made great progress toward controlling this longstanding and serious problem. To allow so-called temporary workers to cross the border now would undermine all the success we have achieved.

A new guestworker program is unwarranted for several reasons:

- It would increase illegal immigration.
- It would reduce work opportunities for U.S. citizens and other legal residents.
- It would depress wages and work standards for American workers.

When these programs were tried in the past, many temporary guestworkers stayed permanently—and illegally—in this country. Hundreds of thousands of immigrants now residing in the U.S. first came as temporary workers, and their presence became a magnet for other illegal immigrants.

If our crackdown on illegal immigration contributes to labor shortages—especially for perishable crops that require large numbers of workers for short periods of time—I will direct the Departments of Labor and Agriculture to work cooperatively to improve and enhance existing programs to meet the labor requirements of our vital agricultural industry consistent with our obligations to American workers.

Statement on the Death of Jonas Salk
June 23, 1995

Hillary and I want to extend our deepest sympathies to the family and friends of Dr. Jonas Salk, a man whose indefatigable pursuit of solutions made this world a better place to live. The victory of this medical pioneer over a dreaded disease continues to touch many, from the students who study his work to the countless individuals whose lives have been saved by his efforts. His polio vaccine opened the door to a society in which good health was taken for granted. And, over the last decade, his efforts to find a cure for AIDS gave us all hope. He was a true leader, and we will miss him greatly.

The President's Radio Address
June 24, 1995

Good morning. Today I'm talking to you from the Convention Center in Pine Bluff, Arkansas. The Arkansas firefighters are meeting here, and I'm the first sitting President ever to visit Pine Bluff. Zachary Taylor planned to come in 1849, but he had to cancel. It's a record I'm proud to set. I'm also proud to be here with Dr. Henry Foster, who was born here and grew up here.

Just under 5 months ago, I nominated this fine man to be our Surgeon General. And this week, a majority of the United States Senate was clearly prepared to confirm him as Surgeon General. But he wasn't confirmed. He wasn't confirmed because the Senate was never even allowed to vote on his confirmation, because they were blocked by a group, a minority group, of willful Senators who abused the procedure to keep his nomination from coming to a vote for their own political ends.

Let me tell you a little bit about Dr. Foster. He's been a doctor for 38 years, including 3 years in the United States Air Force. He has delivered thousands of babies and trained hundreds of young doctors. He's ridden dusty country roads in Alabama to bring health care to people who never would have gotten it otherwise. He has labored to reduce teen pregnancy, to reduce the number of abortions, to tell young people without other role models, in a disciplined, organized way: you shouldn't have sex before you're married; you should stay off drugs; you should stay in school and do a good job with your life. His efforts to give a future to young people without one were recognized first not by me but by my Republican predecessor, President Bush.

Let me tell you something: If more people in America lived their lives like Henry Foster, there would be fewer kids on drugs, fewer teen pregnancies, fewer abortions, fewer broken families. This is a man our country should be proud to call our own.

So why was a group of Senators determined to stop Dr. Foster? A minority of the Senate blocked a vote on him in a calculated move to showcase their desire to take away a woman's right to choose. Dr. Foster has faithfully performed his duties as a doctor for 38 years. Although he has delivered thousands of babies, when the law permitted it, the patient requested it, and after appropriate counseling, he did perform an average of about one abortion per year.

Now, I know it is easy to condemn abortion. It's easy to put on divisive television ads or pass out inflammatory materials. But it is very hard to actually work with children and look at them face to face, kids that nobody pays any attention to, and look at them and tell them they ought not to have sex, they ought not to get pregnant, they ought not to do drugs. That's hard. That's why most of us don't do it. But Henry Foster did.

Unfortunately, in Washington today, pure political correctness and raw political power count a whole lot more than actually doing something to reduce the tragedies of teen pregnancy and the high number of abortions.

You know, I believe it is clear what the law of the land is, and I believe that abortion should be rare but it should be legal and safe. The extreme right wing in our country wants to impose its views on all the rest of Americans. They killed this nomination with the help of the Republican leadership who did as they were told. And they're just getting started.

This week, the House passed a bill which would prevent women who serve in our military or who are on military bases with their servicemen husbands from getting abortions at base hospitals, even if they pay for it and no matter what the circumstances. Imagine a servicewoman in a foreign country, a remote location without good medical facilities or even a safe blood supply. This House bill would say, "If you can spend thousands of dollars to fly back to the United States for a safe and legal procedure, you're all right; otherwise you may have to risk your life in a hospital far from home." Why? Because she voluntarily enlisted to serve her country. So that a woman who's willing to risk her life for her country should also have

to risk her life for a legal medical procedure. This seems to me to be too extreme.

In a few days, the House will actually try to cut off Federal funds for abortions for poor women that arise from rape or incest. Even those with strong antiabortion feelings know this is a tough issue, and most people think it ought to be left to individual citizens. It's one thing to say that the taxpayers should not pay for a legal abortion that arises from a poor woman's own decision. That's one thing. Quite another to say that the same rules apply to rape and incest.

This is a big, diverse country. We are deeply divided over many issues, none more than the painful and difficult issue of abortion. The law now is that the woman, not the Government, makes a decision until the third trimester when a baby can live independently of his mother and therefore the Government can prohibit abortions.

There are some who believe that America now must toe their line and that every woman must live by their rules, even though the Constitution, as interpreted by the Supreme Court, says exactly the reverse. They'll stop at nothing to get their way. And this week it looks like the Republican leaders in Congress have given them the keys to the store. Looks like they'll vote for any bill, oppose any nomination, allow any intrusion into people's lives if they get orders to do so from these groups.

Many, many Americans oppose abortion. And everyone agrees it's a tragedy. I believe we should all work to reduce the number of abortions through vigorous campaigns to promote abstinence among young people; reduce out-of-wedlock pregnancy, especially among teenagers; and promote more adoptions. I believe, in short, that we ought to all do more of the kind of things that Henry Foster has been doing for decades.

If people in Washington spent less time using abortion to divide the country for their own political ends and more time following Dr. Foster's example of fighting these problems, there would be a lot fewer abortions in America and we'd be a lot stronger as a country.

We need more citizens like Henry Foster willing to commit their time, their energy, and love to fighting for our children, our families, and our future.

Thanks for listening.

NOTE: The President spoke at 9:06 a.m. from the Pine Bluff Convention Center in Pine Bluff, AR.

Interview With Susan Yoachum of the San Francisco Chronicle in Pine Bluff, Arkansas
June 24, 1995

The President. Hello.

Ms. Yoachum. Hello, Mr. President.

The President. How are you?

Ms. Yoachum. I'm fine. It's very good of you to call, so I'll get right to it.

The President. Where are you?

Ms. Yoachum. I'm in Portsmouth, New Hampshire.

The President. It's a great town.

United Nations

Ms. Yoachum. Actually, it is. I'm following around one of your newest—well, not your newest rivals but one of the newest candidates for President on the Republican side, Pete Wilson.

So let me begin by asking you about your speech on Monday concerning the 50th anniversary of the United Nations. How do you plan to outline ways for the U.N. to reconstitute itself for the next 50 years?

The President. Well, I think we have to, first of all, recognize that—I think there are two fundamental realities we have to recognize. Number one is that the end of the cold war gives the U.N. the possibility of living up to the dreams of its founders in ways that were simply impossible when the world was divided into two large blocs. And so I think there should be a lot of hope about the U.N.

The second thing I think we have to recognize is that in order for that hope to be realized, the U.N. has got to be properly run and, in particular, the peacekeeping operations have to be properly run. And the United States has spent a lot of time, because we pay a lot of the costs of the U.N., analyzing how the overall operations can be more efficient and cost-effective and inspire more confidence in the countries that are paying the bills and, in particular, looking at the peacekeeping operations and setting up systems to make sure that we use peacekeeping when it will work, that we restrain it when the situation is not right, and that the command-and-control operations are absolutely clear, that we don't have any kind of mixed signals and crossed lines that have sometimes happened in the past.

I think those are the two fundamental realities you start with. And then when you look ahead into the future, I think it's clear that the new problems of the 21st century are likely to be rooted in ethnic, religious, and other internal problems within countries and across borders; dealing with or helping to avoid natural disasters that are brought on by a combination of population explosion and natural problems like the inability to produce food; and the rise of terrorism and the danger of proliferation of biological, chemical, and small-scale nuclear weapons.

I think—and so I want to talk about kind of the threats to the future security of the members of the United Nations and how we have a new set of threats, an unprecedented opportunity, and we have to clean up our—operate—clean up implies—that has the wrong implication. I don't want to imply that there's anything unsavory about it, but it's just that the operation, I think, really needs to be streamlined and reformed in order to inspire confidence in all the member nations.

As you know, both our—the last two Congresses, one was a Democratic Congress and this Republican Congress, expressed varying levels of opposition to some of the U.N. operations. But the last Congress was far more focused on getting the U.N. to work right, not having America walk away from its responsibilities and became more isolationist.

So—and therefore, the message—that will be the message. But I will also say back to my fellow Americans and to the Congress that we should continue to support the United Nations, that they do a lot of work in the world that the United States might have to do alone or might eventually be pulled into doing, because they keep problems from becoming as bad as they would otherwise be.

Ms. Yoachum. Mr. President, given the difficulties, the highly publicized difficulties, of course, with the U.N. peacekeeping forces in Bosnia and other U.N. difficulties, doesn't it make it more difficult for you to try to sell this to Americans, and don't you run some political risk in trying to do so?

The President. Well, I suppose there's—in a time like this, when a lot of people are bewildered almost by all the things that are going on in the world and the apparent conflicts of all the good forces and the troubling forces rising up at once, there's some political risk in everything. But you have to do what you think is right.

I think the—I think it's important not to define the—first of all, I think it's important not to define the U.N. solely in terms of Bosnia. I mean, there was also—I'd ask the United States to remember that we went into Haiti with a multinational force that restored the Aristide government and democracy, but we were able to hand it off to a U.N. force with even more nations involved, where there were more countries paying for it.

I think most Americans know that there are going to be problems all around the world that affect United States interests and that can affect United States citizens, and it's better to have a larger number of nations working on those problems and a larger number of nations paying for the solutions to those problems.

Bosnia is a unique circumstance because it's in the heart of Europe, but there's a war that's been going on there for 4 years. But if you look at it, the people in Northern Ireland fought for 25 years, the people in the Middle East fought for more than four decades before there was any peace progress there. And for all the frustration people in our country have with the problems in Bosnia, the casualty rates have gone way, way down since the U.N. forces went on the ground there and since the United States began to support them with massive humanitarian airlifts and with our operation to keep the war from going into the air. That's what Captain O'Grady was doing when he was shot down; he was enforcing the no-fly zone. And I think it's important never to forget that. Before the United Nations became involved and before we became as aggressive as we were in trying to provide air help, in 1992, there were about

130,000 people killed in that civil war. In 1994, the death rate was down to under—about 3,500. So I think that it's important, even in Bosnia, to keep this in perspective.

The United Nations did not succeed in ending the war in Bosnia. The United Nations did not go in there to militarily defeat the Bosnian Serbs, and they're not capable of doing that, and that was never what they were established—that's not what they were sent there to do. But the war has become less violent and has been at least contained to Bosnia and has not spread beyond its borders. So with all of our frustrations, I think it's important to remember that.

Ms. Yoachum. You'll be doing a number of things in your speech on Monday, which has been, I think, widely anticipated around the world. And certainly, the patron saint of the U.N. 50 celebration, Walter Shorenstein, says that it's a real opportunity for you to give a world-class speech. Having said that, and you having said that you're going to outline your hope for the U.N. given the changing circumstances of the world, what part of your speech—what will you say in your speech to address some of the criticisms, particularly by key Republicans, of the United States' involvement in 1995 in the U.N.?

The President. Well, I will—consider the alternatives. I mean, here the United States is, the world's only superpower militarily, with other countries becoming increasingly wealthy, where there are other countries willing to put their troops on the ground in their own trouble spots and not asking us to do it, like Bosnia, and willing to pay an increasingly large share of running the United Nations. And now we have people in our country and, most importantly, people in our Congress, who want to walk away from our global responsibilities and walk away from the opportunity to cooperate with people in ways that permit others to carry some share of the load.

You know, sometimes I get the feeling that some of the critics of our cooperation with other countries want it both ways. They want to be able to run the world and tell everybody exactly how to behave, and then not have to cooperate with anybody when they have a slight difference of opinion from us or even if they're willing to put their troops on the ground and put their money up.

That's the case in Bosnia, where the Europeans said, "We'll take the lead. We'll put our troops on the ground. This will be paid for through the United Nations, so you won't have to pay for any more than your regular assessment. We ask you for your air power and the support of the NATO, but we're going to follow the prescribed United Nations policy. We're not going to let the U.S. dictate policy, especially when it's our troops and our lives that are at risk."

And I think we cannot have it both ways. We can't become an isolationist country, and we can't dictate every other country's course. We can't become the world's policemen. And it's better for us to be a leader within the framework of the United Nations, which means that from time to time we will have to cooperate with people and agree on a policy that may reflect more of a consensus than our absolute best desires. But that's what the United Nations was set up to do.

The U.S. is still clearly the dominant country in the United Nations. We still are able to do the things we need to do to be—for example, to keep a firm hand with Serbia; we've been able to keep other countries from lifting the sanctions off Iraq; we've been able to get a tougher line—in many ways, we were able to have our policy in Haiti prevail. But the United Nations is about working with other countries and shared sacrifice, shared contribution, shared decisionmaking, where the U.S. leads but can't control everything. And I think that's the way the world ought to be going forward.

Ms. Yoachum. And so in your speech on Monday, despite the criticism of the U.S. involvement in the U.N., you'll not be backing away from the U.N., but at the same time, you'll also be offering suggestions for reforming it?

The President. Absolutely. I don't intend to back away at all. But I do intend to say that this is going to be a 21st century organization, that it's more than a debating forum and—that involves a collective decision by the community of free nations to deploy people all across the world, not just in military situations, like peacekeeping, but in other ways, where it's going to have to be run very well and it's going to have to be able to inspire the confidence of taxpaying citizens not only in the United States but throughout the world.

But I think—I still think the fundamental fact is that the end of the cold war permits the U.N. to live up to its full potential; that we ought to become—we ought to stay involved,

we ought to pay our fair share, and we ought to be very grateful that there are other countries that are willing to spend their money and actually put their people at risk in places where either we wouldn't do it or we don't now have to do it all, we don't have to carry the whole load; and that we ought to be willing to lead in an atmosphere in which we also have to cooperate from time to time, especially when others are making a greater sacrifice and when the problem's in their backyard. And that is—that's the sort of future we ought to want.

And we also ought to be mature enough to recognize that as long as human beings are alive on the Earth, bad things will happen, problems will exist, and that there will never be a complete and easy solution to all the problems in the world. This is not—the world will never be problem-free. But far better this course into the future than either having the nuclear cloud hang over the world, as it did in the cold war, or having the U.S. become an isolationist power, as we did between the wars, and run the risk of other terrible things happening all around the world which would drag us back into another war in the future.

In other words, the course that I advocate is not problem-free because as long as there are people and as long as bad people can get political power in various places, there will always be problems in the world. But it is far better than the alternative, better than what we went through in the cold war and better than having an American isolationism.

Military Base Closings

Ms. Yoachum. Sir, one question away from the U.N., and that is the subject of military bases. One of your political allies, Senator Boxer, has asked you to consider sparing some of the bases in California slated to be closed. At the same time, one of your political opponents, Pete Wilson, plans to attack the administration in a speech this evening in New Hampshire for what he says are artificially low target levels that OMB has given the Department of Defense, which has resulted in a need to close more military bases than necessary to meet the budget targets. I'm wondering first, on the political ally side, if there is any chance that you would spare any of the bases in California, and on the political opponent side, what you would say to that criticism by Governor Wilson?

The President. Well, first of all, let's deal with the base issue. The way the base closings works is—the way the base closing process works is that the commission votes on which bases to close. Then they send it to me in a package, which they will do on July 1st. Then I have three options: I can accept it, in which case it goes to Congress, and unless Congress rejects it, it goes into law; the second option is I can reject it out of hand, in which case there are no base closings; the third option is that I can send it back to the commission with recommended changes. Are you still on?

Ms. Yoachum. Yes, sir.

The President. And I have to tell you that with regard to California, as you know, the McClellan Air Base was not on our list. And it was not on our list, basically—it was not on the Pentagon list for two reasons, both of which I thought were good reasons. One was that California had about 20 percent of the defense investment for the country, but it sustained 40 percent of the base cuts in the first two rounds. Before I became President I thought that was more than enough, and the law provides for economic impact to be considered. The other is that the Pentagon thought that a better way to deal with the problem of over-capacity in what is done at McClellan and down at Kelly Air Force Base in Texas was to shave some of the capacity off all five of the sites around the country and presented a plan to do that. So I'm concerned specifically—I'm concerned about the decision made by the Base Closing Commission there, but I have to be careful about further comment until they send them all to me.

Now secondly, Governor Wilson is just wrong about what he said about defense. Basically, my defense numbers have been about the same as the Republicans of Congress have recommended and what the Pentagon has asked for. And the truth is that the Army people—all the military people but particularly the Army—will tell you that we have brought the force structure down, we have reduced defense in real dollar terms about 40 percent since 1987 and we have reduced the size of the military by about 40 percent, and we've reduced our base structure, oh, about less than half that, considerably less than half that. So most of the military experts will tell you that the reduction of base structure in the United States and throughout the world has lagged far behind the reduction in numbers of people in the military.

And I have tried to be very sensitive since I've been in office to the economic impact of this, to trying to give these bases a chance to do alternative things like help to develop a civilian mission as well as a military mission, and a lot of that work is being done at McClellan and in some other places as well in California and throughout the country.

But it's just not true to say that inadequate budgets have led to the closing of more bases than were necessary. That's just absolutely untrue. We have, in fact, tried to keep more open than the strict, harsh numbers would dictate, given how much the size of our forces have been reduced. So that's just—it's just not true. I'm sure it's good politics for him to say that in New Hampshire or wherever else, but it's simply not true.

Ms. Yoachum. Sir, one last question. That is——

Deputy Press Secretary Ginny Terzano. Susan, we're going to have to stop this because we now have to depart for our next meeting.

Aid to California and 1996 Election

Ms. Yoachum. Okay, I'm sorry. I was just going to ask the President if Governor Wilson really is the candidate he fears most and if there's any chance that McClellan will or may not open?

The President. Well, first of all, let me just say those two questions are totally independent of one another. From the day I became President I worked hard to help California, and I think the people of California know that. We have given aid because of the earthquakes and the fires on more generous terms than had previously been the case. Thirty-three percent of our defense conversion money to develop new technologies from old defense technologies in the commercial sector have gone into California, a disproportionate amount. An enormous amount of investment has been put into the State because I was so concerned that the California economy had been overly hurt by the defense cutbacks before I showed up and by the global recession. I have also done far more than my two Republican predecessors did to try to combat illegal immigration. And so the record is clear and unambiguous and will not be subject to distortion by anybody between now and 1996.

And in terms of who I fear most, the truth is I don't have a clue. I don't know who's going to win. And I have observed this process for 30 years now at close hand, and one thing I'm absolutely convinced of is that you cannot predict who would be the strongest or the weakest candidate or what the dynamics are going to be. People think—and I don't waste any time thinking about it. I haven't given it 5 minutes thought. Because the Republicans have to pick their nominee, and then whomever is picked will be the nominee, and then I'll launch the election. And I also have to be nominated. So

I'm just worrying about doing my job as President, doing the best I can, and we'll see who gets nominated.

Ms. Terzano. Susan, thank you.

Ms. Yoachum. Mr. President, thank you very much.

The President. Goodbye.

NOTE: The President spoke at 11:10 a.m. by telephone while en route to Taylor Field. During the interview, Ms. Yoachum referred to Walter H. Shorenstein, chairman, U.N. 50 National Committee.

Interview with Gary Matthews of ESPN in Pine Bluff
June 24, 1995

Mr. Matthews. Thank you very much, Mr. President. Thank you for coming in. I understand that you're a great amateur baseball fan. Did you have the opportunity to play when you were growing up here in Arkansas?

The President. I did. Everybody did when I was a boy, but I was never as good as these guys are.

Mr. Matthews. Well, I'm sure you, like other fans across the country—and having played major league baseball myself—are happy that the strike is over. It's just so good to see so many fans here in Pine Bluff come out and support amateur sports.

The President. It is. I was delighted when the strike was over. As you know, I did what I could to help bring it to an end, and I think it kind of keeps the spirits of baseball fans up all across America. But the real heart and soul of baseball in our country are people like this, all these fans out here in stands like this all over America today and all these young people that are doing it in this way. They build the

spirit of baseball, and they make it possible for a few people like you to rise to the top and have the career that you had.

Mr. Matthews. Well, thank you. I really appreciate that. I understand that you're the first President to come to Pine Bluff in over 100 years. What took you so long?

The President. I was here a lot before I became President. These people in this county were as good to me as any people in our entire State. They carried me on their shoulders through 12 years as Governor and I owed them a trip back here, and I'm honored to be here today.

Mr. Matthews. Well, thank you, Mr. President. Enjoy the game today.

The President. Thank you.

NOTE: The interview began at 1:21 p.m. at Taylor Field, where the President threw the first pitch at the National Amateur All Star Baseball Tournament. Mr. Matthews was a former Chicago Cubs baseball player.

Remarks at the Dedication Ceremony for the Mahlon Martin Apartments in Little Rock, Arkansas
June 25, 1995

Thank you very much, Mr. Grogan; Mr. Brimberry; my good friend Gary Smith; and all those who helped to make this day possible: Governor Tucker; Congressman Thornton;

Mayor Dailey; Mayor Hays; Judge Villines; our secretary of state, Sharon Priest, and state treasurer, Jimmie Lou Fisher; prosecuting attorney Mark Stoler, who drove me in my first campaign 21 years ago; Senator Walker; to the fine young AmeriCorps volunteers here who are participating in this event.

Let me say a word to all of you but especially to those who have come from Washington with me. This is a hometown event, all right, for my friend Mahlon Martin and his wonderful wife, Cheryl. A lot of us have come down here for it, the Federal Highway Administrator, Rodney Slater, and Mr. Lindsey and others. But this is an event of national significance because this is a concrete, specific example of what I have been trying to say to the American people now for 2½ years, which is, there is nothing wrong with this country that cannot be solved with what is right with this country, that the best thing to do is not to have a big argument about whether the Government or the private sector ought to solve all our problems, because neither can do it and what we need is a partnership.

I want to thank Mr. Lupberger. I see Mr. Brimberry up here with Mr. Smith—all the people who have been involved with all the banks and all the corporations who have helped in this endeavor. But before I go back to the programs, let me just remind you what this is going to do. These facilities are going to do two things. Most importantly, they are going to give homes to working people who don't have enough money to get by. The real heroes in American society today are the people who get up every day, work a full week, raise their kids the best they can, and do not have enough money to get by. And they deserve a place to live, health care for their kids, decent schools, and safe streets. And if we had it, this country would be in better shape.

Now, that is what this is all about. People are going to be able to afford to live in these places who are out there working for somewhere between $15,000 and $18,000 a year and doing their best to raise their kids, give them a chance to be well-educated and safe and drug-free and have a future. And they deserve this kind of chance. And it happened because practical people developed partnerships which made it possible. And that happens from programs, and it happens from people.

The second thing I want to say is more personal. As a longtime citizen of this city, I used to run by this street almost every day of my life, by these two buildings. Every day, when laziness didn't get the better of me, I would run by these two buildings, and I would think how beautiful they were and what a shame it was that they weren't being used in a productive way.

These buildings will give an example, a sense of pride, a sense of hope, a sense of possibility to other people. They will make people more proud. They will change the way people think about this neighborhood, this downtown area, and this city. And I want all the people who live here to make sure you take good care of them and to make people proud of them and to prove that this effort was worth doing.

I thank you for the mention of the low-income housing tax credit. It was part of the economic development plan in 1993. The other thing we did in 1993 is to cut the income taxes of all the people who will live in this building who have children, because we don't believe people who work 40 hours a week and have kids in their homes should bring those children up in poverty. If you work full-time, your children ought to be able to live above the poverty line.

We've done other things that make this partnership more possible. We've continued the community development block grants, and the city put about 20 percent of the money into this project because of the community development block grants. It's threatened today in Washington. I hope we can save it. We can cut a lot of spending back, but we're going to have to invest some money back in our people and their future.

We also tried to improve the Community Reinvestment Act to give banks better incentives and better support in reinvesting in the community. And we tried to establish a whole national network of community development banks like the Elk Horn Bank in Arkadelphia which the First Lady and Mahlon and so many others, including the Rockefeller Foundation before Mahlon went there, had to do with establishing. We thank you for making Arkansas a national model in that, and we're trying to do that all around the country. We created over 100 empowerment zones and enterprise communities, of which Little Rock is one, to give people incentives for these kind of partnerships.

Now, most voters can never remember the acronym of LISC, and if you told them what a local initiative support corporation was they wouldn't understand what that is either. But most Americans have enough common sense to know that we don't need to get into an ideological debate and you don't have to be a genius to understand that if people are working for a living and trying to raise their children, they ought to have a decent place to live. And the best way to do it is not to have a huge ideological debate in Washington about whether the Government ought to do it or the private sector ought to do it. The best way to do it is to roll up your sleeves, have a practical partnership, and empower people at the grassroots level to make the most of their own lives.

But I also want to say it requires people. And this is the last point I will make in this brief address on a hot day. I'm not sure I would be President today if it weren't for Mahlon Martin. I remember once when I went to Montreal to give a speech to the international convention of city managers, a fellow from another State— Michigan, I think—came up to me and said, "You know, Mahlon Martin when he was city manager of Little Rock was one of the 10 best city managers in the entire United States of America." Mahlon Martin once wanted to be a pro baseball player. He wound up going to Philander Smith and deferring that dream, and instead he spent his life helping the rest of us live out our dreams. In a way, I know he misses baseball and I know he was glad when the strike was settled, but I think that there are very few baseball players which will have helped as many people live out their dreams as Mahlon Martin has helped in our State, in this community.

In 1983, when I persuaded him to become head of the department of finance and administration, we took office with the State broke, in an illegal financial condition. And the first thing that we had to do to make Mahlon and the Governor immensely popular was to cut spending one percent across the board, for everything, just to come into compliance with the State law. It was a wonderful way to begin an administration. [*Laughter*]

Then a couple of years later, Governor, in one budget period, Mahlon had to cut spending in one of our budget cycles six times during the recession of the eighties, six times cutting back on things that we desperately wanted to spend more money on, including education.

I used to tell everybody that when I was Governor, Mahlon Martin was the government, and I made the speeches. I never saw a fellow who could tell people no and make them like it better than he did. [*Laughter*] And I think it's because they always knew he wanted to say yes and that he was trying to preserve the financial integrity of the State and the management integrity of the State in ways that would command the confidence of the taxpayers of Arkansas and make it possible for us to do as much for people in their lives as we possibly could.

And when he left the administration and went on to run the Rockefeller Foundation, I think he was actually doing what he was really put on this Earth to do, which was to find new and different and innovative ways for ordinary people to live extraordinary lives. And I can tell you that I have now served with thousands and thousands of remarkable people all across this country. I have had the privilege of knowing more exceptional Americans than almost anyone of my time, solely because of my position. I have never met a finer American or a more gifted public servant than the person we honor today, our friend Mahlon Martin.

This is a plaque presented to Mahlon Martin in grateful appreciation for his 2 years of outstanding service and dedication to the Local Initiative Support Corporation that provided these opportunities that we celebrate today. The most important thing on the plaque is a quote that could have been about Mahlon Martin from Margaret Meade: "Never doubt that a small group of thoughtful, committed citizens can change the world. Indeed, it's the only thing that ever has."

NOTE: The President spoke at 10:25 a.m. at the Mahlon Martin Apartments. In his remarks, he referred to Paul Grogan, president, Local Initiative Support Corp. (LISC); Ron Brimberry, president, Downtown Little Rock Community Development Corp.; Gary Smith, executive vice president, Boatman's Bank; Gov. Jim Guy Tucker of Arkansas; Mayor Jim Dailey of Little Rock, AR; Mayor Patrick Henry Hays of North Little Rock, AR; Floyd G. (Buddy) Villines, Pulaski County judge; and Edwin Lupberger, chairman and chief executive officer, Entergy.

Statement on the Death of Warren Burger
June 25, 1995

Hillary and I are deeply saddened to learn of Justice Burger's passing. Today the Nation mourns the loss of a great public servant.

Justice Burger was a strong, powerful, and visionary Chief Justice who opened the doors of opportunity. As Chief Justice, he was concerned with the administration of the Court, serving with enthusiasm and always making sure it was above reproach.

He also presided over the most important anniversary of our Nation by serving as Chair of the Bicentennial Commission on the Constitution.

His expansive view of the Constitution and his tireless service will leave a lasting imprint on the Court and our Nation. Our prayers are with his family and friends during this time.

Remarks on the 50th Anniversary of the United Nations Charter in San Francisco, California
June 26, 1995

Thank you very much. Secretary Christopher, Mr. Secretary-General, Ambassador Albright, Bishop Tutu. My good friend Maya Angelou, thank you for your magnificent poem. Delegates to the Charter Conference, distinguished members of the diplomatic corps, the President of Poland, Members of Congress, honored guests, Mayor Jordan, Mr. Shorenstein, people of San Francisco, and friends of the United Nations: The 800 delegates from 50 nations who came here 50 years ago to lift the world from the ashes of war and bring life to the dreams of peacemakers included both giants of diplomacy and untested leaders of infant nations. They were separated by tradition, race, and language, sharing only a vision of a better, safer future. On this day 50 years ago, the dream President Roosevelt did not live to see of a democratic organization of the world was launched.

The charter the delegates signed reflected the harsh lessons of their experience, the experience of the thirties in which the world watched and reacted too slowly to fascist aggression, bringing millions sacrificed on the battlefields and millions more murdered in the death chambers. Those who had gone through this and the Second World War knew that celebrating victory was not enough, that merely punishing the enemy was self-defeating, that instead the world needed an effective and permanent system to promote peace and freedom for everyone.

Some of those who worked at that historic conference are still here today, including our own Senator Claiborne Pell, who to this very day, every day, carries a copy of the U.N. Charter in his pocket. I would last like to ask all of the delegates to the original conference who are here today to rise and be recognized. Would you please stand? [*Applause*]

San Francisco gave the world renewed confidence and hope for the future. On that day President Truman said, "This is proof that nations, like men, can state their differences, can face them, and then can find common ground on which to stand." Five decades later, we see how very much the world has changed. The cold war has given way to freedom and cooperation. On this very day, a Russian spacecraft and an American spacecraft are preparing to link in orbit some 240 miles above the Earth. From Jericho to Belfast, ancient enemies are searching together for peace. On every continent, nations are struggling to embrace democracy, freedom, and prosperity. New technologies move people and ideas around the world, creating vast new reservoirs of opportunity.

Yet we know that these new forces of integration also carry within them the seeds of disintegration and destruction. New technologies and greater openness make all our borders more vulnerable to terrorists, to dangerous weapons, to drug traffickers. Newly independent nations offer ripe targets for international criminals and nuclear smugglers. Fluid capital markets make it easier for nations to build up their economies but also make it much easier for one nation's troubles first to be exaggerated, then to spread to other nations.

Today, to be sure, we face no Hitler, no Stalin, but we do have enemies, enemies who share their contempt for human life and human dignity and the rule of law, enemies who put lethal technology to lethal use, who seek personal gains in age-old conflicts and new divisions.

Our generation's enemies are the terrorists and their outlaw nation sponsors, people who kill children or turn them into orphans, people who target innocent people in order to prevent peace, people who attack peacemakers, as our friend President Mubarak was attacked just a few hours ago, people who in the name of nationalism slaughter those of different faiths or tribes and drive their survivors from their own homelands. Their reach is increased by technology. Their communication is abetted by global media. Their actions reveal the age-old lack of conscience, scruples, and morality which have characterized the forces of destruction throughout history.

Today, the threat to our security is not in an enemy silo but in the briefcase or the car bomb of a terrorist. Our enemies are also international criminals and drug traffickers who threaten the stability of new democracies and the future of our children. Our enemies are the forces of natural destruction, encroaching deserts that threaten the Earth's balance, famines that test the human spirit, deadly new diseases that endanger whole societies.

So, my friends, in this increasingly interdependent world, we have more common opportunities and more common enemies than ever before. It is, therefore, in our interest to face them together as partners, sharing the burdens and costs and increasing our chances of success.

Just months before his death, President Roosevelt said, "We have learned that we cannot live alone at peace, that our own well-being is dependent on the well-being of other nations far away." Today, more than ever, those words ring true. Yet some here in our own country, where the United Nations was founded, dismissed Roosevelt's wisdom. Some of them acknowledge that the United States must play a strong role overseas but refuse to supply the nonmilitary resources our Nation needs to carry

on its responsibilities. Others believe that outside our border America should only act alone.

Well, of course the United States must be prepared to act alone when necessary, but we dare not ignore the benefits that coalitions bring to this Nation. We dare not reject decades of bipartisan wisdom. We dare not reject decades of bipartisan support for international cooperation. Those who would do so, these new isolationists, dismiss 50 years of hard evidence.

In those years we've seen the United Nations compile a remarkable record of progress that advances our Nation's interest and, indeed, the interest of people everywhere. From President Truman in Korea to President Bush in the Persian Gulf, America has built United Nations military coalitions to contain aggressors. U.N. forces also often pick up where United States troops have taken the lead.

As the Secretary of State said, we saw it just yesterday, when Haiti held parliamentary and local elections with the help of U.N. personnel. We saw the U.N. work in partnership with the United States and the people of Haiti, as they labor to create a democracy. And they have now been given a second chance to renew that promise.

On every continent, the United Nations has played a vital role in making people more free and more secure. For decades, the U.N. fought to isolate South Africa, as that regime perpetuated apartheid. Last year, under the watchful eyes of U.N. observers, millions of South Africans who had been disenfranchised for life cast their first votes for freedom.

In Namibia, Mozambique, and soon we hope in Angola, the United Nations is helping people to bury decades of civil strife and turn their energies into building new democratic nations. In Cambodia, where a brutal regime left more than one million dead in the killing fields, the U.N. helped hundreds of thousands of refugees return to their native land and stood watch over democratic elections that brought 90 percent of the people to the polls. In El Salvador, the U.N. brokered an end to 12 years of bloody civil war and stayed on to help reform the army, bring justice to the citizens, and open the doors of democracy.

From the Persian Gulf to the Caribbean, U.N. economic and political sanctions have proved to be a valuable means short of military action to isolate regimes and to make aggressors and terrorists pay at least a price for their actions:

in Iraq, to help stop that nation from developing weapons of mass destruction or threatening its neighbors again; in the Balkans, to isolate aggressors; in North Africa, to pressure Libya to turn over for trial those indicted in the bombing of Pan Am flight 103.

The record of the United Nations includes a proud battle for child survival and against human suffering and disease of all kinds. Every year, UNICEF oral vaccines save the lives of 3 million children. Last year alone the World Food Program, using the contributions of many governments including our own, fed 57 million hungry people. The World Health Organization has eliminated smallpox from the face of the Earth and is making great strides in its campaign to eliminate polio by the year 2000. It has helped to contain fatal diseases like the Ebola virus that could have threatened an entire continent.

To millions around the world, the United Nations is not what we see on our news programs at night. Instead it's the meal that keeps a child from going to bed hungry, the knowledge that helps a farmer coax strong crops from hard land, the shelter that keeps a family together when they're displaced by war or natural disasters.

In the last 50 years, these remarkable stories have been too obscured and the capacity of the United Nations to act too limited by the cold war. As colonial rule broke down, differences between developing and industrialized nations and regional rivalries added new tensions to the United Nations so that too often there was too much invective and too little debate in the General Assembly.

But now the end of the cold war, the strong trend toward democratic ideals among all nations, the emergence of so many problems that can best be met by collective action, all these things enable the United Nations at this 50-year point finally to fulfill the promise of its founders.

But if we want the U.N. to do so, we must face the fact that for all its successes and all its possibilities, it does not work as well as it should. The United Nations must be reformed. In this age of relentless change, successful governments and corporations are constantly reducing their bureaucracies, setting clearer priorities, focusing on targeted results. In the United States we have eliminated hundreds of programs, thousands of regulations. We're reducing our Government to its smallest size since President Kennedy served here, while increasing our efforts in areas most critical to our future. The U.N. must take similar steps.

Over the years it has grown too bloated, too often encouraging duplication, and spending resources on meetings rather than results. As its board of directors, all of us, we, the member states, must create a U.N. that is more flexible, that operates more rapidly, that wastes less and produces more, and most importantly, that inspires confidence among our governments and our people. In the last few years we have seen some good reforms: a new oversight office to hold down costs, a new system to review personnel, a start toward modernization and privatization. But we must do more.

The United Nations supports the proposal of the President of the General Assembly, Mr. Essy, who spoke so eloquently here earlier this morning, to prepare a blueprint for renewing the U.N. and to approve it before the 50th General Assembly finishes its work next fall.

We must consider major structural changes. The United Nations simply does not need a separate agency with its own acronym, stationery, and bureaucracy for every problem. The new U.N. must peel off what doesn't work and get behind what will.

We must also realize, in particular, the limits to peacekeeping and not ask the Blue Helmets to undertake missions they cannot be expected to handle. Peacekeeping can only succeed when the parties to a conflict understand they cannot profit from war. We have too often asked our peacekeepers to work miracles while denying them the military and political support required and the modern command-and-control systems they need to do their job as safely and effectively as possible. Today's U.N. must be ready to handle tomorrow's challenges. Those of us who most respect the U.N. must lead the charge of reform.

Not all the critics of today's United Nations are isolationists. Many are supporters who gladly would pay for the U.N.'s essential work if they were convinced their money was being well-spent. But I pledge to all of you, as we work together to improve the United Nations, I will continue to work to see that the United States takes the lead in paying its fair share of our common load.

Meanwhile, we must all remember that the United Nations is a reflection of the world it represents. Therefore, it will remain far from perfect. It will not be able to solve all problems. But even those it cannot solve, it may well be able to limit in terms of the scope and reach of the problem, and it may well be able to limit the loss of human life until the time for solution comes.

So just as withdrawing from the world is impossible, turning our backs on the U.N. is no solution. It would be shortsighted and self-destructive. It would strengthen the forces of global disintegration. It would threaten the security, the interest, and the values of the American people. So I say especially to the opponents of the United Nations here in the United States, turning our back on the U.N. and going it alone will lead to far more economic, political, and military burdens on our people in the future and would ignore the lessons of our own history.

Instead, on this 50th anniversary of the charter signing, let us renew our vow to live together as good neighbors. And let us agree on a new United Nations agenda to increase confidence and ensure support for the United Nations, and to advance peace and prosperity for the next 50 years.

First and foremost, the U.N. must strengthen its efforts to isolate states and people who traffic in terror and support those who continue to take risks for peace in the face of violence. The bombing in Oklahoma City, the deadly gas attack in Tokyo, the struggles to establish peace in the Middle East and in Northern Ireland, all of these things remind us that we must stand against terror and support those who move away from it. Recent discoveries of laboratories working to produce biological weapons for terrorists demonstrate the dangerous link between terrorism and the weapons of mass destruction.

In 1937, President Roosevelt called for a quarantine against aggressions, to keep the infection of fascism from seeping into the bloodstream of humanity. Today, we should quarantine the terrorists, the terrorist groups, and the nations that support terrorism. Where nations and groups honestly seek to reform, to change, to move away from the killing of innocents, we should support them. But when they are unrepentant in the delivery of death, we should stand tall against them. My friends, there is no easy way around the hard question: If nations and groups are not willing to move away from the delivery of death, we should put aside short-term profits for the people in our countries to stop, stop, stop their conduct.

Second, the U.N. must continue our efforts to stem the proliferation of weapons of mass destruction. There are some things nations can do on their own. The U.S. and Russia today are destroying our nuclear arsenals rapidly, but the U.N. must also play a role. We were honored to help secure an indefinite extension of the Nuclear Non-Proliferation Treaty under U.N. auspices. We rely on U.N. agencies to monitor nations bent on acquiring nuclear capabilities. We must work together on the Chemical Weapons Convention. We must strengthen our common efforts to fight biological weapons. We must do everything we can to limit the spread of fissile materials. We must work on conventional weapons like the land mines that are the curse of children the world over. And we must complete a comprehensive nuclear test ban treaty.

Third, we must support through the United Nations the fight against manmade and natural forces of disintegration, from crime syndicates and drug cartels to new diseases and disappearing forests. These enemies are elusive; they cross borders at will. Nations can and must oppose them alone. But we know, and the Cairo conference reaffirmed, that the most effective opposition requires strong international cooperation and mutual support.

Fourth, we must reaffirm our commitment to strengthen U.N. peacekeeping as an important tool for deterring, containing, and ending violent conflict. The U.N. can never be an absolute guarantor of peace, but it can reduce human suffering and advance the odds of peace.

Fifth—you may clap for that. [*Applause*] Fifth, we must continue what is too often the least noticed of the U.N.'s missions, its unmatched efforts on the frontlines of the battle for child survival and against disease and human suffering.

And finally, let us vow to make the United Nations an increasing strong voice for the protection of fundamental human dignity and human rights. After all, they were at the core of the founding of this great organization.

Today we honor the men and women who gave shape to the United Nations. We celebrate 50 years of achievement. We commit ourselves to real reforms. We reject the siren song of the new isolationists. We set a clear agenda worthy of the vision of our founders. The measure of our generation will be whether we give up because we cannot achieve a perfect world or strive on to build a better world.

Fifty years ago today, President Truman reminded the delegates that history had not ended with Hitler's defeat. He said, it is easier to remove tyrants and destroy concentration camps than it is to kill the ideas which give them birth. Victory on the battlefield was essential, but it is not good enough for a lasting, good peace.

Today we know that history has not ended with the cold war. We know, and we have learned from painful evidence, that as long as there are people on the face of the Earth, imperfection and evil will be a part of human nature; there will be killing, cruelty, self-destructive abuse of our natural environment, denial of the problems that face us all. But we also know that here today, in this historic chamber, the challenge of building a good and lasting peace is in our hands and success is within our reach.

Let us not forget that each child saved, each refugee housed, each disease prevented, each barrier to justice brought down, each sword turned into a plowshare, brings us closer to the vision of our founders, closer to peace, closer to freedom, closer to dignity.

So my fellow citizens of the world, let us not lose heart. Let us gain renewed strength and energy and vigor from the progress which has been made and the opportunities which are plainly before us. Let us say no to isolation; yes to reform; yes to a brave, ambitious new agenda; most of all, yes to the dream of the United Nations.

Thank you.

NOTE: The President spoke at 11:17 a.m. in the War Memorial Opera House. In his remarks, he referred to United Nations Secretary-General Boutros Boutros-Ghali; Bishop Desmond Tutu of South Africa; poet Maya Angelou; President Lech Walesa of Poland; Mayor Frank Jordan of San Francisco; Walter H. Shorenstein, chairman, U.N. 50 National Committee; and President Hosni Mubarak of Egypt.

Exchange With Reporters Prior to Discussions With United Nations Secretary-General Boutros Boutros-Ghali in San Francisco
June 26, 1995

Q. Mr. Secretary-General, will you accept the President's suggestions for reforms of the United Nations?

Secretary-General Boutros-Ghali. Yes, certainly.

Q. Do you think he has a point?

Secretary-General Boutros-Ghali. Yes.

Q. Mr. President, you referred to the new isolationists in your speech. Could you be more specific about who you might mean?

President Clinton. What I've been saying for months now. I think you all know what I mean.

Q. Could you be specific, name who exactly you mean?

Q. Mr. President—*[inaudible]*—the RTC report has vindicated you and the First Lady in Whitewater?

The President. No, I haven't.

NOTE: The exchange began at 12:03 p.m. in the Herbst Auditorium at the War Memorial Veterans Building. A tape was not available for verification of the content of this exchange.

Statement on the Attempted Assassination of President Hosni Mubarak of Egypt
June 26, 1995

On behalf of the American people, I wish to express my outrage at the attempt made today by terrorists to assassinate President Mubarak of Egypt. I am relieved that President Mubarak was not harmed and has now returned safely to Cairo.

The United States stands by Egypt—our partner for peace and prosperity in the Middle East and around the world—at this moment. The enemies of peace will not be allowed to thwart the peaceful hopes of the peoples of the region, and the efforts of President Mubarak and the peace makers to make those hopes a reality.

Statement on the Supreme Court Decision on the Student Athlete Drug Testing Case
June 26, 1995

Today's decision by the Supreme Court in the *Vernonia School District* v. *Acton* case sends exactly the right message to parents and students: drug use will not be tolerated in our schools. The decision reinforces the point that young people should not use drugs.

I applaud the decision of the Supreme Court which upholds the right of the Vernonia (Oregon) School District to conduct random drug testing of school athletes as one effort by local school authorities to reduce drug use among students.

The Solicitor General argued strongly in support of the school district's position. My administration's support for the right of school officials to properly test their high school athletes is part of our overall strategy to make schools places where young people can be safe and drug-free. I believe that to be a good student or a good athlete a student cannot use drugs. Drug use at schools will not and should not be tolerated.

Letter to Congressional Leaders Transmitting a Report on Cyprus
June 26, 1995

Dear Mr. Speaker: (Dear Mr. Chairman:)

In accordance with Public Law 95–384 (22 U.S.C. 2373(c)), I submit to you this report on progress toward a negotiated settlement of the Cyprus question. The previous report covered progress through March 31, 1995. The current report covers April 1, 1995 through May 31, 1995.

The central event of this period was the May 21–23 exploratory talks between Greek Cypriots and Turkish Cypriots. These talks were held in London and facilitated by Presidential Emissary Beattie and Special Cyprus Coordinator Wil-

liams. The talks laid the groundwork for a second visit to the island by Mr. Beattie to explore possible areas of agreement between Greek-Cypriot leader Clerides and Turkish-Cypriot leader Denktash.

Sincerely,

WILLIAM J. CLINTON

NOTE: Identical letters were sent to Newt Gingrich, Speaker of the House of Representatives, and Jesse Helms, chairman, Senate Committee on Foreign Relations.

Message to the Senate Transmitting the Mongolia-United States Investment Treaty
June 26, 1995

To the Senate of the United States:

With a view to receiving the advice and consent of the Senate to ratification, I transmit herewith the Treaty Between the United States of America and Mongolia Concerning the Encouragement and Reciprocal Protection of Investment, with Annex and Protocol, signed at Washington on October 6, 1994. Also transmitted for the information of the Senate is the report of the Department of State with respect to the Treaty, with Annex and Protocol.

The bilateral investment Treaty (BIT) with Mongolia will protect U.S. investors and assist Mongolia in its efforts to develop its economy by creating conditions more favorable for U.S. private investment and thus strengthening the development of the private sector.

The Treaty is fully consistent with U.S. policy toward international and domestic investment. A specific tenet of U.S. policy, reflected in this Treaty, is that U.S. investment abroad and foreign investment in the United States should receive national treatment. Under this Treaty, the Parties also agree to international law standards for expropriation and compensation for expropriation; free transfer of funds associated with investments; freedom of investments from performance requirements; fair, equitable, and most-favored-nation treatment; and the investor's or investment's freedom to choose to resolve disputes with the host government through international arbitration.

I recommend that the Senate consider this Treaty as soon as possible, and give its advice and consent to ratification of the Treaty, with Annex and Protocol, at an early date.

WILLIAM J. CLINTON

The White House,
June 26, 1995.

Remarks to the Cuban-American Community
June 27, 1995

I want to speak with you today about my administration's plans to press forward with our efforts to promote a peaceful transition to democracy in Cuba. A little more than a month ago, I took steps to stop the dangerous and illegal flow of Cubans attempting to enter the United States by sea. I want to report to you on the results of these steps and why I believe it was the right thing to do. But first, let me be clear: our commitment to a better future for the Cuban people remains as strong as ever.

Throughout our hemisphere, a powerful wave of democracy is bringing new respect for human rights, free elections, and free markets. Thirty-four of the thirty-five countries in this region have embraced democratic change. Only one nation resists this trend, Cuba.

Cuba's system is at a dead end politically, economically, and spiritually. The Castro regime denies Cubans their most basic rights. They cannot speak freely. They cannot organize to protest. They cannot choose their own leaders. At the same time, economic collapse threatens the well-being of every man, woman, and child in Cuba.

The pressure of our embargo and the withdrawal of Soviet support have forced Cuba to adopt some economic measures of reform in the last 2 years. We haven't seen that before. But economic change remains slow, stubborn, and painfully inadequate. The denial of basic rights and opportunities has driven tens of thousands of Cubans to desperation.

In the summer of 1994, thousands took to treacherous waters in unseaworthy rafts, seeking to reach our shores; an undetermined number actually lost their lives. In response, I ordered Cubans rescued at sea to be taken to safe haven at our naval base at Guantanamo and, for a time, in Panama. But this could not be a long-term solution. Last fall, I ordered that the young, the old, and the infirm and their imme-

953

diate families be admitted to our country. Thousands entered the United States in this way. Still, that left tens of thousands of young men at Guantanamo who were becoming increasingly frustrated and desperate. Senior United States military officials warned me that unrest and violence this summer were likely, threatening both those in the camps and our own dedicated soldiers.

But to admit those remaining in Guantanamo without doing something to deter new rafters risked unleashing a new, massive exodus of Cubans, many of whom would perish seeking to reach the United States. To prevent that situation and to settle the migration issue, I took action. The Cuban rafters who were brought to Guantanamo last summer will be admitted to the United States, except those found to be inadmissible under U.S. law. Those Cubans rescued at sea while illegally trying to enter the United States will be taken back to Cuba. Under our generous program of legal immigration, 20,000 Cubans from Cuba will be allowed to enter and reside in the United States every year from now on. And we'll continue to provide assistance to Florida to help resettle those Cuban migrants.

I know that many of you have questions about aspects of this policy. Yet, the simple truth is that there is no realistic alternative. We simply cannot admit all Cubans who seek to come here. We cannot let people risk their lives on open seas in unseaworthy rafts. And we cannot sentence thousands of young men to live in limbo at Guantanamo.

Our new policy is working. Since its beginning on May 2d, few Cubans have been intercepted at sea. We cannot know how many lives have been saved by the deterrent effect of this policy. But consider this: In May of last year, some 700 Cubans were picked up and many others were lost at sea. Our new policy can help to avoid uncontrolled migration, and it's already saving lives.

At the same time, we are making every effort to protect those at risk in Cuba. We will not return rafters who we believe would suffer reprisals back in Cuba. The U.S. Interests Section in Havana is carefully monitoring those sent home, visiting each of them individually to ensure they are not harassed. And thanks to our legal migration programs, over 15,000 Cubans have been approved to enter the United States since September 1994 as immigrants, parolees,

and refugees. That is 3 times more than in any previous year.

In short, the actions we took address the serious humanitarian problem at Guantanamo, deter illegal and unsafe migration, protect political refugees, and expand opportunities for legal admission from Cuba. They serve our national interests.

Regularizing Cuban migration also helps our efforts to promote a peaceful transition to democracy on the island. For too long, Castro has used the threat of uncontrolled migration to distract us from this fundamental objective. With the steps I have taken, we are now able to devote ourselves fully to our real, long-term goal.

Our policy is rooted in the Cuban Democracy Act, which I endorsed some 3 years ago and which subsequently passed the Congress with bipartisan support. Consistent with the act, the United States will maintain the economic embargo against the Cuban regime. This is an important way to promote change in Cuba, and it will remain in place until we see far-reaching political and economic reform. As provided in the act, if Cuba takes steps in the direction of meaningful change, we are also prepared to respond with our own carefully calibrated responses.

The Cuban Democracy Act also calls on us to support the Cuban people in their struggle for democracy and economic well-being. We believe that reaching out today will nurture and strengthen the fledgling civil society that will be the backbone of tomorrow's democratic Cuba. We will continue to help Cuba's democratic opposition and the churches, human rights organizations, and others seeking to exercise the political and economic rights that should belong to all Cubans.

Throughout the Americas, dictatorships have given way to democracy. They are following the path of reconciliation and forgiveness preached by Cuba's first Cardinal, Jaime Ortega, during his recent visit here to the United States. Cuba will follow this course of its neighbors. With the support of the American people and their representatives in Congress, we can move forward toward our common goal of a peaceful transition to democracy in Cuba. I hope that it will be my privilege as President to welcome a free Cuba back into the community of democratic nations.

NOTE: The President's remarks were videotaped at noon on June 7 in the Oval Office at the White House for later broadcast, and they were released by the Office of the Press Secretary on June 27.

Remarks at the Opening Session of the Pacific Rim Economic Conference in Portland, Oregon
June 27, 1995

Thank you very much. Mayor Katz, Governor Kitzhaber; I want to thank the people of Portland who have done so much to make us feel at home here; Secretary Peña for cosponsoring the conference; all the members of the Cabinet and the administration who get to do their jobs in Portland, in the real world today instead of back in Washington; President Ramaley; Congresswoman Furse; Governor Lowry. Let me also thank the Coast Guard for all the work that they have done to help us succeed here.

Let me begin by saying I wanted some heated exchanges here today, but I have already overdone it. [*Laughter*]. This is a working conference. We will not be offended if you take your jackets off, roll your sleeves up. It would suit me if the gentlemen here present want to take your ties off. I won't be offended. I think you better stop there. [*Laughter*]

I have really looked forward to this for quite some time. I had a wonderful experience when we came to Portland shortly after I became President for the timber conference. And a lot of ideas were generated out of that which clearly affected the work of our administration in terms of getting an aid package through Congress to help to pay for economic conversion in disadvantaged communities and a lot of other very specific things.

When I was Governor, I used to go out across my State secure in the knowledge that even in every State there is no such thing as a State economy, that within each State the regions are dramatically different in their possibilities and their problems. And I do not believe that our National Government can have a sound economic policy without continuing to establish partnerships and to listen to people who live in various regions of the United States. And that's why we're doing this series of conferences today.

I also think that, as all of you know, as a former Governor, that a lot of the best ideas in the country are not in Washington and don't get there unless you go out and find them. In preparation for this conference, I was given a remarkable biography of the remarkable Oregon Governor Tom McCall, that was written by a man that works for the Oregonian, Brent Walth, and now, according to—I know that no one in the press ever gets it wrong, so I'm sure this book was right in every respect. [*Laughter*] The most impressive thing about the book to me, maybe because of my own experiences with my own mother, was that once Governor McCall's mother was having trouble getting a hold of him, so she called the White House because she heard that the White House could get in touch with anybody, and she actually got President Johnson on the phone and said that she needed to talk to her son. And President Johnson called the Governor and told him to call his mother. [*Laughter*]

Now, that is the kind of full-service Federal Government I have sought to bring to the American people. [*Laughter*] And that is the tradition we are trying to build on.

As the Vice President said, we are here to, first of all review the facts about the region's economy, the good things and the bad things, the barriers to progress, and the possibilities. We are here to determine the impact of the present policies of our administration on that and to get as many new, clear, specific suggestions as possible for where we should go together.

I think it is important to do these things because too often the further you get away from the grassroots in America, the more theoretical and the less practical the debates become. And that is especially true now because we're at an historic watershed period in American history. We won the cold war, but we no longer have a common enemy and a common way of organizing ourselves and thinking about how we should relate to the rest of the world.

So yesterday I went to San Francisco to the 50th anniversary of the United Nations, to try to talk about why we, more than ever, should be working with other countries in partnerships to advance our values and our interests and our security.

And today I say to you that a lot of our economy was organized around our responsibilities in the cold war. And today we know it has to be organized around the realities of a global economy, the information age, and the fact that for many decades, before the end of the cold war, we financed our continuing leadership in that war and our needs at home with massive deficits, which lowered savings rates, lowered investment rates, and put us into some very difficult circumstances, which mean today that we're in the second decade in which most Americans are working a longer work week than they were 20 years ago for about the same or lower wages and at which all these wonderful changes that we find thrilling and exciting, the global society, the rapid movement of money and information, the constant downsizing of big organizations, but the explosion of new ones—because even though we have downsizing of big corporations, in '93 and '94 both we set new records for the incorporation of new businesses—all these things in the aggregate are quite exciting. But if you're just someone caught up in a very new world, who has to worry about paying a mortgage and educating your children and taking care of your parents' health care, they can be very threatening as well.

And over and over and over again we hear all over the country people say, "Well, I know these numbers look good, I know we've got almost 7 million new jobs, but I'm still worried about losing mine. It may be that the economy is growing, but I haven't gotten a raise. I know we've got the best health care in the world, but I lost my coverage at my job last year. I know we have to grow the economy, but how can we do it and preserve our precious environmental heritage so that America as we know it will still be around for our grandchildren?"

These questions are coming at us. They also come from the other way. They say, "Well, we're caught in a bind; I know we have to preserve the economy, but I've got to feed my family tomorrow. I know that we have to advance the environment and I'm worried about other people's economic interests, but what about mine?"

In other words, this is an interesting time in which the clear, simple, monolithic way we used to look at the world, the cold war abroad, constant economic progress at home, steady, slow, certain resolution of our social difficulties, all those things are kind of out the window. And there are more possibilities than ever before, but it's pretty confusing for folks out there. And a lot of people are genuinely scared and worried. And what we have to do is to chart a new course based on our fundamental values.

I personally believe that the debate that has gone on in Washington is understandable, given the national confusion and frustration, but it's way too extreme. We're debating things that I thought were resolved 70 years ago. To me, the issue is not, would we be better off if the Government solved all our problems? Nobody believes that can be done anymore. But it is certainly not, wouldn't we be better off if the Government did nothing but national defense, cut taxes, and balance the budget tomorrow without regard to consequences?

The clear thing it seems to me is we ought to be asking ourselves, how do we have to change our Government to get the kind of policies that advance the American dream, that grow the middle class, shrink the under class, enhance our security and our quality of life, deal with the issues of the day in practical fashion? What kind of partnerships do we need?

That's the way I tend to look at the world, probably because I was a Governor before I became President. But it's also the thing I think that will work. You heard what the Vice President said: In the last 2 years we have cut the deficit by a trillion dollars over 7 years; we have seen a lot of new jobs. Even in some rural counties in Oregon, the unemployment rate has gone down, notwithstanding the difficulties caused by the timber issues.

We have tried to expand trade in unprecedented ways. We have had more than 80 new trade agreements, the big ones like NAFTA and GATT and others on specific things that permit us to sell everything from Washington apples to California rice to software and cellular telephones in Japan for the first time.

And I believe it is clear to everybody that what we have to focus on is reducing the deficit, expanding trade but also increasing the capacity of the American people to make the most of their own lives and enhancing our own security. So that's why I have also focused on the need to invest more in education, training, and research and the need to dramatically improve the ability of the Government to do its job, because if we're going to cut back and cut back and cut back it becomes even more important what we do spend money on.

That's why we try to support things like the Oregon initiative. That's why we've given now 29 States permission to get out from under Federal rules to try their own hand at reforming the welfare system, to move people from welfare to work. That's why we abolished another 16,000 governmental regulations the other day. And these are things that are profoundly important to all of you.

As we look ahead, I just want to say a couple of things and then I want to hear from the panel. We're going to have a big debate this year about what should be done about our budget deficit. I believe it's important to balance the budget. I believe it's important to have a clear path to get there. And I think it's important for two reasons. One is we never had a permanent structural deficit in the United States until 1981. Now, we ran a deficit all during the 1970's because of the oil price problems and because we had something called stagflation. And those of you who were of age in those years understand what happened to our economy. So conventional economic theory called for us to try to keep stimulating the economy a little bit in those years.

But we never had a big, permanent deficit until 1981, when there was a sort of unspoken agreement between the major party leaders in Washington. The Republicans didn't want to raise taxes to get rid of the deficit and the Democrats didn't want to cut too much spending, and besides that, both of them knew that economic growth in America fueled by investment and productivity had reached a very low level and the only way to keep the economy going was through a big deficit. But we have paid a terrible price for it.

Meanwhile, the private sector is much more productive now, much more competitive. And we cannot afford to continue to run our economic business with a permanent deficit, in my opinion. On the other hand, there is a right way and a wrong way to do it. An economic study recently done by the Wharton School of Business in Pennsylvania pointed out that if we reduce the deficit too fast and specifically analyze the Senate proposal, that it could bring

on a recession, increase unemployment to 8.6 percent, and basically undermine what we want to do.

That's why I proposed balancing the budget over 10 years, doing it in a way that increases investment in education, medical research, and technology, not reduces it; cuts everything else in the nondefense area about 20 percent across the board; and reduces Medicare and Medicaid inflation more moderately than the Republican proposals, so that we don't have to cut services primarily to elderly people who don't have enough money to live on as it is.

In order to get to my budget, you have to have a much smaller tax cut; focus it on education, childrearing, and the middle class; and take 10 years instead of 7. But this is the sort of debate I think we ought to be having, in other words, not some big theoretical debate about what's good and evil in some theory but how is this going to affect the American people?

Same thing—I'll just give you one other example about the environment. We'll have a chance to talk about this today. It seems to me what we ought to be focused on here and what you all—most of you at least—said you wanted when I came out here to the forest conference is, how can we guarantee long-term sustainable development that preserves the natural resources, that makes people want to live here in the first place, but enables the maximum number of people to make a decent living in the most diverse and acceptable ways to sustain the environment?

In Washington, the debate often gets so theoretical that you got some people saying, "I think it's a very nice thing if the environment's preserved, but the Government would mess up a one-car parade, so we ought to get out of it anyway." The other day we had a congressional subcommittee actually vote to repeal the ban on offshore oil drilling for every part of America—Florida, New Jersey, California, everybody—no analysis, no nothing. Why? It was pure ideology. Yesterday they reversed the vote after they heard from the people. But you see what I'm saying. In other words, it's—one of the things that I really want to come out of this is a practical sense of what we should be doing.

Finally, let me say, there's one other big issue in the news today that affects the Pacific Northwest, and I want to mention that. That, of course, is the question of our trade talks with Japan. First, let me say there's nobody who's done more than our administration to try to open opportunities for Americans to sell in Japan. And I have also kept a very open door to Japanese products in America. We are, as I mentioned earlier, we're selling apples, rice, software, cellular telephones, computer technology previously prohibited by cold war legislation, all these things we're selling in Japan and the rest of Asia, many of them for the very first time.

I supported the GATT trade agreement. I supported NAFTA. I believe in this. I understand that Japanese cars are made now in Oregon and sent back to Japan for sale. I know all that. I know that Washington State is the most trade-sufficient State in the United States in dealing with the Pacific Rim. This is the future I want.

But you also have to understand in the context of this negotiation, we still have a huge and persistent trade deficit with Japan. More than half of it is in autos and auto parts. We have a trade surplus in auto parts with the rest of the world because we are the low-cost, high-quality producer of auto parts in the world, but we still have a $12.5 billion trade deficit with Japan, partly because they make carburetors in Japan and sell them for 3 times as much in Japan as they do here.

The luxury car issue you've heard talked about, that's the sanction that I propose, unless we can reach an agreement here, of tariffs on luxury cars—those cars are selling—made in Japan—selling for $9,000 more there than here. We have to seek fair trade. No matter how many jobs are created by a country's trade, if they have a $100 billion trade surplus by constantly closing the economic channels of access, more is lost than gained. And this is not good for Japan. They're awash in cash, but they can't have any economic growth. They have no inflation, no growth, and they're moving toward negative interest rates in the Japanese economy. The average Japanese working person looks like

they have a huge income, but they can't afford housing and their consumer costs are almost 40 percent higher than Americans for virtually everything. So they are paying a terrible price.

I want to tell you, the people of the Pacific Northwest, I am not trying to launch a new era of protectionism, but we have tried now for two or three decades to open this market, and this is the last major block to developing a sensible global economic policy. If the United States is going to lower its deficit in ways that promote growth and raise incomes, then the rest of the world has to also make their economic adjustments because we can't deficit-spend the world into prosperity any more. Others have to do their part as well.

That is what this is about. The bottom line is we want to open the markets for American products. And we will take action if necessary in the form of sanctions. We hope it will not be necessary. We hope it will not have an adverse effect in the short run on anyone. But over the long run, if we're going to build the kind of global economic system we want, everyone must change.

Meanwhile, I will get back to basics here. It is not enough for this country to produce impressive economic numbers. It must be manifest in the lives of the people of America. So I ask you to give us your best thoughts about where we are and where we're going and what you think we should do to renew the American dream and to maintain our leadership in a new and exciting world that is full of opportunities and challenges.

Thank you very much.

NOTE: The President spoke at approximately 9:45 a.m. in Smith Memorial Center at Portland State University. In his remarks, he referred to Mayor Vera Katz of Portland; Gov. John A. Kitzhaber of Oregon; Judith A. Ramaley, president, Portland State University; and Gov. Mike Lowry of Washington.

Remarks at the Closing Session of the Pacific Rim Economic Conference in Portland
June 27, 1995

First of all, let me thank this panel and—all of them. I do have to say one thing in deference to Quincy Jones' humor and modesty. You should all know, if you don't, that in the aggregate, I think second only to airplanes, entertainment is our second biggest export. So when all these folks are talking about piracy and opening markets to nontraditional things you don't normally think about being exported, that's a huge deal in the American entertainment industry. It generates untold thousands of jobs, and they're not just the kind of jobs you think about—every time you look at a movie and you see all the people at the end that work on a movie and you imagine what their incomes are like, what their lives are like, just remember, those people, their ability to keep their jobs over a constant long period of time depends upon our ability to be effective in exporting that product as well.

One of the things that we tried to do—and Tom was talking about this—after we took office, was to identify those things where—like apples from Washington—where we knew good and well there would be a consumer market in other countries if only we could pierce them. So there wasn't some sort of theoretical thing. We knew that.

And finally let me say again, this relates to higher wage jobs, because export-related jobs on balance pay about 15 percent higher than jobs where the total nature of the economic activity is within the border of the United States.

Let me give you this thought in closing. Agricultural exports have gone up $9 billion, to over $50 billion a year, since this administration took office. And we've got a surplus of about $20 billion, as I said. Exports to Asia alone reached a record of $18.6 billion—that's 45,000 jobs. That's just agriculture. The Washington Apple Commission has tripled exports. And Washington apple exports to Asia increased 37 percent last year alone. That's just one example.

Now, I'll close with a general point I want to make. I came out here because I really believe that this is what public life should be about—not just this panel, but all three of them—not the kind of rhetorical and highly par-

tisan divisions that normally come to you across the airwaves from a distant National Government.

Also I believe—if you think about it, when World War II was over, we had a remarkable thing happen with President Truman and the Republican leaders of the Congress where we set up NATO, we set up the Marshall Plan, we set up—we really filled out and finished the work of the United Nations. And we had this bipartisan foreign policy, because everybody thought we could be destroyed by nuclear war or by the success of communism over democratic capitalism.

So we fought like crazy about all kinds of domestic issues, but we basically organized ourselves around the issues that were critical to our survival. I think you could argue that in the world toward which we're moving, our survival, our security as a people relate very closely to the issues discussed by these three panels today. And we need to find a way to go beyond partisanship to reach some national consensus on issues of trade and innovation, on issues of education and training, on issues of organizing work and family and education in a way that enables people to make the most of their own lives and on the question of pushing more and more decisions down to the community level but using the National Government as a partner to spark economic activity and get us through tough economic transitions.

That is what I am trying to do. As you can see, the results are mixed from time to time. But it's clear that that's what the country needs to do. You would not run a family, a business, a charitable organization, a local project in the way our national politics is too often run, at a highly theoretical, highly rhetorical, highly ideological level, when what we're really trying to do is to find new patterns in which people can make more of their own lives.

So I ask all of you to think about that. How would you define our security, moving into the 21st century? And if you believe it relates to innovation, to education, to training, to exports, to all these things, then I ask you: Do what you can to help us to build a bipartisan consensus that will take this country into the next century in the way that all these fine people that were on all these panels plainly deserve.

Thank you very much.

NOTE: The President spoke at 3:37 p.m. in Smith Memorial Center at Portland State University. In his remarks, he referred to musician Quincy Jones.

Remarks to Students at Portland State University in Portland
June 27, 1995

Thank you very much. First, President Ramaley, thank you for having us here at this wonderful campus. You know, I used to be a college teacher. My wife and I started out our married life teaching at the University of Arkansas in the Ozark Mountains. And I was looking at all of you under these beautiful trees, thinking there are a lot of days when I might like to be back here working for you here. This is a very wonderful place, and I thank you for having us here.

Thank you, Congresswoman Elizabeth Furse, for being here with us today and for your leadership, your vision, and your conscience. I can tell you all you are very, very fortunate to be represented by one of the most truly extraordinary individuals in the United States House of Representatives in Elizabeth Furse.

I want to thank Governor Kitzhaber, and I want to thank Mayor Katz, who I believe is over there—thank you, Vera, you've been great. And Portland has been wonderful to us. I've never had a bad day in Portland, Oregon, and I certainly didn't today. This is wonderful.

And you know, the Vice President really is funny, isn't he? [*Laughter*] You should have seen him back here when Elizabeth was introducing him and saying how intelligent he was and how energetic he was and how funny he was. And I whispered in his ear right before he came up, I said, "Next thing she's going to say is how pretty you are." [*Laughter*] But she restrained herself, and he was able to compose himself and give that wonderful speech. Let me say that our Nation has been very lucky because there's no doubt that in the entire history of the Republic, Al Gore is the most effective, influential person ever to be Vice President of the United States.

Let me tell you just for a minute what we were really doing here today at this regional economic conference. We were worried about what Oregon and what the Pacific Northwest will be like for all you young people here in the audience. We were worried about how we can guarantee a future, how we can move into the next century with the American dream alive and well and with the leadership and values of our country secure, in a world that is full of possibility and full of uncertainty.

You know, most of us who are my age and older, we've lived most of our lives and our course is pretty well set. And we have been very, very blessed to grow up in a country and to have the opportunities that America has offered for all the decades since the end of the Second World War.

Now, at the end of the cold war, the dawn of the global economy, the information age, moving into a new century, into a new millennium, we look out at a world that is changing so rapidly, that is full of untold possibilities but also some pretty troubling developments; a world that has left a lot of people feeling robust and secure and hopeful and eager for the future and a world that has left a lot of people feeling at a minimum kind of confused and uncertain and concerned about their future.

If you go back and ask yourself, what is the responsibility of the President and what is the responsibility of the citizenry of the United States, you can do no better than to go back to the documents of our Founders, who believed that we are all created equal and endowed by our Creator with the rights to life, liberty, and the pursuit of happiness. That means that at any point in history, but particularly at those points of great change, our responsibility is to do what is necessary to help us make the most of our lives. All of us, without regard to race or region or income or background or religion, have the right to make the most of our own lives. That is the challenge that is facing us here today.

And I believe that that challenge requires us, number one, to create more economic opportunity, more jobs, and higher incomes; number two, to give people the tools they need to develop their God-given abilities; number three, to promote the security of the United States at home and abroad; number four, to preserve the natural heritage of the United States that has brought us to this point and that we want to pass on to our children, our grandchildren, and our grandchildren's grandchildren.

And finally, in a world which is increasingly fast-changing and decentralized, it requires those of us in the National Government, to use the Vice President's term, to literally reinvent the way the Government works, to set a course, to pursue the right priorities, but to make sure that people at the grassroots level can make the fundamental decisions affecting their own lives and can look across the table at people who are different from themselves and work out those differences in a spirit of genuine friendship and good citizenship.

These are the thing we have tried to do in the last 2½ years, and these are the things that will take America into the 21st century.

I just want to close by asking you to think about one or two very important issues. We're in a big debate in Washington now, not only about how to balance the budget—that's the good news; most people agree that we should do it—but about the fundamental purposes of Government. There are those who say today that the Government is intrinsically destructive of our way of life and has no role other than national defense, tax cuts, and eliminating whatever you have to to balance the budget as quickly as possible.

There are those of us who beg to differ, who believe that the Government is nothing more than the expression of the American people and that when it works best, its fundamental duty is the duty of partnership, to help people do things together that they cannot do on their own. That is a debate I hope you will side with us on.

There are those who believe, for example, that it's a very nice thing if you can preserve the environment but not worth getting the Government involved. And then there are those of us who believe we have to find the best grassroots way we can to enable the American people to make a decent living for themselves and their children but to do it while preserving the herit-age that God has given to Oregon, to the Pacific Northwest, and to our entire country, indeed, to our planet.

There are those who believe that all of our problems are personal and cultural. That is, if we would just get together and get our act together and do what is right and stop messing up, that we wouldn't have any problems in this old world. And there are others who believe that our problems are basically economic and political and the Government has to step in and do something.

Now, if you look at the Scouts, the VISTA, the MESA, all the groups that are here, what do all these groups do? What are all these young people doing? Why does national service work? Because we know at some level, unless people are raised with good values and unless they can take responsibility for themselves and do the right things and make the most of their own lives, there is nothing anyone else can do to give it to them. No one can give you a good life inside. No one can give you good values. No one can give you the discipline to do the right thing and—[*applause*]—you have to do that for yourself. So we all know that.

Let me tell you, I'm sure that no one would dispute me when I say that all of us have been given things in life that maybe we didn't even deserve. We've all been given a hand up from time to time. No person here today more than me knows that you do not achieve anything completely alone. So it is not either/or. We still need a country that cares about those of us who need a helping hand to do the right thing, who need a helping hand to make the most of their own lives, who need a sense of partnership to get through the difficult times that our country faces.

Now, over the next 3 or 4 months, you will see a lot of the things that we talked about here today debated in your Nation's Capital. And I want you to think about what I have said and what you have felt today. Should we balance the budget? Yes, we should. Why? Because there's a difference in borrowing money to invest in business or to finance your college education or to buy a home, and borrowing money just because you want to go out to dinner at night. We've been borrowing money for both, and we've been so mixed up we couldn't tell the difference for too long. And as a result, we've been too dependent on other countries for funds. We have saved too little. We have invested too little. And we have had lower incomes because we have run ourselves into too much debt.

But there is a right way and a wrong way to balance the budget, because the Government's deficit is not the only problem in this country. There is also an education deficit in this country. There's a safe streets deficit in this country. There's an adequate affordable health care deficit in this country. There's a welfare reform deficit in this country. There are other deficits.

Our proposal to balance the budget says don't cut education because that's important to our future as well. If we want good jobs and higher incomes, we should increase our investment in education, from college loans to Head Start, while we balance the budget.

Our proposal says, of course we can't continue to increase health care expenditures at 2 and 3 times the rate of inflation; we have to slow it down. But be careful because there are a lot of people, the elderly, the disabled, the poorest children in our country, who depend upon Medicare and Medicaid for their medical care, and we dare not put them in a position to have to either give up health care or pay something they can't afford to pay when they don't have enough money to live on in the first place.

And so we say, yes, let's have big cuts in other things; let's balance the budget. But if you balance the budget in 10 years instead of 7, if you cut the size of the tax cuts and target them to middle class people for education and raising children and not just give tax cuts to people like me, who don't really need it, if you do that, you can balance the budget and increase our investment in education, be kind to the people who need health care help, from the smallest children to the disabled to elderly folks who don't have enough to live on, and still bring the American economy back and go

into the 21st century with good jobs, higher incomes, and an educated citizenry, including all the little children in this audience today.

You know, we all have preconceptions, and sometimes preconceptions can be bad things. They can be stereotypes about people and places. I always had a preconception abut Oregon that I think has been confirmed by all my trips out here. I always felt that the people of Oregon had an astonishing ability to maintain their idealism and be practical, to be practical and idealistic at the same time. That's why we were pleased to give Oregon permission to get out from under all kinds of Federal rules and regulations, to change its welfare programs to move people to work, to change all kinds of other programs, because we knew this was a State where people had good values and common sense.

And so, I ask all of you join us in the fight to preserve education and balance the budget. Join us in the fight to develop the economy and preserve the environment. Join us in the fight to encourage people to be better citizens and to behave better and to have better values but also to give people who deserve it a helping hand and a hand up. In other words, keep your idealism intact. Bring your common sense to the table. Give power back to communities so that the young people here can have the kind of future, can have the kind of American dream that my generation took for granted.

The 21st century will be the most exciting time in all of human history, especially for the American people, if we can bring to the task today the compassion, the values, and the common sense that I believe is at the heart of what it means to be a citizen of this great State.

Thank you, and God bless you all.

NOTE: The President spoke at 4:10 p.m. in the Courtyard at Portland State University.

Remarks on the Japan-United States Trade Agreement
June 28, 1995

Thank you very much, Wolf [Wolf Blitzer, CNN], for that introduction. [*Laughter*]

Ladies and gentlemen, for 2½ years, I have worked hard to open markets and expand trade

around the world for one simple reason: It is good for America. When we open new markets, millions of new consumers buy American products. And when we sell more American products, we create more American jobs. We created the largest market in the world with NAFTA. We passed GATT, the most comprehensive trade agreement ever.

The plain truth is, our products are now the best in the world, high quality, low cost. And our job here, and my job as President, is to make sure they can be sold fairly and freely throughout the world. That's how we create prosperity here at home.

One of the largest obstacles to free and fair trade has been the artificial barriers erected by Japan, especially around its auto and auto parts markets. For over 20 years, Presidents have tried to fix this problem without success. This unfair situation had to end.

After 20 months of negotiations, I ordered my Trade Representative, Ambassador Kantor, to impose sanctions on Japan unless they agreed to open these markets. Today Japan has agreed that it will begin to truly open its auto and auto parts markets to American companies.

This agreement is specific. It is measurable. It will achieve real, concrete results. And I have insisted on it from the start. In 1993, the Japanese and I agreed at our meeting in Japan on specific negotiating goals in the framework agreement. We have now achieved those goals. Now, through 2 years of steady and determined negotiations, we have done what we set out to do 2½ years ago.

Trade must be a two-way street. After 20 years, we finally have an agreement that will move cars and parts both ways between the United States and Japan. This breakthrough is a major step toward free trade throughout the world.

Japan will take specific steps that we expect will increase the number of dealers selling non-Japanese cars by 200 next year and 1,000 over the next 5 years. In the United States, 80 percent of our car dealers sell foreign cars right next to American cars. But in Japan, only 7 percent of car dealers sell American cars or any non-Japanese cars. That is unfair, and this agreement makes a strong start in fixing it.

Japan will begin to undo the rigid regulations of its market for repair parts. This agreement breaks the stranglehold Japanese manufacturers have had over repair shops and garages. It means more U.S. parts will be sold in Japan.

Finally, Japanese carmakers will expand their production in the United States and buy more American parts both here and in Japan. These measurable plans should increase purchases of American car parts by almost $9 billion in 3 years, a 50 percent increase. Japan is going to make half a million more new cars in the United States by 1998, an increase of 25 percent.

Sixty percent of our entire trade deficit with Japan is the result of a car and car parts deficit. This agreement helps to close the gap. This commitment means thousands of new jobs for American workers, jobs for Americans making parts sold to Japan, jobs for Americans making parts for Japanese cars manufactured here, jobs for Americans making American cars now sold in Japan, and jobs for Americans making Japanese models made in the United States, which will increase substantially in number over the next few years. It is therefore a victory for our hardworking families. But make no mistake, it is also a victory for Japanese consumers, because it will mean lower prices for good products for them.

I want to commend the leaders of Japanese auto parts companies and auto companies and the leaders of the Japan Government for the courage and vision it took for them to reach this agreement. I personally want to thank Prime Minister Murayama and Minister Hashimoto for their leadership. And I especially want to thank Ambassador Mickey Kantor and his extraordinary team for the exhaustive efforts they have made to reach this successful conclusion.

In just a few moments, as soon as I conclude here, Ambassador Kantor and Minister Hashimoto will have a statement in detail about this agreement and will answer questions about it. I'm sure you can understand that they are in a better position to answer detailed questions than I am.

I had a long conversation with Ambassador Kantor about an hour ago, and I congratulated him.

I want all of you to understand that there is still much to be done. This agreement will not solve every problem in our relationship. But for today we have proved that hard bargaining and good faith can overcome apparently insurmountable conflict. This is important. And what it means is that sanctions are not necessary because we have achieved our goals. I am very proud of this negotiating team. I want to say that again. We set out a strategy, we held firm to our principles, and we achieved our goals. And those goals will lead to more jobs for Americans. Discipline at the negotiating table once again has proved that we can be successful.

And I want to say finally, again, this is a great victory for the American people. It is also a victory for the Japanese people. We both won. And as a result, the global economy and American jobs are better off.

Thank you.

Q. Is this a voluntary agreement, or are there any guarantees, Mr. President?

The President. Mr. Kantor will be speaking in just a moment, and he'll answer all the questions.

NOTE: The President spoke at 12:20 p.m. in the Briefing Room at the White House. In his remarks, he referred to Ryutaro Hashimoto, Japanese Minister of International Trade and Industry.

Memorandum on the Combined Federal Campaign
June 28, 1995

Memorandum for the Heads of Executive Departments and Agencies

I am delighted that Secretary of Health and Human Services Donna Shalala has agreed to serve as the chair of the 1995 Combined Federal Campaign of the National Capital Area. I ask you to support the campaign by personally chairing it in your Agency and appointing a top official as your vice chair.

The Combined Federal Campaign is an important way for Federal employees to support thousands of worthy charities. This year our goal again is to raise more than $38 million. Public servants not only contribute to the campaign, but assume leadership roles to ensure its success.

Your personal support and enthusiasm will help guarantee another successful campaign this year.

WILLIAM J. CLINTON

Memorandum on Upgrading Security at Federal Facilities
June 28, 1995

Memorandum for Executive Departments and Agencies

Subject: Upgrading Security at Federal Facilities

I have received from the Department of Justice a study entitled, "Vulnerability Assessment of Federal Facilities." In order to ensure adequate security for Federal facilities, I am adopting immediately a number of the recommendations of the Department of Justice Study.

I hereby direct that:

1. Each Federal facility shall, where feasible, be upgraded to the minimum security standards recommended for its security level by the Department of Justice Study;

2. All executive departments and agencies ("agencies") shall immediately begin upgrading their facilities to meet the recommended minimum security standards, to the extent possible within currently available funding;

3. By October 15, 1995, the General Services Administration (GSA), those agencies with facilities in Security Level IV GSA space, and the Office of Management and Budget (OMB) shall identify funding, no later than in the FY97 budget cycle, for the cost of upgrading Level IV facilities to the minimum security standards recommended by the Department of Justice Study;

4. By February 1, 1996, GSA and all agencies shall consult with OMB regarding funding mechanisms for upgrading all remaining Federal facilities to the minimum security standards recommended by the Department of Justice Study; and

5. All agencies shall adhere to the attached timetable for implementing this directive.

I also have directed OMB to review the remaining recommendations of the Department of Justice Study, and to advise me within 30 days from the date of this memorandum concerning the implementation of those recommendations.

WILLIAM J. CLINTON

Timetable for Upgrading Security at Federal Facilities

- All agencies shall immediately begin upgrading their facilities to meet recommended minimum security standards, to the extent possible within currently available funding—Immediate
- GSA shall establish Building Security committees for all Level IV GSA facilities—7/15/95
- GSA shall establish building Security Committees for all Level I–III GSA facilities—8/31/95
- Agencies with non-GSA space shall establish programs for upgrading their facilities to appropriate security standards—8/31/95

- Level IV Committees shall make requests to GSA for security upgrades to meet recommended minimum security standards—9/1/95
- GSA shall review and determine appropriateness of Level IV Committee requests; GSA shall advise Level IV tenant agencies of portion of approved requests that will be charged to their agencies through increased rents—10/1/95
- GSA, Level IV tenant agencies and OMB shall identify funding, no later than in the FY97 budget cycle, for the cost of upgrading security for Level IV facilities—10/15/95
- Level I–III Committees shall make requests to GSA for security upgrades to meet recommended minimum security standards—12/31/95
- GSA shall consult with Level I–III tenant agencies, and with OMB, regarding funding mechanisms for security upgrades—2/1/96
- Agencies with non-GSA space shall consult with OMB regarding funding mechanisms for security upgrades for their facilities—2/1/96

Letter to Congressional Leaders on the Plan To Balance the Budget
June 28, 1995

Dear Mr. Speaker: (Dear Mr. Leader:)
We share the goal of balancing the federal budget, and I look forward to working with you on this important matter.

But as we work together to reach our shared goal, we must ensure that we do so the right way—the way that will raise the standards of living for average Americans.

My plan to balance the budget over 10 years will help raise average living standards by cutting unnecessary spending while investing in education and training, targeting tax relief to middle-income Americans, and taking incremental but serious steps toward health care reform. By contrast, the conference agreement cuts too deeply into Medicare and Medicaid and cuts education and training both to pay for a tax cut that is too large for too many who don't need it, and to meet the 7 year time frame.

Though I am determined to work with you to balance the budget, I cannot accept legislation that will threaten the living standards of American families.

I hope we can work together and avoid a situation in which I would have no choice but to use my veto authority broadly. The American people want us to work together to balance the budget and to do it the right way. I am ready to do that.

Sincerely,

BILL CLINTON

NOTE: Identical letters were sent to Newt Gingrich, Speaker of the House of Representatives, and Bob Dole, Senate majority leader.

Message to the Senate Transmitting Documents on the Ukraine-United States Taxation Convention
June 28, 1995

To the Senate of the United States:

I transmit herewith an exchange of notes dated at Washington May 26 and June 6, 1995, for Senate advice and consent to ratification in connection with the Senate's consideration of the Convention Between the Government of the United States of America and the Government of Ukraine for the Avoidance of Double Taxation and the Prevention of Fiscal Evasion with Respect to Taxes on Income and Capital, together with a related Protocol, signed at Washington on March 4, 1994 ("the Taxation Convention"). Also transmitted for the information of the Senate is the report of the Department of State with respect to the exchange of notes.

This exchange of notes addresses the interaction between the Taxation Convention and other treaties that have tax provisions, including in particular the General Agreement on Trade in Services (GATS), annexed to the Agreement Establishing the World Trade Organization, done at Marrakesh April 15, 1994.

I recommend that the Senate give favorable consideration to this exchange of notes and give its advice and consent to ratification in connection with the Taxation Convention.

WILLIAM J. CLINTON

The White House,
June 28, 1995.

Message to the Congress Transmitting the Report of the Corporation for Public Broadcasting
June 28, 1995

To the Congress of the United States:

As required by section 19(3) of the Public Telecommunications Act of 1992 (Public Law 102–356), I transmit herewith the report of the Corporation for Public Broadcasting.

WILLIAM J. CLINTON

The White House,
June 28, 1995.

Remarks at a Democratic National Committee Fundraiser
June 28, 1995

Thank you very much, Chairman Fowler, for your introduction. Thank you, Congressman Clyburn, for being here tonight and for your leadership. I thank our friend Truman Arnold for his leadership of our finance efforts. I thank particularly Dan Dutko and Peter Knight and all others who raised funds for this important evening. This was the most successful DNC finance dinner ever, thanks to you. And we thank you for that.

I don't keep up with this too much, you know, because I have to spend most of my time being President, but I keep reading these stories that those of you who give to our party are threatened with your lives. If that's true, we appreciate the risk you took in being here. We'll try to make it worth your while for the future. You are living proof that there are a lot of Americans who want to do well themselves and to do good for themselves and for others, and we appreciate that.

I want to thank Senator Dodd. If he'd gotten any hotter tonight, he'd have set off the fire alarm. [*Laughter*] I hope America is listening.

I also want to thank you all for the response you gave when the mention of our agreement with Japan on autos and auto parts was mentioned. I thank you for that. It occurred in typically dramatic circumstances, going up to the 11th hour. Last night I got home and sort of semi woke Hillary up about a quarter to 3 in the morning. I flew in from Portland, Oregon, where we had a wonderful economic conference yesterday on the five States of the Pacific Rim and their future in the 21st century. And I was being kind of kept up with a blow-by-blow description all the way on the airplane, going all the way across the country, about how we were doing with the Japanese and was it going to come apart or was it going to be put back together. And when I got off the plane in what was for us the middle of the night, I was told that it appeared that we were going to be able to do this, but I would still have to go to sleep, and they would wake me up at some point in the future if it all worked out. So this morning they woke me up, and I got to make the announcement that the agreement had been reached.

I start with that because I want to make a point. There are some people who say that our message is not clear or they don't know the difference between Republicans and Democrats. I can tell you one thing—there are two differences: One is, they may talk better, but we do more; we do more. The other is, we try to do what we do in a way that benefits everybody, not just those who are going to do all right if we don't lift a finger anyway. And that makes a big difference.

This is not class warfare. I am proud of the fact that under our administration we've had more new businesses started and more new millionaires than at any previous point in American history. We want more and more people to do very well. But we want everyone to do well because the country is being lifted up, because we're growing the middle class, because we're shrinking the under class. So we do things that are sometimes more difficult, because otherwise it won't work out that way.

And I want to talk to you about that tonight because when you leave here, if somebody asks you, what does it mean to be a Democrat in 1995, I want you to be able to give an answer.

That's really important. It's really important. And if you look at this Japanese trade agreement, you will see one of the answers.

Now today, both parties say they're for free trade; but in 2½ years, we have negotiated 80 trade agreements, 15 with Japan. We're selling apples and rice and cellular telephones and now automobiles and auto parts to Japan. I'm proud of that.

There is no time in our history when we have had so much expansion of trade in such a short time. Why? Because we're living in a global economy. We have open markets. If we don't expand trade, we still get the downside, those countries that import into our country where their people are struggling to lift their own living standards and still working for wages our people can't live on. But when we open markets and we can sell high-quality, low-cost American products around the world, then we create jobs here that pay, on average, 15 percent above average wages in America. We give our people a way to promote the ideals of freedom and democracy and to do well while doing good.

But in order to do that, trade has to become increasingly more free and increasingly more fair. Therefore, when we negotiated the NAFTA agreement, we also wanted a commitment that we would make a long-term effort working together with Mexico and with Canada to protect the environment and to lift labor standards so that ordinary people in Mexico, as well as ordinary people in the United States, would do well if we expanded trade. That is the kind of thing that we try to do.

And we went to the brink with Japan because I know that the United States alone in the 21st century cannot lift the global economy. It will take a cooperation between the United States and Europe and Japan and all of those growing economies. We have to all work together. And I know that a trading system in Japan, which has made the nation fabulously wealthy but also, today, has brought it to the brink of financial trouble because their currency is so overvalued, because no one is investing in the country, their interest rates are almost negative now. And most important, ordinary people there are paying 40 percent more, 40 percent more than they ought to be paying, for consumer products. Those luxury cars we almost had to put tariffs on, made in Japan, cost 9,000 bucks more in Japan than in the United States. We cannot continue to work toward a global economy unless our great partner in Japan is also doing its part. And everything I sought to do in opening their markets, I believe with all my heart, is not only good for our workers but for theirs.

But it's harder than just saying you're for free trade. You also have to be for fair arrangements that create jobs and grow incomes. That's what it means to be a Democrat in 1995. You've got to be for jobs and incomes and a fair global system.

You know, the Secretary of the Treasury and I and the Vice President—who is, by the way, in Russia tonight; and he's sorry that he and Tipper can't be here with Hillary and me, but he's doing very important work—we were in the Treasury Department the other day to announce one of our reinventing Government initiatives. And this initiative was about how businesses and individuals in 32 States next year are going to be able to file their taxes, State and Federal, at the same time electronically. And in the course of that, billions of dollars will be saved in compliance costs with the tax systems. And eventually, of course, we'll get to 50 States. But we're going to 32 next year.

And to illustrate this, we invited what I would call a real American, who happened to be in Washington for the White House Small Business Conference, to come and talk about how his circumstance would be changed. And the fellow we invited was a man named Paul Condit from west Texas, a John Deere dealer from west Texas. And old Paul Condit showed up with all of his papers that he was going to get to throw in the trashcan now that he could file electronically. And he looked at me—and this is why we're all here tonight—and he said, "Mr. President," he said, "you and the Vice President here have done a great job of reinventing Government. What you need to do now is reinvent communications because it ain't getting out in the heartland." And I think that's true.

Sometimes I feel like that old country song when I watch the evening news. Remember that country song that said, "They changed everything about me but my name"? [*Laughter*]

So tonight I want you to think about this: Why are you here? What will you do tomorrow? How do you intend to spend the next year to fulfill the mission that Senator Dodd and Chairman Fowler put before us tonight?

First, let's face facts. One of the reasons that our friends in the other party tend to do well is that they are great at giving simple answers

to complicated questions. And this is a confusing time to people. Why shouldn't people be confused about public issues? They're confused about the way their own lives are working out in this world. It seems to be the best of times and the worst of times.

The good news: 6.7 million new jobs. I'm proud of that. The good news: record numbers of new businesses, record numbers of new millionaires. That's great. But how do you explain that fact that we drove down unemployment, drove up jobs, have the lowest combined rates of unemployment and inflation in 30 years, have the lowest African-American unemployment in 20 years, and the median income in America has dropped by one percent in the last 2 years? And more and more people feel insecure in their own jobs with all the downsizing that's coming along.

So there is this ambivalence about the global economy. They say, "Hey, this is great, America creates jobs, but I may not get a raise." And more than half of the workers in this country are working for about the same wage they were making 10 years ago, and they're working a longer work week. And they're feeling more insecure.

And our Nation is the only one—they may criticize me until the cows come home for trying to do something about health care, Hillary and me, but I'll tell you one thing, we are the only country, the only one, where there are a smaller percentage of people today under the age of 65 with health insurance than there were 10 years ago. You'd be insecure, too, if that happened to you.

So, the good news and the bad news: crime. Look at crime. The crime rate is going down in almost every city in the country. And our crime bill will help it to go down further. But the crime rate is going up among very young teenagers; and random violence among our future citizens, going up.

I'll give you another example: technology. Technology is a blessing beyond all belief. I just was home, Hillary and I went home for 2 or 3 days, and I got to thinking about it. A kid in a rural school district in the Ozark Mountains with only five or six people in the senior class can get on the Internet now and hook into a library in Australia and do a research paper on volcanoes, thanks to technology. Incredible, utterly incredible!

But that same technology can expose that child's younger brother or sister to unbelievable pornography and can teach a deranged person who's smart enough to use a computer how to make a bomb, just like the one that blew up Oklahoma City. Technology means now that radical groups can develop little vials of sarin gas and walk into a subway in Japan and break it open and kill innocent people. It means other fanatic groups are now operating secret laboratories where they are searching for the ability to make biological warfare weapons, little germ warfare mechanisms that will kill people in the same sort of way.

So it's a good news/bad news story. After a while, people just get a headache and say, "Just tell me a simple answer so I can go on with my life." So if somebody says, "Well, vote for us. The Government's causing all your problems. We're for less Government, lower taxes. We'll be tough on crime, welfare, and immigration. We're your ticket." Sounds pretty good to me. "We'll balance the budget. And you don't get anything out of the Government but an occasional audit and a bad regulation anyway." [*Laughter*] Sounds pretty good to me. Right? I mean, that's what we're dealing with. And then the whispered message is, besides that, "Contribute enough, we'll let you write the legislation. We'll just kind of sit there in front for you." [*Laughter*] I think some of you are here tonight because you still want us to do some of the work. You don't want to have to do it all yourselves. [*Laughter*]

So it sounds good. What's wrong with it? First of all, for all the joking I'm saying, we are really—we're in a period of such profound change that we are being now asked by our people and forced by the press of events to debate fundamental questions. You heard Don Fowler stand up and say the Democratic Party rests on two principles; middle class economics and mainstream values is essentially what he said. We try to grow the middle class, help poor people work their way into the middle class. We try to offer a society in which people can come together, not be divided. You say that as if you take that for granted. That is not to be taken for granted any more.

Look what we're debating today in Washington: the first principles of what we are as a people, the first principles. And let me just give you some examples. We used to debate—from the end of the cold war until the last few years,

we debated the difference between Republicans and Democrats in a range sort of like this. Now the range is about this big. All things are back on the table now. Why? The cold war is over. We don't have an organized rationale for how we relate to the rest of the world. And the global economy and the information age have all kinds of apparently conflicting impacts. It's confusing to people and all these questions are open. So let's go back to the basic questions, and when you walk out of here tonight, you'll either know why you're a Democrat or you'll be ready to switch. But at least it'll be a matter of principle, not convenience. Now, let's think about that.

Issue number one: There are now a lot of folks in this town—and Senator Dodd had a funny joke about it tonight: guns don't kill people, movies do—[*laughter*]—there are a lot of people here who believe that all of our problems are personal and cultural, as opposed to the old view that most of our common problems were economic and political. Now, if you think all of our problems are personal and cultural, that really lets you off the hook; you don't have to do much heavy lifting. You just say, "Look, if everybody would just go out and behave and get up tomorrow and do the right thing, we wouldn't have any problems anyway," take your tax cut, and leave town. [*Laughter*] Think about it. If you believe that, if you believe that, you don't have to do much. You can spend all your time exhorting people to behave as individuals and attacking the influence centers in the culture who make movies you don't agree with or music you don't agree with or whatever.

Now, let me tell you what I think, and what I think has to be the credo of the Democratic Party. At a certain level, that is self-evidently true. That is, we know that there is nothing Government can do for anybody they're not prepared to do for themselves. If people will not take responsibility for their own lives, for their children, for their education, for making the most of their own lives, there's nothing we can do. That is self-evidently true. There's not a single soul here tonight who can afford the price of a ticket to be here because somebody just gave you something. You all had to do something back. That's what the Democratic Party was founded on, hard work. And at a certain level, we all know that there are influence centers in our culture, entertainment, sports, the media, business, labor, you name it, that are beyond government and politics. That's true, too.

I'd like you to remember, however, that some of us were raising questions about this long before the Presidential election started. Tipper Gore, 18 years ago, was talking about whether lyrics in music were good for children and how we should discuss this. I was dealing with these issues with Hillary long before I ever thought I was running for President. This should not be an issue for a political season. But that's true. But you know what? If you use that as an excuse to walk away, then you don't have to vote for the family and medical leave law. Let me tell you something, it's a lot easier to be a good person and a good parent if you don't lose your job when you have to go home when your baby is born and your parent is sick. So there are political and economic issues here, as well.

And all those people that came home from World War II, that built the greatest middle class the world had ever known, they did it because they were great patriots and good parents and good workers. And they were good citizens. They also did it because they had the GI bill.

So don't let anybody tell you—the first thing I would tell you is, I believe if you're a Democrat, you don't agree that all of our problems are exclusively personal and cultural, you think there are economic and political dimensions to the challenges we face, and you don't want to take a dive on it.

The second issue flows out of the first. What about the role of Government? What is the role of Government? If you believe that all the problems are personal and cultural, then the role of Government is fund the defense, balance the budget as quick as you can, consistent with giving a big tax cut.

But if you believe that the role of Government is to help people make the most of their own lives and that in every age and time we have common challenges that can best be met in this way, then that changes everything. Then you say, "Yes, well, we ought to balance the budget, but guess what, there's an education deficit, too. And I don't want to cut off my nose to spite my face. And I don't believe that we should give tax cuts unless it will grow the economy and raise incomes, unless people need it, unless it supports education, unless it supports the economic challenges we face. So let's

balance the budget in a way that increases investment in our people so that we get both benefits, a balanced budget and helping people make the most of their own lives, because the objective is to raise incomes and bring the American people together."

I'll give you another example. Look at the crime debate. If you believe all the problems are personal and cultural, then you couldn't possibly support the Brady bill or the assault weapons ban because that represents a minor inconvenience to the law-abiding people who for whatever reason want an assault weapon or the far larger number of law-abiding people who genuinely want to buy handguns and are somehow discomforted if they have to wait a few days while there's a background check. Because if all the problems are personal and cultural, just catch the wrongdoers, throw them in jail, throw the key away, and forget about it.

But if you live in the real world instead of the world of ideological extremes, and you think that some of our problems are political and that we have an obligation to work together, then you say, well, a law-abiding person who wants to buy a handgun really won't object to this minor inconvenience to help a few more police officers and a few more innocent children stay alive. You say to yourself that law-abiding people will find other ways to satisfy their desire for sporting activities with guns, even if they have to give up these assault weapons so we can get the Uzis out of the high schools. That's the kind of thing you say to yourself.

Now, this has—I submit to you, this has nothing to do with the right to keep and bear arms—nothing, nothing. This has to do with whether you think our problems are just isolated personal things or bad culture, or whether you believe that we have to band together, to work together to find practical solutions to solve our problems.

Now, all the law enforcement people say, "We live with this problem, and it's not just as simple as locking people up and throwing away the key. Punishment is important. Please punish bad people. But meanwhile, please pass the Brady bill. Please pass the assault weapons ban. Please spend some money on prevention so our kids have something to say yes to as well as something to say no to." That's what people in law enforcement say, who live with this every day. Why? Because they know that our problems are both personal and cultural and they are political and economic and social. And if we don't pull together and try to solve them, we will never make much progress. We'll just have a lot of elections with hot air, 30-second ads, driving people's emotion through the roof but never really getting down to the business of moving America forward. So I say if you're a Democrat, you say it is both, not one.

Let me just give you one final example. Look at the environment. Look at the environment. Look what has happened. We even had a subcommittee the other day vote to lift the ban on all offshore oil drilling. "Never mind how small the proven reserves are, never mind what it would do to the retirees or the tourists in Florida or California, or never mind what might happen off the New Jersey coast. Government is bad; what is private is good. If somebody can get up enough money to sink an oilwell anywhere in this country offshore, let them do it. And even if there are unfortunate consequences, we are philosophically opposed to doing anything that would interfere with that." These are the people that want to let all the environmental law be rewritten by those who want to get rid of them. And they're doing a pretty good job of that. Now, but to be fair to them, that's the way they think. In other words, they think it's a nice enough thing if you can preserve the environment, but not if the price of preserving the environment, God forbid, is having Government pass a law.

This is the debate that's going on. You laugh. Don't tell me you don't know the difference between our party and the other party. This is the debate that is going on in Washington. But let's be fair to them. They honestly believe that it is wrong for the Government to protect our common heritage because the Government would mess up a one-car parade; the Government might interfere with something someone wants to do to make a dollar in the short run; and the Government, being a fallible institution, will mess up now and again and do really dumb things. Now this is a first principle.

I say to you, any institution comprised of human beings will err. And Government should be restrained because it has power. And that's why we've got the Constitution we've got. But I'll say this too: Unless we preserve our fundamental natural environment and find a way to grow the economy while protecting the environment, then our grandchildren and their grandchildren will not know the America that we have grown up in and come to love.

And again—so you want to know what the difference is? I believe the purpose of Government is to help people to make the most of their own lives. I believe the purpose of Government is to grow the economy in ways that creates more entrepreneurs and more millionaires but also raises incomes for the middle class and shrinks the under class. I believe our business here is to find a way to solve our problems in practical ways that bring us together and don't drive us apart. I believe ideological extremism is the bane of America's progress. It has been for 200 years, and it still is. We cannot put political correctness ahead of advancing the lives of the American people. That's what I believe.

You know, you take every single one of the other party's themes—they say, "We want less Government." Sounds great. Our party, our administration, 2½ years, has reduced the size of the Federal Government by 150,000. If we don't pass another budget, we'll still have the smallest Government we've had since President Kennedy was in office. But you know what? I also know that downsizing, while it is necessary, is threatening to real people. And so look how we did it. We didn't just throw people in the street. We gave them good early retirement incentives. We tried to take time to do this in a reasoned way, because there are people involved and there are practical realities involved.

I want to cut the size of Government. I want to cut regulation. The other day we cut 16,000 regulations at the White House Conference on Small Business. They want to get rid of the Department of Commerce. Why? Because ideologically the Government obviously can never do anything to help the private sector. Never mind the fact that Ron Brown has created more jobs in the private sector than any Secretary of Commerce in history with the partnerships and the efforts that have been made.

I could go on and on and on. But if you strip apart, take it all away, you see an honest, huge debate. They say all of our problems are personal and cultural; private is good, public is bad; balance the budget as quickly as possible; give the biggest tax cut you can; don't worry about anything but defense. We say in the post-cold-war world of the global economy in the 21st century, the most important thing is whether people can make the most of their own lives, whether they can compete and win in the global economy, and whether we can do it in a way that keeps the American dream alive, where more people are moving into the middle class, where people are rewarded for their efforts, and where we find a way to make our diversity a strength, not a weakness. That is the difference. That is enough difference for me to stand on until kingdom come. I am proud to be here with the Democratic Party tonight, and I hope you are, too.

Now, let me say these two brief points in closing. First of all, I have said this so that you would know where I stand and so you could help to determine where you stand. But that does not mean that I believe we would be better off if we were more partisan. I think the American people are sick of partisanship, just for the sake of partisanship.

The other night I was out in San Francisco— I want to tell you this story. And I'll tell you— because I want you to think about this. I think these people are pretty representative of our country. And I saw a couple about my age having dinner, and they said, "Mr. President, would you come shake hands with us?" So I did. And even though they were about my age, they told me they were celebrating their first anniversary—celebrating their first anniversary—and I said, "Well, Hillary and I are about to celebrate our 20th anniversary." And it was—you know, people will sometimes tell you anything when you're President. So this man in this very touching—this man got this sort of faraway look in his eye, and he said, "You know, I'd be celebrating my 20th anniversary, too, this year, but my wife passed away, and I met this wonderful woman." And then the woman smiled, and she said, "My husband didn't pass away. He was a jerk." [*Laughter*] And she said—it's a true story—and she said, "And I met this wonderful man." [*Laughter*]

And then they—I couldn't believe this. I'm just standing here, you know, listening to this. This is America. This is not Washington, DC, now. [*Laughter*] This is America. So then, then they go on to tell me that he is a Republican, and she is a Democrat; that he owns a fast food restaurant chain, and she's a schoolteacher; that she voted for me, and he didn't. They tell me all this in about 5 minutes. I'm listening to this whole thing. [*Laughter*] But let me tell you what they said. Here's the point I want to make. Here's the point I want to make. They were just out there in San Francisco, and they didn't live in California. They were out there

celebrating their first anniversary. And he said to me—he said, and she said amen—he said, "You know, we come from different parties. We look at a lot of things in different ways, but we think what happened to Dr. Foster was a crying shame." That's what they said. And they said, "We just think there's too much partisanship in Washington."

So let me tell you what I'm trying to do. That's why I went to that wonderful little town in New Hampshire, where Hillary and I fell in love with the folks in 1992, and had that conversation with the Speaker of the House. A lot of people said, "This is crazy, don't do it," whatever. I decided that it would be better to try to honestly tell the American people what the real differences are and then see if there is some honest way we can bridge those differences to move forward. That's what I decided we ought to do, because I believe that the American people will listen and think with their heads and their hearts, with their ears open instead of being all torn up and upset by their genuine confusion and uncertainty about the future. We will do fine, because most people run the rest of their lives the way we believe our country ought to be run.

And the only reason that things seem so out of whack today is that everything is changing and people are confused and uncertain, so they are vulnerable to easy answers to complex problems. And what we have to say is, when you hear all this stuff, will it raise incomes? Will it generate jobs? Will it bring people together? Will it make us a stronger country? Will it bring us into the future in better shape? So when we ask ourselves how should we balance the budget, I say if it takes a little longer and you have to have a little smaller tax cut, if you can take care of all these old folks on Medicare and you can increase education instead of cut it, let's do that, because that is the kind of America that we ought to have. That is the kind of America that we ought to have.

What I want to say to you is that I am now convinced that we have an enormous opportunity if we can be clear and unambiguous. We don't have to even attack. We just need to try to honestly explain. I have tried tonight to honestly explain to you where I believe many of them are on their issues and where we are. I have tried to be as honest as I could. But we have an opportunity here. Oklahoma City, as tragic and awful as it was, took a lot of the meanness out of this country. It made us all think again about what it is that we share as human beings across all the divides. And when Captain O'Grady survived those 6 days in Bosnia and came home, it gave a little lift back to our country, and it made us think about all the things we're proud of about America, that brings us together across all the divides.

And I leave you with this: The Democrats— the Democrats believe that we're here to help each other make the most of our own lives, that there will never be a time when Government can do anything for people they won't do for themselves, but that it is simply an evasion of our common responsibility to say our problems are only personal problems, only cultural problems. And it is self-defeating to believe we can move into the 21st century without find-

ing a way to go there together—to go there together.

This is a very great country. And the American people are now listening and looking. And we have an opportunity to be what we are. We are not negative. We are not wreckers. We are builders. Do not run away from that because of the power of the negative forces of recent years. Instead, embrace it. Go out and tell people what you believe, why you believe it, and why we ought to be returned in 1996, not for our sake but for the future of our country.

Thank you, and God bless you all.

NOTE: The President spoke at 9:50 p.m. at the Sheraton Washington Hotel. In his remarks, he referred to Donald L. Fowler, chairman, and Truman Arnold, acting national finance chair, Democratic National Committee.

Remarks Announcing Community Policing Grants
June 29, 1995

Thank you. Commissioner, I need this around here these days. [*Laughter*] I'm delighted to have it. Thank you very much.

Thank you, Madam Attorney General. I thank all the law enforcement officials who are here, the representatives of the victims group, Mrs. Brady, and the others who have supported and led the fight for the passage of the Brady bill and the assault weapons ban. We're glad to see the mayors here: Mayor Giuliani, Mayor Cleaver, Mayor Barry, and others. And I thank the Members of Congress for coming: Senators Biden and Boxer and Pell, and Congressman LaFalce, Congresswoman Maloney, Congressman Schumer, Congresswoman Eleanor Holmes Norton, and I think Congressman Kennedy is here, Congresswoman Harman. I miss anybody? I want to thank all of them, you know, because if it hadn't been for them—and especially I thank you, Senator Biden, for making sure we actually got this crime bill passed last year through all the political fog and the 6 years of debate.

I want to say this is a day—I was thinking— on the way in we had a little television out here in the anteroom, and we were watching the American and the Russian spaceships who

are hooking up in space. And they were going back and forth and kind of playing games with each other in space, and I said, "Well, I guess this really means the cold war is over." It's a source of celebration. Today, as this is going on, the Vice President is in Moscow talking with Prime Minister Chernomyrdin about a whole range of issues between our country.

Yesterday we celebrated what I believe is a very, very strong trade agreement with Japan that will create jobs for American workers. And I feel good about that. And I think in so many ways the United States is taking full advantage of this global society of ours, of the end of the cold war. Of course, there are still problems; there will be problems until the end of time. But in so many ways, we're taking full advantage of it. And yet, I think one of the things that all of us has to recognize, all of us who love our country and want the best for it, is that we must find ways for the American people to feel more secure as they move into a world that is changing more and more.

Part of it is economic security. We have to find ways not only to create jobs but to raise people's incomes and to give them a better chance to either keep the job they've got or to know they can get another one if they have to lose it in this wave of downsizing that's sweeping the entire world. And a lot of it is what you do. It's what you have to do every day. The first responsibility any of us have in public life is to preserve order and law and security.

When I ran for President, I had the opportunity to travel all over this country and visit with police officers and walk the streets of our largest cities and some of our small towns and talk to people about crime and drugs and what was happening to young people and the rising tide of violence in our country. And I pledged at that time that if I were elected, I would do everything I could to put another 100,000 police officers on the street and to pay for it by reducing the size of the Federal Government by 100,000.

The Congress has voted already to reduce the size of the Federal Government by 272,000. And I can report to you that today we're over halfway there. There are 150,000 fewer people working for this Government today than there were on the day I took the oath of office as President. We have done it in what I think is a very humane way. We had packages to give people incentives for early retirement. We've tried not to be guilty of cruel downsizing. And we've tried not to forget that those people served our country and served our country well.

But we need to reallocate the resources from the Federal Government to the streets of America to increase the sense of security people have. And I feel very, very strongly that this has worked because of all of you and because of people like you around the country. The crime bill and the COPS MORE Program, in particular, are running on time, as the Attorney General said, and ahead of schedule, and in fact, we're slightly even under budget. I hesitate to say that because someone will find a way to get us up over it before you know it. [*Laughter*]

This partnership really works. We give communities the resources that they need to put more police officers on the streets. Communities, in return, take responsibility to train and deploy those officers. In turn, the officers help ordinary citizens to find the commitment and the courage to do their part to fight against crime. That is the genius of community policing. It's a fight for the habits of our lives and the habits of our heart.

We can't make our streets truly safe until everybody really is committed to doing their part, until you have the help you need from parents and teachers and friends and neighbors and from the role models that young people look up to, from actors, athletes, and others. Our responsibilities, of course, have to begin with our children.

The evidence suggests today that you are making a lot of headway with the resources that your folks are giving you at the local level and with the crime bill. And I'm encouraged by that. In almost every major city in the country, the crime rate is down. In many major areas, the crime rate is down dramatically. In many smaller and medium sized cities, the crime rate is down.

But we cannot be too optimistic because there are some troubling signs. First of all, in some major areas where the crime rate has gone down because you've been able to deploy more police resources, the crime rate has shifted into areas that aren't as well organized and aren't as well prepared for it. That's one of the reasons that, when the Congress passed the crime bill, they said we had to deploy these resources fairly and evenly across the country, not just in the bigger areas but in the smaller ones as well, because they knew this would happen. And sure enough, it has in some places.

The other thing I want to point out is that even though the overall crime rate has gone down, the rate of random violence among young teenagers is going up. And I might say—I'm concerned about it—that the rate of casual drug use among teenagers is going up, even as the Justice Department has had unparalleled success in breaking big drug gangs and interrupting big drug sales and doing things that are a cause for great celebration. There is this troubling undertow because so many of our kids are still getting in trouble out there. And it's something we need to face.

And I think it is a product, in part, of the chaos of modern times, from the breakdown of the family to the breakdown of order on the streets. And again I say, we have to find a way to take advantage of all these dramatic changes, which make us want to stay glued to the TV and watch the spaceships connect, which make us want to have free but fair trade with Japan and all other countries so all of us can benefit from that, but which have also brought so much disruption to the lives of Americans all over our country.

That's really what this is about. And it's going to require some level of contribution by every citizen. You know, I have listened to this debate, for example, over the Brady bill and over the assault weapons ban, from now to kingdom come. I could close my eyes and give you both sides of it in excruciating detail. But the truth is, it doesn't have anything to do with the right to keep and bear arms. It really has more to do with the way you view what it means to be an American in 1995. That is, some of our people really believe that the only problems we have in this country are personal misconduct and bad cultural trends, and if everybody would just shape up and behave, we'd be fine.

Well, at one level that's true, isn't it? I mean, it's self-evidently true. And it's something we shouldn't minimize because nothing we can do, any of us, will really have any impact on the lives of our people unless more people do the right thing. But to pretend that there are no actions we can take as a people in common that will make a difference is pure folly.

And a lot of the people that object to the Brady bill and the assault weapons ban are people who say things like, "Well, I'm not a criminal. I ought to have a right to have any kind of weapon I want, and I ought not to have to wait 5 minutes for it, much less 5 days. Just punish wrongdoers. Put them in jail. Throw away the key." But that ignores the fact that we have common responsibilities. And you see this running through every single contentious debate. "Why should I wear a helmet when I get on my motorcycle? I'm not going to do anything dumb," or "If I want to, if I want to put myself in danger, I ought to have the right to do it. Never mind what it does to the health care system. Never mind how it might traumatize somebody who might hit me by accident and paralyze me for life."

You see, this is the debate that's going on in our country all the time. And it's a big deal now. There's a huge number of people who believe that since all problems are purely personal or cultural, we don't have any common obligations. This is not a Republican-Democratic deal. It's not a liberal or conservative deal. It is really a—we're back to debating first principles in our country.

And those of you who are in law enforcement, you can really help, because almost all Americans really respect you for what you do. They know you put lives on the line. They know you

stick your necks out. They know you're doing something that you'll never get rich doing because you believe that it's the right thing to do.

And you need to take every opportunity you can to say, "Hey, you know, that's right. We need to punish wrongdoers. And we need to tell everybody to do the right thing, but there are things we can do in common that make a difference. And frankly, everybody who wants a handgun who's a law-abiding citizen ought to be willing to be put out the minor inconvenience it takes to wait a while so we can check and find the others who aren't."

You know, it is a small price to pay for being an American citizen living in the greatest country in the world and making a few more people safe. And people who are interested in sporting weapons ought to be willing to give up these assault weapons to get the Uzis out of the high schools. It is a small price to pay for living in the greatest country in the world and recognizing that we all have common responsibilities. We just don't all get to have our way simply because we're law-abiding.

Now, that is the debate that's going on in this country today. And that's why this community policing is so important. It is a small price to pay to prevent things from going wrong so we don't have to punish even more kids who might have been more law-abiding had community policing been there in the first place. Yes, it's true that you also catch criminals quicker, but the real genius of community policing is that over the long run it helps to prevent crime. But it only works if we have a common decision to do something in common as a people.

I cannot tell you how important I think this is. And of course, these problems have a very human face. Tomorrow I'm going to Chicago to honor one officer named Daniel Doffyn who was killed in the line of duty by a TEK–9, an assault weapon banned now by the assault weapons ban. I realize there may be some people out there who would like to have had these weapons. They're still better off being in America, and they can still have a whole arsenal in their homes, and it is a minor price to pay to be an American at this time facing our problems.

You know, if we had mass starvation in this country because we couldn't grow enough food, we could all say, "Well, everybody should be more responsible," but we'd find some common response to that. When they have an earthquake in California, everybody wants to go help them because we know that requires a common response. We have to start thinking about our persistent problems in this same way. That is really the fundamental debate we're having here in Washington today, goes way beyond partisan politics to how we are going to live as a people.

And so I would say to you that—I'll give you another example, and this is controversial. A lot of people in my party and a lot of my friends don't agree with this. I think the Supreme Court did the right thing this week by upholding the right of schools to do drug testing on student athletes—I don't—because drug use is going up. Now, I believe that not because I think we should assume that kids are using drugs—most kids are good kids, and they've got enough problems as it is without us looking down on them—not because I don't think they're entitled to their constitutional rights but because we know as an objective fact that casual drug use is going up among young people again. And it's wrong. It's crazy. It's not just illegal, it is dangerous for them.

And you know, you don't have a right to be on the football team or the basketball team or in the band or do anything else. So I think it's like the Brady bill. It's like, "Look, this is a hassle for you. We're asking you to do this for your country. We're not assuming you're a drug user. We're asking you to do this for your country. Do this because we need our kids to be drug-free."

And so, I'm proud of all of you. I am proud to be a part of this. I am proud that we are doing this today, and I am proud we've got over 20,000 police officers. And we're on time; we're actually a little ahead of schedule.

But I want you to go home and realize that this community policing debate and this debate about the assault weapons and this debate about the Brady bill is part of a huge, huge question that is now the dominant question every time they go to the floor to vote in the Congress on a controversial bill; this issue is behind almost every one of them. Because our problems at one level are personal and cultural, but they are also common: they are political; they are economic; they are social. And what we have to do is to find the right balance.

And we cannot, any of us, go off in some sanctimonious huff, saying that just because we don't do anything wrong, we shouldn't be asked to contribute to our country. And I'm not just talking about paying taxes. Whether it's obeying the speed limit or wearing a helmet or obeying these gun laws, we all ought to recognize that what—we have to define the challenges of America at this time.

And one of the biggest challenges is to make the American people feel more secure in a time of very rapid change. There is more opportunity out there for our people than ever before. But a lot of Americans are scared to death, for economic reasons and because of crime problems and other things. You, you are making a huge difference to them.

But when people see you with your uniforms, when they see you with these badges, then all these theoretical debates become very real. They know what you are. They know who you are. They know you're sticking up for them.

And the more you can make the community policing program work, the more you can make people understand that you're not trying to take their liberties away by asking them to wait to check on the handguns ownership or by dealing with the assault weapons ban, the more we can bring the American people back into a consensus again that we have more personal liberty in this country than any other democracy in the world but that all of us have to pay a price to maintain our liberties, to maintain our freedom, to meet the challenges of this day.

And frankly, when you look at it clearheadedly, it is a very small price indeed for the benefit of taking this country into the 21st century still the strongest country in the world. That's what the community policing is all about; that's what the Brady law is about; it's what the assault weapons ban is all about; it's what testing those kids in that school district is all about, for drugs; it's what a lot of these controversial issues we're trying to deal with are all about.

So I ask you to go home and tell your folks that we want to preserve our liberties, we want to preserve our freedom, we want to enhance their security, but they have to make some modest contributions to this as well. That's what you're doing, and that's what we have to do.

Thank you very much.

NOTE: The President spoke at 11:33 a.m. in Room 450 of the Old Executive Office Building. In his remarks, he referred to R. Gil Kerlikowske, Buffalo, NY, police commissioner who presented the

President with a Buffalo City Police Department shield; Mayor Rudolph Giuliani of New York City; Mayor Emanuel Cleaver II of Kansas City, MO; and Mayor Marion Barry of Washington, DC.

Statement on the Observance of Independence Day, 1995
June 29, 1995

I am delighted to join my fellow Americans in celebrating Independence Day.

Commemorating the birth of the greatest democracy in the world, the Fourth of July is a testament to all that is unique about America. Born of the courage of our founders and sustained by the spirit and sacrifice of every generation since, our nation has built a proud legacy of liberty. On this day, millions of our citizens join friends and loved ones at picnics and parades to rejoice in the blessings of freedom. People of all backgrounds unite in celebrating the energy and optimism that have always defined us as a people.

We are blessed that our country is better able than any other to face the trials and embrace the opportunities of the next century. Holding fast to the noble principles on which America was founded, we must look toward tomorrow with the same love of freedom, faith in justice, and firm commitment to moving forward together. These ideals, which have seen us through more than two centuries of challenge and change, will bring us ever closer to a future of hope, prosperity, and peace.

Best wishes to all for a wonderful celebration.

BILL CLINTON

NOTE: An identical message was also made available by the White House.

Statement on the Supreme Court Decision on the Georgia Congressional Redistricting Case
June 29, 1995

I am disappointed by the Supreme Court decision in the Georgia congressional redistricting case. The decision is a setback in the struggle to ensure that all Americans participate fully in the electoral process, and it threatens to undermine the promise of the Voting Rights Act.

My administration remains firmly committed to full enforcement of the Voting Rights Act. We will continue working to ensure that minority citizens in racially polarized areas have an effective remedy against the unlawful dilution of their votes and against impairment of their ability to participate in the electoral process. Congress, on a bipartisan basis, passed the Voting Rights Act to fulfill the constitutional guarantees of full political rights for all citizens, regardless of race. The Justice Department will continue its vigorous enforcement of the law.

We have traveled a long road to fulfill the promise of political rights for all citizens. Today is a difficult day on that journey, but the road does not end here. While the ruling in the Georgia case is unfortunate, I am gratified that the Court's statements and actions make clear that race properly may be considered in the drawing of legislative districts.

Despite today's setback, we will not let this decision turn back the clock. We will not abandon those citizens who look to the Voting Rights Act to protect their constitutional rights.

Statement on Agreement With Congress on Budget Rescissions Legislation
June 29, 1995

I am pleased that we have reached an agreement with Republicans and Democrats in the Congress on the rescissions bill.

I vetoed the original rescissions bill because it reduced the deficit the wrong way. The new bill achieves the same amount of deficit reduction as the previous bill, but it does so the right way, by protecting investments in children, education, national service, job training, and the environment that Congress wanted to cut. These are the kind of balanced priorities that make sense for our country as we enter the difficult budget debates ahead.

Specifically, the new legislation restores $733 million in these critical areas, including $220 million for the safe and drug-free schools program, $60 million for training teachers and other reforms under Goals 2000, $105 million for AmeriCorps, and $225 million for the safe drinking water program.

Like the original bill, the legislation contains over $16 billion in spending cuts, and it provides supplemental funds I requested for disaster relief activities of the Federal Emergency Management Agency, the Federal response to the bombing in Oklahoma City, increased antiterrorism efforts, and debt relief to Jordan to facilitate progress toward a Middle East peace settlement.

We have now achieved a bill that I am prepared to sign. This is essential legislation, and I hope the Congress will act on it quickly. While on balance I believe we made such significant changes that I am able to sign the legislation, the bill does contain provisions I do not support.

I still do not believe this bill should contain any of the provisions relating to timber. I opposed the timber salvage rider because I believe that it threatens once again to lead to legal gridlock and to impair, rather than promote, sustainable economic activity. I continue to have that concern. But the conferees did accept important changes in the language that preserve our ability to implement the current forest plans and their standards and to protect other resources such as clean water and fisheries.

Furthermore, Chairman Hatfield insists that the timber salvage provisions provide complete discretion for the administration to implement these provisions according to our best judgment.

I take Senator Hatfield at his word. Therefore, after signing the rescissions bill into law, I will direct the Secretary of Agriculture, the Secretary of the Interior, and all other Federal agencies to carry out timber salvage activities consistent with the spirit and intent of our forest plans and all existing environmental laws.

We will abide by the balanced goals of our forest plans, and we will not violate our environmental standards. Both are too important to protecting our quality of life and our economy.

Message to the Congress on District of Columbia Budget Legislation
June 29, 1995

To the Congress of the United States:

In accordance with section 446 of the District of Columbia Self-Government and Governmental Reorganization Act, I am transmitting the District of Columbia's Proposed FY 1995 Second Supplemental Budget and Rescissions of Authority Request Act and the Proposed FY 1996 Budget Request Act.

The Proposed FY 1996 Budget has not been reviewed or approved by the District of Columbia Financial Responsibility and Management Assistance Authority, created by Public Law 104–8, the District of Columbia Financial Responsibility and Management Assistance Act of 1995 (the "Act"). It will be subject to such review and approval pursuant to section 208 of the Act.

WILLIAM J. CLINTON

The White House,
June 29, 1995.

Remarks at a Fundraiser in Chicago, Illinois
June 29, 1995

Thank you very much. Mr. Mayor, thank you for your introduction, your support, the power of your leadership. Thank you, Bill Daley, for being willing to leave Chicago and come to Washington, which is prima facie evidence of some loss of sanity—*[laughter]*—to help us pass NAFTA. And thank you for your long friendship and your support.

Thank you, Father Wall, for getting us off on the right start. Maybe we'll be a little less partisan, a little less like the Republicans tonight since you prayed over us to start. I thank you all for being here and for your support.

When Hillary was making her remarks I was looking at her, imagining her here, thinking about the first time I ever came to Chicago to see my wife, before we were married. I believe I was in her house 3 hours before her father came down and said hello to me. *[Laughter]* It was sort of like running for President; you just can't get discouraged; you have to keep going and—*[laughter]*—you're laughing, but that's the truth, that story I'm telling. And I owe so much to this city and to this State.

Last Saturday I was home in Arkansas, in a little town called Pine Bluff. I took Dr. Henry Foster back there because he was born there, he grew up there. And that's still a place where people judge you by what you do instead of what you say. And I think we'd be better off if the rest of America were more like that. But anyway, we went home to Pine Bluff. And while we were there, it turned out that in this baseball park four blocks from where Henry Foster was born and where he learned to play baseball, there was a phenomenal amateur baseball tournament going on with all the major amateur leagues there in a playoff. And it was on ESPN. And two of the players were drafted right out there to the majors. And I went to throw out the first pitch, since I was there. And I was interviewed by none other than Gary "The Sarge" Matthews. You all remember him. He took the Cubs to one of those playoffs. So he said to me, "Now, come on, Mr. President, who's your favorite baseball team?" I said, "When I married my wife, I inherited two things, a wonderful family of in-laws and the Chicago Cubs." And I expect to get lots of mail.

After I met the Daleys, I got to go to White Sox games, which made me feel very good about that.

On the wall of my private little office in the White House, just off of the Oval Office, I have one of my most treasured pictures, a picture of Hillary and me on March 17th, Saint Patrick's Day, 1992, in the confetti in Chicago on the night that we won the Democratic primary in Illinois and virtually assured the nomination victory. And for all of that, I thank you all very, very much.

Since then this administration has had a remarkable partnership with this State and this city, in the ways that the mayor mentioned, fighting for the crime bill, bringing the Democratic Convention here, Chicago winning a fair and open contest to be one of the six cities in America to get one of our empowerment zones, to prove that we can have a partnership between Government and the private sector to rebuild the poorest parts of America and give people opportunity and free enterprise again in every part of the country. And I congratulate Chicago on that.

I have strongly supported the mayor's efforts at school reform, something that I care desperately about. If we cannot make our schools work, we're going to have a very hard time prevailing in the 21st century with the American dream. And you know, over 90 percent of all the funds for education in America come from the State and local government. We can do some things at the national level, and our Secretary of Education, Dick Riley, has done a great job. But unless there are people at the grassroots who are committed to making the schools work so that children learn, they learn things they need to know, they are useful, they are effective, we are going to have a very difficult time. There is no more important battle, and I congratulate him on waging that battle.

And finally, I'd like to say a word of appreciation to the city for being willing to work with us in good faith through Secretary Cisneros and the Department of Housing and Urban Development in an attempt to reform and really improve the Chicago public housing. We are committed to that. The mayor is committed to that.

We are going to prove some things that most people in America don't think can be done. And we are going to do it right here in Chicago, thanks to you. And we appreciate you for that.

And we are very much looking forward to being here for the convention. Debra DeLee is here. We've all got our feet on the ground. It was David Wilhelm's parting gift to his neighbor State before he left the Democratic Party in Washington with our strong support.

I thank the mayor for what he said about the things that we had done. I just want to say one word about that. I've done a lot of things that were controversial in this last 2½ years. But I haven't done anything I didn't think was right for America. What I'm trying to do is to test the outer limits of leadership, I think. But I think that's important at a time of profound change. But I'm trying to learn the balance, you know, like the mayor said, balancing the budget in 10 years instead of 7. I want to talk more about the other day—that in a minute.

But I heard a story the other day about the limits of leadership which I think about now before I do something really controversial, about the famous Louisiana Governor and later Senator, Huey Long, who as some of you know was a very great politician and was Franklin Roosevelt's chief rival for the affections of the Democratic Party before he was assassinated in the early thirties. And when Huey Long was a Governor, one day he was out on a country crossroads in the depths of the Depression where people had no money, nothing, no jobs. It was terrible, particularly in our part of the country.

And he had a big crowd of people out there in the country. And he started giving a speech. And his whole platform was share the wealth, you know, that nobody had very much money, and we ought to share what we had. So he looked at this crowd of people, these poor people and farmers in the country, and he said, "You know, we have got to share the wealth." And he spotted a farmer that he knew out in the crowd. And he said, "Farmer Jones, if you had three Cadillacs, wouldn't you give up one of them so we could drive it around here in the county and pick up all the kids and take them to school during the week and take them to church on Sunday?" He said, "Of course I would." He said, "And if you had $3 million, wouldn't you give up a million dollars so we could put a roof on everybody's house and feed all the children in this county?" He said, "Of course I would." He said, "And if you had three hogs——" And the farmer said, "Now, wait a minute, Governor. I've got three hogs." [Laughter] So I'm trying to learn what the limits of leadership are.

This has been a good day for America. We're celebrating the trade agreement with Japan, which all of you were kind enough to applaud. I want to tell you a little about it. It is different from and better than any similar trade agreement we've ever concluded. Most of our trade deficit in the world is with Japan, and 60 percent of our Japanese trade deficit is in autos and auto parts. We have a big surplus in auto parts in the rest of the world and a big deficit with them. This agreement will allow us to improve our position, not to guarantee us results, but it will give us a chance to compete and to be treated fairly and to create American jobs.

And coincidentally, it will be good for Japan, because their more closed economic system has led to the unbelievable anomaly of their being the richest country in the world on paper but not in fact, because their working people are paying 40 percent more—40 percent more—for basic consumer products than Americans are because their markets are closed. We lose jobs, they get money, but they can't do anything with it except spend more for the same stuff.

This is going to be a good thing for America. But it's going to be good for Japan, and it's going to be good for the world. And we were right to be firm and strong and go to the 11th hour, because this is one of the kind of difficult changes we're going to have to make if the world is going to be as it should in the next century.

This was also a good day for America because of the hookup of the Soviet—the Russian and the American space vehicles. Did you see that on television? And you saw them laughing and having a good time together and tumbling around in space. You know, it's amazing when you think about it, all that's happened, just from the last 5 or 6 years. That partnership with Russia that you saw in space today is also being mirrored on the ground.

In Russia today, the Vice President is over there working with the Prime Minister of Russia, Mr. Chernomyrdin. They have established an unprecedented partnership that has helped us to work to continue to reduce the threat of nuclear weapons, to reduce the threat of weapons being stolen or smuggled or nuclear material being smuggled out of Russia, to try to deal with the whole raft of problems that they have that will help our country, to work with them to build their democracy and their economy in the years ahead.

One of the things that I am proudest of is that during our administration, for the first time since the dawn of the nuclear age, there are no Russian missiles pointed at the people of the United States of America. So we're celebrating.

And I also want to talk a little bit about why we're here. When the mayor went through the record, you know, that unemployment's down and jobs are up, and we passed the crime bill, and we passed more trade legislation than anybody in the history of the country, and we've dealt with a lot of important issues, we have been able to play a constructive role for peace in the Middle East and Northern Ireland, lots of other important places in the world—you might ask yourself, if that all happened, well, why isn't everybody happy? What happened in the '94 elections? What's going to happen in the '96 elections? That's what I want to talk to you about tonight.

I want to talk to you about what I believe about this country and what I hope you believe about this country and why we are having the debate that we are having in Washington, DC, today. The truth is that for most Americans this exciting new world toward which we are moving, that has caught us all up, is a mixed bag. It is confusing, and they are confused. And that's why politics seems confusing. And it's why sometimes our adversaries do very well, because they are great at giving simple answers to hard questions. They're usually wrong, but it sounds good. It sounds good.

But I want you to think about what the world looks like from the point of view of the average American family. Let's just take the changes that are going on. Look at the economy. Consider this: In the last 2½ years, we've had 6.7 million new jobs, a big drop in the unemployment rate; the African-American unemployment rate has gone below 10 percent for the first time in 20 years; we have the lowest combined rates of unemployment and inflation in 30 years—that's very, very impressive; we've had the biggest expansion of trade ever in a 2-year period; the deficit has been cut, using the 7-year term

now favored by the congressional majority, by a trillion dollars over 7 years. But the median income in the United States has dropped one percent.

Now, if anybody had ever told you that jobs would go up, trade would go up, productivity would go up, inflation would go down, and the person in the middle would actually have a one percent decline in their income, you wouldn't have an increase in income—it doesn't seem to compute. What happened? How did that happen?

In the last 2 years, we've had more new businesses formed in '93 and '94 than in any 2-year period in American history; more new people have become millionaires in '93 and '94 than in any comparable period in American history. But more than half of the people of this country, 60 percent to be exact, are working a longer work week today than they were 10 years ago for the same or lower wages once you adjust for inflation. It doesn't figure.

What caused all this? It's good news and bad news. Part of it was the global economy. Part of it is the information and technology revolution, which means fewer people can do more work. Part of it was wrong-headed policies in our own Government. But it's happening.

So I get letters all the time from people that say, "I know that things are going well, but I don't feel more secure." I got a letter the other day from a guy that I went to grade school with, came from a very poor family, made himself an engineer, got a job with a Fortune 500 company, and now, after working there for 25 years, was one of three 49- and 50-year-old engineers who was laid off, and thinks he will never again find another job at remotely the same income or benefits. He's very excited for all these good things that are happening to the American economy, but how does he send his kids to college?

So, it's like a good news/bad news story. I'll give you another example: the technology revolution. Do you know what technology means in education? It means that a child in a poor mountain hamlet in the hills of the Arkansas Ozarks can get on the Internet and hook into a library in Australia to get direct information about volcanoes down there to do a research project. It's incredible. That's what it means.

It means that—the technology revolution means that all of you, if you have a computer, can hook into the White House and get all the facts on the budget. We were getting 50,000 people an hour for a few hours after we announced our new budget. It's incredible, what it means.

It means a lot of other things that all of you know, I'm sure. But let me tell you what it also means. It means that our children can get on the Internet, and now, without even paying any money, can be exposed to hardcore porn. It also means that a person who's smart enough to work a computer but is slightly deranged and paranoid can hook into the right people and learn how to make a bomb just like the one that blew up the Federal building in Oklahoma City. It also means that clever radical groups in places like Japan can have little vials of sarin gas they can go into subway systems and break open and kill a lot of innocent people. It means that here in our own country we've found radical groups experimenting with biological weapons, germ warfare. Technology: good news and bad news.

Foreign policy: The good news is no Russian missiles pointed at the United States. The good news is the cold war is over, and there's no serious threat to our security. The bad news is that once you strip the veneer of Communist control off of Russia with nothing to replace it, within 5 years half the banks are run by organized crime.

Hillary and I went to the Baltic States, to Riga, Latvia, and had tens of thousands of people in the streets thanking us for helping to get the Russian troops out of there for the first time since before the Second World War, people weeping in the streets. We went inside to a meeting, and the first thing the Presidents of the country asked us for was an FBI office, because now that there was no communism and no soldiers, they were worried that the port was going to become a center for drug traffickers.

The crime problem: Every major city in the country that's taken an aggressive stance against crime sees the crime rate going down, and that's the good news. But there are so many young people in this country that don't have strong family situations, don't have good community situations, that the rate of random violence among young teenagers is still going up. The rate of random drug use among young teenagers has started going up again, which means unless we figure out something to do about it, in 5

or 6 years, there's going to be an awful price to pay.

So there's all these wonderful things going on and all these troubling things going on. Is it surprising that people would look at all this and be confused and frustrated and anxiety-ridden and feel somewhat insecure?

Now, let me tell you, I believe with all my heart that the United States is better positioned for the 21st century than any nation in the world. I believe that the good news outweighs the bad. And I believe that the future's going to be fine if we will face these challenges.

But I have spent a lot of time in the last few months thinking about how to explain this to my fellow citizens. I ran for President for two reasons. I wanted to restore the American dream, because I did not want my child to be part of the first generation of Americans to do worse than their parents, because I did not want to see all these young people in our cities and isolated rural areas growing up in poverty with nothing to look forward to. And I wanted to unite the country. I wanted to bring us together. The diversity of America, the diversity of Chicago, the racial, religious, ethnic diversity we have in this country, unique among all the large countries of the world, is our meal ticket to the global economy if we can figure out what to do about it.

And if you ask me to give myself a grade on the first 2½ years, I would say I did a very good job on the first part of that, because we have really worked hard on the economy and on crime and on the other major issues facing us. But now, as President, I have to work harder on the second part, how to bring the American people together, how we can understand what it is we are facing.

Because I can tell you right now in Washington—the Members of Congress who are here will tell you—we are debating fundamental questions that we thought were resolved 50, 60, 70 years ago now. All these changes in the economy and all these changes in the way we live and work have led to a sense of unsettling and have led us to a composition in the Congress of people who literally are prepared to debate the first principles of our society. And you better be part of the debate if you want it to come out in the way you believe.

I now believe our ability to restore the American dream and to get this country going economically, to grow the middle class and shrink the under class, our ability to face all these other problems, depends upon our ability to have some understanding about how we relate to each other as a community and what this country's all about. And I just want to give you two or three examples of the profound debates going on in Washington today and why I come down where I do and why I hope you will understand how important this election is.

Debate number one in Washington: Are the problems we have as Americans primarily personal and cultural, or are they primarily political and economic? There are a whole lot of people in the Congress today who believe there's really nothing for the Government to do about our problems and nothing for them to do in their private capacity because most of our problems are personal and cultural. So if everybody would just wake up every day and do the right thing and stop misbehaving, and if people would stop putting out bad movies and CD's, we would have Nirvana. Everything would be fine. [*Laughter*]

Now, you're laughing, but I'm serious. I am serious. There are people who honestly believe that. And let us give them their due. At a certain level, it is true. That is, there is nothing I can do for you if you're not prepared to do the right thing yourself. You will all concede that. You didn't have enough money to come to this fundraiser tonight because somebody just gave you something. You had to live your life in a certain way. So at a certain level, that is true.

It is also true that the influence centers in our culture, whether it's entertainment or media or sports or you name it, have great influence in our society independent of politics and business and economics. That's also true.

But what bothers me is, that is—if that's all you say about it, it's just an excuse to walk away from our common problems and pretend we're not one country. What I believe is that our problems are both personal and cultural and political and economic. And I don't intend to use the personal and cultural nature of our problems as an excuse to walk away from our common responsibilities to do better.

And I'll try to give you a simple example of every one. Example number one: the family and medical leave law. There were people who opposed the family and medical leave law. They said, "It is wrong to impose any burden on the private sector at all. It will be terrible for

them. And besides that, we are philosophically opposed to it."

I believe that, on the personal and cultural side, if every kid in this country had two parents taking care of her or him and loving them and giving them discipline and giving them direction, we'd have about a third of the problems we've got in this country today. Most of them would be gone. I believe that. Now, I also believe that, economically, most people who are adults in this country have to work to make a living, whether they live alone or whether they're in a single-parent or a two-parent family. Therefore, the most important thing we can do, arguably, is to enable our fellow citizens to succeed as parents and to succeed as workers. Therefore, people ought to be able to take a little time off without losing their job if their child is sick or their parent is sick or a baby is born or something terrible happens to their family. So I supported that.

Now, that is the kind of fundamental debate we're having. You've got to decide where you stand. I say it's both, both personal and economic and political. And I hope you believe that. But a lot of people don't.

Let me give you another example. The mayor mentioned the crime bill. You know, I'm the only President—it's sort of—maybe this is not a compliment to me, but I'm the only sitting President, as opposed to somebody who gets out of office and does it, who has ever opposed the National Rifle Association in the Senate. [*Applause*]

I hate to say what I'm about to say now that you clapped. [*Laughter*] The truth is that I have agreed with them on many things. When I was a Governor, I worked with the NRA a lot. I liked their hunter education programs. I liked the fact that they tried to help me resolve some very difficult problems relating to people in rural areas and where you could hunt and where you couldn't and all of that. I don't oppose everything they want. What I oppose is this world view. This is not about the right to keep and bear arms, not the Brady bill and not the assault weapons ban.

There is one view that says, look, the crime problem is a personal problem. It is people doing wrong, right? Their slogan: "Guns don't kill people, people do," right? It's a personal problem. So find the wrongdoer, put him in jail, and throw the key away. This is politics, economics aside—has nothing to do with this.

This is about personal wrongdoing. And therefore, don't you dare inconvenience me one bit because of something somebody else did. I shouldn't have to wait 5 days to get my handgun, because I haven't done anything wrong. If I want to carry a TEK–9 around, I haven't done anything wrong. And who are you to judge me if I want to take it to target practice? That's what this is about. I'm not doing—just find the people who are doing wrong, and punish them. This is all individual.

The problem is, if you talk to the police officers of the country, if you talk to the prosecutors and the former prosecutors, like the mayor, they will tell you that this is like all of our other problems: If we will all take some responsibility for it, we can make progress.

So I have no objection, and I don't think anybody should, to saying to the citizens of this country, it is your responsibility to go through the minor inconvenience of waiting 5 days so we can keep people who have got no business buying guns from buying guns. It is a minor sacrifice for a major good. I don't have any problem telling those guys that you—it may break your heart not to have one of these TEK–9's, but it's worth it to get the Uzis out of the high schools. Sacrifice a little bit for a greater good.

I'll tell you—this may be an unpopular statement here—I agree with this decision the Supreme Court made saying that that school had the right to drug-test the kids who wanted to play on the sports teams. And I'll tell you why. Not because I think most kids do drugs; they don't. Not because I think most of our kids are bad; they're not, they're good. But our young people are pretty smart, and they know this drug deal is a big problem in our country. And I think it's worth saying to them, "It's a privilege to be on an athletic team. It's a privilege to be in music. It's a privilege to do extracurricular activities. This is something you ought to do for your country. Help us get rid of the scourge of drugs in our schools. Be willing to be tested as an example and to help us catch the people who are doing it. Don't cry about having your rights infringed, when all we're asking you to do is to band together and assume a little bit of responsibility and go through a little bit of inconvenience to move this country forward and help us deal with our problems." That's what we ought to be doing.

And I come now to the third example, the budget. Let's give the Republicans credit. First, they wanted to do the balanced budget amendment. And it failed by a vote because a lot of people thought it was a dodge and because a lot of people feared that sometime we might need to run a deficit in a recession and we couldn't do it. But then they came up with a balanced budget. And it adds up, and it's a credible budget.

And I want you to know, I think they're entitled to credit for that. Why? Because I believe it's important to balance the budget. Now, I know a lot of people don't. But let me remind you, this country never—never—had a permanent, structural deficit before 1981—never. We ran rather modest deficits all during the seventies, because those of you who were around then will remember that we had something called stagflation and the economy was weak, and we needed to do it for sound economic reasons. But we never had a permanent, huge deficit.

In 1981, we adopted those big tax cuts. We never really got over it. And then there was sort of a bipartisan agreement in Washington because the Democrats were not about to cut spending as much as it would take to balance the budget and the Republican Presidents didn't want to raise anybody's taxes because it violated their ideology.

So I got to be President 2½ years ago with the debt quadrupled in 12 years. And I'll tell you how severe it is: Our budget would be balanced today but for the interest we have to pay on the debt run up in the 12 years before I became President. I'll tell you how severe it is: Next year, interest payments on the debt will exceed the defense budget. You want more money for the Chicago schools? You want me to help educate more kids? You want me to invest in your efforts to clean up the environment and grow the economy? We won't have it unless we do something to change our spending priorities. So it matters.

When we brought the deficit down 2 years ago, that's how we got the economy going again, because we drove interest rates down and we got this economy spurred. So it is important. But there's a right way and a wrong way to do it.

What is the difference between my budget and theirs? It rests on a simple philosophical difference. They believe—this is honest. I'm not being critical; I'm telling you what they honestly believe. In the heart—when you strip it all away, they believe that the purpose of the Government is national defense, tax cuts on capital, and balance the budget as quick as possible because the Government would mess up a one-car parade otherwise. It's not good for anything. And we don't have any public responsibilities that should be manifest that way. That's what they believe. That's their honest conviction.

Now, I believe that the purpose of Government is to help people make the most of their own lives—that's what I believe—and to meet the challenges of the moment and to provide security for people who have done what they're supposed to do. That's what I believe.

So our budget says, look, if you balance the budget in 10 years instead of 7, if you cut this tax cut by more than half and you don't give it to people who don't really need it and you focus the tax breaks on education and childrearing, the two most important jobs in our society, then you don't have to gut Medicare and Medicaid. You can shave them in a modest way without worrying about whether you're going to close urban hospitals or close rural hospitals or hurt elderly people who don't have enough money to live on as it is. And not only that, you don't have to cut education at all. You can increase education. You can increase Head Start. You can increase apprenticeships for kids that don't go to college. You can increase student loans. You can increase our investment in technology and research. That is the difference.

My belief is we should balance the budget, but we should also grow the economy. The purpose of balancing the budget is to raise incomes, to create jobs, to bring us closer together, to enable us to meet our challenges. So I think my budget is better. But it all rests on a philosophical difference. You have to decide which side of the divide you're on.

I believe our Government's purpose is to help people make the most of their own lives. And let me just point out, there's a lot of people in that Congress who are there because we did that. The GI bill after World War II built the greatest middle class in the history of the world because the Government tried to help people make the most of their own lives. And that's the kind of thing we ought to be doing now.

So our budget proposes a "GI bill" for America's workers. It proposes the kind of thing that

they ought to be for, collapsing all the separate training programs of the Government, putting it in a big voucher. If you lose your job, you call the Government, say, "I'm enrolling at the local community college." We send $2,600 a year for 2 years and let people get a re-education or retraining program to get a new job and a better income and a new start in life. That's the kind of thing I think is worth spending money on. You have to decide where you stand on that.

These are the big, fundamental issues we're debating in Washington today. I believe time is on our side now. And I believe it for a couple of reasons. First of all, as hideous and awful and heartbreaking as the bomb in Oklahoma City was, it took a lot of the meanness out of this country. It brought us together. It made us all think about the impact of our words and our feelings and how we've been conducting ourselves.

And then when Captain O'Grady survived that magnificent, terrible 6 days in Bosnia and he was rescued, it put a little zip back in our step and made us realize what was best about this country. And I think our heads are kind of getting on straighter today as a people.

But I want you to know, I'm going to spend the next year determined to continue to move the country forward economically, to continue to deal with all these problems we've talked about. But we've got to get ourselves together.

I am telling you, this is a great country. If we can get ourselves together, if we can understand we have certain common responsibilities, if we can understand it is a phony political debate to try to say problems are personal and cultural as opposed to political and economic when they are both, if we can have a conversation with each other again about what it's really going to take to help people make the most of their own lives and give every American a chance to succeed, then we are going to do just fine. That is what the 1996 elections are all about.

Thank you, and God bless you all.

NOTE: The President spoke at 8:46 p.m. in the International Ballroom at the Chicago Hilton and Towers. In his remarks, he referred to Mayor Richard M. Daley of Chicago; former Special Counsel to the President for NAFTA William

Daley; Rev. Jack Wall, pastor, Old St. Patrick's Church; Debra DeLee, chair, Democratic National Convention; and David Wilhelm, former chairman, Democratic National Committee.

Letter to the Speaker of the House of Representatives on Emergency Salvage Timber Sale Legislation
June 29, 1995

Dear Mr. Speaker:

I am pleased to be able to address myself to the question of the Emergency Salvage Timber Sale Program in H.R. 1944. I want to make it clear that my Administration will carry out this program with its full resources and a strong commitment to achieving the goals of the program.

I do appreciate the changes that the Congress has made to provide the Administration with the flexibility and authority to carry this program out in a manner that conforms to our existing environmental laws and standards. These changes are also important to preserve our ability to implement the current forest plans and their standards and to protect other natural resources.

The agencies responsible for this program will, under my direction, carry the program out to achieve the timber sales volume goals in the legislation to the fullest possible extent. The financial resources to do that are already available through the timber salvage sale fund.

I would hope that by working together we could achieve a full array of forest health, timber salvage and environmental objectives appropriate for such a program.

Sincerely,

BILL CLINTON

NOTE: This letter was made available by the Office of the Press Secretary on June 30, but was not issued as a White House press release.

Remarks on Receiving the Abraham Lincoln Courage Award in Chicago
June 30, 1995

Thank you so much, Mike Robbins. Thank you for your presentation. Thank you much more for your courage and for your willingness to come back to work after being wounded 11 times. A lot of Americans wouldn't do that, and we appreciate you for doing it.

We thank you, Officer Jackson, Officer Bubalo. We thank the representatives of the Fraternal Order of Police who are here from Chicago and the State of Illinois, Bill Nolan and Sgt. Keith Turney. Thank you, Commander O'Shield. I hope you don't decide to run for President anytime soon after that reception you got when you were introduced—[*laughter*]—or mayor or anything else. [*Laughter*]

I want to thank Mark Karlin for what he said and for his long and often lonely battle against handgun violence.

The First Lady and I are delighted to be here with you today. I do want to introduce just one person of the many who came with me today because he carries on our part of the bargain fighting for law enforcement and against violence in Washington, Under Secretary of the Treasury Ron Noble, who is back here with me. Ron, stand up. Thank you very much.

I thank Superintendent Rodriguez for his outstanding leadership. Senator, thank you for what you said and for what you have done. To all the other distinguished officials who are here, I thank you. I want to say a special word of thanks to the mayor for his leadership and for his willingness to roll up his sleeves and actually solve problems.

You know, I like listening to the mayor talk because he never tries to be flowery, he just says what he has to say. [*Laughter*] But when he gets finished talking, you don't have any doubt about what he just said. [*Laughter*] And I like it because he's interested in doing things and giving other people the power to do things and bringing people together. That means a lot to me. We need more in Washington of what you have here in Chicago and in this Austin neighborhood.

I thank the other dignitaries who are here. Congressman, Bishop, thank you for coming. And ladies and gentlemen, I want to say a special word of thanks to some young people who are here from the "I Have A Dream" Program and the AmeriCorps volunteers who are working with them. Where are they? They're over there.

The "I Have A Dream" Program was founded in New York by a friend of Hillary's and mine named Eugene Lange, who believed that if you would reach young people in grade school and tell them that if they'd stay in school and stay off drugs and make their grades, you'd guarantee them that they could go all the way through college. That's what the "I Have A Dream" Program is about. And those kids in this neighborhood are part of that, and our national service program is helping. And I'm proud of them.

Ladies and gentlemen, it's already been said by Officer Robbins and others, but really this award ought to be given today to the officer who was killed here just a few months ago, Daniel Doffyn, and to his partner, and to Mike Robbins and his partner, and to all those who are willing to put their lives upon the line.

You heard the superintendent say it a moment ago, but Officer Doffyn and his partner, Officer Bubalo, were standing just where we stand today, getting ready to go to work, when they heard a call on the radio that said men were breaking into an apartment building just across the street. They were rookie officers who answered the call. They found gang members from another neighborhood who had come to disrupt this neighborhood. They were stopping one of the suspects when another came upon them. He murdered Officer Doffyn. He critically wounded his partner. He did it with a TEK–9 semiautomatic, one of the weapons banned in the 1994 crime bill.

Officer Doffyn was like me in one important respect, the most important of all: He had a daughter, an 8-year-old daughter who now will have to live with the memory of her father and his sacrifice.

When we talk about these issues and the decisions we ought to make on them, we're a long way, in Washington, DC, from the streets of Austin neighborhood. We'd be a lot better off if we had to vote on issues in front of the place where the police officer was killed.

I know that even from the worst tragedies, some good can spring. After the awful, awful bombing in Oklahoma City a lot of the meanness went out of America, and we all began to ask ourselves again, what can we do to do a better job for our country? What can we do to reach across the lines that are dividing us? What can we do to minimize the hatred and extremism in our own country?

I'm told that after Officer Doffyn was killed, children from Howe Elementary School across the street came to the police station to make sure their favorite police officers were safe, and that some of the officers took the children home in squad cars to reassure them and make sure they were okay. Now, outside this neighborhood that might surprise some people, but I've learned enough from the mayor and others about what you're doing here to know that you've been working for a long time to build that kind of community. Your mission statement—I wish every neighborhood in America had a mission statement—your mission statement says you want to make your neighborhood safe, prosperous, secure, productive, and proud. That's what I want for America.

In this neighborhood the words "community" and "policing" mean the same thing because the men and women of the 15th are the community and they understand that the best way to lower the crime rate is to prevent crime, to stop it from happening in the first place. They are working with you to set up a drug court to help people who get in trouble find a way to get out of trouble and go on to productive lives, not just go to prison. They are working with you to reach out to your children, to help them stay off drugs and stay out of gangs. They are watching out for you as you watch out for one another.

So many of you have taken responsibility for this neighborhood and your lives, and you are getting results. Crime is down across the board. I drove through these streets today and I saw homes, schools, businesses, churches, police stations, all doing their part to keep you safe and pull you together.

Despite the sadness that we all feel today, you should all be very proud. And you should be committed to keeping this community strong and to saving the lives and futures of these children.

When I ran for President, I promised that I would do everything I could to help you in this effort. Part of it was trying to restore the economy and bring opportunities to places that had been too long denied them, which is why I worked with the mayor and others to put an empowerment zone in Chicago, to try to prove that we could bring jobs and incomes and a future to people. But a big part of it was just trying to restore a simple sense of security to people who work hard and obey the law and are doing the best with their own lives.

The mayor referred to this, and Senator Simon knows it well because he was there for the whole time, but the Congress actually debated a crime bill for 6 years without doing anything about it, because there was always some political objection on the right or the left for getting together and doing something that would make a lot of sense at the grassroots level a long way from Washington. Well, we passed the crime bill, and it was largely written by the police officers of America. And it had a requirement that we put 100,000 more police on the street, a 20 percent increase of people walking the beat, working in the neighborhoods, helping to prevent crime in the first place.

I can tell you, that bill just passed late last year, but we are already—we already have given law enforcement agencies in this country enough grants to hire more than 20,000 new police. We're moving ahead of schedule to do that.

The second thing we did was to try and give law enforcement and community officials the tools they need to help save kids, to give children something to say yes to as well as something to say no to. The law enforcement people in this country knew that we needed tougher punishment, we needed greater protection. We passed the "three strikes and you're out" law. We passed the law strengthening the death penalty provisions, especially for people who kill law enforcement officers in the line of duty. But we also did what the law enforcement officers told us to do, which is to give them and community activists the tools to reach children early, to get them on the right path in life, to give them schools and jobs and opportunities and a future.

And yes, we took on the gun issue. And I want to say a little more about that in a minute, but it's been mentioned already. We passed the Brady law, which requires people to wait 5 days while we check the criminal and mental health histories of people who want to buy handguns, unless there is a computerized instant record check in place in a State. And we did ban 19 kinds of assault weapons and any identical copycats that might be made of them, for the obvious reasons you know.

I'll never forget—Mayor, you probably remember this—but we came here in 1994, and we sat at a panel in which people from your health care institutions told us that the mortality rate from gunshot wounds was dramatically increasing because the average victim had more bullets in his body when they showed up at the hospital. Why? Because of these assault weapons. I learned that in a hearing in Chicago from people who make a living working in emergency rooms, seeing people like Officers Robbins and Jackson every day. So yes, we did that.

And as we remember Officer Doffyn, I say there is at least one more thing we must do. Today I am announcing support for legislation that will ban armor-piercing bullets of all kinds.

Senator Simon referred to what we are trying to keep—and he's right, we do ban some kinds of armor-piercing bullets, thanks to him and others. But you need to know the law is written, in my opinion, in the wrong way. Today the law is written to ban ammunition based on what it's made of. If it contains certain materials, then it's off the street. Now, that's a good thing, but it's not good enough because clever people have figured out how to design ammunition made from common materials that do just as much damage. This legislation will change that. It will see to it that we judge ammunition not based on what it's made of but based on how much harm it can do. That should be the test. And the test should be simple and straightforward. If a bullet can rip through a bulletproof vest like a knife through hot butter, then it ought to be history. We should ban it.

Many Members of the United States Congress, Senator Moynihan, Senator Biden, Bradley, Kohl, Congressman Schumer from New York, have joined Senator Simon and others for a long time in trying to deal with these issues. Now, I know this will be controversial among some, just like the Brady bill was, just like the assault weapons ban was. But I want to tell you something, folks. There's a reason that I decided that I should be the first President ever to take on these issues while in office rather than later. [*Laughter*] And I say that—I'm grateful for the support we've received from former Presidents. I'm grateful that Ronald Reagan stood up for the Brady bill and Jim Brady. I am grateful that President Bush resigned from the NRA when they called Federal officials "jackbooted thugs." We should applaud them. [*Applause*] We should applaud them.

But I want you to know the reason I decided to do it, apart from just—first of all, I was sick and tired of reading stories about young children in tough neighborhoods who were straight-A students, being gunned down standing by a bus stop. I got tired of reading that. You know, I got tired of reading all these high school kids and junior high school kids thinking about what kind of funerals they were going to have because they knew so many kids that had been shot. I got tired of reading about it.

But there's another reason. I come from a place where more than half the people live in towns of 10,000 or less, where more than half the people have never been to a city as big as Chicago, and more than half the people have a hunting or a fishing license or both. When I was—long before I was a teenager, I had fired a .22 at cans and birds in bird season. I grew up thinking of guns as a part of my culture and not something evil or bad that would ever be used to kill people.

I understand the kind of folks who have formed the basis of a lot of the opposition to this gun legislation because they never see what you live with every day. They literally don't experience it. So I understood that. But you know, what my position is, is very different. I don't think this is—I don't think the Brady bill or the assault weapons ban or the cop-killer bullet legislation is about the right to keep and bear arms. I think it's about whether we as Americans are willing, those of us who are law-abiding, to undergo some minor inconveniences so we can solve our problems together and keep our kids alive and have a safer future and be fair to our police officers. That's what this is about.

And it's interesting, you know, most of the people who oppose the Brady bill and oppose the assault weapons ban, they don't mind walking through an airport metal detector. But I'm old enough to remember when those metal detectors were first put in when you walk through

an airport. Now, we don't think about it today, do we? Even though most of us would never consider carrying a gun on an airplane, much less a bomb, we go through the metal detectors, and we don't think anything about it. Why? Because it is a minor sacrifice to get on a safe airplane.

There was a decision made by the Supreme Court the other day that's somewhat controversial, but I support it. I want to tell you about it because it's the same point. The Supreme Court said it was all right for a school district to require young people who wanted to be on the football team to undergo drug testing, not because we think most kids are bad—they're not—not because most of them are using drugs—they're not—but because drugs are tearing the heart out of the children of America. It is a privilege to play on a sports team or be in the school band or do anything else like that, and it is a minor inconvenience for young people to take a stand to help to get drugs out of our schools.

Now, that's what I think about this. So I say to all the people who own guns and don't feel like they're ever going to do anything wrong and just want us to punish criminals, it is no big deal if you have to wait a few days to get the next handgun. You will survive. And it's a good thing.

And I say to all the people who love to hunt and shoot in shooting contests, you will be able to do it, and you will find a way to do it even without the TEK-9's. It's worth it to get the Uzis out of the high schools and off the streets, and the bullets out of the bodies of these police officers we celebrate today. It is worth it. It is worth it.

Nobody is interfering with your right to hunt or to enter into any kind of sporting contest or to do whatever else you want to do. But this is a minor, minor change that's good for all of us. And sooner or later, those of us who live in disparate areas of the country with different experiences have got to realize we have common obligations to the common good. And everybody in the smallest rural hamlet in my State is going to be better off if kids don't get killed on the streets of Chicago and police officers don't get gunned down because we got rid of assault weapons and we got rid of cop-killer bullets. We're going to be better off if that happens.

And you know, let me just say one other thing to everybody who objects to this today. I'm almost 50 years old. I have never seen a deer, a duck, or a wild turkey wearing a Kevlar vest in my life. You do not need—[*laughter*]—you do not need these bullets.

So I ask you all to support this. I ask you to oppose the efforts of the lobbies in Washington to lift the ban on assault weapons. I ask you to oppose their efforts to roll back the crime bill; oppose their efforts to keep us from getting all these horrible police-killing bullets out of our lives; and, as Senator Simon said, oppose their efforts to indiscriminately say all felons can have their guns back.

We live in the freest nation the world has ever known, because over 219 years we have found ways to agree on discipline, restraint, and order, to preserve our liberty. And all, all systems of discipline, restraint, and order affect the law-abiding and the lawless equally. That is the point.

So I ask you all today to remember that. I accept this award today, even though I don't feel like I deserve it, because I just did my duty. And I knew because of my childhood and the life I live and the State I governed what the issues were, what the stakes were, and what the forces in play were in this battle over the Brady bill, the assault weapons ban, and the cop-killer bullet issue.

Most of the people on the other side of this issue are good people. But they don't have your experience. And it is time for them to think about you. It is time for them to make minor concessions so that you can have major advances in safety, in security, in the future of your chil-

dren, in the security of your police officers, in the Austin neighborhood, in Chicago, Illinois, and throughout the United States of America. It is time for us to pull together on this issue and do the right thing.

Abraham Lincoln, who saved our Republic, said something very important in his first inaugural. When the country was coming apart at the seams over the issue of slavery and we were headed smack-dab into a Civil War, and when half the people in the country hated him and he'd been elected President with only 39 percent of the vote, he had the understanding to say, "We are not enemies, but friends. We must not be enemies."

So I say to you today, my friends: Let us stand up for the future of our children. Let us stand up for the security of our police forces and their ability to work with us. And let us say to those who disagree, we ask you for a minor contribution to a major public good. Let us not be enemies but friends.

Thank you, and God bless you all.

NOTE: The President spoke at 10:05 a.m. at the 15th District Police Headquarters. In his remarks, he referred to Mike Robbins, Talmadge Jackson, and Milan Bubalo, Chicago police officers wounded in the line of duty; Bill Nolan, president, Chicago Fraternal Order of Police; Sgt. Keith Turney, chairman of the trustees, Illinois State Fraternal Order of Police; Leroy O'Shield, commander, 15th District, Chicago Police Department; Mark Karlin, president, Illinois Council Against Handgun Violence, which sponsored the award; Matt Rodriguez, Chicago Superintendent of Police; and Bishop Shepard Little, Church of God in Christ.

Message to the Congress Transmitting Legislation To Limit the Availability of Certain Handgun Ammunition
June 30, 1995

To the Congress of the United States:

Today I am transmitting for your immediate consideration and passage the "Saving Law Enforcement Officers' Lives Act of 1995." This Act would limit the manufacture, importation, and distribution of handgun ammunition that serves little sporting purpose, but which kills law enforcement officers. The details of this proposal

are described in the enclosed section-by-section analysis.

Existing law already provides for limits on ammunition based on the specific materials from which it is made. It does not, however, address the problem of excessively powerful ammunition based on its performance.

Criminals should not have access to handgun ammunition that will pierce the bullet-proof vests worn by law enforcement officers. That is the standard by which so-called "cop-killer" bullets are judged. My proposal would limit the availability of this ammunition.

The process of designating such ammunition should be a careful one and should be undertaken in close consultation with all those who are affected, including representatives of law enforcement, sporting groups, the industries that manufacture bullet-proof vests and ammunition, and the academic research community. For that reason, the legislation requires the Secretary of the Treasury to consult with the appropriate groups before regulations are promulgated. The legislation also provides for congressional review of the proposed regulations before they take effect.

This legislation will save the lives of law enforcement officers without affecting the needs of legitimate sporting enthusiasts. I urge its prompt and favorable consideration by the Congress.

WILLIAM J. CLINTON

The White House,
June 30, 1995.

Remarks to the American Association of Physicians From India in Chicago
June 30, 1995

Thank you so much, Dr. Khedkar. Thank you, Dr. Ahuja. And thank you, Dr. Lalmalani, for that terrific speech. I was just sitting here watching you speak with such energy and enthusiasm. And I was thinking to myself, I hope he stays in medicine and out of politics until I'm through. [*Laughter*] Dr. Rupani, thank you for welcoming us to Illinois. To my good friend, B.K. Agnihotri, it's good to see you, and out of the South, where we normally see each other. We're delighted here with the presence of the Indian Health Minister, Minister Antulay. Thank you very much for coming from such a long way. And I am especially delighted to see the Indian Ambassador to the United States, Mr. Ambassador Ray. Thank you so much. Thank you. We're delighted to see you.

As I think all of you know. I have been very interested in education and in health care for a long time. But I must say I was certainly humbled when young Dr. Ambati was introduced at 17 years old. Then it was whispered in my ear that his brother became a doctor at the ripe old age of 19. [*Laughter*] Is that right? There he is. He was so old he hardly had any years left to practice at 19. [*Laughter*]

That's remarkable. You know, when I was elected Governor at 32, they said I was too young. When I was a college professor at 26, they said I was too young. When I was elected the third youngest President at the age of 46, they said I was too young. Where were you guys when I needed you? [*Laughter*] Well, your families and your friends and, indeed, all of us should be very, very proud. And congratulations to you, to both of you.

I know that Hillary would want me also to say, since I am the one doing the speaking today, that she and our daughter Chelsea had a magnificent time on their trip to India and, indeed, throughout South Asia. As I said to your board of directors a few moments ago, they came home laden with photographs, with films, with books, with all kinds of gifts. You could go to some places in the White House and some corners, and all of you would think you were back home. You would not even recognize— [*laughter*]—that you were in the President's residence.

But it was a remarkable experience for her, a transforming experience for our daughter, and a great learning experience for me by extension. I can also say I am very, very proud of the strengthening relationships between the United States and India since I have been President. We have been fortunate, thanks to the end of the cold war, to be able to bind these two great democracies more closely together, to support the economic reform efforts in India, to support a closer political relationship, to look toward a 21st century in which together we can advocate freedom for all the peoples of the world, and all the peoples of Asia in particular.

I also want to say I am deeply indebted to the Asian-Indian Americans who are serving in our administration. I cannot name them all, but I would like to mention Arati Prabhakar, who is the Director of the National Institute of Science and Technology, something important to all of you; Dave Sharma, who heads the Research and Special Programs Administration at the Department of Transportation—both of them have done a fine job; Dr. Sam Shekar, a member of AAPI, who's the Director of the Health Care Financing Administration's Practicing Physicians Advisory Council—we need more advice from practicing physicians and less from bureaucrats; and Niranjan Shah, who is here, is on the Goldwater Scholarship Foundation. There are others, but I want to thank all of you who have contributed to this administration.

I want to thank the AAPI for many things, for all the work you do, which your leader has already outlined, the work you have done in our country, the work you have done in India. But most recently, I am indebted to your association for your support of the nomination of Dr. Foster to be the Surgeon General. I thank you for that very much.

I think many of you could identify with him in many ways but perhaps most important that he was a man who had spent almost 40 years doing what other people talk about doing. He had brought health care to people who would not have had it otherwise. He had delivered thousands of babies. He had trained hundreds of doctors. He had actually looked many troubled young people in the eye and told them that they should stay off drugs, they should stay in school, they should not have sex, they should be against teen pregnancy, they should start a better life for themselves. He had actually done these things. And a lot of people who condemned him, I think, missed a terrific opportunity to give a real practicing physician a chance to change the lives of more young people in America. You saw that. You stood by him. And I will never ever forget it. I thank you very much.

I also want to thank you for something else, something more profound that you do every day, many of you without even knowing it. I ran for President for two reasons. One, I thought our country was drifting and not facing the challenges of the moment and that we were at risk of raising the first generation of Americans to do worse than their parents, when it was not necessary. So I wanted to restore the American dream of economy and prosperity for those who work hard.

Second, I thought our country was on the edge of either becoming the greatest country in the world for the 21st century again or being divided in ways that will weaken us. The enormous racial and religious and ethnic diversity of America is the meal ticket of the United States to the future if we can come together, instead of permitting ourselves to be divided by those who seek short-term political advantage from the differences among us. And I want this country to pull together. And I want you to lead the way.

It is obvious that both these objectives become imperative when you consider the realities of the world we face. We are no longer divided by the cold war. The geopolitical realities of India from time to time forced you and the United States to make decisions which divided our two great democracies because of the cold war, even though we were both democracies. The end of the cold war means that we don't have to divide the world up in that way anymore. The dawn of the information age and the technological revolution means that people can move ideas and technology and funds around the world in a split second, that all of us can move more rapidly than ever before.

Therefore, this is a time of enormous human potential. But it is also full of challenges. It is full of economic challenges, because the global economy means that if America wants to continue not only to be a wealthy country but to have everybody able to work hard and be rewarded, that all those people that live within our borders now must compete with people beyond our borders. It means education is more important than ever before. It means personal productivity is more important than ever before. It means the strength of a family's work habits are more important than ever before if we want to lift all Americans up, because now we are not isolated behind our own borders.

That is why so many Americans are frustrated today. They see our economy growing, unemployment is down, 6.7 million new jobs. But still more than half of our working people are working longer work weeks without getting a raise, under the pressure of the global economy. So that is the irony of America. We have more new businesses in the last 2 years than at any time in our history. We have more new millionaires in the last 2 years than at any time in our history, and most people stuck in a rut. So our challenge is to keep all these good things going and lift the rest of Americans who are in the rut out of it.

The same thing is true—[*applause*]—thank you. The same thing is true about making the most of our diversity. The cold war is over. That means we don't have to worry about nuclear annihilation. For the first time since the dawn of the nuclear age, there are no Russian missiles pointed at Americans, no American missiles pointed at Russians. Our space ships linked up yesterday; many of you must have seen it on television. How exciting it was. But when you take the heavy hand of authoritarianism away, you see the horrible conflict in Bosnia, where centuries old religious animosities flare up again today once there is no Yugoslavia run by a Tito to control people. Even in Russia, as it becomes more democratic, you see the ethnic fighting in a place like Chechnya consuming the energies of the nation and threatening the values of the nation.

And in our country, with no iron hand of fear of something outside us to keep us together, you see now resurgent religious and ethnic differences manifesting themselves even across the United States. This is folly. We must find a way to live together, sharing the values of the American Constitution, respecting our different religious heritages, our different ethnic heritages, our different racial heritages. We have counties in the United States now with more than 100 different ethnic groups; Los Angeles County now has more than 150 different. And I say good; this is good for America. This is a good thing if we can use it to come together. It means we can trade with every country in the world. It means some of us can speak to people in every place in the world.

What other nation could have done what we did in Haiti, liberating them from the long night of dictatorship, and doing it by putting 200 Americans in military uniform on the ground in Haiti to speak Creole because they were Haitian-Americans? That's the great thing about this country.

We are a land, and we are a set of ideas and convictions. We are not a single ethnic group. That is the magic of our democracy. We are a land, and we are a single set of convictions, rooted in the simple but powerful words of our Constitution and its Bill of Rights and our devotion to freedom and to competition and to openness. That is our meal ticket to the future. That is what will make it possible for us, not only to succeed economically but to live in harmony, if we can be faithful to it. And that has been the purpose of my Presidency.

Now, what I want to say to you today is to echo a few words that your leader just spoke. We are having a great debate in the United States today, largely because we are at the end of the cold war, largely because we are in a new economic time, largely because all these changes have forced Americans both to change the way they live and work and to try to think of how we should organize ourselves into the future.

And there are many people in the Nation's Capital who believe something that I think a lot of you do not believe. And that's one of the reasons I'm here. They say—and many of them who disagree with me would use you as an example, a good example—they would say all of the problems in America today are personal problems, individual failures; they are cultural problems. Why, if everybody would just wake up tomorrow and work hard and have a good family, we wouldn't have any other problems. And they would say if they were here arguing, they would say, look at all those Indian doctors and their families who come to our country. Many people come to our country without any money at all, and they become very successful. Why? Because they work like crazy and they have good family values and they transmit them to their children. And I agree with that. I mean, I agree with that. By definition—you know, no one can become anything just because someone else gives them something. We all have to work and build ourselves inside. That is true; at one level that is true.

But then they take another step. And that is the debate in Washington with which I do not agree. The next step is, if all of our problems are personal and cultural and can be solved by people working harder and having stronger families, we therefore have no problems that are economic, political, and social. And therefore, there is nothing for us to do together, no public response required, no governmental action required. Now, that is what I don't agree with.

Our country became the strongest in the world after World War II and grew the biggest middle class in the world after World War II because we recognized that our challenge was both personal and public. And when the soldiers came home after the Second World War and built the America that many of you wished to come to, they did it because the Congress passed something called the GI bill of rights, which enabled them to go to school, to buy a home for the first time, that gave us over two-thirds of our people owning their own home, something unheard of in virtually any country in the world, because there was public action. So we had personal responsibility and public action.

When you go out and practice medicine to people who don't have any way to see a doctor, unless you see them and you get paid because of Medicare or Medicaid, that's personal responsibility by you and public action by your country. And so what I say to you is that this debate, which I, too, want you to be a part of, about the future of health care, is one facet of this huge debate we're having in America today about how we're going to organize ourselves for the future.

And I believe America should come down firmly on the side of saying yes, we have to have more personal responsibility and family strength, but we also need to face our problems together, because we cannot solve the education problem unless we solve it together. We cannot solve the crime problem unless we're all willing to make some sacrifices to solve it together. We certainly cannot solve the health care problem if we let every individual in America go his or her own way. We're going to have a lot of older people and a lot of innocent children in dire straits in America. We need to do some things together. That is the way we're going to succeed in the 21st century, by working together.

On health care alone, let me just make a few observations. We have a big problem in America with our budget deficit. You all know that. What I want you to know is just how big a problem it is and where it's located. Our budget would be in balance today but for the interest we pay on the debt we ran up in the 12 years before I became President. It would be in balance today. Not only that, it's still such a big problem that next year the interest we

pay on that debt will be larger than our defense budget.

We have not increased anything much in our budget in the last few years except Medicare and Medicaid had been growing at two and three times, sometimes more than three times, the rate of inflation. Part of that is because more people have been going onto the program. Part of that is because as older people live longer and longer and longer, they have to access medical services more and more, as many of you know.

But the truth is, if we are going to have money in the United States Treasury to invest in education, to invest in technology, to invest in medical research, something you all believe in, we are going to have to reduce this——

[*At this point, the sound system malfunctioned.*]

Did it come on? Is it on? What about now? Can you hear me in the back?

Audience members. Yes!

The President. Someone said, "No, and I'm sure glad." [*Laughter*] Well, anyway, I'll talk louder, and we'll do the best we can. Something happened to it. I didn't touch it. It just happened. [*Laughter*] Eventually they'll get it back.

If we're going to do this, we're going to have to bring that deficit down, which means as Dr. Lalmalani said, we're going to have to change the way we do health care. But there is a huge difference in making a deliberate change over a reasonable period of time and just cutting the budget out of Medicare and Medicaid to meet an arbitrary date to balance the budget for an arbitrary huge tax cut to a lot of folks who don't need that as much as they need a country with good health care, strong education, safe streets, and a balanced budget.

What I want to say to you is, yes, we will have to slow the growth of Medicare and Medicaid, but we should do it in a fair way. If you balance the budget in 10 years instead of 7, if you have a much smaller tax cut and you target it to the things we already said we believed in, childrearing and education, if we involve the physicians and other health care professionals in our country in making the decisions instead of just making arbitrary cuts in these medical costs, we can get where we need to go as a country and still provide decent health care and still provide a good quality of life and not divide our people even further by income and by region and by race. Now, that's what we can do.

A lot of you know this because of your own practice, but if we cut too much without understanding the circumstances, we will isolate more elderly people, we will isolate more racial minorities, we will disadvantage more young children who will suffer intellectually because of the health care they don't have when they're very young. So this is a very important part of rebuilding America.

[The sound system produced a loud feedback sound.]

Better none at all than that. *[Laughter]*

So I say to you, in the next 4 or 5 months, we will chart a major part of America's health care course for the future. And my commitment to you is, I will work with you. I do not want to see these decisions made without working with you. *[Applause]* Thank you.

But keep in mind, the health care debate is an example of the larger debate I talked to you about. And you can have a huge impact on Members of Congress in both parties if you simply show up and say, "Look, I know America first and foremost is a place where individual effort and family values count. That's why I am successful. But I live in the real America, not in Washington, DC. And I know we need a public response to society's problems if more people are going to become like me." That's what I want you to say to the Congress. And you can do that.

And then I want you to be involved. And I want you to say, don't wait until the day before you pass this budget to point out what the changes will be in Medicare and Medicaid. Let's say it well in advance. Don't wait until one day or two days or even a week before and then jam it through. Let's say right now, if we're going to cut Medicare and Medicaid projected expenditures by the amount you say, what changes will be made in Medicare and Medicaid. Then let us tell you—I don't want anybody to get hysterical or angry or anything—let us tell you what the consequences of those changes will be. And then let's work together to do

something that is good for America. We should do what is right here.

And it is not necessary—I will say again—it is not necessary to dramatically undermine Medicare and Medicaid. It is not necessary to hurt defenseless children or elderly people who don't have enough to live on as it is to balance the budget. We do not have to do that. It is certainly not necessary to undermine the medical practice. It is not—also, it is not necessary to undermine the integrity of the doctor-patient relationship. It is not necessary.

And I certainly agree with you. I think—I am all for managed care plans if people voluntarily join them and if every physician who is willing to meet the requirements of the plan has a chance to practice to maintain choice for consumers.

So I want to make this point again. This budget debate, because it's part of a larger social debate, can empower all of you as citizens far beyond voting, contributing to candidates, being active in political campaigns. This budget debate can empower you because every one of you can be heard by your Member of Congress. And you can say, "I accept what you're saying that our problems require harder work, more discipline, stronger families. But it is not enough. It also requires us to work together. And I want to be heard in the health care debate. And I want you to enable America to balance the budget and meet its responsibilities to bring us together and move us forward." If you'll do that, I'll be grateful.

Thank you, and God bless you all.

NOTE: The President spoke at 1:35 p.m. in the Sheraton Chicago. In his remarks, he referred to Dr. Nanda Khedkar and Dr. Satya Ahuja, convention cochairmen; Dr. Gopal Lalmalani, association national president; Dr. Prem Rupani, president, India Medical Association of Illinois; B.K. Agnihotri, chancellor, Southern University Law Center, Baton Rouge, LA; A.R. Antulay, Indian Minister of Health and Family Welfare; S.S. Ray, Indian Ambassador to the U.S.; and convention participants Dr. Balamurali Ambati and his brother, Dr. Jayakrishna Ambati.

Statement on the Nomination of General John M. Shalikashvili To Be Chairman of the Joint Chiefs of Staff
June 30, 1995

I am pleased to announce that I have nominated General John M. Shalikashvili, U.S. Army, for reappointment as Chairman of the Joint Chiefs of Staff for a 2-year term.

As I said when I nominated General Shalikashvili for Chairman in 1993, he is a shining symbol of what is best about the United States and best about our armed services. He has again proven that over the past 20 months by maintaining the strongest military in the world, with the equipment and trained force to fight and win when we must, even as he completed the post-cold-war drawdown of our forces. From morale to readiness, General Shalikashvili has provided the sound leadership needed to keep our military strong while shaping the Armed Forces for the 21st century. I look forward to the next 2 years with General Shalikashvili as Chairman, to his wise and reasoned counsel, and to his advocacy for the men and women in the Armed Forces in support of the national security of the United States.

Message to the Congress on Trade With Russia
June 30, 1995

To the Congress of the United States:

On September 21, 1994, I determined and reported to the Congress that the Russian Federation is in full compliance with the freedom of emigration criteria of sections 402 and 409 of the Trade Act of 1974. This action allowed for the continuation of most-favored-nation (MFN) status for Russia and certain other activities without the requirement of a waiver.

As required by law, I am submitting an updated Report to Congress concerning the emigration laws and policies of the Russian Federation. You will find that the report indicates continued Russian compliance with U.S. and international standards in the area of emigration.

WILLIAM J. CLINTON

The White House,
June 30, 1995.

Appendix A—Digest of Other White House Announcements

The following list includes the President's public schedule and other items of general interest announced by the Office of the Press Secretary and not included elsewhere in this book.

January 1

In the afternoon, the President and Hillary Clinton returned to Washington, DC, from Hilton Head, NC.

January 2

In the morning, the President and Hillary Clinton traveled to Little Rock, AR.

January 4

In the morning, the President and Hillary Clinton returned to Washington, DC.

The President announced his intention to appoint Ambler H. Moss, Jr., as a member of the Panama Canal Consultative Committee.

The President announced that he recess-appointed Kathleen A. McGinty to chair the Council on Environmental Quality and that he submitted her name to the Senate for confirmation.

The President announced his intention to appoint Daryl L. Jones as a member of the U.S. Air Force Academy Board of Visitors.

The President announced his intention to nominate Denis J. Hauptly to be Chairman of the Special Panel on Appeals.

The White House announced that the President recess-appointed Robert Talcott Francis II as a member of the National Transportation Safety Board.

January 5

The President announced that Adm. William O. Studeman, Deputy Director of the Central Intelligence Agency, will serve as the Acting Director of Central Intelligence until a new Director has been confirmed by the Senate. His appointment will become effective January 10.

The President announced the appointment of Richard I. Beattie to be U.S. Special Presidential Emissary for Cyprus. He will travel to the region January 22.

The President announced his intention to appoint Shirley Humphrey to the National Nutrition Monitoring Advisory Council.

The President announced his intention to appoint Margaret Vanderhye as a member of the National Capital Planning Commission.

The President announced his intention to nominate Janie Ledlow Shores to be a member of the Board of Directors of the State Justice Institute.

January 6

The White House announced that the President invited President Fernando Henrique Cardoso of Brazil to the United States for a state visit beginning April 20.

The President announced his intention to appoint Robin Corathers to be a member of the Ohio River Valley Sanitation Compact Commission.

The President announced his intention to appoint Denice Wheeler as Chair and Federal Representative to the Bear River Commission.

The President announced his appointment of John M. Deutch and John D. Podesta to the Commission on Protecting and Reducing Government Secrecy.

The President announced his intention to nominate Wilma A. Lewis as Inspector General of the Department of the Interior.

January 10

In the morning, the President traveled to Galesburg, IL, where he participated in an informal discussion with area students, graduates, and employers at Carl Sandburg Community College. In the afternoon, he returned to Washington, DC.

The White House announced that the President invited President Mircea Snegur of Moldova to meet with him at the White House on January 30.

The White House announced that the President, at the invitation of the Canadian Government, will make his first state visit to Ottawa on February 23–24.

January 11

The President announced that he nominated Sheila C. Cheston to be General Counsel of the U.S. Air Force.

January 12

In the evening, the President and Hillary and Chelsea Clinton attended a performance of "Tommy" at the John F. Kennedy Center for the Performing Arts.

The President announced his intention to appoint Kay Dickersin to the National Cancer Advisory Board.

The President announced his intention to appoint Timothy Finchem and Al Mead to the President's Council on Physical Fitness and Sports.

The President announced his intention to appoint Samuel J. Simmons to the Policy Committee of the White House Conference on Aging.

The President announced his intention to designate William T. Esrey to be Chairman and Charles R. Lee to be Vice Chairman of the President's National Security Telecommunications Advisory Committee.

The President announced his intention to nominate Lawrence Harrington to be Alternate Executive Director of the Inter-American Development Bank.

January 13
In the morning, the President traveled to Cleveland, OH, where he met with a group of Central and Eastern European-Americans and with representatives of Central and Eastern European news organizations at the Stouffer Renaissance Hotel.

In the afternoon, the President met with participants in the White House Conference on Trade and Investment in Central and Eastern Europe. He then went to Cleveland-Hopkins International Airport where he met with the editorial board of the Cleveland Plain Dealer in the conference room at the IX Jet Center. He then returned to Washington, DC.

In the evening, the President and Hillary and Chelsea Clinton went to Camp David, MD, for the weekend.

The White House announced that the President moved the effective date of the latest California flood disaster from January 6 to January 3.

The President announced his intention to appoint S. David Fineman to the Board of Governors of the U.S. Postal Service.

The President announced his intention to appoint James R. Houghton, Vera Katz, Marc S. Tucker, and Alan L. Wurtzel to the National Skill Standards Board.

January 14
In the afternoon, the President met with a group of writers, professors, and political scientists at Camp David to discuss the future role of Government.

January 16
In the morning, the President returned from Camp David to Andrews Air Force Base, MD, and then traveled to Denver, CO. Following his arrival, he met with a group of officials from the natural gas industry at Denver Stapleton International Airport.

In the afternoon, the President traveled to Los Angeles, CA.

January 17
In the late morning, the President met with rescue workers at the Swift Water Rescue Unit at Fire Station 88 to discuss the recent flooding in southern California. Following the meeting, he traveled to Roseville, CA, where he toured flood-damaged areas and visited with victims.

In the afternoon, the President departed for Washington, DC, returning in the late evening.

The President announced his intention to appoint John J. Sweeney to the National Commission on Employment Policy.

The White House announced that Richard Schifter will assume a broader assignment at the National Security Council as Special Assistant to the President and Counselor and that Daniel Fried will succeed Mr. Schifter as Special Assistant to the President for

National Security Affairs and Senior Director for Central and Eastern Europe.

The White House announced the appointment of Coit D. Blacker as Special Assistant to the President and Senior Director for Russian, Ukrainian, and Eurasian Affairs, National Security Council.

The President announced his intention to appoint the following individuals as members of the Advisory Council of the Border Environment Cooperation Commission:

Thomas L. Soto;
Kathleen Marr;
Dan Eckstrom;
Sandra Ferniza;
Travis Johnson; and
Cynthia Ann Miscikowski.

January 19
The White House announced that the President will attend a ceremony in San Francisco, CA, in June and a special commemorative meeting of the U.N. General Assembly in New York City in October to celebrate the 50th anniversary of the founding of the United Nations.

The White House announced that the President invited Prime Minister Benazir Bhutto of Pakistan to Washington, DC, for an official working visit on April 11.

The President announced his intention to appoint the following individuals to the Advisory Committee on the Arts for the John F. Kennedy Center for the Performing Arts, Smithsonian Institution:

Wayne Cranford, Chair;
John C. Barsness;
Kathie Bartlett;
Anne Boyle;
Diana Carlin;
Arthur Chapa;
Bethine Church;
Leon Cohan;
Darrell Dorgan;
Pamela Eakes;
Sim Farar;
Hartina Flournoy;
Joseph Fuchs;
John Grisham;
Mary Gail Gwaltney;
Sharon Harrington;
Margaret Dunne Hartigan;
Steve Hicks;
Kenneth Jacobsen;
Susan Roach Kelly;
Zina Kramer;
Betty Oxendine-Mangum;
Bonnie Milenthal;
Sandra Montrone;
Leslie Moonves;
Kenneth Pentony;
Deborah Dozier Potter;

John Raffaelli;
Mary Stoner Rauh;
Mary Lou Reed;
Alice Richmond;
Susan Roberts;
Linda Kapuniai Rosehill;
Elaine Schuster;
Diane Meyer Simon;
Gary Smith;
Sally Troyer;
Michael Turpen;
Joseph Walsh;
Donna Axum Whitworth;
Caryl Yontz; and
Robert P. Zimmerman.

January 20
The President announced his intention to appoint Harriet Mayor Fulbright, Alan H. Schechter, and Caroline A. Matano Yang to the J. William Fulbright Foreign Scholarship Board.

The President announced his intention to appoint Harriett Woods to be a member of the Board of Directors of the Federal Home Loan Mortgage Corporation.

The President announced his intention to nominate Clifford Gregory Stewart to be General Counsel of the Equal Employment Opportunity Commission.

The President announced his intention to appoint the following individuals to the Advisory Committee for Trade Policy and Negotiations:

George Ariyoshi;
W.L. Lyons Brown, Jr.;
Ralph Gerson;
Dean R. Kleckner;
Lewis E. Platt; and
Jeannette S. Wagner.

January 23
In the afternoon, the President had a telephone conversation with President Ernesto Zedillo of Mexico to discuss the Mexican economic situation and U.S. loan guarantee legislation.

The President announced his intention to nominate Marianne C. Spraggins to be a member of the Board of Directors of the Securities Investor Protection Corporation.

January 24
The President announced his intention to appoint Miguel Angel Corzo to be a member of the Cultural Property Advisory Committee.

The President announced his intention to appoint Paul Cole, Terrance L. Craney, Yvette Herrera, and Esteban Soriano to the National Skill Standards Board.

January 25
In the morning, the President traveled to Kutztown, PA, where he met with students, teachers, and area business people and residents in the Keystone Gym-

nasium at Kutztown University. In the afternoon, he returned to Washington, DC.

The President appointed Nobel laureate Elie Wiesel to head the Presidential delegation to the commemoration on January 26–27 in Krakow, Poland, marking the 50th anniversary of the liberation of the Auschwitz-Birkenau concentration and death camp.

The White House announced that the President invited Chancellor Helmut Kohl of Germany to make an official visit on February 9.

The White House announced that the President will meet with President Isaias Afworki of Eritrea on February 1 at the White House.

The President announced his intention to appoint the following individuals to be members of the Panel of Arbitrators and/or Conciliators of the International Centre for Settlement of Investment Disputes:

Antonio J. Colorado, Conciliator;
Frederick Frank, Conciliator;
O. Jerome Green, Conciliator;
D. Holly Hammonds, Conciliator;
David Michael Ifshin, Arbitrator;
Carolyn B. Lamm, Arbitrator;
Lawrence B. Low, Arbitrator; and
Robert B. Owen, Arbitrator.

January 26
The President announced his intention to nominate Kirsten S. Moy as the administrator of the Community Development Financial Institutions Fund.

The White House announced that the President made the following appointments to the White House staff:

Kathryn O'Leary (Kitty) Higgins, as Cabinet Secretary, with the title of Assistant to the President for Cabinet Affairs;
Bob J. Nash, as Assistant to the President and Director of Presidential Personnel;
Rahm Emanuel, as Director of Special Projects;
John B. Emerson, as Deputy Assistant to the President and Deputy Director of Intergovernmental Affairs; and
Stephen B. Silverman, as Deputy Cabinet Secretary, with the title Deputy Assistant to the President for Cabinet Affairs.

January 27
The White House announced that the President directed a team of U.S. disaster experts to travel to Japan on January 30 to tour areas affected by the recent earthquake.

The President announced his intention to appoint Frank J. Biondi, Jr., to be a member of the President's Export Council.

The President announced his intention to appoint Stephanie Gonzales to the President's Commission on White House Fellowships.

The President announced his intention to appoint Clayton Lukow as Chair and Federal Representative of the Big Blue River Compact Commission.

The President announced his intention to appoint the following members of the Advisory Committee for the 1995 White House Conference on Aging:

James E. Birren;
David K. Brown;
Robert Butler;
Karyl Eckles;
Charles J. Fahey;
Evelynn C. Gioiella;
Lou Glasse;
Ed Haas;
Henry Jay Hannigan;
James Santiago Hena;
Carmela Lacayo;
John E. Lyle;
Martha A. McSteen;
Mary Mulvey;
Ron Pollack;
Steve Protulis;
Eugene Rinaldi;
Teresa Scannelli;
E. Percil Stanford;
Jeannette C. Takamura;
Eric G. Tangalos; and
Don Watanabe.

January 28
In the morning, the President attended a meeting at Blair House with Cabinet members, Members of Congress, Governors, and State and local officials to discuss welfare reform.

In the evening, the President and Hillary Clinton attended the Alfalfa Club dinner at the Capital Hilton.

January 30
In a ceremony in the Oval Office, the President received diplomatic credentials from Ambassadors Eunice M. Bulane of Lesotho, Tedo Djaparidze of the Republic of Georgia, and Amdemicael Kahsai of Eritrea.

The President announced his intention to nominate Bill Burton as a member of the Board of the U.S. Enrichment Corporation.

The President announced the appointment of Guillermo Linares to the President's Advisory Commission on Educational Excellence for Hispanic Americans.

The President announced his intention to nominate Rae E. Unzicker and Ela Yazzie-King to the National Council on Disability.

January 31
In the afternoon, the President traveled to Boston, MA. In the evening, he returned to Washington, DC.

The White House announced that the President invited Prime Minister Vaclav Klaus of the Czech Republic to make a working visit to Washington, DC, on May 4.

The White House announced that the President will meet with Prime Minister James Bolger of New Zealand on March 27 at the White House.

The President announced the appointment of the following individuals to the President's Advisory Board on Arms Proliferation Policy:

Janne Nolan, Chair;
Paul C. Warnke;
Edward Randolph Jayne II;
Ronald F. Lehman II; and
David E. McGiffert.

February 2
The President announced his intention to nominate Mary S. Furlong as a member of the National Commission on Libraries and Information Science.

The President announced his intention to appoint Joseph A. Cari, Jr., as a member of the Board of Trustees of the Woodrow Wilson International Center for Scholars.

The President announced his intention to appoint John T. Smith and Hugh B. Price to the National Skill Standards Board.

The President announced his intention to appoint Karl Stauber as the Department of Agriculture Federal Representative to the Rural Telephone Bank Board.

February 3
In the afternoon, the President hosted a working lunch for Prime Minister Lamberto Dini of Italy.

The President announced his intention to nominate Jeffrey M. Lang to be Deputy U.S. Trade Representative.

The President announced the appointment of James K. Huhta as a member of the Advisory Council on Historic Preservation.

February 4
In the afternoon, the President and Chelsea Clinton attended a basketball game at George Washington University.

February 5
The President directed the Immigration and Naturalization Service to immediately send 62 Border Patrol agents to Nogales, AZ, to combat an unprecedented rise in illegal border crossings there.

February 7
The White House announced that the President invited King Hassan II of Morocco to Washington for a state visit on March 15.

The President announced his intention to nominate Herbert F. Collins to be a member of the Thrift Depositor Protection Oversight Board.

The President announced his intention to nominate the following individuals to be members of the Defense Base Closure and Realignment Commission:

Al Cornella;

Rebecca G. Cox;
Gen. J.B. Davis;
S. Lee Kling;
Benjamin F. Montoya;
Wendi L. Steele; and
Michael P.W. Stone.

February 9

The President announced his intention to appoint Fredric K. Schroeder to the Committee for Purchase From People Who Are Blind or Severely Disabled.

The President announced his intention to appoint Peggy Montaño as Chair and Federal Representative on the Sabine River Compact Commission.

The President announced his intention to appoint Marcia Devins Greenberger to the National Skill Standards Board.

The President announced his intention to appoint Alice Kilham to be Chair of the Klamath River Compact Commission.

February 10

The President announced his intention to nominate Sheryl R. Marshall to be a member of the Federal Retirement Thrift Investment Board.

The President announced his intention to appoint the following members to the Advisory Committee on the Arts of the John F. Kennedy Center for the Performing Arts, Smithsonian Institution:

Lucy Madden Buntain;
Michael Driver;
Pete Flaherty;
Robin Greenspun; and
Nancy Blount.

February 11

In the afternoon, the President hosted a working lunch for Prime Minister Jean-Luc Dehaene of Belgium.

February 13

In the afternoon, the President had a telephone conversation with President Boris Yeltsin of Russia, to express strong U.S. support for the continuation of reform in Russia.

The President announced his intention to nominate Gloria Rose Ott and Harvey Sigelbaum to the Board of Directors of the Overseas Private Investment Corporation (OPIC). He also announced his intention to renominate George Kourpias and John Chrystal to full 3-year terms.

The President announced his intention to nominate John Goglia to the National Transportation Safety Board.

February 14

In the morning, the President traveled to San Francisco, CA. In the afternoon, he traveled to San Bernardino, CA, where he participated in a roundtable discussion on education at San Bernardino Valley College. In the evening, he traveled to Palm Springs, CA.

The President announced his intention to appoint the following individuals to the Federal Salary Council:

Anthony F. Ingrassia, Vice Chair;
John F. Leyden;
Leslie E. Nulty;
John N. Sturdivant;
Peter A. Tchirkow; and
Robert M. Tobias.

The President announced his intention to name the following members to the Advisory Committee for the 1995 White House Conference on Aging:

Liz Carpenter;
Elsie Frank;
Anita Freedman;
Elinor Guggenheimer;
Daniel P. Perry;
Ruth Shepherd; and
James T. Sykes.

February 15

In the evening, the President returned to Washington, DC.

February 16

In the afternoon, the President met with presidents of historically black colleges and universities in the Cabinet Room at the White House.

The White House announced that the President named Douglas B. Sosnik as Assistant to the President and Director of Political Affairs.

February 17

The President made available an additional $145 million in emergency funding to assist communities in Georgia, Florida, and Alabama in their continuing recovery from flooding and damage caused by Tropical Storm Alberto.

February 18

In the afternoon, the President and Hillary Clinton went to Camp David, MD.

February 19

In the morning, the President and Hillary Clinton traveled to Arlington, VA. In the afternoon, they returned to Camp David, MD.

February 20

In the afternoon, the President returned to Washington, DC, and later attended the Georgetown-Villanova basketball game at the USAir Arena in Landover, MD.

February 21

The White House announced that the President named William E. Curry, Jr., as Counselor to the President.

February 23

In the morning, the President and Hillary Clinton traveled to Ottawa, Canada.

In the late afternoon, the President had meetings with Reform Party leader Preston Manning and Bloc Quebecois leader Lucien Bouchard at the U.S. Ambassador's residence.

In the evening, the President and Hillary Clinton toured the History Hall at the Museum of Civilization.

The President announced his intention to appoint Ken Grotewiel as Presiding Officer and Commissioner and Max Holloway as Alternate Commissioner of the Kansas-Oklahoma Arkansas River Compact Commission.

February 24

In the morning, the President met with Prime Minister Jean Chrétien at the Parliament.

In the afternoon, the President and Hillary Clinton attended a lunch at the Canal Ritz. Following the lunch, they returned to Washington, DC.

The President announced his intention to nominate Edmundo A. Gonzales as Chief Financial Officer of the Department of Labor.

The President announced his intention to nominate John D. Kemp to the National Council on Disability.

The President announced his appointment of former Senator Dennis DeConcini to the board of directors of the Federal Home Loan Mortgage Corporation (Freddie Mac).

The President announced his intention to appoint Deborah Kastrin as a member of the Advisory Council of the Border Environment Cooperation Commission.

The President announced his intention to appoint Jamie S. Gorelick, Matt L. Rodriguez, and Robert T. Scully to be members of the National Commission To Support Law Enforcement.

February 27

The President announced his intention to appoint Hector Villa III as U.S. Representative to the Pecos River Commission.

February 28

The President announced his nomination of Josue (Joe) Robles, Jr., to serve on the Defense Base Closure and Realignment Commission.

The President announced his intention to appoint Harvey Gantt as a member and Chair and Robert Gaines as a member of the National Capital Planning Commission.

March 2

In the morning, the President met with Prince Saud, Foreign Minister of Saudi Arabia. Later in the morning, he had a telephone conversation with Prime Minister Yitzhak Rabin of Israel.

In the afternoon, the President had lunch with Members of Congress in the President's West Wing Dining Room.

The White House announced that the President invited President Jerry Rawlings of Ghana for an official working visit at the White House on March 9.

The President announced the appointment of the following individuals to be members of the U.S. Holocaust Memorial Council:

Allen I. Bildner;
Stanley M. Chesley;
Michael C. Gelman;
John F. Kordek;
Leo Melamed;
Ruth R. Miller; and
Set Charles Momjian.

March 6

In the afternoon, the President met with the NCAA Division I–AA champion Youngstown State University football team.

March 7

The White House announced that the President invited Prime Minister Gyula Horn of Hungary for a working visit to Washington, DC, on June 6.

March 8

In the evening, the President attended a Democratic Leadership Council event at Union Station.

The White House announced that the President will visit Haiti at the invitation of President Jean-Bertrand Aristide on March 31.

March 9

In the afternoon, the President hosted a working luncheon for President Jerry John Rawlings of Ghana.

The President announced his nomination of Daniel Mica and Harriet Zimmerman to the Board of Directors of the U.S. Institute of Peace.

The White House announced the appointment of Jan H. Kalicki, Counselor to the Department of Commerce specializing in international trade and investment, as the administration's Ombudsman for Energy and Commercial Cooperation with the New Independent States of the Former Soviet Union.

March 10

In the afternoon, the President hosted a luncheon for Members of Congress.

The President announced the renomination of James J. Hoecker to be a member of the Federal Energy Regulatory Commission.

March 11

The White House announced that the President directed U.S. Executive Director of the World Bank Jan Piercy to recommend that the World Bank Board of Directors elect James D. Wolfensohn as the next President of the World Bank.

March 12

The President declared a major disaster in California and ordered Federal aid to supplement State and local recovery efforts in the areas struck by winter storms that caused flooding, landslides, and mud debris flows beginning February 13.

March 13

In the afternoon, in an Oval Office ceremony, the President received the Boy Scout Report to the Nation from Boy Scouts of America representatives.

March 14

The President declared a major disaster in South Dakota and ordered Federal aid to supplement State and local recovery efforts in the areas struck by severe winter storms for the period of January 13–February 10.

The President announced his intention to appoint Paul Warnke, Albert Carnesale, Mike Mochizuki, and Gregory van der Vink to be members of the Scientific and Policy Advisory Committee of the Arms Control and Disarmament Agency.

The President announced his intention to appoint LeRoy F. Saunders to the Committee for Purchase From People Who Are Blind or Severely Disabled.

March 15

In the morning, the President met with California State legislators in the Roosevelt Room to discuss flood relief efforts.

March 16

In the afternoon, the President attended a St. Patrick's Day luncheon at the Capitol. Later in the afternoon, in the Roosevelt Room, he met briefly with Franjo Tudjman, President of Croatia; Kresimir Zubak, President, and Ejup Ganic, Vice President, Federation of Bosnian Muslims and Croats; and Tatjana Ljujic-Mijatovic, Presidency Member, Republic of Bosnia-Herzegovina. He then met with President Tudjman in the Oval Office.

The President declared nine additional counties in California as major disaster areas following winter storms which caused flooding and mud slides.

March 17

In the evening, the President and Hillary Clinton hosted a St. Patrick's Day reception on the State Floor.

The President announced his intention to appoint Linda Alvarado to the President's Advisory Commission on Educational Excellence for Hispanic Americans.

The President announced his intention to appoint Mary Houghton as a member of the Board of Directors of the Credit Standards Advisory Committee.

The President announced his intention to appoint Louis V. Gerstner, Jr., and John A. Georges to be members of the Advisory Committee for Trade Policy and Negotiations.

March 19

In the morning, the President had a telephone conversation with Prime Minister John Major of the United Kingdom.

March 20

In an afternoon ceremony in the Oval Office, the President received diplomatic credentials from Ambassadors Abdallah bin Muhammad al-Dhahab of Oman, Jorge G. Prieto of Paraguay, Franklin Sonn of South Africa, Mahamat Saleh Ahmat of Chad, Jayantha C.B. Dhanapala of Sri Lanka, Kun Woo Park of South Korea, Courtney N.M. Blackman of Barbados, Corentino Virgillio Santos of Cape Verde, Severin Ntahomvukiye of Burundi, Jesus Silva Herzog of Mexico, Hadj Osmane Bencherif of Algeria, Willie Chokani of Malawi, and Basudev Prasad Dhungana of Nepal.

The President announced that he will lead a National Rural Conference on the future of America's rural communities in Ames, IA, on April 25.

The President announced his intention to nominate Jerome A. Stricker to be a member of the Federal Retirement Thrift Investment Board.

The White House announced that the President will visit Russia and Ukraine on May 9–11 to attend ceremonies marking the 50th anniversary of V–E Day and for bilateral discussions with President Boris Yeltsin of Russia and President Leonid Kuchma of Ukraine.

The White House announced that the President invited Prime Minister John Major of the United Kingdom to make an official working visit to Washington, DC, on April 3–4.

March 21

The President announced his intention to appoint Peter Chase Neumann as a member of the Tahoe Regional Planning Agency.

The President announced his intention to appoint Joseph T. Gorman and Richard Notebaert to be members of the President's Export Council.

The President announced his intention to appoint the following individuals to be members of the National Selective Service Appeal Board:

Betsy Levine;
Leo M. Romero;
James Roosevelt, Jr.;
Jan Craig Scruggs; and
Barbara W. White.

March 22

The President announced his intention to appoint Anne-Lee Verville to the National Skill Standards Board.

The President announced his intention to appoint Kitty Dukakis to the U.S. Holocaust Memorial Council.

The President announced the appointment of Secretary of Defense William J. Perry as Chairman of the 1995 Interagency Savings Bonds Committee.

The White House announced that the President made available $57.8 million in emergency funding to provide assistance to Georgia and Florida in recovering from the damage caused by Tropical Storm Alberto and subsequent flooding.

March 23

The White House announced the appointment of William C. Danvers as Special Assistant to the President and Senior Director for Legislative Affairs at the National Security Council.

The President announced his intention to appoint Walter Parker as the Academic Representative to the Arctic Research Commission.

The President announced his intention to appoint the following individuals to be members of the Advisory Committee on the Arts of the John F. Kennedy Center for the Performing Arts, Smithsonian Institution:

Ann M. DeLaney;
Patricia Staunton Etchart;
Meghan Zanolli Holbrook;
John P. Manning;
Cherri D. Roden; and
Kandy Stroud.

March 24

In the morning, the President had a routine physical examination at the National Naval Medical Center in Bethesda, MD.

The President announced his intention to appoint Jimmie Lou Fisher to be a public member of the Rural Telephone Bank Board.

March 27

In the morning, the President met with Prime Minister James Bolger of New Zealand.

March 28

In the afternoon, the President traveled to Atlanta, GA, where he attended a reception for Southern Regional Economic Conference participants at the residence of Gov. Zell Miller of Georgia.

March 29

In the evening, the President traveled to Tallahassee, FL.

The President announced his intention to nominate Tommy Edward Jewell III as a member of the Board of Directors of the State Justice Institute.

The President announced his intention to designate Shirley A. Jackson to be Chair of the Nuclear Regulatory Commission following her confirmation as a Commissioner.

March 30

In the morning, the President went to the Florida State Capitol, where he met with direct student loan recipients, police officers, and welfare-to-work mothers in the Senate President's Conference Room. He then met with Democratic leadership members in the House Rules Committee Room.

In the afternoon, the President traveled to Tampa Bay, FL, and later to Palm Beach, FL.

The President announced his intention to nominate Kenneth H. Bacon to be Assistant Secretary of Defense for Public Affairs.

The President announced his intention to reappoint Zvi Kestenbaum and to appoint Bernyce Adler, Fred Hochberg, and Lee Seeman as members of the Commission for the Preservation of America's Heritage Abroad.

The White House announced that the President asked the Intelligence Oversight Board to conduct a governmentwide review of the allegations surrounding the 1990 death of Michael Devine and the 1992 disappearance of Efrain Bamaca Velasquez in Guatemala.

March 31

In the morning, the President traveled to Port-au-Prince, Haiti.

In the afternoon, the President met with United Nations Secretary-General Boutros Boutros-Ghali and attended a reception at the National Palace.

In the early evening, the President met with U.S. troops at Warrior Base. Later in the evening, he met with embassy staff at the U.S. Embassy. He then traveled to Little Rock, AR.

The President announced his intention to appoint Karen Lau Sullivan to be U.S. Alternate Representative to the South Pacific Commission.

The President announced his intention to nominate Vera Alexander as a member of the Marine Mammal Commission.

April 4

In the morning, the President returned to Washington, DC, from a weekend stay in Little Rock, AR.

In the afternoon, the President hosted a working lunch for Prime Minister John Major of the United Kingdom in the Residence.

In the evening, the President attended a fundraising dinner at Senator Edward M. Kennedy's residence in McLean, VA. Following the dinner, he met with Prime Minister Major at Georgia Brown's restaurant.

The President announced his intention to appoint the following individuals to the Community Adjustment and Investment Program Advisory Committee for the North American Development Bank:

William Podlich, Chairman;
Loretta Armenta;
Glenn Biggs;
Linda Griego;
Dionicio Morales; and
Penny Pritzker.

April 5

In the afternoon, the President hosted a working lunch for President Hosni Mubarak of Egypt in the Residence.

The President announced his intention to appoint the following individuals to the Advisory Committee on the Arts of the John F. Kennedy Center for the Performing Arts, Smithsonian Institution:

Judith Aronson;
A. Arthur Davis;
Sandra Stillman Gartner;
June S. Hamra;
James H. Newberry, Jr.;
Neal K. Okabayashi;
Sally R. Peltz;
Edna Louise Saffy;
Bettylu K. Saltzman; and
Carol T. Toussaint.

April 6
In the morning, the President met with members of the House Southwestern Regional Democratic Caucus in the Roosevelt Room.

April 7
In the morning, the President traveled to Dallas, TX.

In the afternoon, the President attended a luncheon at the Mansion at Turtle Creek. He then traveled to Sacramento, CA.

In the evening, the President attended a California State Democratic Party fundraiser at a private residence.

April 8
In the morning, the President traveled to Los Angeles, CA. In the evening, he attended a Democratic National Committee fundraiser at a private residence.

April 9
In the afternoon, the President and Hillary Clinton returned to Washington, DC.

April 10
The President announced his intention to appoint Patrick D. Cannon, Chester R. Helms and June Isaacson Kailes to the Architectural and Transportation Barriers Compliance Board.

The President announced his intention to nominate Marilyn Moon and Stephen G. Kellison to be public members of the Board of Trustees of the Federal Old-Age and Survivors Insurance Trust Fund and the Federal Disability Insurance Trust Fund (Social Security). They will also be nominated to be public members of the Boards of Trustees of the Federal Hospital Insurance Trust Fund and the Federal Supplementary Medical Insurance Trust Fund (Medicare).

April 11
In the afternoon, the President hosted a working lunch for Prime Minister Benazir Bhutto of Pakistan.

The President announced his intention to appoint Wayne Shackelford as a member of the Federal Advisory Committee on Greenhouse Gas Emissions From Personal Motor Vehicles.

The President announced his intention to appoint Leland D. Tillman as Chairman and U.S. Commissioner of the Canadian River Commission.

The White House announced that the President invited President Kim Yong-Sam of South Korea to the United States for a state visit on July 25–28.

April 12
In the morning, the President traveled to Fort Benning, GA, and then to Warm Springs, GA.

In the afternoon, the President returned to Washington, DC.

April 13
The President announced his intention to appoint Beverly Byron and Vernon Weaver as members of the U.S. Naval Academy Board of Visitors.

April 14
In the afternoon, the President and Hillary and Chelsea Clinton traveled to Camp David, MD, for the Easter weekend.

The President announced his intention to appoint John L. Hall to the Board of Directors of the Mickey Leland National Urban Air Toxics Research Center.

The President announced his intention to appoint Anthony Williams as a Department of Agriculture Federal Representative to the Rural Telephone Bank Board.

The President announced his intention to appoint Joseph C. Swift as a member of the Federal Advisory Committee on Greenhouse Gas Emissions From Personal Motor Vehicles.

April 16
In the evening, the President and Hillary and Chelsea Clinton returned to the White House from a weekend stay at Camp David, MD.

April 18
The President announced his intention to nominate Ira S. Shapiro for the rank of Ambassador during his tenure of service as Senior Counsel and Negotiator in the Office of the U.S. Trade Representative.

The White House announced that the President granted waivers for welfare reform to Missouri and Montana.

April 19
The President announced his intention to appoint Art Trujillo and Rick Reyes as members of the Advisory Council of the Border Environment Cooperation Commission established under the North American Free Trade Agreement.

April 20
The President announced his intention to nominate Larry C. Napper to be Ambassador to Latvia.

The President announced his intention to nominate Lawrence Palmer Taylor to be Ambassador to Estonia.

The President announced his intention to nominate Peter Tomsen to be Ambassador to Armenia.

The President announced his intention to nominate Jenonne Walker to be Ambassador to the Czech Republic.

The President announced his intention to nominate R. Grant Smith to be Ambassador to Tajikistan.

The President announced the appointment of Panamanian citizens Fernando Cardoze, Moises Mizrachi, Emmanuel Gonzales Revilla, and Jorge Ritter as members of the Board of the Panama Canal Commission.

April 21

In the morning, the President traveled to Havre de Grace, MD, where he met with environmental activists at the Duck Decoy Museum. In the afternoon, he returned to Washington, DC.

The White House announced that the President met with U.S. Ambassador to Burundi Robert Krueger to discuss ethnic tensions in Burundi.

The President declared a major disaster in Alabama and ordered Federal aid to supplement State and local recovery efforts in the area struck by severe storms, tornadoes, and flooding on February 15–20.

The President announced his intention to nominate Patrick Nickolas Theros to be Ambassador to Qatar.

The President announced his intention to nominate A. Peter Burleigh to be Ambassador to Sri Lanka and to Maldives.

The President announced his intention to appoint Frederick Calhoun James and Huel D. Perkins to the President's Board of Advisors on Historically Black Colleges and Universities.

The President announced his intention to appoint Helen Roth to the Advisory Committee to the White House Conference on Aging.

The President announced his intention to reappoint Dennis DeConcini, Jerry M. Hultin, James B. Nutter, and Harriett Woods as members of the Board of Directors of the Federal Home Loan Mortgage Corporation.

April 23

In the morning, the President and Hillary Clinton helped plant a tree on the South Lawn in memory of those killed or injured in the Oklahoma City bombing. They then traveled to Oklahoma City, OK.

Following their arrival in the afternoon, the President and Hillary Clinton went to the State Fair Grounds Arena, where they met with members of search and rescue teams and later with families affected by the bombing.

In the evening, the President traveled to Minneapolis, MN.

April 24

In the morning, the President met with community college students at the Minneapolis Convention Center.

In the afternoon, the President traveled to Des Moines, IA, where he met with the editorial board of the Des Moines Register.

The President announced his intention to nominate Lannon Walker to be Ambassador to Cote d'Ivoire.

The President announced his intention to nominate David C. Litt to be Ambassador to the United Arab Emirates.

The President announced his intention to nominate James Alan Williams for the rank of Ambassador during his tenure of service as Special Coordinator for Cyprus.

The President announced his intention to nominate Mosina H. Jordan to be Ambassador to the Central African Republic.

The President announced his intention to nominate Donald K. Steinberg to be Ambassador to Angola.

April 25

In the evening, the President returned to Washington, DC.

The President announced his intention to nominate Sandra J. Kristoff for the rank of Ambassador during her tenure of service as U.S. Coordinator for Asia-Pacific Economic Cooperation.

The President announced his intention to appoint Frank E. (Sam) Maynes as the U.S. Commissioner of the Upper Colorado River Commission.

The President named the following individuals to serve as delegates to the White House Conference on Aging:

Fidel Aguilar;
Frank Alexander;
Samuel Amorose;
Lena Archuleta;
Norma Asnes;
Judy Basham;
Theressa Burns;
Shirley Cagle;
Helen Carlstrom;
Amelia Castillo;
George Chassey;
Harvey Cohen;
Victoria Cowell;
Erica Goode;
Pauline Gore;
Helene Grossman;
Harry Guenther;
Richard Gunther;
Lars Hennum;
Sherrye Henry;
Peggy Houston;
Laura Hyatt;
Theresa McKenna;
Matthew McNulty;
Herbert McTaggart;
Cecil Malone;
Rose Marie Meridith;
Wesley Parrott;
Madeline Parsons;

Nancy Peace;
Charlie Peritore;
Frederick Perkins;
Mike Rankin;
Linda Rhodes;
Kay Ryder;
Janice Schakowsky;
Lynn Williams Shipp;
Eleanor Slater;
Alan Solomont;
Viston Taylor;
Norman Vaughan;
Fredda Vladeck;
Diana Wiley;
Norma Wisor; and
Ken Worley.

April 26

In the morning, the President and Hillary Clinton attended funeral services for Alan G. Whicher, a Secret Service agent killed in the Oklahoma City bombing, at St. Patrick's Catholic Church in Rockville, MD.

The President asked all Federal workers to join in observing a national moment of silence at 10:02 a.m., to remember and honor the victims of the Oklahoma City bombing.

The President declared a major disaster in Oklahoma City, OK, following the bombing of the Alfred P. Murrah Federal Building on April 19, making Federal aid available to affected individuals in Oklahoma County.

The President announced his intention to nominate David W. Burke as Chairman and Edward E. Kaufman, Tom C. Korologos, and Bette Bao Lord as members of the Broadcasting Board of Governors for the International Bureau of Broadcasting.

April 27

In the morning, the President met with Foreign Minister Andrey Kozyrev of Russia. Following the meeting, he had a telephone conversation with President Boris Yeltsin of Russia.

The President announced his intention to nominate Richard J. Stern to the National Council on the Arts.

The President announced his intention to nominate William H. LeBlanc III to the Postal Rate Commission.

April 28

The President announced his intention to appoint Susan Albert Loewenberg and William E. Morgan as members of the Board of Directors of the Federal Prison Industries Corporation.

The President announced his intention to reappoint William M. Daley, Thomas Leonard, John R. Sasso, and Jose Villarreal to the Federal National Mortgage Association.

April 29

In the morning, the President traveled to Williamsburg, VA, where he attended the Democratic Policy Committee annual retreat at the Kingsmill Resort Conference Center. In the afternoon, he returned to Washington, DC.

April 30

In the morning, the President traveled to New York City. In the evening, he returned to Washington, DC.

May 1

The President announced his intention to appoint Paul Calabresi to the President's Cancer Panel.

The President announced his intention to appoint Ronald W. Drach and Sylvia Walker as Vice Chairs of the President's Committee on Employment of People With Disabilities.

May 2

The President announced his intention to nominate Timothy Michael Carney as Ambassador to Sudan.

The White House announced that the President will send a delegation led by Secretary of Commerce Ron Brown to the Third African-American Summit in Dakar, Senegal, May 1–5.

May 3

The President announced the selection of H. Martin Lancaster as Special Adviser to the President and U.S. Arms Control and Disarmament Agency Director on the Chemical Weapons Convention.

May 4

In the morning, the President met with Prime Minister Vaclav Klaus of the Czech Republic.

The President announced his intention to nominate Robert F. Rider as a member of the Board of Governors of the U.S. Postal Service.

May 5

In the morning, the President traveled to East Lansing, MI. In the afternoon, he returned to Washington, DC.

In the evening, the President and Hillary Clinton attended a benefit for the Southwest Voter Education Registration Project at the Washington Hilton. They then attended a premiere showing of the movie "Mi Familia" at the Embassy Theater.

The President announced his intention to nominate Andrew Fois as Assistant Attorney General of the Office of Legislative Affairs at the Department of Justice.

The President announced the appointment of Michael V. Dunn to serve as a Federal Representative and Robert Lee Stanton to serve as a Public Representative to the Rural Telephone Bank Board.

The President amended his April 26 declaration of a major disaster in Oklahoma City, OK, as a result of the bombing at the Alfred P. Murrah Federal Building on April 19 to make Federal funding available to affected State and local governments for the repair or replacement of public facilities damaged by the explosion.

May 8

In the morning, the President participated in a wreath-laying ceremony at Arlington National Cemetery in Arlington, VA, commemorating the 50th anniversary of V–E Day.

In the afternoon, the President and Hillary Clinton traveled to Moscow, Russia. While en route to Moscow, the President had a telephone conversation with President-elect Jacques Chirac of France.

The President announced his intention to nominate Leo K. Goto to be a member of the Civil Liberties Public Education Fund Board of Directors.

The President announced his intention to nominate Marc B. Nathanson as a member of the Broadcasting Board of Governors for the International Bureau of Broadcasting.

May 9

Following their arrival in Moscow in the early morning, the President and Hillary Clinton went to the Kremlin, where they participated in a wreath-laying ceremony at the Tomb of the Unknowns. They then viewed the veterans parade at Red Square.

In the afternoon, the President and Hillary Clinton toured the Central Museum of the Great Patriotic War at Poklonnaya Gora. Later in the afternoon, they attended a reception for U.S. veterans of World War II at the Radisson Slavjanskaya Hotel.

In the early evening, the President and Hillary Clinton toured the Novedevichy Convent. Following a reception for heads of state at St. George's Hall, they attended a state dinner hosted by President Boris Yeltsin of Russia at the Palace of Congresses in the Kremlin.

The President announced his intention to nominate John White to be Deputy Secretary of Defense.

May 10

In the morning, the President met with President Yeltsin in St. Catherine's Room at the Kremlin.

In the evening, the President and Hillary Clinton attended a dinner in the Hall of Facets at the Kremlin.

The President declared a major disaster in Louisiana and ordered Federal aid to supplement State and local recovery efforts in the area struck by severe storms, tornadoes, and flooding on May 8–9.

The White House announced that the President invited President Robert Mugabe of Zimbabwe to the White House for an official working visit on May 18.

May 11

In the morning, the President and Hillary Clinton met with staff at the U.S. Embassy compound.

In the afternoon, the President and Hillary Clinton toured a Coca-Cola plant. Following the tour, they traveled to Kiev, Ukraine, where the President met with President Leonid Kuchma of Ukraine at Mariinsky Palace.

In the evening, the President and Hillary Clinton attended a state dinner hosted by President Kuchma at Mariinsky Palace.

The White House announced that the President asked a delegation led by Deputy Secretary of Veterans Affairs Hershel Gober, Assistant Secretary of State Winston Lord, and Deputy Assistant Secretary of Defense for POW/MIA Affairs James Wold to travel to Vietnam, May 13–16, and Laos, May 17–18, to facilitate the fullest possible accounting of American POW/MIA's.

The President announced his intention to appoint Michael L. Beatty to be the U.S. Representative to the Western Interstate Nuclear Board.

The President announced his intention to appoint the following individuals to the Advisory Committee on the Arts of the John F. Kennedy Center for the Performing Arts, Smithsonian Institution:

Don Anselmi;
Gregory Carr;
David Cofrin;
Susan Gelman;
Mary C. Hansen;
Gary Hindes;
Sherry K. Jelsma;
Michael Pannos; and
Gail Rosene Smith.

May 12

In the morning, the President and Hillary Clinton participated in a wreath-laying ceremony at the World War II Memorial.

In the afternoon, following a departure ceremony at Mariinsky Palace and tours of St. Andrew's Church and Kyyevo-Pecherska Lavra monastery, the President and Hillary Clinton returned to Washington, DC.

The President declared a major disaster in Mississippi and ordered Federal aid to supplement State and local recovery efforts in the area struck by severe storms, tornadoes, and flooding beginning May 8.

The President announced his intention to appoint Thomas L. Blair to the Advisory Board of the National Air and Space Museum.

The President selected the following individuals to serve as delegates to the White House Conference on Small Business:

Peggy Hernandez Anastos;
George A. Beach;
Kenneth C. Blair, Jr.;
Roderick Blount;
William D. Budinger;
C. Michael Davenport;
Tony Davidow;
Ned Densmore;
Kenneth Eakes;
Sandra Fowler;
Betty Franklin-Hammonds;
Zdenka Gast;
John Paul Giere;

Marina Grant;
Betty Hall;
R. Alan Hall;
Ada S. Hollingsworth;
Nat Hyman;
Morris Kaplan;
Michael W. Kempner;
Phyllis Gutierrez Kenney;
William C. Kimball;
Sandra K. Lee;
Carmen Orta;
Indira B. Patel;
Wayne Patrick;
Derron Pierson;
Alice Rickel;
Barbara Serna;
Donald J. Sterhan;
Soundra Johnson Temple;
Mary Touris;
Carolyn Warner;
Robert A. Weygand;
Alan L. White;
Phyllis Williams;
Edward Zetick; and
George Zoffinger.

May 13
In the afternoon, the President and Hillary Clinton went to Camp David, MD, for the weekend.

May 14
In the late evening, the President and Hillary Clinton returned to the White House from Camp David.

May 15
In the morning, the President met with Foreign Minister Farouk al-Shara of Syria.

May 16
In the afternoon, the President received diplomatic credentials from Ambassadors Fernando Andresen Guimaraes of Portugal and Juergen Chrobog of Germany. He then met with delegates from the U.S.-Mexico Binational Commission.

The White House announced the President invited President Ernesto Zedillo of Mexico for a state visit on October 10.

The President announced his intention to appoint Gov. Roy Romer of Colorado as a member of the Advisory Council on Historic Preservation.

The President announced his intention to appoint the following individuals to the President's National Security Telecommunications Advisory Committee:

Stanley C. Beckelman;
Bobby A. Boaldin;
Louis V. Gerstner, Jr.;
Arthur E. Johnson;
Donald J. Schuenke; and
Martin A. Stein.

May 17
In the morning, the President traveled to White Plains, MD, where he viewed a demonstration of a school-to-work project at Automated Graphic Systems, Inc. In the afternoon, he returned to Washington, DC.

May 18
In the afternoon, the President hosted a luncheon for President Robert Mugabe of Zimbabwe in the Old Family Dining Room.

The President announced his intention to appoint James H. Bilbray to be a member of the U.S. Military Academy Board of Visitors.

The President announced his intention to appoint Robert B. Shapiro to be a member of the Advisory Committee for Trade Policy and Negotiations.

The President announced his intention to nominate Maria Luisa M. Haley to a new term as a member of the Board of Directors of the Export-Import Bank of the United States.

May 19
The President nominated John D. Hawke, Jr., as Under Secretary of the Treasury for Domestic Finance.

The President announced his intention to nominate George J. Tenet to be Deputy Director of Central Intelligence at the Central Intelligence Agency.

The President announced his intention to appoint Randall Franke to the Advisory Commission on Intergovernmental Relations.

The President announced his selection of the following individuals to serve as delegates to the White House Conference on Small Business, June 11–15:

Thomas A. Antoon;
Anthony A. Armstrong;
Thomas Baker;
Richard Bertsch;
Darwin Bromley;
Paul Condit;
Margarita R. Delgado;
Darlene D. Drake;
Patrick Geho;
Carolyn Jean Hawks;
Lance Herndon;
Sam Kapourales;
John R. McKeehan;
Jeffrey Newbauer;
Robert J. Shell;
Orna Shulman; and
Richard J. Whouley.

May 22
The President announced the nomination of Dwight P. Robinson as Deputy Secretary of the Department of Housing and Urban Development.

The President announced his intention to reappoint Jean Kennedy Smith to the Board of Trustees of the

John F. Kennedy Center for the Performing Arts, Smithsonian Institution.

The White House announced that the President will meet with Jacques Santer, President of the European Commission, and President Jacques Chirac of France, President of the European Council, at a summit in Washington, DC, on June 14.

May 24

In the afternoon, the President and Hillary Clinton hosted a tea for King Juan Carlos I and Queen Sophia of Spain in the Yellow Oval Room.

The President announced his intention to appoint Rose Dobrof to the Federal Council on the Aging.

The President nominated Linda L. Robertson to be Assistant Secretary of the Treasury for Legislative Affairs.

The President announced his intention to nominate Peggy A. Nagae to be a member of the Civil Liberties Public Education Fund Board of Directors.

May 25

The President announced the appointment of Richard Nuccio as Special Adviser to the President and Secretary of State for Cuba.

The President named Melvin E. Clark, Jr., and Charles A. Docter to the Pennsylvania Avenue Development Corporation Board of Directors.

May 26

The President declared a major disaster in South Dakota and ordered Federal funds to supplement State and local recovery efforts in communities struck by severe storms, flooding, and ground saturation due to high water tables, beginning March 1.

The President announced his intention to appoint Phyllis Middleton Jackson to the Board of Trustees of the John F. Kennedy Center for the Performing Arts, Smithsonian Institution.

The President announced the appointment of the following individuals to be members of the Presidential Advisory Committee on Gulf War Veterans' Illnesses:

Joyce Lashof, Chair;
John Baldeschwieler;
Arthur Caplan;
Donald Custis;
Frederick M. Franks, Jr.;
David A. Hamburg;
James A. Johnson;
Marguerite Knox;
Philip Landrigan;
Elaine L. Larson;
Rolando Rios; and
Andrea Kidd Taylor.

The President announced that he selected the following individuals to serve as delegates to the White House Conference on Small Business to be held in Washington, DC, on June 11–15:

Sarah Barela;
John Burgess;
Robert Calcaterra;
Lorrie J. Carey;
Mary Ann Carlson;
Barbara L. Cash;
Audrey L. Davis;
Deborah D. Dolman;
Charles J. Dorame;
Sue Ling Gin;
Omar M. Kader;
Kathy Kemp;
Nadine Mathis;
Urban Miyares;
Ann L. Mulholland;
Kathy Neal;
Harry Posey;
Barbara Skelton;
Edward I. Weisiger, Jr.; and
Buck W. Wong.

May 29

In the morning, the President visited Arlington National Cemetery in Arlington, VA, where he placed a wreath at the Tomb of the Unknowns.

May 30

In the afternoon, the President had a telephone conversation with President Fernando Henrique Cardoso of Brazil.

The President declared a major disaster in Illinois and ordered Federal funds to supplement State and local recovery efforts in communities recently struck by severe storms and flooding.

May 31

In the morning, the President traveled to Colorado Springs, CO. In the afternoon, he traveled to Billings, MT.

The President named Andrew F. Brimmer as Chairman and Joyce Ladner and Constance B. Newman as members of the District of Columbia Financial Responsibility and Management Assistance Authority.

June 1

In the morning, the President went horseback riding at the Intermountain Equestrian Center. In the early afternoon, he toured the Leslie Auer wheat farm.

The President announced the appointment of Philip W. Pillsbury, Jr., and reappointment of Gary S. Hartshorn to the Panama Canal Joint Commission on the Environment.

The President announced his intention to nominate William J. Hughes to be Ambassador to Panama.

The President announced his intention to nominate David L. Hobbs to be Ambassador to Guyana.

The President announced his intention to appoint Joseph W. Cornelison as Deputy Administrator of the Panama Canal Commission.

The President announced his intention to appoint Richard K. Glenn as the Indigenous Representative to the Arctic Research Commission.

June 2

In the early morning, the President returned to Washington, DC. In the afternoon, he hosted a working luncheon with Democratic Governors in the Old Family Dining Room.

The President declared a major disaster in Missouri and ordered Federal funds to supplement State and local recovery efforts in communities struck by severe storms, hail, tornadoes, and flooding beginning May 13 and continuing.

The President announced his intent to nominate Tracey Dean Conwell and Jeanne R. Ferst to the National Museum Services Board.

The President announced his intention to appoint Larry E. Trujillo, Sr., as the Chair and Federal Representative to the Arkansas River Compact Administration between the States of Colorado and Kansas.

The White House announced that the President sent fiscal year 1996 budget amendments to the Congress for the Departments of Defense, Education, Interior, Transportation, and the Railroad Retirement Board.

June 5

The President announced his intention to nominate C. Richard Allen as a Managing Director of the Corporation for National and Community Service.

The President announced his intention to appoint Joyce A. Savocchio to the Board of Trustees of the Christopher Columbus Fellowship Foundation.

June 6

In the morning, the President met with Prime Minister Gyula Horn of Hungary.

In the afternoon, the President traveled to Baltimore, MD. Later in the afternoon, he returned to Washington, DC.

The President named Stephen D. Harlan and Edward A. Singletary to the District of Columbia Financial Responsibility and Management Assistance Authority.

The President announced his intention to nominate Beth Susan Slavet to be Vice Chair and member of the Merit Systems Protection Board.

The White House announced that the President appointed Jeremy Ben-Ami as Deputy Assistant to the President for Domestic Policy.

June 7

The President named Betsy Myers as Deputy Assistant to the President and Director of Women's Initiatives.

The President named Frank Herrera and Mary Jo Waits as members of the Community Adjustment and Investment Program Advisory Committee for the North American Development Bank.

The President announced his intention to nominate John J. Callahan to be Assistant Secretary for Management and Budget at the Department of Health and Human Services.

June 8

In the afternoon, the President had a telephone conversation with Capt. Scott F. O'Grady, USAF, the pilot who was rescued after having been shot down and stranded in western Bosnia.

The President selected the following individuals to serve as delegates to the White House Conference on Small Business:

Pedro Alfonso;
James Burke;
Paula Calimafde;
Sharon Casey;
Judith A. Clark;
John H. French;
Gail S. Messerman;
Mary Ann Mitchell;
James W. Mozley;
Santiago J. Negre;
Edward M. Nigro;
R. Donahue Peebles;
William Petrocelli;
Joan Y. Phillips;
Carlos Portes;
John C. Rennie; and
Amy Zisook.

June 9

The President announced his intention to appoint Richard Garwin and Edwin Smith as members of the U.S. Arms Control and Disarmament Agency's Scientific and Policy Advisory Committee.

The President announced his intention to appoint Joyce Keller, K. Charlie Lakin, and Jacquelyn B. Victorian to the President's Committee on Mental Retardation.

The President selected the following additional individuals to serve as delegates to the White House Conference on Small Business:

Brenda Garrand;
Wayne Granquist;
James T. Hamilton;
Richard C. Herring;
Donna Jean Rainville;
George Shanklin; and
William Worley.

June 11

In the morning, the President traveled to Hanover, NH.

In the afternoon, the President held interviews with the Union Leader of Manchester, NH, and WMUR Television in the Dickey Room of Baker Library at Dartmouth College. Following the interviews, he attended a private reception at the library. He then traveled to Claremont, NH.

In the evening, the President traveled to Boston, MA. Later in the evening, he returned to Washington, DC.

June 12

In the late morning, the President met in the Oval Office with rescued pilot Capt. Scott O'Grady, USAF. He then hosted a luncheon in the Residence for Captain O'Grady and his family.

The President announced his intention to nominate James E. Goodby for the rank of Ambassador during his tenure of service as Principal Negotiator and Special Representative of the President for Nuclear Safety and Dismantlement.

The President announced his intention to appoint Gerald T. Garvey, Courtney Riordan, and Reginal Spiller to the Geologic Mapping Advisory Committee.

The President announced his intention to nominate the following individuals to the following ambassadorial posts:

Michael William Cotter, Ambassador to Turkmenistan;
Victor Jackovich, Ambassador to Slovenia;
Elizabeth Jones, Ambassador to Kazakhstan;
John Raymond Malott, Ambassador to Malaysia;
John K. Menzies, Ambassador to Bosnia and Herzegovina;
Kenneth Michael Quinn, Ambassador to Cambodia; and
John Todd Stewart, Ambassador to Moldova.

June 13

The President announced his intention to nominate Under Secretary of the Treasury for International Affairs Lawrence Summers as Deputy Treasury Secretary.

The President declared a major disaster in Kentucky and ordered Federal funds to supplement State and local recovery efforts in communities struck by tornadoes, severe wind and hail storms, torrential rain, and flooding on May 13–19.

The President declared a major disaster in Texas and ordered Federal funds to supplement State and local recovery efforts in communities struck by severe thunderstorms, flooding, hail, and tornadoes on May 28–31.

The President took action to protect life and property from the threat of rising water in North Dakota's Devil Lake Basin by determining that certain Federal-aid roads in the basin area are eligible for assistance from the Federal Highway Administration emergency fund.

The President announced his intention to appoint the following members to the Board for International Food and Agricultural Development:

Ada Demb;
Walter Falcon;
Miles Goggans;
Alan Kligerman;

Edward Schuh; and
Goro Uehara.

June 14

In the evening, the President and Hillary Clinton hosted a dinner in the State Dining Room for Jacques Santer, President of the European Commission, and his wife, Daniele, and President Jacques Chirac of France, President of the European Council, and his wife, Bernadette.

June 15

In the morning, the President and Hillary Clinton traveled to Shearwater Military Base, Nova Scotia, Canada. Following an arrival ceremony, they boarded the H.M.S. *Sir William Alexander* and traveled to Halifax, where they participated in an arrival ceremony at the Historic Halifax Dock.

In the afternoon, the President met with Prime Minister Tomiichi Murayama of Japan in the Board Room at Dalhousie University.

In the evening, the President attended a welcoming reception and dinner for the Group of Seven leaders at Government House.

The President announced his intention to nominate John W. Hechinger, Sr., to the National Security Education Board.

The President announced his intention to appoint Scott Bernstein as a member of the Federal Advisory Committee on Greenhouse Gas Emissions From Personal Motor Vehicles.

The President announced his intention to appoint Jared L. Cohon, John W. Arendt, and Jeffrey J. Wong as members of the Nuclear Waste Technical Review Board.

The President announced his intention to nominate the following individuals to the following ambassadorial posts:

Edward Brynn, Ambassador to Ghana;
Peggy Blackford, Ambassador to Guinea-Bissau;
John Hirsch, Ambassador to Sierra Leone;
Vicki Huddleston, Ambassador to Madagascar;
Elizabeth Raspolic, Ambassador to Sao Tome and Principe; and
Daniel Howard Simpson, Ambassador to Zaire.

The President announced that Secretary of Health and Human Services Donna Shalala will appoint the following individuals to serve on the Presidential Advisory Council on HIV/AIDS:

Terje Anderson;
Regina Aragon;
Mary Boland;
Nicholas Bollman;
Robert L. Fogel;
Debra Frazer-Howze;
Kathleen M. Gerus;
Edward Gould;
Phyllis Greenberger;
Bob Hattoy;

R. Scott Hitt;
Carole laFavor;
Jeremy Landau;
Alexandra Mary Levine;
Steve Lew;
Altagracia Perez;
H. Alexander Robinson;
Debbie Runions;
Benjamin Schatz;
Denise Stokes;
Sandra Thurman;
Charles Quincy Troupe; and
Bruce G. Weniger.

June 16

In the morning, the President attended a G–7 leaders meeting at Summit Place. He then met with Prime Minister John Major of Great Britain and attended a working lunch with G–7 leaders.

In the afternoon, the President met with Chancellor Helmut Kohl at Summit Place and then attended the first plenary session of the G–7 summit at the Maritime Museum of the Atlantic. Following the meeting, he participated in a press conference with the G–7 leaders at Sackville Landing.

In the evening, the President attended a reception and working dinner with G–7 leaders at the Waegwoltic Boat Club. He then went to Harbourfront, where he and Hillary Clinton attended a brief reception, a performance by Cirque du Soleil, and a fireworks display.

The President announced his intention to nominate Ernest J. Moniz as Associate Director for Science at the Office of Science and Technology Policy.

The President announced his intention to appoint Luis J. Lauredo as the U.S. Representative to the Southern States Energy Board.

June 17

In the morning, the President attended the plenary session of the G–7 summit at the Maritime Museum in Halifax, Nova Scotia. Later in the morning, he went to Summit Place where he participated in a G–7 leaders meeting and a press conference.

In the afternoon, the President attended a farewell luncheon at the World Trade Club.

In the evening, the President and Hillary Clinton returned to Washington, DC.

June 20

The President announced his intention to nominate Derrick L. Forrister as Assistant Secretary for Congressional, Intergovernmental and Public Liaison at the Department of Energy.

The President announced his intention to nominate Alberto Mora as a member of the Broadcasting Board of Governors for the International Broadcasting Bureau.

The President announced that Theodore C. Sorensen, Harrison J. Goldin, and Jules B. Kroll were

named to serve on the Board of Directors of the Central Asian-American Enterprise Fund.

The President announced that James C. Rosapepe was named to serve on the Board of Directors of the Albanian-American Enterprise Fund.

The President announced his intention to nominate William H. Itoh as Ambassador to Thailand.

June 21

In the morning, the President met with Members of Congress in the Oval Office.

The President announced his intention to nominate John T. Conway as Chairman and member of the Defense Nuclear Facilities Safety Board.

The President announced his intention to appoint A. Huda Farouki to the Advisory Committee on the Arts of the John F. Kennedy Center for the Performing Arts, Smithsonian Institution.

The President announced his intention to appoint Norman R. Augustine as Principal Officer of the Board of Governors of the American National Red Cross.

June 22

In the afternoon, the President and Hillary Clinton traveled to Edison, NJ, where they toured the assembly line at the Ford Motor Co. plant. In the late afternoon, they traveled to Somerset, NJ.

In the evening, the President and Hillary Clinton traveled to Little Rock, AR.

The President announced his intention to renominate Stephen D. Potts as Director of the Office of Government Ethics.

June 23

The President announced his intention to nominate Jill L. Long as Under Secretary for Rural, Economic and Community Development at the Department of Agriculture.

The President announced his intention to appoint former Senator Birch Bayh to be a member of the J. William Fulbright Foreign Scholarship Board.

June 24

In the morning, the President traveled to Pine Bluff, AR, where he met with community leaders in the Banquet Hall at the Pine Bluff Convention Center. In the late afternoon, he returned to Little Rock.

June 25

In the afternoon, the President traveled to San Francisco, CA.

June 26

In the afternoon, the President met with President Lech Walesa of Poland in the foyer at Herbst Theater.

In the evening, the President attended a dinner hosted by U.N. 50 National Committee chairman Walter Shorenstein at his residence. Following the dinner, he traveled to Portland, OR.

The President announced his intention to nominate Eluid Levi Martinez as Commissioner of the Bureau of Reclamation at the Department of the Interior.

The President announced his intention to appoint Richard L. Bloch and Stanley S. Shuman to the President's Foreign Intelligence Advisory Board.

The President declared a major disaster in Oklahoma and ordered Federal aid to supplement State and local recovery efforts in the area struck by severe storms, flooding, and tornadoes beginning May 26.

June 27

In the evening, the President returned to Washington, DC.

The President announced his intention to nominate George D. Milidrag to serve as a member of the Advisory Board of the Saint Lawrence Seaway Development Corporation.

June 28

The President announced that he designated Joseph Stiglitz as Chair and that he intends to nominate Alicia Munnell as a member of the Council of Economic Advisers.

The President announced his intention to nominate the following individuals to the following ambassadorial posts:

Frances D. Cook, Ambassador to Oman;

J. Stapleton Roy, Ambassador to Indonesia;

Thomas W. Simons, Jr., Ambassador to Pakistan; and

John M. Yates, Ambassador to Benin.

June 29

In the afternoon, the President attended a memorial service for former Supreme Court Chief Justice Warren E. Burger at the National Presbyterian Church.

In the late afternoon, the President and Hillary Clinton traveled to Chicago, IL.

The President announced his intention to nominate Stanley A. Riveles for the rank of Ambassador during his tenure of service as U.S. Commissioner on the Standing Consultative Commission.

The President announced his intention to nominate William Harrison Courtney as Ambassador to the Republic of Georgia.

June 30

In the afternoon, the President and Hillary Clinton traveled to Miami, FL.

The President announced his intention to nominate Howard M. Schloss to be Assistant Secretary for Public Affairs at the Department of the Treasury.

The President announced his intention to nominate John W. Douglass to be Assistant Secretary of the Navy for Research, Development and Acquisition.

The President announced his intention to appoint Arva Moore Parks to the Advisory Council on Historic Preservation.

The President named White House Deputy Staff Secretary Todd Stern to be Assistant to the President and Staff Secretary. Mr. Stern will be replaced as Deputy Staff Secretary by Special Assistant to the President Philip Caplan, of the White House Cabinet Affairs Office.

Appendix B—Nominations Submitted to the Senate

The following list does not include promotions of members of the Uniformed Services, nominations to the Service Academies, or nominations of Foreign Service officers.

Submitted January 4

Robert E. Rubin,
of New York, to be Secretary of the Treasury, vice Lloyd Bentsen, resigned.

Robert E. Rubin,
of New York, to be U.S. Governor of the International Monetary Fund for a term of 5 years; U.S. Governor of the International Bank for Reconstruction and Development for a term of 5 years; U.S. Governor of the Inter-American Development Bank for a term of 5 years; U.S. Governor of the African Development Bank for a term of 5 years; U.S. Governor of the Asian Development Bank; U.S. Governor of the African Development Fund; U.S. Governor of the European Bank for Reconstruction and Development.

Ronna Lee Beck,
of the District of Columbia, to be an Associate Judge of the Superior Court of the District of Columbia for the term of 15 years, vice Bruce D. Beaudin, resigned.

Linda Kay Davis,
of the District of Columbia, to be an Associate Judge of the Superior Court of the District of Columbia for the term of 15 years, vice Gladys Kessler, elevated.

Eric T. Washington,
of the District of Columbia, to be an Associate Judge of the Superior Court of the District of Columbia for the term of 15 years, vice Ricardo M. Urbina, elevated.

Submitted January 5

Terrence B. Adamson,
of the District of Columbia, to be a member of the Board of Directors of the State Justice Institute for a term expiring September 17, 1997 (reappointment).

Yerker Andersson,
of Maryland, to be a member of the National Council on Disability for a term expiring September 17, 1996, vice Anne C. Seggerman, term expired.

Martin Neil Baily,
of Maryland, to be a member of the Council of Economic Advisers, vice Alan S. Blinder, resigned.

Calton Windley Bland,
of North Carolina, to be U.S. Marshal for the Eastern District of North Carolina for a term of 4 years, vice William I. Berryhill, Jr.

Robert G. Breunig,
of Arizona, to be a member of the National Museum Services Board for a term expiring December 6, 1998 (reappointment).

Robert Clarke Brown,
of New York, to be a member of the Board of Directors of the Metropolitan Washington Airports Authority for a term of 6 years, vice Jack Edwards, term expired.

Howard W. Cannon,
of Nevada, to be a member of the Board of Trustees of the Barry Goldwater Scholarship and Excellence in Education Foundation for a term expiring March 3, 1998 (reappointment).

Herschelle Challenor,
of Georgia, to be a member of the National Security Education Board for a term of 4 years, vice Steven Muller.

Sheila Cheston,
of the District of Columbia, to be General Counsel of the Department of the Air Force, vice Gilbert F. Casellas.

Kinshasha Holman Conwill,
of New York, to be a member of the National Museum Services Board for a term expiring December 6, 1997, vice Willard L. Boyd, term expired.

Juan Abran DeHerrera,
of Wyoming, to be U.S. Marshal for the District of Wyoming for the term of 4 years, vice Delaine Roberts.

G. Edward DeSeve,
of Pennsylvania, to be Controller, Office of Federal Financial Management, Office of Management and Budget, vice Edward Joseph Mazur, resigned.

Robert F. Drinan,
of Massachusetts, to be a member of the Board of Directors of the Civil Liberties Public Education Fund for a term of 3 years (new position).

Dennis M. Duffy,
of Pennsylvania, to be an Assistant Secretary of Veterans Affairs (Policy and Planning), vice Victor P. Raymond.

Jay C. Ehle,
of Ohio, to be a member of the Advisory Board of the Saint Lawrence Seaway Development Corporation, vice Conrad Fredin.

Maurice B. Foley,
of California, to be a Judge of the U.S. Tax Court for a term expiring 15 years after he takes office, vice Charles E. Clapp II, retired.

John A. Gannon,
of Ohio, to be a member of the National Council on Disability for a term expiring September 17, 1995 (reappointment).

E. Gordon Gee,
of Ohio, to be a member of the Board of Trustees of the Harry S Truman Scholarship Foundation for a term expiring December 10, 1999, vice Gary Eugene Wood, term expired.

Peggy Goldwater-Clay,
of California, to be a member of the Board of Trustees of the Barry Goldwater Scholarship and Excellence in Education Foundation for a term expiring June 5, 2000, vice Barry M. Goldwater, Jr., term expired.

Sanford D. Greenberg,
of the District of Columbia, to be a member of the National Science Board, National Science Foundation, for a term expiring May 10, 2000, vice Warren J. Baker, term expired.

Susan Hayase,
of California, to be a member of the Board of Directors of the Civil Liberties Public Education Fund for a term of 3 years (new position).

Steve M. Hays,
of Tennessee, to be a member of the Board of Directors of the National Institute of Building Sciences for a term expiring September 7, 1997, vice Dianne E. Ingels, term expired.

Eleanor Hill,
of Virginia, to be Inspector General, Department of Defense, vice Susan J. Crawford.

Kenneth Byron Hipp,
of Hawaii, to be a member of the National Mediation Board for a term expiring July 1, 1997, vice Patrick J. Cleary, resigned.

Charles Hummel,
of Delaware, to be a member of the National Museum Services Board for a term expiring December 6, 1999, vice Marilyn Logsdon Mennello, term expired.

Norwood J. Jackson, Jr.,
of Virginia, to be Inspector General, Federal Deposit Insurance Corporation (new position).

Shirley Ann Jackson,
of New Jersey, to be a member of the Nuclear Regulatory Commission for a term of 5 years expiring June 30, 1999, vice Forrest J. Remick, term expired.

Ayse Manyas Kenmore,
of Florida, to be a member of the National Museum Services Board for the remainder of the term expiring December 6, 1995, vice Daphne Wood Murray, resigned.

Jerome F. Kever,
of Illinois, to be a member of the Railroad Retirement Board for a term expiring August 28, 1998 (reappointment).

Cherry T. Kinoshita,
of Washington, to be a member of the Board of Directors of the Civil Liberties Public Education Fund for a term of 2 years (new position).

Elsa H. Kudo,
of Hawaii, to be a member of the Board of Directors of the Civil Liberties Public Education Fund for a term of 2 years (new position).

Yeiichi Kuwayama,
of the District of Columbia, to be a member of the Board of Directors of the Civil Liberties Public Education Fund for a term of 3 years (new position).

Charles T. Manatt,
of the District of Columbia, to be a member of the Board of Directors of the Communications Satellite Corporation until the date of the annual meeting of the Corporation in 1997, vice Rudy Boschwitz.

Charles L. Marinaccio,
of the District of Columbia, to be a Director of the Securities Investor Protection Corporation for a term expiring December 31, 1996, vice George H. Pfau, Jr., term expired.

Nancy Marsiglia,
of Louisiana, to be a member of the National Museum Services Board for a term expiring December 6, 1998, vice George S. Rosborough, Jr., term expired.

Marciene S. Mattleman,
of Pennsylvania, to be a member of the National Institute for Literacy Advisory Board for the remainder of the term expiring October 12, 1995, vice Jim Edgar, resigned.

Audrey L. McCrimon,
of Illinois, to be a member of the National Council on Disability for a term expiring September 17, 1997, vice Robert S. Mueller, term expired.

Eve L. Menger,
of New York, to be a member of the National Science Board, National Science Foundation, for a term expiring May 10, 2000, vice Arden L. Bement, Jr., term expired.

Dale Minami,
of California, to be a member of the Board of Directors of the Civil Liberties Public Education Fund for a term of 3 years (new position).

Claudia I. Mitchell-Kernan,
of California, to be a member of the National Science Board, National Science Foundation, for a term expiring May 10, 2000, vice Daniel C. Drucker, term expired.

Thomas Hill Moore,
of Florida, to be a Commissioner of the Consumer Product Safety Commission for the remainder of the term expiring October 26, 1996, vice Jacqueline Jones-Smith, resigned.

Bruce A. Morrison,
of Connecticut, to be a Director of the Federal Housing Finance Board for a term expiring February 27, 2000, vice William C. Perkins, resigned.

Don T. Nakanishi,
of California, to be a member of the Board of Directors of the Civil Liberties Public Education Fund for a term of 2 years (new position).

Diana S. Natalicio,
of Texas, to be a member of the National Science Board, National Science Foundation, for a term expiring May 10, 2000, vice Charles L. Hosler, Jr., term expired.

J. Timothy O'Neill,
of Virginia, to be a Director of the Federal Housing Finance Board for the remainder of the term expiring February 27, 1997, vice Marilyn R. Seymann, resigned.

Rose Ochi,
of California, to be an Associate Director for National Drug Control Policy, vice Kay Coles James, resigned.

Joe Bradley Pigott,
of Mississippi, to be U.S. Attorney for the Southern District of Mississippi for the term of 4 years, vice George L. Phillips.

Robert Pitofsky,
of Maryland, to be a Federal Trade Commissioner for the term of 7 years from September 26, 1994, vice Deborah Kaye Owen, resigned.

Lilliam Rangel Pollo,
of Florida, to be a member of the National Council on Disability for a term expiring September 17, 1996, vice Helen Wilshire Walsh, term expired.

Lt. Gen. William W. Quinn, USA (Ret.),
of Maryland, to be a member of the Board of Trustees of the Barry Goldwater Scholarship and Excellence in Education Foundation for a term expiring October 13, 1999 (reappointment).

Debra Robinson,
of Pennsylvania, to be a member of the National Council on Disability for a term expiring September 17, 1997, vice Anthony Hurlbutt Flack, term expired.

Arthur Rosenblatt,
of New York, to be a member of the National Museum Services Board for a term expiring December 6, 1997, vice Richard J. Schwartz, term expired.

Vincent Reed Ryan, Jr.,
of Texas, to be a member of the Board of Directors of the Panama Canal Commission, vice Walter J. Shea.

Lynda Hare Scribante,
of Nebraska, to be a member of the Board of Trustees of the Barry Goldwater Scholarship and Excellence in Education Foundation for a term expiring October 13, 1999, vice Dean Burch.

Niranjan Shamalbhai Shah,
of Illinois, to be a member of the Board of Trustees of the Barry Goldwater Scholarship and Excellence in Education Foundation for a term expiring August 11, 1998, vice Timothy W. Tong, term expired.

Stanley K. Sheinbaum,
of California, to be a member of the National Security Education Board for a term of 4 years, vice John P. Roche, resigned.

Robert M. Solow,
of Massachusetts, to be a member of the National Science Board, National Science Foundation, for a term expiring May 10, 2000, vice Peter H. Raven, term expired.

Virgil M. Speakman,
of Ohio, to be a member of the Railroad Retirement Board for a term expiring August 28, 1999 (reappointment).

Catherine Baker Stetson,
of New Mexico, to be a member of the Board of Trustees of the Institute of American Indian and Alaska Native Culture and Arts Development for a term expiring May 19, 2000, vice James D. Santini, term expired.

Joseph E. Stevens, Jr.,
of Missouri, to be a member of the Board of Trustees of the Harry S Truman Scholarship Foundation for a term expiring December 10, 1997, vice Truman McGill Hobbs, term expired.

Robert M. Sussman,
of the District of Columbia, to be a member of the Nuclear Regulatory Commission for a term of 5 years expiring June 30, 1998, vice James R. Curtiss, term expired.

Ruth Y. Tamura,
of Hawaii, to be a member of the National Museum Services Board for a term expiring December 6, 1996, vice James H. Duff, term expired.

Juan F. Vasquez,
of Texas, to be a Judge of the U.S. Tax Court for a term expiring 15 years after he takes office, vice Perry Shields, retired.

Lynne C. Waihee,
of Hawaii, to be a member of the National Institute for Literacy Advisory Board for a term of 3 years (new position).

Warren M. Washington,
of Colorado, to be a member of the National Science Board, National Science Foundation, for a term expiring May 10, 2000, vice Roland W. Schmitt, term expired.

John A. White, Jr.,
of Georgia, to be a member of the National Science Board, National Science Foundation, for a term expiring May 10, 2000, vice Benjamin S. Shen, term expired.

Townsend Wolfe,
of Arkansas, to be a member of the National Museum Services Board for a term expiring December 6, 1995, vice Rosemary G. McMillan, term expired.

Steven L. Zinter,
of South Dakota, to be a member of the Board of Trustees of the Harry S Truman Scholarship Foundation for a term expiring December 10, 1997, vice Richard J. Fitzgerald, resigned.

Dan M. Berkovitz,
of the District of Columbia, to be a member of the Nuclear Regulatory Commission for the term expiring June 30, 2000, vice E. Gail de Planque, term expiring.

Deborah Dudley Branson,
of Texas, to be a Director of the Securities Investor Protection Corporation for a term expiring December 31, 1996, vice Jesse D. Winzenreid, term expired.

Eugene Branstool,
of Ohio, to be a member of the Board of Directors of the Federal Agricultural Mortgage Corporation, vice John R. Dahl.

Martin James Burke,
of New York, to be U.S. Marshal for the Southern District of New York for the term of 4 years, vice Romolo J. Imundi.

Joan Challinor,
of the District of Columbia, to be a member of the National Commission on Libraries and Information Science for a term expiring July 19, 1999, vice Elinor H. Swaim, term expired.

Shirley Sears Chater,
of Texas, to be Commissioner of Social Security for the term expiring January 19, 2001 (new position).

Albert James Dwoskin,
of Virginia to be a Director of the Securities Investor Protection Corporation for a term expiring December 31, 1995, vice Frank G. Zarb, term expired.

J. Don Foster,
of Alabama, to be U.S. Attorney for the Southern District of Alabama for the term of 4 years, vice J. B. Sessions III, resigned.

Robert Talcott Francis II,
of Massachusetts, to be a member of the National Transportation Safety Board for the term expiring December 31, 1999, vice John K. Lauber, term expired, to which position he was appointed during the last recess of the Senate.

Phillip Frost,
of Florida, to be a member of the National Museum Services Board for a term expiring December 6, 1996, vice Arthur C. Beale, term expired.

Denis J. Hauptly,
of Minnesota, to be Chairman of the Special Panel on Appeals for a term of 6 years, vice Barbara Jean Mahone, term expired.

Wilma A. Lewis,
of the District of Columbia, to be Inspector General, Department of the Interior, vice James R. Richards, resigned.

Kathleen A. McGinty,
of Pennsylvania, to be a member of the Council on Environmental Quality, vice Michael R. Deland, resigned, to which position she was appointed during the last recess of the Senate.

George K. McKinney,
of Maryland, to be U.S. Marshal for the District of Maryland for the term of 4 years, vice Scott Alan Sewell.

Tony Scallon,
of Minnesota, to be a member of the Board of Directors of the National Consumer Cooperative Bank for a term of 3 years, vice John K. Stewart, term expired.

Janie L. Shores,
of Alabama, to be a member of the Board of Directors
of the State Justice Institute for a term expiring September 17, 1997, vice Vivi L. Dilweg, term expired.

Sheila Anne Smith,
of Illinois, to be a member of the Board of Directors
of the National Consumer Cooperative Bank for a
term of 3 years, vice Frank B. Sollars, term expired.

William L. Wilson,
of Minnesota, to be a member of the Advisory Board
of the Saint Lawrence Seaway Development Corporation, vice Virgil E. Brown, resigned.

Submitted January 10

Ray L. Caldwell,
of Virginia, a career member of the Senior Foreign
Service, class of Minister-Counselor, for the rank of
Ambassador during his tenure of service as Deputy
Assistant Secretary of State for Burdensharing.

Johnnie Carson,
of Illinois, a career member of the Senior Foreign
Service, class of Minister-Counselor, to be Ambassador
Extraordinary and Plenipotentiary of the United States
of America to the Republic of Zimbabwe.

Herman E. Gallegos,
of California, to be an Alternate Representative of
the United States of America to the 49th Session
of the General Assembly of the United Nations.

Lawrence Harrington,
of Tennessee, to be U.S. Alternate Executive Director
of the Inter-American Development Bank, vice Richard C. Houseworth, resigned.

Lee C. Howley,
of Ohio, to be a Representative of the United States
of America to the 49th Session of the General Assembly of the United Nations.

Jeanette W. Hyde,
of North Carolina, to serve concurrently and without
additional compensation as Ambassador Extraordinary
and Plenipotentiary of the United States of America
to Antigua and Barbuda, and as Ambassador Extraordinary and Plenipotentiary of the United States of
America to St. Kitts and Nevis, and as Ambassador
Extraordinary and Plenipotentiary of the United States
of America to Grenada.

Martin S. Indyk,
of the District of Columbia, to be Ambassador Extraordinary and Plenipotentiary of the United States
of America to Israel.

Isabelle Leeds,
of New York, to be an Alternate Representative of
the United States of America to the 49th Session
of the General Assembly of the United Nations.

Bismarck Myrick,
of Virginia, a career member of the Senior Foreign
Service, class of Counselor, to be Ambassador Extraordinary and Plenipotentiary of the United States of
America to the Kingdom of Lesotho.

Philip C. Wilcox, Jr.,
of Maryland, a career member of the Senior Foreign
Service, class of Minister-Counselor, for the rank of
Ambassador during his tenure of service as Coordinator for Counter Terrorism.

Jacquelyn L. Williams-Bridgers,
of Maryland, to be Inspector General, Department
of State, vice Sherman M. Funk, resigned.

Frank G. Wisner,
of the District of Columbia, a career member of the
Senior Foreign Service, class of Career Minister, for
the personal rank of Career Ambassador in recognition
of especially distinguished service over a sustained period.

Submitted January 11

Sandra L. Lynch,
of Massachusetts, to be U.S. Circuit Judge for the
First Circuit, vice Stephen G. Breyer, elevated.

David Folsom,
of Texas, to be U.S. District Judge for the Eastern
District of Texas, vice Sam B. Hall, Jr., deceased.

Thadd Heartfield,
of Texas, to be U.S. District Judge for the Eastern
District of Texas, vice Robert M. Parker, elevated.

John D. Snodgrass,
of Alabama, to be U.S. District Judge for the Northern
District of Alabama, vice E.B. Haltom, Jr., retired.

Sidney H. Stein,
of New York, to be U.S. District Judge for the Southern District of New York, vice Pierre N. Leval, elevated.

Lacy H. Thornburg,
of North Carolina, to be U.S. District Judge for the
Western District of North Carolina, vice Robert D.
Potter, retired.

Submitted January 18

S. David Fineman,
of Pennsylvania, to be a Governor of the U.S. Postal
Service for the term expiring December 8, 2003, vice
Norma Pace, term expired.

Submitted January 23

Janet Bond Arterton,
of Connecticut, to be U.S. District Judge for the District of Connecticut, vice Jose A. Cabranes, elevated.

Willis B. Hunt, Jr.,
of Georgia, to be U.S. District Judge for the Northern District of Georgia, vice Horace T. Ward, retired.

Susan Y. Illston,
of California, to be U.S. District Judge for the Northern District of California, vice Barbara A. Caulfield, resigned.

Charles B. Kornmann,
of South Dakota, to be U.S. District Judge for the District of South Dakota, vice John B. Jones, retired.

John L. Bryant, Jr.,
of the District of Columbia, to be a member of the National Museum Services Board for a term expiring December 6, 1997, vice Helmuth J. Naumer, term expired.

Submitted January 24

Maxine M. Chesney,
of California, to be U.S. District Judge for the Northern District of California, vice John P. Vukasin, Jr., deceased.

Karen Nelson Moore,
of Ohio, to be U.S. Circuit Judge for the Sixth Circuit, vice Robert B. Krupansky, retired.

Marianne C. Spraggins,
of New York, to be a Director of the Securities Investor Protection Corporation for a term expiring December 31, 1997, vice Thomas J. Healey, term expired.

Submitted January 31

James L. Dennis,
of Louisiana, to be U.S. Circuit Judge for the Fifth Circuit, vice Charles Clark, retired.

Rae E. Unzicker,
of North Dakota, to be a member of the National Council on Disability for a term expiring September 17, 1997, vice Mary Ann Mobley-Collins, term expired.

Hughey Walker,
of South Carolina, to be a member of the National Council on Disability for a term expiring September 17, 1996, vice Ellis B. Bodron, term expired.

Ela Yazzie-King,
of Arizona, to be a member of the National Council on Disability for a term expiring September 17, 1996, vice Linda Allison, term expired.

Submitted February 3

Eldon E. Fallon,
of Louisiana, to be U.S. District Judge for the Eastern District of Louisiana, vice Adrian G. Duplantier, retired.

Submitted February 8

Alton W. Cornella,
of South Dakota, to be a member of the Defense Base Closure and Realignment Commission for a term expiring at the end of the first session of the 104th Congress, vice Peter B. Bowman, term expired.

Rebecca G. Cox,
of California, to be a member of the Defense Base Closure and Realignment Commission for a term expiring at the end of the first session of the 104th Congress (reappointment).

Gen. James B. Davis, USAF (Ret.),
of Florida, to be a member of the Defense Base Closure and Realignment Commission for a term expiring at the end of the first session of the 104th Congress, vice Beverly Butcher Byron, term expired.

S. Lee Kling,
of Maryland, to be a member of the Defense Base Closure and Realignment Commission for a term expiring at the end of the first session of the 104th Congress, vice Hansford T. Johnson, term expired.

Benjamin F. Montoya,
of New Mexico, to be a member of the Defense Base Closure and Realignment Commission for a term expiring at the end of the first session of the 104th Congress, vice Arthur Levitt, Jr., term expired.

Wendi Louise Steele,
of Texas, to be a member of the Defense Base Closure and Realignment Commission for a term expiring at the end of the first session of the 104th Congress, vice Harry C. McPherson, Jr., term expired.

Submitted February 13

Curtis L. Collier,
of Tennessee, to be U.S. District Judge for the Eastern District of Tennessee (new position).

Submitted February 22

John Chrystal,
of Iowa, to be a member of the Board of Directors of the Overseas Private Investment Corporation for a term expiring December 17, 1997 (reappointment).

George J. Kourpias,
of Maryland, to be a member of the Board of Directors of the Overseas Private Investment Corporation for a term expiring December 17, 1997 (reappointment).

Gloria Rose Ott,
of California, to be a member of the Board of Directors of the Overseas Private Investment Corporation for a term expiring December 17, 1996, vice Weldon W. Case, term expired.

Harvey Sigelbaum,
of New York, to be a member of the Board of Directors of the Overseas Private Investment Corporation for a term expiring December 17, 1996, vice Carolyn D. Leavens, term expired.

Inez Smith Reid,
of the District of Columbia, to be an Associate Judge of the District of Columbia Court of Appeals for the term of 15 years, vice Emmet G. Sullivan.

Submitted February 24

Kirsten S. Moy,
of New York, to be Administrator of the Community Development Financial Institutions Fund (new position).

Submitted February 26

Edmundo A. Gonzales,
of Colorado, to be Chief Financial Officer, Department of Labor (new position).

John D. Kemp,
of the District of Columbia, to be a member of the National Council on Disability for a term expiring September 17, 1997, vice Mary Matthews Raether, term expired.

Submitted February 27

Josue Robles, Jr.,
of Texas, to be a member of the Defense Base Closure and Realignment Commission for a term expiring at the end of the first session of the 104th Congress, vice Robert D. Stuart, Jr., term expired.

Submitted February 28

Henry W. Foster, Jr.,
of Tennessee, to be Medical Director in the Regular Corps of the Public Health Service, subject to qualifications therefor as provided by law and regulations, and to be Surgeon General of the Public Health Service, for a term of 4 years, vice M. Joycelyn Elders, resigned.

Peter C. Economus,
of Ohio, to be U.S. District Judge for the Northern District of Ohio, vice Frank J. Battisti, resigned.

Joseph Robert Goodwin,
of West Virginia, to be U.S. District Judge for the Southern District of West Virginia, vice Robert J. Staker, retired.

Submitted March 3

Charles William Burton,
of Texas, to be a member of the Board of Directors of the U.S. Enrichment Corporation for the remainder of the term expiring February 24, 1996, vice Frank G. Zarb, resigned.

Submitted March 6

John Goglia,
of Massachusetts, to be a member of the National Transportation Safety Board for the term expiring December 31, 1998, vice Susan M. Coughlin, resigned.

Clifford Gregory Stewart,
of New Jersey, to be General Counsel of the Equal Employment Opportunity Commission for a term of 4 years, vice Donald R. Livingston, resigned.

Submitted March 9

Daniel A. Mica,
of Virginia, to be a member of the Board of Directors of the U.S. Institute of Peace for a term expiring January 19, 1997, vice W. Scott Thompson, term expired.

Harriet M. Zimmerman,
of Florida, to be a member of the Board of Directors of the U.S. Institute of Peace for a term expiring January 19, 1999, vice William R. Kintner, term expired.

Submitted March 10

Daniel Robert Glickman,
of Kansas, to be Secretary of Agriculture, vice Mike Espy, resigned.

Submitted March 14

Mary Beck Briscoe,
of Kansas, to be U.S. Circuit Judge for the Tenth Circuit, vice James K. Logan, retired.

Submitted March 23

Mary S. Furlong,
of California, to be a member of the National Commission on Libraries and Information Science for a term expiring July 19, 1999, vice Daniel W. Casey, term expired.

Jeffrey M. Lang,
of Maryland, to be Deputy United States Trade Representative, with the rank of Ambassador, vice Rufus Hawkins Yerxa, resigned.

Jerome A. Stricker,
of Kentucky, to be a member of the Federal Retirement Thrift Investment Board for a term expiring

September 25, 1998, vice Shirley Chilton-O'Dell, term expired.

Carlos F. Lucero,
of Colorado, to be U.S. Circuit Judge for the Tenth Circuit (new position).

Wenona Y. Whitfield,
of Illinois, to be U.S. District Judge for the Southern District of Illinois, vice William L. Beatty, retired.

Submitted March 28

James John Hoecker,
of Virginia, to be a member of the Federal Energy Regulatory Commission for the term expiring June 30, 2000 (reappointment).

John M. Deutch,
of Massachusetts, to be Director of Central Intelligence, vice R. James Woolsey, resigned.

Withdrawn March 30

Catherine Baker Stetson,
of New Mexico, to be a member of the Board of Trustees of the Institute of American Indian and Alaska Native Culture and Arts Development for a term expiring May 19, 2000, vice James D. Santini, term expired, which was sent to the Senate on January 5, 1995.

Submitted March 30

Catherine Baker Stetson,
of New Mexico, to be a member of the Board of Trustees of the Institute of American Indian and Alaska Native Culture and Arts Development for a term expiring May 19, 2000, vice LaDonna Harris, resigned.

Submitted March 31

Michele Driscoll Alioto,
of California, to be a member of the National Council on Disability for a term expiring September 17, 1996, vice Michael B. Unhjem, term expired.

Wiley Y. Daniel,
of Colorado, to be U.S. District Judge for the District of Colorado, vice Sherman G. Finesilver, retired.

Tommy Edward Jewell III,
of New Mexico, to be a member of the Board of Directors of the State Justice Institute for a term expiring September 17, 1995, vice Janice L. Gradwohl, term expired.

Tommy Edward Jewell III,
of New Mexico, to be a member of the Board of Directors of the State Justice Institute for a term expiring September 17, 1998 (reappointment).

Diane P. Wood,
of Illinois, to be U.S. Circuit Judge for the Seventh Circuit, vice William J. Bauer, retired.

Submitted April 3

Vera Alexander,
of Alaska, to be a member of the Marine Mammal Commission for a term expiring May 13, 1997, vice Jack Warren Lentfer, term expired.

Submitted April 4

Nancy Friedman Atlas,
of Texas, to be U.S. District Judge for the Southern District of Texas, vice James DeAnda, retired.

John Garvan Murtha,
of Vermont, to be U.S. District Judge for the District of Vermont, vice Franklin S. Billings, Jr., retired.

George A. O'Toole, Jr.,
of Massachusetts, to be U.S. District Judge for the District of Massachusetts (additional position).

Leland M. Shurin,
of Missouri, to be U.S. District Judge for the Western District of Missouri, vice Scott O. Wright, retired.

Submitted April 6

Roberta L. Gross,
of the District of Columbia, to be Inspector General, National Aeronautics and Space Administration, vice Bill D. Colvin, resigned.

Karl N. Stauber,
of Minnesota, to be Under Secretary of Agriculture for Research, Education, and Economics (new position).

A. Wallace Tashima,
of California, to be U.S. Circuit Judge for the Ninth Circuit, vice Arthur L. Alarcon, retired.

Submitted April 24

A. Peter Burleigh,
of California, a career member of the Senior Foreign Service, class of Minister-Counselor, to be Ambassador Extraordinary and Plenipotentiary of the United States of America to the Democratic Socialist Republic of Sri Lanka, and to serve concurrently and without additional compensation as Ambassador Extraordinary and Plenipotentiary of the United States of America to the Republic of Maldives.

David C. Litt,
of Florida, a career member of the Senior Foreign Service, class of Counselor, to be Ambassador Extraordinary and Plenipotentiary of the United States of America to the United Arab Emirates.

Larry C. Napper,
of Texas, a career member of the Senior Foreign Service, class of Minister-Counselor, to be Ambassador Extraordinary and Plenipotentiary of the United States of America to Latvia.

Ira S. Shapiro,
of Maryland, for the rank of Ambassador during his tenure of service as Senior Counsel and Negotiator in the Office of the United States Trade Representative.

R. Grant Smith,
of New Jersey, a career member of the Senior Foreign Service, class of Minister-Counselor, to be Ambassador Extraordinary and Plenipotentiary of the United States of America to the Republic of Tajikistan.

Donald K. Steinberg,
of California, a career member of the Senior Foreign Service, class of Minister-Counselor, to be Ambassador Extraordinary and Plenipotentiary of the United States of America to the Republic of Angola.

Lawrence Palmer Taylor,
of Pennsylvania, a career member of the Senior Foreign Service, class of Minister-Counselor, to be Ambassador Extraordinary and Plenipotentiary of the United States of America to the Republic of Estonia.

Patrick Nickolas Theros,
of the District of Columbia, a career member of the Senior Foreign Service, class of Minister-Counselor, to be Ambassador Extraordinary and Plenipotentiary of the United States of America to the State of Qatar.

Peter Tomsen,
of California, a career member of the Senior Foreign Service, class of Minister-Counselor, to be Ambassador Extraordinary and Plenipotentiary of the United States of America to the Republic of Armenia.

Jenonne R. Walker,
of the District of Columbia, to be Ambassador Extraordinary and Plenipotentiary of the United States of America to the Czech Republic.

James Alan Williams,
of Virginia, a career member of the Senior Foreign Service, class of Minister-Counselor, to be rank of Ambassador during his tenure of service as the Special Coordinator for Cyprus.

Stephen G. Kellison,
of Texas, to be a member of the Board of Trustees of the Federal Old-Age and Survivors Insurance Trust Fund and the Federal Disability Insurance Trust Fund for a term of 4 years, vice David M. Walker, term expired.

Marilyn Moon,
of Maryland, to be a member of the Board of Trustees of the Federal Old-Age and Survivors Insurance Trust Fund and the Federal Disability Insurance Trust Fund for a term of 4 years, vice Stanford G. Ross.

Submitted April 25

Terence T. Evans,
of Wisconsin, to be U.S. Circuit Judge for the Seventh Circuit, vice Richard D. Cudahy, retired.

William A. Fletcher,
of California, to be U.S. Circuit Judge for the Ninth Circuit, vice William Albert Norris, retired.

Sandra J. Kristoff,
of Virginia, for the rank of Ambassador during her tenure of service as U.S. Coordinator for Asia-Pacific Economic Cooperation (APEC).

Mosina H. Jordan,
of New York, a career member of the Senior Foreign Service, class of Minister-Counselor, to be Ambassador Extraordinary and Plenipotentiary of the United States of America to the Central African Republic.

Lannon Walker,
of Maryland, a career member of the Senior Foreign Service, class of Career Minister, to be Ambassador Extraordinary and Plenipotentiary of the United States of America to the Republic of Cote d'Ivoire.

Submitted April 27

George H. King,
of California, to be U.S. District Judge for the Central District of California (new position).

Donald C. Nugent,
of Ohio, to be U.S. District Judge for the Northern District of Ohio, vice Thomas D. Lambros, retired.

Submitted May 2

William H. LeBlanc III,
of Louisiana, to be a Commissioner of the Postal Rate Commission for a term expiring November 22, 2000 (reappointment).

Jacob Joseph Lew,
of New York, to be Deputy Director of the Office of Management and Budget, vice Alice Rivlin.

Richard J. Stern,
of Illinois, to be a member of the National Council on the Arts for a term expiring September 3, 2000, vice Catherine Yi-yu Cho Woo, term expired.

Submitted May 4

Catherine C. Blake,
of Maryland, to be U.S. District Judge for the District of Maryland, vice John M. Hargrove, retired.

Andre M. Davis,
of Maryland, to be U.S. District Judge for the District of Maryland, vice Walter E. Black, Jr., retired.

Herbert F. Collins,
of Massachusetts, to be a member of the Thrift Depositor Protection Oversight Board for a term of 3 years, vice Philip C. Jackson, Jr., term expired.

Submitted May 5

John W. Carlin,
of Kansas, to be Archivist of the United States, vice Don W. Wilson, resigned.

Robert F. Rider,
of Delaware, to be a Governor of the U.S. Postal Service for the remainder of the term expiring December 8, 1995, vice John N. Griesemer.

Robert F. Rider,
of Delaware, to be a Governor of the U.S. Postal Service for the term expiring December 8, 2004 (reappointment).

Submitted May 8

Leo K. Goto,
of Colorado, to be a member of the Board of Directors of the Civil Liberties Public Education Fund for a term of 2 years (new position).

Patrick M. Ryan,
of Oklahoma, to be U.S. Attorney for the Western District of Oklahoma, vice Vicki Miles-LaGrange, resigned.

Submitted May 9

John P. White,
of Massachusetts, to be Deputy Secretary of Defense, vice John M. Deutch.

Submitted May 11

Karl N. Stauber,
of Minnesota, to be a member of the Board of Directors of the Commodity Credit Corporation, vice Daniel A. Sumner, resigned.

Submitted May 19

Andrew Fois,
of New York, to be an Assistant Attorney General, vice Sheila Foster Anthony, resigned.

Maria Luisa Mabilangan Haley,
of Arkansas, to be a member of the Board of Directors of the Export-Import Bank of the United States for a term expiring January 20, 1999 (reappointment).

John D. Hawke, Jr.,
of New York, to be Under Secretary of the Treasury, vice Frank N. Newman.

George J. Tenet,
of Maryland, to be Deputy Director of Central Intelligence, vice Adm. William O. Studeman.

Dwight P. Robinson,
of Michigan, to be Deputy Secretary of Housing and Urban Development, vice Terrence R. Duvernay, Sr., resigned.

Submitted May 24

Linda Lee Robertson,
of Oklahoma, to be a Deputy Under Secretary of the Treasury, vice Michael B. Levy, resigned.

Joseph H. McKinley, Jr.,
of Kentucky, to be U.S. District Judge for the Western District of Kentucky, vice Ronald E. Meredith, deceased.

Robert H. Whaley,
of Washington, to be U.S. District Judge for the Western District of Washington, vice Justin L. Quackenbush, retired.

B. Lynn Winmill,
of Idaho, to be U.S. District Judge for the District of Idaho, vice Harold L. Ryan, retired.

Submitted May 25

Kenneth H. Bacon,
of the District of Columbia, to be an Assistant Secretary of Defense (new position).

Sheryl R. Marshall,
of Massachusetts, to be a member of the Federal Retirement Thrift Investment Board for a term expiring October 11, 1998, vice Stephen Norris, term expired.

Peggy A. Nagae,
of Oregon, to be a member of the Board of Directors of the Civil Liberties Public Education Fund for a term of 3 years (new position).

Submitted June 5

Tracey D. Conwell,
of Texas, to be a member of the National Museum Services Board for a term expiring December 6, 1996, vice Fay S. Howell, term expired.

Albert James Dwoskin,
of Virginia, to be a Director of the Securities Investor Protection Corporation for a term expiring December 31, 1998 (reappointment).

David L. Hobbs,
of California, a career member of the Senior Foreign Service, class of Minister-Counselor, to be Ambassador Extraordinary and Plenipotentiary of the United States of America to the Cooperative Republic of Guyana.

William J. Hughes,
of New Jersey, to be Ambassador Extraordinary and Plenipotentiary of the United States of America to the Republic of Panama.

Submitted June 6

C. Richard Allen,
of Maryland, to be a Managing Director of the Corporation for National and Community Service (new position).

Chris Evert,
of Florida, to be a member of the Board of Directors of the Corporation for National and Community Service for a term of 3 years (new position).

Christine Hernandez,
of Texas, to be a member of the Board of Directors of the Corporation for National and Community Service for a term of 2 years (new position).

Submitted June 7

John Joseph Callahan,
of Massachusetts, to be an Assistant Secretary of Health and Human Services, vice Kenneth S. Apfel, resigned.

Stephen G. Kellison,
of Texas, to be a member of the Board of Trustees of the Federal Hospital Insurance Trust Fund for a term of 4 years, vice David M. Walker, term expired.

Stephen G. Kellison,
of Texas, to be a member of the Board of Trustees of the Federal Supplementary Medical Insurance Trust Fund for a term of 4 years, vice David M. Walker, term expired.

Marilyn Moon,
of Maryland, to be a member of the Board of Trustees of the Federal Hospital Insurance Trust Fund for a term of 4 years, vice Stanford G. Ross, term expired.

Marilyn Moon,
of Maryland, to be a member of the Board of Trustees of the Federal Supplementary Medical Insurance Trust Fund for a term of 4 years, vice Stanford G. Ross, term expired.

Submitted June 13

Edward Scott Blair,
of Tennessee, to be U.S. Marshal for the Middle District of Tennessee, vice Charles F. Goggin III.

Michael William Cotter,
of the District of Columbia, a career member of the Senior Foreign Service, class of Counselor, to be Ambassador Extraordinary and Plenipotentiary of the United States of America to the Republic of Turkmenistan.

James E. Goodby,
of the District of Columbia, for the rank of Ambassador during his tenure of service as Principal Negotiator for the Safe and Secure Dismantlement of Nuclear Weapons.

Victor Jackovich,
of Iowa, a career member of the Senior Foreign Service, class of Minister-Counselor, to be Ambassador Extraordinary and Plenipotentiary of the United States of America to the Republic of Slovenia.

A. Elizabeth Jones,
of Maryland, a career member of the Senior Foreign Service, class of Minister-Counselor, to be Ambassador Extraordinary and Plenipotentiary of the United States of America to the Republic of Kazakhstan.

John Raymond Malott,
of Virginia, a career member of the Senior Foreign Service, class of Minister-Counselor, to be Ambassador Extraordinary and Plenipotentiary of the United States of America to Malaysia.

John K. Menzies,
of Virginia, a career member of the Senior Foreign Service, class of Counselor, to be Ambassador Extraordinary and Plenipotentiary of the United States of America to the Republic of Bosnia and Herzegovina.

Kenneth Michael Quinn,
of Iowa, a career member of the Senior Foreign Service, class of Minister-Counselor, to be Ambassador Extraordinary and Plenipotentiary of the United States of America to Cambodia.

John Todd Stewart,
of California, a career member of the Senior Foreign Service, class of Minister-Counselor, to be Ambassador Extraordinary and Plenipotentiary of the United States of America to the Republic of Moldova.

Submitted June 14

Beth Susan Slavet,
of Massachusetts, to be a member of the Merit Systems Protection Board for the term of 7 years expiring March 1, 2002, vice Jessica L. Parks, term expired.

Submitted June 21

John T. Conway,
of New York, to be a member of the Defense Nuclear Facilities Safety Board for a term expiring October 18, 1999 (reappointment).

Submitted June 26

Derrick L. Forrister,
of Tennessee, to be an Assistant Secretary of Energy (Congressional and Intergovernmental Affairs), vice William J. Taylor III, resigned.

Submitted June 27

Todd J. Campbell,
of Tennessee, to be U.S. District Judge for the Middle District of Tennessee, vice Thomas A. Wiseman, Jr., retired.

James M. Moody,
of Arkansas, to be U.S. District Judge for the Eastern District of Arkansas, vice Henry Woods, retired.

Alberto J. Mora,
of Florida, to be a member of the Broadcasting Board of Governors for a term of 2 years (new position).

Evan J. Wallach,
of Nevada, to be a Judge of the U.S. Court of International Trade, vice Edward D. Re, retired.

Submitted June 28

George D. Milidrag,
of Michigan, to be a member of the Advisory Board of the Saint Lawrence Seaway Development Corporation, vice L. Steven Reimers.

Lawrence H. Summers,
of Massachusetts, to be Deputy Secretary of the Treasury, vice Frank N. Newman, resigned.

Frances D. Cook,
of Florida, a career member of the Senior Foreign Service, class of Minister-Counselor, to be Ambassador Extraordinary and Plenipotentiary of the United States of America to the Sultanate of Oman.

J. Stapleton Roy,
of Pennsylvania, a career member of the Senior Foreign Service, class of Career Minister, to be Ambassador Extraordinary and Plenipotentiary of the United States of America to the Republic of Indonesia.

Thomas W. Simons, Jr.,
of the District of Columbia, a career member of the Senior Foreign Service, class of Career Minister, to be Ambassador Extraordinary and Plenipotentiary of the United States of America to the Islamic Republic of Pakistan.

John M. Yates,
of Washington, a career member of the Senior Foreign Service, class of Minister-Counselor, to be Ambassador Extraordinary and Plenipotentiary of the United States of America to the Republic of Benin.

Submitted June 29

R. Guy Cole, Jr.,
of Ohio, to be U.S. Circuit Judge for the Sixth Circuit, vice Nathaniel R. Jones, retired.

John Raymond Garamendi,
of California, to be Deputy Secretary of the Interior, vice Frank A. Bracken, resigned.

Submitted June 30

Ernest W. DuBester,
of New Jersey, to be a member of the National Mediation Board for a term expiring July 1, 1998 (reappointment).

Richard Henry Jones,
of Nebraska, a career member of the Senior Foreign Service, class of Counselor, to be Ambassador Extraordinary and Plenipotentiary of the United States of America to the Republic of Lebanon.

William Harrison Courtney,
of West Virginia, a career member of the Senior Foreign Service, class of Minister-Counselor, to be Ambassador Extraordinary and Plenipotentiary of the United States of America to the Republic of Georgia.

Barry Ted Moskowitz,
of California, to be U.S. District Judge for the Southern District of California (new position).

Stephen M. Orlofsky,
of New Jersey, to be U.S. District Judge for the District of New Jersey, vice Dickinson Richards Debevoise, retired.

Donald C. Pogue,
of Connecticut, to be a Judge of the U.S. Court of International Trade, vice James L. Watson, retired.

Howard Monroe Schloss,
of Louisiana, to be an Assistant Secretary of the Treasury, vice Joan Logue-Kinder.

William K. Sessions III,
of Vermont, to be U.S. District Judge for the District of Vermont, vice Fred I. Parker, elevated.

Ortrie D. Smith,
of Missouri, to be U.S. District Judge for the Western District of Missouri, vice Howard F. Sachs, retired.

Appendix C—Checklist of White House Press Releases

The following list contains releases of the Office of the Press Secretary which are not included in this book.

Released January 3

Statement by White House Counsel Abner Mikva on release of the U.S. Senate Banking Committee Report on the Washington aspects of Whitewater

Released January 4

Announcement of nomination for three District of Columbia Superior Court Judges

Released January 6

Statement by Press Secretary Mike McCurry announcing the upcoming state visit of President Fernando Henrique Cardoso of Brazil

Transcript of a press briefing by Secretary of Labor Robert Reich and Council of Economic Advisers Chair Laura D'Andrea Tyson on the economy

Released January 9

Announcement on release of funds for earthquake assistance to California

Released January 10

Statement by Press Secretary Mike McCurry announcing the upcoming visit of President Mircea Snegur of Moldova

Statement by Press Secretary Mike McCurry on the President's upcoming state visit to Canada

Transcript of a press briefing by Secretary of Labor Robert Reich and Secretary of Education Richard Riley on the middle class bill of rights

Released January 11

Statement by Press Secretary Mike McCurry on the upcoming White House Conference on Trade and Investment in Ireland

Transcript of a press briefing on the President's meeting with Prime Minister Tomiichi Murayama of Japan by U.S. Ambassador to Japan Walter Mondale, Deputy Assistant to the President for Economic Policy Bo Cutter, and National Security Council Senior Director for Asian Affairs Stanley Roth

Text of a report to the President and Prime Minister Tomiichi Murayama of Japan entitled "Common Agenda for Cooperation in Global Perspective"

Transcript of a press briefing on the middle class bill of rights by Secretary of Education Richard Riley, Secretary of Commerce Ron Brown, and Secretary of Housing and Urban Development Henry Cisneros

Released January 12

Transcript of a press briefing by Press Secretary Mike McCurry

Transcript of a press briefing by Federal Emergency Management Agency Director James Lee Witt on the flooding in California

List of Democratic freshman Members of Congress meeting with the President

List of retired military officers attending a luncheon meeting with the President

Released January 13

White House statement on the White House Conference on Trade and Investment in Central and Eastern Europe

White House statement on Ex-Im Bank's expansion of programs with Central and Eastern Europe

Released January 16

Transcript of a press briefing by Corporation for National and Community Service President Eli Segal on the King Holiday and Service Act of 1994

Released January 17

Statement by Press Secretary Mike McCurry announcing National Security Council personnel changes

Statement by Press Secretary Mike McCurry on National Security Adviser Anthony Lake's announcement of National Security Council personnel changes

Released January 19

Transcript of a press briefing by Press Secretary Mike McCurry

Statement by Press Secretary Mike McCurry announcing events commemorating the 50th anniversary of the founding of the United Nations

Statement by Press Secretary Mike McCurry in response to a letter from Speaker of the House of Representatives Newt Gingrich regarding the proposed balanced budget constitutional amendment

Statement by Press Secretary Mike McCurry on the upcoming visit of Prime Minister Benazir Bhutto of Pakistan

White House statement on the President's record of accomplishment on the 2 year anniversary of his inauguration

Released January 20

Transcript of a press briefing by Press Secretary Mike McCurry

Transcript of a press briefing on loan guarantees for Mexico by Secretary of the Treasury Robert Rubin, Council of Economic Advisers Chair Laura D'Andrea Tyson, Senator Daniel Patrick Moynihan, and Representative Sander M. Levin

Released January 23

Transcript of a press briefing by Press Secretary Mike McCurry

Statement by Press Secretary Mike McCurry on the President's telephone conversation with President Ernesto Zedillo of Mexico

Announcement of nomination for four U.S. District Court Judges

Released January 24

Transcript of a press briefing by Chief of Staff Leon Panetta on the State of the Union Address

Statement by Press Secretary Mike McCurry on the President's action against terrorists who threaten to disrupt the Middle East peace process

Fact sheet on the Executive order on transactions with terrorists who threaten to disrupt the Middle East peace process

Announcement on travel by Cabinet members and other administration officials to discuss the middle class bill of rights

Released January 25

Statement by Press Secretary Mike McCurry on the visit of Chancellor Helmut Kohl of Germany

Statement by Press Secretary Mike McCurry on the visit of President Isaias Afworki of Eritrea

Statement by Press Secretary Mike McCurry on rescheduling the White House Conference on Trade and Investment in Ireland for May 24–26

White House statement on the Presidential delegation to the 50th anniversary commemoration of the liberation of Auschwitz

Released January 26

Transcript of a press briefing by Press Secretary Mike McCurry

Statement by Press Secretary Mike McCurry on the constitutional requirements of a balanced budget

Released January 27

Transcript of a press briefing by Press Secretary Mike McCurry

Transcript of a press briefing by Council of Economic Advisers Chair Laura D'Andrea Tyson on the economy

Transcript of a press briefing by Secretary of Health and Human Services Donna Shalala on welfare reform

Fact sheet on the President's record on welfare reform

Statement by Press Secretary Mike McCurry on the visit of U.S. disaster experts to Japan

Announcement on the President's meeting with members of the U.S. Conference of Mayors

Released January 28

Transcript of a press conference by participants in the working session on welfare reform

Statement by Press Secretary Mike McCurry on attacks by the Burmese army in Mannerplaw

Released January 30

Transcript of a press briefing by Press Secretary Mike McCurry

Released January 31

Statement by Press Secretary Mike McCurry on the withdrawal of Robert Pastor's nomination to be Ambassador to Panama

Statement by Press Secretary Mike McCurry on the visit of Prime Minister Vaclav Klaus of the Czech Republic

Statement by Press Secretary Mike McCurry on the visit of Prime Minister James Bolger of New Zealand

Transcript of a press briefing by Secretary of State Warren Christopher and Secretary of the Treasury Robert Rubin on loan guarantees for Mexico

Released February 1

Transcript of a press briefing by Press Secretary Mike McCurry

Statement by Press Secretary Mike McCurry on the visit of Prime Minister Lamberto Dini of Italy

Statement by Press Secretary Mike McCurry on the President's meeting with President Isaias Afworki of Eritrea

Released February 2

Transcript of a press briefing by Press Secretary Mike McCurry

Statement by Press Secretary Mike McCurry on the President's letter to President Alberto Fujimori of Peru and President Sixto Duran-Ballen of Ecuador on hostilities between the two countries

Fact sheet on the naming of aircraft carriers CVN–75 and CVN–76

Released February 3

Transcript of a press briefing by Press Secretary Mike McCurry

Transcript of a press briefing by Secretary of Labor Robert Reich and Council of Economic Advisers Chair Laura D'Andrea Tyson on the minimum wage and unemployment

Announcement of nomination for U.S. District Court Judge for the Eastern District of Louisiana

Announcement of administration briefings on the fiscal year 1996 budget

Released February 5

Statement by Press Secretary Mike McCurry on the President's action to combat illegal border crossings in Nogales, AZ

Released February 6

Transcript of a press briefing by Press Secretary Mike McCurry

Transcript of a press briefing on the fiscal year 1996 budget by Vice President Albert Gore, Secretary of the Treasury Robert Rubin, Council of Economic Advisers Chair Laura D'Andrea Tyson, and Office of Management and Budget Director Alice Rivlin

Released February 7

Transcripts of press briefings by Press Secretary Mike McCurry

Transcript of a press briefing by Secretary of Labor Robert Reich and former Secretary of Labor William Usery on the major league baseball strike

Statement by Press Secretary Mike McCurry on the upcoming visit of King Hassan of Morocco

Transcript of a press briefing on the illegal immigration initiative by Attorney General Janet Reno, Immigration and Naturalization Service Commissioner Doris Meissner, Secretary of Labor Robert Reich, El Paso Chief Border Patrol Agent Silvestre Reyes, and Immigration and Naturalization Service Western Region Director Gus de la Vina

Released February 8

Transcript of a press briefing by Press Secretary Mike McCurry

Transcript of a press briefing by Associate Attorney General John Schmidt and COPS Program Director Chief Joseph Brann on community policing grants

Released February 10

Transcript of a press briefing by Press Secretary Mike McCurry

Statement by Press Secretary Mike McCurry on Chief of Staff Leon Panetta's letter to Secretary of Defense William Perry on Department of Defense spending for breast cancer and AIDS research

White House statement on the President's decision that the United States will sign the United Nations Convention on the Rights of the Child

Fact sheet on the proposed "Omnibus Counterterrorism Act of 1995"

Released February 11

Statement by Press Secretary Mike McCurry on National Security Adviser Anthony Lake's meeting with representatives of the transitional Government of Ethiopia

Transcript of a press briefing on anticrime legislation by Attorney General Janet Reno, National Drug Control Policy Director Lee Brown, Associate Attorney General John Schmidt, and COPS Program Director Chief Joseph Brann

Letter from the Law Enforcement Steering Committee to the President and Members of Congress on anticrime legislation

Released February 12

Transcript of a press briefing by Secretary of State Warren Christopher on the President's meeting with Middle Eastern leaders

Released February 13

Transcript of a press briefing by Press Secretary Mike McCurry

Statement by Press Secretary Mike McCurry on the President's telephone conversation with President Boris Yeltsin of Russia

Fact sheet on the proposed "Middle-Class Bill of Rights Tax Relief Act of 1995"

Announcement of nomination for U.S. District Court Judge for the Eastern District of Tennessee

Released February 14

Statement by Press Secretary Mike McCurry on National Security Adviser Anthony Lake's announcement of the appointment of the National Security Council Executive Director

Transcript of a press briefing by Deputy Assistant to the President for Economic Policy Gene Sperling on the President's remarks to the American Council on Education

Fact sheet on the President's remarks to the American Council on Education

Excerpts of the President's remarks to the American Council on Education

Released February 15

Statement by Press Secretary Mike McCurry on the administration's determination that the U.S. Information Agency, the Agency for International Development, and the U.S. Arms Control and Disarmament Agency should continue as independent agencies

Released February 16

Transcript of a press briefing by Press Secretary Mike McCurry

Statement by Press Secretary Mike McCurry on the appointment of an Assistant to the President and Director of Political Affairs

Released February 17

Transcript of a press briefing by Press Secretary Mike McCurry

Transcript of a press briefing by U.S. Ambassador to Canada James Johnston Blanchard on the President's upcoming visit to Canada

Statement by Press Secretary Mike McCurry on the Ecuador-Peru peace declaration

Statement by Press Secretary Mike McCurry on conventional arms transfer policy

Fact sheet on conventional arms transfer policy

Fact sheet on criteria for decisionmaking on U.S. arms exports

Released February 21

Transcript of a press briefing by Press Secretary Mike McCurry

Transcript of a press briefing by OMB Office of Information and Regulatory Affairs Administrator Sally Katzen and Senior Policy Adviser to the Vice President Elaine Kamarck on regulatory reform

Statement by Press Secretary Mike McCurry on National Security Adviser Anthony Lake's meeting with Northern Ireland Ulster Unionist Party officials

Released February 22

Transcript of a press briefing by Press Secretary Mike McCurry

Transcript of a press briefing on the Republican proposal to abolish the school lunch program by Chief of Staff Leon Panetta, Secretary of Health and Human Services Donna Shalala, Secretary of Education Richard Riley, and Assistant Secretary of Agriculture for Food and Consumer Services Ellen Haas

Statement by Press Secretary Mike McCurry on the establishment of Presidential Emergency Board No. 226

Released February 23

Transcript of a press briefing by Press Secretary Mike McCurry

Statement by Press Secretary Mike McCurry on the President's request that Ambassador to the United Nations Madeleine Albright visit U.N. Security Council capitals to consult on Iraq

Transcript of remarks by Dr. Chris Carruthers, Dr. Paul Deneault, and Dr. Andreas Laupacis on the medical condition of Secretary of State Warren Christopher

Announcement of nomination for a District of Columbia Court of Appeals Judge

Released February 24

Transcript of a press briefing on the balanced budget amendment by Secretary of the Treasury Robert Rubin, National Economic Adviser Laura D'Andrea Tyson, Office of Management and Budget Director Alice Rivlin, and White House Counsel Abner Mikva

Released February 27

Transcript of a press briefing by Press Secretary Mike McCurry

Released February 28

Transcript of a press briefing by Press Secretary Mike McCurry

Statement by Press Secretary Mike McCurry on the Albanian-American Enterprise Fund

Announcement of nomination for two U.S. District Court Judges

March 1

Transcript of a press briefing by Press Secretary Mike McCurry

Statement by Press Secretary Mike McCurry on the appointment of a Special Assistant to the President and National Security Council Senior Director for African Affairs

Transcript of a press briefing by National Security Adviser Anthony Lake on the President's remarks to the Nixon Center for Peace and Freedom Policy Conference

Excerpts from the President's remarks to the Nixon Center for Peace and Freedom Policy Conference

Transcript of remarks by the First Lady at the Child Welfare League 75th anniversary dinner

March 2

Transcript of a press briefing by Press Secretary Mike McCurry

Statement by Press Secretary Mike McCurry on the Vice President's and the First Lady's attendance at the United Nations World Summit for Social Development in Copenhagen, Denmark

Statement by Press Secretary Mike McCurry on the Presidential business development mission to Haiti

Statement by Press Secretary Mike McCurry on the President's letter to congressional leaders on child support enforcement

Released March 6

Transcript of a press briefing by Press Secretary Mike McCurry

Fact sheet entitled "Gulf War Veterans' Illnesses: New Initiatives"

Fact sheet entitled "Gulf War Veterans' Illnesses: Ongoing Initiatives"

Released March 7

Transcript of a press briefing by Press Secretary Mike McCurry

Statement by Press Secretary Mike McCurry on the visit of Prime Minister Gyula Horn of Hungary

Statement by Press Secretary Mike McCurry on the appointment of a Special Assistant to the President and National Security Council Senior Director for Near East and South Asian Affairs

Released March 8

Transcripts of press briefings by Press Secretary Mike McCurry

Statement by Press Secretary Mike McCurry announcing the President's upcoming visit to Haiti

Transcript of remarks by Hillary Clinton at a celebration of International Women's Day in Copenhagen, Denmark

Released March 9

Transcript of a press briefing by Chief of Staff Leon Panetta and Press Secretary Mike McCurry

Statement by Press Secretary Mike McCurry on the President's meeting with President Jerry John Rawlings of Ghana

Released March 10

Transcript of a press briefing by Press Secretary Mike McCurry

Transcript of a press briefing by Secretary of Labor Robert Reich and National Economic Adviser Laura D'Andrea Tyson on the economy

Released March 13

Transcript of a press briefing by Press Secretary Mike McCurry

Released March 14

Transcripts of press briefings by Press Secretary Mike McCurry

Statement by Press Secretary Mike McCurry on the President's intention to issue an Executive order prohibiting certain transactions with respect to development of Iranian petroleum resources

Statement by Press Secretary Mike McCurry announcing that the Department of Justice will join an appeal of the decision in a Federal District Court in Texas on the Religious Freedom Restoration Act

Announcement of nomination for a U.S. Court of Appeals Judge for the Tenth Circuit

Released March 15

Transcript of a press briefing by Press Secretary Mike McCurry

Statement by Press Secretary Mike McCurry on reinventing Government

White House statement on the Department of Health and Human Services survey on State use of license revocation as a child support enforcement measure

Released March 16

Transcript of a press briefing by Press Secretary Mike McCurry

Transcript of a press briefing on regulatory reform by Senior Policy Adviser to the Vice President Elaine Kamarck, Environmental Protection Agency Administrator Carol Browner, Small Business Administrator Phil Lader, and Commissioner of Food and Drugs David Kessler

Statement by Press Secretary Mike McCurry on the President's meeting with Bosnian and Croatian leaders

Advance text of remarks by Surgeon General nominee Henry Foster to the National Newspaper Publishers Association

Released March 17

Transcript of a press briefing by Press Secretary Mike McCurry

Transcript of a press briefing by Secretary of Health and Human Services Donna Shalala on child support enforcement

White House statement on child support enforcement

Listing of Democratic Senators meeting with the President

Released March 19

Statement by Press Secretary Mike McCurry on the President's telephone conversation with Prime Minister John Major of the United Kingdom

death of Michael Devine and the disappearance of Efrain Bamaca Velasquez

Released March 31

Transcript of remarks by Ambassador to the United Nations Madeleine Albright and Agency for International Development Administrator Brian Atwood to the pool

Announcement of nomination for U.S. Court of Appeals and U.S. District Court Judges

Transcript of a press briefing by U.S. Ambassador to Haiti William L. Swing on the situation in Haiti

Released April 3

Transcript of a press briefing by Secretary Mike McCurry

Released April 4

Transcript of a press briefing by William J. Crowe, Jr., U.S. Ambassador to the Court of St. James, and Senior Director for West European Affairs Alexander Vershbow on the President's meeting with Prime Minister John Major of the United Kingdom

Released April 5

Transcript of a press briefing by Assistant Secretary of State for Near Eastern Affairs Robert Pelletreau and National Security Council Assistant Director for Near Eastern and South Asian Affairs David Satterfield on the visit of President Hosni Mubarak of Egypt

Released April 6

Transcript of a press briefing by Press Secretary Mike McCurry

Statement by Press Secretary Mike McCurry on the appointment of the Special Adviser to the President and the Secretary of State on Assistance to the New Independent States of the Former Soviet Union

List of members of the Southwest Regional Democratic Caucus meeting with the President

Released April 7

Statement by Press Secretary Mike McCurry on The Netherlands decision to purchase U.S. helicopters

Transcript of a press briefing by Secretary of Education Richard Riley on funding for education

Released April 8

Excerpts of remarks to the California Democratic Party in Sacramento, CA

Released April 10

Transcript of a press briefing by Press Secretary Mike McCurry

Memorandum from National Security Adviser Anthony Lake to Intelligence Oversight Board Chairman Anthony S. Harrington on the governmentwide review of allegations surrounding the death of Michael Devine and the disappearance of Efrain Bamaca Velasquez

Transcript of a press briefing by Secretary of Labor Robert Reich and Women's Bureau Director Karen Nussbaum on initiatives for working women

Released April 11

Transcript of a press briefing by Press Secretary Mike McCurry

Transcript of a press briefing by Assistant Secretary of State for South Asian Affairs Robin Raphel and National Security Council Director for Near East and South Asian Affairs Ellen Laipson on the President's meeting with Prime Minister Benazir Bhutto of Pakistan

Statement by Press Secretary Mike McCurry announcing the upcoming visit of President Kim Yong-sam of South Korea

Statement by Press Secretary Mike McCurry on the appointment of the Executive Director of UNICEF

Released April 12

Announcement by Vice President Albert Gore on reinvention of Social Security operations

Released April 13

Transcript of a press briefing by Press Secretary Mike McCurry

Released April 14

Transcript of a press briefing by Press Secretary Mike McCurry

Statement by Press Secretary Mike McCurry on the President and Hillary Clinton's 1994 Federal income tax return

Released April 18

Transcript of a press briefing by Press Secretary Mike McCurry

Released April 19

Transcript of a press briefing by Press Secretary Mike McCurry

Transcript of a press briefing on the visit of Prime Minister Tansu Ciller of Turkey by U.S. Ambassador to Turkey Marc Grossman, National Security Council Senior Director for European Affairs Alexander Vershbow, and Assistant Secretary of State for European and Canadian Affairs Richard Holbrooke

Transcript of a press briefing by Attorney General Janet Reno on the bombing in Oklahoma City, OK

Statement by Press Secretary Mike McCurry on the President's meeting with Prime Minister Vaclav Klaus of the Czech Republic

Announcement of nomination for two U.S. District Court Judges

Released May 6

Transcript of remarks by National Security Adviser Anthony Lake to the Annual Interaction Forum on May 2

Transcript of remarks by National Security Adviser Anthony Lake to the American Center for International Leadership on May 3

Released May 7

Advance text of remarks to the American Israel Public Affairs Committee Policy Conference

Statement by Press Secretary Mike McCurry on the election of Jacques Chirac as President of France

Released May 8

Statement by Press Secretary Mike McCurry on the May 6 meeting between President Jose Eduardo dos Santos of Angola and UNITA president Jonas Savimbi in Lusaka, Zambia

Statement by Press Secretary Mike McCurry announcing the Executive order imposing new economic sanctions on Iran

Announcement of nomination for U.S. Attorney for the Western District of Oklahoma

Released May 9

Transcript of a press briefing by Press Secretary Mike McCurry and Department of State Spokesman Nick Burns

Released May 10

Transcript of a press briefing by Press Secretary Mike McCurry

Transcript of a press briefing on trade with Japan by U.S. Trade Representative Mickey Kantor, National Economic Adviser Laura D'Andrea Tyson, and Secretary of Commerce Ron Brown

Transcript of a press briefing on Republican budget proposals by Chief of Staff Leon Panetta, Office of Management and Budget Director Alice Rivlin, Secretary of Health and Human Services Donna Shalala, and National Economic Adviser Laura D'Andrea Tyson

Statement by Press Secretary Mike McCurry announcing the upcoming visit of President Robert Mugabe of Zimbabwe

Statement by Press Secretary Mike McCurry on the Senate version of product liability legislation

Fact sheet on the proposed "Gun-Free School Zones Amendments Act of 1995"

Fact sheet on U.S. bilateral assistance to Russia

Fact sheet on the establishment of a civilian research and development foundation

Fact sheet on U.S.-Russian trade and investment

Released May 11

Transcript of a press briefing on the impact of Republican budget proposals on education by Chief of Staff Leon Panetta, Office of Management and Budget Director Alice Rivlin, Secretary of Labor Robert Reich, and Secretary of Education Richard Riley

Transcript of a press briefing on the President's meeting with President Leonid Kuchma of Ukraine by Secretary of State Warren Christopher, Secretary of the Treasury Robert Rubin, and National Security Adviser Anthony Lake

Fact sheet on U.S.-Ukraine overview

Fact sheet on U.S.-Ukraine space cooperation

Fact sheet on U.S.-Ukraine trade and investment

Fact sheet on U.S. bilateral economic assistance to Ukraine

Fact sheet on U.S.-Ukraine cooperation on dismantlement and nonproliferation assistance

Fact sheet on the Chernobyl/G–7 action plan

Statement by Press Secretary Mike McCurry announcing the delegation to Vietnam and Laos

Released May 12

Transcript of a press briefing by Press Secretary Mike McCurry

Released May 15

Transcript of a press briefing by Press Secretary Mike McCurry

Statement by Press Secretary Mike McCurry on the underground nuclear test by China at Lop Nur

Released May 16

Transcript of a press briefing by Press Secretary Mike McCurry

Transcript of a press briefing on the National Performance Review by Secretary of Labor Robert Reich, Assistant Secretary of Labor for Occupational Safety and Health Joseph Dear, and Senior Policy Adviser to the Vice President Elaine Kamarck

White House statement announcing reinvention of worker safety and health regulation

Statement by Press Secretary Mike McCurry on the upcoming visit of President Ernesto Zedillo of Mexico

Statement by White House Counsel Abner Mikva on the President's Public Financial Disclosure Report

Released May 17

Transcript of a press briefing by Press Secretary Mike McCurry

Transcript of a press briefing by Chief of Staff Leon Panetta and Office of Management and Budget Director Alice Rivlin on budget proposals

Statement by Press Secretary Mike McCurry on scheduled Senate Whitewater hearings

Released May 18

Transcript of a press briefing by Press Secretary Mike McCurry

Statement by Press Secretary Mike McCurry on the visit of President Robert Mugabe of Zimbabwe

Statement by Press Secretary Mike McCurry on the House budget proposal

Released May 19

Transcript of a press briefing by Press Secretary Mike McCurry

Statement by Press Secretary Mike McCurry announcing a letter from Chief of Staff Leon Panetta to House Appropriations Committee chair Bob Livingston

Released May 22

Transcript of a press briefing by Press Secretary Mike McCurry

Statement by Press Secretary Mike McCurry announcing the upcoming European Union-U.S. summit in Washington, DC

Released May 23

Transcript of a press briefing by Press Secretary Mike McCurry

Statement by Press Secretary Mike McCurry on the May 22 meeting with National Security Adviser Anthony Lake, Deputy National Security Adviser Nancy Soderberg, and the Northern Ireland Ulster Unionist Party delegation

Statement by Chief of Staff Leon Panetta on the Senate budget bill

Fact sheet on the proposed "American Overseas Interests Act of 1995" (H.R. 1561)

Released May 24

Transcript of a press briefing by Press Secretary Mike McCurry

Announcement of nomination for three U.S. District Court Judges

Released May 25

Transcript of a press briefing by Press Secretary Mike McCurry

Statement by Press Secretary Mike McCurry on the appointment of a Special Adviser to the President and Secretary of State for Cuba

Statement by Chief of Staff Leon Panetta on the Senate budget bill

Released May 26

Transcript of a press briefing by Press Secretary Mike McCurry

Released May 28

Advance text of remarks by National Security Adviser Anthony Lake at the University of Massachusetts commencement

Released May 30

Transcript of a press briefing by Press Secretary Mike McCurry

Released May 31

Transcript of a press briefing by Press Secretary Mike McCurry

Released June 1

Statement by Press Secretary Mike McCurry on the President's telephone conversation with President Fernando Henrique Cardoso of Brazil

Released June 2

Transcript of a press briefing by Press Secretary Mike McCurry

Statement by Press Secretary Mike McCurry on most-favored-nation trade status for China

Statement by Press Secretary Mike McCurry on consolidation of the Russian-American Enterprise Fund and the Fund for Large Enterprises in Russia

Released June 5

Transcript of a press briefing by Press Secretary Mike McCurry

Statement by Press Secretary Mike McCurry on the President's initiatives supporting peace in Northern Ireland

Released June 6

Transcript of a press briefing by Press Secretary Mike McCurry

Statement by Press Secretary Mike McCurry on the President's meeting with Prime Minister Gyula Horn of Hungary

Statement by Press Secretary Mike McCurry on the appointment of the Deputy Assistant to the President for Domestic Policy

Released June 7

Transcript of a press briefing by Press Secretary Mike McCurry

Statement by Press Secretary Mike McCurry on American overseas interests legislation (H.R. 1561)

Statement by Special Associate Counsel Mark Fabiani on the indictment of Gov. Jim Guy Tucker of Arkansas

Released June 8

Transcripts of press briefings by Press Secretary Mike McCurry

Released June 9

Transcript of a press briefing by Press Secretary Mike McCurry

Statement by Press Secretary Mike McCurry on the capture of Cali drug kingpin Gilberto Rodriguez Orejuela

Transcript of a press briefing on the upcoming Group of Seven summit in Halifax, Canada by Deputy National Security Adviser Samuel Berger, Assistant Secretary of State for Economic and Business Affairs Dan Tarullo, and Under Secretary of the Treasury for International Affairs Lawrence Summers

White House announcement on initiatives to streamline wage and income reporting requirements for small business owners and individuals

Released June 11

Transcript of remarks by Press Secretary Mike McCurry in Lebanon, NH

Released June 12

Transcript of a press briefing by Press Secretary Mike McCurry

Released June 13

Transcript of a press briefing by Press Secretary Mike McCurry

Statement by Press Secretary Mike McCurry on the announcement that France will resume nuclear testing

Transcript of a press briefing by Secretary of State Warren Christopher and Secretary of the Treasury Robert Rubin on the Group of Seven summit in Halifax, Canada

Transcript of a press briefing on the President's plan to balance the budget by Chief of Staff Leon Panetta, National Economic Adviser Laura D'Andrea Tyson, Office of Management and Budget Director Alice Rivlin, and Secretary of the Treasury Robert Rubin

Released June 14

Joint statement with European Union leaders

Transcript of a press briefing by Press Secretary Mike McCurry

Transcript of a press briefing by Office of Management and Budget Director Alice Rivlin and Secretary of Health and Human Services Donna Shalala on the President's plan to balance the budget

Released June 15

Transcript of a press briefing by Secretary of State Warren Christopher and Secretary of the Treasury Robert Rubin on Japan-U.S. bilateral meetings in Halifax, Canada

White House statement on Senate action on S. 652

White House statement on the Presidential Advisory Council on HIV/AIDS

Released June 16

Transcript of a press briefing by Press Secretary Mike McCurry and Department of State Spokesman Dave Johnson on the Group of Seven summit in Halifax, Canada

Fact sheet on financial reforms

Fact sheet on United Nations reforms

Fact sheet on Halifax economic communique highlights

Transcript of a press briefing on the Group of Seven summit by Under Secretary of State for Economic and Agricultural Affairs Joan Spero, Assistant Secretary of State for Economic and Business Affairs Daniel Tarullo, Under Secretary of the Treasury for International Affairs Lawrence Summers, and Press Secretary Mike McCurry

Released June 17

Transcript of a press briefing by Press Secretary Mike McCurry

Transcript of a press briefing on the Group of Seven summit by Press Secretary Mike McCurry, Under Secretary of State for Political Affairs Peter Tarnoff, and Deputy National Security Adviser Samuel Berger

Released June 19

Transcript of a press briefing by Press Secretary Mike McCurry

White House statement on fiscal year 1996 budget amendments for the Department of Housing and Urban Development and the Small Business Administration

Released June 20

Transcript of a press briefing by Press Secretary Mike McCurry

Statement by National Economic Adviser Laura D'Andrea Tyson on the President's plan to balance the budget

Released June 21

Transcript of a press briefing by Press Secretary Mike McCurry

Transcript of a press briefing by National Economic Adviser Laura D'Andrea Tyson and Deputy Assistant to the President for Intergovernmental Affairs John Emerson on the Pacific Rim Economic Conference

Statement by Press Secretary Mike McCurry on Nigeria's arrest and detention of former President Gen. Olusegun Obasanjo

Statement by Press Secretary Mike McCurry on the refusal of the regime in Rangoon to reach an acceptable arrangement on access for the International Committee of the Red Cross

Announcement of nomination for Peace Corps Director

Released June 22

Statement by Chief of Staff Leon Panetta on the President's plan to balance the budget

Statement by Press Secretary Mike McCurry on the U.S. delegation to observe the elections in Haiti

Statement by Press Secretary Mike McCurry on the U.S.-Russia Joint Commission on POW/MIA's

Fact sheet on the U.S.-Russia Joint Commission on POW/MIA's

Interim Report of the U.S.-Russia Joint Commission on POW/MIA's

Announcement of nomination for U.S. District Court Judge for the District of Utah

Released June 23

Fact sheet on the elections in Haiti

Released June 25

Transcript of a press briefing by National Security Adviser Anthony Lake on the elections in Haiti

Released June 26

Transcript of remarks by the First Lady at a PBS event

Transcript of remarks by the First Lady at an American newswomen press conference

Released June 27

Announcement of nomination for U.S. District Court and U.S. Court of International Trade Judges

Released June 28

Transcript of a press briefing by Press Secretary Mike McCurry

Transcript of a press briefing by Chief of Staff Leon Panetta on the appointment of the Chairman of the Council of Economic Advisers

Statement by Press Secretary Mike McCurry announcing the President's letter to congressional leaders on the plan to balance the budget

Transcript of a press briefing by Special Associate Counsel to the President Mark Fabiani on Webster Hubbell

Released June 29

Transcript of a press briefing by Press Secretary Mike McCurry

Statement by Press Secretary Mike McCurry on the President's meeting with Syrian Chief of Staff Lt. Gen. Hikmat al-Shihabi and Israeli Chief of Staff Lt. Gen. Amnon Shahak

Announcement of nomination for a U.S. Court of Appeals Judge for the Sixth Circuit

Released June 30

Statement by Press Secretary Mike McCurry on lifting trade sanctions against Taiwan and major steps towards protection of endangered species

Announcement of nomination for U.S. District Court and U.S. Court of International Trade Judges

Statement by Chief of Staff Leon Panetta on rescission legislation

Fact sheet on the proposed "Saving Law Enforcement Officers' Lives Act of 1995"

Appendix D—Presidential Documents Published in the Federal Register

This appendix lists Presidential documents released by the Office of the Press Secretary and published in the
Federal Register. The texts of the documents are printed in the Federal Register (F.R.) at the citations listed
below. The documents are also printed in title 3 of the Code of Federal Regulations and in the Weekly Compilation of Presidential Documents.

PROCLAMATIONS

PROCLAMATIONS—Continued

EXECUTIVE ORDERS

OTHER PRESIDENTIAL DOCUMENTS

Subject Index

Congress—Continued
    Speaker of the House of Representatives—100, 848, 900, 986
Congressional Accountability Act of 1995—59, 73
Connecticut, University of—802
Conoco Co.—616
Conservation
    See also Environment
    Federal lands—776
    Floodplain management, report—312
    Forest preservation—473, 698, 776, 826, 829, 978, 986
    Payment to property owners for protected lands—480, 500, 565
    Wilderness and wildlife preservation—801
Corporation. *See* other part of subject
Cote d'Ivoire, U.S. Ambassador—1006
Council. *See* other part of subject
Counties, National Association of—313
Createc Forestry Systems—256
Credit Standards Advisory Committee—1003
Crime. *See* Law enforcement and crime
Croatia
    President—281, 298, 1003
    United Nations peacekeeping forces—281, 298
    U.S. military, role—298, 745
Cuba
    Democracy and freedom—533, 953
    Economic sanctions—483, 534, 954
    Human rights—954
    Immigration agreement with U.S.—954
    President, Council of State—954
    Refugees—483, 953
Cuban Democracy Act of 1992—533, 954
Cultural Property Advisory Committee—999
Custom Print—358
Customs Service, U.S. *See* Treasury, Department of the
Cyprus
    Conflict resolution—312, 605, 952
    President—952
    Turkish Cypriot leader—312, 952
    U.S. Special Coordinator—312, 605, 952, 1006
    U.S. Special Emissary—312, 605, 952, 997
Czech Republic
    President—847
    Prime Minister—1000, 1007
    U.S. Ambassador—1006

Dartmouth College—844
Day. *See* other part of subject
Defense and national security
    See also Arms and munitions; Nuclear weapons
    Counterterrorism efforts—74, 83, 186, 190, 557, 568, 575-577, 605, 608, 615, 621, 633, 635, 641, 643, 657, 689, 720, 722, 757, 767, 806, 812, 830, 832
    Energy security—215
    Intelligence capability—155
    Military strength and deterrence—83, 308, 515, 523, 769, 771-773, 818
    National security information, reform of classification system—540

Defense and national security—Continued
    National security strategy, report—281
    Terrorists threatening Middle East peace efforts, U.S. national emergency—74, 83, 616
Defense Base Closure and Realignment Commission—943, 1000, 1002
Defense, Department of
    See also specific military department; Armed Forces, U.S.
    Arms Proliferation Policy, President's Advisory Board on—1000
    Assistant Secretary—1004
    Budget—144, 515, 523, 770, 773, 942, 1011
    Deputy Assistant Secretary—1008
    Deputy Secretary—144, 332, 1008
    Environmental satellite systems program—744
    Joint Chiefs of Staff—55, 801, 996
    Persian Gulf conflict veterans, undiagnosed illnesses—310
    Procurement—422
    Secretary—72, 116, 144, 310, 488, 516, 736, 801
Defense Nuclear Facilities Safety Board—1013
Deficit, Federal. *See* Budget, Federal
Delaware
    Governor—129, 657, 929
    Welfare reform—657
Democracy, National Endowment for—313
Democratic Governors Association—120
Democratic Leadership Council—1002
Democratic National Committee—39, 66, 966, 1005
Democratic Party
    Congressional dinner—739
    General Chairman—39, 968
    Governors, meetings with President—926, 1011
    National Chairman—39, 968
    Presidential dinners and galas—137
    State party organizations, fundraisers, etc. *See* specific State
Democratic Policy Committee—1007
Department. *See* other part of subject
Deposit Insurance Corporation, Federal—553
Des Moines Register—1006
Detroit Free Press—634
Development Bank, Inter-American—998
Development Cooperation Agency, U.S. International, Overseas Private Investment Corporation (OPIC)—45, 354, 671, 1001
Disability, National Council on—1000, 1002
Disaster assistance
    Alabama flooding—1001, 1006
    California earthquake—56, 213
    California flooding—31, 32, 38, 47, 55, 58, 333, 998, 1002, 1003
    Floodplain management—312
    Florida flooding—1001, 1004
    Georgia flooding—1001, 1004
    Illinois storms and flooding—1010
    Japan earthquake—72, 999
    Kentucky tornadoes and flooding—1012
    Louisiana storms and flooding—1008
    Mississippi storms and flooding—1008

Name Index

Adams, Eileen—623
Adams, Gerry—368, 369, 452, 738
Adamson, Terrence B.—1015
Adler, Bernyce,—1004
Agee, Arthur—444, 448
Aguilar, Fidel—1006
Ahmat, Mahamat Saleh—1003
Albright, Madeleine K.—2, 323, 325, 699, 736, 895
Alexander, Frank—1006
Alexander, Les—224
Alexander, Vera—1004, 1022
Alfonso, Pedro—1011
Alioto, Michele Driscoll—1022
Allen, C. Richard—1011, 1025
Allen, Lew, Jr.—155
Allen, Robert E.—249
Altman, Roger C.—297
Alvardo, Linda—1003
Amdemicael Kahsai—1000
Amorose, Samuel—1006
Anastos, Peggy Hernandez—1008
Anderson, Rebecca—607
Anderson, Terje—1012
Andersson, Yerker—1015
Annenberg, Lee—834, 835
Annenberg, Walter—835
Anselmi, Don—1008
Antoon, Thomas—1009
Apponte, Jose Garcia—436
Arafat, Yasser—616, 652, 811
Aragon, Regina—1012
Archuleta, Lena—1006
Arendt, John W.—1012
Aristide, Jean-Bertrand—158, 432, 437, 439, 1002
Ariyoshi, George—999
Armenta, Loretta—1004
Armey, Richard K.—130, 529
Armstrong, Anthony A.—1009
Aronson, Judith—1005
Arterton, Janet Bond—1020
Asad, Hafiz al- —467, 545, 811
Asnes, Norma—1006
Aspin, Les—155, 174, 332, 730, 732, 733, 769, 876
Atkins, Chet—701
Atlas, Nancy Friedman—1022
Auer, Les—785
Augustine, Norman R.—1013
Auriemma, Geno—802, 803
Aviles, Jessica—580, 584

Bacon, Kenneth H.—1004, 1024
Baily, Martin Neil—194, 1015
Baird, Zoe—155

Baker, Thomas—1009
Baldeschwieler, John—1010
Bamaca Velasquez, Efrain—1004
Barela, Sarah—1010
Barry, Marion—539
Barsness, John C.—998
Bartlett, Kathie—998
Basham, Judy—1006
Bassa, Marjorie—439
Baucus, Max—776, 784, 793
Bayh, Birch—1013
Bayh, Evan—928
Beach, George A.—1008
Beattie, Richard I.—312, 605, 952, 997
Beatty, Michael L.—1008
Beck, Ronna Lee—1015
Beckelman, Stanley C.—1009
Bellamy, Carol—912
Bellamy, Michelle—423
Ben-Ami, Jeremy—1011
Bencherif, Hadj Osmane—1003
Bennett, William—728
Bentsen, Lloyd—140
Berkovitz, Dan M.—1018
Berndt, Martin—870
Bernstein, Scott—1012
Bersoff, Ed—733
Bertsch, Richard—1009
Bettman, Gary—370
Bhutto, Benazir—516, 998, 1005
Biden, Joseph R., Jr.—832, 988
Bieber, Owen—871
Biggs, Glenn—1004
Bilbray, James H.—1009
Bildner, Allen I.—1002
Biondi, Frank J., Jr.—999
Birren, James E.—1000
Bishop, Stephen—85
Blacker, Coit D.—998
Blackford, Peggy—1012
Blackman, Courtney N.M.—1003
Blair, Edward Scott—1025
Blair, Kenneth C., Jr.—1008
Blair, Thomas—1008
Blake, Catherine C.—1024
Blanchard, James J.—259
Bland, Calton Windley—1015
Bliley, Thomas J., Jr.—20
Blitzer, Wolf—527
Bloch, Richard L.—1014
Bloom, Brent—606
Blount, Nancy—1001
Blount, Roderick—1008

Document Categories List